Introductory Mathematical Analysis

5TH EDITION

Introductory Mathematical Analysis

For Business, Economics, and the Life and Social Sciences

Ernest F. Haeussler, Jr.

Richard S. Paul

The Pennsylvania State University

PRENTICE-HALL, Inc., Englewood Cliffs, New Jersey 07632

Library of Congress Cataloging in Publication Data

HAEUSSLER, ERNEST F.
  Introductory mathematical analysis for business,
economics, and the life and social sciences.

  Rev. ed. of: Introductory mathematical analysis
for students of business and economics. 4th ed. 1983.
  Bibliography: p.
  Includes index.
  1. Mathematical analysis. 2. Economics, Mathe-
matical.   3. Business mathematics. I. Paul, Richard S.
II. Haeussler, Ernest F. Introductory mathematical
analysis for students of business and economics.
III. Title.
QA300.H33   1987   515   86-25374
ISBN 0-13-501941-9

Editorial/production supervision: Fay Ahuja and John Morgan
Interior and cover design: Janet Schmid
Cover photograph: © 1986 Geoff Gove
Manufacturing buyer: John Hall
Page layout: Irene Poth and Marty Behan

Printed in the United States of America

10 9 8 7 6 5 4 3 2 1

ISBN 0-13-501941-9   01

Prentice-Hall International (UK) Limited, *London*
Prentice-Hall of Australia Pty. Limited, *Sydney*
Prentice-Hall Canada Inc., *Toronto*
Prentice-Hall Hispanoamericana, S.A., *Mexico*
Prentice-Hall of India Private Limited, *New Delhi*
Prentice-Hall of Japan, Inc., *Tokyo*
Prentice-Hall of Southeast Asia Pte. Ltd., *Singapore*
Editora Prentice-Hall do Brasil, Ltda., *Rio de Janeiro*

Contents

Preface

The fifth edition of *Introductory Mathematical Analysis* provides a mathematical foundation for students in business, economics, and the life and social sciences. It begins with noncalculus topics such as equations, functions, mathematics of finance, probability, matrix algebra, and linear programming. Then it progresses through both single variable and multivariable calculus, including continuous random variables.

An abundance and variety of applications for the intended audience are blended throughout the book so that students continually see ways in which the mathematics they are learning can be used. While the applications in previous editions were primarily in business and economics, the fifth edition also includes applications from such diverse areas as biology, sociology, psychology, ecology, statistics, and archeology. Many applied problems are drawn from literature and are documented by references. In some the background and context are given in order to stimulate interest. However, the text is virtually self-contained in the sense that it assumes no prior exposure to the concepts on which the applications are based.

Besides expanding the range of applications, we have made other changes for this edition. All noncalculus topics, including matrix algebra and linear programming, appear in the first half of the book. Probability has been divided into two chapters: discrete random variables in Chapter 7 and continuous random variables in Chapter 16. Permutations and combination are now included (Sec. 7.1). Exponential and logarithmic functions are now considered in separate sections. Continuity is treated more intuitively than before. Curve sketching is now a separate chapter. Differential equations has been expanded to two sections (Secs. 15.6 and 15.7). Many sections have been rewritten to afford greater clarity. Some exercise sets have been revised; many challenging problems have been added. Chapter summaries are now included.

Interspersed throughout the text are many warnings to the student that point out commonly made errors. These warnings are indicated under the heading "Pitfall."

With the exception of Chapter 0, each chapter ends with a section called

"Review," which contains a list of important terms and symbols, a chapter summary, and numerous review problems.

Answers to odd-numbered problems appear at the end of the book. For many of the differentiation problems in Chapter 11, the answers appear in both unsimplified and simplified forms.

Because instructors plan a course outline to serve the individual needs of a particular class and curriculum, we shall not attempt to provide sample outlines. However, depending on the background of the students, some instructors will choose to omit Chapter 0 (Algebra Refresher) and Chapter 1 (Equations). Others may exclude the topics of matrix algebra and linear programming. Certainly there are other sections of chapters that may be omitted at the discretion of the instructor. As an aid to planning a course outline, perhaps a few comments may be helpful. Section 2.1 introduces some business terms, such as total revenue, fixed cost, variable cost, and profit. Section 4.2 introduces the notion of supply and demand equations, and Sec. 4.6 discusses the equilibrium point. Some sections that are optional and will not cause problems if they are omitted are: 9.3, 9.5, 15.1, 15.2, 17.4, 17.6, 17.9, 17.10. Section 8.9 may be omitted if 8.10 is not covered. Section 15.8 may be omitted if Chapter 16 is not covered.

Available from the publisher is an extensive instructor's manual that includes answers to all problems and detailed solutions to a great many of them. Also available is a test bank and a student's solution manual.

We express our appreciation to the following colleagues who contributed comments and suggestions that were valuable to us in developing the manuscript for either this edition or a previous edition:

R. M. Alliston *(Pennsylvania State University)*, R. A. Alo *(University of Houston)*, M. N. de Arce *(University of Puerto Rico)*, G. R. Bates *(Western Illinois University)*, D. E. Bennett *(Murray State University)*, C. Bernett *(Harper College)*, A. Bishop *(Western Illinois University)*, S. A. Book *(California State University)*, A. Brink *(St. Cloud State University)*, R. Brown *(York University)*, R. W. Brown *(University of Alaska)*, S. D. Bulman-Fleming *(Wilfrid Laurier University)*, D. Calvetti *(National College)*, K. S. Chung *(Kapiolani Community College)*, D. N. Clark *(University of Georgia)*, E. L. Cohen *(University of Ottawa)*, J. Dawson *(Pennsylvania State University)*, A. Dollins *(Pennsylvania State University)*, G. A. Earles *(St. Cloud State University)*, B. H. Edwards *(University of Florida)*, J. R. Elliott *(Wilfrid Laurier University)*, J. Fitzpatrick *(University of Texas at El Paso)*, M. J. Flynn *(Rhode Island Junior College)*, G. J. Fuentes *(University of Maine)*, G. Goff *(Oklahoma State University)*, J. Goldman *(DePaul University)*, L. Griff *(Pennsylvania State University)*, F. H. Hall *(Pennsylvania State University)*, V. E. Hanks *(Western Kentucky University)*, J. N. Henry *(California State University)*, W. U. Hodgson *(West Chester State College)*, B. C. Horne, Jr. *(Virginia Polytechnic Institute and State University)*, J. Hradnansky *(Pennsylvania State University)*, C. Hurd *(Pennsylvania State University)*, J. A. Jimenez *(Pennsylvania State University)*, W. C. Jones *(Western Kentucky University)*, R. M. King *(Gettysburg College)*, M. M. Kostreva *(University of Maine)*, G. A. Kraus *(Gannon University)*, M. R. Latina *(Rhode*

Island Junior College), J. F. Longman *(Villanova University)*, I. Marshak *(Loyola University of Chicago)*, F. B. Mayer *(Mt. San Antonio College)*, P. McDougle *(University of Miami)*, F. Miles *(California State University)*, E. Mohnike *(Mt. San Antonio College)*, C. Monk *(University of Richmond)*, J. G. Morris *(University of Wisconsin—Madison)*, J. C. Moss *(Paducah Community College)*, D. Mullin *(Pennsylvania State University)*, E. Nelson *(Pennsylvania State University)*, S. A. Nett *(Western Illinois University)*, R. H. Oehmke *(University of Iowa)*, Y. Y. Oh *(Pennsylvania State University)*, N. B. Patterson *(Pennsylvania State University)*, E. Pemberton *(Wilfrid Laurier University)*, M. Perkel *(Wright State University)*, D. B. Priest *(Harding College)*, J. R. Provencio *(University of Texas)*, L. R. Pulsinelli *(Western Kentucky University)*, M. Racine *(University of Ottawa)*, N. M. Rice *(Queen's University)*, A. Santiago *(University of Puerto Rico)*, W. H. Seybold, Jr. *(West Chester State College)*, J. R. Schaefer *(University of Wisconsin—Milwaukee)*, S. Sehgal *(Ohio State University)*, S. Singh *(Pennsylvania State University)*, E. Smet *(Huron College)*, M. Stoll *(University of South Carolina)*, B. Toole *(University of Maine)*, J. W. Toole *(University of Maine)*, D. H. Trahan *(Naval Postgraduate School)*, J. P. Tull *(Ohio State University)*, L. O. Vaughan, Jr. *(University of Alabama in Birmingham)*, L. A. Vercoe *(Pennsylvania State University)*, M. Vuilleumier *(Ohio State University)*, B. K. Waits *(Ohio State University)*, A. Walton *(Virginia Polytechnic Institute and State University)*, H. Walum *(Ohio State University)*, A. J. Weidner *(Pennsylvania State University)*, L. Weiss *(Pennsylvania State University)*, N. A. Weigmann *(California State University)*, C. R. B. Wright *(University of Oregon)*, C. Wu *(University of Wisconsin—Milwaukee)*.

Finally, a special word of thanks is due to John Morgan and Fay Ahuja, our production editors, and to the entire Prentice-Hall staff for their efficiency, competent assistance, and enthusiastic cooperation.

Ernest F. Haeussler, Jr.

Richard S. Paul

Algebra Refresher

0.1 PURPOSE

This chapter is designed to give you a brief review of some terms and methods of manipulative mathematics. No doubt you have been exposed to much of this material before. However, because these topics are important in handling the mathematics that comes later, perhaps an immediate second exposure to them would be beneficial. Devote whatever time is necessary to those sections in which you need review.

0.2 SETS AND REAL NUMBERS

In simplest terms, a *set* is a collection of objects. For example, we can speak of the set of even numbers between 5 and 11, namely 6, 8, and 10. An object in a set is called a *member* or *element* of that set.

One way to specify a set is by listing its members, in any order, inside braces. For example, the previous set is {6, 8, 10}, which we can denote by a letter such as A. A set A is said to be a **subset** of a set B if and only if every element of A is also an element of B. For example, if $A = \{6, 8, 10\}$ and $B = \{6, 8, 10, 12\}$, then A is a subset of B.

Certain sets of numbers have special names. The numbers 1, 2, 3, and so on, form the set of **positive integers** (or **natural numbers**):

$$\begin{array}{c} \textit{set of} \\ \textit{positive integers} \end{array} = \{1, 2, 3, \ldots\}.$$

The three dots mean that the listing of elements is unending, although we know what the elements are.

The positive integers together with 0 and the **negative integers** -1, -2, -3, . . . form the set of **integers:**

$$\begin{array}{c} set\ of \\ integers \end{array} = \{ \ldots, -3, -2, -1, 0, 1, 2, 3, \ldots \}.$$

The set of **rational numbers** consists of numbers, such as $\frac{1}{2}$ and $\frac{5}{3}$, which can be written as a ratio (quotient) of two integers. That is, a rational number is one that can be written as p/q, where p and q are integers and $q \neq 0$. (The symbol "$\neq$" is read "is not equal to.") **We cannot divide by zero.** The numbers $\frac{19}{20}$, $\frac{-2}{7}$, and $\frac{-6}{-2}$ are rational. The integer 2 is rational since $2 = \frac{2}{1}$. In fact, every integer is rational. We point out that $\frac{2}{4}$, $\frac{1}{2}$, $\frac{3}{6}$, $\frac{-4}{-8}$, and 0.5 all represent the same rational number.

All rational numbers can be represented by decimal numbers that *terminate,* such as $\frac{3}{4} = 0.75$ and $\frac{3}{2} = 1.5$, or by *nonterminating repeating* decimals (a group of digits repeats without end), such as $\frac{2}{3} = 0.666 \ldots$, $\frac{-4}{11} = -0.3636 \ldots$, and $\frac{2}{15} = 0.1333 \ldots$. Numbers represented by *nonterminating nonrepeating* decimals are called **irrational numbers.** An irrational number cannot be written as an integer divided by an integer. The numbers π (pi) and $\sqrt{2}$ are irrational.

Together, the rational numbers and irrational numbers form the set of **real numbers.** Real numbers can be represented by points on a line. To do this we first choose a point on the line to represent zero. This point is called the *origin* (see Fig. 0.1). Then a standard measure of distance, called a "unit distance," is

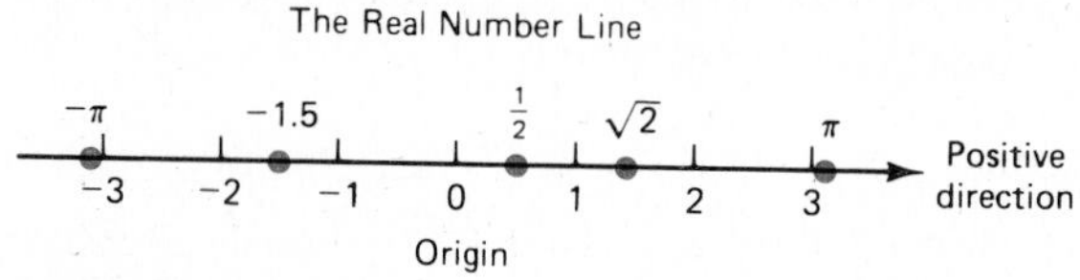

The Real Number Line

FIGURE 0.1

chosen and is successively marked off both to the right and to the left of the origin. With each point on the line we associate a directed distance, or *signed number,* which depends on the position of the point with respect to the origin. Positions to the right of the origin are considered positive $(+)$, and positions to the left are negative $(-)$. For example, with the point $\frac{1}{2}$ unit to the right of the origin there corresponds the signed number $\frac{1}{2}$, which is called the **coordinate** of that point. Similarly, the coordinate of the point 1.5 units to the left of the origin is -1.5. In Fig. 0.1 the coordinates of some points are marked. The arrowhead indicates that the direction to the right along the line is considered the positive direction.

To each point on the line there corresponds a unique real number, and to each real number there corresponds a unique point on the line. For this reason we say that there is a *one-to-one correspondence* between points on the line and real numbers. We call this line a **coordinate line** or the **real number line.** We feel free to treat real numbers as points on a real number line, and vice versa.

EXERCISE 0.2

In Problems **1–12,** *classify the statement as either true or false. If false, give a reason.*

1. -7 is an integer.

2. $\frac{1}{6}$ is rational.

3. -3 is a natural number.

4. 0 is not rational.

5. 5 is rational.

6. $\frac{7}{0}$ is a rational number.

7. $\frac{4}{2}$ is not a positive integer.

8. π is a real number.

9. $\frac{0}{6}$ is rational.

10. 0 is a natural number.

11. -3 is to the right of -4 on the real number line.

12. Every integer is positive or negative.

0.3   SOME PROPERTIES OF REAL NUMBERS

If a, b, and c are real numbers, here are a few important properties of the real numbers.

---

1. THE TRANSITIVE PROPERTY OF EQUALITY

If $a = b$ and $b = c$, then $a = c$.

Thus two numbers that are both equal to a third number are equal to each other. For example, if $x = y$ and $y = 7$, then $x = 7$.

---

2. THE COMMUTATIVE PROPERTIES OF ADDITION AND MULTIPLICATION

$$a + b = b + a \quad \text{and} \quad ab = ba.$$

This means that we can add or multiply two real numbers in any order. For example, $3 + 4 = 4 + 3$ and $7(-4) = (-4)(7)$.

---

3. THE ASSOCIATIVE PROPERTIES OF ADDITION AND MULTIPLICATION

$$a + (b + c) = (a + b) + c \quad \text{and} \quad a(bc) = (ab)c.$$

This means that in addition or multiplication, numbers can be grouped in any order. For example, $2 + (3 + 4) = (2 + 3) + 4$. Also, $6(\frac{1}{3} \cdot 5) = (6 \cdot \frac{1}{3}) \cdot 5$ and $2x + (x + y) = (2x + x) + y$.

4. THE INVERSE PROPERTIES

a. For each real number a, there is a unique real number denoted $-a$ such that

$$a + (-a) = 0.$$

The number $-a$ is called the **additive inverse,** or **negative,** of a.

For example, since $6 + (-6) = 0$, the additive inverse of 6 is -6. The additive inverse of a number is not necessarily a negative number. For example, the additive inverse of -6 is 6, since $(-6) + (6) = 0$. That is, the negative of -6 is 6.

b. For each real number a, except 0, there is a unique real number denoted a^{-1} such that

$$a \cdot a^{-1} = 1.$$

The number a^{-1} is called the **multiplicative inverse** of a.

Thus all numbers except 0 have a multiplicative inverse. You may recall that a^{-1} can be written $\dfrac{1}{a}$ and is also called the *reciprocal* of a. For example, the multiplicative inverse of 3 is $\frac{1}{3}$, since $3(\frac{1}{3}) = 1$. Thus $\frac{1}{3}$ is the reciprocal of 3. The reciprocal of $\frac{1}{3}$ is 3, since $(\frac{1}{3})(3) = 1$. **The reciprocal of 0 is not defined.**

5. THE DISTRIBUTIVE PROPERTIES

$$a(b + c) = ab + ac \qquad \text{and} \qquad (b + c)a = ba + ca.$$

For example,

$$2(3 + 4) = 2(3) + 2(4) = 6 + 8 = 14,$$

$$(2 + 3)(4) = 2(4) + 3(4) = 8 + 12 = 20,$$

$$x(z + 4) = x(z) + x(4) = xz + 4x.$$

The distributive property can be extended to the form $a(b + c + d) = ab + ac + ad$. In fact, it can be extended to sums involving any number of terms.

It is by the additive inverse property that we formally define *subtraction:*

$a - b$ means $a + (-b)$, where $-b$ is the additive inverse of b. Thus $6 - 8$ means $6 + (-8)$. Subtraction is therefore defined in terms of addition.

In a similar way we define *division* in terms of multiplication. If $b \neq 0$, then $a \div b$, or $\dfrac{a}{b}$, is defined by

$$\frac{a}{b} = a(b^{-1}).$$

Since $b^{-1} = \dfrac{1}{b}$,

$$\frac{a}{b} = a(b^{-1}) = a\left(\frac{1}{b}\right).$$

Thus $\frac{3}{5}$ means 3 times $\frac{1}{5}$, where $\frac{1}{5}$ is the multiplicative inverse of 5. Sometimes we refer to $a \div b$ or $\dfrac{a}{b}$ as the *ratio* of a to b.

The following examples show some manipulations involving the above properties.

EXAMPLE 1

a. $x(y - 3z + 2w) = (y - 3z + 2w)x$, by the commutative property of multiplication.

b. By the associative property of multiplication, $3(4 \cdot 5) = (3 \cdot 4)5$. Thus the result of multiplying 3 by the product of 4 and 5 is the same as the result of multiplying the product of 3 and 4 by 5. In either case the result is 60.

c. By the definition of subtraction, $2 - \sqrt{2} = 2 + (-\sqrt{2})$. However, by the commutative property of addition, $2 + (-\sqrt{2}) = -\sqrt{2} + 2$. Thus, by the transitive property, $2 - \sqrt{2} = -\sqrt{2} + 2$. More concisely, we can write

$$2 - \sqrt{2} = 2 + (-\sqrt{2}) = -\sqrt{2} + 2.$$

d.
$$(8 + x) - y = (8 + x) + (-y) \qquad \text{(definition of subtraction)}$$
$$= 8 + [x + (-y)] \qquad \text{(associative property)}$$
$$= 8 + (x - y) \qquad \text{(definition of subtraction)}.$$

Hence, by the transitive property,

$$(8 + x) - y = 8 + (x - y).$$

e. By the definition of division,

$$\frac{ab}{c} = (ab) \cdot \frac{1}{c} \quad \text{for} \quad c \neq 0.$$

But by the associative property,

$$(ab) \cdot \frac{1}{c} = a\left(b \cdot \frac{1}{c}\right).$$

However, by the definition of division, $b \cdot \dfrac{1}{c} = \dfrac{b}{c}$. Thus

$$\frac{ab}{c} = a\left(\frac{b}{c}\right).$$

We can also show that $\dfrac{ab}{c} = \left(\dfrac{a}{c}\right)b.$

EXAMPLE 2

a. *Show that* $3(4x + 2y + 8) = 12x + 6y + 24.$

By the distributive property,

$$3(4x + 2y + 8) = 3(4x) + 3(2y) + 3(8).$$

But by the associative property of multiplication,

$$3(4x) = (3 \cdot 4)x = 12x \quad \text{and similarly} \quad 3(2y) = 6y.$$

Thus $3(4x + 2y + 8) = 12x + 6y + 24.$

b. *Show that* $x(y - z) = xy - xz.$

By the definition of subtraction and the distributive property,

$$x(y - z) = x[y + (-z)]$$
$$= xy + x(-z).$$

Recalling that $-z = (-1)z$, we can then say that $x(-z)(= x[(-1)z]$. By the associative and commutative properties, $x[(-1)z] = [x(-1)]z = [(-1)x]z = (-1)(xz)$. Hence

$$x(y - z) = xy + x(-z)$$
$$= xy + (-1)(xz)$$
$$= xy + [-(xz)].$$

Referring again to the definition of subtraction, we have $x(y - z) = xy - xz.$

c. *Show that if* $c \neq 0$, *then* $\dfrac{a + b}{c} = \dfrac{a}{c} + \dfrac{b}{c}.$

By the definition of division and the distributive property,

$$\frac{a + b}{c} = (a + b)\frac{1}{c} = a \cdot \frac{1}{c} + b \cdot \frac{1}{c}.$$

However,

$$a \cdot \frac{1}{c} + b \cdot \frac{1}{c} = \frac{a}{c} + \frac{b}{c}.$$

Hence

$$\frac{a + b}{c} = \frac{a}{c} + \frac{b}{c}.$$

This important result **does not** mean that $\dfrac{a}{b + c} = \dfrac{a}{b} + \dfrac{a}{c}$, a very common error. For example,

$$\frac{3}{2 + 1} \neq \frac{3}{2} + \frac{3}{1}.$$

Finding the product of several numbers can be done only by considering products of numbers taken two at a time. For example, to find the product of x, y, and z we could first multiply x by y and then multiply that product by z, or alternatively we could multiply x by the product of y and z. The associative property of multiplication says that both results are identical, regardless of how the numbers are grouped. Thus it is not ambiguous to write xyz. This concept can be extended to more than three numbers and applies equally well to addition.

One final comment before we end this section. Not only should you be aware of the manipulative aspects of the properties of the real numbers, but you should also be aware of and familiar with the terminology involved.

EXERCISE 0.3

In Problems **1–10,** *classify the statements as either true or false.*

1. Every real number has a reciprocal.

2. The reciprocal of $\frac{2}{5}$ is $\frac{5}{2}$.

3. The additive inverse of 5 is $\frac{1}{5}$.

4. $2(3 \cdot 4) = (2 \cdot 3)(2 \cdot 4)$.

5. $-x + y = y - x$.

6. $(x + 2)(4) = 4x + 8$.

7. $\dfrac{x + 2}{2} = \dfrac{x}{2} + 1$.

8. $3\left(\dfrac{x}{4}\right) = \dfrac{3x}{4}$.

9. $x + (y + 5) = (x + y) + (x + 5)$.

10. $8(9x) = 72x$.

In Problems **11–20,** *state which properties of the real numbers are being used.*

11. $2(x + y) = 2x + 2y$.

12. $(x + 5) + y = y + (x + 5)$.

13. $2(3y) = (2 \cdot 3)y$.

14. $\frac{6}{7} = 6 \cdot \frac{1}{7}$.

15. $2(x - y) = (x - y)(2)$.

16. $x + (x + y) = (x + x) + y$.

17. $8 - y = 8 + (-y)$.

18. $5(4 + 7) = 5(7 + 4)$.

19. $(7 + x)y = 7y + xy$.

20. $(-1)[-3 + 4] = (-1)(-3) + (-1)(4)$.

In Problems **21–26,** *show that the statements are true by using properties of the real numbers.*

21. $5a(x + 3) = 5ax + 15a$.

22. $(2 - x) + y = 2 + (y - x)$.

23. $(x - y)(2) = 2x - 2y.$

24. $2[27 + (x + y)] = 2[(y + 27) + x].$

25. $x[(2y + 1) + 3] = 2xy + 4x.$

26. $(x + 1)(y + 1) = xy + x + y + 1.$

27. Show that $a(b + c + d) = ab + ac + ad.$ [*Hint:* $b + c + d = (b + c) + d.$]

0.4 OPERATIONS WITH REAL NUMBERS

Listed below are important properties of real numbers which you should study thoroughly. Being able to manipulate real numbers is essential to your success in mathematics. A numerical example follows each property. All denominators are different from zero. A knowledge of addition and subtraction of real numbers is assumed.

PROPERTY	EXAMPLE
1. $a - b = a + (-b).$	$2 - 7 = 2 + (-7) = -5.$
2. $a - (-b) = a + b.$	$2 - (-7) = 2 + 7 = 9.$
3. $-a = (-1)(a).$	$-7 = (-1)(7).$
4. $a(b + c) = ab + ac.$	$6(7 + 2) = 6 \cdot 7 + 6 \cdot 2 = 54.$
5. $a(b - c) = ab - ac.$	$6(7 - 2) = 6 \cdot 7 - 6 \cdot 2 = 30.$
6. $-(a + b) = -a - b.$	$-(7 + 2) = -7 - 2 = -9.$
7. $-(a - b) = -a + b.$	$-(2 - 7) = -2 + 7 = 5.$
8. $-(-a) = a.$	$-(-2) = 2.$
9. $a(0) = (-a)(0) = 0.$	$2(0) = (-2)(0) = 0.$
10. $(-a)(b) = -(ab) = a(-b).$	$(-2)(7) = -(2 \cdot 7) = 2(-7).$
11. $(-a)(-b) = ab.$	$(-2)(-7) = 2 \cdot 7 = 14.$
12. $\dfrac{a}{1} = a.$	$\dfrac{7}{1} = 7, \dfrac{-2}{1} = -2.$
13. $\dfrac{a}{b} = a\left(\dfrac{1}{b}\right).$	$\dfrac{2}{7} = 2\left(\dfrac{1}{7}\right).$
14. $\dfrac{a}{-b} = -\dfrac{a}{b} = \dfrac{-a}{b}.$	$\dfrac{2}{-7} = -\dfrac{2}{7} = \dfrac{-2}{7}.$
15. $\dfrac{-a}{-b} = \dfrac{a}{b}.$	$\dfrac{-2}{-7} = \dfrac{2}{7}.$
16. $\dfrac{0}{a} = 0$ when $a \neq 0.$	$\dfrac{0}{7} = 0.$
17. $\dfrac{a}{a} = 1$ when $a \neq 0.$	$\dfrac{2}{2} = 1, \dfrac{-5}{-5} = 1.$

18. $a\left(\dfrac{b}{a}\right) = b.$ $2\left(\dfrac{7}{2}\right) = 7.$

19. $a \cdot \dfrac{1}{a} = 1$ when $a \neq 0.$ $2 \cdot \dfrac{1}{2} = 1.$

20. $\dfrac{a}{b} \cdot \dfrac{c}{d} = \dfrac{ac}{bd}.$ $\dfrac{2}{3} \cdot \dfrac{4}{5} = \dfrac{2 \cdot 4}{3 \cdot 5} = \dfrac{8}{15}.$

21. $\dfrac{ab}{c} = \left(\dfrac{a}{c}\right)b = a\left(\dfrac{b}{c}\right).$ $\dfrac{2 \cdot 7}{3} = \dfrac{2}{3} \cdot 7 = 2 \cdot \dfrac{7}{3}.$

22. $\dfrac{a}{bc} = \left(\dfrac{a}{b}\right)\left(\dfrac{1}{c}\right) = \left(\dfrac{1}{b}\right)\left(\dfrac{a}{c}\right).$ $\dfrac{2}{3 \cdot 7} = \dfrac{2}{3} \cdot \dfrac{1}{7} = \dfrac{1}{3} \cdot \dfrac{2}{7}.$

23. $\dfrac{a}{b} = \left(\dfrac{a}{b}\right)\left(\dfrac{c}{c}\right) = \dfrac{ac}{bc}$ $\dfrac{2}{7} = \left(\dfrac{2}{7}\right)\left(\dfrac{5}{5}\right) = \dfrac{2 \cdot 5}{7 \cdot 5}.$

when $c \neq 0.$

24. $\dfrac{a}{b(-c)} = \dfrac{a}{(-b)(c)} = \dfrac{-a}{bc} =$ $\dfrac{2}{3(-5)} = \dfrac{2}{(-3)(5)} = \dfrac{-2}{3(5)} =$

$\dfrac{-a}{(-b)(-c)} = -\dfrac{a}{bc}.$ $\dfrac{-2}{(-3)(-5)} = -\dfrac{2}{3(5)} = -\dfrac{2}{15}.$

25. $\dfrac{a}{c} + \dfrac{b}{c} = \dfrac{a+b}{c}.$ $\dfrac{2}{9} + \dfrac{3}{9} = \dfrac{2+3}{9} = \dfrac{5}{9}.$

26. $\dfrac{a}{c} - \dfrac{b}{c} = \dfrac{a-b}{c}.$ $\dfrac{2}{9} - \dfrac{3}{9} = \dfrac{2-3}{9} = \dfrac{-1}{9}.$

27. $\dfrac{a}{b} + \dfrac{c}{d} = \dfrac{ad+bc}{bd}.$ $\dfrac{4}{5} + \dfrac{2}{3} = \dfrac{4 \cdot 3 + 5 \cdot 2}{5 \cdot 3} = \dfrac{22}{15}.$

28. $\dfrac{a}{b} - \dfrac{c}{d} = \dfrac{ad-bc}{bd}.$ $\dfrac{4}{5} - \dfrac{2}{3} = \dfrac{4 \cdot 3 - 5 \cdot 2}{5 \cdot 3} = \dfrac{2}{15}.$

29. $\dfrac{\dfrac{a}{b}}{\dfrac{c}{d}} = \dfrac{a}{b} \div \dfrac{c}{d} = \dfrac{a}{b} \cdot \dfrac{d}{c} = \dfrac{ad}{bc}.$ $\dfrac{\dfrac{2}{3}}{\dfrac{7}{5}} = \dfrac{2}{3} \div \dfrac{7}{5} = \dfrac{2}{3} \cdot \dfrac{5}{7} = \dfrac{10}{21}.$

30. $\dfrac{a}{\dfrac{b}{c}} = a \div \dfrac{b}{c} = \dfrac{ac}{b}.$ $\dfrac{2}{\dfrac{3}{5}} = 2 \div \dfrac{3}{5} = \dfrac{2 \cdot 5}{3} = \dfrac{10}{3}.$

31. $\dfrac{\dfrac{a}{b}}{c} = \dfrac{a}{b} \div c = \dfrac{a}{bc}.$ $\dfrac{\dfrac{2}{3}}{5} = \dfrac{2}{3} \div 5 = \dfrac{2}{3 \cdot 5} = \dfrac{2}{15}.$

Property 23 is essentially the **fundamental principle of fractions,** which states that *multiplying or dividing both the numerator and denominator of a fraction by the same number, except 0, results in a fraction which is equivalent to (that is, it has the same value as) the original fraction.* Thus

$$\frac{7}{\frac{1}{8}} = \frac{7 \cdot 8}{\frac{1}{8} \cdot 8} = \frac{56}{1} = 56.$$

By Properties 27 and 23 we have

$$\frac{2}{5} + \frac{4}{15} = \frac{2 \cdot 15 + 5 \cdot 4}{5 \cdot 15} = \frac{50}{75} = \frac{2 \cdot 25}{3 \cdot 25} = \frac{2}{3}.$$

We can also do this problem by converting $\frac{2}{5}$ and $\frac{4}{15}$ into equivalent fractions that have the same denominators and then using Property 25. The fractions $\frac{2}{5}$ and $\frac{4}{15}$ can be written with a common denominator of $5 \cdot 15$: $\frac{2}{5} = \frac{2 \cdot 15}{5 \cdot 15}$ and $\frac{4}{15} = \frac{4 \cdot 5}{15 \cdot 5}$. However, 15 is the *least* such common denominator and is called the *least common denominator* (L.C.D.) of $\frac{2}{5}$ and $\frac{4}{15}$. Thus

$$\frac{2}{5} + \frac{4}{15} = \frac{2 \cdot 3}{5 \cdot 3} + \frac{4}{15} = \frac{6}{15} + \frac{4}{15} = \frac{10}{15} = \frac{2}{3}.$$

Similarly,

$$\frac{3}{8} - \frac{5}{12} = \frac{3 \cdot 3}{8 \cdot 3} - \frac{5 \cdot 2}{12 \cdot 2} \qquad (\text{L.C.D.} = 24)$$

$$= \frac{9}{24} - \frac{10}{24} = \frac{9 - 10}{24}$$

$$= -\frac{1}{24}.$$

EXERCISE 0.4

Simplify each of the following if possible.

1. $-2 + (-4)$.
2. $-6 + 2$.
3. $6 + (-4)$.
4. $7 - 2$.

5. $7 - (-4)$.
6. $-7 - (-4)$.
7. $-8 - (-6)$.
8. $(-2)(9)$.

9. $7(-9)$.
10. $(-2)(-12)$.
11. $(-1)6$.
12. $-(-9)$.

13. $-(-6 + x)$.
14. $-7(x)$.
15. $-12(x - y)$.
16. $-[-6 + (-y)]$.

17. $-2 \div 6$.
18. $-2 \div (-4)$.
19. $4 \div (-2)$.
20. $2(-6 + 2)$.

21. $3[-2(3) + 6(2)]$.
22. $(-2)(-4)(-1)$.
23. $(-5)(-5)$.
24. $x(0)$.

25. $3(x - 4)$.
26. $4(5 + x)$.
27. $-(x - 2)$.
28. $0(-x)$.

29. $8\left(\frac{1}{11}\right)$.
30. $\frac{7}{1}$.
31. $\frac{-5x}{7y}$.
32. $\frac{3}{-2x}$.

33. $\dfrac{2}{3} \cdot \dfrac{1}{x}$.

34. $\dfrac{x}{y}(2z)$.

35. $(2x)\left(\dfrac{3}{2x}\right)$.

36. $\dfrac{-15x}{-3y}$.

37. $\dfrac{7}{y} \cdot \dfrac{1}{x}$.

38. $\dfrac{2}{x} \cdot \dfrac{5}{y}$.

39. $\dfrac{1}{2} + \dfrac{1}{3}$.

40. $\dfrac{5}{12} + \dfrac{3}{4}$.

41. $\dfrac{3}{10} - \dfrac{7}{15}$.

42. $\dfrac{2}{3} + \dfrac{7}{3}$.

43. $\dfrac{x}{9} - \dfrac{y}{9}$.

44. $\dfrac{3}{2} - \dfrac{1}{4} + \dfrac{1}{6}$.

45. $\dfrac{2}{3} - \dfrac{5}{8}$.

46. $\dfrac{\dfrac{6}{x}}{y}$.

47. $\dfrac{\dfrac{x}{6}}{y}$.

48. $\dfrac{\dfrac{-7}{2}}{\dfrac{5}{8}}$.

49. $\dfrac{7}{0}$.

50. $\dfrac{0}{7}$.

51. $\dfrac{0}{0}$.

52. $0 \cdot 0$.

0.5 EXPONENTS AND RADICALS

The product $x \cdot x \cdot x$ is abbreviated x^3. In general, for n a positive integer, x^n is the abbreviation for the product of n x's. The letter n in x^n is called the *exponent* and x is called the *base*. More specifically, if n is a positive integer we have:

---

1. $x^n = \underbrace{x \cdot x \cdot x \cdot \ldots \cdot x}_{n \text{ factors}}$.

2. $x^{-n} = \dfrac{1}{x^n} = \dfrac{1}{\underbrace{x \cdot x \cdot x \cdot \ldots \cdot x}_{n \text{ factors}}}$.

3. $\dfrac{1}{x^{-n}} = x^n$.

4. $x^0 = 1$ if $x \neq 0$. 0^0 is not defined.

EXAMPLE 1

a. $\left(\dfrac{1}{2}\right)^4 = \left(\dfrac{1}{2}\right)\left(\dfrac{1}{2}\right)\left(\dfrac{1}{2}\right)\left(\dfrac{1}{2}\right) = \dfrac{1}{16}$.

b. $3^{-5} = \dfrac{1}{3^5} = \dfrac{1}{3 \cdot 3 \cdot 3 \cdot 3 \cdot 3} = \dfrac{1}{243}$.

c. $\dfrac{1}{3^{-5}} = 3^5 = 243$.

d. $2^0 = 1$, $\pi^0 = 1$, $(-5)^0 = 1$.

e. $x^1 = x$.

If $r^n = x$ where n is a positive integer, then r is an nth *root* of x. For example, $3^2 = 9$ and so 3 is a second root (usually called a *square root*) of 9. Since $(-3)^2 = 9$, -3 is also a square root of 9. Similarly, -2 is a *cube root* of -8 since $(-2)^3 = -8$.

Some numbers do not have an nth root that is a real number. For example, since the square of any real number is nonnegative, there is no real number that is a square root of -4.

The **principal nth root** of x is that nth root of x which is positive if x is positive, and is negative if x is negative and n is odd. We denote it by $\sqrt[n]{x}$. Thus

$$\sqrt[n]{x} \text{ is } \begin{cases} \text{positive if } x \text{ is positive,} \\ \text{negative if } x \text{ is negative and } n \text{ is odd.} \end{cases}$$

For example, $\sqrt[2]{9} = 3$, $\sqrt[3]{-8} = -2$, and $\sqrt[3]{\frac{1}{27}} = \frac{1}{3}$. We define $\sqrt[n]{0} = 0$.

The symbol $\sqrt[n]{x}$ is called a **radical.** Here n is the *index*, x is the *radicand*, and $\sqrt{}$ is the *radical sign*. With principal square roots we usually omit the index and write $\sqrt{x}$ instead of $\sqrt[2]{x}$. Thus $\sqrt{9} = 3$.

Pitfall

Although 2 and -2 are square roots of 4, the **principal** square root of 4 is 2, not -2. Hence $\sqrt{4} = 2$.

If x is positive, the expression $x^{p/q}$, where p and q are integers and q is positive, is defined to be $\sqrt[q]{x^p}$. Thus

$$x^{3/4} = \sqrt[4]{x^3}; \qquad 8^{2/3} = \sqrt[3]{8^2} = \sqrt[3]{64} = 4;$$
$$4^{-1/2} = \sqrt[2]{4^{-1}} = \sqrt{\tfrac{1}{4}} = \tfrac{1}{2}.$$

Here are the basic laws of exponents and radicals.*

LAW	EXAMPLE
1. $x^m \cdot x^n = x^{m+n}$.	$2^3 \cdot 2^5 = 2^8 = 256$; $\quad x^2 \cdot x^3 = x^5$.
2. $x^0 = 1$ if $x \neq 0$.	$2^0 = 1$.
3. $x^{-n} = \dfrac{1}{x^n}$.	$2^{-3} = \dfrac{1}{2^3} = \dfrac{1}{8}$.
4. $\dfrac{1}{x^{-n}} = x^n$.	$\dfrac{1}{2^{-3}} = 2^3 = 8$; $\quad \dfrac{1}{x^{-5}} = x^5$.

* Although some laws involve restrictions, they are not vital to our discussion.

5. $\dfrac{x^m}{x^n} = x^{m-n} = \dfrac{1}{x^{n-m}}.$ $\dfrac{2^{12}}{2^8} = 2^4 = 16;$ $\dfrac{x^8}{x^{12}} = \dfrac{1}{x^4}.$

6. $\dfrac{x^m}{x^m} = 1.$ $\dfrac{2^4}{2^4} = 1.$

7. $(x^m)^n = x^{mn}.$ $(2^3)^5 = 2^{15};$ $(x^2)^3 = x^6.$

8. $(xy)^n = x^n y^n.$ $(2 \cdot 4)^3 = 2^3 \cdot 4^3 = 8 \cdot 64.$

9. $\left(\dfrac{x}{y}\right)^n = \dfrac{x^n}{y^n}.$ $\left(\dfrac{2}{3}\right)^3 = \dfrac{2^3}{3^3};$ $\left(\dfrac{1}{3}\right)^5 = \dfrac{1^5}{3^5} = \dfrac{1}{3^5} = 3^{-5}.$

10. $\left(\dfrac{x}{y}\right)^{-n} = \left(\dfrac{y}{x}\right)^n.$ $\left(\dfrac{3}{4}\right)^{-2} = \left(\dfrac{4}{3}\right)^2 = \dfrac{16}{9}.$

11. $x^{1/n} = \sqrt[n]{x}.$ $3^{1/5} = \sqrt[5]{3}.$

12. $x^{-1/n} = \dfrac{1}{x^{1/n}} = \dfrac{1}{\sqrt[n]{x}}.$ $4^{-1/2} = \dfrac{1}{4^{1/2}} = \dfrac{1}{\sqrt{4}} = \dfrac{1}{2}.$

13. $\sqrt[n]{x}\,\sqrt[n]{y} = \sqrt[n]{xy}.$ $\sqrt[3]{9}\,\sqrt[3]{2} = \sqrt[3]{18}.$

14. $\dfrac{\sqrt[n]{x}}{\sqrt[n]{y}} = \sqrt[n]{\dfrac{x}{y}}.$ $\dfrac{\sqrt[3]{90}}{\sqrt[3]{10}} = \sqrt[3]{\dfrac{90}{10}} = \sqrt[3]{9}.$

15. $\sqrt[m]{\sqrt[n]{x}} = \sqrt[mn]{x}.$ $\sqrt[3]{\sqrt[4]{2}} = \sqrt[12]{2}.$

16. $x^{m/n} = \sqrt[n]{x^m} = (\sqrt[n]{x})^m.$ $8^{2/3} = \sqrt[3]{8^2} = (\sqrt[3]{8})^2 = 2^2 = 4.$

17. $(\sqrt[m]{x})^m = x.$ $(\sqrt[8]{7})^8 = 7.$

EXAMPLE 2

a. By Law 1,

$$x^6 x^8 = x^{6+8} = x^{14},$$
$$a^3 b^2 a^5 b = a^3 a^5 b^2 b = a^8 b^3,$$
$$x^{11} x^{-5} = x^{11-5} = x^6,$$
$$z^{2/5} z^{3/5} = z^1 = z,$$
$$x x^{1/2} = x^1 x^{1/2} = x^{3/2}.$$

b. By Law 16,

$$\left(\dfrac{1}{4}\right)^{3/2} = \left(\sqrt{\dfrac{1}{4}}\right)^3 = \left(\dfrac{1}{2}\right)^3 = \dfrac{1}{8}.$$

c. $\left(-\dfrac{8}{27}\right)^{4/3} = \left(\sqrt[3]{\dfrac{-8}{27}}\right)^4 = \left(\dfrac{\sqrt[3]{-8}}{\sqrt[3]{27}}\right)^4$ (Laws 16 and 14)

$$= \left(\dfrac{-2}{3}\right)^4$$

$$= \dfrac{(-2)^4}{3^4} = \dfrac{16}{81}$$ (Law 9).

d. $(64a^3)^{2/3} = 64^{2/3}(a^3)^{2/3}$ (Law 8)

$$= (\sqrt[3]{64})^2 a^2$$ (Laws 16 and 7)

$$= (4)^2 a^2 = 16a^2.$$

Rationalizing the denominator of a fraction is a procedure in which a fraction having a radical in its denominator is expressed as an equivalent fraction without a radical in its denominator. We use the fundamental principle of fractions.

EXAMPLE 3   Rationalize the denominators.

a. $\dfrac{2}{\sqrt{5}} = \dfrac{2}{5^{1/2}} = \dfrac{2 \cdot 5^{1/2}}{5^{1/2} \cdot 5^{1/2}} = \dfrac{2 \cdot 5^{1/2}}{5^1} = \dfrac{2\sqrt{5}}{5}.$

b. $\dfrac{2}{\sqrt[6]{3x^5}} = \dfrac{2}{\sqrt[6]{3} \cdot \sqrt[6]{x^5}} = \dfrac{2}{3^{1/6}x^{5/6}} = \dfrac{2 \cdot 3^{5/6}x^{1/6}}{3^{1/6}x^{5/6} \cdot 3^{5/6}x^{1/6}}$

$$= \dfrac{2(3^5 x)^{1/6}}{3x} = \dfrac{2\sqrt[6]{3^5 x}}{3x}.$$

The following examples illustrate various applications of the laws of exponents and radicals.

EXAMPLE 4

a. Eliminate negative exponents in $\dfrac{x^{-2}y^3}{z^{-2}}$.

$$\dfrac{x^{-2}y^3}{z^{-2}} = x^{-2} \cdot y^3 \cdot \dfrac{1}{z^{-2}} = \dfrac{1}{x^2} \cdot y^3 \cdot z^2 = \dfrac{y^3 z^2}{x^2}.$$

By comparing our answer with the original expression, we can bring a factor of the numerator down to the denominator, and vice versa, by changing the sign of the exponent.

b. Simplify $\dfrac{x^2 y^7}{x^3 y^5}$.

$$\dfrac{x^2 y^7}{x^3 y^5} = \dfrac{y^{7-5}}{x^{3-2}} = \dfrac{y^2}{x}.$$

c. *Eliminate negative exponents in $x^{-1} + y^{-1}$ and simplify.*

$$x^{-1} + y^{-1} = \frac{1}{x} + \frac{1}{y} = \frac{y + x}{xy}. \qquad \left(\text{Note: } x^{-1} + y^{-1} \neq \frac{1}{x + y}.\right)$$

d. *Simplify $x^{3/2} - x^{1/2}$ by using the distributive law.*

$$x^{3/2} - x^{1/2} = x^{1/2}(x - 1).$$

e. *Simplify $(x^5 y^8)^5$.*

$$(x^5 y^8)^5 = (x^5)^5 (y^8)^5 = x^{25} y^{40}.$$

f. *Simplify $(x^{5/9} y^{4/3})^{18}$.*

$$(x^{5/9} y^{4/3})^{18} = (x^{5/9})^{18} (y^{4/3})^{18} = x^{10} y^{24}.$$

g. *Simplify $\left(\dfrac{x^{1/5} y^{6/5}}{z^{2/5}}\right)^5$.*

$$\left(\frac{x^{1/5} y^{6/5}}{z^{2/5}}\right)^5 = \frac{(x^{1/5} y^{6/5})^5}{(z^{2/5})^5} = \frac{xy^6}{z^2}.$$

h. *Eliminate negative exponents in $7x^{-2} + (7x)^{-2}$.*

$$7x^{-2} + (7x)^{-2} = \frac{7}{x^2} + \frac{1}{(7x)^2} = \frac{7}{x^2} + \frac{1}{49x^2}.$$

i. *Eliminate negative exponents in $(x^{-1} - y^{-1})^{-2}$.*

$$(x^{-1} - y^{-1})^{-2} = \left(\frac{1}{x} - \frac{1}{y}\right)^{-2} = \left(\frac{y - x}{xy}\right)^{-2}$$

$$= \left(\frac{xy}{y - x}\right)^2 = \frac{x^2 y^2}{(y - x)^2}.$$

j. *Apply the distributive law to $x^{2/5}(y^{1/2} + 2z^{6/5})$.*

$$x^{2/5}(y^{1/2} + 2x^{6/5}) = x^{2/5} y^{1/2} + 2x^{8/5}.$$

k. *Simplify $\dfrac{x^3}{y^2} \div \dfrac{x^6}{y^5}$.*

$$\frac{x^3}{y^2} \div \frac{x^6}{y^5} = \frac{x^3}{y^2} \cdot \frac{y^5}{x^6} = \frac{y^3}{x^3}.$$

EXAMPLE 5

a. *Simplify $\sqrt[4]{48}$.*

$$\sqrt[4]{48} = \sqrt[4]{16 \cdot 3} = \sqrt[4]{16} \; \sqrt[4]{3} = 2\sqrt[4]{3}.$$

b. *Rewrite $\sqrt{2 + 5x}$ without using a radical sign.*

$$\sqrt{2 + 5x} = (2 + 5x)^{1/2}.$$

c. *Rationalize the denominator of* $\dfrac{\sqrt[5]{2}}{\sqrt[3]{6}}$ *and simplify.*

$$\frac{\sqrt[5]{2}}{\sqrt[3]{6}} = \frac{2^{1/5} \cdot 6^{2/3}}{6^{1/3} \cdot 6^{2/3}} = \frac{2^{3/15}6^{10/15}}{6} = \frac{(2^3 6^{10})^{1/15}}{6} = \frac{\sqrt[15]{2^3 6^{10}}}{6}.$$

d. *Simplify* $\dfrac{\sqrt{20}}{\sqrt{5}}$.

$$\frac{\sqrt{20}}{\sqrt{5}} = \sqrt{\frac{20}{5}} = \sqrt{4} = 2.$$

e. *Simplify* $\sqrt[3]{x^6 y^4}$.

$$\sqrt[3]{x^6 y^4} = \sqrt[3]{(x^2)^3 y^3 y} = \sqrt[3]{(x^2)^3} \cdot \sqrt[3]{y^3} \cdot \sqrt[3]{y}$$
$$= x^2 y \sqrt[3]{y}.$$

f. *Simplify* $\sqrt{\dfrac{2}{7}}$.

$$\sqrt{\frac{2}{7}} = \sqrt{\frac{2}{7} \cdot \frac{7}{7}} = \sqrt{\frac{14}{7^2}} = \frac{\sqrt{14}}{\sqrt{7^2}} = \frac{\sqrt{14}}{7}.$$

g. *Simplify* $\sqrt{250} - \sqrt{50} + 15\sqrt{2}$.

$$\sqrt{250} - \sqrt{50} + 15\sqrt{2} = \sqrt{25 \cdot 10} - \sqrt{25 \cdot 2} + 15\sqrt{2}$$
$$= 5\sqrt{10} - 5\sqrt{2} + 15\sqrt{2}$$
$$= 5\sqrt{10} + 10\sqrt{2}.$$

h. *If x is any real number, simplify* $\sqrt{x^2}$.

$$\sqrt{x^2} = \begin{cases} x, & \text{if } x \text{ is positive,} \\ -x, & \text{if } x \text{ is negative,} \\ 0, & \text{if } x = 0. \end{cases}$$

Thus $\sqrt{2^2} = 2$ and $\sqrt{(-3)^2} = -(-3) = 3$.

EXERCISE 0.5

In Problems **1–14,** *simplify and express all answers in terms of positive exponents.*

1. $(2^3)(2^2)$.

2. $x^6 x^9$.

3. $w^4 w^8$.

4. $x^6 x^4 x^3$.

5. $\dfrac{x^2 x^6}{y^7 y^{10}}$.

6. $(x^{12})^4$.

7. $\dfrac{(x^2)^5}{(y^5)^{10}}$.

8. $\left(\dfrac{x^2}{y^3}\right)^5$.

9. $(2x^2 y^3)^3$.

10. $\left(\dfrac{w^2 s^3}{y^2}\right)^2$.

11. $\dfrac{x^8}{x^2}$.

12. $\left(\dfrac{2x^2}{4x^4}\right)^3$.

13. $\dfrac{(x^3)^6}{x(x^3)}$.

14. $\dfrac{(x^2)^3 (x^3)^2}{(x^3)^4}$.

In Problems **15–28,** *evaluate the expressions.*

15. $\sqrt{25}$.

16. $\sqrt[3]{64}$.

17. $\sqrt[5]{-32}$.

18. $\sqrt{.04}$.

19. $\sqrt[4]{\frac{1}{16}}$.

20. $\sqrt[3]{-\frac{8}{27}}$.

21. $(100)^{1/2}$.

22. $(64)^{1/3}$.

23. $4^{3/2}$.

24. $(25)^{-3/2}$.

25. $(32)^{-2/5}$.

26. $(0.09)^{-1/2}$.

27. $\left(\frac{1}{16}\right)^{5/4}$.

28. $\left(-\frac{27}{64}\right)^{2/3}$.

In Problems **29–38,** *simplify the expressions.*

29. $\sqrt{32}$.

30. $\sqrt[3]{24}$.

31. $\sqrt[3]{2x^3}$.

32. $\sqrt{4x}$.

33. $\sqrt{16x^4}$.

34. $\sqrt[4]{x/16}$.

35. $(9z^4)^{1/2}$.

36. $(16y^8)^{3/4}$.

37. $\left(\frac{27t^3}{8}\right)^{2/3}$.

38. $\left(\frac{1000}{a^9}\right)^{-2/3}$.

In Problems **39–50,** *write the expressions in terms of positive exponents only. Avoid all radicals in the final form. For example,*
$$y^{-1}\sqrt{x} = \frac{x^{1/2}}{y}.$$

39. $\frac{x^3 y^{-2}}{z^2}$.

40. $\sqrt[5]{x^2 y^3 z^{-10}}$.

41. $2x^{-1}x^{-3}$.

42. $x + y^{-1}$.

43. $(3t)^{-2}$.

44. $(3 - z)^{-4}$.

45. $\sqrt[3]{7s^2}$.

46. $(x^{-2}y^2)^{-2}$.

47. $\sqrt{x} - \sqrt{y}$.

48. $\frac{x^{-2}y^{-6}z^2}{xy^{-1}}$.

49. $x^2\sqrt[4]{xy^{-2}z^3}$.

50. $\left(\sqrt[5]{xy^{-3}}\right)x^{-1}y^{-2}$.

In Problems **51–56,** *write the exponential forms in equivalent forms involving radicals.*

51. $(8x - y)^{4/5}$.

52. $(ab^2c^3)^{3/4}$.

53. $x^{-4/5}$.

54. $2x^{1/2} - (2y)^{1/2}$.

55. $2x^{-2/5} - (2x)^{-2/5}$.

56. $[(x^{-4})^{1/5}]^{1/6}$.

In Problems **57–66,** *rationalize the denominators.*

57. $\frac{3}{\sqrt{7}}$.

58. $\frac{5}{\sqrt{11}}$.

59. $\frac{4}{\sqrt{2x}}$.

60. $\frac{y}{\sqrt{2y}}$.

61. $\frac{1}{\sqrt[3]{3x}}$.

62. $\frac{4}{3\sqrt[3]{x^2}}$.

63. $\frac{\sqrt{32}}{\sqrt{2}}$.

64. $\frac{\sqrt{18}}{\sqrt{2}}$.

65. $\frac{\sqrt[4]{2}}{\sqrt[3]{xy^2}}$.

66. $\frac{\sqrt{2}}{\sqrt[3]{3}}$.

In Problems **67–88,** *simplify. Express all answers in terms of positive exponents. Rationalize the denominator where necessary to avoid fractional exponents in the denominator.*

67. $2x^2 y^{-3} x^4$.

68. $\frac{2}{x^{3/2} y^{1/3}}$.

69. $\sqrt{\sqrt[3]{t^4}}$.

70. $\{[(2x^2)^3]^{-4}\}^{-1}$.

71. $\frac{2^0}{(2^{-2}x^{1/2}y^{-2})^3}$.

72. $\frac{\sqrt{s^5}}{\sqrt[3]{s^2}}$.

73. $\sqrt[3]{x^2yz^3}\sqrt[3]{xy^2}.$

74. $(\sqrt[5]{2})^{10}.$

75. $3^2(27)^{-4/3}.$

76. $(\sqrt[5]{x^2y})^{2/5}.$

77. $(2x^{-1}y^2)^2.$

78. $\dfrac{3}{\sqrt[3]{y}\sqrt[4]{x}}.$

79. $\sqrt{x}\sqrt{x^2y^3}\sqrt{xy^2}.$

80. $\sqrt{75k^4}.$

81. $\dfrac{(x^2y^{-1}z)^{-2}}{(xy^2)^{-4}}.$

82. $\sqrt{6(6)}.$

83. $\dfrac{(x^2)^3}{x^4} \div \left[\dfrac{x^3}{(x^3)^2}\right]^{-2}.$

84. $\sqrt{(-6)(-6)}.$

85. $-\dfrac{8s^{-2}}{2s^3}.$

86. $(x^{-1}y^{-2}\sqrt{z})^4.$

87. $(2x^2y \div 3y^3z^{-2})^2.$

88. $\dfrac{1}{\left(\dfrac{\sqrt{2x^{-2}}}{\sqrt{16x^3}}\right)^2}.$

0.6 OPERATIONS WITH ALGEBRAIC EXPRESSIONS

If numbers, represented by symbols, are combined by the operations of addition, subtraction, multiplication, division, or extraction of roots, then the resulting expression is called an *algebraic expression*.

EXAMPLE 1

a. $\sqrt[3]{\dfrac{3x^3 - 5x - 2}{10 - x}}$ is an algebraic expression in the variable x.

b. $10 - 3\sqrt{y} + \dfrac{5}{7 + y^2}$ is an algebraic expression in the variable y.

c. $\dfrac{(x + y)^3 - xy}{y} + 2$ is an algebraic expression in the variables x and y.

The algebraic expression $5ax^3 - 2bx + 3$ consists of three *terms:* $+5ax^3$, $-2bx$, and $+3$. Some of the *factors* of the first term $5ax^3$ are 5, a, x, x^2, x^3, $5ax$, and ax^2. Also, $5a$ is the *coefficient* of x^3 and 5 is the *numerical coefficient* of ax^3. If a and b represent fixed numbers throughout a discussion, then a and b are called *constants*.

Algebraic expressions with exactly one term are called *monomials*. Those having exactly two terms are *binomials*, and those with exactly three terms are *trinomials*. Algebraic expressions with more than one term are called *multinomials*. Thus the multinomial $2x - 5$ is a binomial; the multinomial $3\sqrt{y} + 2y - 4y^2$ is a trinomial.

A *polynomial in x* is an algebraic expression of the form*

$$c_n x^n + c_{n-1} x^{n-1} + \cdots + c_1 x + c_0,$$

where n is a nonnegative integer and the coefficients $c_0, c_1, \ldots, c_n$ are constants with $c_n \neq 0$. We call n the *degree* of the polynomial. Hence $4x^3 - 5x^2 + x - 2$ is a polynomial in x of degree 3, and $y^5 - 2$ is a polynomial in y of degree 5. A nonzero constant is a polynomial of degree zero; thus 5 is a polynomial of degree zero. The constant 0 is considered to be a polynomial; however, no degree is assigned to it.

EXAMPLE 2   *Simplify* $(3x^2 y - 2x + 1) + (4x^2 y + 6x - 3)$.

We shall first remove the parentheses. Next, using the commutative property of addition, we gather all similar terms together. *Similar terms* are those terms which differ only by their numerical coefficients. In our case, $3x^2 y$ and $4x^2 y$ are similar, as are the pairs $-2x$ and $6x$, and 1 and -3. Thus

$$(3x^2 y - 2x + 1) + (4x^2 y + 6x - 3)$$
$$= 3x^2 y - 2x + 1 + 4x^2 y + 6x - 3$$
$$= 3x^2 y + 4x^2 y - 2x + 6x + 1 - 3.$$

By the distributive property,

$$3x^2 y + 4x^2 y = (3 + 4)x^2 y = 7x^2 y$$

and $-2x + 6x = (-2 + 6)x = 4x.$

Hence

$$(3x^2 y - 2x + 1) + (4x^2 y + 6x - 3) = 7x^2 y + 4x - 2.$$

EXAMPLE 3   *Simplify* $(3x^2 y - 2x + 1) - (4x^2 y + 6x - 3)$.

Here we apply the definition of subtraction and the distributive property:

$$(3x^2 y - 2x + 1) - (4x^2 y + 6x - 3)$$
$$= (3x^2 y - 2x + 1) + (-1)(4x^2 y + 6x - 3)$$
$$= (3x^2 y - 2x + 1) + (-4x^2 y - 6x + 3)$$
$$= 3x^2 y - 2x + 1 - 4x^2 y - 6x + 3$$
$$= 3x^2 y - 4x^2 y - 2x - 6x + 1 + 3$$
$$= (3 - 4)x^2 y + (-2 - 6)x + 1 + 3$$
$$= -x^2 y - 8x + 4.$$

---

* The three dots indicate the terms that are understood to be included in the sum.

EXAMPLE 4   *Simplify* $3\{2x[2x + 3] + 5[4x^2 - (3 - 4x)]\}$.

We shall first remove the innermost grouping symbols (parentheses) by using the distributive property. Then we repeat the process until all grouping symbols are removed—combining similar terms whenever possible.

$$3\{2x[2x + 3] + 5[4x^2 - (3 - 4x)]\}$$
$$= 3\{2x[2x + 3] + 5[4x^2 - 3 + 4x]\}$$
$$= 3\{4x^2 + 6x + 20x^2 - 15 + 20x\}$$
$$= 3\{24x^2 + 26x - 15\}$$
$$= 72x^2 + 78x - 45.$$

The distributive property is the key tool in multiplying expressions. For example, to multiply $ax + c$ by $bx + d$ we can consider $ax + c$ as a single number and then use the distributive property.

$$(ax + c)(bx + d) = (ax + c)bx + (ax + c)d.$$

Using the distributive property again, we have

$$(ax + c)bx + (ax + c)d = abx^2 + cbx + adx + cd$$
$$= abx^2 + (ad + cb)x + cd.$$

Thus $(ax + c)(bx + d) = abx^2 + (ad + cb)x + cd$. In particular, if $a = 2$, $b = 1$, $c = 3$, and $d = -2$, then

$$(2x + 3)(x - 2) = 2(1)x^2 + [2(-2) + 3(1)]x + 3(-2)$$
$$= 2x^2 - x - 6.$$

Below is a list of special products which may be obtained from the distributive property and are useful in multiplying algebraic expressions.

SPECIAL PRODUCTS

1. $x(y + z) = xy + xz$ (distributive property).

2. $(x + a)(x + b) = x^2 + (a + b)x + ab$.

3. $(ax + c)(bx + d) = abx^2 + (ad + cb)x + cd$.

4. $(x + a)^2 = x^2 + 2ax + a^2$ (square of a binomial).

5. $(x - a)^2 = x^2 - 2ax + a^2$ (square of a binomial).

6. $(x + a)(x - a) = x^2 - a^2$ (product of sum and difference).

7. $(x + a)^3 = x^3 + 3ax^2 + 3a^2x + a^3$ (cube of a binomial).

8. $(x - a)^3 = x^3 - 3ax^2 + 3a^2x - a^3$ (cube of a binomial).

EXAMPLE 5

a. By Rule 2, $(x + 2)(x - 5) = [x + 2][x + (-5)]$

$$= x^2 + (2 - 5)x + 2(-5)$$
$$= x^2 - 3x - 10.$$

b. By Rule 3, $(3z + 5)(7z + 4) = 3 \cdot 7z^2 + (3 \cdot 4 + 5 \cdot 7)z + 5 \cdot 4$

$$= 21z^2 + 47z + 20.$$

c. By Rule 5, $(x - 4)^2 = x^2 - 2(4)x + 4^2$

$$= x^2 - 8x + 16.$$

d. By Rule 6,

$$(\sqrt{y^2 + 1} + 3)(\sqrt{y^2 + 1} - 3) = (\sqrt{y^2 + 1})^2 - 3^2$$
$$= (y^2 + 1) - 9$$
$$= y^2 - 8.$$

e. By Rule 7,

$$(3x + 2)^3 = (3x)^3 + 3(2)(3x)^2 + 3(2)^2(3x) + (2)^3$$
$$= 27x^3 + 54x^2 + 36x + 8.$$

EXAMPLE 6   *Multiply:* $(2t - 3)(5t^2 + 3t - 1)$.

We treat $2t - 3$ as a single number and apply the distributive property twice.

$$(2t - 3)(5t^2 + 3t - 1) = (2t - 3)5t^2 + (2t - 3)3t - (2t - 3)1$$
$$= 10t^3 - 15t^2 + 6t^2 - 9t - 2t + 3$$
$$= 10t^3 - 9t^2 - 11t + 3.$$

In Example 2(c) of Sec. 0.3 we showed that $\dfrac{a + b}{c} = \dfrac{a}{c} + \dfrac{b}{c}$. Similarly,

$\dfrac{a - b}{c} = \dfrac{a}{c} - \dfrac{b}{c}$. Using these results, we can divide a multinomial by a mon-

omial by dividing each term in the multinomial by the monomial.

EXAMPLE 7

a. $\dfrac{x^3 + 3x}{x} = \dfrac{x^3}{x} + \dfrac{3x}{x} = x^2 + 3.$

b. $\dfrac{4z^3 - 8z^2 + 3z - 6}{2z} = \dfrac{4z^3}{2z} - \dfrac{8z^2}{2z} + \dfrac{3z}{2z} - \dfrac{6}{2z}$

$$= 2z^2 - 4z + \frac{3}{2} - \frac{3}{z}.$$

To divide a polynomial by a polynomial, we use so-called "long division" when the degree of the divisor is less than or equal to the degree of the dividend, as the next example shows.

EXAMPLE 8   *Divide $2x^3 - 14x - 5$ by $x - 3$.*

Here $2x^3 - 14x - 5$ is the *dividend* and $x - 3$ is the *divisor*. To avoid errors it is best to write the dividend as $2x^3 + 0x^2 - 14x - 5$. Note that the powers of x are in decreasing order.

$$
\begin{array}{r}
2x^2 + 6x + 4 \leftarrow \text{quotient} \\
x - 3 \overline{)\, 2x^3 + 0x^2 - 14x - 5} \\
\underline{2x^3 - 6x^2} \\
6x^2 - 14x \\
\underline{6x^2 - 18x} \\
4x - 5 \\
\underline{4x - 12} \\
7 \leftarrow \text{remainder.}
\end{array}
$$

Here we divided x (the first term of the divisor) into $2x^3$ and got $2x^2$. Then we multiplied $2x^2$ by $x - 3$, getting $2x^3 - 6x^2$. After subtracting $2x^3 - 6x^2$ from $2x^3 + 0x^2$, we obtained $6x^2$ and then "brought down" the term $-14x$. This process is continued until we arrive at 7, the *remainder*. We always stop when the remainder is 0 or is a polynomial whose degree is less than the degree of the divisor. Our answer may be written as

$$2x^2 + 6x + 4 + \frac{7}{x - 3}.$$

A way of checking a division is to verfiy that

$$\text{(quotient)(divisor)} + \text{remainder} = \text{dividend.}$$

By using this equation you should verify the result of the example.

EXERCISE 0.6

Perform the indicated operations and simplify.

1. $(8x - 4y + 2) + (3x + 2y - 5)$.

2. $(6x^2 - 10xy + 2) + (2z - xy + 4)$.

3. $(8t^2 - 6s^2) + (4s^2 - 2t^2 + 6)$.

4. $(\sqrt{x} + 2\sqrt{x}) + (\sqrt{x} + 3\sqrt{x})$.

5. $(\sqrt{x} + \sqrt{2}y) + (\sqrt{x} + \sqrt{3}z)$.

6. $(3x + 2y - 5) - (8x - 4y + 2)$.

7. $(6x^2 - 10xy + \sqrt{2}) - (2z - xy + 4)$.

8. $(\sqrt{x} + 2\sqrt{x}) - (\sqrt{x} + 3\sqrt{x})$.

9. $(\sqrt{x} + \sqrt{2}y) - (\sqrt{x} + \sqrt{3}z)$.

10. $4(2z - w) - 3(w - 2z)$.

11. $3(3x + 2y - 5) - 2(8x - 4y + 2)$.

12. $(2s + t) - 3(s - 6) + 4(1 - t)$.

13. $3(x^2 + y^2) - x(y + 2x) + 2y(x + 3y)$.

14. $2 - [3 + 4(s - 3)]$.

15. $2\{3[3(x^2 + 2) - 2(x^2 - 5)]\}$.

16. $4\{3(t + 5) - t[1 - (t + 1)]\}$.

17. $-3\{4x(x + 2) - 2[x^2 - (3 - x)]\}$.

18. $-\{-2[2a + 3b - 1] + 4[a - 2b] - a[2(b - 3)]\}$.

19. $(x + 4)(x + 5)$.

20. $(x + 3)(x + 2)$.

21. $(x + 3)(x - 2)$.

22. $(z - 7)(z - 3)$.

23. $(2x + 3)(5x + 2)$.

24. $(y - 4)(2y + 3)$.

25. $(x + 3)^2$.

26. $(2x - 1)^2$.

27. $(x - 5)^2$.

28. $(\sqrt{x} - 1)(2\sqrt{x} + 5)$.

29. $(\sqrt{2y} + 3)^2$.

30. $(y - 3)(y + 3)$.

31. $(2s - 1)(2s + 1)$.

32. $(z^2 - 3w)(z^2 + 3w)$.

33. $(x^2 - 3)(x + 4)$.

34. $(x + 1)(x^2 + x + 3)$.

35. $(x^2 - 1)(2x^2 + 2x - 3)$.

36. $(2x - 1)(3x^3 + 7x^2 - 5)$.

37. $x\{3(x - 1)(x - 2) + 2[x\{x + 7\}]\}$.

38. $[(2z + 1)(2z - 1)](4z^2 + 1)$.

39. $(x + y + 2)(3x + 2y - 4)$.

40. $(x^2 + x + 1)^2$.

41. $(x + 5)^3$.

42. $(x - 2)^3$.

43. $(2x - 3)^3$.

44. $(x + 2y)^3$.

45. $\dfrac{z^2 - 4z}{z}$.

46. $\dfrac{2x^3 - 7x + 4}{x}$.

47. $\dfrac{6x^5 + 4x^3 - 1}{2x^2}$.

48. $\dfrac{(3x - 4) - (x + 8)}{4x}$.

49. $(x^2 + 3x - 1) \div (x + 3)$.

50. $(x^2 - 5x + 4) \div (x - 4)$.

51. $(3x^3 - 2x^2 + x - 3) \div (x + 2)$.

52. $(x^4 + 2x^2 + 1) \div (x - 1)$.

53. $t^2 \div (t - 8)$.

54. $(4x^2 + 6x + 1) \div (2x - 1)$.

55. $(3x^2 - 4x + 3) \div (3x + 2)$.

56. $(z^3 + z^2 + z) \div (z^2 - z + 1)$.

0.7 FACTORING

If two or more expressions are multiplied together, the expressions are called *factors* of the product. Thus if $c = ab$, then a and b are both factors of the product c. The process by which an expression is written as a product of its factors is called *factoring*.

Listed below are factorization rules, most of which arise from the special products discussed in Sec. 0.6. The right side of each identity is the factored form of the left side.

FACTORING RULES

1. $xy + xz = x(y + z)$ (common factor).

2. $x^2 + (a + b)x + ab = (x + a)(x + b)$.

3. $abx^2 + (ad + cb)x + cd = (ax + c)(bx + d)$.

4. $x^2 + 2ax + a^2 = (x + a)^2$ (perfect-square trinominal).

5. $x^2 - 2ax + a^2 = (x - a)^2$ (perfect-square trinomial).

6. $x^2 - a^2 = (x + a)(x - a)$ (difference of two squares).

7. $x^3 + a^3 = (x + a)(x^2 - ax + a^2)$ (sum of two cubes).

8. $x^3 - a^3 = (x - a)(x^2 + ax + a^2)$ (difference of two cubes).

When factoring a polynomial we usually choose factors which themselves are polynomials. For example, $x^2 - 4 = (x + 2)(x - 2)$. We shall not write $x - 4$ as $(\sqrt{x} + 2)(\sqrt{x} - 2)$.

Always factor completely. For example,

$$2x^2 - 8 = 2(x^2 - 4) = 2(x + 2)(x - 2).$$

EXAMPLE 1   *Completely factor the expressions.*

a. $3k^2x^2 + 9k^3x$.

Since $3k^2x^2 = (3k^2x)(x)$ and $9k^3x = (3k^2x)(3k)$, each term of the original expression contains the common factor $3k^2x$. Thus, by Rule 1,

$$3k^2x^2 + 9k^3x = 3k^2x(x + 3k).$$

Note that although $3k^2x^2 + 9k^3x = 3(k^2x^2 + 3k^3x)$, we do not say that the expression is completely factored since $k^2x^2 + 3k^3x$ can yet be factored.

b. $8a^5x^2y^3 - 6a^2b^3yz - 2a^4b^4xy^2z^2$.

$$8a^5x^2y^3 - 6a^2b^3yz - 2a^4b^4xy^2z^2$$
$$= 2a^2y(4a^3x^2y^2 - 3b^3z - a^2b^4xyz^2).$$

c. $3x^2 + 6x + 3$.

$$3x^2 + 6x + 3 = 3(x^2 + 2x + 1)$$
$$= 3(x + 1)^2   \text{(Rule 4)}.$$

EXAMPLE 2   *Completely factor the expressions.*

a. $x^2 - x - 6$.

If this trinomial factors into the form $x^2 - x - 6 = (x + a)(x + b)$, which is a product of two binomials, then we must determine the values of a and b. Since $(x + a)(x + b) = x^2 + (a + b)x + ab$, then

$$x^2 + (-1)x + (-6) = x^2 + (a + b)x + ab.$$

By equating corresponding coefficients, we want

$$a + b = -1 \quad \text{and} \quad ab = -6.$$

If $a = -3$ and $b = 2$, then both conditions are met and hence

$$x^2 - x - 6 = (x - 3)(x + 2).$$

b. $x^2 - 7x + 12$.

$$x^2 - 7x + 12 = (x - 3)(x - 4).$$

EXAMPLE 3   Listed below are expressions that are completely factored. The numbers in parentheses refer to the rules used.

a. $x^2 + 8x + 16 = (x + 4)^2$ (4).

b. $9x^2 + 9x + 2 = (3x + 1)(3x + 2)$ (3).

c. $6y^3 + 3y^2 - 18y = 3y(2y^2 + y - 6)$ (1)

$$= 3y(2y - 3)(y + 2) \qquad (3).$$

d. $x^2 - 6x + 9 = (x - 3)^2$ (5).

e. $z^{1/4} + z^{5/4} = z^{1/4}(1 + z)$ (1).

f. $x^4 - 1 = (x^2 + 1)(x^2 - 1)$ (6)

$$= (x^2 + 1)(x + 1)(x - 1) \qquad (6).$$

g. $x^{2/3} - 5x^{1/3} + 4 = (x^{1/3} - 1)(x^{1/3} - 4)$ (2).

h. $ax^2 - ay^2 + bx^2 - by^2 = (ax^2 - ay^2) + (bx^2 - by^2)$

$$= a(x^2 - y^2) + b(x^2 - y^2) \qquad (1)$$

$$= (x^2 - y^2)(a + b) \qquad (1)$$

$$= (x + y)(x - y)(a + b) \qquad (6).$$

i. $8 - x^3 = (2)^3 - (x)^3 = (2 - x)(4 + 2x + x^2)$ (8).

j. $x^6 - y^6 = (x^3)^2 - (y^3)^2 = (x^3 + y^3)(x^3 - y^3)$ (6)

$$= (x + y)(x^2 - xy + y^2)(x - y)(x^2 + xy + y^2) \qquad (7),\ (8).$$

Note in Example 3(f) that $x^2 - 1$ is factorable but $x^2 + 1$ is not. In Example 3(h) we factored by making use of grouping.

EXERCISE 0.7

Completely factor the expressions.

1. $6x + 4$.

2. $6y^2 - 4y$.

3. $10xy + 5xz$.

4. $3x^2y - 9x^3y^3$.

5. $8a^3bc - 12ab^3cd + 4b^4c^2d^2$.

6. $6z^2t^3 + 3zst^4 - 12z^2t^3$.

7. $x^2 - 25$.

8. $x^2 + 3x - 4$.

9. $p^2 + 4p + 3$.

10. $s^2 - 6s + 8$.

11. $16x^2 - 9$.

12. $x^2 + 5x - 24$.

13. $z^2 + 6z + 8$.

14. $4t^2 - 9s^2$.

15. $x^2 + 6x + 9$.

16. $y^2 - 15y + 50$.

17. $2x^2 + 12x + 16$.

18. $2x^2 + 7x - 15$.

19. $3x^2 - 3$.

20. $4y^2 - 8y + 3$.

21. $6y^2 + 13y + 2$.

22. $4x^2 - x - 3$.

23. $12s^3 + 10s^2 - 8s$.

24. $9z^2 + 24z + 16$.

25. $x^{2/3}y - 4x^{8/3}y^3$.

26. $9x^{4/7} - 1$.

27. $2x^3 + 2x^2 - 12x$.

28. $x^2y^2 - 4xy + 4$.

29. $(4x + 2)^2$.

30. $3s^2(3s - 9s^2)^2$.

31. $x^3y^2 - 10x^2y + 25x$.

32. $(3x^2 + x) + (6x + 2)$.

33. $(x^3 - 4x) + (8 - 2x^2)$.

34. $(x^2 - 1) + (x^2 - x - 2)$.

35. $(y^{10} + 8y^6 + 16y^2) - (y^8 + 8y^4 + 16)$.

36. $x^3y - xy + z^2x^2 - z^2$.

37. $x^3 + 8$.

38. $x^3 - 1$.

39. $x^6 - 1$.

40. $27 + 8x^3$.

41. $(x + 3)^3(x - 1) + (x + 3)^2(x - 1)^2$.

42. $(x + 5)^2(x + 1)^3 + (x + 5)^3(x + 1)^2$.

43. $P(1 + r) + P(1 + r)r$.

44. $(x - 3)(2x + 3) - (2x + 3)(x + 5)$.

45. $x^4 - 16$.

46. $81x^4 - y^4$.

47. $y^8 - 1$.

48. $t^4 - 4$.

49. $x^4 + x^2 - 2$.

50. $x^4 - 5x^2 + 4$.

51. $x^5 - 2x^3 + x$.

52. $4x^3 - 6x^2 - 4x$.

0.8   FRACTIONS _____

By using the fundamental principle of fractions (Sec. 0.4), we may be able to simplify fractions. That principle allows us to multiply or divide both the numerator and the denominator of a fraction by the same nonzero quantity. The resulting fraction will be equivalent to the original one. The fractions that we shall consider are assumed to have nonzero denominators.

EXAMPLE 1   *Simplify.*

a. $\dfrac{x^2 - x - 6}{x^2 - 7x + 12}$.

First, we completely factor the numerator and denominator.

$$\frac{x^2 - x - 6}{x^2 - 7x + 12} = \frac{(x - 3)(x + 2)}{(x - 3)(x - 4)}.$$

Dividing both numerator and denominator by the common factor $x - 3$, we have

$$\frac{(x - 3)(x + 2)}{(x - 3)(x - 4)} = \frac{1(x + 2)}{1(x - 4)} = \frac{x + 2}{x - 4}.$$

Usually, we just write

$$\frac{x^2 - x - 6}{x^2 - 7x + 12} = \frac{\overset{1}{\cancel{(x - 3)}}(x + 2)}{\underset{1}{\cancel{(x - 3)}}(x - 4)} = \frac{x + 2}{x - 4}$$

or

$$\frac{x^2 - x - 6}{x^2 - 7x + 12} = \frac{(x - 3)(x + 2)}{(x - 3)(x - 4)} = \frac{x + 2}{x - 4}.$$

The process we have used here is commonly referred to as "cancellation."

b. $\dfrac{2x^2 + 6x - 8}{8 - 4x - 4x^2}$.

$$\frac{2x^2 + 6x - 8}{8 - 4x - 4x^2} = \frac{2(x^2 + 3x - 4)}{4(2 - x - x^2)} = \frac{2(x - 1)(x + 4)}{4(1 - x)(2 + x)}$$

$$= \frac{2(x - 1)(x + 4)}{2(2)[(-1)(x - 1)](2 + x)}$$

$$= \frac{x + 4}{-2(2 + x)} = -\frac{x + 4}{2(x + 2)}.$$

If we wish to multiply $\dfrac{a}{b}$ by $\dfrac{c}{d}$, then

$$\frac{a}{b} \cdot \frac{c}{d} = \frac{ac}{bd}.$$

To divide $\dfrac{a}{b}$ by $\dfrac{c}{d}$, where $c \neq 0$, we have

$$\frac{a}{b} \div \frac{c}{d} = \frac{\dfrac{a}{b}}{\dfrac{c}{d}} = \frac{a}{b} \cdot \frac{d}{c}.$$

EXAMPLE 2

a. $\dfrac{x}{x + 2} \cdot \dfrac{x + 3}{x - 5} = \dfrac{x(x + 3)}{(x + 2)(x - 5)}.$

b. $\dfrac{x^2 - 4x + 4}{x^2 + 2x - 3} \cdot \dfrac{6x^2 - 6}{x^2 + 2x - 8} = \dfrac{[(x - 2)^2][6(x + 1)(x - 1)]}{[(x + 3)(x - 1)][(x + 4)(x - 2)]}$

$$= \frac{6(x - 2)(x + 1)}{(x + 3)(x + 4)}.$$

c. $\dfrac{x}{x + 2} \div \dfrac{x + 3}{x - 5} = \dfrac{x}{x + 2} \cdot \dfrac{x - 5}{x + 3} = \dfrac{x(x - 5)}{(x + 2)(x + 3)}.$

d. $\dfrac{\dfrac{x - 5}{x - 3}}{2x} = \dfrac{\dfrac{x - 5}{x - 3}}{\dfrac{2x}{1}} = \dfrac{x - 5}{x - 3} \cdot \dfrac{1}{2x} = \dfrac{x - 5}{2x(x - 3)}.$

e. $\dfrac{\dfrac{4x}{x^2 - 1}}{\dfrac{2x^2 + 8x}{x - 1}} = \dfrac{4x}{x^2 - 1} \cdot \dfrac{x - 1}{2x^2 + 8x} = \dfrac{4x(x - 1)}{[(x + 1)(x - 1)][2x(x + 4)]}$

$$= \frac{2}{(x + 1)(x + 4)}.$$

Sometimes a denominator of a fraction has two terms and involves square roots, such as $2 - \sqrt{3}$ or $\sqrt{5} + \sqrt{2}$. The denominator may be rationalized by multiplying by an expression that makes the denominator a difference of two squares. For example,

$$\frac{4}{\sqrt{5} + \sqrt{2}} = \frac{4}{\sqrt{5} + \sqrt{2}} \cdot \frac{\sqrt{5} - \sqrt{2}}{\sqrt{5} - \sqrt{2}}$$

$$= \frac{4(\sqrt{5} - \sqrt{2})}{(\sqrt{5})^2 - (\sqrt{2})^2} = \frac{4(\sqrt{5} - \sqrt{2})}{5 - 2}$$

$$= \frac{4(\sqrt{5} - \sqrt{2})}{3}.$$

EXAMPLE 3   *Rationalize the denominators.*

a. $\dfrac{x}{\sqrt{2} - 6} = \dfrac{x}{\sqrt{2} - 6} \cdot \dfrac{\sqrt{2} + 6}{\sqrt{2} + 6} = \dfrac{x(\sqrt{2} + 6)}{(\sqrt{2})^2 - 6^2}$

$$= \dfrac{x(\sqrt{2} + 6)}{2 - 36} = -\dfrac{x(\sqrt{2} + 6)}{34}.$$

b. $\dfrac{\sqrt{5} - \sqrt{2}}{\sqrt{5} + \sqrt{2}} = \dfrac{\sqrt{5} - \sqrt{2}}{\sqrt{5} + \sqrt{2}} \cdot \dfrac{\sqrt{5} - \sqrt{2}}{\sqrt{5} - \sqrt{2}}$

$$= \dfrac{(\sqrt{5} - \sqrt{2})^2}{5 - 2} = \dfrac{5 - 2\sqrt{5}\sqrt{2} + 2}{3} = \dfrac{7 - 2\sqrt{10}}{3}.$$

In Example 2(c) of Sec 0.3, it was shown that $\dfrac{a}{c} + \dfrac{b}{c} = \dfrac{a + b}{c}$. That is, if we add two fractions having a common denominator, then the result is a fraction whose denominator is the common denominator. The numerator is the sum of the numerators of the original fractions. Similarly, $\dfrac{a}{c} - \dfrac{b}{c} = \dfrac{a - b}{c}$.

EXAMPLE 4

a. $\dfrac{p^2 - 5}{p - 2} + \dfrac{3p + 2}{p - 2} = \dfrac{(p^2 - 5) + (3p + 2)}{p - 2}$

$$= \dfrac{p^2 + 3p - 3}{p - 2}.$$

b. $\dfrac{x^2 - 5x + 4}{x^2 + 2x - 3} - \dfrac{x^2 + 2x}{x^2 + 5x + 6}$

$$= \dfrac{(x - 1)(x - 4)}{(x - 1)(x + 3)} - \dfrac{x(x + 2)}{(x + 2)(x + 3)}$$

$$= \dfrac{x - 4}{x + 3} - \dfrac{x}{x + 3} = \dfrac{(x - 4) - x}{x + 3} = -\dfrac{4}{x + 3}.$$

c. $\dfrac{x^2 + x - 5}{x - 7} - \dfrac{x^2 - 2}{x - 7} + \dfrac{-4x + 8}{x^2 - 9x + 14}$

$$= \dfrac{x^2 + x - 5}{x - 7} - \dfrac{x^2 - 2}{x - 7} + \dfrac{-4(x - 2)}{(x - 2)(x - 7)}$$

$$= \dfrac{(x^2 + x - 5) - (x^2 - 2) + (-4)}{x - 7}$$

$$= \dfrac{x - 7}{x - 7} = 1.$$

To add (or subtract) two fractions with different denominators, use the fundamental principle of fractions to rewrite the fractions as equivalent fractions that have the same denominator. Then proceed with the addition (or subtraction) by the method described above.

For example, to find

$$\frac{2}{x^3(x-3)} + \frac{3}{x(x-3)^2},$$

we can convert the first fraction into an equivalent fraction by multiplying the numerator and denominator by $x - 3$:

$$\frac{2(x-3)}{x^3(x-3)^2};$$

we can convert the second fraction by multiplying the numerator and denominator by x^2:

$$\frac{3x^2}{x^3(x-3)^2}.$$

These fractions have the same denominator. Hence

$$\frac{2}{x^3(x-3)} + \frac{3}{x(x-3)^2} = \frac{2(x-3)}{x^3(x-3)^2} + \frac{3x^2}{x^3(x-3)^2}$$

$$= \frac{3x^2 + 2x - 6}{x^3(x-3)^2}.$$

We could have converted the original fractions into equivalent fractions with any common denominator. However, we chose to convert them into fractions with the denominator $x^3(x-3)^2$. This is the **least common denominator** **(L.C.D.)** of the fractions $2/[x^3(x-3)]$ and $3/[x(x-3)^2]$.

In general, to find the L.C.D. of two or more fractions, first factor each denominator completely. *The L.C.D. is the product of each of the distinct factors appearing in the denominators, each raised to the highest power to which it occurs in any single denominator.*

EXAMPLE 5

a. *Subtract:* $\dfrac{t}{3t+2} - \dfrac{4}{t-1}.$

The L.C.D. is $(3t+2)(t-1)$.

$$\frac{t}{3t+2} - \frac{4}{t-1} = \frac{t(t-1)}{(3t+2)(t-1)} - \frac{4(3t+2)}{(3t+2)(t-1)}$$

$$= \frac{t(t-1) - 4(3t+2)}{(3t+2)(t-1)}$$

$$= \frac{t^2 - t - 12t - 8}{(3t + 2)(t - 1)} = \frac{t^2 - 13t - 8}{(3t + 2)(t - 1)}.$$

b. $\dfrac{4}{q - 1} + 3 = \dfrac{4}{q - 1} + \dfrac{3(q - 1)}{q - 1}$

$$= \frac{4 + 3(q - 1)}{q - 1} = \frac{3q + 1}{q - 1}.$$

EXAMPLE 6

$$\frac{x - 2}{x^2 + 6x + 9} - \frac{x + 2}{2(x^2 - 9)}$$

$$= \frac{x - 2}{(x + 3)^2} - \frac{x + 2}{2(x + 3)(x - 3)} \qquad [\text{L.C.D.} = 2(x + 3)^2(x - 3)]$$

$$= \frac{(x - 2)(2)(x - 3)}{(x + 3)^2(2)(x - 3)} - \frac{(x + 2)(x + 3)}{2(x + 3)(x - 3)(x + 3)}$$

$$= \frac{(x - 2)(2)(x - 3) - (x + 2)(x + 3)}{2(x + 3)^2(x - 3)}$$

$$= \frac{2(x^2 - 5x + 6) - (x^2 + 5x + 6)}{2(x + 3)^2(x - 3)}$$

$$= \frac{2x^2 - 10x + 12 - x^2 - 5x - 6}{2(x + 3)^2(x - 3)}$$

$$= \frac{x^2 - 15x + 6}{2(x + 3)^2(x - 3)}.$$

EXAMPLE 7

$$\frac{\dfrac{1}{x + h} - \dfrac{1}{x}}{h} = \frac{\dfrac{x}{x(x + h)} - \dfrac{x + h}{x(x + h)}}{h} = \frac{\dfrac{x - (x + h)}{x(x + h)}}{h}$$

$$= \frac{\dfrac{-h}{x(x + h)}}{\dfrac{h}{1}} = \frac{-h}{x(x + h)h} = -\frac{1}{x(x + h)}.$$

The original fraction can also be simplified by multiplying the numerator and denominator by $x(x + h)$:

$$\frac{\dfrac{1}{x+h}-\dfrac{1}{x}}{h} = \frac{x(x+h)\left[\dfrac{1}{x+h}-\dfrac{1}{x}\right]}{x(x+h)h}$$

$$= \frac{x-(x+h)}{x(x+h)h} = \frac{-h}{x(x+h)h} = -\frac{1}{x(x+h)}.$$

EXERCISE 0.8

In Problems **1–42,** *perform the operations and simplify as much as possible.*

1. $\dfrac{y^2}{y-3}\cdot\dfrac{-1}{y+2}.$

2. $\dfrac{z^2-4}{z^2+2z}\cdot\dfrac{z^2}{z-2}.$

3. $\dfrac{2x-3}{x-2}\cdot\dfrac{2-x}{2x+3}.$

4. $\dfrac{x^2-y^2}{x+y}\cdot\dfrac{x^2+2xy+y^2}{y-x}.$

5. $\dfrac{2x-2}{x^2-2x-8}\div\dfrac{x^2-1}{x^2+5x+4}.$

6. $\dfrac{x^2+2x}{3x^2-18x+24}\div\dfrac{x^2-x-6}{x^2-4x+4}.$

7. $\dfrac{\dfrac{x^2}{6}}{\dfrac{x}{3}}.$

8. $\dfrac{\dfrac{4x^3}{9x}}{\dfrac{x}{18}}.$

9. $\dfrac{\dfrac{2m}{n^3}}{\dfrac{4m}{n^2}}.$

10. $\dfrac{\dfrac{c+d}{c}}{\dfrac{c-d}{2c}}.$

11. $\dfrac{\dfrac{4x}{3}}{2x}.$

12. $\dfrac{\dfrac{4x}{3}}{2x}.$

13. $\dfrac{\dfrac{-9x^3}{x}}{3}.$

14. $\dfrac{\dfrac{-9x^3}{x}}{3}.$

15. $\dfrac{\dfrac{x-5}{x^2-7x+10}}{x-2}.$

16. $\dfrac{\dfrac{x^2+6x+9}{x}}{x+3}.$

17. $\dfrac{\dfrac{10x^3}{x^2-1}}{\dfrac{5x}{x+1}}.$

18. $\dfrac{\dfrac{x^2-4}{x^2+2x-3}}{\dfrac{x^2-x-6}{x^2-9}}.$

19. $\dfrac{\dfrac{x^2+7x+10}{x^2-2x-8}}{\dfrac{x^2+6x+5}{x^2-3x-4}}.$

20. $\dfrac{\dfrac{(x+2)^2}{3x-2}}{\dfrac{9x+18}{4-9x^2}}.$

21. $\dfrac{\dfrac{4x^2-9}{x^2+3x-4}}{\dfrac{2x-3}{1-x^2}}.$

22. $\dfrac{\dfrac{6x^2y+7xy-3y}{xy-x+5y-5}}{\dfrac{x^3y+4x^2y}{xy-x+4y-4}}.$

23. $\dfrac{x^2}{x+3}+\dfrac{5x+6}{x+3}.$

24. $\dfrac{2}{x+2}+\dfrac{x}{x+2}.$

25. $\dfrac{1}{t}+\dfrac{2}{3t}.$

26. $\dfrac{4}{x^2}-\dfrac{1}{x}.$

27. $1-\dfrac{p^2}{p^2-1}.$

28. $\dfrac{4}{s+4}+s.$

29. $\dfrac{4}{2x-1}+\dfrac{x}{x+3}.$

30. $\dfrac{x+1}{x-1}-\dfrac{x-1}{x+1}.$

31. $\dfrac{1}{x^2-x-2}+\dfrac{1}{x^2-1}.$

32. $\dfrac{y}{3y^2-5y-2}-\dfrac{2}{3y^2-7y+2}.$

33. $\dfrac{4}{x-1} - 3 + \dfrac{-3x^2}{5 - 4x - x^2}.$

34. $\dfrac{2x-3}{2x^2 + 11x - 6} - \dfrac{3x+1}{3x^2 + 16x - 12} + \dfrac{1}{3x-2}.$

35. $(1 + x^{-1})^2.$

36. $(x^{-1} + y^{-1})^2.$

37. $(x^{-1} - y)^{-1}.$

38. $(x - y^{-1})^{-2}.$

39. $\dfrac{1 + \dfrac{1}{x}}{3}.$

40. $\dfrac{\dfrac{x+3}{x}}{x - \dfrac{9}{x}}.$

41. $\dfrac{3 - \dfrac{1}{2x}}{x + \dfrac{x}{x+2}}.$

42. $\dfrac{\dfrac{x-1}{x^2 + 5x + 6} - \dfrac{1}{x+2}}{3 + \dfrac{x-7}{3}}.$

In Problems **43** *and* **44,** *perform the indicated operations, but do not rationalize the denominators.*

43. $\dfrac{2}{\sqrt{x+h}} - \dfrac{2}{\sqrt{x}}.$

44. $\dfrac{x\sqrt{x}}{\sqrt{1+x}} + \dfrac{1}{\sqrt{x}}.$

In Problems **45–54,** *simplify and express your answer in a form that is free of radicals in the denominator.*

45. $\dfrac{1}{2 + \sqrt{3}}.$

46. $\dfrac{1}{1 - \sqrt{2}}.$

47. $\dfrac{\sqrt{2}}{\sqrt{3} - \sqrt{6}}.$

48. $\dfrac{5}{\sqrt{6} + \sqrt{7}}.$

49. $\dfrac{2\sqrt{2}}{\sqrt{2} - \sqrt{3}}.$

50. $\dfrac{2\sqrt{3}}{\sqrt{5} - \sqrt{2}}.$

51. $\dfrac{1}{x + \sqrt{5}}.$

52. $\dfrac{x-3}{\sqrt{x} - 1} + \dfrac{4}{\sqrt{x} - 1}.$

53. $\dfrac{5}{1 + \sqrt{3}} - \dfrac{4}{2 - \sqrt{2}}.$

54. $\dfrac{4}{\sqrt{x} + 2} \cdot \dfrac{x^2}{3}.$

Equations

Even beginning students in many areas of study are soon faced with solving elementary equations. In this chapter we shall develop techniques to accomplish this task. These methods will be applied in the next chapter to some practical situations.

1.1 LINEAR EQUATIONS

An **equation** is a statement that two expressions are equal. The two expressions that make up an equation are called its **sides** or **members.** They are separated by the **equality sign** "$=$."

EXAMPLE 1   *The following are equations.*

a. $x + 2 = 3$.

b. $x^2 + 3x + 2 = 0$.

c. $\dfrac{y}{y - 5} = 7$.

d. $w = 7 - z$.

In Example 1 each equation contains at least one variable. A **variable** is a symbol that can be replaced by any one of a set of different numbers. The most popular symbols for variables are letters from the latter part of the alphabet, such as x, y, z, w, and t. Hence equations (a) and (c) are said to be in the variables x and y, respectively. Equation (d) is in the variables w and z. In the equation $x + 2 = 3$, the numbers 2 and 3 are called *constants*. They are fixed numbers.

We never allow a variable to have a value for which any expression in the equation is undefined. Thus in $y/(y - 5) = 7$, y cannot be 5 since this would result in a denominator of 0.

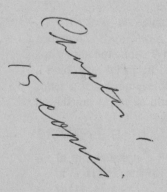

n means to find all values of its variables for which the
ues are called *solutions* of the equation and are said to
only one variable is involved, a solution is also called
ons is called the **solution set** of the equation. Some-
n unknown quantity in an equation is simply called
these terms.

the variable x is the unknown. The only value
ion is 1. Hence 1 is a root and the solution set

.....on in two unknowns. One solution is the pair of
and $z = 3$. However, there are infinitely many solutions. Can
....nk of another?

c. -2 is a root of $x^2 + 3x + 2 = 0$ because substituting -2 for x makes the
equation true: $(-2)^2 + 3(-2) + 2 = 0$.

In solving an equation we want any operation on it to result in another
equation having exactly the same solutions as the given equation. When this
occurs, the equations are said to be **equivalent.** There are three operations that
guarantee equivalence:

> **1.** Adding (subtracting) the same polynomial* to (from) both
> sides of an equation, where the polynomial is in the same
> variable as that occurring in the equation.

For example, if $3x = 5 - 6x$, then adding $6x$ to both sides gives the equivalent
equation $3x + 6x = 5 - 6x + 6x$, or $9x = 5$.

> **2.** Multiplying (dividing) both sides of an equation by the same
> constant, except by zero.

For example, if $10x = 5$, then dividing both sides by 10 gives the equivalent
equation $\dfrac{10x}{10} = \dfrac{5}{10}$, or $x = \dfrac{1}{2}$.

> **3.** Replacing either side of an equation by an equal expression.

* See Sec. 0.6 for a definition of a polynominal.

For example, if $x(x + 2) = 3$, then replacing the left side by the equal expression $x^2 + 2x$ gives the equivalent equation $x^2 + 2x = 3$.

We repeat: Applying operations 1–3 guarantees that the resulting equation is equivalent to the given one. However, sometimes in solving an equation we have to apply operations other than 1–3. These operations may *not* necessarily result in equivalent equations. They include:

> **4.** Multiplying both sides of an equation by an expression involving the variable;
>
> **5.** Dividing both sides of an equation by an expression involving the variable;
>
> **6.** Raising both sides of an equation to equal powers.

Let us illustrate the last three operations. For example, by inspection the only root of $x - 1 = 0$ is 1. Multiplying each side by x (operation 4) gives $x^2 - x = 0$, which is satisfied if x is 0 or 1 (check this by substitution). But 0 *does not* satisfy the *original* equation. Thus the equations are not equivalent.

Continuing, you may check that $(x - 4)(x - 3) = 0$ is satisfied when x is 4 or 3. Dividing both sides by $x - 4$ (operation 5) gives $x - 3 = 0$, whose only root is 3. Again, we do not have equivalence since, in this case, a root has been "lost." Note that when x is 4, division by $x - 4$ implies division by 0, an invalid operation.

Finally, squaring each side of the equation $x = 2$ (operation 6) gives $x^2 = 4$, which is true if $x = 2$ or -2. But -2 is not a root of the given equation.

From our discussion it is clear that when operations 4–6 are performed, we must be careful about drawing conclusions concerning the roots of a given equation. Operations 4 and 6 *can* produce an equation with more roots. Thus you should check whether or not each "solution" obtained by these operations satisfies the *original* equation. Operation 5 *can* produce an equation with fewer roots. In this case, any "lost" root may never be determined. Thus, avoid operation 5 whenever possible.

In summary, an equation may be thought of as a set of restrictions on any variable in the equation. Operations 4–6 may increase or decrease the restrictions, giving different solutions from the original equation. However, operations 1–3 never affect the restrictions.

The principles presented so far will now be demonstrated in the solution of a *linear equation*.

Definition

*A **linear equation** in the variable x is an equation that can be written in the form*

$$ax + b = 0, \tag{1}$$

where a and b are constants and $a \neq 0$.

A linear equation is also called a *first-degree equation* or an *equation of degree one,* since the highest power of the variable that occurs in Eq. (1) is the first.

To solve a linear equation we perform operations on it until we have an equivalent equation whose solutions are *obvious*. This means an equation in which the variable is isolated on one side, as the following examples show.

EXAMPLE 3   *Solve $5x - 6 = 3x$.*

We begin by getting the terms involving x on one side and the constants on the other.

$$5x - 6 = 3x,$$

$$5x - 6 + (-3x) = 3x + (-3x) \quad \text{(adding } -3x \text{ to both sides)},$$

$$2x - 6 = 0 \quad \text{(simplifying, that is, operation 3)},$$

$$2x - 6 + 6 = 0 + 6 \quad \text{(adding 6 to both sides)},$$

$$2x = 6 \quad \text{(simplifying)},$$

$$\frac{2x}{2} = \frac{6}{2} \quad \text{(dividing both sides by 2)},$$

$$x = 3.$$

Clearly, 3 is the only root of the last equation. Since each equation is equivalent to the one before it, we conclude that 3 must be the only root of $5x - 6 = 3x$. That is, the solution set is {3}. We can describe the first step in the solution as moving a term from one side of an equation to the other while changing its sign; this is commonly called *transposing*. Note that since the original equation can be put in the form $2x + (-6) = 0$, it is a linear equation.

EXAMPLE 4   *Solve $2(p + 4) = 7p + 2$.*

First, we remove parentheses.

$$2(p + 4) = 7p + 2,$$

$$2p + 8 = 7p + 2 \quad \text{(distributive property)},$$

$$2p = 7p - 6 \quad \text{(subtracting 8 from both sides)},$$

$$-5p = -6 \quad \text{(subtracting } 7p \text{ from both sides)},$$

$$p = \frac{-6}{-5} \quad \text{(dividing both sides by } -5),$$

$$p = \frac{6}{5}.$$

EXAMPLE 5   *Solve* $\dfrac{7x + 3}{2} - \dfrac{9x - 8}{4} = 6.$

We first clear of fractions by multiplying *both* sides by the least common denominator (L.C.D.),* which is 4.

$$4\left(\frac{7x + 3}{2} - \frac{9x - 8}{4}\right) = 4(6),$$

$$4 \cdot \frac{7x + 3}{2} - 4 \cdot \frac{9x - 8}{4} = 24 \qquad \text{(distributive property)},$$

$$2(7x + 3) - (9x - 8) = 24 \qquad \text{(simplifying)},$$

$$14x + 6 - 9x + 8 = 24 \qquad \text{(distributive property)},$$

$$5x + 14 = 24 \qquad \text{(simplifying)},$$

$$5x = 10 \qquad \text{(subtracting 14 from both sides)},$$

$$x = 2. \qquad \text{(dividing both sides by 5)}.$$

Each equation in Examples 3–5 has one and only one root. This is typical of every linear equation in one variable.

Equations in which some of the constants are represented by letters are called **literal equations.** For example, in the literal equation $x + a = 4b$ we consider a and b to be unspecified constants. Formulas, such as $I = Prt$, which express a relationship between certain quantities, may be regarded as literal equations. If we want to express a particular letter in a formula in terms of the others, this letter is considered the unknown.

EXAMPLE 6

a. *The equation $I = Prt$ is the formula for the simple interest I on a principal of P dollars at the annual interest rate of r for a period of t years. Express r in terms of I, P, and t.*

Here we consider r to be the unknown. To isolate r we divide both sides by Pt.

$$I = Prt,$$

$$\frac{I}{Pt} = \frac{Prt}{Pt},$$

$$\frac{I}{Pt} = r \qquad \text{or} \qquad r = \frac{I}{Pt}.$$

When we divided both sides by Pt, we assumed $Pt \neq 0$ since we cannot divide by 0. Similar assumptions will be made in solving other literal equations.

---

* The *least common denominator* of two or more fractions is the smallest number with all the denominators as factors. That is, the L.C.D. is the least common multiple of all the denominators.

b. *The equation $S = P + Prt$ is the formula for the value S of an investment of a principal of P dollars at a simple annual interest rate of r for a period of t years. Solve for P.*

$$S = P + Prt,$$

$$S = P(1 + rt) \qquad \text{(factoring)},$$

$$\frac{S}{1 + rt} = P \qquad \text{(dividing both sides by } 1 + rt).$$

c. *Solve $(a + c)x + x^2 = (x + a)^2$ for x.*

We shall first simplify the equation and then get all terms involving x on one side.

$$(a + c)x + x^2 = (x + a)^2,$$

$$ax + cx + x^2 = x^2 + 2ax + a^2,$$

$$ax + cx = 2ax + a^2,$$

$$cx - ax = a^2,$$

$$x(c - a) = a^2,$$

$$x = \frac{a^2}{c - a}.$$

EXERCISE 1.1

In Problems **1–6,** *determine by substitution which of the given numbers, if any, satisfy the given equation.*

1. $9x - x^2 = 0$; 1, 0.

2. $20 - 9x = -x^2$; 5, 4.

3. $y + 2(y - 3) = 4$; $\frac{10}{3}$, 1.

4. $2x + x^2 - 8 = 0$; 2, -4.

5. $x(7 + x) - 2(x + 1) - 3x = -2$; -3.

6. $x(x + 1)^2(x + 2) = 0$; 0, -1, 2.

In Problems **7–16,** *determine what operations were applied to the first equation to obtain the second. State whether or not the operations* **guarantee** *that the equations are equivalent. Do not solve the equations.*

7. $x - 5 = 4x + 10$; $x = 4x + 15$.

8. $8x - 4 = 16$; $x - \frac{1}{2} = 2$.

9. $x = 4$; $x^2 = 16$.

10. $\frac{1}{2}x^2 + 3 = x - 9$; $x^2 + 6 = 2x - 18$.

11. $x^2 - 2x = 0$; $x - 2 = 0$.

12. $\dfrac{2}{x - 2} + x = x^2$; $2 + x(x - 2) = x^2(x - 2)$.

13. $\dfrac{x^2 - 1}{x - 1} = 3$; $x^2 - 1 = 3(x - 1)$.

14. $x(x + 5)(x + 9) = x(x + 1)$; $(x + 5)(x + 9) = x + 1$.

15. $\dfrac{x(x + 1)}{x - 5} = x(x + 9)$; $x + 1 = (x + 9)(x - 5)$.

16. $2x^2 - 9 = x$; $x^2 - \frac{1}{2}x = \frac{9}{2}$.

In Problems **17–46,** *solve the equations.*

17. $4x = 10$.

18. $0.2x = 5$.

19. $3y = 0$.

20. $2x - 4x = -5$.

21. $-5x = 10 - 15$.

22. $3 - 2x = 4$.

23. $5x - 3 = 9$.

24. $\sqrt{2}\, x + 3 = 8$.

25. $7x + 7 = 2(x + 1)$.

26. $6z + 5z - 3 = 41$.

27. $2(p - 1) - 3(p - 4) = 4p$.

28. $t = 2 - 2[2t - 3(1 - t)]$.

29. $\dfrac{x}{5} = 2x - 6$.

30. $\dfrac{5y}{7} - \dfrac{6}{7} = 2 - 4y$.

31. $5 + \dfrac{4x}{9} = \dfrac{x}{2}$.

32. $\dfrac{x}{3} - 4 = \dfrac{x}{5}$.

33. $q = \dfrac{3}{2}q - 4$.

34. $\dfrac{x}{2} + \dfrac{x}{3} = 7$.

35. $3x + \dfrac{x}{5} - 5 = \dfrac{1}{5} + 5x$.

36. $y - \dfrac{y}{2} + \dfrac{y}{3} - \dfrac{y}{4} = \dfrac{y}{5}$.

37. $\dfrac{2y - 3}{4} = \dfrac{6y + 7}{3}$.

38. $\dfrac{p}{3} + \dfrac{3}{4}p = \dfrac{9}{2}(p - 1)$.

39. $w + \dfrac{w}{2} - \dfrac{w}{3} + \dfrac{w}{4} = 5$.

40. $\dfrac{7 + 2(x + 1)}{3} = \dfrac{8x}{5}$.

41. $\dfrac{x + 2}{3} - \dfrac{2 - x}{6} = x - 2$.

42. $\dfrac{x}{5} + \dfrac{2(x - 4)}{10} = 7$.

43. $\dfrac{9}{5}(3 - x) = \dfrac{3}{4}(x - 3)$.

44. $\dfrac{2y - 7}{3} + \dfrac{8y - 9}{14} = \dfrac{3y - 5}{21}$.

45. $\dfrac{3}{2}(4x - 3) = 2[x - (4x - 3)]$.

46. $(3x - 1)^2 - (5x - 3)^2 = -(4x - 2)^2$.

In Problems 47–54, express the indicated symbol in terms of the remaining symbols.

47. $I = Prt$; P.

48. $ax + b = 0$; x.

49. $p = 8q - 1$; q.

50. $p = -3q + 6$; q.

51. $S = P(1 + rt)$; r.

52. $r = \dfrac{2mI}{B(n + 1)}$; m.

53. $S = \dfrac{n}{2}(a_1 + a_n)$; a_1.

54. $S = \dfrac{R[(1 + i)^n - 1]}{i}$; R.

55. If you purchase an item for business use, in preparing your income tax you may be able to spread out its expense over the life of the item. This is called *depreciation*. One method of depreciation is *straight-line depreciation*, in which the annual depreciation is computed by dividing the cost of the item, less its estimated salvage value, by its useful life. Suppose the cost is C dollars, the useful life is N years, and there is no salvage value. Then the value V (in dollars) of the item at the end of n years is given by

$$V = C\left(1 - \frac{n}{N}\right).$$

Suppose new office furniture is purchased for $1600, has a useful life of 8 years, and has no salvage value. After how many years will it have a value of $1000?

56. When radar is used on a highway to determine the speed of a car, a radar beam is sent out and reflected from the moving car. The difference F (in cycles per second) in frequency between the original and reflected beams is given by

$$F = \frac{vf}{334.8},$$

where v is the speed of the car in miles per hour (mi/h) and f is the frequency of the original beam (in megacycles per second).

Suppose you are driving along a highway with a speed limit of 55 mi/h. A police officer aims a radar beam with a frequency of 2450 (megacycles per second) at your car, and the officer observes the difference in frequency to be 420 (cycles per second). Can the officer claim that you were speeding?

57. To study a predator-prey relationship, an experiment* was conducted in which a blindfolded subject, the "predator," stood in front of a 3-ft-square table on which uniform sandpaper discs, the "prey," were placed. For 1 minute the "predator" searched for the discs by tapping with a finger. Whenever a disc was found, it was removed and searching resumed. The experiment was repeated for various disc densities (number of discs per 9 ft^2). If y is the number of discs picked up in 1 minute when x discs are on the table, it was estimated that

$$y = a(1 - by)x,$$

where a and b are constants. Solve this equation for y.

1.2 EQUATIONS LEADING TO LINEAR EQUATIONS

Some equations that are not linear do not have any solutions. In this case we say that the solution set is the **empty set** or **null set,** which we denote by $\{\ \ \}$ or $\varnothing$. The following examples illustrate that solving a nonlinear equation may lead to a linear equation.

EXAMPLE 1   *Solve the following equations.*

a. $\dfrac{5}{x - 4} = \dfrac{6}{x - 3}.$

This is called a *fractional equation* because the unknown is in a denominator. To solve it we shall first write it in a form that is free of fractions. Multiplying both sides by the L.C.D., $(x - 4)(x - 3)$, we have

$$(x - 4)(x - 3)\left(\frac{5}{x - 4}\right) = (x - 4)(x - 3)\left(\frac{6}{x - 3}\right),$$

$$5(x - 3) = 6(x - 4) \qquad \text{[linear equation]},$$

$$5x - 15 = 6x - 24,$$

$$9 = x.$$

In the first step we multiplied each side by an expression involving the *variable* x. As we mentioned in Sec. 1.1, this means that we are not guaranteed that the last equation is equivalent to the *original* equation. Thus we must check whether or not 9 satisfies the *original* equation. If 9 is substituted for x in that equation, the left side is

$$\frac{5}{9 - 4} = \frac{5}{5} = 1$$

and the right side is

$$\frac{6}{9 - 3} = \frac{6}{6} = 1.$$

Since both sides are equal, 9 is a root.

* C. S. Holling, "Some Characteristics of Simple Types of Predation and Parasitism," *The Canadian Entomologist,* XCI, no. 7 (1959), 385–98.

b. $\dfrac{3x + 4}{x + 2} - \dfrac{3x - 5}{x - 4} = \dfrac{12}{x^2 - 2x - 8}.$

Since $x^2 - 2x - 8 = (x + 2)(x - 4)$, the L.C.D. is $(x + 2)(x - 4)$. Multiplying both sides by the L.C.D., we have

$$(x - 4)(3x + 4) - (x + 2)(3x - 5) = 12,$$

$$3x^2 - 8x - 16 - (3x^2 + x - 10) = 12,$$

$$3x^2 - 8x - 16 - 3x^2 - x + 10 = 12,$$

$$-9x - 6 = 12,$$

$$-9x = 18,$$

$$x = -2.$$

However, the *original* equation is not defined for $x = -2$ (we cannot divide by zero), so there are no roots. The solution set is $\varnothing$.

c. $\dfrac{4}{x - 5} = 0.$

The only way a fraction can equal zero is if the numerator is 0 and the denominator is different from 0. Since the numerator, 4, is never 0, the solution set is $\varnothing$.

EXAMPLE 2   *Solve* $\sqrt{x^2 + 33} - x = 3.$

This is called a *radical equation,* since a variable occurs in a radicand. To solve it we raise both sides to the same power to eliminate the radical. This operation does *not* guarantee equivalence, so we must check any resulting "solutions." We begin by isolating the radical on one side.

$$\sqrt{x^2 + 33} = x + 3,$$

$$x^2 + 33 = (x + 3)^2 \quad \text{(squaring both sides)},$$

$$x^2 + 33 = x^2 + 6x + 9,$$

$$24 = 6x,$$

$$4 = x.$$

You should show by substitution that 4 is indeed a root.

You may have to raise both sides of a radical equation to the same power more than once, as Example 3 shows.

EXAMPLE 3   *Solve* $\sqrt{y - 3} - \sqrt{y} = -3.$

When an equation has two terms involving radicals, first write the equation so that one radical is on each side, if possible.

$$\sqrt{y - 3} = \sqrt{y} - 3,$$

$$y - 3 = y - 6\sqrt{y} + 9 \qquad \text{(squaring both sides)},$$

$$6\sqrt{y} = 12,$$

$$\sqrt{y} = 2,$$

$$y = 4 \qquad \text{(squaring both sides)}.$$

Substituting 4 into the left side of the *original* equation gives $\sqrt{1} - \sqrt{4}$, which is -1. Since this does not equal the right side, -3, there is no solution. That is, the solution set is $\varnothing$.

EXERCISE 1.2

In Problems **1–34**, *solve the equations.*

1. $\dfrac{5}{x} = 25.$

2. $\dfrac{4}{x - 1} = 2.$

3. $\dfrac{3}{7 - x} = 0.$

4. $\dfrac{5x - 2}{x + 1} = 0.$

5. $\dfrac{4}{8 - x} = \dfrac{3}{4}.$

6. $\dfrac{x + 3}{x} = \dfrac{2}{5}.$

7. $\dfrac{q}{3q - 4} = 3.$

8. $\dfrac{4p}{7 - p} = 1.$

9. $\dfrac{1}{p - 1} = \dfrac{2}{p - 2}.$

10. $\dfrac{2x - 3}{4x - 5} = 6.$

11. $\dfrac{1}{x} + \dfrac{1}{5} = \dfrac{4}{5}.$

12. $\dfrac{4}{t - 3} = \dfrac{3}{t - 4}.$

13. $\dfrac{3x - 2}{2x + 3} = \dfrac{3x - 1}{2x + 1}.$

14. $\dfrac{x + 2}{x - 1} + \dfrac{x + 1}{2 - x} = 0.$

15. $\dfrac{y - 6}{y} - \dfrac{6}{y} = \dfrac{y + 6}{y - 6}.$

16. $\dfrac{y - 3}{y + 3} = \dfrac{y - 3}{y + 2}.$

17. $\dfrac{-4}{x - 1} = \dfrac{7}{2 - x} + \dfrac{3}{x + 1}.$

18. $\dfrac{1}{x - 3} - \dfrac{3}{x - 2} = \dfrac{4}{1 - 2x}.$

19. $\dfrac{9}{x - 3} = \dfrac{3x}{x - 3}.$

20. $\dfrac{x}{x + 3} - \dfrac{x}{x - 3} = \dfrac{3x - 4}{x^2 - 9}.$

21. $\sqrt{x + 6} = 3.$

22. $\sqrt{z - 2} = 3.$

23. $\sqrt{5x - 6} - 16 = 0.$

24. $6 - \sqrt{2x + 5} = 0.$

25. $\sqrt{\dfrac{x}{2} + 1} = \dfrac{2}{3}.$

26. $(x + 6)^{1/2} = 7.$

27. $\sqrt{4x - 6} = \sqrt{x}.$

28. $\sqrt{7 - 2x} = \sqrt{x - 1}.$

29. $(x - 3)^{3/2} = 8.$

30. $\sqrt{y^2 - 9} = 9 - y.$

31. $\sqrt{y} + \sqrt{y + 2} = 3.$

32. $\sqrt{x} - \sqrt{x + 1} = 1.$

33. $\sqrt{z^2 + 2z} = 3 + z.$

34. $\sqrt{\dfrac{1}{w}} - \sqrt{\dfrac{2}{5w - 2}} = 0.$

In Problems **35–38,** *express the indicated letter in terms of the remaining letters.*

35. $r = \dfrac{d}{1 - dt}$; d.

36. $\dfrac{x - a}{b - x} = \dfrac{x - b}{a - x}$; x.

37. $r = \dfrac{2mI}{B(n + 1)}$; n.

38. $\dfrac{1}{p} + \dfrac{1}{q} = \dfrac{1}{f}$; q.

39. In a certain wildlife preserve, the number y of prey consumed by an individual predator over a given period of time is given by

$$y = \frac{10x}{1 + 0.1x},$$

where x is *prey density* (the number of prey per unit of area). What prey density would allow a predator to survive if it needs to consume 50 prey over the given time period?

40. There are several rules for determining doses of medicine for children when the adult dose has been specified. Such rules may be based on weight, height, and so on. If A = age of child, d = adult dose, and c = child's dose, then here are two rules.

$$\text{Young's rule: } c = \frac{A}{A + 12}d.$$

$$\text{Cowling's rule: } c = \frac{A + 1}{24}d.$$

At what age are the children's doses the same under both rules? Round your answer to the nearest year.

41. Police have used the formula $s = \sqrt{30fd}$ to estimate the speed s (in miles per hour) of a car if it skidded d feet when stopping. The literal number f is the coefficient of friction determined by the kind of road (such as concrete, asphalt, gravel, or tar) and whether the road is wet or dry. Some values of f are given in the table below. At 40 mi/h, about how many feet will a car skid on a dry concrete road? Give your answer to the nearest foot.

	CONCRETE	TAR
Wet	0.4	0.5
Dry	0.8	1.0

1.3   QUADRATIC EQUATIONS

To learn how to solve more complicated problems, we turn to methods of solving *quadratic equations.*

Definition
*A **quadratic equation** in the variable x is an equation that can be written in the form*

$$ax^2 + bx + c = 0,$$

where a, b, and c are constants and $a \neq 0$.

A quadratic equation is also called a *second-degree equation* or an *equation of degree two,* since the highest power of the variable that occurs is the second.

Whereas a linear equation has only one root, some quadratic equations have two different roots.

A useful method of solving quadratic equations is based on factoring $ax^2 + bx + c$, as the following example shows.

EXAMPLE 1   *Solve the following quadratic equations.*

a. $x^2 + x - 12 = 0$.

The left side factors easily:

$$(x - 3)(x + 4) = 0.$$

Think of this as two quantities, $x - 3$ and $x + 4$, whose product is zero. **Whenever a product of two or more quantities is zero, at least one of the quantities *must* be zero.** This means that either $x - 3 = 0$ or $x + 4 = 0$. Solving these gives $x = 3$ and $x = -4$. The roots are 3 and -4 and the solution set is $\{3, -4\}$.

b. $6w^2 = 5w$.

We *do not* divide both sides by w (a variable) since equivalence is not guaranteed and we may "lose" a root. Instead, we write the equation as

$$6w^2 - 5w = 0.$$

Factoring gives

$$w(6w - 5) = 0.$$

Setting each factor equal to 0, we have

$$w = 0 \quad \text{and} \quad 6w - 5 = 0.$$

Thus the roots are $w = 0$ and $w = \frac{5}{6}$. Note that if we had divided both sides of $6w^2 = 5w$ by w and obtained $6w = 5$, our only solution would be $w = \frac{5}{6}$. That is, we would lose the root $w = 0$. This confirms our discussion of operation 5 in Sec. 1.1.

Some equations that are not quadratic may be solved by factoring, as Example 2 shows.

EXAMPLE 2   *Solve the following equations.*

a. $4x - 4x^3 = 0$.

This is called a *third-degree equation*.

$$4x - 4x^3 = 0,$$
$$4x(1 - x^2) = 0,$$
$$4x(1 - x)(1 + x) = 0.$$

Setting each factor equal to 0 gives $4 = 0$ (impossible), $x = 0$, $1 - x = 0$, or $1 + x = 0$. Thus

$$x = 0, 1, -1,$$

which we can write as $x = 0, \pm 1$.

b. $x(x + 2)^2(x + 5) + x(x + 2)^3 = 0$.

Since the factor $x(x + 2)^2$ is common to both terms in the left side, we have

$$x(x + 2)^2[(x + 5) + (x + 2)] = 0,$$

$$x(x + 2)^2(2x + 7) = 0.$$

Hence $x = 0$, $x + 2 = 0$, or $2x + 7 = 0$, from which we conclude that $x = 0, -2, -\frac{7}{2}$.

EXAMPLE 3   *Solve* $(3x - 4)(x + 1) = -2$.

Pitfall

You should approach a problem like this with caution. If the product of two quantities is equal to -2, it is not true that at least one of the quantities must be -2. Why? You should **not** set each factor equal to -2; doing so will not provide solutions to the given equation.

We first multiply the factors in the left side:

$$3x^2 - x - 4 = -2.$$

Rewriting so that 0 appears on one side, we have

$$3x^2 - x - 2 = 0.$$

Factoring gives

$$(3x + 2)(x - 1) = 0.$$

Thus

$$x = -\tfrac{2}{3}, 1.$$

EXAMPLE 4   *Solve* $\dfrac{y + 1}{y + 3} + \dfrac{y + 5}{y - 2} = \dfrac{7(2y + 1)}{y^2 + y - 6}$.   (1)

Multiplying both sides by the L.C.D., $(y + 3)(y - 2)$, we get

$$(y - 2)(y + 1) + (y + 3)(y + 5) = 7(2y + 1). \tag{2}$$

Since Eq. (1) was multiplied by an expression involving the variable y, remember (from Sec. 1.1) that Eq. (2) is not necessarily equivalent to Eq. (1). After simplifying Eq. (2) we have

$$2y^2 - 7y + 6 = 0,$$

$$(2y - 3)(y - 2) = 0.$$

Thus $\frac{3}{2}$ and 2 are *possible* roots of the given equation. But 2 cannot be a root of Eq. (1) since substitution leads to a denominator of 0. However, you should check that $\frac{3}{2}$ does indeed satisfy the *original* equation. Thus its only root is $\frac{3}{2}$.

EXAMPLE 5   *Solve $x^2 = 3$.*

This equation is equivalent to

$$x^2 - 3 = 0.$$

Factoring, we obtain

$$(x - \sqrt{3})(x + \sqrt{3}) = 0.$$

Thus $x - \sqrt{3} = 0$ or $x + \sqrt{3} = 0$. The roots are $\pm\sqrt{3}$.

A more general form of the equation $x^2 = 3$ is $u^2 = k$. In the same manner as above, we can show the following:

$$\boxed{\text{If } u^2 = k, \quad \text{then} \quad u = \pm\sqrt{k}.}$$

Solving quadratic equations by factoring can be quite difficult, as is evident by trying that method on $0.7x^2 - \sqrt{2}x - 8\sqrt{5} = 0$. However, there is a formula called the *quadratic formula** that gives the roots of any quadratic equation:

QUADRATIC FORMULA

If $ax^2 + bx + c = 0$, where a, b, and c are constants and $a \neq 0$, then

$$x = \frac{-b \pm \sqrt{b^2 - 4ac}}{2a}.$$

These values of x are the roots of the quadratic equation above.

EXAMPLE 6   *Solve $4x^2 - 17x + 15 = 0$ by the quadratic formula.*

Here $a = 4$, $b = -17$, and $c = 15$.

$$x = \frac{-b \pm \sqrt{b^2 - 4ac}}{2a} = \frac{-(-17) \pm \sqrt{(-17)^2 - 4(4)(15)}}{2(4)}$$

$$= \frac{17 \pm \sqrt{49}}{8} = \frac{17 \pm 7}{8}.$$

The roots are $\dfrac{17 + 7}{8} = \dfrac{24}{8} = 3$ and $\dfrac{17 - 7}{8} = \dfrac{10}{8} = \dfrac{5}{4}$.

---

* A derivation of the quadratic formula appears in Sec. 1.4 as a supplement.

EXAMPLE 7   *Solve $2 + 6\sqrt{2}y + 9y^2 = 0$ by the quadratic formula.*

Look at the arrangement of the terms. Here $a = 9$, $b = 6\sqrt{2}$, and $c = 2$.

$$y = \frac{-b \pm \sqrt{b^2 - 4ac}}{2a} = \frac{-6\sqrt{2} \pm \sqrt{0}}{2(9)}.$$

Thus $y = \dfrac{-6\sqrt{2} + 0}{18} = -\dfrac{\sqrt{2}}{3}$ or $y = \dfrac{-6\sqrt{2} - 0}{18} = -\dfrac{\sqrt{2}}{3}$. Therefore, the

only root is $-\dfrac{\sqrt{2}}{3}$.

EXAMPLE 8   *Solve $z^2 + z + 1 = 0$ by the quadratic formula.*

Here $a = 1$, $b = 1$, and $c = 1$. The roots are

$$\frac{-b \pm \sqrt{b^2 - 4ac}}{2a} = \frac{-1 \pm \sqrt{-3}}{2}.$$

Now, $\sqrt{-3}$ denotes a number whose square is -3. However, no such real number exists since the square of any real number is nonnegative. Thus the equation has no real roots.*

Pitfall

Be certain that you use the quadratic formula correctly.

$$x \neq -b \pm \frac{\sqrt{b^2 - 4ac}}{2a}.$$

From Examples 6–8 you can see that a quadratic equation has either two different real roots, exactly one real root, or no real roots, depending on whether $b^2 - 4ac$ is > 0, $= 0$, or < 0.

EXERCISE 1.3

*In Problems **1–30,** solve by factoring.*

1. $x^2 - 4x + 4 = 0$.

2. $t^2 + 3t + 2 = 0$.

3. $y^2 - 7y + 12 = 0$.

4. $x^2 + x - 12 = 0$.

5. $x^2 - 2x - 3 = 0$.

6. $x^2 - 16 = 0$.

7. $x^2 - 12x = -36$.

8. $3w^2 - 12w + 12 = 0$.

9. $x^2 - 4 = 0$.

* $\dfrac{-1 \pm \sqrt{-3}}{2}$ can be expressed as $\dfrac{-1 \pm i\sqrt{3}}{2}$, where $i\, (= \sqrt{-1})$ is called the imaginary unit.

10. $2x^2 + 4x = 0$.

11. $z^2 - 8z = 0$.

12. $x^2 + 9x = -14$.

13. $4x^2 + 1 = 4x$.

14. $2z^2 + 7z = 4$.

15. $y(2y + 3) = 5$.

16. $8 + 2x - 3x^2 = 0$.

17. $-x^2 + 3x + 10 = 0$.

18. $\frac{1}{7}y^2 = \frac{3}{7}y$.

19. $2p^2 = 3p$.

20. $-r^2 - r + 12 = 0$.

21. $x(x - 1)(x + 2) = 0$.

22. $(x - 2)^2(x + 1)^2 = 0$.

23. $x^3 - 64x = 0$.

24. $x^3 - 4x^2 - 5x = 0$.

25. $6x^3 + 5x^2 - 4x = 0$.

26. $(x + 1)^2 - 5x + 1 = 0$.

27. $(x + 3)(x^2 - x - 2) = 0$.

28. $3(x^2 + 2x - 8)(x - 5) = 0$.

29. $p(p - 3)^2 - 4(p - 3)^3 = 0$.

30. $x^4 - 3x^2 + 2 = 0$.

In Problems **31–44,** *find all real roots by using the quadratic formula.*

31. $x^2 + 2x - 24 = 0$.

32. $x^2 - 2x - 15 = 0$.

33. $4x^2 - 12x + 9 = 0$.

34. $p^2 + 2p = 0$.

35. $p^2 - 5p + 3 = 0$.

36. $2 - 2x + x^2 = 0$.

37. $4 - 2n + n^2 = 0$.

38. $2x^2 + x = 5$.

39. $6x^2 + 7x - 5 = 0$.

40. $w^2 - 2\sqrt{2}w + 2 = 0$.

41. $2x^2 - 3x = 20$.

42. $0.01x^2 + 0.2x - 0.6 = 0$.

43. $2x^2 + 4x = 5$.

44. $-2x^2 - 6x + 5 = 0$.

In Problems **45–66,** *solve by any method.*

45. $x^2 = \dfrac{x + 3}{2}$.

46. $\dfrac{x}{3} = \dfrac{6}{x} - 1$.

47. $\dfrac{3}{x - 4} + \dfrac{x - 3}{x} = 2$.

48. $\dfrac{2}{x - 1} - \dfrac{6}{2x + 1} = 5$.

49. $\dfrac{6x + 7}{2x + 1} - \dfrac{6x + 1}{2x} = 1$.

50. $\dfrac{6(w + 1)}{2 - w} + \dfrac{w}{w - 1} = 3$.

51. $\dfrac{2}{r - 2} - \dfrac{r + 1}{r + 4} = 0$.

52. $\dfrac{2x - 3}{2x + 5} + \dfrac{2x}{3x + 1} = 1$.

53. $\dfrac{y + 1}{y + 3} + \dfrac{y + 5}{y - 2} = \dfrac{14y + 7}{y^2 + y - 6}$.

54. $\dfrac{3}{t + 1} + \dfrac{4}{t} = \dfrac{12}{t + 2}$.

55. $\dfrac{2}{x^2 - 1} - \dfrac{1}{x(x - 1)} = \dfrac{2}{x^2}$.

56. $5 - \dfrac{3(x + 3)}{x^2 + 3x} = \dfrac{1 - x}{x}$.

57. $\sqrt{x + 2} = x - 4$.

58. $3\sqrt{x + 4} = x - 6$.

59. $q + 2 = 2\sqrt{4q - 7}$.

60. $x + \sqrt{x - 2} = 0$.

61. $\sqrt{x + 7} - \sqrt{2x - 1} = 0$.

62. $\sqrt{x} - \sqrt{2x - 8} - 2 = 0$.

63. $\sqrt{x} - \sqrt{2x + 1} + 1 = 0$.

64. $\sqrt{y - 2} + 2 = \sqrt{2y + 3}$.

65. $\sqrt{x + 5} + 1 = 2\sqrt{x}$.

66. $\sqrt{\sqrt{x} + 2} = \sqrt{2x - 4}$.

67. On page 354 of Samuelson's *Economics** it is stated that one root of the equation

$$\overline{M} = \frac{Q(Q + 10)}{44}$$

is $-5 + \sqrt{25 + 44\overline{M}}$. Verify this by using the quadratic formula to solve for Q in terms of $\overline{M}$. Here Q is real income and $\overline{M}$ is level of money supply.

* From Paul A. Samuelson, *Economics,* 10th ed. (New York: McGraw-Hill Book Company, 1976).

68. A group of biologists studied the nutritional effects on rats that were fed a diet containing 10% protein.* The protein was made up of yeast and corn flour. By changing the percentage P (expressed as a decimal) of yeast in the protein mix, the group estimated that the average weight gain g (in grams) of a rat over a period of time was given by

$$g = -200P^2 + 200P + 20.$$

What percentage of yeast gave an average weight gain of 70 grams?

69. In a discussion of a delivered price of a good from a mill to a customer, DeCanio† arrives at and solves the following two quadratic equations:

1. $(2n - 1)v^2 - 2nv + 1 = 0,$

2. $nv^2 - (2n + 1)v + 1 = 0,$

where $n > 0$.

(a) Solve the first equation for v.
(b) Solve the second equation for v if $v \le 2$.

1.4 SUPPLEMENT

The following is a derivation of the quadratic formula.

Suppose $ax^2 + bx + c = 0$ is a quadratic equation. Since $a \ne 0$, we can divide both sides by a:

$$x^2 + \frac{b}{a}x + \frac{c}{a} = 0,$$

$$x^2 + \frac{b}{a}x = -\frac{c}{a}.$$

If we add $\left(\dfrac{b}{2a}\right)^2$ to both sides,

$$x^2 + \frac{b}{a}x + \left(\frac{b}{2a}\right)^2 = \left(\frac{b}{2a}\right)^2 - \frac{c}{a},$$

then the left side factors into $\left(x + \dfrac{b}{2a}\right)^2$ and the right side simplifies into $\dfrac{b^2 - 4ac}{4a^2}$. Thus

$$\left(x + \frac{b}{2a}\right)^2 = \frac{b^2 - 4ac}{4a^2}.$$

* Adapted from R. Bressani, "The Use of Yeast in Human Foods," in *Single-Cell Protein*, ed. R. I. Mateles and S. R. Tannenbaum, (Cambridge, Mass.: MIT Press, 1968).

† S. J. DeCanio, "Delivered Pricing and Multiple Basing Point Equilibria: A Revolution," *The Quarterly Journal of Economics*, XCIX, no. 2 (1984), 329–49.

This equation has the form $u^2 = k$, where $u = x + \dfrac{b}{2a}$ and $k = \dfrac{b^2 - 4ac}{4a^2}$. By Example 5 of Sec. 1.3 we have

$$x + \frac{b}{2a} = \pm\sqrt{\frac{b^2 - 4ac}{4a^2}} = \pm\frac{\sqrt{b^2 - 4ac}}{2a}.$$

Solving for x gives

$$x = -\frac{b}{2a} \pm \frac{\sqrt{b^2 - 4ac}}{2a} = \frac{-b \pm \sqrt{b^2 - 4ac}}{2a}.$$

In summary, the roots of the quadratic equation $ax^2 + bx + c = 0$ are given by the **quadratic formula:**

$$x = \frac{-b \pm \sqrt{b^2 - 4ac}}{2a}.$$

1.5 REVIEW

Important Terms and Symbols

Section 1.1   equation   side (member) of equation   variable   root of equation   solution set
equivalent equations   linear (first-degree) equation   literal equation

Section 1.2   empty set, $\varnothing$ fractional equation   radical equation

Section 1.3   quadratic (second-degree) equation   quadratic formula

Summary

When solving an equation we may apply rules to it that give equivalent equations, that is, equations with exactly the same solutions as the given equation. These rules include adding (or subtracting) the same number to (from) both sides as well as multiplying (or dividing) both sides by the same constant, except 0.

A linear equation (in x) is of the first degree and has the form $ax + b = 0$, where $a \neq 0$. Every linear equation has exactly one root. To solve a linear equation we apply operations on it until we obtain an equivalent equation in which the unknown is isolated on one side.

A quadratic equation (in x) is of the second degree and has the form $ax^2 + bx + c = 0$, where $a \neq 0$. It has either two different real roots, exactly one real root, or no real roots. A quadratic equation may be solved by either factoring or by the quadratic formula:

$$x = \frac{-b \pm \sqrt{b^2 - 4ac}}{2a}.$$

When solving a fractional equation or a radical equation, one often applies operations to it that do not guarantee that the resulting equation is equivalent to the given equation. These operations include multiplying both sides by an expression containing the variable and raising both sides to the same power. In such cases all solutions obtained at the end of such procedures must be checked by substituting them into the given equation.

Review Problems

Solve the following equations.

1. $4 - 3x = 2 + 5x$.

2. $\frac{5}{7}x - \frac{2}{3}x = \frac{3}{21}x$.

3. $3[2 - 4(1 + x)] = 5 - 3(3 - x)$.

4. $3(x + 4)^2 + 6x = 3x^2 + 7$.

5. $2 - w = 3 + w$.

6. $x = 2x$.

7. $x = 2x - (7 + x)$.

8. $3x - 8 = 4(x - 2)$.

9. $2(4 - \frac{3}{5}p) = 5$.

10. $\frac{5}{7}x - \frac{2}{3}x = \frac{3}{21}$.

11. $\dfrac{3x - 1}{x + 4} = 0$.

12. $\dfrac{5}{p + 3} - \dfrac{2}{p + 3} = 0$.

13. $\dfrac{2x}{x - 3} - \dfrac{x + 1}{x + 2} = 1$.

14. $\dfrac{t + 3t + 4}{7 - t} = 14$.

15. $3x^2 + 2x - 5 = 0$.

16. $x^2 - 2x - 2 = 0$.

17. $5q^2 = 7q$.

18. $2x^2 - x = 0$.

19. $x^2 - 10x + 25 = 0$.

20. $r^2 + 10r - 25 = 0$.

21. $3x^2 - 5 = 0$.

22. $x(x - 9) = 0$.

23. $(8t - 5)(2t + 6) = 0$.

24. $2(x^2 - 1) + 2x = x^2 - 6x + 1$.

25. $-3x^2 + 5x - 1 = 0$.

26. $y^2 = 6$.

27. $x(x^2 - 9) = 4(x^2 - 9)$.

28. $4x^2(x - 5) - 9(x - 5) = 0$.

29. $\dfrac{6w + 7}{2w + 1} - \dfrac{6w + 1}{2w} = 1$.

30. $\dfrac{3}{x + 1} + \dfrac{4}{x} - \dfrac{12}{x + 2} = 0$.

31. $\dfrac{2}{x^2 - 9} - \dfrac{3x}{x + 3} = \dfrac{1}{x - 3}$.

32. $\dfrac{3}{x^2 - 4} + \dfrac{2}{x^2 + 4x + 4} - \dfrac{4}{x + 2} = 0$.

33. $\sqrt{2x + 5} = 5$.

34. $\sqrt{3x - 4} = \sqrt{2x + 5}$.

35. $\sqrt[3]{11x + 9} = 4$.

36. $\sqrt{x^2 + 5x + 25} = x + 4$.

37. $\sqrt{y} + 6 = 5$.

38. $\sqrt{z^2 + 9} = 5$.

39. $\sqrt{x - 1} + \sqrt{x + 6} = 7$.

40. $\sqrt{2x + 1} = x - 7$.

41. $x + 2 = 2\sqrt{4x - 7}$.

42. $\sqrt{3z} - \sqrt{5z + 1} + 1 = 0$.

Applications of Equations and Inequalities

2.1 APPLICATIONS OF EQUATIONS

In most cases, to solve practical problems you must translate the relationships stated in the problems into mathematical symbols. This is called *modeling*. The following examples illustrate basic techniques and concepts. Examine each of them carefully before going to the exercises.

In the first example we shall refer to some business terms relative to a manufacturing firm. **Fixed cost** (or *overhead*) is the sum of all costs that are independent of the level of production, such as rent, insurance, and so on. This cost must be paid whether or not output is produced. **Variable cost** is the sum of all costs that are dependent on the level of output, such as labor and material. **Total cost** is the sum of variable cost and fixed cost:

$$\text{total cost } = \text{ variable cost } + \text{ fixed cost.}$$

Total revenue is the money that the manufacturer receives for selling the output. It is given by:

$$\text{total revenue } = \text{ (price per unit)(number of units sold).}$$

Profit is total revenue minus total cost:

$$\boxed{\text{profit} = \text{total revenue} - \text{total cost.}}$$

EXAMPLE 1   *The Anderson Company produces a product for which the variable cost per unit is $6 and fixed cost is $80,000. Each unit has a selling price of $10. Determine the number of units that must be sold for the company to earn a profit of $60,000.*

Let q be the number of units which must be sold. (In many business problems, q represents quantity.) Then the variable cost (in dollars) is $6q$. The *total* cost for the business is therefore $6q + 80,000$. The total revenue from the sale of q units is $10q$. Since

$$\text{profit} = \text{total revenue} - \text{total cost,}$$

our model for this problem is

$$60,000 = 10q - (6q + 80,000).$$

Solving gives

$$60,000 = 10q - 6q - 80,000,$$
$$140,000 = 4q,$$
$$35,000 = q.$$

Thus 35,000 units must be sold to earn a profit of $60,000.

EXAMPLE 2   *A company manufactures women's sportswear and is planning to sell its new line of slacks sets to retail outlets. The cost to the retailer will be $33 per set. As a convenience to the retailer, the manufacturer will attach a price tag to each set. What amount should be marked on the price tag so that the retailer may reduce this price by 20% during a sale and still make a profit of 15% on the cost?*

Here we use the fact that

$$\text{selling price} = \text{cost per set} + \text{profit per set.}$$

Let p be the tag price per set in dollars. During the sale the retailer receives $p - 0.2p$. This must equal the cost, 33, plus the profit, $(0.15)(33)$. Hence

$$\text{selling price} = \text{cost} + \text{profit.}$$
$$p - 0.2p = 33 + (0.15)(33),$$
$$0.8p = 37.95,$$
$$p = 47.4375.$$

From a practical point of view, the company should mark the price tag at $47.44.

EXAMPLE 3   *A total of $10,000 was invested in two business ventures, A and B. At the end of the first year, A and B yielded returns of 6% and $5\frac{3}{4}$%, respectively, on the original investments. How was the original amount allocated if the total amount earned was $588.75?*

Let x be the amount (in dollars) invested at 6%. Then $10,000 - x$ was invested at $5\frac{3}{4}$%. The interest earned was $(0.06)(x)$ and $(0.0575)(10,000 - x)$, which total 588.75. Hence

$$(0.06)x + (0.0575)(10,000 - x) = 588.75,$$

$$0.06x + 575 - 0.0575x = 588.75,$$

$$0.0025x = 13.75,$$

$$x = 5500.$$

Thus $5500 was invested at 6%, and $10,000 - $5500 = 4500 was invested at $5\frac{3}{4}$%.

EXAMPLE 4   *The board of directors of a corporation agrees to redeem some of its bonds in 2 years. At that time $1,102,500 will be required. Suppose they presently set aside $1,000,000. At what annual rate of interest, compounded annually, will this money have to be invested in order that its future value be sufficient to redeem the bonds?*

Let r be the required annual rate of interest. At the end of the first year, the accumulated amount will be $1,000,000 plus the interest $1,000,000r$, for a total of

$$1,000,000 + 1,000,000r = 1,000,000(1 + r).$$

Under compound interest, at the end of the second year the accumulated amount will be $1,000,000(1 + r)$ plus the interest on this which is $[1,000,000(1 + r)]r$. Thus the total value at the end of the second year will be $1,000,000(1 + r) + 1,000,000(1 + r)r$. This must equal $1,102,500$:

$$1,000,000(1 + r) + 1,000,000(1 + r)r = 1,102,500. \qquad (1)$$

Since $1,000,000(1 + r)$ is a common factor of both terms on the left side, we have

$$1,000,000(1 + r)(1 + r) = 1,102,500,$$

$$1,000,000(1 + r)^2 = 1,102,500,$$

$$(1 + r)^2 = \frac{1,102,500}{1,000,000} = \frac{11,025}{10,000} = \frac{441}{400},$$

$$1 + r = \pm\sqrt{\frac{441}{400}} = \pm\frac{21}{20},$$

$$r = -1 \pm \frac{21}{20}.$$

Thus $r = -1 + (21/20) = 0.05$ or $r = -1 - (21/20) = -2.05$. Although 0.05 and -2.05 are roots of Eq. (1), we reject -2.05 since we want r to be positive. Hence $r = 0.05$, so the desired rate is 5%.

At times there may be more than one way to model a word problem, as Example 5 shows.

EXAMPLE 5   *A real estate firm owns the Parklane Garden Apartments, which consist of 70 apartments. At $250 per month every apartment can be rented. However, for each $10 per month increase there will be two vacancies with no possibility of filling them. The firm wants to receive $17,980 per month from rents. What rent should be charged for each apartment?*

Method I.   Suppose r is the rent (in dollars) to be charged per apartment. Then the increase over the $250 level is $r - 250$. Thus the number of $10 increases is $\dfrac{r - 250}{10}$. Since each $10 increase results in two vacancies, the total number of vacancies will be $2\left(\dfrac{r - 250}{10}\right)$. Hence the total number of apartments rented will be $70 - 2\left(\dfrac{r - 250}{10}\right)$. Since

$$\text{total rent} = (\text{rent per apartment})(\text{number of apartments rented}),$$

we have

$$17,980 = r\left[70 - \frac{2(r - 250)}{10}\right],$$

$$17,980 = r\left[70 - \frac{r - 250}{5}\right],$$

$$17,980 = r\left[\frac{350 - r + 250}{5}\right],$$

$$89,900 = r[600 - r].$$

Thus,

$$r^2 - 600r + 89,000 = 0.$$

By the quadratic formula,

$$r = \frac{600 \pm \sqrt{(-600)^2 - 4(1)(89,900)}}{2(1)}$$

$$= \frac{600 \pm \sqrt{400}}{2} = \frac{600 \pm 20}{2} = 300 \pm 10.$$

Thus the rent for each apartment should be $310 or $290.

Method II.   Suppose n is the number of $10 increases. Then the increase in rent per apartment will be $10n$ and there will be $2n$ vacancies. Since

$$\text{total rent} = (\text{rent per apartment})(\text{number of apartments rented}),$$

we have

$$17{,}980 = (250 + 10n)(70 - 2n),$$
$$17{,}980 = 17{,}500 + 200n - 20n^2,$$
$$20n^2 - 200n + 480 = 0,$$
$$n^2 - 10n + 24 = 0,$$
$$(n - 6)(n - 4) = 0.$$

Thus $n = 6$ or $n = 4$. The rent charged should be either $250 + 10(6) = \$310$ or $250 + 10(4) = \$290$.

EXERCISE 2.1

1. The Geometric Products Company produces a product at a variable cost per unit of $2.20. If fixed costs are $95,000 and each unit sells for $3, how many units must be sold for the company to have a profit of $50,000?

2. The Clark Company management would like to know the total sales units that are required for the company to earn a profit of $100,000. The following data are available: unit selling price of $20; variable cost per unit of $15; total fixed cost of $600,000. From these data determine the required sales units.

3. A person wishes to invest $20,000 in two enterprises so that the total income per year will be $1440. One enterprise pays 6% annually; the other has more risk and pays $7\frac{1}{2}\%$ annually. How much must be invested in each?

4. A person invested $20,000: part at an interest rate of 6% annually and the remainder at 7% annually. The total interest at the end of 1 year was equivalent to an annual $6\frac{3}{4}\%$ rate on the entire $20,000. How much was invested at each rate?

5. The cost of a product to a retailer is $3.40. If the retailer wishes to make a profit of 20% on the selling price, at what price should the product be sold?

6. In 2 years a company will require $1,123,600 in order to retire some bonds. If the company now invests $1,000,000 for this purpose, what annual rate of interest, compounded annually, must it receive on this amount in order to retire the bonds?

7. In 2 years a company will begin an expansion program. It has decided to invest $2,000,000 now so that in 2 years the total value of the investment will be $2,163,200, the amount required for the expansion. What is the annual rate of interest, compounded annually, that the company must receive to achieve its purpose?

8. A company finds that if it produces and sells q units of a product, its total sales revenue in dollars is $100\sqrt{q}$. If the variable cost per unit is $2 and the fixed cost is $1200, find the values of q for which

$$\text{total sales revenue} = \text{variable cost} + \text{fixed cost}$$

(that is, profit is zero).

9. A college dormitory houses 210 students. This fall, rooms are available for 76 freshmen. On the average, 95% of those freshmen who request room applications actually reserve a room. How many room applications should the college send out if it wants to receive 76 reservations?

10. A group of people were polled and 20%, or 700, of them favored a new product over the best-selling brand. How many people were polled?

11. It was reported that in a certain women's jail, women prison guards, called matrons, received 30% (or $200) a month less than their male counterparts, deputy sheriffs. Find the yearly salary of a deputy sheriff. Give your answer to the nearest dollar.

12. A few years ago, cement drivers were on strike for 46 days. Before the strike, these drivers earned $7.50 per hour and worked 260 eight-hour days a year. What percentage increase is needed in yearly income to make up for the lost time within 1 year?

13. A manufacturer of video-game cartridges sells each cartridge for $19.95. The manufacturing cost of each cartridge is $14.95. Monthly fixed costs are $8000. During the first month of sales of a new game, how many cartridges must be sold in order for the manufacturer to break even (that is, in order that total revenue equal total cost)?

14. An investment club bought a bond of an oil corporation for $5000. The bond yields 8% per year. The club now wants to buy shares of stock in a hospital supply company. The stock sells at $20 per share and earns a dividend of $0.50 per share per year. How many shares should the club buy so that its total investment in stocks and bonds yields 5% per year?

15. As a fringe benefit for its employees, a company established a vision-care plan. Under this plan, each year the company will pay the first $10 of an employee's vision-care expenses and 80% of all additional vision-

care expenses up to a maximum *total* benefit payment of $60. For an employee, find the total annual vision-care expenses covered by this program.

16. Over a period of time, the manufacturer of a caramel-center candy bar found that 2% of the bars were rejected for imperfections.
   (a) If c candy bars are made in a year, how many would the manufacturer expect to be rejected?
   (b) This year, annual consumption of this candy is projected to be 2,000,000 bars. Approximately how many bars will have to be made if rejections are taken into consideration?

17. Suppose that consumers will purchase q units of a product when the price is $(80 - q)/4$ dollars *each*. How many units must be sold in order that sales revenue be $400?

18. How long would it take to double an investment at simple interest with a rate of 5% per year? [*Hint:* See Example 6(a) of Sec. 1.1 and express 5% as 0.05.]

19. The inventor of a new toy offers the Kiddy Toy Company exclusive rights to manufacture and sell the toy for a lump-sum payment of $25,000. After estimating that future sales possibilities beyond 1 year are nonexistent, the company management is reviewing the following alternate proposal: to give a lump-sum payment of $2000 plus a royalty of $0.50 for each unit sold. How many units must be sold the first year to make this alternative as economically attractive to the inventor as the original request? (*Hint:* Determine when the incomes under both proposals are the same.)

20. A company parking lot is 120 ft long and 80 ft wide. Due to an increase in personnel, it is decided to double the area of the lot by adding strips of equal width to one end and one side. Find the width of one such strip.

21. You are the chief financial advisor to a corporation which owns an office complex consisting of 50 suites. At $400 per month every suite can be rented. However,

for each $20 per month increase there will be two va-
cancies with no possibility of filling them. The corporation wants to receive a total of $20,240 per month
from rents in the complex. You are asked to determine
the rent that should be charged for each suite. What is
your reply?

22. Six months ago an investment company had a
$3,000,000 portfolio consisting of blue chip and glamor
stocks. Since then, the value of the blue chip investment increased by $\frac{1}{10}$, while the value of the glamor
stocks decreased by $\frac{1}{10}$. The current value of the portfolio is $3,140,000. What is the *current* value of the
blue chip investment?

23. The monthly revenue R of a certain company is given
by $R = 800p - 7p^2$, where p is the price in dollars of
the product they manufacture. At what price will the
revenue be $10,000 if the price must be greater than
$50?

24. The *price-earning ratio* (*P/E* ratio) of a company is the
ratio of the market value of one share of its outstanding
common stock to the earnings per share. If the *P/E* ratio
increases by 10% and the earnings per share increase by
20%, determine the percentage increase in the market
value per share of the common stock.

25. When the price of a product is p dollars each, suppose
that a manufacturer will supply $2p - 8$ units of the
product to the market and that consumers will demand
to buy $300 - 2p$ units. At the value of p for which
supply equals demand, the market is said to be in equilibrium. Find this value of p.

26. Repeat Problem 25 for the following conditions: at a
price of p dollars each, the supply is $3p^2 - 4p$ and the
demand is $24 - p^2$.

27. For security reasons a company will enclose a rectangular area of 11,200 ft^2 in the rear of its plant. One side
will be bounded by the building and the other three
sides by fencing (see Fig. 2.1). If 300 ft of fencing will
be used, what will be the dimensions of the

rectangular area?

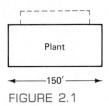

FIGURE 2.1

28. A company is designing a package for its product. One
part of the package is to be an open box made from a
square piece of aluminum by cutting out a 3-in. square
from each corner and folding up the sides (see Fig.
2.2). The box is to contain 75 in.^{3}. What are the dimensions of the square piece of aluminum that must be
used?

FIGURE 2.2

29. A candy company makes the popular Dandy Bar. The
rectangular-shaped bar is 10 centimeters (cm) long, 5
cm wide, and 2 cm thick (see Fig. 2.3). Because of
increasing costs, the company has decided to cut the
volume of the bar by a drastic 28%. The thickness will
be the same, but the length and width will be reduced
by equal amounts. What will be the length and width
of the new bar?

FIGURE 2.3

30. A candy company makes a washer-shaped candy (a
candy with a hole in it); see Fig. 2.4. Because of increasing costs, the company will cut the volume of

candy in each piece by 20%. To do this they will keep the same thickness and outer radius, but will make the inner radius larger. At present the thickness is 2 millimeters (mm), the inner radius is 2 mm, and the outer radius is 7 mm. Find the inner radius of the new-style candy. (*Hint:* The volume V of a solid disc is $\pi r^2 h$, where r is the radius and h is the thickness.)

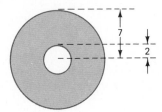

FIGURE 2.4

31. A *compensating balance* refers to that practice wherein a bank requires a borrower to maintain on deposit a certain portion of a loan during the term of the loan. For example, if a firm makes a $100,000 loan which requires a compensating balance of 20%, it would have to leave $20,000 on deposit and would have the use of $80,000. To meet the expenses of retooling, the Victor Manufacturing Company must borrow $95,000. The Third National Bank, with whom they have had no prior association, requires a compensating balance of 15%. To the nearest thousand dollars, what must be the amount of the loan to obtain the needed funds?

32. A machine company has an incentive plan for its salespeople. For each machine that a salesperson sells, the commission is $20. The commission for *every* machine sold will increase by $0.02 for each machine sold over 600. For example, the commission on each of 602 machines sold is $20.04. How many machines must a salesperson sell in order to earn $15,400?

33. A land investment company purchased a parcel of land for $7200. After having sold all but 20 acres at a profit of $30 per acre, the entire cost of the parcel had been regained. How many acres were sold?

34. The *margin of profit* of a company is the net income divided by the total sales. A company's margin of profit increased by 0.02 from last year. In that year the company sold its product at $3.00 each and had a net income of $4500. This year it increased the price of its product by $0.50 each, sold 2000 more, and had a net income of $7140. The company never has had a margin of profit greater than 0.15. How many of its product were sold last year and how many were sold this year?

35. A company manufactures products A and B. The cost of producing each unit of A is $2 more than that of B. The costs of production of A and B are $1500 and $1000, respectively, and 25 more units of A are produced than of B. How many of each are produced?

2.2 LINEAR INEQUALITIES

Suppose a and b are two points on the real number line. Then either a and b coincide, or a lies to the left of b, or a lies to the right of b (see Fig. 2.5).

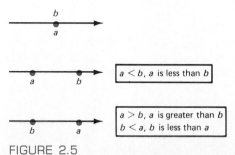

FIGURE 2.5

If a and b coincide, then $a = b$. If a lies to the left of b, we say a is less than b and write $a < b$, where the *inequality symbol* "$<$" is read "is less than." On the other hand, if a lies to the right of b, we say a is greater than b, written $a > b$. To write $a > b$ is equivalent to writing $b < a$.

Another inequality symbol "$\leq$" is read "is less than or equal to" and is defined: $a \leq b$ if and only if $a < b$ or $a = b$. Similarly, the symbol "$\geq$" is defined: $a \geq b$ if and only if $a > b$ or $a = b$. In this case we say "a is greater than or equal to b."

We shall use the words *real numbers* and *points* interchangeably, since there is a one-to-one correspondence between real numbers and points on a line. Thus we can speak of the points -5, -2, 0, 7, and 9, and can write $7 < 9$, $-2 > -5$, $7 \leq 7$, and $7 \geq 0$ (see Fig. 2.6). Clearly, if $a > 0$, then a is positive; if $a < 0$, then a is negative.

FIGURE 2.6

Suppose that $a < b$ and x is between a and b (see Fig. 2.7). Then not only is $a < x$, but also $x < b$. We indicate this by writing $a < x < b$. For example, $0 < 7 < 9$ (see Fig. 2.6).

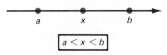

FIGURE 2.7

In defining an inequality below we shall use the less than relation ($<$), but the others ($>$, $\geq$, $\leq$) would also apply.

Definition

*An **inequality** is a statement that one number is less than another number.*

Of course we represent inequalities by means of inequality symbols. If two inequalities have their inequality symbols pointing in the same direction, then the inequalities are said to have the *same sense*. If not, they are said to be *opposite in sense* or one is said to have the *reverse sense* of the other. Hence $a < b$ and $c < d$ have the same sense, but $a < b$ has the reverse sense of $c > d$.

Solving an inequality, such as $2(x - 3) < 4$, means to find all values of the variable for which the inequality is true. This involves the application of certain rules which we now state.

1. *If the same number is added to or subtracted from both sides of an inequality, the resulting inequality has the same sense as the original inequality.* Symbolically,

$$\text{if } a < b, \text{ then } a + c < b + c \text{ and } a - c < b - c.$$

For example, $7 < 10$ and $7 + 3 < 10 + 3$.

2. *If both sides of an inequality are multiplied or divided by the same **positive** number, the resulting inequality has the same sense as the original inequality. Symbolically,*

$$\text{if } a < b \text{ and } c > 0, \text{ then } ac < bc \text{ and } \frac{a}{c} < \frac{b}{c}.$$

For example, since $3 < 7$ and $2 > 0$, then $3(2) < 7(2)$. Also, $\frac{3}{2} < \frac{7}{2}$.

3. *If both sides of an inequality are multiplied or divided by the same **negative** number, then the resulting inequality has the **reverse** sense of the original inequality. Symbolically,*

$$\text{if } a < b \text{ and } c > 0, \text{ then } a(-c) > b(-c) \text{ and } \frac{a}{-c} > \frac{b}{-c}.$$

For example, $4 < 7$ but $4(-2) > 7(-2)$. Also $\frac{4}{-2} > \frac{7}{-2}$.

4. *Any side of an inequality can be replaced by an expression equal to it. Symbolically,*

$$\text{if } a < b \text{ and } a = c, \text{ then } c < b.$$

For example, if $x < 2$ and $x = y + 4$, then $y + 4 < 2$.

5. *If the sides of an inequality are either both positive or both negative, then their respective reciprocals* are unequal in the **reverse** sense. For example,* $2 < 4$ but $\frac{1}{2} > \frac{1}{4}$.

6. *If both sides of an inequality are positive and we raise each side to the same positive power, then the resulting inequality has the same sense as the original inequality. Thus if* $a > b > 0$ *and* $n > 0$, *then*

$$a^n > b^n \qquad \text{and} \qquad \sqrt[n]{a} > \sqrt[n]{b}.$$

For example, $9 > 4$ and so $9^2 > 4^2$ and $\sqrt{9} > \sqrt{4}$.

The result of applying rules 1–4 to an inequality is called an *equivalent inequality*. It is an inequality whose solution is exactly the same as that of the original inequality. We shall apply these rules to a *linear inequality*.

Definition
*A **linear inequality** in the variable x is an inequality which can be written in the form*

$$ax + b < 0 \quad or \quad ax + b \le 0,$$

where a and b are constants and $a \ne 0$.

---

* The *reciprocal* of a nonzero number a is defined to be $\dfrac{1}{a}$.

In the following examples of solving linear inequalities, the property used is indicated to the right. In each step the given inequality will be replaced by an equivalent one until the solution is evident.

EXAMPLE 1   *Solve the following inequalities.*

a. $2(x - 3) < 4$.

$$2(x - 3) < 4,$$
$$2x - 6 < 4 \qquad (4),$$
$$2x - 6 + 6 < 4 + 6 \qquad (1),$$
$$2x < 10 \qquad (4),$$
$$\frac{2x}{2} < \frac{10}{2} \qquad (2),$$
$$x < 5.$$

$x < 5$

5

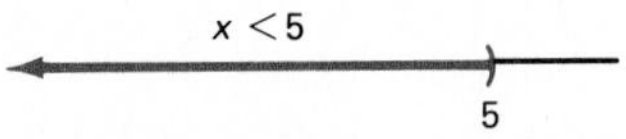

FIGURE 2.8

All of the inequalities are equivalent. Thus the original inequality is true for *all* real numbers x such that $x < 5$. We shall write our solution simply as $x < 5$. Geometrically, we may represent this by the bold line segment in Fig. 2.8. The parenthesis indicates that 5 *is not included* in the solution.

b. $3 - 2x \le 6$.

$$3 - 2x \le 6,$$
$$-2x \le 3 \qquad (1)$$
$$x \ge -\frac{3}{2} \qquad (3)$$

$x \ge -\frac{3}{2}$

$-\frac{3}{2}$

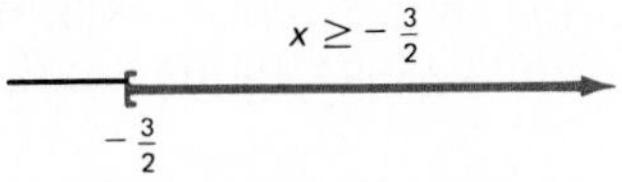

FIGURE 2.9

The solution is $x \ge -\frac{3}{2}$. This is represented geometrically in Fig. 2.9. The square bracket indicates that $-\frac{3}{2}$ *is included* in the solution.

EXAMPLE 2   *Solve $\frac{3}{2}(s - 2) + 1 > -2(s - 4)$.*

$$\frac{3}{2}(s - 2) + 1 > -2(s - 4),$$
$$2[\frac{3}{2}(s - 2) + 1] > 2[-2(s - 4)] \qquad (2),$$
$$3(s - 2) + 2 > -4(s - 4),$$
$$3s - 4 > -4s + 16,$$
$$7s > 20 \qquad (1),$$
$$s > \frac{20}{7} \qquad (2).$$

$s > \frac{20}{7}$

$\frac{20}{7}$

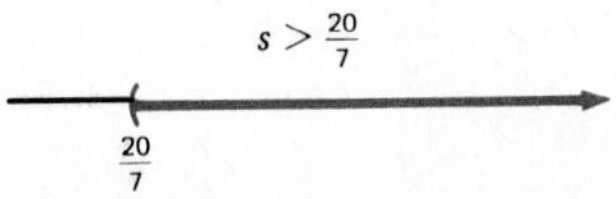

FIGURE 2.10

See Fig. 2-10.

Closed interval [a, b]

Open interval (a, b)

FIGURE 2.12

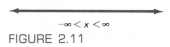

FIGURE 2.13

EXAMPLE 3   *Solve the following inequalities.*

a. $2(x - 4) - 3 > 2x - 1$.

$$2(x - 4) - 3 > 2x - 1,$$
$$2x - 8 - 3 > 2x - 1,$$
$$-11 > -1.$$

Since it is never true that $-11 > -1$, there is no solution and the solution set is $\varnothing$.

b. $2(x - 4) - 3 < 2x - 1$.

Proceeding in the same manner as in (a), we obtain $-11 < -1$. This is true for all real numbers x. We write our solution as $-\infty < x < \infty$ (see Fig. 2.11). The symbols $-\infty$ and ∞ are not numbers, but are merely a convenience for indicating that the solution is all real numbers.

$$\overleftarrow{}\rightarrow$$
$$-\infty < x < \infty$$

FIGURE 2.11

Frequently, we shall use the term *interval* to describe certain sets of real numbers. For example, the set of all numbers x for which $a \leq x \leq b$ is called a **closed interval** and includes the *endpoints* a and b. We denote it by $[a, b]$. The set of all x for which $a < x < b$ is called an **open interval** and is denoted by (a, b). The endpoints are *not* part of this set (see Fig. 2.12).

Extending these concepts, we have the intervals shown in Fig. 2.13, where the symbols ∞ and $-\infty$ are not numbers but merely a convenience for indicating that an interval extends indefinitely in some direction.

EXERCISE 2.2

In Problems **1–34,** *solve the inequalities and indicate your answers geometrically on the real number line.*

1. $3x > 12$.

2. $4x < -2$.

3. $4x - 13 \leq 7$.

4. $3x \geq 0$.

5. $-4x \geq 2$.

6. $2y + 1 > 0$.

7. $3 - 5s > 5$.

8. $4s - 1 < -5$.

9. $3 < 2y + 3$.

10. $6 \leq 5 - 3y$.

11. $2x - 3 \leq 4 + 7x$.

12. $-3 \geq 8(2 - x)$.

13. $3(2 - 3x) > 4(1 - 4x)$.

14. $8(x + 1) + 1 < 3(2x) + 1$.

15. $2(3x - 2) > 3(2x - 1)$.

16. $3 - 2(x - 1) \leq 2(4 + x)$.

17. $x + 2 < \sqrt{3} - x$.

18. $\sqrt{2}\,(x + 2) > \sqrt{8}\,(3 - x)$.

19. $\dfrac{5}{3}x < 10$.

20. $-\dfrac{1}{2}x > 6$.

21. $\dfrac{9y + 1}{4} \leq 2y - 1$.

22. $\dfrac{4y - 3}{2} \geq \dfrac{1}{3}$.

23. $4x - 1 \geq 4(x - 2) + 7$.

24. $0x \leq 0$.

25. $\dfrac{1 - t}{2} < \dfrac{3t - 7}{3}.$

26. $\dfrac{3(2t - 2)}{2} > \dfrac{6t - 3}{5} + \dfrac{t}{10}.$

27. $2x + 3 \geq \dfrac{1}{2}x - 4.$

28. $4x - \dfrac{1}{2} \leq \dfrac{3}{2}x.$

29. $\dfrac{2}{3}r < \dfrac{5}{6}r.$

30. $\dfrac{7}{4}t > -\dfrac{2}{3}t.$

31. $\dfrac{y}{2} + \dfrac{y}{3} > y + \dfrac{y}{5}.$

32. $9 - 0.1x \leq \dfrac{2 - 0.01x}{0.2}.$

33. $0.1(0.03x + 4) \geq 0.02x + 0.434.$

34. $\dfrac{5y - 1}{-3} < \dfrac{7(y + 1)}{-2}.$

35. Each month last year, a company had earnings that were greater than \$37,000 but less than \$53,000. If S represents the total earnings for the year, describe S by using inequalities.

36. Using inequalities, symbolize the statement: The number of labor hours x to produce a product is not less than $2\frac{1}{2}$ nor more than 4.

2.3 APPLICATIONS OF INEQUALITIES

Solving word problems may sometimes involve inequalities, as the following examples illustrate.

EXAMPLE 1   *For a manufacturer of thermostats, the combined cost for labor and material is \$5 per thermostat. Fixed costs (costs incurred in a given time period, regardless of output) are \$60,000. If the selling price of a thermostat is \$7, how many must be sold for the company to earn a profit?*

Let q be the number of thermostats that must be sold. Then their cost is $5q$. The total cost for the company is therefore $5q + 60,000$. The total revenue from the sale of q thermostats will be $7q$. Now,

$$\text{profit} = \text{total revenue} - \text{total cost},$$

and we want profit > 0. Thus

$$\text{total revenue} - \text{total cost} > 0.$$

$$7q - (5q + 60,000) > 0,$$

$$2q > 60,000,$$

$$q > 30,000.$$

Therefore, at least 30,001 thermostats must be sold for the company to earn a profit.

EXAMPLE 2   *A builder must decide whether to rent or buy an excavating machine. If he were to rent the machine, the rental fee would be \$600 per month (on a yearly basis), and the daily cost (gas, oil, and driver) would be \$60 for each day it is used. If he were to buy it, his fixed annual cost would be \$4000, and daily operating and maintenance costs would be \$80 for each day the machine is used. What is the least number of days each year that he would have to use the machine to justify renting it rather than buying it?*

Let d be the number of days each year that the machine is used. If the machine is rented, the total yearly cost consists of rental fees, which are $(12)(600)$, and daily charges of $60d$. If the machine is purchased, the cost per year is $4000 + 80d$. We want

$$\text{cost}_{\text{rent}} < \text{cost}_{\text{purchase}},$$

$$12(600) + 60d < 4000 + 80d,$$

$$7200 + 60d < 4000 + 80d,$$

$$3200 < 20d,$$

$$160 < d.$$

Thus the builder must use the machine at least 161 days to justify renting it.

EXAMPLE 3   The *current ratio* of a business is the ratio of its current assets (such as cash, merchandise inventory, and accounts receivable) to its current liabilities (such as short-term loans and taxes payable).

After consulting with the comptroller, the president of the Ace Sports Equipment Company decides to make a short-term loan to build up its inventory. The company has current assets of $350,000 and current liabilities of $80,000. How much can they borrow if they want their current ratio to be no less than 2.5? (Note: The funds they receive are considered as current assets and the loan as a current liability.)

Let x denote the amount which the company can borrow. Then their current assets will be $350,000 + x$, and their current liabilities will be $80,000 + x$. Thus

$$\text{current ratio} = \frac{\text{current assets}}{\text{current liabilities}} = \frac{350,000 + x}{80,000 + x}.$$

We want

$$\frac{350,000 + x}{80,000 + x} \geq 2.5.$$

Since x is positive, so is $80,000 + x$. Thus we can multiply both sides of the inequality by $80,000 + x$ and the sense of the inequality will remain the same.

$$350,000 + x \geq 2.5(80,000 + x),$$

$$150,000 \geq 1.5x,$$

$$100,000 \geq x.$$

Hence they may borrow as much as $100,000 and yet maintain a current ratio of no less than 2.5.

EXAMPLE 4   *A publishing company finds that the cost of publishing each copy of a certain magazine is $0.38. The revenue from dealers is $0.35 per copy. The advertising revenue is 10% of the revenue received from dealers for all copies sold beyond 10,000. What is the least number of copies which must be sold so as to have a profit for the company?*

Let q be the number of copies that are sold. The revenue from dealers is $0.35q$ and the revenue from advertising is $(0.10)[(0.35)(q - 10,000)]$. The total cost of publication is $0.38q$. Since profit = total revenue $-$ total cost, we want

$$\text{total revenue} - \text{total cost} > 0.$$

$$0.35q + (0.10)[(0.35)(q - 10,000)] - 0.38q > 0,$$

$$0.35q + 0.035q - 350 - 0.38q > 0,$$

$$0.005q - 350 > 0,$$

$$0.005q > 350,$$

$$q > 70,000.$$

Thus the total number of copies must be greater than 70,000. That is, at least 70,001 copies must be sold to guarantee a profit.

EXERCISE 2.3

1. The Davis Company manufactures a product that has a unit selling price of $20 and a unit cost of $15. If fixed costs are $600,000, determine the least number of units that must be sold for the company to have a profit.

2. To produce 1 unit of a new product, a company determines that the cost for material is $2.50 and the cost of labor is $4. The constant overhead, regardless of sales volume, is $5000. If the cost to a wholesaler is $7.40 per unit, determine the least number of units that must be sold by the company to realize a profit.

3. A businesswoman wants to determine the difference between the costs of owning and renting an automobile. She can rent a small car for $135 per month (on an annual basis). Under this plan the cost per mile (gas and oil) is $0.05. If she were to purchase the car, the fixed annual expense would be $1000 and other costs would amount to $0.10 per mile. What is the least number of miles she would have to drive per year to make renting no more expensive than purchasing?

4. A shirt manufacturer produces N shirts at a total labor cost (in dollars) of $1.2N$ and a total material cost of $0.3N$. The constant overhead for the plant is $6000. If each shirt sells for $3, how many must be sold by the company to realize a profit?

5. The cost of publication of each copy of a magazine is $0.65. It is sold to dealers for $0.60 each, and the amount received for advertising is 10% of the amount received for all magazines issued beyond 10,000. Find the least number of magazines that can be published without loss, that is, such that profit ≥ 0. (Assume that all issues will be sold.)

6. A company produces alarm clocks. During the regular workweek, the labor cost for producing one clock is $2.00. However, if a clock is produced in overtime the labor cost is $3.00. Management has decided to spend no more than a total of $25,000 per week for labor. The company must produce 11,000 clocks this week. What is the minimum number of clocks that must be produced during the regular workweek?

7. A company invests a total of $30,000 of surplus funds at two annual rates of interest: 5% and $6\frac{3}{4}$%. It wishes an annual yield of no less than $6\frac{1}{2}$%. What is the least amount of money that it must invest at the $6\frac{3}{4}$% rate?

8. The current ratio of Precision Machine Products is 3.8. If their current assets are $570,000, what are their current liabilities? To raise additional funds, what is the maximum amount they can borrow on a short-term basis if they want their current ratio to be no less than 2.6? (See Example 3 for an explanation of current ratio.)

9. A manufacturer presently has 2500 units of product in stock. The product is now selling at $4 per unit. Next month the unit price will increase by $0.50. The manufacturer wants the total revenue received from the sale of the 2500 units to be no less than $10,750. What is the maximum number of units that can be sold this month?

10. Suppose that consumers will purchase q units of a product at a price of $\dfrac{100}{q} + 1$ dollars per unit. What is the minimum number of units that must be sold in order that sales revenue be greater than $5000?

11. Painters are often paid either by the hour or on a per-job basis. The rate they receive can affect their working speed. For example, suppose they can work for $8.50 per hour, or for $300 plus $3 for each hour less than 40 if they complete the job in less than 40 hours. Suppose the job will take t hours. If $t \geq 40$, clearly the hourly rate is better. If $t < 40$, for what values of t is the hourly rate the better pay scale?

12. Suppose a company offers you a sales position with your choice of two methods of determining your yearly salary. One method pays $12,600 plus a bonus of 2% of your yearly sales. The other method pays a straight 8% commission of your sales. For what yearly sales' level is it better to choose the first method?

13. The dean of student affairs of a college is arranging for a rock group to perform a concert on campus. Their charge is a flat fee of $2440 or, instead, a fee of $1000 plus 40% of the gate. It is likely that 800 students will attend. At most, how much could the dean charge for a ticket so that the second arrangement is no more costly than the flat fee? If this maximum is charged, how much money will be left over to pay for publicity, guards, and other concert expenses?

2.4 ABSOLUTE VALUE

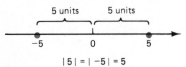

5 units   5 units

−5   0   5

$|5| = |−5| = 5$

FIGURE 2.14

Sometimes it is useful to consider, on the real number line, the distance between a number x and 0. We call this distance the **absolute value** of x and denote it by $|x|$. For example, $|5| = 5$ and $|−5| = 5$ because both 5 and $−5$ are 5 units from 0 (see Fig. 2.14). Similarly, $|0| = 0$.

If x is positive, clearly $|x| = x$. Just as $|−5| = 5 = −(−5)$, it should not be difficult to convince yourself that if x is any negative number, then $|x|$ is the positive number $−x$. The minus sign indicates that we have changed the sign of x. Thus, aside from its geometrical interpretation, absolute value can be defined as follows:

Definition
*The **absolute value** of a real number x, written $|x|$, is*

$$|x| = \begin{cases} x, & \text{if } x \geq 0, \\ -x, & \text{if } x < 0. \end{cases}$$

Applying the definition, we have $|3| = 3$; $|−8| = −(−8) = 8$; $|\frac{1}{2}| = \frac{1}{2}$; $−|2| = −2$; and $−|−2| = −2$. Notice that $|x|$ is always positive or zero; that is, $|x| \geq 0$.

Pitfall

$\sqrt{x^2}$ is not necessarily x, but $\sqrt{x^2} = |x|$. For example, $\sqrt{(-2)^2} = |-2| = 2$, not -2. This agrees with the fact that $\sqrt{(-2)^2} = \sqrt{4} = 2$. Also, $|-x| \neq x$ and $|-x - 1| \neq x + 1$. For example, if we let $x = -3$, then $|-(-3)| \neq -3$ and $|-(-3) - 1| \neq -3 + 1$.

EXAMPLE 1   *Solve each equation for x.*

a. $|x - 3| = 2$.

This equation states that $x - 3$ is a number 2 units from 0. Thus either

$$x - 3 = 2 \quad \text{or} \quad x - 3 = -2.$$

Solving these gives $x = 5$ and $x = 1$.

b. $|7 - 3x| = 5$.

The equation is true if $7 - 3x = 5$ or if $7 - 3x = -5$. Solving these gives $x = \frac{2}{3}$ and $x = 4$.

c. $|x - 4| = -3$.

The absolute value of a number is never negative. Thus the solution set is $\emptyset$.

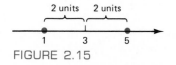

2 units   2 units

1   3   5

FIGURE 2.15

The numbers 5 and 9 are 4 units apart. Also,

$$|9 - 5| = |4| = 4,$$
$$|5 - 9| = |-4| = 4.$$

In general, we may interpret $|a - b|$ or $|b - a|$ as the distance between a and b.

For example, the equation $|x - 3| = 2$ states that the distance between x and 3 is 2 units. Thus x can be 1 or 5, as shown in Example 1(a) and Fig. 2.15.

Let us turn now to inequalities. If $|x| < 3$, then x is less than 3 units from 0. Thus x must lie between -3 and 3. That is, $-3 < x < 3$ [see Fig. 2.16(a)]. On the other hand, if $|x| > 3$, then x must be greater than 3 units from 0. Thus there are two cases: either $x > 3$ or $x < -3$ [see Fig. 2.16(b)]. We can extend these ideas. If $|x| \leq 3$, then $-3 \leq x \leq 3$. If $|x| \geq 3$, then $x \geq 3$ or $x \leq -3$.

In general, the solution of $|x| < d$ or $|x| \leq d$, where d is a positive number, consists of one interval, namely $-d < x < d$ or $-d \leq x \leq d$. However, when $|x| > d$ or $|x| \geq d$ there are two intervals in the solution, namely $x < -d$ and $x > d$, or $x \leq -d$ and $x \geq d$.

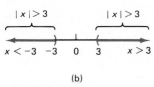

$|x| < 3;\ -3 < x < 3$

-3 0   3

(a)

$|x| > 3$ $|x| > 3$

$x < -3$ -3 0   3 $x > 3$

(b)

FIGURE 2.16

EXAMPLE 2   *Solve each inequality for x.*

a. $|x - 2| < 4$.

The number $x - 2$ must be less than 4 units from 0. From our discussion above, this means that $-4 < x - 2 < 4$. We may set up the procedure for solving this inequality as follows:

$$-4 < x - 2 < 4,$$

$$-4 + 2 < x < 4 + 2 \qquad \text{(adding 2 to each member)},$$

$$-2 < x < 6.$$

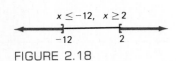

$-2 < x < 6$

−2   6

FIGURE 2.17

Thus the solution is $-2 < x < 6$. This means that all numbers between -2 and 6 satisfy the original inequality (see Fig. 2.17).

b. $|3 - 2x| \leq 5.$

$$-5 \leq 3 - 2x \leq 5,$$

$$-5 - 3 \leq -2x \leq 5 - 3 \qquad \text{(subtracting 3 from each member)},$$

$$-8 \leq -2x \leq 2,$$

$$4 \geq x \geq -1 \qquad \text{(dividing each member by } -2\text{)},$$

$$-1 \leq x \leq 4 \qquad \text{(rewriting)}.$$

Note that the sense of the original inequality was *reversed* when we divided by a negative number.

EXAMPLE 3   *Solve each inequality for x.*

$x \leq -12, \quad x \geq 2$

−12   2

FIGURE 2.18

a. $|x + 5| \geq 7.$

Here $x + 5$ must be *at least* 7 units from 0. Thus, either $x + 5 \leq -7$ or $x + 5 \geq 7$. This means that either $x \leq -12$ or $x \geq 2$ (see Fig. 2.18).

b. $|3x - 4| > 1.$

Either $3x - 4 < -1$ or $3x - 4 > 1$. Thus either $3x < 3$ or $3x > 5$. Therefore, $x < 1$ or $x > \frac{5}{3}$.

EXAMPLE 4   *Using absolute value notation, express the following statements:*

a. x is less than 3 units from 5.

$$|x - 5| < 3.$$

b. x differs from 6 by at least 7.

$$|x - 6| \geq 7.$$

c. $x < 3$ and $x > -3$ simultaneously.

$$|x| < 3.$$

d. x is more than 1 unit from -2.

$$|x - (-2)| > 1,$$

$$|x + 2| > 1.$$

e. x is less than σ (a Greek letter read "sigma") units from μ (a Greek letter read "mu").

$$|x - \mu| < \sigma.$$

Three basic properties of absolute value are

$$\textbf{1. } |ab| = |a| \cdot |b|.$$

$$\textbf{2. } \left|\frac{a}{b}\right| = \frac{|a|}{|b|}.$$

$$\textbf{3. } |a - b| = |b - a|.$$

EXAMPLE 5

a. $|(-7) \cdot 3| = |-7| \cdot |3| = 21;\ |(-7)(-3)| = |-7| \cdot |-3| = 21.$

b. $|4 - 2| = |2 - 4| = 2.$

c. $|7 - x| = |x - 7|.$

d. $\left|\dfrac{-7}{3}\right| = \dfrac{|-7|}{|3|} = \dfrac{7}{3};\ \left|\dfrac{-7}{-3}\right| = \dfrac{|-7|}{|-3|} = \dfrac{7}{3}.$

e. $\left|\dfrac{x-3}{-5}\right| = \dfrac{|x-3|}{|-5|} = \dfrac{|x-3|}{5}.$

EXERCISE 2.4

In Problems **1–10**, *write an equivalent form without the absolute value symbol.*

1. $|-13|.$

2. $|2^{-1}|.$

3. $|8 - 2|.$

4. $|(-4 - 6)/2|.$

5. $|3(-\frac{5}{3})|.$

6. $|2 - 7| - |7 - 2|.$

7. $|x| < 3.$

8. $|x| < 10.$

9. $|2 - \sqrt{5}|.$

10. $|\sqrt{5} - 2|.$

11. Using the absolute value symbol, express each fact.
  a. x is less than 3 units from 7.
  b. x differs from 2 by less than 3.
  c. x is no more than 5 units from 7.
  d. The distance between 7 and x is 4.
  e. $x + 4$ is less than 2 units from 0.
  f. x is between -3 and 3, but is not equal to 3 or -3.
  g. $x < -6$ or $x > 6$.
  h. $x - 6 > 4$ or $x - 6 < -4$.
  i. The number x of hours that a machine will operate efficiently differs from 105 by less than 3.
  j. The average monthly income x (in dollars) of a family differs from 850 by less than 100.

12. Use absolute value notation to indicate that x and μ differ by no more than σ.

13. Use absolute value notation to indicate that the prices p_1 and p_2 of two products may differ by no more than 2 (dollars).

14. Find all values of x such that $|x - \mu| \leq 2\sigma$.

In Problems **15–36,** *solve the given equation or inequality.*

15. $|x| = 7.$

16. $|-x| = 2.$

17. $\left|\dfrac{x}{3}\right| = 2.$

18. $\left|\dfrac{4}{x}\right| = 8.$

19. $|x - 5| = 8.$

20. $|4 + 3x| = 2.$

21. $|5x - 2| = 0.$

22. $|7x + 3| = x.$

23. $|7 - 4x| = 5.$

24. $|1 - 2x| = 1.$

25. $|x| < 4.$

26. $|-x| < 3.$

27. $\left|\dfrac{x}{4}\right| > 2.$

28. $\left|\dfrac{x}{3}\right| > \dfrac{1}{2}.$

29. $|x + 7| < 2.$

30. $|5x - 1| < -6.$

31. $|x - \frac{1}{2}| > \frac{1}{2}.$

32. $|1 - 3x| > 2.$

33. $|5 - 2x| \leq 1.$

34. $|4x - 1| \geq 0.$

35. $\left|\dfrac{3x - 8}{2}\right| \geq 4.$

36. $\left|\dfrac{x - 8}{4}\right| \leq 2.$

37. In statistical analysis, the Chebyshev inequality asserts that if x is a random variable, μ its mean, and σ its standard deviation, then

$$(\text{probability that } |x - \mu| > h\sigma) \leq \frac{1}{h^2}.$$

Find those values of x such that $|x - \mu| > h\sigma.$

38. In the manufacture of widgets, the average dimension of a part is 0.01 cm. Using the absolute value symbol, express the fact that an individual measurement x of a part does not differ from the average by more than 0.005 cm.

2.5 REVIEW

Important Terms and Symbols

Section 2.1	fixed cost	overhead	variable cost	total cost	total revenue	profit

Section 2.2 $a < b$ $a \leq b$ $a > b$ $a \geq b$ $a < x < b$ inequality
sense of inequality   equivalent inequality   linear inequality $-\infty < x < \infty$
open interval   closed interval

Section 2.4   absolute value, $|x|$

Summary

With a word problem, an equation is not handed to you. Instead, you must set it up by translating verbal statements into an equation (or inequality). This is *mathematical modeling*. It is important that you first read the problem more than once so that you clearly understand what facts are given and what you are asked to find. Then choose a letter to represent the unknown quantity that you want to find. Use the relationships and facts given in the problem and translate them into an equation involving the letter. Finally, solve the equation and see if your solution answers what was asked. Sometimes the solution to the *equation* will not be the answer to the *problem,* but it may be useful in obtaining that answer.

Some basic relationships that are used in solving business problems are:

$$\text{total cost} = \text{variable cost} + \text{fixed cost,}$$

$$\text{total revenue} = (\text{price per unit})(\text{number of units sold}).$$

$$\text{profit} = \text{total revenue} - \text{total cost.}$$

The inequality symbols $<$, $\leq$, $>$, and $\geq$ are used to represent an inequality, which is a statement that one number is, for example, less than another number. Three basic operations that, when applied to an inequality, guarantee an equivalent inequality are:

1. Adding (or subtracting) the same number to (or from) both sides.

2. Multiplying (or dividing) both sides by the same positive number.

3. Multiplying (or dividing) both sides by the same negative number and reversing the sense of the inequality.

These operations are useful in solving a linear inequality (one that can be put in the form $ax + b < 0$ or $ax + b \leq 0$, where $a \neq 0$).

An algebraic definition of absolute value is:

$$|x| = x, \text{ if } x \geq 0 \qquad \text{and} \qquad |x| = -x, \text{ if } x < 0.$$

We interpret $|a - b|$ or $|b - a|$ as the distance between a and b. If $d > 0$, then the solution to the inequality $|x| < d$ is the interval given by $-d < x < d$. The solution to $|x| > d$ consists of two intervals, namely the intervals given by $x < -d$ and $x > d$. Three basic properties of absolute value are:

1. $|ab| = |a| \cdot |b|$,

2. $\left|\dfrac{a}{b}\right| = \dfrac{|a|}{|b|}$,

3. $|a - b| = |b - a|$.

Review Problems

In Problems **1–15**, *solve the equation or inequality.*

1. $3x - 8 \geq 4(x - 2)$.

2. $2x - (7 + x) \leq x$.

3. $-(5x + 2) < -(2x + 4)$.

4. $-2(x + 6) > x + 4$.

5. $3p(1 - p) > 3(2 + p) - 3p^2$.

6. $2(4 - \frac{3}{5}q) < 5$.

7. $\dfrac{x + 1}{3} - \dfrac{1}{2} \leq 2$.

8. $\dfrac{x}{2} + \dfrac{x}{3} < \dfrac{x}{4}$.

9. $\dfrac{1}{4}s - 3 \leq \dfrac{1}{8}(3 + 2s)$.

10. $\dfrac{1}{3}(t + 2) \geq \dfrac{1}{4}t + 4$.

11. $|3 - 2x| = 7$.

12. $\left|\dfrac{5x - 8}{13}\right| = 0$.

13. $|4t - 1| < 1$.

14. $4 < \left|\dfrac{2}{3}x + 5\right|$.

15. $|3 - 2x| \geq 4$.

16. A profit of 40% on the selling price of a product is equivalent to what percent profit on the cost?

17. On a certain day, there were 1132 different issues traded on the New York Stock Exchange. There were 48 more issues showing an increase than showing a decline and no issues remained the same. How many issues suffered a decline?

18. The sales tax in a certain state is 6%. If a total of $3017.29 in purchases, including tax, is made in the course of a year, how much of it is tax?

19. A company will manufacture a total of 10,000 units of its product at plants A and B. Available data are shown in the table below.

	PLANT A	PLANT B
Unit cost for labor and material	$5	$5.50
Fixed costs	$30,000	$35,000

Between the two plants the company has decided to allot no more than $117,000 for total costs. What is the minimum number of units that must be produced at plant A?

20. A company is replacing two cylindrical oil-storage tanks with one new tank. The old tanks are each 16 ft high. One has a radius of 15 ft and the other a radius of 20 ft. The new tank will also be 16 ft high. Find its radius if it is to have the same volume as the old tanks combined. (*Hint:* The volume V of a cylindrical tank is $V = \pi r^2 h$, where r is the radius and h is the height.)

Functions and Graphs

3.1 FUNCTIONS

In the seventeenth century, Gottfried Wilhelm Leibniz, one of the inventors of calculus, introduced the term *function* into the mathematical vocabulary. The concept of a function is one of the most basic in all of mathematics, and it is essential to the study of calculus.

Briefly, a function is a special type of input-output relation that expresses how one quantity (the *output*) depends on another quantity (the *input*). For example, when money is invested at some interest rate, the interest I (output) depends on the length of time t (input) that the money is invested. To express this dependence, we say that "I is a function of t." Functional relations like this are usually specified by a formula that shows what must be done to the input to find the output.

To illustrate, suppose \$100 earns simple interest at an annual rate of 6%. Then it can be shown that interest and time are related by the formula

$$I = 100(0.06)t, \tag{1}$$

where I is in dollars and t is in years. For example,

$$\text{if } t = \tfrac{1}{2}, \quad \text{then} \quad I = 100(0.06)(\tfrac{1}{2}) = 3. \tag{2}$$

Thus Formula (1) assigns to the input $\tfrac{1}{2}$ the output 3. We can think of Formula (1) as defining a *rule:* Multiply t by 100(0.06). The rule assigns to each input number t exactly one output number I, which we symbolize by the following arrow notation:

$$t \rightarrow I \quad \text{or} \quad t \rightarrow 100(0.06)t.$$

This rule is an example of a *function* in the following sense:

Definition

*A **function** is a rule that assigns to each input number exactly one output number. The set of all input numbers to which the rule applies is called the **domain** of the function. The set of all output numbers is called the **range**.*

For the interest function defined by Formula (1), the input number t cannot be negative because negative time makes no sense. Thus the domain consists of all nonnegative numbers; that is, all $t \geq 0$. From (2) we see that, when the input is $\frac{1}{2}$, the output is 3. Thus 3 is in the range.

We have been using the term *function* in a restricted sense because, in general, the inputs or outputs do not have to be numbers. For example, a list of states and their capitals assigns to each state its capital (exactly one output). Thus a function is implied. However, for the time being we shall consider only functions whose domains and ranges consist of real numbers.

A variable that represents input numbers for a function is called an **independent variable**. A variable that represents output numbers is called a **dependent variable** because its value *depends* on the value of the independent variable. We say that the dependent variable is a *function of* the independent variable. That is, output is a function of input. Thus for the interest formula $I = 100(0.06)t$, the independent variable is t, the dependent variable is I, and I is a function of t.

As another example, the equation (or formula)

$$y = x + 2 \tag{3}$$

defines y as a function of x. It gives the rule: Add 2 to x. This rule assigns to each input x exactly one output $x + 2$, which is y. Thus if $x = 1$, then $y = 3$; if $x = -4$, then $y = -2$. The independent variable is x and the dependent variable is y.

Not all equations in x and y define y as a function of x. For example, let $y^2 = x$. If x is 9, then $y^2 = 9$, so $y = \pm 3$. Thus to the input 9 there are assigned not one but *two* output numbers, 3 and -3. This violates the definition of a function, so y is **not** a function of x.

On the other hand, some equations in two variables define either variable as a function of the other variable. For example, if $y = 2x$, then for each input x there is exactly one output, $2x$. Thus y is a function of x. However, solving the equation for x gives $x = y/2$. For each input y there is exactly one output, $y/2$. Thus x is a function of y.

Usually, the letters f, g, h, F, G, and so on are used to represent function rules. For example, Eq. (3) above ($y = x + 2$) defines y as a function of x, where the rule is add 2 to the input. Suppose we let f represent this rule. Then we say that f is the function. To indicate that f assigns to the input 1 the output 3, we write $f(1) = 3$, which is read "f of 1 equals 3." Similarly, $f(-4) = -2$. More generally, if x is any input, we have the following notation:

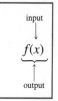

f(x), which is read "f of x," means the output number in the range of f that corresponds to the input number x in the domain.

Thus the output $f(x)$ is the same as y. But since $y = x + 2$, we may write $y = f(x) = x + 2$ or simply

$$f(x) = x + 2.$$

For example, to find $f(3)$, which is the output corresponding to the input 3, we replace each x in $f(x) = x + 2$ by 3:

$$f(3) = 3 + 2 = 5.$$

Likewise,

$$f(8) = 8 + 2 = 10,$$

$$f(-4) = -4 + 2 = -2.$$

Output numbers such as $f(-4)$ are called **function values** (or functional values). Keep in mind that they are in the range of f.

Pitfall
$f(x)$ does **not** mean f times x.

Quite often, functions are defined by "functional notation." For example, the equation $g(x) = x^3 + x^2$ defines the function g that assigns to an input number x the output number $x^3 + x^2$.

$$g: \quad x \rightarrow x^3 + x^2.$$

Thus g adds the cube and the square of an input number. Some function values are

$$g(2) = 2^3 + 2^2 = 12,$$

$$g(-1) = (-1)^3 + (-1)^2 = -1 + 1 = 0,$$

$$g(t) = t^3 + t^2,$$

$$g(x + 1) = (x + 1)^3 + (x + 1)^2.$$

Note that $g(x + 1)$ was found by replacing each x in $x^3 + x^2$ by the input $x + 1$.

When we refer to the function g defined by $g(x) = x^3 + x^2$, we shall feel free to call the equation itself a function. Thus we speak of "the function $g(x) = x^3 + x^2$," and similarly, "the function $y = x + 2$."

Let's be specific about the domain of a function that is given by an equation. Unless otherwise stated, the domain consists of all real numbers for which that equation makes sense and gives function values that are real numbers. For example, suppose

$$h(x) = \frac{1}{x - 6}.$$

Here any real number can be used for x except 6 because the denominator is 0 when x is 6 (we cannot divide by zero). Thus the domain of h is understood to be all real numbers except 6.

EXAMPLE 1   *Find the domain of each function.*

a. $f(x) = \dfrac{x}{x^2 - x - 2}.$

We cannot divide by zero, so we must find any values of x that make the denominator 0. These *cannot* be input numbers. Thus we set the denominator equal to 0 and solve for x.

$$x^2 - x - 2 = 0 \qquad \text{(quadratic equation)},$$

$$(x - 2)(x + 1) = 0 \qquad \text{(factoring)},$$

$$x = 2, -1.$$

Therefore, the domain of f is all real numbers *except* 2 and -1.

b. $g(t) = \sqrt{2t - 1}.$

We cannot have function values that involve imaginary numbers. To avoid square roots of negative numbers, $2t - 1$ must be greater than or equal to 0.

$$2t - 1 \geq 0,$$

$$2t \geq 1 \qquad \text{(adding 1 to both sides)},$$

$$t \geq \frac{1}{2} \qquad \text{(dividing both sides by 2)}.$$

Thus the domain is all real numbers t such that $t \geq \frac{1}{2}$.

EXAMPLE 2   *Domain and functional notation.*

Let $g(x) = 3x^2 - x + 5.$

Any real number can be used for x, so the domain of g is all real numbers.

$$g(x) = 3x^2 - x + 5.$$

Find $g(z)$: $g(z) = 3(z)^2 - z + 5 = 3z^2 - z + 5.$

Find $g(r^2)$: $g(r^2) = 3(r^2)^2 - r^2 + 5 = 3r^4 - r^2 + 5.$

Find $g(x + h)$: $g(x + h) = 3(x + h)^2 - (x + h) + 5$

$$= 3(x^2 + 2hx + h^2) - x - h + 5$$

$$= 3x^2 + 6hx + 3h^2 - x - h + 5.$$

Pitfall

Don't be confused by notation. In Example 2 we found $g(x + h)$ by replacing each x in $g(x) = 3x^2 - x + 5$ by the input $x + h$. **Don't** write the function and then add h. That is, $g(x + h) \neq g(x) + h$.

$$g(x + h) \neq 3x^2 - x + 5 + h.$$

Also, **don't** use the distributive law on $g(x + h)$. It does **not** stand for multiplication.

$$g(x + h) \neq g(x) + g(h).$$

EXAMPLE 3   *If* $f(x) = x^2$, *find* $\dfrac{f(x + h) - f(x)}{h}$.

Here the numerator is a difference of function values.

$$\frac{f(x + h) - f(x)}{h} = \frac{(x + h)^2 - x^2}{h}$$

$$= \frac{x^2 + 2hx + h^2 - x^2}{h} = \frac{2hx + h^2}{h}$$

$$= \frac{h(2x + h)}{h} = 2x + h.$$

In some cases the domain of a function is restricted for physical or economic reasons. For example, the previous interest function $I = 100(0.06)t$ has $t \geq 0$ because t represents time. Example 4 will give another illustration.

EXAMPLE 4   Suppose that the equation $p = 100/q$ describes the relationship between the price per unit, p, of a certain product and the number of units, q, of that product that consumers will buy (that is, demand) per week at that price. This equation is called a *demand equation* for the product. If q is an input number, then to each value of q there is assigned exactly one output number p:

$$q \to \frac{100}{q} = p.$$

For example,

$$20 \to \frac{100}{20} = 5;$$

that is, when q is 20, then p is 5. Thus price p is a function of quantity de-manded, q. Here q is the independent variable and p is the dependent variable. Since q cannot be 0 (division by 0 is not defined) and cannot be negative (q represents quantity), the domain is all values of q such that $q > 0$. This function is called a **demand function.**

EXERCISE 3.1

In Problems **1–12**, give the domain of each function.

1. $f(x) = \dfrac{3}{x}$.

2. $g(x) = \dfrac{x}{3}$.

3. $h(x) = \sqrt{x - 5}$.

4. $H(z) = \dfrac{1}{\sqrt{z}}$.

5. $F(t) = 3t^2 + 5$.

6. $H(x) = \dfrac{x}{x + 2}$.

7. $f(x) = \dfrac{3x - 1}{2x + 5}$.

8. $g(x) = \sqrt{4x + 3}$.

9. $G(y) = \dfrac{4}{y^2 - y}$.

10. $f(x) = \dfrac{x + 1}{x^2 + 6x + 5}$.

11. $h(s) = \dfrac{4 - s^2}{2s^2 - 7s - 4}$.

12. $G(r) = \dfrac{2}{r^2 + 1}$.

In Problems **13–24**, find the function values for each function.

13. $f(x) = 5x$; $f(0)$, $f(3)$, $f(-4)$.

14. $H(s) = s^2 - 3$; $H(4)$, $H(\sqrt{2})$, $H(\tfrac{2}{3})$.

15. $G(x) = 2 - x^2$; $G(-8)$, $G(u)$, $G(u^2)$.

16. $f(x) = 7x$; $f(s)$, $f(t + 1)$, $f(x + 3)$.

17. $g(u) = u^2 + u$; $g(-2)$, $g(2v)$, $g(-x^2)$.

18. $h(v) = \dfrac{1}{\sqrt{v}}$; $h(16)$, $h\left(\dfrac{1}{4}\right)$, $h(1 - x)$.

19. $f(x) = x^2 + 2x + 1$; $f(1)$, $f(-1)$, $f(x + h)$.

20. $H(x) = (x + 4)^2$; $H(0)$, $H(2)$, $H(t - 4)$.

21. $g(x) = \dfrac{x - 5}{x^2 + 4}$; $g(5)$, $g(3x)$, $g(x + h)$.

22. $H(x) = \sqrt{4 + x}$; $H(-4)$, $H(-3)$, $H(x + 1) - H(x)$.

23. $f(x) = x^{4/3}$; $f(0)$, $f(64)$, $f(\tfrac{1}{8})$.

24. $g(x) = x^{2/5}$; $g(32)$, $g(-64)$, $g(t^{10})$.

In Problems **25–28**, find (a) $f(x + h)$ and (b) $\dfrac{f(x + h) - f(x)}{h}$; simplify your answers.

25. $f(x) = 3x - 4$.

26. $f(x) = \dfrac{x}{2}$.

27. $f(x) = x^2 + 2x$.

28. $f(x) = 2x^2 - 3x - 5$.

In Problems **29–32**, is y a function of x? Is x a function of y?

29. $y - 3x - 4 = 0$.

30. $x^2 + y = 0$.

31. $y = 7x^2$.

32. $x^2 + y^2 = 1$.

33. The formula for the area A of a circle of radius r is $A = \pi r^2$. Is the area a function of the radius?

34. Suppose $f(b) = ab^2 + a^2b$. (a) Find $f(a)$. (b) Find $f(ab)$.

35. A business with an original capital of $10,000 has income and expenses each week of $2000 and $1600, respectively. If all profits are retained in the business, express the value V of the business at the end of t weeks as a function of t.

36. If a $30,000 machine depreciates 2% of its original value each year, find a function f that expresses its value V after t years have elapsed.

37. If q units of a certain product are sold (q is nonnegative), the profit P is given by the equation $P = 1.25q$. Is P a function of q? What is the dependent variable; the independent variable?

38. An insurance company examined the records of a group of individuals hospitalized for a particular illness. It was found that the total proportion who had been discharged at the end of t days of hospitalization is given by $f(t)$, where

$$f(t) = 1 - \left(\frac{300}{300 + t}\right)^3.$$

Evaluate (a) $f(0)$, (b) $f(100)$, and (c) $f(300)$. (d) At the end of how many days was 0.999 of the group discharged?

39. A psychophysical experiment was conducted to analyze human response to electrical shocks.* The subjects received a shock of a certain intensity. They were told to assign a magnitude of 10 to this particular shock, called the standard stimulus. Then other shocks (stimuli) of various intensities were given. For each one the response R was to be a number that indicated the perceived magnitude of the shock relative to that of the standard stimulus. It was found that R was a function of the intensity I of the shock (I in microamperes) and was estimated by

$$R = f(I) = \frac{I^{4/3}}{2500}, \qquad 500 \leq I \leq 3500.$$

Evaluate (a) $f(1000)$ and (b) $f(2000)$. (c) Suppose I_0 and $2I_0$ are in the domain of f. Express $f(2I_0)$ in terms of $f(I_0)$. What effect does the doubling of intensity have on response?

40. In a paired-associate learning experiment,† the probability of a correct response as a function of the number n of trials has the form

$$P(n) = 1 - \frac{1}{2}(1 - c)^{n-1}, \qquad n \geq 1,$$

where the estimated value of c is 0.344. Find $P(1)$ and $P(2)$ by using this value of c.

3.2 SPECIAL FUNCTIONS

In this section we shall look at functions having special forms and representations. We begin with perhaps the simplest type of function there is: a *constant function*.

EXAMPLE 1   Let $h(x) = 2$. The domain of h is all real numbers. All function values are 2. For example,

$$h(10) = 2, \qquad h(-387) = 2, \qquad h(x + 3) = 2.$$

We call h a *constant function*. More generally, we have this definition:

* Adapted from H. Babkoff, "Magnitude Estimation of Short Electrocutaneous Pulses," *Psychological Research*, 39, no. 1 (1976), 39–49.

† D. Laming, *Mathematical Psychology* (New York: Academic Press, Inc., 1973).

> A function of the form $h(x) = c$, where c is a *constant*, is called a **constant function.**

A constant function belongs to a broader class of functions, called *polynomial functions,* as Example 2 shows.

EXAMPLE 2   A function of the form

$$f(x) = c_n x^n + c_{n-1} x^{n-1} + \cdots + c_1 x + c_0,$$

where n is a nonnegative integer and $c_n, c_{n-1}, \ldots, c_0$ are constants with $c_n \neq 0$, is called a **polynomial function** (in x). The number n is called the **degree** of the function, and c_n is the **leading coefficient.** Thus $f(x) = 3x^2 - 8x + 9$ is a polynomial function of degree 2 with leading coefficient 3. Likewise, $g(x) = 4 - 2x$ has degree 1 and leading coefficient -2. Polynomial functions of degree 1 or 2 are called **linear** or **quadratic functions,** respectively. Hence $g(x) = 4 - 2x$ is linear and $f(x) = 3x^2 - 8x + 9$ is quadratic. Note that a nonzero constant function, such as $f(x) = 5$, has degree 0. The constant function $f(x) = 0$ is also considered a polynomial function but has no degree assigned to it. The domain of any polynomial function is all real numbers.

Sometimes more than one equation is needed to define a function, as Example 3 shows.

EXAMPLE 3   Let

$$F(s) = \begin{cases} 1, & \text{if } -1 \leq s < 1, \\ 0, & \text{if } 1 \leq s \leq 2, \\ s - 3, & \text{if } 2 < s \leq 3 \end{cases}$$

This is called a **compound function** because it is defined by more than one equation. Here s is the independent variable and the domain of F is all s such that $-1 \leq s \leq 3$. The value of s determines which equation to use.

Find $F(0)$:   Since $-1 \leq 0 < 1$, we have $F(0) = 1$.

Find $F(2)$:   Since $1 \leq 2 \leq 2$, we have $F(2) = 0$.

Find $F(\frac{9}{4})$:   Since $2 < \frac{9}{4} \leq 3$, we substitute $\frac{9}{4}$ for s in $s - 3$.

$$F(\tfrac{9}{4}) = \tfrac{9}{4} - 3 = -\tfrac{3}{4}.$$

EXAMPLE 4   The function $f(x) = |x|$ is called the *absolute value function.* Recall that the **absolute value,** or **magnitude,** of a real number x is denoted $|x|$ and is defined by

$$|x| = \begin{cases} x, & \text{if } x \geq 0, \\ -x, & \text{if } x < 0. \end{cases}$$

Thus the domain of f is all real numbers. Some function values are

$$f(16) = |16| = 16,$$

$$f(-\tfrac{4}{3}) = |-\tfrac{4}{3}| = -(-\tfrac{4}{3}) = \tfrac{4}{3},$$

$$f(0) = |0| = 0.$$

EXAMPLE 5   *Suppose two black guinea pigs are bred and produce exactly five offspring. Under certain conditions it can be shown that the probability P that exactly r of the offspring will be brown and the others black is a function of r, say P = P(r), where*

$$P(r) = \frac{5!(\tfrac{1}{4})^r(\tfrac{3}{4})^{5-r}}{r!(5-r)!}, \qquad r = 0, 1, 2, \ldots, 5.$$

*The letter P in P = P(r) is used in two ways. On the right side, P represents the function rule. On the left side, P represents the dependent variable. The domain of P is all integers from 0 to 5 inclusive. The symbol r!, where r is a positive integer, is read "**r factorial.**" It represents the product of the first r positive integers: r! = 1 · 2 · 3 ··· r. For example, 5! = 1 · 2 · 3 · 4 · 5 = 120. We define 0! to be 1. Find the probability that exactly three guinea pigs will be brown.*

We want to find $P(3)$.

$$P(3) = \frac{5!(\tfrac{1}{4})^3(\tfrac{3}{4})^2}{3!2!} = \frac{120(\tfrac{1}{64})(\tfrac{9}{16})}{6(2)} = \frac{45}{512}.$$

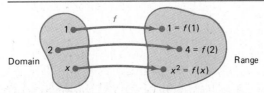

FIGURE 3.1

We have seen that a function is essentially a *correspondence* whereby to each input number in the domain there is assigned exactly one output number in the range. For the correspondence given by $f(x) = x^2$, some sample assignments are shown by the arrows in Fig. 3.1. The next example shows a functional correspondence that is not given by an algebraic formula.

EXAMPLE 6   The table in Fig. 3.2 is a *supply schedule*. It gives a correspondence between the price p of a certain product and the quantity q the producers will supply per week at that price. For each price there corresponds exactly one quantity, and vice versa.

Supply schedule

p	q
Price per unit in dollars	Quantity supplied per week
500	11
600	14
700	17
800	20

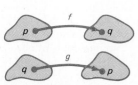

FIGURE 3.2

If p is the independent variable, then q is a function of p, say $q = f(p)$, and

$$f(500) = 11, \quad f(600) = 14, \quad f(700) = 17, \quad \text{and} \quad f(800) = 20.$$

Similarly, if q is the independent variable, then p is a function of q, say $p = g(q)$, and

$$g(11) = 500, \quad g(14) = 600, \quad g(17) = 700, \quad \text{and} \quad g(20) = 800.$$

We speak of f and g as **supply functions.** Notice from the supply schedule that, as price per unit increases, the producers are willing to supply more units per week.

EXERCISE 3.2

In Problems **1–4,** *find the domain of each function.*

1. $H(z) = 10$.

2. $f(t) = \pi$.

3. $f(x) = \begin{cases} 2x, & \text{if } x > 1, \\ 3, & \text{if } x \leq 1. \end{cases}$

4. $f(x) = \begin{cases} 4, & \text{if } x = 3, \\ x^2, & \text{if } 1 \leq x < 3. \end{cases}$

In Problems **5–8,** *state (a) the degree and (b) the leading coefficient of the given polynomial function.*

5. $F(x) = 2x^3 - 5x^2 + 6$.

6. $f(x) = x$.

7. $f(x) = 2 - 3x^4 + 2x$.

8. $f(x) = 9$.

In Problems **9–14,** *find the function values for each function.*

9. $f(x) = 12$; $f(2)$, $f(t + 8)$, $f(-\sqrt{17})$.

10. $g(x) = |x - 3|$; $g(10)$, $g(3)$, $g(-3)$.

11. $F(t) = \begin{cases} 1, & \text{if } t > 0 \\ 0, & \text{if } t = 0; \\ -1, & \text{if } t < 0 \end{cases}$ $F(10)$, $F(-\sqrt{3})$, $F(0)$, $F(-\tfrac{18}{5})$.

12. $f(x) = \begin{cases} 4, & \text{if } x \geq 0 \\ 3, & \text{if } x < 0 \end{cases}$; $f(3)$, $f(-4)$, $f(0)$.

13. $G(x) = \begin{cases} x, & \text{if } x \geq 3 \\ 2 - x, & \text{if } x < 3 \end{cases}$; $G(8)$, $G(3)$, $G(-1)$, $G(1)$.

14. $h(r) = \begin{cases} 3r - 1, & \text{if } r > 2 \\ r^2 - 4r + 7, & \text{if } r < 2 \end{cases}$; $h(3)$, $h(-3)$, $h(2)$.

15. In manufacturing a component for a machine, the initial cost of a die is $850 and all other additional costs are $3 per unit produced. (a) Express the total cost C (in dollars) as a linear function of the number q of units produced. (b) How many units are produced if the total cost is $1600?

16. If a principal of P dollars is invested at a simple annual interest rate of r for t years, express the total accumulated amount of the principal and interest as a function of t. Is your result a linear function of t?

17. Under certain conditions, if two brown-eyed parents have exactly three children, the probability P that there will be exactly r blue-eyed children is given by the function $P = P(r)$, where

$$P(r) = \frac{3!(\frac{1}{4})^r(\frac{3}{4})^{3-r}}{r!(3-r)!}, \qquad r = 0, 1, 2, 3.$$

Find the probability that exactly two of the children will be blue-eyed.

18. In Example 5 find the probability that all five offspring will be brown.

19. Bacteria are growing in a culture. The time t (in hours) for the number of bacteria to double in number (generation time) is a function of the temperature T (in °C) of the culture. If this function is given by*

$$t = f(T) = \begin{cases} \frac{1}{24}T + \frac{11}{4}, & \text{if } 30 \le T \le 36, \\ \frac{4}{3}T - \frac{175}{4}, & \text{if } 36 < T \le 39, \end{cases}$$

(a) determine the domain of f, and (b) find $f(30)$, $f(36)$, and $f(39)$.

20. The table below is called a *demand schedule*. It gives a correspondence between the price p of a product and the quantity q that consumers will demand (that is, purchase) at that price. (a) If $p = f(q)$, list the numbers in the domain of f. Find $f(2900)$ and $f(3000)$. (b) If $q = g(p)$, list the numbers in the domain of g. Find $g(10)$ and $g(17)$.

PRICE PER UNIT, p	QUANTITY DEMANDED PER WEEK, q
$10	3000
12	2900
17	2300
20	2000

3.3 COMBINATIONS OF FUNCTIONS

There are different ways of combining two functions to create a new function. Suppose f and g are the functions given by

$$f(x) = x^2 \quad \text{and} \quad g(x) = 3x.$$

Adding $f(x)$ and $g(x)$ gives

$$f(x) + g(x) = x^2 + 3x.$$

This operation defines a new function called the **sum** of f and g, denoted **$f + g$**. Its function value at x is $f(x) + g(x)$. That is,

$$(f + g)(x) = f(x) + g(x) = x^2 + 3x.$$

For example,

$$(f + g)(2) = 2^2 + 3(2) = 10.$$

* Adapted from F. K. E. Imrie and A. J. Vlitos, "Production of Fungal Protein from Carob," in *Single-Cell Protein II*, ed. S. R. Tannenbaum and D. I. C. Wang (Cambridge, Mass.: MIT Press, 1975).

Similarly, we define the **difference** $f - g$, **product** fg, and **quotient** $\dfrac{f}{g}$ as follows:*

$$(f - g)(x) = f(x) - g(x) = x^2 - 3x,$$

$$(fg)(x) = f(x) \cdot g(x) = x^2(3x) = 3x^3,$$

$$\frac{f}{g}(x) = \frac{f(x)}{g(x)} = \frac{x^2}{3x} = \frac{x}{3}, \qquad \text{for } x \neq 0.$$

EXAMPLE 1   *If $f(x) = 3x - 1$ and $g(x) = x^2 + 3x$, find (a) $(f + g)(x)$, (b) $(f - g)(x)$, (c) $(fg)(x)$, and (d) $\dfrac{f}{g}(x)$.*

a. $(f + g)(x) = f(x) + g(x) = (3x - 1) + (x^2 + 3x) = x^2 + 6x - 1.$

b. $(f - g)(x) = f(x) - g(x) = (3x - 1) - (x^2 + 3x) = -1 - x^2.$

c. $(fg)(x) = f(x)g(x) = (3x - 1)(x^2 + 3x) = 3x^3 + 8x^2 - 3x.$

d. $\dfrac{f}{g}(x) = \dfrac{f(x)}{g(x)} = \dfrac{3x - 1}{x^2 + 3x}.$

We may also combine two functions by first applying one function to a number and then applying the other function to the result. For example, suppose $f(x) = x^2$, $g(x) = 3x$, and $x = 2$. Then $g(2) = 3(2) = 6$. Thus g sends the input 2 into the output 6:

$$2 \xrightarrow{g} 6.$$

Next, we let the output 6 become input to f.

$$f(6) = 6^2 = 36,$$

so f sends 6 into 36.

$$6 \xrightarrow{f} 36.$$

By first applying g and then f, we send 2 into 36.

$$2 \xrightarrow{g} 6 \xrightarrow{f} 36.$$

To be more general, let's replace the 2 by x, where x is in the domain of g (see Fig. 3.3). Applying g to x, we get the number $g(x)$, which we shall assume is in the domain of f. By applying f to $g(x)$, we get $f(g(x))$, read "f of g of x," which is in the range of f. This operation of applying g and then f defines a so-called "composite" function denoted $f \circ g$. This function assigns to the input number x the output number $f(g(x))$ [see the bottom arrow in Fig. 3.3]. Thus $(f \circ g)(x) = f(g(x))$. We can think of $f(g(x))$ as a function of a function.

---

* In each of the four combinations, we assume that x is in the domains of both f and g. In the quotient we also do not allow any value of x for which $g(x)$ is 0.

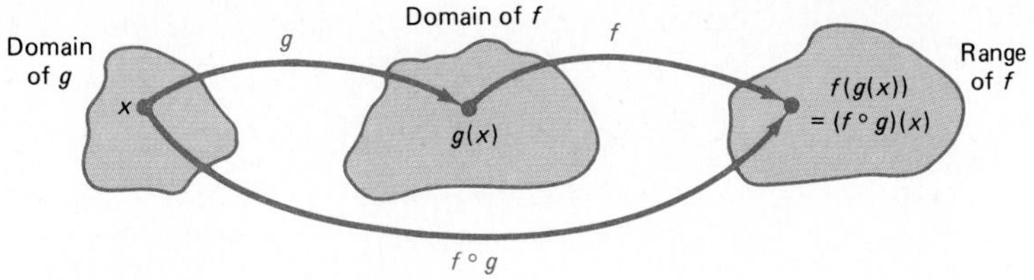

FIGURE 3.3

Definition

*If f and g are functions, the **composition of f with g** is the function f ∘ g defined by*

$$(f \circ g)(x) = f(g(x)),$$

where the domain of f ∘ g is the set of all x in the domain of g such that g(x) is in the domain of f.

For $f(x) = x^2$ and $g(x) = 3x$, we can get a simple form for $f \circ g$:

$$(f \circ g)(x) = f(g(x)) = f(3x) = (3x)^2 = 9x^2.$$

For example, $(f \circ g)(2) = 9(2)^2 = 36$, as we saw before.

EXAMPLE 2   *Let $f(x) = \sqrt{x}$ and $g(x) = x + 1$. Find (a) $(f \circ g)(x)$ and (b) $(g \circ f)(x)$.*

a. $(f \circ g)(x)$ is $f(g(x))$ and f takes the square root of an input number, which is $g(x)$ or $x + 1$. Thus

$$(f \circ g)(x) = f(g(x)) = f(x + 1) = \sqrt{x + 1}.$$

The domain of g is all real numbers x, and the domain of f is all nonnegative reals. Hence the domain of the composition is all x for which $g(x) = x + 1$ is nonnegative. That is, the domain is all $x \geq -1$.

b. $(g \circ f)(x)$ is $g(f(x))$ and g adds 1 to an input number, which is $f(x)$ or $\sqrt{x}$. Thus g adds 1 to $\sqrt{x}$.

$$(g \circ f)(x) = g(f(x)) = g(\sqrt{x}) = \sqrt{x} + 1.$$

The domain of f is all $x \geq 0$ and the domain of g is all reals. Hence the domain of the composition is all $x \geq 0$ for which $f(x) = \sqrt{x}$ is real, namely all $x \geq 0$.

Pitfall

Generally, $f \circ g \neq g \circ f$. In Example 2, $(f \circ g)(x) = \sqrt{x + 1}$, but $(g \circ f)(x) = \sqrt{x} + 1$. Also, do not confuse $f(g(x))$ with the product $f(x)g(x)$. Here

$$f(g(x)) = \sqrt{x + 1}$$

but $$f(x)g(x) = \sqrt{x}(x + 1).$$

EXAMPLE 3   If $F(p) = p^2 + 4p - 3$ and $G(p) = 2p + 1$, find (a) $F(G(p))$ and (b) $G(F(1))$.

a. $F(G(p)) = F(2p + 1) = (2p + 1)^2 + 4(2p + 1) - 3 = 4p^2 + 12p + 2$.

b. $G(F(1)) = G(1^2 + 4 \cdot 1 - 3) = G(2) = 2 \cdot 2 + 1 = 5$.

In calculus it is necessary at times to think of a particular function as being a composition of two simpler functions, as the next example shows.

EXAMPLE 4   The function $h(x) = (2x - 1)^3$ can be considered to be a composition. We note that $h(x)$ is obtained by finding $2x - 1$ and cubing the result. Suppose we let $g(x) = 2x - 1$ and $f(x) = x^3$. Then

$$h(x) = (2x - 1)^3 = [g(x)]^3 = f(g(x)) = (f \circ g)(x),$$

which gives h as a composition of two functions.

EXERCISE 3.3

1. If $f(x) = x + 1$ and $g(x) = x + 4$, find the following.

   a. $(f + g)(x)$.
   b. $(f + g)(0)$.
   c. $(f - g)(x)$.

   d. $(fg)(x)$.
   e. $(fg)(-2)$.
   f. $\dfrac{f}{g}(x)$.

   g. $(f \circ g)(x)$.
   h. $(f \circ g)(3)$.
   i. $(g \circ f)(x)$.

2. If $f(x) = 8x$ and $g(x) = 8 + x$, find the following.

   a. $(f + g)(x)$.
   b. $(f - g)(x)$.
   c. $(f - g)(4)$.

   d. $(fg)(x)$.
   e. $\dfrac{f}{g}(x)$.
   f. $\dfrac{f}{g}(2)$.

   g. $(f \circ g)(x)$.
   h. $(g \circ f)(x)$.
   i. $(g \circ f)(2)$.

3. If $f(x) = x^2$ and $g(x) = x^2 + x$, find the following.

   a. $(f + g)(x)$.
   b. $(f - g)(x)$.
   c. $(f - g)(-\tfrac{1}{2})$.

   d. $(fg)(x)$.
   e. $\dfrac{f}{g}(x)$.
   f. $\dfrac{f}{g}(-\tfrac{1}{2})$.

   g. $(f \circ g)(x)$.
   h. $(g \circ f)(x)$.
   i. $(g \circ f)(-3)$.

4. If $f(x) = x^2 - 1$ and $g(x) = 4$, find the following.

   a. $(f + g)(x)$.
   b. $(f + g)(\tfrac{1}{2})$.
   c. $(f - g)(x)$.

   d. $(fg)(x)$.
   e. $(fg)(4)$.
   f. $\dfrac{f}{g}(x)$.

   g. $(f \circ g)(x)$.
   h. $(f \circ g)(100)$.
   i. $(g \circ f)(x)$.

5. If $f(x) = 2x^2 + 3$ and $g(x) = 1 - 3x$, find $f(g(2))$ and $g(f(2))$.

6. If $f(p) = \dfrac{4}{p}$ and $g(p) = \dfrac{p - 2}{3}$, find $(f \circ g)(p)$ and $(g \circ f)(p)$.

7. If $F(t) = t^2 + 3t + 1$ and $G(t) = \dfrac{2}{t - 1}$, find $(F \circ G)(t)$ and $(G \circ F)(t)$.

8. If $F(s) = \sqrt{s}$ and $G(t) = 3t^2 + 4t + 2$, find $(F \circ G)(t)$ and $(G \circ F)(s)$.

9. If $f(w) = \dfrac{1}{w^2 + 1}$ and $g(v) = \sqrt{v + 2}$, find $(f \circ g)(v)$ and $(g \circ f)(w)$.

10. If $f(x) = x^2 + 3$, find $(f \circ f)(x)$.

In Problems **11–16,** *find functions f and g such that* $h(x) = f(g(x))$.

11. $h(x) = (3x + 1)^4$.

12. $h(x) = \sqrt{x^2 - 2}$.

13. $h(x) = \dfrac{1}{x^2 - 2}$.

14. $h(x) = (3x^3 - 2x)^3 - (3x^3 - 2x)^2 + 7$.

15. $h(x) = \sqrt[5]{\dfrac{x + 1}{3}}$.

16. $h(x) = \dfrac{x + 1}{(x + 1)^2 + 2}$.

17. A manufacturer determines that the total number of units of output per day, q, is a function of the number of employees, m, where $q = f(m) = (40m - m^2)/4$. The total revenue, r, that is received for selling q units is given by the function g, where $r = g(q) = 40q$. Determine $(g \circ f)(m)$. What does this composition function describe?

18. Studies have been conducted concerning the statistical relations between a person's status, education, and income.* Let S denote a numerical value of status based on annual income I. For a certain population, suppose

$$S = f(I) = 0.45(I - 1000)^{0.53}.$$

Furthermore, suppose a person's income I is a function of the number of years of education E, where

$$I = g(E) = 7202 + 0.29E^{3.68}.$$

Find $(f \circ g)(E)$. What does this function describe?

3.4 GRAPHS IN RECTANGULAR COORDINATES ⎯⎯⎯⎯⎯⎯⎯⎯⎯

A **rectangular** (or **Cartesian**) **coordinate system** allows us to specify and locate points in a plane. It also provides a geometric way to represent equations in two variables as well as functions.

In a plane two real number lines, called *coordinate axes,* are constructed perpendicular to each other so that their origins coincide as in Fig. 3.4. Their point of intersection is called the *origin* of the coordinate system. For now we shall call the horizontal line the *x-axis* and the vertical line the *y-axis*. The unit distance on the *x*-axis need not necessarily be the same as on the *y*-axis.

* R. K. Leik and B. F. Meeker, *Mathematical Sociology* (Englewood Cliffs, N.J.: Prentice-Hall, Inc., 1975).

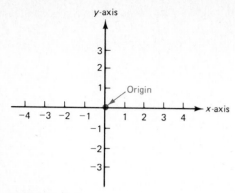

FIGURE 3.4

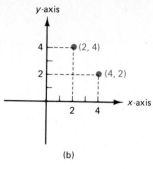

FIGURE 3.5

(a)

(b)

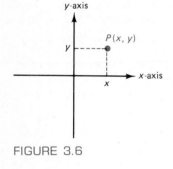

FIGURE 3.6

The plane on which the coordinate axes are placed is called a *rectangular coordinate plane* or, more simply, an *x,y-plane*. Every point in the *x,y*-plane can be labeled to indicate its position. To label point P in Fig. 3.5(a) we draw perpendiculars from P to the *x*-axis and *y*-axis. They meet these axes at 4 and 2, respectively. Thus P determines two numbers, 4 and 2. We say that the **rectangular coordinates** of P are given by the **ordered pair** (4, 2). The word "ordered" is important. In Fig. 3.5(b) the point corresponding to (4, 2) is not the same as that for (2, 4):

$$(4, 2) \neq (2, 4).$$

In general, if P is any point, then its rectangular coordinates will be given by an ordered pair of the form (x, y) (see Fig. 3.6). We call x the *abscissa* or *x-coordinate* of P, and y the *ordinate* or *y-coordinate* of P.

Thus with each point in a given coordinate plane we can associate exactly one ordered pair (x, y) of real numbers. Also, it should be clear that with each ordered pair (x, y) of real numbers we can associate exactly one point in that plane. Since there is a *one-to-one correspondence* between the points in the plane and all ordered pairs of real numbers, we shall refer to a point P with abscissa x and ordinate y simply as the point (x, y), or as $P(x, y)$. Moreover, we shall use the words "point" and "ordered pair" interchangeably.

In Fig. 3.7 the coordinates of various points are indicated. For example, the point $(1, -4)$ is located one unit to the right of the *y*-axis and four units

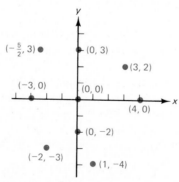

FIGURE 3.7

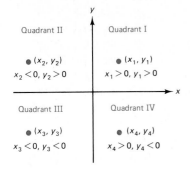

FIGURE 3.8

below the x-axis. The origin is $(0, 0)$. The x-coordinate of every point on the y-axis is 0, and the y-coordinate of every point on the x-axis is 0.

The coordinate axes divide the plane into four regions called *quadrants* (Fig. 3.8). For example, quadrant I consists of all points (x_1, y_1) with $x_1 > 0$ and $y_1 > 0$. The points on the axes do not lie in any quadrant.

Using a rectangular coordinate system, we can geometrically represent equations in two variables. For example, let us consider

$$y = x^2 + 2x - 3.$$

A solution of this equation is a value of x and a value of y that make the equation true. For example,

$$\text{if } x = 1, \quad \text{then} \quad y = 1^2 + 2(1) - 3 = 0.$$

Thus $x = 1$, $y = 0$ is a solution. Similarly,

$$\text{if } x = -2, \quad \text{then} \quad y = (-2)^2 + 2(-2) - 3 = -3,$$

and so $x = -2$, $y = -3$ is also a solution. By choosing other values for x we can get more solutions [see Fig. 3.9(a)]. It should be clear that there are infinitely many solutions.

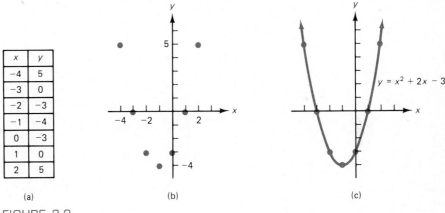

x	y
-4	5
-3	0
-2	-3
-1	-4
0	-3
1	0
2	5

(a)   (b)   (c)

FIGURE 3.9

Each solution gives rise to a point (x, y). For example, to $x = 1$ and $y = 0$ corresponds $(1, 0)$. The **graph** of $y = x^2 + 2x - 3$ is the geometric representation of all its solutions. In Fig. 3.9(b) we have plotted the points corresponding to the solutions in the table.

Since the equation has infinitely many solutions, it seems impossible to determine its graph precisely. However, we are concerned only with the graph's general shape. For this reason we plot enough points so that we may intelligently guess its proper shape. Then we join these points by a smooth curve wherever conditions permit. We start with the point having the least x-coordinate, namely $(-4, 5)$, and progress through the points having increasingly larger x-coordi-

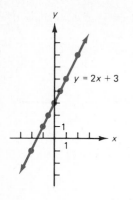

x	0	$\frac{1}{2}$	$-\frac{1}{2}$	1	-1	2	-2
y	3	4	2	5	1	7	-1

FIGURE 3.10

nates. We finish with the point having the greatest x-coordinate, namely (2, 5) [see Fig. 3.9(c)]. Of course, the more points we plot, the better our graph is. Here we assume that the graph extends indefinitely upward, which is indicated by arrows. The point $(0, -3)$ where the curve intersects the y-axis is called the **y-intercept.** It is found by solving the equation for y when $x = 0$. The y-intercept is a convenient point to plot because it is usually easy to find. The points $(-3, 0)$ and $(1, 0)$ where the curve intersects the x-axis are called the **x-intercepts.** They are found by solving the equation for x when $y = 0$.

In a later chapter you will see that calculus is a *great* aid in graphing because it helps determine the shape of a graph. It provides powerful techniques for determining whether or not a curve "wiggles" between points.

EXAMPLE 1   *Graph $y = 2x + 3$.*

See Fig. 3.10.

EXAMPLE 2   *Graph $s = \dfrac{100}{t}$.*

Using t for the horizontal axis and s for the vertical, we get Fig. 3.11. The graph has no point corresponding to $t = 0$ because division by zero is not defined. Thus there is no s-intercept. In general, the graph of $s = k/t$, where k is a nonzero constant, is called a *hyperbola*.

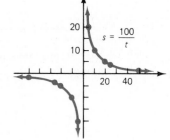

t	5	-5	10	-10	20	-20	25	-25	50	-50
s	20	-20	10	-10	5	-5	4	-4	2	-2

FIGURE 3.11

EXAMPLE 3   *Graph $x = 3$.*

We can think of this as an equation in the variables x and y if we write it as $x = 3 + 0y$. Here y can be any value, but x must be 3 (see Fig. 3.12).

We can also represent functions in a coordinate plane. If f is a function with independent variable x and dependent variable y, then the graph of f is simply the graph of the equation $y = f(x)$. It consists of all points (x, y), or $(x, f(x))$, where x is in the domain of f. The vertical axis can be labeled either y or $f(x)$ and is referred to as the **function-value axis.** *We always label the horizontal axis with the independent variable.*

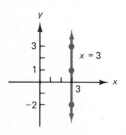

x	3	3	3
y	1	3	-2

FIGURE 3.12

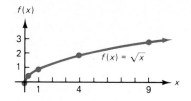

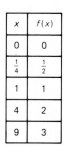

FIGURE 3.13

EXAMPLE 4   *Graph* $f(x) = \sqrt{x}$.

See Fig. 3.13. We label the vertical axis as $f(x)$. Recall that $\sqrt{x}$ denotes the *principal* square root of x. Thus $f(9) = \sqrt{9} = 3$, not ± 3. Also, we cannot choose negative values for x because we don't want imaginary numbers for $\sqrt{x}$. That is, we must have $x \geq 0$.

EXAMPLE 5   *Graph* $p = G(q) = |q|$ (*absolute value function*).

We use the independent variable q to label the horizontal axis. The function-value axis can be labeled either $G(q)$ or p (see Fig. 3.14).

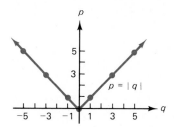

q	0	1	−1	3	−3	5	−5
p	0	1	1	3	3	5	5

FIGURE 3.14

Figure 3.15 shows the graph of some function $y = f(x)$. Corresponding to the input number x on the horizontal axis is the output number $f(x)$ on the vertical axis. For example, corresponding to the input 4 is the output 3, so $f(4) = 3$. From the shape of the graph, it seems reasonable to assume that, for any value of x, there is an output number, so the domain of f is all real numbers. Notice that the set of all y-coordinates of points on the graph is the set of all nonnegative numbers. Thus the range of f is all $y \geq 0$. This shows that we can make an "educated" guess about the domain and range of a function by looking at its graph. In general, the domain consists of all x-values that are included in the

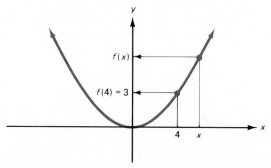

FIGURE 3.15

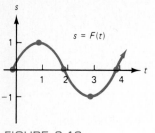

FIGURE 3.16

graph, and the range is all y-values that are included. For example, Fig. 3.13 implies that both the domain and range of $f(x) = \sqrt{x}$ are all nonnegative numbers. From Fig. 3.14 it is clear that the domain of $p = G(q) = |q|$ is all real numbers and the range is all $p \geq 0$.

EXAMPLE 6   Figure 3.16 shows the graph of a function F. To the right of 4 assume that the graph repeats itself indefinitely. Thus the domain of F is all $t \geq 0$. The range is $-1 \leq s \leq 1$. Some function values are

$$F(0) = 0, \qquad F(1) = 1, \qquad F(2) = 0, \qquad F(3) = -1.$$

EXAMPLE 7   *Graph the compound function*

$$f(x) = \begin{cases} x, & \text{if } 0 \leq x < 3, \\ x - 1, & \text{if } 3 \leq x \leq 5, \\ 4, & \text{if } 5 < x \leq 7. \end{cases}$$

The domain of f is $0 \leq x \leq 7$. The graph is given in Fig. 3.17, where the *hollow dot* means that the point is *not* included in the graph. Notice that the range of f is all real numbers y such that $0 \leq y \leq 4$.

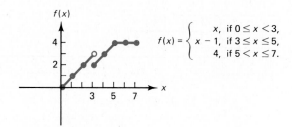

x	0	1	2	3	4	5	6	7
$f(x)$	0	1	2	2	3	4	4	4

FIGURE 3.17

There is an easy way to tell whether or not a curve is the graph of a function. In the leftmost diagram in Fig. 3.18, notice that with the given x there are associated *two* values of y—namely y_1 and y_2. Thus the curve is *not* the graph of

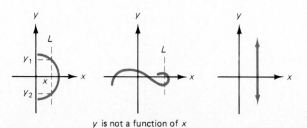

y is not a function of x

FIGURE 3.18

a function of x. Looking at it another way, we have the following general rule, called the **vertical-line test.** If a *vertical* line L can be drawn that intersects a curve in at least two points, then the curve is *not* the graph of a function of x. When no such vertical line can be drawn, the curve *is* the graph of a function of x. Thus the curves in Fig. 3.18 do not represent functions of x, but those in Fig. 3.19 do.

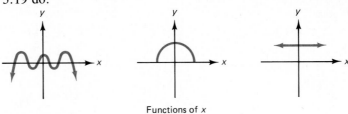

Functions of x

FIGURE 3.19

EXAMPLE 8   *Graph $x = 2y^2$.*

Here it is easier to choose values of y and then find the corresponding values of x. The equation does *not* define a function of x (see Fig. 3.20).

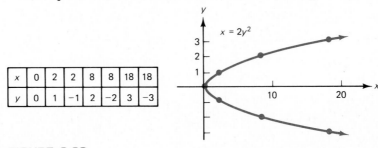

x	0	2	2	8	8	18	18
y	0	1	-1	2	-2	3	-3

FIGURE 3.20

EXERCISE 3.4

In Problems **1** *and* **2,** *locate and label each of the points and give the quadrant, if possible, in which each point lies.*

1. $(2, 7)$, $(8, -3)$, $(-\frac{1}{2}, -2)$, $(0, 0)$.

2. $(-4, 5)$, $(3, 0)$, $(1, 1)$, $(0, -6)$.

3. Figure 3.21(a) shows the graph of $y = f(x)$. (a) Estimate $f(0)$, $f(2)$, $f(4)$, and $f(-2)$. (b) What is the domain of f? (c) What is the range of f?

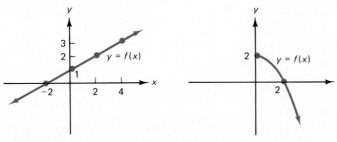

(a)   (b)

FIGURE 3.21

4. Figure 3.21(b) shows the graph of $y = f(x)$.
   (a) Estimate $f(0)$ and $f(2)$.
   (b) What is the domain of f?
   (c) What is the range of f?

5. Figure 3.22(a) shows the graph of $y = f(x)$.
   (a) Estimate $f(0)$, $f(1)$, and $f(-1)$.
   (b) What is the domain of f?
   (c) What is the range of f?

6. Figure 3.22(b) shows the graph of $y = f(x)$.
   (a) Estimate $f(0)$, $f(2)$, $f(3)$, and $f(4)$.
   (b) What is the domain of f?
   (c) What is the range of f?

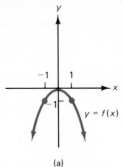

(a)

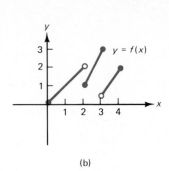

(b)

FIGURE 3.22

In Problems **7–20**, graph each equation. Based on your graph, is y a function of x and if so, what are the domain and range?

7. $y = x$.

8. $y = x + 1$.

9. $y = 3x - 5$.

10. $y = 3 - 2x$.

11. $y = x^2$.

12. $y = \dfrac{3}{x}$.

13. $x = 0$.

14. $y = x^2 - 9$.

15. $y = x^3$.

16. $x = -4$.

17. $x = -3y^2$.

18. $x^2 = y^2$.

19. $2x + y - 2 = 0$.

20. $x + y = 1$.

In Problems **21–38**, graph each function and give the domain and range.

21. $s = f(t) = 4 - t^2$.

22. $f(x) = 5 - 2x^2$.

23. $y = g(x) = 2$.

24. $G(s) = -8$.

25. $y = h(x) = x^2 - 4x + 1$.

26. $y = f(x) = x^2 + 2x - 8$.

27. $f(t) = -t^3$.

28. $p = h(q) = q(2 - q)$.

29. $s = F(r) = \sqrt{r - 5}$.

30. $F(r) = -\dfrac{1}{r}$.

31. $f(x) = |2x - 1|$.

32. $v = H(u) = |u - 3|$.

33. $F(t) = \dfrac{16}{t^2}$.

34. $y = f(x) = \dfrac{2}{x - 4}$.

35. $c = g(p) = \begin{cases} p, & \text{if } 0 \le p < 2, \\ 2, & \text{if } p \ge 2. \end{cases}$

36. $f(x) = \begin{cases} 2x + 1, & \text{if } -1 \le x < 2, \\ 9 - x^2, & \text{if } x \ge 2. \end{cases}$

37. $g(x) = \begin{cases} x + 6, & \text{if } x \ge 3, \\ x^2, & \text{if } x < 3. \end{cases}$

38. $f(x) = \begin{cases} x + 1, & \text{if } 0 < x \le 3, \\ 4, & \text{if } 3 < x \le 5, \\ x - 1, & \text{if } x > 5. \end{cases}$

39. Which of the graphs in Fig. 3.23 represent functions of x?

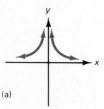

(a)

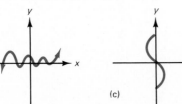

(b)   (c)

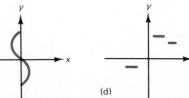

(d)

FIGURE 3.23

40. Given the supply schedule below (see Example 6 of Sec. 3.2), plot each quantity-price pair by choosing the horizontal axis for the possible quantities. Approximate the points in between the data by connecting the data points with a smooth curve. Thus you get a *supply curve*. From the graph, determine the relationship between price and supply. (That is, as price increases, what happens to the quantity supplied?) Is price per unit a function of quantity supplied?

QUANTITY SUPPLIED PER WEEK, q	PRICE PER UNIT, p
30	$10
100	20
150	30
190	40
210	50

41. The following table is called a *demand schedule*. It indicates the quantities of brand X that consumers will demand (that is, purchase) each week at certain prices per unit (in dollars). Plot each quantity-price pair by choosing the vertical axis for the possible prices. Connect the points with a smooth curve. In this way we approximate points in between the given data. The result is called a *demand curve*. From the graph, determine the relationship between the price of brand X and the amount that will be demanded. (That is, as price decreases, what happens to the quantity demanded?) Is price per unit a function of quantity demanded?

QUANTITY DEMANDED, q	PRICE PER UNIT, p
5	$20
10	10
20	5
25	4

42. Sketch the graph of

$$y = f(x) = \begin{cases} -100x + 600, & \text{if } 0 \le x < 5, \\ -100x + 1100, & \text{if } 5 \le x < 10, \\ -100x + 1600, & \text{if } 10 \le x < 15. \end{cases}$$

A function such as this might describe the inventory y of a company at time x.

43. In a psychological experiment on visual information, a subject briefly viewed an array of letters and was then asked to recall as many letters as possible from the array. The procedure was repeated several times. Suppose that y is the average number of letters recalled from arrays with x letters. The graph of the results approximately fits the graph of

$$y = f(x) = \begin{cases} x, & \text{if } 0 \le x \le 4, \\ \frac{1}{2}x + 2, & \text{if } 4 < x \le 5, \\ 4.5, & \text{if } 5 < x \le 12. \end{cases}$$

Graph this function.*

3.5 REVIEW

Important Terms and Symbols

Section 3.1	function	domain	range	independent variable	dependent variable	$f(x)$
	function value		demand function			

* Adapted from G. R. Loftus and E. F. Loftus, *Human Memory: The Processing of Information* (New York: Lawrence Erlbaum Associates, Inc., distributed by the Halsted Press, Division of John Wiley & Sons, Inc. 1976).

Section 3.2	constant function	polynomial function	linear function	quadratic function
	compound function	absolute value, $|x|$	factorial, $r!$	supply function

Section 3.3	$f + g$	$f - g$	fg	f/g	$f \circ g$	composition function

Section 3.4	rectangular coordinate system		coordinate axes	origin	x, y-plane	
	ordered pair, (x, y)	coordinates of a point		x-coordinate	y-coordinate	abscissa
	ordinate	quadrant	graph of equation	y-intercept	x-intercept	
	graph of function	function-value axis		vertical-line test		

Summary

A function f is a rule of correspondence that assigns to each input number x exactly one output number $f(x)$. Usually, a function is specified by an equation that indicates what must be done to an input x to obtain $f(x)$. To obtain a particular function value $f(a)$, we replace each x in the equation by a.

The domain of a function consists of all input numbers, and the range consists of all output numbers. Unless otherwise specified, the domain of f consists of all values of x for which $f(x)$ is a real number.

Some special types of functions are constant functions and polynomial functions. A function that is defined by more than one equation is called a compound function.

Two functions, f and g, can be combined to form a sum, difference, product, quotient, or composition as follows:

$$(f + g)(x) = f(x) + g(x),$$

$$(f - g)(x) = f(x) - g(x),$$

$$(fg)(x) = f(x)g(x),$$

$$\frac{f}{g}(x) = \frac{f(x)}{g(x)},$$

$$(f \circ g)(x) = f(g(x)).$$

A rectangular coordinate system allows us to geometrically represent equations in two variables, as well as functions. The graph of an equation in x and y consists of all points (x, y) that correspond to the solutions to the equation. We plot a sufficient number of points and connect them (where appropriate) so that the basic shape of the graph is apparent. One important point to include is the y-intercept, which is found by letting x be 0 and solving for y.

The graph of a function f is the graph of the equation $y = f(x)$ and consists of all points $(x, f(x))$. The graph should make it clear what the domain and range are.

The fact that a graph represents a function can be determined by using the vertical-line test. A vertical line cannot cut the graph of a function at more than one point.

In economics, supply functions and demand functions give a correspondence between the price p of a product and the number of units q of the product that producers (or consumers) will supply (or buy) at that price.

Review Problems

*In Problems **1–6**, give the domain of each function.*

1. $f(x) = \dfrac{x}{x^2 - 3x + 2}$.

2. $g(x) = x^2 + 3x$.

3. $F(t) = 7t + 4t^2$.

4. $G(x) = 18$.

5. $h(x) = \dfrac{\sqrt{x}}{x - 1}$.

6. $H(s) = \dfrac{\sqrt{s - 5}}{4}$.

In Problems **7–14,** *find the function values for the given function.*

7. $f(x) = 3x^2 - 4x + 7$; $f(0)$, $f(-3)$, $f(5)$, $f(t)$.

8. $g(x) = 4$; $g(4)$, $g(\frac{1}{100})$, $g(-156)$, $g(x + 4)$.

9. $G(x) = \sqrt{x - 1}$; $G(1)$, $G(10)$, $G(t + 1)$, $G(x^2)$.

10. $F(x) = \dfrac{x - 3}{x + 4}$; $F(-1)$, $F(0)$, $F(5)$, $F(x + 3)$.

11. $h(u) = \dfrac{\sqrt{u + 4}}{u}$; $h(5)$, $h(-4)$, $h(x)$, $h(u - 4)$.

12. $H(s) = \dfrac{(s - 4)^2}{3}$; $H(-2)$, $H(7)$, $H(\frac{1}{2})$, $H(x^2)$.

13. $f(x) = \begin{cases} 4, & \text{if } x < 2 \\ 8 - x^2, & \text{if } x > 2 \end{cases}$; $f(4)$, $f(-2)$, $f(0)$, $f(10)$.

14. $h(q) = \begin{cases} q, & \text{if } -1 \le q < 0 \\ 3 - q, & \text{if } 0 \le q < 3 \\ 2q^2, & \text{if } 3 \le q \le 5 \end{cases}$; $h(0)$, $h(4)$, $h(-\frac{1}{2})$, $h(\frac{1}{2})$.

In Problems **15** *and* **16,** *find (a)* $f(x + h)$, *and (b)* $\dfrac{f(x + h) - f(x)}{h}$, *and simplify your answers.*

15. $f(x) = 3 - 7x$.

16. $f(x) = x^2 + 4$.

17. If $f(x) = 3x - 1$ and $g(x) = 2x + 3$, find the following.

   a. $(f + g)(x)$.

   b. $(f + g)(4)$.

   c. $(f - g)(x)$.

   d. $(fg)(x)$.

   e. $(fg)(1)$.

   f. $\dfrac{f}{g}(x)$.

   g. $(f \circ g)(x)$.

   h. $(f \circ g)(5)$.

   i. $(g \circ f)(x)$.

18. If $f(x) = x^2$ and $g(x) = 2x + 1$, find the following.

   a. $(f + g)(x)$.

   b. $(f - g)(x)$.

   c. $(f - g)(-3)$.

   d. $(fg)(x)$.

   e. $\dfrac{f}{g}(x)$.

   f. $\dfrac{f}{g}(2)$.

   g. $(f \circ g)(x)$.

   h. $(g \circ f)(x)$.

   i. $(g \circ f)(-4)$.

In Problems **19–22,** *find* $(f \circ g)(x)$ *and* $(g \circ f)(x)$.

19. $f(x) = \dfrac{1}{x}$, $g(x) = x - 1$.

20. $f(x) = \dfrac{x + 1}{4}$, $g(x) = \sqrt{x}$.

21. $f(x) = x + 2$, $g(x) = x^3$.

22. $f(x) = 2$, $g(x) = 3$.

In Problems **23** *and* **24,** *graph the equations.*

23. $y = 9 - x^2$.

24. $y = 3x - 7$.

In Problems **25–29,** *graph each function and give its domain and range.*

25. $G(u) = \sqrt{u + 4}$.

26. $f(x) = |x| + 1$.

27. $y = f(x) = \begin{cases} 1 - x, & \text{if } x \le 0, \\ 1, & \text{if } x > 0. \end{cases}$

28. $g(t) = \sqrt{4t}$.

29. $y = g(t) = \dfrac{2}{t - 4}$.

30. The projected annual sales S (in dollars) of a new product is given by the equation $S = 150,000 + 3000t$, where t is the time in years from 1986. Such an equation is called a *trend equation*. Find the projected annual sales for 1991. Is S a function of t?

31. In Fig. 3.24, which graphs represent functions of x?

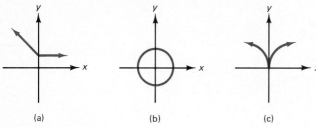

(a)   (b)   (c)

FIGURE 3.24

Lines, Parabolas and Systems

4.1 LINES

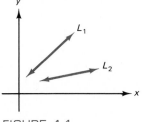

FIGURE 4.1

Many relationships between quantities can be represented conveniently by straight lines. One feature of a straight line is its "steepness." For example, in Fig. 4.1 line L_1 rises faster as it goes from left to right than does line L_2. In this sense L_1 is steeper.

To measure the steepness of a line, we use the notion of *slope*. In Fig. 4.2, as we move along line L from (2, 1) to (4, 5), the x-coordinate increases from 2 to 4 and the y-coordinate increases from 1 to 5. The average rate of change of y with respect to x is the ratio

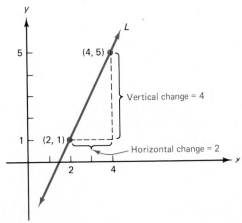

FIGURE 4.2

$$\frac{\text{change in } y}{\text{change in } x} = \frac{5 - 1}{4 - 2} = \frac{4}{2} = 2.$$

This means that for each 1-unit increase in x, there is a 2-unit *increase* in y. Thus the line must *rise* from left to right. We say that the *slope* of the line is 2. Choosing two other different points on L would also give a slope of 2. In general we have the following.

Definition

*Let (x_1, y_1) and (x_2, y_2) be two points on a line where $x_1 \neq x_2$. The **slope** of the line is the number m given by*

$$m = \frac{y_2 - y_1}{x_2 - x_1} \quad \left(= \frac{\text{vertical change}}{\text{horizontal change}} \right). \tag{1}$$

Slope is not defined for a vertical line because any two points on such a line must have $x_1 = x_2$ (see Fig. 4.3). Thus the denominator in (1) is zero. For a horizontal line, any two points must have $y_1 = y_2$. Thus the numerator in (1) is zero, so $m = 0$.

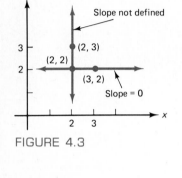

FIGURE 4.3

EXAMPLE 1   *The line in Fig. 4.4 shows the relationship between the price p of a widget (in dollars) and the quantity q of widgets (in thousands) that consumers will buy at that price. Find and interpret the slope.*

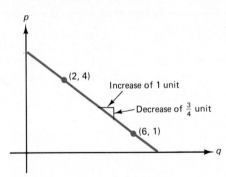

FIGURE 4.4

In the slope formula (1) we replace the x's by q's and the y's by p's. Either point in Fig. 4.4 may be chosen as (q_1, p_1). Letting $(2, 4) = (q_1, p_1)$ and $(6, 1) = (q_2, p_2)$, we have

$$m = \frac{p_2 - p_1}{q_2 - q_1} = \frac{1 - 4}{6 - 2} = \frac{-3}{4} = -\frac{3}{4}.$$

The slope is negative, $-\frac{3}{4}$. This means that for each 1-unit increase in quantity (one thousand widgets), there corresponds a **decrease** in price of $\frac{3}{4}$ (dollars per widget). Due to this decrease, the line **falls** from left to right.

In summary, we can characterize the orientation of a line by its slope:

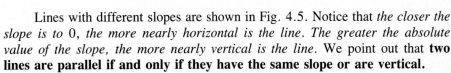

Zero slope: horizontal line,
Undefined slope: vertical line,
Positive slope: line rises from left to right,
Negative slope: line falls from left to right.

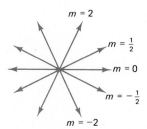

FIGURE 4.5

Lines with different slopes are shown in Fig. 4.5. Notice that *the closer the slope is to 0, the more nearly horizontal is the line. The greater the absolute value of the slope, the more nearly vertical is the line.* We point out that **two lines are parallel if and only if they have the same slope or are vertical.**

Suppose that line L has slope m and passes through the point (x_1, y_1). If (x, y) is *any* other point on L (see Fig. 4.6), we can find an algebraic relationship between x and y. Using the slope formula on the points (x_1, y_1) and (x, y), we must have

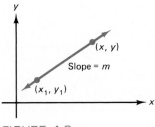

FIGURE 4.6

$$\frac{y - y_1}{x - x_1} = m,$$

$$y - y_1 = m(x - x_1). \tag{2}$$

That is, every point on L satisfies Eq. (2). It is also true that every point satisfying Eq. (2) must lie on L. Thus Eq. (2) is an equation for L and is given a special name:

$$y - y_1 = m(x - x_1)$$

is the **point-slope form** of an equation of the line through (x_1, y_1) with slope m.

EXAMPLE 2   *Find an equation of the line that has slope 2 and passes through* $(1, -3)$.

Here $m = 2$ and $(x_1, y_1) = (1, -3)$. Using the point-slope form, we have

$$y - (-3) = 2(x - 1),$$

$$y + 3 = 2x - 2.$$

We can rewrite our answer as

$$2x - y - 5 = 0.$$

An equation of the line passing through two given points can be found easily, as Example 3 shows.

EXAMPLE 3   *Find an equation of the line passing through* $(-3, 8)$ *and* $(4, -2)$.

The line has slope

$$m = \frac{-2 - 8}{4 - (-3)} = -\frac{10}{7}.$$

Choosing $(-3, 8)$ as (x_1, y_1) in a point slope form gives

$$y - 8 = -\tfrac{10}{7}[x - (-3)],$$

$$y - 8 = -\tfrac{10}{7}(x + 3).$$

$$7y - 56 = -10x - 30,$$

or

$$10x + 7y - 26 = 0.$$

Choosing $(4, -2)$ as (x_1, y_1) would give an equivalent result.

Recall that a point $(0, b)$ where a graph intersects the y-axis is called a y-intercept (Fig. 4.7). Sometimes we simply say that the number b is the y-intercept. If the slope and y-intercept of a line are known, an equation for the line is (by using the point-slope form)

$$y - b = m(x - 0).$$

Solving for y gives $y = mx + b$, called the *slope-intercept form* of an equation of the line.

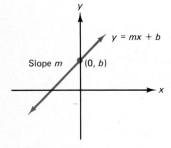

FIGURE 4.7

$$y = mx + b$$

is the **slope-intercept form** of an equation of the line with slope m and y-intercept b.

EXAMPLE 4

a. An equation of the line with slope 3 and y-intercept -4 is

$$y = mx + b,$$

$$y = 3x + (-4),$$

$$y = 3x - 4.$$

b. The equation $y = 5(x - 3)$ can be written $y = 5x - 15$, which has the form $y = mx + b$ with $m = 5$ and $b = -15$. Thus its graph is a line with slope 5 and y-intercept -15.

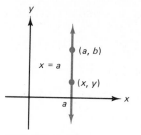

FIGURE 4.8

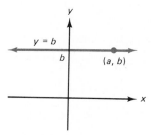

FIGURE 4.9

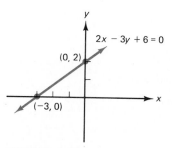

FIGURE 4.10

If a *vertical* line passes through (a, b) (see Fig. 4.8), then any other point (x, y) lies on the line if and only if $x = a$. The y-coordinate can have any value. Hence an equation of the line is $x = a$. Similarly, an equation of the *horizontal* line passing through (a, b) is $y = b$ (see Fig. 4.9). Here the x-coordinate can have any value.

EXAMPLE 5

a. An equation of the vertical line through $(-2, 3)$ is $x = -2$. An equation of the horizontal line through $(-2, 3)$ is $y = 3$.

b. The x- and y-axes are horizontal and vertical lines, respectively. Since $(0, 0)$ lies on both axes, an equation of the x-axis is $y = 0$ and an equation of the y-axis is $x = 0$.

From our discussions we can show that every straight line is the graph of an equation of the form $Ax + By + C = 0$, where A, B, and C are constants and A and B are not both zero. We call this a **general linear equation** (or *an equation of the first degree*) **in the variables x and y,** and x and y are said to be **linearly related.** For example, a general linear equation for $y = 7x - 2$ is $(-7)x + (1)y + (2) = 0$. Conversely, the graph of a general linear equation is a straight line. For example, $3x + 4y + 5 = 0$ is equivalent to $y = (-\frac{3}{4})x + (-\frac{5}{4})$, so its graph is a straight line with slope $-\frac{3}{4}$ and y-intercept $-\frac{5}{4}$.

EXAMPLE 6   *Sketch the graph of $2x - 3y + 6 = 0$.*

Since this is a general linear equation, its graph is a straight line. Thus we need only determine two different points on the graph in order to sketch it. If $x = 0$, then $y = 2$. If $y = 0$, then $x = -3$. We now draw the line passing through $(0, 2)$ and $(-3, 0)$ (see Fig. 4.10). The point $(-3, 0)$ is an x-intercept of the graph.

Table 4.1 gives the various forms of equations of straight lines.

TABLE 4.1
Forms of Equations of Straight Lines

Point-slope form	$y - y_1 = m(x - x_1)$
Slope-intercept form	$y = mx + b$
General linear form	$Ax + By + C = 0$
Vertical line	$x = a$
Horizontal line	$y = b$

EXERCISE 4.1

In Problems **1–8,** *find the slope of the straight line that passes through the given points.*

1. $(1, 2)$, $(4, 8)$.   **2.** $(-1, 9)$, $(1, 5)$.   **3.** $(6, -3)$, $(-7, 5)$.   **4.** $(2, -4)$, $(3, -4)$.

5. $(-2, 4)$, $(-2, 8)$.   **6.** $(0, -6)$, $(3, 0)$.   **7.** $(5, -2)$, $(4, -2)$.   **8.** $(1, -6)$, $(1, 0)$.

In Problems **9–24,** *find a general linear equation* $(Ax + By + C = 0)$ *of the straight line that has the indicated properties and sketch each line.*

9. Passes through $(1, 2)$ and has slope 6.

10. Passes through origin and has slope -5.

11. Passes through $(-2, 5)$ and has slope $-\frac{1}{4}$.

12. Passes through $(\frac{1}{2}, 6)$ and has slope $\frac{1}{3}$.

13. Passes through $(1, 4)$ and $(8, 7)$.

14. Passes through $(7, 1)$ and $(7, -5)$.

15. Passes through $(3, -1)$ and $(-2, -9)$.

16. Passes through $(0, 0)$ and $(2, 3)$.

17. Has slope 2 and y-intercept 4.

18. Has slope 7 and y-intercept -5.

19. Has slope $-\frac{1}{2}$ and y-intercept -3.

20. Has slope 0 and y-intercept $-\frac{1}{2}$.

21. Is horizontal and passes through $(-3, -2)$.

22. Is vertical and passes through $(-1, 4)$.

23. Passes through $(2, -3)$ and is vertical.

24. Passes through the origin and is horizontal.

In Problems **25–34,** *find, if possible, the slope and y-intercept of the straight line determined by the equation and sketch the graph.*

25. $y = 2x - 1$.

26. $x - 1 = 5$.

27. $x + 2y - 3 = 0$.

28. $y + 4 = 7$.

29. $x = -5$.

30. $x - 1 = 5y + 3$.

31. $y = 3x$.

32. $y - 7 = 3(x - 4)$.

33. $y = 1$.

34. $2y - 3 = 0$.

In Problems **35–40,** *find a general linear form and the slope-intercept form of the given equation.*

35. $x = -2y + 4$.

36. $3x + 2y = 6$.

37. $4x + 9y - 5 = 0$.

38. $2(x - 3) - 4(y + 2) = 8$.

39. $\dfrac{x}{2} - \dfrac{y}{3} = -4$.

40. $y = \dfrac{1}{300}x + 8$.

41. A straight line passes through $(1, 2)$ and $(-3, 8)$. Find the point on it that has a first coordinate of 5.

42. A straight line has slope 2 and y-intercept $(0, 1)$. Does the point $(-1, -1)$ lie on the line?

4.2 APPLICATIONS AND LINEAR FUNCTIONS _____

Many situations in economics can be described by using straight lines, as Example 1 shows.

EXAMPLE 1   Suppose that a manufacturer has 100 lb of material from which he can produce two products, A and B, which require 4 lb and 2 lb of material per unit, respectively. If x and y denote the number of units produced of A and B, respectively, then all levels of production are given by the combinations of x and y that satisfy the equation

$$4x + 2y = 100, \qquad \text{where } x, y \geq 0.$$

Thus the levels of production of A and B are linearly related. Solving for y, we get the slope-intercept form

$$y = -2x + 50,$$

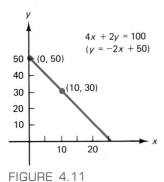

FIGURE 4.11

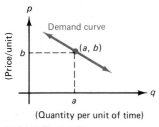

(Quantity per unit of time)

FIGURE 4.12

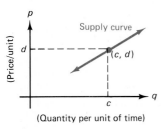

(Quantity per unit of time)

FIGURE 4.13

and hence the slope is -2. The slope reflects the rate of change of the level of production of B with respect to the level of production of A. For example, if 1 more unit of A is to be produced, it will require 4 more pounds of material, resulting in $\frac{4}{2} = 2$ *fewer* units of B. Thus as x increases by 1 unit, the corresponding value of y decreases 2 units. To sketch the graph of $y = -2x + 50$, we can use the y-intercept $(0, 50)$ and the fact that when $x = 10$, then $y = 30$ (see Fig. 4.11).

For each price level of a product there is a corresponding quantity of that product that consumers will demand (that is, purchase) during some time period. Usually, the higher the price, the smaller the quantity demanded; as the price falls, the quantity demanded increases. If the price per unit of the product is given by p and the corresponding quantity (in units) is given by q, then an equation relating p and q is called a **demand equation.** Its graph is called a **demand curve.**

Figure 4.12 shows a demand curve which is a straight line; it is called a *linear* demand curve. There, p and q are linearly related. In keeping with the practice of most economists, the horizontal axis is the q-axis and the vertical axis is the p-axis. We shall assume that the price per unit is given in dollars and the time period is 1 week. Thus the point (a, b) in Fig. 4.12 indicates that, at a price of b dollars per unit, consumers will demand a units per week. Since negative prices or quantities are not meaningful, both a and b must be nonnegative. For most products, an increase in the quantity demanded corresponds to a decrease in price. Thus a linear demand curve typically has negative slope, as in Fig. 4.12.

In response to various prices, there is a corresponding quantity of product that *producers* are willing to supply to the market during some time period. Usually, the higher the price per unit, the larger the quantity that producers are willing to supply; as the price falls, so will the quantity supplied. If p denotes the price per unit and q denotes the corresponding quantity, then an equation relating p and q is called a **supply equation** and its graph is called a **supply curve.** Figure 4.13 shows a *linear* supply curve. If p is in dollars and the time period is 1 week, then the point (c, d) indicates that, at a price of d dollars each, producers will supply c units per week. As before, c and d are nonnegative. A linear supply curve usually rises from left to right, that is, has a positive slope. This indicates that a producer will supply more of a product at higher prices.

EXAMPLE 2   *Suppose the demand per week for a product is* 100 *units when the price is* $58 *per unit, and* 200 *units at* $51 *each. Determine the demand equation, assuming that it is linear.*

Since the demand equation is linear, the demand curve must be a straight line. We are given that quantity q and price p are linearly related such that $p = 58$ when $q = 100$, and $p = 51$ when $q = 200$. Thus the given data can be represented in a q,p-coordinate plane (see Fig. 4.12) by the points $(100, 58)$ and $(200, 51)$, which lie on a line with slope

$$m = \frac{51 - 58}{200 - 100} = -\frac{7}{100}.$$

An equation of the line (point-slope form) is

$$p - p_1 = m(q - q_1),$$

$$p - 58 = -\frac{7}{100}(q - 100).$$

Simplifying gives the demand equation

$$p = -\frac{7}{100}q + 65. \tag{1}$$

Customarily, a demand equation (as well as a supply equation) expresses p in terms of q and actually defines a function of q. For example, Eq. (1) defines p as a function of q and is called the *demand function* for the product.

In Sec. 3.2 (Example 2) a *linear function* was described. More formally, we have the following definition.

Definition
*A function f is a **linear function** if and only if $f(x)$ can be written in the form $f(x) = ax + b$, where a and b are constants and $a \neq 0$.*

Suppose f is a linear function and we let $y = f(x)$. Then $y = ax + b$, which is an equation of a straight line with slope a and y-intercept b. Thus **the graph of a linear function is a straight line.** We say that the function $f(x) = ax + b$ has slope a.

EXAMPLE 3   *Graph the following functions.*

a. $f(x) = 2x - 1$.

Here f is a linear function (with slope 2), so its graph is a straight line. Since two points determine a straight line, we need only plot two points and then draw a line through them [see Fig. 4.14(a)]. Note that one of the points plotted is the vertical-axis intercept -1 that occurs when $x = 0$.

b. $g(t) = \dfrac{15 - 2t}{3}$.

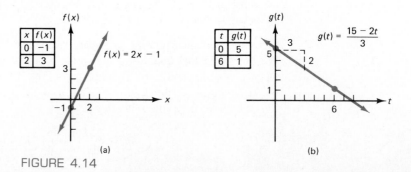

(a)   (b)

FIGURE 4.14

Notice that

$$g(t) = \frac{15 - 2t}{3} = \frac{15}{3} - \frac{2t}{3} = -\frac{2}{3}t + 5.$$

Thus g is a linear function [see Fig. 4.14(b)]. Observe that since the slope is $-\frac{2}{3}$, then as t increases by 3 units, $g(t)$ decreases by 2.

EXAMPLE 4   *Suppose f is a linear function with slope 2 and $f(4) = 8$. Find $f(x)$.*

Since f is linear it has the form $f(x) = ax + b$. The slope is 2, so $a = 2$:

$$f(x) = 2x + b. \tag{2}$$

Now we determine b. Since $f(4) = 8$, in Eq. (2) we replace x by 4 and solve for b.

$$f(4) = 2(4) + b,$$
$$8 = 8 + b,$$
$$0 = b.$$

Hence $f(x) = 2x$.

EXAMPLE 5   *If $y = f(x)$ is a linear function such that $f(-2) = 6$ and $f(1) = -3$, find $f(x)$.*

The condition that $f(-2) = 6$ means that when $x = -2$, then $y = 6$. Thus $(-2, 6)$ lies on the graph of f, which is a straight line. Similarly, $f(1) = -3$ implies that $(1, -3)$ also lies on the line. If $(x_1, y_1) = (-2, 6)$ and $(x_2, y_2) = (1, -3)$, then the slope of the line is

$$m = \frac{y_2 - y_1}{x_2 - x_1} = \frac{-3 - 6}{1 - (-2)} = \frac{-9}{3} = -3.$$

We can find an equation of the line by using a point-slope form.

$$y - y_1 = m(x - x_1),$$
$$y - 6 = -3[x - (-2)],$$
$$y - 6 = -3x - 6.$$
$$y = -3x.$$

Because $y = f(x)$, $f(x) = -3x$.

In many studies data are collected and plotted on a coordinate system. An analysis of the results may indicate a functional relationship between the variables involved. For example, the data points may be approximated by points on a straight line. This would indicate a linear functional relationship, such as the one in Example 6 below.

EXAMPLE 6   *In testing an experimental diet for hens, it was determined that the average live weight* w *(in grams) of a hen was statistically a linear function of the number of days* d *after the diet was begun, where* $0 \le d \le 50$. *Suppose the average weight of a hen beginning the diet was 40 grams and 25 days later it was 675 grams.*

a. *Determine w as a linear function of d.*

b. *Find the average weight of a hen when* $d = 10$.

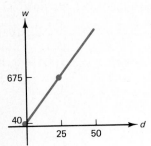

FIGURE 4.15

a. Since w is a linear function of d, its graph is a straight line. When $d = 0$ (the beginning of the diet) then $w = 40$. Thus $(0, 40)$ lies on the graph (see Fig. 4.15). Similarly, $(25, 675)$ lies on the graph. If $(d_1, w_1) = (0, 40)$ and $(d_2, w_2) = (25, 675)$, then the slope of the line is

$$m = \frac{w_2 - w_1}{d_2 - d_1} = \frac{675 - 40}{25 - 0} = \frac{635}{25} = \frac{127}{5}.$$

Using the point-slope form, we have

$$w - w_1 = m(d - d_1),$$

$$w - 40 = \frac{127}{5}(d - 0),$$

$$w - 40 = \frac{127}{5}d,$$

$$w = \frac{127}{5}d + 40,$$

which expresses w as a linear function of d.

b. When $d = 10$, then $w = \frac{127}{5}(10) + 40 = 254 + 40 = 294$. Thus the average weight of a hen 10 days after the beginning of the diet is 294 grams.

EXERCISE 4.2

In Problems **1–6,** *find the slope and vertical-axis intercept of the linear function and sketch the graph.*

1. $y = f(x) = -4x.$

2. $y = f(x) = x + 1.$

3. $g(t) = 2t - 4.$

4. $g(t) = 2(4 - t).$

5. $h(q) = \dfrac{7 - q}{2}.$

6. $h(q) = 0.5q + 0.25.$

In Problems **7–14,** *find* $f(x)$ *if* f *is a linear function that has the given properties.*

7. slope $= 5$, $f(3) = 1.$

8. $f(0) = 4$, $f(2) = -6.$

9. $f(2) = 3$, $f(-1) = 12.$

10. slope $= -6$, $f(\frac{1}{2}) = -2.$

11. slope $= -\frac{1}{2}$, $f(-\frac{1}{2}) = 4.$

12. $f(1) = 1$, $f(2) = 2.$

13. $f(-1) = -2$, $f(-3) = -4.$

14. slope $= 0.01$, $f(0.1) = 0.01.$

15. Suppose consumers will demand 40 units of a product when the price is $12 per unit and 25 units when the price is $18 each. Find the demand equation assuming that it is linear. Find the price per unit when 30 units are demanded.

16. Suppose a manufacturer of shoes will place on the market 50 (thousand pairs) when the price is 35 (dollars per pair) and 35 when the price is 30. Find the supply equation, assuming that price p and quantity q are linearly related.

17. Suppose the cost to produce 10 units of a product is $40 and the cost of 20 units is $70. If cost c is linearly related to output q, find a linear equation relating c and q. Find the cost to produce 35 units.

18. A cancer patient is to receive drug and radiation therapies. Each cubic centimeter of the drug to be used contains 200 curative units, and each minute of radiation exposure gives 300 curative units. The patient requires 2400 curative units. If d cubic centimeters of the drug and r minutes of radiation are administered, determine an equation relating d and r. Graph the equation for $d \geq 0$ and $r \geq 0$; label the horizontal axis as d.

19. Suppose the value of a piece of machinery decreases each year by 10% of its original value. If the original value is $8000, find an equation that expresses the value v of the machinery after t years of purchase, where $0 \leq t \leq 10$. Sketch the equation, choosing t as the horizontal axis and v as the vertical axis. What is the slope of the resulting line? This method of considering the value of equipment is called *straight-line depreciation*.

20. For sheep maintained at high environmental temperatures, respiratory rate r (per minute) increases as wool length l (in centimeters) decreases.* Suppose sheep with a wool length of 2 cm have an (average) respiratory rate of 160, and those with a wool length of 4 cm have a respiratory rate of 125. Assume that r and l are linearly related. (a) Find an equation that gives r in terms of l. (b) Find the respiratory rate of sheep with a wool length of 1 cm.

21. In production analysis, an *isocost line* is a line whose points represent all combinations of two factors of production that can be purchased for the same amount. Suppose a farmer has allocated $20,000 for the purchase of x tons of fertilizer (costing $200 per ton) and y acres of land (costing $2000 per acre). Find an equation of the isocost line which describes the various combinations that can be purchased for $20,000. Observe that neither x nor y can be negative.

22. A manufacturer produces products X and Y for which the profits per unit are $4 and $6, respectively. If x units of X and y units of Y are sold, then the total profit P is given by $P = 4x + 6y$, where $x, y \geq 0$. (a) Sketch the graph of this equation for $P = 240$. The result is called an *isoprofit line* and its points represent all combinations of sales that produce a profit of $240. (b) Determine the slope for $P = 240$. (c) If $P = 600$, determine the slope. (d) Are isoprofit lines for products X and Y parallel?

23. For reasons of comparison, a professor wants to rescale the scores on a set of test papers so that the maximum score is still 100 but the mean (average) is 80 instead of 56. (a) Find a linear equation that will do this. [Hint: You want 56 to become an 80 and 100 to remain 100. Consider the points (56, 80) and (100, 100) and, more generally, (x, y), where x is the old score and y is the new score. Find the slope and use a point-slope form. Express y in terms of x.] (b) If 60 on the new scale is the lowest passing score, what was the lowest passing score on the original scale?

24. The result of Sternberg's psychological experiment† on information retrieval is that a person's reaction time R, in milliseconds, is statistically a linear function of memory set size N as follows:

$$R = 38N + 397.$$

Sketch the graph for $1 \leq N \leq 5$. What is the slope?

* Adapted from G. E. Folk, Jr., *Textbook of Environmental Physiology*, 2nd ed. (Philadelphia: Lea & Febiger, 1974).

† G. R. Loftus and E. F. Loftus, *Human Memory: The Processing of Information* (New York: Lawrence Erlbaum Associates, Inc., distributed by the Halsted Press, Division of John Wiley & Sons, Inc., 1976).

25. In a certain learning experiment involving repetition and memory,* the proportion p of items recalled was estimated to be linearly related to effective study time t (in seconds), where t is between 5 and 9. For an effective study time of 5 seconds, the proportion of items recalled was 0.32. For each 1-second increase in study time, the proportion recalled increased by 0.059. (a) Find an equation that gives p in terms of t. (b) What proportion of items was recalled with 9 seconds of effective study time?

26. In testing an experimental diet for pigs, it was determined that the (average) live weight w (in kilograms) of a pig was statistically a linear function of the number of days d after the diet was initiated, where

$0 \le d \le 100$. If the weight of a pig beginning the diet was 20 kg and thereafter the pig gained 6.6 kg every 10 days, determine w as a function of d and find the weight of a pig 50 days after the beginning of the diet.

27. Biologists have found that the number of chirps made per minute by crickets of a certain species is related to the temperature. The relationship is very close to being linear. At 68°F, those crickets chirp about 124 times a minute. At 80°F, they chirp about 172 times a minute. (a) Find an equation that gives Fahrenheit temperature t in terms of the number of chirps c per minute. (b) If you count chirps for only 15 seconds, how can you quickly estimate the temperature?

4.3 QUADRATIC FUNCTIONS

Parabola: $y = f(x) = ax^2 + bx + c$

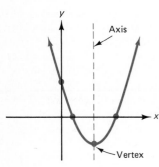

$a > 0$, opens upward

(a)

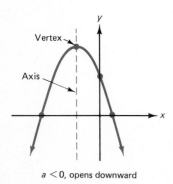

$a < 0$, opens downward

(b)

FIGURE 4.16

In Sec. 3.2 (Example 2) a *quadratic function* was described as a polynomial function of degree 2. Here is a formal definition.

Definition
*A function f is a **quadratic function** if and only if f(x) can be written in the form f(x) = ax² + bx + c, where a, b, and c are constants and a ≠ 0.*

For example, the functions $f(x) = x^2 - 3x + 2$ and $F(t) = -3t^2$ are quadratic. However, $g(x) = \dfrac{1}{x^2}$ is *not* quadratic because it cannot be written in the form $g(x) = ax^2 + bx + c$.

The graph of the quadratic function $y = f(x) = ax^2 + bx + c$ is called a **parabola** and has a shape like the curves in Fig. 4.16. If $a > 0$, the graph extends upward indefinitely and we say that the parabola *opens upward* [Fig. 4.16(a)]. If $a < 0$, the parabola *opens downward* [Fig. 4.16(b)].

Each parabola in Fig. 4.16 is *symmetric* about a vertical line, called the **axis of symmetry** of the parabola. That is, if the page were folded on one of these lines, then the two halves of the corresponding parabola would coincide. The axis (of symmetry) is *not* part of the parabola.

Figure 4.16 also shows points labeled **vertex,** where the axis cuts the parabola. If $a > 0$, the vertex is the "lowest" point on the parabola. This means that $f(x)$ has a minimum value at this point. By performing algebraic manipulations on $ax^2 + bx + c$ (referred to as *completing the square*), we can determine not only this minimum value, but also where it occurs.

$$f(x) = ax^2 + bx + c = (ax^2 + bx) + c.$$

* D. L. Hintzman, "Repetition and Learning," in *The Psychology of Learning*, Vol. 10, ed. G. H. Bower (New York: Academic Press, Inc., 1976), p. 77.

Adding and subtracting $\dfrac{b^2}{4a}$ give

$$f(x) = \left(ax^2 + bx + \frac{b^2}{4a}\right) + c - \frac{b^2}{4a}$$

$$= a\left(x^2 + \frac{b}{a}x + \frac{b^2}{4a^2}\right) + c - \frac{b^2}{4a}.$$

$$f(x) = a\left(x + \frac{b}{2a}\right)^2 + c - \frac{b^2}{4a}.$$

Since $\left(x + \dfrac{b}{2a}\right)^2 \geq 0$ and $a > 0$, it follows that $f(x)$ has a minimum value when

$x + \dfrac{b}{2a} = 0$, that is, when $x = -\dfrac{b}{2a}$. The minimum value is $c - \dfrac{b^2}{4a}$. Thus the

vertex is the point $\left(-\dfrac{b}{2a}, c - \dfrac{b^2}{4a}\right)$. Since the y-coordinate of this point is

$f\left(-\dfrac{b}{2a}\right)$, we have

$$\text{vertex} = \left(-\frac{b}{2a}, f\left(-\frac{b}{2a}\right)\right).$$

This is also the vertex of a parabola that opens downward ($a < 0$), but in this

case $f\left(-\dfrac{b}{2a}\right)$ is the *maximum* value of $f(x)$ [see Fig. 4.16(b)].

The point where the parabola $y = ax^2 + bx + c$ intersects the y-axis (that is, the y-intercept) occurs when $x = 0$. The y-coordinate of this point is c, so the y-intercept is $(0, c)$ or, more simply, c. In summary, we have the following.

The graph of the quadratic function $y = f(x) = ax^2 + bx + c$ is a parabola.

1. If $a > 0$, the parabola opens upward.
   If $a < 0$, it opens downward.

2. The vertex is $\left(-\dfrac{b}{2a}, f\left(-\dfrac{b}{2a}\right)\right)$.

3. The y-intercept is c.

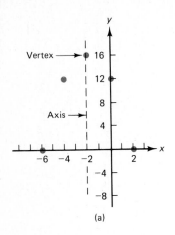

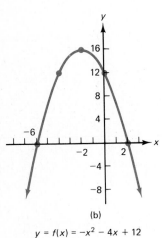

$$y = f(x) = -x^2 - 4x + 12$$

FIGURE 4.17

We can quickly sketch the graph of a quadratic function by first locating the vertex, the *y*-intercept, and a few other points like those where the parabola intersects the *x*-axis. These *x-intercepts* are found by setting $y = 0$ and solving for *x*. Once the intercepts and vertex are found, it is then relatively easy to pass the appropriate parabola through these points. In the event that the *x*-intercepts are very close to the vertex, or that no *x*-intercepts exist, we find a point on each side of the vertex so that we can give a reasonable sketch of the parabola. Keep in mind that passing a (broken) vertical line through the vertex gives the axis of symmetry. By plotting points to one side of the axis, we can use symmetry and obtain corresponding points on the other side.

EXAMPLE 1   *Graph the quadratic function* $y = f(x) = -x^2 - 4x + 12$.

Here $a = -1$, $b = -4$, and $c = 12$. Since $a < 0$, the parabola opens downward. The *x*-coordinate of the vertex is

$$-\frac{b}{2a} = -\frac{-4}{2(-1)} = -2.$$

The *y*-coordinate is $f(-2) = -(-2)^2 - 4(-2) + 12 = 16$. Thus the vertex (highest point) is $(-2, 16)$. Since $c = 12$, the *y*-intercept is 12. To find the *x*-intercepts, we let *y* be 0 in $y = -x^2 - 4x + 12$ and solve for *x*.

$$0 = -x^2 - 4x + 12,$$
$$0 = -(x^2 + 4x - 12),$$
$$0 = -(x + 6)(x - 2).$$

Thus $x = -6$ or $x = 2$, so the *x*-intercepts are -6 and 2. Now we plot the vertex, axis of symmetry, and intercepts [see Fig. 4.17(a)]. Since $(0, 12)$ is *two* units to the *right* of the axis, there is a corresponding point *two* units to the *left* of the axis with the same *y*-coordinate. Thus we get the point $(-4, 12)$. Through all points we draw a parabola opening downward [see Fig. 4.17(b)].

EXAMPLE 2   *Graph* $p = 2q^2$.

Here *p* is a quadratic function of *q*, where $a = 2$, $b = 0$, and $c = 0$. Since $a > 0$, the parabola opens upward. The *q*-coordinate of the vertex is

$$-\frac{b}{2a} = -\frac{0}{2(2)} = 0,$$

and the *p*-coordinate is $2(0)^2 = 0$. Thus the vertex is $(0, 0)$. In this case the *p*-axis is the axis of symmetry. A parabola opening upward with vertex at $(0, 0)$ cannot have any other intercepts. Hence to draw a reasonable graph we plot a point on each side of the vertex. If $q = 2$, then $p = 8$. This gives the point $(2, 8)$ and, by symmetry, the point $(-2, 8)$ (see Fig. 4.18).

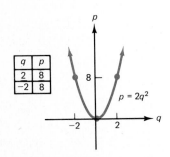

FIGURE 4.18

EXAMPLE 3   *Graph $g(x) = x^2 - 6x + 7$.*

Here g is a quadratic function, where $a = 1$, $b = -6$, and $c = 7$. The parabola opens upward because $a > 0$. The x-coordinate of the vertex is

$$-\frac{b}{2a} = -\frac{-6}{2(1)} = 3,$$

and $g(3) = 3^2 - 6(3) + 7 = -2$. Thus the vertex is $(3, -2)$. Since $c = 7$, the vertical-axis intercept is 7. To find x-intercepts, we set $g(x) = 0$.

$$0 = x^2 - 6x + 7.$$

The right side does not factor easily, so we shall use the quadratic formula to solve for x.

$$x = \frac{-b \pm \sqrt{b^2 - 4ac}}{2a} = \frac{-(-6) \pm \sqrt{(-6)^2 - 4(1)(7)}}{2(1)}$$

$$= \frac{6 \pm \sqrt{8}}{2} = \frac{6 \pm \sqrt{4 \cdot 2}}{2} = \frac{6 \pm 2\sqrt{2}}{2}$$

$$= \frac{6}{2} \pm \frac{2\sqrt{2}}{2} = 3 \pm \sqrt{2}.$$

Thus the x-intercepts are $3 + \sqrt{2}$ and $3 - \sqrt{2}$. After plotting the vertex, intercepts, and (by symmetry) the point $(6, 7)$, we draw a parabola opening upward in Fig. 4.19.

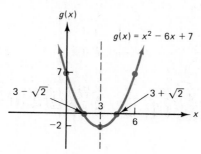

FIGURE 4.19

EXAMPLE 4   *Graph $y = f(x) = 2x^2 + 2x + 3$ and find the range of f.*

This function is quadratic with $a = 2$, $b = 2$, and $c = 3$. Since $a > 0$, the graph is a parabola opening upward. The x-coordinate of the vertex is

$$-\frac{b}{2a} = -\frac{2}{2(2)} = -\frac{1}{2},$$

and the y-coordinate is $2(-\frac{1}{2})^2 + 2(-\frac{1}{2}) + 3 = \frac{5}{2}$. Thus the vertex is $(-\frac{1}{2}, \frac{5}{2})$. Since $c = 3$, the y-intercept is 3. A parabola opening upward with its vertex above the x-axis has no x-intercepts. In Fig. 4.20 we plotted the y-intercept, the vertex, and an additional point $(-2, 7)$ to the left of the vertex. By symmetry, we also get the point $(1, 7)$. Passing a parabola through these points gives the desired graph. From Fig. 4.20 we see that the range of f is all $y \geq \frac{5}{2}$.

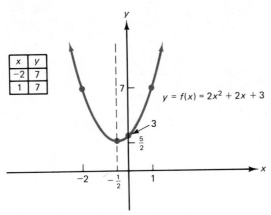

x	y
-2	7
1	7

$y = f(x) = 2x^2 + 2x + 3$

FIGURE 4.20

EXAMPLE 5   *The demand function for a manufacturer's product is p =* *1000 − 2q, where p is the price (in dollars) per unit when q units are demanded* *(per week) by consumers. Find the level of production that will maximize the* *manufacturer's total revenue, and determine this revenue.*

Total revenue r is given by

total revenue = (price)(quantity).

$$r = pq$$
$$= (1000 - 2q)q$$
$$r = 1000q - 2q^2.$$

Note that r is a quadratic function of q, with $a = -2$, $b = 1000$, and $c = 0$. Since $a < 0$ (parabola opens downward), r is maximum when

$$q = -\frac{b}{2a} = -\frac{1000}{2(-2)} = 250.$$

The maximum value of r is

$$r = 1000(250) - 2(250)^2$$
$$= 250,000 - 125,000 = 125,000.$$

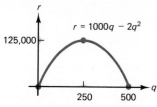

FIGURE 4.21

Thus the maximum revenue that the manufacturer can receive is $125,000, which occurs at a production level of 250 units. Figure 4.21 shows the graph of the revenue function. Only that portion for which $q \geq 0$ and $r \geq 0$ is drawn, since quantity and revenue cannot be negative.

EXERCISE 4.3

In Problems **1–8,** *state whether or not the function is quadratic.*

1. $f(x) = 26 - 3x.$

2. $g(x) = (7 - x)^2.$

3. $g(x) = 4x^2.$

4. $h(s) = 6(4s + 1).$

5. $h(q) = \dfrac{1}{2q - 4}.$

6. $f(t) = 2t(3 - t) + 4t.$

7. $f(s) = \dfrac{s^2 - 4}{2}.$

8. $g(t) = (t^2 - 1)^2.$

In Problems **9–12,** *do not include a graph.*

9. For the parabola $y = f(x) = -4x^2 + 8x + 7$, (a) find the vertex. (b) Does the vertex correspond to the highest point, or the lowest point, on the graph?

10. Repeat Problem 9 if $y = f(x) = 8x^2 + 4x - 1.$

11. For the parabola $y = f(x) = x^2 + 2x - 8$, find (a) the y-intercept, (b) the x-intercepts, and (c) the vertex.

12. Repeat Problem 11 if $y = f(x) = 3 + x - 2x^2.$

In Problems **13–22,** *graph each function. Give the vertex and intercepts, and state the range.*

13. $y = f(x) = x^2 - 6x + 5.$

14. $y = f(x) = -3x^2.$

15. $y = g(x) = -2x^2 - 6x.$

16. $y = f(x) = x^2 - 1.$

17. $s = h(t) = t^2 + 2t + 1.$

18. $s = h(t) = 2t^2 + 3t - 2.$

19. $y = f(x) = -9 + 8x - 2x^2.$

20. $y = H(x) = 1 - x - x^2.$

21. $t = f(s) = s^2 - 8s + 13.$

22. $t = f(s) = s^2 + 6s + 11.$

In Problems **23–26,** *state whether $f(x)$ has a maximum value or a minimum value, and find that value.*

23. $f(x) = 100x^2 - 20x + 25.$

24. $f(x) = -2x^2 - 16x + 3.$

25. $f(x) = 4x - 50 - 0.1x^2.$

26. $f(x) = x(x + 3) - 12.$

27. The demand function for a manufacturer's product is $p = f(q) = 1200 - 3q$, where p is the price (in dollars) per unit when q units are demanded (per week). Find the level of production that maximizes the manufacturer's total revenue and determine this revenue.

28. A marketing firm estimates that n months after the introduction of a client's new product, $f(n)$ thousand households will use it, where

$$f(n) = \tfrac{10}{9} n(12 - n), \qquad 0 \leq n \leq 12.$$

Estimate the maximum number of households that will use the product.

29. Biologists studied the nutritional effects on rats that were fed a diet containing 10% protein.* The protein consisted of yeast and corn flour. By varying the percentage P of yeast in the protein mix, the group estimated that the average weight gain (in grams) of a rat over a period of time was $f(P)$, where

$$f(P) = -\tfrac{1}{50}P^2 + 2P + 20, \qquad 0 \le P \le 100.$$

Find the maximum weight gain.

30. The height s of a ball thrown vertically upward from the ground is given by

$$s = -4.9t^2 + 58.8t,$$

where s is in meters and t is elapsed time in seconds. After how many seconds will the ball reach its maximum height? What is the maximum height?

4.4 SYSTEMS OF LINEAR EQUATIONS

When a situation must be described mathematically, it is not unusual for a *set* of equations to arise. For example, suppose that the manager of a factory is setting up a production schedule for two models of a new product. The first model requires 4 widgets and 9 klunkers. The second requires 5 widgets and 14 klunkers. From its suppliers, the factory gets 335 widgets and 850 klunkers each day. How many of each model should the manager plan to make each day so that all the widgets and klunkers are used?

It's a good idea to construct a table that summarizes the important information. Table 4.2 shows the number of widgets and klunkers required for each model, as well as the total number available.

TABLE 4.2

	FIRST MODEL	SECOND MODEL	TOTAL AVAILABLE
Widgets	4	5	335
Klunkers	9	14	850

Suppose we let x be the number of first models made each day and y be the number of second models. Then these require a total of $4x + 5y$ widgets and $9x + 14y$ klunkers. Since 335 widgets and 850 klunkers are available, we have

$$\begin{cases} 4x + 5y = 335, & (1) \\ 9x + 14y = 850. & (2) \end{cases}$$

We call this set of equations a **system** of two linear equations in the variables (or unknowns) x and y. The problem is to find values of x and y for which *both* equations are true *simultaneously*. These are called *solutions* of the system.

Since Eqs. (1) and (2) are linear, their graphs are straight lines; call them L_1 and L_2. Now, the coordinates of any point on a line satisfy the equation of that line; that is, they make the equation true. Thus the coordinates of any point

---

* Adapted from R. Bressani, "The Use of Yeast in Human Foods," in *Single-Cell Protein,* ed. R. I. Mateles and S. R. Tannenbaum (Cambridge, Mass.: MIT Press, 1968).

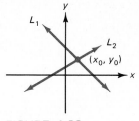

FIGURE 4.22

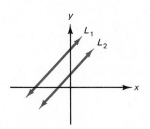

FIGURE 4.23

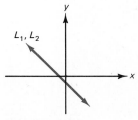

FIGURE 4.24

of intersection of L_1 and L_2 will satisfy both equations. This means that a point of intersection gives a solution of the system.

If L_1 and L_2 are drawn on the same plane, they will appear in one of three ways.

1. L_1 and L_2 may meet at exactly one point, say (x_0, y_0) (see Fig. 4.22). Thus the system has the solution $x = x_0$ and $y = y_0$.

2. L_1 and L_2 may be parallel and have no points in common (see Fig. 4.23). Thus there is no solution.

3. L_1 and L_2 may be the same line (see Fig. 4.24). Thus the coordinates of any point on the line are a solution of the system. Consequently, there are infinitely many solutions.

Our main concern here is algebraic methods of solving a system of linear equations. Essentially, we successively replace the system by other systems which have the same solution (that is, by *equivalent systems*), but whose equations have a progressively more desirable form for determining the solution. More precisely, we seek an equivalent system containing an equation in which one of the variables does not appear (that is, one of the variables is *eliminated*). We shall illustrate this procedure.

In the problem originally posed,

$$\begin{cases} 4x + 5y = 335, & (3) \\ 9x + 14y = 850, & (4) \end{cases}$$

we shall obtain an equivalent system in which x does not appear in one equation. First we find an equivalent system in which the coefficients of the x-terms in each equation are the same except for sign. Multiplying Eq. (3) by 9 [that is, multiplying both sides of Eq. (3) by 9] and multiplying Eq. (4) by -4 give

$$\begin{cases} 36x + 45y = 3015, & (5) \\ -36x - 56y = -3400. & (6) \end{cases}$$

The left and right sides of Eq. (6) are equal, so each side can be *added* to the corresponding side of Eq. (5). This gives

$$-11y = -385,$$

which has only one variable, as planned. Solving gives

$$y = 35,$$

so we obtain the equivalent system

$$\begin{cases} y = 35, & (7) \\ -36x - 56y = -3400. & (8) \end{cases}$$

Replacing y in Eq. (8) by 35, we get

$$-36x - 56(35) = -3400,$$
$$-36x - 1960 = -3400,$$
$$-36x = -1440,$$
$$x = 40.$$

Thus the original system is equivalent to

$$\begin{cases} y = 35, \\ x = 40. \end{cases}$$

We can check our answer by substituting $x = 40$ and $y = 35$ into *both* of the original equations. In Eq. (3) we get $4(40) + 5(35) = 335$, or $335 = 335$. In Eq. (4) we get $9(40) + 14(35) = 850$, or $850 = 850$. Thus the solution is

$$x = 40 \qquad \text{and} \qquad y = 35.$$

Each day the manager should plan to make 40 of the first model and 35 of the second. Our procedure is referred to as **elimination by addition.** Although we chose to eliminate x first, we could have done the same for y by a similar procedure.

EXAMPLE 1   *Use elimination by addition to solve the system*

$$\begin{cases} 3x - 4y = 13, \\ 3y + 2x = 3. \end{cases}$$

Aligning the x- and y-terms for convenience gives

$$\begin{cases} 3x - 4y = 13, & \quad (9) \\ 2x + 3y = 3. & \quad (10) \end{cases}$$

To eliminate y, we multiply Eq. (9) by 3 and Eq. (10) by 4:

$$\begin{cases} 9x - 12y = 39, & \quad (11) \\ 8x + 12y = 12. & \quad (12) \end{cases}$$

Adding Eq. (11) to Eq. (12) gives $17x = 51$, from which $x = 3$. We have the equivalent system

$$\begin{cases} 9x - 12y = 39, & \quad (13) \\ \quad\quad x = 3. & \quad (14) \end{cases}$$

Replacing x by 3 in Eq. (13) gives

$$9(3) - 12y = 39,$$
$$-12y = 12,$$
$$y = -1,$$

so the original system is equivalent to

$$\begin{cases} y = -1, \\ x = 3. \end{cases}$$

The solution is $x = 3$ and $y = -1$. Figure 4.25 shows a graph of the system.

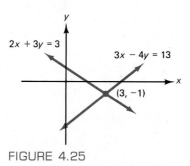

FIGURE 4.25

There's another way to solve the system in Example 1:

$$\begin{cases} 3x - 4y = 13, & \text{(15)} \\ 2x + 3y = 3. & \text{(16)} \end{cases}$$

We first choose one of the equations, for example Eq. (15), and solve it for one unknown in terms of the other, say x in terms of y. Hence Eq. (15) is equivalent to $3x = 4y + 13$ or

$$x = \frac{4}{3}y + \frac{13}{3},$$

and we obtain

$$\begin{cases} x = \dfrac{4}{3}y + \dfrac{13}{3}, & \text{(17)} \\ \\ 2x + 3y = 3. & \text{(18)} \end{cases}$$

Substituting the right side of Eq. (17) for x in Eq. (18) gives

$$2\left(\frac{4}{3}y + \frac{13}{3}\right) + 3y = 3. \qquad \text{(19)}$$

Thus x has been eliminated. Solving Eq. (19) we have

$$\frac{8}{3}y + \frac{26}{3} + 3y = 3,$$

$$8y + 26 + 9y = 9 \qquad \text{(clearing of fractions)},$$

$$17y = -17,$$

$$y = -1.$$

Replacing y in Eq. (17) by -1 gives $x = 3$, and the original system is equivalent to

$$\begin{cases} x = & 3 \\ y = & -1, \end{cases}$$

as before. This method is called **elimination by substitution.**

EXAMPLE 2   *Use elimination by substitution to solve the system*

$$\begin{cases} x + 2y - 8 = 0, \\ 2x + 4y + 4 = 0. \end{cases}$$

It is easy to solve the first equation for x. This gives the equivalent system

$$\begin{cases} x = -2y + 8, & \text{(20)} \\ 2x + 4y + 4 = 0. & \text{(21)} \end{cases}$$

Substituting $-2y + 8$ for x in Eq. (21) gives

$$2(-2y + 8) + 4y + 4 = 0,$$

$$-4y + 16 + 4y + 4 = 0.$$

This simplifies to $20 = 0$.

$$\begin{cases} x = -2y + 8, & \text{(22)} \\ 20 = 0. & \text{(23)} \end{cases}$$

Since Eq. (23) is *never* true, there is **no solution** to the original system. The reason is clear if we observe that the original equations can be written in slope-intercept form as

$$y = -\frac{1}{2}x + 4$$

and

$$y = -\frac{1}{2}x - 1.$$

These equations represent straight lines having slopes of $-\frac{1}{2}$ but different y-intercepts, 4 and -1. That is, they determine different parallel lines (see Fig. 4.26).

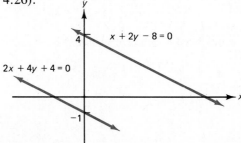

FIGURE 4.26

EXAMPLE 3   *Solve*

$$x + 5y = 2, \tag{24}$$

$$\frac{1}{2}x + \frac{5}{2}y = 1. \tag{25}$$

Multiplying Eq. (25) by -2, we have

$$x + 5y = 2, \tag{26}$$

$$-x - 5y = -2. \tag{27}$$

Adding Eq. (26) to Eq. (27) gives

$$x + 5y = 2, \tag{28}$$

$$0 = 0. \tag{29}$$

Because Eq. (29) is *always* true, any solution of Eq. (28) is a solution of the system. Looking at it another way, by writing Eqs. (24) and (25) in their slope-intercept forms, we get the equivalent system

$$y = -\frac{1}{5}x + \frac{2}{5},$$

$$y = -\frac{1}{5}x + \frac{2}{5}$$

in which both equations represent the same line. Hence the lines coincide (Fig. 4.27), and Eqs. (24) and (25) are equivalent. The solution to the system consists of the coordinates of any point on the line $x + 5y = 2$, and so there are infinitely many solutions. For example, $x = 0$ and $y = \frac{2}{5}$ is one solution.

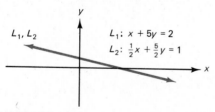

L_1, L_2

L_1: $x + 5y = 2$
L_2: $\frac{1}{2}x + \frac{5}{2}y = 1$

FIGURE 4.27

An equation of the form $Ax + By + Cz = D$, where A, B, C, and D are constants and A, B, and C are not all zero, is called a **general linear equation in the variables x, y, and z.** Example 4 shows how to solve a system of three such equations.

EXAMPLE 4   *Solve*

$$2x + y + z = 3, \tag{30}$$

$$-x + 2y + 2z = 1, \tag{31}$$

$$x - y - 3z = -6. \tag{32}$$

This system consists of three linear equations in three variables. From Eq. (32), $x = y + 3z - 6$. By substituting for x in Eqs. (30) and (31), we obtain

$$\begin{cases} 2(y + 3z - 6) + y + z = 3, \\ -(y + 3z - 6) + 2y + 2z = 1, \\ \qquad\qquad x = y + 3z - 6. \end{cases}$$

Simplifying gives

$$\begin{cases} 3y + 7z = 15, & (33) \\ \quad y - z = -5, & (34) \\ \quad x = y + 3z - 6. & (35) \end{cases}$$

Note that x does not appear in Eqs. (33) and (34). Since any solution of the original system must satisfy Eqs. (33) and (34), we shall consider their solution first:

$$\begin{cases} 3y + 7z = \quad 15, & (33) \\ \quad y - \quad z = -5. & (34) \end{cases}$$

From Eq. (34), $y = z - 5$. This means we can replace Eq. (33) by $3(z - 5) + 7z = 15$ or $z = 3$. Since z is 3, we can replace Eq. (34) with $y = -2$. Hence the above system is equivalent to

$$\begin{cases} z = \quad 3, \\ y = -2. \end{cases}$$

The original system becomes

$$\begin{cases} z = 3, \\ y = -2, \\ x = y + 3z - 6, \end{cases}$$

from which $x = 1$. The solution is $x = 1$, $y = -2$, and $z = 3$, which you may verify.

EXAMPLE 5   *Solve*

$$\begin{cases} 2x + y + z = -2, & (36) \\ \quad x - 2y = \dfrac{13}{2}, & (37) \\ 3x + 2y - 2z = -\dfrac{9}{2}. & (38) \end{cases}$$

Since Eq. (37) can be written $x - 2y + 0z = \frac{13}{2}$, we can view Eqs. (36) to (38) as a system of three linear equations in the variables x, y, and z. From Eq. (37), $x = 2y + \frac{13}{2}$. By substituting for x in Eqs. (36) and (38) and simplifying, we obtain

$$\begin{cases} 5y + z = -15, & \quad (39) \\ \\ x = 2y + \dfrac{13}{2}, & \quad (40) \\ \\ 4y - z = -12. & \quad (41) \end{cases}$$

Solving the system formed by Eqs. (39) and (41),

$$\begin{cases} 5y + z = -15, \\ 4y - z = -12, \end{cases}$$

we find that $y = -3$ and $z = 0$. Substituting these values in Eq. (40) gives $x = \frac{1}{2}$. Hence the solution of the original system is $x = \frac{1}{2}$, $y = -3$, and $z = 0$.

EXAMPLE 6   *A chemical manufacturer wishes to fill a request for 500 liters of a 25% acid solution (25% by volume is acid). If solutions of 30 and 18% are available in stock, how many liters of each must be mixed to fill the order?*

Let x and y, respectively, be the number of liters of the 30 and 18% solutions which should be mixed. Then

$$x + y = 500. \qquad (42)$$

See Fig. 4.28. In 500 liters of a 25% solution, there will be $0.25(500) = 125$ liters of acid. This acid comes from two sources: $0.30x$ liters of it come from the 30% solution and $0.18y$ liters of it come from the 18% solution. Hence

$$0.30x + 0.18y = 125. \qquad (43)$$

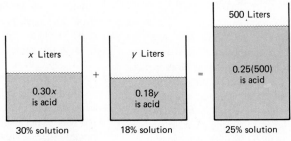

FIGURE 4.28

Equations (42) and (43) form a system of two linear equations in two unknowns. Solving Eq. (42) for x gives $x = 500 - y$. Substituting in Eq. (43) gives

$$0.30(500 - y) + 0.18y = 125. \qquad (44)$$

Solving Eq. (44) for y, we find $y = 208\frac{1}{3}$ liters. Thus $x = 500 - 208\frac{1}{3} = 291\frac{2}{3}$ liters.

EXERCISE 4.4

In Problems **1–16**, *solve the systems algebraically*.

1. $\begin{cases} 3x + y = 7, \\ 2x + 2y = -2. \end{cases}$

2. $\begin{cases} 2x - y = -11, \\ y + 5x = -7. \end{cases}$

3. $\begin{cases} 3x - 4y = 13, \\ 2x + 3y = 3. \end{cases}$

4. $\begin{cases} 2x - y = 1, \\ -x + 2y = 7. \end{cases}$

5. $\begin{cases} 5v + 2w = 36, \\ 8v - 3w = -54. \end{cases}$

6. $\begin{cases} p + q = 3, \\ 3p + 2q = 19. \end{cases}$

7. $\begin{cases} 4x - 3y - 2 = 3x - 7y, \\ x + 5y - 2 = y + 4. \end{cases}$

8. $\begin{cases} 5x + 7y + 2 = 9y - 4x + 6, \\ \frac{21}{2}x - \frac{4}{3}y - \frac{11}{4} = \frac{3}{2}x + \frac{2}{3}y + \frac{5}{4}. \end{cases}$

9. $\begin{cases} \frac{2}{3}x + \frac{1}{2}y = 2, \\ \frac{3}{8}x + \frac{5}{6}y = -\frac{11}{2}. \end{cases}$

10. $\begin{cases} \frac{1}{2}z - \frac{1}{4}w = \frac{1}{6}, \\ z + \frac{1}{2}w = \frac{2}{3}. \end{cases}$

11. $\begin{cases} 4p + 12q = 6, \\ 2p + 6q = 3. \end{cases}$

12. $\begin{cases} 5x - 3y = 2, \\ -10x + 6y = 4. \end{cases}$

13. $\begin{cases} 2x + y + 6z = 3, \\ x - y + 4z = 1, \\ 3x + 2y - 2z = 2. \end{cases}$

14. $\begin{cases} x + y + z = -1, \\ 3x + y + z = 1, \\ 4x - 2y + 2z = 0. \end{cases}$

15. $\begin{cases} 5x - 7y + 4z = 2, \\ 3x + 2y - 2z = 3, \\ 2x - y + 3z = 4. \end{cases}$

16. $\begin{cases} 3x - 2y + z = 0, \\ -2x + y - 3z = 15, \\ \frac{3}{2}x + \frac{4}{5}y + 4z = 10. \end{cases}$

17. A chemical manufacturer wishes to fill an order for 700 gallons of a 24% acid solution. Solutions of 20% and 30% are in stock. How many gallons of each solution must be mixed to fill the order?

18. A company has taxable income of $312,000. The federal tax is 25% of that portion left after the state tax has been paid. The state tax is 10% of that portion left after the federal tax has been paid. Find the federal and state taxes.

19. A manufacturer of dining-room sets produces two styles, early American and contemporary. From past experience management has determined that 20% more of the early American styles can be sold than the contemporary styles. A profit of $250 is made on each early American sold, while one of $350 is made on each contemporary. If, in the forthcoming year, management desires a total profit of $130,000, how many units of each style must be sold?

20. National Surveys was awarded a contract to perform a product rating survey for Crispy Crackers. A total of 250 people were interviewed. National Surveys reported that 62.5% more people liked Crispy Crackers than disliked them. However, the report did not indicate that 16% of those interviewed had no comment. How many of those surveyed liked Crispy Crackers? How many disliked them? How many had no comment?

21. United Products Co. manufactures calculators and has plants in the cities of Exton and Whyton. At the Exton plant, fixed costs are $7000 per month, and the cost of producing each calculator is $7.50. At the Whyton plant, fixed costs are $8800 per month, and each calculator costs $6.00 to produce. Next month, United Products must produce 1500 calculators. How many must be made at each plant if the total cost at each plant is to be the same?

22. A coffee wholesaler blends together three types of coffee that sell for $2.20, $2.30, and $2.60 per pound so as to obtain 100 lb of coffee worth $2.40 per pound. If the wholesaler uses the same amount of the two higher-priced coffees, how much of each type must be used in the blend?

23. A company pays its salespeople on a basis of a certain percentage of the first $100,000 in sales, plus a certain percentage of any amount over $100,000 in sales. If one salesperson earned $8500 on sales of $175,000 and another salesperson earned $14,800 on sales of $280,000, find the two percentages.

24. In news reports, profits of a company this year (T) are often compared with those of last year (L), but actual values of T and L are not always given. This year a company had profits of $20 million more than last year. The profits were up 25%. Determine T and L from these data.

25. Universal Control Co. makes industrial control units. Their new models are the Argon I and the Argon II. To make each Argon I unit, they use 6 doodles and 3 skeeters. To make each Argon II unit, they use 10 doodles and 8 skeeters. The company receives a total of 760 doodles and 500 skeeters each day from its supplier. How many units of each model of the Argon can the company make each day? Assume that all the parts are used.

26. A person made two investments and the percentage return per year on each was the same. Of the total amount invested, $\frac{3}{10}$ of it plus $600 was invested in one venture and at the end of 1 year the person received a return of $384 from that venture. If the total return after 1 year was $1120, find the total amount invested.

27. A company makes three types of patio furniture: chairs, rockers, and chaise lounges. Each requires wood, plastic, and aluminum, as given in the table below. The company has in stock 400 units of wood, 600 units of plastic, and 1500 units of aluminum. For its end-of-the-season production run, the company wants to use up all the stock. To do this, how many chairs, rockers, and chaise lounges should it make?

	WOOD	PLASTIC	ALUMINUM
Chair	1 unit	1 unit	2 units
Rocker	1 unit	1 unit	3 units
Chaise lounge	1 unit	2 units	5 units

28. A total of $35,000 was invested at three interest rates: 7, 8, and 9%. The interest for the first year was $2830, which was not reinvested. The second year the amount originally invested at 9% earned 10% instead, and the other rates remained the same. The total interest the second year was $2960. How much was invested at each rate?

29. A company pays skilled workers in its assembly department $8 per hour. Semiskilled workers in that department are paid $4 per hour. Shipping clerks are paid $5 per hour. Because of an increase in orders, the company needs to employ a total of 70 workers in the assembly and shipping departments. It will pay a total of $370 per hour to these employees. Because of a union contract, twice as many semiskilled workers as skilled workers must be employed. How many semiskilled workers, skilled workers, and shipping clerks should the company hire?

30. A 10,000-gallon railroad tank car is to be filled with solvent from two storage tanks, A and B. Solvent from A is pumped at the rate of 20 gal/min. Solvent from B is pumped at 30 gal/min. Usually, both pumps operate at the same time. However, because of a blown fuse the pump on A is delayed 10 minutes. How many gallons from each storage tank will be used to fill the car?

4.5 NONLINEAR SYSTEMS

A system of equations in which at least one equation is not linear is called a **nonlinear system.** Solutions of such systems may often be found algebraically by substitution, as was done with linear systems. The following examples illustrate.

EXAMPLE 1   *Solve*

$$\begin{cases} x^2 - 2x + y - 7 = 0, & (1) \\ 3x - y + 1 = 0. & (2) \end{cases}$$

Solving Eq. (2) for y gives

$$y = 3x + 1. \qquad (3)$$

Substituting in Eq. (1) and simplifying, we have

$$x^2 - 2x + (3x + 1) - 7 = 0,$$
$$x^2 + x - 6 = 0,$$
$$(x + 3)(x - 2) = 0,$$
$$x = -3 \quad \text{or} \quad x = 2.$$

From Eq. (3), if $x = -3$, then $y = -8$; if $x = 2$, then $y = 7$. You should verify that each pair of values satisfies the given system. Hence the solutions are $x = -3, y = -8$ and $x = 2, y = 7$. These solutions can be seen geometrically in the graph of the system in Fig. 4.29. Notice that the graph of Eq. (1) is a parabola and the graph of Eq. (2) is a line. The solutions correspond to the intersection points $(-3, -8)$ and $(2, 7)$.

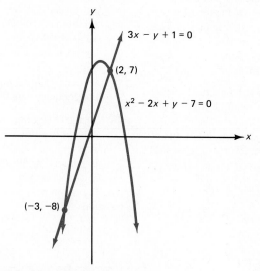

FIGURE 4.29

EXAMPLE 2   *Solve*

$$\begin{cases} y = \sqrt{x + 2}, \\ x + y = 4. \end{cases}$$

Solving the second equation for y gives

$$y = 4 - x. \tag{4}$$

Substituting gives

$$4 - x = \sqrt{x + 2},$$
$$16 - 8x + x^2 = x + 2 \qquad \text{(squaring both sides),}$$

$$x^2 - 9x + 14 = 0,$$

$$(x - 2)(x - 7) = 0.$$

Thus $x = 2$ or $x = 7$. From Eq. (4), if $x = 2$, then $y = 2$; if $x = 7$, then $y = -3$. Although $x = 2$ and $y = 2$ satisfy the original equations, this is not the case for $x = 7$ and $y = -3$. Thus the solution is $x = 2$, $y = 2$.

EXERCISE 4.5

Solve the following nonlinear systems.

1. $\begin{cases} y = 4 - x^2, \\ 3x + y = 0. \end{cases}$

2. $\begin{cases} y = x^3, \\ x - y = 0. \end{cases}$

3. $\begin{cases} p^2 = 4 - q, \\ p = q + 2. \end{cases}$

4. $\begin{cases} y^2 - x^2 = 28, \\ x - y = 14. \end{cases}$

5. $\begin{cases} x = y^2, \\ y = x^2. \end{cases}$

6. $\begin{cases} p^2 - q = 0, \\ 3q - 2p - 1 = 0. \end{cases}$

7. $\begin{cases} y = 4x - x^2 + 8, \\ y = x^2 - 2x. \end{cases}$

8. $\begin{cases} x^2 - y = 8, \\ y - x^2 = 0. \end{cases}$

9. $\begin{cases} p = \sqrt{q}, \\ p = q^2. \end{cases}$

10. $\begin{cases} z = 4/w, \\ 3z = 2w + 2. \end{cases}$

11. $\begin{cases} x^2 = y^2 + 14, \\ y = x^2 - 16. \end{cases}$

12. $\begin{cases} x^2 + y^2 - 2xy = 1, \\ 3x - y = 5. \end{cases}$

13. $\begin{cases} y = \dfrac{x^2}{x - 1} + 1, \\ y = \dfrac{1}{x - 1}. \end{cases}$

14. $\begin{cases} x = y + 6, \\ y = 3\sqrt{x} + 4. \end{cases}$

4.6 APPLICATIONS OF SYSTEMS OF EQUATIONS

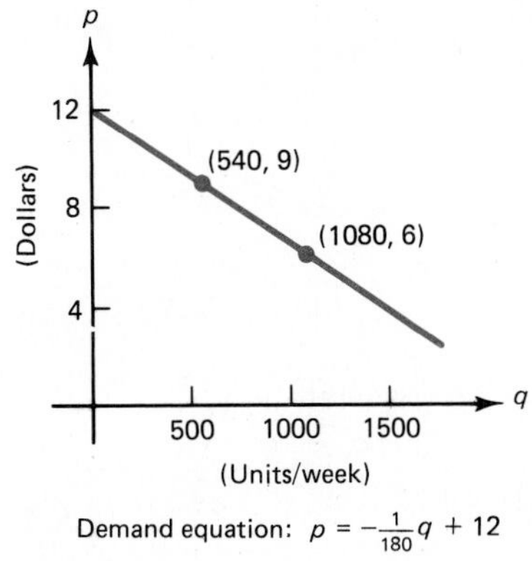

Demand equation: $p = -\frac{1}{180}q + 12$

FIGURE 4.30

Recall from Sec. 4.2 that an equation that relates price per unit and quantity demanded (supplied) is called a *demand equation (supply equation)*. Suppose that the linear demand equation for product Z is

$$p = -\frac{1}{180}q + 12 \tag{1}$$

and its linear supply equation is

$$p = \frac{1}{300}q + 8, \tag{2}$$

where $q, p \geq 0$. The demand and supply curves defined by Eqs. (1) and (2) are given in Figs. 4.30 and 4.31. In analyzing Fig. 4.30, we see that consumers will purchase 540 units per week when the price is $9 per unit; 1080 units when the price is $6; and so on. Figure 4.31 shows that when the price is $9 per unit, producers will place 300 units per week on the market; at $10 they will supply 600 units; and so on.

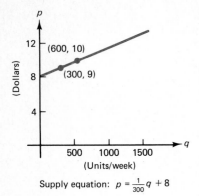

Supply equation: $p = \frac{1}{300}q + 8$

FIGURE 4.31

When the demand and supply curves of a product are represented on the same coordinate plane, the point $(m,\ n)$ where the curves intersect is called the **point of equilibrium** (see Fig. 4.32). The price n, called the **equilibrium price,** is the price at which consumers will purchase the same quantity of a product that producers wish to sell at that price. In short, n is the price at which stability in the producer-consumer relationship occurs. The quantity m is called the **equilibrium quantity.**

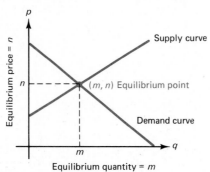

FIGURE 4.32

To determine precisely the equilibrium point, we solve the system formed by the supply and demand equations. Let us do this for our previous data, namely the system

$$\begin{cases} p = -\dfrac{1}{180}q + 12 & \text{(demand equation)}, \\[2mm] p = \dfrac{1}{300}q + 8 & \text{(supply equation)}. \end{cases}$$

By substituting $\frac{1}{300}q + 8$ for p in the demand equation, we get

$$\frac{1}{300}q + 8 = -\frac{1}{180}q + 12,$$

$$\left(\frac{1}{300} + \frac{1}{180}\right)q = 4,$$

$$q = 450 \qquad \text{(equilibrium quantity)}.$$

Thus

$$p = \frac{1}{300}(450) + 8$$

$$= 9.50 \qquad \text{(equilibrium price)},$$

and the equilibrium point is (450, 9.50). Therefore, at the price of $9.50 per unit, manufacturers will produce exactly the quantity (450) of units per week that consumers will purchase at that price (see Fig. 4.33).

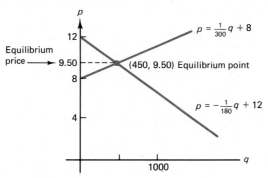

FIGURE 4.33

EXAMPLE 1   *Let $p = \frac{8}{100}q + 50$ be the supply equation for a certain manufacturer and suppose the demand equation for his product is $p = -\frac{7}{100}q + 65$.*

a. *If a tax of $1.50 per unit is to be imposed on the manufacturer, how will the original equilibrium price be affected if the demand remains the same?*

b. *Determine the total revenue obtained by the manufacturer at the equilibrium point both before and after the tax.*

a. Before the tax, the equilibrium price is obtained by solving the system

$$\begin{cases} p = \dfrac{8}{100}q + 50, \\[2mm] p = -\dfrac{7}{100}q + 65. \end{cases}$$

By substitution,

$$-\frac{7}{100}q + 65 = \frac{8}{100}q + 50,$$

$$15 = \frac{15}{100}q,$$

$$100 = q,$$

and

$$p = \frac{8}{100}(100) + 50 = 58.$$

Thus \$58 is the original equilibrium price. Before the tax the manufacturer supplies q units at a price of $p = \frac{8}{100}q + 50$ per unit. After the tax he will sell the same q units for an additional \$1.50 per unit. The price per unit will be $(\frac{8}{100}q + 50) + 1.50$ and the new supply equation is $p = \frac{8}{100}q + 51.50$. Solving the system

$$\begin{cases} p = \dfrac{8}{100}q + 51.50, \\ \\ p = -\dfrac{7}{100}q + 65 \end{cases}$$

will give the new equilibrium price.

$$\frac{8}{100}q + 51.50 = -\frac{7}{100}q + 65,$$

$$\frac{15}{100}q = 13.50,$$

$$q = 90,$$

$$p = \frac{8}{100}(90) + 51.50 = 58.70.$$

The tax of \$1.50 per unit increases the equilibrium price by \$0.70 (Fig. 4.34). Note that there is also a decrease in the equilibrium quantity from $q = 100$ to $q = 90$ because of the change in the equilibrium price. (In the exercises, you are asked to find the effect of a subsidy given to the manufacturer which will reduce the price of the product.)

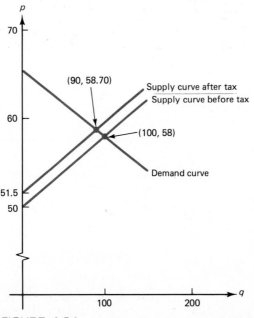

FIGURE 4.34

b. If q units of a product are sold at a price of p dollars each, then the total revenue, which we shall denote by y_{TR}, is given by

$$y_{TR} = pq.$$

Before the tax the revenue at (100, 58) is (in dollars)

$$y_{TR} = (58)(100) = 5800.$$

After the tax it is

$$y_{TR} = (58.70)(90) = 5283,$$

which is a decrease.

EXAMPLE 2   *Find the equilibrium point if the supply and demand equations of a product are $p = \dfrac{q}{40} + 10$ and $p = \dfrac{8000}{q}$, respectively.*

Here the demand equation is not linear. Solving the system

$$\begin{cases} p = \dfrac{q}{40} + 10, \\[2mm] p = \dfrac{8000}{q} \end{cases}$$

by substitution gives

$$\frac{8000}{q} = \frac{q}{40} + 10,$$

$$320,000 = q^2 + 400q,$$

$$q^2 + 400q - 320,000 = 0,$$

$$(q + 800)(q - 400) = 0,$$

$$q = -800 \quad \text{or} \quad q = 400.$$

We disregard $q = -800$, since q represents quantity. Choosing $q = 400$, then we have $p = (8000/400) = 20$ and the required point is (400, 20) (see Fig. 4.35).

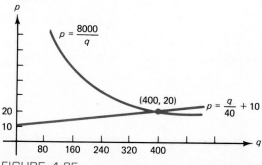

FIGURE 4.35

Suppose a manufacturer produces product A and sells it at $8.00 per unit. Then the total revenue y_{TR} received (in dollars) from selling q units is

$$y_{TR} = 8q \qquad \text{(total revenue).}$$

The difference between the total revenue received for q units and the total cost of q units is the manufacturer's profit (or loss if the difference is negative):

profit (or loss) = total revenue − total cost.

Total cost, y_{TC}, is the sum of total variable costs y_{VC} and total fixed costs y_{FC}.

$$y_{TC} = y_{VC} + y_{FC}.$$

Fixed costs are those costs that under normal conditions do not depend on the level of production; that is, over some period of time they remain constant at all levels of output (examples are rent, officers' salaries and normal maintenance). **Variable costs** are those costs that vary with the level of production (such as cost of materials, labor, maintenance due to wear and tear, etc.). For q units of product A, suppose that

$$y_{FC} = 5000 \qquad \text{(fixed cost)}$$

$$\text{and} \qquad y_{VC} = \frac{22}{9}q \qquad \text{(variable cost).}$$

Then

$$y_{TC} = \frac{22}{9}q + 5000 \qquad \text{(total cost).}$$

The graphs of fixed cost, total cost, and total revenue appear in Fig. 4.36. The horizontal axis represents level of production q, and the vertical axis represents the total dollar value, be it revenue or costs. The **break-even point** is the point at which total revenue = total cost ($TR = TC$). It occurs when the levels of production and sales result in neither a profit nor a loss to the manufacturer. In the diagram, called a *break-even chart*, it is the point (m, n) at which the graphs of $y_{TR} = 8q$ and $y_{TC} = \frac{22}{9}q + 5000$ intersect. We call m the **break-even**

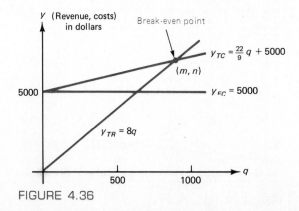

FIGURE 4.36

quantity and n the **break-even revenue.** When variable costs and revenue are linearly related to output, as in our case, any production level greater than m units will produce a profit, while any level less than m units will produce a loss. At an output of m units the profit is zero. In the following example we shall examine our data in more detail.

EXAMPLE 3   *A manufacturer sells a product at $8 per unit, selling all that is produced. Fixed cost is $5000 and variable cost per unit is $\frac{22}{9}$ (dollars). Find the following.*

a. *Total output and revenue at the break-even point.*

b. *Profit when* 1800 *units are produced.*

c. *Loss when* 450 *units are produced.*

d. *Output required to obtain a profit of* $10,000.

a. At an output level of q units, the variable cost is $y_{VC} = \frac{22}{9}q$ and the total revenue is $y_{TR} = 8q$. Hence

$$y_{TR} = 8q,$$

$$y_{TC} = y_{VC} + y_{FC} = \frac{22}{9}q + 5000.$$

At the break-even point, total revenue = total cost. Thus we solve the system formed by the equations above. Since

$$y_{TR} = y_{TC},$$

we have

$$8q = \frac{22}{9}q + 5000,$$

$$\frac{50}{9}q = 5000,$$

$$q = 900.$$

Thus the desired output is 900 units, resulting in a total revenue (in dollars) of

$$y_{TR} = 8(900) = 7200.$$

b. Since profit = total revenue − total cost, when $q = 1800$ we have

$$y_{TR} - y_{TC} = 8(1800) - \left[\frac{22}{9}(1800) + 5000\right]$$

$$= 5000.$$

The profit when 1800 units are produced and sold is $5000.

c. When $q = 450$,

$$y_{TR} - y_{TC} = 8(450) - \left[\frac{22}{9}(450) + 5000\right] = -2500.$$

A loss of $2500 occurs when the level of production is 450 units.

d. In order to obtain a profit of $10,000, we have

$$\text{profit} = \text{total revenue} - \text{total cost}.$$

$$10,000 = 8q - \left(\frac{22}{9}q + 5000\right),$$

$$15,000 = \frac{50}{9}q,$$

$$q = 2700.$$

Thus 2700 units must be produced.

EXAMPLE 4   *Determine the break-even quantity of XYZ Manufacturing Co. given the following data: total fixed cost, $1200; variable cost per unit, $2; total revenue for selling q units,* $y_{TR} = 100\sqrt{q}$.

For q units of output,

$$y_{TR} = 100\sqrt{q},$$

$$y_{TC} = 2q + 1200.$$

Equating total revenue to total cost gives

$$100\sqrt{q} = 2q + 1200,$$

$$50\sqrt{q} = q + 600.$$

Squaring both sides, we have

$$2500q = q^2 + 1200q + (600)^2,$$

$$0 = q^2 - 1300q + 360,000.$$

By the quadratic formula

$$q = \frac{1300 \pm \sqrt{250,000}}{2},$$

$$q = \frac{1300 \pm 500}{2},$$

$$q = 400 \quad \text{or} \quad q = 900.$$

Although both $q = 400$ and $q = 900$ are break-even quantities, observe in Fig. 4.37 that there will always be a loss when $q > 900$. Thus producing more than the break-even quantity does not necessarily guarantee a profit.

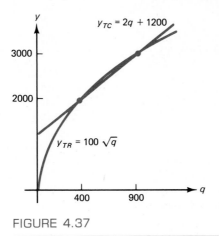

FIGURE 4.37

EXERCISE 4.6

In Problems 1–8, the first equation is a supply equation and the second is a demand equation for a product. If p represents price per unit in dollars and q represents the number of units per unit of time, find the equilibrium point. In Problems 1 and 2 sketch the system.

1. $p = \frac{3}{100}q + 2$,
   $p = -\frac{7}{100}q + 12$.

2. $p = \frac{1}{2000}q + 3$,
   $p = -\frac{1}{2500}q + \frac{42}{5}$.

3. $35q - 2p + 250 = 0$,
   $65q + p - 537.5 = 0$.

4. $246p - 3.25q - 2460 = 0$,
   $410p + 3q - 14{,}452.5 = 0$.

5. $p = 2q + 20$,
   $p = 200 - 2q^2$.

6. $p = (q + 10)^2$,
   $p = 388 - 16q - q^2$.

7. $p = \sqrt{q + 10}$,
   $p = 20 - q$.

8. $p = \frac{1}{5}q + 5$,
   $p = \dfrac{3000}{q + 20}$.

In Problems 9–14, y_{TR} represents total revenue in dollars and y_{TC} represents total cost in dollars for a manufacturer. If q represents both the number of units produced and the number of units sold, find the break-even quantity. Sketch a break-even chart in Problems 9 and 10.

9. $y_{TR} = 3q$,
   $y_{TC} = 2q + 4500$.

10. $y_{TR} = 14q$,
    $y_{TC} = \frac{40}{3}q + 1200$.

11. $y_{TR} = 0.05q$,
    $y_{TC} = 0.85q + 600$.

12. $y_{TR} = 0.25q$,
    $y_{TC} = 0.16q + 360$.

13. $y_{TR} = 100 - \dfrac{1000}{q + 10}$,
    $y_{TC} = q + 40$.

14. $y_{TR} = 0.1q^2 + 7q$,
    $y_{TC} = 2q + 500$.

15. Supply and demand equations for a certain product are $3q - 200p + 1800 = 0$ and $3q + 100p - 1800 = 0$, respectively, where p represents the price per unit in dollars, and q represents the number of units per time period.

    a. Find the equilibrium price algebraically, and derive it graphically.
    b. Find the equilibrium price when a tax of 27 cents per unit is imposed on the supplier.

16. A manufacturer of a product sells all that is produced. The total revenue is given by $y_{TR} = 7q$ and the total cost is given by $y_{TC} = 6q + 800$, where q represents the number of units produced and sold.
   a. Find the level of production at the break-even point and draw the break-even chart.
   b. Find the level of production at the break-even point if the total cost increases by 5%.

17. A manufacturer sells a product at $8.35 per unit, selling all produced. The fixed cost is $2116 and the variable cost is $7.20 per unit. At what level of production will there be a profit of $4600? At what level of production will there be a loss of $1150? At what level of production will the break-even point occur?

18. The market equilibrium point for a product occurs when 13,500 units are produced at a price of $4.50 per unit. The producer will supply no units at $1 and the consumers will demand no units at $20. Find the supply and demand equations if they are both linear.

19. A manufacturer of widgets will break even at a sales volume of $200,000. Fixed costs are $40,000 and each unit of output sells for $5. Determine the variable cost per unit.

20. The Footsie Sandal Co. manufactures sandals for which the material cost is $0.80 per pair and the labor cost is $0.90 per pair. Additional variable costs amount to $0.30 per pair. Fixed costs are $70,000. If each pair sells for $2.50, how many pairs must be sold for the company to break even?

21. Find the break-even point for company Z, which sells all it produces, if the variable cost per unit is $2, fixed costs are $1050, and $y_{TR} = 50\sqrt{q}$, where q is the number of units of output.

22. A company has determined that the demand equation for its product is $p = 1000/q$, where p is the price per unit for q units in some time period. Determine the quantity demanded when the price per unit is: (a) $4; (b) $2; and (c) $0.50. For each of these prices, determine the total revenue that the company will receive. What will be the revenue regardless of the price? (*Hint:* find the revenue when the price is p dollars.)

23. By using the data in Example 1, determine how the original equilibrium price will be affected if the company is given a government subsidy of $1.50 per unit.

24. The Monroe Forging Company sells a corrugated steel product to the Standard Manufacturing Company and is in competition on such sales with other suppliers of the Standard Manufacturing Co. The vice president of sales of Monroe Forging Co. believes that by reducing the price of the product, a 40% increase in the volume of units sold to the Standard Manufacturing Co. could be secured. As the manager of the cost and analysis department, you have been asked to analyze the proposal of the vice president and submit your recommendations as to whether it is financially beneficial to the Monroe Forging Co.

You are specifically requested to determine the following.

(1) Net profit or loss based on the pricing proposal.

(2) Unit sales volume under the proposed price that is required to make the same $40,000 profit that is now earned at the current price and unit sales volume.

Use the following data in your analysis.

	CURRENT OPERATIONS	PROPOSAL OF VICE PRESIDENT OF SALES
Unit price	$2.50	$2.00
Unit sales volume	200,000 units	280,000 units
Variable cost		
Total	$350,000	
Per Unit	$1.75	$1.75
Fixed cost	$110,000	$110,000
Profit	$40,000	?

25. Suppose products A and B have demand and supply equations that are related to each other. If q_A and q_B are quantities of A and B, respectively, and p_A and p_B are their respective prices, the demand equations are

$$q_A = 8 - p_A + p_B$$

and $$q_B = 26 + p_A - p_B,$$

and the supply equations are

$$q_A = -2 + 5p_A - p_B$$

and $$q_B = -4 - p_A + 3p_B.$$

Eliminate q_A and q_B to get the equilibrium prices.

4.7 REVIEW

Important Terms and Symbols

Section 4.1   slope of a line   point-slope form   slope-intercept form
general linear equation in x and y linearly related

Section 4.2   demand equation   demand curve   supply equation   supply curve   linear function

Section 4.3   quadratic function   parabola   axis of symmetry   vertex

Section 4.4   system of equations   equivalent systems   elimination by addition
elimination by substitution   general linear equation in x, y, and z

Section 4.5   nonlinear system

Section 4.6   point of equilibrium   equilibrium price   equilibrium quantity   profit   total cost
fixed cost   variable cost   break-even point   break-even quantity
break-even revenue

Summary

The orientation of a nonvertical line is characterized by the slope m of the line:

$$m = \frac{y_2 - y_1}{x_2 - x_1},$$

where (x_1, y_1) and (x_2, y_2) are two different points on the line. The slope of a vertical line is not defined, and the slope of a horizontal line is zero. Rising (falling) lines have positive (negative) slopes, and lines with the same slope are parallel. Basic forms of equations of lines are:

$$y - y_1 = m(x - x_1) \quad \text{(point-slope form)},$$
$$y = mx + b \quad \text{(slope-intercept form)},$$
$$x = a \quad \text{(vertical line)},$$
$$y = b \quad \text{(horizontal line)},$$
$$Ax + By + C = 0. \quad \text{(general)}.$$

The linear function $f(x) = ax + b$ ($a \neq 0$) has a straight line for its graph.

In economics, supply functions and demand functions have the form $p = f(q)$ and play an important role. Each gives a correspondence between the price p of a product and the number of units q of the product that manufacturers (or consumers) will supply (or purchase) at that price during some time period.

A quadratic function has the form

$$f(x) = ax^2 + bx + c \qquad (a \neq 0).$$

Its graph is a parabola that opens upward if $a > 0$ and downward if $a < 0$. The vertex is

$$\left(-\frac{b}{2a}, f\left(-\frac{b}{2a} \right) \right),$$

and the y-intercept is c. The axis of symmetry as well as the x- and y-intercepts are useful in sketching the graph.

A system of linear equations may be solved with the methods of elimination by addition and elimination by substitution. Substitution is also useful in solving nonlinear systems.

Solving a system formed by the supply and demand equations for a product gives the equilibrium point, which indicates the price at which consumers will purchase the same quantity of a product that producers wish to sell at that price.

Profit is total revenue − total cost, where total cost is the sum of fixed costs and variable costs. The break-even point is the point where total revenue = total cost.

Review Problems

1. The slope of the line through $(2, 5)$ and $(3, k)$ is 4. Find k.

2. The slope of the line through $(2, 3)$ and $(k, 3)$ is 0. Find k.

In Problems 3–7, determine the slope-intercept form and a general linear form of an equation of the straight line that has the indicated properties.

3. Passes through $(3, -2)$ and has y-intercept 1.

4. Passes through $(-1, -1)$ and is parallel to the line $y = 3x - 4$.

5. Passes through $(10, 4)$ and has slope $\frac{1}{2}$.

6. Passes through $(3, 5)$ and is vertical.

7. Passes through $(-2, 4)$ and is horizontal.

8. Determine whether the point $(0, -7)$ lies on the line through $(1, -3)$ and $(4, 9)$.

In Problems 9–12, write each line in slope-intercept form and sketch. What is the slope of the line?

9. $3x - 2y = 4.$ 10. $x = -3y + 4.$ 11. $4 - 3y = 0.$ 12. $y = 2x.$

In Problems 13–22, graph each function. For those that are linear, also give the slope and the vertical-axis intercept. For those that are quadratic, give all intercepts and the vertex.

13. $y = f(x) = 4 - 2x.$

14. $s = g(t) = 8 - 2t - t^2.$

15. $y = f(x) = 9 - x^2.$

16. $y = f(x) = 3x - 7.$

17. $y = h(t) = t^2 - 4t - 5.$

18. $y = h(t) = 1 + 3t.$

19. $p = g(t) = 3t.$

20. $y = F(x) = (2x - 1)^2.$

21. $y = F(x) = -(x^2 + 2x + 3).$

22. $y = f(x) = \dfrac{x}{3} - 2.$

In Problems **23–32,** *solve the given system.*

23. $\begin{cases} 2x - y = 6, \\ 3x + 2y = 5. \end{cases}$

24. $\begin{cases} 8x - 4y = 7, \\ y = 2x - 4. \end{cases}$

25. $\begin{cases} 4x + 5y = 3, \\ 3x + 4y = 2. \end{cases}$

26. $\begin{cases} 3x + 6y = 9, \\ 4x + 8y = 12. \end{cases}$

27. $\begin{cases} \frac{1}{4}x - \frac{3}{2}y = -4, \\ \frac{3}{4}x + \frac{1}{2}y = 8. \end{cases}$

28. $\begin{cases} \frac{1}{3}x - \frac{1}{4}y = \frac{1}{12}, \\ \frac{3}{4}x + 3y = \frac{5}{3}. \end{cases}$

29. $\begin{cases} 3x - 2y + z = -2, \\ 2x + y + z = 1, \\ x + 3y - z = 3. \end{cases}$

30. $\begin{cases} x + \dfrac{2y + x}{6} = 14, \\ y + \dfrac{3x + y}{4} = 20. \end{cases}$

31. $\begin{cases} x^2 - y + 2x = 7, \\ x^2 + y = 5. \end{cases}$

32. $\begin{cases} y = \dfrac{18}{x + 4}, \\ x - y + 7 = 0. \end{cases}$

33. Suppose a and b are linearly related so that $a = 1$ when $b = 2$, and $a = 2$ when $b = 1$. Find a general linear form of an equation that relates a and b. Also, find a when $b = 3$.

34. When the temperature T (in degrees Celsius) of a cat is reduced, the cat's heart rate r (in beats per minute) decreases. Under laboratory conditions, a cat at a temperature of 37°C had a heart rate of 220, and at a temperature of 32°C its heart rate was 150. If r is linearly related to T, where T is between 26 and 38, (a) determine an equation for r in terms of T, and (b) determine the heart rate at a temperature of 28°C.

35. Suppose f is a linear function such that $f(1) = 5$ and $f(x)$ decreases by 4 units for every 3-unit increase in x. Find $f(x)$.

36. If f is a linear function such that $f(-1) = 8$ and $f(2) = 5$, find $f(x)$.

37. The demand function for a manufacturer's product is $p = f(q) = 200 - 2q$, where p is the price (in dollars) per unit when q units are demanded. Find the level of production that maximizes the manufacturer's total revenue and determine this revenue.

38. The difference in price of two items before a 5% sales tax is imposed is $4. The difference in price after the sales tax is imposed is $4.20. Find the price of each item before the sales tax.

39. If the supply and demand equations of a certain product are $125p - q - 250 = 0$ and $100p + q - 1100 = 0$, respectively, find the equilibrium price.

40. A manufacturer of a certain product sells all that is produced. Determine the break-even point if the product is sold at $16 per unit, fixed cost is $10,000, and variable cost is given by $y_{VC} = 8q$, where q is the number of units produced (y_{VC} expressed in dollars).

41. In psychology the term *semantic memory* refers to our knowledge of the meaning and relationships of words as well as the means by which we store and retrieve such information.* In a network model of semantic memory, there is a hierarchy of levels at which information is stored. In an experiment by Collins and Quillian based on a network model, data were obtained on the reaction time to respond to simple questions about nouns. The graph of the results shows that, on the average, reaction time R (in milliseconds) is a linear function of the level L at which a characterizing property of the noun is stored. At level 0 the reaction time is 1310; at level 2 the reaction time is 1460. (a) Find the linear function. (b) Find the reaction time at level 1. (c) Find the slope and determine its significance.

42. Celsius temperature C is a linear function of Fahrenheit temperature F. Use the facts that 32°F is the same as 0°C and 212°F is the same as 100°C to find this function. Also find C when F = 50.

* G. R. Loftus and E. F. Loftus, *Human Memory: The Processing of Information* (New York: Lawrence Erlbaum Associates, Inc., distributed by the Halsted Press, Division of John Wiley & Sons, Inc., 1976).

Exponential and Logarithmic Functions

5.1 EXPONENTIAL FUNCTIONS

There is a function that has an important role not only in mathematics but in business, economics, and other areas of study. It involves a constant raised to a variable power, such as $f(x) = 2^x$. We call this an *exponential function*.

Definition

The function f defined by

$$f(x) = b^x,$$

*where $b > 0$, $b \neq 1$, and the exponent x is any real number, is called an **exponential function** to the base b.**

Do not confuse the exponential function $y = 2^x$ with the *power function* $y = x^2$, which has a variable base and a constant exponent.

Since the exponent in b^x can be any real number, you may wonder how we assign a value to something like $2^{\sqrt{2}}$. Stated simply, we use approximations. First, $2^{\sqrt{2}}$ is approximately $2^{1.4} = 2^{7/5} = \sqrt[5]{2^7}$, which *is* defined. Better approximations are $2^{1.41} = 2^{141/100} = \sqrt[100]{2^{141}}$, and so on. In this way the meaning of $2^{\sqrt{2}}$ becomes clear.

When you work with exponential functions, it may be necessary to apply

---

* If $b = 1$, then $f(x) = 1^x = 1$. This function is so uninteresting that we do not call it an exponential function.

rules for exponents. These rules are as follows, where m and n are real numbers and a and b are positive.

1. $a^m a^n = a^{m+n}$.

2. $\dfrac{a^m}{a^n} = a^{m-n}$.

3. $(a^m)^n = a^{mn}$.

4. $(ab)^n = a^n b^n$.

5. $\left(\dfrac{a}{b}\right)^n = \dfrac{a^n}{b^n}$.

6. $a^1 = a$.

7. $a^0 = 1$.

8. $a^{-n} = \dfrac{1}{a^n}$.

Some functions that do not appear to have the exponential form b^x can be put in that form by applying the rules above. For example, $2^{-x} = 1/(2^x) = (\tfrac{1}{2})^x$ and $3^{2x} = (3^2)^x = 9^x$.

Graphs of some exponential functions are shown in Fig. 5.1. Notice the following:

1. The domain of an exponential function is all real numbers.

2. The range is all positive real numbers.

3. Since $b^0 = 1$ for every base b, each graph has y-intercept $(0, 1)$. There is no x-intercept.

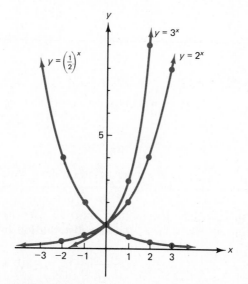

x	2^x	3^x	$\left(\dfrac{1}{2}\right)^x$
-2	$\frac{1}{4}$	$\frac{1}{9}$	4
-1	$\frac{1}{2}$	$\frac{1}{3}$	2
0	1	1	1
1	2	3	$\frac{1}{2}$
2	4	9	$\frac{1}{4}$
3	8	27	$\frac{1}{8}$

FIGURE 5.1

We also see in Fig. 5.1 that $y = b^x$ has two basic shapes, depending on whether $b > 1$ or $0 < b < 1$.

4. If $b > 1$, then the graph of $y = b^x$ *rises* from left to right. That is, as x increases, y also increases. But y can also take on values very close to zero. (Look in quadrant II.) Notice also that in quadrant I, the greater the value of b, the more quickly the graph rises. (Compare the graphs of $y = 2^x$ and $y = 3^x$.)

5. If $0 < b < 1$, then the graph of $y = b^x$ *falls* from left to right. [See the graph of $y = (\frac{1}{2})^x$.] As x increases, then y *decreases* and takes on values close to 0.

One of the numbers most useful for a base in an exponential function is a certain irrational number denoted by the letter e in honor of the Swiss mathematician Leonhard Euler (1707–1783):

$$e \text{ is approximately } 2.71828.$$

Although e may seem to be a strange base for an exponential function, it arises quite naturally in calculus (as you will see later). It also occurs in economic analysis and problems involving natural growth (or decay), such as compound interest and population studies. A table of (approximate) values of e^x and e^{-x} is in Appendix B. These values can also be obtained with many calculators. The graph of $y = e^x$ is shown in Fig. 5.2.

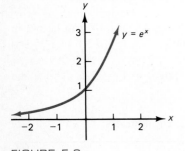

FIGURE 5.2

EXAMPLE 1   *The projected population P of a city is given by*

$$P = 100{,}000e^{0.05t},$$

where t is the number of years after 1985. Predict the population for the year 2005.

The number of years from 1985 to 2005 is 20, so let $t = 20$. Then

$$P = 100{,}000e^{0.05(20)} = 100{,}000e^1 = 100{,}000e.$$

Since $e \approx 2.71828$,

$$P \approx 100{,}000(2.71828) = 271{,}828.$$

Many economic forecasts are based on population studies.

In statistics an important function used as a model in describing events occurring in nature is the **Poisson distribution function:**

$$f(x) = \frac{e^{-\mu}\mu^x}{x!}, \quad x = 0, 1, 2, \ldots .$$

The symbol μ (read "mu") is a Greek letter. In certain situations $f(x)$ gives the probability that exactly x events will occur in an interval of time or space. The constant μ is the mean, or average number, of occurrences in the interval. The next example illustrates the Poisson distribution.

EXAMPLE 2   *A hemacytometer is a counting chamber divided into squares and is used in studying the number of microscopic structures in a liquid. In a well-known experiment,* yeast cells were diluted and thoroughly mixed in a liquid, and the mixture was placed in a hemacytometer. With a microscope the number of yeast cells on each square were counted. The probability that there were exactly x yeast cells on a hemacytometer square was found to fit a Poisson distribution with $\mu = 1.8$. Find the probability that there were exactly four cells per square.*

We use the Poisson distribution function with $\mu = 1.8$ and $x = 4$.

$$f(x) = \frac{e^{-\mu}\mu^x}{x!}.$$

$$f(4) = \frac{e^{-1.8}(1.8)^4}{4!}.$$

From the table in Appendix B, $e^{-1.8} \approx 0.16530$, so

$$f(4) \approx \frac{(0.16530)(10.4976)}{24} \approx 0.072.$$

This means that in 400 squares we would *expect* $400(0.072) \approx 29$ squares to contain exactly 4 cells. (In the experiment the actual number observed was 30.)

EXERCISE 5.1

In Problems 1–6, graph each function.

1. $y = f(x) = 4^x$.

2. $y = f(x) = (\frac{1}{3})^x$.

3. $y = f(x) = 2(\frac{1}{4})^x$.

4. $y = f(x) = \frac{1}{2}(3^{x/2})$.

5. $y = f(x) = 2^x - 1$.

6. $y = f(x) = 2^{x-1}$.

In Problems 7–10, use the table in Appendix B to find the approximate value of each expression.

7. $e^{1.5}$.

8. $e^{3.4}$.

9. $e^{-0.4}$.

10. $e^{-3/4}$.

11. The projected population P of a city is given by $P = 125{,}000(1.12)^{t/20}$, where t is the number of years after 1985. What is the projected population in 2005?

12. For a certain city the population P grows at the rate of 2% per year. The formula $P = 1{,}000{,}000(1.02)^t$ gives the population t years after 1980. Find the population in (a) 1981 and (b) 1982.

* R. R. Sokal and F. J. Rohlf, *Introduction to Biostatistics* (San Francisco: W. H. Freeman and Company, Publishers, 1973).

13. The probability P that a telephone operator will receive exactly x calls during a certain time period is given by

$$P = \frac{e^{-3}3^x}{x!}.$$

Find the probability that the operator will receive exactly three calls. Give your answer to four decimal places.

14. Express e^{kt} in the form b^t.

15. An important function used in economic and business decisions is the *normal distribution density function*, which in standard form is

$$f(x) = \frac{1}{\sqrt{2\pi}}e^{-x^2/2}.$$

Evaluate $f(0), f(-1)$, and $f(1)$ by using $\dfrac{1}{\sqrt{2\pi}} = 0.399$.

Give your answers to three decimal places.

16. A mail-order company advertises in a national magazine. The company finds that of all small towns, the percentage (given as a decimal) in which exactly x people respond to an ad fits a Poisson distribution with $\mu = 0.5$. From what percentage of small towns can the company expect exactly two people to respond? Give your answer to four decimal places.

17. Suppose that the number of patients admitted into a hospital emergency room during a certain hour of the day has a Poisson distribution with mean 4. Find the probability that during that hour there will be exactly two emergency patients. Give your answer to four decimal places.

18. In a psychological experiment involving learning,* subjects were asked to give particular responses after being shown certain stimuli. Each stimulus was a pair of letters, and each response was either the digit 1 or 2. After each response the subject was told the correct answer. In this so-called *paired-associate* learning experiment, the theoretical probability P that a subject makes a correct response on the nth trial is given by

$$P = 1 - \tfrac{1}{2}(1 - c)^{n-1}, \qquad n \geq 1, 0 < c < 1.$$

Find P when $n = 1$.

19. At a certain time there are 100 milligrams of a radioactive substance. It decays so that after t years the number of milligrams present, A, is given by $A = 100e^{-0.035t}$. How many milligrams are present after 20 years? Give your answer to the nearest milligram.

20. The demand equation for a new toy is $q = 10{,}000(0.95123)^p$. It is desired to evaluate q when $p = 10$. To convert the equation into a more desirable computational form, use Appendix B to show that $q = 10{,}000e^{-0.05p}$. Then evaluate and give your answer to the nearest integer. (*Hint:* Find a number x such that $0.95123 \approx e^{-x}$.)

5.2 LOGARITHMIC FUNCTIONS

The second function of interest to us in this chapter is a *logarithmic function*, which is related to an exponential function. Figure 5.3(a) shows the graph of the exponential function $s = f(t) = 2^t$. Here f sends an input number t into a *positive* output number s:

$$f: \quad t \to s \quad \text{where} \quad s = 2^t.$$

For example, f sends 2 into 4.

* D. Laming, *Mathematical Psychology* (New York: Academic Press, Inc., 1973).

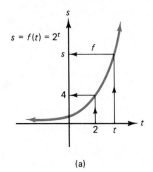

$s = f(t) = 2^t$

(a)

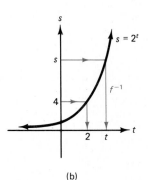

$s = 2^t$

(b)

FIGURE 5.3

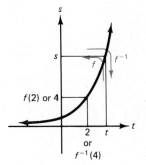

$f(2)$ or 4

or

$f^{-1}(4)$

FIGURE 5.4

Looking at the same curve in Fig. 5.3(b), you can see from the small arrows that, with each positive number s on the vertical axis, we can associate exactly one value of t. With $s = 4$ we associate $t = 2$. By thinking of s as an input and t as an output, we have a function that sends s's into t's. We shall denote this function by f^{-1} (read "f inverse"):*

$$f^{-1}: \quad s \to t, \qquad \text{where } s = 2^t.$$

Thus $f^{-1}(s) = t$. The domain of f^{-1} is the range of f (all positive real numbers), and the range of f^{-1} is the domain of f (all real numbers).

The functions f and f^{-1} are related. Figure 5.4 shows that f^{-1} *reverses* the action of f, and vice versa. For example,

$$f \text{ sends 2 into 4} \qquad \text{and} \qquad f^{-1} \text{ sends 4 into 2.}$$

More generally, $f(t) = s$ and $f^{-1}(s) = t$. In terms of composition, when either $f^{-1} \circ f$ or $f \circ f^{-1}$ is applied to an input number, that number is obtained for output because of the reversing effects of f and f^{-1}. That is,

$$(f^{-1} \circ f)(t) = f^{-1}(f(t)) = f^{-1}(s) = t$$

$$\text{and} \qquad (f \circ f^{-1})(s) = f(f^{-1}(s)) = f(t) = s.$$

We give a special name to f^{-1}. It is called the **logarithmic function with base 2** and is written as $\log_2$ [read "logarithm (or log) base 2"]. Thus $f^{-1}(4) = \log_2 4 = 2$, and we say that the *logarithm* base 2 of 4 is 2.

In summary,

$$\text{if} \quad s = 2^t, \quad \text{then} \quad t = \log_2 s. \tag{1}$$

We now generalize our discussion to other bases. In Eq. (1), replacing 2 by b, s by x, and t by y gives the following definition.

Definition

*The **logarithmic function** with base b, where $b > 0$ and $b \neq 1$, is denoted by $\log_b$ and is defined by*

$$y = \log_b x \quad \text{if and only if} \quad b^y = x.$$

The domain of $\log_b$ is all positive real numbers and the range is all real numbers.

The logarithmic function reverses the action of the exponential function, and vice versa. Because of this we say that the logarithmic function is the *inverse* of the exponential function, and the exponential function is the inverse of the logarithmic function.

Always remember: When we say that the log base b of x is y, we mean that b raised to the y power is x.

$$y = \log_b x \quad \text{means} \quad b^y = x.$$

---

* The -1 in f^{-1} is not an exponent, so f^{-1} does *not* mean $\dfrac{1}{f}$.

In this sense, *a logarithm of a number is an exponent.* It is the power to which we must raise the base to get the number. For example,

$$\log_2 8 = 3 \quad \text{because} \quad 2^3 = 8.$$

We say that $\log_2 8 = 3$ is the **logarithmic form** of the **exponential form** $2^3 = 8$.

EXAMPLE 1

	EXPONENTIAL FORM		LOGARITHMIC FORM
a. Since	$5^2 = 25,$	then	$\log_5 25 = 2.$
b. Since	$3^4 = 81,$	then	$\log_3 81 = 4.$
c. Since	$10^0 = 1,$	then	$\log_{10} 1 = 0.$

EXAMPLE 2

LOGARITHMIC FORM		EXPONENTIAL FORM
a. $\log_{10} 1000 = 3$	means	$10^3 = 1000.$
b. $\log_{64} 8 = \dfrac{1}{2}$	means	$64^{1/2} = 8.$
c. $\log_2 \dfrac{1}{16} = -4$	means	$2^{-4} = \dfrac{1}{16}.$

EXAMPLE 3   *Graph the function* $y = \log_2 x.$

It can be awkward to substitute values of x and then find corresponding values of y. For example, if $x = 3$, then $y = \log_2 3$, which is not easily determined. An easier way to plot points is to use the equivalent exponential form $x = 2^y$. We choose values of y and find the corresponding values of x. For example, if $y = 0$, then $x = 1$. This gives the point $(1, 0)$. Other points are shown in Fig. 5.5. From the graph you can see that the domain is all positive real numbers.

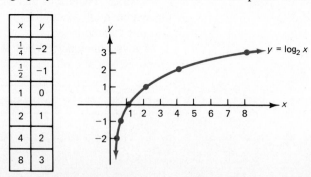

x	y
$\frac{1}{4}$	-2
$\frac{1}{2}$	-1
1	0
2	1
4	2
8	3

$y = \log_2 x$

FIGURE 5.5

Thus negative numbers and 0 do not have logarithms. The range is all real numbers. Numbers between 0 and 1 have negative logarithms, and the closer a number is to 0, the more negative is its logarithm. The log of 1 is 0, which corresponds to the intercept (1, 0). There is no y-intercept. This graph is typical for a logarithmic function with $b > 1$.

Logarithms to the base 10 are called **common logarithms.** They were frequently used for computational purposes before the calculator age. The subscript 10 is usually omitted from the notation:

$$\log x \quad \text{means} \quad \log_{10} x.$$

Important in calculus are logarithms to the base e, called **natural logarithms.** We use the notation ''ln'' for such logarithms:

$$\ln x \quad \text{means} \quad \log_e x.$$

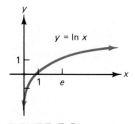

FIGURE 5.6

The symbol $\ln x$ may be read ''ell-en of x.'' Appendix C gives a table of approximate values of natural logarithms and instructions on how to use the table. For example, you can see that $\ln 2 \approx 0.69315$. This means that $e^{0.69315} \approx 2$. Figure 5.6 shows the graph of $y = \ln x$. It has the same shape as does Fig. 5.5. Natural and common logarithms can be found with many calculators.

EXAMPLE 4   *Find each of the following.*

a. log 100.
   Here the base is 10. Thus log 100 is the power to which we must raise 10 to get 100. Since $10^2 = 100$, log 100 = 2.

b. ln 1.
   Here the base is e. Because $e^0 = 1$, ln 1 = 0.

c. log 0.1.
   Since $0.1 = \frac{1}{10} = 10^{-1}$, log 0.1 = -1.

d. $\ln e^{-1}$.
   Since $\ln e^{-1}$ is the power to which e must be raised to get e^{-1}, clearly $\ln e^{-1} = -1$.

e. $\log_{36} 6$.
   Because $36^{1/2}$ (or $\sqrt{36}$) is 6, $\log_{36} 6 = \frac{1}{2}$.

EXAMPLE 5   *Solve each equation for x.*

a. $\log_2 x = 4$.
   In exponential form, $2^4 = x$, so $x = 16$.

b. $\ln (x + 1) = 7$.

The exponential form gives $e^7 = x + 1$. Thus $x = e^7 - 1$.

c. $\log_x 49 = 2$.

In exponential form, $x^2 = 49$, so $x = 7$. We rejected $x = -7$ in solving $x^2 = 49$ because a negative number cannot be a base of a logarithmic function.

d. $e^{5x} = 4$.

In logarithmic form, $\ln 4 = 5x$. Thus $x = \dfrac{\ln 4}{5}$.

e. $12 = 5 + 3(4)^{x-1}$.

$$12 = 5 + 3(4)^{x-1},$$

$$7 = 3(4)^{x-1},$$

$$\tfrac{7}{3} = 4^{x-1}.$$

This means that the logarithm base 4 of $\tfrac{7}{3}$ is $x - 1$:

$$x - 1 = \log_4 \tfrac{7}{3},$$

$$x = 1 + \log_4 \tfrac{7}{3}.$$

EXERCISE 5.2

In Problems **1–8**, *express each logarithmic form exponentially and each exponential form logarithmically.*

1. $10^4 = 10,000$.

2. $2 = \log_{12} 144$.

3. $\log_2 64 = 6$.

4. $8^{2/3} = 4$.

5. $e^2 = 7.3891$.

6. $e^{0.33647} = 1.4$.

7. $\ln 3 = 1.09861$.

8. $\log 5 = 0.6990$.

In Problems **9 and 10**, *graph the functions.*

9. $y = f(x) = \log_3 x$.

10. $y = f(x) = \log_{1/2} x$.

In Problems **11–22**, *evaluate.*

11. $\log_6 36$.

12. $\log_2 32$.

13. $\log_3 27$.

14. $\log_{16} 4$.

15. $\log_7 7$.

16. $\log 10,000$.

17. $\log 0.01$.

18. $\log_2 \sqrt{2}$.

19. $\log_5 1$.

20. $\log_5 \tfrac{1}{25}$.

21. $\log_2 \tfrac{1}{8}$.

22. $\log_4 \sqrt[5]{4}$.

In Problems **23–40**, *find x.*

23. $\log_3 x = 2$.

24. $\log_2 x = 4$.

25. $\log_5 x = 3$.

26. $\log_4 x = 0$.

27. $\log x = -1$.

28. $\ln x = 1$.

29. $\ln x = 2$.

30. $\log_x 100 = 2$.

31. $\log_x 8 = 3$.

32. $\log_x 3 = \tfrac{1}{2}$.

33. $\log_x \tfrac{1}{6} = -1$.

34. $\log_x y = 1$.

35. $\log_3 x = -4$.

36. $\log_x(2x - 3) = 1$.

37. $\log_x(6 - x) = 2$.

38. $\log_8 64 = x - 1$.

39. $2 + \log_2 4 = 3x - 1$.

40. $\log_3(x + 2) = -2$.

*In Problems **41–48**, find x and express your answer in terms of logarithms.*

41. $2^x = 5$.

42. $4^{x+3} = 7$.

43. $e^{3x} = 2$.

44. $\dfrac{8}{3^x} = 4$.

45. $5(3^x - 6) = 10$.

46. $0.1e^{0.1x} = 0.5$.

47. $e^{2x-5} + 1 = 4$.

48. $3e^{2x} - 1 = \frac{1}{2}$.

*In Problems **49–52**, use Appendix C to find the approximate value of each expression.*

49. $\ln 5$.

50. $\ln 3.12$.

51. $\ln 7.39$.

52. $\ln 9.98$.

53. The cost c for a firm producing q units of a product is given by the cost equation $c = (2q \ln q) + 20$. Evaluate the cost when $q = 6$. (Give your answer to two decimal places.)

54. A manufacturer's supply equation is $p = \log[10 + (q/2)]$, where q is the number of units supplied at a price p per unit. At what price will the manufacturer supply 1980 units?

55. The magnitude M of an earthquake and its energy E are related by the equation*

$$1.5M = \log\left(\frac{E}{2.5 \times 10^{11}}\right).$$

Here M is given in terms of Richter's preferred scale of 1958 and E is in ergs. Solve the equation for E.

56. For a certain population of cells, the number N of cells at time t is given by $N = N_0(2^{t/k})$, where N_0 is the number of cells at $t = 0$ and k is a positive constant. (a) Find N when $t = k$. (b) What is the significance of k? (c) Show that the time it takes to have population N_1 can be written $t = k \log_2(N_1/N_0)$.

57. On the surface of a glass slide is a grid that divides the surface into 225 equal squares. Suppose a blood sample containing N red cells is spread on the slide and the cells are randomly distributed. Then the number of squares containing no cells is (approximately) given by $225e^{-N/225}$. If 100 of the squares contain no cells, estimate the number of cells the blood sample contained.

58. Suppose that the daily output of units, q, of a new product on the tth day of a production run is given by $q = 500(1 - e^{-0.2t})$. Such an equation is called a *learning equation* and indicates that as time progresses, output per day will increase. This may be due to the gain of the workers' proficiencies at their jobs. Determine to the nearest complete unit the output on the (a) first day, and (b) tenth day after the start of a production run. (c) After how many days will a daily production run of 400 units be reached? Assume that $\ln 0.2 = -1.6$.

59. In a discussion of an inferior good, Persky[†] solves an equation of the form

$$u_0 = A \ln(x_1) + \frac{x_2^2}{2}$$

for x_1, where x_1 and x_2 are quantities of two products, u_0 is a measure of utility, and A is a positive constant. Determine x_1.

60. In a discussion of market penetration by new products, Hurter and Rubenstein[‡] refer to the function

* K. E. Bullen, *An Introduction to the Theory of Seismology* (Cambridge at the University Press, 1963).

† A. L. Persky, "An Inferior Good and a Novel Indifference Map," *The American Economist*, XXIX, no. 1 (Spring 1985).

‡ A. P. Hurter, Jr., A. H. Rubenstein, et al., "Market Penetration by New Innovations: The Technological Literature," *Technological Forecasting and Social Change*, 11 (1978), 197–221.

$$F(t) = \frac{q - pe^{-(t+C)(p+q)}}{q[1 + e^{-(t+C)(p+q)}]},$$

where p, q, and C are constants. They claim that if

$F(0) = 0$, then

$$C = -\frac{1}{p+q}\ln\frac{q}{p}.$$

Show that their claim is true.

5.3 PROPERTIES OF LOGARITHMS

The logarithmic function has many important properties. For example, the logarithm of a product of two numbers is the sum of the logarithms of the numbers. Symbolically, $\log_b(mn) = \log_b m + \log_b n$. To prove this, we let $x = \log_b m$ and $y = \log_b n$. Then $b^x = m$, $b^y = n$, and

$$mn = b^x b^y = b^{x+y}.$$

Thus $mn = b^{x+y}$. In logarithmic form, this means that $\log_b(mn) = x + y$. Therefore $\log_b(mn) = \log_b m + \log_b n$.

---

1. $\log_b(mn) = \log_b m + \log_b n$.

The logarithm of a product is a sum of logarithms.

We shall not prove the next two properties, since their proofs are similar to that of Property 1.

---

2. $\log_b \dfrac{m}{n} = \log_b m - \log_b n$.

The logarithm of a quotient is a difference of logarithms.

3. $\log_b m^r = r \log_b m$.

The logarithm of a power of a number is the exponent times a logarithm.

Pitfall

Make sure that you clearly understand Properties 1–3. They do not apply to the log of a sum $[\log_b(m + n)]$, log of a difference $[\log_b(m - n)]$, or quotient of logs $\left[\dfrac{\log_b m}{\log_b n}\right]$.

For example,

$$\log_b(m + n) \neq \log_b m + \log_b n,$$

$$\log_b(m - n) \neq \log_b m - \log_b n,$$

$$\frac{\log_b m}{\log_b n} \neq \log_b(m - n),$$

$$\text{and} \qquad \frac{\log_b m}{\log_b n} \neq \log_b\left(\frac{m}{n}\right).$$

Table 5.1 gives values of a few common logarithms. Most entries are approximate. For example, $\log 4 \approx 0.6021$, which means $10^{0.6021} \approx 4$. We shall use this table in some of the examples and exercises that follow.

TABLE 5.1
Common Logarithms

x	$\log x$	x	$\log x$
2	0.3010	7	0.8451
3	0.4771	8	0.9031
4	0.6021	9	0.9542
5	0.6990	10	1.0000
6	0.7782	e	0.4343

EXAMPLE 1   *Find the following logarithms.*

a. log 56.

Log 56 is not in Table 5.1. But we can write 56 as the product $8 \cdot 7$. Thus by Property 1,

$$\log 56 = \log(8 \cdot 7) = \log 8 + \log 7 \approx 0.9031 + 0.8451 = 1.7482.$$

b. $\log \frac{9}{2}$.

By Property 2,

$$\log \tfrac{9}{2} = \log 9 - \log 2 \approx 0.9542 - 0.3010 = 0.6532.$$

c. log 64.

Since $64 = 8^2$, then by Property 3.

$$\log 64 = \log 8^2 = 2 \log 8 \approx 2(0.9031) = 1.8062.$$

d. $\log \sqrt{5}$.

$$\log\sqrt{5} = \log 5^{1/2} = \tfrac{1}{2} \log 5 \approx \tfrac{1}{2}(0.6990) = 0.3495.$$

e. $\log \dfrac{16}{21}$.

$$\log \frac{16}{21} = \log 16 - \log 21 = \log(4^2) - \log(3 \cdot 7)$$

$$= 2 \log 4 - [\log 3 + \log 7]$$

$$\approx 2(0.6021) - [0.4771 + 0.8451] = -0.1180.$$

You should note the use of brackets in the second line. It is wrong to write $2 \log 4 - \log 3 + \log 7$.

EXAMPLE 2   *Write the following in terms of* $\log x$.

a. $\log \dfrac{1}{x^2}$.

$$\log \frac{1}{x^2} = \log x^{-2} = -2 \log x \qquad \text{(Property 3)}.$$

b. $\log \dfrac{1}{x}$.

By Property 3,

$$\log \frac{1}{x} = \log x^{-1} = -1 \log x = -\log x.$$

In general, $\log_b \dfrac{m}{n} = -\log_b \dfrac{n}{m}$ because $\log_b \dfrac{m}{n} = \log_b \left(\dfrac{n}{m}\right)^{-1} = -\log_b \dfrac{n}{m}$.

EXAMPLE 3

a. *Write* $\ln \dfrac{x}{zw}$ *in terms of* $\ln x$, $\ln z$, *and* $\ln w$.

$$\ln \frac{x}{zw} = \ln x - \ln(zw) \qquad \text{(Property 2)}$$
$$= \ln x - (\ln z + \ln w) \qquad \text{(Property 1)}$$
$$= \ln x - \ln z - \ln w.$$

b. *Write* $\ln \sqrt[3]{\dfrac{x^5(x-2)^8}{x-3}}$ *in terms of* $\ln x$, $\ln(x-2)$, *and* $\ln(x-3)$.

$$\sqrt[3]{\frac{x^5(x-2)^8}{x-3}} = \ln\left[\frac{x^5(x-2)^8}{x-3}\right]^{1/3} = \frac{1}{3}\ln \frac{x^5(x-2)^8}{x-3}$$
$$= \frac{1}{3}\{\ln[x^5(x-2)^8] - \ln(x-3)\}$$
$$= \frac{1}{3}[\ln x^5 + \ln(x-2)^8 - \ln(x-3)]$$
$$= \frac{1}{3}[5 \ln x + 8 \ln(x-2) - \ln(x-3)].$$

EXAMPLE 4   *Write as a single logarithm.*

a. $\ln x - \ln(x + 3)$.

$$\ln x - \ln(x + 3) = \ln\frac{x}{x + 3} \qquad \text{(Property 2)}.$$

b. $\ln 3 + \ln 7 - \ln 2 - 2 \ln 4$.

$$\ln 3 + \ln 7 - \ln 2 - 2 \ln 4$$

$$= \ln 3 + \ln 7 - \ln 2 - \ln(4^2) \qquad \text{(Property 3)}$$

$$= \ln 3 + \ln 7 - [\ln 2 + \ln(4^2)]$$

$$= \ln(3 \cdot 7) - \ln(2 \cdot 4^2) \qquad \text{(Property 1)}$$

$$= \ln 21 - \ln 32$$

$$= \ln\frac{21}{32} \qquad \text{(Property 2)}.$$

Since $b^0 = 1$ and $b^1 = b$, by converting to logarithmic forms we have the following properties:

---

4. $\log_b 1 = 0$.

5. $\log_b b = 1$.

By Property 3, $\log_b b^r = r \log_b b$. But by Property 5, $\log_b b = 1$. Thus we have the next property.

---

6. $\log_b b^r = r$.

EXAMPLE 5   *Find the following logarithms.*

a. $\ln e^{3x}$.

By Property 6 with $b = e$, we have $\ln e^{3x} = 3x$. Alternatively, by Properties 3 and 5,

$$\ln e^{3x} = 3x \ln e = 3x(1) = 3x.$$

b. $\log 1 + \log 1000$.

By Property 4, $\log 1 = 0$. Thus

$$\log 1 + \log 1000 = 0 + \log 10^3$$

$$= 3 \log 10 \qquad \text{(Property 3)}$$

$$= 3(1) = 3 \qquad \text{(Property 5)}.$$

c. $\log 10^c$.

$$\log 10^c = \log_{10} 10^c = c \qquad \text{(Property 6).}$$

d. $\log_7 \sqrt[9]{7^8}$.

$$\log_7 \sqrt[9]{7^8} = \log_7 7^{8/9} = \tfrac{8}{9}.$$

e. $\log_3(\tfrac{27}{81})$.

$$\log_3\left(\frac{27}{81}\right) = \log_3\left(\frac{3^3}{3^4}\right) = \log_3(3^{-1}) = -1.$$

f. $\ln e + \log \tfrac{1}{10}$.

$$\ln e + \log \tfrac{1}{10} = \ln e + \log 10^{-1}$$
$$= 1 + (-1) = 0.$$

Do not confuse $\ln x^2$ with $(\ln x)^2$. We have

$$\ln x^2 = \ln(x \cdot x),$$

but $\qquad (\ln x)^2 = (\ln x)(\ln x),$

which can be written as $\ln^2 x$. Thus in $\ln x^2$ we square x; in $(\ln x)^2$, or $\ln^2 x$, we square $\ln x$.

For many functions f, if $f(m) = f(n)$, this does not imply that $m = n$. For example, if $f(x) = x^2$ and $m = 2$ and $n = -2$, then $f(m) = f(n)$, but $m \neq n$. This is not the case for the logarithmic function. It is obvious in Fig. 5.7 that if x_1 and x_2 are different, then their logarithms (y-values) are different. This means that if $\log_2 m = \log_2 n$, then $m = n$. Generalizing to base b, we have the following property:

> **7.** *If $\log_b m = \log_b n$, then $m = n$.*

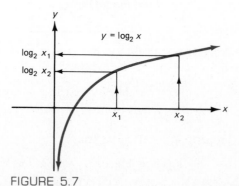

FIGURE 5.7

There is a similar property for exponentials:

---

8. If $b^m = b^n$, then $m = n$.

EXAMPLE 6   *An experiment was conducted with a particular type of small animal.* The logarithm of the amount of oxygen consumed per hour was determined for a number of the animals and was plotted against the logarithms of the weights of the animals. It was found that*

$$\log y = \log 5.934 + 0.885 \log x,$$

where y was the number of microliters of oxygen consumed per hour, and x was the weight of the animal (in grams). Solve for y.

We first combine the terms on the right side into a single logarithm.

$$\log y = \log 5.934 + 0.885 \log x$$
$$= \log 5.934 + \log x^{0.885} \qquad \text{(Property 3)}.$$
$$\log y = \log(5.934x^{0.885}) \qquad \text{(Property 1)}.$$

By Property 7, we have

$$y = 5.934x^{0.885}.$$

EXAMPLE 7   *Find x if* $(25)^{x+2} = 5^{3x-4}$.

Since $25 = 5^2$, we can express both sides of the equation as powers of 5.

$$(25)^{x+2} = 5^{3x-4},$$
$$(5^2)^{x+2} = 5^{3x-4},$$
$$5^{2x+4} = 5^{3x-4},$$
$$2x + 4 = 3x - 4 \qquad \text{(Property 8)},$$
$$x = 8.$$

Our next property is:

---

9. $b^{\log_b m} = m$ and, in particular, $10^{\log x} = x$ and $e^{\ln x} = x$.

Property 9 is true because it states, in logarithmic form, that $\log_b m = \log_b m$.

* R. W. Poole, *An Introduction to Quantitative Ecology* (New York: McGraw-Hill Book Company, 1974).

EXAMPLE 8

a. *Find $e^{\ln x^2}$.*

By Property 9, $e^{\ln x^2} = x^2$.

b. *Solve $10^{\log x^2} = 25$ for x.*

$$10^{\log x^2} = 25,$$

$$x^2 = 25 \qquad \text{(Property 9)},$$

$$x = \pm 5.$$

EXAMPLE 9   *Find $\log_5 2$.*

Let $x = \log_5 2$. Then $5^x = 2$, and by taking common logarithms of both sides we get

$$\log 5^x = \log 2,$$

$$x \log 5 = \log 2,$$

$$x = \frac{\log 2}{\log 5} \approx \frac{0.3010}{0.6990} \approx 0.4306.$$

If we had taken natural logarithms of both sides, the result would be $x = (\ln 2)/(\ln 5) \approx 0.69315/1.60944 \approx 0.43068$. This differs from our previous result due to the accuracy of the tables involved.

Generalizing the method used in Example 9, we have:

$$\boxed{\text{10. } \log_b m = \frac{\log_a m}{\log_a b}.}$$

Property 10 is called the **change of base formula.** It allows conversion of logarithms from one base (a) to another (b).

EXAMPLE 10   *Express $\log x$ in terms of natural logarithms.*

We must transform from base 10 into base e. Thus we use the change of base formula (Property 10) with $b = 10$, $m = x$, and $a = e$.

$$\log x = \frac{\ln x}{\ln 10}.$$

EXAMPLE 11   *A demand equation for a product is $p = 12^{1-0.1q}$. Use common logarithms to express q in terms of p.*

Taking common logarithms of both sides of $p = 12^{1-0.1q}$ gives

$$\log p = \log(12^{1-0.1q}),$$

$$\log p = (1 - 0.1q) \log 12,$$

$$\frac{\log p}{\log 12} = 1 - 0.1q,$$

$$0.1q = 1 - \frac{\log p}{\log 12},$$

$$q = 10\left(1 - \frac{\log p}{\log 3 + \log 4}\right),$$

$$q \approx 10\left(1 - \frac{\log p}{1.0792}\right).$$

EXERCISE 5.3

In Problems **1–18,** *find the given values. Where necessary, use Table* 5.1.

1. $\log 15$.

2. $\log 16$.

3. $\log \frac{8}{3}$.

4. $\log \frac{7}{10}$.

5. $\log 36$.

6. $\log 0.0001$.

7. $\log 2000$.

8. $\log 900$.

9. $\log_7 7^{48}$.

10. $\log_5(5\sqrt{5})^5$.

11. $\ln e^{5x}$.

12. $\log_7 4$.

13. $\log_2 3$.

14. $\ln e$.

15. $\ln \dfrac{1}{e}$.

16. $\log_2 4$.

17. $\log 10 + \ln e^3$.

18. $e^{\ln 6}$.

In Problems **19–30,** *write the expression in terms of* $\ln x$, $\ln(x + 1)$, *and / or* $\ln(x + 2)$.

19. $\ln[x(x + 1)^2]$.

20. $\ln\dfrac{\sqrt{x}}{x + 1}$.

21. $\ln\dfrac{x^2}{(x + 1)^3}$.

22. $\ln[x(x + 1)]^3$.

23. $\ln\left(\dfrac{x}{x + 1}\right)^3$.

24. $\ln\sqrt{x(x + 1)}$.

25. $\ln\dfrac{x}{(x + 1)(x + 2)}$.

26. $\ln\dfrac{x^2(x + 1)}{x + 2}$.

27. $\ln\dfrac{\sqrt{x}}{(x + 1)^2(x + 2)^3}$.

28. $\ln\dfrac{1}{x(x + 1)(x + 2)}$.

29. $\ln\left[\dfrac{1}{x + 2}\sqrt[5]{\dfrac{x^2}{x + 1}}\right]$.

30. $\ln\sqrt{\dfrac{x^4(x + 1)^3}{x + 2}}$.

In Problems **31–38,** *express each of the given forms as a single logarithm.*

31. $\log 7 + \log 4$.

32. $\log_3 10 - \log_3 5$.

33. $\log_2(2x) - \log_2(x + 1)$.

34. $2 \log x - \frac{1}{2} \log(x - 2)$.

35. $9 \log 7 + 5 \log 23$.

36. $3 (\log x + \log y - 2 \log z)$.

37. $2 + 10 \log 1.05$.

38. $\frac{1}{2}(\log 215 + 8 \log 6 - 3 \log 121)$.

*In Problems **39–52**, find x.*

39. $e^{2x} \cdot e^{5x} = e^{14}$.

40. $(e^{5x+1})^2 = e$.

41. $(16)^{3x} = 2$.

42. $(27)^{2x+1} = \frac{1}{3}$.

43. $e^{\ln(2x)} = 5$.

44. $4^{\log_4 x + \log_4 2} = 3$.

45. $10^{\log x^2} = 4$.

46. $e^{3 \ln x} = 8$.

47. $\log(2x + 1) = \log(x + 6)$.

48. $\log x + \log 3 = \log 5$.

49. $\log x - \log(x - 1) = \log 4$.

50. $\log_2 x + 3 \log_2 2 = \log_2(2/x)$.

51. $\log(x + 2)^2 = 2$, where $x > 0$.

52. $\ln x = \ln(3x + 1) + 1$.

*In Problems **53** and **54**, write each expression in terms of natural logarithms.*

53. $\log(x + 8)$.

54. $\log_2 x$.

55. In statistics, the sample regression equation $y = ab^x$ is reduced to a linear form by taking logarithms of both sides. Find $\log y$.

56. In a study of military enlistments, Brown* considers total military compensation C as the sum of basic military compensation B (which includes the value of allowances, tax advantages, and base pay) and educational benefits E. Thus $C = B + E$. Brown states that

$$\ln C = \ln B + \ln\left(1 + \frac{E}{B}\right).$$

Verify this.

57. In a study of rooted plants in a certain geographic region,† it was determined that on plots of size A (in square meters), the average number of species that occurred was S. When $\log S$ was graphed as a function of $\log A$, the result was a straight line given by

$$\log S = \log 12.4 + 0.26 \log A.$$

Solve for S.

58. According to Richter‡ the magnitude M of an earthquake occurring 100 km from a certain type of seismometer is given by $M = \log(A) + 3$, where A is the recorded trace amplitude (in millimeters) of the quake.

(a) Find the magnitude of an earthquake that records a trace amplitude of 1 mm. (b) If a particular earthquake has amplitude A_1 and magnitude M_1, determine the magnitude of a quake with amplitude $100A_1$. Express your answer to (b) in terms of M_1.

59. The demand equation for a consumer product is $q = 80 - 2^p$. Solve for p and express your answer in terms of common logarithms as in Example 11. Evaluate p to two decimal places when $q = 60$.

60. After t years the number of units, q, of a product sold per year is given by $q = 1000(\frac{1}{2})^{0.8^t}$. Such an equation is called a *Gompertz equation* and describes natural growth in many areas of study. Solve this equation for t in the same manner as in Example 11 and show that

$$t = \frac{\log \dfrac{3 - \log q}{\log 2}}{(3 \log 2) - 1}.$$

61. In an article, Taagepera and Hayes refer to an equation of the form

$$\log T = 1.7 + 0.2068 \log P - 0.1334 \log^2 P.$$

Here T is the percentage of a country's gross national product (GNP) that corresponds to foreign trade (ex-

---

* C. Brown, "Military Enlistments: What Can We Learn from Geographic Variation?" *The American Economic Review*, 75, no. 1 (1985), 228–34.

† R. W. Poole, *An Introduction to Quantitative Ecology* (New York: McGraw-Hill Book Company, 1974).

‡ C. F. Richter, *Elementary Seismology* (San Francisco: W. H. Freeman and Company, Publishers, 1958).

ports plus imports), and P is the country's population (in units of 100,000).* Verify the claim that

$$T = 50P^{(0.2068 - 0.1334 \log P)}.$$

You may assume that $\log 50 = 1.7$.

62. In a discussion of the rate of cooling of isolated portions of the body when they are exposed to low temperatures, the following equation occurs:†

$$T_t - T_e = (T_t - T_e)_o e^{-at},$$

where T_t is temperature of the portion at time t, T_e is environmental temperature, the subscript o refers to initial temperature difference, and a is a constant. Show that

$$a = \frac{1}{t} \ln \frac{(T_t - T_e)_o}{T_t - T_e}.$$

5.4 REVIEW

Important Terms and Symbols

Section 5.1	exponential function, b^x $\quad$ e
Section 5.2	logarithmic function, $\log_b x$ $\quad$ common logarithm, $\log x$ $\quad$ natural logarithm, $\ln x$
Section 5.3	change of base formula

Summary

An exponential function has the form $f(x) = b^x$. A frequently used base in an exponential function is the irrational number e, where $e \approx 2.71828$. This base occurs in economic analysis and many situations involving growth or decay, such as population studies.

The logarithmic function is the inverse function for the exponential function, and vice versa. The logarithmic function with base b is denoted $\log_b$, and $y = \log_b x$ if and only if $b^y = x$. Logarithms with base e are called natural logarithms and are denoted ln; those with base 10 are called common logarithms and are denoted log. Some important properties of logarithms are:

$$\log_b(mn) = \log_b m + \log_b n, \qquad \log_b \frac{m}{n} = \log_b m - \log_b n,$$

$$\log_b m^r = r \log_b m, \qquad \log_b 1 = 0,$$

$$\log_b b = 1, \qquad \log_b b^r = r,$$

$$b^{\log_b m} = m, \qquad \log_b m = \frac{\log_a m}{\log_a b}.$$

* R. Taagepera and J. P. Hayes, "How Trade/GNP Ratio Decreases with Country Size," *Social Science Research,* 6 (1977), 108–32.

† R. W. Stacy et al., *Essentials of Biological and Medical Physics* (New York: McGraw-Hill Book Company, 1955).

Review Problems

1. Convert $3^4 = 81$ to logarithmic form.

2. Convert $\log_5 \frac{1}{5} = -1$ to exponential form.

In Problems **3–8,** *find the value.*

3. $\log_5 125$.

4. $\log_4 16$.

5. $\log_2 \frac{1}{16}$.

6. $\log_{1/3} \frac{1}{9}$.

7. $\log_{1/3} 9$.

8. $\log_4 2$.

In Problems **9–16,** *find x.*

9. $\log_5 125 = x$.

10. $\log_x \frac{1}{8} = -3$.

11. $\log x = -2$.

12. $\ln \frac{1}{e} = x$.

13. $\log_x(2x + 3) = 2$.

14. $\log(4x + 1) = \log(x + 2)$.

15. $e^{\ln(x+4)} = 7$.

16. $\log x + \log 2 = 1$.

17. Suppose that $\log_2 19 = 4.2479$ and $\log_2 5 = 2.3219$. Find $\log_5 19$.

18. Find the value of $\log 2500$.

In Problems **19–24,** *write each expression as a single logarithm.*

19. $2 \log 5 - 3 \log 3$.

20. $6 \ln x + 4 \ln y$.

21. $2 \ln x + \ln y - 3 \ln z$.

22. $\log_6 2 - \log_6 4 - 2 \log_6 3$.

23. $\frac{1}{2} \log_2 x + 2 \log_2(x^2) - 3 \log_2(x + 1) - 4 \log_2(x + 2)$.

24. $3 \log x + \log y - 2(\log z + \log w)$.

In Problems **25–30,** *write the expression in terms of* $\ln x$, $\ln y$, *and* $\ln z$.

25. $\ln \frac{x^2 y}{z^3}$.

26. $\ln \frac{\sqrt{x}}{(yz)^2}$.

27. $\ln \sqrt[3]{xyz}$.

28. $\ln \left[\frac{xy^3}{z^2} \right]^4$.

29. $\ln \left[\frac{1}{x} \sqrt{\frac{y}{z}} \right]$.

30. $\ln \left[\left(\frac{x}{y} \right)^2 \left(\frac{x}{z} \right)^3 \right]$.

31. If $\log 3 = x$ and $\log 4 = y$, express $\log(16\sqrt{3})$ in terms of x and y.

32. Express $\log \dfrac{x^2\sqrt{x + 1}}{\sqrt[3]{x^2 + 2}}$ in terms of $\log x$, $\log(x + 1)$, and $\log(x^2 + 2)$.

33. Simplify $e^{\ln x} + \ln e^x + \ln 1$.

34. Simplify $\log 10^2 + \log 1000 - 5$.

35. If $\ln y = x^2 + 2$, find y.

36. Sketch the graphs of $y = 3^x$ and $y = \log_3 x$.

37. Due to ineffective advertising, the Kleer-Kut Razor Company finds its annual revenues have been cut sharply. Moreover, the annual revenue R at the end of t years of business satisfies the equation $R = 200,000e^{-0.2t}$. Find the annual revenue at the end of 2 years; at the end of 3 years.

38. A marketing-research company needs to determine how people adapt to the taste of a new cough drop. In one experiment, a person was given a cough drop and was asked periodically to assign a number, on a scale from 0 to 10, to the perceived taste. This number was called the *response magnitude*. The number 10 was assigned to the initial taste. After conducting the experiment several times, the company estimated that the response magnitude, R, is given by

$$R = 10e^{-t/40},$$

where t is the number of seconds after the person is given the cough drop. (a) Find the response magnitude after 20 seconds. Give your answer to the nearest integer. (b) After how many seconds does a person have a response magnitude of 5? Give your answer to the nearest second.

Mathematics of Finance

6.1 COMPOUND INTEREST

In this chapter we shall model selected topics in finance that deal with the time value of money, such as investments, loans, and so on. In later chapters, when more mathematics is at our disposal, certain topics will be revisited and expanded.

Practically everyone is familiar with **compound interest,** whereby the interest earned by an invested amount of money (or **principal**) is reinvested so that it too earns interest. That is, the interest is converted (or *compounded*) into principal and hence there is "interest on interest."

For example, suppose that $100 is invested at the rate of 5% compounded annually. At the end of the first year, the value of the investment is the original principal ($100) plus the interest on the principal [100(0.05)]:

$$100 + 100(0.05) = \$105.$$

This is the amount on which interest is earned for the second year. At the end of the second year, the value of the investment is the principal at the end of the first year ($105) plus the interest on that sum [105(0.05)]:

$$105 + 105(0.05) = \$110.25.$$

Thus each year the principal increases by 5%. The $110.25 represents the original principal plus all accrued interest; it is called the **accumulated amount** or **compound amount.** The difference between the compound amount and the original principal is called the **compound interest.** Thus the compound interest is $110.25 - 100 = \$10.25$.

More generally, if a principal of P dollars is invested at a rate of $100r$ percent compounded annually (for example, at 5%, r is 0.05), the compound amount after 1 year is $P + Pr$ or $P(1 + r)$. At the end of the second year the compound amount is

$$P(1 + r) + [P(1 + r)]r$$

$$= P(1 + r)[1 + r] \qquad \text{(factoring)}$$

$$= P(1 + r)^2.$$

This pattern continues. After 3 years the compound amount is $P(1 + r)^3$. In general, **the compound amount S of a principal P at the end of n years at the rate of r compounded annually** is given by

$$S = P(1 + r)^n. \qquad (1)$$

Some approximate values of $(1 + r)^n$ are given in Appendix D.

EXAMPLE 1   *Suppose $1000 is invested for 10 years at 6% compounded annually.*

a. *Find the compound amount.*

We use Eq. (1) with $P = 1000$, $r = 0.06$, and $n = 10$.

$$S = 1000(1 + 0.06)^{10} = 1000(1.06)^{10}.$$

In Appendix D we find that $(1.06)^{10} \approx 1.790848$. Thus

$$S \approx 1000(1.790848) \approx \$1790.85.$$

b. *Find the compound interest.*

Using the result from part (a), we have

$$\text{compound interest} = S - P$$

$$= 1790.85 - 1000$$

$$= \$790.85.$$

Suppose the principal of $1000 in Example 1 is invested for 10 years as before, but this time the compounding takes place every 3 months (that is, *quarterly*) at the rate of $1\frac{1}{2}\%$ *per quarter*. Then there are four **interest periods** or **conversion periods** per year, and in 10 years there are $10(4) = 40$ interest periods. Thus the compound amount with $r = 0.015$ is now

$$1000(1.015)^{40} \approx 1000(1.814018)$$

$$\approx \$1814.02,$$

and the compound interest is $814.02. Usually, the interest rate per conversion period is stated as an annual rate. Here we would speak of an annual rate of 6% compounded quarterly so that the rate per interest period, or the **periodic rate,** is 6%/4 = 1.5%. This *quoted* annual rate of 6% is called the **nominal rate** or the **annual percentage rate (A.P.R.).** Unless otherwise stated, all interest rates will be assumed to be annual (nominal) rates. Thus a rate of 15% compounded monthly corresponds to a periodic rate of 15%/12 = 1.25%.

On the basis of our discussion, we can generalize Eq. (1). The formula

$$S = P(1 + r)^n \qquad\qquad (2)$$

gives **the compound amount S of a principal P at the end of n interest periods at the periodic rate of r.**

You have seen that for a principal of $1000 at a nominal rate of 6% over a period of 10 years, annual compounding results in compound interest of $790.85, and with quarterly compounding the compound interest is $814.02. It is typical that for a given nominal rate, the more frequent the compounding, the greater is the compound interest. However, as the number of interest periods increases, the effect tends to be less meaningful. For example, with weekly compounding the compound interest is

$$1000\left(1 + \frac{0.06}{52}\right)^{10(52)} - 1000 \approx \$821.49,$$

and with daily compounding it is

$$1000\left(1 + \frac{0.06}{365}\right)^{10(365)} - 1000 \approx \$822.03.$$

The difference is not too significant here.

Pitfall

A nominal rate of 6% annually does not necessarily mean that an investment increases in value by 6% in a year's time.

Sometimes the phrase "money is worth" is used to express an annual interest rate. Thus, saying that money is worth 6% compounded quarterly refers to an annual (nominal) rate of 6% compounded quarterly.

EXAMPLE 2   *The sum of $3000 is placed in a savings account. If money is worth 6% compounded semiannually, what is the balance in the account after 7 years? (Assume no other deposits and no withdrawals.)*

Here P = 3000. With two interest periods per year, we have n = 7(2) = 14, and the periodic rate r is 0.06/2 = 0.03. By Eq. (2) we have

$$S = 3000(1.03)^{14} \approx 3000(1.512590) = \$4537.77.$$

EXAMPLE 3   *How long will it take for* $600 *to amount to* $900 *at an annual rate of 8% compounded quarterly?*

The periodic rate is $r = 0.08/4 = 0.02$. Let n be the number of interest periods it takes for a principal of $P = 600$ to amount to $S = 900$. Then from Eq. (2),

$$900 = 600(1.02)^n,$$

$$(1.02)^n = \frac{900}{600},$$

$$(1.02)^n = 1.5.$$

To solve for n we first take the natural logarithms of both sides.

$$\ln(1.02)^n = \ln 1.5,$$

$$n \ln 1.02 = \ln 1.5 \qquad (\text{since } \ln m^r = r \ln m),$$

$$n = \frac{\ln 1.5}{\ln 1.02} \approx \frac{0.40547}{0.01980} \approx 20.478.$$

The number of years that corresponds to 20.478 quarterly interest periods is $20.478/4 = 5.1195$, which is slightly more than 5 years and 1 month. Actually, the principal doesn't amount to $900 until $5\frac{1}{4}$ years pass because interest is compounded quarterly.

EXAMPLE 4   *Calculator Problem.*

At what nominal rate of interest, compounded yearly, will money double in 8 years?

Let r be the desired rate at which a principal of P doubles in 8 years. Then the compound amount is $2P$. Thus

$$P(1 + r)^8 = 2P,$$

$$(1 + r)^8 = 2,$$

$$1 + r = \sqrt[8]{2},$$

$$r = \sqrt[8]{2} - 1,$$

$$r \approx 1.0905 - 1 = 0.0905.$$

Thus the desired rate is 9.05%.

EXAMPLE 5   *Calculator Problem.*

Suppose that $500 *amounted to* $588.38 *in a savings account after 3 years. If interest was compounded semiannually, find the nominal rate of interest, compounded semiannually, that was earned by the money.*

Let r be the semiannual rate. There are six interest periods. Thus

$$500(1 + r)^6 = 588.38,$$

$$(1 + r)^6 = \frac{588.38}{500},$$

$$1 + r = \sqrt[6]{\frac{588.38}{500}},$$

$$r = \sqrt[6]{\frac{588.38}{500}} - 1,$$

$$r \approx 1.0275 - 1 = 0.0275.$$

Thus the semiannual rate was 2.75%, so the nominal rate was $5\frac{1}{2}$% compounded semiannually.

If $1 is invested at a nominal rate of 8% compounded quarterly for 1 year, the dollar will earn more than 8% that year. The compound interest is $S - P = 1(1.02)^4 - 1 \approx 1.082432 - 1 = \$0.082432$, which is about 8.24% of the original dollar. That is, 8.24% is the rate of interest *compounded annually* that is actually obtained, and it is called the **effective rate.** Following this procedure, we can show that the **effective rate which is equivalent to a nominal rate of r compounded n times a year** is given by

$$\text{effective rate} = \left(1 + \frac{r}{n}\right)^n - 1. \qquad (3)$$

EXAMPLE 6   *What effective rate is equivalent to a nominal rate of 6% compounded (a) semiannually and (b) quarterly?*

a. From Eq. (3) the effective rate is

$$\left(1 + \frac{0.06}{2}\right)^2 - 1 = (1.03)^2 - 1 = 0.0609 \quad \text{or} \quad 6.09\%.$$

b. The effective rate is

$$\left(1 + \frac{0.06}{4}\right)^4 - 1 = (1.015)^4 - 1 \approx 0.061364 \quad \text{or} \quad 6.14\%.$$

EXAMPLE 7   *To what amount will $12,000 accumulate in 15 years if invested at an effective rate of 5%?*

Since an effective rate is the actual rate compounded annually, we have

$$S = 12{,}000(1.05)^{15} \approx 12{,}000(2.078928)$$

$$\approx \$24{,}947.14.$$

EXAMPLE 8   *How many years will it take for money to double at the effective rate of r?*

Let n be the number of years it takes for a principal of P to double. Then the compound amount is $2P$. Thus

$$2P = P(1 + r)^n,$$

$$2 = (1 + r)^n,$$

$$\ln 2 = n \ln(1 + r) \qquad \text{(taking logs of both sides).}$$

Hence

$$n = \frac{\ln 2}{\ln(1 + r)} \approx \frac{0.69315}{\ln(1 + r)}.$$

For example, if $r = 0.06$, the number of years it takes to double a principal is approximately

$$\frac{0.69315}{\ln 1.06} \approx \frac{0.69315}{0.05827} \approx 11.9 \text{ years.}$$

We remark that effective rates are used to compare different interest rates, that is, which is "best." For example, if you had a choice of investing money at 6% compounded daily or $6\frac{1}{8}\%$ compounded semiannually, which is the better choice? The respective equivalent effective rates are

$$\left(1 + \frac{0.06}{365}\right)^{365} - 1 \approx 0.061831 \approx 6.18\%$$

and

$$\left(1 + \frac{0.06125}{4}\right)^{4} - 1 \approx 0.062671 \approx 6.27\%.$$

Clearly, the second choice is the better, although the notion of daily compounding may appear to be more appealing.

EXERCISE 6.1

In Problems **1–10,** *find (a) the compound amount and (b) the compound interest for the given investment and annual rate.*

1. $4000 for 7 years at 6% compounded annually.

2. $5000 for 20 years at 5% compounded annually.

3. $700 for 15 years at 7% compounded semiannually.

4. $4000 for 12 years at 6% compounded semiannually.

5. $10,000 for $8\frac{1}{2}$ years at 8% compounded quarterly.

6. $900 for 11 years at 10% compounded quarterly.

7. $5000 for $2\frac{1}{2}$ years at 9% compounded monthly.

8. $1000 for $3\frac{3}{4}$ years at 6% compounded monthly.

9. $6000 for 8 years at an effective rate of 8%.

10. $750 for 12 months at an effective rate of 10%.

In Problems **11–14,** *use a calculator to find the compound amount for the given investment.*

11. $4000 for 15 years at $8\frac{1}{2}$% compounded quarterly.

12. $500 for 5 years at 11% compounded semiannually.

13. $8000 for 3 years at $6\frac{1}{4}$% compounded daily.

14. $1000 for 2 years at 12% compounded hourly.

In Problems **15–18,** *find the effective rate that corresponds to the given nominal rate. Use a calculator for Problems* **17** *and* **18** *and give these answers to five decimal places.*

15. 8% compounded quarterly.

16. 12% compounded monthly.

17. 8% compounded daily.

18. 12% compounded daily.

In Problems **19** *and* **20,** *find how many years it would take to double a principal at the given effective rate. Give your answer to one decimal place.*

19. 8%.

20. 5%.

21. A $6000 certificate of deposit is purchased for $6000 and is held 7 years. If the certificate earns 8% compounded quarterly, what is it worth at the end of that period?

22. How many years will it take for money to triple at the effective rate of *r*?

23. Suppose the 1984–1985 costs for a resident student to attend a four-year private college are $9000. This includes tuition, room, and board. Assuming an effective 6% inflation rate for these costs, determine what these college costs will be in the 1994–1995 school year.

24. Repeat Problem 23 for an inflation rate of 6% compounded semiannually.

25. A major credit-card company has a finance charge of $1\frac{1}{2}$% per month on the outstanding indebtedness. (a) What is the nominal rate compounded monthly? (b) What is the effective rate?

26. How long would it take for a principal of *P* to double if money is worth 12% compounded monthly? Give your answer to the nearest month.

27. To what sum will $2000 amount in 8 years if invested at a 6% effective rate for the first 4 years and 6% compounded semiannually thereafter?

28. How long will it take for $500 to amount to $700 if it is invested at 8% compounded quarterly?

29. An investor has a choice of investing a sum of money at 8% compounded annually, or at 7.8% compounded semiannually. Which is the better of the two rates?

30. *Calculator Problem.* What nominal rate of interest compounded quarterly corresponds to an effective rate of 4%?

31. *Calculator Problem.* A bank advertises that it pays interest on savings accounts at the rate of $5\frac{1}{4}$% compounded daily. Find the effective rate if the bank assumes that a year consists of (a) 360 days or (b) 365 days in determining the *daily rate*. Assume that compounding occurs 365 times a year and give your answer to four decimal places.

32. *Calculator Problem.* Suppose that $700 amounted to $801.06 in a savings account after 2 years. If interest was compounded quarterly, find the nominal rate of interest compounded quarterly that was earned by the money.

33. *Calculator Problem.* As a hedge against inflation, an investor purchased a painting in 1976 for $100,000. It was sold in 1986 for $300,000. At what effective rate did the painting appreciate in value?

34. *Calculator Problem.* If the rate of inflation for certain goods is $7\frac{1}{4}$% compounded daily, how many years will it take for the average price of such a good to double?

35. *Calculator Problem.* A *zero-coupon bond* is a bond that
is sold for less than its face value (that is, it is *discounted*) and has no periodic interest payments. Instead, the bond is redeemed for its face value at maturity. Thus in this sense, interest is paid at maturity.

Suppose that a zero-coupon bond sells for $220 and can
be redeemed in 14 years for its face value of $1000.
The bond earns interest at what nominal rate, compounded semiannually?

6.2 PRESENT VALUE

Suppose that $100 is deposited in a savings account that pays 6% compounded
annually. Then at the end of 2 years the account is worth $100(1.06)^2 = 112.36.
To describe this we say that the compound amount $112.36 is the *future value*
of the $100, and $100 is the *present value* of the $112.36. In general, there are
times when we may know the future value of an investment and wish to find the
present value. To obtain a formula for this we solve the equation $S = P(1 + r)^n$
for P. This gives $P = S/(1 + r)^n$. Thus

$$P = S(1 + r)^{-n} \tag{1}$$

gives **the principal P which must be invested at the periodic rate of r for n
interest periods so that the compound amount is S.** We call P the **present
value** of S. Approximate values of $(1 + r)^{-n}$ are given in Appendix D.

EXAMPLE 1   *Find the present value of $1000 due after 3 years if the
interest rate is 9% compounded monthly.*

We use Eq. (1) with $S = 1000$, $r = 0.09/12 = 0.0075$, and $n = 3(12) = 36$.
$$P = 1000(1.0075)^{-36} \approx 1000(0.764149)$$
$$\approx \$764.15.$$

If the interest rate in Example 1 were 10% compounded monthly, the present value would be

$$P = 1000\left(1 + \frac{0.1}{12}\right)^{-36} \approx \$741.74,$$

which is less than before. It is typical that the present value decreases as the
interest rate per conversion period increases.

EXAMPLE 2   *A trust fund for a child's education is being set up by a
single payment so that at the end of 15 years there will be $24,000. If the fund
earns interest at the rate of 7% compounded semiannually, how much money
should be paid into the fund initially?*

We want the present value of $24,000 due in 15 years. From Eq. (1) with $S = 24,000$, $r = 0.07/2 = 0.035$, and $n = 15(2) = 30$, we have

$$P = 24{,}000(1.035)^{-30} \approx 24{,}000(0.356278)$$

$$\approx \$8550.67.$$

Suppose that Mr. Smith owes Mr. Jones two sums of money: $1000 due in 2 years and $600 due in 5 years. If Mr. Smith wishes to pay off the total debt now by a single payment, how much should the payment be? Assume an interest rate of 8% compounded quarterly.

The single payment x due now must be such that it would grow and eventually pay off the debts when they are due. That is, it must equal the sum of the present values of the future payments. As shown in Fig. 6.1, we have

$$x = 1000(1.02)^{-8} + 600(1.02)^{-20} \tag{2}$$

$$\approx 1000(0.853490) + 600(0.672971)$$

$$= 853.490 + 403.78260$$

$$\approx \$1257.27.$$

Thus the single payment due now is $1257.27. Let us now analyze the situation

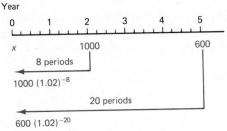

FIGURE 6.1

in more detail. There are two methods of payment of the debt: a single payment now, or two payments in the future. Notice that Eq. (2) indicates that the value *now* of all payments under one method must equal the value *now* of all payments under the other method. In general, this is true not just *now* but at *any time*. For example, if we multiply both sides of Eq. (2) by $(1.02)^{20}$, we get

$$x(1.02)^{20} = 1000(1.02)^{12} + 600. \tag{3}$$

The left side of Eq. (3) gives the value 5 years from now of the single payment (see Fig. 6.2), while the right sides gives the value 5 years from now of all payments under the other method. Solving Eq. (3) for x gives the same result, $x = \$1257.27$. Each of Eqs. (2) and (3) is called an **equation of value.** They illustrate that when one is considering two methods of paying a debt (or other transaction), *at any time* the value of all payments under one method must equal the value of all payments under the other method.

In certain situations one equation of value may be more convenient to use than another, as Example 3 will illustrate.

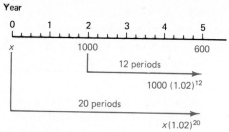

FIGURE 6.2

EXAMPLE 3 *A debt of* $3000, *which is due 6 years from now, is instead to be paid off by three payments:* $500 *now,* $1500 *in 3 years, and a final payment at the end of 5 years. What would this payment be if an interest rate of 6% compounded annually is assumed?*

Let x be the final payment due in 5 years. For computational convenience we shall set up an equation of value to represent the situation at the end of 5 years, for in that way the coefficient of x will be 1, as seen in Fig. 6.3. Notice that at year 5 we compute the future values of $500 and $1500, and the present value of $3000. The equation of value is

$$500(1.06)^5 + 1500(1.06)^2 + x = 3000(1.06)^{-1},$$

$$500(1.338226) + 1500(1.123600) + x \approx 3000(0.943396),$$

$$x \approx \$475.68.$$

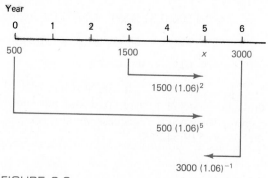

FIGURE 6.3

When one is considering a choice of two investments, a comparison should be made of the value of each investment at a certain time, as Example 4 shows.

EXAMPLE 4 *Suppose that you had the opportunity of investing* $4000 *in a business such that the value of the investment after 5 years would be* $5300. *On the other hand, you could instead put the* $4000 *in a savings account that pays 6% compounded semiannually. Which investment is better?*

Let us consider the value of each investment at the end of 5 years. At that time the business investment would have a value of \$5300, while the savings account would have a value of $4000(1.03)^{10} \approx \$5375.66$. Clearly, the better choice is putting the money in the savings account.

If an initial investment will bring in payments at future times, the payments are called **cash flows.** The **net present value,** denoted NPV, of the cash flows is defined to be the sum of the present values of the cash flows, minus the initial investment. If $NPV > 0$, then the investment is profitable; if $NPV < 0$, the investment is not profitable.

EXAMPLE 5   *Suppose that you can invest \$20,000 in a business that guarantees you the following cash flows at the end of the indicated years:*

YEAR	CASH FLOW
2	\$10,000
3	8,000
5	6,000

Assume an interest rate of 7% compounded annually and find the net present value of the cash flows.

Subtracting the initial investment from the sum of the present values of the cash flows gives

$$NPV = 10,000(1.07)^{-2} + 8000(1.07)^{-3} + 6000(1.07)^{-5} - 20,000$$

$$\approx 10,000(0.873439) + 8000(0.816298) + 6000(0.712986) - 20,000$$

$$= 8734.39 + 6530.384 + 4277.916 - 20,000$$

$$= -\$457.31.$$

Note that since $NPV < 0$, the business venture is not profitable if one considers the time value of money. It would be better to invest the \$20,000 in a bank paying 7%, since the business venture is equivalent to only investing $20,000 - 457.31 = \$19,542.69$.

EXERCISE 6.2

In Problems **1–8,** *find the present value of the given future payment at the specified interest rate.*

1. \$6000 due in 20 years at 5% compounded annually.

2. \$3500 due in 8 years at 6% effective.

3. \$4000 due in 12 years at 7% compounded semiannually.

4. \$2500 due in 15 months at 8% compounded quarterly.

5. \$2000 due in $2\frac{1}{2}$ years at 9% compounded monthly.

6. \$750 due in 3 years at 18% compounded monthly.

7. \$8000 due in $7\frac{1}{2}$ years at 6% compounded quarterly.

8. \$6000 due in $6\frac{1}{2}$ years at 10% compounded semiannually.

In Problems **9–12,** *use a calculator to find the present value of the given future payment at the specified interest rate.*

9. $8000 due in 5 years at 10% compounded monthly.

10. $500 due in 3 years at $8\frac{3}{4}$% compounded quarterly.

11. $10,000 due in 4 years at $9\frac{1}{2}$% compounded daily.

12. $1250 due in $1\frac{1}{2}$ years at $13\frac{1}{2}$% compounded weekly.

13. A trust fund for a 10-year-old child is being set up by a single payment so that at age 21 the child will receive $27,000. Find how much the payment is if an interest rate of 6% compounded semiannually is assumed.

14. A debt of $550 due in four years and $550 due in 5 years is to be repaid by a single payment now. Find how much the payment is if an interest rate of 10% compounded quarterly is assumed.

15. A debt of $600 due in three years and $800 due in 4 years is to be repaid by a single payment 2 years from now. If the interest rate is 8% compounded semiannually, how much is the payment?

16. A debt of $5000 due in 5 years is to be repaid by a payment of $2000 now and a second payment at the end of 6 years. How much should the second payment be if the interest rate is 6% compounded quarterly?

17. A debt of $5000 due 5 years from now and $5000 due 10 years from now is to be repaid by a payment of $2000 in 2 years, a payment of $4000 in 4 years, and a final payment at the end of 6 years. If the interest rate is 7% compounded annually, how much is the final payment?

18. A debt of $2000 due in 3 years and $3000 due in 7 years is to be repaid by a single payment of $1000 now and two equal payments which are due 1 year from now and 4 years from now. If the interest rate is 6% compounded annually, how much are each of the equal payments?

19. An initial investment of $25,000 in a business guarantees the following cash flows.

YEAR	CASH FLOW
3	$ 8,000
4	$10,000
6	$14,000

Assume an interest rate of 5% compounded semiannually.
a. Find the net present value of the cash flows.
b. Is the investment profitable?

20. Repeat Problem 19 for the interest rate of 6% compounded semiannually.

21. Suppose that a person has the following choices of investing $10,000:
a. placing it in a savings account paying 6% compounded semiannually;
b. investing in a business such that the value of the investment after 8 years is $16,000.
Which is the better choice?

22. A owes B two sums of money: $1000 plus interest at 7% compounded annually, which is due in 5 years, and $2000 plus interest at 8% compounded semiannually, which is due in 7 years. If both debts are to be paid off by a single payment at the end of 6 years, find the amount of the payment if money is worth 6% compounded quarterly.

23. *Calculator Problem.* A jewelry store advertises that for every $1000 spent on diamond jewelry, the purchaser receives a $1000 bond at absolutely no cost. In reality, the $1000 is the full maturity value of a zero-coupon bond (see Problem 35 of Exercise 6.1), which the store purchases at a heavily reduced price. If the bond earns interest at the rate of 11.5% compounded quarterly and matures after 20 years, how much does the bond cost the store?

24. *Calculator Problem.* Find the present value of $3000 due in 2 years at a bank rate of 8% compounded daily. Assume that the bank uses 360 days in determining the daily rate and that there are 365 days in a year, that is, compounding occurs 365 times in a year.

25. *Calculator Problem.* A *(promissory) note* is a written statement agreeing to pay a sum of money either on demand or at a definite future time. When a note is purchased for its present value at a given interest rate, the note is said to be *discounted* and the interest rate is called the *discount rate.* Suppose a $10,000 note due 8 years from now is sold to a financial institution for $4700. What is the nominal discount rate with quarterly compounding?

6.3   ANNUITIES

In mathematics we use the word **sequence** to describe a list of numbers, called *terms,* that are arranged in a definite order. For example, the list

$$2, 4, 6, 8$$

is a (finite) sequence. The first term is 2, the second is 4, and so on.

In the sequence

$$3, 6, 12, 24, 48,$$

each term, after the first, can be obtained by multiplying the preceding term by 2:

$$6 = 3(2), \qquad 12 = 6(2), \qquad \text{and so on.}$$

This means that the *ratio* of every two consecutive terms is 2:

$$\frac{6}{3} = 2, \qquad \frac{12}{6} = 2, \qquad \text{and so on.}$$

We call the sequence a *geometric sequence* with *common ratio* 2. Note that it can be written as

$$3, 3(2), 3(2)(2), 3(2)(2)(2), 3(2)(2)(2)(2)$$

or in the form

$$3, 3(2), 3(2^2), 3(2^3), 3(2^4).$$

More generally, if a geometric sequence has n terms such that the first term is a and the common ratio is the constant r, then the sequence has the form

$$a, ar, ar^2, ar^3, \ldots, ar^{n-1}.$$

Note that the nth term in the sequence is ar^{n-1}.

Definition
The sequence of n numbers

$$a, ar, ar^2, \ldots, ar^{n-1}, \qquad \text{where } a \neq 0,*$$

*is called a **geometric sequence** with **first term** a and **common ratio** r.*

---

* If $a = 0$, the sequence is $0, 0, 0, \ldots, 0$. We shall not consider this uninteresting case.

EXAMPLE 1

a. The geometric sequence with $a = 3$, common ratio $\frac{1}{2}$, and $n = 5$ is

$$3, \ 3(\tfrac{1}{2}), \ 3(\tfrac{1}{2})^2, \ 3(\tfrac{1}{2})^3, \ 3(\tfrac{1}{2})^4,$$

or $\qquad 3, \ \tfrac{3}{2}, \ \tfrac{3}{4}, \ \tfrac{3}{8}, \ \tfrac{3}{16}.$

b. The numbers

$$1, \ 0.1, \ 0.01, \ 0.001$$

form a geometric sequence with $a = 1$, $r = 0.1$, and $n = 4$.

EXAMPLE 2

If \$100 is invested at the rate of 6% compounded annually, then the list of compound amounts at the end of each year for 8 years is

$$100(1.06), \quad 100(1.06)^2, \quad 100(1.06)^3, \quad \ldots, \quad 100(1.06)^8.$$

This is a geometric sequence with common ratio 1.06.

The indicated sum of the terms of the geometric sequence $a, ar, ar^2, \ldots, ar^{n-1}$ is called a **geometric series:**

$$a + ar + ar^2 + \cdots + ar^{n-1}. \tag{1}$$

For example,

$$1 + \tfrac{1}{2} + (\tfrac{1}{2})^2 + \cdots + (\tfrac{1}{2})^6$$

is a geometric series with $a = 1$, common ratio $r = \frac{1}{2}$, and $n = 7$.

Let us compute the sum s of the geometric series in (1):

$$s = a + ar + ar^2 + \cdots + ar^{n-1}. \tag{2}$$

We can express s in a more compact form. Multiplying both sides by r gives

$$rs = ar + ar^2 + ar^3 + \cdots + ar^n. \tag{3}$$

Subtracting corresponding sides of Eq. (3) from Eq. (2) gives

$$s - rs = a - ar^n,$$

$$s(1 - r) = a(1 - r^n) \qquad \text{(factoring)}.$$

Dividing both sides by $1 - r$, we have

$$s = \frac{a(1 - r^n)}{1 - r}, \tag{4}$$

which gives **the sum s of a geometric series* of n terms with first term a and common ratio r.**

EXAMPLE 3   *Find the sum of the geometric series*

$$1 + \tfrac{1}{2} + (\tfrac{1}{2})^2 + \cdots + (\tfrac{1}{2})^6.$$

Here $a = 1$, $r = \tfrac{1}{2}$, and $n = 7$ (not 6). From Eq. (4) we have

$$s = \frac{a(1 - r^n)}{1 - r} = \frac{1[1 - (\tfrac{1}{2})^7]}{1 - \tfrac{1}{2}} = \frac{\tfrac{127}{128}}{\tfrac{1}{2}} = \frac{127}{64}.$$

EXAMPLE 4   *Find the sum of the geometric series*

$$3^5 + 3^6 + 3^7 + \cdots + 3^{11}.$$

Here $a = 3^5$, $r = 3$, and $n = 7$. From Eq. (4),

$$s = \frac{3^5(1 - 3^7)}{1 - 3} = \frac{243(1 - 2187)}{-2} = 265{,}599.$$

The notion of a geometric series is the basis of the mathematical model of an *annuity*. Basically, an **annuity** is a sequence of payments made at fixed periods of time over a given time interval. The fixed period is called the **payment period,** and the given time interval is the **term** of the annuity. An example of an annuity is the depositing of $100 in a savings account every 3 months for a year.

The **present value of an annuity** is the sum of the *present values* of all the payments. It represents the amount that must be invested now to purchase the payments due in the future. Unless otherwise specified, we assume that each payment is made at the *end* of a payment period; that is called an **ordinary annuity.** We also assume that interest is computed at the end of each payment period.

Let us consider an annuity of n payments of R (dollars) each, where the interest rate *per period* is r (see Fig. 6.4) and the first payment is due one period from now. The present value A of the annuity is given by

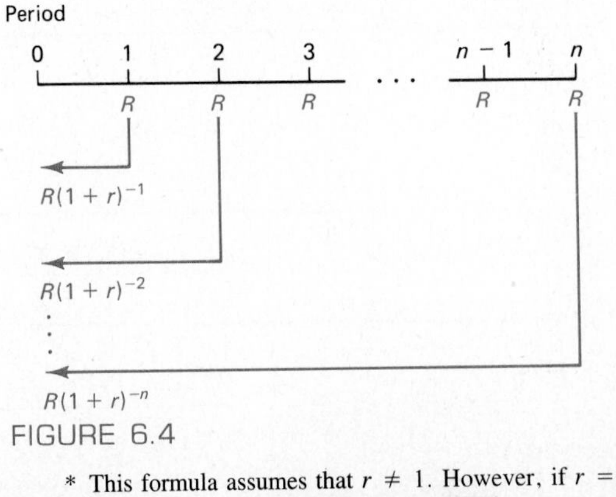

FIGURE 6.4

* This formula assumes that $r \neq 1$. However, if $r = 1$, then $s = a + a + \cdots + a = na$.

$$A = R(1 + r)^{-1} + R(1 + r)^{-2} + \cdots + R(1 + r)^{-n}.$$

This is a geometric series of n terms with first term $R(1 + r)^{-1}$ and common ratio $(1 + r)^{-1}$. Hence from Eq. (4) we have

$$A = \frac{R(1 + r)^{-1}[1 - (1 + r)^{-n}]}{1 - (1 + r)^{-1}}$$

$$= \frac{R[1 - (1 + r)^{-n}]}{(1 + r)[1 - (1 + r)^{-1}]} = \frac{R[1 - (1 + r)^{-n}]}{(1 + r) - 1}.$$

Thus the formula

$$A = R\frac{1 - (1 + r)^{-n}}{r} \tag{5}$$

gives **the present value A of an annuity of R (dollars) per payment period for n periods at the rate of r per period.** The expression $[1 - (1 + r)^{-n}]/r$ is denoted $a_{\overline{n}|r}$ and [letting $R = 1$ in Eq. (5)] represents the present value of an annuity of \$1 per period. The symbol $a_{\overline{n}|r}$ is read "a angle n at r." Selected values of $a_{\overline{n}|r}$ are given in Appendix D (most are approximate). Thus Eq. (5) can be written

$$A = Ra_{\overline{n}|r}. \tag{6}$$

EXAMPLE 5   *Find the present value of an annuity of \$100 per month for $3\frac{1}{2}$ years at an interest rate of 6% compounded monthly.*

In Eq. (6) we let $R = 100$, $r = 0.06/12 = 0.005$, and $n = (3\frac{1}{2})(12) = 42$. Thus

$$A = 100a_{\overline{42}|0.005}.$$

From Appendix D, $a_{\overline{42}|0.005} \approx 37.798300$. Hence

$$A \approx 100(37.798300) = \$3779.83.$$

EXAMPLE 6   *Given an interest rate of 5% compounded annually, find the present value of the following annuity: \$2000 due at the end of each year for 3 years, and \$5000 due thereafter at the end of each year for 4 years (see Fig. 6.5).*

Period

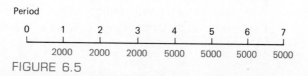

FIGURE 6.5

The present value is obtained by summing the present values of all payments:

$$2000(1.05)^{-1} + 2000(1.05)^{-2} + 2000(1.05)^{-3} + 5000(1.05)^{-4} +$$
$$5000(1.05)^{-5} + 5000(1.05)^{-6} + 5000(1.05)^{-7}.$$

Rather than evaluating this expression, we can simplify our work by considering the payments to be an annuity of $5000 for 7 years, minus an annuity of $3000 for 3 years so that the first three payments are $2000 each. Thus the present value is

$$5000a_{\overline{7}|0.05} - 3000a_{\overline{3}|0.05}$$

$$\approx 5000(5.786373) - 3000(2.723248)$$

$$\approx \$20{,}762.12.$$

EXAMPLE 7   *If $10,000 is used to purchase an annuity consisting of equal payments at the end of each year for the next 4 years and the interest rate is 6% compounded annually, find the amount of each payment.*

Here $A = \$10{,}000$, $n = 4$, $r = 0.06$, and we want to find R. From Eq. (6),

$$10{,}000 = Ra_{\overline{4}|0.06}.$$

Solving for R gives

$$R = \frac{10{,}000}{a_{\overline{4}|0.06}} \approx \frac{10{,}000}{3.465106} \approx \$2885.91.$$

In general, the formula

$$R = \frac{A}{a_{\overline{n}|r}}$$

gives the periodic payment R of an annuity whose present value is A.

EXAMPLE 8   *The premiums on an insurance policy are $50 a quarter, payable at the beginning of each quarter. If the policyholder wishes to pay 1 year's premiums in advance, how much should be paid provided that the interest rate is 4% compounded quarterly?*

We want the present value of an annuity of $50 per period for four periods at a rate of 1% per period. However, each payment is due at the *beginning* of a payment period. Such an annuity is called an **annuity due.** The given annuity can be thought of as an initial payment of $50 followed by an ordinary annuity of $50 for three periods. Thus the present value is

$$50 + 50a_{\overline{3}|0.01} \approx 50 + 50(2.940985) \approx \$197.05.$$

We remark that the general formula for the **present value of an annuity due** is $A = R + Ra_{\overline{n-1}|r}$, or

$$A = R(1 + a_{\overline{n-1}|r}).$$

The **amount** (or **future value**) **of an annuity** is the value, at the end of the term, of all payments. That is, it is the sum of the compound amounts of all payments. Let us consider an ordinary annuity of n payments of R (dollars) each, where the interest rate per period is r. The compound amount of the last payment is R, since it occurs at the end of the last interest period and hence does not accrue interest (see Fig. 6.6). The $(n - 1)$th payment earns interest for one period, and so on, and the first payment earns interest for $n - 1$ periods. Hence the future value of the annuity is

$$R + R(1 + r) + R(1 + r)^2 + \cdots + R(1 + r)^{n-1}.$$

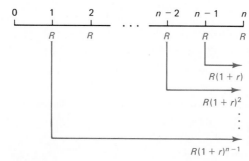

Period

FIGURE 6.6

This is a geometric series of n terms with first term R and common ratio $1 + r$. Hence its sum S is [by using Eq. (4)]

$$S = \frac{R[1 - (1 + r)^n]}{1 - (1 + r)} = R\frac{1 - (1 + r)^n}{-r}$$

$$= R\frac{(1 + r)^n - 1}{r}.$$

Thus the formula

$$S = R\frac{(1 + r)^n - 1}{r} \qquad (7)$$

gives **the amount S of an annuity of R (dollars) per payment period for n periods at the rate of r per period.** The expression $[(1 + r)^n - 1]/r$ is abbreviated $s_{\overline{n}|r}$ and approximate values of $s_{\overline{n}|r}$ are given in Appendix D. Thus

$$S = Rs_{\overline{n}|r}. \tag{8}$$

EXAMPLE 9   *Find the amount of an annuity consisting of payments of $50 at the end of every 3 months for 3 years at the rate of 6% compounded quarterly. Also find the compound interest.*

To find the amount of the annuity we use Eq. (8) with $R = 50$, $n = 4(3) = 12$, and $r = 0.06/4 = 0.015$:

$$S = 50s_{\overline{12}|0.015} \approx 50(13.041211) \approx \$652.06.$$

The compound interest is the difference between the amount of the annuity and the sum of the payments, namely

$$652.06 - 12(50) = 652.06 - 600 = \$52.06.$$

EXAMPLE 10   *At the beginning of each quarter, $50 is deposited into a savings account that pays 6% compounded quarterly. Find the balance in the account at the end of 3 years.*

Since the deposits are made at the beginning of a payment period, we want the amount of an *annuity due* as defined in Example 8 (see Fig. 6.7). The given

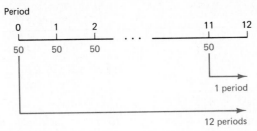

FIGURE 6.7

annuity can be thought of as an ordinary annuity of $50 for 13 periods minus the final payment of $50. Thus the amount is

$$50s_{\overline{13}|0.015} - 50 \approx 50(14.236830) - 50 \approx \$661.84.$$

The formula for the **future value of an annuity due** is $S = Rs_{\overline{n+1}|r} - R$ or

$$S = R(s_{\overline{n+1}|r} - 1).$$

EXAMPLE 11   *A **sinking fund** is a fund into which periodic payments are made in order to satisfy a future obligation. Suppose a machine costing $7000 is to be replaced at the end of 8 years, at which time it will have a salvage value*

*of $700. In order to provide money at that time for a new machine costing the
same amount, a sinking fund is set up. The amount in the fund at that time is to
be the difference between the replacement cost and salvage value. If equal payments are placed in the fund at the end of each quarter and the fund earns 8%
compounded quarterly, what should each payment be?*

The amount needed after 8 years is $7000 - 700 = \$6300$. Let R be the quarterly
payment. The payments into the sinking fund form an annuity with $n = 4(8) =
32$, $r = 0.08/4 = 0.02$, and $S = 6300$. Thus, from Eq. (8) we have

$$6300 = Rs_{\overline{32}|0.02},$$

$$R = \frac{6300}{s_{\overline{32}|0.02}} \approx \frac{6300}{44.227030} \approx \$142.45.$$

In general, the formula

$$R = \frac{S}{s_{\overline{n}|r}}$$

gives the periodic payment R of an annuity which is to amount to S.

EXAMPLE 12   *A rental firm estimates that, if purchased, a machine will
yield an annual net return of $1000 for 6 years, after which the machine would
be worthless. How much should the firm pay for the machine if it wants to earn
7% on its investment and also set up a sinking fund to replace the purchase
price. For the fund, assume annual payments and a rate of 5% compounded
annually.*

Let x be the purchase price. Each year the return on the investment is $0.07x$.
Since the machine gives a return of $1000 a year, the amount left to be placed
into the fund each year is $1000 - 0.07x$. These payments must accumulate to x.
Hence

$$(1000 - 0.07x)s_{\overline{6}|0.05} = x,$$

$$1000s_{\overline{6}|0.05} - 0.07xs_{\overline{6}|0.05} = x,$$

$$1000s_{\overline{6}|0.05} = x(1 + 0.07s_{\overline{6}|0.05}),$$

$$\frac{1000s_{\overline{6}|0.05}}{1 + 0.07s_{\overline{6}|0.05}} = x,$$

$$x \approx \frac{1000(6.801913)}{1 + 0.07(6.801913)}$$

$$\approx \$4607.92.$$

Another way to look at the problem is as follows. Each year the $1000 must account for a return of $0.07x$ and also a payment of $\dfrac{x}{s_{\overline{6}|0.05}}$ into the sinking fund.

Hence $1000 = 0.07x + \dfrac{x}{s_{\overline{6}|0.05}}$, which when solved gives the same result.

EXERCISE 6.3

In Problems 1–4, write the geometric sequence satisfying the given conditions. Simplify the terms.

1. $a = 64$, $r = \frac{1}{2}$, $n = 5$.
2. $a = 2$, $r = -3$, $n = 4$.
3. $a = 100$, $r = 1.02$, $n = 3$.
4. $a = 81$, $r = 3^{-1}$, $n = 4$.

In Problems 5–8, find the sum of the given geometric series by using Eq. (4) of this section.

5. $\frac{2}{3} + (\frac{2}{3})^2 + \cdots + (\frac{2}{3})^5$.
6. $1 + \frac{1}{4} + (\frac{1}{4})^2 + \cdots + (\frac{1}{4})^5$.
7. $1 + 0.1 + (0.1)^2 + \cdots + (0.1)^5$.
8. $(1.1)^{-1} + (1.1)^{-2} + \cdots + (1.1)^{-6}$.

In Problems 9–12, use Appendix D and find the value of the given expression.

9. $a_{\overline{35}|0.04}$.
10. $a_{\overline{15}|0.07}$.
11. $s_{\overline{8}|0.0075}$.
12. $s_{\overline{12}|0.005}$.

In Problems 13–16, find the present value of the given (ordinary) annuity.

13. $500 per year for 5 years at the rate of 7% compounded annually.
14. $1000 every 6 months for 4 years at the rate of 10% compounded semiannually.
15. $2000 per quarter for $4\frac{1}{2}$ years at the rate of 8% compounded quarterly.
16. $1500 per month for 15 months at the rate of 9% compounded monthly.

In Problems 17 and 18, find the present value of the given annuity due.

17. $800 paid at the beginning of each 6-month period for 6 years at the rate of 7% compounded semiannually.
18. $100 paid at the beginning of each quarter for 5 years at the rate of 6% compounded quarterly.

In Problems 19–22, find the future value of the given (ordinary) annuity.

19. $2000 per month for 3 years at the rate of 15% compounded monthly.
20. $600 per quarter for 4 years at the rate of 8% compounded quarterly.
21. $5000 per year for 20 years at the rate of 7% compounded annually.
22. $2000 every 6 months for 10 years at the rate of 6% compounded semiannually.

In Problems 23 and 24, find the future value of the given annuity due.

23. $1200 each year for 12 years at the rate of 8% compounded annually.
24. $500 every quarter for $5\frac{3}{4}$ years at the rate of 5% compounded quarterly.

25. For an interest rate of 6% compounded monthly, find the present value of an annuity of $50 at the end of each month for 6 months and $75 thereafter at the end of each month for 2 years.

26. A company wishes to lease temporary office space for a period of 6 months. The rental fee is $500 a month payable in advance. Suppose that the company wants to make a lump-sum payment, at the beginning of the

rental period, to cover all rental fees due over the 6-month period. If money is worth 9% compounded monthly, how much should the payment be?

27. An annuity consisting of equal payments at the end of each quarter for 3 years is to be purchased for $5000. If the interest rate is 6% compounded quarterly, how much is each payment?

28. A machine is purchased for $3000 down and payments of $250 at the end of every 6 months for 6 years. If interest is at 8% compounded semiannually, find the corresponding cash price of the machine.

29. Suppose $50 is placed in a savings account at the end of each month for 4 years. If no further deposits are made, (a) how much is in the account after 6 years and (b) how much of this is compound interest? Assume that the savings account pays 6% compounded monthly.

30. The beneficiary of an insurance policy has the option of receiving a lump-sum payment of $35,000 or 10 equal yearly payments, where the first payment is due at once. If interest is at 4% compounded annually, find the yearly payment.

31. In 10 years a $40,000 machine will have a salvage value of $4000. A new machine at that time is expected to sell for $52,000. In order to provide funds for the difference between the replacement cost and the salvage value, a sinking fund is set up into which equal pay-

ments are placed at the end of each year. If the fund earns 7% compounded annually, how much should each payment be?

32. A paper company is considering the purchase of a forest that is estimated to yield an annual return of $50,000 for 10 years, after which the forest will have no value. The company wants to earn 8% on its investment and also set up a sinking fund to replace the purchase price. If money is placed in the fund at the end of each year and earns 6% compounded annually, find the price the company should pay for the forest. Give your answer to the nearest hundred dollars.

33. In order to replace a machine in the future, a company is placing equal payments into a sinking fund at the end of each year so that after 10 years the amount in the fund is $25,000. The fund earns 6% compounded annually. After 6 years, the interest rate increases and the fund pays 7% compounded annually. Because of the higher interest rate, the company decreases the amount of the remaining payments. Find the amount of the new payment. Give your answer to the nearest dollar.

34. A owes B the sum of $5000 and agress to pay B the sum of $1000 at the end of each year for 5 years and a final payment at the end of the sixth year. How much should the final payment be if interest is at 8% compounded annually?

In Problems **35–41**, use the following formulas.

$$a_{\overline{n}|r} = \frac{1 - (1 + r)^{-n}}{r},$$

$$s_{\overline{n}|r} = \frac{(1 + r)^n - 1}{r},$$

$$R = \frac{A}{a_{\overline{n}|r}} = \frac{Ar}{1 - (1 + r)^{-n}} = \frac{Ar(1 + r)^n}{(1 + r)^n - 1},$$

$$R = \frac{S}{s_{\overline{n}|r}} = \frac{Sr}{(1 + r)^n - 1}.$$

35. *Calculator Problem.* Find $s_{\overline{60}|0.017}$ to five decimal places.

36. *Calculator Problem.* Find $a_{\overline{10}|0.073}$ to five decimal places.

37. *Calculator Problem.* Find $700a_{\overline{360}|0.0125}$ to two decimal places.

38. *Calculator Problem.* Find $1000s_{\overline{120}|0.01}$ to two decimal places.

39. *Calculator Problem.* Equal payments are to be deposited in a savings account at the end of each quarter for 5 years so that at the end of that time there will be $3000. If interest is at $5\frac{1}{2}$% compounded quarterly, find the quarterly payment.

40. *Calculator Problem.* Suppose that insurance proceeds of $25,000 are used to purchase an annuity of equal payments at the end of each month for 5 years. If interest is at the rate of 10% compounded monthly, find the amount of each payment.

41. *Calculator Problem.* Mary Jones wins a state $1,000,000 lottery and will receive a check for $50,000 now and a similar one each year for the next 19 years. To provide these 20 payments, the State Lottery Com- mission purchases an annuity due at the interest rate of 12% compounded annually. How much does the annu- ity cost the Commission?

6.4 AMORTIZATION OF LOANS

Suppose that a bank lends you $1500. This amount plus interest is to be repaid by equal payments of R dollars at the end of each month for 3 months. Further more, let us assume that the bank charges interest at the nominal rate of 12% compounded monthly. Essentially, for $1500 the bank is purchasing an annuity of three payments of R each. Using the formula from Example 7 of the preceding section, we find that the monthly payment R is given by

$$R = \frac{A}{a_{\overline{n}|r}} = \frac{1500}{a_{\overline{3}|0.01}} \approx \frac{1500}{2.940985} \approx \$510.03.$$

The bank can consider each payment as consisting of two parts: (1) interest on the outstanding loan, and (2) repayment of part of the loan. This is called **am- ortizing.** A loan is **amortized** when part of each payment is used to pay interest and the remaining part is used to reduce the outstanding principal. Since each payment reduces the outstanding principal, the interest portion of a payment de- creases as time goes on. Let us analyze the loan described above.

At the end of the first month, you pay $510.03. The interest on the out- standing principal is 0.01(1500) = $15. The balance of the payment, 510.03 − 15 = $495.03, is then applied to reduce the principal. Hence the principal out- standing is now 1500 − 495.03 = $1004.97. At the end of the second month, the interest is 0.01(1004.97) ≈ $10.05. Thus the amount of the loan repaid is 510.03 − 10.05 = $499.98, and the outstanding balance is 1004.97 − 499.98 = $504.99. The interest due at the end of the third and final month is 0.01(504.99) ≈ $5.05, so the amount of the loan repaid is 510.03 − 5.05 = $504.98. Hence the outstanding balance is 504.99 − 504.98 = $0.01. Actually, the debt should now be paid off, and the balance of $0.01 is due to rounding. Of- ten, banks will change the amount of the last payment to offset this. In the case above, the final payment would be $510.04. An analysis of how each payment in the loan is handled can be given in a table called an **amortization schedule** (see Table 6.1).

TABLE 6.1
Amortization Schedule

PERIOD	PRINCIPAL OUTSTANDING AT BEGINNING OF PERIOD	INTEREST FOR PERIOD	PAYMENT AT END OF PERIOD	PRINCIPAL REPAID AT END OF PERIOD
1	$1500	$15	$ 510.03	$ 495.03
2	1004.97	10.05	510.03	499.98
3	504.99	5.05	510.03	504.98
Total		30.10	1530.09	1499.99

The total interest paid is $30.10, which is often called the **finance charge.** As mentioned before, the total of the entries in the last column would equal the original principal were it not for rounding errors.

When one is amortizing a loan, at the beginning of any period the principal outstanding is the present value of the remaining payments. Using this fact together with our previous development, we obtain the formulas listed in Table 6.2 that describe the amortization of an interest-bearing loan of A dollars, at a rate r per period, by n equal payments of R dollars each and such that a payment is made at the end of each period. Notice below that the formula for the periodic payment R involves $a_{\overline{n}|r}$, which, as you recall, is defined as $[1 - (1 + r)^{-n}]/r$.

TABLE 6.2
Amortization Formulas

1. Periodic payment: $R = \dfrac{A}{a_{\overline{n}|r}} = A\dfrac{r}{1 - (1 + r)^{-n}}$

2. Principal outstanding at beginning of kth period:

$$Ra_{\overline{n-k+1}|r} = R\frac{1 - (1 + r)^{-n+k-1}}{r}$$

3. Interest in kth payment: $Rra_{\overline{n-k+1}|r}$

4. Principal contained in kth payment: $R[1 - ra_{\overline{n-k+1}|r}]$

5. Total interest paid: $R(n - a_{\overline{n}|r})$ or $nR - A$

EXAMPLE 1   *Calculator Problem.*

A person amortizes a loan of $30,000 for a new home by obtaining a 20-year mortgage at the rate of 9% compounded monthly. Find (a) the monthly payment, (b) the total interest charges, and (c) the principal remaining after 5 years.

a. The number of payment periods is $n = 12(20) = 240$, the interest rate per period is $r = 0.09/12 = 0.0075$, and $A = 30,000$. From Formula 1 in Table 6.2, the monthly payment R is $30,000/a_{\overline{240}|0.0075}$. Since $a_{\overline{240}|0.0075}$ is not in Appendix D, we use the following equivalent formula and a calculator.

$$R = 30,000\left[\frac{0.0075}{1 - (1.0075)^{-240}}\right]$$

$$\approx 30,000\left[\frac{0.0075}{1 - (0.166413)}\right]$$

$$\approx \$269.92.$$

b. From Formula 5 the total interest charges are

$$240(269.92) - 30,000 = 64,780.80 - 30,000$$

$$= \$34,780.80.$$

This is more than the loan itself.

c. After 5 years we are at the beginning of the 61st period. Using Formula 2 with $n - k + 1 = 240 - 61 + 1 = 180$, we find that the principal remaining is

$$269.92\left[\frac{1 - (1.0075)^{-180}}{0.0075}\right] \approx \$26,612.33.$$

Prior to the 1980s, a very common type of installment loan involved the "add-on method" of determining the finance charge. With that method the finance charge is found by applying a quoted annual interest rate (under simple interest, that is, noncompounded) to the borrowed amount of the loan. The charge is then added to the principal, and the total is divided by the number of *months* of the loan to determine the monthly installment payment. In loans of this type, the borrower may not immediately realize that the true annual rate is significantly higher than the quoted rate, as the next example shows.

EXAMPLE 2   *A $1000 loan is taken for 1 year at 9% interest under the add-on method. Estimate the true annual interest rate if monthly compounding is assumed.*

The finance charge for $1000 at 9% simple interest for 1 year is $0.09(1000) = \$90$. Adding this to the loan amount gives $1000 + 90 = \$1090$. Thus the monthly installment payment is $1090/12 \approx \$90.83$. We thus have a loan of $1000 with 12 equal payments of $90.83. From Formula 1 in Table 6.2 we have

$$R = \frac{A}{a_{\overline{n}|\,r}},$$

$$90.83 = \frac{1000}{a_{\overline{12}|\,r}},$$

$$a_{\overline{12}|\,r} = \frac{1000}{90.83} \approx 11.009578.$$

Solving $a_{\overline{12}|r} = 11.009578$ for the monthly rate r is not so easy to do. Instead, we examine Appendix D along the rows corresponding to $n = 12$ and find that the value 11.009578 lies between the entries $a_{\overline{12}|\,0.0125} = 11.079312$ and $a_{\overline{12}|\,0.015} = 10.907505$. Therefore, r lies between 0.0125 and 0.015, which correspond to annual rates of $12(0.0125) = 0.15$ and $12(0.015) = 0.18$. Thus the true annual rate lies between 15 and 18% (and is actually 16.22%). Federal regulations concerning truth-in-lending laws have made add-on loans virtually obsolete.

The annuity formula

$$A = R\frac{1 - (1 + r)^{-n}}{r}$$

can be solved for n to give the number of periods of a loan. Multiplying both sides by $\dfrac{r}{R}$ gives

$$\frac{Ar}{R} = 1 - (1 + r)^{-n},$$

$$(1 + r)^{-n} = 1 - \frac{Ar}{R} = \frac{R - Ar}{R},$$

$$-n \ln(1 + r) = \ln\left(\frac{R - Ar}{R}\right) \qquad \text{(taking logs of both sides),}$$

$$n = -\frac{\ln\left(\dfrac{R - Ar}{R}\right)}{\ln(1 + r)}.$$

Using properties of logarithms, we eliminate the minus sign by inverting the quotient in the numerator.

$$n = \frac{\ln\left(\dfrac{R}{R - Ar}\right)}{\ln(1 + r)}. \tag{1}$$

EXAMPLE 3   *Mr. Smith purchases a stereo system for $1500 and agrees to pay it off by monthly payments of $75. If the store charges interest at the rate of 12% compounded monthly, how many months will it take to pay off the debt?*

From Eq. (1),

$$n = \frac{\ln\left[\dfrac{75}{75 - 1500(0.01)}\right]}{\ln(1.01)}$$

$$= \frac{\ln(1.25)}{\ln(1.01)} \approx \frac{0.22314}{0.00995} \approx 22.4 \text{ months.}$$

In reality there will be 23 payments; however, the final payment will be less than $75.

EXERCISE 6.4

1. A person borrows $2000 from a bank and agrees to pay it off by equal payments at the end of each month for 3 years. If interest is at 15% compounded monthly, how much is each payment?

2. A person wishes to make a 3-year loan and can afford payments of $50 at the end of each month. If interest is at 12% compounded monthly, how much can the person afford to borrow?

3. Determine the finance charge on a 36-month $8000 auto loan with monthly payments if interest is at the rate of 12% compounded monthly.

4. For a 1-year loan of $500 at the rate of 15% compounded monthly, find (a) the monthly installment payment and (b) the finance charge.

5. A person is amortizing a 36-month car loan of $7500 with interest at the rate of 12% compounded monthly.

Find (a) the monthly payment, (b) the interest in the first month, and (c) the principal repaid in the first payment.

6. A person is amortizing a 48-month loan of $10,000 for a house lot. If interest is at the rate of 9% compounded monthly, find (a) the monthly payment, (b) the interest in the first payment, and (c) the principal repaid in the first payment.

In Problems 7–10, construct an amortization schedule for the indicated debts.

7. $5000 repaid by four equal yearly payments with interest at 7% compounded annually.

8. $8000 repaid by six equal semiannual payments with interest at 8% compounded semiannually.

9. $900 repaid by five equal quarterly payments with interest at 10% compounded quarterly.

10. $10,000 repaid by five equal monthly payments with interest at 9% compounded monthly.

11. A loan of $1000 is being paid off by quarterly payments of $100. If interest is at the rate of 8% compounded quarterly, how many *full* payments will be made?

12. A loan of $2000 is being amortized over 48 months at an interest rate of 12% compounded monthly. Find:
   a. the monthly payment;
   b. the principal outstanding at the beginning of the 36th month;
   c. the interest in the 36th payment;
   d. the principal in the 36th payment;
   e. the total interest paid.

13. A debt of $10,000 is being repaid by 10 equal semiannual payments with the first payment to be made 6 months from now. Interest is at the rate of 8% compounded semiannually. However, after 2 years the interest rate increases to 10% compounded semiannually. If the debt must be paid off on the original date agreed upon, find the new annual payment. Give your answer to the nearest dollar.

14. *Calculator Problem.* A person borrows $2000 and will pay off the loan by equal payments at the end of each month for 5 years. If interest is at the rate of 16.8% compounded monthly, how much is each payment?

15. *Calculator Problem.* A $45,000 mortgage for 25 years for a new home is obtained at the rate of 10.2% compounded monthly. Find (a) the monthly payment, (b) the interest in the first payment, (c) the principal repaid in the first payment, and (d) the finance charge.

16. *Calculator Problem.* An automobile loan of $8500 is to be amortized over 48 months at an interest rate of 13.2% compounded monthly. Find (a) the monthly payment and (b) the finance charge.

17. *Calculator Problem.* A person purchases furniture for $2000 and agrees to pay off this amount by monthly payments of $100. If interest is charged at the rate of 18% compounded monthly, how many *full* payments will there be?

18. *Calculator Problem.* Find the monthly payment of a 5-year loan for $7000 if interest is at 12.12% compounded monthly.

19. *Calculator Problem.* Bob and Mary Rodgers want to purchase a new house and feel that they can afford a mortgage payment of $600 a month. They are able to obtain a 30-year 12.6% mortgage (compounded monthly), but must put down 25% of the cost of the house. Assuming they have enough savings for the down payment, how expensive a house can they afford? Give your answer to the nearest dollar.

20. *Calculator Problem.* Suppose you have the choice of taking out an $80,000 mortgage at 12% compounded monthly for either 15 years or 30 years. How much savings is there in the finance charge if you were to choose the 15-year mortgage?

21. *Calculator Problem.* On a $25,000 five-year loan, how much less is the monthly payment if the loan were at the rate of 12% compounded monthly rather than at 15% compounded monthly?

6.5 REVIEW

Important Terms and Symbols

Section 6.1   compound interest   principal   compound amount   interest period   conversion period
periodic rate   nominal rate   effective rate

Section 6.2   present value   future value   equation of value   cash flows   net present value

Section 6.3   geometric sequence   geometric series   common ratio   annuity   ordinary annuity
annuity due   present value of annuity, $a_{\overline{n}|r}$ amount of annuity, $s_{\overline{n}|r}$

Section 6.4   amortizing   amortization schedule   finance charge

Summary

The concept of compound interest lies at the heart of any discussion dealing with the time value of money, that is, the present value of money due in the future or the future value of money presently invested. Under compound interest, interest is converted into principal and earns interest itself. The basic compound interest formulas are:

$$S = P(1 + r)^n \quad \text{(future value)},$$

$$P = S(1 + r)^{-n} \quad \text{(present value)},$$

where S = compound amount (future value),

P = principal (present value),

r = periodic rate,

n = number of conversion periods.

Interest rates are usually quoted as an annual rate called the nominal rate. The periodic rate is obtained by dividing the nominal rate by the number of conversion periods each year. The effective rate is the annual simple interest rate that is equivalent to the nominal rate of r compounded n times a year and is given by

$$\left(1 + \frac{r}{n}\right)^n - 1 \quad \text{(effective rate)}.$$

Effective rates are used to compare different interest rates.

An annuity is a sequence of payments made at fixed periods of time over some time interval. The mathematical basis for the formulas dealing with annuities is the notion of the sum of a geometric series:

$$s = \frac{a(1 - r^n)}{1 - r} \quad \text{(sum of geometric series)},$$

where s = sum,
a = first term,
r = common ratio,
n = number of terms.

An ordinary annuity is one in which each payment is made at the *end* of a payment period, while an annuity due is one in which each payment is made at the *beginning* of a payment period. The basic formulas dealing with ordinary annuities are:

$$A = R\frac{1 - (1 + r)^{-n}}{r} = Ra_{\overline{n}|r} \qquad \text{(present value)},$$

$$S = R\frac{(1 + r)^n - 1}{r} = Rs_{\overline{n}|r} \qquad \text{(future value)},$$

where $A =$ present value of annuity,

$S =$ amount (future value) of annuity,

$R =$ amount of each payment,

$n =$ number of payment periods,

$r =$ periodic rate.

For an annuity due the corresponding formulas are:

$$A = R(1 + a_{\overline{n-1}|r}) \qquad \text{(present value)},$$

$$S = R(s_{\overline{n+1}|r} - 1) \qquad \text{(future value)}.$$

A loan, such as a mortgage, is amortized when part of each installment payment is used to pay interest and the remaining part is used to reduce the principal. A complete analysis of each payment is given in an amortization schedule. The following formulas deal with amortizing a loan of A dollars, at the periodic rate of r, by n equal payments of R dollars each and such that a payment is made at the end of each period.

Periodic payment: $R = \dfrac{A}{a_{\overline{n}|r}} = A\dfrac{r}{1 - (1 + r)^{-n}}.$

Principal outstanding at beginning of kth period:

$$Ra_{\overline{n-k+1}|r} = R\frac{1 - (1 + r)^{-n+k-1}}{r}.$$

Interest in kth payment: $Rra_{\overline{n-k+1}|r}.$

Principal contained in kth payment: $R[1 - ra_{\overline{n-k+1}|r}].$

Total interest paid: $R(n - a_{\overline{n}|r})$ or $nR - A.$

Review Problems

1. Find the sum of the geometric series

$$2 + \tfrac{1}{2} + \tfrac{1}{8} + \cdots + 2(\tfrac{1}{4})^5.$$

2. Find the nominal rate that corresponds to a periodic rate of $1\tfrac{1}{6}\%$ per month.

3. If \$2600 is invested for $6\tfrac{1}{2}$ years at 6% compounded quarterly, find (a) the compound amount and (b) the compound interest.

4. Find the effective rate that corresponds to a nominal rate of 6% compounded quarterly.

5. An investor has a choice of investing a sum of money at either 8.5% compounded annually or 8.2% compounded semiannually. Which is the better choice?

6. Find the net present value of the following cash flows, which can be purchased by an initial investment of \$7000. Assume that interest is at 7% compounded semiannually.

YEAR	CASH FLOW
2	$3400
4	3500

7. A debt of $1200 due in 4 years and $1000 due in 6 years is to be repaid by a payment of $1000 now and a second payment at the end of 2 years. How much should the second payment be if interest is at 8% compounded semiannually?

8. Find the present value of an annuity of $250 at the end of each month for 4 years if interest is at 6% compounded monthly.

9. For an annuity of $200 at the end of every 6 months for $6\frac{1}{2}$ years, find (a) the present value and (b) the future value at an interest rate of 8% compounded semiannually.

10. Find the amount of an annuity due which consists of 10 yearly payments of $100 provided that the interest rate is 6% compounded annually.

11. Suppose $100 is initially placed in a savings account and $100 is deposited at the end of every 6 months for the next 4 years. If interest is at 7% compounded semiannually, how much is in the account at the end of 4 years?

12. A savings account pays interest at the rate of 5% compounded semiannually. What amount must be deposited now so that $250 can be withdrawn at the end of every 6 months for the next 10 years?

13. A company borrows $5000 on which it will pay interest at the end of each year at the annual rate of 11%. In addition, a sinking fund is set up so that the loan can be repaid at the end of 5 years. Equal payments are placed in the fund at the end of each year, and the fund earns interest at the effective rate of 6%. Find the annual payment in the *sinking fund*.

14. A debtor is to amortize a $7000 car loan by making equal payments at the end of each month for 36 months. If interest is at 12% compounded monthly, find (a) the amount of each payment and (b) the finance charge.

15. A person has debts of $500 due in 3 years with interest at 5% compounded annually, and $500 due in 4 years with interest at 6% compounded semiannually. The debtor wants to pay off these debts by making two payments: the first payment now, and the second, which is double the first payment, at the end of the third year. If money is worth 7% compounded annually, how much is the first payment?

16. Construct an amortization schedule for a loan of $2000 repaid by three monthly payments with interest at 12% compounded monthly.

17. Construct an amortization schedule for a loan of $15,000 repaid by five monthly payments with interest at 9% compounded monthly.

18. *Calculator Problem*. Find the compound amount of an investment of $4000 for 5 years at the rate of 11% compounded monthly.

19. *Calculator Problem*. Find the present value of an ordinary annuity of $540 every month for 7 years at the rate of 10% compounded monthly.

20. *Calculator Problem*. Determine the finance charge for a 48-month auto loan for $11,000 with monthly payments at the rate of 13.5% compounded monthly.

7

Introduction to Probability

The term *probability* is familiar to most of us. It is not uncommon to hear such phrases as "the probability of precipitation," "the probability of flooding," and "the probability of receiving an A in a course." Loosely speaking, probability refers to a number that indicates the degree of likelihood that some future event will have a particular outcome. For example, before tossing a well-balanced coin, you do not know with certainty whether a head or a tail will show. However, if the coin were tossed a large number of times, approximately half of the tosses would give heads. Thus we say that the probability that a head occurs on any toss is $\frac{1}{2}$ or 50%. In this chapter we shall be concerned with the fundamentals of probability. Section 7.1 will involve some counting principles.

7.1 PERMUTATIONS AND COMBINATIONS

Some problems in probability are simplified if we have some efficient methods of counting the objects in a set. To this end, we shall consider some counting principles.

Suppose a manufacturer wants to produce coffee brewers in 2-, 8-, and 10-cup capacities, with each capacity available in the colors of white, beige, red, and green. How many types of coffee brewers must the manufacturer produce? Since there are four colors for each capacity, and there are three capacities, the number of types is the product $3 \cdot 4$, or 12. We can systematically list the different types by using a **tree diagram,** as illustrated in Fig. 7.1. From the starting point, there are three branches that indicate the possible capacities. From each of these branches are four more branches that indicate the possible colors. This tree determines 12 paths, each beginning at the starting point and ending at a tip. Each path determines a type of coffee brewer.

Tree Diagram

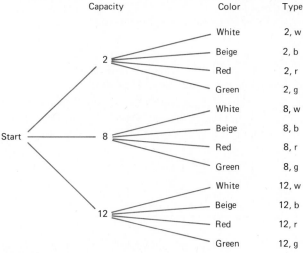

FIGURE 7.1

We can view the listing of the types of coffee brewers as a procedure that involves a sequence of two processes. In the first process we indicate a capacity, and in the second we indicate the color. The number of types of coffee brewers is the number of ways the first process can occur (3), times the number of ways the second process can occur (4), which yields $3 \cdot 4 = 12$. This multiplication procedure can be generalized into a basic counting principle.

BASIC COUNTING PRINCIPLE

Suppose that a procedure involves a sequence of k processes. Let n_1 be the number of ways the first can occur and n_2 be the number of ways the second can occur after the first process has occurred. Continuing in this way, let n_k be the number of ways the kth process can occur after the first $k - 1$ processes have occurred. Then the total number of ways the procedure can occur is $n_1 \cdot n_2 \cdots n_k$.

EXAMPLE 1   *Two roads connect cities* A *and* B, *four roads connect* B *and* C, *and five roads connect cities* C *and* D. *To drive from* A, *to* B, *to* C, *and then to city* D, *how many different routes are possible?*

To select a route we must first choose one of the two roads from A to B. Then we choose one of the four roads from B to C. Finally, we choose one of the five roads from C to D. By the basic counting principle, the total number of routes is $2 \cdot 4 \cdot 5 = 40$.

EXAMPLE 2   *Using all of the letters a, b, and c, how many horizontal arrangements are possible if no repetition of letters is allowed?*

Two possible arrangements are

$$abc \quad \text{and} \quad bca.$$

To form an arrangement, there are three choices for the first letter; after that letter is chosen, there are two choices for the second letter; after the second letter is chosen, there remains only one letter for the third position. By the basic counting principle, the total number of arrangements is $3 \cdot 2 \cdot 1 = 6$. The six arrangements are

$$abc, \quad acb,$$
$$bac, \quad bca,$$
$$cab, \quad cba.$$

In Example 2 we were concerned with arranging the letters a, b, and c in an order (that is, there was a first letter, a second letter, and a third letter), and no letter was repeated. Such an arrangement is called a *permutation*.

Definition

*An ordered arrangement of n distinct objects without repetition is called a **permutation** of the objects.*

From Example 2 we conclude that the number of permutations of three objects is $3 \cdot 2 \cdot 1$, or, in factorial notation,* $3!$. Similarly, the number of permutations of 5 objects is $5 \cdot 4 \cdot 3 \cdot 2 \cdot 1$, or $5!$. In general, we have the following result.

> The number of permutations of n objects is $n!$

If we select three letters from the five letters a, b, c, d, and e, and arrange them in an order, the result is called a *permutation of the five letters taken three at a time*. Two examples are

$$ade \quad \text{and} \quad cab.$$

Definition

*An ordered arrangement of r objects selected from n objects is called a **permutation of n objects taken r at a time**. The number of such permutations is denoted $P_{n,r}$.*

* Factorials are discussed in Example 5 of Sec. 3.2.

It is easy to determine $P_{n,r}$. In selecting an ordered arrangement of n objects taken r at a time, for the first item we may choose any one of the n objects (see Fig. 7.2). After the first item is selected, there are $n - 1$ objects that may be

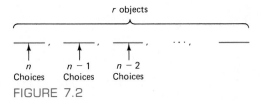

FIGURE 7.2

chosen for the second item in the arrangement. After the second item is selected, there are $n - 2$ objects that may be chosen for the third item. By continuing in this way and by using the basic counting principle, we have

$$P_{n,r} = \underbrace{n(n - 1)(n - 2) \cdots}_{r \text{ factors}} \qquad (1)$$

We can express the formula for $P_{n,r}$ in another way. It can be shown that the last factor in Eq. (1) is $n - r + 1$. Thus

$$P_{n,r} = n(n - 1)(n - 2) \cdots (n - r + 1). \qquad (2)$$

Multiplying the right side of Eq. (2) by

$$\frac{(n - r)(n - r - 1) \cdots 1}{(n - r)(n - r - 1) \cdots 1}$$

gives

$$P_{n,r} = \frac{n(n - 1)(n - 2) \cdots (n - r + 1) \cdot (n - r)(n - r - 1) \cdots 1}{(n - r)(n - r - 1) \cdots 1}.$$

The numerator is simply $n!$ and the denominator is $(n - r)!$ Thus

$$P_{n,r} = \frac{n!}{(n - r)!}. \qquad (3)$$

EXAMPLE 3   *A club has 20 members. The offices of president, vice president, secretary, and treasurer are to be filled and no member may serve in two offices. How many different slates of candidates are possible?*

We shall consider a slate in the order of president, vice president, secretary, and treasurer. Any ordered arrangement of four members constitutes a slate, so the number of possible slates is $P_{20,4}$. By Eq. (1),

$$P_{20,4} = 20 \cdot 19 \cdot 18 \cdot 17 = 116{,}280.$$

Alternatively, using Eq. (3) gives

$$P_{20,4} = \frac{20!}{(20-4)!} = \frac{20!}{16!} = \frac{20 \cdot 19 \cdot 18 \cdot 17 \cdot 16!}{16!}$$

$$= 20 \cdot 19 \cdot 18 \cdot 17 = 116{,}280.$$

Note the large number of slates that are possible!

In Example 3, suppose members A, B, C, and D were chosen for a slate of president, vice president, secretary, and treasurer, respectively. We can represent this slate by

ABCD.

A different slate is

BACD.

Now, instead of considering slates of candidates, suppose we consider four-person committees that may be formed from the 20 members. Then

ABCD   and   BACD

represent the *same* committee. Here the order of listing the members is of no concern. Such arrangements are called *combinations*.

Definition

An arrangement of r objects, without regard to order and without repetition, selected from n distinct objects is called a **combination of n objects taken r at a time.** *The number of such combinations is denoted $C_{n,r}$.*

EXAMPLE 4   *List all combinations and all permutations of*

a,   b,   c,   and   d

taken three at a time.

The combinations of a, b, c, and d taken three at a time are

abc,   abd,   acd,   bcd.

There are four combinations and thus $C_{4,3} = 4$.

The permutations of a, b, c, and d taken three at a time are

abc,   abd,   acd,   bcd,

acb,   adb,   adc,   bdc,

bac,   bad,   cad,   cbd,

bca,   bda,   cda,   cdb,
cab,   dab,   dac,   dbc,
cba,   dba,   dca,   dcb.

In Example 4, notice that the permutations of four objects taken three at a time may be found by considering all of the permutations of each combination. Each column gives the permutations for a particular combination. With this observation we can determine a formula for $C_{n,r}$—the number of combinations of n objects taken r at a time. Suppose one such combination is

$$x_1 \, x_2 \, . \, . \, . \, x_r.$$

The number of permutations of these r objects is $r!$. If we listed all other such combinations, and then listed all permutations of these combinations, we would obtain a complete list of permutations of the n objects taken r at a time. Thus

$$C_{n,r} \cdot r! = P_{n,r}.$$

Solving for $C_{n,r}$ gives

$$C_{n,r} = \frac{P_{n,r}}{r!}$$

$$= \frac{n!/(n-r)!}{r!} \qquad \text{[by Eq. (3)]}.$$

Therefore,

$$C_{n,r} = \frac{n!}{r!(n-r)!}.$$

EXAMPLE 5   *From an ordinary deck of 52 playing cards, a five-card hand is dealt. How many hands are possible?*

One possible hand is

2 of hearts,   3 of diamonds,   6 of clubs,
4 of spades,   king of hearts,

which we can abbreviate as

2H,   3D,   6C,   4S,   KH.

The order in which the cards are dealt does not matter, so the hand above is the same as

KH,   4S,   6C,   3D,   2H.

Thus to find the number of possible hands, we can find the number of ways that five cards can be selected from 52, without regard to order. That is, we have a combination problem and want to find $C_{52,5}$.

$$C_{52,5} = \frac{52!}{5!(52 - 5)!} = \frac{52!}{5!47!}$$

$$= \frac{52 \cdot 51 \cdot 50 \cdot 49 \cdot 48 \cdot 47!}{5 \cdot 4 \cdot 3 \cdot 2 \cdot 1 \cdot 47!}$$

$$= \frac{52 \cdot 51 \cdot 50 \cdot 49 \cdot 48}{5 \cdot 4 \cdot 3 \cdot 2} = 2,598,960.$$

It is important to remember that if a selection of objects is made and *order is important,* then *permutations* should be considered. If *order is not important,* consider *combinations.*

EXAMPLE 6   *A promotion committee at a college consists of five members. In how many ways can the committee reach a majority decision?*

A majority decision is reached if, and only if,

exactly three members vote the same way,

or   exactly four members vote the same way,

or   all five members vote the same way.

To determine the total number of ways to reach a majority decision, we *add* the number of ways that each of the votes above can occur.

Suppose exactly three members vote the same way. The order of the members is of no concern and thus we can think of these members as forming a combination. Hence the number of ways three of the five members can have the same vote is $C_{5,3}$. Similarly, the number of ways exactly four members can have the same vote is $C_{5,4}$, and the number of ways all five members can have the same vote is $C_{5,5}$ (which, of course, is 1). Adding $C_{5,3}$, $C_{5,4}$, and $C_{5,5}$ gives the number of ways to reach a majority decision:

$$C_{5,3} + C_{5,4} + C_{5,5} = \frac{5!}{3!(5 - 3)!} + \frac{5!}{4!(5 - 4)!} + \frac{5!}{5!(5 - 5)!}$$

$$= \frac{5!}{3!2!} + \frac{5!}{4!1!} + \frac{5!}{5!0!}$$

$$= \frac{5 \cdot 4 \cdot 3!}{3! \cdot 2 \cdot 1} + \frac{5 \cdot 4!}{4! \cdot 1} + 1$$

$$= 10 + 5 + 1 = 16.$$

EXAMPLE 7   *A politician sends a questionnaire to his constituents to determine their concerns about unemployment,*

environment,

taxes,

interest rates,

national defense,

and   social security.

A respondent is to select four categories of concern and place the numbers 1, 2, 3, or 4 after each selected category to indicate the degree of concern, with 1 indicating the greatest concern and 4 the least. In how many ways can a respondent reply to the questionnaire?

A respondent is to rank four of the six categories. Thus we can consider a reply as an ordered arrangement of six items taken four at a time, where the first item is the category with rank 1, the second is the category with rank 2, and so on. Hence we have a permutation problem and the number of possible replies is $P_{6,4}$.

$$P_{6,4} = \frac{6!}{(6-4)!} = \frac{6!}{2!} = \frac{6 \cdot 5 \cdot 4 \cdot 3 \cdot 2!}{2!}$$

$$= 6 \cdot 5 \cdot 4 \cdot 3 = 360.$$

EXAMPLE 8   *When a coin is tossed, a head* (H) *or a tail* (T) *may show. If a die is rolled, a 1, 2, 3, 4, 5, or 6 may show. Suppose a coin is tossed twice and then a die is rolled, and the results are observed. How many different results can occur?*

Tossing a coin twice and then rolling a die can be considered as a sequence of three processes. Each of the first two processes (tossing the coin) has two possible outcomes. The third process (rolling the die) has six possible outcomes. By the basic counting principle, the number of different results for the procedure is

$$2 \cdot 2 \cdot 6 = 24.$$

EXERCISE 7.1

1. In a production process, a product goes through one of the assembly lines A, B, or C, and then goes through one of the finishing lines D or E. Draw a tree diagram that indicates the possible production routes for a unit of the product.

2. A die is rolled and then a coin is tossed. Draw a tree diagram to indicate the possible results.

*In Problems **3–10**, determine the values.*

3. $P_{5,2}$.

4. $P_{100,1}$.

5. $P_{6,6}$.

6. $P_{9,4}$.

7. $C_{6,4}$.

8. $C_{6,2}$.

9. $C_{100,100}$.

10. $P_{3,2} \cdot C_{3,2}$.

11. Show that $C_{n,r} = C_{n,n-r}$.

12. Determine $P_{n,n}$.

13. A student must take a science course and a humanities course. The science courses that are available are biology, chemistry, physics, computer science, and mathematics. The courses available in the humanities are English, history, speech communications, and classics. For the two courses, the student has how many selections?

14. A person lives in city A and commutes by automobile to city B. There are four roads connecting A and B. (a) How many routes are possible for a round trip? (b) How many routes are possible if a different road is to be used for the return trip?

15. At a restaurant a complete dinner consists of an appetizer, an entrée, a dessert, and a beverage. For the appetizer, the choices are soup or juice; for the entrée, the choices are chicken, fish, steak, or lamb; for the dessert, the choices are cherries jubilee, fresh peach cobbler, chocolate truffle cake, or blueberry rolypoly; for the beverage, the choices are coffee, tea, or milk. How many complete dinners are possible?

16. In how many ways is it possible to answer a six-question multiple-choice examination if each question has four choices and one choice is selected for each question?

17. In how many ways is it possible to answer a 10-question true-false examination?

18. If a softball league has seven teams, how many different end-of-the-season rankings are possible? Assume that there are no ties.

19. For a contest, in how many ways can a judge award first, second, and third prizes if there are eight contestants?

20. A coin is tossed four times. How many results are possible if the order of the tosses is considered?

21. A die is rolled three times. How many results are possible if the order of the rolls is considered?

22. In how many ways can a five-member committee be formed from a group of 15 people?

23. In how many ways can five of seven books be arranged on a bookshelf? In how many ways can all seven books be arranged on the shelf?

24. In a merchandise catalog, a blanket is available in the colors of blue, pink, yellow, and beige. When placing an order, a first and a second choice for color are to be indicated. In how many ways can this be done?

25. On a 12-question mathematics examination, a student must answer any 10 questions. In how many ways can the 10 questions be chosen (without regard to order)?

26. In a horserace, a horse is said to finish in the money if it finishes in first, second, or third place. For an eight-horse race, in how many ways can the horses finish in the money? Assume no ties.

27. A company must hire two workers for the assembly department. If there are 10 equally qualified applicants for the jobs, in how many ways can the company fill the positions?

28. From a deck of 52 playing cards, in how many ways can a three-card hand be dealt?

29. On a 10-question examination, each question is worth 10 points and is graded right or wrong. Considering the individual questions, in how many ways can a student score 80 or better?

30. A lecture hall has five doors. (a) In how many ways can a student enter the hall by one door and exit by a different door? (b) Exit by any door?

31. A poker hand consists of five cards from a deck of 52 playing cards. The hand is called "four of a kind" if four of the cards have the same face value. For example, hands with four 10's or four jacks or four 2's are four of a kind hands. How many such hands are possible?

32. Suppose a fraternity is named by three Greek letters. (There are 24 letters in the Greek alphabet.) (a) How many names are possible? (b) How many names are possible if no letter can be used more than one time?

33. A club has 12 members. In how many ways can the offices of president, vice president, secretary, and treasurer be filled if no member can serve in two offices? In how many ways can the offices be filled if the president and vice president must be different members?

34. The director of research and development for a company has eight scientists that are equally qualified to work on project A or project B. In how many ways can the director assign four scientists to each project?

35. Four colored flags, red, green, yellow, and blue, when arranged vertically on a flagpole indicate a signal (or message). Different arrangements give different signals. (a) How many different signals are possible if all four flags are used? (b) How many different signals are possible if at least one flag is used?

36. In how many ways can a baseball manager assign positions to his nine-member team if two of the players are qualified to pitch and all are qualified at all other positions?

37. A manufacturer places a five-symbol code on each unit of product. The code consists of a letter followed by four numbers, the first of which is not 0. How many codes are possible?

38. In how many ways can three men and two women line up for a group photograph? In how many ways can they line up if a woman is to be at each end?

39. A financial advisor wants to create a portfolio consisting of eight stocks and four bonds. If 12 stocks and seven bonds are acceptable for the portfolio, in how many ways can the portfolio be created?

40. A personnel director of a company must hire five people; three will work in the assembly department and two will work in the shipping department. There are 10 applicants and each is qualified to work in each department. In how many ways can the personnel director fill the positions?

7.2 SAMPLE SPACES AND EVENTS

Inherent in any discussion of probability is the performance of an *experiment* involving chance. By an experiment we mean a procedure whose results, or *outcomes,* are clearly defined. For example, rolling two dice and observing the numbers that turn up (on the top faces) is an experiment. Another experiment is drawing one card at random from an ordinary deck of 52 playing cards (and observing what card it is).

Consider the experiment of tossing a coin and observing whether it lands heads upward (H) or lands tails upward (T). (We assume that the coin does not land on an edge.) The actual outcome is determined by chance. We can write the set of all possible outcomes as

$$\{H, T\},$$

which is called the *sample space* for this experiment. The elements H and T are called *sample points*.

Definition
*The **sample space** S of an experiment is the set of all possible outcomes of the experiment. The elements of the sample space are called **sample points**. A sample space with a finite number of sample points is called a **finite sample space**.*

EXAMPLE 1   *A die is rolled and the number that turns up is observed. Determine the sample space of this experiment.*

The only possible outcomes are that 1, 2, 3, 4, 5, or 6 turns up. Thus the sample space is

$$S = \{1, 2, 3, 4, 5, 6\}.$$

EXAMPLE 2   *Two coins are tossed and the result (H or T) for each coin is observed. Determine the sample space.*

One possible outcome is H on the first coin and H on the second coin. We can indicate this sample point by the ordered pair (H, H) or, more simply, by HH. Another outcome is a head on the first coin and a tail on the second, HT, and so on. The sample space is

$$S = \{HH, HT, TH, TT\}.$$

A tree diagram is given in Fig. 7.3. We remark that this experiment of tossing two coins gives the same sample space as does the experiment of tossing a single coin twice in succession. In fact, these two experiments can be considered as being one in the same.

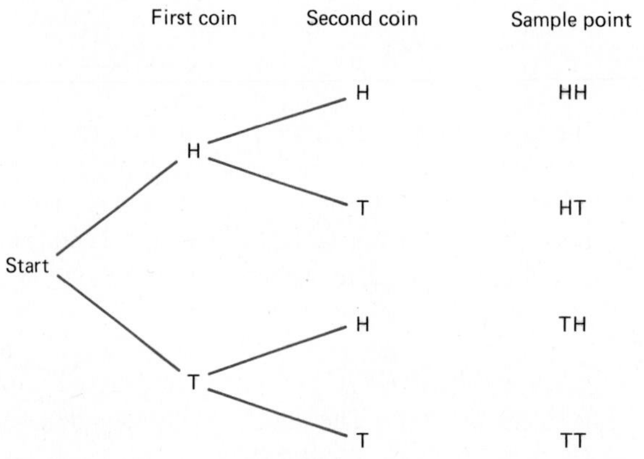

FIGURE 7.3

EXAMPLE 3   *A coin is tossed three times and the result of each toss is observed. Determine the number of points in the sample space and then give the sample space.*

On each toss there are two possible ways the coin can fall (H or T), and the result of one toss does not affect the result of another toss. Because three tosses are involved, by the basic counting principle the total number of sample points is $2 \cdot 2 \cdot 2 = 2^3 = 8$. The sample space is

$$S = \{HHH, HHT, HTH, HTT, THH, THT, TTH, TTT\}.$$

A tree diagram appears in Fig. 7.4.

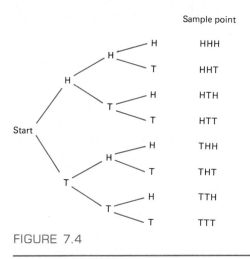

FIGURE 7.4

EXAMPLE 4   *An urn contains four colored marbles: one red, one white, one blue, and one yellow.*

a. *A marble is selected at random and its color is noted. After the marble is replaced in the urn, a second marble is selected at random and its color noted. Determine the number of sample points in the sample space.*

In this experiment we say that two marbles are drawn from the urn in succession **with replacement.** Let R, W, B, and Y denote drawing red, white, blue, and yellow marbles, respectively. We can represent, for example, the selection of a red and then a white marble by RW. The sample points are RW, RB, WR, WW, and so on. For the first selection there are four possibilities: R, W, B, or Y. Since the first marble is replaced in the urn, there are also four possibilities for the second selection. By the basic counting principle, the number of sample points is $4 \cdot 4 = 16$.

b. *Determine the number of sample points in the sample space if two marbles are selected in succession **without replacement** and the colors are noted.*

The first marble drawn can be any of four colors. Since it is *not* returned to the urn, the second marble drawn can have any of the *three* colors that remain. Thus the number of sample points is $4 \cdot 3 = 12$. Alternatively, the number of sample points is $P_{4,2} = 12$.

EXAMPLE 5   *From a deck of 52 playing cards a five-card hand (a poker hand) is dealt. Determine the number of sample points in the sample space.*

From Example 5 of Sec. 7.1, the number of sample points is $C_{52,5} = 2,598,960$.

EXAMPLE 6   *Two dice are rolled once and the numbers that turn up are observed. Determine the number of points in the sample space.*

Think of the dice as being distinguishable, as if one were red and the other green. Then the outcome of 2 on one die and 3 on the other, (2, 3), is different from the outcome (3, 2). Since each die can turn up in six ways, by the basic counting principle there are a total of $6 \cdot 6 = 36$ outcomes.

At times we are concerned with those outcomes of an experiment that satisfy a particular relationship. For example, we may be interested in whether the outcome of tossing a die is an even number—that is 2, 4, or 6. This relationship can be considered to be the set of outcomes {2, 4, 6}, which is a subset of the sample space {1, 2, 3, 4, 5, 6}. In general, any subset of a sample space is called an *event* for the experiment. Thus

{2, 4, 6} is the event that an even number appears,

which can also be described by

{an even number appears}.

Note that although an event is a set, it can be described verbally. Usually, an event is denoted by E: when several events are involved in a discussion they may be denoted by E_1, E_2, E_3, and so on.

Definition
*Any subset E of the sample space of an experiment is called an **event** for the experiment. If the outcome of the experiment is a sample point in E, then event E is said to **occur.***

For the experiment of rolling a die, the sample space is $S = \{1, 2, 3, 4, 5, 6\}$. We saw that {2, 4, 6} is an event. Thus if a 2 shows, the event {2, 4, 6} occurs. Some other events are

$$E_1 = \{1, 3, 5\} = \{\text{an odd number shows}\},$$

$$E_2 = \{3, 4, 5, 6\} = \{\text{a number} \geq 3 \text{ shows}\},$$

$$E_3 = \{1\} = \{1 \text{ shows}\}.$$

An event, such as E_3, that consists of a single outcome of an experiment is called a **simple event.** Moreover, because the sample space S is a subset of itself, S is an event called the **certain event.** It must occur no matter what the outcome. We can also consider an event such as "7 appears." Because no outcome meets this condition, this event is the empty set $\varnothing$ (the set with no elements in it). Sometimes $\varnothing$ is called the **impossible event** because it can never occur.

EXAMPLE 7   *A coin is tossed three times and the result of each toss is observed. Determine the following events.*

a. $E_1 = \{$one head and two tails$\}$.

$$E_1 = \{HTT, THT, TTH\}.$$

b. $E_2 = \{$at least two heads$\}$.

$$E_2 = \{HHT, HTH, THH, HHH\}.$$

c. $E_3 = \{$all heads$\}$.

$$E_3 = \{HHH\}.$$

d. $E_4 = \{$head on first toss$\}$.

$$E_4 = \{HHT, HHH, HTH, HTT\}.$$

Sometimes it is convenient to represent the sample space S and an event E for an experiment by a *Venn diagram*, as in Fig. 7.5. The points inside the rectangle represent the sample points in S. (The sample points are not specifically shown.) The sample points in E are represented by the points inside the circle. Because E is a subset of S, the circular region cannot extend outside the rectangle.

With Venn diagrams it is easy to see how events for an experiment can be used to form other events. Figure 7.6 shows sample space S and event E. The

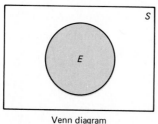

Venn diagram
FIGURE 7.5

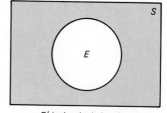

E' is the shaded region
FIGURE 7.6

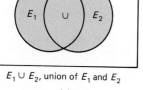

$E_1 \cup E_2$, union of E_1 and E_2

(a)

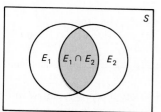

$E_1 \cap E_2$, intersection of E_1 and E_2

(b)

FIGURE 7.7

shaded region represents the set of all sample points in S that are not in E. This set is an event called the *complement of E* and denoted by E'. Figure 7.7(a) shows two events, E_1 and E_2. The shaded region represents the set of all sample points either in E_1, or in E_2, or in both E_1 and E_2. This set is an event called the *union of E_1 and E_2* and denoted by $E_1 \cup E_2$. The shaded region in Fig. 7.7(b) represents the event that consists of all sample points that are common to both E_1 and E_2. This event is called the *intersection of E_1 and E_2* and is denoted by $E_1 \cap E_2$. In summary, we have the following definitions.

Definition

Let S be the sample space of an experiment with events E, E_1, and E_2. The **complement of E,** *denoted by E', is the event consisting of all sample points in S that are not in E. The* **union of E_1 and E_2,** *denoted by $E_1 \cup E_2$, is the event consisting of all sample points that are either in E_1, or in E_2, or in both E_1 and E_2. The* **intersection of E_1 and E_2,** *denoted by $E_1 \cap E_2$, is the event consisting of all sample points that are common to both E_1 and E_2.*

EXAMPLE 8   *Given the sample space $S = \{1, 2, 3, 4, 5, 6\}$ for the rolling of a die, let E_1, E_2, and E_3 be the events*

$$E_1 = \{1, 3, 5\}, \qquad E_2 = \{3, 4, 5, 6\}, \qquad E_3 = \{1\}.$$

Determine each of the following events.

a. E_1'.

We must find those sample points in S that are not in E_1.

$$E_1' = \{2, 4, 6\}.$$

Thus E_1' is the event that an even number appears.

b. $E_1 \cup E_2$.

We want the sample points in E_1, or E_2, or both.

$$E_1 \cup E_2 = \{1, 3, 4, 5, 6\}.$$

c. $E_1 \cap E_2$.

The sample points common to both E_1 and E_2 are 3 and 5. Thus

$$E_1 \cap E_2 = \{3, 5\}.$$

d. $E_2 \cap E_3$.

Since E_2 and E_3 have no sample point in common,

$$E_2 \cap E_3 = \varnothing.$$

e. $E_1 \cup E_1'$.

By using the result of part (a), we have

$$E_1 \cup E_1' = \{1, 3, 5\} \cup \{2, 4, 6\} = \{1, 2, 3, 4, 5, 6\} = S.$$

f. $E_1 \cap E_1'$.

$$E_1 \cap E_1' = \{1, 3, 5\} \cap \{2, 4, 6\} = \varnothing.$$

The results of Examples 8(e) and 8(f) can be generalized.

If E is any event for an experiment with sample space S, then

$$E \cup E' = S \quad \text{and} \quad E \cap E' = \varnothing.$$

When two events have no sample point in common, they are called *mutually exclusive events*.

Definition

Events E_1 and E_2 for an experiment are **mutually exclusive events** *if and only if $E_1 \cap E_2 = \varnothing$.*

For example, in the tossing of a die the events {2, 4, 6} and {1} are mutually exclusive. Moreover, an event and its complement are mutually exclusive, since $E \cap E' = \varnothing$. When two events are mutually exclusive, the occurrence of one event means that the other event does not occur.

EXERICISE 7.2

In Problems **1–6,** *determine the sample space of the given experiment.*

1. A card is drawn from a four-card deck consisting of the 9 of diamonds, 9 of hearts, 9 of clubs, and 9 of spades.

2. A coin is tossed four times in succession and the faces showing are observed.

3. A die is rolled and then a coin is tossed.

4. Two dice are rolled and the sum of the numbers that turn up is observed.

5. Two different letters are selected in succession from the letters in the word "love."

6. The sexes of the first, second, and third children of a three-children family are noted. (Let, for example, BGB denote that the first, second, and third children are boy, girl, boy, respectively.)

In Problems **7–12,** *determine the number of sample points in the sample space of the given experiment.*

7. A coin is tossed six times in succession and the faces showing are observed.

8. Four dice are rolled and the numbers that turn up are observed.

9. A card is drawn from an ordinary deck of 52 cards and then a die is rolled.

10. From an urn containing eight different balls, four balls are drawn successively without replacement.

11. A 13-card hand is dealt from a deck of 52 cards. Do not simplify your answer.

12. A four-letter "word" is formed by choosing any four letters from the alphabet in succession with replacement.

Suppose that $S = \{1, 2, 3, 4, 5, 6, 7, 8, 9, 10\}$ *is the sample space for an experiment with events*

$$E_1 = \{1, 3, 5\}, \quad E_2 = \{3, 5, 7, 9\}, \quad and \quad E_3 = \{2, 4, 6, 8\}.$$

In Problems **13–20,** *determine the indicated events.*

13. $E_1 \cup E_2$.

14. E_3'.

15. $E_1 \cap E_2$.

16. $E_1 \cap E_3$.

17. E_2'.

18. $(E_1 \cup E_2)'$.

19. $(E_2 \cap E_3)'$.

20. $(E_1 \cup E_3) \cap E_2'$.

21. Of the following events, which pairs are mutually exclusive?

$$E_1 = \{1, 2, 3\}, \quad E_2 = \{3, 4, 5\},$$
$$E_3 = \{1, 2,\}, \quad E_4 = \{5, 6, 7\}.$$

22. From a standard deck of 52 playing cards, two cards are drawn without replacement. Suppose E_A is the event that both cards are aces, E_H is the event that both cards are hearts, and E_2 is the event that both cards are 2's. Which pairs of these events are mutually exclusive?

23. An urn contains three colored marbles: one red, one white, and one blue. Determine the sample space if (a) two marbles are selected with replacement and (b) two marbles are selected without replacement.

24. A company makes a product that goes through three processes during its manufacture. The first is an assembly line, the second is a finishing line, and the third is an inspection line. There are three assembly lines (A, B, and C), two finishing lines (D and E), and two inspection lines (F and G). For each process the company chooses a line at random. Determine the sample space.

25. A coin is tossed three times in succession and the results are observed. Determine each of the following.
    a. Sample space S.
    b. Event E_1 that at least one head occurs.
    c. Event E_2 that at least one tail occurs.
    d. $E_1 \cup E_2$.
    e. $E_1 \cap E_2$.
    f. $(E_1 \cup E_2)'$.
    g. $(E_1 \cap E_2)'$.

26. A husband and wife have two children. The outcome of the first child being a boy and the second a girl can be represented by BG. Determine each of the following.
    a. Sample space that describes all the orders of the possible sexes of the children.
    b. Event that at least one child is a girl.
    c. Event that at least one child is a boy.
    d. Is the event in part (c) the complement of the event in part (b)?

27. Persons A, B, and C enter a building at different times. The outcome of A arriving first, B second, and C third can be indicated by ABC. Determine each of the following.
    a. Sample space involved for the arrivals.
    b. Event that A arrives first.
    c. Event that A does not arrive first.

28. A manufacturer can order electronic components from suppliers U, V, W, or X and mechanical components from suppliers U, V, Y, or Z. The manufacturer selects one supplier for each type of component. The outcome of U being selected for electronic components and V for mechanical components can be represented by UV.
    a. Determine the sample space.
    b. Determine the event E that the suppliers are different.
    c. Determine E' and give a verbal description of this event.

7.3 PROBABILITY

Suppose a well-balanced die is tossed once and the number that turns up is observed. Then the sample space is $S = \{1, 2, 3, 4, 5, 6\}$. Before the experiment is performed, we cannot predict with certainty which of these six outcomes will occur. But it does seem reasonable that each outcome has the same chance of occurring, that is, the outcomes are *equally likely*. This does not mean that in six tosses each number must turn up once. Rather, it means that if the experiment were performed a large number of times, each outcome would occur about $\frac{1}{6}$ of the time.

To be more specific, let the experiment be performed n times. Each performance of an experiment is called a **trial.** Suppose that we are interested in the event of obtaining a 1 (that is, the simple event consisting of the sample point 1). If 1 occurs in k of these n trials, then the proportion of times that 1 occurs is k/n. This ratio is called the **relative frequency** of the event. Because getting a 1 is just one out of six possible equally likely outcomes, we expect that in the long run a 1 will occur $\frac{1}{6}$ of the time. That is, as n becomes very large, we expect the relative frequency k/n to approach $\frac{1}{6}$. The number $\frac{1}{6}$ is taken to be the probability of getting a 1 on the toss of a well-balanced die, which is denoted $P(1)$. Thus $P(1) = \frac{1}{6}$. Similarly, $P(2) = \frac{1}{6}$, $P(3) = \frac{1}{6}$, and so on.

In this experiment all of the simple events in the sample space were understood to be equally likely to occur. To describe this we say that S is an *equiprobable space*.

Definition

*A sample space S is called an **equiprobable space** if and only if the simple events are equally likely to occur.*

We remark that besides the phrase "equally likely," other words and phrases used in the context of an equiprobable space are "well-balanced," "fair," "unbiased," and "at random." For example, we may have a *well-balanced* die (as above), a *fair* coin, *unbiased* dice, or we may select a marble *at random* from an urn.

We can generalize our probability results for the well-balanced die experiment to other (finite) equiprobable spaces.

Definition

*If S is an equiprobable sample space with N outcomes, $s_1, s_2, \ldots, s_N$, then the **probability of the simple event** $\{s_i\}$ is given by*

$$P(s_i) = \frac{1}{N},$$

for $i = 1, 2, \ldots, N$.

$P(s_i)$ can be interpreted as the relative frequency of $\{s_i\}$ occurring in the long run.

We can also assign probabilities to events that are not simple. For example, in the well-balanced die experiment, consider the event E of a 1 or a 2 turning up:

$$E = \{1, 2\}.$$

In n trials, where n is large, 1 should turn up approximately $\frac{1}{6}$ of the time, and 2 should turn up approximately $\frac{1}{6}$ of the time. Thus 1 or 2 should turn up approximately $\frac{1}{6} + \frac{1}{6}$ of the time, namely $\frac{2}{6}$ of the time. Hence it is reasonable to assume that the long-run relative frequency of E is $\frac{2}{6}$. We say that this number is the probability of E and denote it $P(E)$.

$$P(E) = \tfrac{1}{6} + \tfrac{1}{6} = \tfrac{2}{6}.$$

Note that $P(E)$ is the sum of the probabilities of the simple events that form E. Equivalently, $P(E)$ is the ratio of the number of outcomes in E (two) to the number of outcomes in the sample space (six).

Definition

*If S is a finite equiprobable space and $E = \{s_1, s_2, \ldots, s_j\}$, then the **probability of E** is denoted by $P(E)$ and is given by*

$$P(E) = P(s_1) + P(s_2) + \cdots + P(s_j).$$

Equivalently,

$$P(E) = \frac{n(E)}{n(S)},$$

where $n(E)$ is the number of outcomes in E and $n(S)$ is the number of outcomes in S.

Note that we can think of P as a function that associates with each event E the probability of E, namely $P(E)$. The probability of E can be interpreted as the relative frequency of E occurring in the long run.

EXAMPLE 1   *Two fair coins are tossed. Determine the probability that* (a) *two heads occur, and* (b) *at least one head occurs.*

The sample space is

$$S = \{HH, HT, TH, TT\},$$

which has four equally likely outcomes, so S is equiprobable.

a. If $E = \{HH\}$, then E is a simple event, so

$$P(E) = \tfrac{1}{4}.$$

b. Let $E = \{$at least one head$\}$. Then

$$E = \{HH, HT, TH\},$$

which has three outcomes. Thus

$$P(E) = \frac{n(E)}{n(S)} = \frac{3}{4}.$$

Alternatively,

$$P(E) = P(HH) + P(HT) + P(TH)$$
$$= \tfrac{1}{4} + \tfrac{1}{4} + \tfrac{1}{4} = \tfrac{3}{4}.$$

Suppose that S is an equiprobable sample space with N outcomes. (We assume a finite sample space throughout this section.) That is, $n(S) = N$. If E is an event, then $0 \le n(E) \le N$. Dividing each member by $n(S)$, or N, gives

$$0 \le \frac{n(E)}{n(S)} \le \frac{N}{N},$$

$$0 \le P(E) \le 1.$$

In particular, if $E = \varnothing$, then $\dfrac{n(\varnothing)}{n(S)} = \dfrac{0}{N} = 0$; thus

$$P(\varnothing) = 0.$$

If $E = S$, then $\dfrac{n(S)}{n(S)} = \dfrac{N}{N} = 1$, so

$$P(S) = 1.$$

That is, the probability of an event is a number between 0 and 1 inclusive. The probability of an impossible event is 0, and the probability of a certain event is 1.

Because $P(S) = 1$ and $P(S)$ is the sum of the probabilities of the outcomes in the sample space, we conclude that the sum of the probabilities of all the simple events in a sample space is 1.

Furthermore, if E_1 and E_2 are events, then $P(E_1 \cup E_2) = n(E_1 \cup E_2)/n(S)$. You might think that $n(E_1 \cup E_2) = n(E_1) + n(E_2)$. But this is not necessarily the case. Since $E_1 \cap E_2$ is contained in both E_1 and E_2 (see Fig. 7.8), if we were to add $n(E_1)$ and $n(E_2)$, the sum would include $n(E_1 \cap E_2)$ twice. By subtracting $N(E_1 \cap E_2)$ from $n(E_1) + n(E_2)$, we obtain $n(E_1 \cup E_2)$.

$$n(E_1 \cup E_2) = n(E_1) + n(E_2) - n(E_1 \cap E_2).$$

Dividing both sides by $n(S)$ gives the following result.

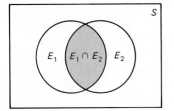

FIGURE 7.8

If E_1 and E_2 are events, then
$$P(E_1 \cup E_2) = P(E_1) + P(E_2) - P(E_1 \cap E_2). \quad (1)$$

For example, if a die is rolled, let E_1 be $\{1, 3, 5\}$ and E_2 be $\{1, 2, 3\}$. Then $E_1 \cap E_2 = \{1, 3\}$, so

$$P(E_1 \cup E_2) = P(E_1) + P(E_2) - P(E_1 \cap E_2)$$
$$= \tfrac{3}{6} + \tfrac{3}{6} - \tfrac{2}{6} = \tfrac{2}{3}.$$

Alternatively, since $E_1 \cup E_2 = \{1, 2, 3, 5\}$, $P(E_1 \cup E_2) = \tfrac{4}{6} = \tfrac{2}{3}$.

If E_1 and E_2 are mutually exclusive events, then $E_1 \cap E_2 = \varnothing$, so we have $P(E_1 \cap E_2) = P(\varnothing) = 0$. Thus, from Eq. (1) we can conclude the following:

If E_1 and E_2 are *mutually exclusive* events, then
$$P(E_1 \cup E_2) = P(E_1) + P(E_2).$$

In particular, if $E_1 = E$ and $E_2 = E'$, the complement of E, then $E \cap E' = \varnothing$, so

$$P(E \cup E') = P(E) + P(E').$$

But $E \cup E' = S$. Thus

$$P(S) = P(E) + P(E').$$

Since $P(S) = 1$, we have

$$P(E') = 1 - P(E),$$

or, equivalently,

$$P(E) = 1 - P(E').$$

Thus, if we know the probability of an event, then we can easily find the probability of its complement, and vice versa. For example, if $P(E) = \frac{1}{4}$, then $P(E') = 1 - \frac{1}{4} = \frac{3}{4}$.

EXAMPLE 2   *From a production run of* 5000 *light bulbs,* 2% *of which are defective, one bulb is selected at random. What is the probability that the bulb is defective? What is the probability that it is not defective?*

The sample space S consists of the 5000 bulbs. Since a bulb is selected at random, the possible outcomes are equally likely. Let E be the event of selecting a defective bulb. The number of outcomes in E is $0.02 \cdot 5000$, or 100. Thus

$$P(E) = \frac{n(E)}{n(S)} = \frac{100}{5000} = \frac{1}{50} = 0.02.$$

Alternatively, since the probability of selecting a particular bulb is $\frac{1}{5000}$ and E contains 100 sample points, by summing probabilities we have

$$P(E) = 100 \cdot \tfrac{1}{5000} = 0.02.$$

The event that the bulb selected is *not* defective is E'. Hence

$$P(E') = 1 - P(E) = 1 - 0.02 = 0.98.$$

EXAMPLE 3   *A pair of well-balanced dice are rolled. Determine the probability that the sum of the numbers that turn up is* (a) 7, (b) 7 *or* 11, *and* (c) *greater than* 3.

Since each die can roll any of six ways, the total number of sample points in the sample space is $6 \cdot 6 = 36$. The sample points can be considered as ordered pairs:

$$(1, 1), \quad (1, 2), \quad (1, 3), \quad (1, 4), \quad (1, 5), \quad (1, 6),$$
$$(2, 1), \quad (2, 2), \quad (2, 3), \quad (2, 4), \quad (2, 5), \quad (2, 6),$$
$$(3, 1), \quad (3, 2), \quad (3, 3), \quad (3, 4), \quad (3, 5), \quad (3, 6),$$

$$(4, 1), \quad (4, 2), \quad (4, 3), \quad (4, 4), \quad (4, 5), \quad (4, 6),$$
$$(5, 1), \quad (5, 2), \quad (5, 3), \quad (5, 4), \quad (5, 5), \quad (5, 6),$$
$$(6, 1), \quad (6, 2), \quad (6, 3), \quad (6, 4), \quad (6, 5), \quad (6, 6).$$

Since the dice are well balanced, the outcomes are equally likely. Thus the probability of any outcome is $\frac{1}{36}$.

a. Let E_7 be the event that the sum of the numbers appearing is 7. Then

$$E_7 = \{(1, 6), (2, 5), (3, 4), (4, 3), (5, 2), (6, 1)\}.$$

which has six outcomes. Thus

$$P(E_7) = \tfrac{6}{36} = \tfrac{1}{6}.$$

b. Let $E_{7 \text{ or } 11}$ be the event that the sum is 7 or 11. If E_{11} is the event that the sum is 11, then

$$E_{11} = \{(5, 6), (6, 5)\}.$$

which has two outcomes. Since $E_{7 \text{ or } 11} = E_7 \cup E_{11}$ and E_7 and E_{11} are mutually exclusive, we have

$$P(E_{7 \text{ or } 11}) = P(E_7) + P(E_{11}) = \tfrac{6}{36} + \tfrac{2}{36} = \tfrac{8}{36} = \tfrac{2}{9}.$$

Alternatively, we can determine $P(E_{7 \text{ or } 11})$ by counting the number of outcomes in $E_{7 \text{ or } 11}$.

$$E_{7 \text{ or } 11} = \{(1, 6), (2, 5), (3, 4), (4, 3), (5, 2), (6, 1), (5, 6), (6, 5)\},$$

which has eight outcomes. Thus

$$P(E_{7 \text{ or } 11}) = \tfrac{8}{36} = \tfrac{2}{9}.$$

c. Let E be the event that the sum is greater than 3. The number of outcomes in E is relatively large. Thus, to determine $P(E)$, it is easier to find E', rather than E, and then use the formula $P(E) = 1 - P(E')$. Here E' is the event that the sum is 2 or 3. Thus

$$E' = \{(1, 1), (1, 2), (2, 1)\},$$

which has three outcomes. Hence

$$P(E) = 1 - P(E') = 1 - \tfrac{3}{36} = \tfrac{11}{12}.$$

EXAMPLE 4   *From a standard deck of 52 playing cards, two cards are drawn in succession and at random without replacement. Find P(E), where E is the event that one card is a 2 and the other is a 3.*

Disregarding order, we can select two cards from 52 cards in $C_{52,2}$ ways. This is $n(S)$. A 2 can be drawn in 4 ways, and a 3 can be drawn in 4 ways. Thus a 2 and a 3 can be drawn in $4 \cdot 4$ ways. This is $n(E)$. Thus

$$P(E) = \frac{4 \cdot 4}{C_{52,2}} = \frac{16}{1326} = \frac{8}{663}.$$

EXAMPLE 5   *Find the probability of drawing four of a kind in a five-card poker hand (for example, four 10's and one 4).*

We have

$$n(S) = C_{52,5}.$$

Since there are 13 face values, four cards with the same face value can be selected in 13 ways. Once such a selection is made, there are 48 possible selections for the fifth card. Thus

$$P(4 \text{ of a kind}) = \frac{13 \cdot 48}{C_{52,5}} = \frac{13 \cdot 48}{2,598,960} \approx 0.00024.$$

Alternatively, all four suits with a particular face value can be drawn in $C_{4,4}$ ways, and there are 13 face values. Thus four cards consisting of four of a kind can be drawn in $13 \cdot C_{4,4}$ ways. The fifth card can be drawn in $C_{48,1}$ ways. Thus

$$P(4 \text{ of a kind}) = \frac{13 \cdot C_{4,4} \cdot C_{48,1}}{C_{52,5}} = \frac{13 \cdot 1 \cdot 48}{2,598,960} \approx 0.00024.$$

Many of the properties of equiprobable spaces carry over to sample spaces that are not equiprobable. To illustrate such a space, consider the experiment of tossing two fair coins and observing the number of heads. The coins can fall in the following four ways:

$$\text{HH, HT, TH, TT,}$$

which correspond to two heads, one head, one head, and zero heads, respectively. Because we are interested in the number of heads, the sample space is

$$S = \{0, 1, 2\}.$$

However, the simple events in S are not equally likely to occur because of the four possible ways in which the coins can fall: two of these ways correspond to the one-head outcome, while only one corresponds to the two-head outcome and similarly for the zero-head outcome. In the long run, it is reasonable to expect repeated trials to result in one head about $\frac{2}{4}$ of the time, zero heads about $\frac{1}{4}$ of the time, and two heads about $\frac{1}{4}$ of the time. If we were to assign probabilities to these simple events, it is natural to have

$$P(0) = \tfrac{1}{4}, \qquad P(1) = \tfrac{2}{4}, \qquad P(2) = \tfrac{1}{4}.$$

These probabilities lie between 0 and 1 inclusive, and their sum is 1. This is consistent with what was stated for an equiprobable space.

Based on our discussion, we can consider a *probability function* that relates to sample spaces in general.

Definition
*Let $S = \{s_1, s_2, \ldots, s_N\}$ be a sample space for an experiment. The function P is called a **probability function** if*

1. $0 \le P(s_i) \le 1$ *for* $i = 1$ *to* N.

2. $P(s_1) + P(s_2) + \cdots + P(s_N) = 1$.

3. *If E is an event, then P(E) is the sum of the probabilities of the sample points in E.*

4. $P(\emptyset) = 0$.

In general, for any probability function defined on a sample space (finite or infinite), it can be shown that

$$P(E') = 1 - P(E),$$

$$P(S) = 1,$$

and

$$P(E_1 \cup E_2) = P(E_1) + P(E_2) \qquad \text{if } E_1 \cap E_2 = \emptyset.$$

EXAMPLE 6   *A die is biased such that* $P(1) = \frac{3}{10}$, $P(2) = P(5) = \frac{2}{10}$, *and* $P(3) = P(4) = P(6) = \frac{1}{10}$. *If the die is tossed, find P(even number).*

We have {even number} = {2, 4, 6}. By the definition of a probability function,

$$P(\text{even number}) = P(2) + P(4) + P(6)$$

$$= \tfrac{2}{10} + \tfrac{1}{10} + \tfrac{1}{10} = \tfrac{4}{10} = \tfrac{2}{5}.$$

EXERCISE 7.3

1. A pair of well-balanced dice are tossed. Find the probability that the sum of the numbers is (a) 8, (b) 2 or 3, (c) 3, 4, or 5, (d) 12 or 13, (e) even, (f) odd, and (g) less than 10.

2. A pair of fair dice are tossed. Determine the probability that at least one die shows a 2.

3. A card is randomly selected from a standard deck of 52 playing cards. Determine the probability that the card is (a) a king of hearts, (b) a diamond, (c) a jack, (d) red, (e) a heart or a club, (f) a club and a 4, (g) a club or a 4, (h) red and a king, and (i) a spade and a heart.

4. A fair coin and a fair die are tossed. Find the probability that (a) a head and a 5 show, (b) a head shows, (c) a 3 shows, and (d) a head and an even number show.

5. A fair coin and a fair die are tossed and a card is randomly selected from a standard deck of 52 playing cards. Determine the probability that the coin, die, and card respectively show (a) a tail, a 3, the queen of hearts, (b) a tail, a 3, and a queen, (c) a head, a 2 or 3, and a queen, and (d) a head, an even number, and a diamond.

6. Three fair coins are tossed. Find the probability that (a) three heads show, (b) exactly one tail shows, (c) no more than two heads show, and (d) no more than one tail shows.

7. Two cards from a standard deck of 52 playing cards are successively drawn at random without replacement. Find the probability that (a) both cards are kings and (b) one card is a diamond and the other is a heart.

8. Two cards from a standard deck of 52 playing cards are successively drawn at random with replacement. Find the probability that (a) both cards are kings and (b) one card is a king and the other is a heart.

9. Assuming that the sex of a person is determined at random, determine the probabilitiy that a family with three children has (a) three girls, (b) exactly one boy, (c) no girls, and (d) at least one girl.

10. A marble is randomly drawn from an urn that contains seven red, five white, and eight blue marbles. Find the probability that the marble is (a) blue, (b) not red, (c) red or white, (d) neither red nor blue, (e) yellow, and (f) red or yellow.

11. When a biased die is tossed, the probabilities of 1, 3, and 5 showing are the same. The probabilities of 2, 4, and 6 showing are also the same, but are twice those of 1, 3 and 5. Determine $P(1)$.

12. For the sample space {a, b, c, d, e}, suppose that the probabilities of a, b, c, and d are the same. Is it possible to determine $P(e)$?

13. A stock is selected at random from a list of 60 utility stocks, 48 of which have an annual dividend yield of 10% or more. Find the probability that the stock pays an annual dividend that yields (a) 10% or more and (b) less than 10%.

14. A clothing store maintains its inventory of suits so that 25% are 100% pure wool. If a suit is selected at random, what is the probability that it is (a) 100 percent pure wool and (b) not 100% pure wool?

15. On an examination given to 40 students, 10% received an A, 25% a B, 35% a C, 25% a D, and 5% an F. If a student is selected at random, what is the probability that the student (a) received an A, (b) received an A or B, (c) received neither a D nor an F, and (d) did not receive an F? (e) Answer questions (a)–(d) if the number of students that were given the examination is unknown.

16. Two urns contain colored marbles. Urn 1 contains three red and two green marbles and urn 2 contains four red and five green marbles. A marble is selected at random from each urn. Find the probability that (a) both marbles are red and (b) one marble is red and the other is green.

17. From a group of two women and three men, two persons are selected at random to form a committee. Find the probability that the committee consists of women only.

18. For the committee selection in Problem 17, find the probability that the committee consists of a man and a woman.

19. A student answers each question on a 10-question true-false examination in a random fashion. If each question is worth 10 points, what is the probability that the student scores (a) 100 points and (b) 90 or more points.

20. On a five-question, multiple-choice examination there are four choices for each question, only one of which is correct. If a student answers each question in a random fashion, find the probability that the student answers (a) each question correctly and (b) exactly four questions correctly.

21. Find the probability of being dealt a full-house in a poker game. A full-house is three of one kind and two of another, such as three queens and two 10's. Express your answer using the symbol $C_{n,r}$.

7.4 DISCRETE RANDOM VARIABLES

With some experiments we are interested in events associated with numbers. For example, if two coins are tossed, our interest may be in the *number* of heads that occur. Thus we consider the events

0 heads show,   1 head shows,   2 heads show.

If we let X be a variable that represents the number of heads that occur, then the only values that X can assume are 0, 1, and 2. The value of X is determined by the outcome of the experiment, and hence by chance. In general, a variable whose values depend on the outcome of a random process is called a **random variable.** Usually, random variables are denoted by capital letters such as X, Y, or Z, and the values that these variables assume may be denoted by corresponding lower case letters (x, y, z). Thus, for the number of heads (X) that occur in the tossing of two coins, we may indicate the possible values by writing

$$X = x \quad \text{where} \quad x = 0, 1, 2,$$

or, more simply,

$$X = 0, 1, 2.$$

EXAMPLE 1

a. Suppose a die is rolled and X is the number that turns up. Then X is a random variable and $X = 1, 2, 3, 4, 5, 6$.

b. Suppose a coin is successively tossed until a head appears. If Y is the number of such tosses, then Y is a random variable and $Y = y$, where $y = 1, 2, 3, 4, \ldots$. Note that Y may assume infinitely many values.

c. A student is taking an exam with a 1-hour time limit. If X is the number of minutes it takes to complete the exam, then X is a random variable. The values that X may assume form the interval $(0, 60]$. That is, $0 < X \leq 60$.

A random variable is called a **discrete random variable** if it may assume only a finite number of values or if its values can be placed in one-to-one correspondence with the positive integers. In Example 1(a) and 1(b), X and Y are discrete. A random variable is called a **continuous random variable** if it may assume any value in some interval or intervals, such as X does in Example 1(c). In this chapter we shall be concerned with discrete random variables; Chapter 16 deals with those that are continuous.

If X is a random variable, the probability of the event that X assumes the value x is denoted $P(X = x)$. Similarly, we can consider the probabilities of events such as $X \leq x$ and $X > x$. If X is discrete, then the function f that assigns the number $P(X = x)$ to each possible value of X is called the **probability function,** the **probability distribution,** or—more simply—the **distribution** of the random variable X. Thus,

$$f(x) = P(X = x).$$

EXAMPLE 2   *Suppose that X is the number of heads that appear on the toss of two well-balanced coins. Determine the distribution of X.*

We must find the probabilities of the events $X = 0$, $X = 1$, and $X = 2$. The sample space is

$$S = \{HH, HT, TH, TT\},$$

where the four outcomes are equally likely.

The event $X = 0$ is $\{TT\}$.

The event $X = 1$ is $\{HT, TH\}$.

The event $X = 2$ is $\{HH\}$.

The probability for each of these events is

$$\frac{\text{number of outcomes in the event}}{4}$$

and is given in the following **probability table.**

x	$P(X = x)$
0	$\frac{1}{4}$
1	$\frac{2}{4} = \frac{1}{2}$
2	$\frac{1}{4}$

If f is the distribution for X, that is, $f(x) = P(X = x)$, then

$$f(0) = \tfrac{1}{4}, \qquad f(1) = \tfrac{1}{2}, \quad \text{and} \quad f(2) = \tfrac{1}{4}.$$

In Example 2, the distribution f was indicated by the listing

$$f(0) = \tfrac{1}{4}, \qquad f(1) = \tfrac{1}{2}, \quad \text{and} \quad f(2) = \tfrac{1}{4}.$$

However, the probability table for X gives the same information and is an acceptable way of expressing the distribution. Another way is by its graph, as shown in Fig. 7.9. The vertical lines from the x-axis to the points on the graph merely emphasize the heights of the points. Another representation for the distribution of X is the rectangle diagram in Fig. 7.10, called the **probability histogram** for X. Here each rectangle is centered over the corresponding value of X.

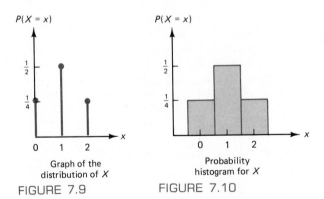

Graph of the
distribution of X

FIGURE 7.9

Probability
histogram for X

FIGURE 7.10

The rectangle above x has width 1 and height $P(X = x)$. Thus its *area* is the probability $P(X = x)$. This interpretation of probability as an area is important in the next section.

Note that in Example 2, the sum of $f(0)$, $f(1)$, and $f(2)$ is 1:

$$f(0) + f(1) + f(2) = \tfrac{1}{4} + \tfrac{1}{2} + \tfrac{1}{4} = 1.$$

This must be the case because any two of the events $X = 0$, $X = 1$, and $X = 2$ are mutually exclusive and the union of all three is the sample space [and $P(S) = 1$]. We can conveniently indicate the sum $f(0) + f(1) + f(2)$ by the notation

$$\sum_x f(x),$$

which is called *sigma notation** because the Greek letter Σ (sigma) is used. Here $\sum_x f(x)$ means that we are to sum all terms of the form $f(x)$ for all values of x, which in this case are 0, 1, and 2. Thus

$$\sum_x f(x) = f(0) + f(1) + f(2).$$

In general, for any probability distribution f, the sum of all function values is 1. Therefore,

$$\sum_x f(x) = 1.$$

This means that in any probability histogram, the sum of the areas of the rectangles is 1.

The probability distribution for a random variable X gives the relative frequencies of the values of X in the long run. However, it is often useful to determine the "average" value of X in the long run. In Example 2 for instance, suppose that the two coins were tossed n times, in which $X = 0$ occurred k_0 times, $X = 1$ occurred k_1 times, and $X = 2$ occurred k_2 times. Then the average value of X for these n tosses is

$$\frac{0 \cdot k_0 + 1 \cdot k_1 + 2 \cdot k_2}{n}$$

or, equivalently,

$$0 \cdot \frac{k_0}{n} + 1 \cdot \frac{k_1}{n} + 2 \cdot \frac{k_2}{n}.$$

But the fractions k_0/n, k_1/n, and k_2/n are the relative frequencies of the events $X = 0$, $X = 1$, and $X = 2$, respectively, that occur in the n tosses. If n is very large, then these relative frequencies approach the probabilities of the events $X = 0$, $X = 1$, and $X = 2$. Thus it seems reasonable that the average value of X in the long run is

$$0 \cdot f(0) + 1 \cdot f(1) + 2 \cdot f(2) \tag{1}$$

$$= 0 \cdot \tfrac{1}{4} + 1 \cdot \tfrac{1}{2} + 2 \cdot \tfrac{1}{4} = 1.$$

This means that if we tossed the coins many times, the average number of heads appearing per toss is very close to 1. We define the sum in Eq. (1) to be the *mean, expected value,* or *expectation of X* and denote it by μ (the Greek letter

---

* A more thorough discussion of sigma notation occurs in Sec. 14.4.

"mu") or $E(X)$. The mean does not necessarily have to be an outcome of the experiment. Note that from Eq. (1), μ has the form $\sum\limits_{x} xf(x)$. In general, we have the following definition.

Definition

*If X is a discrete random variable with probability distribution f, then the **mean** (or **expected value** or **expectation**) of X, denoted by μ, or $E(X)$, is given by*

$$\mu = E(X) = \sum_{x} xf(x).$$

The mean of X can be interpreted as the average value of X in the long run.

EXAMPLE 3   *An insurance company offers a $80,000 catastrophic fire insurance policy to homeowners of a certain type of house. The policy provides protection in the event that such a house is totally destroyed by fire in a 1-year period. The company has determined that the probability of such an event is 0.0002. If the annual policy premium is $52, find the expected gain to the company.*

If an insured house does not suffer a catastrophic fire, the company gains $52. However, if there is such a fire, the company loses $80,000 − $52 (insured value of house minus premium), or $79,948. Let X be the gain (in dollars) to the company. Then X is a random variable that may assume the values 52 and −79,948 (a loss is considered a negative gain). If f is the probability function for X, then

$$f(-79{,}948) = P(X = -79{,}948) = 0.0002$$

and

$$f(52) = P(X = 52) = 1 - 0.0002 = 0.9998.$$

The expected gain to the company is the expected value of X.

$$E(X) = \sum_{x} xf(x) = -79{,}948\, f(-79{,}948) + 52\, f(52)$$

$$= -79{,}948(0.0002) + 52(0.9998) = 36.$$

Thus if the company sold many policies, it could expect to gain approximately $36 per policy, which could be applied to such expenses as advertising, overhead, and profit.

Since $E(X)$ is the average value of X in the long run, it is a measure of the central tendency of X. However, $E(X)$ does not indicate the dispersion or spread of X from the mean in the long run. For example, Fig. 7.11 shows the graphs of two probability distributions, f and g, for the random variables X and Y. It can easily be shown that both X and Y have the same mean: $E(X) = 2$ and $E(Y) = 2$. You should verify these results. But from Fig. 7.11, X is more likely to assume the values 1 or 3 than is Y, because $f(1)$ and $f(3)$ are $\frac{2}{5}$, while $g(1)$ and

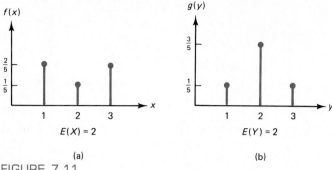

FIGURE 7.11

$g(3)$ are $\frac{1}{5}$. Thus X has more likelihood of assuming values away from the mean than does Y, so there is more dispersion for X in the long run.

There are various ways to measure dispersion for a random variable X. One way is to determine the long run average of the absolute values of the deviations from the mean μ, that is $E(|X - \mu|)$:

$$E(|X - \mu|) = \sum_x |x - \mu|\, f(x).*$$

However, since $|x - \mu|$ is involved, $E(|X - \mu|)$ is a mathematically awkward expression.

Although many other measures of dispersion can be considered, two are most widely accepted. One is *variance* and the other (which is related to variance) is *standard deviation*. The **variance of X,** denoted by Var(X), is the long-run average of the *squares* of the deviations of X from μ.

VARIANCE OF X

$$\text{Var}(X) = E[(X - \mu)^2] = \sum_x (x - \mu)^2 f(x). \dagger \qquad (2)$$

Since $(X - \mu)^2$ is involved in Var(X) and both X and μ have the same units of measurement, the units for Var(X) are those of X^2. For instance, in Example 3, X is in dollars; thus Var(X) has units of dollars squared. It is convenient to have a measure of dispersion in the same units as X. Such a measure is $\sqrt{\text{Var}(X)}$, which is called the **standard deviation of X** and is denoted by σ (the Greek letter "sigma").

STANDARD DEVIATION OF X

$$\sigma = \sqrt{\text{Var}(X)}.$$

---

* It can be shown that if $Y = g(X)$, then $E(Y) = \sum_x g(x)f(x)$, where f is the probability function for X. For example, if $Y = |X - \mu|$ then $E(|X - \mu|) = \sum_x |x - \mu|f(x)$.

$\dagger$ By the preceding footnote, if $Y = (X - \mu)^2$, then $E[(X - \mu)^2] = \sum_x (x - \mu)^2 f(x)$.

Note that σ has the property that

$$\sigma^2 = \text{Var}(X).$$

Both Var(X) [or σ^2] and σ are measures of the dispersion of X. The greater the value of Var(X), or σ, the greater the dispersion. One result of a famous theorem, *Chebyshev's inequality*, is that the probability of X falling within two standard deviations of the mean is at least $\frac{3}{4}$.

We can write the formula for variance in Eq. (2) in a different way. Suppose the possible values of X are x_1 and x_2, and f is the probability function for X. By Eq. (2),

$$\text{Var}(X) = \sum_x (x - \mu)^2 f(x)$$

$$= (x_1 - \mu)^2 f(x_1) + (x_2 - \mu)^2 f(x_2)$$

$$= (x_1^2 - 2x_1\mu + \mu^2) f(x_1) + (x_2^2 - 2x_2\mu + \mu^2) f(x_2)$$

$$= x_1^2 f(x_1) - 2x_1\mu f(x_1) + \mu^2 f(x_1) + x_2^2 f(x_2) -$$

$$2x_2\mu f(x_2) + \mu^2 f(x_2).$$

By regrouping and factoring, we have

$$\text{Var}(X) = [x_1^2 f(x_1) + x_2^2 f(x_2)] - 2\mu[x_1 f(x_1) + x_2 f(x_2)] +$$

$$\mu^2[f(x_1) + f(x_2)]$$

$$= \sum_x x^2 f(x) - 2\mu \sum_x x f(x) + \mu^2 \sum_x f(x).$$

But $\sum_x x^2 f(x) = E(X^2)$,* $\sum_x x f(x) = \mu$, and $\sum_x f(x) = 1$. Therefore,

$$\text{Var}(X) = \sigma^2 = E(X^2) - 2\mu^2 + \mu^2,$$

or

$$\boxed{\begin{array}{c} \text{Var}(X) = \sigma^2 = E(X^2) - \mu^2 \\ = \sum_x x^2 f(x) - \mu^2. \end{array}} \qquad (3)$$

This formula for variance is quite useful since it usually simplifies computations.

EXAMPLE 4   *An urn contains ten marbles, each of which shows a number. Five marbles show 1, two show 2, and three show 3. A marble is drawn at random. If X is the number that shows, determine μ, Var(X), and σ.*

* This is a consequence of a preceding footnote.

The sample space consists of 10 equally likely outcomes (the marbles). The values that X can assume are 1, 2, and 3. The events $X = 1$, $X = 2$, and $X = 3$ contain 5, 2, and 3 sample points, respectively. Thus if f is the probability function for X,

$$f(1) = P(X = 1) = \tfrac{5}{10} = \tfrac{1}{2},$$

$$f(2) = P(X = 2) = \tfrac{2}{10} = \tfrac{1}{5},$$

$$f(3) = P(X = 3) = \tfrac{3}{10}.$$

Calculating the mean μ gives

$$\mu = \sum_x xf(x) = 1 \cdot f(1) + 2 \cdot f(2) + 3 \cdot f(3)$$

$$= 1 \cdot \tfrac{5}{10} + 2 \cdot \tfrac{2}{10} + 3 \cdot \tfrac{3}{10} = \tfrac{18}{10} = \tfrac{9}{5}.$$

To find Var(X), either Eq. (2) or Eq. (3) can be used. Both will be used here so that we can compare the arithmetical computations involved. By Eq. (2),

$$\text{Var}(X) = \sum_x (x - \mu)^2 f(x)$$

$$= \left(1 - \frac{9}{5}\right)^2 f(1) + \left(2 - \frac{9}{5}\right)^2 f(2) + \left(3 - \frac{9}{5}\right)^2 f(3)$$

$$= \left(-\frac{4}{5}\right)^2 \cdot \frac{5}{10} + \left(\frac{1}{5}\right)^2 \cdot \frac{2}{10} + \left(\frac{6}{5}\right)^2 \cdot \frac{3}{10}$$

$$= \frac{16}{25} \cdot \frac{5}{10} + \frac{1}{25} \cdot \frac{2}{10} + \frac{36}{25} \cdot \frac{3}{10}$$

$$= \frac{80 + 2 + 108}{250} = \frac{190}{250} = \frac{19}{25}.$$

By Eq. (3),

$$\text{Var}(X) = \sum_x x^2 f(x) - \mu^2$$

$$= 1^2 \cdot f(1) + 2^2 \cdot f(2) + 3^2 \cdot f(3) - \left(\frac{9}{5}\right)^2$$

$$= 1 \cdot \frac{5}{10} + 4 \cdot \frac{2}{10} + 9 \cdot \frac{3}{10} - \frac{81}{25}$$

$$= \frac{5 + 8 + 27}{10} - \frac{81}{25} = \frac{40}{10} - \frac{81}{25}$$

$$= 4 - \frac{81}{25} = \frac{19}{25}.$$

Notice that Eq. (2) involves $(x - \mu)^2$, but Eq. (3) involves x^2. Because of this, it is often easier to compute variance by Eq. (3) than by Eq. (2).

Since $\sigma^2 = \text{Var}(X) = \frac{19}{25}$, the standard deviation σ is

$$\sigma = \sqrt{\text{Var}(X)} = \sqrt{\frac{19}{25}} = \frac{\sqrt{19}}{5}.$$

EXERCISE 7.4

In Problems **1–4,** *the distribution of the random variable X is given. Determine μ, Var(X), and σ. In Problem* **1,** *construct the probability histogram. In Problem* **2,** *graph the distribution.*

1. $f(0) = 0.1$, $f(1) = 0.4$, $f(2) = 0.2$, $f(3) = 0.3$.

2. $f(4) = 0.4$, $f(5) = 0.6$.

3.

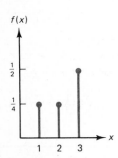

FIGURE 7.12

4.

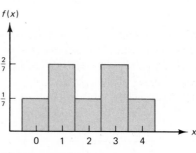

FIGURE 7.13

In Problems **5–8,** *determine E(X), σ^2, and σ for the random variable X.*

5. Three fair coins are tossed. Let X be the number of heads that occur.

6. An urn contains six marbles, each of which shows a number. Four marbles show a 1 and two show a 2. A marble is randomly selected and the number that shows, X, is observed.

7. From a group of two women and three men, two persons are selected at random to form a committee. Let X be the number of women on the committee.

8. An urn contains two red and three green marbles. Two marbles are randomly drawn in succession with replacement and the number of red marbles, X, is observed.

9. A landscaper earns $200 per day when working and loses $30 per day when not working. If the probability of working on any day is $\frac{4}{7}$, find the landscaper's expected daily earnings.

10. A fast-food chain estimates that if it opens a restaurant in a shopping center, the probability that the restaurant is successful is 0.65. To the chain, a successful restaurant earns an annual profit of $75,000; one that is not loses $20,000. What is the expected gain to the chain if it opens a restaurant in a shopping center?

11. An insurance company offers a hospitalization policy to individuals in a certain group. For a 1-year period, the company will pay $100 per day, to a maximum of 5 days, for each day the policyholder is hospitalized. The company estimates that the probability that any person in this group is hospitalized for exactly 1 day is 0.001; for exactly 2 days, 0.002; for exactly 3 days, 0.003; for exactly 4 days, 0.004; and for 5 or more days, 0.008. Find the expected gain per policy to the company if the annual premium is $10.

12. The table below gives the probability that X units of a company's product are demanded weekly. Determine the expected weekly demand.

x	0	1	2	3	4	5
$P(X = x)$	0.05	0.20	0.40	0.24	0.10	0.01

13. In Example 3, if the company wants an expected gain of $50 per policy, determine the annual premium.

14. In the game of roulette, there is a wheel with 37 slots numbered with the integers from 0 to 36, inclusive. A player bets $1 (for example) and chooses a number. The wheel is spun and a ball rolls on the wheel. If the ball lands in the slot showing the chosen number, the player receives the $1 bet plus $35. Otherwise, the player loses the $1 bet. Assume that all numbers are equally likely and determine the expected gain or loss per play.

15. Suppose that you pay $1.25 to play a game in which two fair coins are tossed. You receive the number of dollars equal to the number of heads that occur. What is your expected gain (or loss) on each play? The game is said to be *fair* to you when your expected gain is $0. What should you pay to play if this is to be a fair game?

7.5 THE BINOMIAL DISTRIBUTION

Later in this section you will see that the terms in the expansion of a power of a binomial are useful in describing the probability distributions of certain random variables. It is worthwhile, therefore, to first discuss the *binomial theorem*, which is a formula for expanding $(a + b)^n$, where n is a positive integer.

Regardless of n, there are patterns in the expansion of $(a + b)^n$. To illustrate, we shall consider the *cube* of the binomial $a + b$. By successively applying the distributive law, we have

$$
\begin{aligned}
(a + b)^3 &= [(a + b)(a + b)](a + b) \\
&= [a(a + b) + b(a + b)](a + b) \\
&= [aa + ab + ba + bb](a + b) \\
&= aa(a + b) + ab(a + b) + ba(a + b) + bb(a + b) \\
&= aaa + aab + aba + abb + baa + bab + bba + bbb \quad (1) \\
&= a^3 + 3a^2b + 3ab^2 + b^3. \quad (2)
\end{aligned}
$$

First, notice that the number of terms in Eq. (2) is four, which is one more than the power to which $a + b$ is raised. Second, the first and last terms in Eq. (2) are the *cubes* of a and b; the powers of a *decrease* from left to right (from 3 to 0), and the powers of b *increase* (from 0 to 3). Third, for each term the sum of the exponents of a and b is 3, the power to which $a + b$ is raised.

Let us now focus on the coefficients of the terms in Eq. (2). Consider the coefficient of the ab^2-term. It is the number of terms in Eq. (1) that involve exactly two b's, namely 3. But let us see *why* there are three terms that involve two b's. Notice in Eq. (1) that each term is the product of three numbers, each of which is either a or b. Because of the distributive law, each of the three $a + b$ factors in $(a + b)^3$ contributes either an a or b to the term. Thus to supply exactly two b's to a term, the b's in two of the three $a + b$ factors must be involved. Now, the number of ways of choosing two of the three factors is $C_{3,2}$.

Thus the coefficient of the ab^2-term is $C_{3,2} = \dfrac{3!}{2!1!} = 3$. Similarly,

the coefficient of the a^3-term is $C_{3,0}$,

the coefficient of the a^2b-term is $C_{3,1}$,

and   the coefficient of the b^3-term is $C_{3,3}$.

By generalizing our results, we obtain a formula for expanding $(a + b)^n$, called the *binomial theorem*.

BINOMIAL THEOREM

If n is a positive integer, then

$$(a + b)^n = C_{n,0}a^n + C_{n,1}a^{n-1}b + C_{n,2}a^{n-2}b^2$$
$$+ \cdots + C_{n,n-1}ab^{n-1} + C_{n,n}b^n.$$

The coefficients $C_{n,r}$ are called **binomial coefficients.**

EXAMPLE 1   *Use the binomial theorem to expand $(q + p)^4$.*

Here $n = 4$, $a = q$, and $b = p$.

$$(q + p)^4 = C_{4,0}q^4 + C_{4,1}q^3p + C_{4,2}q^2p^2 + C_{4,3}qp^3 + C_{4,4}p^4$$

$$= \frac{4!}{0!4!}q^4 + \frac{4!}{1!3!}q^3p + \frac{4!}{2!2!}q^2p^2 + \frac{4!}{3!1!}qp^3 + \frac{4!}{4!0!}p^4.$$

Recalling that $0! = 1$, we have

$$(q + p)^4 = q^4 + 4q^3p + 6q^2p^2 + 4qp^3 + p^4.$$

Before applying the binomial theorem to a distribution, we shall consider probabilities associated with repetitions, or **trials,** of an experiment such that the trials are *independent* of each other. By **independent trials** we mean that the outcome of any single trial does not effect the outcome of any other trial. An example of two independent trials of an experiment is tossing a coin twice in succession. Suppose the coin is biased so that the probability a head occurs on any toss is $\frac{1}{3}$. Thus the probability that a tail occurs on any toss is $1 - \frac{1}{3} = \frac{2}{3}$. Let us determine $P(HT)$. If tossing the coin twice is performed n times, where n is a large number, we should expect that heads occur approximately $\frac{1}{3}n$ times on the first toss. Because what occurs on the first toss in no way influences what occurs on the second, we should expect that a tail on the second toss occurs approximately $\frac{2}{3}$ of these $\frac{1}{3}n$ times. Thus in n performances, the number of times we get HT is about $\frac{2}{3}(\frac{1}{3}n)$. Therefore, the relative frequency of HT is approximately

$$\frac{\frac{2}{3}(\frac{1}{3}n)}{n} = \frac{2}{3} \cdot \frac{1}{3}.$$

Since n is large, we conclude that

$$P(\text{HT}) = \tfrac{1}{3} \cdot \tfrac{2}{3} = P(\text{H}) \cdot P(\text{T}),$$

where $P(\text{H})$ is the probability of a head on the first toss and $P(\text{T})$ is the probability of a tail on the second toss. Notice that $P(\text{HT})$ is the product of two probabilities, $P(\text{H})$ and $P(\text{T})$. This result can be generalized to n independent trials of an experiment.

MULTIPLICATION RULE FOR n INDEPENDENT TRIALS

Let there be n independent trials of an experiment and let a_i be a possible outcome of the ith trial. Then

$$P(a_1, a_2, \ldots, a_n) = P(a_1)P(a_2) \cdots P(a_n).$$

EXAMPLE 2   *A fair die is tossed three times. Find the probability of the event of getting* 1 *on the first toss,* 3 *on the second toss, and* 5 *on the third toss.*

Here we have three independent trials of tossing a coin. The probability of a particular number showing on any toss $\tfrac{1}{6}$. By the multiplication rule,

$$P(1, 3, 5) = P(1) \cdot P(3) \cdot P(5) = \tfrac{1}{6} \cdot \tfrac{1}{6} \cdot \tfrac{1}{6} = \tfrac{1}{216}.$$

We shall now consider independent trials of an experiment such that each trial has only *two* possible outcomes. For example, tossing a coin has two possible outcomes, H or T. For a particular coin, suppose that $P(\text{H}) = p$ and $P(\text{T}) = q = 1 - p$. Let the coin be tossed twice. The sample space is

$$\{\text{TT, TH, HT, HH}\}$$

By using the multiplication rule, we can determine the probabilities of the simple events.

$$P(\text{TT}) = qq = q^2,$$
$$P(\text{TH}) = qp,$$
$$P(\text{HT}) = pq,$$
$$P(\text{HH}) = pp = p^2.$$

If X is the number of heads that occur on the two trials, then $X = 0$, 1, or 2. The distribution f for X is given by

$$f(0) = P(X = 0) = P(\text{TT}) = q^2,$$
$$f(1) = P(X = 1) = P(\text{TH}) + P(\text{HT}) = qp + pq = 2qp,$$
$$f(2) = P(X = 2) = P(\text{HH}) = p^2.$$

We can generate the sample space and distribution of X in another, but interesting, way. If we think of T and H as numbers, then the terms in the expansion of the square of the binomial T + H can be interpreted as the points in the sample space:

$$(T + H)^2 = (T + H)(T + H) = T(T + H) + H(T + H)$$
$$= TT + TH + HT + HH. \tag{3}$$
$$(T + H)^2 = T^2 + 2TH + H^2. \tag{4}$$

Notice that the terms in Eq. (3) indicate all possible outcomes. The terms TH and HT each refer to one head occurring. Thus in Eq. (4), the coefficient 2 of 2TH indicates that one head can occur *two* ways (TH and HT). Both TH and HT have the same probability of occurring: qp (or pq). Thus $P(X = 1) = 2(qp)$. We can obtain this probability from the term 2TH in Eq. (4) by replacing T by q and H by p. Similarly, in Eq. (4) the coefficient 1 of T^2 indicates that there is only *one* way that no heads can occur. Replacing T by q here gives $P(X = 0)$, or q^2. Also, the coefficient 1 of H^2 indicates that there is only *one* way that two heads can occur. Replacing H by p gives the corresponding probability $P(X = 2)$, which is p^2. In summary, replacing T by q and H by p in Eq. (4) completely describes the distribution of X. That is, the distribution of X (number of heads that occur) is given by the terms in the square of the binomial $q + p$.

This pattern holds for any number of trials. For example, if the coin is tossed three times, then we get the distribution for X from the terms in the *cube* of $q + p$:

$$(q + p)^3 = q^3 + 3q^2p + 3qp^2 + p^3.$$

If we think of q's as T's and p's as H's, then q^3 is the probability of three tails, that is, $P(X = 0)$. Similarly, $3q^2p$ is the probability of two tails and one head, that is, $P(X = 1)$. Thus

$$P(X = 0) = q^3,$$
$$P(X = 1) = 3q^2p,$$
$$P(X = 2) = 3qp^2,$$
$$P(X = 3) = p^3.$$

We shall now generalize our results so that they apply to n independent trials of an experiment in which each trial has only two possible outcomes—call them *success* and *failure*—and the probability of success in each trial remains the same. Such trials are called **Bernoulli trials.** Because the sample space and the distribution of the number of successes correspond to the expansion of a power of a binomial, the experiment is called a **binomial experiment** and the distribution of the number of successes is called a **binomial distribution.**

> ## BINOMIAL DISTRIBUTION
>
> If X is the number of successes in n independent trials of a binomial experiment with probability p of success and q of failure on any trial, then the distribution f for X is given by
>
> $$f(x) = P(X = x) = C_{n,x}\, p^x q^{n-x},$$
>
> where x is an integer such that $0 \le x \le n$, and $q = 1 - p$. Any random variable with this distribution is called a **binomial random variable** and is said to have a **binomial distribution.** The mean and standard deviation of X are given, respectively, by
>
> $$\mu = np, \qquad \sigma = \sqrt{npq}.$$

EXAMPLE 3   *Suppose X is a binomial random variable with $n = 4$ and $p = \frac{1}{3}$. Find the distribution for X.*

Here $q = 1 - p = 1 - \frac{1}{3} = \frac{2}{3}$.

$$P(X = x) = C_{n,x}\, p^x q^{n-x}, \qquad x = 0, 1, 2, 3, 4.$$

Thus

$$P(X = 0) = C_{4,0}\left(\frac{1}{3}\right)^0\left(\frac{2}{3}\right)^4 = \frac{4!}{0!\,4!} \cdot 1 \cdot \frac{16}{81} = 1 \cdot 1 \cdot \frac{16}{81} = \frac{16}{81}.$$

$$P(X = 1) = C_{4,1}\left(\frac{1}{3}\right)^1\left(\frac{2}{3}\right)^3 = \frac{4!}{1!\,3!} \cdot \frac{1}{3} \cdot \frac{8}{27} = 4 \cdot \frac{1}{3} \cdot \frac{8}{27} = \frac{32}{81}.$$

$$P(X = 2) = C_{4,2}\left(\frac{1}{3}\right)^2\left(\frac{2}{3}\right)^2 = \frac{4!}{2!\,2!} \cdot \frac{1}{9} \cdot \frac{4}{9} = 6 \cdot \frac{1}{9} \cdot \frac{4}{9} = \frac{8}{27}.$$

$$P(X = 3) = C_{4,3}\left(\frac{1}{3}\right)^3\left(\frac{2}{3}\right)^1 = \frac{4!}{3!\,1!} \cdot \frac{1}{27} \cdot \frac{2}{3} = 4 \cdot \frac{1}{27} \cdot \frac{2}{3} = \frac{8}{81}.$$

$$P(X = 4) = C_{4,4}\left(\frac{1}{3}\right)^4\left(\frac{2}{3}\right)^0 = \frac{4!}{4!\,0!} \cdot \frac{1}{81} \cdot 1 = 1 \cdot \frac{1}{81} \cdot 1 = \frac{1}{81}.$$

The probability histogram for X is given in Fig. 7.14. Note that the mean μ for X is $np = 4(\frac{1}{3}) = \frac{4}{3}$, and the standard deviation σ is

$$\sqrt{npq} = \sqrt{4 \cdot \frac{1}{3} \cdot \frac{2}{3}} = \sqrt{\frac{8}{9}} = \frac{2\sqrt{2}}{3}.$$

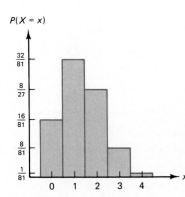

$P(X = x)$

FIGURE 7.14

EXAMPLE 4   *A fair coin is tossed eight times. Find the probability of getting at least two heads.*

If X is the number of heads that occur, then X has a binomial distribution with $n = 8$, $p = \frac{1}{2}$ and $q = \frac{1}{2}$. To simplify our work, we use the fact that

$$P(X \geq 2) = 1 - P(X < 2).$$

Now

$$P(X < 2) = P(X = 0) + P(X = 1)$$

$$= C_{8,0}\left(\frac{1}{2}\right)^0\left(\frac{1}{2}\right)^8 + C_{8,1}\left(\frac{1}{2}\right)^1\left(\frac{1}{2}\right)^7$$

$$= \frac{8!}{0!8!} \cdot 1 \cdot \frac{1}{256} + \frac{8!}{1!7!} \cdot \frac{1}{2} \cdot \frac{1}{128}$$

$$= 1 \cdot 1 \cdot \frac{1}{256} + 8 \cdot \frac{1}{2} \cdot \frac{1}{128} = \frac{9}{256}.$$

Thus

$$P(X \geq 2) = 1 - \frac{9}{256} = \frac{247}{256}.$$

A probability histogram for X is given in Fig. 7.15.

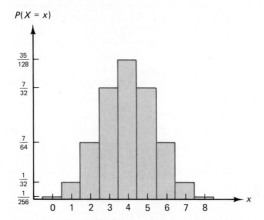

FIGURE 7.15

EXAMPLE 5   *For a particular group of individuals, 20% of their income tax returns are audited each year. Of five randomly chosen individuals, what is the probability that exactly two will have their returns audited?*

We shall consider this to be a binomial experiment with five trials (selecting an individual). Actually, the experiment is not truly binomial because selecting an individual from this group affects the probability that another individual's return will be audited. For example, if there are 5000 individuals, then 20% or 1000, will be audited. The probability that the first individual selected will be audited is $\frac{1000}{5000}$. If that event occurs, the probability that the second individual selected will be audited is $\frac{999}{4999}$. Thus the trials are not independent. However, we assume that the number of individuals is large, so that for practical purposes the probability of auditing an individual remains constant from trial to trial.

For each trial, the two outcomes are *being audited* or *not being audited*. Here we shall define a success as being audited. Letting X be the number of returns audited, $p = 0.2$, and $q = 1 - 0.2 = 0.8$, we have

$$P(X = 2) = C_{5,2}(0.2)^2(0.8)^3 = \frac{5!}{2!3!}(0.04)(0.512)$$

$$= 10(0.04)(0.512) = 0.2048.$$

EXERCISE 7.5

In Problems **1** and **2**, determine the distribution f for the binomial random variable X if the number of trials is n and the probability of success on any trial is p. Also find μ and σ.

1. $n = 2$, $p = \frac{1}{4}$.

2. $n = 3$, $p = \frac{1}{2}$.

In Problems **3** and **4**, determine the given probability if X is a binomial random variable, n is the number of trials, and p is the probability of success on any trial.

3. $P(X = 5)$; $n = 6$, $p = 0.2$.

4. $P(X = 3)$; $n = 5$, $p = \frac{2}{3}$.

5. A biased coin is tossed three times in succession. The probability of heads on any toss is $\frac{1}{4}$. Find the probability that (a) exactly two heads occur and (b) two or three heads occur.

6. A fair coin is tossed 10 times. What is the probability that exactly eight heads occur?

7. If a family has five children, find the probability that at least two are girls. (Assume the probability that a child is a girl is $\frac{1}{2}$.)

8. From a deck of 52 playing cards, three cards are randomly selected in succession with replacement. Determine the probability that exactly two cards are aces.

9. An urn contains four red and six green marbles, and four marbles are randomly drawn in succession with replacement. Determine the probability that exactly one marble is green.

10. A financial advisor claims that 60% of the stocks that he recommends for purchase increase in value. From a list of 200 recommended stocks, a client selects four at random. Determine, to two decimal places, the probability that two of the chosen stocks increase in value. Assume that the selections of the stocks are independent trials and that the number of stocks that increase in value has a binomial distribution.

11. A manufacturer produces electrical switches, of which 2% are defective. From a production run of 50,000 switches, four are randomly selected and each is tested. Determine, to three decimal places, the probability that the sample contains exactly two defective switches. Assume that the four trials are independent and that the number of defective switches in the sample has a binomial distribution.

7.6 REVIEW

Important Terms and Symbols

Section 7.1	tree diagram	basic counting principle	permutation, $P_{n,r}$	combination, $C_{n,r}$
Section 7.2	sample space	sample point	finite sample space	certain event	impossible event
	simple event	Venn diagram	complement, E'	union, $\cup$	intersection, $\cap$
	mutually exclusive events				

Section 7.3   equally likely outcomes   trial   relative frequency   equiprobable space
probability of event, $P(E)$ probability function

Section 7.4   discrete random variable   continuous random variable   probability function
probability distribution   probability histogram   sigma notation, $\sum_x f(x)$

mean, μ expected value, $E(X)$ variance, $\text{Var}(X)$, σ^2 standard deviation, σ

Section 7.5   binomial theorem   binomial coefficients   independent trials   Bernoulli trials
binomial experiment   binomial distribution

Summary

It is important to know the number of ways a procedure can occur. Suppose a procedure involves a sequence of k processes. Let n_1 be the number of ways the first process can occur, and let n_i be the number of ways the ith process can occur after the first $i - 1$ processes have occurred, for $i = 2, 3, \ldots, k$. Then the number of ways the procedure can occur is

$$n_1 \cdot n_2 \cdots n_k.$$

This result is called the basic counting principle.

An ordered arrangement of r objects selected from n objects is called a permutation of the n objects taken r at a time. The number of such permutations is denoted $P_{n,r}$ and

$$P_{n,r} = \underbrace{n(n - 1)(n - 2) \cdots}_{r \text{ factors}} = \frac{n!}{(n - r)!}.$$

If the arrangement is made without regard to order, then it is called a combination of n objects taken r at a time. The number of such combinations is denoted $C_{n,r}$ and

$$C_{n,r} = \frac{n!}{r!(n - r)!}.$$

The sample space of an experiment is the set S of all possible outcomes of the experiment. These outcomes are called sample points. A subset E of S is called an event. Two special events are the sample space itself, which is the certain event, and the empty set, which is the impossible event. An event consisting of a single sample point is called a simple event.

A sample space whose outcomes are equally likely is called an equiprobable space. If E is an event for such a space, then

$$P(E) = \frac{n(E)}{n(S)}.$$

Some properties are

$$P(E_1 \cup E_2) = P(E_1) + P(E_2) - P(E_1 \cap E_2),$$

$$P(E') = 1 - P(E),$$

$$P(S) = 1,$$

$$P(\varnothing) = 0.$$

If X is a discrete random variable and f is the function such that $f(x) = P(X = x)$, then f is called the probability function, or probability distribution, of X. In general

$$\sum_x f(x) = 1.$$

The mean, or expected value, of X is the long-run average of X and is denoted μ or $E(X)$:

$$\mu = E(X) = \sum_x xf(x).$$

The mean can be interpreted as a measure of the central tendency of X in the long run. A measure of the dispersion of X is variance, denoted $\text{Var}(X)$, and is given by

$$\text{Var}(X) = \sum_x (x - \mu)^2 f(x),$$

or, equivalently, by

$$\text{Var}(X) = \sum_x x^2 f(x) - \mu^2.$$

Another measure of dispersion of X is the standard deviation σ, where

$$\sigma = \sqrt{\text{Var}(X)}.$$

If an experiment is repeated several times, then each performance of the experiment is called a trial. The trials are independent when the outcome of any single trial does not effect the outcome of any other. For n independent trials, if a_i is a possible outcome on the ith trial, then

$$P(a_1, a_2, \ldots, a_n) = P(a_1)P(a_2) \cdots P(a_n).$$

If there are only two possible outcomes (success or failure) for each independent trial, and the probabilities of success or failure do not change from trial to trial, then the experiment is called a binomial experiment. For such an experiment, if X is the number of successes in n trials, then the distribution f of X is called a binomial distribution and

$$f(x) = P(X = x) = C_{n,x} p^x q^{n-x},$$

where p is the probability of success on any trial and $q = 1 - p$ (the probability of failure). The mean μ and standard deviation σ of X are given by

$$\mu = np \quad \text{and} \quad \sigma = \sqrt{npq}.$$

A binomial distribution is intimately connected with the binomial theorem, which is a formula for expanding the nth power of a binomial:

$$(a + b)^n = C_{n,0} a^n + C_{n,1} a^{n-1} b + \cdots + C_{n,n-1} ab^{n-1} + C_{n,n} b^n,$$

where n is a positive integer.

Review Problems

In Problems 1–4, determine the values.

1. $P_{8,3}$.

2. $P_{20,1}$.

3. $C_{9,7}$.

4. $C_{12,4}$.

5. A five-symbol license plate consists of two letters followed by three numbers, the first of which is not 0. How many different license plates are possible?

6. In a restaurant, a complete dinner consists of one appetizer, one entrée, and one dessert. The choices for the appetizer are soup and juice; for the entrée, chicken, steak, lobster, and veal; for the dessert, ice cream, pie, and pudding. How many complete dinners are possible?

7. The transmitter for an electric garage door opener transmits a coded signal to a receiver. The code is determined by five switches, each of which is either in an "on" or "off" position. Determine the number of different codes that may be transmitted.

8. A baseball manager must determine a batting order for his nine-member team. How many batting orders are possible?

9. A softball league has seven teams. In terms of first, second, and third place, in how many ways can the season end? Assume that there are no ties.

10. In a trophy case, nine different trophies are to be placed—two on the top shelf, three on the middle, and four on the bottom. Considering the order of arrangement on each shelf, in how many ways can the trophies be placed in the case?

11. Because of crowding, five of eight people can enter an elevator. How many different groups can enter?

12. From a 52-card deck of playing cards, a three-card hand is dealt. In how many ways can two of the cards be of the same face value and the other of a different face value?

13. A carton contains 24 light bulbs, one of which is defective. (a) In how many ways can three bulbs be selected? (b) In how many ways can three bulbs be selected if one is defective?

14. Each question of a 10-question multiple-choice examination has four choices, only one of which is correct, and is worth 10 points. By guessing, in how many ways is it possible to receive a score of 90 or better?

15. Suppose $S = \{1, 2, 3, 4, 5, 6, 7, 8\}$ is the sample space and $E_1 = \{1, 2, 3, 4, 5, 6\}$ and $E_2 = \{4, 5, 6, 7\}$ are events for an experiment. Determine (a) $E_1 \cup E_2$, (b) $E_1 \cap E_2$, (c) $E_1' \cup E_2$, (d) $E_1 \cap E_1'$, and (e) $(E_1 \cap E_2')'$. (f) Are E_1 and E_2 mutually exclusive?

16. A die is rolled and then a coin is tossed. (a) Determine the sample space for this experiment. Determine the events that (b) a 2 shows and (c) a head and an even number show.

17. Three urns, labeled 1, 2, and 3, each contain two marbles, one red and the other green. A marble is selected at random from each urn. (a) Determine the sample space for this experiment. Determine the events that (b) exactly two marbles are red and (c) the marbles are the same color.

18. Suppose E_1 and E_2 are events for an experiment with a finite number of sample points. If $P(E_1) = 0.6$, $P(E_1 \cup E_2) = 0.7$, and $P(E_1 \cap E_2) = 0.2$, find $P(E_2)$.

19. A manufacturer of computer chips packages 10 chips to a box. For quality control, two chips are selected at random from each box and tested. If any one of the chips is defective, the entire box of chips is rejected for sale. For a box that contains exactly one defective chip, what is the probability that the box is rejected?

20. Each of 80 white mice was injected with one of four drugs, A, B, C, or D. Drug A was given to 25%, B to 20%, and C to 20%. If a mouse is chosen at random, determine the probability that it was injected with either C or D.

21. An urn contains four red and six green marbles.
    a. If two marbles are randomly selected in succession with replacement, determine the probability that both are red.
    b. If the selection is made without replacement, determine the probability that both are red.

22. A pair of fair dice are rolled. Determine the probability that the sum of the numbers is (a) 4 or 5, (b) a multiple of 4, and (c) no less than 5.

23. Two cards from a standard deck of 52 playing cards are randomly drawn in succession with replacement. Determine the probability that (a) both cards are red and (b) one card is red and the other is a club.

24. Two cards from a standard deck of 52 playing cards are randomly drawn in succession without replacement. Determine the probability that (a) both are hearts and (b) one is an ace and the other is a red king.

In Problems **25** *and* **26,** *the distribution for the random variable X is given. Construct the probability histogram and determine* μ, *Var(X), and* σ.

25. $f(1) = 0.7, f(2) = 0.1, f(3) = 0.2.$

26. $f(0) = \frac{1}{2}, f(1) = \frac{1}{8}, f(2) = \frac{3}{8}.$

27. A fair coin and a fair die are tossed. Let X be the sum of the number of heads and the number of dots that show. Determine (a) the distribution f for X and (b) $E(X)$.

28. Two cards from a standard deck of 52 playing cards are randomly drawn in succession without replacement and the number of aces, X, is observed. Determine (a) the distribution f for X and (b) $E(X)$.

29. In a game, a player pays $0.25 to randomly draw two cards, with replacement, from a standard deck of 52 playing cards. For each 10 that appears, the player receives $1. What is the player's expected gain or loss? Give your answer to the nearest cent.

30. An oil company determines that the probability that a gas station located along an interstate highway is successful is 0.45. A successful station earns an annual profit of $40,000; one that is not loses $10,000 annually. What is the expected gain to the company if it locates a station along an interstate highway?

31. Determine the distribution of the binomial random variable X for three trials if the probability of success on any trial is 0.1. Also, determine the mean and standard deviation of X.

32. If X is a binomial random variable with six trials, and the probability of success on any trial is $\frac{2}{3}$, determine $P(X > 2)$.

33. A biased coin is tossed four times. The probability that a head occurs on any toss is $\frac{1}{3}$. Find the probability that at least two heads occur.

34. The probability that a certain type of seed germinates is 0.8. If five seeds are planted, what is the probability that none will germinate?

CHAPTER 8

Matrix Algebra

8.1 MATRICES

Finding ways to describe many situations in mathematics and economics leads to the study of rectangular arrays of numbers. Consider, for example, the system of linear equations

$$
\begin{cases}
3x + 4y + 3z = 0, \\
2x + y - z = 0, \\
9x - 6y + 2z = 0.
\end{cases}
$$

The features that characterize this system are the numerical coefficients in the equations, together with their relative positions. For this reason the system can be described by the rectangular array

$$
\begin{bmatrix}
3 & 4 & 3 \\
2 & 1 & -1 \\
9 & -6 & 2
\end{bmatrix},
$$

which is called a *matrix* (plural: *matrices,* pronounced may'tri sees). We shall consider such rectangular arrays to be objects in themselves and our custom, as shown above, will be to enclose them by brackets. Parentheses ( ) are also commonly used.

Pitfall

Do not use vertical bars, | |, instead of brackets or parentheses, for they have a different meaning.

In symbolically representing matrices, we shall use bold capital letters such as **A, B, C,** and so on.

In economics it is often convenient to use matrices in formulating problems and displaying data. For example, a manufacturer who produces products A, B,

238

and C could represent the units of labor and material involved in one week's production of these items as in Table 8.1. More simply, these data can be rep-

TABLE 8.1

	PRODUCT		
	A	B	C
Labor	10	12	16
Material	5	9	7

resented by the matrix

$$\mathbf{A} = \begin{bmatrix} 10 & 12 & 16 \\ 5 & 9 & 7 \end{bmatrix}.$$

The horizontal rows of a matrix are numbered consecutively from top to bottom, and the vertical columns are numbered from left to right. For matrix **A** above we have

$$\begin{array}{ccc} \text{column 1} & \text{column 2} & \text{column 3} \end{array}$$

$$\begin{array}{c} \text{row 1} \\ \text{row 2} \end{array} \begin{bmatrix} 10 & 12 & 16 \\ 5 & 9 & 7 \end{bmatrix} = \mathbf{A}.$$

Since **A** has two rows and three columns, we say **A** has *order* 2×3 (read "2 by 3"), where the number of rows is specified first. Similarly, the matrices

$$\mathbf{B} = \begin{bmatrix} 1 & 6 & -2 \\ 5 & 1 & -4 \\ -3 & 5 & 0 \end{bmatrix} \quad \text{and} \quad \mathbf{C} = \begin{bmatrix} 1 & 2 \\ -3 & 4 \\ 5 & 6 \\ 7 & -8 \end{bmatrix}$$

have orders 3×3 and 4×2, respectively.

The numbers in a matrix are called its **entries** or **elements.** To denote arbitrary entries in a matrix, say one of order 2×3, there are two common methods. First, we may use different letters:

$$\begin{bmatrix} a & b & c \\ d & e & f \end{bmatrix}.$$

Second, a single letter may be used, say *a,* along with appropriate *double* subscripts to indicate position:

$$\begin{bmatrix} a_{11} & a_{12} & a_{13} \\ a_{21} & a_{22} & a_{23} \end{bmatrix}.$$

For the entry a_{12} (read "*a* sub one-two"), the first subscript 1 specifies the row and the second subscript 2, the column in which the entry appears. Similarly, the entry a_{23} (read ''a sub two-three'') is the entry in the second row and the third column. Generalizing, we say that the symbol a_{ij} denotes the entry in the ith row and jth column.

Our concern in this chapter is the manipulation and application of various types of matrices. For completeness, we now give a formal definition of a matrix.

Definition

*A rectangular array of numbers consisting of **m** rows and **n** columns,*

$$\begin{bmatrix} a_{11} & a_{12} & \cdots & a_{1n} \\ a_{21} & a_{22} & \cdots & a_{2n} \\ \cdot & \cdot & \cdots & \cdot \\ \cdot & \cdot & \cdots & \cdot \\ \cdot & \cdot & \cdots & \cdot \\ a_{m1} & a_{m2} & \cdots & a_{mn} \end{bmatrix},$$

*is called an **m × n matrix** or a **matrix of order m × n**. For the entry a_{ij}, i is the row subscript and j the column subscript.*

In general, $m \times n$ matrices have mn entries. For brevity, an $m \times n$ matrix can be denoted by the symbol $[a_{ij}]_{m \times n}$ or more simply $[a_{ij}]$, where the order is understood to be that which is appropriate for the given context. This notation merely indicates what types of symbols we are using to denote the general entry.

Pitfall

Do not confuse the general entry a_{ij} with the matrix $[a_{ij}]$.

A matrix that has exactly one row, such as

$$\mathbf{A} = [1 \quad 7 \quad 12 \quad 3],$$

is called a **row matrix**. Here $\mathbf{A}$ has order 1×4. Similarly, a matrix consisting of a single column, such as the 5×1 matrix

$$\mathbf{B} = \begin{bmatrix} 1 \\ -2 \\ 15 \\ 9 \\ 16 \end{bmatrix},$$

is called a **column matrix**.

EXAMPLE 1   The matrices

$$\mathbf{A} = [1 \quad 2 \quad 0], \qquad \mathbf{B} = \begin{bmatrix} 1 & -6 \\ 5 & 1 \\ 9 & 4 \end{bmatrix}, \qquad \mathbf{C} = [7],$$

$$\mathbf{D} = \begin{bmatrix} 1 & 3 & 7 & -2 & 4 \\ 9 & 11 & 5 & 6 & 8 \\ 6 & -2 & -1 & 1 & 1 \end{bmatrix}$$

have orders 1×3, 3×2, 1×1, and 3×5, respectively.

EXAMPLE 2

a. *Construct a three-entry column matrix such that $a_{21} = 6$ and $a_{ij} = 0$ otherwise.*

The matrix is given by

$$\begin{bmatrix} 0 \\ 6 \\ 0 \end{bmatrix}.$$

b. *If $\mathbf{A} = [a_{ij}]$ has order 3×4 and $a_{ij} = i + j$, find $\mathbf{A}$.*

Here $i = 1, 2, 3$ and $j = 1, 2, 3, 4$, and $\mathbf{A}$ has $(3)(4) = 12$ entries. Since $a_{ij} = i + j$, the entry in row i and column j is obtained by adding the numbers i and j. Hence $a_{11} = 1 + 1 = 2$, $a_{12} = 1 + 2 = 3$, $a_{13} = 1 + 3 = 4$, and so on. Thus

$$\mathbf{A} = \begin{bmatrix} 1+1 & 1+2 & 1+3 & 1+4 \\ 2+1 & 2+2 & 2+3 & 2+4 \\ 3+1 & 3+2 & 3+3 & 3+4 \end{bmatrix} = \begin{bmatrix} 2 & 3 & 4 & 5 \\ 3 & 4 & 5 & 6 \\ 4 & 5 & 6 & 7 \end{bmatrix}.$$

c. *Construct the 3×3 matrix $\mathbf{I}$ given that $a_{11} = a_{22} = a_{33} = 1$ and $a_{ij} = 0$ otherwise.*

The matrix is given by

$$\mathbf{I} = \begin{bmatrix} 1 & 0 & 0 \\ 0 & 1 & 0 \\ 0 & 0 & 1 \end{bmatrix}.$$

Definition

*Two matrices are **equal** if and only if they have the same order and corresponding entries are equal.*

For example,

$$\begin{bmatrix} 1+1 & \frac{2}{2} \\ 2 \cdot 3 & 0 \end{bmatrix} = \begin{bmatrix} 2 & 1 \\ 6 & 0 \end{bmatrix},$$

but

$$[1 \quad 1] \neq \begin{bmatrix} 1 \\ 1 \end{bmatrix},$$

and

$$[1 \quad 1] \neq [1 \quad 1 \quad 1].$$

By the definition of equality, for the matrix equation

$$\begin{bmatrix} x & y+1 \\ 2z & 5w \end{bmatrix} = \begin{bmatrix} 2 & 7 \\ 4 & 2 \end{bmatrix}$$

to be a true statement, it must be equivalent to the system

$$\begin{cases} x = 2, \\ y + 1 = 7, \\ 2z = 4, \\ 5w = 2. \end{cases}$$

Solving gives $x = 2$, $y = 6$, $z = 2$, and $w = \frac{2}{5}$. It is a significant fact that a matrix equation can define a system of linear equations as has been shown above.

Certain types of matrices play important roles in matrix theory. We now consider three such types.

An $m \times n$ matrix whose entries are all 0 is called the $m \times n$ **zero matrix,** denoted $\mathbf{O}_{m \times n}$ or, more simply, $\mathbf{O}$. Thus the 2×3 zero matrix is

$$\mathbf{O} = \begin{bmatrix} 0 & 0 & 0 \\ 0 & 0 & 0 \end{bmatrix},$$

and in general

$$\mathbf{O} = \begin{bmatrix} 0 & 0 & \cdots & 0 \\ 0 & 0 & \cdots & 0 \\ \cdot & \cdot & \cdots & \cdot \\ \cdot & \cdot & \cdots & \cdot \\ \cdot & \cdot & \cdots & \cdot \\ 0 & 0 & \cdots & 0 \end{bmatrix}.$$

Pitfall
Do not confuse the matrix $\mathbf{O}$ with the real number 0.

A matrix having the same number of columns as rows, for example n rows and n columns, is called a **square matrix** of order n. That is, an $m \times n$ matrix is square if and only if $m = n$. Thus

$$\begin{bmatrix} -2 & 7 & 4 \\ 6 & 2 & 0 \\ 4 & 6 & 1 \end{bmatrix} \qquad \text{and} \qquad [3]$$

are square matrices of orders 3 and 1, respectively.

In a square matrix of order n, the entries $a_{11}, a_{22}, a_{33}, \ldots, a_{nn}$ which lie on the diagonal extending from the upper left corner to the lower right corner are called the *main diagonal* entries, or more simply the **main diagonal.** Thus in the matrix

$$\begin{bmatrix} 1 & 2 & 3 \\ 4 & 5 & 6 \\ 7 & 8 & 9 \end{bmatrix},$$

the main diagonal consists of $a_{11} = 1$, $a_{22} = 5$, and $a_{33} = 9$.

A square matrix is said to be an **upper (lower) triangular matrix** if all entries below (above) the main diagonal are zeros. Thus

$$\begin{bmatrix} 5 & 1 & 1 \\ 0 & -3 & 7 \\ 0 & 0 & 4 \end{bmatrix} \quad \text{and} \quad \begin{bmatrix} 7 & 0 & 0 & 0 \\ -3 & 2 & 0 & 0 \\ 6 & 5 & -4 & 0 \\ 1 & 6 & 0 & 1 \end{bmatrix}$$

are upper and lower triangular matrices, respectively.

EXERCISE 8.1

1. Given the matrices

$$A = \begin{bmatrix} 1 & -6 & 2 \\ -4 & 2 & 1 \end{bmatrix}, \quad B = \begin{bmatrix} 1 & 2 & 3 \\ 4 & 5 & 6 \\ 7 & 8 & 9 \end{bmatrix}, \quad C = \begin{bmatrix} 1 & 1 \\ 2 & 2 \\ 3 & 3 \end{bmatrix}, \quad D = \begin{bmatrix} 1 & 0 \\ 2 & 3 \end{bmatrix},$$

$$E = \begin{bmatrix} 1 & 2 & 3 & 4 \\ 0 & 1 & 6 & 0 \\ 0 & 0 & 2 & 0 \\ 0 & 0 & 6 & 1 \end{bmatrix}, \quad F = [6 \quad 2], \quad G = \begin{bmatrix} 5 \\ 6 \\ 1 \end{bmatrix}, \quad H = \begin{bmatrix} 1 & 6 & 2 \\ 0 & 0 & 0 \\ 0 & 0 & 0 \end{bmatrix}, \quad J = [4],$$

a. State the order of each matrix.

b. Which matrices are square?

c. Which matrices are upper triangular? lower triangular?

d. Which are row matrices?

e. Which are column matrices?

In Problems 2–9, let

$$A = [a_{ij}] = \begin{bmatrix} 7 & -2 & 14 & 6 \\ 6 & 2 & 3 & -2 \\ 5 & 4 & 1 & 0 \\ 8 & 0 & 2 & 0 \end{bmatrix}.$$

2. What is the order of A?

Find the following entries.

3. a_{43}.   4. a_{12}.   5. a_{32}.   6. a_{34}.   7. a_{14}.   8. a_{55}.

9. What are the main diagonal entries?

10. Write the upper triangular matrix of order 5 given that all entries which are not required to be 0 are equal to 1.

11. Write $A = [a_{ij}]$ if A is 3×4 and $a_{ij} = 2i + 3j$.

12. Write $B = [b_{ij}]$ if B is 2×2 and $b_{ij} = (-1)^{i+j}(i^2 + j^2)$.

13. If $\mathbf{A} = [a_{ij}]$ is 12×10, how many entries does $\mathbf{A}$ have? If $a_{ij} = 1$ for $i = j$, and $a_{ij} = 0$ for $i \neq j$, find a_{33}, a_{52}, $a_{10,10}$, and $a_{12,10}$.

14. List the main diagonal of

$$\text{a.} \begin{bmatrix} 1 & 4 & -2 & 0 \\ 7 & 0 & 4 & -1 \\ -6 & 6 & -5 & 1 \\ 2 & 1 & 7 & 2 \end{bmatrix}, \qquad \text{b.} \begin{bmatrix} x & 1 & y \\ 9 & y & 7 \\ y & 0 & z \end{bmatrix}.$$

15. Write the zero matrix of order (a) 4; (b) 6.

In Problems 16–19, solve the matrix equation.

16. $\begin{bmatrix} 2x & y \\ z & 3w \end{bmatrix} = \begin{bmatrix} 4 & 6 \\ 0 & 7 \end{bmatrix}.$

17. $\begin{bmatrix} 6 & 2 \\ x & 7 \\ 3y & 2z \end{bmatrix} = \begin{bmatrix} 6 & 2 \\ 6 & 7 \\ 2 & 7 \end{bmatrix}.$

18. $\begin{bmatrix} 4 & 2 & 1 \\ 3x & y & 3z \\ 0 & w & 7 \end{bmatrix} = \begin{bmatrix} 4 & 2 & 1 \\ 6 & 7 & 9 \\ 0 & 9 & 8 \end{bmatrix}.$

19. $\begin{bmatrix} 2x & 7 \\ 7 & 2y \end{bmatrix} = \begin{bmatrix} y & 7 \\ 7 & y \end{bmatrix}.$

20. A stock broker sold a customer 200 shares of stock A, 300 shares of stock B, 500 shares of stock C, and 300 shares of stock D. Write a row matrix that gives the number of shares of each stock sold. If the stocks sell for $20, $30, $45, and $100 per share, respectively, write this information as a column matrix.

21. The Widget Company has its monthly sales reports given by means of matrices whose rows, in order, represent the number of regular, deluxe, and super-duper models sold, and the columns, in order, give the number of red, white, blue, and purple units sold. The matrices for January (**J**) and February (**F**) are

$$\mathbf{J} = \begin{bmatrix} 2 & 6 & 1 & 2 \\ 0 & 1 & 3 & 5 \\ 2 & 7 & 6 & 0 \end{bmatrix}, \qquad \mathbf{F} = \begin{bmatrix} 0 & 2 & 4 & 4 \\ 2 & 3 & 3 & 2 \\ 4 & 0 & 2 & 6 \end{bmatrix}.$$

(a) How many white super-duper models were sold in January? (b) How many blue deluxe models were sold in February? (c) In which month were more purple regular models sold? (d) Which model and color sold the same number of units in both months? (e) In which month were more deluxe models sold? (f) In which month were more red widgets sold? (g) How many widgets were sold in January?

22. Input-output matrices, which were developed by W. W. Leontief, indicate the interrelationships that exist among the various sectors of an economy during some period of time. A hypothetical example for a simplified economy is given by matrix **M** below. The consuming sectors are the same as the producing sectors and can be thought of as manufacturers, government, steel, agriculture, households, and so on. Each row shows how the output of a given sector is consumed by the four sectors. For example, of the total output of industry A, 50 went to industry A itself, 70 to B, 200 to C, and 360 to all others. The sum of the entries in row 1, namely 680, gives the total output of A for a given time period. Each column gives the output of each sector that is consumed by a given sector. For example, in producing 680 units, industry A consumed 50 units of A, 90 of B, 120 of C, and 420 from all other producers. For each column, find the sum of the entries. Do the same for each row. What do you observe in comparing these totals? Suppose sector A increases its output by 20%, namely by 136 units. Assuming this results in a uniform 20% increase of all its inputs, by how many units will sector B have to increase its output? Answer the same question for C and D.

CONSUMERS

	Industry A	Industry B	Industry C	All Other Consumers
PRODUCERS				

$$M = \begin{array}{l} \text{Industry A} \\ \text{Industry B} \\ \text{Industry C} \\ \text{All Other Producers} \end{array} \begin{bmatrix} 50 & 70 & 200 & 360 \\ 90 & 30 & 270 & 320 \\ 120 & 240 & 100 & 1{,}050 \\ 420 & 370 & 940 & 4{,}960 \end{bmatrix}$$

8.2 MATRIX ADDITION AND SCALAR MULTIPLICATION

Consider a snowmobile dealer who sells two models, Deluxe and Super. Each is available in one of two colors, red and blue. Suppose that the sales for January and February are represented by the sales matrices

$$\begin{array}{cc} & \text{Deluxe} \quad \text{Super} \end{array}$$

$$J = \begin{array}{l} \text{red} \\ \text{blue} \end{array} \begin{bmatrix} 1 & 2 \\ 3 & 5 \end{bmatrix}, \qquad F = \begin{bmatrix} 3 & 1 \\ 4 & 2 \end{bmatrix}.$$

Each row of J and F gives the number of each model sold for a given color. Each column gives the number of each color sold for a given model. A matrix representing total sales for each model and color for both months can be obtained by adding the corresponding entries in J and F:

$$\begin{bmatrix} 4 & 3 \\ 7 & 7 \end{bmatrix}.$$

This situation provides some motivation for introducing the operation of matrix addition for two matrices of the same order.

Definition

If A and B are both $m \times n$ matrices, then $A + B$ is the $m \times n$ matrix obtained by adding corresponding entries of A and B.

Thus if

$$A = \begin{bmatrix} a_{11} & a_{12} & a_{13} \\ a_{21} & a_{22} & a_{23} \end{bmatrix} \quad \text{and} \quad B = \begin{bmatrix} b_{11} & b_{12} & b_{13} \\ b_{21} & b_{22} & b_{23} \end{bmatrix},$$

then A and B have the same order (2×3) and

$$A + B = \begin{bmatrix} a_{11} + b_{11} & a_{12} + b_{12} & a_{13} + b_{13} \\ a_{21} + b_{21} & a_{22} + b_{22} & a_{23} + b_{23} \end{bmatrix}.$$

EXAMPLE 1

a. $\begin{bmatrix} 1 & 2 \\ 3 & 4 \\ 5 & 6 \end{bmatrix} + \begin{bmatrix} 7 & -2 \\ -6 & 4 \\ 3 & 0 \end{bmatrix} = \begin{bmatrix} 1+7 & 2-2 \\ 3-6 & 4+4 \\ 5+3 & 6+0 \end{bmatrix} = \begin{bmatrix} 8 & 0 \\ -3 & 8 \\ 8 & 6 \end{bmatrix}.$

b. $\begin{bmatrix} 1 & 2 \\ 3 & 4 \end{bmatrix} + \begin{bmatrix} 2 \\ 1 \end{bmatrix}$ is not defined since the matrices do not have the same order.

If **A**, **B**, **C**, and **O** have the same order, then the following properties hold for matrix addition:

---

1. **A** + **B** = **B** + **A**   (commutative property),
2. **A** + (**B** + **C**) = (**A** + **B**) + **C**   (associative property),
3. **A** + **O** = **O** + **A** = **A**   (identity property).

These properties are illustrated in the following example.

EXAMPLE 2   Let

$$\mathbf{A} = \begin{bmatrix} 1 & 2 & 1 \\ -2 & 0 & 1 \end{bmatrix}, \qquad \mathbf{B} = \begin{bmatrix} 0 & 1 & 2 \\ 1 & -3 & 1 \end{bmatrix},$$

$$\mathbf{C} = \begin{bmatrix} -2 & 1 & -1 \\ 0 & -2 & 1 \end{bmatrix}, \quad \mathbf{O} = \begin{bmatrix} 0 & 0 & 0 \\ 0 & 0 & 0 \end{bmatrix}.$$

a. $\mathbf{A} + \mathbf{B} = \begin{bmatrix} 1 & 3 & 3 \\ -1 & -3 & 2 \end{bmatrix}; \qquad \mathbf{B} + \mathbf{A} = \begin{bmatrix} 1 & 3 & 3 \\ -1 & -3 & 2 \end{bmatrix}.$

b. $\mathbf{A} + (\mathbf{B} + \mathbf{C}) = \mathbf{A} + \begin{bmatrix} -2 & 2 & 1 \\ 1 & -5 & 2 \end{bmatrix} = \begin{bmatrix} -1 & 4 & 2 \\ -1 & -5 & 3 \end{bmatrix},$

$(\mathbf{A} + \mathbf{B}) + \mathbf{C} = \begin{bmatrix} 1 & 3 & 3 \\ -1 & -3 & 2 \end{bmatrix} + \mathbf{C} = \begin{bmatrix} -1 & 4 & 2 \\ -1 & -5 & 3 \end{bmatrix}.$

c. $\mathbf{A} + \mathbf{O} = \begin{bmatrix} 1 & 2 & 1 \\ -2 & 0 & 1 \end{bmatrix} + \begin{bmatrix} 0 & 0 & 0 \\ 0 & 0 & 0 \end{bmatrix} = \begin{bmatrix} 1 & 2 & 1 \\ -2 & 0 & 1 \end{bmatrix} = \mathbf{A}.$

Thus the zero matrix plays the same role in matrix addition as the number zero does in addition of real numbers.

Returning to the snowmobile dealer, recall that February sales were given by the matrix

$$\mathbf{F} = \begin{bmatrix} 3 & 1 \\ 4 & 2 \end{bmatrix}.$$

If in March the dealer doubles February's sales of each model and color of snowmobile, the sales matrix $\mathbf{M}$ for March could be obtained by multiplying each entry in $\mathbf{F}$ by 2:

$$\mathbf{M} = \begin{bmatrix} 2 \cdot 3 & 2 \cdot 1 \\ 2 \cdot 4 & 2 \cdot 2 \end{bmatrix}.$$

It seems reasonable to write this operation as

$$\mathbf{M} = 2\mathbf{F} = 2\begin{bmatrix} 3 & 1 \\ 4 & 2 \end{bmatrix} = \begin{bmatrix} 2 \cdot 3 & 2 \cdot 1 \\ 2 \cdot 4 & 2 \cdot 2 \end{bmatrix} = \begin{bmatrix} 6 & 2 \\ 8 & 4 \end{bmatrix},$$

which is thought of as multiplying a matrix by a real number. Indeed, we have the following definition.

Definition

If $\mathbf{A}$ is an $m \times n$ matrix and k is a real number (also called a scalar), then by $k\mathbf{A}$ we denote the $m \times n$ matrix obtained by multiplying each entry in $\mathbf{A}$ by k. This operation is called **scalar multiplication.**

Thus if

$$\mathbf{A} = \begin{bmatrix} a_{11} & a_{12} \\ a_{21} & a_{22} \end{bmatrix},$$

then

$$k\mathbf{A} = \begin{bmatrix} ka_{11} & ka_{12} \\ ka_{21} & ka_{22} \end{bmatrix}.$$

EXAMPLE 3   *Let*

$$\mathbf{A} = \begin{bmatrix} 1 & 2 \\ 4 & -2 \end{bmatrix}, \quad \mathbf{B} = \begin{bmatrix} 3 & -4 \\ 7 & 1 \end{bmatrix}, \quad \mathbf{O} = \begin{bmatrix} 0 & 0 \\ 0 & 0 \end{bmatrix}.$$

Find the following matrices.

a. $4\mathbf{A}$.

$$4\mathbf{A} = 4\begin{bmatrix} 1 & 2 \\ 4 & -2 \end{bmatrix} = \begin{bmatrix} 4 \cdot 1 & 4 \cdot 2 \\ 4 \cdot 4 & 4 \cdot (-2) \end{bmatrix} = \begin{bmatrix} 4 & 8 \\ 16 & -8 \end{bmatrix}.$$

b. $-\dfrac{2}{3}\mathbf{B}$.

$$-\frac{2}{3}\mathbf{B} = \begin{bmatrix} -\frac{2}{3}(3) & -\frac{2}{3}(-4) \\ -\frac{2}{3}(7) & -\frac{2}{3}(1) \end{bmatrix} = \begin{bmatrix} -2 & \frac{8}{3} \\ -\frac{14}{3} & -\frac{2}{3} \end{bmatrix}.$$

c. $\frac{1}{2}\mathbf{A} + 3\mathbf{B}$.

$$\frac{1}{2}\mathbf{A} + 3\mathbf{B} = \frac{1}{2}\begin{bmatrix} 1 & 2 \\ 4 & -2 \end{bmatrix} + 3\begin{bmatrix} 3 & -4 \\ 7 & 1 \end{bmatrix}$$

$$= \begin{bmatrix} \frac{1}{2} & 1 \\ 2 & -1 \end{bmatrix} + \begin{bmatrix} 9 & -12 \\ 21 & 3 \end{bmatrix} = \begin{bmatrix} \frac{19}{2} & -11 \\ 23 & 2 \end{bmatrix}.$$

d. $0\mathbf{A}$.

$$0\mathbf{A} = 0\begin{bmatrix} 1 & 2 \\ 4 & -2 \end{bmatrix} = \begin{bmatrix} 0 & 0 \\ 0 & 0 \end{bmatrix} = \mathbf{O}.$$

e. $k\mathbf{O}$.

$$k\mathbf{O} = k\begin{bmatrix} 0 & 0 \\ 0 & 0 \end{bmatrix} = \begin{bmatrix} 0 & 0 \\ 0 & 0 \end{bmatrix} = \mathbf{O}.$$

If $\mathbf{A}$, $\mathbf{B}$, and $\mathbf{O}$ have the same order, then for any scalars k, k_1, and k_2 we have the following properties of scalar multiplication:

1. $k(\mathbf{A} + \mathbf{B}) = k\mathbf{A} + k\mathbf{B}$,
2. $(k_1 + k_2)\mathbf{A} = k_1\mathbf{A} + k_2\mathbf{A}$,
3. $k_1(k_2\mathbf{A}) = (k_1 k_2)\mathbf{A}$,
4. $0\mathbf{A} = \mathbf{O}$,
5. $k\mathbf{O} = \mathbf{O}$.

Properties 4 and 5 were illustrated in Example 3(d) and (e); the others will be illustrated in the exercises. Remember that $\mathbf{O} \neq 0$, for 0 is a *scalar* and $\mathbf{O}$ is a zero *matrix*.

For the case that $k = -1$, then $k\mathbf{A} = (-1)\mathbf{A}$, which will be denoted by simply writing $-\mathbf{A}$, called the *negative* of $\mathbf{A}$. Thus if

$$\mathbf{A} = \begin{bmatrix} 3 & 1 \\ -4 & 5 \end{bmatrix},$$

then

$$-\mathbf{A} = (-1)\begin{bmatrix} 3 & 1 \\ -4 & 5 \end{bmatrix} = \begin{bmatrix} -3 & -1 \\ 4 & -5 \end{bmatrix}.$$

Note that $-\mathbf{A}$ is the matrix obtained by multiplying each entry of $\mathbf{A}$ by -1.
Subtraction of matrices can now be defined.

Definition
If $\mathbf{A}$ and $\mathbf{B}$ have the same order, then by $\mathbf{A} - \mathbf{B}$ we mean $\mathbf{A} + (-\mathbf{B})$.

EXAMPLE 4

a. $\begin{bmatrix} 2 & 6 \\ -4 & 1 \\ 3 & 2 \end{bmatrix} - \begin{bmatrix} 6 & -2 \\ 4 & 1 \\ 0 & 3 \end{bmatrix} = \begin{bmatrix} 2 & 6 \\ -4 & 1 \\ 3 & 2 \end{bmatrix} + (-1)\begin{bmatrix} 6 & -2 \\ 4 & 1 \\ 0 & 3 \end{bmatrix}$

$$= \begin{bmatrix} 2 & 6 \\ -4 & 1 \\ 3 & 2 \end{bmatrix} + \begin{bmatrix} -6 & 2 \\ -4 & -1 \\ 0 & -3 \end{bmatrix}$$

$$= \begin{bmatrix} 2-6 & 6+2 \\ -4-4 & 1-1 \\ 3+0 & 2-3 \end{bmatrix} = \begin{bmatrix} -4 & 8 \\ -8 & 0 \\ 3 & -1 \end{bmatrix}.$$

More simply, to find $\mathbf{A} - \mathbf{B}$ we can subtract each entry in $\mathbf{B}$ from the corresponding entry in $\mathbf{A}$.

b. $\begin{bmatrix} 6 & -4 & 7 & 1 \\ -1 & 6 & 0 & -4 \\ 2 & -1 & 3 & 1 \end{bmatrix} - \begin{bmatrix} 2 & -3 & 3 & 2 \\ 4 & 2 & 1 & 3 \\ 1 & 0 & -1 & -4 \end{bmatrix}$

$$= \begin{bmatrix} 6-2 & -4+3 & 7-3 & 1-2 \\ -1-4 & 6-2 & 0-1 & -4-3 \\ 2-1 & -1-0 & 3+1 & 1+4 \end{bmatrix} = \begin{bmatrix} 4 & -1 & 4 & -1 \\ -5 & 4 & -1 & -7 \\ 1 & -1 & 4 & 5 \end{bmatrix}.$$

EXAMPLE 5   Solve $2\begin{bmatrix} x_1 \\ x_2 \end{bmatrix} - \begin{bmatrix} 3 \\ 4 \end{bmatrix} = 5\begin{bmatrix} 5 \\ -4 \end{bmatrix}.$

$$2\begin{bmatrix} x_1 \\ x_2 \end{bmatrix} - \begin{bmatrix} 3 \\ 4 \end{bmatrix} = 5\begin{bmatrix} 5 \\ -4 \end{bmatrix},$$

$$\begin{bmatrix} 2x_1 \\ 2x_2 \end{bmatrix} - \begin{bmatrix} 3 \\ 4 \end{bmatrix} = \begin{bmatrix} 25 \\ -20 \end{bmatrix},$$

$$\begin{bmatrix} 2x_1 - 3 \\ 2x_2 - 4 \end{bmatrix} = \begin{bmatrix} 25 \\ -20 \end{bmatrix}.$$

By equality of matrices we must have $2x_1 - 3 = 25$, which gives $x_1 = 14$; from $2x_2 - 4 = -20$ we get $x_2 = -8$.

EXAMPLE 6   Consider a simplified hypothetical economy having three industries, say coal, electricity, and steel, and three consumers 1, 2, and 3. Moreover, assume each consumer may use some of the output of each industry, and also that each industry uses some of the output of each other industry. The needs of each consumer and industry can be represented by a (row) demand matrix whose entries, in order, give the amount of coal, electricity, and steel needed by the consumer or industry in some convenient units. For example, the demand matrices for the consumers might be

$$\mathbf{D_1} = [3 \quad 2 \quad 5], \qquad \mathbf{D_2} = [0 \quad 17 \quad 1], \qquad \mathbf{D_3} = [4 \quad 6 \quad 12],$$

and for the industries they might be

$$\mathbf{D_C} = [0 \quad 1 \quad 4], \qquad \mathbf{D_E} = [20 \quad 0 \quad 8], \qquad \mathbf{D_S} = [30 \quad 5 \quad 0],$$

where the subscripts C, E, and S stand for coal, electricity, and steel, respectively. The total demand for these goods by the consumers is given by the sum

$$\mathbf{D_1} + \mathbf{D_2} + \mathbf{D_3} = [3 \quad 2 \quad 5] + [0 \quad 17 \quad 1] + [4 \quad 6 \quad 12] = [7 \quad 25 \quad 18].$$

The total industrial demand is given by the sum

$$\mathbf{D_C} + \mathbf{D_E} + \mathbf{D_S} = [0 \quad 1 \quad 4] + [20 \quad 0 \quad 8] + [30 \quad 5 \quad 0] = [50 \quad 6 \quad 12].$$

Therefore, the total overall demand is given by

$$[7 \quad 25 \quad 18] + [50 \quad 6 \quad 12] = [57 \quad 31 \quad 30].$$

Thus the coal industry sells a total of 57 units, the total units of electricity sold is 31, and the total units of steel which are sold is 30.*

EXERCISE 8.2

In Problems **1–12,** *perform the indicated operations.*

1. $\begin{bmatrix} 2 & 0 & -3 \\ -1 & 4 & 0 \\ 1 & -6 & 5 \end{bmatrix} + \begin{bmatrix} 2 & -3 & 4 \\ -1 & 6 & 5 \\ 9 & 11 & -2 \end{bmatrix}.$

2. $\begin{bmatrix} 2 & -7 \\ -6 & 4 \end{bmatrix} + \begin{bmatrix} 7 & -4 \\ -2 & 1 \end{bmatrix} + \begin{bmatrix} 2 & 7 \\ 7 & 2 \end{bmatrix}.$

3. $\begin{bmatrix} 1 & 4 \\ -2 & 7 \\ 6 & 9 \end{bmatrix} - \begin{bmatrix} 6 & -1 \\ 7 & 2 \\ 1 & 0 \end{bmatrix}.$

4. $2\begin{bmatrix} 3 & -1 & 4 \\ 2 & 1 & -1 \\ 0 & 0 & 2 \end{bmatrix}.$

---

* This example, as well as some others in this chapter, are from John G. Kemeny, J. Laurie Snell, and Gerald L. Thompson, *Introduction to Finite Mathematics*, 3rd ed, © 1974. Reprinted by permission of Prentice-Hall, Inc., Englewood Cliffs, New Jersey.

5. $3[1 \quad -3 \quad 2 \quad 1] + 2[-6 \quad 1 \quad 0 \quad 4] - 0[-2 \quad 7 \quad 6 \quad 4]$.

6. $[7 \quad 7] + 66$.

7. $\begin{bmatrix} 1 & 2 \\ 3 & 4 \end{bmatrix} + \begin{bmatrix} 5 \\ 6 \end{bmatrix}$.

8. $\begin{bmatrix} 2 & -1 \\ 7 & 4 \end{bmatrix} + 3\begin{bmatrix} 0 & 0 \\ 0 & 0 \end{bmatrix}$.

9. $-6\begin{bmatrix} 2 & -6 & 7 & 1 \\ 7 & 1 & 6 & -2 \end{bmatrix}$.

10. $\begin{bmatrix} 1 & -1 \\ 2 & 0 \\ 3 & -6 \\ 4 & 9 \end{bmatrix} - 3\begin{bmatrix} -6 & 9 \\ 2 & 6 \\ 1 & -2 \\ 4 & 5 \end{bmatrix}$.

11. $\begin{bmatrix} 2 & -4 & 0 \\ 0 & 6 & -2 \\ -4 & 0 & 10 \end{bmatrix} + \dfrac{1}{3}\begin{bmatrix} 9 & 0 & 3 \\ 0 & 3 & 0 \\ 3 & 9 & 9 \end{bmatrix}$.

12. $2\begin{bmatrix} 1 & 0 & 0 \\ 0 & 1 & 0 \\ 0 & 0 & 1 \end{bmatrix} - 3\left(\begin{bmatrix} 2 & 1 & 0 \\ 1 & -2 & 3 \\ 1 & 0 & 0 \end{bmatrix} - \begin{bmatrix} 6 & -2 & 1 \\ -5 & 1 & -2 \\ 0 & 1 & 3 \end{bmatrix}\right)$.

In Problems **13–24**, compute the required matrices if

$$\mathbf{A} = \begin{bmatrix} 2 & 1 \\ 3 & -3 \end{bmatrix}, \quad \mathbf{B} = \begin{bmatrix} -6 & -5 \\ 2 & -3 \end{bmatrix}, \quad \mathbf{C} = \begin{bmatrix} -2 & -1 \\ -3 & 3 \end{bmatrix}, \quad \mathbf{O} = \begin{bmatrix} 0 & 0 \\ 0 & 0 \end{bmatrix}.$$

13. $-\mathbf{B}$.

14. $-(\mathbf{A} - \mathbf{B})$.

15. $2\mathbf{O}$.

16. $\mathbf{A} + \mathbf{B} - \mathbf{C}$.

17. $2(\mathbf{A} - 2\mathbf{B})$.

18. $0(\mathbf{A} + \mathbf{B})$.

19. $3(\mathbf{A} - \mathbf{C}) + 6$.

20. $\mathbf{A} + (\mathbf{C} + 2\mathbf{O})$.

21. $2\mathbf{B} - 3\mathbf{A} + 2\mathbf{C}$.

22. $3\mathbf{C} - 2\mathbf{B}$.

23. $\tfrac{1}{2}\mathbf{A} - 2(\mathbf{B} + 2\mathbf{C})$.

24. $2\mathbf{A} - \tfrac{1}{2}(\mathbf{B} - \mathbf{C})$.

For matrices **A, B,** and **C** above, verify that:

25. $3(\mathbf{A} + \mathbf{B}) = 3\mathbf{A} + 3\mathbf{B}$.

26. $(2 + 3)\mathbf{A} = 2\mathbf{A} + 3\mathbf{A}$.

27. $k_1(k_2\mathbf{A}) = (k_2 k_2)\mathbf{A}$.

28. $k(\mathbf{A} + \mathbf{B} + \mathbf{C}) = k\mathbf{A} + k\mathbf{B} + k\mathbf{C}$.

29. Express the matrix equation

$$x\begin{bmatrix} 2 \\ 1 \end{bmatrix} - y\begin{bmatrix} -3 \\ 5 \end{bmatrix} = 2\begin{bmatrix} 8 \\ 11 \end{bmatrix}$$

as a system of linear equations and solve.

30. In the reverse of the manner used in Problem 29, write the system

$$\begin{cases} 3x + 5y = 16 \\ 2x - 6y = -4 \end{cases}$$

as a matrix equation.

In Problems **31–34**, solve the matrix equations.

31. $3\begin{bmatrix} x \\ y \end{bmatrix} - 3\begin{bmatrix} -2 \\ 4 \end{bmatrix} = 4\begin{bmatrix} 6 \\ -2 \end{bmatrix}$.

32. $3\begin{bmatrix} x \\ 2 \end{bmatrix} - 4\begin{bmatrix} 7 \\ -y \end{bmatrix} = \begin{bmatrix} -x \\ 2y \end{bmatrix}$.

33. $\begin{bmatrix} 2 \\ 4 \\ 6 \end{bmatrix} + 2 \begin{bmatrix} x \\ y \\ 4z \end{bmatrix} = \begin{bmatrix} -10 \\ -24 \\ 14 \end{bmatrix}.$

34. $x \begin{bmatrix} 2 \\ 0 \\ 3 \end{bmatrix} + 2 \begin{bmatrix} -1 \\ 0 \\ 6 \end{bmatrix} + y \begin{bmatrix} 0 \\ 2 \\ -3 \end{bmatrix} = \begin{bmatrix} 8 \\ 4 \\ 3x + 12 - 3y \end{bmatrix}.$

35. Suppose the price of products A, B, and C are given, in that order, by the price matrix

$$\mathbf{P} = [p_1 \quad p_2 \quad p_3].$$

If the prices are to be increased by 10%, the matrix of the new prices can be obtained by multiplying $\mathbf{P}$ by what scalar?

8.3 MATRIX MULTIPLICATION

Besides the operations of matrix addition and scalar multiplication, the product $\mathbf{AB}$ of matrices $\mathbf{A}$ and $\mathbf{B}$ can be defined under certain conditions, namely that the number of columns of $\mathbf{A}$ is equal to the number of rows of $\mathbf{B}$.

Definition
Let $\mathbf{A}$ be an $m \times n$ matrix and $\mathbf{B}$ be an $n \times p$ matrix. Then the product $\mathbf{AB}$ is the $m \times p$ matrix $\mathbf{C}$ whose entry c_{ij} in the ith row and jth column is obtained as follows: sum the products formed by multiplying, in order, each entry (that is, first, second, etc.) in the ith row of $\mathbf{A}$ by the "corresponding" entry (that is, first, second, etc.) in the jth column of $\mathbf{B}$.

Three points must be completely understood concerning the above definition of $\mathbf{AB}$. First, the condition that $\mathbf{A}$ be $m \times n$ and $\mathbf{B}$ be $n \times p$ is equivalent to saying that the number of columns of $\mathbf{A}$ must be equal to the number of rows of $\mathbf{B}$. Second, the product will be a matrix of order $m \times p$; it will have as many rows as $\mathbf{A}$ and as many columns as $\mathbf{B}$. Third, the definition refers to the product $\mathbf{AB}$, *in that order;* $\mathbf{A}$ is the left factor and $\mathbf{B}$ is the right factor. For $\mathbf{AB}$ we say $\mathbf{B}$ is *premultiplied* by $\mathbf{A}$, or $\mathbf{A}$ is *postmultiplied* by $\mathbf{B}$.

To apply the definition, let us find the product

$$\mathbf{AB} = \begin{bmatrix} 2 & 1 & -6 \\ 1 & -3 & 2 \end{bmatrix} \begin{bmatrix} 1 & 0 & -3 \\ 0 & 4 & 2 \\ -2 & 1 & 1 \end{bmatrix}.$$

The number of columns of $\mathbf{A}$ is equal to the number of rows of $\mathbf{B}$, so the product is defined. Since $\mathbf{A}$ is 2×3 ($m \times n$) and $\mathbf{B}$ is 3×3 ($n \times p$), the product $\mathbf{C}$ will have order 2×3 ($m \times p$):

$$\mathbf{C} = \begin{bmatrix} c_{11} & c_{12} & c_{13} \\ c_{21} & c_{22} & c_{23} \end{bmatrix}.$$

The entry c_{11} is obtained by summing the products of each entry in row 1 of $\mathbf{A}$ by the "corresponding" entry in column 1 of $\mathbf{B}$. That is,

row 1 entries of $\mathbf{A}$

$$c_{11} = (2)(1) + (1)(0) + (-6)(-2) = 14.$$

column 1 entries of $\mathbf{B}$

Similarly, for c_{21} we use the entries in row 2 of **A** and those in column 1 of **B**:

$$\overset{\text{row 2 entries of A}}{c_{21} = (1)(1) + (-3)(0) + (2)(-2) = -3.}$$

$$\underset{\text{column 1 entries of B}}{}$$

Also,

$$c_{12} = (2)(0) + (1)(4) + (-6)(1) = -2,$$

$$c_{22} = (1)(0) + (-3)(4) + (2)(1) = -10,$$

$$c_{13} = (2)(-3) + (1)(2) + (-6)(1) = -10,$$

$$c_{23} = (1)(-3) + (-3)(2) + (2)(1) = -7.$$

Thus

$$\mathbf{AB} = \begin{bmatrix} 2 & 1 & -6 \\ 1 & -3 & 2 \end{bmatrix} \begin{bmatrix} 1 & 0 & -3 \\ 0 & 4 & 2 \\ -2 & 1 & 1 \end{bmatrix} = \begin{bmatrix} 14 & -2 & -10 \\ -3 & -10 & -7 \end{bmatrix}.$$

If we reverse the order of the factors, then

$$\mathbf{BA} = \begin{bmatrix} 1 & 0 & -3 \\ 0 & 4 & 2 \\ -2 & 1 & 1 \end{bmatrix} \begin{bmatrix} 2 & 1 & -6 \\ 1 & -3 & 2 \end{bmatrix}.$$

This product is *not* defined since the number of columns of **B** does *not* equal the number of rows of **A.** This shows that matrix multiplication is not commutative. That is, for any matrices **A** and **B** it is usually the case that $\mathbf{AB} \neq \mathbf{BA}$ (even if both products are defined).

EXAMPLE 1   *Determine*

$$\mathbf{AB} = \begin{bmatrix} 2 & -4 & 2 \\ 0 & 1 & -3 \end{bmatrix} \begin{bmatrix} 2 & 1 \\ 0 & 4 \\ 2 & 2 \end{bmatrix}.$$

Since **A** is 2×3 and **B** is 3×2, the product **AB** is defined and will have order 2×2. By simultaneously moving the index finger of your left hand along the rows of **A** and the index finger of your right hand along the columns of **B,** you can find mentally the entries of the product.

$$\begin{bmatrix} 2 & -4 & 2 \\ 0 & 1 & -3 \end{bmatrix} \begin{bmatrix} 2 & 1 \\ 0 & 4 \\ 2 & 2 \end{bmatrix} = \begin{bmatrix} 8 & -10 \\ -6 & -2 \end{bmatrix}.$$

EXAMPLE 2   *Evaluate each of the following.*

a. $[1 \quad 2 \quad 3]\begin{bmatrix} 4 \\ 5 \\ 6 \end{bmatrix}$.

The product has order 1×1:

$$[1 \quad 2 \quad 3]\begin{bmatrix} 4 \\ 5 \\ 6 \end{bmatrix} = [32].$$

b. $\begin{bmatrix} 1 \\ 2 \\ 3 \end{bmatrix}[1 \quad 6]$.

The product has order 3×2:

$$\begin{bmatrix} 1 \\ 2 \\ 3 \end{bmatrix}[1 \quad 6] = \begin{bmatrix} 1 & 6 \\ 2 & 12 \\ 3 & 18 \end{bmatrix}.$$

c. $\begin{bmatrix} 1 & 3 & 0 \\ -2 & 2 & 1 \\ 1 & 0 & -4 \end{bmatrix}\begin{bmatrix} 1 & 0 & 2 \\ 5 & -1 & 3 \\ 2 & 1 & -2 \end{bmatrix} = \begin{bmatrix} 16 & -3 & 11 \\ 10 & -1 & 0 \\ -7 & -4 & 10 \end{bmatrix}.$

d. $\begin{bmatrix} a_{11} & a_{12} \\ a_{21} & a_{22} \end{bmatrix}\begin{bmatrix} b_{11} & b_{12} \\ b_{21} & b_{22} \end{bmatrix} = \begin{bmatrix} a_{11}b_{11} + a_{12}b_{21} & a_{11}b_{12} + a_{12}b_{22} \\ a_{21}b_{11} + a_{22}b_{21} & a_{21}b_{12} + a_{22}b_{22} \end{bmatrix}.$

EXAMPLE 3   *Find* **AB** *and* **BA** *if*

$$\mathbf{A} = \begin{bmatrix} 2 & -1 \\ 3 & 1 \end{bmatrix} \quad and \quad \mathbf{B} = \begin{bmatrix} -2 & 1 \\ 1 & 4 \end{bmatrix}.$$

We have

$$\mathbf{AB} = \begin{bmatrix} 2 & -1 \\ 3 & 1 \end{bmatrix}\begin{bmatrix} -2 & 1 \\ 1 & 4 \end{bmatrix} = \begin{bmatrix} -5 & -2 \\ -5 & 7 \end{bmatrix},$$

$$\mathbf{BA} = \begin{bmatrix} -2 & 1 \\ 1 & 4 \end{bmatrix}\begin{bmatrix} 2 & -1 \\ 3 & 1 \end{bmatrix} = \begin{bmatrix} -1 & 3 \\ 14 & 3 \end{bmatrix}.$$

Although both **AB** and **BA** are defined, **AB** $\neq$ **BA.**

Matrix multiplication satisfies the following properties if it is assumed that all sums and products are defined:

$$
\begin{array}{ll}
\textbf{1. A(BC)} = \textbf{(AB)C} & \text{(associative property)} \\
\textbf{2. A(B + C)} = \textbf{AB + AC,} & \\
\quad \textbf{(A + B)C} = \textbf{AC + BC} & \text{(distributive properties)}
\end{array}
$$

EXAMPLE 4   *If*

$$
\mathbf{A} = \begin{bmatrix} 1 & -2 \\ -3 & 4 \end{bmatrix}, \quad \mathbf{B} = \begin{bmatrix} 3 & 0 & -1 \\ 1 & 1 & 2 \end{bmatrix}, \quad and \quad \mathbf{C} = \begin{bmatrix} 1 & 0 \\ 0 & 2 \\ 1 & 1 \end{bmatrix},
$$

find **ABC** *in two ways.*

$$
\mathbf{A(BC)} = \begin{bmatrix} 1 & -2 \\ -3 & 4 \end{bmatrix} \left(\begin{bmatrix} 3 & 0 & -1 \\ 1 & 1 & 2 \end{bmatrix} \begin{bmatrix} 1 & 0 \\ 0 & 2 \\ 1 & 1 \end{bmatrix} \right)
$$

$$
= \begin{bmatrix} 1 & -2 \\ -3 & 4 \end{bmatrix} \begin{bmatrix} 2 & -1 \\ 3 & 4 \end{bmatrix} = \begin{bmatrix} -4 & -9 \\ 6 & 19 \end{bmatrix}.
$$

$$
\mathbf{(AB)C} = \left(\begin{bmatrix} 1 & -2 \\ -3 & 4 \end{bmatrix} \begin{bmatrix} 3 & 0 & -1 \\ 1 & 1 & 2 \end{bmatrix} \right) \begin{bmatrix} 1 & 0 \\ 0 & 2 \\ 1 & 1 \end{bmatrix}
$$

$$
= \begin{bmatrix} 1 & -2 & -5 \\ -5 & 4 & 11 \end{bmatrix} \begin{bmatrix} 1 & 0 \\ 0 & 2 \\ 1 & 1 \end{bmatrix}
$$

$$
= \begin{bmatrix} -4 & -9 \\ 6 & 19 \end{bmatrix}.
$$

EXAMPLE 5   *Verify that* **A(B + C)** = **AB + AC** *if*

$$
\mathbf{A} = \begin{bmatrix} 1 & 0 \\ 2 & 3 \end{bmatrix}, \quad \mathbf{B} = \begin{bmatrix} -2 & 0 \\ 1 & 3 \end{bmatrix}, \quad and \quad \mathbf{C} = \begin{bmatrix} -2 & 1 \\ 0 & 2 \end{bmatrix}.
$$

$$
\mathbf{A(B + C)} = \begin{bmatrix} 1 & 0 \\ 2 & 3 \end{bmatrix} \left(\begin{bmatrix} -2 & 0 \\ 1 & 3 \end{bmatrix} + \begin{bmatrix} -2 & 1 \\ 0 & 2 \end{bmatrix} \right)
$$

$$
= \begin{bmatrix} 1 & 0 \\ 2 & 3 \end{bmatrix} \begin{bmatrix} -4 & 1 \\ 1 & 5 \end{bmatrix} = \begin{bmatrix} -4 & 1 \\ -5 & 17 \end{bmatrix}.
$$

$$
\mathbf{AB + AC} = \begin{bmatrix} 1 & 0 \\ 2 & 3 \end{bmatrix} \begin{bmatrix} -2 & 0 \\ 1 & 3 \end{bmatrix} + \begin{bmatrix} 1 & 0 \\ 2 & 3 \end{bmatrix} \begin{bmatrix} -2 & 1 \\ 0 & 2 \end{bmatrix}
$$

$$= \begin{bmatrix} -2 & 0 \\ -1 & 9 \end{bmatrix} + \begin{bmatrix} -2 & 1 \\ -4 & 8 \end{bmatrix} = \begin{bmatrix} -4 & 1 \\ -5 & 17 \end{bmatrix}.$$

Thus $\mathbf{A}(\mathbf{B} + \mathbf{C}) = \mathbf{AB} + \mathbf{AC}$.

A square matrix of order n whose main diagonal entries are all 1's and all of whose other entries are 0's is called the **identity matrix** of order n. It is denoted by $\mathbf{I}$. For example, the identity matrices of orders 3 and 4, respectively, are

$$\mathbf{I} = \begin{bmatrix} 1 & 0 & 0 \\ 0 & 1 & 0 \\ 0 & 0 & 1 \end{bmatrix} \quad \text{and} \quad \mathbf{I} = \begin{bmatrix} 1 & 0 & 0 & 0 \\ 0 & 1 & 0 & 0 \\ 0 & 0 & 1 & 0 \\ 0 & 0 & 0 & 1 \end{bmatrix}.$$

If $\mathbf{A}$ is a square matrix and both $\mathbf{A}$ and $\mathbf{I}$ have the same order, then

$$\boxed{\mathbf{AI} = \mathbf{IA} = \mathbf{A}.}$$

Thus the identity matrix plays the same role in matrix multiplication as does the number 1 in the multiplication of real numbers. For example,

$$\begin{bmatrix} 2 & 4 \\ 1 & 5 \end{bmatrix} \begin{bmatrix} 1 & 0 \\ 0 & 1 \end{bmatrix} = \begin{bmatrix} 2 & 4 \\ 1 & 5 \end{bmatrix}$$

and

$$\begin{bmatrix} 1 & 0 \\ 0 & 1 \end{bmatrix} \begin{bmatrix} 2 & 4 \\ 1 & 5 \end{bmatrix} = \begin{bmatrix} 2 & 4 \\ 1 & 5 \end{bmatrix}.$$

EXAMPLE 6   *If*

$$\mathbf{A} = \begin{bmatrix} 3 & 2 \\ 1 & 4 \end{bmatrix}, \quad \mathbf{B} = \begin{bmatrix} \frac{2}{5} & -\frac{1}{5} \\ -\frac{1}{10} & \frac{3}{10} \end{bmatrix},$$

$$\mathbf{I} = \begin{bmatrix} 1 & 0 \\ 0 & 1 \end{bmatrix}, \quad and \quad \mathbf{O} = \begin{bmatrix} 0 & 0 \\ 0 & 0 \end{bmatrix},$$

determine each of the following.

a. $\mathbf{I} - \mathbf{A}$.

$$\mathbf{I} - \mathbf{A} = \begin{bmatrix} 1 & 0 \\ 0 & 1 \end{bmatrix} - \begin{bmatrix} 3 & 2 \\ 1 & 4 \end{bmatrix} = \begin{bmatrix} -2 & -2 \\ -1 & -3 \end{bmatrix}.$$

b. $3(\mathbf{A} - 2\mathbf{I})$.

$$3(\mathbf{A} - 2\mathbf{I}) = 3\left(\begin{bmatrix} 3 & 2 \\ 1 & 4 \end{bmatrix} - 2\begin{bmatrix} 1 & 0 \\ 0 & 1 \end{bmatrix}\right)$$

$$= 3\left(\begin{bmatrix} 3 & 2 \\ 1 & 4 \end{bmatrix} - \begin{bmatrix} 2 & 0 \\ 0 & 2 \end{bmatrix}\right)$$

$$= 3\begin{bmatrix} 1 & 2 \\ 1 & 2 \end{bmatrix} = \begin{bmatrix} 3 & 6 \\ 3 & 6 \end{bmatrix}.$$

c. $\mathbf{AO}$.

$$\mathbf{AO} = \begin{bmatrix} 3 & 2 \\ 1 & 4 \end{bmatrix}\begin{bmatrix} 0 & 0 \\ 0 & 0 \end{bmatrix} = \begin{bmatrix} 0 & 0 \\ 0 & 0 \end{bmatrix} = \mathbf{O}.$$

d. $\mathbf{AB}$.

$$\mathbf{AB} = \begin{bmatrix} 3 & 2 \\ 1 & 4 \end{bmatrix}\begin{bmatrix} \frac{2}{5} & -\frac{1}{5} \\ -\frac{1}{10} & \frac{3}{10} \end{bmatrix} = \begin{bmatrix} 1 & 0 \\ 0 & 1 \end{bmatrix} = \mathbf{I}.$$

Systems of linear equations can be represented by using matrix multiplication. Consider the left side of the matrix equation

$$\begin{bmatrix} a_{11} & a_{12} \\ a_{21} & a_{22} \end{bmatrix}\begin{bmatrix} x_1 \\ x_2 \end{bmatrix} = \begin{bmatrix} c_1 \\ c_2 \end{bmatrix}. \tag{1}$$

The product on the left side has order 2×1 and hence is a column matrix:

$$\begin{bmatrix} a_{11}x_1 + a_{12}x_2 \\ a_{21}x_1 + a_{22}x_2 \end{bmatrix} = \begin{bmatrix} c_1 \\ c_2 \end{bmatrix}.$$

By equality of matrices we must have

$$\begin{cases} a_{11}x_1 + a_{12}x_2 = c_1, \\ a_{21}x_1 + a_{22}x_2 = c_2. \end{cases}$$

Hence a system of linear equations can be defined by a matrix equation. We usually describe Eq. (1) by saying it has the form

$$\boxed{\mathbf{AX} = \mathbf{C}.}$$

EXAMPLE 7   *Represent the system*

$$\begin{cases} 2x_1 + 5x_2 = 4, \\ 8x_1 + 3x_2 = 7 \end{cases}$$

in terms of matrix multiplication.

If

$$\mathbf{A} = \begin{bmatrix} 2 & 5 \\ 8 & 3 \end{bmatrix}, \quad \mathbf{X} = \begin{bmatrix} x_1 \\ x_2 \end{bmatrix}, \quad and \quad \mathbf{C} = \begin{bmatrix} 4 \\ 7 \end{bmatrix},$$

then the given system is equivalent to

$$\mathbf{AX} = \mathbf{C}$$

or

$$\begin{bmatrix} 2 & 5 \\ 8 & 3 \end{bmatrix}\begin{bmatrix} x_1 \\ x_2 \end{bmatrix} = \begin{bmatrix} 4 \\ 7 \end{bmatrix}.$$

EXAMPLE 8   Suppose that the prices (in dollars per unit) for products A, B, and C are represented by the price matrix

Price of
A B C
$$\mathbf{P} = [2 \quad 3 \quad 4].$$

If the quantities (in units) of A, B, and C that are purchased are given by the column matrix

$$\mathbf{Q} = \begin{bmatrix} 7 \\ 5 \\ 11 \end{bmatrix} \begin{matrix} \text{units of A} \\ \text{units of B} \\ \text{units of C,} \end{matrix}$$

then the total cost (in dollars) of the purchases is given by the entry in **PQ**:

$$\mathbf{PQ} = [2 \ 3 \ 4]\begin{bmatrix} 7 \\ 5 \\ 11 \end{bmatrix} = [(2 \cdot 7) + (3 \cdot 5) + (4 \cdot 11)] = [73].$$

EXAMPLE 9   Suppose that a building contractor has accepted orders for five ranch-style houses, seven Cape Cod-style houses, and 12 colonial-style houses. Then his orders can be represented by the row matrix

$$\mathbf{Q} = [5 \quad 7 \quad 12].$$

Furthermore, suppose that the "raw materials" that go into each type of house are steel, wood, glass, paint, and labor. The entries in the matrix **R** below give the number of units of each raw material going into each type of house. (The entries are not necessarily realistic, but are chosen for convenience.)

	Steel	Wood	Glass	Paint	Labor
Ranch	5	20	16	7	17
Cape Cod	7	18	12	9	21
Colonial	6	25	8	5	13

= **R**.

Each row indicates the amount of each raw material needed for a given kind of house; each column indicates the amount of a given raw material needed for each type of house. Suppose now that the contractor wishes to compute the amount of each raw material needed to fulfill his contracts. Then such information is given by **QR**:

$$\mathbf{QR} = [5 \quad 7 \quad 12] \begin{bmatrix} 5 & 20 & 16 & 7 & 17 \\ 7 & 18 & 12 & 9 & 21 \\ 6 & 25 & 8 & 5 & 13 \end{bmatrix}$$

$$= [146 \quad 526 \quad 260 \quad 158 \quad 388].$$

Thus the contractor should order 146 units of steel, 526 units of wood, 260 units of glass, and so on.

The contractor is also interested in the costs he will have to pay for these materials. Suppose steel costs $1500 per unit, wood costs $800 per unit, and glass, paint, and labor cost $500, $100, and $1000 per unit, respectively. These data can be written as the column cost matrix

$$\mathbf{C} = \begin{bmatrix} 1500 \\ 800 \\ 500 \\ 100 \\ 1000 \end{bmatrix}.$$

Then **RC** gives the cost of each type of house:

$$\mathbf{RC} = \begin{bmatrix} 5 & 20 & 16 & 7 & 17 \\ 7 & 18 & 12 & 9 & 21 \\ 6 & 25 & 8 & 5 & 13 \end{bmatrix} \begin{bmatrix} 1500 \\ 800 \\ 500 \\ 100 \\ 1000 \end{bmatrix} = \begin{bmatrix} 49{,}200 \\ 52{,}800 \\ 46{,}500 \end{bmatrix}.$$

Thus the cost of materials for the ranch-style house is $49,200, for the Cape Cod house, $52,800, and for the colonial house, $46,500.

The total cost of raw materials for all the houses is given by

$$\mathbf{QRC} = \mathbf{Q(RC)} = [5 \quad 7 \quad 12] \begin{bmatrix} 49{,}200 \\ 52{,}800 \\ 46{,}500 \end{bmatrix} = [1{,}173{,}600].$$

The total cost is $1,173,600.

EXAMPLE 10   In Example 6 of Sec. 8.2, suppose that the price of coal is $10,000 per unit, the price of electricity is $20,000 per unit, and the price of steel is $40,000 per unit. These prices can be represented by the (column) price matrix

$$P = \begin{bmatrix} 10{,}000 \\ 20{,}000 \\ 40{,}000 \end{bmatrix}.$$

Consider the steel industry. It sells a total of 30 units of steel at \$40,000 per unit and its total income is therefore \$1,200,000. Its costs for the various goods are given by the matrix product

$$\mathbf{D_sP} = [30 \quad 5 \quad 0] \begin{bmatrix} 10{,}000 \\ 20{,}000 \\ 40{,}000 \end{bmatrix} = [400{,}000].$$

Hence the profit for the steel industry is \$1,200,000 − \$400,000 = \$800,000.

EXERCISE 8.3

If $\mathbf{A} = \begin{bmatrix} 1 & 3 & -2 \\ -2 & 1 & -1 \\ 0 & 4 & 3 \end{bmatrix}$, $\mathbf{B} = \begin{bmatrix} 0 & -2 & 3 \\ -2 & 4 & -2 \\ 3 & 1 & -1 \end{bmatrix}$, and $\mathbf{AB} = \mathbf{C}$, find each of the following.

1. c_{11}.
2. c_{23}.
3. c_{32}.
4. c_{33}.
5. c_{22}.
6. c_{13}.

If $\mathbf{A}$ is 2×3, $\mathbf{B}$ is 3×1, $\mathbf{C}$ is 2×5, $\mathbf{D}$ is 4×3, $\mathbf{E}$ is 3×2, and $\mathbf{F}$ is 2×3, find the order and number of entries of each of the following.

7. **AE.**
8. **DE.**
9. **EC.**
10. **DB.**
11. **FB.**

12. **BA.**
13. **EA.**
14. **E(AE).**
15. **E(FB).**
16. **(F + A)B.**

Write the identity matrix that has the following order.

17. 4.
18. 6.

In Problems **19–36**, perform the indicated operations.

19. $\begin{bmatrix} 2 & -4 \\ 3 & 2 \end{bmatrix} \begin{bmatrix} 3 & 0 \\ -1 & 4 \end{bmatrix}$.

20. $\begin{bmatrix} -1 & 1 \\ 0 & 4 \\ 2 & 1 \end{bmatrix} \begin{bmatrix} 1 & -2 \\ 3 & 4 \end{bmatrix}$.

21. $\begin{bmatrix} 2 & 0 & 3 \\ -1 & 4 & 5 \end{bmatrix} \begin{bmatrix} 1 \\ 4 \\ 7 \end{bmatrix}$.

22. $[1 \quad 0 \quad 6 \quad 2] \begin{bmatrix} 0 \\ 1 \\ 2 \\ 3 \end{bmatrix}$.

23. $\begin{bmatrix} 1 & 4 & -1 \\ 0 & 0 & 2 \\ -2 & 1 & 1 \end{bmatrix} \begin{bmatrix} -2 & 1 & 0 \\ 0 & 1 & 1 \\ 1 & 1 & 2 \end{bmatrix}$.

24. $\begin{bmatrix} 3 & 2 & -1 \\ 4 & 10 & 0 \\ 0 & 1 & 2 \end{bmatrix} \begin{bmatrix} 2 & 0 & 1 & 0 \\ 0 & 1 & 0 & 0 \\ 0 & 1 & 0 & 1 \end{bmatrix}$.

25. $[-1 \quad 2 \quad 3] \begin{bmatrix} 3 & 1 & -1 & 2 \\ 0 & 4 & 3 & 1 \\ -1 & 3 & 1 & -2 \end{bmatrix}$.

26. $[1 \quad -4] \begin{bmatrix} -2 & 1 \\ 0 & 5 \\ 1 & 0 \end{bmatrix}$.

27. $\begin{bmatrix} 2 \\ 3 \\ -4 \\ 1 \end{bmatrix} [2 \quad 3 \quad -2 \quad 3]$.

28. $\begin{bmatrix} 0 & 1 \\ 2 & 3 \end{bmatrix} \left(\begin{bmatrix} 1 & 0 & 1 \\ 0 & 1 & 0 \end{bmatrix} + \begin{bmatrix} 0 & 1 & 0 \\ 0 & 0 & 1 \end{bmatrix} \right)$.

29. $3 \left(\begin{bmatrix} -2 & 0 & 2 \\ 3 & -1 & 1 \end{bmatrix} + 2 \begin{bmatrix} -1 & 0 & 2 \\ 1 & 1 & -2 \end{bmatrix} \right) \begin{bmatrix} 1 & 2 \\ 3 & 4 \\ 5 & 6 \end{bmatrix}$.

30. $\begin{bmatrix} -1 & 3 \\ -1 & 0 \end{bmatrix} \begin{bmatrix} -1 & 0 & 2 & -1 \\ 2 & 1 & -3 & -2 \end{bmatrix}$.

31. $\begin{bmatrix} 1 & 2 \\ 3 & 4 \end{bmatrix} \left(\begin{bmatrix} 2 & 0 \\ 1 & 0 \end{bmatrix} \begin{bmatrix} 1 \\ -2 \end{bmatrix} \begin{bmatrix} 1 & -2 \\ 2 & 1 \\ 3 & 0 \end{bmatrix} \right)$.

32. $3 \begin{bmatrix} 1 & 2 \\ -1 & 4 \end{bmatrix} - 4 \left(\begin{bmatrix} 1 & 0 \\ 0 & 1 \end{bmatrix} \begin{bmatrix} -2 & 4 \\ 6 & 1 \end{bmatrix} \right)$.

33. $\begin{bmatrix} 1 & 0 & 0 \\ 0 & 1 & 0 \\ 0 & 0 & 1 \end{bmatrix} \begin{bmatrix} x \\ y \\ z \end{bmatrix}$.

34. $\begin{bmatrix} a_{11} & a_{12} \\ a_{21} & a_{22} \end{bmatrix} \begin{bmatrix} x_1 \\ x_2 \end{bmatrix}$.

35. $\begin{bmatrix} 2 & 1 & 3 \\ 4 & 9 & 7 \end{bmatrix} \begin{bmatrix} x_1 \\ x_2 \\ x_3 \end{bmatrix}$.

36. $\begin{bmatrix} 1 & -2 \\ 0 & 1 \\ 3 & 2 \end{bmatrix} \begin{bmatrix} x_1 \\ x_2 \end{bmatrix}$.

In Problems **37–51,** compute the required matrices if

$$A = \begin{bmatrix} 1 & -2 \\ 0 & 3 \end{bmatrix}, \qquad B = \begin{bmatrix} -2 & 3 & 0 \\ 1 & -4 & 1 \end{bmatrix}, \qquad C = \begin{bmatrix} -1 & 1 \\ 0 & 3 \\ 2 & 4 \end{bmatrix},$$

$$D = \begin{bmatrix} 1 & 0 & 0 \\ 0 & 1 & 1 \\ 1 & 2 & 1 \end{bmatrix}, \qquad E = [1 \quad 2 \quad 4], \qquad F = \begin{bmatrix} 2 \\ 1 \end{bmatrix},$$

$$G = \begin{bmatrix} 3 & 0 & 0 \\ 0 & 6 & 0 \\ 0 & 0 & 3 \end{bmatrix}, \qquad H = \begin{bmatrix} \frac{1}{3} & 0 & 0 \\ 0 & \frac{1}{6} & 0 \\ 0 & 0 & \frac{1}{3} \end{bmatrix}, \qquad I = \begin{bmatrix} 1 & 0 & 0 \\ 0 & 1 & 0 \\ 0 & 0 & 1 \end{bmatrix}.$$

37. **AB.**

38. **BD.**

39. **CF.**

40. **FE − 3B.**

41. **DG.**

42. **D² (= DD).**

43. **EC.**

44. **GC.**

45. **DI − ⅓G.**

46. **B(D + G).**

47. **3A − 2BC.**

48. **G(2D − 3I).**

49. **2I − ½GH.**

50. **A(BC).**

51. **(DC)A.**

In Problems **52–55,** represent the given system by using matrix multiplication.

52. $\begin{cases} 2x - y = 4, \\ 3x + y = 5. \end{cases}$

53. $\begin{cases} 3x + y = 6, \\ 7x - 2y = 5. \end{cases}$

54. $\begin{cases} x + y + z = 6, \\ x - y + z = 2, \\ 2x - y + 3z = 6. \end{cases}$

55. $\begin{cases} 4r - s + 3t = 9, \\ 3r \quad - t = 7, \\ 3s + 2t = 15. \end{cases}$

56. A stockbroker sold a customer 200 shares of stock A, 300 shares of stock B, 500 shares of stock C, and 250 shares of stock D. The prices per share of A, B, C, and D are $100, $150, $200, and $300, respectively. Write

a row matrix representing the number of shares of each stock bought. Write a column matrix representing the price per share of each stock. Using matrix multiplication, find the total cost of the stocks.

57. In Example 9 assume that the contractor is to build seven ranch-style, three Cape Cod, and five colonial-style houses. Compute, using matrix multiplication, the total cost of raw materials.

58. In Example 9 assume that the contractor wishes to take into account the cost of transporting raw materials to the building site as well as the purchasing cost. Suppose the costs are given in the matrix below.

$$
\mathbf{C} = \begin{array}{c} \\ \\ \\ \\ \\ \\ \end{array}
\begin{array}{cc} \text{Purchase} & \text{Transport} \\ \begin{bmatrix} 1500 & 45 \\ 800 & 20 \\ 500 & 30 \\ 100 & 5 \\ 1000 & 0 \end{bmatrix} & \begin{array}{l} \text{Steel} \\ \text{Wood} \\ \text{Glass} \\ \text{Paint} \\ \text{Labor.} \end{array} \end{array}
$$

a. By computing **RC**, find a matrix whose entries give the purchase and transportation costs of the materials for each type of house.

b. Find the matrix **QRC** whose first entry gives the total purchase price and whose second entry gives the total transportation cost.

c. Let $\mathbf{Z} = \begin{bmatrix} 1 \\ 1 \end{bmatrix}$ and then compute **QRCZ**, which gives the total cost of materials and transportation for all houses being built.

59. Perform the following calculations for Example 10:
   a. Compute the amount that each industry and each consumer have to pay for the goods they receive.
   b. Compute the profit earned by each industry.
   c. Find the total amount of money that is paid out by all the industries and consumers.
   d. Find the proportion of the total amount of money found in (c) paid out by the industries. Find the proportion of the total amount of money found in (c) that is paid out by the consumers.

8.4 METHOD OF REDUCTION

In this section we shall illustrate a method by which matrices can be used to solve a system of linear equations, *the method of reduction*. In introducing the method we shall first solve a system in the usual way. Then we shall obtain the same solution by using matrices.

Let us consider the system

$$
\begin{cases} 3x - y = 1, & (1) \\ x + 2y = 5 & (2) \end{cases}
$$

consisting of two linear equations in two unknowns, x and y. Although this system can be solved by various algebraic methods, we shall solve it by a method which is readily adapted to matrices.

For reasons that will be obvious later, we begin by replacing Eq. (1) by Eq. (2), and Eq. (2) by Eq. (1), thus obtaining the equivalent system

$$
\begin{cases} x + 2y = 5, & (3) \\ 3x - y = 1. & (4) \end{cases}
$$

In $x + 2y = 5$, multiplying both sides by -3 gives $-3x - 6y = -15$. Adding the left and right sides of this equation to the corresponding sides of Eq. (4) gives the equivalent system

$$\begin{cases} x + 2y = 5, & (5) \\ 0x - 7y = -14. & (6) \end{cases}$$

Multiplying both sides of Eq. (6) by $-\frac{1}{7}$ gives the equivalent system

$$\begin{cases} x + 2y = 5, & (7) \\ 0x + y = 2. & (8) \end{cases}$$

By Eq. (8), $y = 2$ and hence $-2y = -4$. Adding the sides of $-2y = -4$ to the corresponding sides of Eq. (7), we get the equivalent system

$$\begin{cases} x + 0y = 1, \\ 0x + y = 2. \end{cases}$$

Therefore, $x = 1$ and $y = 2$, and the original system is solved.

Before showing a method of solving

$$\begin{cases} 3x - y = 1, \\ x + 2y = 5 \end{cases}$$

by matrices, we first define some terms. We say that the matrix

$$\begin{bmatrix} 3 & -1 \\ 1 & 2 \end{bmatrix}$$

is the **coefficient matrix** of this system. The entries in the first column correspond to the coefficients of the x's in the equations. For example, the entry in the first row and first column corresponds to the coefficient of x in the first equation; the entry in the second row and first column corresponds to the coefficient of x in the second equation. Similarly, the entries in the second column correspond to the coefficients of the y's.

Another matrix associated with this system is called the **augmented coefficient matrix** and is given by

$$\begin{bmatrix} 3 & -1 & \vdots & 1 \\ 1 & 2 & \vdots & 5 \end{bmatrix}.$$

The first and second columns are the first and second columns, respectively, of the coefficient matrix. The entries in the third column correspond to the constant terms in the system: the entry in the first row of this column is the constant term of the first equation, while the entry in the second row is the constant term of the second equation. Although it is not necessary to include the broken line in the augmented coefficient matrix, it serves to remind us that the 1 and the 5 are the constant terms that appear on the right sides of the equations. The augmented coefficient matrix itself completely describes the system of equations.

The procedure that was used to solve the original system involved a number of equivalent systems. With each of these systems we can associate its augmented coefficient matrix. Listed below are the systems that were involved, together with their corresponding augmented coefficient matrices, which we have labeled **A**, **B**, **C**, **D**, and **E**.

$$\begin{cases} 3x - y = 1, \\ x + 2y = 5. \end{cases} \quad \begin{bmatrix} 3 & -1 & \vdots & 1 \\ 1 & 2 & \vdots & 5 \end{bmatrix} = \mathbf{A}.$$

$$\begin{cases} x + 2y = 5, \\ 3x - y = 1. \end{cases} \quad \begin{bmatrix} 1 & 2 & \vdots & 5 \\ 3 & -1 & \vdots & 1 \end{bmatrix} = \mathbf{B}.$$

$$\begin{cases} x + 2y = 5, \\ 0x - 7y = -14. \end{cases} \quad \begin{bmatrix} 1 & 2 & \vdots & 5 \\ 0 & -7 & \vdots & -14 \end{bmatrix} = \mathbf{C}.$$

$$\begin{cases} x + 2y = 5, \\ 0x + y = 2. \end{cases} \quad \begin{bmatrix} 1 & 2 & \vdots & 5 \\ 0 & 1 & \vdots & 2 \end{bmatrix} = \mathbf{D}.$$

$$\begin{cases} x + 0y = 1, \\ 0x + y = 2. \end{cases} \quad \begin{bmatrix} 1 & 0 & \vdots & 1 \\ 0 & 1 & \vdots & 2 \end{bmatrix} = \mathbf{E}.$$

Let us see how these matrices are related.

B can be obtained from **A** by interchanging the first and second rows of **A**. This operation corresponds to the interchanging of the two equations in the original system.

C can be obtained from **B** by adding to each entry in the second row of **B**, -3 times the corresponding entry in the first row of **B**.

$$\mathbf{C} = \begin{bmatrix} 1 & 2 & \vdots & 5 \\ 3 + (-3)(1) & -1 + (-3)(2) & \vdots & 1 + (-3)(5) \end{bmatrix}$$

$$= \begin{bmatrix} 1 & 2 & \vdots & 5 \\ 0 & -7 & \vdots & -14 \end{bmatrix}.$$

This operation is described as the addition of -3 times the first row of **B** to the second row of **B**.

D can be obtained from **C** by multiplying each entry in the second row of **C** by $-\frac{1}{7}$. This operation is referred to as multiplying the second row of **C** by $-\frac{1}{7}$.

E can be obtained from **D** by adding -2 times the second row of **D** to the first row of **D**.

Observe that **E**, which essentially gives the solution, can be obtained from **A** by a series of operations which include:

1. interchanging two rows of a matrix;

2. adding a multiple of one row of a matrix to a different row of that matrix;

3. multiplying a row of a matrix by a nonzero scalar.

We refer to these operations as **elementary row operations.** Whenever a matrix can be obtained from another by one or more elementary row operations, we say that the matrices are **equivalent.** Thus **A** is equivalent to **E,** and we write **A ~ E.**

We are now ready to describe a matrix procedure for solving a system of linear equations. First, form the augmented coefficient matrix of the system; then, by means of elementary row operations, determine an equivalent matrix that clearly indicates the solution. Let us be quite specific as to what we mean by a matrix that clearly indicates the solution. It is a matrix, called a **reduced matrix,** such that

---

1. the first nonzero entry in each row is 1 while all other entries in the column in which the 1 appears are zeros,

2. the first nonzero entry in each row is to the right of the first nonzero entry of each preceding row,

3. each row that consists entirely of zeros is below each row that contains a nonzero entry.*

In other words, to solve the system we must find a reduced matrix such that the augmented coefficient matrix is equivalent to it. Note that **E** above,

$$\mathbf{E} = \begin{bmatrix} 1 & 0 & \vdots & 1 \\ 0 & 1 & \vdots & 2 \end{bmatrix},$$

is a reduced matrix.

EXAMPLE 1   *For each matrix below, determine whether it is reduced or not reduced.*

a. $\begin{bmatrix} 1 & 0 \\ 0 & 3 \end{bmatrix}$.

b. $\begin{bmatrix} 1 & 0 & 0 \\ 0 & 1 & 0 \end{bmatrix}$.

c. $\begin{bmatrix} 0 & 1 \\ 1 & 0 \end{bmatrix}$.

d. $\begin{bmatrix} 0 & 0 & 0 \\ 0 & 0 & 0 \end{bmatrix}$.

e. $\begin{bmatrix} 1 & 0 & 0 \\ 0 & 0 & 0 \\ 0 & 1 & 0 \end{bmatrix}$.

f. $\begin{bmatrix} 0 & 1 & 0 & 3 \\ 0 & 0 & 1 & 2 \\ 0 & 0 & 0 & 0 \end{bmatrix}$.

a. Not a reduced matrix, since the first nonzero entry in the second row is not 1.

b. Reduced matrix.

* From Paul C. Shields, *Elementary Linear Algebra*, 2nd ed. (New York: Worth Publishers, Inc., 1973), p. 7.

c. Not a reduced matrix, since the first nonzero entry in the second row is not to the right of the first nonzero entry in the first row.

d. Reduced matrix.

e. Not a reduced matrix, since the second row, consisting entirely of zeros, is not below each row which contains nonzero entries.

f. Reduced matrix.

The method of reduction described for solving our original system can be generalized to systems consisting of m linear equations in n unknowns.

To solve such a system as

$$\begin{cases} a_{11}x_1 + a_{12}x_2 + \cdots + a_{1n}x_n = c_1, \\ a_{21}x_1 + a_{22}x_2 + \cdots + a_{2n}x_n = c_2, \\ \phantom{a_{m1}x_1}\vdots \phantom{+ a_{m2}x_2 + \cdots + a_{mn}x_n} \vdots \\ a_{m1}x_1 + a_{m2}x_2 + \cdots + a_{mn}x_n = c_m \end{cases}$$

involves

1. determining the augmented coefficient matrix of the system:

$$\begin{bmatrix} a_{11} & a_{12} & \cdots & a_{1n} & \vdots & c_1 \\ a_{21} & a_{22} & \cdots & a_{2n} & \vdots & c_2 \\ \vdots & \vdots & & \vdots & \vdots & \vdots \\ a_{m1} & a_{m2} & \cdots & a_{mn} & \vdots & c_m \end{bmatrix}$$

and

2. determining a reduced matrix such that the augmented coefficient matrix is equivalent to it.

Frequently, step 2 is called *reducing the augmented coefficient matrix.*

EXAMPLE 2   *By using matrix reduction, solve the system*

$$\begin{cases} 2x + 3y = -1, \\ 2x + y = 5, \\ x + y = 1. \end{cases}$$

The augmented coefficient matrix of the system is

$$\begin{bmatrix} 2 & 3 & \vdots & -1 \\ 2 & 1 & \vdots & 5 \\ 1 & 1 & \vdots & 1 \end{bmatrix}.$$

Reducing this matrix, we have

$$\begin{bmatrix} 2 & 3 & \vdots & -1 \\ 2 & 1 & \vdots & 5 \\ 1 & 1 & \vdots & 1 \end{bmatrix}$$

$$\sim \begin{bmatrix} 1 & 1 & \vdots & 1 \\ 2 & 1 & \vdots & 5 \\ 2 & 3 & \vdots & -1 \end{bmatrix} \qquad \text{(by interchanging the first and third rows)}$$

$$\sim \begin{bmatrix} 1 & 1 & \vdots & 1 \\ 0 & -1 & \vdots & 3 \\ 2 & 3 & \vdots & -1 \end{bmatrix} \qquad \text{(by adding } -2 \text{ times the first row to the second)}$$

$$\sim \begin{bmatrix} 1 & 1 & \vdots & 1 \\ 0 & -1 & \vdots & 3 \\ 0 & 1 & \vdots & -3 \end{bmatrix} \qquad \text{(by adding } -2 \text{ times the first row to the third)}$$

$$\sim \begin{bmatrix} 1 & 1 & \vdots & 1 \\ 0 & 1 & \vdots & -3 \\ 0 & 1 & \vdots & -3 \end{bmatrix} \qquad \text{(by multiplying the second row by } -1)$$

$$\sim \begin{bmatrix} 1 & 0 & \vdots & 4 \\ 0 & 1 & \vdots & -3 \\ 0 & 1 & \vdots & -3 \end{bmatrix} \qquad \text{(by adding } -1 \text{ times the second row to the first)}$$

$$\sim \begin{bmatrix} 1 & 0 & \vdots & 4 \\ 0 & 1 & \vdots & -3 \\ 0 & 0 & \vdots & 0 \end{bmatrix} \qquad \text{(by adding } -1 \text{ times the second row to the third).}$$

The last matrix is reduced and corresponds to the system

$$\begin{cases} x + 0y = 4, \\ 0x + y = -3, \\ 0x + 0y = 0. \end{cases}$$

Since the original system is equivalent to this system, it has a unique solution, namely

$$x = 4,$$

$$y = -3.$$

We point out that the sequence of steps that are used to reduce a matrix is not unique.

EXAMPLE 3   *Using matrix reduction, solve*

$$\begin{cases} x + 2y + 4z - 6 = 0, \\ 2z + y - 3 = 0, \\ x + y + 2z - 1 = 0. \end{cases}$$

Rewriting the system so that the variables are aligned and the constant terms appear on the right sides of the equations, we have

$$\begin{cases} x + 2y + 4z = 6, \\ \phantom{x + {}} y + 2z = 3, \\ x + y + 2z = 1. \end{cases}$$

Reducing the augmented coefficient matrix, we have

$$\begin{bmatrix} 1 & 2 & 4 & \vdots & 6 \\ 0 & 1 & 2 & \vdots & 3 \\ 1 & 1 & 2 & \vdots & 1 \end{bmatrix}$$

$$\sim \begin{bmatrix} 1 & 2 & 4 & \vdots & 6 \\ 0 & 1 & 2 & \vdots & 3 \\ 0 & -1 & -2 & \vdots & -5 \end{bmatrix}$$ (by adding -1 times the first row to the third)

$$\sim \begin{bmatrix} 1 & 0 & 0 & \vdots & 0 \\ 0 & 1 & 2 & \vdots & 3 \\ 0 & 0 & 0 & \vdots & -2 \end{bmatrix}$$ (by adding -2 times the second row to the first, and adding the second row to the third)

$$\sim \begin{bmatrix} 1 & 0 & 0 & \vdots & 0 \\ 0 & 1 & 2 & \vdots & 3 \\ 0 & 0 & 0 & \vdots & 1 \end{bmatrix}$$ (by multiplying the third row by $-\frac{1}{2}$)

$$\sim \begin{bmatrix} 1 & 0 & 0 & \vdots & 0 \\ 0 & 1 & 2 & \vdots & 0 \\ 0 & 0 & 0 & \vdots & 1 \end{bmatrix}$$ (by adding -3 times the third row to the second).

The last matrix is reduced and corresponds to

$$\begin{cases} x = 0, \\ y + 2z = 0, \\ 0 = 1. \end{cases}$$

Since $0 \neq 1$, there are no values of x, y, and z for which all equations are satisfied simultaneously. Thus the original system has no solution.

EXAMPLE 4   *Using matrix reduction, solve*

$$\begin{cases} 2x + 3x_2 + 2x_3 + 6x_4 = 10, \\ \phantom{2x + 3x_2 + {}} x_2 + 2x_3 + x_4 = 2, \\ 3x_1 \phantom{ + 3x_2 + {}} - 3x_3 + 6x_4 = 9. \end{cases}$$

Reducing the augmented coefficient matrix, we have

$$\begin{bmatrix} 2 & 3 & 2 & 6 & \vdots & 10 \\ 0 & 1 & 2 & 1 & \vdots & 2 \\ 3 & 0 & -3 & 6 & \vdots & 9 \end{bmatrix}$$

$$\sim \begin{bmatrix} 1 & \frac{3}{2} & 1 & 3 & \vdots & 5 \\ 0 & 1 & 2 & 1 & \vdots & 2 \\ 3 & 0 & -3 & 6 & \vdots & 9 \end{bmatrix}$$

(by multiplying the first row by $\frac{1}{2}$)

$$\sim \begin{bmatrix} 1 & \frac{3}{2} & 1 & 3 & \vdots & 5 \\ 0 & 1 & 2 & 1 & \vdots & 2 \\ 0 & -\frac{9}{2} & -6 & -3 & \vdots & -6 \end{bmatrix}$$

(by adding -3 times the first row to the third)

$$\sim \begin{bmatrix} 1 & 0 & -2 & \frac{3}{2} & \vdots & 2 \\ 0 & 1 & 2 & 1 & \vdots & 2 \\ 0 & 0 & 3 & \frac{3}{2} & \vdots & 3 \end{bmatrix}$$

(by adding $-\frac{3}{2}$ times the second row to the first, and adding $\frac{9}{2}$ times the second row to the third)

$$\sim \begin{bmatrix} 1 & 0 & -2 & \frac{3}{2} & \vdots & 2 \\ 0 & 1 & 2 & 1 & \vdots & 2 \\ 0 & 0 & 1 & \frac{1}{2} & \vdots & 1 \end{bmatrix}$$

(by multiplying the third row by $\frac{1}{3}$)

$$\sim \begin{bmatrix} 1 & 0 & 0 & \frac{5}{2} & \vdots & 4 \\ 0 & 1 & 0 & 0 & \vdots & 0 \\ 0 & 0 & 1 & \frac{1}{2} & \vdots & 1 \end{bmatrix}$$

(by adding 2 times the third row to the first, and adding -2 times the third row to the second).

The last matrix is reduced and corresponds to the system

$$\begin{cases} x_1 + \frac{5}{2}x_4 = 4, \\ x_2 = 0, \\ x_3 + \frac{1}{2}x_4 = 1. \end{cases}$$

Thus

$$x_1 = -\frac{5}{2}x_4 + 4, \tag{9}$$

$$x_2 = 0, \tag{10}$$

$$x_3 = -\frac{1}{2}x_4 + 1, \tag{11}$$

$$x_4 = x_4. \tag{12}$$

If x_4 is any real number, then Eqs. (9)–(12) determine a particular solution to the original system. For example, if $x_4 = 0$, then a *particular* solution is $x_1 = 4$, $x_2 = 0$, $x_3 = 1$, and $x_4 = 0$. If $x_4 = 2$, then $x_1 = -1$, $x_2 = 0$, $x_3 = 0$, and $x_4 = 2$ is a particular solution. The variable x_4, on which x_1 and x_3 depend, is called a *parameter*. Clearly, there are an infinite number of solutions to the system—one corresponding to each value of the parameter. We say that the *general* solution of the original system is given by Eqs. (9)–(12).

EXERCISE 8.4

In each of Problems 1–6, determine whether the matrix is reduced or not reduced.

1. $\begin{bmatrix} 1 & 2 \\ 3 & 0 \end{bmatrix}$.

2. $\begin{bmatrix} 1 & 0 & 0 & 3 \\ 0 & 0 & 1 & 2 \end{bmatrix}$.

3. $\begin{bmatrix} 1 & 0 & 0 \\ 0 & 1 & 0 \\ 0 & 0 & 1 \end{bmatrix}$.

4. $\begin{bmatrix} 1 & 1 \\ 0 & 1 \\ 0 & 0 \\ 0 & 0 \end{bmatrix}$

5. $\begin{bmatrix} 0 & 0 & 0 & 0 \\ 0 & 1 & 0 & 0 \\ 0 & 0 & 1 & 0 \\ 0 & 0 & 0 & 0 \end{bmatrix}$

6. $\begin{bmatrix} 0 & 0 & 5 \\ 1 & 0 & 4 \\ 0 & 1 & 2 \\ 0 & 0 & 0 \end{bmatrix}$

In each of Problems 7–12, reduce the given matrix.

7. $\begin{bmatrix} 1 & 3 \\ 4 & 0 \end{bmatrix}$.

8. $\begin{bmatrix} 0 & -2 & 0 & 1 \\ 1 & 2 & 0 & 4 \end{bmatrix}$.

9. $\begin{bmatrix} 2 & 4 & 6 \\ 1 & 2 & 3 \\ 1 & 2 & 3 \end{bmatrix}$.

10. $\begin{bmatrix} 2 & 3 \\ 1 & -6 \\ 4 & 8 \\ 1 & 7 \end{bmatrix}$.

11. $\begin{bmatrix} 2 & 0 & 3 & 1 \\ 1 & 4 & 2 & 2 \\ -1 & 3 & 1 & 4 \\ 0 & 2 & 1 & 0 \end{bmatrix}$.

12. $\begin{bmatrix} 0 & 0 & 2 \\ 2 & 0 & 3 \\ 0 & -1 & 0 \\ 0 & 4 & 1 \end{bmatrix}$.

Solve Problems 13–26 by the method of reduction.

13. $\begin{cases} 2x + 3y = 5, \\ x - 2y = -1. \end{cases}$

14. $\begin{cases} x - 3y = -11, \\ 4x + 3y = 9. \end{cases}$

15. $\begin{cases} 3x + y = 4, \\ 12x + 4y = 2. \end{cases}$

16. $\begin{cases} x + 2y - 3z = 0, \\ -2x - 4y + 6z = 1. \end{cases}$

17. $\begin{cases} x + 2y + z - 4 = 0, \\ 3x + 2z - 5 = 0. \end{cases}$

18. $\begin{cases} x + 2y + 5z - 1 = 0, \\ x + y + 3z - 2 = 0. \end{cases}$

19. $\begin{cases} x_1 - 3x_2 = 0, \\ 2x_1 + 2x_2 = 3, \\ 5x_1 - x_2 = 1. \end{cases}$

20. $\begin{cases} x_1 + 3x_2 = 5, \\ 2x_1 + x_2 = 5, \\ x_1 + x_2 = 3. \end{cases}$

21. $\begin{cases} x - y - 3z = -4, \\ 2x - y - 4z = -7, \\ x + y - z = -2. \end{cases}$

22. $\begin{cases} x + y - z = 6, \\ 2x - 3y - 2z = 2, \\ x - y - 5z = 18. \end{cases}$

23. $\begin{cases} 2x - 4z = 8, \\ x - 2y - 2z = 14, \\ x + y - 2z = -1, \\ 3x + y + z = 0. \end{cases}$

24. $\begin{cases} x + 3z = -1, \\ 3x + 2y + 11z = 1, \\ x + y + 4z = 1, \\ 2x - 3y + 3z = -8. \end{cases}$

25. $\begin{cases} x_1 + x_2 - x_3 + x_4 + x_5 = 0, \\ x_1 + x_2 + x_3 - x_4 + x_5 = 0, \\ x_1 - x_2 - x_3 + x_4 - x_5 = 0, \\ x_1 + x_2 - x_3 - x_4 - x_5 = 0. \end{cases}$

26. $\begin{cases} x_1 + x_2 - x_3 + x_4 = 0, \\ x_1 + x_2 + x_3 - x_4 = 0, \\ x_1 - x_2 - x_3 + x_4 = 0, \\ x_1 + x_2 - x_3 - x_4 = 0. \end{cases}$

Solve Problems 27–31 by using matrix reduction.

27. A company has taxable income of $312,000. The federal tax is 25% of that portion which is left after the state tax has been paid. The state tax is 10% of that portion which is left after the federal tax has been paid. Find the federal and state taxes.

28. A manufacturer produces two products, A and B. For each unit of A sold the profit is $8, and for each unit of B sold the profit is $11. From past experience it has been found that 25% more of A can be sold than of B. Next year the manufacturer desires a total profit of $42,000. How many units of each product must be sold?

29. A manufacturer produces three products, A, B, and C. The profits for each unit sold of A, B, and C are $1, 2, and $3, respectively. Fixed costs are $17,000 per year and the costs of producing each unit of A, B, and C are $4, $5, and $7, respectively. Next year, a total of 11,000 units of all three products is to be produced and sold, and a total profit of $25,000 is to be realized. If total cost is to be $80,000, how many units of each of the products should be produced next year?

30. National Desk Co. has plants for producing desks on both the east and west coasts. At the east coast plant, fixed costs are $16,000 per year and the cost of producing each desk is $90. At the west coast plant, fixed costs are $20,000 per year and the cost of producing each desk is $80. Next year the company wants to produce a total of 800 desks. Determine the production or-

der for each plant for the forthcoming year if the total cost for each plant is to be the same.

31. A person is ordered by a doctor to take 10 units of vitamin A, 9 units of vitamin D, and 19 units of vitamin E each day. The person can choose from three brands of vitamin pills. Brand X contains 2 units of vitamin A, 3 units of vitamin D, and 5 units of vitamin E; brand Y has 1, 3, and 4 units, respectively; and brand Z has 1 unit of vitamin A, none of vitamin D, and 1 of vitamin E.

   a. Find all possible combinations of pills that will provide exactly the required amounts of vitamins.
   b. If brand X costs 1 cent a pill, brand Y 6 cents, and brand Z 3 cents, are there any combinations in part (a) costing exactly 15 cents a day?
   c. What is the least expensive combination in part (a)? The most expensive?

8.5 METHOD OF REDUCTION (CONTINUED)*

As we saw in Sec. 8.4, a system of linear equations may have a unique solution, no solution, or infinitely many solutions. When there are infinitely many, the general solution is expressed in terms of at least one parameter. For example, the general solution in Example 4 was given in terms of the parameter x_4:

$$x_1 = -\tfrac{5}{2}x_4 + 4,$$

$$x_2 = 0,$$

$$x_3 = -\tfrac{1}{2}x_4 + 1,$$

$$x_4 = x_4.$$

At times, more than one parameter is necessary, as the following example shows.

EXAMPLE 1   *Using matrix reduction, solve*

$$\begin{cases} x_1 + 2x_2 + 5x_3 + 5x_4 = -3, \\ x_1 + x_2 + 3x_3 + 4x_4 = -1, \\ x_1 - x_2 - x_3 + 2x_4 = 3. \end{cases}$$

The augmented coefficient matrix is

$$\begin{bmatrix} 1 & 2 & 5 & 5 & \vdots & -3 \\ 1 & 1 & 3 & 4 & \vdots & -1 \\ 1 & -1 & -1 & 2 & \vdots & 3 \end{bmatrix},$$

* This section may be omitted.

which is equivalent to the reduced matrix

$$\begin{bmatrix} 1 & 0 & 1 & 3 & \vdots & 1 \\ 0 & 1 & 2 & 1 & \vdots & -2 \\ 0 & 0 & 0 & 0 & \vdots & 0 \end{bmatrix}.$$

Hence

$$\begin{cases} x_1 + x_3 + 3x_4 = 1, \\ x_2 + 2x_3 + x_4 = -2. \end{cases}$$

Thus the general solution can be given by

$$x_1 = 1 - x_3 - 3x_4,$$

$$x_2 = -2 - 2x_3 - x_4,$$

$$x_3 = x_3,$$

$$x_4 = x_4,$$

where parameters x_3 and x_4 are involved. By assigning specific values to x_3 and x_4, we get particular solutions. For example, if $x_3 = 1$ and $x_4 = 2$, then the corresponding particular solution is $x_1 = -6$, $x_2 = -6$, $x_3 = 1$, and $x_4 = 2$.

It is customary to classify a system of linear equations as being either *homogeneous* or *nonhomogeneous*. The appropriate classification depends on the constant terms, as the following definition indicates.

Definition
The system

$$\begin{cases} a_{11}x_1 + a_{12}x_2 + \cdots + a_{1n}x_n = c_1, \\ a_{21}x_1 + a_{22}x_2 + \cdots + a_{2n}x_n = c_2, \\ \phantom{a_{21}x_1} \cdot \phantom{a_{22}x_2 + \cdots} \cdot \\ \phantom{a_{21}x_1} \cdot \phantom{a_{22}x_2 + \cdots} \cdot \\ \phantom{a_{21}x_1} \cdot \phantom{a_{22}x_2 + \cdots} \cdot \\ a_{m1}x_1 + a_{m2}x_2 + \cdots + a_{mn}x_n = c_m \end{cases}$$

*is a **homogenous system** if $c_1 = c_2 = \cdots = c_m = 0$. The system is a **nonhomogeneous system** if at least one of the c's is not equal to 0.*

EXAMPLE 2   The system

$$\begin{cases} 2x + 3y = 4, \\ 3x - 4y = 0 \end{cases}$$

is nonhomogeneous because of the 4 in the top equation. The system

$$\begin{cases} 2x + 3y = 0, \\ 3x - 4y = 0 \end{cases}$$

is homogeneous.

If the homogeneous system

$$\begin{cases} 2x + 3y = 0, \\ 3x - 4y = 0 \end{cases}$$

were solved by the method of reduction, first the augmented coefficient matrix would be written

$$\begin{bmatrix} 2 & 3 & \vdots & 0 \\ 3 & -4 & \vdots & 0 \end{bmatrix}.$$

Observe that the last column consists entirely of zeros. This is typical of the augmented coefficient matrix of any homogeneous system. We would then reduce this matrix by using elementary row operations:

$$\begin{bmatrix} 2 & 3 & \vdots & 0 \\ 3 & -4 & \vdots & 0 \end{bmatrix} \sim \cdots \sim \begin{bmatrix} 1 & 0 & \vdots & 0 \\ 0 & 1 & \vdots & 0 \end{bmatrix}.$$

The last column of the reduced matrix also consists only of zeros. This does not occur by chance. When any elementary row operation is performed on a matrix that has a column consisting entirely of zeros, the corresponding column of the resulting matrix will also be all zeros. For convenience it will be our custom when solving a homogeneous system by matrix reduction to delete the last column of the matrices involved. That is, we shall reduce only the *coefficient matrix* of the system. For the system above we would have

$$\begin{bmatrix} 2 & 3 \\ 3 & -4 \end{bmatrix} \sim \cdots \sim \begin{bmatrix} 1 & 0 \\ 0 & 1 \end{bmatrix}.$$

Here the reduced matrix, called the *reduced coefficient matrix*, corresponds to

$$\begin{cases} x + 0y = 0, \\ 0x + \ y = 0, \end{cases}$$

so the solution is $x = 0$ and $y = 0$.

Let us now consider the number of solutions of the homogeneous system

$$\begin{cases} a_{11} x_1 + a_{12} x_2 + \cdots + a_{1n} x_n = 0, \\ a_{21} x_1 + a_{22} x_2 + \cdots + a_{2n} x_n = 0, \\ \quad \vdots \qquad\quad \vdots \qquad\qquad\quad \vdots \qquad \vdots \\ a_{m1} x_1 + a_{m2} x_2 + \cdots + a_{mn} x_n = 0. \end{cases}$$

One solution always occurs when $x_1 = 0$, $x_2 = 0$, . . . , and $x_n = 0$ since each equation is satisfied for these values. This solution, called the **trivial solution,** is a solution of *every* homogeneous system.

There is a theorem which allows us to determine whether a homogeneous system has a unique solution (the trivial solution only) or infinitely many solutions. The theorem is based on the number of nonzero rows that appear in the reduced coefficient matrix of the system. A *nonzero row* is a row that does not consist entirely of zeros.

Theorem.   Let **A** be the *reduced* coefficient matrix of a homogeneous system of m linear equations in n unknowns. If **A** has exactly k nonzero rows, then $k \le n$. Moreover,

  a. if $k < n$, the system has infinitely many solutions;
  and
  b. if $k = n$, the system has a unique solution (the trivial solution).

If a homogeneous system consists of m equations in n unknowns, then the coefficient matrix of the system has order $m \times n$. Thus if $m < n$ and k is the number of nonzero rows in the reduced coefficient matrix, then $k \le m$ and hence $k < n$. By the theorem, the system must have infinitely many solutions. Consequently we have the following.

Corollary.   A homogeneous system of linear equations with fewer equations than unknowns has infinitely many solutions.

EXAMPLE 3   *Determine whether the system*

$$\begin{cases} x + y - 2z = 0, \\ 2x + 2y - 4z = 0 \end{cases}$$

has a unique solution or infinitely many solutions.

There are two equations in this homogeneous system and this number is less than the number of unknowns (three). Thus, by the corollary above, the system has infinitely many solutions.

Pitfall

The theorem and corollary above apply only to **homogeneous systems** of linear equations. For example, consider the system

$$\begin{cases} x + y - 2z = 3, \\ 2x + 2y - 4x = 4, \end{cases}$$

which consists of two linear equations in three unknowns. We **cannot** conclude that this system has infinitely many solutions, since it is not homogeneous. Indeed, you should verify that it has no solution.

EXAMPLE 4   *Determine whether the following homogeneous systems have a unique solution or infinitely many solutions; then solve the system.*

a.
$$\begin{cases} x - 2y + z = 0, \\ 2x - y + 5z = 0, \\ x + y + 4z = 0. \end{cases}$$

Reducing the coefficient matrix, we have

$$\begin{bmatrix} 1 & -2 & 1 \\ 2 & -1 & 5 \\ 1 & 1 & 4 \end{bmatrix} \sim \cdots \sim \begin{bmatrix} 1 & 0 & 3 \\ 0 & 1 & 1 \\ 0 & 0 & 0 \end{bmatrix}.$$

The number of nonzero rows (2) in the reduced coefficient matrix is less than the number of unknowns (3) in the system. By the theorem above, there are infinitely many solutions.

Since the reduced coefficient matrix corresponds to

$$\begin{cases} x + 3z = 0, \\ y + z = 0, \end{cases}$$

the solution may be given by

$$x = -3z,$$
$$y = -z,$$
$$z = z,$$

where z is any real number.

b.
$$\begin{cases} 3x + 4y = 0, \\ x - 2y = 0, \\ 2x + y = 0, \\ 2x + 3y = 0. \end{cases}$$

Reducing the coefficient matrix, we have

$$\begin{bmatrix} 3 & 4 \\ 1 & -2 \\ 2 & 1 \\ 2 & 3 \end{bmatrix} \sim \cdots \sim \begin{bmatrix} 1 & 0 \\ 0 & 1 \\ 0 & 0 \\ 0 & 0 \end{bmatrix}.$$

The number of nonzero rows (2) in the reduced coefficient matrix equals the number of unknowns in the system. By the theorem the system must have a unique solution, namely the trivial solution $x = 0$, $y = 0$.

EXERCISE 8.5

In Problems **1–8,** *solve the systems by using matrix reduction.*

1.
$$\begin{cases} w - x - y + 4z = 5, \\ 2w - 3x - 4y + 9z = 13, \\ 2w + x + 4y + 5z = 1. \end{cases}$$

2.
$$\begin{cases} 3w - x + 12y + 18z = -4, \\ w - 2x + 4y + 11z = -13, \\ w + x + 4y + 2z = 8. \end{cases}$$

3.
$$\begin{cases} 3w - x - 3y - z = -2, \\ 2w - 2x - 6y - 6z = -4, \\ 2w - x - 3y - 2z = -2, \\ 3w + x + 3y + 7z = 2. \end{cases}$$

4.
$$\begin{cases} w + x + 5z = 1, \\ w + y + 2z = 1, \\ w - 3x + 4y - 7x = 1, \\ x - y + 3z = 0. \end{cases}$$

5.
$$\begin{cases} w + x + 3y - z = 2, \\ 2w + x + 5y - 2z = 0, \\ 2w - x + 3y - 2z = -8, \\ 3w + 2x + 8y - 3z = 2, \\ w + 2y - z = -2. \end{cases}$$

6.
$$\begin{cases} w + x + y + 2z = 4, \\ 2w + x + 2y + 2z = 7, \\ w + 2x + y + 4z = 5, \\ 3w - 2x + 3y - 4z = 7, \\ 4w - 3x + 4y - 6z = 9. \end{cases}$$

7.
$$\begin{cases} 4x_1 - 3x_2 + 5x_3 - 10x_4 + 11x_5 = -8, \\ 2x_1 + x_2 + 5x_3 + 3x_5 = 6. \end{cases}$$

8.
$$\begin{cases} x_1 + 2x_3 + x_4 + 4x_5 = 1, \\ x_2 + x_3 - 3x_4 = -2. \\ 4x_1 - 3x_2 + 5x_3 + 13x_4 + 16x_5 = 10, \\ x_1 + 2x_2 + 4x_3 - 5x_4 + 4x_5 = -3. \end{cases}$$

For each of Problems **9–14,** *determine whether the system has infinitely many solutions or only the trivial solution. Do not solve the systems.*

9.
$$\begin{cases} 0.07x + 0.3y + 0.02z = 0, \\ 0.053x - 0.4y + 0.08z = 0. \end{cases}$$

10.
$$\begin{cases} 3w + 5x - 4y + 2z = 0, \\ 7w - 2x + 9y + 3z = 0. \end{cases}$$

11.
$$\begin{cases} 3x - 4y = 0, \\ x + 5y = 0, \\ 4x - y = 0. \end{cases}$$

12.
$$\begin{cases} 2x + 3y + 12z = 0, \\ 3x - 2y + 5z = 0, \\ 4x + y + 14z = 0. \end{cases}$$

13.
$$\begin{cases} x + y + z = 0, \\ x - z = 0, \\ x - 2y - 5z = 0. \end{cases}$$

14.
$$\begin{cases} 2x + 5y = 0, \\ x + 4y = 0, \\ 3x - 2y = 0. \end{cases}$$

Solve each of the following systems.

15.
$$\begin{cases} x + y = 0, \\ 3x - 4y = 0. \end{cases}$$

16.
$$\begin{cases} 2x - 5y = 0, \\ 8x - 20y = 0. \end{cases}$$

17.
$$\begin{cases} x + 6y - 2z = 0, \\ 2x - 3y + 4z = 0. \end{cases}$$

18.
$$\begin{cases} 4x + 7y = 0, \\ 2x + 3y = 0. \end{cases}$$

19.
$$\begin{cases} x + y = 0, \\ 3x - 4y = 0, \\ 5x - 8y = 0. \end{cases}$$

20.
$$\begin{cases} 4x - 3y + 2z = 0, \\ x + 2y + 3z = 0, \\ x + y + z = 0. \end{cases}$$

21.
$$\begin{cases} x + y + z = 0, \\ 5x - 2y - 9z = 0, \\ 3x + y - z = 0, \\ 3x - 2y - 7z = 0. \end{cases}$$

22.
$$\begin{cases} x + y + 7z = 0, \\ x - y - z = 0, \\ 2x - 3y - 6z = 0, \\ 3x + y + 13z = 0. \end{cases}$$

23. $\begin{cases} w + x + y + 4z = 0, \\ w + x \quad\;\; + 5z = 0, \\ 2w + x + 3y + 4z = 0, \\ w - 3x + 2y - 9z = 0. \end{cases}$

24. $\begin{cases} w + x + 2y + 7z = 0, \\ w - 2x - y + z = 0, \\ w + 2x + 3y + 9z = 0, \\ 2w - 3x - y + 4z = 0. \end{cases}$

8.6 INVERSES

We have seen how useful the method of reduction is for solving systems of linear equations. But it is by no means the only method which uses matrices. In this section we shall discuss a different method that applies to many systems of n linear equations in n unknowns.

To introduce the general technique, we consider the system

$$\begin{cases} a_{11}x_1 + a_{12}x_2 = c_1, \\ a_{21}x_1 + a_{22}x_2 = c_2. \end{cases}$$

We know from Sec. 8.3 that this system can be represented by the matrix equation

$$\begin{bmatrix} a_{11} & a_{12} \\ a_{21} & a_{22} \end{bmatrix} \begin{bmatrix} x_1 \\ x_2 \end{bmatrix} = \begin{bmatrix} c_1 \\ c_2 \end{bmatrix}. \tag{1}$$

Note that the 2×2 matrix in Eq. (1), which we shall denote by $\mathbf{A}$, is the coefficient matrix of the system. Let us assume that there exists a 2×2 matrix $\mathbf{B}$,

$$\mathbf{B} = \begin{bmatrix} p & q \\ r & s \end{bmatrix},$$

such that $\mathbf{B}$ times $\mathbf{A}$ is the identity matrix:

$$\begin{bmatrix} p & q \\ r & s \end{bmatrix} \begin{bmatrix} a_{11} & a_{12} \\ a_{21} & a_{22} \end{bmatrix} = \begin{bmatrix} 1 & 0 \\ 0 & 1 \end{bmatrix}.$$

If both sides of Eq. (1) are premultiplied by $\mathbf{B}$, we have

$$\begin{bmatrix} p & q \\ r & s \end{bmatrix} \begin{bmatrix} a_{11} & a_{12} \\ a_{21} & a_{22} \end{bmatrix} \begin{bmatrix} x_1 \\ x_2 \end{bmatrix} = \begin{bmatrix} p & q \\ r & s \end{bmatrix} \begin{bmatrix} c_1 \\ c_2 \end{bmatrix},$$

$$\begin{bmatrix} 1 & 0 \\ 0 & 1 \end{bmatrix} \begin{bmatrix} x_1 \\ x_2 \end{bmatrix} = \begin{bmatrix} p & q \\ r & s \end{bmatrix} \begin{bmatrix} c_1 \\ c_2 \end{bmatrix},$$

$$\begin{bmatrix} x_1 \\ x_2 \end{bmatrix} = \begin{bmatrix} pc_1 + qc_2 \\ rc_1 + sc_2 \end{bmatrix}.$$

Thus $x_1 = pc_1 + qc_2$, $x_2 = rc_1 + sc_2$, and the system is solved.

Summarizing our procedure, we first express the system as a matrix equation of the form

$$\mathbf{AX} = \mathbf{C}. \tag{2}$$

Then, provided there exists a matrix **B** such that **BA** = **I**, we premultiply both sides of Eq. (2) by **B**:

$$\mathbf{BAX} = \mathbf{BC}.$$

Simplifying, we have

$$\mathbf{IX} = \mathbf{BC},$$
$$\mathbf{X} = \mathbf{BC}. \tag{3}$$

Thus the solution is given by **X** = **BC**. This procedure is based on our assuming the existence of a matrix **B** such that **BA** = **I**. When such a matrix does exist, we say that it is an *inverse* matrix of **A**.

Definition
If **A** *and* **B** *are* $n \times n$ *matrices, then* **B** *is an* **inverse matrix** *of* **A** *(or* **B** *is an inverse of* **A***) if and only if* **BA** = **I**.

EXAMPLE 1   Let $\mathbf{A} = \begin{bmatrix} 1 & 2 \\ 3 & 7 \end{bmatrix}$ and $\mathbf{B} = \begin{bmatrix} 7 & -2 \\ -3 & 1 \end{bmatrix}$. Since

$$\mathbf{BA} = \begin{bmatrix} 7 & -2 \\ -3 & 1 \end{bmatrix}\begin{bmatrix} 1 & 2 \\ 3 & 7 \end{bmatrix} = \begin{bmatrix} 1 & 0 \\ 0 & 1 \end{bmatrix},$$

B is an inverse matrix of **A**.

It can be shown that if **B** is an inverse matrix of **A**, then that inverse is unique. Thus in Example 1, **B** is the *only* matrix that has the property that **BA** = **I**. In keeping with common practice, we denote *the* inverse of a matrix **A** by $\mathbf{A}^{-1}$. Hence $\mathbf{B} = \mathbf{A}^{-1}$ and

$$\mathbf{A}^{-1}\mathbf{A} = \mathbf{I}.$$

We may now write Eq. (3) as

$$\boxed{\mathbf{X} = \mathbf{A}^{-1}\mathbf{C}. \tag{4}}$$

It is also true that $\mathbf{A}^{-1}\mathbf{A} = \mathbf{AA}^{-1}$. When $\mathbf{A}^{-1}$ does exist, we say **A** is **invertible** (or **nonsingular**).

Not all square matrices are invertible. For example, if

$$\mathbf{A} = \begin{bmatrix} 0 & 1 \\ 0 & 1 \end{bmatrix},$$

then

$$\begin{bmatrix} a & b \\ c & d \end{bmatrix} \begin{bmatrix} 0 & 1 \\ 0 & 1 \end{bmatrix} = \begin{bmatrix} 0 & a+b \\ 0 & c+d \end{bmatrix} \neq \begin{bmatrix} 1 & 0 \\ 0 & 1 \end{bmatrix}.$$

Hence there is no matrix which when postmultiplied by $\mathbf{A}$ yields the identity matrix. Thus $\mathbf{A}$ is not invertible.

Before discussing a procedure for finding the inverse of an invertible matrix, we introduce the concept of *elementary matrices*. An $n \times n$ **elementary matrix** is a matrix obtained from the $n \times n$ identity matrix $\mathbf{I}$ by an elementary row operation. Thus there are three basic types of elementary matrices:

ELEMENTARY MATRICES

1. one obtained by interchanging two rows of $\mathbf{I}$;

2. one obtained by multiplying a row of $\mathbf{I}$ by a nonzero scalar; and

3. one obtained by adding a multiple of one row of $\mathbf{I}$ to another.

EXAMPLE 2   The matrices

$$\mathbf{E}_1 = \begin{bmatrix} 1 & 0 & 0 \\ 0 & 0 & 1 \\ 0 & 1 & 0 \end{bmatrix}, \qquad \mathbf{E}_2 = \begin{bmatrix} -4 & 0 \\ 0 & 1 \end{bmatrix}, \quad \text{and} \quad \mathbf{E}_3 = \begin{bmatrix} 1 & 0 \\ 3 & 1 \end{bmatrix}$$

are elementary matrices. $\mathbf{E}_1$ is obtained from the 3×3 identity matrix by interchanging the second and third rows. $\mathbf{E}_2$ is obtained from the 2×2 identity matrix by multiplying the first row by -4. $\mathbf{E}_3$ is obtained from the 2×2 identity matrix by adding 3 times the first row to the second.

Suppose that $\mathbf{E}$ is an $n \times n$ elementary matrix obtained from $\mathbf{I}$ by a certain elementary row operation, and $\mathbf{A}$ is an $n \times n$ matrix. Then it can be shown that the product $\mathbf{EA}$ is equal to the matrix that is obtained from $\mathbf{A}$ by applying the same elementary row operation to $\mathbf{A}$. For example, let

$$\mathbf{A} = \begin{bmatrix} 1 & 2 \\ 3 & 4 \end{bmatrix}, \qquad \mathbf{E}_1 = \begin{bmatrix} 0 & 1 \\ 1 & 0 \end{bmatrix},$$

$$\mathbf{E}_2 = \begin{bmatrix} 1 & 0 \\ 0 & 2 \end{bmatrix}, \quad \text{and} \quad \mathbf{E}_3 = \begin{bmatrix} 1 & -2 \\ 0 & 1 \end{bmatrix}.$$

$\mathbf{E}_1$, $\mathbf{E}_2$, and $\mathbf{E}_3$ are elementary matrices. $\mathbf{E}_1$ is obtained by interchanging the first and second rows of $\mathbf{I}$. Likewise, the product

$$\mathbf{E}_1\mathbf{A} = \begin{bmatrix} 0 & 1 \\ 1 & 0 \end{bmatrix} \begin{bmatrix} 1 & 2 \\ 3 & 4 \end{bmatrix} = \begin{bmatrix} 3 & 4 \\ 1 & 2 \end{bmatrix}$$

is the matrix obtained from $\mathbf{A}$ by interchanging the first and second rows of $\mathbf{A}$. $\mathbf{E}_2$ is obtained by multiplying the second row of $\mathbf{I}$ by 2. Accordingly, the product

$$E_2A = \begin{bmatrix} 1 & 0 \\ 0 & 2 \end{bmatrix}\begin{bmatrix} 1 & 2 \\ 3 & 4 \end{bmatrix} = \begin{bmatrix} 1 & 2 \\ 6 & 8 \end{bmatrix}$$

is the matrix obtained by multiplying the second row of A by 2. E_3 is obtained by adding -2 times the second row of I to the first row. The product

$$E_3A = \begin{bmatrix} 1 & -2 \\ 0 & 1 \end{bmatrix}\begin{bmatrix} 1 & 2 \\ 3 & 4 \end{bmatrix} = \begin{bmatrix} -5 & -6 \\ 3 & 4 \end{bmatrix}$$

is the matrix obtained from A by the same elementary row operation.

If we wanted to reduce the matrix

$$A = \begin{bmatrix} 1 & 0 \\ 2 & 2 \end{bmatrix},$$

we might proceed through a sequence of steps as follows:

$$A = \begin{bmatrix} 1 & 0 \\ 2 & 2 \end{bmatrix}$$

$$\sim \begin{bmatrix} 1 & 0 \\ 0 & 2 \end{bmatrix} \qquad \text{(by adding } -2 \text{ times the first row to the second)}$$

$$\sim \begin{bmatrix} 1 & 0 \\ 0 & 1 \end{bmatrix} \qquad \text{(by multiplying the second row by } \tfrac{1}{2}\text{)}.$$

Since this involves elementary row operations, it seems natural that elementary matrices can be used to reduce A. If A is premultiplied by the elementary matrix $E_1 = \begin{bmatrix} 1 & 0 \\ -2 & 1 \end{bmatrix}$, then E_1A is the matrix obtained from A by adding -2 times the first row to the second row:

$$E_1A = \begin{bmatrix} 1 & 0 \\ -2 & 1 \end{bmatrix}\begin{bmatrix} 1 & 0 \\ 2 & 2 \end{bmatrix} = \begin{bmatrix} 1 & 0 \\ 0 & 2 \end{bmatrix}.$$

Premultiplying E_1A by the elementary matrix $E_2 = \begin{bmatrix} 1 & 0 \\ 0 & \tfrac{1}{2} \end{bmatrix}$ gives the matrix obtained by multiplying the second row of E_1A by $\tfrac{1}{2}$:

$$E_2(E_1A) = \begin{bmatrix} 1 & 0 \\ 0 & \tfrac{1}{2} \end{bmatrix}\begin{bmatrix} 1 & 0 \\ 0 & 2 \end{bmatrix} = \begin{bmatrix} 1 & 0 \\ 0 & 1 \end{bmatrix} = I.$$

Thus we have reduced A by multiplying A by a product of elementary matrices.

Since $(E_2E_1)A = E_2(E_1A) = I$, the product E_2E_1 is A^{-1}. However, $A^{-1} = E_2E_1 = (E_2E_1)I = E_2(E_1I)$. Thus A^{-1} can be obtained by applying the same elementary row operations, beginning with I, that were used to reduce A to I.

$$I = \begin{bmatrix} 1 & 0 \\ 0 & 1 \end{bmatrix}$$

$$\sim \begin{bmatrix} 1 & 0 \\ -2 & 1 \end{bmatrix} \qquad \text{(by adding } -2 \text{ times the first row to the second)}$$

$$\sim \begin{bmatrix} 1 & 0 \\ -1 & \frac{1}{2} \end{bmatrix} \qquad \text{(by multiplying the second row by } \tfrac{1}{2}\text{).}$$

Therefore,

$$\mathbf{A}^{-1} = \begin{bmatrix} 1 & 0 \\ -1 & \frac{1}{2} \end{bmatrix}.$$

Our result can be verified by showing $\mathbf{A}^{-1}\mathbf{A} = \mathbf{I}$:

$$\mathbf{A}^{-1}\mathbf{A} = \begin{bmatrix} 1 & 0 \\ -1 & \frac{1}{2} \end{bmatrix}\begin{bmatrix} 1 & 0 \\ 2 & 2 \end{bmatrix} = \begin{bmatrix} 1 & 0 \\ 0 & 1 \end{bmatrix} = \mathbf{I}.$$

In summary, to find $\mathbf{A}^{-1}$ we apply the identical elementary row operations, beginning with $\mathbf{I}$ and proceeding in the same order, as those that were used to reduce $\mathbf{A}$ to $\mathbf{I}$. Finding $\mathbf{A}^{-1}$ by this technique can be done conveniently by using the following format. First, we write the matrix

$$[\mathbf{A} \mid \mathbf{I}] = \begin{bmatrix} 1 & 0 & \vdots & 1 & 0 \\ 2 & 2 & \vdots & 0 & 1 \end{bmatrix}.$$

Then we apply elementary row operations until $[\mathbf{A} \quad \mathbf{I}]$ is equivalent to a matrix which has $\mathbf{I}$ as its first two columns. The last two columns of this matrix will be $\mathbf{A}^{-1}$. Thus

$$[\mathbf{A} \mid \mathbf{I}] = \begin{bmatrix} 1 & 0 & \vdots & 1 & 0 \\ 2 & 2 & \vdots & 0 & 1 \end{bmatrix} \sim \begin{bmatrix} 1 & 0 & \vdots & 1 & 0 \\ 0 & 2 & \vdots & -2 & 1 \end{bmatrix}$$

$$\sim \begin{bmatrix} 1 & 0 & \vdots & 1 & 0 \\ 0 & 1 & \vdots & -1 & \frac{1}{2} \end{bmatrix} = [\mathbf{I} \mid \mathbf{A}^{-1}].$$

Note that the first two columns of $[\mathbf{I} \mid \mathbf{A}^{-1}]$ form a reduced matrix.

This procedure can be extended to find the inverse of *any* invertible $n \times n$ matrix. If $\mathbf{M}$ is such a matrix, form the $n \times (2n)$ matrix $[\mathbf{M} \mid \mathbf{I}]$. Then perform elementary row operations until the first n columns form a reduced matrix equal to $\mathbf{I}$. The last n columns will be $\mathbf{M}^{-1}$.

$$[\mathbf{M} \mid \mathbf{I}] \sim \cdots \sim [\mathbf{I} \mid \mathbf{M}^{-1}].$$

If a matrix $\mathbf{M}$ does not reduce to $\mathbf{I}$, then $\mathbf{M}^{-1}$ does not exist.

EXAMPLE 3   *Determine $\mathbf{A}^{-1}$ if $\mathbf{A}$ is invertible.*

a. $\mathbf{A} = \begin{bmatrix} 1 & 0 & -2 \\ 4 & -2 & 1 \\ 1 & 2 & -10 \end{bmatrix}.$

$$[\mathbf{A} \mid \mathbf{I}] = \begin{bmatrix} 1 & 0 & -2 & \vdots & 1 & 0 & 0 \\ 4 & -2 & 1 & \vdots & 0 & 1 & 0 \\ 1 & 2 & -10 & \vdots & 0 & 0 & 1 \end{bmatrix}$$

$$\sim \cdots \sim \begin{bmatrix} 1 & 0 & 0 & \vdots & -9 & 2 & 2 \\ 0 & 1 & 0 & \vdots & -\frac{41}{2} & 4 & \frac{9}{2} \\ 0 & 0 & 1 & \vdots & -5 & 1 & 1 \end{bmatrix}.$$

The first three columns of the last matrix form **I**. Thus **A** is invertible and

$$\mathbf{A}^{-1} = \begin{bmatrix} -9 & 2 & 2 \\ \frac{41}{2} & 4 & \frac{9}{2} \\ -5 & 1 & 1 \end{bmatrix}.$$

b. $\mathbf{A} = \begin{bmatrix} 3 & 2 \\ 6 & 4 \end{bmatrix}.$

$$[\mathbf{A} \mid \mathbf{I}] = \begin{bmatrix} 3 & 2 & \vdots & 1 & 0 \\ 6 & 4 & \vdots & 0 & 1 \end{bmatrix} \sim \begin{bmatrix} 3 & 2 & \vdots & 1 & 0 \\ 0 & 0 & \vdots & -2 & 1 \end{bmatrix}$$

$$\sim \begin{bmatrix} 1 & \frac{2}{3} & \vdots & \frac{1}{3} & 0 \\ 0 & 0 & \vdots & -2 & 1 \end{bmatrix}.$$

The first two columns of the last matrix form a reduced matrix different from **I**. Thus **A** is not invertible.

Now we shall solve a system by using an inverse matrix.

EXAMPLE 4   *Solve each system by finding the inverse of the coefficient matrix.*

a. $\begin{cases} x_1 + 2x_2 = 0, \\ 4x_1 + 9x_2 = 1. \end{cases}$

The system can be expressed as the matrix equation $\mathbf{AX} = \mathbf{C}$, where **A** is the coefficient matrix of the system.

$$\begin{bmatrix} 1 & 2 \\ 4 & 9 \end{bmatrix} \begin{bmatrix} x_1 \\ x_2 \end{bmatrix} = \begin{bmatrix} 0 \\ 1 \end{bmatrix}.$$

Since $\mathbf{AX} = \mathbf{C}$, then $\mathbf{A}^{-1}\mathbf{AX} = \mathbf{A}^{-1}\mathbf{C}$, so our solution is given by

$$\mathbf{X} = \mathbf{A}^{-1}\mathbf{C},$$

which, you may recall, is Eq. (4). Thus we need to find $\mathbf{A}^{-1}$.

$$\begin{bmatrix} 1 & 2 & \vdots & 1 & 0 \\ 4 & 9 & \vdots & 0 & 1 \end{bmatrix} \sim \cdots \sim \begin{bmatrix} 1 & 0 & \vdots & 9 & -2 \\ 0 & 1 & \vdots & -4 & 1 \end{bmatrix}.$$

$$\mathbf{A}^{-1} = \begin{bmatrix} 9 & -2 \\ -4 & 1 \end{bmatrix}.$$

Hence

$$\mathbf{X} = \begin{bmatrix} x_1 \\ x_2 \end{bmatrix} = \mathbf{A}^{-1}\mathbf{C} = \begin{bmatrix} 9 & -2 \\ -4 & 1 \end{bmatrix}\begin{bmatrix} 0 \\ 1 \end{bmatrix} = \begin{bmatrix} -2 \\ 1 \end{bmatrix}.$$

Therefore, $x_1 = -2$ and $x_2 = 1$.

b. $\begin{cases} x_1 & - & 2x_3 & = & 1, \\ 4x_1 & - 2x_2 + & x_3 & = & 2, \\ x_1 & + 2x_2 - & 10x_3 & = & -1. \end{cases}$

The coefficient matrix of the system is

$$\mathbf{A} = \begin{bmatrix} 1 & 0 & -2 \\ 4 & -2 & 1 \\ 1 & 2 & -10 \end{bmatrix}.$$

By example 3(a),

$$\mathbf{A}^{-1} = \begin{bmatrix} -9 & 2 & 2 \\ -\frac{41}{2} & 4 & \frac{9}{2} \\ -5 & 1 & 1 \end{bmatrix}.$$

Thus the solution is given by $\mathbf{X} = \mathbf{A}^{-1}\mathbf{C}$:

$$\begin{bmatrix} x_1 \\ x_2 \\ x_3 \end{bmatrix} = \begin{bmatrix} 9 & 2 & 2 \\ -\frac{41}{2} & 4 & \frac{9}{2} \\ -5 & 1 & 1 \end{bmatrix}\begin{bmatrix} 1 \\ 2 \\ -1 \end{bmatrix} = \begin{bmatrix} -7 \\ -17 \\ -4 \end{bmatrix}.$$

Consequently, $x_1 = -7$, $x_2 = -17$, and $x_3 = -4$.

It can be shown that a system of n linear equations in n unknowns has a unique solution if and only if the coefficient matrix is invertible. Indeed, in both parts of the last example the coefficient matrices were invertible and unique solutions did in fact exist. When the coefficient matrix is not invertible, the system will have either no solution or infinitely many solutions.

EXAMPLE 5   *Solve the system*

$$\begin{cases} x - 2y + z = 0, \\ 2x - y + 5z = 0, \\ x + y + 4z = 0. \end{cases}$$

The coefficient matrix is

$$\begin{bmatrix} 1 & -2 & 1 \\ 2 & -1 & 5 \\ 1 & 1 & 4 \end{bmatrix}.$$

Since

$$\begin{bmatrix} 1 & -2 & 1 & \vdots & 1 & 0 & 0 \\ 2 & -1 & 5 & \vdots & 0 & 1 & 0 \\ 1 & 1 & 4 & \vdots & 0 & 0 & 1 \end{bmatrix} \sim \cdots \sim \begin{bmatrix} 1 & 0 & 3 & \vdots & -\frac{1}{3} & \frac{2}{3} & 0 \\ 0 & 1 & 1 & \vdots & -\frac{2}{3} & \frac{1}{3} & 0 \\ 0 & 0 & 0 & \vdots & 1 & -1 & 1 \end{bmatrix},$$

the coefficient matrix is not invertible. Hence the system *cannot* be solved by inverses. Another method must be used. In Example 4(a) of Sec. 8.5, the solution was found to be $x = -3z$, $y = -z$, $z = z$.

EXERCISE 8.6

In each of Problems **1–18,** *if the given matrix is invertible, find its inverse.*

1. $\begin{bmatrix} 6 & 1 \\ 5 & 1 \end{bmatrix}$.

2. $\begin{bmatrix} 2 & 8 \\ 3 & 12 \end{bmatrix}$.

3. $\begin{bmatrix} 1 & 1 \\ 1 & 1 \end{bmatrix}$.

4. $\begin{bmatrix} 4 & 9 \\ 0 & -6 \end{bmatrix}$.

5. $\begin{bmatrix} 1 & 0 & 0 \\ 0 & -3 & 0 \\ 0 & 0 & 4 \end{bmatrix}$.

6. $\begin{bmatrix} 2 & 0 & 8 \\ -1 & 4 & 0 \\ 2 & 1 & 0 \end{bmatrix}$.

7. $\begin{bmatrix} 1 & 2 & 3 \\ 0 & 0 & 4 \\ 0 & 0 & 5 \end{bmatrix}$.

8. $\begin{bmatrix} 2 & 0 & 0 \\ 0 & 0 & 0 \\ 0 & 0 & -4 \end{bmatrix}$.

9. $\begin{bmatrix} 2 & 4 \\ 8 & 1 \\ 6 & 3 \end{bmatrix}$.

10. $\begin{bmatrix} 0 & 0 & 0 \\ 0 & 0 & 0 \\ 0 & 0 & 0 \end{bmatrix}$.

11. $\begin{bmatrix} 1 & 1 & 1 \\ 0 & 1 & 1 \\ 0 & 0 & 1 \end{bmatrix}$.

12. $\begin{bmatrix} 1 & 2 & -1 \\ 0 & 1 & 4 \\ 1 & -1 & 2 \end{bmatrix}$.

13. $\begin{bmatrix} 7 & 0 & -2 \\ 0 & 1 & 0 \\ -3 & 0 & 1 \end{bmatrix}$.

14. $\begin{bmatrix} 7 & -8 & 5 \\ -4 & 5 & -3 \\ 1 & -1 & 1 \end{bmatrix}$.

15. $\begin{bmatrix} 2 & 1 & 0 \\ 4 & -1 & 5 \\ 1 & -1 & 2 \end{bmatrix}$.

16. $\begin{bmatrix} -5 & 4 & -3 \\ 10 & -7 & 6 \\ 8 & -6 & 5 \end{bmatrix}$.

17. $\begin{bmatrix} 1 & 2 & 3 \\ 1 & 3 & 5 \\ 1 & 5 & 12 \end{bmatrix}$.

18. $\begin{bmatrix} 2 & -1 & 3 \\ 0 & 2 & 0 \\ 2 & 1 & 1 \end{bmatrix}$.

For each of Problems **19–32,** *if the coefficient matrix of the system is invertible, solve the system by using the inverse. If not, solve the system by the method of reduction.*

19. $\begin{cases} 6x + 5y = 2, \\ x + y = -3. \end{cases}$

20. $\begin{cases} 2x + 3y = 4, \\ -x + 5y = -2. \end{cases}$

21. $\begin{cases} 2x + y = 5, \\ 3x - y = 0. \end{cases}$

22. $\begin{cases} 3x + 2y = 26, \\ 4x + 3y = 37. \end{cases}$

23. $\begin{cases} 2x + 6y = 2, \\ 3x + 9y = 3. \end{cases}$

24. $\begin{cases} 2x + 8y = 3, \\ 3x + 12y = 6. \end{cases}$

25. $\begin{cases} x + 2y + z = 4, \\ 3x + z = 2, \\ x - y + z = 1. \end{cases}$

26. $\begin{cases} x + y + z = 2, \\ x - y + z = -2, \\ x - y - z = 0. \end{cases}$

27. $\begin{cases} x + y + z = 2, \\ x - y + z = 1, \\ x - y - z = 0. \end{cases}$

28. $\begin{cases} 2x \quad + 8z = 8, \\ -x + 4y \quad = 36, \\ 2x + y \quad = 9. \end{cases}$

29. $\begin{cases} x + 3y + 3z = 7, \\ 2x + y + z = 4, \\ x + y + z = 4. \end{cases}$

30. $\begin{cases} x + 3y + 3z = 7, \\ 2x + y + z = 4, \\ x + y + z = 3. \end{cases}$

31. $\begin{cases} w \quad + 2y + z = 4, \\ w - x \quad + 2z = 12, \\ 2w + x \quad + z = 12, \\ w + 2x + y + z = 12. \end{cases}$

32. $\begin{cases} w + x \quad + z = 2, \\ w \quad + y \quad = 0, \\ x + y + z = 4, \\ y + z = 1. \end{cases}$

Find $(\mathbf{I} - \mathbf{A})^{-1}$ for each of the following matrices $\mathbf{A}$.

33. $\begin{bmatrix} 2 & -1 \\ 1 & 3 \end{bmatrix}.$

34. $\begin{bmatrix} -3 & 2 \\ 4 & 3 \end{bmatrix}.$

35. Solve the following problems by using the inverse of the matrix involved.

a. An automobile factory produces two models. The first requires 1 labor hour to paint and $\frac{1}{2}$ labor hour to polish; the second requires 1 labor hour for each process. During each hour that the assembly line is operating, there are 100 labor hours available for painting and 80 labor hours for polishing. How many of each model can be produced each hour if all the labor hours available are to be utilized?

b. Suppose each car of the first type requires 10 widgets and 14 shims, and each car of the second type requires 7 widgets and 10 shims. The factory can obtain 800 widgets and 1130 shims each hour. How many cars of each model can it produce while utilizing all the parts available?

8.7 DETERMINANTS

We now introduce a new function, the *determinant function*. Here our inputs will be *square* matrices, but our outputs will be real numbers. If $\mathbf{A}$ is a square matrix, then the determinant function associates with $\mathbf{A}$ exactly one real number called the *determinant* of $\mathbf{A}$. Denoting the determinant of $\mathbf{A}$ by $|\mathbf{A}|$ (that is, using vertical bars), we can think of the determinant function as a correspondence:

$$\begin{matrix} \mathbf{A} & \to & |\mathbf{A}| \\ \text{square} & & \text{real} \\ \text{matrix} & & \text{number} \end{matrix} = \begin{matrix} \text{determinant} \\ \text{of } \mathbf{A} \end{matrix}$$

The use of determinants in solving systems of linear equations will be discussed later. Turning to how a real number is assigned to a square matrix, we shall first consider the special cases of matrices of orders 1 and 2. Then we shall extend the definition to matrices of order n.

Definition
If $\mathbf{A} = [a_{11}]$ *is a square matrix of order* 1, *then* $|\mathbf{A}| = a_{11}$.

That is, the determinant function assigns to the one-entry matrix $[a_{11}]$ the number a_{11}. Hence if $\mathbf{A} = [6]$, then $|\mathbf{A}| = 6$.

Definition
If $\mathbf{A} = \begin{bmatrix} a_{11} & a_{12} \\ a_{21} & a_{22} \end{bmatrix}$ *is a square matrix of order* 2, *then*

$$|\mathbf{A}| = a_{11}a_{22} - a_{12}a_{21}.$$

That is, the determinant of a 2×2 matrix is obtained by taking the product of the entries in the main diagonal and subtracting from it the product of the entries in the other diagonal. We speak of the determinant of a 2×2 matrix as a *determinant of order 2*.

EXAMPLE 1   *Find $|\mathbf{A}|$ if $\mathbf{A}$ =*

a. $\begin{bmatrix} 2 & 1 \\ 3 & -4 \end{bmatrix}$.   b. $\begin{bmatrix} -3 & -2 \\ 0 & 1 \end{bmatrix}$.   c. $\begin{bmatrix} 1 & 0 \\ 0 & 1 \end{bmatrix}$.   d. $\begin{bmatrix} x & 0 \\ y & 1 \end{bmatrix}$.

We have

a. $|\mathbf{A}| = \begin{vmatrix} 2 & 1 \\ 3 & -4 \end{vmatrix} = (2)(-4) - (1)(3) = -8 - 3 = -11.$

b. $|\mathbf{A}| = \begin{vmatrix} -3 & -2 \\ 0 & 1 \end{vmatrix} = (-3)(1) - (-2)(0) = -3 - 0 = -3.$

c. $|\mathbf{A}| = \begin{vmatrix} 1 & 0 \\ 0 & 1 \end{vmatrix} = (1)(1) - (0)(0) = 1.$

d. $|\mathbf{A}| = \begin{vmatrix} x & 0 \\ y & 1 \end{vmatrix} = (x)(1) - (0)(y) = x.$

The determinant of a square matrix $\mathbf{A}$ of order n ($n > 2$) is defined in the following manner. With a given entry of $\mathbf{A}$ we associate the square matrix of order $n - 1$ obtained by deleting the entries in the row and column in which the given entry lies. For example, given the matrix

$$\begin{bmatrix} a_{11} & a_{12} & a_{13} \\ a_{21} & a_{22} & a_{23} \\ a_{31} & a_{32} & a_{33} \end{bmatrix},$$

with entry a_{21} we delete the entries in row 2 and column 1,

$$\begin{bmatrix} a_{11} & a_{12} & a_{13} \\ a_{21} & a_{22} & a_{23} \\ a_{31} & a_{32} & a_{33} \end{bmatrix},$$

leaving the matrix of order 2,

$$\begin{bmatrix} a_{12} & a_{13} \\ a_{32} & a_{33} \end{bmatrix}.$$

The *determinant* of this matrix is called the **minor** of a_{21}. Similarly, the minor of a_{22} is

$$\begin{vmatrix} a_{11} & a_{13} \\ a_{31} & a_{33} \end{vmatrix},$$

and for a_{23} it is

$$\begin{vmatrix} a_{11} & a_{12} \\ a_{31} & a_{32} \end{vmatrix}.$$

With each entry a_{ij} we also associate a number determined by the subscript of the entry:

$$(-1)^{i+j},$$

where $i + j$ is the sum of the row number i and column number j in which the entry lies. With a_{21} we associate $(-1)^{2+1} = -1$, with a_{22} the number $(-1)^{2+2} = 1$, and with a_{23} the number $(-1)^{2+3} = -1$. The **cofactor** c_{ij} of the entry a_{ij} is the product of $(-1)^{i+j}$ and the minor of a_{ij}. For example, the cofactor of a_{21} is

$$c_{21} = (-1)^{2+1} \begin{vmatrix} a_{12} & a_{13} \\ a_{32} & a_{33} \end{vmatrix}.$$

The only difference between a cofactor and a minor is the factor $(-1)^{i+j}$.

To find the determinant of any square matrix **A** of order n, select *any* row (or column) of **A** and multiply each entry in the row (column) by its cofactor. The sum of these products is defined to be the determinant of **A** and is called a **determinant of order** n.

Let us find the determinant of

$$\begin{bmatrix} 2 & -1 & 3 \\ 3 & 0 & -5 \\ 2 & 1 & 1 \end{bmatrix}$$

by applying the rule above to the first row (sometimes referred to as "expanding along the first row"). For

$$a_{11} \text{ we obtain } (2)(-1)^{1+1} \begin{vmatrix} 0 & -5 \\ 1 & 1 \end{vmatrix} = (2)(1)(5) = 10,$$

$$a_{12} \text{ we obtain } (-1)(-1)^{1+2} \begin{vmatrix} 3 & -5 \\ 2 & 1 \end{vmatrix} = (-1)(-1)(13) = 13,$$

$$a_{13} \text{ we obtain } (3)(-1)^{1+3} \begin{vmatrix} 3 & 0 \\ 2 & 1 \end{vmatrix} = 3(1)(3) = 9.$$

Hence

$$\begin{vmatrix} 2 & -1 & 3 \\ 3 & 0 & -5 \\ 2 & 1 & 1 \end{vmatrix} = 10 + 13 + 9 = 32.$$

If we had expanded along the second column, then

$$\begin{vmatrix} 2 & -1 & 3 \\ 3 & 0 & -5 \\ 2 & 1 & 1 \end{vmatrix} = (-1)(-1)^{1+2}\begin{vmatrix} 3 & -5 \\ 2 & 1 \end{vmatrix} + 0 + (1)(-1)^{3+2}\begin{vmatrix} 2 & 3 \\ 3 & -5 \end{vmatrix}$$

$$= 13 + 0 + 19 = 32 \quad \text{as before.}$$

It can be shown that the determinant of a matrix is unique and does not depend on the row or column chosen for its evaluation. In the problem above, the second expansion is preferable since the 0 in column 2 contributed nothing to the sum, thus simplifying the calculation.

EXAMPLE 2   *Find* $|\mathbf{A}|$ *if*

a. $\mathbf{A} = \begin{bmatrix} 12 & -1 & 3 \\ -3 & 1 & -1 \\ -10 & 2 & -3 \end{bmatrix}$.

Expanding along the first row, we have

$$|\mathbf{A}| = 12(-1)^{1+1}\begin{vmatrix} 1 & -1 \\ 2 & -3 \end{vmatrix} + (-1)(-1)^{1+2}\begin{vmatrix} -3 & -1 \\ -10 & -3 \end{vmatrix} +$$

$$3(-1)^{1+3}\begin{vmatrix} -3 & 1 \\ -10 & 2 \end{vmatrix}$$

$$= 12(1)(-1) + (-1)(-1)(-1) + 3(1)(4) = -1.$$

b. $\mathbf{A} = \begin{bmatrix} 0 & 1 & 1 \\ 2 & 3 & 2 \\ 0 & -1 & 3 \end{bmatrix}$.

Expanding along column 1 for convenience, we have

$$|\mathbf{A}| = 0 + 2(-1)^{2+1}\begin{vmatrix} 1 & 1 \\ -1 & 3 \end{vmatrix} + 0 = 2(-1)(4) = -8.$$

EXAMPLE 3   *Evaluate*

$$|\mathbf{A}| = \begin{vmatrix} 2 & 0 & 0 & 1 \\ 0 & 1 & 0 & 3 \\ 0 & 0 & 1 & 2 \\ 1 & 2 & 3 & 0 \end{vmatrix}$$

by expanding along the first row.

$$|\mathbf{A}| = 2(-1)^{1+1}\begin{vmatrix} 1 & 0 & 3 \\ 0 & 1 & 2 \\ 2 & 3 & 0 \end{vmatrix} + 1(-1)^{1+4}\begin{vmatrix} 0 & 1 & 0 \\ 0 & 0 & 1 \\ 1 & 2 & 3 \end{vmatrix}.$$

We have now expressed $|\mathbf{A}|$ in terms of determinants of order three. Expanding each of these along the first row, we have

$$|\mathbf{A}| = 2(1)\left[1(-1)^{1+1}\begin{vmatrix} 1 & 2 \\ 3 & 0 \end{vmatrix} + 3(-1)^{1+3}\begin{vmatrix} 0 & 1 \\ 2 & 3 \end{vmatrix}\right] + 1(-1)\left[1(-1)^{1+2}\begin{vmatrix} 0 & 1 \\ 1 & 3 \end{vmatrix}\right]$$

$$= 2[1(1)(-6) + 3(1)(-2)] + (-1)[(1)(-1)(-1)] = -25.$$

The evaluation of determinants is often simplified by the use of various properties, some of which we now list. In each case $\mathbf{A}$ denotes a square matrix.

1. **If each of the entries in a row (or column) of A is 0, then $|\mathbf{A}| = 0$.**
   Thus
   $$\begin{vmatrix} 6 & 2 & 5 \\ 7 & 1 & 4 \\ 0 & 0 & 0 \end{vmatrix} = 0.$$

2. **If two rows (or columns) of A are identical, $|\mathbf{A}| = 0$.**
   Thus
   $$\begin{vmatrix} 2 & 5 & 2 & 1 \\ 2 & 6 & 2 & 3 \\ 2 & 4 & 2 & 1 \\ 6 & 5 & 6 & 1 \end{vmatrix} = 0, \quad \text{since column 1} = \text{column 3}.$$

3. **If all the entries below (or above) the main diagonal of A are zeros, then $|\mathbf{A}|$ is equal to the product of the main diagonal entries.**
   Thus
   $$\begin{vmatrix} 2 & 6 & 1 & 0 \\ 0 & 5 & 7 & 6 \\ 0 & 0 & -2 & 5 \\ 0 & 0 & 0 & 1 \end{vmatrix} = (2)(5)(-2)(1) = -20.$$

   From this property we conclude that the determinant of an identity matrix is 1.

4. **If B is the matrix obtained by adding a multiple of one row (or column) of A to another row (column), then $|\mathbf{B}| = |\mathbf{A}|$.**
   Thus if
   $$\mathbf{A} = \begin{bmatrix} 2 & 4 & 2 & 6 \\ 1 & 3 & 5 & 2 \\ 1 & 2 & 1 & 3 \\ 0 & 5 & 6 & 2 \end{bmatrix}$$

and **B** is the matrix obtained from **A** by adding -2 times row 3 to row 1, then

$$|\mathbf{A}| = \begin{vmatrix} 2 & 4 & 2 & 6 \\ 1 & 3 & 5 & 2 \\ 1 & 2 & 1 & 3 \\ 0 & 5 & 6 & 2 \end{vmatrix} = \begin{vmatrix} 0 & 0 & 0 & 0 \\ 1 & 3 & 5 & 2 \\ 1 & 2 & 1 & 3 \\ 0 & 5 & 6 & 2 \end{vmatrix} = |\mathbf{B}|.$$

By property 1, $|\mathbf{B}| = 0$ and hence $|\mathbf{A}| = 0$.

5. **If B is the matrix obtained by interchanging two rows (or columns) of A, then $|\mathbf{A}| = -|\mathbf{B}|$.**
Thus if

$$\mathbf{A} = \begin{vmatrix} 2 & 2 & 1 & 6 \\ 0 & 0 & 0 & 1 \\ 0 & 0 & 2 & 0 \\ 0 & 1 & -3 & 4 \end{vmatrix}$$

and **B** is obtained from **A** by interchanging rows 2 and 4, then

$$|\mathbf{A}| = \begin{vmatrix} 2 & 2 & 1 & 6 \\ 0 & 0 & 0 & 1 \\ 0 & 0 & 2 & 0 \\ 0 & 1 & -3 & 4 \end{vmatrix} = - \begin{vmatrix} 2 & 2 & 1 & 6 \\ 0 & 1 & -3 & 4 \\ 0 & 0 & 2 & 0 \\ 0 & 0 & 0 & 1 \end{vmatrix} = -|\mathbf{B}|.$$

By property 3, $|\mathbf{B}| = 4$ and hence $|\mathbf{A}| = -4$.

6. **If B is the matrix obtained by multiplying each entry of a row (or column) of A by the same number k, then $|\mathbf{B}| = k|\mathbf{A}|$.**
Thus

$$\begin{vmatrix} 2 \cdot 3 & 2 \cdot 5 & 2 \cdot 7 \\ 5 & 2 & 1 \\ 6 & 4 & 3 \end{vmatrix} = 2 \begin{vmatrix} 3 & 5 & 7 \\ 5 & 2 & 1 \\ 6 & 4 & 3 \end{vmatrix}.$$

Essentially, a number can be "factored out" of one row or column.

7. **The determinant of the product of two matrices of order n is the product of their determinants. That is, $|\mathbf{AB}| = |\mathbf{A}||\mathbf{B}|$.**
Thus if

$$\mathbf{A} = \begin{bmatrix} 1 & 2 \\ 3 & 4 \end{bmatrix} \quad \text{and} \quad \mathbf{B} = \begin{bmatrix} 1 & 2 \\ 0 & 3 \end{bmatrix},$$

then

$$|\mathbf{AB}| = |\mathbf{A}| \cdot |\mathbf{B}| = \begin{vmatrix} 1 & 2 \\ 3 & 4 \end{vmatrix} \cdot \begin{vmatrix} 1 & 2 \\ 0 & 3 \end{vmatrix} = (-2)(3) = -6.$$

EXAMPLE 4   *Evaluate*

$$|\mathbf{A}| = \begin{vmatrix} 1 & 1 & 0 & 5 \\ 1 & 2 & 1 & 0 \\ 0 & 2 & 1 & 1 \\ 3 & 0 & 0 & -4 \end{vmatrix}.$$

We shall express **A** in upper triangular form (we say that we "triangulate") and then, by property 3, take the product of the main diagonal.

$$\begin{vmatrix} 1 & 1 & 0 & 5 \\ 1 & 2 & 1 & 0 \\ 0 & 2 & 1 & 1 \\ 3 & 0 & 0 & -4 \end{vmatrix} = \begin{vmatrix} 1 & 1 & 0 & 5 \\ 0 & 1 & 1 & -5 \\ 0 & 2 & 1 & 1 \\ 0 & -3 & 0 & -19 \end{vmatrix}$$

(by adding -1 times row 1 to row 2; adding -3 times row 1 to row 4)

$$= \begin{vmatrix} 1 & 1 & 0 & 5 \\ 0 & 1 & 1 & -5 \\ 0 & 0 & -1 & 11 \\ 0 & 0 & 3 & -34 \end{vmatrix}$$

(by adding -2 times row 2 to row 3; adding 3 times row 2 to row 4)

$$= \begin{vmatrix} 1 & 1 & 0 & 5 \\ 0 & 1 & 1 & -5 \\ 0 & 0 & -1 & 11 \\ 0 & 0 & 0 & -1 \end{vmatrix}$$

(by adding 3 times row 3 to row 4)

$$= (1)(1)(-1)(-1) = 1.$$

EXERCISE 8.7

Evaluate the determinants in Problems 1–6.

1. $\begin{vmatrix} 2 & 1 \\ 3 & 2 \end{vmatrix}.$

2. $\begin{vmatrix} 3 & 2 \\ -5 & -4 \end{vmatrix}.$

3. $\begin{vmatrix} -2 & -3 \\ -4 & -6 \end{vmatrix}.$

4. $\begin{vmatrix} -3 & 1 \\ -a & b \end{vmatrix}.$

5. $\begin{vmatrix} 1 & x \\ 0 & y \end{vmatrix}.$

6. $\begin{vmatrix} -2 & -a \\ -a & 2 \end{vmatrix}.$

In Problems 7 and 8, evaluate the given expressions.

7. $\dfrac{\begin{vmatrix} 1 & 2 \\ 3 & 4 \end{vmatrix}}{\begin{vmatrix} 2 & 1 \\ 5 & 6 \end{vmatrix}}.$

8. $\dfrac{\begin{vmatrix} 6 & 2 \\ 1 & 5 \end{vmatrix}}{\begin{vmatrix} 2 & -6 \\ 5 & 3 \end{vmatrix}}.$

9. Solve for k if $\begin{vmatrix} 2 & 3 \\ 4 & k \end{vmatrix} = 12.$

If $\mathbf{A} = \begin{bmatrix} 1 & 2 & 3 \\ 4 & 5 & 6 \\ 7 & 8 & 9 \end{bmatrix}$, *determine each of the following.*

10. The minor of a_{31}.   **11.** The minor of a_{22}.   **12.** The cofactor of a_{23}.   **13.** The cofactor of a_{32}.

14. If $\mathbf{A} = [a_{ij}]$ is 50×50 and the minor of $a_{43,47}$ equals 20, what is the value of the cofactor of $a_{43,47}$?

If $\mathbf{A} = \begin{bmatrix} a_{11} & a_{12} & a_{13} & a_{14} \\ a_{21} & a_{22} & a_{23} & a_{24} \\ a_{31} & a_{32} & a_{33} & a_{34} \\ a_{41} & a_{42} & a_{43} & a_{44} \end{bmatrix}$, *write each of the following.*

15. The minor of a_{32}.   **16.** The minor of a_{24}.   **17.** The cofactor of a_{13}.   **18.** The cofactor of a_{43}.

In Problems **19–34**, *evaluate the determinant. Use properties of determinants if possible.*

19. $\begin{vmatrix} 2 & 1 & 3 \\ 2 & 0 & 1 \\ -4 & 0 & 6 \end{vmatrix}$.

20. $\begin{vmatrix} 3 & 2 & 1 \\ 1 & -2 & 3 \\ -1 & 3 & 2 \end{vmatrix}$.

21. $\begin{vmatrix} 1 & 2 & -3 \\ 4 & 5 & 4 \\ 3 & -2 & 1 \end{vmatrix}$.

22. $\begin{vmatrix} 1 & 0 & -1 \\ 0 & 1 & 0 \\ 1 & -1 & 1 \end{vmatrix}$.

23. $\begin{vmatrix} 2 & 1 & 5 \\ -3 & 4 & -1 \\ 0 & 6 & -1 \end{vmatrix}$.

24. $\begin{vmatrix} 1 & 2 & 3 \\ 4 & 5 & 4 \\ 3 & 2 & 1 \end{vmatrix}$.

25. $\begin{vmatrix} 2 & -1 & 3 \\ 1 & 1 & -1 \\ 1 & 2 & -3 \end{vmatrix}$.

26. $\begin{vmatrix} 1 & 2 & 3 \\ 4 & 5 & 6 \\ 7 & 8 & 9 \end{vmatrix}$.

27. $\begin{vmatrix} \frac{1}{2} & \frac{2}{3} & -\frac{1}{2} \\ -1 & \frac{1}{3} & \frac{2}{3} \\ 3 & -4 & 1 \end{vmatrix}$.

28. $\begin{vmatrix} -\frac{1}{3} & \frac{1}{4} & 4 \\ \frac{3}{2} & \frac{3}{8} & -2 \\ -\frac{1}{8} & \frac{9}{2} & 1 \end{vmatrix}$.

29. $\begin{vmatrix} 1 & 0 & 3 & 2 \\ 4 & -1 & 0 & 1 \\ 2 & 1 & 0 & 3 \\ -1 & 2 & 3 & -1 \end{vmatrix}$.

30. $\begin{vmatrix} 7 & 6 & 0 & 5 \\ -3 & 2 & 0 & 1 \\ 4 & -3 & 0 & 2 \\ 1 & 0 & 0 & 6 \end{vmatrix}$.

31. $\begin{vmatrix} 1 & 7 & -3 & 8 \\ 0 & 1 & -5 & 4 \\ 0 & 0 & 1 & 7 \\ 0 & 0 & 0 & 1 \end{vmatrix}$.

32. $\begin{vmatrix} 1 & 2 & -3 & 4 \\ 3 & -1 & 2 & 4 \\ -2 & -4 & 6 & -8 \\ 0 & 3 & -1 & 2 \end{vmatrix}$.

33. $\begin{vmatrix} 1 & 0 & 0 & 0 \\ 0 & -2 & 0 & 0 \\ 0 & 0 & 4 & 0 \\ 0 & 0 & 0 & -3 \end{vmatrix}$.

34. $\begin{vmatrix} 1 & -3 & 2 & 6 & 4 \\ 0 & 13 & 0 & 1 & 5 \\ -2 & 1 & 2 & 3 & 4 \\ 1 & 1 & 4 & 5 & 9 \end{vmatrix}$.

In Problems **35** *and* **36**, *solve for x.*

35. $\begin{vmatrix} x & -2 \\ 7 & 7-x \end{vmatrix} = 26$.

36. $\begin{vmatrix} 3 & x & 2x \\ 0 & x & 99 \\ 0 & 0 & x-1 \end{vmatrix} = 60$.

37. If $\mathbf{A}$ is of order 4×4 and $|\mathbf{A}| = 12$, what is the value of the determinant obtained by multiplying every element in $\mathbf{A}$ by 2?

8.8 CRAMER'S RULE

Determinants can be applied to solving a system of n linear equations in n un-knowns. In fact, it is from the analysis of such systems that the study of deter-minants took its origin. Although the method of reduction is more practical for systems involving a large number of unknowns, the method of solution by deter-minants is interesting enough to warrant some attention here and it also allows us to solve for one unknown without having to solve for the others. We shall first consider a system of two linear equations in two unknowns. Then the results will be extended to include more general situations.

Let us solve

$$\begin{cases} a_{11}x + a_{12}y = c_1, \\ a_{21}x + a_{22}y = c_2. \end{cases} \tag{1}$$

To find an explicit formula for x, we look at $x\begin{vmatrix} a_{11} & a_{12} \\ a_{21} & a_{22} \end{vmatrix}$.

$$x\begin{vmatrix} a_{11} & a_{12} \\ a_{21} & a_{22} \end{vmatrix} = \begin{vmatrix} a_{11}x & a_{12} \\ a_{21}x & a_{22} \end{vmatrix} \qquad \text{(property 6 of Sec. 8.7)}$$

$$= \begin{vmatrix} a_{11}x + a_{12}y & a_{12} \\ a_{21}x + a_{22}y & a_{22} \end{vmatrix} \qquad \text{(adding } y \text{ times column 2 to column 1)}$$

$$= \begin{vmatrix} c_1 & a_{12} \\ c_2 & a_{22} \end{vmatrix} \qquad \text{[from Eq. (1)].}$$

Thus

$$x\begin{vmatrix} a_{11} & a_{12} \\ a_{21} & a_{22} \end{vmatrix} = \begin{vmatrix} c_1 & a_{12} \\ c_2 & a_{22} \end{vmatrix},$$

so

$$x = \frac{\begin{vmatrix} c_1 & a_{12} \\ c_2 & a_{22} \end{vmatrix}}{\begin{vmatrix} a_{11} & a_{12} \\ a_{21} & a_{22} \end{vmatrix}}. \tag{2}$$

To find a formula for y, we look at $y\begin{vmatrix} a_{11} & a_{12} \\ a_{21} & a_{22} \end{vmatrix}$.

$$y\begin{vmatrix} a_{11} & a_{12} \\ a_{21} & a_{22} \end{vmatrix} = \begin{vmatrix} a_{11} & a_{12}y \\ a_{21} & a_{22}y \end{vmatrix} \qquad \text{(property 6 of Sec. 8.7)}$$

$$= \begin{vmatrix} a_{11} & a_{11}x + a_{12}y \\ a_{21} & a_{21}x + a_{22}y \end{vmatrix} \qquad \text{(adding } x \text{ times column 1 to column 2)}$$

$$= \begin{vmatrix} a_{11} & c_1 \\ a_{21} & c_2 \end{vmatrix} \qquad \text{[from Eq. (1)].}$$

Thus

$$y \begin{vmatrix} a_{11} & a_{12} \\ a_{21} & a_{22} \end{vmatrix} = \begin{vmatrix} a_{11} & c_1 \\ a_{21} & c_2 \end{vmatrix},$$

so

$$y = \frac{\begin{vmatrix} a_{11} & c_1 \\ a_{21} & c_2 \end{vmatrix}}{\begin{vmatrix} a_{11} & a_{12} \\ a_{21} & a_{22} \end{vmatrix}}. \tag{3}$$

Note that in Eqs. (2) and (3) the denominators are the same, namely the determinant of the coefficient matrix of the given system. In finding x, the numerator in Eq. (2) is the determinant of the matrix obtained by replacing the "x-column" (that is, column 1) of the coefficient matrix by the column of constants $\begin{smallmatrix} c_1 \\ c_2 \end{smallmatrix}$. Similarly, the numerator in Eq. (3) is the determinant of the matrix obtained from the coefficient matrix when the "y-column" (that is, column 2) is replaced by $\begin{smallmatrix} c_1 \\ c_2 \end{smallmatrix}$. Provided that the determinant of the coefficient matrix is not zero, the original system will have a unique solution. However, if this determinant is zero, the procedure is not applicable and the system may have either no solution or infinitely many solutions. In such cases previous methods should be used to solve the system.

We shall illustrate the results above by solving the system

$$\begin{cases} 2x + y + 5 = 0, \\ 3y + x = 6. \end{cases}$$

First, the system is written in the appropriate form:

$$\begin{cases} 2x + y = -5. \\ x + 3y = 6. \end{cases}$$

The determinant Δ of the coefficient matrix is

$$\Delta = \begin{vmatrix} 2 & 1 \\ 1 & 3 \end{vmatrix} = 2(3) - 1(1) = 5.$$

Since $\Delta \neq 0$, there is a unique solution. Solving for x, we have

$$x = \frac{\begin{vmatrix} -5 & 1 \\ 6 & 3 \end{vmatrix}}{\Delta} = \frac{-21}{5} = -\frac{21}{5}.$$

Solving for y, we obtain

$$y = \frac{\begin{vmatrix} 2 & -5 \\ 1 & 6 \end{vmatrix}}{\Delta} = \frac{17}{5}.$$

Thus the solution is $x = -\frac{21}{5}$ and $y = \frac{17}{5}$.

The method described above can be extended to systems of n linear equations in n unknowns and is referred to as *Cramer's rule*.

Cramer's Rule

Let a system of n linear equations in n unknowns be given by

$$\begin{cases} a_{11}x_1 & + & a_{12}x_2 & + \cdots + & a_{1n}x_n & = c_1, \\ a_{21}x_1 & + & a_{22}x_2 & + \cdots + & a_{2n}x_n & = c_2, \\ \cdot & & \cdot & & \cdot & \cdot \\ \cdot & & \cdot & & \cdot & \cdot \\ \cdot & & \cdot & & \cdot & \cdot \\ a_{n1}x_1 & + & a_{n2}x_2 & + \cdots + & a_{nn}x_n & = c_n. \end{cases}$$

If the determinant Δ of the coefficient matrix $\mathbf{A}$ is different from 0, then the system has a unique solution. Moreover, the solution is given by

$$x_1 = \frac{\Delta_1}{\Delta}, \qquad x_2 = \frac{\Delta_2}{\Delta}, \qquad \ldots, \qquad x_n = \frac{\Delta_n}{\Delta},$$

where Δ_k, the numerator of x_k, is the determinant of the matrix obtained by replacing the kth column of $\mathbf{A}$ by the column of constants.

EXAMPLE 1   *Solve the following system by Cramer's rule.*

$$\begin{cases} 2x + y + z = 0, \\ 4x + 3y + 2z = 2, \\ 2x - y - 3z = 0. \end{cases}$$

The determinant of the coefficient matrix is

$$\Delta = \begin{vmatrix} 2 & 1 & 1 \\ 4 & 3 & 2 \\ 2 & -1 & -3 \end{vmatrix} = -8.$$

Since $\Delta \neq 0$, there is a unique solution. Solving for x, we obtain

$$x = \frac{\begin{vmatrix} 0 & 1 & 1 \\ 2 & 3 & 2 \\ 0 & -1 & -3 \end{vmatrix}}{\Delta} = \frac{4}{-8} = -\frac{1}{2}.$$

Similarly,

$$y = \frac{\begin{vmatrix} 2 & 0 & 1 \\ 4 & 2 & 2 \\ 2 & 0 & -3 \end{vmatrix}}{\Delta} = \frac{-16}{-8} = 2,$$

$$z = \frac{\begin{vmatrix} 2 & 1 & 0 \\ 4 & 3 & 2 \\ 2 & -1 & 0 \end{vmatrix}}{\Delta} = \frac{8}{-8} = -1.$$

The solution is $x = -\frac{1}{2}$, $y = 2$, and $z = -1$.

EXAMPLE 2   *Solve the following system for z by using Cramer's rule.*

$$\begin{cases} x + y & + 5w = 6, \\ x + 2y + z & = 4, \\ 2y + z + w = 6, \\ 3x & - 4w = 2. \end{cases}$$

We have

$$\Delta = \begin{vmatrix} 1 & 1 & 0 & 5 \\ 1 & 2 & 1 & 0 \\ 0 & 2 & 1 & 1 \\ 3 & 0 & 0 & -4 \end{vmatrix} = \begin{vmatrix} 1 & 1 & 0 & 5 \\ 0 & 1 & 1 & -5 \\ 0 & 0 & -1 & 11 \\ 0 & 0 & 0 & -1 \end{vmatrix} = 1.$$

Here we transformed into upper-triangular form and found the product of the main diagonal entries (Sec. 8.7, Example 4). In a similar fashion we obtain

$$\Delta_z = \begin{vmatrix} 1 & 1 & 6 & 5 \\ 1 & 2 & 4 & 0 \\ 0 & 2 & 6 & 1 \\ 3 & 0 & 2 & -4 \end{vmatrix} = \begin{vmatrix} 1 & 1 & 6 & 5 \\ 0 & 1 & -2 & -5 \\ 0 & 0 & 10 & 11 \\ 0 & 0 & 0 & -\frac{49}{5} \end{vmatrix} = -98.$$

Hence $z = \Delta_z/\Delta = -98/1 = -98$.

EXERCISE 8.8

Solve each of the following. Use Cramer's rule, if possible.

1. $\begin{cases} 2x - y = 4, \\ 3x + y = 5. \end{cases}$

2. $\begin{cases} 3x + y = 6, \\ 7x - 2y = 5. \end{cases}$

3. $\begin{cases} -2x = 4 - 3y, \\ y = 6x - 1. \end{cases}$

4. $\begin{cases} x + 2y - 6 = 0, \\ y - 1 = 3x. \end{cases}$

5. $\begin{cases} 3(x + 2) = 5, \\ 6(x + y) = -8. \end{cases}$

6. $\begin{cases} w - 2z = 4, \\ 3w - 4z = 6. \end{cases}$

7. $\begin{cases} \frac{3}{2}x - \frac{1}{4}z = 1, \\ \frac{1}{3}x + \frac{1}{2}z = 2. \end{cases}$

8. $\begin{cases} 0.6x - 0.7y = 0.33, \\ 2.1x - 0.9y = 0.69. \end{cases}$

9. $\begin{cases} x + y + z = 6, \\ x - y + z = 2, \\ 2x - y + 3z = 6. \end{cases}$

10. $\begin{cases} 2x - y + 3z = 12, \\ x + y - z = -3, \\ x + 2y - 3z = -10. \end{cases}$

11. $\begin{cases} 2x - 3y + 4z = 0, \\ x + y - 3z = 4, \\ 3x + 2y - z = 0. \end{cases}$

12. $\begin{cases} 3r - t = 7, \\ 4r - s + 3t = 9, \\ 3s + 2t = 15. \end{cases}$

13. $\begin{cases} x - 2y + z = 3, \\ 2x + y + 2z = 6, \\ x + 8y + z = 3. \end{cases}$

14. $\begin{cases} 2x + y + z = 1, \\ x - y + z = 4, \\ 5x + y + 3z = 5. \end{cases}$

15. $\begin{cases} 2x - 3y + z = -2, \\ x - 6y + 3z = -2, \\ 3x + 3y - 2z = 2. \end{cases}$

16. $\begin{cases} x - z = 14, \\ y + z = 21, \\ x - y + z = -10. \end{cases}$

In each of the following solve for the indicated unknowns.

17. $\begin{cases} x - y + 3z + w = -14, \\ x + 2y - 3w = 12, \\ 2x + 3y + 6z + w = 1, \\ x + y + z + w = 6. \end{cases}$ $y, w.$

18. $\begin{cases} x + y + 5z = 6, \\ x + 2y + w = 4, \\ 2y + z + w = 6, \\ 3x - 4z = 2. \end{cases}$ $x, y.$

19. Show that Cramer's rule does *not* apply to

$$\begin{cases} 2 - y = x, \\ 3 + x = -y, \end{cases}$$

but that from geometrical considerations there is no solution.

8.9 INVERSES USING THE ADJOINT

Determinants and cofactors can be used to find the inverse of a matrix, if it exists. To begin we need the idea of the *transpose* of a matrix.

Definition
The **transpose** of an $m \times n$ matrix $\mathbf{A}$, denoted $\mathbf{A}^T$, is the $n \times m$ matrix whose i-th row is the i-th column of $\mathbf{A}$.

EXAMPLE 1   *If* $\mathbf{A} = \begin{bmatrix} 1 & 2 & 3 \\ 4 & 5 & 6 \\ 7 & 8 & 9 \end{bmatrix}$, *find* $\mathbf{A}^T$.

Column 1 of $\mathbf{A}$ becomes row 1 of $\mathbf{A}^T$, column 2 becomes row 2, and column 3 becomes row 3. Thus

$$\mathbf{A}^T = \begin{bmatrix} 1 & 4 & 7 \\ 2 & 5 & 8 \\ 3 & 6 & 9 \end{bmatrix}.$$

Definition

*The **adjoint** of a square matrix* **A**, *denoted* adj **A**, *is the tranpose of the matrix obtained by replacing each entry* a_{ij} *in* **A** *by its cofactor* c_{ij}. *That is, it is the transpose of the cofactor matrix* $[c_{ij}]$.

EXAMPLE 2   *If* $\mathbf{A} = \begin{bmatrix} 2 & -1 & 3 \\ 3 & 0 & -5 \\ 2 & 1 & 1 \end{bmatrix}$, *find* adj **A.**

We first find the cofactor c_{ij} of each entry a_{ij} in **A.**

$$c_{11} = (-1)^{1+1}\begin{vmatrix} 0 & -5 \\ 1 & 1 \end{vmatrix} = (1)(5) = 5.$$

$$c_{12} = (-1)^{1+2}\begin{vmatrix} 3 & -5 \\ 2 & 1 \end{vmatrix} = (-1)(13) = -13.$$

$$c_{13} = (-1)^{1+3}\begin{vmatrix} 3 & 0 \\ 2 & 1 \end{vmatrix} = (1)(3) = 3.$$

$$c_{21} = (-1)^{2+1}\begin{vmatrix} -1 & 3 \\ 1 & 1 \end{vmatrix} = (-1)(-4) = 4.$$

$$c_{22} = (-1)^{2+2}\begin{vmatrix} 2 & 3 \\ 2 & 1 \end{vmatrix} = (1)(-4) = -4.$$

$$c_{23} = (-1)^{2+3}\begin{vmatrix} 2 & -1 \\ 2 & 1 \end{vmatrix} = (-1)(4) = -4.$$

$$c_{31} = (-1)^{3+1}\begin{vmatrix} -1 & 3 \\ 0 & -5 \end{vmatrix} = (1)(5) = 5.$$

$$c_{32} = (-1)^{3+2}\begin{vmatrix} 2 & 3 \\ 3 & -5 \end{vmatrix} = (-1)(-19) = 19.$$

$$c_{33} = (-1)^{3+3}\begin{vmatrix} 2 & -1 \\ 3 & 0 \end{vmatrix} = (1)(3) = 3.$$

The cofactor matrix $[c_{ij}]$ is thus

$$[c_{ij}] = \begin{bmatrix} 5 & -13 & 3 \\ 4 & -4 & -4 \\ 5 & 19 & 3 \end{bmatrix}.$$

The adjoint is

$$\text{adj } \mathbf{A} = [c_{ij}]^{\mathrm{T}} = \begin{bmatrix} 5 & 4 & 5 \\ -13 & -4 & 19 \\ 3 & -4 & 3 \end{bmatrix}.$$

It can be shown that if $|\mathbf{A}| \neq 0$, then $\mathbf{A}^{-1}$ exists and

$$\mathbf{A}^{-1} = \frac{1}{|\mathbf{A}|} \text{ adj } \mathbf{A}.$$

EXAMPLE 3   *If* $\mathbf{A} = \begin{bmatrix} 2 & -1 & 3 \\ 3 & 0 & -5 \\ 2 & 1 & 1 \end{bmatrix}$, *find* $\mathbf{A}^{-1}$.

We find that

$$|\mathbf{A}| = 32 \neq 0.$$

Thus $\mathbf{A}^{-1}$ exists. Also, from Example 2,

$$\text{adj } \mathbf{A} = \begin{bmatrix} 5 & 4 & 5 \\ -13 & -4 & 19 \\ 3 & -4 & 3 \end{bmatrix}.$$

Thus

$$\mathbf{A}^{-1} = \frac{1}{|\mathbf{A}|} \text{ adj } \mathbf{A}$$

$$= \frac{1}{32} \begin{bmatrix} 5 & 4 & 5 \\ -13 & -4 & 19 \\ 3 & -4 & 3 \end{bmatrix}$$

$$= \begin{bmatrix} \frac{5}{32} & \frac{1}{8} & \frac{5}{32} \\ -\frac{13}{32} & -\frac{1}{8} & \frac{19}{32} \\ \frac{3}{32} & -\frac{1}{8} & \frac{3}{32} \end{bmatrix}.$$

You should verify that $\mathbf{A}^{-1}\mathbf{A} = \mathbf{I}$.

EXAMPLE 4   *Find* $\mathbf{A}^{-1}$ *if* $\mathbf{A} = \begin{bmatrix} 1 & 0 & -2 \\ 4 & -2 & 1 \\ 1 & 2 & -10 \end{bmatrix}$.

We first find the cofactors of $\mathbf{A}$.

$$c_{11} = (-1)^2 \begin{vmatrix} -2 & 1 \\ 2 & -10 \end{vmatrix} = 18.$$

$$c_{12} = (-1)^3 \begin{vmatrix} 4 & 1 \\ 1 & -10 \end{vmatrix} = 41.$$

$$c_{13} = (-1)^4 \begin{vmatrix} 4 & -2 \\ 1 & 2 \end{vmatrix} = 10.$$

$$c_{21} = (-1)^3 \begin{vmatrix} 0 & -2 \\ 2 & -10 \end{vmatrix} = -4.$$

$$c_{22} = (-1)^4 \begin{vmatrix} 1 & -2 \\ 1 & -10 \end{vmatrix} = -8.$$

$$c_{23} = (-1)^5 \begin{vmatrix} 1 & 0 \\ 1 & 2 \end{vmatrix} = -2.$$

$$c_{31} = (-1)^4 \begin{vmatrix} 0 & -2 \\ -2 & 1 \end{vmatrix} = -4.$$

$$c_{32} = (-1)^5 \begin{vmatrix} 1 & -2 \\ 4 & 1 \end{vmatrix} = -9.$$

$$c_{33} = (-1)^6 \begin{vmatrix} 1 & 0 \\ 4 & -2 \end{vmatrix} = -2.$$

Since the inverse of $\mathbf{A}$ involves $|\mathbf{A}|$, we compute $|\mathbf{A}|$ next. We already have the cofactors, so we shall find $|\mathbf{A}|$ by expanding along the first row.

$$|\mathbf{A}| = (1)(18) + 0 + (-2)(10) = -2.$$

The cofactor matrix is

$$[c_{ij}] = \begin{bmatrix} 18 & 41 & 10 \\ -4 & -8 & -2 \\ -4 & -9 & -2 \end{bmatrix},$$

and the adjoint is $[c_{ij}]^{\mathrm{T}}$:

$$\mathrm{adj}\ \mathbf{A} = \begin{bmatrix} 18 & -4 & -4 \\ 41 & -8 & -9 \\ 10 & -2 & -2 \end{bmatrix}.$$

Thus

$$\mathbf{A}^{-1} = \frac{1}{|\mathbf{A}|}\ \mathrm{adj}\ \mathbf{A}$$

$$= \frac{1}{-2} \begin{bmatrix} 18 & -4 & -4 \\ 41 & -8 & -9 \\ 10 & -2 & -2 \end{bmatrix}$$

$$= \begin{bmatrix} -9 & 2 & 2 \\ -\frac{41}{2} & 4 & \frac{9}{2} \\ -5 & 1 & 1 \end{bmatrix}$$

This result was also obtained by reduction in Example 3(a) of Sec. 8.6.

EXAMPLE 5   *Find* $\mathbf{A}^{-1}$ *if* $\mathbf{A} = \begin{bmatrix} \frac{4}{5} & -\frac{1}{3} \\ -\frac{3}{10} & \frac{13}{15} \end{bmatrix}$.

Since $|\mathbf{A}| = (\frac{4}{5})(\frac{13}{15}) - (-\frac{1}{3})(-\frac{3}{10}) = \frac{89}{150} \neq 0$, $\mathbf{A}^{-1}$ exists. The cofactors are (the vertical bars here denote determinants, not absolute value)

$$c_{11} = (-1)^2 |\tfrac{13}{15}| = \tfrac{13}{15}, \quad c_{12} = (-1)^3 |-\tfrac{3}{10}| = \tfrac{3}{10},$$

$$c_{21} = (-1)^3 |-\tfrac{1}{3}| = \tfrac{1}{3}, \quad c_{22} = (-1)^4 |\tfrac{4}{5}| = \tfrac{4}{5}.$$

The cofactor matrix is

$$[c_{ij}] = \begin{bmatrix} \frac{13}{15} & \frac{3}{10} \\ \frac{1}{3} & \frac{4}{5} \end{bmatrix},$$

and the adjoint is

$$\text{adj } \mathbf{A} = [c_{ij}]^{\mathrm{T}} = \begin{bmatrix} \frac{13}{15} & \frac{1}{3} \\ \frac{3}{10} & \frac{4}{5} \end{bmatrix}.$$

Hence

$$\mathbf{A}^{-1} = \frac{1}{|\mathbf{A}|} \text{ adj } \mathbf{A} = \frac{150}{89} \begin{bmatrix} \frac{13}{15} & \frac{1}{3} \\ \frac{3}{10} & \frac{4}{5} \end{bmatrix}$$

$$= \begin{bmatrix} \frac{130}{89} & \frac{50}{89} \\ \frac{45}{89} & \frac{120}{89} \end{bmatrix}.$$

EXERCISE 8.9

For the following, use adjoints to find the inverses.

1. $\begin{bmatrix} 3 & -2 \\ 1 & 2 \end{bmatrix}$.

2. $\begin{bmatrix} 2 & -1 \\ 1 & 3 \end{bmatrix}$.

3. $\begin{bmatrix} \frac{1}{4} & \frac{3}{8} \\ 0 & \frac{1}{6} \end{bmatrix}$.

4. $\begin{bmatrix} \frac{1}{2} & \frac{1}{4} \\ \frac{1}{3} & \frac{2}{3} \end{bmatrix}$.

5. $\begin{bmatrix} 2 & 3 & -1 \\ 1 & 2 & 1 \\ -1 & -1 & 3 \end{bmatrix}$.

6. $\begin{bmatrix} -1 & 2 & -3 \\ 2 & 1 & 0 \\ 4 & -2 & 5 \end{bmatrix}$.

7. $\begin{bmatrix} 1 & -\frac{2}{3} & \frac{5}{3} \\ -1 & \frac{4}{3} & -\frac{10}{3} \\ -1 & 1 & -2 \end{bmatrix}$.

8. $\begin{bmatrix} 1 & 2 & 3 \\ 1 & 3 & 5 \\ 1 & 5 & 12 \end{bmatrix}$.

9. $\begin{bmatrix} -\frac{1}{4} & -\frac{1}{2} & \frac{3}{4} \\ 0 & \frac{1}{2} & 0 \\ \frac{1}{2} & \frac{1}{2} & -\frac{1}{2} \end{bmatrix}$.

10. $\begin{bmatrix} \frac{11}{2} & -\frac{5}{2} & -\frac{3}{2} \\ -4 & 2 & 1 \\ -\frac{7}{2} & \frac{3}{2} & \frac{1}{2} \end{bmatrix}$.

11. $\begin{bmatrix} \frac{2}{5} & -\frac{1}{5} & \frac{9}{15} \\ \frac{4}{15} & \frac{1}{5} & -\frac{4}{15} \\ -\frac{1}{15} & \frac{1}{5} & \frac{1}{15} \end{bmatrix}$.

12. $\begin{bmatrix} 0 & -\frac{1}{9} & \frac{4}{9} \\ 0 & \frac{2}{9} & \frac{1}{9} \\ \frac{1}{8} & \frac{1}{36} & -\frac{1}{9} \end{bmatrix}$.

8.10   INPUT-OUTPUT ANALYSIS

Input-output matrices, which were developed by Wassily W. Leontief* of Harvard, indicate the supply and demand interrelationships that exist between the various sectors of an economy during some time period. The phrase "input-output" is used because the matrices show the values of outputs of each industry that are sold as inputs to each industry and for final use by consumers.

A hypothetical example for an oversimplified two-industry economy is given by the input-output matrix below. Before we explain the matrix, let us say that the *industrial* sectors can be thought of as manufacturing, steel, agriculture, coal, and so on. The *other production factors* sector consists of costs to the respective industries such as labor, profits, and so on. The *final demand* sector could be consumption by households, government, and so on.

	Consumers (input)			
	Industry A	Industry B	Final Demand	Totals
Producers (output):				
Industry A	240	500	460	1200
Industry B	360	200	940	1500
Other Production Factors	600	800	—	
Totals	1200	1500		

Each industry appears in a row and column. The row shows the purchases of an industry's output by the industrial sectors and by consumers for final use (hence the term "final demand"). The entries represent the value of the products and might be in units of millions of dollars of product. For example, of the total output of industry A, 240 went as input to industry A itself (for internal use), 500 to industry B, and 460 went direct to the final demand sector. The total output of A is the sum of industrial demand and final demand ($240 + 500 + 460 = 1200$).

Each industry column gives the value of what the industry purchased for input from each industry as well as what it spent for other costs. For example, in order to produce its 1200 units, A purchased 240 units of output from itself, 360 of B's output, and had labor and other costs of 600 units.

Note that for each industry, the sum of the entries in its row is equal to the sum of the entries in its column. That is, the value of total output of A is equal to the value of total input to A.

Input-output analysis allows us to estimate the total production of each *industrial* sector if there is a change in final demand *as long as the basic structure of the economy remains the same.* This important assumption means that for each industry, the amount spent on each input for each dollar's worth of output must remain fixed.

* Leontief won the 1973 Nobel prize in economic science for the development of the "input-output" method and its applications to economic problems.

For example, in producing 1200 units worth of product, industry A purchases 240 units' worth from industry A, 360 units' worth from B, and spends 600 units on other costs. Thus for each dollar's worth of output, industry A spends $\frac{240}{1200} = \frac{1}{5} (= \$0.20)$ on A, $\frac{360}{1200} = \frac{3}{10} (= \$0.30)$ on B, and $\frac{600}{1200} = \frac{1}{2} (= \$0.50)$ on other costs. Combining these fixed ratios of industry A with those of industry B, we can give the input requirements per dollar of output for each industry.

$$
\begin{array}{cc}
 & \begin{array}{cc} A & B \end{array} \\
\begin{array}{c} A \\ B \\ \\ \text{Other} \end{array} &
\left[\begin{array}{cc}
\frac{240}{1200} & \frac{500}{1500} \\
\frac{360}{1200} & \frac{200}{1500} \\
\hline
\frac{600}{1200} & \frac{800}{1500}
\end{array} \right]
\end{array}
=
\begin{array}{cc}
\begin{array}{cc} A & B \end{array} \\
\left[\begin{array}{cc}
\frac{1}{5} & \frac{1}{3} \\
\frac{3}{10} & \frac{2}{15} \\
\hline
\frac{1}{2} & \frac{8}{15}
\end{array} \right]
\begin{array}{c} A \\ B \\ \\ \text{Other} \end{array}
\end{array}
$$

The entries in the matrix are called *input-output coefficients*. The sum of each column is 1.

Now, suppose the value of final demand changes from 460 to 500 for industry A and from 940 to 1200 for industry B. We would like to estimate the value of *total* output that A and B must produce for both industry and final demand to meet this goal, provided the structure in the preceding matrix remains the same.

Let the new values of total outputs for industries A and B be X_A and X_B, respectively. Since

$$
\begin{array}{c} \text{total value of} \\ \text{output of A} \end{array} = \begin{array}{c} \text{value consumed} \\ \text{by A} \end{array} + \begin{array}{c} \text{value consumed} \\ \text{by B} \end{array} + \begin{array}{c} \text{value consumed} \\ \text{by final demand}' \end{array}
$$

we have

$$ X_A = \tfrac{1}{5}X_A + \tfrac{1}{3}X_B + 500. $$

Similarly,

$$ X_B = \tfrac{3}{10}X_A + \tfrac{2}{15}X_B + 1200. $$

In matrix notation,

$$
\begin{bmatrix} X_A \\ X_B \end{bmatrix} = \begin{bmatrix} \frac{1}{5} & \frac{1}{3} \\ \frac{3}{10} & \frac{2}{15} \end{bmatrix} \begin{bmatrix} X_A \\ X_B \end{bmatrix} + \begin{bmatrix} 500 \\ 1200 \end{bmatrix}. \tag{1}
$$

Let

$$
\mathbf{X} = \begin{bmatrix} X_A \\ X_B \end{bmatrix}, \quad \mathbf{A} = \begin{bmatrix} \frac{1}{5} & \frac{1}{3} \\ \frac{3}{10} & \frac{2}{15} \end{bmatrix}, \quad \text{and} \quad \mathbf{C} = \begin{bmatrix} 500 \\ 1200 \end{bmatrix}.
$$

We call $\mathbf{X}$ the **output matrix,** $\mathbf{A}$ the **coefficient matrix,** and $\mathbf{C}$ the **final demand matrix.** From Eq. (1)

$$ \mathbf{X} = \mathbf{AX} + \mathbf{C}, $$
$$ \mathbf{X} - \mathbf{AX} = \mathbf{C}. $$

If **I** is the 2 × 2 identity matrix, then

$$IX - AX = C,$$

$$(I - A)X = C.$$

If $(I - A)^{-1}$ exists, then

$$X = (I - A)^{-1}C.$$

The matrix $I - A$ is called the Leontief matrix. Now,

$$I - A = \begin{bmatrix} 1 & 0 \\ 0 & 1 \end{bmatrix} - \begin{bmatrix} \frac{1}{5} & \frac{1}{3} \\ \frac{3}{10} & \frac{2}{15} \end{bmatrix}$$

$$= \begin{bmatrix} \frac{4}{5} & -\frac{1}{3} \\ -\frac{3}{10} & \frac{13}{15} \end{bmatrix}.$$

From Example 5 of Sec. 8.9,

$$(I - A)^{-1} = \begin{bmatrix} \frac{130}{89} & \frac{50}{89} \\ \frac{45}{89} & \frac{120}{89} \end{bmatrix}.$$

Hence the output matrix is

$$X = (I - A)^{-1}C = \begin{bmatrix} \frac{130}{89} & \frac{50}{89} \\ \frac{45}{89} & \frac{120}{89} \end{bmatrix} \begin{bmatrix} 500 \\ 1200 \end{bmatrix}$$

$$= \begin{bmatrix} 1404.49 \\ 1870.79 \end{bmatrix}.$$

Thus to meet the goal, industry A must produce 1404.49 units of value and industry B must produce 1870.79. If we were interested in the value of other production factors for A, then

$$P_A = \tfrac{1}{2}X_A = 702.25.$$

EXAMPLE 1   *Given the input-output matrix below, suppose final demand changes to 77 for A, 154 for B, and 231 for C. Find the output matrix for the economy. (The entries are in millions of dollars.)*

		Industry		Final Demand
	A	B	C	
Industry: A	240	180	144	36
B	120	36	48	156
C	120	72	48	240
Other	120	72	240	—

We separately add the entries in the first three rows. The total value of output for industries A, B, and C are 600, 360, and 480, respectively. To get the coefficient matrix, we divide the industry entries in each industry column by the total value of output for that industry.

$$\mathbf{A} = \begin{bmatrix} \frac{240}{600} & \frac{180}{360} & \frac{144}{480} \\ \frac{120}{600} & \frac{36}{360} & \frac{48}{480} \\ \frac{120}{600} & \frac{72}{360} & \frac{48}{480} \end{bmatrix} = \begin{bmatrix} \frac{2}{5} & \frac{1}{2} & \frac{3}{10} \\ \frac{1}{5} & \frac{1}{10} & \frac{1}{10} \\ \frac{1}{5} & \frac{1}{5} & \frac{1}{10} \end{bmatrix}.$$

Thus, if $\mathbf{I}$ is the 3×3 identity matrix,

$$\mathbf{I} - \mathbf{A} = \begin{bmatrix} \frac{3}{5} & -\frac{1}{2} & -\frac{3}{10} \\ -\frac{1}{5} & \frac{9}{10} & -\frac{1}{10} \\ -\frac{1}{5} & -\frac{1}{5} & \frac{9}{10} \end{bmatrix}.$$

We shall find $(\mathbf{I} - \mathbf{A})^{-1}$ by using the adjoint. Computing the cofactors, we have

$$c_{11} = (-1)^{1+1} \begin{vmatrix} \frac{9}{10} & -\frac{1}{10} \\ -\frac{1}{5} & \frac{9}{10} \end{vmatrix} = \frac{79}{100},$$

$$c_{12} = (-1)^{1+2} \begin{vmatrix} -\frac{1}{5} & -\frac{1}{10} \\ -\frac{1}{5} & \frac{9}{10} \end{vmatrix} = \frac{1}{5},$$

$$c_{13} = (-1)^{1+3} \begin{vmatrix} -\frac{1}{5} & \frac{9}{10} \\ -\frac{1}{5} & -\frac{1}{5} \end{vmatrix} = \frac{11}{50}.$$

At this stage we can evaluate $|\mathbf{I} - \mathbf{A}|$ along row 1 by using cofactors.

$$|\mathbf{I} - \mathbf{A}| = \tfrac{3}{5}(\tfrac{79}{100}) - \tfrac{1}{2}(\tfrac{1}{5}) - \tfrac{3}{10}(\tfrac{11}{50}) = \tfrac{77}{250}.$$

Continuing, we obtain

$$c_{21} = (-1)^{2+1} \begin{vmatrix} -\frac{1}{2} & -\frac{3}{10} \\ -\frac{1}{5} & \frac{9}{10} \end{vmatrix} = \frac{51}{100},$$

$$c_{22} = (-1)^{2+2} \begin{vmatrix} \frac{3}{5} & -\frac{3}{10} \\ -\frac{1}{5} & \frac{9}{10} \end{vmatrix} = \frac{12}{25},$$

$$c_{23} = (-1)^{2+3} \begin{vmatrix} \frac{3}{5} & -\frac{1}{2} \\ -\frac{1}{5} & -\frac{1}{5} \end{vmatrix} = \frac{11}{50},$$

$$c_{31} = (-1)^{3+1} \begin{vmatrix} -\frac{1}{2} & -\frac{3}{10} \\ \frac{9}{10} & -\frac{1}{10} \end{vmatrix} = \frac{8}{25},$$

$$c_{32} = (-1)^{3+2} \begin{vmatrix} \frac{3}{5} & -\frac{3}{10} \\ -\frac{1}{5} & -\frac{1}{10} \end{vmatrix} = \frac{3}{25},$$

$$c_{33} = (-1)^{3+3} \begin{vmatrix} \frac{3}{5} & -\frac{1}{2} \\ -\frac{1}{5} & \frac{9}{10} \end{vmatrix} = \frac{11}{25}.$$

Thus

$$(\mathbf{I} - \mathbf{A})^{-1} = \frac{1}{|\mathbf{I} - \mathbf{A}|} \operatorname{adj}(\mathbf{I} - \mathbf{A})$$

$$= \frac{250}{77}\begin{bmatrix} \frac{79}{100} & \frac{51}{100} & \frac{8}{25} \\ \frac{1}{5} & \frac{12}{25} & \frac{3}{25} \\ \frac{11}{50} & \frac{11}{50} & \frac{11}{25} \end{bmatrix} = \begin{bmatrix} \frac{395}{154} & \frac{255}{154} & \frac{80}{77} \\ \frac{50}{77} & \frac{120}{77} & \frac{30}{77} \\ \frac{5}{7} & \frac{5}{7} & \frac{10}{7} \end{bmatrix}.$$

Hence

$$X = (I - A)^{-1}C$$

$$= \begin{bmatrix} \frac{395}{154} & \frac{255}{154} & \frac{80}{77} \\ \frac{50}{77} & \frac{120}{77} & \frac{30}{77} \\ \frac{5}{7} & \frac{5}{7} & \frac{10}{7} \end{bmatrix}\begin{bmatrix} 77 \\ 154 \\ 231 \end{bmatrix} = \begin{bmatrix} 692.5 \\ 380 \\ 495 \end{bmatrix}.$$

EXERCISE 8.10

1. Given the input-output matrix below, find the output matrix if final demand changes to 600 for A and 805 for B. Find the total value of other production costs that this involves.

	Industry A	Industry B	Final Demand
Industry: A	200	500	500
B	400	200	900
Other	600	800	—

2. Given the input-output matrix below, find the output matrix if final demand changes to (a) 200 for A and 300 for B; (b) 64 for A and 64 for B.

	Industry A	Industry B	Final Demand
Industry: A	40	120	40
B	120	90	90
Other	40	90	—

3. Given the input-ouput matrix below, find the output matrix if final demand changes to (a) 50 for A, 40 for B, and 30 for C; (b) 10 for A, 10 for B, and 24 for C.

	Industry			Final
	A	B	C	Demand
Industry: A	18	30	45	15
B	27	30	60	3
C	54	40	60	26
Other	9	20	15	—

4. Given the input-output matrix below, find the output matrix if final demand changes to 300 for A, 200 for B, and 400 for C.

	Industry			Final
	A	B	C	Demand
Industry: A	100	400	240	260
B	100	80	480	140
C	300	160	240	500
Other	500	160	240	—

8.11 REVIEW

Important Terms and Symbols

Section 8.1	matrix order entry a_{ij} $[a_{ij}]$ row matrix column matrix
	equality of matrices zero matrix, **O** square matrix main diagonal
	upper (lower) triangular matrix
Section 8.2	scalar multiplication addition and subtraction of matrices
Section 8.3	matrix multiplication identity matrix, **I**
Section 8.4	coefficient matrix augmented coefficient matrix elementary row operation
	equivalent matrices reduced matrix parameter
Section 8.5	homogeneous system nonhomogeneous system trivial solution
Section 8.6	inverse matrix invertible (nonsingular) matrix elementary matrix
Section 8.7	determinant of matrix minor of entry cofactor of entry
Section 8.8	Cramer's rule
Section 8.9	transpose of matrix, $\mathbf{A}^T$ adjoint of matrix, adj **A**
Section 8.10	input-output matrix

Summary

A matrix is a rectangular array of numbers enclosed within brackets. Three special types are a zero matrix **O**, square matrix, and identity matrix **I**. Besides the basic operation of scalar multiplication, there are the operations of matrix addition and subtraction, which apply to matrices of the same order. The product **AB** is defined when the number of columns of **A** is equal to the number of rows of **B**. Although matrix addition is commutative, matrix multiplication is not. By using matrix multiplication, we can express a system of linear equations as the matrix equation **AX = C**.

A system of linear equations may have a unique solution, no solution, or infinitely many solutions. Three methods of solving a system of linear equations are: (1) by using the three elementary row operations, (2) by using an inverse matrix, and (3) with determinants. The first method involves applying elementary row operations to the augmented coefficient matrix of the system until an equivalent reduced matrix is obtained. The reduced matrix makes the solution(s) to the system obvious (assuming solutions exist). If there are infinitely many solutions, the general solution involves at least one parameter.

The second method of solving a system of linear equations involves inverses. The inverse (if it exists) of a square matrix A is a matrix A^{-1} such that $A^{-1}A = I$. If A is invertible, we can find A^{-1} by augmenting A with I and applying elementary row operations until A is reduced to I. The result of applying the same elementary row operations to I is A^{-1}. The inverse of a matrix can be used to solve a system of n equations in n unknowns given by $AX = C$, provided the coefficient matrix A is invertible. The unique solution is given by $X = A^{-1}C$. If A is not invertible, the system has either no solution or infinitely many solutions.

The third method of solving a system of linear equations makes use of determinants and is known as Cramer's rule. It applies to a system of n equations in n unknowns when the determinant of the coefficient matrix is not zero.

Determinants and adjoints can be used to find the inverse of a matrix. If $|A| \neq 0$, then A^{-1} exists and

$$A^{-1} = \frac{1}{|A|} \text{ adj } A.$$

Our final application of matrices dealt with the interrelationships that exist between the various sectors of an economy and is known as input-output analysis.

Review Problems

In Problems 1–6, simplify.

1. $3\begin{bmatrix} 3 & 4 \\ -5 & 1 \end{bmatrix} - 2\begin{bmatrix} 1 & 0 \\ 2 & 4 \end{bmatrix}$.

2. $5\begin{bmatrix} 1 & 2 \\ 7 & 0 \end{bmatrix} - 6\begin{bmatrix} 1 & 0 \\ 0 & 1 \end{bmatrix}$.

3. $\begin{bmatrix} 1 & 7 \\ 2 & -3 \\ 1 & 0 \end{bmatrix}\begin{bmatrix} 1 & 0 & -2 \\ 0 & 5 & 1 \end{bmatrix}$.

4. $[1 \quad 4 \quad 5]\begin{bmatrix} 2 & 1 \\ 0 & -1 \\ 8 & 1 \end{bmatrix}$.

5. $\begin{bmatrix} 1 & 0 \\ -1 & 4 \end{bmatrix}\left(\begin{bmatrix} 1 & 4 \\ 6 & 5 \end{bmatrix} - \begin{bmatrix} 2 & 6 \\ 5 & 0 \end{bmatrix}\right)$.

6. $-\left(\begin{bmatrix} 2 & 0 \\ 7 & 8 \end{bmatrix} + 2\begin{bmatrix} 0 & -5 \\ 6 & -4 \end{bmatrix}\right)$.

In Problems 7 and 8, solve for x and y.

7. $\begin{bmatrix} 5 \\ 2 \end{bmatrix}[x] = \begin{bmatrix} 15 \\ y \end{bmatrix}$.

8. $\begin{bmatrix} 1 & x \\ 2 & y \end{bmatrix}\begin{bmatrix} 2 & 1 \\ x & 3 \end{bmatrix} = \begin{bmatrix} 3 & 4 \\ 3 & y \end{bmatrix}$.

In Problems 9–12, reduce the given matrices.

9. $\begin{bmatrix} 1 & 4 \\ 5 & 8 \end{bmatrix}$.

10. $\begin{bmatrix} 0 & 0 & 4 \\ 0 & 3 & 5 \end{bmatrix}$.

11. $\begin{bmatrix} 2 & 4 & 3 \\ 1 & 2 & 3 \\ 4 & 8 & 6 \end{bmatrix}$.

12. $\begin{bmatrix} 0 & 0 & 0 & 1 \\ 0 & 0 & 0 & 0 \\ 1 & 0 & 0 & 0 \end{bmatrix}$.

In Problems 13–16, solve each of the systems by the method of reduction.

13. $\begin{cases} 2x - 5y = 0, \\ 4x + 3y = 0. \end{cases}$

14. $\begin{cases} x - y + 2z = 3, \\ 3x + y + z = 5. \end{cases}$

15. $\begin{cases} x + y + 2z = 1, \\ 3x - 2y - 4z = -7, \\ 2x - y - 2z = 2. \end{cases}$ 16. $\begin{cases} x - y - z - 2 = 0, \\ x + y + 2z + 5 = 0, \\ 2x + z + 3 = 0. \end{cases}$

In Problems **17–20,** *find the inverses of the matrices by using reduction.*

17. $\begin{bmatrix} 1 & 5 \\ 3 & 9 \end{bmatrix}.$ 18. $\begin{bmatrix} 0 & 1 \\ 1 & 0 \end{bmatrix}.$

19. $\begin{bmatrix} 1 & 3 & -2 \\ 4 & 1 & 0 \\ 3 & -2 & 2 \end{bmatrix}.$ 20. $\begin{bmatrix} 1 & 0 & 0 \\ 2 & 3 & -1 \\ 1 & -1 & 2 \end{bmatrix}.$

In Problems **21** *and* **22,** *solve the given system by finding the inverse of the coefficient matrix.*

21. $\begin{cases} 3x + y + 4z = 1, \\ x + z = 0, \\ 2y + z = 2. \end{cases}$ 22. $\begin{cases} 2x + y - z = 0, \\ 3x + z = 0, \\ x - y + z = 0. \end{cases}$

In Problems **23–28,** *evaluate the determinants.*

23. $\begin{vmatrix} 2 & -1 \\ 4 & 7 \end{vmatrix}.$ 24. $\begin{vmatrix} 5 & 8 \\ 3 & 0 \end{vmatrix}.$

25. $\begin{vmatrix} 1 & 2 & -1 \\ 0 & 1 & 4 \\ 1 & 2 & 2 \end{vmatrix}.$ 26. $\begin{vmatrix} 2 & 0 & 3 \\ 1 & 4 & 6 \\ -1 & 2 & -1 \end{vmatrix}.$

27. $\begin{vmatrix} r & p & q & a \\ 0 & i & j & m \\ 0 & 0 & c & n \\ 0 & 0 & 0 & h \end{vmatrix}.$ 28. $\begin{vmatrix} e & 0 & 0 & 0 \\ a & r & 0 & 0 \\ p & j & n & 0 \\ s & k & t & i \end{vmatrix}.$

Solve the systems in Problems **29** *and* **30** *by using Cramer's rule.*

29. $\begin{cases} 3x - y = 1, \\ 2x + 3y = 8. \end{cases}$ 30. $\begin{cases} x + 2y - z = 0, \\ y + 4z = 0, \\ x + 2y + 2z = 0. \end{cases}$

In Problems **31** *and* **32,** *use the adjoint to find the inverse of each matrix.*

31. $\begin{bmatrix} 1 & 1 & 1 \\ 0 & 2 & 1 \\ 1 & 3 & 1 \end{bmatrix}.$ 32. $\begin{bmatrix} 2 & 1 & -1 \\ 1 & 1 & 3 \\ -1 & 1 & -1 \end{bmatrix}.$

33. Given the input-output matrix below, find the output matrix if final demand changes to 2 for A and 2 for B. (Data are in tens of billions of dollars.)

	Industry A	Industry B	Final Demand
Industry: A	0	2	1
B	1	0	3
Other	2	2	—

Linear Programming

9.1 LINEAR INEQUALITIES IN TWO VARIABLES

Suppose a consumer receives a fixed income of $60 per week and uses it all to purchase products A and B. If x kilograms of A cost $2 per kilogram and y kilograms of B cost $3 per kilogram, then the possible combinations of A and B that can be purchased must satisfy the consumer's *budget equation*

$$2x + 3y = 60, \qquad \text{where } x, y \geq 0.$$

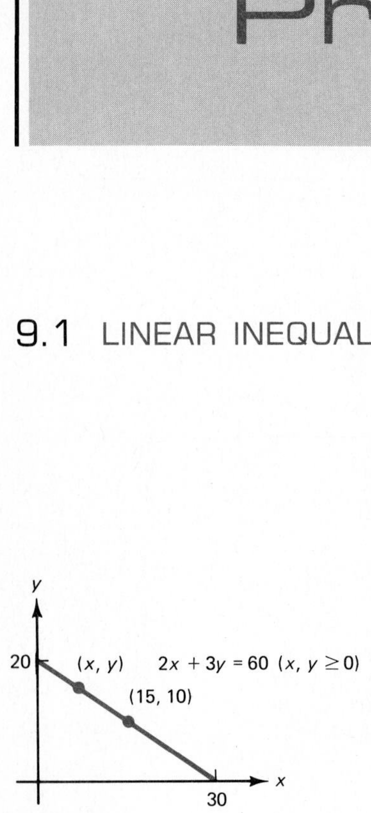

The solution is represented by the *budget line* in Fig. 9.1. For example, if 15 kg of A are purchased at a total cost of $30, then 10 kg of B must be bought at a total cost of $30. Thus (15, 10) lies on the line.

On the other hand, suppose the consumer does not necessarily wish to spend his *total* income. In this case the possible combinations are described by the inequality

$$2x + 3y \leq 60, \quad \text{where } x, y \geq 0. \tag{1}$$

When inequalities in one variable were discussed in Chapter 2, their solutions were represented geometrically by *intervals* on the real number line. However, for an inequality in two variables, as in inequality (1), the solution is usually represented by a *region* in the coordinate plane. We shall find the region corresponding to inequality (1) after considering such inequalities in general.

FIGURE 9.1

Definition
A **linear inequality** in the variables x and y is an inequality that can be written in the form

$$ax + by + c < 0 \quad (or \leq 0, \geq 0, > 0),$$

where a, b, and c are constants and a and b are not both zero.

Geometrically, the solution of a linear inequality in x and y consists of all points in the plane whose coordinates satisfy the inequality. In particular, the graph of a nonvertical line $y = mx + b$ separates the plane into three distinct parts (Fig. 9.2):

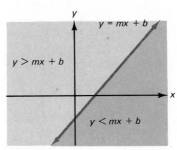

FIGURE 9.2

1. the line itself, consisting of all points (x, y) whose coordinates satisfy $y = mx + b$;

2. the region above the line, consisting of all points (x, y) which satisfy $y > mx + b$;

3. the region below the line, consisting of all points (x, y) satisfying $y < mx + b$.

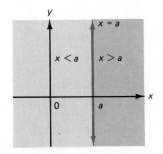

FIGURE 9.3

For a vertical line $x = a$, we speak of regions to the right ($x > a$) or to the left ($x < a$) of the line (Fig. 9.3).

To apply these facts we shall solve $2x + y < 5$. The corresponding *line* $2x + y = 5$ is first sketched by choosing two points on it, for instance the intercepts $(\frac{5}{2}, 0)$ and $(0, 5)$ [Fig. 9.4]. By writing the inequality in the equivalent form $y < 5 - 2x$, we conclude from (3) above that the solution consists of all points below the line. Part of this region is shaded in the diagram. Thus if (x_0, y_0) is *any* point in this region, then its ordinate y_0 is less than the number $5 - 2x_0$ (Fig. 9.5). For example, $(-2, -1)$ is in the region and $-1 < 5 - 2(-2)$. If we had required that $y \leq 5 - 2x$, the line $y = 5 - 2x$ would also have been included in the solution as indicated by the solid line in Fig. 9.6. We shall adopt

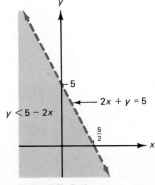

FIGURE 9.4

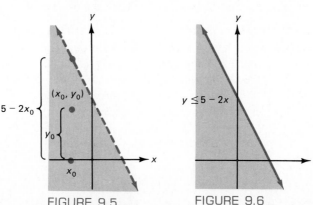

FIGURE 9.5   FIGURE 9.6

the conventions that **a solid line *is* included in the solution, and a dashed line *is not*.**

EXAMPLE 1

a. *Find the region described by* $y \leq 5$.

Since x does not appear, the inequality is assumed to be true for all values of x. The solution consists of the line $y = 5$ *and* the region below it (see Fig. 9.7), since the y-coordinate of each point in that region is less than 5.

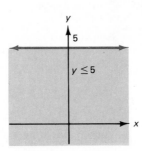

FIGURE 9.7

b. *Solve* $2(2x - y) < 2(x + y) - 4$.

The inequality is equivalent to

$$4x - 2y < 2x + 2y - 4,$$
$$-4y < -2x - 4,$$
$$y > \frac{x}{2} + 1.$$

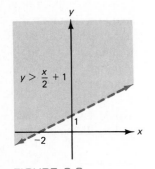

FIGURE 9.8

In the last step, both sides were divided by -4 and the sense of the inequality was reversed. We now sketch the line $y = (x/2) + 1$ by noting that its intercepts are $(0, 1)$ and $(-2, 0)$. Then we shade the region above it (see Fig. 9.8). Every point in this region is a solution.

The solution of a *system* of inequalities consists of all points whose coordinates simultaneously satisfy all of the given inequalities. Geometrically, it is the region which is common to all the regions determined by the given inequalities. For example, let us solve the system

$$\begin{cases} 2x + y > 3, \\ x \geq y, \\ 2y - 1 > 0. \end{cases}$$

This system is equivalent to

$$\begin{cases} y > -2x + 3, \\ y \le x, \\ y > \frac{1}{2}. \end{cases}$$

Note that each inequality has been written so that y is isolated. Thus the appropriate regions with respect to the corresponding lines will be apparent. We first sketch the lines $y = -2x + 3$, $y = x$, and $y = \frac{1}{2}$ and then shade the region that is simultaneously above the first line, on or below the second line, and above the third line (see Fig. 9.9). This region is the solution. When one is sketching the lines, **it is best to draw dashed lines everywhere until it is clear which portions are to be included in the solution.**

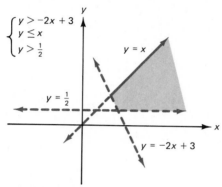

FIGURE 9.9

EXAMPLE 2 *Solve*

$$\begin{cases} y \ge -2x + 10, \\ y \ge x - 2. \end{cases}$$

The solution consists of all points that are simultaneously on or above $y = -2x + 10$ and on or above $y = x - 2$. It is the shaded region in Fig. 9.10.

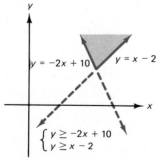

FIGURE 9.10

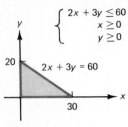

$$\begin{cases} 2x + 3y \le 60 \\ x \ge 0 \\ y \ge 0 \end{cases}$$

$2x + 3y = 60$

FIGURE 9.11

EXAMPLE 3   *Find the region described by*

$$\begin{cases} 2x + 3y \le 60, \\ x \ge 0, \\ y \ge 0. \end{cases}$$

This system relates to inequality (1) in the discussion of budget lines at the beginning of this section. The latter two inequalities restrict the solution to points which are both on or to the right of the y-axis *and* also on or above the x-axis. The desired region is shaded in Fig. 9.11.

EXERCISE 9.1

In Problems 1–24, sketch the region described by the inequalities.

1. $2x + 3y > 6$.

2. $3x - 2y \ge 12$.

3. $x + 2y \le 7$.

4. $y > 6 - 2x$.

5. $-x \le 2y - 4$.

6. $2x + y \ge 10$.

7. $3x + y < 0$.

8. $x + 5y < -5$.

9. $\begin{cases} 3x - 2y < 6, \\ x - 3y > 9. \end{cases}$

10. $\begin{cases} 2x + 3y > -6, \\ 3x - y < 6. \end{cases}$

11. $\begin{cases} 2x + 3y \le 6, \\ x \ge 0. \end{cases}$

12. $\begin{cases} 2y - 3x < 6, \\ x < 0. \end{cases}$

13. $\begin{cases} y - 3x < 6, \\ x - y > -3. \end{cases}$

14. $\begin{cases} x - y < 1, \\ y - x < 1. \end{cases}$

15. $\begin{cases} 2x - 2 \ge y, \\ 2x \le 3 - 2y. \end{cases}$

16. $\begin{cases} 2y < 4x + 2, \\ y < 2x + 1. \end{cases}$

17. $\begin{cases} x - y > 4, \\ x < 2, \\ y > -5. \end{cases}$

18. $\begin{cases} 2x + y < -1, \\ y > -x, \\ 2x + 6 < 0. \end{cases}$

19. $\begin{cases} y < 2x + 4, \\ x \ge -2, \\ y < 1. \end{cases}$

20. $\begin{cases} 4x + 3y \ge 12, \\ y \ge x, \\ 2y \le 3x + 6. \end{cases}$

21. $\begin{cases} x + y > 1, \\ 3x - 5 \le y, \\ y < 2x. \end{cases}$

22. $\begin{cases} 2x - 3y > -12, \\ 3x + y > -6, \\ y > x. \end{cases}$

23. $\begin{cases} 3x + y > -6, \\ x - y > -5, \\ x \ge 0. \end{cases}$

24. $\begin{cases} 5y - 2x \le 10, \\ 4x - 6y \le 12, \\ y \ge 0. \end{cases}$

If a consumer wants to spend no more than P dollars to purchase quantities x and y of two products having prices of p_1 and p_2 dollars per unit, respectively, then $p_1x + p_2y \le P$, where x, y $\ge$ 0. In Problems 25 and 26, find geometrically the possible combinations of purchases by determining the solution of this system for the given values of p_1, p_2, and P.

25. $p_1 = 5, p_2 = 3, P = 15$.

26. $p_1 = 6, p_2 = 4, P = 24$.

27. If a manufacturer wishes to purchase a *total* of no more than 100 lb of product Z from suppliers A and B, set up a system of inequalities which describes the possible combinations of quantities that can be purchased from each supplier. Sketch the solution in the plane.

9.2 LINEAR PROGRAMMING _____

Sometimes it is desired to maximize or minimize a function subject to certain restrictions (or *constraints*). For example, a manufacturer may want to maximize a profit function subject to production restrictions imposed by limitations on the use of machinery and labor.

We shall now consider how to solve such problems when the function to be maximized or minimized is *linear*. A **linear function in x and y** has the form

$$Z = ax + by,$$

where a and b are constants. We shall also require that the corresponding constraints be represented by a system of linear inequalities (involving "$\leq$" or "$\geq$") or linear equations in x and y, and that all variables be nonnegative. A problem involving all of these conditions is called a *linear programming problem*.

Linear programming was developed by George B. Danzig in the late 1940s, and was first used by the U.S. Air Force as an aid in decision making. Today it has wide application in industrial and economic analysis.

In a linear programming problem, the function to be maximized or minimized is called the **objective function.** Although there are usually infinitely many solutions to the system of constraints (these are called **feasible solutions** or **feasible points**), the aim is to find one such solution that is an **optimum solution** (that is, one that gives the maximum or minimum value of the objective function).

We shall now give a geometrical approach to linear programming. In Sec. 9.4 a matrix approach will be discussed that will enable us to work with more than two variables and, hence, a wider range of problems.

Suppose a company produces two types of widgets, manual and electric. Each requires in its manufacture the use of three machines: A, B, and C. A manual widget requires the use of machine A for 2 hours, machine B for 1 hour, and machine C for 1 hour. An electric widget requires 1 hour on A, 2 hours on B, and 1 hour on C. Furthermore, suppose the maximum numbers of hours available per month for the use of machines A, B, and C are 180, 160, and 100, respectively. The profit on a manual widget is $4 and on an electric widget it is $6. (See Table 9.1 for a summary of data.) If the company can sell all the widgets it can produce, how many of each type should it make in order to maximize the monthly profit?

TABLE 9.1

	A	B	C	PROFIT/UNIT
Manual	2 hr	1 hr	1 hr	$4
Electric	1 hr	2 hr	1 hr	6
Hours available	180	160	100	

To answer the question we let x and y denote the number of manual and electric widgets, respectively, that are made in a month. Since the number of widgets made is not negative, we have

$$x \geq 0, \qquad y \geq 0.$$

For machine A, the time needed for working on x manual widgets is $2x$ hours, and the time needed for working on y electric widgets is $1y$ hours. The sum of these times cannot be greater than 180, so we have

$$2x + y \leq 180.$$

Similarly, the restrictions for machines B and C give

$$x + 2y \leq 160 \qquad \text{and} \qquad x + y \leq 100.$$

The profit P is a function of x and y and is given by the *profit function*

$$P = 4x + 6y.$$

Summarizing, we want to maximize the *objective function*

$$P = 4x + 6y \tag{1}$$

subject to the condition that x and y must be a solution to the system of constraints

$$\begin{cases} x \geq 0, & (2) \\ y \geq 0, & (3) \\ 2x + y \leq 180, & (4) \\ x + 2y \leq 160, & (5) \\ x + y \leq 100. & (6) \end{cases}$$

Thus we have a linear programming problem. Constraints (2) and (3) are called **nonnegativity conditions.** The region simultaneously satisfying constraints (2)–(6) is shaded in Fig. 9.12. Each point in this region represents a feasible solution, and the region is called the **feasible region.** Although there are infinitely many feasible solutions, we must find one that maximizes the profit function.

Since $P = 4x + 6y$ is equivalent to

$$y = -\frac{2}{3}x + \frac{P}{6},$$

it defines a so-called "family" of parallel lines, each having a slope of $-2/3$ and y-intercept $(0, P/6)$. For example, if $P = 600$, then we obtain the line $y = -\frac{2}{3}x + 100$ shown in Fig. 9.13. This line, called an **isoprofit line,** gives all possible combinations of x and y that yield the same profit, $600. Note that this isoprofit line has no point in common with the feasible region, whereas the isoprofit line for $P = 300$ has infinitely many such points. Let us look for the member of the family that contains a feasible point and whose P-value is maximum. *It will be the line whose y-intercept is furthest from the origin (this gives a maximum value of P) and which has at least one point in common with the feasible region.* It is not difficult to observe that such a line will contain the

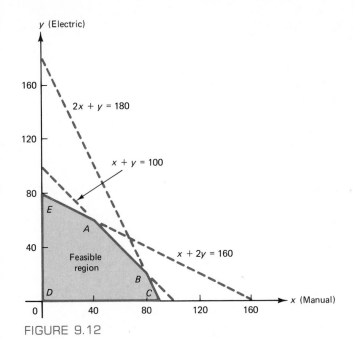

FIGURE 9.12

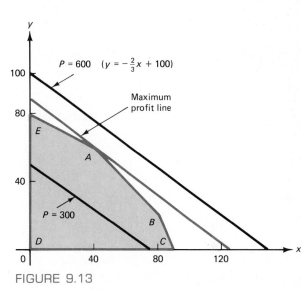

FIGURE 9.13

corner point A. Any isoprofit line with a greater profit will contain no points of the feasible region.

From Fig. 9.12, *A* lies on both the line $x + y = 100$ and the line $x + 2y = 160$. Thus its coordinates may be found by solving the system

$$\begin{cases} x + y = 100, \\ x + 2y = 160. \end{cases}$$

This gives $x = 40$ and $y = 60$. Substituting these values in $P = 4x + 6y$, we find that the maximum profit subject to the constraints is $520, which is obtained by producing 40 manual widgets and 60 electric widgets per month.

If a feasible region can be contained within a circle, such as the region in Fig. 9.13, it is called a **bounded feasible region.** Otherwise, it is **unbounded.** When a feasible region contains at least one point, it is said to be **nonempty.** Otherwise, it is **empty.** Thus the region in Fig. 9.13 is a nonempty bounded feasible region.

It can be shown that:

> A linear function defined on a nonempty bounded feasible region has a maximum (minimum) value, and this value can be found at a corner point.

This statement gives us a way of finding an optimum solution without drawing isoprofit lines as we did above. We could evaluate the objective function at each of the corner points of the feasible region and then choose a corner point at which the function is optimum.

For example, in Fig. 9.13 the corner points are A, B, C, D, and E. We found A before to be $(40, 60)$. To find B, we see from Fig. 9.12 that we must solve $2x + y = 180$ and $x + y = 100$ simultaneously. This gives the point $B = (80, 20)$. In a similar way we obtain all the corner points:

$$A = (40, 60), \qquad B = (80, 20), \qquad C = (90, 0),$$
$$D = (0, 0), \qquad E = (0, 80).$$

We now evaluate the objective function $P = 4x + 6y$ at each point:

$$P(A) = 4(40) + 6(60) = 520,$$

$$P(B) = 4(80) + 6(20) = 440,$$

$$P(C) = 4(90) + 6(0) = 360,$$

$$P(D) = 4(0) + 6(0) = 0,$$

$$P(E) = 4(0) + 6(80) = 480.$$

Thus P has a maximum value of 520 at A, where $x = 40$ and $y = 60$.

The optimum solution to a linear programming problem is given by the point where the optimum value of the objective function occurs. We shall also include the optimum value of the objective function.

EXAMPLE 1   *Maximize the objective function $Z = 3x + y$ subject to the constraints*

$$2x + y \le 8,$$

$$2x + 3y \le 12,$$

$$x \ge 0,$$

$$y \ge 0.$$

In Fig. 9.14 the feasible region is nonempty and bounded. Thus Z is maximum at one of the four corner points. The coordinates of A, B, and D are obvious on inspection. To find C we solve the equations $2x + y = 8$ and $2x + 3y = 12$ simultaneously, which gives $x = 3$, $y = 2$. Thus,

$$A = (0, 0), \qquad B = (4, 0), \qquad C = (3, 2), \qquad D = (0, 4).$$

Evaluating Z at these points, we obtain

$$Z(A) = 3(0) + 0 = 0,$$

$$Z(B) = 3(4) + 0 = 12,$$

$$Z(C) = 3(3) + 2 = 11,$$

$$Z(D) = 3(0) + 4 = 4.$$

Hence the maximum value of Z, subject to the constraints, is 12 and it occurs when $x = 4$ and $y = 0$.

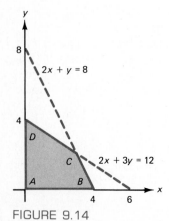

FIGURE 9.14

EXAMPLE 2 *Minimize the objective function* $Z = 8x - 3y$ *subject to the constraints*

$$-x + 3y = 21,$$
$$x + y \le 5,$$
$$x \ge 0,$$
$$y \ge 0.$$

Notice that the first constraint $-x + 3y = 21$ is an *equality*. The portions of the lines $-x + 3y = 21$ and $x + y = 5$ for which $x \ge 0$ and $y \ge 0$ are shown in Fig. 9.15. They will remain dashed lines until we determine whether or not they are to be included in the feasible region. A feasible point (x, y) must have $x \ge 0$, $y \ge 0$, and must lie both on the top dashed line and on or below the bottom dashed line. However, no such point exists. Hence the feasible region is *empty* and thus this problem has *no* optimum solution.

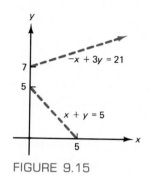

FIGURE 9.15

The result in Example 2 can be made more general:

> Whenever the feasible region of a linear programming problem is empty, no optimum solution exists.

Suppose a feasible region is defined by

$$y = 2, \quad x \ge 0, \quad \text{and} \quad y \ge 0.$$

This region is the portion of the horizontal line $y = 2$ indicated in Fig. 9.16.

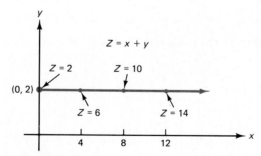

FIGURE 9.16

Since the region cannot be contained within a circle, it is *unbounded*. Let us consider maximizing

$$Z = x + y$$

subject to the constraints above. Since $y = 2$, then $Z = x + 2$. Clearly, as x increases without bound, so does Z. Thus no feasible point maximizes Z, so no

optimum solution exists. In this case we say that the solution is "unbounded."
On the other hand, suppose we want to *minimize Z* $= x + y$ over the same
region. Since $Z = x + 2$, then Z is minimum when x is as small as possible,
namely when $x = 0$. This gives a minimum value of $Z = x + y = 0 + 2 = 2$, and the optimum solution is the corner point $(0, 2)$.

In general, it can be shown that:

> If a feasible region is unbounded, and if the objective function
> has a maximum (or minimum) value, then that value occurs at a
> corner point.

EXAMPLE 3   *A produce grower is purchasing fertilizer containing three
nutrients, A, B, and C. The minimum needs are 160 units of A, 200 units of B,
and 80 units of C. There are two popular brands of fertilizer on the market. Fast
Grow, costing $4 a bag, contains 3 units of A, 5 units of B, and 1 unit of C.
Easy Grow, costing $3 a bag, contains 2 units of each nutrient. If the grower
wishes to minimize cost while still maintaining the nutrients required, how many
bags of each brand should be bought? The information is summarized as follows.*

	A	B	C	COST/BAG
Fast Grow	3 units	5 units	1 unit	$4
Easy Grow	2 units	2 units	2 units	3
Units required	160	200	80	

Let x be the number of bags of Fast Grow that are bought and y the number of
bags of Easy Grow that are bought. Then we wish to *minimize* the cost function

$$C = 4x + 3y \tag{7}$$

subject to the constraints

$$x \geq 0, \tag{8}$$

$$y \geq 0, \tag{9}$$

$$3x + 2y \geq 160, \tag{10}$$

$$5x + 2y \geq 200, \tag{11}$$

$$x + 2y \geq 80. \tag{12}$$

The feasible region satisfying constraints (8)–(12) is shaded in Fig. 9.17, along
with *isocost lines* for $C = 200$ and $C = 300$. The feasible region is unbounded.
The member of the family of lines $C = 4x + 3y$ which gives a minimum cost,
subject to the constraints, intersects the feasible region at corner point B. Here
we chose the isocost line whose y-intercept was *closest* to the origin and which

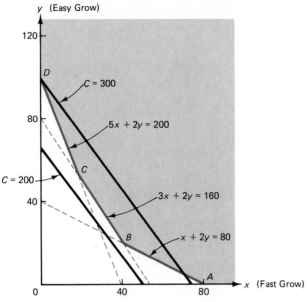

FIGURE 9.17

had at least one point in common with the feasible region. The coordinates of B are found by solving the system

$$\begin{cases} 3x + 2y = 160, \\ x + 2y = 80. \end{cases}$$

Thus $x = 40$ and $y = 20$, which gives a minimum cost of $220. The produce grower should buy 40 bags of Fast Grow and 20 bags of Easy Grow.

In Example 3 we found that the function $C = 4x + 3y$ has a minimum value at a corner point of the unbounded feasible region. On the other hand, suppose we want to *maximize* C over that region and take the approach of evaluating C at all corner points. These points are

$$A = (80, 0), \quad B = (40, 20), \quad C = (20, 50), \quad D = (0, 100),$$

from which

$$C(A) = 4(80) + 3(0) = 320,$$

$$C(B) = 4(40) + 3(20) = 220,$$

$$C(C) = 4(20) + 3(50) = 230,$$

$$C(D) = 4(0) + 3(100) = 300.$$

A hasty conclusion is that the maximum value of C is 320. This is *false!* There is *no* maximum value, since isocost lines with arbitrarily large values of C intersect the feasible region.

Pitfall

When working with an unbounded feasible region, do not simply conclude that an optimum solution exists at a corner point, since there may not be an optimum solution!

EXERCISE 9.2

1. Maximize
$$P = 10x + 12y$$
subject to
$$x + y \le 60,$$
$$x - 2y \ge 0,$$
$$x, y \ge 0.$$

2. Maximize
$$P = 5x + 6y$$
subject to
$$x + y \le 80,$$
$$3x + 2y \le 220,$$
$$2x + 3y \le 210,$$
$$x, y \ge 0.$$

3. Maximize
$$Z = 4x - 6y$$
subject to
$$y \le 7,$$
$$3x - y \le 3,$$
$$x + y \ge 5,$$
$$x, y \ge 0.$$

4. Minimize
$$Z = x + y$$
subject to
$$x - y \ge 0,$$
$$4x + 3y \ge 12,$$
$$9x + 11y \le 99,$$
$$x \le 8,$$
$$x, y \ge 0.$$

5. Maximize
$$Z = 4x - 10y$$
subject to
$$x - 4y \ge 4,$$
$$2x - y \le 2,$$
$$x, y \ge 0.$$

6. Minimize
$$Z = 20x + 30y$$
subject to
$$2x + y \le 10,$$
$$3x + 4y \le 24,$$
$$8x + 7y \ge 56,$$
$$x, y \ge 0.$$

7. Minimize
$$Z = 7x + 3y$$
subject to
$$3x - y \ge -2,$$
$$x + y \le 9,$$
$$x - y = -1,$$
$$x, y \ge 0.$$

8. Maximize
$$Z = 0.5x - 0.3y$$
subject to
$$x - y \ge -2,$$
$$2x - y \le 4,$$
$$2x + y = 8,$$
$$x, y \ge 0.$$

9. Minimize
$$C = 2x + y$$
subject to
$$3x + y \ge 3,$$
$$4x + 3y \ge 6,$$
$$x + 2y \ge 2,$$
$$x, y \ge 0.$$

10. Minimize
$$C = 2x + 2y$$
subject to
$$x + 2y \ge 80,$$
$$3x + 2y \ge 160,$$
$$5x + 2y \ge 200,$$
$$x, y \ge 0.$$

11. Maximize
$$Z = 10x + 2y$$
subject to
$$x + 2y \ge 4,$$
$$x - 2y \ge 0,$$
$$x, y \ge 0.$$

12. Minimize
$$Z = y - x$$
subject to
$$x \ge 3,$$
$$x + 3y \ge 6,$$
$$x - 3y \ge -6,$$
$$x, y \ge 0.$$

13. A toy manufacturer preparing a production schedule for two new toys, widgets and wadgits, must use the information concerning their construction times given in the table below. For example, each widget requires 2 hours on machine A. The available employee hours per week are as follows: for operating machine A, 70 hours; for B, 40 hours; for finishing, 90 hours. If the profits on each widget and wadgit are $4 and $6, respectively, how many of each toy should be made per week in order to maximize profit? What would the maximum profit be?

	MACHINE A	MACHINE B	FINISHING
Widgets	2 hr	1 hr	1 hr
Wadgits	1 hr	1 hr	3 hr

14. A manufacturer produces two types of barbecue grills, Old Smokey and Blaze Away. During production the grills require the use of two machines, A and B. The number of hours needed on both are indicated in the table below. If each machine can be used 24 hours a day, and the profits on the Old Smokey and Blaze Away models are $4 and $6, respectively, how many of each type of grill should be made per day to obtain maximum profit? What is the maximum profit?

	MACHINE A	MACHINE B
Old Smokey	2 hr	4 hr
Blaze Away	4 hr	2 hr

15. A diet is to contain at least 16 units of carbohydrates and 20 units of protein. Food A contains 2 units of carbohydrates and 4 of protein; food B contains 2 units of carbohydrates and 1 of protein. If food A costs $1.20 per unit and food B costs $0.80 per unit, how many units of each food should be purchased in order to minimize cost? What is the minimum cost?

16. A produce grower is purchasing fertilizer containing three nutrients: A, B, and C. The minimum weekly requirements are 80 units of A, 120 of B, and 240 of C. There are two popular blends of fertilizer on the market. Blend I, costing $4 a bag, contains 2 units of A, 6 of B, and 4 of C. Blend II, costing $5 a bag, contains 2 units of A, 2 of B, and 12 of C. How many bags of each blend should the grower buy each week to minimize the cost of meeting the nutrient requirements?

17. A company extracts minerals from ore. The number of pounds of minerals A and B that can be extracted from each ton of ores I and II are given in the table below together with the costs per ton of the ores. If the company must produce at least 3000 lb of A and 2500 lb of B, how many tons of each ore should be processed in order to minimize cost? What is the minimum cost?

	ORE I	ORE II
Mineral A	100 lb	200 lb
Mineral B	200 lb	50 lb
Cost per ton	$50	$60

9.3 MULTIPLE OPTIMUM SOLUTIONS*

Sometimes an objective function attains its optimum value at more than one feasible point, in which case **multiple optimum solutions** are said to exist. Example 1 will illustrate.

* This section can be omitted.

EXAMPLE 1   *Maximize Z = 2x + 4y subject to the constraints*

$$x - 4y \leq -8,$$

$$x + 2y \leq 16,$$

$$x \geq 0, \quad y \geq 0.$$

The feasible region appears in Fig. 9.18. Since the region is nonempty and

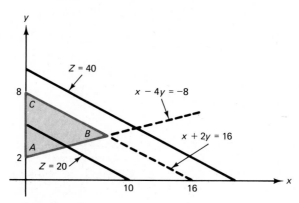

FIGURE 9.18

bounded, Z has a maximum value at a corner point. The corner points are

$$A = (0, 2), \quad B = (8, 4), \quad C = (0, 8).$$

Evaluating the objective function at A, B, and C gives

$$Z(A) = 2(0) + 4(2) = 8,$$

$$Z(B) = 2(8) + 4(4) = 32,$$

$$Z(C) = 2(0) + 4(8) = 32.$$

Thus the maximum value of Z over the region is 32, and it occurs at *two* corner points, B and C. In fact, this maximum value also occurs at *all* points on the line segment *joining* B and C, for the following reason. Each member of the family of lines $Z = 2x + 4y$ has slope $-\frac{1}{2}$. Moreover, the constraint line $x + 2y = 16$, which contains B and C, also has slope $-\frac{1}{2}$, and hence is parallel to each member of $Z = 2x + 4y$. Figure 9.18 shows lines for $Z = 20$ and $Z = 40$. Thus the member of the family that maximizes Z contains not only B and C but also all points on the line segment BC. It thus has infinitely many points in common with the feasible region. Hence this linear programming problem has infinitely many optimum solutions. In fact, it can be shown that:

If (x_1, y_1) and (x_2, y_2) are two corner points at which an objective function is optimum, then the function will also be optimum at all points (x, y) where

$$x = (1 - t)x_1 + tx_2,$$

$$y = (1 - t)y_1 + ty_2,$$

and $0 \leq t \leq 1$.

In our case, if $(x_1, y_1) = B = (8, 4)$ and $(x_2, y_2) = C = (0, 8)$, then Z is maximum at any point (x, y) where

$$x = (1 - t)8 + t \cdot 0 = 8(1 - t),$$

$$y = (1 - t)4 + t \cdot 8 = 4(1 + t),$$

and $0 \leq t \leq 1$.

These equations give the coordinates of any point on the line segment BC. In particular, if $t = 0$, then $x = 8$ and $y = 4$, which gives the corner point $B = (8, 4)$. If $t = 1$, we get the corner point $C = (0, 8)$. The value $t = \frac{1}{2}$ gives the point $(4, 6)$. Notice that at $(4, 6)$, $Z = 2(4) + 4(6) = 32$, which is the maximum value of Z.

EXERCISE 9.3

1. Minimize
$$Z = 3x + 9y$$
subject to
$$y \geq -\tfrac{3}{2}x + 6,$$
$$y \geq -\tfrac{1}{3}x + \tfrac{11}{3},$$
$$y \geq x - 3,$$
$$x, y \geq 0.$$

2. Maximize
$$Z = 3x + 6y$$
subject to
$$x - y \geq -3,$$
$$2x - y \leq 4,$$
$$x + 2y = 12,$$
$$x, y \geq 0.$$

3. Maximize
$$Z = 18x + 9y$$
subject to
$$2x + 3y \leq 12,$$
$$2x + y \leq 8,$$
$$x, y \geq 0.$$

9.4 THE SIMPLEX METHOD

Up to now we have solved linear programming problems by a geometric method. This method will not be handy when the number of variables increases to three, and will not be possible beyond that. Now we shall look at a different technique—the **simplex method,** whose name is linked in more advanced discussions to a geometrical object called a simplex.

The simplex method begins with a feasible solution and tests whether or not it is optimum. If not optimum, the method proceeds to a *better* solution. We say "better" in the sense that the new solution brings you closer to optimization of the objective function.* Should this new solution not be optimum, then we repeat the procedure. Eventually the simplex method leads to an optimum solution, if one exists.

Besides being efficient, there are other advantages to the simplex method. It is completely mechanical (we use matrices, elementary row operations, and basic arithmetic). Moreover, no geometry is involved. This allows us to solve linear programming problems having any number of constraints and variables.

In this section we shall consider only so-called **standard linear programming problems.** These can be put in the form:

$$\text{maximize } Z = c_1x_1 + c_2x_2 + \cdots + c_nx_n$$

such that

$$\left. \begin{array}{c} a_{11}x_1 + a_{12}x_2 + \cdots + a_{1n}x_n \le b_1, \\ a_{21}x_1 + a_{22}x_2 + \cdots + a_{2n}x_n \le b_2, \\ \cdot \qquad \cdot \qquad \qquad \cdot \qquad \cdot \\ \cdot \qquad \cdot \qquad \qquad \cdot \qquad \cdot \\ \cdot \qquad \cdot \qquad \qquad \cdot \qquad \cdot \\ a_{m1}x_1 + a_{m2}x_2 + \cdots + a_{mn}x_n \le b_m, \end{array} \right\} \tag{1}$$

where $x_1, x_2, \ldots, x_n$ and $b_1, b_2, \ldots, b_m$ are nonnegative.

Note that one feasible solution to a standard linear programming problem is always $x_1 = 0$, $x_2 = 0$, $\ldots$, $x_n = 0$. Other types of linear programming problems will be discussed in Sec. 9.6 and 9.7.

We shall now apply the simplex method to the problem in Example 1 of Sec. 9.2 that has the form:

$$\text{maximize } Z = 3x_1 + x_2$$

subject to the constraints

$$2x_1 + x_2 \le 8 \tag{2}$$

$$\text{and} \qquad 2x_1 + 3x_2 \le 12, \tag{3}$$

where $x_1 \ge 0$ and $x_2 \ge 0$. This problem is of standard form. We begin by expressing constraints (2) and (3) as equations. In (2), $2x_1 + x_2$ will *equal* 8 if we add some nonnegative number s_1 to $2x_1 + x_2$:

$$2x_1 + x_2 + s_1 = 8, \quad \text{where } s_1 \ge 0.$$

We call s_1 a **slack variable** since it makes up for the "slack" on the left side of (2) so that we have equality. Similarly, inequality (3) can be written as an equation by using the slack variable s_2:

$$2x_1 + 3x_2 + s_2 = 12, \quad \text{where } s_2 \ge 0.$$

The variables x_1 and x_2 are called **structural variables.**

---

* In most cases this is true. In some situations, however, the new solution may be just as good as the previous one. Example 2 will illustrate this.

Now we can restate the problem in terms of equations:

$$\text{maximize } Z = 3x_1 + x_2 \tag{4}$$

such that

$$2x_1 + x_2 + s_1 = 8 \tag{5}$$

$$\text{and} \quad 2x_1 + 3x_2 + s_2 = 12, \tag{6}$$

where x_1, x_2, s_1, and s_2 are nonnegative.

From Sec. 9.2 we know that the optimum solution occurs at a corner point of the feasible region in Fig. 9.19. At each of these points at least *two* of the variables x_1, x_2, s_1, and s_2 are 0.

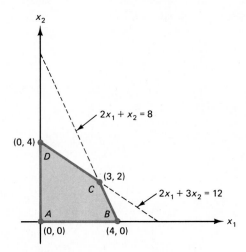

FIGURE 9.19

1. At A, we have $x_1 = 0$ and $x_2 = 0$.

2. At B, $x_1 = 4$ and $x_2 = 0$. But from Eq. (5), $2(4) + 0 + s_1 = 8$. Thus $s_1 = 0$.

3. At C, $x_1 = 3$ and $x_2 = 2$. But from Eq. (5), $2(3) + 2 + s_1 = 8$. Thus $s_1 = 0$. From Eq. (6), $2(3) + 3(2) + s_2 = 12$. Thus $s_2 = 0$.

4. At D, $x_1 = 0$ and $x_2 = 4$. From Eq. (6), $2(0) + 3(4) + s_2 = 12$. Thus $s_2 = 0$.

It can also be shown that any solution to Eqs. (5) and (6), such that at least *two* of the four variables x_1, x_2, s_1, and s_2 are zero, corresponds to a corner point. Any such solution where at least two of these variables are zero is called a **basic feasible solution** (abbreviated B.F.S.). This number, 2, is determined by the expression $n - m$, where m is the number of constraints (excluding the nonnegativity conditions) and n is the number of variables that occur after these constraints are converted to equations. In our case $n = 4$ and $m = 2$. For any particular B.F.S., the two variables held at zero value are called **nonbasic variables,** while the others are called **basic variables** for that B.F.S. Thus, for the B.F.S. corresponding to discussion (3) above, s_1 and s_2 are the nonbasic variables, but for the B.F.S. corresponding to (4) the nonbasic variables are x_1 and s_2. We eventually want to find a B.F.S. that maximizes Z.

We shall first find an initial B.F.S. and then determine whether the corresponding value of Z can be increased by a different B.F.S. Since $x_1 = 0$ and $x_2 = 0$ is a feasible solution to this standard linear programming problem, let us initially find the B.F.S. where the structural variables x_1 and x_2 are nonbasic. That is, we choose $x_1 = 0$ and $x_2 = 0$ and find the corresponding values of s_1, s_2, and Z. This can be done most conveniently by matrix techniques, based on the methods developed in Chapter 8.

If we write Eq. (4) as $-3x_1 - x_2 + Z = 0$, then Eqs. (5), (6), and (4) form the system

$$\begin{cases} 2x_1 + x_2 + s_1 & = 8, \\ 2x_1 + 3x_2 + s_2 & = 12, \\ -3x_1 - x_2 + Z = 0. \end{cases}$$

In terms of an augmented coefficient matrix (also called a **simplex tableau**), we have

$$\begin{array}{c} \quad\;\; x_1 \quad x_2 \quad s_1 \quad s_2 \quad Z \\ \begin{array}{c} s_1 \\ s_2 \\ \\ Z \end{array} \left[\begin{array}{ccccc|c} 2 & 1 & 1 & 0 & 0 & 8 \\ 2 & 3 & 0 & 1 & 0 & 12 \\ \hline -3 & -1 & 0 & 0 & 1 & 0 \end{array} \right]. \end{array}$$

The first two rows correspond to the constraints, and the last row corresponds to the objective equation—thus the dashed horizontal separating line. Notice that if $x_1 = 0$ and $x_2 = 0$, then from rows 1, 2, and 3 we can directly read off the values of s_1, s_2, and Z; $s_1 = 8$, $s_2 = 12$, and $Z = 0$. That is why we placed the letters s_1, s_2, and Z to the left of the rows. (We remind you that s_1 and s_2 are the basic variables.) Thus our initial basic feasible solution is

$$x_1 = 0, \qquad x_2 = 0, \qquad s_1 = 8, \qquad s_2 = 12,$$

at which $Z = 0$. Let us see if we can find a B.F.S. that gives a larger value of Z.

The variables x_1 and x_2 are nonbasic in the B.F.S. above. We shall now look for a B.F.S. in which one of these variables is basic while the other remains nonbasic. Which one should we choose as the basic variable? Let us examine the possibilities. From the Z-row of the matrix above, $Z = 3x_1 + x_2$. If x_1 is allowed to become basic, then x_2 remains at 0 and $Z = 3x_1$; thus, for each one-unit increase in x_1, Z increases by three units. On the other hand, if x_2 is allowed to become basic, then x_1 remains at 0 and $Z = x_2$; thus, for each one-unit increase in x_2, Z increases by one unit. Hence we get a *greater* increase in the value of Z if x_1, rather than x_2, enters the basic variable category. In this case we call x_1 an

entering variable. Thus, in terms of the simplex tableau below (which is the same as the matrix above except for some additional labeling) the entering variable can be found by looking at the "most negative" of the numbers enclosed by the brace in the Z-row. Since that number is -3 and appears in the x_1-column, x_1 is the entering variable. The numbers in the brace are sometimes called **indicators**.

$$
\begin{array}{c c}
& \begin{array}{c c c c c}
x_1 & x_2 & s_1 & s_2 & Z
\end{array} \\
\begin{array}{c}
s_1 \\
s_2 \\
\\
Z
\end{array}
&
\left[
\begin{array}{c c c c c | c}
2 & 1 & 1 & 0 & 0 & 8 \\
2 & 3 & 0 & 1 & 0 & 12 \\
\hline
-3 & -1 & 0 & 0 & 1 & 0
\end{array}
\right].
\end{array}
$$

$\underbrace{\qquad\qquad\qquad}_{\text{indicators}}$

$\uparrow$

entering
variable

Let us summarize the information that can be obtained from this tableau. It gives a B.F.S. where s_1 and s_2 are the basic variables and x_1 and x_2 are nonbasic. The B.F.S. is $s_1 = 8$ ($=$ the right-hand side of the s_1-row), $s_2 = 12$ ($=$ the right-hand side of the s_2-row), $x_1 = 0$, and $x_2 = 0$. The -3 in the x_1-column of the Z-row indicates that if x_2 remains 0, then Z increases three units for each one-unit increase in x_1. The -1 in the x_2-column of the Z-row indicates that if x_1 remains 0, then Z increases one unit for each one-unit increase in x_2. The column in which the most negative indicator -3 lies gives the entering variable x_1, that is, the variable that should become basic in the next B.F.S.

In our new B.F.S., the larger the increase in x_1 (from $x_1 = 0$), the larger the increase in Z. Now, by how much can we increase x_1? Since x_2 is still held at 0, from rows 1 and 2 of the simplex tableau above it follows that

$$s_1 = 8 - 2x_1$$

and $\qquad s_2 = 12 - 2x_1.$

Since s_1 and s_2 are nonnegative, we have

$$8 - 2x_1 \geq 0$$

and $\qquad 12 - 2x_1 \geq 0.$

From the first inequality, $x_1 \leq \frac{8}{2} = 4$; from the second, $x_1 \leq \frac{12}{2} = 6$. Thus x_1 must be less than or equal to the smaller of the quotients $\frac{8}{2}$ and $\frac{12}{2}$, which is $\frac{8}{2}$. Hence x_1 can increase at most by 4. However, in a B.F.S. two variables must be 0. We already have $x_2 = 0$. Since $s_1 = 8 - 2x_1$, s_1 must be 0 for $x_1 = 4$. Thus we have a new B.F.S. with x_1 replacing s_1 as a basic variable. That is, s_1 will *depart* from the category of basic variables in the previous B.F.S. and will be nonbasic in the new B.F.S. We say that s_1 is the **departing variable** for the previous B.F.S. In summary, for our new B.F.S. we want x_1 and s_2 as basic variables with $x_1 = 4$, and x_2 and s_1 as nonbasic variables ($x_2 = 0$, $s_1 = 0$).

Before proceeding, let us update our tableau. To the right of the tableau below, the quotients $\frac{8}{2}$ and $\frac{12}{2}$ are indicated. They are obtained by dividing each entry in the first two rows of the b-column by the entry in the corresponding row of the entering variable column. Notice that the departing variable is in the same row as the *smaller* quotient $8 \div 2$.

$$
\begin{array}{ccccccc}
 & x_1 & x_2 & s_1 & s_2 & Z & b \\
\text{departing} \rightarrow s_1 & 2 & 1 & 1 & 0 & 0 & 8 \\
\text{variable} \quad\; s_2 & 2 & 3 & 0 & 1 & 0 & 12 \\
\hline
Z & -3 & -1 & 0 & 0 & 1 & 0
\end{array}
$$

$$
\begin{array}{c}
\uparrow \\
\text{entering variable}
\end{array}
$$

Quotients

$8 \div 2 = 4.$
$12 \div 2 = 6.$

Since x_1 and s_2 will be basic variables in our new B.F.S., it would be convenient to change our previous tableau by elementary row operations into a form where the values of x_1, s_2, and Z can be read off with ease (just as we were able to do with the solution corresponding to $x_1 = 0$ and $x_2 = 0$). To do this we want to find a matrix which is equivalent to the tableau above but which has the form

$$
\begin{array}{ccccc}
x_1 & x_2 & s_1 & s_2 & Z \\
\begin{bmatrix}
1 & ? & ? & 0 & 0 & ? \\
0 & ? & ? & 1 & 0 & ? \\
\hline
0 & ? & ? & 0 & 1 & ?
\end{bmatrix}
\end{array}
$$

where the question marks represent numbers to be determined. Notice here that if $x_2 = 0$ and $s_1 = 0$, then x_1 equals the number in row 1 of the last column, s_2 equals the number in row 2, and Z is the number in row 3. Thus we must transform the tableau

$$
\begin{array}{ccccccc}
 & x_1 & x_2 & s_1 & s_2 & Z & \\
\text{departing} \rightarrow s_1 & ② & 1 & 1 & 0 & 0 & 8 \\
\text{variable} \quad\; s_2 & 2 & 3 & 0 & 1 & 0 & 12 \\
\hline
Z & -3 & -1 & 0 & 0 & 1 & 0
\end{array} \tag{7}
$$

$$
\begin{array}{c}
\uparrow \\
\text{entering variable}
\end{array}
$$

into an equivalent matrix that has a 1 where the circle appears and 0's elsewhere in the x_1-column. The entry in the circle is called the **pivot entry**—it is in the column of the entering variable and the row of the departing variable. By elementary row operations, we have

$$
\begin{array}{ccccc}
x_1 & x_2 & s_1 & s_2 & Z \\
\begin{bmatrix}
② & 1 & 1 & 0 & 0 & 8 \\
2 & 3 & 0 & 1 & 0 & 12 \\
\hline
-3 & -1 & 0 & 0 & 1 & 0
\end{bmatrix}
\end{array}
$$

$$\sim \begin{bmatrix} 1 & \frac{1}{2} & \frac{1}{2} & 0 & 0 & \vdots & 4 \\ 2 & 3 & 0 & 1 & 0 & \vdots & 12 \\ \hdashline -3 & -1 & 0 & 0 & 1 & \vdots & 0 \end{bmatrix} \qquad \text{(by multiplying first row by } \tfrac{1}{2}\text{)}$$

$$\sim \begin{bmatrix} 1 & \frac{1}{2} & \frac{1}{2} & 0 & 0 & \vdots & 4 \\ 0 & 2 & -1 & 1 & 0 & \vdots & 4 \\ \hdashline 0 & \frac{1}{2} & \frac{3}{2} & 0 & 1 & \vdots & 12 \end{bmatrix} \qquad \begin{array}{l}\text{(by adding } -2 \text{ times first row} \\ \text{to the second, and adding 3} \\ \text{times first row to the third).}\end{array}$$

Thus we have a new simplex tableau:

$$\begin{array}{c} \begin{array}{cccccc} x_1 & x_2 & s_1 & s_2 & Z & \end{array} \\ \begin{array}{c} x_1 \\ s_2 \\ \\ Z \end{array}\begin{bmatrix} 1 & \frac{1}{2} & \frac{1}{2} & 0 & 0 & \vdots & 4 \\ 0 & 2 & -1 & 1 & 0 & \vdots & 4 \\ \hdashline 0 & \frac{1}{2} & \frac{3}{2} & 0 & 1 & \vdots & 12 \end{bmatrix} \\ \underbrace{}_{\text{indicators}} \end{array} \qquad (8)$$

For $x_2 = 0$ and $s_1 = 0$, then from the first row we have $x_1 = 4$; from the second, $s_2 = 4$. These values give us the new B.F.S. Note that we replaced the s_1 located to the left of the initial tableau in (7) by x_1 in our new tableau (8)—thus s_1 *departed* and x_1 *entered*. From row 3, for $x_2 = 0$ and $s_1 = 0$ we get $Z = 12$, which is a larger value than we had before (it was $Z = 0$).

In our present B.F.S., x_2 and s_1 are nonbasic variables ($x_2 = 0$, $s_1 = 0$). Suppose we look for another B.F.S. that gives a larger value of Z and such that one of x_2 or s_1 is basic. The equation corresponding to the Z-row is given by $\frac{1}{2}x_2 + \frac{3}{2}s_1 + Z = 12$ or

$$Z = 12 - \tfrac{1}{2}x_2 - \tfrac{3}{2}s_1. \qquad (9)$$

If x_2 becomes basic and therefore s_1 remains nonbasic, then

$$Z = 12 - \tfrac{1}{2}x_2 \qquad \text{(since } s_1 = 0\text{)}.$$

Here, each one-unit increase in x_2 *decreases* Z by $\frac{1}{2}$ unit. Thus any increase in x_2 would make Z smaller than before. On the other hand, if s_1 becomes basic and x_2 remains nonbasic, then from Eq. (9),

$$Z = 12 - \tfrac{3}{2}s_1 \qquad \text{(since } x_2 = 0\text{)}.$$

Here each one-unit increase in s_1 *decreases* Z by $\frac{3}{2}$ units. Thus any increase in s_1 would make Z smaller than before. We cannot move to a better B.F.S. In short, no B.F.S. gives a larger value of Z than the B.F.S. $x_1 = 4$, $s_2 = 4$, $x_2 = 0$, $s_1 = 0$ (which gives $Z = 12$).

In fact, since $x_2 \geq 0$ and $s_1 \geq 0$ and the coefficients of x_2 and s_1 in Eq. (9) are negative, then Z is maximum when $x_2 = 0$ and $s_1 = 0$. That is, in (8), *having all nonnegative indicators means that we have an optimum solution.*

In terms of our original problem, if

$$Z = 3x_1 + x_2,$$

such that

$$2x_1 + x_2 \le 8, \qquad 2x_1 + 3x_2 \le 12, \qquad x_1 \ge 0, \quad \text{and} \quad x_2 \ge 0,$$

then Z is maximum when $x_1 = 4$ and $x_2 = 0$, and the maximum value of Z is 12 (this confirms our result in Example 1 of Sec. 9.2). Note that the values of s_1 and s_2 do not have to appear here.

Let us outline the simplex method for a standard linear programming problem with three structural variables and four constraints not counting nonnegativity conditions. This is to imply how the simplex method works for any number of structural variables and constraints.

SIMPLEX METHOD

Problem:

$$\text{maximize } Z = c_1 x_1 + c_2 x_2 + c_3 x_3$$

such that

$$a_{11}x_1 + a_{12}x_2 + a_{13}x_3 \le b_1,$$

$$a_{21}x_1 + a_{22}x_2 + a_{23}x_3 \le b_2,$$

$$a_{31}x_1 + a_{32}x_2 + a_{33}x_3 \le b_3,$$

$$a_{41}x_1 + a_{42}x_2 + a_{43}x_3 \le b_4,$$

where x_1, x_2, x_3 and b_1, b_2,b_3, b_4 are nonnegative.

Method:

1. Set up the initial simplex tableau.

	x_1	x_2	x_3	s_1	s_2	s_3	s_4	Z	b
s_1	a_{11}	a_{12}	a_{13}	1	0	0	0	0	b_1
s_2	a_{21}	a_{22}	a_{23}	0	1	0	0	0	b_2
s_3	a_{31}	a_{32}	a_{33}	0	0	1	0	0	b_3
s_4	a_{41}	a_{42}	a_{43}	0	0	0	1	0	b_4
Z	$-c_1$	$-c_2$	$-c_3$	0	0	0	0	1	0

$$\underbrace{}_{\text{indicators}}$$

There are four slack variables, s_1, s_2, s_3, and s_4—one for each constraint.

2. If all the indicators in the last row are nonnegative, then Z has a maximum when $x_1 = 0$, $x_2 = 0$, and $x_3 = 0$. The maximum value is 0.
If there are any negative indicators, locate the column in which the most negative indicator appears. This column gives the entering variable.

3. Divide each *positive** entry above the dashed line in the entering variable column *into* the corresponding value of b.

*This will be discussed after Example 1.

4. Place a circle around the entry in the entering variable column that corresponds to the smallest quotient in step 3. This is the pivot entry. The departing variable is the one to the left of the pivot entry row.

5. Use elementary row operations to transform the tableau into a new equivalent tableau that has a 1 where the pivot entry was and 0's elsewhere in that column.

6. On the left side of this tableau the entering variable replaces the departing variable.

7. If the indicators of the new tableau are all nonnegative, you have an optimum solution. The maximum value of Z is the entry in the last row and last column. It occurs when the variables to the left of the tableau are equal to the corresponding entries in the last column. All other variables are 0.
   If at least one of the indicators is negative, repeat the process beginning with step 2 applied to the new tableau.

As an aid in understanding the simplex method, you should be able to interpret certain entries in a tableau. Suppose that we obtain a tableau where the last row is indicated below.

$$
\begin{array}{c}
\begin{array}{cccccccc}
x_1 & x_2 & x_3 & s_1 & s_2 & s_3 & s_4 & Z
\end{array} \\
\left[
\begin{array}{cccccccc|c}
\vdots & \vdots & \vdots & \vdots & \vdots & \vdots & \vdots & \vdots & \vdots \\
\vdots & \vdots & \vdots & \vdots & \vdots & \vdots & \vdots & \vdots & \vdots \\
\hline
Z \quad a & b & c & d & e & f & g & 1 & h
\end{array}
\right].
\end{array}
$$

We can interpret the entry b, for example, as follows. If x_2 is nonbasic and were to become basic, then for each 1 unit increase in x_2,

if $b < 0$, Z *increases* by $|b|$ units;

if $b > 0$, Z *decreases* by b units;

if $b = 0$, there is no change in Z.

EXAMPLE 1   *Maximize Z = $5x_1 + 4x_2$ subject to*

$$x_1 + x_2 \leq 20,$$

$$2x_1 + x_2 \leq 35,$$

$$-3x_1 + x_2 \leq 12,$$

and $x_1 \geq 0$, $x_2 \geq 0$.

This linear programming problem fits the standard form. The initial simplex tableau is

$$
\begin{array}{c}
\begin{array}{cccccccc}
& x_1 & x_2 & s_1 & s_2 & s_3 & Z & b
\end{array} \\
\begin{array}{c}
s_1 \\
\text{departing} \rightarrow s_2 \\
\text{variable} \quad s_3 \\
Z
\end{array}
\left[
\begin{array}{ccccccc|c}
1 & 1 & 1 & 0 & 0 & 0 & 20 \\
② & 1 & 0 & 1 & 0 & 0 & 35 \\
-3 & 1 & 0 & 0 & 1 & 0 & 12 \\
\hline
-5 & -4 & 0 & 0 & 0 & 1 & 0
\end{array}
\right]
\begin{array}{l}
\textit{Quotients} \\
20 \div 1 = 20. \\
35 \div 2 = \frac{35}{2}. \\
\text{no quotient since} \\
-3 \text{ is not positive.}
\end{array}
\end{array}
$$

↑   indicators
entering
variable

The most negative indicator, -5, occurs in the x_1-column. Thus x_1 is the entering variable. The smaller quotient is $\frac{35}{2}$, so s_2 is the departing variable. The pivot entry is 2. Using elementary row operations to get a 1 in the pivot position and 0's elsewhere in its column, we have

$$
\begin{array}{c}
\begin{array}{ccccccc}
x_1 & x_2 & s_1 & s_2 & s_3 & Z & b
\end{array} \\
\left[
\begin{array}{ccccccc|c}
1 & 1 & 1 & 0 & 0 & 0 & 20 \\
② & 1 & 0 & 1 & 0 & 0 & 35 \\
-3 & 1 & 0 & 0 & 1 & 0 & 12 \\
\hline
-5 & -4 & 0 & 0 & 0 & 1 & 0
\end{array}
\right]
\end{array}
$$

$$
\sim
\left[
\begin{array}{ccccccc|c}
1 & 1 & 1 & 0 & 0 & 0 & 20 \\
1 & \frac{1}{2} & 0 & \frac{1}{2} & 0 & 0 & \frac{35}{2} \\
-3 & 1 & 0 & 0 & 1 & 0 & 12 \\
\hline
-5 & -4 & 0 & 0 & 0 & 1 & 0
\end{array}
\right]
\qquad \text{(by multiplying row two by } \tfrac{1}{2})
$$

$$
\sim
\left[
\begin{array}{ccccccc|c}
0 & \frac{1}{2} & 1 & -\frac{1}{2} & 0 & 0 & \frac{5}{2} \\
1 & \frac{1}{2} & 0 & \frac{1}{2} & 0 & 0 & \frac{35}{2} \\
0 & \frac{5}{2} & 0 & \frac{3}{2} & 1 & 0 & \frac{129}{2} \\
\hline
0 & -\frac{3}{2} & 0 & \frac{5}{2} & 0 & 1 & \frac{175}{2}
\end{array}
\right]
\qquad
\begin{array}{l}
\text{(by adding } -1 \text{ times row two} \\
\text{to row one; adding 3 times} \\
\text{row two to row three; adding} \\
5 \text{ times row two to row four).}
\end{array}
$$

Our new tableau is

$$
\begin{array}{c}
\begin{array}{cccccccc}
& x_1 & x_2 & s_1 & s_2 & s_3 & Z & b
\end{array} \\
\begin{array}{c}
\text{departing} \rightarrow s_1 \\
\text{variable} \quad x_1 \\
s_3 \\
Z
\end{array}
\left[
\begin{array}{ccccccc|c}
0 & ①\!\!\frac{1}{2} & 1 & -\frac{1}{2} & 0 & 0 & \frac{5}{2} \\
1 & \frac{1}{2} & 0 & \frac{1}{2} & 0 & 0 & \frac{35}{2} \\
0 & \frac{5}{2} & 0 & \frac{3}{2} & 1 & 0 & \frac{129}{2} \\
\hline
0 & -\frac{3}{2} & 0 & \frac{5}{2} & 0 & 1 & \frac{175}{2}
\end{array}
\right]
\begin{array}{l}
\textit{Quotients} \\
\frac{5}{2} \div \frac{1}{2} = 5. \\
\frac{35}{2} \div \frac{1}{2} = 35. \\
\frac{129}{2} \div \frac{5}{2} = 25\frac{4}{5}.
\end{array}
\end{array}
$$

indicators
↑
entering
variable

Note that on the left side, x_1 replaced s_2. Since $-\frac{3}{2}$ is the most negative indicator, we must continue our process. The entering variable is now x_2. The smallest quotient is 5. Thus s_1 is the departing variable and $\frac{1}{2}$ is the pivot entry. Using elementary row operations we have

$$
\begin{array}{ccccccc}
x_1 & x_2 & s_1 & s_2 & s_3 & Z & b \\
\end{array}
$$

$$
\left[
\begin{array}{cccccc|c}
0 & \boxed{\tfrac{1}{2}} & 1 & -\tfrac{1}{2} & 0 & 0 & \tfrac{5}{2} \\
1 & \tfrac{1}{2} & 0 & \tfrac{1}{2} & 0 & 0 & \tfrac{35}{2} \\
0 & \tfrac{5}{2} & 0 & \tfrac{3}{2} & 1 & 0 & \tfrac{129}{2} \\
\hline
0 & -\tfrac{3}{2} & 0 & \tfrac{5}{2} & 0 & 1 & \tfrac{175}{2}
\end{array}
\right]
$$

$$
\sim
\left[
\begin{array}{cccccc|c}
0 & \tfrac{1}{2} & 1 & -\tfrac{1}{2} & 0 & 0 & \tfrac{5}{2} \\
1 & 0 & -1 & 1 & 0 & 0 & 15 \\
0 & 0 & -5 & 4 & 1 & 0 & 52 \\
\hline
0 & 0 & 3 & 1 & 0 & 1 & 95
\end{array}
\right]
$$

(by adding -1 times row one to row two; adding -5 times row one to row three; adding 3 times row one to row four)

$$
\sim
\left[
\begin{array}{cccccc|c}
0 & 1 & 2 & -1 & 0 & 0 & 5 \\
1 & 0 & -1 & 1 & 0 & 0 & 15 \\
0 & 0 & -5 & 4 & 1 & 0 & 52 \\
\hline
0 & 0 & 3 & 1 & 0 & 1 & 95
\end{array}
\right]
$$

(by multiplying row one by 2).

Our new tableau is

$$
\begin{array}{c}
\begin{array}{ccccccc}
& x_1 & x_2 & s_1 & s_2 & s_3 & Z \quad b \\
\end{array} \\
\begin{array}{c}
x_2 \\ x_1 \\ s_3 \\ \\ Z
\end{array}
\left[
\begin{array}{cccccc|c}
0 & 1 & 2 & -1 & 0 & 0 & 5 \\
1 & 0 & -1 & 1 & 0 & 0 & 15 \\
0 & 0 & -5 & 4 & 1 & 0 & 52 \\
\hline
0 & 0 & 3 & 1 & 0 & 1 & 95
\end{array}
\right]
\end{array},
$$

$$\underbrace{}_{\text{indicators}}$$

where x_2 replaced s_1 on the left side. Since all indicators are nonnegative, the maximum value of Z is 95 and occurs when $x_2 = 5$ and $x_1 = 15$ (and $s_3 = 52$, $s_1 = 0$, and $s_2 = 0$).

It is interesting to see how the values of Z got progressively ''better'' in successive tableaus in Example 1. These are the entries in the last row and column of each tableau. In the initial tableau we had $Z = 0$. From then on we obtained $Z = \frac{175}{2} = 87\frac{1}{2}$ and then $Z = 95$, the maximum.

In Example 1, you may wonder why no quotient is considered in the third row of the initial tableau. The B.F.S. for this tableau is

$$s_1 = 20, \qquad s_2 = 35, \qquad s_3 = 12, \qquad x_1 = 0, \qquad x_2 = 0,$$

where x_1 is the entering variable. The quotients 20 and $\frac{35}{2}$ reflect that for the next B.F.S., we have $x_1 \le 20$ and $x_1 \le \frac{35}{2}$. Since the third row represents the equation $s_3 = 12 + 3x_1 - x_2$, and $x_2 = 0$, then $s_3 = 12 + 3x_1$. But $s_3 \ge 0$, so $12 + 3x_1 \ge 0$, which implies $x_1 \ge -\frac{12}{3} = -4$. Thus we have

$$x_1 \le 20, \qquad x_1 \le \tfrac{35}{2}, \quad \text{and} \quad x_1 \ge -4.$$

Hence x_1 can increase at most by $\frac{35}{2}$. The condition $x_1 \ge -4$ has no influence in determining the maximum increase in x_1. That is why the quotient $12/(-3) =$

-4 is not considered in row 3. In general, *no quotient is considered for a row if the entry in the entering variable column is negative (or, of course, 0).*

Although the simplex procedure that has been developed in this section applies only to linear programming problems of standard form, other forms may be adapted to fit this form. Suppose that a constraint has the form

$$a_1 x_1 + a_2 x_2 + \cdots + a_n x_n \geq -b,$$

where $b > 0$. Here the inequality symbol is "$\geq$" and the constant on the right side is *negative*. Thus the constraint is not in standard form. However, multiplying both sides by -1 gives

$$-a_1 x_1 - a_2 x_2 - \cdots - a_n x_n \leq b,$$

which *does* have the proper form. Thus it may be necessary to rewrite a constraint before proceeding with the simplex method.

In a simplex tableau, several indicators may "tie" for being most negative. In this case, choose any one of these indicators to give the column for the entering variable. Likewise, there may be several quotients that "tie" for being the smallest. You may choose any one of these quotients to give you the departing variable and pivot entry. Example 2 will illustrate this. When a tie for the smallest quotient exists, then along with the nonbasic variables a B.F.S. will have a basic variable that is 0. In this case we say that the B.F.S. is *degenerate* or that the linear programming problem has a *degeneracy*. More will be said about this in Sec. 9.5.

EXAMPLE 2　　*Maximize* $Z = 3x_1 + 4x_2 + \frac{3}{2}x_3$ *subject to*

$$
\begin{aligned}
-x_1 - 2x_2 &\geq -10, \\
2x_1 + 2x_2 + x_3 &\leq 10,
\end{aligned}
\tag{10}
$$

and $x_1, x_2, x_3 \geq 0$.

Constraint (10) does not fit the standard form. However, multiplying both sides of (10) by -1 gives

$$x_1 + 2x_2 \leq 10,$$

which *does* have the proper form. Thus our initial simplex tableau is tableau I.

SIMPLEX TABLEAU I

	x_1	x_2	x_3	s_1	s_2	Z	b	Quotients
departing variable → s_1	1	②	0	1	0	0	10	$10 \div 2 = 5.$
s_2	2	2	1	0	1	0	10	$10 \div 2 = 5.$
Z	-3	-4	$-\frac{3}{2}$	0	0	1	0	

indicators

↑

entering variable

The entering variable is x_2. Since there is a tie for the smallest quotient, we can choose either s_1 or s_2 as the departing variable. Let us choose s_1. The pivot entry is circled. Using elementary row operations, we get tableau II.

SIMPLEX TABLEAU II

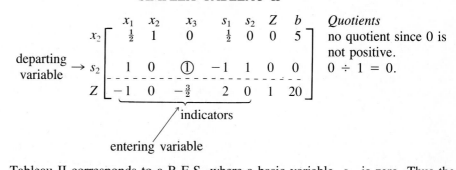

Tableau II corresponds to a B.F.S. where a basic variable, s_2, is zero. Thus the B.F.S. is degenerate. Since there are negative indicators, we continue. The entering variable is now x_3, the departing variable is s_2, and the pivot is circled. Using elementary row operations, we get tableau III.

SIMPLEX TABLEAU III

$$
\begin{array}{c c c c c c c c}
 & x_1 & x_2 & x_3 & s_1 & s_2 & Z & b \\
x_2 & \frac{1}{2} & 1 & 0 & \frac{1}{2} & 0 & 0 & 5 \\
x_3 & 1 & 0 & 1 & -1 & 1 & 0 & 0 \\
\hline
Z & \frac{1}{2} & 0 & 0 & \frac{1}{2} & \frac{3}{2} & 1 & 20
\end{array}
$$

indicators

Since all indicators are nonnegative, Z is maximum when $x_2 = 5$ and $x_3 = 0$, and $x_1 = s_1 = s_2 = 0$. The maximum value is $Z = 20$. Note that this value is the same as that value of Z corresponding to tableau II. In degenerate problems it is possible to arrive at the same value of Z at various stages of the simplex process. In Exercise 9.4 you are asked to solve this example problem by using s_2 as the departing variable in the initial tableau.

Because of its mechanical nature, the simplex procedure is readily adaptable to computers to solve linear programming problems involving many variables and constraints.

EXERCISE 9.4   *Use the simplex method to solve the following problems.*

1. Maximize
$$Z = x_1 + 2x_2$$
subject to
$$2x_1 + x_2 \le 8,$$
$$2x_1 + 3x_2 \le 12,$$
$$x_1, x_2 \ge 0.$$

2. Maximize
$$Z = 2x_1 + x_2$$
subject to
$$-x_1 + x_2 \le 4,$$
$$x_1 + x_2 \le 6,$$
$$x_1, x_2 \ge 0.$$

3. Maximize
$$Z = -x_1 + 3x_2$$
subject to
$$x_1 + x_2 \le 6,$$
$$-x_1 + x_2 \le 4,$$
$$x_1, x_2 \ge 0.$$

4. Maximize
$$Z = 3x_1 + 8x_2$$
subject to
$$x_1 + 2x_2 \le 8,$$
$$x_1 + 6x_2 \le 12,$$
$$x_1, x_2 \ge 0$$

5. Maximize
$$Z = 8x_1 + 2x_2$$
subject to
$$x_1 - x_2 \le 1,$$
$$x_1 + 2x_2 \le 8,$$
$$x_1 + x_2 \le 5,$$
$$x_1, x_2 \ge 0.$$

6. Maximize
$$Z = 2x_1 - 6x_2$$
subject to
$$x_1 - x_2 \le 4,$$
$$-x_1 + x_2 \le 4,$$
$$x_1 + x_2 \le 6,$$
$$x_1, x_2 \ge 0.$$

7. Solve the problem in Example 2 by choosing s_2 as the departing variable in tableau I.

8. Maximize
$$Z = 2x_1 - x_2 + x_3$$
subject to
$$2x_1 + x_2 - x_3 \le 4,$$
$$x_1 + x_2 + x_3 \le 2,$$
$$x_1, x_2, x_3 \ge 0.$$

9. Maximize
$$Z = 2x_1 + x_2 - x_3$$
subject to
$$x_1 + x_2 \le 1,$$
$$x_1 - 2x_2 - x_3 \ge -2,$$
$$x_1, x_2, x_3 \ge 0.$$

10. Maximize
$$Z = -x_1 + 2x_2$$
subject to
$$x_1 + x_2 \le 1,$$
$$x_1 - x_2 \le 1,$$
$$x_1 - x_2 \ge -2,$$
$$x_1 \le 2,$$
$$x_1, x_2 \ge 0.$$

11. Maximize
$$Z = x_1 + x_2$$
subject to
$$x_1 - x_2 \le 4,$$
$$-x_1 + x_2 \le 4,$$
$$8x_1 + 5x_2 \le 40,$$
$$2x_1 + x_2 \le 6,$$
$$x_1, x_2 \ge 0.$$

12. Maximize
$$W = 2x_1 + x_2 - 2x_3$$
subject to
$$-2x_1 + x_2 + x_3 \ge -2,$$
$$x_1 - x_2 + x_3 \le 4,$$
$$x_1 + x_2 + 2x_3 \le 6,$$
$$x_1, x_2, x_3 \ge 0.$$

13. Maximize
$$W = x_1 - 12x_2 + 4x_3$$
subject to
$$4x_1 + 3x_2 - x_3 \le 1,$$
$$x_1 + x_2 - x_3 \ge -2,$$
$$-x_1 + x_2 + x_3 \ge -1,$$
$$x_1, x_2, x_3 \ge 0.$$

14. Maximize
$$W = 4x_1 + 0x_2 - x_3$$
subject to
$$x_1 + x_2 + x_3 \le 6,$$
$$x_1 - x_2 + x_3 \le 10,$$
$$x_1 - x_2 - x_3 \le 4,$$
$$x_1, x_2, x_3 \ge 0.$$

15. Maximize
$$Z = 60x_1 + 0x_2 + 90x_3 + 0x_4$$
subject to
$$x_1 - 2x_2 \le 2,$$
$$x_1 + x_2 \le 5,$$
$$x_3 + x_4 \le 4,$$
$$x_3 - 2x_4 \le 7,$$
$$x_1, x_2, x_3, x_4 \ge 0.$$

16. Maximize
$$Z = 4x_1 + 10x_2 - 6x_3 - x_4$$
subject to
$$x_1 + x_3 - x_4 \le 1,$$
$$x_1 - x_2 + x_4 \le 2,$$
$$x_1 + x_2 - x_3 + x_4 \le 4,$$
$$x_1, x_2, x_3, x_4 \ge 0.$$

17. A freight company handles shipments by two corporations, A and B, that are located in the same city. Corporation A ships boxes that each weigh 3 lb and have a volume of 2 ft³; B ships 1 ft³ boxes that weigh 5 lb each. Both A and B ship to the same destination. The transporation cost for each box from A is $0.75, and from B it is $0.50. The freight company has a truck with 2400 ft³ of cargo space and a maximum capacity of 9200 lb. In one haul, how many boxes from each corporation should be transported by this truck so that the freight company receives maximum revenue? What is the maximum revenue?

18. A company manufactures three products: X, Y, and Z. Each product requires machine time and finishing time as given in the table below. The numbers of hours of machine time and finishing time available per month are 900 and 5000, respectively. The unit profit on X, Y, and Z is $3, $4, and $6, respectively. What is the maximum profit per month that can be obtained?

	MACHINE TIME	FINISHING TIME
X	1 hr	4 hr
Y	2 hr	4 hr
Z	3 hr	8 hr

19. A company manufactures three types of patio furniture: chairs, rockers, and chaise lounges. Each requires

wood, plastic, and aluminum as given in the table below. The company has available 400 units of wood, 500 units of plastic, and 1450 units of aluminum. Each chair, rocker, and chaise lounge sells at $7, $8, and $12, respectively. Assuming that all furniture can be sold, determine a production order so that total revenue will be maximum. What is the maximum revenue?

	WOOD	PLASTIC	ALUMINUM
Chair	1 unit	1 unit	2 units
Rocker	1 unit	1 unit	3 units
Chaise lounge	1 unit	2 units	5 units

9.5 DEGENERACY, UNBOUNDED SOLUTIONS, MULTIPLE OPTIMUM SOLUTIONS*

In the preceding section we stated that a basic feasible solution is **degenerate** if along with one of the nonbasic variables one of the basic variables is 0. Suppose x_1, x_2, x_3, and x_4 are the variables in a degenerate B.F.S., where x_1 and x_2 are basic with $x_1 = 0$, and x_3 and x_4 are nonbasic, and x_3 is the entering variable. The corresponding simplex tableau has the form

$$\begin{array}{c} \text{departing} \\ \text{variable} \end{array} \rightarrow \begin{array}{c} x_1 \\ x_2 \\ \\ Z \end{array} \begin{bmatrix} \begin{array}{cccc|cc} x_1 & x_2 & x_3 & x_4 & Z & b \\ 1 & 0 & \boxed{a_{13}} & a_{14} & 0 & 0 \\ 0 & 1 & a_{23} & a_{24} & 0 & a \\ \hline 0 & 0 & d_1 & d_2 & 1 & d_3 \end{array} \end{bmatrix} 0 \div a_{13} = 0.$$

indicators

entering variable

Thus the B.F.S. is

$$x_1 = 0, \qquad x_2 = a, \qquad x_3 = 0, \qquad x_4 = 0.$$

Suppose $a_{13} > 0$. Then the smaller quotient is 0 and we can choose a_{13} as the pivot entry. Thus x_1 is the departing variable. Elementary row operations give the following tableau, where the question marks represent numbers to be determined.

* This section may be omitted.

$$\begin{array}{c c} & \begin{array}{cccccc} x_1 & x_2 & x_3 & x_4 & Z & b \end{array} \\ \begin{array}{c} x_3 \\ x_2 \\ \\ Z \end{array} & \left[\begin{array}{cccccc} ? & 0 & 1 & ? & 0 & 0 \\ ? & 1 & 0 & ? & 0 & a \\ \hline ? & 0 & 0 & ? & 1 & d_3 \end{array} \right] \end{array}$$

For the B.F. S. corresponding to this tableau, x_3 and x_2 are basic variables, and x_1 and x_4 are nonbasic. The B.F.S. is

$$x_3 = 0, \qquad x_2 = a, \qquad x_1 = 0, \qquad x_4 = 0,$$

which is the same B.F.S. as before. Actually, these are usually considered different B.F.S.'s, where the only distinction is that x_1 is basic in the first B.F.S., while in the second it is nonbasic. The value of Z for both B.F.S.'s is the same, d_3. Thus no "improvement" in Z is obtained.

In a degenerate situation, some problems may develop in the simplex procedure. It is possible to obtain a sequence of tableaus that correspond to B.F.S.'s which give the same Z value. Moreover, we may eventually return to the first tableau in the sequence. In Fig. 9.20 we arrive at B.F.S.$_1$, proceed to B.F.S.$_2$, then B.F.S.$_3$, and finally return to B.F.S.$_1$. This is called *cycling*. When cycling occurs, it is possible that we may never obtain the optimum value of Z. This phenomenon rarely is encountered in practical linear programming problems. However, there are techniques (which will not be considered in this text) for resolving such difficulties.

A degenerate B.F.S. will occur when two quotients in a simplex tableau tie for being the smallest. For example, consider the following (partial) tableau:

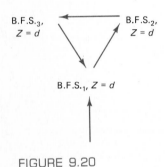

FIGURE 9.20

$$\begin{array}{c c} & \begin{array}{cc} x_3 & \qquad\qquad \textit{Quotients} \end{array} \\ \begin{array}{c} x_1 \\ x_2 \end{array} & \left[\begin{array}{cc} \boxed{q_1} & \quad p_1 \\ q_2 & \quad p_2 \end{array} \right] \begin{array}{c} p_1/q_1. \\ p_2/q_2. \end{array} \end{array}$$

Here x_1 and x_2 are basic variables. Suppose x_3 is nonbasic and entering, and p_1/q_1 and p_2/q_2 are equal and also the smallest quotients involved. Choosing q_1 as the pivot entry, by elementary row operations we obtain

$$\begin{array}{c c} & \begin{array}{c} x_3 \end{array} \\ \begin{array}{c} x_3 \\ \\ x_2 \end{array} & \left[\begin{array}{cc} 1 & \quad p_1/q_1 \\ \\ 0 & \quad p_2 - q_2 \dfrac{p_1}{q_1} \end{array} \right] \end{array}$$

Since $p_1/q_1 = p_2/q_2$, then $p_2 - q_2(p_1/q_1) = 0$. Thus the B.F.S. corresponding to this tableau has $x_2 = 0$, which gives a *degenerate* B.F.S. Although such a B.F.S. may produce cycling, we shall not encounter such situations in this book.

We now turn our attention to "unbounded problems." In Sec. 9.2 you saw that a linear programming problem may have no maximum value because the feasible region is such that the objective function may become arbitrarily large therein. In this case the problem is said to have an **unbounded solution.** This is a way of saying specifically that no optimum solution exists. Such a situation occurs when no quotients are possible in a simplex tableau for an entering variable. For example, consider the following tableau:

$$
\begin{array}{c}
\quad\ \ \begin{matrix} x_1 & x_2 & x_3 & x_4 & Z & b \end{matrix} \\
\begin{matrix} x_1 \\ x_3 \\ \\ Z \end{matrix}
\left[
\begin{array}{ccccc|c}
1 & -3 & 0 & 2 & 0 & 5 \\
0 & 0 & 1 & 4 & 0 & 1 \\
\hline
0 & -5 & 0 & -2 & 1 & 10
\end{array}
\right]
\begin{matrix} \text{no quotient.} \\ \text{no quotient.} \\ \\ \\ \end{matrix}
\end{array}
$$

$$\underbrace{\qquad\qquad\qquad}$$
↑ indicators
entering
variable

Here x_2 is the entering variable and for each one-unit increase in x_2, Z increases by 5. Since there are no positive entries in the first two rows of the x_2 column, no quotients exist. From rows 1 and 2 we get

$$x_1 = 5 + 3x_2 - 2x_4$$

and $x_3 = 1 - 4x_4.$

In the B.F.S. for this tableau, $x_4 = 0$. Thus $x_1 = 5 + 3x_2$ and $x_3 = 1$. Since $x_1 \geq 0$, then $x_2 \geq -\frac{5}{3}$. Thus there is no upper bound on x_2. Hence Z can be arbitrarily large and we have an unbounded solution. In general:

If no quotients exist in a simplex tableau, then the linear programming problem has an unbounded solution.

EXAMPLE 1   *Maximize $Z = x_1 + 4x_2 - x_3$ subject to*

$$-5x_1 + 6x_2 - 2x_3 \leq 30,$$

$$-x_1 + 3x_2 + 6x_3 \leq 12,$$

and $x_1, x_2, x_3 \geq 0.$

The initial simplex tableau is

$$
\begin{array}{c}
\qquad\qquad \begin{matrix} x_1 & x_2 & x_3 & s_1 & s_2 & Z & b \end{matrix} \\
\begin{matrix} s_1 \\ s_2 \\ \\ Z \end{matrix}
\left[
\begin{array}{cccccc|c}
-5 & 6 & -2 & 1 & 0 & 0 & 30 \\
-1 & ③ & 6 & 0 & 1 & 0 & 12 \\
\hline
-1 & -4 & 1 & 0 & 0 & 1 & 0
\end{array}
\right]
\begin{matrix} 30 \div 6 = 5. \\ 12 \div 3 = 4. \\ \\ \\ \end{matrix}
\end{array}
$$

departing → (at s_2 row)
variable

Quotients (above right)

$$\underbrace{\qquad\qquad\qquad}$$
↑ indicators
entering
variable

The second tableau is

$$
\begin{array}{c}
\quad\quad x_1 \quad x_2 \quad x_3 \quad s_1 \quad s_2 \quad Z \quad b \\
\begin{array}{c} s_1 \\ x_2 \\ \\ Z \end{array}
\left[
\begin{array}{cccccc|c}
-3 & 0 & -14 & 1 & -2 & 0 & 6 \\
-\frac{1}{3} & 1 & 2 & 0 & \frac{1}{3} & 0 & 4 \\
\hline
-\frac{7}{3} & 0 & 9 & 0 & \frac{4}{3} & 1 & 16
\end{array}
\right]
\begin{array}{l} \text{no quotient.} \\ \text{no quotient.} \end{array}
\end{array}
$$

$$\underset{\substack{\uparrow \\ \text{entering variable}}}{\text{indicators}}$$

Here the entering variable is x_1. Since the entries in the first two rows of the x_1-column are negative, no quotients exist. Hence the problem has an unbounded solution.

We conclude this section with a discussion of "multiple optimum solutions." Suppose that

$$x_1 = a_1, \quad x_2 = a_2, \quad \ldots, \quad x_n = a_n$$

$$\text{and} \quad x_1 = b_1, \quad x_2 = b_2, \quad \ldots, \quad x_n = b_n$$

are two *different* B.F.S.'s for which a linear programming problem is optimum. By "different B.F.S.'s" we mean that $a_i \neq b_i$ for some i, where $1 \le i \le n$. It can be shown that the values

$$x_1 = (1 - t)a_1 + tb_1,$$

$$x_2 = (1 - t)a_2 + tb_2,$$

$$\vdots \tag{1}$$

$$x_n = (1 - t)a_n + tb_n,$$

$$\text{for any } t \text{ where } 0 \le t \le 1,$$

also give an optimum solution (although it may not necessarily be a B.F.S.). Thus there are *multiple (optimum) solutions* to the problem.

We can determine the possibility of multiple optimum solutions from a simplex tableau that gives an optimum solution, such as the (partial) tableau below:

$$
\begin{array}{c}
\quad\quad x_1 \quad x_2 \quad x_3 \quad x_4 \quad Z \\
\begin{array}{c} x_1 \\ x_2 \\ \\ Z \end{array}
\left[
\begin{array}{ccccc|c}
& & & & & p_1 \\
& & & & & q_1 \\
\hline
0 & 0 & a & 0 & 1 & r
\end{array}
\right].
\end{array}
$$

$$\text{indicators}$$

Here a must be nonnegative. The corresponding B.F.S. is

$$x_1 = p_1, \quad x_2 = q_1, \quad x_3 = 0, \quad x_4 = 0,$$

and the maximum value of Z is r. If x_4 were to become basic, the indicator 0 in the x_4-column means that for each one-unit increase in x_4, Z does not change. Thus we can find a B.F.S. in which x_4 is basic and the corresponding Z-value is the same as before. This is done by treating x_4 as an entering variable in the tableau above. If, for instance, x_1 is the departing variable, the new B.F.S. has the form

$$x_1 = 0, \qquad x_2 = q_2, \qquad x_3 = 0, \qquad x_4 = p_2.$$

If this B.F.S. is different from the previous one, multiple solutions exist. In fact, from Eqs. (1) an optimum solution is given by any values of x_1, x_2, x_3, and x_4 such that

$$x_1 = (1 - t)p_1 + t \cdot 0 = (1 - t)p_1,$$

$$x_2 = (1 - t)q_1 + tq_2,$$

$$x_3 = (1 - t) \cdot 0 + t \cdot 0 = 0,$$

$$x_4 = (1 - t) \cdot 0 + tp_2 = tp_2,$$

$$\text{where} \quad 0 \le t \le 1.$$

Note that when $t = 0$ we get the first optimum B.F.S.; when $t = 1$ we get the second. Of course, it may be possible to repeat the procedure by using the tableau corresponding to the last B.F.S. and obtain more optimum solutions by using Eqs. (1).

In general:

> In a tableau that gives an optimum solution, a zero indicator for a nonbasic variable suggests the possibility of multiple optimum solutions.

EXAMPLE 2   *Maximize $Z = -x_1 + 4x_2 + 6x_3$ subject to*

$$x_1 + 2x_2 + 3x_3 \le 6,$$

$$-2x_1 - 5x_2 + x_3 \le 10,$$

and $x_1, x_2, x_3 \ge 0$.

Our initial simplex tableau is

		x_1	x_2	x_3	s_1	s_2	Z	b	Quotients
departing →	s_1	1	2	③	1	0	0	6	$6 \div 3 = 2.$
variable	s_2	-2	-5	1	0	1	0	10	$10 \div 1 = 10.$
	Z	1	-4	-6	0	0	1	0	

↗ indicators
entering variable

Since there is a negative indicator, we continue.

$$
\begin{array}{c}
\begin{array}{cccccccc}
& x_1 & x_2 & x_3 & s_1 & s_2 & Z & b \\
\end{array} \\
\begin{array}{c}
\text{departing} \rightarrow x_3 \\
\text{variable} \quad s_2 \\
\\
Z
\end{array}
\left[
\begin{array}{ccccccc|c}
\frac{1}{3} & \tfrac{2}{3} & 1 & \frac{1}{3} & 0 & 0 & 2 \\
-\frac{7}{3} & -\frac{17}{3} & 0 & -\frac{1}{3} & 1 & 0 & 8 \\
\hline
3 & 0 & 0 & 2 & 0 & 1 & 12
\end{array}
\right]
\end{array}
$$

$$
\begin{array}{l}
\text{Quotients} \\
2 \div \tfrac{2}{3} = 3. \\
\text{no quotient.}
\end{array}
$$

indicators
entering variable

All indicators are nonnegative and hence an optimum solution occurs for the B.F.S.

$$
x_3 = 2, \qquad s_2 = 8, \qquad x_1 = 0, \qquad x_2 = 0, \qquad s_1 = 0,
$$

and the maximum value of Z is 12. However, since x_2 is a nonbasic variable and its indicator is 0, we shall check for multiple solutions. Treating x_2 as an entering variable, we obtain the following tableau:

$$
\begin{array}{c}
\begin{array}{cccccccc}
& x_1 & x_2 & x_3 & s_1 & s_2 & Z & b \\
\end{array} \\
\begin{array}{c}
x_2 \\
s_2 \\
\\
Z
\end{array}
\left[
\begin{array}{ccccccc|c}
\frac{1}{2} & 1 & \frac{3}{2} & \frac{1}{2} & 0 & 0 & 3 \\
\frac{1}{2} & 0 & \frac{17}{2} & \frac{5}{2} & 1 & 0 & 25 \\
\hline
3 & 0 & 0 & 2 & 0 & 1 & 12
\end{array}
\right]
\end{array}
$$

The B.F.S. here is

$$
x_2 = 3, \qquad s_2 = 25, \qquad x_1 = 0, \qquad x_3 = 0, \qquad s_1 = 0
$$

(for which $Z = 12$, as before) and is different from the previous one. Thus multiple solutions exist. Since we are concerned only with values of the structural variables, we have an optimum solution

$$
x_1 = (1 - t) \cdot 0 + t \cdot 0 = 0,
$$

$$
x_2 = (1 - t) \cdot 0 + t \cdot 3 = 3t,
$$

$$
x_3 = (1 - t) \cdot 2 + t \cdot 0 = 2(1 - t)
$$

for each value of t where $0 \le t \le 1$. (For example, if $t = \frac{1}{2}$, then $x_1 = 0$, $x_2 = \frac{3}{2}$, and $x_3 = 1$ is an optimum solution.)

In the last B.F.S., x_3 is nonbasic and its indicator is 0. However, if we repeated the process for determining other optimum solutions, we would return to the second tableau. Thus our procedure gives no other optimum solutions.

EXERCISE 9.5

In each of Problems 1 and 2, does the linear programming problem associated with the given tableau have a degeneracy? If so, why?

1.
$$
\begin{array}{c}
\begin{array}{cccccc}
& x_1 & x_2 & s_1 & s_2 & Z \\
\end{array} \\
\begin{array}{c}
x_1 \\
s_2 \\
\\
Z
\end{array}
\left[
\begin{array}{ccccc|c}
1 & 2 & 4 & 0 & 0 & 6 \\
0 & 1 & 1 & 1 & 0 & 3 \\
\hline
0 & -3 & -2 & 0 & 1 & 10
\end{array}
\right].
\end{array}
$$

indicators

2.
$$
\begin{array}{c}
\begin{array}{ccccccc}
& x_1 & x_2 & x_3 & s_1 & s_2 & Z \\
\end{array} \\
\begin{array}{c}
s_1 \\
x_2 \\
\\
Z
\end{array}
\left[
\begin{array}{cccccc|c}
2 & 0 & 2 & 1 & 1 & 0 & 4 \\
3 & 1 & 1 & 0 & 1 & 0 & 0 \\
\hline
-5 & 0 & 1 & 0 & -3 & 1 & 2
\end{array}
\right].
\end{array}
$$

indicators

In Problems 3–11, use the simplex method.

3. Maximize
$$Z = 2x_1 + 7x_2$$
subject to
$$4x_1 - 3x_2 \le 4,$$
$$3x_1 - x_2 \le 6,$$
$$5x_1 \qquad \le 8,$$
$$x_1, x_2 \ge 0.$$

4. Maximize
$$Z = x_1 + x_2$$
subject to
$$x_1 - x_2 \le 4,$$
$$-x_1 + x_2 \le 4,$$
$$8x_1 + 5x_2 \le 40,$$
$$x_1 + x_2 \le 6,$$
$$x_1, x_2 \ge 0.$$

5. Maximize
$$Z = 3x_1 - 3x_2$$
subject to
$$x_1 - x_2 \le 4,$$
$$-x_1 + x_2 \le 4,$$
$$x_1 + x_2 \le 6,$$
$$x_1, x_2 \ge 0.$$

6. Maximize
$$Z = 4x_1 + x_2 + 2x_3$$
subject to
$$x_1 - x_2 + 4x_3 \le 6,$$
$$x_1 - x_2 - x_3 \ge -4,$$
$$x_1 - 6x_2 + x_3 \le 8,$$
$$x_1, x_2, x_3 \ge 0.$$

7. Maximize
$$Z = 5x_1 + 6x_2 + x_3$$
subject to
$$9x_1 + 3x_2 - 2x_3 \le 5,$$
$$4x_1 + 2x_2 - x_3 \le 2,$$
$$x_1 - 4x_2 + x_3 \le 3,$$
$$x_1, x_2, x_3 \ge 0.$$

8. Maximize
$$Z = 2x_1 + x_2 - 4x_3$$
subject to
$$6x_1 + 3x_2 - 3x_3 \le 10,$$
$$x_1 - x_2 + x_3 \le 1,$$
$$2x_1 - x_2 + 2x_3 \le 12,$$
$$x_1, x_2, x_3 \ge 0.$$

9. Maximize
$$Z = 6x_1 + 2x_2 + x_3$$
subject to
$$2x_1 + x_2 + x_3 \le 7,$$
$$-4x_1 - x_2 \qquad \ge -6,$$
$$x_1, x_2, x_3 \ge 0.$$

10. Maximize
$$P = 4x_1 + 3x_2 + 2x_3 + x_4$$
subject to
$$x_1 - x_2 \qquad\qquad \le 5,$$
$$x_2 - x_3 \qquad \le 2,$$
$$x_2 - 2x_3 + x_4 \le 4,$$
$$x_1, x_2, x_3, x_4 \ge 0.$$

11. A company manufactures three types of patio furniture: chairs, rockers, and chaise lounges. Each requires wood, plastic, and aluminum as given in the table below. The company has available 400 units of wood, 600 units of plastic, and 1500 units of aluminum. Each chair, rocker, and chaise lounge sells at $6, $8, and $12, respectively. Assuming that all furniture can be sold, what is the maximum total revenue that can be obtained? Determine the possible production orders that will generate this revenue.

	WOOD	PLASTIC	ALUMINUM
Chair	1 unit	1 unit	2 units
Rocker	1 unit	1 unit	3 units
Chaise lounge	1 unit	2 units	5 units

9.6 ARTIFICIAL VARIABLES

To initiate the simplex method, a basic feasible solution is required. For a standard linear programming problem, we begin with the B.F.S. in which all structural variables are zero. However, for a maximization problem that is not of standard form, such a B.F.S. may not exist. In this section you will see how the simplex method is used in such situations.

Let us consider the following problem:

$$\text{maximize } Z = x_1 + 2x_2$$

subject to

$$x_1 + x_2 \leq 9, \tag{1}$$

$$x_1 - x_2 \geq 1, \tag{2}$$

and $x_1, x_2 \geq 0$. Since constraint (2) can not be written as $a_1 x_1 + a_2 x_2 \leq b$, where b is nonnegative, this problem cannot be put into standard form. Note that $(0, 0)$ is not a feasible point. To solve this problem, we begin by writing constraints (1) and (2) as equations. Constraint (1) becomes

$$x + x_2 + s_1 = 9, \tag{3}$$

where s_1 is a slack variable and $s_1 \geq 0$. For constraint (2), $x_1 - x_2$ will equal 1 if we *subtract* a nonnegative slack variable s_2 from $x_1 - x_2$. That is, by subtracting s_2 we are making up for the "surplus" on the left side of (2) so that we have equality. Thus

$$x_1 - x_2 - s_2 = 1, \tag{4}$$

where $s_2 \geq 0$. We can now restate the problem:

$$\text{maximize } Z = x_1 + 2x_2 \tag{5}$$

subject to

$$x_1 + x_2 + s_1 = 9, \tag{6}$$

$$x_1 - x_2 - s_2 = 1, \tag{7}$$

and $x_1, x_2, s_1, s_2 \geq 0$.

Since $(0, 0)$ is not in the feasible region, we do not have a B.F.S. in which $x_1 = x_2 = 0$. In fact, if $x_1 = 0$ and $x_2 = 0$ are substituted into Eq. (7), then $0 - 0 - s_2 = 1$, which gives $s_2 = -1$. But this contradicts the condition that $s_2 \geq 0$.

To get the simplex method started, we need an initial B.F.S. Although none is obvious, there is an ingenious method to arrive at one *artificially*. It requires that we consider a related linear programming problem called the *artificial problem*. First, a new equation is formed by adding a nonnegative variable t to the left side of the equation in which the coefficient of the slack variable is -1. The variable t is called an **artificial variable.** In our case, we replace Eq. (7) by $x_1 - x_2 - s_2 + t = 1$. Thus Eqs. (6) and (7) become

$$x_1 + x_2 + s_1 = 9, \tag{8}$$

$$x_1 - x_2 - s_2 + t = 1, \tag{9}$$

where $x_1, x_2, s_1, s_2, t \geq 0$.

An obvious solution to Eqs. (8) and (9) is found by setting x_1, x_2, and s_2 equal to 0. This gives

$$x_1 = x_2 = s_2 = 0, \qquad s_1 = 9, \qquad t = 1.$$

Note that these values do not satisfy Eqs. (6) and (7). However, it is clear that any solution of Eqs. (8) and (9) for which $t = 0$ will give a solution to Eqs. (6) and (7), and conversely.

We can eventually force t to be 0 if we alter the original objective function. We define the **artificial objective function** to be

$$W = Z - Mt = x_1 + 2x_2 - Mt, \tag{10}$$

where the constant M is a large positive number. We shall not worry about the particular value of M and shall proceed to maximize W by the simplex method. Since there are $m = 2$ constraints (excluding the nonnegativity conditions) and $n = 5$ variables in Eqs. (8) and (9), any B.F.S. must have at least $n - m = 3$ variables equal to zero. We start with the following B.F.S.:

$$x_1 = x_2 = s_2 = 0, \qquad s_1 = 9, \qquad t = 1. \tag{11}$$

In this initial B.F.S., the nonbasic variables are the structural variables and the slack variable with coefficient -1 in Eqs. (8) and (9). The corresponding value of W is $W = x_1 + 2x_2 - Mt = -M$, which is "extremely" negative. A significant improvement in W will occur if we can find another B.F.S. for which $t = 0$. Since the simplex method seeks better values of W at each stage, we shall apply it until we reach such a B.F.S., if possible. That solution will be an initial B.F.S. for the original problem.

To apply the simplex method to the artificial problem, we first write Eq. (10) as

$$-x_1 - 2x_2 + Mt + W = 0. \tag{12}$$

The augmented coefficient matrix of Eqs. (8), (9), and (12) is

$$\begin{array}{c} \\ s_1 \\ t \\ \\ \end{array} \begin{array}{cccccc} x_1 & x_2 & s_1 & s_2 & t & W \\ \left[\begin{array}{cccccc|c} 1 & 1 & 1 & 0 & 0 & 0 & 9 \\ 1 & -1 & 0 & -1 & 1 & 0 & 1 \\ \hline -1 & -2 & 0 & 0 & M & 1 & 0 \end{array} \right]. \end{array} \tag{13}$$

An initial B.F.S. is given by (11). Notice that from row 1, when $x_1 = x_2 = s_2 = 0$, we can directly read the value of s_1, namely $s_1 = 9$. From row 2 we get $t = 1$. From row 3, $MT + W = 0$. Since $t = 1$, then $W = -M$. But in a simplex tableau we want the value of W to appear in the last row and last column. This is not so in (13), and thus we modify that matrix.

To do this we transform (13) into an equivalent matrix whose last row has the form

$$\begin{array}{cccccc} x_1 & x_2 & s_1 & s_2 & t & W \\ ? & ? & 0 & ? & 0 & 1 \end{array} \quad ?$$

That is, the M in the t-column is replaced by 0. As a result, if $x_1 = x_2 = s_2 = 0$, then W equals the last entry. Proceeding to obtain such a matrix, we have

$$
\begin{array}{ccccccc}
x_1 & x_2 & s_1 & s_2 & t & W & \\
\end{array}
$$

$$
\left[\begin{array}{cccccc|c}
1 & 1 & 1 & 0 & 0 & 0 & 9 \\
1 & -1 & 0 & -1 & 1 & 0 & 1 \\
\hline
-1 & -2 & 0 & 0 & M & 1 & 0
\end{array}\right]
$$

$$
\begin{array}{ccccccc}
x_1 & x_2 & s_1 & s_2 & t & W & \\
\end{array}
$$

$$
\sim \left[\begin{array}{cccccc|c}
1 & 1 & 1 & 0 & 0 & 0 & 9 \\
1 & -1 & 0 & -1 & 1 & 0 & 1 \\
\hline
-1-M & -2+M & 0 & M & 0 & 1 & -M
\end{array}\right]
$$

(by adding $-M$ times row 2 to row 3).

Let us now check things out. If $x_1 = 0$, $x_2 = 0$, and $s_2 = 0$, then from row 1 we get $s_1 = 9$; from row 2, $t = 1$; and from row 3, $W = -M$. Thus we now have initial simplex tableau I.

SIMPLEX TABLEAU I

$$
\begin{array}{c}
\text{departing} \\
\text{variable}
\end{array} \to
\begin{array}{c}
\\ s_1 \\ t \\ \\ W
\end{array}
\begin{array}{ccccccc}
x_1 & x_2 & s_1 & s_2 & t & W & \\
\end{array}
\left[\begin{array}{cccccc|c}
1 & 1 & 1 & 0 & 0 & 0 & 9 \\
① & -1 & 0 & -1 & 1 & 0 & 1 \\
\hline
-1-M & -2+M & 0 & M & 0 & 1 & -M
\end{array}\right]
\begin{array}{l}
\textit{Quotients} \\
9 \div 1 = 9. \\
1 \div 1 = 1.
\end{array}
$$

↑   indicators

entering
variable

From this point we can use the procedures of Sec. 9.4. Since M is a large positive number, the most negative indicator is $-1 - M$. Thus the entering variable is x_1. From the quotients we choose t as the departing variable. The pivot entry is circled. Using elementary row operations to get 1 in the pivot position and 0's elsewhere in that column, we get tableau II.

SIMPLEX TABLEAU II

$$
\begin{array}{c}
\text{departing} \to \\
\text{variable}
\end{array}
\begin{array}{c}
\\ s_1 \\ x_1 \\ \\ W
\end{array}
\begin{array}{ccccccc}
x_1 & x_2 & s_1 & s_2 & t & W & \\
\end{array}
\left[\begin{array}{cccccc|c}
0 & ② & 1 & 1 & -1 & 0 & 8 \\
1 & -1 & 0 & -1 & 1 & 0 & 1 \\
\hline
0 & -3 & 0 & -1 & M+1 & 1 & 1
\end{array}\right]
\begin{array}{l}
\textit{Quotients} \\
8 \div 2 = 4. \\
\text{(no quotient, since} \\
-1 \text{ is not positive).}
\end{array}
$$

↑ indicators

entering
variable

From tableau II, we have the following B.F.S.:

$$
s_1 = 8, \qquad x_1 = 1, \qquad x_2 = 0, \qquad s_2 = 0, \qquad t = 0.
$$

Since $t = 0$, the values $s_1 = 8$, $x_1 = 1$, $x_2 = 0$, and $s_2 = 0$ form an initial B.F.S. for the *original* problem! The artificial variable has served its purpose. For succeeding tableaus we shall delete the t-column (since we want to solve the original problem) and change the W's to Z's (since $W = Z$ for $t = 0$). From tableau II, the entering variable is x_2, the departing variable is s_1, and the pivot entry is circled. Using elementary row operations (omitting the t-column), we get tableau III.

SIMPLEX TABLEAU III

$$
\begin{array}{c}
\begin{array}{cccccc}
x_1 & x_2 & s_1 & s_2 & Z & \\
\end{array} \\
\begin{array}{c}
x_2 \\
x_1 \\
\\
Z
\end{array}
\left[
\begin{array}{ccccc|c}
0 & 1 & \frac{1}{2} & \frac{1}{2} & 0 & 4 \\
1 & 0 & \frac{1}{2} & -\frac{1}{2} & 0 & 5 \\
\hline
0 & 0 & \frac{3}{2} & \frac{1}{2} & 1 & 13
\end{array}
\right]
\end{array}
$$

indicators

Since all the indicators are nonnegative, the maximum value of Z is 13. It occurs when $x_1 = 5$ and $x_2 = 4$.

It is worthwhile to review the steps we performed to solve our problem:

$$\text{maximize } Z = x_1 + 2x_2$$

subject to

$$x_1 + x_2 \le 9, \tag{14}$$

$$x_1 - x_2 \ge 1, \tag{15}$$

and $x_1 \ge 0$, $x_2 \ge 0$. We write (14) as

$$x_1 + x_2 + s_1 = 9. \tag{16}$$

Since (15) involves the symbol $\ge$ and the constant on the right side is nonnegative, we write (15) in a form having both a slack variable (with coefficient -1) and an artificial variable.

$$x_1 - x_2 - s_2 + t = 1. \tag{17}$$

The artificial objective equation to consider is $W = x_1 + 2x_2 - Mt$, or equivalently,

$$-x_1 - 2x_2 + Mt + W = 0. \tag{18}$$

The augmented coefficient matrix of the system formed by Eqs. (16)–(18) is

$$
\begin{array}{c}
\begin{array}{cccccc}
x_1 & x_2 & s_1 & s_2 & t & W \\
\end{array} \\
\left[
\begin{array}{cccccc|c}
1 & 1 & 1 & 0 & 0 & 0 & 9 \\
1 & -1 & 0 & -1 & 1 & 0 & 1 \\
\hline
-1 & -2 & 0 & 0 & M & 1 & 0
\end{array}
\right].
\end{array}
$$

Next we remove the M from the artificial variable column and replace it by 0 by using elementary row operations. The resulting simplex tableau I corresponds to the initial B.F.S. of the artificial problem in which the structural variables, x_1 and x_2, and the slack variable s_2 (the one associated with the constraint involving the symbol $\ge$) are each 0.

SIMPLEX TABLEAU I

$$
\begin{array}{c c}
& \begin{array}{c c c c c c c} x_1 & x_2 & s_1 & s_2 & t & W & \end{array} \\
\begin{array}{c} s_1 \\ t \\[4pt] W \end{array} &
\left[\begin{array}{c c c c c c | c}
1 & 1 & 1 & 0 & 0 & 0 & 9 \\
1 & -1 & 0 & -1 & 1 & 0 & 1 \\
\hline
-1-M & -2+M & 0 & M & 0 & 1 & -M
\end{array} \right].
\end{array}
$$

The basic variables s_1 and t on the left side of the tableau correspond to the nonstructural variables in Eqs. (16) and (17) that have positive coefficients. We now apply the simplex method until we obtain a B.F.S. in which the artificial variable t equals 0. Then we can delete the artificial variable column, change the W's to Z's, and continue the procedure until the maximum value of Z is obtained.

EXAMPLE 1   *Use the simplex method to maximize $Z = 2x_1 + x_2$ subject to*

$$x_1 + x_2 \le 12, \tag{19}$$

$$x_1 + 2x_2 \le 20, \tag{20}$$

$$-x_1 + x_2 \ge 2, \tag{21}$$

and $x_1 \ge 0$, $x_2 \ge 0$.

The equations for (19)–(21) will involve a total of three slack variables: s_1, s_2, and s_3. Since (21) contains the symbol $\ge$ and the constant on the right side is nonnegative, its equation will also involve an artificial variable t, and the coefficient of its slack variable s_3 will be -1.

$$x_1 + x_2 + s_1 \qquad\qquad = 12, \tag{22}$$

$$x_1 + 2x_2 \qquad + s_2 \qquad\qquad = 20, \tag{23}$$

$$-x_1 + x_2 \qquad\qquad - s_3 + t = 2. \tag{24}$$

We consider $W = Z - Mt = 2x_1 + x_2 - Mt$ as the artificial objective equation, or equivalently,

$$-2x_1 - x_2 + Mt + W = 0, \tag{25}$$

where M is a large positive number. Now we construct the augmented coefficient matrix of Eqs. (22)–(25).

$$
\begin{array}{c}
\begin{array}{c c c c c c c} x_1 & x_2 & s_1 & s_2 & s_3 & t & W \end{array} \\
\left[\begin{array}{c c c c c c c | c}
1 & 1 & 1 & 0 & 0 & 0 & 0 & 12 \\
1 & 2 & 0 & 1 & 0 & 0 & 0 & 20 \\
-1 & 1 & 0 & 0 & -1 & 1 & 0 & 2 \\
\hline
-2 & -1 & 0 & 0 & 0 & M & 1 & 0
\end{array} \right].
\end{array}
$$

To get simplex tableau I, we replace the M in the artificial variable column by zero by adding $-M$ times row 3 to row 4.

SIMPLEX TABLEAU I

$$
\begin{array}{c}
\\
\text{departing} \rightarrow \\
\text{variable}
\end{array}
\begin{array}{c}
s_1 \\
s_2 \\
t \\
\\
W
\end{array}
\left[
\begin{array}{ccccccc|c}
x_1 & x_2 & s_1 & s_2 & s_3 & t & W & \\
1 & 1 & 1 & 0 & 0 & 0 & 0 & 12 \\
1 & 2 & 0 & 1 & 0 & 0 & 0 & 20 \\
-1 & \textcircled{1} & 0 & 0 & -1 & 1 & 0 & 2 \\
\hline
-2+M & -1-M & 0 & 0 & M & 0 & 1 & -2M
\end{array}
\right]
\begin{array}{c}
Quotients \\
12 \div 1 = 12. \\
20 \div 2 = 10. \\
2 \div 1 = 2.
\end{array}
$$

↑ indicators
entering
variable

The variables s_1, s_2, and t on the left side of tableau I are the nonstructural variables with positive coefficients in Eqs. (22)–(24). Since M is a large positive number, $-1 - M$ is the most negative indicator. The entering variable is x_2, the departing variable is t, and the pivot entry is circled. Proceeding, we get tableau II.

SIMPLEX TABLEAU II

$$
\begin{array}{c}
\text{departing} \rightarrow \\
\text{variable}
\end{array}
\begin{array}{c}
s_1 \\
s_2 \\
x_2 \\
\\
W
\end{array}
\left[
\begin{array}{ccccccc|c}
x_1 & x_2 & s_1 & s_2 & s_3 & t & W & \\
\textcircled{2} & 0 & 1 & 0 & 1 & -1 & 0 & 10 \\
3 & 0 & 0 & 1 & 2 & -2 & 0 & 16 \\
-1 & 1 & 0 & 0 & -1 & 1 & 0 & 2 \\
\hline
-3 & 0 & 0 & 0 & -1 & 1+M & 1 & 2
\end{array}
\right]
\begin{array}{c}
Quotients \\
10 \div 2 = 5. \\
16 \div 3 = 5\frac{1}{3}.
\end{array}
$$

↑ indicators
entering
variable

The B.F.S. corresponding to tableau II has $t = 0$. Thus we shall delete the t-column and change W's to Z's in succeeding tableaus. Continuing, we obtain tableau III.

SIMPLEX TABLEAU III

$$
\begin{array}{c}
x_1 \\
s_2 \\
x_2 \\
\\
Z
\end{array}
\left[
\begin{array}{cccccc|c}
x_1 & x_2 & s_1 & s_2 & s_3 & Z & \\
1 & 0 & \frac{1}{2} & 0 & \frac{1}{2} & 0 & 5 \\
0 & 0 & -\frac{3}{2} & 1 & \frac{1}{2} & 0 & 1 \\
0 & 1 & \frac{1}{2} & 0 & -\frac{1}{2} & 0 & 7 \\
\hline
0 & 0 & \frac{3}{2} & 0 & \frac{1}{2} & 1 & 17
\end{array}
\right]
$$

indicators

All indicators are nonnegative. Thus the maximum value of Z is 17. It occurs when $x_1 = 5$ and $x_2 = 7$.

When an *equality* constraint of the form

$$a_1x_1 + a_2x_2 + \ldots + a_nx_n = b, \quad \text{where } b \geq 0,$$

occurs in a linear programming problem, artificial variables are used in the simplex method. To illustrate, consider the following problem:

$$\text{maximize } Z = x_1 + 3x_2 - 2x_3$$

subject to

$$x_1 + x_2 - x_3 = 6, \tag{26}$$

and x_1, x_2, $x_3 \geq 0$. Constraint (26) is already expressed as an equation, so no slack variable is necessary. Since $x_1 = x_2 = x_3 = 0$ is not a feasible solution, we do not have an obvious starting point for the simplex procedure. Thus we create an artificial problem by first adding an artificial variable t to the left side of Eq. (26):

$$x_1 + x_2 - x_3 + t = 6.$$

Here an obvious B.F.S. is $x_1 = x_2 = x_3 = 0$, $t = 6$. The artificial objective function is

$$W = Z - Mt = x_1 + 3x_2 - 2x_3 - Mt,$$

where M is a large positive number. The simplex procedure is applied to this artificial problem until we obtain a B.F.S. in which $t = 0$. This solution will give an initial B.F.S. for the original problem and we then proceed as before.

In general, the simplex method may be used to

$$\text{maximize } Z = c_1x_1 + c_2x_2 + \cdots + c_nx_n$$

subject to

$$\left. \begin{array}{l} a_{11}x_1 + a_{12}x_2 + \cdots + a_{1n}x_n \; \{\leq, \geq, =\} \; b_1, \\ a_{21}x_1 + a_{22}x_2 + \cdots + a_{2n}x_n \; \{\leq, \geq, =\} \; b_2, \\ \quad \vdots \qquad \vdots \qquad \qquad \vdots \qquad \qquad \vdots \\ a_{m1}x_1 + a_{m2}x_2 + \cdots + a_{mn}x_n \; \{\leq, \geq, =\} \; b_m, \end{array} \right\} \tag{27}$$

where x_1, x_2, . . . , x_n and b_1, b_2, . . . , b_m are nonnegative. The symbolism $\{\leq, \geq, =\}$ means that one of the relations "$\leq$," "$\geq$," or "$=$" exists for a constraint. If all constraints involve "$\leq$," the problem is of standard form and the simplex techniques of the previous sections apply. If any constraint involves "$\geq$" or "$=$," we begin with an artificial problem, which is obtained as follows.

Each constraint that contains "$\leq$" is written as an equation involving a slack variable s_i with coefficient $+1$:

$$a_{i1}x_1 + a_{i2}x_2 + \cdots + a_{in}x_n + s_i = b_i.$$

Each constraint that contains "$\geq$" is written as an equation involving a slack variable s_j with coefficient -1 and an artificial variable t_j:

$$a_{j1}x_1 + a_{j2}x_2 + \cdots + a_{jn}x_n - s_j + t_j = b_j.$$

A nonnegative artificial variable t_k is inserted into each equality constraint:

$$a_{k1}x_1 + a_{k2}x_2 + \cdots + a_{kn}x_n + t_k = b_k.$$

Should the artificial variables involved in this problem be, for example, t_1, t_2, t_3, then the artificial objective function is

$$W = Z - Mt_1 - Mt_2 - Mt_3,$$

where M is a large positive number. An initial B.F.S. occurs when $x_1 = x_2 = \ldots = x_n = 0$ and each slack variable with a coefficient of -1 equals 0. After obtaining an initial simplex tableau, we apply the simplex procedure until we arrive at a tableau that corresponds to a B.F.S. in which *all* artificial variables are 0. We then delete the artificial variable columns, change W's to Z's, and continue by using the procedures of the previous sections.

EXAMPLE 2   *Use the simplex method to maximize* $Z = x_1 + 3x_2 - 2x_3$ *subject to*

$$-x_1 - 2x_2 - 2x_3 = -6, \tag{28}$$

$$-x_1 - x_2 + x_3 \leq -2, \tag{29}$$

and $x_1, x_2, x_3 \geq 0.$

Constraints (28) and (29) will have the forms indicated in (27) [that is, b's positive] if we multiply both sides of each constraint by -1:

$$x_1 + 2x_2 + 2x_3 = 6, \tag{30}$$

$$x_1 + x_2 - x_3 \geq 2. \tag{31}$$

Since constraints (30) and (31) involve "$=$" and "$\geq$," two artificial variables, t_1 and t_2, will occur. The equations for the artificial problem are

$$x_1 + 2x_2 + 2x_3 \qquad + t_1 \qquad = 6 \tag{32}$$

$$\text{and} \qquad x_1 + x_2 - x_3 - s_2 \qquad + t_2 = 2. \tag{33}$$

Here the subscript 2 on s_2 reflects the order of the equations. The artificial objective function is $W = Z - Mt_1 - Mt_2$, or equivalently,

$$-x_1 - 3x_2 + 2x_3 + Mt_1 + Mt_2 + W = 0, \tag{34}$$

where M is a large positive number. The augmented coefficient matrix of Eqs. (32)–(34) is

$$\begin{array}{ccccccc}
x_1 & x_2 & x_3 & s_2 & t_1 & t_2 & W \\
\end{array}$$
$$\left[\begin{array}{ccccccc|c}
1 & 2 & 2 & 0 & 1 & 0 & 0 & 6 \\
1 & 1 & -1 & -1 & 0 & 1 & 0 & 2 \\
\hline
-1 & -3 & 2 & 0 & M & M & 1 & 0
\end{array} \right].$$

We now use elementary row operations to remove the M's from *all* the artificial variable columns. By adding $-M$ times row 1 to row 3 and adding $-M$ times row 2 to row 3, we get initial simplex tableau I.

SIMPLEX TABLEAU I

$$
\begin{array}{c c}
& \begin{array}{c c c c c c c}
\ \ x_1 & x_2 & x_3 & s_2 & t_1 & t_2 & W
\end{array} \\
\begin{array}{r}
\\
\text{departing} \rightarrow t_1 \\
\text{variable} \ \ \ \ t_2 \\
\\
W
\end{array}
&
\left[
\begin{array}{c c c c c c c | c}
1 & 2 & 2 & 0 & 1 & 0 & 0 & 6 \\
1 & ① & -1 & -1 & 0 & 1 & 0 & 2 \\
\hline
-1-2M & -3-3M & 2-M & M & 0 & 0 & 1 & -8M
\end{array}
\right]
\end{array}
$$

$\qquad\qquad\qquad$ *Quotients*
$\qquad\qquad\qquad$ $6 \div 2 = 3.$
$\qquad\qquad\qquad$ $2 \div 1 = 2.$

$\uparrow$ indicators
entering
variable

Proceeding, we obtain simplex tableaus II and III.

SIMPLEX TABLEAU II

$$
\begin{array}{c c}
& \begin{array}{c c c c c c c}
\ \ x_1 & x_2 & x_3 & s_2 & t_1 & t_2 & W
\end{array} \\
\begin{array}{r}
\text{departing} \rightarrow t_1 \\
\text{variable} \ \ \ \ x_2 \\
\\
W
\end{array}
&
\left[
\begin{array}{c c c c c c c | c}
-1 & 0 & ④ & 2 & 1 & -2 & 0 & 2 \\
1 & 1 & -1 & -1 & 0 & 1 & 0 & 2 \\
\hline
2+M & 0 & -1-4M & -3-2M & 0 & 3+3M & 1 & 6-2M
\end{array}
\right]
\end{array}
$$

$\qquad\qquad\qquad$ *Quotients*
$\qquad\qquad\qquad$ $2 \div 4 = \frac{1}{2}.$

$\diagup$ indicators
entering variable

SIMPLEX TABLEAU III

$$
\begin{array}{c c}
& \begin{array}{c c c c c c c}
\ \ x_1 & x_2 & x_3 & s_2 & t_1 & t_2 & W
\end{array} \\
\begin{array}{r}
\text{departing} \rightarrow x_3 \\
\text{variable} \ \ \ \ x_2 \\
\\
W
\end{array}
&
\left[
\begin{array}{c c c c c c c | c}
-\frac{1}{4} & 0 & 1 & ⑫ & \frac{1}{4} & -\frac{1}{2} & 0 & \frac{1}{2} \\
\frac{3}{4} & 1 & 0 & -\frac{1}{2} & \frac{1}{4} & \frac{1}{2} & 0 & \frac{5}{2} \\
\hline
\frac{7}{4} & 0 & 0 & -\frac{5}{2} & \frac{1}{4}+M & \frac{5}{2}+M & 1 & \frac{13}{2}
\end{array}
\right]
\end{array}
$$

$\qquad\qquad\qquad$ *Quotients*
$\qquad\qquad\qquad$ $\frac{1}{2} \div \frac{1}{2} = 1.$

indicators $\uparrow$
entering variable

For the B.F.S. corresponding to tableau III, the artificial variables t_1 and t_2 are both 0. We now can delete the t_1- and t_2- columns and change W's to Z's. Continuing, we obtain simplex tableau IV.

SIMPLEX TABLEAU IV

$$
\begin{array}{c c}
& \begin{array}{c c c c c}
\ \ x_1 & x_2 & x_3 & s_2 & Z
\end{array} \\
\begin{array}{r}
s_2 \\
x_2 \\
\\
Z
\end{array}
&
\left[
\begin{array}{c c c c c | c}
-\frac{1}{2} & 0 & 2 & 1 & 0 & 1 \\
\frac{1}{2} & 1 & 1 & 0 & 0 & 3 \\
\hline
\frac{1}{2} & 0 & 5 & 0 & 1 & 9
\end{array}
\right].
\end{array}
$$

indicators

Since all indicators are nonnegative, we have reached the final tableau. The maximum value of Z is 9 and it occurs when $x_1 = 0$, $x_2 = 3$, and $x_3 = 0$.

It is possible that the simplex procedure terminates and not all artificial variables are 0. It can be shown that in this situation *the feasible region of the original problem is empty* and hence there is *no optimum solution*. The following example will illustrate.

EXAMPLE 3   *Use the simplex method to maximize* $Z = 2x_1 + x_2$ *subject to*

$$-x_1 + x_2 \geq 2, \tag{35}$$

$$x_1 + x_2 \leq 1,$$

and $x_1, x_2 \geq 0$.

Since constraint (35) is of the form $a_{11}x_1 + a_{12}x_2 \geq b_1$ where $b_1 \geq 0$, an artificial variable will occur. The equations to consider are

$$-x_1 + x_2 - s_1 \qquad + t_1 = 2 \tag{36}$$

$$\text{and} \quad x_1 + x_2 \qquad + s_2 \qquad = 1, \tag{37}$$

where s_1 and s_2 are slack variables and t_1 is artificial. The artificial objective function is $W = Z - Mt_1$ or, equivalently,

$$-2x_1 - x_2 + Mt_1 + W = 0. \tag{38}$$

The augmented coefficient matrix of Eqs. (36)–(38) is

$$
\begin{array}{cccccc}
x_1 & x_2 & s_1 & s_2 & t_1 & W \\
\end{array}
$$

$$
\left[
\begin{array}{cccccc|c}
-1 & 1 & -1 & 0 & 1 & 0 & 2 \\
1 & 1 & 0 & 1 & 0 & 0 & 1 \\
\hline
-2 & -1 & 0 & 0 & M & 1 & 0 \\
\end{array}
\right]
$$

The simplex tableaus appear below.

SIMPLEX TABLEAU I

	x_1	x_2	s_1	s_2	t_1	W		Quotients
t_1	-1	1	-1	0	1	0	2	$2 \div 1 = 2.$
departing → s_2	1	①	0	1	0	0	1	$1 \div 1 = 1.$
W	$-2+M$	$-1-M$	M	0	0	1	$-2M$	

indicators

entering variable

SIMPLEX TABLEAU II

	x_1	x_2	s_1	s_2	t_1	W	
t_1	-2	0	-1	-1	1	0	1
x_2	1	1	0	1	0	0	1
W	$-1+2M$	0	M	$1+M$	0	1	$1-M$

indicators

Since M is a large positive number, the indicators in simplex tableau II are non-negative, so the simplex procedure terminates. The value of the artificial variable t_1 is 1. Therefore, as previously stated the feasible region of the original problem is empty and hence no solution exists. This result can be obtained geometrically. Figure 9.21 shows the graphs of $-x_1 + x_2 = 2$ and $x_1 + x_2 = 1$ for x_1, $x_2 \geq$

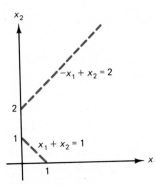

FIGURE 9.21

0. Since there is no point (x_1, x_2) that simultaneously lies above $-x_1 + x_2 = 2$ and below $x_1 + x_2 = 1$ such that x_1, $x_2 \geq 0$, the feasible region is empty and thus no solution exists.

In the next section we shall use the simplex method on minimization problems.

EXERCISE 9.6

Use the simplex method to solve the following problems.

1. Maximize
$$Z = 2x_1 + x_2$$
subject to
$$x_1 + x_2 \leq 6,$$
$$-x_1 + x_2 \geq 4,$$
$$x_1, x_2 \geq 0.$$

2. Maximize
$$Z = 3x_1 + 4x_2$$
subject to
$$x_1 + 2x_2 \leq 8,$$
$$x_1 + 6x_2 \geq 12,$$
$$x_1, x_2 \geq 0.$$

3. Maximize
$$Z = 2x_1 + x_2 - x_3$$
subject to
$$x_1 + 2x_2 + x_3 \leq 5,$$
$$-x_1 + x_2 + x_3 \geq 1,$$
$$x_1, x_2, x_3 \geq 0.$$

4. Maximize
$$Z = x_1 - x_2 + 4x_3$$
subject to
$$x_1 + x_2 + x_3 \leq 9,$$
$$x_1 - 2x_2 + x_3 \geq 6,$$
$$x_1, x_2, x_3 \geq 0.$$

5. Maximize
$$Z = 4x_1 + x_2 + 2x_3$$
subject to
$$2x_1 + x_2 + 3x_3 \leq 10,$$
$$x_1 - x_2 + x_3 = 4,$$
$$x_1, x_2, x_3 \geq 0.$$

6. Maximize
$$Z = x_1 + 2x_2 + 3x_3$$
subject to
$$x_2 - 2x_3 \geq 5,$$
$$x_1 + x_2 + x_3 = 8,$$
$$x_1, x_2, x_3 \geq 0.$$

7. Maximize
$$Z = x_1 - 10x_2$$
subject to
$$x_1 - x_2 \leq 1,$$
$$x_1 + 2x_2 \leq 8,$$
$$x_1 + x_2 \geq 5,$$
$$x_1, x_2 \geq 0.$$

8. Maximize
$$Z = x_1 + 4x_2 - x_3$$
subject to
$$x_1 + x_2 - x_3 \geq 5,$$
$$x_1 + x_2 + x_3 \leq 3,$$
$$x_1 - x_2 + x_3 = 7,$$
$$x_1, x_2, x_3 \geq 0.$$

9. Maximize
$$Z = 3x_1 - 2x_2 + x_3$$
subject to
$$x_1 + x_2 + x_3 \leq 1,$$
$$x_1 - x_2 + x_3 \geq 2,$$
$$x_1 - x_2 - x_3 \leq -6,$$
$$x_1, x_2, x_3 \geq 0.$$

10. Maximize
$$Z = x_1 + 4x_2$$
subject to
$$x_1 + 2x_2 \leq 8,$$
$$x_1 + 6x_2 \geq 12,$$
$$x_2 \geq 2,$$
$$x_1, x_2 \geq 0.$$

11. Maximize
$$Z = -3x_1 + 2x_2$$
subject to
$$x_1 - x_2 \leq 4,$$
$$-x_1 + x_2 = 4,$$
$$x_1 \geq 6,$$
$$x_1, x_2 \geq 0.$$

12. Maximize
$$Z = x_1 - 5x_2$$
subject to
$$x_1 - 2x_2 \geq -13,$$
$$-x_1 + x_2 \geq 3,$$
$$x_1 + x_2 \geq 11,$$
$$x_1, x_2 \geq 0.$$

13. A company manufactures two models of kitchen tables: Contemporary and Traditional. Each model requires assembly and finishing times as given in the table below. The profit on each set is also indicated. The number of hours available per week in the assembly department is 400, and in the finishing department it is 510. Because of a union contract, the finishing department is guaranteed at least 240 hours of work per week. How many tables of each model should the company produce each week to maximize profit?

	ASSEMBLY TIME	FINISHING TIME	PROFIT PER SET
Contemporary	1 hr	2 hr	$10
Traditional	2 hr	3 hr	12

14. A company manufactures three products: X, Y, and Z. Each product requires the use of machine time on machines A and B as given in the table below. The numbers of hours per week that A and B are available for production are 40 and 30, respectively. The profit per unit on X, Y, and Z is $50, $60, and $75, respectively. At least five units of Z must be produced next week. What should be the production order for that period if maximum profit is to be achieved? What is the maximum profit?

	MACHINE A	MACHINE B
Product X	1 hr	1 hr
Product Y	2 hr	1 hr
Product Z	2 hr	2 hr

15. The prospectus of an investment fund states that all money is invested in bonds that are rated A, AA, and AAA; no more than 30% of the total investment is in A and AA bonds, and at least 50% is in AA and AAA bonds. The A, AA, and AAA bonds respectively yield 8%, 7%, and 6% annually. Determine the percentages of the total investment that should be committed to each type of bond so that the fund maximizes its annual yield. What is this yield?

9.7 MINIMIZATION

So far we have used the simplex method to *maximize* objective functions. In general, to *minimize* a function it suffices to maximize the negative of the function. To understand why, consider the function $f(x) = x^2 - 4$. In Fig. 9.22(a) observe that the minimum value of f is -4 and it occurs when $x = 0$. Figure 9.22(b) shows the graph of $g(x) = -f(x) = -(x^2 - 4)$. This graph is the

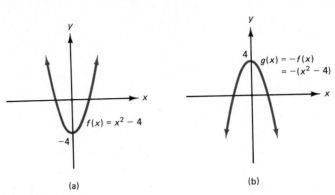

(a)   (b)

FIGURE 9.22

reflection through the x-axis of the graph of f. Notice that the maximum value of g is 4 and occurs when $x = 0$. Thus the minimum value of $x^2 - 4$ is the negative of the maximum value of $-(x^2 - 4)$. That is,

$$\min f = -\max(-f).$$

EXAMPLE 1   *Use the simplex method to minimize* $Z = x_1 + 2x_2$ *subject to*

$$-2x_1 + x_2 \geq 1, \tag{1}$$

$$-x_1 + x_2 \geq 2, \tag{2}$$

and $x_1, x_2 \geq 0$.

To minimize Z we can maximize $-Z = -x_1 - 2x_2$. Note that constraints (1) and (2) each have the form $a_1x_1 + a_2x_2 \geq b$, where $b \geq 0$. Thus their equations involve two slack variables s_1 and s_2, each with coefficient -1, and two artificial variables t_1 and t_2.

$$-2x_1 + x_2 - s_1 + t_1 = 1, \tag{3}$$

$$-x_1 + x_2 - s_2 + t_2 = 2. \tag{4}$$

Since there are *two* artificial variables, we maximize the objective function $W = (-Z) - Mt_1 - Mt_2$, where M is a large positive number. Equivalently,

$$x_1 + 2x_2 + Mt_1 + Mt_2 + W = 0. \tag{5}$$

The augmented coefficient matrix of Eqs. (3)–(5) is

$$
\begin{array}{ccccccc}
x_1 & x_2 & s_1 & s_2 & t_1 & t_2 & W \\
\end{array}
$$
$$
\left[
\begin{array}{ccccccc|c}
-2 & 1 & -1 & 0 & 1 & 0 & 0 & 1 \\
-1 & 1 & 0 & -1 & 0 & 1 & 0 & 2 \\
\hline
1 & 2 & 0 & 0 & M & M & 1 & 0
\end{array}
\right].
$$

Proceeding, we obtain tableaus I, II, and III.

SIMPLEX TABLEAU I

$$
\begin{array}{c}
\text{departing} \rightarrow t_1 \\
\text{variable} \quad t_2 \\
 W
\end{array}
\begin{array}{c}
\begin{array}{ccccccc}
x_1 & x_2 & s_1 & s_2 & t_1 & t_2 & W \\
\end{array} \\
\left[
\begin{array}{ccccccc|c}
-2 & ① & -1 & 0 & 1 & 0 & 0 & 1 \\
-1 & 1 & 0 & -1 & 0 & 1 & 0 & 2 \\
\hline
1+3M & 2-2M & M & M & 0 & 0 & 1 & -3M
\end{array}
\right]
\end{array}
\quad
\begin{array}{l}
\textit{Quotients} \\
1 \div 1 = 1. \\
2 \div 1 = 2.
\end{array}
$$

entering variable — indicators

SIMPLEX TABLEAU II

$$
\begin{array}{c}
\text{departing} \quad x_2 \\
\text{variable} \rightarrow t_2 \\
 W
\end{array}
\begin{array}{c}
\begin{array}{ccccccc}
x_1 & x_2 & s_1 & s_2 & t_1 & t_2 & W \\
\end{array} \\
\left[
\begin{array}{ccccccc|c}
-2 & 1 & -1 & 0 & 1 & 0 & 0 & 1 \\
1 & 0 & ① & -1 & -1 & 1 & 0 & 1 \\
\hline
5-M & 0 & 2-M & M & -2+2M & 0 & 1 & -2-M
\end{array}
\right]
\end{array}
\quad
\begin{array}{l}
\textit{Quotients} \\
 \\
1 \div 1 = 1.
\end{array}
$$

entering variable — indicators

SIMPLEX TABLEAU III

$$
\begin{array}{c}
x_2 \\
s_1 \\
W
\end{array}
\begin{array}{c}
\begin{array}{ccccccc}
x_1 & x_2 & s_1 & s_2 & t_1 & t_2 & W \\
\end{array} \\
\left[
\begin{array}{ccccccc|c}
-1 & 1 & 0 & -1 & 0 & 1 & 0 & 2 \\
1 & 0 & 1 & -1 & -1 & 1 & 0 & 1 \\
\hline
3 & 0 & 0 & 2 & M & -2+M & 1 & -4
\end{array}
\right].
\end{array}
$$

indicators

The B.F.S. corresponding to tableau III has both artificial variables equal to 0. Thus the t_1- and t_2-columns are no longer needed. However, the indicators in the x_1-, x_2-, s_1-, and s_2-columns are nonnegative and hence an optimum solution has been reached. Since $W = -Z$ when $t_1 = t_2 = 0$, the maximum value of $-Z$ is -4. Thus the *minimum* value of Z is $-(-4)$ or 4. It occurs when $x_1 = 0$ and $x_2 = 2$.

EXAMPLE 2   *A cement plant produces 2,500,000 barrels of cement per year. The kilns emit 2 lb of dust for each barrel produced. A governmental agency dealing with environmental protection requires that the plant reduce its dust emissions to no more than 800,000 lb per year. There are two emission control devices available, A and B. Device A reduces emissions to $\frac{1}{2}$ lb per barrel and its cost is $0.20 per barrel of cement produced. For device B, emissions are reduced to $\frac{1}{5}$ lb per barrel and the cost is $0.25 per barrel of cement produced. Determine the most economical course of action that the plant should take so* *that it complies with the agency's requirement and also maintains its annual production of* 2,500,000 *barrels of cement.**

We must minimize the annual cost of emission control. Let x_1, x_2, and x_3 be the annual numbers of barrels of cement produced in kilns that use device A, device B, and no device, respectively, Then x_1, x_2, $x_3 \geq 0$ and the annual emission control cost C (in dollars) is

$$C = \tfrac{1}{5}x_1 + \tfrac{1}{4}x_2 + 0x_3. \tag{6}$$

Since 2,500,000 barrels of cement are produced each year,

$$x_1 + x_2 + x_3 = 2{,}500{,}000. \tag{7}$$

The numbers of pounds of dust emitted annually by the kilns that use device A, device B, and no device are $\tfrac{1}{2}x_1$, $\tfrac{1}{5}x_2$, and $2x_3$, respectively. Since the total number of pounds of dust emissions is to be no more than 800,000,

$$\tfrac{1}{2}x_1 + \tfrac{1}{5}x_2 + 2x_3 \leq 800{,}000. \tag{8}$$

To minimize C subject to constraints (7) and (8) where x_1, x_2, $x_3 \geq 0$, we shall first maximize $-C$ by using the simplex method. The equations to consider are

$$x_1 + x_2 + x_3 + t_1 = 2{,}500{,}000 \tag{9}$$

$$\text{and} \quad \tfrac{1}{2}x_1 + \tfrac{1}{5}x_2 + 2x_3 + s_2 = \quad 800{,}000, \tag{10}$$

where t_1 and s_2 are artificial and slack variables, respectively. The artificial objective equation is $W = (-C) - Mt_1$, or equivalently,

$$\tfrac{1}{5}x_1 + \tfrac{1}{4}x_2 + 0x_3 + Mt_1 + W = 0, \tag{11}$$

where M is a large positive number. The augmented coefficient matrix of Eqs. (9)–(11) is

$$
\begin{array}{cccccc}
x_1 & x_2 & x_3 & s_2 & t_1 & W \\
\end{array}
$$

$$
\left[
\begin{array}{cccccc|c}
1 & 1 & 1 & 0 & 1 & 0 & 2{,}500{,}000 \\
\tfrac{1}{2} & \tfrac{1}{5} & 2 & 1 & 0 & 0 & 800{,}000 \\
\hline
\tfrac{1}{5} & \tfrac{1}{4} & 0 & 0 & M & 1 & 0 \\
\end{array}
\right].
$$

After determining our initial simplex tableau, we proceed and obtain (after three additional tableaus) our final tableau:

$$
\begin{array}{c}
 \\
x_2 \\
x_1 \\
\\
-C
\end{array}
\begin{array}{ccccc}
x_1 & x_2 & x_3 & s_2 & -C \\
\end{array}
$$

$$
\begin{array}{c}
x_2 \\
x_1 \\
\\
-C
\end{array}
\left[
\begin{array}{ccccc|c}
0 & 1 & -5 & -\tfrac{10}{3} & 0 & 1{,}500{,}000 \\
1 & 0 & 6 & \tfrac{10}{3} & 0 & 1{,}000{,}000 \\
\hline
0 & 0 & \tfrac{1}{20} & \tfrac{1}{6} & 1 & -575{,}000 \\
\end{array}
\right].
$$

$$\underbrace{\phantom{0 \quad 0 \quad \tfrac{1}{20} \quad \tfrac{1}{6}}}_{\text{indicators}}$$

Notice that W is replaced by $-C$ when $t_1 = 0$. The maximum value of $-C$ is

* This example is adapted from Robert E. Kohn, "A Mathematical Model for Air Pollution Control," *School Science and Mathematics*, 69 (1969),487–94.

$-575,000$ and occurs when $x_1 = 1,000,000$, $x_2 = 1,500,000$, and $x_3 = 0$. Thus the *minimum* annual cost of emission control is $-(-575,000) = \$575,000$. Device A should be installed on kilns producing 1,000,000 barrels of cement annually, and device B should be installed on kilns producing 1,500,000 barrels annually.

EXERCISE 9.7

Use the simplex method to solve the following problems.

1. Minimize

$$Z = 3x_1 + 6x_2$$

subject to

$$-x_1 + x_2 \geq 6,$$
$$x_1 + x_2 \geq 10,$$
$$x_1, x_2 \geq 0.$$

2. Minimize

$$Z = 8x_1 + 12x_2$$

subject to

$$2x_1 + 2x_2 \geq 1,$$
$$x_1 + 3x_2 \geq 2,$$
$$x_1, x_2 \geq 0.$$

3. Minimize

$$Z = 4x_1 + 2x_2 + x_3$$

subject to

$$x_1 - x_2 - x_3 \geq 9,$$
$$x_1, x_2, x_3 \geq 0.$$

4. Minimize

$$Z = x_1 + x_2 + 2x_3$$

subject to

$$x_1 + 2x_2 - x_3 \geq 4,$$
$$x_1, x_2, x_3 \geq 0.$$

5. Minimize

$$Z = 2x_1 + 3x_2 + x_3$$

subject to

$$x_1 + x_2 + x_3 \leq 6,$$
$$x_1 \quad\ - x_3 \leq -4,$$
$$x_2 + x_3 \leq 5,$$
$$x_1, x_2, x_3 \geq 0.$$

6. Minimize

$$Z = 4x_1 + x_2 + 2x_3$$

subject to

$$4x_1 + x_2 - x_3 \leq 3,$$
$$x_1 \quad\ + x_3 \leq 4,$$
$$x_1 + x_2 + x_3 \geq 1,$$
$$x_1, x_2, x_3 \geq 0.$$

7. Minimize

$$Z = x_1 - x_2 - 3x_3$$

subject to

$$x_1 + 2x_2 + x_3 = 4,$$
$$x_2 + x_3 = 1,$$
$$x_1 + x_2 \quad\quad \leq 6,$$
$$x_1, x_2, x_3 \geq 0.$$

8. Minimize

$$Z = x_1 + x_2 - 2x_3$$

subject to

$$x_1 - x_2 + x_3 \leq 4,$$
$$2x_1 + x_2 - 3x_3 \geq 6,$$
$$x_1 - x_2 - 2x_3 = 2,$$
$$x_1, x_2, x_3 \geq 0.$$

9. Minimize

$$Z = x_1 + 8x_2 + 5x_3$$

subject to

$$x_1 + x_2 + x_3 \geq 8,$$
$$-x_1 + 2x_2 + x_3 \geq 2,$$
$$x_1, x_2, x_3 \geq 0.$$

10. Minimize

$$Z = 4x_1 + 4x_2 + 6x_3$$

subject to

$$x_1 - x_2 - x_3 \leq 3,$$
$$x_1 - x_2 + x_3 \geq 3,$$
$$x_1, x_2, x_3 \geq 0.$$

11. A cement plant produces 3,300,000 barrels of cement per year. The kilns emit 2 lb of dust for each barrel produced. The plant must reduce its dust emissions to no more than 1,000,000 lb per year. There are two devices available, A and B, that will control emissions. Device A will reduce emissions to $\frac{1}{2}$ lb per barrel and the cost is \$0.25 per barrel of cement produced. For device B, emissions are reduced to $\frac{1}{4}$ lb per barrel and the cost is \$0.40 per barrel of cement produced. Determine the most economical course of action that the plant should take so that it maintains an annual production of exactly 3,300,000 barrels of cement.

12. Because of increased business, a catering service finds that it must rent additional delivery trucks. The minimum needs are 12 units each of refrigerated and nonrefrigerated space. Two standard types of trucks are available in the rental market. Type A has 2 units of refrigerated space and 1 unit of nonrefrigerated space. Type B has 2 units of refrigerated space and 3 units of nonrefrigerated space. The costs per mile are $0.40 for A and $0.60 for B. How many of each type of truck should be rented so as to minimize total cost per mile? What is the minimum total cost per mile?

13. A retailer has stores in Exton and Whyton, and has warehouses A and B in two other cities. Each store requires delivery of exactly 30 refrigerators. In warehouse A there are 50 refrigerators, and in B there are 20. The transportation costs to ship refrigerators from the warehouses to the stores are given in the table below. For example, the cost to ship a refrigerator from A to the Exton store is $15. How should the retailer order the refrigerators so that the requirements of the stores are met and the total transportation costs are minimized? What is the minimum transportation cost?

	EXTON	WHYTON
Warehouse A	$15	$13
Warehouse B	11	12

14. An auto manufacturer purchases batteries from two suppliers, X and Y. The manufacturer has two plants, A and B, and requires delivery of exactly 6000 batteries to plant A and exactly 4000 to plant B. Supplier X charges $30 and $32 per battery (including transportation cost) to A and B, respectively. For these prices, X requires that the auto manufacturer order at least a total of 2000 batteries. However, X can supply no more than 4000 batteries. Supplier Y charges $34 and $28 per battery to A and B, respectively, and requires a minimum order of 6000 batteries. Determine how the auto manufacturer should order the necessary batteries so that their total cost is a minimum. What is this minimum cost?

15. A paper company stocks its holiday wrapping paper in 48-in.-wide rolls, called stock rolls, and cuts such rolls into smaller widths depending on customers' orders. Suppose that an order for 50 rolls of 15-in.-wide paper and 60 rolls of 10-in.-wide paper is received. From a stock roll the company can cut three 15-in.-wide rolls and one 3-in.-wide roll (see Fig. 9.23). Since the 3-in.-wide roll cannot be used in this order, 3 in. is called the trim loss for this roll. Similarly, from a stock roll,

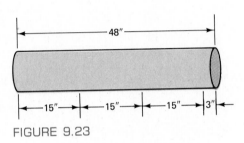

FIGURE 9.23

two 15-in.-wide rolls, one 10-in.-wide roll, and one 8-in.-wide roll could be cut. Here the trim loss would be 8 in. The table below indicates the number of 15-in. and 10-in. rolls, together with trim loss, that can be cut from a stock roll. (a) Complete the last two columns of the table. (b) Assume that the company has a sufficient number of stock rolls to fill the order and that *at least* 50 rolls of 15-in.-wide and 60 rolls of 10-in.-wide wrapping paper will be cut. If x_1, x_2, x_3, and x_4 are the numbers of stock rolls that are cut in a manner described by columns 1–4 of the table, respectively, determine the values of the x's so that the total trim loss is minimized. (c) What is the minimum amount of total trim loss?

Roll width	15 in.	3	2	1	—
	10 in.	0	1	—	—
	Trim loss	3	8	—	—

9.8 THE DUAL

There is a fundamental principle, called *duality,* that allows us to solve a maximization problem by solving a related minimization problem. Let us illustrate.

Suppose that a company produces two types of widgets, manual and electric, and each requires the use of machines A and B in its production. Table 9.2 indicates that a manual widget requires the use of A for 1 hour and B for 1 hour. An electric widget requires A for 2 hours and B for 4 hours. The maximum

TABLE 9.2

	MACHINE *A*	MACHINE *B*	PROFIT/UNIT
Manual	1 hr	1 hr	$10
Electric	2 hr	4 hr	$24
Hours available	120	180	

number of hours available per month for machines A and B are 120 and 180, respectively. The profit on a manual widget is $10 and on an electric widget it is $24. Assuming that the company can sell all the widgets it can produce, we shall determine the maximum monthly profit. If x_1 and x_2 are the number of manual and electric widgets produced per month, respectively, then we want to maximize the monthly profit function

$$P = 10x_1 + 24x_2,$$

subject to

$$x_1 + 2x_2 \le 120, \tag{1}$$

$$x_1 + 4x_2 \le 180, \tag{2}$$

and $x_1, x_2 \ge 0$. Writing constraints (1) and (2) as equations, we have

$$x_1 + 2x_2 + s_1 = 120 \tag{3}$$

and

$$x_1 + 4x_2 + s_2 = 180,$$

where s_1 and s_2 are slack variables. In Eq. (3), $x_1 + 2x_2$ is the number of hours that machine A is used. Since 120 hours on A are available, then s_1 is the number of available hours that are *not* used for production. That is, s_1 represents unused capacity (in hours) for A. Similarly, s_2 represents unused capacity for B. Solving this problem by the simplex method, we find that the final tableau is

$$
\begin{array}{c c}
& \begin{array}{ccccc} x_1 & x_2 & s_1 & s_2 & P \end{array} \\
\begin{array}{c} x_1 \\ x_2 \\ \\ P \end{array} &
\left[
\begin{array}{ccccc|c}
1 & 0 & 2 & -1 & 0 & 60 \\
0 & 1 & -\frac{1}{2} & \frac{1}{2} & 0 & 30 \\
\hline
0 & 0 & 8 & 2 & 1 & 1320
\end{array}
\right].
\end{array}
\tag{4}
$$

$$\underbrace{\qquad\qquad}_{\text{indicators}}$$

Thus the maximum profit per month is $1320, which occurs when $x_1 = 60$ and $x_2 = 30$.

Now, let us look at the situation from a different point of view. Suppose that the company wishes to rent out machines A and B. What is the minimum monthly rental fee they should charge? Certainly if the charge is too high, no one would rent the machines. On the other hand, if the charge is too low, it may not pay the company to rent them at all. Obviously, the minimum rent should be $1320. That is, the minimum the company should charge is the profit it could make by using the machines itself. We can arrive at this minimum rental fee directly by solving a linear programming problem.

Let R be the total monthly rental fee. To determine R, suppose the company assigns values or "worths" to each hour of capacity on machines A and B. Let these worths be y_1 and y_2 dollars, respectively, where y_1, $y_2 \geq 0$. Then the monthly worth of machine A is $120y_1$, and for B it is $180y_2$. Thus

$$R = 120y_1 + 180y_2.$$

The total worth of machine time to produce a manual widget is $1y_1 + 1y_2$. This should be at least equal to the $10 profit the company can earn by producing that widget. If not, the company would make more money by using the machine time to produce a manual widget. Thus

$$1y_1 + 1y_2 \geq 10.$$

Similarly, the total worth of machine time to produce an electric widget should be at least $24:

$$2y_1 + 4y_2 \geq 24.$$

Therefore, the company wants to

$$\text{minimize } R = 120y_1 + 180y_2$$

subject to

$$y_1 + y_2 \geq 10, \tag{5}$$

$$2y_1 + 4y_2 \geq 24, \tag{6}$$

and y_1, $y_2 \geq 0$.

To minimize R, we shall maximize $-R$. Since constraints (5) and (6) have the form $a_1y_1 + a_2y_2 \geq b$, where $b \geq 0$, we consider an artificial problem. If r_1 and r_2 are slack variables, and t_1 and t_2 are artificial variables, then we want to maximize $W = (-R) - Mt_1 - Mt_2$, where M is a large positive number, such that $y_1 + y_2 - r_1 + t_1 = 10$, $2y_1 + 4y_2 - r_2 + t_2 = 24$, and the y's, r's, and t's are nonnegative. The final simplex tableau for this problem (with the artificial variable columns deleted and W changed to $-R$) is

$$\begin{array}{c} \\ y_1 \\ y_2 \\ \\ -R \end{array} \begin{array}{c} y_1 \quad y_2 \quad r_1 \quad r_2 \quad -R \\ \left[\begin{array}{ccccc|c} 1 & 0 & -2 & \frac{1}{2} & 0 & 8 \\ 0 & 1 & 1 & -\frac{1}{2} & 0 & 2 \\ \hline 0 & 0 & 60 & 30 & 1 & -1320 \end{array} \right]. \end{array}$$

indicators

Since the maximimum value of $-R$ is -1320, the *minimum* value of R is $-(-1320) = \$1320$ (as anticipated). It occurs when $y_1 = 8$ and $y_2 = 2$. We have therefore determined the optimum value of one linear programming problem (maximizing profit) by finding the optimum value of another problem (minimizing rental fee).

The values $y_1 = 8$ and $y_2 = 2$ could have been anticipated from the final tableau of the maximization problem. In (4), the indicator 8 in the s_1-column means that at the optimum level of production, if s_1 increases by one unit, then the profit P *decreases* by 8. That is, 1 unused hour of capacity on A decreases the maximum profit by \$8. Thus 1 hour of capacity on A is worth \$8. We say that the **shadow price** or **accounting price** of 1 hour of capacity on A is \$8. Now, recall that y_1 in the rental problem is the worth of 1 hour of capacity on A. Thus y_1 must equal 8 in the optimum solution for that problem. Similarly, since the indicator in the s_2-column is 2, the shadow price of 1 hour of capacity on B is \$2, which is the value of y_2 in the optimum solution of the rental problem.

Let us now analyze the structure of our two linear programming problems:

Maximize	Minimize
$P = 10x_1 + 24x_2$	$R = 120y_1 + 180y_2$
subject to	subject to
$\left. \begin{array}{c} x_1 + 2x_2 \leq 120 \\ x_1 + 4x_2 \leq 180 \end{array} \right\}$ (7)	$\left. \begin{array}{c} y_1 + y_2 \geq 10 \\ 2y_1 + 4y_2 \geq 24 \end{array} \right\}$ (8)
and $x_1, x_2 \geq 0$.	and $y_1, y_2 \geq 0$.

Note that in (7) the inequalities are all $\leq$, but in (8) they are all $\geq$. The coefficients of the objective function in the minimization problem are the constant terms in (7). The constant terms in (8) are the coefficients of the objective function of the maximization problem. The coefficients of the y_1's in (8) are the coefficients of x_1 and x_2 in the first constraint of (7); the coefficients of the y_2's in (8) are the coefficients of x_1 and x_2 in the second constraint of (7). The minimization problem is called the *dual* of the maximization problem and vice versa.

In general, with any given linear programming problem we can associate another linear programming problem called its **dual.** The given problem is called **primal.** If the primal is a maximization problem, then its dual is a minimization problem. Similarly, if the primal involves minimization, then the dual involves maximization.

Any primal maximization problem can be written in the form indicated in Table 9.3. Note that there are no restrictions on the b's.* The corresponding dual minimization problem can be written in the form indicated in Table 9.4. Similarly, any primal minimization problem can be put in the form of Table 9.4 and its dual is the maximization problem in Table 9.3.

---

* If an inequality constraint involves $\geq$, multiplying both sides by -1 yields an inequality involving $\leq$. If a constraint is an equality, it can be written in terms of two inequalities: one involving $\leq$ and one involving $\geq$.

TABLE 9.3
Primal (Dual)

Maximize $Z = c_1 x_1 + c_2 x_2 + \cdots + c_n x_n$

subject to

$$
\left.
\begin{aligned}
a_{11} x_1 + a_{12} x_2 + \cdots + a_{1n} x_n &\le b_1, \\
a_{21} x_1 + a_{22} x_2 + \cdots + a_{2n} x_n &\le b_2, \\
&\ \ \vdots \\
a_{m1} x_1 + a_{m2} x_2 + \cdots + a_{mn} x_n &\le b_m,
\end{aligned}
\right\} \quad (9)
$$

and $x_1, x_2, \ldots, x_n \ge 0.$

TABLE 9.4
Dual (Primal)

Minimize $W = b_1 y_1 + b_2 y_2 + \cdots + b_m y_m$

subject to

$$
\left.
\begin{aligned}
a_{11} y_1 + a_{21} y_2 + \cdots + a_{m1} y_m &\ge c_1, \\
a_{12} y_1 + a_{22} y_2 + \cdots + a_{m2} y_m &\ge c_2, \\
&\ \ \vdots \\
a_{1n} y_1 + a_{2n} y_2 + \cdots + a_{mn} y_m &\ge c_n,
\end{aligned}
\right\} \quad (10)
$$

and $y_1, y_2, \ldots, y_m \ge 0.$

Let us compare the primal and its dual in Tables 9.3 and 9.4. For convenience, when we refer to constraints we shall mean those in (9) or (10); we shall not include the nonnegativity conditions. Observe that if all the constraints in the primal involve $\le$ ($\ge$), then all the constraints in its dual involve $\ge$ ($\le$). The coefficients in the dual's objective function are the constant terms in the primal's constraints. Similarly, the constant terms in the dual's constraints are the coefficients of the primal's objective function. The coefficient matrix of the left sides of the dual's constraints is the *transpose* of the coefficient matrix of the left sides of the primal's constraints. That is, for example,

$$
\begin{bmatrix}
a_{11} & a_{12} & \cdots & a_{1n} \\
a_{21} & a_{22} & \cdots & a_{2n} \\
\vdots & \vdots & & \vdots \\
a_{m1} & a_{m2} & \cdots & a_{mn}
\end{bmatrix}^{\mathrm{T}}
=
\begin{bmatrix}
a_{11} & a_{21} & \cdots & a_{m1} \\
a_{12} & a_{22} & \cdots & a_{m2} \\
\vdots & \vdots & & \vdots \\
a_{1n} & a_{2n} & \cdots & a_{mn}
\end{bmatrix}
$$

If the primal involves n structural variables and m slack variables, then the dual involves m structural variables and n slack variables. It should be noted that the dual of the *dual* is the primal.

There is an important relationship between the primal and its dual:

> If the primal has an optimum solution, then so does the dual, and the optimum value of the primal's objective function is the *same* as that of its dual.

Moreover, suppose that the primal's objective function is $Z = c_1x_1 + c_2x_2 + \cdots + c_nx_n$.

If s_i is the slack variable associated with the ith constraint in the dual, then the indicator in the s_i-column of the final simplex tableau of the dual is the value of x_i in the optimum solution of the primal.

Thus we can solve the primal by merely solving its dual. At times this is more convenient than solving the primal directly.

EXAMPLE 1   *Find the dual of the following:*

$$\text{maximize } Z = 3x_1 + 4x_2 + 2x_3$$

subject to

$$x_1 + 2x_2 + 0x_3 \le 10,$$
$$2x_1 + 2x_2 + x_3 \le 10,$$

and $x_1, x_2, x_3 \ge 0$.

The primal is of the form of Table 9.3. Thus the dual is

$$\text{minimize } W = 10y_1 + 10y_2$$

subject to

$$y_1 + 2y_2 \ge 3,$$
$$2y_1 + 2y_2 \ge 4,$$
$$0y_1 + y_2 \ge 2,$$

and $y_1, y_2 \ge 0$.

EXAMPLE 2   *Find the dual of the following:*

$$\text{minimize } Z = 4x_1 + 3x_2$$

subject to

$$3x_1 - x_2 \ge 2, \tag{11}$$
$$x_1 + x_2 \le 1, \tag{12}$$
$$-4x_1 + x_2 \le 3, \tag{13}$$

and $x_1, x_2 \ge 0$.

Since the primal is a minimization problem, we want constraints (12) and (13) to involve $\geq$ (see Table 9.4). Multiplying both sides of (12) and (13) by -1, we get $-x_1 - x_2 \geq -1$ and $4x_1 - x_2 \geq -3$. Thus constraints (11)–(13) become

$$3x_1 - x_2 \geq \quad 2,$$

$$-x_1 - x_2 \geq -1,$$

$$4x_1 - x_2 \geq -3.$$

The dual is

$$\text{maximize } W = 2y_1 - y_2 - 3y_3$$

subject to

$$3y_1 - y_2 + 4y_3 \leq 4,$$

$$-y_1 - y_2 - \quad y_3 \leq 3,$$

and $y_1, y_2, y_3 \geq 0$.

EXAMPLE 3 *Use the dual and the simplex method to maximize $Z = 4x_1 - x_2 - x_3$ subject to*

$$3x_1 + x_2 - x_3 \leq 4,$$

$$x_1 + x_2 + x_3 \leq 2,$$

and $x_1, x_2, x_3 \geq 0$.

The dual is

$$\text{minimize } W = 4y_1 + 2y_2$$

subject to

$$3y_1 + y_2 \geq 4, \tag{14}$$

$$y_1 + y_2 \geq -1, \tag{15}$$

$$-y_1 + y_2 \geq -1, \tag{16}$$

and $y_1, y_2 \geq 0$. To use the simplex method we must get nonnegative constants in (15) and (16). Multiplying both sides of (15) and (16) by -1 gives

$$-y_1 - y_2 \leq 1, \tag{17}$$

$$y_1 - y_2 \leq 1. \tag{18}$$

Since (14) involves $\geq$, an artificial variable is required. The corresponding equations of (14), (17), and (18) are, respectively,

$$3y_1 + y_2 - s_1 + t_1 = 4,$$

$$-y_1 - y_2 + s_2 \qquad = 1,$$

$$\text{and} \quad y_1 - y_2 + s_3 \qquad = 1,$$

where t_1 is an artificial variable and s_1, s_2, and s_3 are slack variables. To minimize W, we maximize $-W$. The artificial objective function is $U = (-W) - Mt$, where M is a large positive number. After computations we find that the final simplex tableau is

$$
\begin{array}{c}
\begin{array}{c}

\end{array}
\begin{array}{cccccc}
y_1 & y_2 & s_1 & s_2 & s_3 & -W
\end{array}
\\
\begin{array}{c}
y_2 \\ s_2 \\ y_1 \\ \\ -W
\end{array}
\left[
\begin{array}{cccccc|c}
0 & 1 & -\frac{1}{4} & 0 & -\frac{3}{4} & 0 & \frac{1}{4} \\
0 & 0 & -\frac{1}{2} & 1 & -\frac{1}{2} & 0 & \frac{5}{2} \\
1 & 0 & -\frac{1}{4} & 0 & \frac{1}{4} & 0 & \frac{5}{4} \\
\hline
0 & 0 & \frac{3}{2} & 0 & \frac{1}{2} & 1 & -\frac{11}{2}
\end{array}
\right]
\end{array}
$$

$$\underbrace{}_{\text{indicators}}$$

The maximum value of $-W$ is $-\frac{11}{2}$, so the *minimum* value of W is $\frac{11}{2}$. Hence the maximum value of Z is also $\frac{11}{2}$. Note that the indicators in the s_1-, s_2-, and s_3-columns are $\frac{3}{2}$, 0, and $\frac{1}{2}$, respectively. Thus the maximum value of Z occurs when $x_1 = \frac{3}{2}$, $x_2 = 0$, and $x_3 = \frac{1}{2}$.

In Example 1 of Sec. 9.7 we used the simplex method to minimize $Z = x_1 + 2x_2$ such that

$$-2x_1 + x_2 \geq 1,$$

$$-x_1 + x_2 \geq 2,$$

and x_1, $x_1 \geq 0$. The initial simplex tableau had 24 entries and involved two artificial variables. The tableau of the dual has only 18 entries and *no artificial variables,* and is easier to handle, as Example 4 will show. Thus there may be a distinct advantage in solving the dual to determine the solution of the primal.

EXAMPLE 4   *Use the dual and the simplex method to minimize $Z = x_1 + 2x_2$ subject to*

$$-2x_1 + x_2 \geq 1,$$

$$-x_1 + x_2 \geq 2,$$

and x_1, $x_2 \geq 0$.

The dual is

$$\text{maximize } W = y_1 + 2y_2$$

subject to

$$-2y_1 - y_2 \leq 1,$$

$$y_1 + y_2 \leq 2,$$

and y_1, $y_2 \geq 0$. The initial simplex tableau is tableau I.

SIMPLEX TABLEAU I

	y_1	y_2	s_1	s_2	W		Quotients
s_1	-2	-1	1	0	0	1	
s_2	1	①	0	1	0	2	$2 \div 1 = 2.$
W	-1	-2	0	0	1	0	

departing → variable

indicators

entering variable

Continuing, we get tableau II.

SIMPLEX TABLEAU II

	y_1	y_2	s_1	s_2	W	
s_1	-1	0	1	1	0	3
y_2	1	1	0	1	0	2
W	1	0	0	2	1	4

indicators

Since all indicators are nonnegative in tableau II, the maximum value of W is 4. Hence the minimum value of Z is also 4. The indicators 0 and 2 in the s_1- and s_2-columns of tableau II mean that the minimum value of Z occurs when $x_1 = 0$ and $x_2 = 2$.

EXERCISE 9.8

In Problems **1–8**, *find the duals. Do not solve.*

1. Maximize
$$Z = 2x_1 + 3x_2$$
subject to
$$x_1 + x_2 \le 6,$$
$$-x_1 + x_2 \le 4,$$
$$x_1, x_2 \ge 0.$$

2. Maximize
$$Z = 2x_1 + x_2 - x_3$$
subject to
$$x_1 + x_2 \le 1,$$
$$-x_1 + 2x_2 + x_3 \le 2,$$
$$x_1, x_2, x_3 \ge 0.$$

3. Minimize
$$Z = x_1 + 8x_2 + 5x_3$$
subject to
$$x_1 + x_2 + x_3 \ge 8,$$
$$-x_1 + 2x_2 + x_3 \ge 2,$$
$$x_1, x_2, x_3 \ge 0.$$

4. Minimize
$$Z = 8x_1 + 12x_2$$
subject to
$$2x_1 + 2x_2 \ge 1,$$
$$x_1 + 3x_2 \ge 2,$$
$$x_1, x_2 \ge 0.$$

5. Maximize
$$Z = x_1 - x_2$$
subject to
$$-x_1 + 2x_2 \le 13,$$
$$-x_1 + x_2 \ge 3,$$
$$x_1 + x_2 \ge 11,$$
$$x_1, x_2 \ge 0.$$

6. Maximize
$$Z = x_1 - x_2 + 4x_3$$
subject to
$$x_1 + x_2 + x_3 \le 9,$$
$$x_1 - 2x_2 + x_3 \ge 6,$$
$$x_1, x_2, x_3 \ge 0.$$

7. Minimize
$$Z = 4x_1 + 4x_2 + 6x_3$$
subject to
$$x_1 - x_2 - x_3 \le 3,$$
$$x_1 - x_2 + x_3 \ge 3,$$
$$x_1, x_2, x_3 \ge 0.$$

8. Minimize
$$Z = 6x_1 + 3x_2$$
subject to
$$-3x_1 + 4x_2 \ge -12,$$
$$13x_1 - 8x_2 \le 80,$$
$$x_1, x_2 \ge 0.$$

In Problems 9–14, solve by using duals and the simplex method.

9. Minimize
$$Z = 4x_1 + 4x_2 + 6x_3$$
subject to
$$x_1 - x_2 + x_3 \ge 1,$$
$$-x_1 + x_2 + x_3 \ge 2,$$
$$x_1, x_2, x_3 \ge 0.$$

10. Minimize
$$Z = x_1 + x_2$$
subject to
$$x_1 + 4x_2 \ge 28,$$
$$2x_1 - x_2 \ge 2,$$
$$-3x_1 + 8x_2 \ge 16,$$
$$x_1, x_2 \ge 0.$$

11. Maximize
$$Z = 3x_1 + 8x_2$$
subject to
$$x_1 + 2x_2 \le 8,$$
$$x_1 + 6x_2 \le 12,$$
$$x_1, x_2 \ge 0.$$

12. Maximize
$$Z = 2x_1 + 6x_2$$
subject to
$$3x_1 + x_2 \le 12,$$
$$x_1 + x_2 \le 8,$$
$$x_1, x_2 \ge 0.$$

13. Minimize
$$Z = 6x_1 + 4x_2$$
subject to
$$-x_1 + x_2 \le 1,$$
$$x_1 + x_2 \ge 3,$$
$$x_1, x_2 \ge 0.$$

14. Minimize
$$Z = x_1 + x_2 + 2x_3$$
subject to
$$-x_1 - x_2 + x_3 \le 1,$$
$$x_1 - x_2 + x_3 \ge 2,$$
$$x_1, x_2, x_3 \ge 0.$$

15. A firm is comparing the costs of advertising in two media: newspaper and radio. For every dollar's worth of advertising, the table below gives the number of people, by income group, reached by these media. The firm wants to reach at least 8000 persons earning under $20,000 and at least 6000 earning over $20,000. Use the dual and the simplex method to find the amounts that the firm should spend on newspaper and radio advertising so as to reach these numbers of people at a minimum total advertising cost? What is the minimum total advertising cost?

	UNDER $20,000	OVER $20,000
Newspaper	40	100
Radio	50	25

16. Use the dual and the simplex method to find the minimum total cost per mile in Problem 12 of Exercise 9.7.

17. A company pays skilled and semiskilled workers in its assembly department $7 and $4 per hour, respectively. In the shipping department, shipping clerks are paid $5 per hour and shipping clerk apprentices are paid $2 per hour. The company requires at least 90 workers in the assembly department and at least 60 in the shipping department. Because of union agreements, at least twice as many semiskilled workers must be employed as skilled workers. Also, at least twice as many shipping clerks must be employed as shipping clerk apprentices. Use the dual and the simplex method to find the number of each type of worker that the company must employ so that the total hourly wage paid to these employees is a minimum. What is the minimum total hourly wage?

9.9 REVIEW

Important Terms and Symbols

Section 9.1   linear inequality   system of inequalities

Section 9.2   constraints   linear function in x and y linear programming problem
objective function   feasible solution   nonnegativity conditions   feasible region
isoprofit line   corner point   bounded feasible region   unbounded feasible region
nonempty feasible region   empty feasible region   isocost line   unbounded solution

Section 9.3   multiple optimum solution

Section 9.4   standard linear programming problem   slack variable   structural variable
basic feasible solution   nonbasic variable   basic variable   simplex tableau
entering variable   indicator   departing variable   pivot entry   simplex method
degeneracy

Section 9.6   artificial problem   artificial variable   artificial objective function

Section 9.8   shadow price   dual   primal

Summary

The solution to a system of linear inequalities consists of all points whose coordinates simultaneously satisfy all of the inequalities. Geometrically, for two variables it is the region that is common to all of the regions determined by the inequalities.

Linear programming involves maximizing or minimizing a linear function (the objective function) subject to a system of constraints, which are linear inequalities or linear equations. One method shown for finding an optimum solution for a nonempty feasible region was the corner point method. The objective function is evaluated at each of the corner points of the feasible region and we choose a corner point at which the objective function is optimum.

For a problem involving more than two variables, the corner point method is either impractical or impossible. Instead we use a matrix method called the simplex method, which is efficient and completely mechanical.

Review Problems

In Problems **1–10** *solve the given inequality or system of inequalities.*

1. $-3x + 2y > -6$.

2. $x - 2y + 6 \geq 0$.

3. $2y \leq -3$.

4. $-x < 2$.

5. $\begin{cases} y - 3x < 6, \\ x - y > -3. \end{cases}$

6. $\begin{cases} x - 2y > 4, \\ x + y > 1. \end{cases}$

7. $\begin{cases} x - y < 4, \\ y - x < 4. \end{cases}$

8. $\begin{cases} x > y, \\ x + y < 0. \end{cases}$

9. $\begin{cases} 3x + y > -4, \\ x - y > -5, \\ x \geq 0. \end{cases}$

10. $\begin{cases} x - y > 4, \\ x < 2, \\ y < -4. \end{cases}$

In Problems **11–18,** *do not use the simplex method.*

11. Maximize
$Z = x - 2y$
subject to
$y - x \leq 2,$
$x + y \leq 4,$
$x \leq 3,$
$x, y \geq 0.$

12. Maximize
$Z = 4x + 2y$
subject to
$x + 2y \leq 10,$
$x \leq 4,$
$y \geq 1,$
$x, y \geq 0.$

13. Minimize
$Z = 2x - y$
subject to
$x - y \geq -2,$
$x + y \geq 1,$
$x - 2y \leq 2,$
$x, y \geq 0.$

14. Minimize
$$Z = x + y$$
subject to
$$x + 3y \le 15,$$
$$3x + 2y \le 17,$$
$$x - 5y \le 0,$$
$$x, y \ge 0.$$

15. Minimize
$$Z = 4x - 3y$$
subject to
$$x + y \le 3,$$
$$2x + 3y \le 12,$$
$$5x + 8y \ge 40,$$
$$x, y \ge 0.$$

*16. Minimize
$$Z = 2x + 2y$$
subject to
$$x + y \ge 4,$$
$$-x + 3y \le 18,$$
$$x \le 6,$$
$$x, y \ge 0.$$

†17. Maximize
$$Z = 9x + 6y$$
subject to
$$x + 2y \le 8,$$
$$3x + 2y \le 12,$$
$$x, y \ge 0.$$

18. Maximize
$$Z = 4x + y$$
subject to
$$x + 2y \ge 8,$$
$$3x + 2y \ge 12,$$
$$x, y \ge 0.$$

In Problems **19–28,** *use the simplex method.*

19. Maximize
$$Z = 4x_1 + 5x_2$$
subject to
$$x_1 + 6x_2 \le 12,$$
$$x_1 + 2x_2 \le 8,$$
$$x_1, x_2 \ge 0.$$

20. Maximize
$$Z = 18x_1 + 20x_2$$
subject to
$$2x_1 + 3x_2 \le 18,$$
$$4x_1 + 3x_2 \le 24,$$
$$x_2 \le 5,$$
$$x_1, x_2 \ge 0.$$

21. Minimize
$$Z = 2x_1 + 3x_2 + x_3$$
subject to
$$x_1 + 2x_2 + 3x_3 \ge 6,$$
$$x_1, x_2, x_3 \ge 0.$$

22. Minimize
$$Z = x_1 + x_2$$
subject to
$$3x_1 + 4x_2 \ge 24,$$
$$x_2 \ge 3,$$
$$x_1, x_2 \ge 0.$$

23. Maximize
$$Z = x_1 + 2x_2$$
subject to
$$x_1 + x_2 \le 12,$$
$$x_1 + x_2 \ge 5,$$
$$x_1 \le 10,$$
$$x_1, x_2 \ge 0.$$

24. Minimize
$$Z = 2x_1 + x_2$$
subject to
$$x_1 + 2x_2 \le 6,$$
$$x_1 + x_2 \ge 1,$$
$$x_1, x_2 \ge 0.$$

25. Minimize
$$Z = x_1 + 2x_2 + x_3$$
subject to
$$x_1 - x_2 - x_3 \le -1,$$
$$6x_1 + 3x_2 + 2x_3 = 12,$$
$$x_1, x_2, x_3 \ge 0.$$

26. Maximize
$$Z = x_1 + 3x_2 + 2x_3$$
subject to
$$x_1 + x_2 + 4x_3 \ge 6,$$
$$2x_1 + x_2 + 3x_3 \le 4,$$
$$x_1, x_2, x_3 \ge 0.$$

†27. Maximize
$$Z = x_1 + 4x_2 + 2x_3$$
subject to
$$4x_1 - x_2 \le 2,$$
$$-10x_1 + x_2 + 3x_3 \le 1,$$
$$x_1, x_2, x_3 \ge 0.$$

†28. Minimize
$$Z = x_1 + x_2$$
subject to
$$x_1 + x_2 + 2x_3 \le 4,$$
$$x_3 \ge 1,$$
$$x_1, x_2, x_3 \ge 0.$$

* Refers to Sec. 9.3

† Refers to Sec. 9.3 or Sec. 9.5.

In Problems **29** *and* **30,** *solve by using duals and the simplex method.*

29. Minimize
$$Z = 2x_1 + 7x_2 + 8x_3$$
subject to
$$x_1 + 2x_2 + 3x_3 \geq 35,$$
$$x_1 + x_2 + x_3 \geq 25,$$
$$x_1, x_2, x_3 \geq 0.$$

30. Maximize
$$Z = x_1 - 2x_2$$
subject to
$$x_1 - x_2 \leq 3,$$
$$x_1 + 2x_2 \leq 4,$$
$$4x_1 + x_2 \geq 2,$$
$$x_1, x_2, \geq 0.$$

31. A company manufactures three products: X, Y, and Z. Each product requires the use of machine time on machines A and B as given in the table below. The number of hours per week that A and B are available for production are 40 and 34, respectively. The profit per unit on X, Y, and Z is $10, $15, and $22, respectively. What should be the weekly production order if maximum profit is to be obtained? What is the maximum profit?

	MACHINE A	MACHINE B
Product X	1 hr	1 hr
Product Y	2 hr	1 hr
Product Z	2 hr	2 hr

32. Repeat Problem 32 if the company must produce at least a total of 24 units per week.

33. An oil company has storage facilities for heating-fuel in cities A, B, C, and D. Cities C and D are each in need of exactly 500,000 gal of fuel. The company determines that A and B can each sacrifice at most 600,000 gal to satisfy the needs of C and D. The table below gives the costs per gallon to transport fuel between the cities. How should the company distribute the fuel in order to minimize the total transportation cost? What is the minimum transportation cost?

	TO	
FROM	C	D
A	$0.01	$0.02
B	$0.02	$0.04

CHAPTER 10

Limits and Continuity

10.1 LIMITS

Our study of calculus will begin in Chapter 11. Because the notion of a *limit* lies at the foundation of calculus, we must develop not only some understanding of that concept, but also insight. We shall first give you a "feeling" for limits by some examples.

Suppose we examine the function

$$f(x) = 2x - 1$$

when x is "near" 2 but not equal to 2. Some values of $f(x)$ for x less than 2 and then greater than 2 are given in Table 10.1. It is apparent that as x takes on

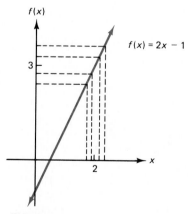

$f(x) = 2x - 1$

FIGURE 10.1

TABLE 10.1

$x < 2$	$x > 2$
$f(1.7) = 2.4$	$f(2.3) = 3.6$
$f(1.8) = 2.6$	$f(2.2) = 3.4$
$f(1.9) = 2.8$	$f(2.1) = 3.2$
$f(1.99) = 2.98$	$f(2.01) = 3.02$
$f(1.999) = 2.998$	$f(2.001) = 3.002$

values closer to 2, regardless of whether x approaches 2 *from the left* $(x < 2)$ or *from the right* $(x > 2)$, the corresponding values of $f(x)$ become closer to one number, 3. This is also clear from the graph of f in Fig 10.1. To express our conclusion we say that 3 is the **limit** of $f(x)$ as x approaches 2, which is written

$$\lim_{x \to 2} (2x - 1) = 3.$$

We can make the number $f(x)$ as close to 3 as we wish by taking x sufficiently close, but not equal, to 2.

You may think that you can find the limit of a function as x approaches some number a by just evaluating the function when x is a. For the function above this is true: $f(2) = 2(2) - 1 = 3$, which is also the limit. But simple substitution does not always work. For example, consider the function

$$g(x) = \begin{cases} 2x - 1, & \text{if } x \neq 2, \\ 1, & \text{if } x = 2. \end{cases}$$

Notice that $g(2) = 1$. Let us find the limit of $g(x)$ as x approaches 2, that is, as $x \rightarrow 2$. From the graph of g in Fig. 10.2, you can see that as x gets closer to 2

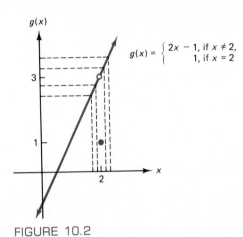

$$g(x) = \begin{cases} 2x - 1, \text{ if } x \neq 2, \\ 1, \text{ if } x = 2 \end{cases}$$

FIGURE 10.2

(but *not equal* to 2), then $g(x)$ gets closer to 3. Thus

$$\lim_{x \to 2} g(x) = 3,$$

which is *not* the same as $g(2)$.

Our results can be generalized to any function f. To say that "the limit of $f(x)$, as x approaches a, is L," written

$$\lim_{x \to a} f(x) = L,$$

means that $f(x)$ will be as close to the number L as we please for all x sufficiently close to the number a but not equal to a. Again, here we are not concerned with what happens to $f(x)$ when x *equals a,* but only what happens to it when x is *close* to a. We emphasize that a limit is independent of the way $x \rightarrow a$. The limit must be the same whether x approaches a from the left or from the right (for $x < a$ or $x > a$, respectively).

We shall now state some properties of limits which may seem reasonable to you.

1. If $f(x) = c$ is a constant function, then $\lim\limits_{x \to a} f(x) = \lim\limits_{x \to a} c = c$.

2. $\lim\limits_{x \to a} x^n = a^n$, for any positive integer n.

EXAMPLE 1

a. $\lim_{x \to 2} 7 = 7;$ $\lim_{x \to -5} 7 = 7.$

b. $\lim_{x \to 6} x^2 = 6^2 = 36.$

c. $\lim_{t \to -2} t^4 = (-2)^4 = 16.$

Some other properties of limits are as follows, where we assume that f and g have limits as $x \to a$.

3. $\displaystyle \lim_{x \to a} [f(x) \pm g(x)] = \lim_{x \to a} f(x) \pm \lim_{x \to a} g(x).$

That is, the limit of a sum or difference is the sum or difference, respectively, of the limits. This property can be extended to the limit of a finite number of sums and differences. Similarly, Property 4 states that the limit of a product is the product of the limits.

4. $\displaystyle \lim_{x \to a} [f(x) \cdot g(x)] = \lim_{x \to a} f(x) \cdot \lim_{x \to a} g(x).$

5. $\displaystyle \lim_{x \to a} [cf(x)] = c \cdot \lim_{x \to a} f(x),$ where c is a constant.

EXAMPLE 2

a. $\displaystyle \lim_{x \to 2} (x^2 + x) = \lim_{x \to 2} x^2 + \lim_{x \to 2} x = 2^2 + 2 = 6$ [Properties 3, 2].

b. $\displaystyle \lim_{q \to -1} (q^3 - q + 1) = \lim_{q \to -1} q^3 - \lim_{q \to -1} q + \lim_{q \to -1} 1$

$$= (-1)^3 - (-1) + 1 = 1.$$

c. $\displaystyle \lim_{x \to 2} [(x + 1)(x - 3)] = \lim_{x \to 2} (x + 1) \cdot \lim_{x \to 2} (x - 3)$ [Property 4]

$$= [\lim_{x \to 2} x + \lim_{x \to 2} 1] \cdot [\lim_{x \to 2} x - \lim_{x \to 2} 3]$$

$$= [2 + 1] \cdot [2 - 3] = 3[-1] = -3.$$

d. $\displaystyle \lim_{x \to -2} 3x^2 = 3 \lim_{x \to -2} x^3 = 3(-2)^3 = -24$ [Properties 5, 2].

EXAMPLE 3   Let $f(x) = c_n x^n + c_{n-1} x^{n-1} + \cdots + c_1 x + c_0$ be a polynomial function f. Then

$$\lim_{x \to a} f(x) = \lim_{x \to a} (c_n x^n + c_{n-1} x^{n-1} + \cdots + c_1 x + c_0)$$

$$= c_n \cdot \lim_{x \to a} x^n + c_{n-1} \cdot \lim_{x \to a} x^{n-1} + \cdots + c_1 \cdot \lim_{x \to a} x + \lim_{x \to a} c_0$$

$$= c_n a^n + c_{n-1} a^{n-1} + \cdots + c_1 a + c_0 = f(a).$$

Thus **if f is a polynomial function, then**

$$\lim_{x \to a} f(x) = f(a).$$

The result of Example 3 allows us to find many limits as $x \to a$ by just substituting a for x. For example,

$$\lim_{x \to -3} (x^3 + 4x^2 - 7) = (-3)^3 + 4(-3)^2 - 7 = 2,$$

$$\lim_{h \to 3} [2(h - 1)] = 2(3 - 1) = 4.$$

Our final two properties will concern limits involving quotients and roots.

6. $\displaystyle \lim_{x \to a} \frac{f(x)}{g(x)} = \frac{\displaystyle \lim_{x \to a} f(x)}{\displaystyle \lim_{x \to a} g(x)}$, **if** $\displaystyle \lim_{x \to a} g(x) \neq 0.$

That is, a limit of a quotient is the quotient of the limits, provided the denominator does not have a limit of 0.

7. $\displaystyle \lim_{x \to a} \sqrt[n]{f(x)} = \sqrt[n]{\lim_{x \to a} f(x)}.$*

EXAMPLE 4

a. $\displaystyle \lim_{x \to 1} \frac{2x^2 + x - 3}{x^3 + 4} = \frac{\displaystyle \lim_{x \to 1} (2x^2 + x - 3)}{\displaystyle \lim_{x \to 1} (x^3 + 4)} = \frac{2 + 1 - 3}{1 + 4} = \frac{0}{5} = 0.$

b. $\displaystyle \lim_{t \to 4} \sqrt{t^2 + 1} = \sqrt{\lim_{t \to 4} (t^2 + 1)} = \sqrt{17}.$

c. $\displaystyle \lim_{x \to 3} \sqrt[3]{x^2 + 7} = \sqrt[3]{\lim_{x \to 3} (x^2 + 7)} = \sqrt[3]{16} = \sqrt[3]{8 \cdot 2} = 2\sqrt[3]{2}.$

EXAMPLE 5   *Find* $\displaystyle \lim_{x \to -1} \frac{x^2 - 1}{x + 1}.$

As $x \to -1$, both numerator and denominator approach zero. Because the limit of the denominator is 0, we cannot use Property 6. However, since what happens to the quotient when x equals -1 is of no concern, we can assume $x \neq -1$ and write

$$\frac{x^2 - 1}{x + 1} = \frac{(x + 1)(x - 1)}{x + 1} = x - 1.$$

---

* If n is even, we require that $\displaystyle \lim_{x \to a} f(x)$ be positive.

This algebraic manipulation on the original function $\dfrac{x^2 - 1}{x + 1}$ yields a new function $x - 1$, which is the same as the original function for $x \neq -1$. Thus

$$\lim_{x \to -1} \frac{x^2 - 1}{x + 1} = \lim_{x \to -1} \frac{(x + 1)(x - 1)}{x + 1} = \lim_{x \to -1} (x - 1) = -2.$$

Notice that, although the original function is not defined at -1, it *does* have a limit as $x \to -1$.

In Example 5 the method of finding a limit by direct substitution does not work. Replacing x by -1 gives 0/0, which has no meaning. When the meaningless form 0/0 arises, algebraic manipulation (as in Example 5) may result in a form for which the limit *can* be determined. In fact, many important limits cannot be evaluated by substitution.

EXAMPLE 6   *If* $f(x) = x^2 + 1$, *find* $\lim\limits_{h \to 0} \dfrac{f(x + h) - f(x)}{h}$.

$$\lim_{h \to 0} \frac{f(x + h) - f(x)}{h} = \lim_{h \to 0} \frac{[(x + h)^2 + 1] - (x^2 + 1)}{h}.$$

Here we treat x as a constant because h, not x, is changing. As $h \to 0$, both the numerator and denominator approach 0. Therefore, we shall try to express the quotient in a different form for $h \neq 0$.

$$\lim_{h \to 0} \frac{[(x + h)^2 + 1] - (x^2 + 1)}{h} = \lim_{h \to 0} \frac{[x^2 + 2xh + h^2 + 1] - x^2 - 1}{h}$$

$$= \lim_{h \to 0} \frac{2xh + h^2}{h} = \lim_{h \to 0} \frac{h(2x + h)}{h}$$

$$= \lim_{h \to 0} (2x + h) = 2x.$$

EXERCISE 10.1

In Problems 1–28, find the limits.

1. $\lim\limits_{x \to 2} 16$.

2. $\lim\limits_{x \to 3} 2x$.

3. $\lim\limits_{x \to 4} (x + 3)$.

4. $\lim\limits_{s \to 1} 2$.

5. $\lim\limits_{t \to -5} (t^2 - 5)$.

6. $\lim\limits_{t \to 1/2} (3t - 5)$.

7. $\lim\limits_{x \to -1} (x^3 - 3x^2 - 2x + 1)$.

8. $\lim\limits_{r \to 9} \dfrac{4r - 3}{11}$.

9. $\lim\limits_{t \to -3} \dfrac{t - 2}{t + 5}$.

10. $\lim\limits_{x \to -6} \dfrac{x^2 + 6}{x - 6}$.

11. $\lim\limits_{h \to 0} \dfrac{h}{h^2 - 7h + 1}$.

12. $\lim\limits_{h \to 0} \dfrac{h^2 - 2h - 4}{h^3 - 1}$.

13. $\lim\limits_{p \to 4} \sqrt{p^2 + p + 5}$.

14. $\lim\limits_{y \to 9} \sqrt{y + 3}$.

15. $\lim\limits_{x \to -2} \dfrac{x^2 + 2x}{x + 2}$.

16. $\lim\limits_{x \to -1} \dfrac{x + 1}{x + 1}$.

17. $\lim\limits_{x \to 2} \dfrac{x^2 - x - 2}{x - 2}$.

18. $\lim\limits_{t \to 0} \dfrac{t^2 + 2t}{t^2 - 2t}$.

19. $\lim\limits_{x \to -1} \dfrac{x^2 + 2x + 1}{x + 1}$.

20. $\lim\limits_{t \to 1} \dfrac{t^2 - 1}{t - 1}$.

21. $\lim\limits_{x \to 3} \dfrac{x - 3}{x^2 - 9}$.

22. $\lim\limits_{x \to 0} \dfrac{x^2 - 2x}{x}$.

23. $\lim\limits_{x \to 4} \dfrac{x^2 - 9x + 20}{x^2 - 3x - 4}$.

24. $\lim\limits_{x \to 2} \dfrac{x^2 - 2x}{x - 2}$.

25. $\lim\limits_{x \to 2} \dfrac{3x^2 - x - 10}{x^2 + 5x - 14}$.

26. $\lim\limits_{x \to -4} \dfrac{x^2 + 2x - 8}{x^2 + 5x + 4}$.

27. $\lim\limits_{h \to 0} \dfrac{(2 + h)^2 - 2^2}{h}$.

28. $\lim\limits_{x \to 0} \dfrac{(x + 2)^2 - 4}{x}$.

29. Find $\lim\limits_{h \to 0} \dfrac{(x + h)^2 - x^2}{h}$ by treating x as a constant.

30. Find $\lim\limits_{h \to 0} \dfrac{2(x + h)^2 + 5(x + h) - 2x^2 - 5x}{h}$ by treating x as a constant.

In Problems **31–34,** *find* $\lim\limits_{h \to 0} \dfrac{f(x + h) - f(x)}{h}$.

31. $f(x) = 4 - x$.

32. $f(x) = 2x + 3$.

33. $f(x) = x^2 - 3$.

34. $f(x) = x^2 + x + 1$.

35. Shonle* indicates that the maximum theoretical efficiency E of a power plant is given by

$$E = \frac{T_h - T_c}{T_h},$$

where T_c and T_h are the respective absolute temperatures of the hotter and colder reservoirs. Find (a) $\lim\limits_{T_c \to 0} E$ and (b) $\lim\limits_{T_c \to T_h} E$.

10.2 LIMITS, CONTINUED

Figure 10.3 shows the graph of a function f. Notice that $f(x)$ is not defined when

---

* J. I. Shonle, *Environmental Applications of General Physics* (Reading, Mass.: Addison-Wesley Publishing Company, Inc., 1975).

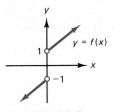

FIGURE 10.3

$x = 0$. As x approaches 0 *from the right*, $f(x)$ approaches 1. We write this as

$$\lim_{x \to 0^+} f(x) = 1.$$

On the other hand, as x approaches 0 *from the left*, $f(x)$ approaches -1 and we write

$$\lim_{x \to 0^-} f(x) = -1.$$

Limits like these are called **one-sided limits.** From the last section we know that the limit of a function as $x \to a$ is independent of the way x approaches a. Thus the limit will exist if and only if both one-sided limits exist and are equal. We therefore conclude that

$$\lim_{x \to 0} f(x) \text{ does not exist.}$$

As another example of a one-sided limit, consider $f(x) = \sqrt{x - 3}$ as x approaches 3 (see Fig. 10.4). Since f is defined only when $x \geq 3$, we may speak

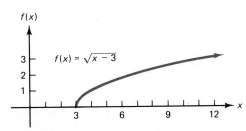

FIGURE 10.4

of the limit as x approaches 3 from the right. If x is slightly greater than 3, then $x - 3$ is a positive number that is close to 0 and thus $\sqrt{x - 3}$ is close to 0. Hence

$$\lim_{x \to 3^+} \sqrt{x - 3} = 0.$$

This limit is also evident from Fig. 10.4.

Now let us consider $y = f(x) = 1/x^2$ near $x = 0$. If x is close to 0, then x^2 is positive and also close to 0, and thus its reciprocal, $1/x^2$, is very large. Figure 10.5 shows a table of values of $f(x)$ for x near 0, together with the graph of the function. Notice that as $x \to 0$, both from the left and from the right, $f(x)$ increases without bound. Hence no limit exists at 0. We say that as $x \to 0$, $f(x)$ becomes positively infinite and symbolially we write

$$\lim_{x \to 0} \frac{1}{x^2} = \infty$$

Pitfall

The use of the "equals" sign in this situation does not mean that the limit exists. On the contrary, the symbolism here (∞) is a way of saying specifically that there is no limit and it indicates **why** there is no limit.

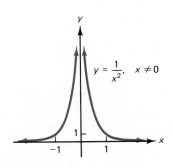

x	$f(x)$
±1	1
±0.5	4
±0.1	100
±0.01	10,000
±0.001	1,000,000

FIGURE 10.5

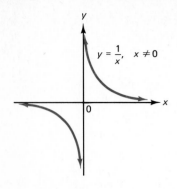

$y = \dfrac{1}{x}, \quad x \neq 0$

x	$f(x)$
0.01	100
0.001	1,000
0.0001	10,000
−0.01	−100
−0.001	−1,000
−0.0001	−10,000

FIGURE 10.6

Consider now the graph of $y = f(x) = 1/x$ for $x \neq 0$ (see Fig. 10.6). As x approaches 0 from the right, $1/x$ becomes positively infinite; as x approaches 0 from the left, $1/x$ becomes negatively infinite. Symbolically, we write

$$\lim_{x \to 0^+} \frac{1}{x} = \infty \qquad \text{and} \qquad \lim_{x \to 0^-} \frac{1}{x} = -\infty.$$

Either one of these facts implies that

$$\lim_{x \to 0} \frac{1}{x} \text{ does not exist.}$$

Now let us examine this function as x becomes infinite, first in a positive sense and then in a negative sense. From Table 10.2 you can see that as x increases

TABLE 10.2

x	$f(x)$	x	$f(x)$
1,000	0.001	−1,000	−0.001
10,000	0.0001	−10,000	−0.0001
100,000	0.00001	−100,000	−0.00001
1,000,000	0.000001	−1,000,000	−0.000001

without bound through positive values, the values of $f(x)$ approach 0. Likewise, as x decreases without bound through negative values, the values of $f(x)$ also approach 0. These observations are also apparent from the graph in Fig. 10.6. Symbolically, we write

$$\lim_{x \to \infty} \frac{1}{x} = 0 \qquad \text{and} \qquad \lim_{x \to -\infty} \frac{1}{x} = 0.$$

EXAMPLE 1   *Find the limit (if it exists).*

a. $\displaystyle \lim_{x \to -1^+} \frac{2}{x + 1}$.

As x approaches -1 from the right, $x + 1$ approaches 0 but is always positive. Since we are dividing 2 by positive numbers approaching 0, the results, $2/(x + 1)$, are positive numbers that are becoming arbitrarily large. Thus

$$\lim_{x \to -1^+} \frac{2}{x + 1} = \infty,$$

and the limit does not exist.

b. $\displaystyle \lim_{x \to 2} \frac{x + 2}{x^2 - 4}$.

As $x \to 2$ the numerator approaches 4 and the denominator approaches 0. Thus we are dividing numbers near 4 by numbers near 0. The results are numbers that become arbitrarily large in magnitude. At this stage we can write

$$\lim_{x \to 2} \frac{x + 2}{x^2 - 4} \text{ does not exist.}$$

However, let us see if we can use the symbol ∞ or $-\infty$ to be more specific about "does not exist." Notice that

$$\lim_{x \to 2} \frac{x + 2}{x^2 - 4} = \lim_{x \to 2} \frac{x + 2}{(x + 2)(x - 2)} = \lim_{x \to 2} \frac{1}{x - 2}.$$

Since

$$\lim_{x \to 2^+} \frac{1}{x - 2} = \infty \quad \text{and} \quad \lim_{x \to 2^-} \frac{1}{x - 2} = -\infty,$$

then $\lim_{x \to 2} \dfrac{x + 2}{x^2 - 4}$ is neither ∞ nor $-\infty$.

c. $\lim_{t \to 2} \dfrac{t - 2}{t^2 - 4}.$

As $t \to 2$ both numerator and denominator approach 0. Thus we first simplify the fraction, as we did in Sec. 10.1.

$$\lim_{t \to 2} \frac{t - 2}{t^2 - 4} = \lim_{t \to 2} \frac{t - 2}{(t + 2)(t - 2)} = \lim_{t \to 2} \frac{1}{t + 2} = \frac{1}{4}.$$

d. $\lim_{x \to \infty} \dfrac{4}{(x - 5)^3}.$

As x becomes very large, so does $x - 5$. Since the cube of a large number is also large, $(x - 5)^3 \to \infty$. Dividing 4 by very large numbers results in numbers near 0. Thus

$$\lim_{x \to \infty} \frac{4}{(x - 5)^3} = 0.$$

In our next discussion we shall need a certain limit, namely, $\lim_{x \to \infty} 1/x^p$ where

$p > 0$. As x becomes very large, so does x^p. Dividing 1 by very large numbers results in numbers near 0. Thus $\lim_{x \to \infty} 1/x^p = 0$. In general,

$$\boxed{\lim_{x \to \infty} \frac{1}{x^p} = 0 \quad \text{and} \quad \lim_{x \to -\infty} \frac{1}{x^p} = 0,}$$

where $p > 0$.*

Let us now find the limit of the function

$$f(x) = \frac{4x^3 + x}{2x^3 + 3}$$

* For $\lim_{x \to -\infty} 1/x^p$, we assume that p is such that $1/x^p$ is defined for $x < 0$.

as $x \to \infty$. This function is a quotient of polynomials and is called a **rational function.** As x gets larger and larger, *both* the numerator and denominator of $f(x)$ become infinite. However, the form of the quotient can be changed so that we can draw a conclusion as to whether or not it has a limit. To do this, we divide both the numerator and denominator by the greatest power of x that occurs in the denominator. Here it is x^3. This gives

$$\lim_{x \to \infty} \frac{4x^3 + x}{2x^3 + 3} = \lim_{x \to \infty} \frac{\dfrac{4x^3 + x}{x^3}}{\dfrac{2x^3 + 3}{x^3}}$$

$$= \lim_{x \to \infty} \frac{\dfrac{4x^3}{x^3} + \dfrac{x}{x^3}}{\dfrac{2x^3}{x^3} + \dfrac{3}{x^3}}$$

$$= \lim_{x \to \infty} \frac{4 + \dfrac{1}{x^2}}{2 + \dfrac{3}{x^3}} = \frac{\lim_{x \to \infty} 4 + \lim_{x \to \infty} \dfrac{1}{x^2}}{\lim_{x \to \infty} 2 + 3 \cdot \lim_{x \to \infty} \dfrac{1}{x^3}}.$$

Since $\lim_{x \to \infty} 1/x^p = 0$ for $p > 0$,

$$\lim_{x \to \infty} \frac{4x^3 + x}{2x^3 + 3} = \frac{4 + 0}{2 + 3(0)} = \frac{4}{2} = 2.$$

Similarly, the limit as $x \to -\infty$ is 2.

There is an easier way to find $\lim_{x \to \infty} f(x)$. For *large* values of x, in the numerator the term involving the greatest power of x, namely $4x^3$, dominates the sum $4x^3 + x$, and the dominant term in the denominator, $2x^3 + 3$, is $2x^3$. Hence to determine the limit of $f(x)$, it suffices to determine the limit of $(4x^3)/(2x^3)$. That is,

$$\lim_{x \to \infty} \frac{4x^3 + x}{2x^3 + 3} = \lim_{x \to \infty} \frac{4x^3}{2x^3} = \lim_{x \to \infty} 2 = 2,$$

as we saw before. In general, we have the following.

If $f(x)$ is a rational function and $a_n x^n$ and $b_m x^m$ are the terms in the numerator and denominator, respectively, with the greatest powers of x, then

$$\lim_{x \to \infty} f(x) = \lim_{x \to \infty} \frac{a_n x^n}{b_m x^m}$$

and $$\lim_{x \to -\infty} f(x) = \lim_{x \to -\infty} \frac{a_n x^n}{b_m x^m}.$$

For example,

$$\lim_{x \to -\infty} \frac{x^4 - 3x}{5 - 2x} = \lim_{x \to -\infty} \frac{x^4}{-2x} = \lim_{x \to -\infty} \left(-\frac{1}{2} x^3 \right) = \infty.$$

(Note that in the next-to-last step, as x becomes very negative, so does x^3; moreover, $-\frac{1}{2}$ times a very negative number is very positive.) Similarly,

$$\lim_{x \to \infty} \frac{x^4 - 3x}{5 - 2x} = \lim_{x \to \infty} \left(-\frac{1}{2} x^3 \right) = -\infty.$$

From this illustration we conclude that *whenever the degree of the numerator of a rational function is greater than the degree of the denominator, the function has no limit as $x \to \infty$ or as $x \to -\infty$.*

EXAMPLE 2   *Find the limit (if it exists).*

a. $\lim\limits_{x \to \infty} \dfrac{x^2 - 1}{7 - 2x + 8x^2}.$

$$\lim_{x \to \infty} \frac{x^2 - 1}{7 - 2x + 8x^2} = \lim_{x \to \infty} \frac{x^2}{8x^2} = \lim_{x \to \infty} \frac{1}{8} = \frac{1}{8}.$$

b. $\lim\limits_{x \to -\infty} \dfrac{6x^2 - 5x}{x^4 + 2x^2 + 1}.$

$$\lim_{x \to -\infty} \frac{6x^2 - 5x}{x^4 + 2x^2 + 1} = \lim_{x \to -\infty} \frac{6x^2}{x^4} = \lim_{x \to -\infty} \frac{6}{x^2} = 6 \lim_{x \to -\infty} \frac{1}{x^2} = 6 \cdot 0 = 0.$$

c. $\lim\limits_{x \to \infty} \dfrac{x^5 - x^4}{x^4 - x^3 + 2}.$

Since the degree of the numerator is greater than that of the denominator, there is no limit. More precisely,

$$\lim_{x \to \infty} \frac{x^5 - x^4}{x^4 - x^3 + 2} = \lim_{x \to \infty} \frac{x^5}{x^4} = \lim_{x \to \infty} x = \infty.$$

Pitfall

To find $\lim\limits_{x \to 0} \dfrac{x^2 - 1}{7 - 2x + 8x^2}$, we do not determine the limit of $x^2/(8x^2)$ because x does not approach ∞ or $-\infty$. We have

$$\lim_{x \to 0} \frac{x^2 - 1}{7 - 2x + 8x^2} = \frac{0 - 1}{7 - 0 + 0} = -\frac{1}{7}.$$

We conclude this section with a note concerning a most important limit, namely

$$\lim_{x \to 0} (1 + x)^{1/x}.$$

Figure 10.7 shows the graph of $f(x) = (1 + x)^{1/x}$. As $x \to 0$, it is clear that the

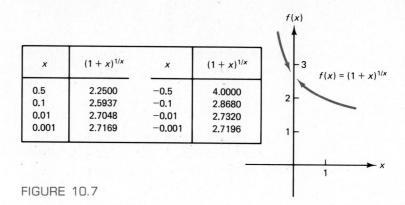

x	$(1 + x)^{1/x}$	x	$(1 + x)^{1/x}$
0.5	2.2500	−0.5	4.0000
0.1	2.5937	−0.1	2.8680
0.01	2.7048	−0.01	2.7320
0.001	2.7169	−0.001	2.7196

FIGURE 10.7

limit of $(1 + x)^{1/x}$ exists. It is approximately 2.71828 and is denoted by the letter e. This you recall, is the base of the system of natural logarithms. The limit

$$\lim_{x \to 0} (1 + x)^{1/x} = e$$

can actually be considered the definition of e.

EXERCISE 10.2

1. For the function f given in Fig. 10.8(a), find the following limits. If the limit does not exist, so state or use the symbol ∞ or $-\infty$ where appropriate.

a. $\lim_{x \to 1^-} f(x)$,   **b.** $\lim_{x \to 1^+} f(x)$,   **c.** $\lim_{x \to 1} f(x)$,   **d.** $\lim_{x \to \infty} f(x)$,

e. $\lim_{x \to -2^-} f(x)$,   **f.** $\lim_{x \to -2^+} f(x)$,   **g.** $\lim_{x \to -2} f(x)$,   **h.** $\lim_{x \to -\infty} f(x)$,

i. $\lim_{x \to -1^-} f(x)$,   **j.** $\lim_{x \to -1^+} f(x)$,   **k.** $\lim_{x \to -1} f(x)$.

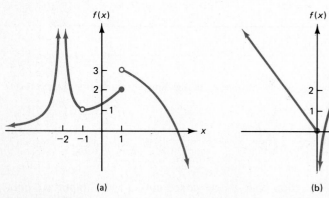

(a)   (b)

FIGURE 10.8

2. For the function f given in Fig. 10.8(b), find the following limits. If the limit does not exist, so state or use the symbol ∞ or $-\infty$ where appropriate.

a. $\lim\limits_{x \to 0^-} f(x)$,   **b.** $\lim\limits_{x \to 0^+} f(x)$,   **c.** $\lim\limits_{x \to 0} f(x)$,   **d.** $\lim\limits_{x \to -\infty} f(x)$,

e. $\lim\limits_{x \to 1} f(x)$,   **f.** $\lim\limits_{x \to 2^-} f(x)$,   **g.** $\lim\limits_{x \to 2^+} f(x)$,   **h.** $\lim\limits_{x \to \infty} f(x)$.

In each of Problems 3–46, find the limit. If the limit does not exist, so state or use the symbol ∞ or $-\infty$ where appropriate.

3. $\lim\limits_{x \to 3^+} (x - 2)$.

4. $\lim\limits_{x \to -1^-} (1 - x^2)$.

5. $\lim\limits_{x \to -\infty} 5x$.

6. $\lim\limits_{x \to \infty} 3$.

7. $\lim\limits_{x \to 0^-} \dfrac{6x}{x^4}$.

8. $\lim\limits_{x \to 0} \dfrac{5}{x - 1}$.

9. $\lim\limits_{x \to -\infty} x^2$.

10. $\lim\limits_{t \to \infty} (t - 1)^3$.

11. $\lim\limits_{h \to 0^+} \sqrt{h}$.

12. $\lim\limits_{h \to 5^-} \sqrt{5 - h}$.

13. $\lim\limits_{x \to 5} \dfrac{3}{x - 5}$.

14. $\lim\limits_{x \to 0^-} 2^{1/2}$.

15. $\lim\limits_{x \to 1^+} (4\sqrt{x - 1})$.

16. $\lim\limits_{x \to 2^+} (x\sqrt{x^2 - 4})$.

17. $\lim\limits_{x \to \infty} \dfrac{x + 2}{x + 3}$.

18. $\lim\limits_{x \to \infty} \dfrac{2x - 4}{3 - 2x}$.

19. $\lim\limits_{x \to -\infty} \dfrac{x^2 - 1}{x^3 + 4x - 3}$.

20. $\lim\limits_{r \to \infty} \dfrac{r^3}{r^2 + 1}$.

21. $\lim\limits_{t \to \infty} \dfrac{5t^2 + 2t + 1}{4t + 7}$.

22. $\lim\limits_{x \to -\infty} \dfrac{2x}{3x^6 - x + 4}$.

23. $\lim\limits_{x \to \infty} \dfrac{7}{2x + 1}$.

24. $\lim\limits_{x \to -\infty} \dfrac{1}{(4x - 1)^3}$.

25. $\lim\limits_{x \to \infty} \dfrac{3 - 4x - 2x^3}{5x^3 - 8x + 1}$.

26. $\lim\limits_{x \to \infty} \dfrac{7 - 2x - x^4}{9 - 3x^4 + 2x^2}$.

27. $\lim\limits_{x \to 3^-} \dfrac{x + 3}{x^2 - 9}$.

28. $\lim\limits_{x \to -2^+} \dfrac{2x}{4 - x^2}$.

29. $\lim\limits_{w \to \infty} \dfrac{2w^2 - 3w + 4}{5w^2 + 7w - 1}$.

30. $\lim\limits_{x \to \infty} \dfrac{4 - 3x^3}{x^3 - 1}$.

31. $\lim\limits_{x \to -5} \dfrac{2x^2 + 9x - 5}{x^2 + 5x}$.

32. $\lim\limits_{t \to 2} \dfrac{t^2 + 2t - 8}{2t^2 - 5t + 2}$.

33. $\lim\limits_{x \to 1} \dfrac{x^2 - 3x + 1}{x^2 + 1}$.

34. $\lim\limits_{x \to -1} \dfrac{3x^3 - x^2}{2x + 1}$.

35. $\lim\limits_{x \to 1^+} \left[1 + \dfrac{1}{x - 1} \right]$.

36. $\lim\limits_{x \to -\infty} \dfrac{x^3 + 2x^2 + 1}{x^3 - 4}$.

37. $\lim\limits_{x \to 0^+} \dfrac{2}{x + x^2}$.

38. $\lim\limits_{x \to \infty} \left(x + \dfrac{1}{x} \right)$.

39. $\lim\limits_{x \to 1} x(x - 1)^{-1}$.

40. $\lim\limits_{x \to 1/2} \dfrac{1}{2x - 1}$.

41. $\lim\limits_{x \to 0^+} \left(-\dfrac{3}{x} \right)$.

42. $\lim\limits_{x \to 0} \left(-\dfrac{3}{x} \right)$.

43. $\lim\limits_{x \to 0} |x|$.

44. $\lim\limits_{x \to 0} \left| \dfrac{1}{x} \right|$.

45. $\lim\limits_{x \to -\infty} \dfrac{x + 1}{x}$.

46. $\lim\limits_{x \to \infty} \left[\dfrac{2}{x} - \dfrac{x^2}{x^2 - 1} \right]$.

In Problems 47–50, sketch the graphs of the functions and find the indicated limits. If the limit does not exist, so state or use the symbol ∞ or $-\infty$ where appropriate.

47. $f(x) = \begin{cases} 2, & \text{if } x \le 2 \\ 1, & \text{if } x > 2 \end{cases}$;   **a.** $\lim\limits_{x \to 2^+} f(x)$,   **b.** $\lim\limits_{x \to 2^-} f(x)$,   **c.** $\lim\limits_{x \to 2} f(x)$,   **d.** $\lim\limits_{x \to \infty} f(x)$,   **e.** $\lim\limits_{x \to -\infty} f(x)$.

48. $f(x) = \begin{cases} x, & \text{if } x \le 1 \\ 2, & \text{if } x > 1 \end{cases}$;   **a.** $\lim\limits_{x \to 1^+} f(x)$,   **b.** $\lim\limits_{x \to 1^-} f(x)$,   **c.** $\lim\limits_{x \to 1} f(x)$,   **d.** $\lim\limits_{x \to \infty} f(x)$,   **e.** $\lim\limits_{x \to -\infty} f(x)$.

49. $g(x) = \begin{cases} x, & \text{if } x < 0 \\ -x, & \text{if } x > 0 \end{cases}$;   **a.** $\lim\limits_{x \to 0^+} g(x)$,   **b.** $\lim\limits_{x \to 0^-} g(x)$,   **c.** $\lim\limits_{x \to 0} g(x)$,   **d.** $\lim\limits_{x \to \infty} g(x)$,   **e.** $\lim\limits_{x \to -\infty} g(x)$.

50. $g(x) = \begin{cases} x^2, & \text{if } x < 0 \\ x, & \text{if } x > 0 \end{cases}$;   **a.** $\lim\limits_{x \to 0^+} g(x)$,   **b.** $\lim\limits_{x \to 0^-} g(x)$,   **c.** $\lim\limits_{x \to 0} g(x)$,   **d.** $\lim\limits_{x \to \infty} g(x)$,   **e.** $\lim\limits_{x \to -\infty} g(x)$.

51. If c is the total cost in dollars to produce q units of a product, then the average cost per unit $\bar{c}$ for an output of q units is given by $\bar{c} = c/q$. Thus, if the total cost equation is $c = 5000 + 6q$, then $\bar{c} = (5000/q) + 6$. For example, the total cost of an output of 5 units is $5030, and the average cost per unit at this level of production is $1006. By finding $\lim\limits_{q \to \infty} \bar{c}$, show that the average cost approaches a level of stability if the producer continually increases output. What is the limiting value of the average cost? Sketch the graph of the average cost function.

52. Repeat Problem 51 given that fixed cost is $12,000 and the variable cost is given by the function $c_v = 7q$.

53. The population N of a certain small city t years from now is predicted to be

$$N = 20,000 + \frac{10,000}{(t + 2)^2}.$$

Determine the population in the long run; that is, find $\lim\limits_{t \to \infty} N$.

(Calculator Problems) In Problems **54** *and* **55,** *evaluate the given function when* $x = 1, 0.5, 0.2, 0.1, 0.01, 0.001,$ *and* 0.0001. *From your results draw a conclusion about* $\lim\limits_{x \to 0^+} f(x)$.

54. $f(x) = x \ln x$.

55. $f(x) = x^{2x}$.

10.3 INTEREST COMPOUNDED CONTINUOUSLY _____

If a principal of P dollars is invested and interest is compounded k times a year at an annual rate of r, then the rate per conversion period is r/k. In t years there are kt periods. From Chapter 6 the compound amount S at the end of t years is

$$S = P\left(1 + \frac{r}{k}\right)^{kt}.$$

If $k \to \infty$, the number of conversion periods increases indefinitely and the length of each period approaches 0. In this case we say that interest is **compounded continuously,** that is, at every instant of time. The compound amount is

$$\lim_{k \to \infty} P\left(1 + \frac{r}{k}\right)^{kt},$$

which may be written

$$P\left[\lim_{k \to \infty} \left(1 + \frac{r}{k}\right)^{k/r}\right]^{rt}.$$

By letting $x = r/k$, then as $k \to \infty$ we have $x \to 0$. Thus the limit inside the brackets has the form $\lim\limits_{x \to 0} (1 + x)^{1/x}$ which, as we saw in Sec. 10.2, is e. Therefore,

$$S = Pe^{rt}$$

is the compound amount S of a principal of P dollars after t years at an annual interest rate r compounded continuously.

EXAMPLE 1   *If $100 is invested at an annual rate of 5% compounded continuously, find the compound amount at the end of (a) 1 year and (b) 5 years.*

a. Here $P = 100$, $r = 0.05$, and $t = 1$.

$$S = Pe^{rt} = 100e^{(0.05)(1)} \approx 100(1.0513) = \$105.13.$$

We can compare this value with the value after 1 year of a $100 investment at an annual rate of 5% compounded semiannually—namely, $100(1.025)^2 \approx$ $105.06. The difference is not significant.

b. Here $P = 100$, $r = 0.05$, and $t = 5$.

$$S = 100e^{(0.05)(5)} = 100e^{0.25} \approx 100(1.2840) = \$128.40.$$

We can find an expression that gives the effective rate which corresponds to an annual rate of r compounded continuously. If i is the corresponding effective rate, then after 1 year a principal P accumulates to $P(1 + i)$. This must equal the accumulated amount under continuous interest, Pe^r. Thus $P(1 + i) = Pe^r$ or $1 + i = e^r$, so $i = e^r - 1$. Therefore,

$$e^r - 1$$

is the **effective rate corresponding to an annual rate of r compounded continuously.**

EXAMPLE 2   *Find the effective rate which corresponds to an annual rate of 5% compounded continuously.*

The effective rate is

$$e^r - 1 = e^{0.05} - 1 \approx 1.0513 - 1 = 0.0513 \quad \text{or} \quad 5.13\%.$$

If we solve $S = Pe^{rt}$ for P, we get $P = S/e^{rt}$ or

$$P = Se^{-rt},$$

which is the **present value of S dollars due at the end of t years at an annual** rate of r compounded continuously. That is, P is the principal that must be invested now so that it will accumulate to S after t years.

EXAMPLE 3   *A trust fund is being set up by a single payment so that at the end of 20 years there will be $25,000 in the fund. If interest is compounded continuously at an annual rate of 7%, how much money should be paid into the fund initially?*

We want the present value of $25,000 due in 20 years.

$$P = Se^{-rt} = 25{,}000e^{-(0.07)(20)}$$

$$= 25{,}000e^{-1.4} \approx 25{,}000(0.24660)$$

$$= 6165.$$

Thus $6165 should be paid initially.

EXERCISE 10.3

In Problems **1** *and* **2**, *find the compound amount and compound interest if $4000 is invested for 6 years and interest is compounded continuously at the given annual rate.*

1. $5\frac{1}{2}\%$.   **2.** 9%.

In Problems **3** *and* **4**, *find the present value of $2500 due 8 years from now if interest is compounded continuously at the given annual rate.*

3. $6\frac{3}{4}\%$.   **4.** 8%.

In Problems **5–8**, *find the effective rate of interest which corresponds to the given annual rate compounded continuously.*

5. 4%.   **6.** 7%.   **7.** 10%.   **8.** 9%.

9. If $100 is deposited in a savings account that earns interest at an annual rate of $5\frac{1}{2}\%$ compounded continuously, what is the value of the account at the end of 2 years?

10. If $1000 is invested at an annual rate of 6% compounded continuously, find the compound amount at the end of 8 years.

11. The board of directors of a corporation agrees to redeem some of its callable preferred stock in 5 years. At that time $1,000,000 will be required. If the corporation can invest money at an annual interest rate of 8% compounded continuously, how much should it presently invest so that the future value is sufficient to redeem the shares?

12. A trust fund is being set up by a single payment so that at the end of 30 years there will be $50,000 in the fund.

If interest is compounded continuously at an annual rate of 5%, how much money should be paid into the fund initially?

13. What annual rate compounded continuously is equivalent to an effective rate of 5%?

14. What annual rate r compounded continuously is equivalent to a nominal rate of 6% compounded semiannually? [*Hint*: First show that $r = 2 \ln (1.03)$.]

15. An annuity in which R dollars are paid each year by uniform payments that are payable continuously is called a *continuous annuity* or a *continuous income stream*. The present value of a continuous annuity for t years is

$$R\frac{1 - e^{-rt}}{r},$$

where r is the annual rate of interest compounded continuously. Find the present value of a continuous annuity of $100 a year for 20 years at 9% compounded continuously. Give your answer to the nearest dollar.

16. Suppose a business has an annual profit of $40,000 for the next 5 years and the profits are earned continuously throughout each year. Then the profits can be thought of as a continuous annuity (see Problem 15). If money is worth 5% compounded continuously, find the present value of the profits.

17. If interest is compounded continuously at an annual rate of 0.07, how many years would it take for a principal P to triple? Give your answer to the nearest year.

18. If interest is compounded continuously, at what annual rate will a principal of P double in 10 years? Give your answer to the nearest percent.

10.4 CONTINUITY

Many functions have the property that there is no "break" in their graphs. For example, compare Figs. 10.9 and 10.10. When $x = 1$ the graph of the function

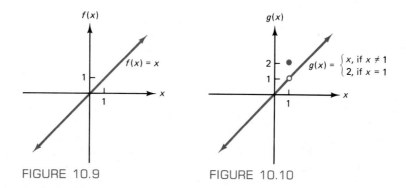

FIGURE 10.9   FIGURE 10.10

f is unbroken, but the graph of g has a break. Stated another way, if you were to trace both graphs with a pencil, you would have to lift the pencil on the graph of g when $x = 1$, but you would not have to lift it on the graph of f. We characterize these situations by saying that f is *continuous* at $x = 1$ and g is *discontinuous* at $x = 1$.

Definition

*A function f is **continuous** at the point $x = a$ (or simply, continuous at a) if and only if there is no break in its graph at $x = a$.* If f is not continuous at a point, then it is said to be **discontinuous** there.*

We say that a function is *continuous on an interval* if it is continuous at each point there. In such a situation, the function has a graph that is connected over the interval.

* This geometric approach to continuity is sufficient for our purposes. A more formal definition of continuity involves limits.

EXAMPLE 1

a. In Fig. 10.11(a) the graph of f has no break, so f is continuous for all values of x. To describe this, we say that f is **continuous everywhere,** or simply f is **continuous.**

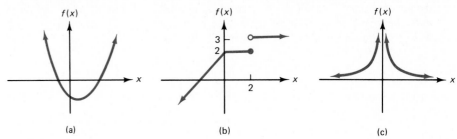

FIGURE 10.11

b. In Fig. 10.11(b) the graph has a break, or *discontinuity* for $x = 2$ only. Thus f is discontinuous at 2 and is continuous on $(-\infty, 2)$ and on $(2, \infty)$.

c. In Fig. 10.11(c) the graph has a break at $x = 0$ only. Thus f is discontinuous at 0 and is continuous otherwise.

EXAMPLE 2   *Determine whether* $f(x) = \dfrac{x^2 - 1}{x - 1}$ *is continuous at 1.*

Because this function is not defined at $x = 1$, its graph has no point there. This causes a break in the graph, so f is discontinuous at 1. In general, *if a function is not defined at $x = a$, it is discontinuous there.* It is interesting to note that

$$f(x) = \frac{x^2 - 1}{x - 1} = \frac{(x + 1)(x - 1)}{x - 1} = x + 1, \qquad x \neq 1.$$

Thus the graph of f is the same as the graph of $y = x + 1$ (which is a straight line) except that it has a hole in it when $x = 1$ (see Fig. 10.12).

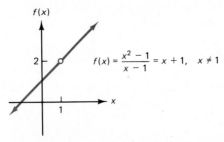

FIGURE 10.12

If a function has a certain form, we can easily determine whether or not it is continuous. It can be shown that:

1. A polynomial function is continuous everywhere.

2. A rational function is discontinuous at points where the denominator is 0 and is continuous otherwise.

EXAMPLE 3   *For each of the following functions, determine all points of discontinuity.*

a. $f(x) = 2x^2 + 5x + 4$.

Since f is a polynomial, it is continuous everywhere and hence has no points of discontinuity.

b. $F(x) = \dfrac{x^2 - 3}{x^2 + 2x - 8}$.

This rational function has denominator

$$x^2 + 2x - 8 = (x + 4)(x - 2),$$

which is 0 when $x = -4$ or $x = 2$. Thus F is discontinuous only at -4 and 2.

c. $h(x) = \dfrac{x + 4}{x^2 + 4}$.

For this rational function, the denominator is never 0 (it is always positive). Thus h has no discontinuity.

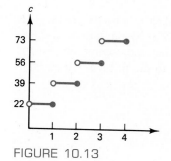

FIGURE 10.13

EXAMPLE 4   The "post-office function"

$$c = f(x) = \begin{cases} 22, & \text{if } 0 < x \le 1, \\ 39, & \text{if } 1 < x \le 2, \\ 56, & \text{if } 2 < x \le 3, \\ 73, & \text{if } 3 < x \le 4 \end{cases}$$

gives the cost c (in cents) of mailing a parcel of weight x (ounces), $0 < x \le 4$, in January 1986. It is clear from its graph in Fig. 10.13 that f has discontinuities at 1, 2, and 3 and is constant for values of x between successive discontinuities. Such a function is called a *step function* because of the appearance of its graph.

EXAMPLE 5   *Find all points of discontinuity of*

$$f(x) = \begin{cases} x + 6, & \text{if } x \ge 3, \\ x^2, & \text{if } x < 3 \end{cases}$$

by sketching its graph.

Figure 10.14 shows the graph of f. Because the graph has no break, there is no

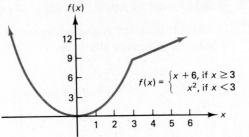

$$f(x) = \begin{cases} x + 6, & \text{if } x \geq 3 \\ x^2, & \text{if } x < 3 \end{cases}$$

FIGURE 10.14

point of discontinuity. The function is continuous everywhere.

Often it is helpful to describe a situation by a by a continuous function. For example, the demand schedule in Table 10.3 indicates the number of units of a

TABLE 10.3
Demand Schedule

PRICE/UNIT, p	QUANTITY PER WEEK, q
$20	0
10	5
5	15
4	20
2	45
1	95

particular product that consumers will demand per week at various prices. This information can be given graphically as in Fig. 10.15(a) by plotting each quantity-price pair as a point. Clearly, this graph does not represent a continuous function. Furthermore, it gives us no information as to the price at which, say,

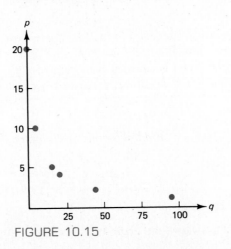

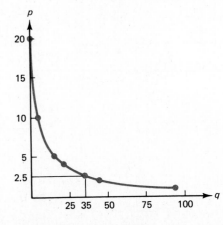

FIGURE 10.15

35 units would be demanded. However, if we connect the points in Fig. 10.15(a) by a smooth curve [see Fig. 10.15(b)], we get a so-called demand curve. From it we could guess that at about $2.50 per unit, 35 units would be demanded.

Frequently it is possible and useful to describe a graph, as in Fig. 10.15(b), by means of an equation that defines a continuous function f. Such a function not only gives us a demand equation, $p = f(q)$, which allows us to anticipate corresponding prices and quantities demanded, it also permits a convenient mathematical analysis of the nature and basic properties of demand. Of course some care must be used in working with equations such as $p = f(q)$. Mathematically, f may be defined when $q = \sqrt{37}$, but from a practical standpoint, a demand of $\sqrt{37}$ units could be meaningless to our particular situation. For example, if a unit is an egg, then a demand of $\sqrt{37}$ eggs makes no sense.

In general, it will be our desire to view practical situations in terms of continuous functions whenever possible so that we may be better able to analyze their nature.

EXERCISE 10.4

In Problems **1–4,** *determine whether the function is continuous at the given points.*

1. $f(x) = \dfrac{x + 4}{x - 2}$; $-2, 0$.

2. $f(x) = \dfrac{x^2 - 4x + 4}{6}$; $2, -2$.

3. $g(x) = \dfrac{x - 3}{x^2 - 9}$; $3, -3$.

4. $h(x) = \dfrac{3}{x^2 + 4}$; $2, -2$.

In Problems **5–8,** *give a reason why the function is continuous everywhere.*

5. $f(x) = 2x^2 - 3$.

6. $f(x) = \dfrac{x + 2}{5}$.

7. $f(x) = \dfrac{x - 1}{x^2 + 4}$.

8. $f(x) = x(1 - x)$.

In Problems **9–20,** *find all points of discontinuity.*

9. $f(x) = 3x^2 - 3$.

10. $h(x) = x - 2$.

11. $f(x) = \dfrac{3}{x - 4}$.

12. $f(x) = \dfrac{x^2 + 3x - 4}{x + 4}$.

13. $g(x) = \dfrac{(x^2 - 1)^2}{5}$.

14. $f(x) = 0$.

15. $f(x) = \dfrac{x^2 + 6x + 9}{x^2 + 2x - 15}$.

16. $g(x) = \dfrac{x - 3}{x^2 + x}$.

17. $h(x) = \dfrac{x - 7}{x^3 - x}$.

18. $f(x) = \dfrac{x}{x}$.

19. $p(x) = \dfrac{x}{x^2 + 1}$.

20. $f(x) = \dfrac{x^4}{x^4 - 1}$.

In Problems **21–24,** *find all points of discontinuity by sketching the graph of the function.*

21. $f(x) = \begin{cases} 1, & \text{if } x \geq 0, \\ -1, & \text{if } x < 0. \end{cases}$

22. $f(x) = \begin{cases} 2x + 1, & \text{if } x \geq -1, \\ 1, & \text{if } x < -1. \end{cases}$

23. $f(x) = \begin{cases} 0, & \text{if } x \leq 1, \\ x - 1, & \text{if } x > 1. \end{cases}$

24. $f(x) = \begin{cases} x - 3, & \text{if } x > 2, \\ 3 - 2x, & \text{if } x < 2. \end{cases}$

25. Suppose the long-distance rate for a telephone call from Hazleton, Pennsylvania, to Los Angeles, California, is $0.29 for the first minute and $0.20 for each additional minute or fraction thereof. If $y = f(t)$ is a function that indicates the total charge y for a call of t minutes' duration, sketch the graph of f for $0 < t \leq 4\frac{1}{2}$. Use your graph to determine the values of t, where $0 < t \leq 4\frac{1}{2}$, at which discontinuities occur.

26. The *greatest integer function*, $f(x) = [x]$, is defined to be the greatest integer less than or equal to x, where x is any real number. For example, $[3] = 3$, $[1.999] =$

1, $[\frac{1}{4}] = 0$, and $[-4.5] = -5$. Sketch the graph of this function for $-3.5 \leq x \leq 3.5$. Use your sketch to determine the values of x at which discontinuities occur.

27. Sketch the graph of

$$y = f(x) = \begin{cases} -100x + 600, & \text{if } 0 \leq x < 5, \\ -100x + 1100, & \text{if } 5 \leq x < 10, \\ -100x + 1600, & \text{if } 10 \leq x < 15. \end{cases}$$

A function such as this might describe the inventory y of a company at time x. If f continous at 2? At 5? At 10?

10.5 CONTINUITY APPLIED TO INEQUALITIES

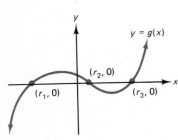

FIGURE 10.16

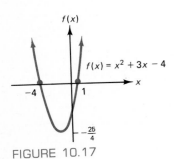

FIGURE 10.17

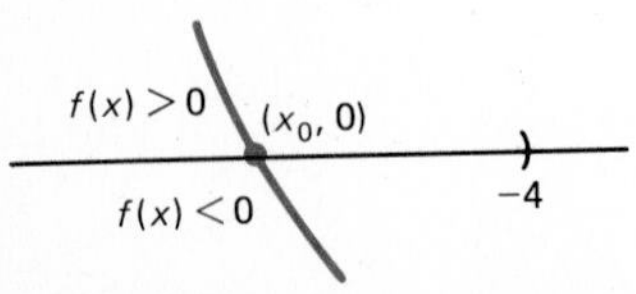

In this section you will see how continuity can be applied to solve inequalities such as $x^2 + 3x - 4 > 0$. But first we must take a moment to provide a framework on which to build our technique.

We wish to draw your attention to the relationship between the x-intercepts of the graph of a function g (that is, the points where the graph meets the x-axis) and the roots of the equation $g(x) = 0$. If the graph of g has an x-intercept $(r, 0)$, then $g(r) = 0$, so r is a root of the equation $g(x) = 0$. Hence, from the graph of $y = g(x)$ in Fig. 10.16, we conclude that r_1, r_2, and r_3 are roots of $g(x) = 0$. On the other hand, if r is any real root of the equation $g(x) = 0$, then $g(r) = 0$ and hence $(r, 0)$ lies on the graph of g. This means that all real roots of the equation $g(x) = 0$ can be represented by the points where the graph of g meets the x-axis. Note also that in Fig. 10.16 these points determine four open intervals on the x-axis:

$$(-\infty, r_1), \ (r_1, r_2), \ (r_2, r_3), \text{ and } (r_3, \infty).$$

Now we are ready to solve inequalities. Returning to $x^2 + 3x - 4 > 0$, we shall let $f(x) = x^2 + 3x - 4 = (x + 4)(x - 1)$. Since f is a polynomial function, it is continuous everywhere. The roots of $f(x) = 0$ are -4 and 1; hence the graph of f has x-intercepts $(-4, 0)$ and $(1, 0)$ (see Fig. 10.17). The roots, or to be more precise the intercepts, determine three intervals on the x-axis:

$$(-\infty, -4), \ (-4, 1), \text{ and } (1, \infty).$$

Consider the interval $(-\infty, -4)$. Since f is continuous on this interval, we claim that either $f(x) > 0$ or $f(x) < 0$ *throughout* the interval. Suppose $f(x)$ did indeed change sign there. Then by the continuity of f there would be a point where the graph intersects the x-axis, for example at $(x_0, 0)$ (see Fig. 10.18). But then x_0 would be a root of the equation $f(x) = 0$. This cannot be, since there is

FIGURE 10.18

no root of $x^2 + 3x - 4 = 0$ that is less than -4. Hence $f(x)$ must be strictly positive or strictly negative on $(-\infty, -4)$ as well as on the other intervals.

To determine the sign of $f(x)$ on any of these intervals, it is sufficient to determine its sign at any point in the interval. For instance, -5 is in $(-\infty, -4)$ and $f(-5) = 6 > 0$. Thus $f(x) > 0$ on $(-\infty, -4)$. Since 0 is in $(-4, 1)$, and $f(0) = -4 < 0$, then $f(x) < 0$ on $(-4, 1)$. Similarly, 3 is in $(1, \infty)$ and $f(3) = 14 > 0$; thus, $f(x) > 0$ on $(1, \infty)$ (see Fig. 10.19). Therefore, $x^2 + 3x - 4 > 0$

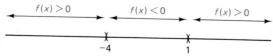

FIGURE 10.19

for $x < -4$ and for $x > 1$, so we have solved the inequality. These results are obvious from the graph in Fig. 10.17.

EXAMPLE 1   *Solve $x(x - 1)(x + 4) \leq 0$.*

If $f(x) = x(x - 1)(x + 4)$, then f is continuous everywhere. The roots of $f(x) = 0$ are 0, 1, and -4, which are shown in Fig. 10.20.

FIGURE 10.20

These roots determine four intervals:

$$(-\infty, -4), \ (-4, 0), \ (0, 1), \ \text{and} \ (1, \infty).$$

Since -5 is in $(-\infty, -4)$, the sign of $f(x)$ on $(-\infty, -4)$ is the same as that of $f(-5)$. Because

$$f(x) = x(x - 1)(x + 4),$$

we have

$$f(-5) = -5(-5 - 1)(-5 + 4) = (-)(-)(-) = (-),$$

so $f(x) < 0$ on $(-\infty, -4)$. For the other intervals we find that

$$f(-2) = (-)(-)(+) = (+), \quad \text{so } f(x) > 0 \text{ on } (-4, 0);$$
$$f(\tfrac{1}{2}) = (+)(-)(+) = (-), \quad \text{so } f(x) < 0 \text{ on } (0, 1);$$
$$\text{and} \quad f(2) = (+)(+)(+) = (+), \quad \text{so } f(x) > 0 \text{ on } (1, \infty).$$

A summary of our results is in the sign chart in Fig. 10.21. Thus

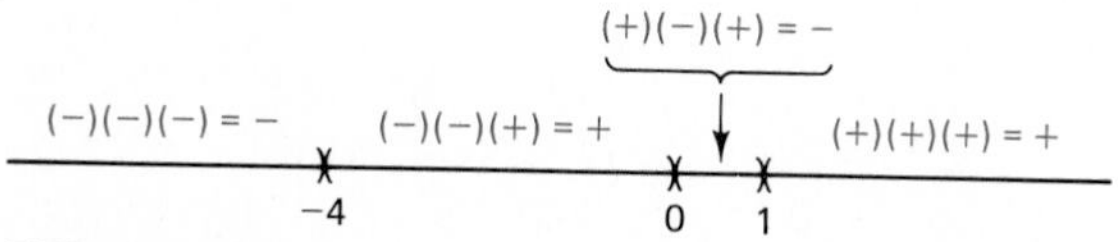

FIGURE 10.21

$x(x - 1)(x + 4) \leq 0$ for $x \leq -4$ and for $0 \leq x \leq 1$. Note that $-4, 0$, and 1 are included in the solution because these roots satisfy the equality ($=$) part of the inequality ($\leq$).

EXAMPLE 2   *Solve* $\dfrac{x^2 - 6x + 5}{x} \geq 0.$

Let $f(x) = \dfrac{x^2 - 6x + 5}{x} = \dfrac{(x - 1)(x - 5)}{x}$. For a quotient we solve the inequality by considering the intervals determined by the roots of $f(x) = 0$, namely 1 and 5, and the points where f is discontinuous. The function is discontinuous at $x = 0$ and continuous otherwise. In Fig. 10.22 we have placed a hollow dot at 0 to indicate that f is not defined there. We thus consider the intervals

$$(-\infty, 0), \ (0, 1), \ (1, 5), \text{ and } (5, \infty).$$

Determining the sign of $f(x)$ at a point in each interval, we find that

$$f(-1) = \frac{(-)(-)}{(-)} = (-), \quad \text{so } f(x) < 0 \text{ on } (-\infty, 0);$$

$$f\left(\frac{1}{2}\right) = \frac{(-)(-)}{(+)} = (+), \quad \text{so } f(x) > 0 \text{ on } (0, 1);$$

$$f(2) = \frac{(+)(-)}{(+)} = (-), \quad \text{so } f(x) < 0 \text{ on } (1, 5);$$

$$\text{and} \quad f(6) = \frac{(+)(+)}{(+)} = (+), \quad \text{so } f(x) > 0 \text{ on } (5, \infty).$$

The sign chart is given in Fig. 10.23. Therefore, $f(x) \geq 0$ for $0 < x \leq 1$ and for $x \geq 5$ (see Fig. 10.24). Why are 1 and 5 included, but 0 excluded?

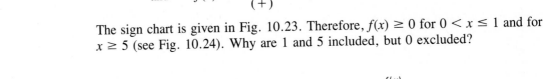

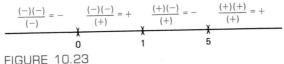

FIGURE 10.23

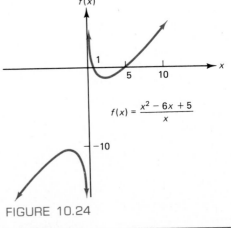

FIGURE 10.24

FIGURE 10.22

To summarize: $f(x)$ may change sign only about points where $f(x) = 0$ or where f has a discontinuity.

EXAMPLE 3   *Solve the following inequalities.*

a. $x^2 + 1 > 0$.

The equation $x^2 + 1 = 0$ has no real roots. Thus the graph of $f(x) = x^2 + 1$ has no x-intercepts. Also, f is continuous everywhere. Thus $f(x)$ is always positive or is always negative. But x^2 is always positive or zero, so $x^2 + 1$ is always positive. Thus the solution of $x^2 + 1 > 0$ is $-\infty < x < \infty$.

b. $x^2 + 1 < 0$.

From part (a), $x^2 + 1$ is always positive, so the inequality $x^2 + 1 < 0$ has no solution.

EXERCISE 10.5

By the technique discussed in this section, solve the following inequalities.

1. $x^2 - 3x - 4 > 0$.

2. $x^2 - 8x + 15 > 0$.

3. $x^2 - 5x + 6 \le 0$.

4. $14 - 5x - x^2 \le 0$.

5. $2x^2 + 11x + 14 < 0$.

6. $x^2 - 4 < 0$.

7. $x^2 + 4 < 0$.

8. $2x^2 - x - 2 \le 0$.

9. $(x + 2)(x - 3)(x + 6) \le 0$.

10. $(x - 5)(x - 2)(x + 3) \ge 0$.

11. $-x(x - 5)(x + 4) > 0$.

12. $(x + 2)^2 > 0$.

13. $x^3 + 4x \ge 0$.

14. $(x + 2)^2(x^2 - 1) < 0$.

15. $x^3 + 2x^2 - 3x > 0$.

16. $x^3 - 4x^2 + 4x > 0$.

17. $\dfrac{x}{x^2 - 1} < 0$.

18. $\dfrac{x^2 - 1}{x} < 0$.

19. $\dfrac{4}{x - 1} \ge 0$.

20. $\dfrac{3}{x^2 - 5x + 6} > 0$.

21. $\dfrac{x^2 - x - 6}{x^2 + 4x - 5} \ge 0$.

22. $\dfrac{x^2 + 2x - 8}{x^2 + 3x + 2} \ge 0$.

23. $\dfrac{3}{x^2 + 6x + 8} \le 0$.

24. $\dfrac{2x + 1}{x^2} \le 0$.

25. $x^2 + 2x \ge 2$.

26. $x^4 - 16 \ge 0$.

27. Suppose that consumers will purchase q units of a product when the price of *each* unit is $20 - 0.1q$ dollars. How many units must be sold in order that sales revenue will be no less than $750?

28. A lumber company owns a forest which is of rectangular shape, 1 mi $\times$ 2 mi. The company wants to cut a uniform strip of trees along the outer edges of the forest. At most how wide can the strip be if the company wants at least $\frac{3}{4}$ mi^2 of forest to remain?

29. A container manufacturer wishes to make an open box by cutting a 4-in. square from each corner of a square sheet of aluminum and then turning up the sides. The box is to contain at least 324 in.^{3}. Find the dimensions of the smallest sheet of aluminum that can be used.

30. Imperial Education Services (I.E.S.) is offering a workshop in data processing to key personnel at Zeta Corporation. The price per person is $50 and Zeta Corporation guarantees that at least 50 persons will attend.

Suppose I.E.S. offers to reduce the charge for *everybody* by $0.50 for each person over the 50 who attends. How should I.E.S. limit the size of the group so that

the total revenue they receive will never be less than that received for 50 persons?

10.6 REVIEW

Important Terms and Symbols

Section 10.1 $\lim_{x \to a} f(x) = L$

Section 10.2   one-sided limits $\lim_{x \to a^-} f(x) = L$ $\lim_{x \to a^+} f(x) = L$ $\lim_{x \to a} f(x) = \infty$ $\lim_{x \to -\infty} f(x) = L$

$\lim_{x \to \infty} f(x) = L$ rational function

Section 10.3   compounding continuously

Section 10.4   continuous   discontinuous   continuous on an interval   continuous everywhere

Summary

The notion of a limit lies at the foundation of calculus. To say that $\lim_{x \to a} f(x) = L$ means that the values of $f(x)$ can be made as close to the number L as we choose by taking x sufficiently close to a. If $\lim_{x \to a} f(x)$ and $\lim_{x \to a} g(x)$ exist and c is a constant, then

1. $\lim_{x \to a} c = c,$

2. $\lim_{x \to a} x^n = a^n,$

3. $\lim_{x \to a} [f(x) \pm g(x)] = \lim_{x \to a} f(x) \pm \lim_{x \to a} g(x),$

4. $\lim_{x \to a} [f(x) \cdot g(x)] = \lim_{x \to a} f(x) \cdot \lim_{x \to a} g(x),$

5. $\lim_{x \to a} [cf(x)] = c \cdot \lim_{x \to a} f(x),$

6. $\lim_{x \to a} \dfrac{f(x)}{g(x)} = \dfrac{\lim_{x \to a} f(x)}{\lim_{x \to a} g(x)}$ if $\lim_{x \to a} g(x) \neq 0,$

7. $\lim_{x \to a} \sqrt[n]{f(x)} = \sqrt[n]{\lim_{x \to a} f(x)},$

8. If f is a polynomial function, then $\lim_{x \to a} f(x) = f(a).$

Property 8 means that the limit of a polynomial function can be found by simply substituting a for x. However, with other functions, substitution may lead to the meaningless form 0/0. In such cases, algebraic manipulation such as factoring may give a form from which the limit can be determined.

If $f(x)$ approaches L as x approaches a from the right, then we write $\lim_{x \to a^+} f(x)$. Similarly, if $f(x)$ approaches L as x approaches a from the left, then we have $\lim_{x \to a^-} f(x)$. These limits are called one-sided limits.

The infinity symbol ∞, which does not represent a number, is used in describing limits. The statement

$$\lim_{x \to \infty} f(x) = L$$

means that as x increases without bound, the values of $f(x)$ approach the number L. A similar statement applies when $x \to -\infty$, which means that x is decreasing without bound. In general, if $p > 0$, then

$$\lim_{x \to \infty} \frac{1}{x^p} = 0 \quad \text{and} \quad \lim_{x \to -\infty} \frac{1}{x^p} = 0.$$

If $f(x)$ increases without bound as $x \to a$, then we write $\lim\limits_{x \to a} f(x) = \infty$. Similarly, if $f(x)$ decreases without bound, we have $\lim\limits_{x \to a} f(x) = -\infty$. To say that the limit of a function is ∞ (or $-\infty$) does not mean that the limit exists. Rather, it is a way of saying that the limit does not exist and tells *why* there is no limit.

There is a rule for evaluating the limit of a rational function (quotient of polynomials) as $x \to \infty$ or $-\infty$. If $f(x)$ is a rational function and $a_n x^n$ and $b_m x^m$ are the terms in the numerator and denominator, respectively, with the greatest powers of x, then

$$\lim_{x \to \infty} f(x) = \lim_{x \to \infty} \frac{a_n x^n}{b_m x^m}$$

and

$$\lim_{x \to -\infty} f(x) = \lim_{x \to -\infty} \frac{a_n x^n}{b_m x^m}.$$

When interest is compounded at every instant of time, we say that it is compounded continuously. Under continuous compounding at an annual rate r for t year, the formula $S = Pe^{rt}$ gives the compound amount S of a principal of P dollars. The formula $P = Se^{-rt}$ gives the present value P of S dollars. The effective rate corresponding to an annual rate r compounded continuously is $e^r - 1$.

A function that has no break in its graph when x is a is said to be continuous at a. Otherwise, it is discontinuous at a. In particular, a function that is not defined when $x = a$ must be discontinuous there. Polynomial functions are continuous everywhere, and rational functions are discontinuous only at points where the denominator is zero.

To solve the inequality $f(x) > 0$ (or $f(x) < 0$), we first find the values of x for which $f(x) = 0$, and the values of x for which f is discontinuous. These values determine intervals, and on each interval, $f(x)$ is either always positive or always negative. To find the sign on any one of these intervals, it suffices to find the sign of $f(x)$ at any point there. After the signs are determined for all intervals, it is then easy to give the solution of $f(x) > 0$ (or $f(x) < 0$).

Review Problems

In Problems 1–22, find the limits if they exist. If the limit does not exist, so state or use the symbol ∞ or $-\infty$ where appropriate.

1. $\lim\limits_{x \to -1} (2x^2 + 6x - 1)$.

2. $\lim\limits_{x \to 0} \dfrac{2x^2 - 3x + 1}{2x^2 - 2}$.

3. $\lim\limits_{x \to 3} \dfrac{x^2 - 9}{x^2 - 3x}$.

4. $\lim\limits_{x \to -2} \dfrac{x + 1}{x^2 - 2}$.

5. $\lim\limits_{h \to 0} (x + h)$.

6. $\lim\limits_{x \to 2} \dfrac{x^2 - 4}{x^2 - 3x + 2}$.

7. $\lim\limits_{x \to -4} \dfrac{x^3 + 4x^2}{x^2 + 2x - 8}$.

8. $\lim\limits_{x \to 1} \dfrac{x^2 + x - 2}{x^2 + 4x - 5}$.

9. $\lim\limits_{x \to \infty} \dfrac{2}{x + 1}$.

10. $\lim\limits_{x \to \infty} \dfrac{x^2 + 1}{x^2}$.

11. $\lim\limits_{x \to \infty} \dfrac{3x - 2}{5x + 3}$.

12. $\lim\limits_{x \to -\infty} \dfrac{1}{x^4}$.

13. $\lim\limits_{t \to 3} \dfrac{2t - 3}{t - 3}$.

14. $\lim\limits_{x \to -\infty} \dfrac{x^6}{x^5}$.

15. $\lim\limits_{x \to -\infty} \dfrac{x + 3}{1 - x}$.

16. $\lim\limits_{x \to 4} \sqrt{4}$.

17. $\lim\limits_{y \to 5^+} \sqrt{y - 5}$.

18. $\lim\limits_{x \to 1} f(x)$ if $f(x) = \begin{cases} x^2, & \text{if } 0 \le x < 1, \\ x, & \text{if } x > 1. \end{cases}$

19. $\lim\limits_{x \to \infty} \dfrac{x^2 - 1}{(3x + 2)^2}$.

20. $\lim\limits_{x \to 1} \dfrac{x^2 + x - 2}{x - 1}$.

21. $\lim\limits_{x \to 3^-} \dfrac{x + 3}{x^2 - 9}$.

22. $\lim\limits_{x \to 2} \dfrac{2 - x}{x - 2}$.

23. For an annual interest rate of 7% compounded continuously, find:
a. the compound amount of $2500 after 14 years.
b. the present value of $2500 due in 14 years.

24. For an annual interest rate of 6% compounded continuously, find:
a. the compound amount of $800 after 9 years.
b. the present value of $800 due in 9 years.

25. Find the effective rate equivalent to an annual rate of 6% compounded continuously.

26. Find the effective rate equivalent to an annual rate of 1% compounded continuously.

27. State whether $f(x) = x/4$ is continuous everywhere. Give a reason for your answer.

28. State whether $f(x) = x^2 - 2$ is continuous everywhere. Give a reason for your answer.

In Problems 29–34, find the points of discontinuity (if any) for each function.

29. $f(x) = \dfrac{x^2}{x + 3}.$

30. $f(x) = \dfrac{0}{x^3}.$

31. $f(x) = \dfrac{x - 1}{2x^2 + 3}.$

32. $f(x) = (3 - 2x)^2.$

33. $f(x) = \dfrac{4 - x^2}{x^2 + 3x - 4}.$

34. $f(x) = \dfrac{2x + 6}{x^3 + x}$

In Problems 35 and 36, find points of discontinuity (if any) by sketching the graph of the function.

35. $f(x) = \begin{cases} x + 4, & \text{if } x > -2, \\ 3x + 6, & \text{if } x \leq -2. \end{cases}$

36. $f(x) = \begin{cases} 1/x, & \text{if } x < 1, \\ 1, & \text{if } x \geq 1. \end{cases}$

In Problems 37–44, solve the given inequalities.

37. $x^2 + 4x - 12 > 0.$

38. $2x^2 - 6x + 4 \leq 0.$

39. $x^3 \geq 2x^2.$

40. $x^3 + 8x^2 + 15x \geq 0.$

41. $\dfrac{x + 5}{x^2 - 1} < 0.$

42. $\dfrac{x(x + 5)(x + 8)}{3} < 0.$

43. $\dfrac{x^2 + 3x}{x^2 + 2x - 8} \geq 0.$

44. $\dfrac{x^2 - 4}{x^2 + 2x + 1} \geq 0.$

CHAPTER 11

Differentiation

Now we begin our study of calculus. The ideas involved in calculus are completely different from those of algebra and geometry. The power and importance of these ideas and their applications will be evident to you later in the text. The objective of this chapter is not only to convey an understanding of what the so-called ''derivative'' of a function is, but also to teach techniques of finding derivatives by properly applying rules.

11.1 THE DERIVATIVE

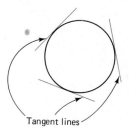

Tangent lines

FIGURE 11.1

One of the main problems with which calculus deals is finding the slope of the *tangent line* at a point on a curve. In geometry you probably thought of a tangent line, or *tangent,* to a circle as a line that meets the circle at exactly one point (Fig. 11.1). Unfortunately, this idea of a tangent is not very useful for other kinds of curves.

For example, in Fig. 11.2(a) the lines L_1 and L_2 intersect the curve at exactly one point. Although we would not think of L_2 as the tangent at this point, it seems natural that L_1 is. In Fig. 11.2(b) we would consider L_3 to be the tangent

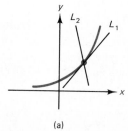

(a)

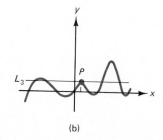

(b)

FIGURE 11.2

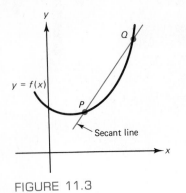

FIGURE 11.3

at point P even though L_3 intersects the curve at other points. From these exam- ples, you can see that we must drop the idea that a tangent is simply a line that intersects a curve at only one point. To develop a suitable definition of tangent line, we use the limit concept.

Look at the graph of the function $y = f(x)$ in Fig. 11.3. Here P and Q are two different points on the curve. The line PQ passing through them is called a **secant line.** If Q moves along the curve and approaches P from the right, typical secant lines are PQ', PQ'', and so on, as shown in Fig. 11.4. As Q approaches P from the left, they are PQ_1, PQ_2, and so on. *In both cases, the secant lines approach the same limiting position.* This common limiting position of the secant lines is defined to be the **tangent line** to the curve at P. This definition seems reasonable and avoids the difficulties mentioned at the beginning of this section.

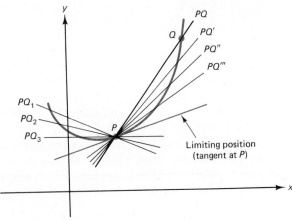

FIGURE 11.4

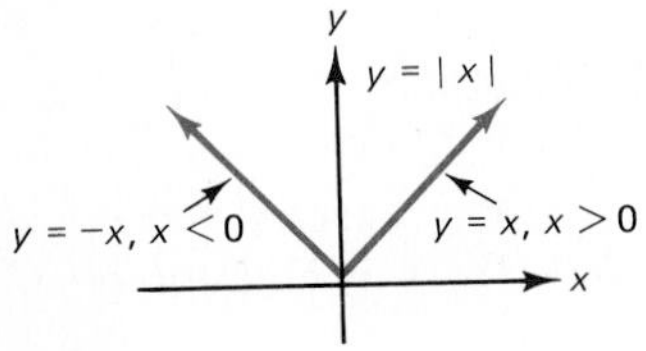

A curve does not necessarily have a tangent at each of its points. For ex- ample, the curve $y = |x|$ does not have a tangent at $(0, 0)$ for the following reason. In Fig. 11.5, a secant line joining $(0, 0)$ to a nearby point to its right must always be the line $y = x$, and one to a nearby point to its left is the line $y = -x$. Since there is no common limiting position, there is no tangent.

Now that we have a suitable definition of a tangent to a curve at a point, we can define the *slope of a curve* at a point.

FIGURE 11.5

Definition
*The **slope of a curve** at a point P is the slope of the tangent line at P.*

Since the tangent at P is a limiting position of secant lines PQ, the slope of the tangent is the limiting value of the slopes of the secant lines as Q ap- proaches P. We shall find an expression for the slope of the curve $y = f(x)$ at point $P = (x_1, f(x_1))$ shown in Fig. 11.6. If $Q = (x_2, f(x_2))$, the slope of the secant line PQ is

$$m_{PQ} = \frac{f(x_2) - f(x_1)}{x_2 - x_1}.$$

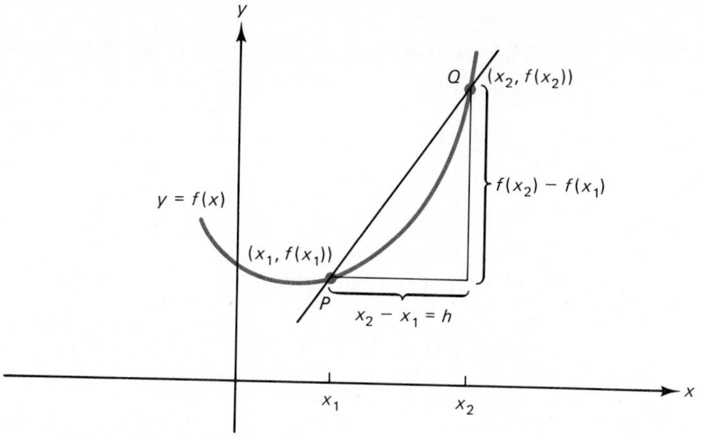

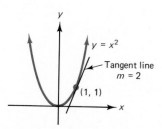

FIGURE 11.6

If the difference $x_2 - x_1$ is called h, then we can write x_2 as $x_1 + h$. Here we have $h \neq 0$, for if $h = 0$ then $x_2 = x_1$ and no secant line exists. Thus

$$m_{PQ} = \frac{f(x_1 + h) - f(x_1)}{(x_1 + h) - x_1} = \frac{f(x_1 + h) - f(x_1)}{h}.$$

As Q moves along the curve toward P, then x_2 approaches x_1. This means that h approaches zero. The limiting value of the slopes of the secant lines—which is the slope of the tangent line at $(x_1, f(x_1))$—is the following limit:

$$m_{\text{tan}} = \lim_{h \to 0} \frac{f(x_1 + h) - f(x_1)}{h}. \tag{1}$$

EXAMPLE 1 *Find the slope of the curve* $y = f(x) = x^2$ *at the point* (1, 1).

The slope is the limit in Eq. (1) with $f(x) = x^2$ and $x_1 = 1$.

$$\lim_{h \to 0} \frac{f(1 + h) - f(1)}{h} = \lim_{h \to 0} \frac{(1 + h)^2 - (1)^2}{h}$$

$$= \lim_{h \to 0} \frac{1 + 2h + h^2 - 1}{h} = \lim_{h \to 0} \frac{2h + h^2}{h}$$

$$= \lim_{h \to 0} \frac{h(2 + h)}{h} = \lim_{h \to 0} (2 + h) = 2.$$

FIGURE 11.7

Thus the tangent line to $y = x^2$ at (1, 1) has slope 2 (Fig. 11.7).

We can generalize Eq. (1) so it applies to any point $(x, f(x))$ on a curve. Replacing x_1 by x gives a function, called the *derivative* of f, whose input is x and whose output is the slope of the tangent line to the curve at $(x, f(x))$. We thus have the following definition, which forms the basis of differential calculus.

Definition

*The **derivative** of a function f is the function denoted f' (read "f prime") and defined by*

$$f'(x) = \lim_{h \to 0} \frac{f(x + h) - f(x)}{h}$$

*(provided this limit exists). If f'(x) can be found, f is said to be **differentiable** and f'(x) is called the derivative of f at x or the derivative of f with respect to x. The process of finding the derivative is called **differentiation**.*

EXAMPLE 2   *If $f(x) = x^2$, find the derivative of f.*

Applying the definition above gives

$$f'(x) = \lim_{h \to 0} \frac{f(x + h) - f(x)}{h}$$

$$= \lim_{h \to 0} \frac{(x + h)^2 - x^2}{h} = \lim_{h \to 0} \frac{x^2 + 2xh + h^2 - x^2}{h}$$

$$= \lim_{h \to 0} \frac{2xh + h^2}{h} = \lim_{h \to 0} \frac{h(2x + h)}{h} = \lim_{h \to 0} (2x + h) = 2x.$$

Observe that in taking the limit we treated x as a constant because it was h, not x, that was changing. Also note that $f'(x) = 2x$ defines a function of x, which we can interpret as giving the slope of the tangent line to the graph of f at (x, f(x)). For example, if $x = 1$, then the slope is $f'(1) = 2(1) = 2$, which confirms the result in Example 1.

Besides $f'(x)$, other notations for the derivative of $y = f(x)$ at x are

$$\frac{dy}{dx} \qquad \text{(pronounced "dee } y, \text{ dee } x\text{"),}$$

$$\frac{d}{dx}[f(x)] \qquad [\text{dee } f(x), \text{ dee } x],$$

$$y' \qquad (y \text{ prime}),$$

$$D_x y \qquad (\text{dee } x \text{ of } y),$$

$$D_x[f(x)] \qquad [\text{dee } x \text{ of } f(x)].$$

Pitfall

$\frac{dy}{dx}$ is not a fraction, but is a single symbol for a derivative. We have not yet attached any meaning to individual symbols such as dy and dx.

If the derivative of $y = f(x)$ can be evaluated at $x = x_1$, the resulting *number $f'(x_1)$ is called the derivative of f at x_1 and f is said to be differentiable* at x_1. Because f' gives the slope of the tangent line,

$$\boxed{f'(x_1) \text{ is the slope of the tangent to } y = f(x) \text{ at } (x_1, f(x_1)).}$$

Other notations for $f'(x_1)$ are

$$\frac{dy}{dx}\bigg|_{x=x_1} \quad \text{and} \quad y'(x_1).$$

EXAMPLE 3 *If $f(x) = 2x^2 + 2x + 3$, find $f'(1)$. Then find an equation of the tangent line to the graph of f at $(1, 7)$.*

We shall find $f'(x)$ and evaluate it at $x = 1$.

$$f'(x) = \lim_{h \to 0} \frac{f(x + h) - f(x)}{h}$$

$$= \lim_{h \to 0} \frac{[2(x + h)^2 + 2(x + h) + 3] - (2x^2 + 2x + 3)}{h}$$

$$= \lim_{h \to 0} \frac{2x^2 + 4xh + 2h^2 + 2x + 2h + 3 - 2x^2 - 2x - 3}{h}$$

$$= \lim_{h \to 0} \frac{4xh + 2h^2 + 2h}{h} = \lim_{h \to 0} (4x + 2h + 2).$$

$$f'(x) = 4x + 2.$$

$$f'(1) = 4(1) + 2 = 6.$$

Thus the tangent to the graph at $(1, 7)$ has slope 6. A point-slope form of the tangent line is $y - 7 = 6(x - 1)$. Simplifying gives $y = 6x + 1$.

Pitfall

In Example 3 it is **not** correct to say that since the derivative is $4x + 2$, the tangent line at $(1, 7)$ is $y - 7 = (4x + 2)(x - 1)$. The derivative must be **evaluated** at the point of tangency to determine the slope of the tangent line.

EXAMPLE 4 *Find the slope of the curve $y = 2x + 3$ at the point where $x = 6$.*

Letting $y = f(x) = 2x + 3$, we have

$$\frac{dy}{dx} = \lim_{h \to 0} \frac{f(x + h) - f(x)}{h} = \lim_{h \to 0} \frac{[2(x + h) + 3] - (2x + 3)}{h}$$

$$= \lim_{h \to 0} \frac{2h}{h} = \lim_{h \to 0} 2 = 2.$$

Since $D_x(2x + 3) = 2$, the slope when $x = 6$, or in fact at any point, is 2. Note that the curve is a straight line and thus has the same slope at each point.

EXAMPLE 5   *Find $D_x(\sqrt{x})$.*

If $f(x) = \sqrt{x}$, then

$$D_x(\sqrt{x}) = \lim_{h \to 0} \frac{f(x + h) - f(x)}{h} = \lim_{h \to 0} \frac{\sqrt{x + h} - \sqrt{x}}{h}.$$

As $h \to 0$, both the numerator and denominator approach zero. This can be avoided by rationalizing the numerator.

$$\frac{\sqrt{x + h} - \sqrt{x}}{h} = \frac{\sqrt{x + h} - \sqrt{x}}{h} \cdot \frac{\sqrt{x + h} + \sqrt{x}}{\sqrt{x + h} + \sqrt{x}} = \frac{(x + h) - x}{h(\sqrt{x + h} + \sqrt{x})}$$

$$= \frac{h}{h(\sqrt{x + h} + \sqrt{x})} = \frac{1}{\sqrt{x + h} + \sqrt{x}}.$$

Thus

$$D_x(\sqrt{x}) = \lim_{h \to 0} \frac{1}{\sqrt{x + h} + \sqrt{x}} = \frac{1}{\sqrt{x} + \sqrt{x}} = \frac{1}{2\sqrt{x}}.$$

Note that the original function, $\sqrt{x}$, is defined for $x \geq 0$. But the derivative, $1/(2\sqrt{x})$, is defined only when $x > 0$. From the graph of $y = \sqrt{x}$ in Fig. 11.8, it is clear that when $x = 0$, the tangent is a vertical line and hence does not have a slope.

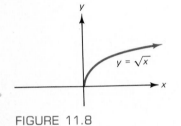

FIGURE 11.8

If a variable, say p, is a function of some variable, say q, then we speak of the derivative of p with respect to q, written dp/dq.

EXAMPLE 6   *If $p = f(q) = \dfrac{1}{2q}$, find $\dfrac{dp}{dq}$.*

$$\frac{dp}{dq} = \frac{d}{dq}\left(\frac{1}{2q}\right) = \lim_{h \to 0} \frac{f(q + h) - f(q)}{h}$$

$$= \lim_{h \to 0} \frac{\dfrac{1}{2(q + h)} - \dfrac{1}{2q}}{h} = \lim_{h \to 0} \frac{\dfrac{q - (q + h)}{2q(q + h)}}{h}$$

$$= \lim_{h \to 0} \frac{q - (q + h)}{h[2q(q + h)]} = \lim_{h \to 0} \frac{-h}{h[2q(q + h)]}$$

$$= \lim_{h \to 0} \frac{-1}{2q(q + h)} = -\frac{1}{2q^2}.$$

Note that when $q = 0$, neither the function nor its derivative exists.

As a final note we point out that the derivative of $y = f(x)$ at x is nothing more than the following limit:

$$\lim_{h \to 0} \frac{f(x + h) - f(x)}{h}.$$

Although we can interpret the derivative as a function that gives the slope of the tangent line to the curve $y = f(x)$ at the point $(x, f(x))$, this interpretation is simply a geometric convenience that assists our understanding. The limit above may exist aside from any geometric consideration at all. As you will see later, there are other useful interpretations.

EXERCISE 11.1

In Problems **1–16,** *use the definition of the derivative to find each of the following.*

1. $f'(x)$ if $f(x) = x$.

2. $f'(x)$ if $f(x) = 4x - 1$.

3. $\dfrac{dy}{dx}$ if $y = 3x + 7$.

4. $\dfrac{dy}{dx}$ if $y = -5x$.

5. $\dfrac{d}{dx}(5 - 4x)$.

6. $\dfrac{d}{dx}\left(2 - \dfrac{x}{4}\right)$.

7. $f'(x)$ if $f(x) = 3$.

8. $f'(x)$ if $f(x) = 7.01$.

9. $D_x(x^2 + 4x - 8)$.

10. $D_x y$ if $y = x^2 + 5$.

11. $\dfrac{dp}{dq}$ if $p = 2q^2 + 5q - 1$.

12. $D_x(x^2 - x - 3)$.

13. $D_x y$ if $y = \dfrac{1}{x}$.

14. $\dfrac{dC}{dq}$ if $C = 7 + 2q - 3q^2$.

15. $f'(x)$ if $f(x) = \sqrt{x + 2}$.

16. $g'(x)$ if $g(x) = \dfrac{2}{x - 3}$.

17. Find the slope of the curve $y = x^2 + 4$ at the point $(-2, 8)$.

18. Find the slope of the curve $y = 2 - 3x^2$ at the point $(1, -1)$.

19. Find the slope of the curve $y = 4x^2 - 5$ when $x = 0$.   **20.** Find the slope of the curve $y = \sqrt{x}$ when $x = 1$.

In Problems **21–26,** *find an equation of the tangent line to the curve at the given point.*

21. $y = x + 4$; $(3, 7)$.

22. $y = 2x^2 - 5$; $(-2, 3)$.

23. $y = 3x^2 + 3x - 4$; $(-1, -4)$.

24. $y = (x - 1)^2$; $(0, 1)$.

25. $y = \dfrac{3}{x + 1}$; $(2, 1)$.

26. $y = \dfrac{5}{1 - 3x}$; $(2, -1)$.

27. Equations may involve derivatives of functions. In an article on interest rate deregulation, Christofi and Agapos* solve the equation

$$r = \left(\frac{\eta}{1 + \eta}\right)\left(r_L - \frac{dC}{dD}\right)$$

for η (the Greek letter "eta"). Here r is the deposit rate paid by commerical banks, r_L is the rate earned by commercial banks, C is the administrative cost of transforming deposits into return-earning assets, D is the savings deposits level, and η is the deposit elasticity with respect to the deposit rate. Find η.

* A. Christofi and A. Agapos, "Interest Rate Deregulation: An Empirical Justification," *Review of Business and Economic Research*, XX, no. 1 (1984), 39–49.

11.2 RULES FOR DIFFERENTIATION

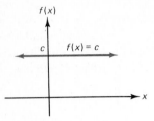

$f(x)$

c $f(x) = c$

x

FIGURE 11.9

You would probably agree that differentiating a function by direct use of the definition of a derivative can be tedious. Fortunately, there are rules that give us completely mechanical and efficient procedures for differentiation. They also avoid direct use of limits. We shall look at some rules in this section.

To begin with, recall that the graph of the constant function $f(x) = c$ is a horizontal line (Fig. 11.9), which has a slope of zero everywhere. This means that $f'(x) = 0$, which is our first rule. We shall give a formal proof.

Rule 1

If c is a constant, then

$$\frac{d}{dx}(c) = 0.$$

That is, the derivative of a constant function is zero.

Proof. If $f(x) = c$, applying the definition of the derivative gives

$$f'(x) = \lim_{h \to 0} \frac{f(x + h) - f(x)}{h} = \lim_{h \to 0} \frac{c - c}{h}$$

$$= \lim_{h \to 0} \frac{0}{h} = \lim_{h \to 0} 0 = 0.$$

EXAMPLE 1

a. $D_x(3) = 0$ because 3 is a constant function.

b. If $g(x) = \sqrt{5}$, then $g'(x) = 0$ because g is a constant function. For example, the derivative of g when $x = 4$ is $g'(4) = 0$.

c. If $s(t) = (1,938,623)^{807.4}$, then $ds/dt = 0$.

To prove the next rule, we must expand a binomial. Recall that

$$(x + h)^2 = x^2 + 2xh + h^2$$

$$\text{and} \quad (x + h)^3 = x^3 + 3x^2h + 3xh^2 + h^3.$$

In both expansions the exponents of x decrease from left to right while those of h increase. This is true for the general case $(x + h)^n$, where n is a positive integer. It can be shown that

$$(x + h)^n = x^n + nx^{n-1}h + (\quad)x^{n-2}h^2 + \cdots + (\quad)xh^{n-1} + h^n,$$

where the missing numbers inside the parentheses are certain constants. This formula is used to prove the next rule, which involves the derivative of x raised to a constant power.

Rule 2

If n is any real number, then

$$\frac{d}{dx}(x^n) = nx^{n-1}.$$

That is, the derivative of a constant power of x is the exponent times x raised to a power one less than the given power.

Proof. We shall give a proof for the case when n is a positive integer. If $f(x) = x^n$, applying the definition of the derivative gives

$$f'(x) = \lim_{h \to 0} \frac{f(x + h) - f(x)}{h} = \lim_{h \to 0} \frac{(x + h)^n - x^n}{h}.$$

By our previous discussion on expanding $(x + h)^n$,

$$f'(x) = \lim_{h \to 0} \frac{x^n + nx^{n-1}h + (\ )x^{n-2}h^2 + \cdots + h^n - x^n}{h}.$$

In the numerator the sum of the first and last terms is 0. Dividing each of the remaining terms by h gives

$$f'(x) = \lim_{h \to 0} [nx^{n-1} + (\ )x^{n-2}h + \cdots + h^{n-1}].$$

Each term after the first has h as a factor and must approach 0 as $h \to 0$. Hence $f'(x) = nx^{n-1}$.

EXAMPLE 2

a. By Rule 2, $D_x(x^2) = 2x^{2-1} = 2x$.

b. If $F(x) = x = x^1$, then $F'(x) = 1 \cdot x^{1-1} = 1 \cdot x^0 = 1$. Thus the derivative of x with respect to x is 1.

c. To differentiate $y = \sqrt{x}$, we write $\sqrt{x}$ as $x^{1/2}$ so that it has the form x^n. Thus

$$\frac{dy}{dx} = \frac{1}{2}x^{(1/2)-1} = \frac{1}{2}x^{-1/2} = \frac{1}{2\sqrt{x}}.$$

d. Let $h(x) = \frac{1}{x\sqrt{x}}$. To apply Rule 2 we *must* write $h(x)$ as $h(x) = x^{-3/2}$ so that it has the form x^n.

$$D_x\left(\frac{1}{x\sqrt{x}}\right) = D_x(x^{-3/2}) = -\frac{3}{2}x^{(-3/2)-1} = -\frac{3}{2}x^{-5/2}.$$

Pitfall

Do not write $\frac{1}{x\sqrt{x}}$ as $\frac{1}{x^{3/2}}$ and then merely differentiate the denominator, that is,

$$D_x\left(\frac{1}{x^{3/2}}\right) \neq \frac{1}{\frac{3}{2}x^{1/2}}.$$

Rule 3

If f is a differentiable function and c is a constant, then

$$\frac{d}{dx}[cf(x)] = cf'(x).$$

That is, the derivative of a constant times a function is the constant times the derivative of the function.

Proof. If $g(x) = cf(x)$, applying the definition of the derivative of g gives

$$g'(x) = \lim_{h \to 0} \frac{g(x + h) - g(x)}{h} = \lim_{h \to 0} \frac{cf(x + h) - cf(x)}{h}$$

$$= \lim_{h \to 0} \left[c \cdot \frac{f(x + h) - f(x)}{h}\right] = c \cdot \lim_{h \to 0} \frac{f(x + h) - f(x)}{h}.$$

But $\lim_{h \to 0} \frac{f(x + h) - f(x)}{h}$ is $f'(x)$, so $g'(x) = cf'(x)$.

EXAMPLE 3   *Differentiate the following functions.*

a. $g(x) = 5x^3$.

Here g is a constant (5) times a function (x^3).

$$\frac{d}{dx}(5x^3) = 5D_x(x^3) \qquad \text{(Rule 3)}$$

$$= 5(3x^{3-1}) = 15x^2 \qquad \text{(Rule 2).}$$

b. $f(q) = \frac{13q}{5}$.

Because $\frac{13q}{5} = \frac{13}{5}q$, f is a constant $\left(\frac{13}{5}\right)$ times a function (q).

$$f'(q) = \frac{13}{5}D_q(q) \qquad \text{(Rule 3)}$$

$$= \frac{13}{5} \cdot 1 = \frac{13}{5} \qquad \text{(Rule 2).}$$

c. $y = \dfrac{0.702}{\sqrt[5]{x^2}} = 0.702x^{-2/5}$.

Note that y can be considered a constant times a function.

$$y' = 0.702D_x(x^{-2/5}) \qquad \text{(Rule 3)}$$

$$= 0.702\left(-\frac{2}{5}x^{-7/5}\right) = -0.2808x^{-7/5} \qquad \text{(Rule 2).}$$

Pitfall

If $f(x) = (4x)^3$, you may be tempted to write $f'(x) = 3(4x)^2$. This is **incorrect!** The reason is that Rule 2 applies to a power of the variable x, **not** a power of an expression involving x such as $4x$. To apply our rules we must get a suitable form for $f(x)$. We can write $(4x)^3$ as 4^3x^3 or $64x^3$. Thus

$$f'(x) = 64D_x(x^3) = 64(3x^2) = 192x^2.$$

The next rule involves derivatives of sums and differences of functions.

Rule 4

If f and g are differentiable functions, then

$$\frac{d}{dx}[f(x) + g(x)] = f'(x) + g'(x)$$

and $\dfrac{d}{dx}[f(x) - g(x)] = f'(x) - g'(x).$

That is, the derivative of the sum (or difference) of two functions is the sum (or difference) of their derivatives.

Proof. For the case of a sum, if $F(x) = f(x) + g(x)$, applying the definition of the derivative of F gives

$$F'(x) = \lim_{h \to 0} \frac{F(x + h) - F(x)}{h}$$

$$= \lim_{h \to 0} \frac{[f(x + h) + g(x + h)] - [f(x) + g(x)]}{h}$$

$$= \lim_{h \to 0} \frac{[f(x + h) - f(x)] + [g(x + h) - g(x)]}{h} \qquad \text{(regrouping)}$$

$$= \lim_{h \to 0} \left[\frac{f(x + h) - f(x)}{h} + \frac{g(x + h) - g(x)}{h}\right].$$

Because the limit of a sum is the sum of the limits,

$$F'(x) = \lim_{h \to 0} \frac{f(x + h) - f(x)}{h} + \lim_{h \to 0} \frac{g(x + h) - g(x)}{h}.$$

But these two limits are $f'(x)$ and $g'(x)$. Thus

$$F'(x) = f'(x) + g'(x).$$

The proof for the derivative of a difference of two functions is similar to the above.

Rule 4 can be extended to the derivative of any number of sums and differences of functions. For example,

$$\frac{d}{dx}[f(x) - g(x) + h(x) + k(x)] = f'(x) - g'(x) + h'(x) + k'(x).$$

EXAMPLE 4   *Differentiate the following functions.*

a. $F(x) = 3x^5 + \sqrt{x}$.

Here F is the sum of two functions, $3x^5$ and $\sqrt{x}$. Thus

$$F'(x) = D_x(3x^5) + D_x(x^{1/2}) \qquad \text{(Rule 4)}$$

$$= 3D_x(x^5) + D_x(x^{1/2}) \qquad \text{(Rule 3)}$$

$$= 3(5x^4) + \frac{1}{2}x^{-1/2} = 15x^4 + \frac{1}{2\sqrt{x}} \qquad \text{(Rule 2)}.$$

b. $f(z) = \dfrac{z^4}{4} - \dfrac{5}{z^{1/3}}$.

Note that we can write $f(z) = \frac{1}{4}z^4 - 5z^{-1/3}$. Since f is the difference of two functions,

$$f'(z) = D_z(\tfrac{1}{4}z^4) - D_z(5z^{-1/3}) \qquad \text{(Rule 4)}$$

$$= \tfrac{1}{4}D_z(z^4) - 5D_z(z^{-1/3}) \qquad \text{(Rule 3)}$$

$$= \tfrac{1}{4}(4z^3) - 5(-\tfrac{1}{3}z^{-4/3}) \qquad \text{(Rule 2)}$$

$$= z^3 + \tfrac{5}{3}z^{-4/3}.$$

c. $y = 6x^3 - 2x^2 + 7x - 8$.

$$\frac{dy}{dx} = D_x(6x^3) - D_x(2x^2) + D_x(7x) - D_x(8)$$

$$= 6D_x(x^3) - 2D_x(x^2) + 7D_x(x) - D_x(8)$$

$$= 6(3x^2) - 2(2x) + 7(1) - 0$$

$$= 18x^2 - 4x + 7.$$

EXAMPLE 5   *Find the derivative of* $f(x) = 2x(x^2 - 5x + 2)$ *when* $x = 2$.

We multiply and then differentiate each term.

$$f(x) = 2x^3 - 10x^2 + 4x.$$

$$f'(x) = 2(3x^2) - 10(2x) + 4(1)$$

$$= 6x^2 - 20x + 4.$$

$$f'(2) = 6(2)^2 - 20(2) + 4 = -12.$$

EXAMPLE 6   *Find an equation of the tangent line to the curve* $y = \dfrac{3x^2 - 2}{x}$ *when* $x = 1$.

By writing y as a difference of two functions, we have $y = \dfrac{3x^2}{x} - \dfrac{2}{x} = 3x - 2x^{-1}$. Thus

$$\frac{dy}{dx} = 3(1) - 2[(-1)x^{-2}] = 3 + \frac{2}{x^2}.$$

The slope of the tangent line to the curve when $x = 1$ is

$$\left.\frac{dy}{dx}\right|_{x=1} = 3 + \frac{2}{1^2} = 5.$$

To find the y-coordinate of the point on the curve where $x = 1$, we substitute this value of x into the equation of the *curve*. This gives $y = [3(1)^2 - 2]/1 = 1$. Hence the point $(1, 1)$ lies on both the curve and the tangent line. Therefore, an equation of the tangent line is

$$y - 1 = 5(x - 1),$$

$$y = 5x - 4.$$

EXERCISE 11.2

In Problems **1–54,** *differentiate the functions.*

1. $f(x) = 5$.

2. $f(x) = (\frac{11}{13})^{4/5}$.

3. $f(x) = x^5$.

4. $f(x) = 0.3x$

5. $f(x) = 8x^4$.

6. $f(x) = \sqrt{2}\,x^{83/4}$.

7. $g(w) = w^{-7}$.

8. $f(t) = 3t^{-2}$.

9. $f(x) = 4x^{-14/5}$.

10. $v(x) = x^e$.

11. $f(x) = 3x - 2$.

12. $f(w) = 5w - 7\ln \frac{4}{5}$.

13. $f(p) = \dfrac{13p}{5} + \dfrac{7}{3}$.

14. $q(x) = \dfrac{5x + 2}{8}$.

15. $g(x) = 3x^2 - 5x - 2$.

16. $f(q) = 7q^2 - 5q + 3$.

17. $f(x) = 14x^3 - 6x^2 + 7x - e^3$.

18. $f(r) = -8r^3 + 9^{2/3}$

19. $f(q) = -3q^3 + \frac{9}{2}q^2 + 9q + 9.$

20. $f(x) = 100x^{-3} - 50x^{-1/2} + 10x - 1.$

21. $f(x) = 2x^{501} - 125x^{100} + 0.2x^{3.4}.$

22. $f(x) = 17 + 8x^{1/7} - 10x^{12} - 3x^{-15}.$

23. $f(x) = 2(13 - x^4).$

24. $f(s) = 5(s^4 - 3).$

25. $g(x) = \dfrac{13 - x^4}{3}.$

26. $f(x) = \dfrac{5(x^4 - 3)}{2}.$

27. $f(x) = x^{-4} - 9x^{1/3} + 5x^{-2/5}.$

28. $f(z) = 3z^{1/4} - 12^2 - 8z^{-3/4}.$

29. $h(x) = -2(27x - 14x^5).$

30. $f(x) = \dfrac{-(1 + x - x^2 + x^3 + x^4 - x^5)}{2}.$

31. $f(x) = -2x^2 + \dfrac{3}{2}x + \dfrac{x^4}{4} + 2.$

32. $p(x) = \dfrac{x^7}{7} + \dfrac{x}{2}.$

33. $f(x) = \dfrac{1}{x}.$

34. $f(x) = \dfrac{7}{x^3}.$

35. $f(s) = \dfrac{1}{4s^5}.$

36. $g(w) = \dfrac{2}{3w^3}.$

37. $f(t) = 4\sqrt{t}.$

38. $f(x) = \dfrac{4}{\sqrt{x}}.$

39. $q(x) = \dfrac{1}{\sqrt[5]{x}}.$

40. $f(x) = \dfrac{3}{\sqrt[4]{x^3}}.$

41. $f(x) = x(3x^2 - 7x + 7).$

42. $f(x) = x^3(3x^6 - 5x^2 + 4).$

43. $g(t) = \dfrac{t^2}{2} - \dfrac{2}{t^2}.$

44. $f(x) = x\sqrt{x}.$

45. $f(x) = x^3(3x)^2.$

46. $f(x) = \sqrt{x}(5 - 6x + 3\sqrt[4]{x}).$

47. $v(x) = x^{-2/3}(x + 5).$

48. $f(x) = x^{3/5}(x^2 + 7x + 1).$

49. $f(q) = \dfrac{4q^3 + 7q - 4}{q}.$

50. $f(w) = \dfrac{w - 5}{w^5}.$

51. $f(x) = (x + 1)(x + 3).$

52. $f(x) = x^2(x - 2)(x + 4).$

53. $w(x) = \dfrac{x^2 + x^3}{x^2}.$

54. $f(x) = \dfrac{7x^3 + x}{2\sqrt{x}}.$

For each curve in Problems **55–58**, *find the slopes at the indicated points.*

55. $y = 3x^2 + 4x - 8;$ $(0, -8), (2, 12), (-3, 7).$

56. $y = 5 - 6x - 2x^3;$ $(0, 5), (\frac{3}{2}, -\frac{43}{4}), (-3, 77).$

57. $y = 4;$ when $x = -4, x = 7, x = 22.$

58. $y = 2x - 3\sqrt{x};$ when $x = 1, x = 16, x = 25.$

In Problems **59** *and* **60**, *find an equation of the tangent line to the curve at the indicated point.*

59. $y = 4x^2 + 5x + 2;$ $(1, 11).$

60. $y = (1 - x^2)/5;$ $(4, -3).$

61. Find an equation of the tangent line to the curve $y = 3 + x - 5x^2 + x^4$ when $x = 0.$

62. Repeat Problem 61 for the curve $y = \dfrac{\sqrt{x}(2 - x^2)}{x}$ when $x = 4.$

63. Find all points on the curve $y = \frac{1}{3}x^3 - x^2$ where the tangent line is horizontal.

64. Find all points on the curve $y = x^2 - 5x + 3$ where the slope is 1.

65. Eswaran and Kotwal* consider agrarian economies in which there are two types of workers, permanent and casual. Permanent workers are employed on long-term contracts and may receive benefits such as holiday gifts and emergency aid. Casual workers are hired on a daily basis and perform routine and menial tasks such as weeding, harvesting, and threshing. The difference z in the present value cost of hiring a permanent worker over that of hiring a casual worker is given by

$$z = (1 + b)w_p - bw_c,$$

where w_p and w_c are wage rates for permanent labor and casual labor, respectively, b is a constant, and w_p is a function of w_c. Eswaran and Kotwal claim that

$$\frac{dz}{dw_c} = (1 + b)\left[\frac{dw_p}{dw_c} - \frac{b}{1 + b}\right].$$

Verify this.

11.3 THE DERIVATIVE AS A RATE OF CHANGE _____

FIGURE 11.10

Historically, an important application of the derivative involves motion in a straight line. It gives us a convenient way to interpret the derivative as a *rate of change*. To denote the change in a variable such as x, the symbol Δx (read "delta x") is commonly used. For example, if x changes from 1 to 3, then the change in x is $\Delta x = 3 - 1 = 2$. The new value of x ($= 3$) is the odd value plus the change, or $1 + \Delta x$. Similarly, if t increases by Δt, the new value is $t + \Delta t$. We shall use Δ-notation in the following discussion.

Suppose a particle moves along the number line in Fig. 11.10 according to the equation

$$s = f(t) = t^2,$$

where s is the position of the particle at time t. This equation is called an *equation of motion*. Assume that t is in seconds and s is in meters. At $t = 1$, the position is $s = f(1) = 1^2 = 1$, and at $t = 3$ the position is $s = f(3) = 3^2 = 9$. Over this 2-second time interval, the particle has a change in position, or a *displacement*, of $9 - 1 = 8$ m, and the *average velocity* (v_{ave}) of the particle is defined as

$$v_{ave} = \frac{displacement}{length \ of \ time \ interval} \tag{1}$$

$$= \frac{8}{2} = 4 \ m/s.$$

More generally, over the time interval from t to $t + \Delta t$, the particle moves from position $f(t)$ to position $f(t + \Delta t)$. Thus its displacement is $f(t + \Delta t) - f(t)$, which is a change in s-values, denoted by Δs:

$$\Delta s = f(t + \Delta t) - f(t).$$

Since the given time interval has length Δt, from Eq. (1) the particle's average velocity is

$$v_{ave} = \frac{\Delta s}{\Delta t} = \frac{f(t + \Delta t) - f(t)}{\Delta t}.$$

* M. Eswaran and A. Kotwal, "A Theory of Two-Tier Labor Markets in Agrarian Economies," *The American Economic Review*, 75, no. 1 (1985), 162–77.

The expression $\Delta s/\Delta t$ is also called the *average rate of change* of s with respect to t over the interval from t to $t + \Delta t$.

If Δt were to become smaller and smaller, the average velocity over the interval from t to $t + \Delta t$ would be close to what we might call the *instantaneous velocity* at time t—that is, the velocity at a *point in time* (t) as opposed to velocity over an *interval* of time. We define the limit of the average velocity as $\Delta t \to 0$ to be the **instantaneous velocity** v at time t, or the **instantaneous rate of change** of s with respect to t.

$$v = \lim_{\Delta t \to 0} v_{\text{ave}} = \lim_{\Delta t \to 0} \frac{\Delta s}{\Delta t} = \lim_{\Delta t \to 0} \frac{f(t + \Delta t) - f(t)}{\Delta t}.$$

The last limit is just the definition of the derivative of f with respect to t because replacing Δt by h gives

$$\lim_{h \to 0} \frac{f(t + h) - f(t)}{h}.$$

Thus

$$v = \frac{ds}{dt}.$$

For the original equation of motion, $s = t^2$, the instantaneous velocity at time t is given by

$$v = \frac{ds}{dt} = 2t.$$

For example, the instantaneous velocity when $t = 1$ is

$$\left.\frac{ds}{dt}\right|_{t=1} = 2(1) = 2 \text{ m/s}.$$

Usually, instantaneous velocity is simply referred to as *velocity*.

EXAMPLE 1   *Suppose the equation of motion of a particle moving along a number line is given by $s = \dfrac{3t^2 + 5}{4}$. Find the velocity when $t = 10$.*

The velocity at any time t is given by

$$v = \frac{ds}{dt} = D_t\left(\frac{3t^2 + 5}{4}\right)$$

$$= \tfrac{1}{4}D_t(3t^2 + 5)$$

$$= \tfrac{1}{4}[6t + 0] = \tfrac{3}{2}t.$$

When $t = 10$,

$$v = \tfrac{3}{2} \cdot 10 = 15.$$

Our discussion of rate of change of s with respect to t applies equally well to *any* function $y = f(x)$. This means as follows.

If $y = f(x)$, then

$$\frac{\Delta y}{\Delta x} = \frac{f(x + \Delta x) - f(x)}{\Delta x} = \begin{cases} \text{average rate of change} \\ \text{of } y \text{ with respect to } x \\ \text{over the interval from} \\ x \text{ to } x + \Delta x \end{cases}$$

and $\quad \dfrac{dy}{dx} = \lim\limits_{\Delta x \to 0} \dfrac{\Delta y}{\Delta x} = \begin{cases} \textbf{instantaneous rate of} \\ \textbf{change of } y \textbf{ with respect to } x. \end{cases}$ $\qquad$ (2)

Because the instantaneous rate of change of $y = f(x)$ at a point is a derivative, it is also the *slope of the tangent line* to the graph of $y = f(x)$ at that point. For convenience we usually refer to instantaneous rate of change simply as *rate of change*.

From Eq. (2), if Δx (a change in x) is close to 0, then $\Delta y/\Delta x$ is close to dy/dx. That is,

$$\frac{\Delta y}{\Delta x} \approx \frac{dy}{dx}.$$

Therefore,

$$\Delta y \approx \frac{dy}{dx}\Delta x.$$

That is, if x changes by Δx, then the change in y, Δy, is approximately dy/dx times the change in x. In particular, if x changes by 1, an estimate in the change in y is dy/dx.

EXAMPLE 2   *Find the rate of change of $y = x^4$ with respect to x. Evaluate the rate when $x = 2$ and when $x = -1$.*

The rate of change is dy/dx:

$$\frac{dy}{dx} = 4x^3.$$

When $x = 2$, then $dy/dx = 4(2)^3 = 32$. This means that if x increases by a small amount, then y increases approximately 32 times as much. More simply, we say that y is increasing 32 times as fast as x does. When $x = -1$, then $dy/dx = 4(-1)^3 = -4$. The significance of the minus sign on -4 is that y is *decreasing* 4 times as fast as x increases.

The interpretation of a derivative as a rate of change has applications to business and economics, as well as other areas.

EXAMPLE 3   *Let $p = 100 - q^2$ be the demand function for a manufacturer's product. Find the rate of change of price p per unit with respect to quan-*

tity q. How fast is the price changing with respect to q when q = 5? Assume that p is in dollars.

The rate of change of p with respect to q is dp/dq.

$$\frac{dp}{dq} = \frac{d}{dq}(100 - q^2) = -2q.$$

$$\left.\frac{dp}{dq}\right|_{q=5} = -2(5) = -10.$$

This means that when 5 units are demanded, an *increase* of one extra unit demanded corresponds to a decrease of approximately $10 in the price per unit that consumers are willing to pay.

EXAMPLE 4   *A sociologist is studying various suggested programs that can aid in the education of preschool-age children in a certain city. The sociologist believes that x years after the beginning of a particular program, f(x) thousand preschoolers will be enrolled, where*

$$f(x) = \frac{10}{9}(12x - x^2), \qquad 0 \le x \le 12.$$

At what rate would enrollment change (a) after 3 years from the start of this program? (b) After 9 years?

The rate of change of $f(x)$ is $f'(x)$:

$$f'(x) = \frac{10}{9}(12 - 2x).$$

a. After 3 years the rate of change is

$$f'(3) = \frac{10}{9}[12 - 2(3)] = \frac{10}{9} \cdot 6 = \frac{20}{3} = 6\frac{2}{3}.$$

Thus enrollment would be increasing at the rate of $6\frac{2}{3}$ thousand preschoolers per year.

b. After 9 years the rate is

$$f'(9) = \frac{10}{9}[12 - 2(9)] = \frac{10}{9}[-6] = -\frac{20}{3} = -6\frac{2}{3}.$$

Thus enrollment would be *decreasing* at the rate of $6\frac{2}{3}$ thousand preschoolers per year.

A manufacturer's **total cost function,** $c = f(q)$, gives the total cost c of producing and marketing q units of a product. The rate of change of c with respect to q is called **marginal cost.** Thus

$$\text{marginal cost} = \frac{dc}{dq}.$$

For example, suppose $c = f(q) = 0.1q^2 + 3$ is a cost function, where c is in dollars and q is in pounds. Then

$$\frac{dc}{dq} = 0.2q.$$

The marginal cost when 4 lb are produced is dc/dq evaluated when $q = 4$:

$$\left.\frac{dc}{dq}\right|_{q=4} = 0.2(4) = 0.80.$$

This means that, if production is increased by 1 lb, from 4 lb to 5 lb, then the change in cost is approximately \$0.80. That is, the additional pound costs about \$0.80. In general, *we interpret marginal cost as the approximate cost of one additional unit of output*. [The actual cost of producing one more pound beyond 4 lb is $f(5) - f(4) = 5.5 - 4.6 = \$0.90$.]

If c is the total cost of producing q units of a product, then the **average cost** per unit, $\bar{c}$, is

$$\bar{c} = \frac{c}{q}. \tag{3}$$

For example, if the total cost of 20 units is \$100, then the average cost per unit is $\bar{c} = 100/20 = \$5$. By multiplying both sides of Eq. (3) by q, we have

$$c = q\bar{c}.$$

That is, total cost is the product of the number of units produced and the average cost per unit.

EXAMPLE 5   *If a manufacturer's average cost equation is*

$$\bar{c} = 0.0001q^2 - 0.02q + 5 + \frac{5000}{q},$$

find the marginal cost function. What is the marginal cost when 50 units are produced?

We first find total cost c. Since $c = q\bar{c}$, then

$$c = q\bar{c}$$

$$= q\left[0.0001q^2 - 0.02q + 5 + \frac{5000}{q}\right].$$

$$c = 0.0001q^3 - 0.02q^2 + 5q + 5000.$$

Differentiating c, we have the marginal cost function:

$$\frac{dc}{dq} = 0.0001(3q^2) - 0.02(2q) + 5(1) + 0$$

$$= 0.0003q^2 - 0.04q + 5.$$

The marginal cost when 50 units are produced is

$$\left.\frac{dc}{dq}\right|_{q=50} = 0.0003(50)^2 - 0.04(50) + 5 = 3.75.$$

If c is in dollars and production is increased by one unit from $q = 50$ to $q = 51$, then the cost of the additional unit is approximately \$3.75. If production is increased by $\frac{1}{3}$ unit from $q = 50$, then the cost of the additional output is approximately $(\frac{1}{3})(3.75) = \$1.25$.

Suppose $r = f(q)$ is the **total revenue function** for a manufacturer. The equation $r = f(q)$ states that the total dollar value received for selling q units of a product is r. The **marginal revenue** is defined as the rate of change of the total dollar value received with respect to the total number of units sold. Hence marginal revenue is merely the derivative of r with respect to q.

$$\textbf{marginal revenue} = \frac{dr}{dq}.$$

Marginal revenue indicates the rate at which revenue changes with respect to units sold. We interpret it as the approximate revenue received from selling one additional unit of output.

EXAMPLE 6   Suppose a manufacturer sells a product at \$2 per unit. If q units are sold, the total revenue is given by

$$r = 2q.$$

The marginal revenue function is

$$\frac{dr}{dq} = \frac{d}{dq}(2q) = 2,$$

which is a constant function. Thus the marginal revenue is 2 regardless of the number of units sold. This is what we would expect because the manufacturer receives \$2 for each unit sold.

For the total revenue function in Example 6, $r = f(q) = 2q$,

$$\frac{dr}{dq} = 2.$$

This means that revenue is changing at the rate of \$2 per unit, regardless of the numbers of units sold. Although this is valuable information, it may be more significant when compared to r itself. For example, if $q = 50$, then $r = 2(50) = \$100$. Thus the rate of change of revenue is $2/100 = 0.02$ **of r.** On the other hand, if $q = 5000$, then $r = 2(5000) = \$10,000$, so the rate of change of r is $2/10,000 = 0.0002$ **of** r. Although r changes at the same rate at each level, when compared to r itself this rate is relatively smaller when $r = 10,000$ than when $r = 100$. By considering the ratio

$$\frac{dr/dq}{r},$$

we have a means of comparing the rate of change of r with r itself. This ratio is called the *relative rate of change* of r. We have shown above that the relative rate of change when $q = 50$ is

$$\frac{dr/dq}{r} = \frac{2}{100} = 0.02,$$

and when $q = 5000$, it is

$$\frac{dr/dq}{r} = \frac{2}{10,000} = 0.0002.$$

By multiplying these relative rates by 100, we obtain so-called *percentage rates of change*. The percentage rate of change when $q = 50$ is $(0.02)(100) = 2\%$; when $q = 5000$ it is $(0.0002)(100) = 0.02\%$. Thus, for example, if an additional unit beyond 50 is sold, then revenue increases by approximately 2%. In general, for any function f we have the following definition.

Definition
*The **relative rate of change** of $f(x)$ is*

$$\frac{f'(x)}{f(x)}.$$

*The **percentage rate of change** of $f(x)$ is*

$$\frac{f'(x)}{f(x)} \cdot 100.$$

EXAMPLE 7   *Determine the relative and percentage rates of change of* $y = f(x) = 3x^2 - 5x + 25$ *when* $x = 5$.

Here

$$f'(x) = 6x - 5.$$

Since $f'(5) = 6(5) - 5 = 25$ and $f(5) = 3(5)^2 - 5(5) + 25 = 75$, the relative rate of change of y when $x = 5$ is

$$\frac{f'(5)}{f(5)} = \frac{25}{75} \approx 0.333.$$

Multiplying 0.333 by 100 gives the percentage rate of change: $(0.333)(100) = 33.3\%$.

EXERCISE 11.3

In each of Problems **1–6,** *an equation of motion is given. For the given value of t, find* (a) *the position and* (b) *the velocity. Assume t is in seconds and s is in meters.*

1. $s = t^2 - 3t$; $t = 4$.

2. $s = \frac{1}{2}t + 1$; $t = 2$.

3. $s = 2t^3 + 6$; $t = 1$.

4. $s = -3t^2 + 2t + 1$; $t = 1$.

5. $s = t^4 - 2t^3 + t$; $t = 2$.

6. $s = t^4 - t^{5/2}$; $t = 0$.

7. Sociologists studied the relation between income and number of years of education for members of a particular urban group. They found that a person with x years of education before seeking regular employment can expect to receive an average yearly income of y dollars per year, where

$$y = 4x^{5/2} + 4900, \qquad 4 \le x \le 16.$$

Find the rate of change of income with respect to number of years of education. Evaluate when $x = 9$.

8. Find the rate of change of the area A of a circle with respect to its radius r if $A = \pi r^2$. Evaluate when $r = 3$ in.

9. The approximate temperature T of the skin in terms of the temperature T_e of the environment is given by

$$T = 32.8 + 0.27(T_e - 20),$$

where T and T_e are in degrees Celsius.* Find the rate of change of T with respect to T_e.

10. The volume V of a spherical cell is given by $V = \frac{4}{3}\pi r^3$, where r is the radius. Find the rate of change of volume with respect to the radius when $r = 6.5 \times 10^{-4}$ cm.

In Problems **11–16,** *cost functions are given where c is the cost of producing q units of a product. In each case find the marginal cost function. What is the marginal cost at the given value(s) of q?*

11. $c = 500 + 10q$; $q = 100$.

12. $c = 5000 + 6q$; $q = 36$.

13. $c = 0.3q^2 + 2q + 850$; $q = 3$.

14. $c = 0.1q^2 + 3q + 2$; $q = 3$.

15. $c = q^2 + 50q + 1000$; $q = 15, q = 16, q = 17$.

16. $c = 0.03q^3 - 0.6q^2 + 4.5q + 7700$; $q = 10, q = 20, q = 100$.

In Problems **17–20,** $\bar{c}$ *represents average cost per unit, which is a function of the number q of units produced. Find the marginal cost function and the marginal cost for the indicated values of q.*

17. $\bar{c} = 0.01q + 5 + \dfrac{500}{q}$; $q = 50, q = 100$.

18. $\bar{c} = 2 + \dfrac{1000}{q}$; $q = 25, q = 235$.

19. $\bar{c} = 0.00002q^2 - 0.01q + 6 + \dfrac{20{,}000}{q}$; $q = 100, q = 500$.

20. $\bar{c} = 0.001q^2 - 0.3q + 40 + \dfrac{7000}{q}$; $q = 10, q = 20$.

In Problems **21–24,** *r represents total revenue and is a function of the number q of units sold. Find the marginal revenue function and the marginal revenue for the indicated values of q.*

21. $r = 0.7q$; $q = 8, q = 100, q = 200$.

22. $r = q(15 - \frac{1}{30}q)$; $q = 5, q = 15, q = 150$.

23. $r = 250q + 45q^2 - q^3$; $q = 5, q = 10, q = 25$.

24. $r = 2q(30 - 0.1q)$; $q = 10, q = 20$.

* R. W. Stacy et al., *Essentials of Biological and Medical Physics* (New York: McGraw-Hill Book Company, 1955).

25. The total cost function for a hosiery mill is estimated by Dean:*

$$c = -10,484.69 + 6.750q - 0.000328q^2,$$

where q is output in dozens of pairs and c is total cost in dollars. Find the marginal cost function and evaluate it when $q = 5000$.

26. The total cost function for an electric light and power plant is estimated by Nordin:†

$$c = 32.07 - 0.79q + 0.02142q^2 - 0.0001q^3,$$
$$20 \le q \le 90,$$

where q is 8-hour total output (as percentage of capacity) and c is total fuel cost in dollars. Find the marginal cost function and evaluate it when $q = 70$.

27. Suppose the 100 largest cities in the United States in 1920 are ranked according to magnitude (areas of cities). From Lotka‡ the following relation approximately holds:

$$PR^{0.93} = 5,000,000,$$

where P is the population of the city having respective rank R. This relation is called the *law of urban concentration* for 1920. Solve for P in terms of R and then find how fast population is changing with respect to rank.

28. Under the straight-line method of depreciation, the value v of a certain machine after t years have elapsed is given by $v = 50,000 - 5000t$ where $0 \le t \le 10$. How fast is v changing with respect to t when $t = 2$? $t = 3$? at any time?

29. A study of the winter moth was made in Nova Scotia (adapted from Embree§). The prepupae of the moth fall onto the ground from host trees. At a distance of x ft from the base of a host tree, the prepupal density (number of prepupae per square foot of soil) was y, where

$$y = 59.3 - 1.5x - 0.5x^2, \qquad 1 \le x \le 9.$$

a. At what rate is the prepupal density changing with respect to distance from the base of the tree when $x = 6$?

b. For what value of x is the prepupal density decreasing at the rate of 6 prepupae per square foot per foot?

30. For the cost function $c = 0.4q^2 + 4q + 5$, find the rate of change of c with respect to q when $q = 2$. Also, what is $\Delta c/\Delta q$ over the interval $[2, 3]$?

In Problems **31–36,** *find (a) the rate of change of y with respect to x, and (b) the relative rate of change of y. At the given value of x, find (c) the rate of change of y, (d) the relative rate of change of y, and (e) the percentage rate of change of y.*

31. $y = f(x) = x + 4;\quad x = 5.$

32. $y = f(x) = 4 - 2x;\quad x = 3.$

33. $y = 3x^2 + 6;\quad x = 2.$

34. $y = 2 - x^2;\quad x = 0.$

35. $y = 8 - x^3;\quad x = 1.$

36. $y = x^2 + 3x - 4;\quad x = -1.$

37. For the cost function $c = 0.2q^2 + 1.2q + 4$, how fast does c change with respect to q when $q = 5$? Determine the percentage rate of change of c with respect to q when $q = 5$.

38. In a discussion of contemporary waters of shallow seas, Odum‖ claims that in such waters the total organic matter y (in milligrams per liter) is a function of species diversity x (in number of species per thousand individ-

* J. Dean, "Statistical Cost Functions of a Hosiery Mill," *Studies in Business Administration,* XI, no. 4 (Chicago: University of Chicago Press, 1941).

† J. A. Nordin, "Note on a Light Plant's Cost Curves," *Econometrica,* 15 (1947), 231–35.

‡ A. J. Lotka, *Elements of Mathematical Biology* (New York: Dover Publications, Inc., 1956).

§ D. G. Embree, "The Population Dynamics of the Winter Moth in Nova Scotia, 1954–1962," *Memoirs of the Entomological Society of Canada,* no. 46 (1965).

‖ H. T. Odum, "Biological Circuits and the Marine Systems of Texas," in *Pollution and Marine Biology,* ed. T. A. Olsen and F. J. Burgess (New York: Interscience Publishers, 1967).

uals). If $y = 100/x$, at what rate is the total organic matter changing with respect to species diversity when $x = 10$? What is the percentage rate of change when $x = 10$?

39. For a certain manufacturer, the revenue r obtained from the sale of q units of a product is given by $r = 30q - 0.3q^2$. (a) How fast does r change with respect to q? When $q = 10$, (b) find the relative rate of change of r, and (c) to the nearest percent, find the percentage rate of change of r.

40. Repeat Problem 39 for the revenue function given by $r = 20q - 0.1q^2$ and $q = 100$.

41. The weight W of a limb of a tree is given by $W = 2t^{0.432}$, where t is time. Find the relative rate of change of W with respect to t.

42. A psychological experiment* was conducted to analyze human response to electrical shocks (stimuli). The sub-

jects received shocks of various intensities. The response R to a shock of intensity I (in microamperes) was to be a number that indicated the perceived magnitude relative to that of a "standard" shock. The standard shock was assigned a magnitude of 10. Two groups of subjects were tested under slightly different conditions. The responses R_1 and R_2 of the first and second groups to a shock of intensity I were given by

$$R_1 = \frac{I^{1.3}}{1855.24}, \qquad 800 \le I \le 3500,$$

and

$$R_2 = \frac{I^{1.3}}{1101.29}, \qquad 800 \le I \le 3500.$$

a. For each group determine the relative rate of change of response with respect to intensity.
b. How do these changes compare?
c. In general, if $f(x) = C_1x^n$ and $g(x) = C_2x^n$, where C_1 and C_2 are constants, how do the relative rates of change of f and g compare?

11.4 DIFFERENTIABILITY AND CONTINUITY

In the next section we shall make use of an important relationship between differentiability and continuity, namely

> If f is differentiable at a, then f is continuous at a.

To establish this result, let us first reconsider the concept of continuity.

If a function f is continuous at a, then the graph of $y = f(x)$ has no break when $x = a$. This means that the graph must have a point when $x = a$, and therefore $f(a)$ must be defined (see Fig. 11.11). In addition, there must be points on the graph for all values of x near a and their function values must be near $f(a)$. In particular, as values of x get closer to a, then $f(x)$ gets closer to $f(a)$. That is

$$\lim_{x \to a} f(x) = f(a). \tag{1}$$

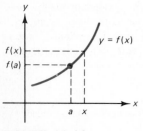

FIGURE 11.11

Let us reformulate this limit in terms of the difference $x - a$ (see Fig. 11.12).

* H. Babkoff, "Magnitude Estimation of Short Electrocutaneous Pulses," *Psychological Research*, 39, no. 1 (1976), 39–49.

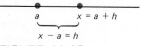

FIGURE 11.12

If $x - a$ is denoted by h, then $x = a + h$. From the diagram, it is clear that as $x \to a$, then $h \to 0$. Restating the limit in Eq. (1), we have the following. If f is continuous at a, then

$$\lim_{h \to 0} f(a + h) = f(a). \tag{2}$$

Conversely, it can also be shown that if Eq. (2) is true, then f is continuous at a. Thus Eq. (2) can be considered a definition of continuity at a.

Now we shall relate differentiability to continuity. Suppose that f is differentiable at a. Then $f'(a)$ exists and

$$\lim_{h \to 0} \frac{f(a + h) - f(a)}{h} = f'(a).$$

Consider the numerator $f(a + h) - f(a)$ as $h \to 0$.

$$\lim_{h \to 0} [f(a + h) - f(a)] = \lim_{h \to 0} \left[\frac{f(a + h) - f(a)}{h} \cdot h \right]$$

$$= \lim_{h \to 0} \frac{f(a + h) - f(a)}{h} \cdot \lim_{h \to 0} h$$

$$= f'(a) \cdot 0 = 0.$$

Thus $\lim_{h \to 0} [f(a + h) - f(a)] = 0$. This means that $f(a + h) - f(a)$ approaches 0 as $h \to 0$. Consequently,

$$\lim_{h \to 0} f(a + h) = f(a),$$

which is Eq. (2). This proves that f is continuous at a when f is differentiable there. More simply, we say that **differentiability at a point implies continuity at that point.**

If a function is not continuous at a point, then it cannot have a derivative there. For example, the function in Fig. 11.13 is discontinuous at a. The curve has no tangent at that point, so the function is not differentiable there.

FIGURE 11.13

EXAMPLE 1

a. Let $f(x) = x^2$. Since $f'(x) = 2x$ is defined for all values of x, then $f(x) = x^2$ must be continuous for all values of x.

b. The function $f(p) = \dfrac{1}{2p}$ is not continuous at $p = 0$ because f is not defined there. Thus the derivative does not exist at $p = 0$.

The converse of the statement that differentiability implies continuity is *false*. In Example 2 you will see a function that is continuous at a point but not differentiable there.

EXAMPLE 2   The function $y = f(x) = |x|$ is continuous at $x = 0$ (see Fig. 11.14). As we mentioned in Sec. 11.1, there is no tangent line at $x = 0$. Thus the derivative does not exist there. This shows that continuity does *not* imply differentiability.

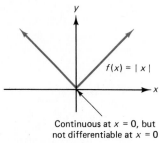

Continuous at $x = 0$, but
not differentiable at $x = 0$

FIGURE 11.14

11.5 PRODUCT AND QUOTIENT RULES

The equation $F(x) = (x^2 + 3x)(4x + 5)$ expresses $F(x)$ as a product of two functions: $x^2 + 3x$ and $4x + 5$. To find $F'(x)$ by using only our previous rules, we first multiply the functions, which gives $F(x) = 4x^3 + 17x^2 + 15x$. Then we differentiate term by term:

$$F'(x) = 12x^2 + 34x + 15. \tag{1}$$

However, in many problems that involve differentiating a product of functions, the multiplication is not as simple as it is here. Often it is not even practical to attempt it. Fortunately, there is a rule for differentiating a product, and the rule avoids such multiplications. Since the derivative of a sum of functions is the sum of their derivatives, you might think that the derivative of a product of two functions is the product of their derivatives. This is **not** the case, as the next rule shows.

Rule 5

PRODUCT RULE. *If f and g are differentiable functions, then*

$$\frac{d}{dx}[f(x)g(x)] = f(x)g'(x) + g(x)f'(x).$$

That is, the derivative of the product of two functions is the first function times the derivative of the second, plus the second function times the derivative of the first.

Proof. If $F(x) = f(x)g(x)$, then by the definition of the derivative of F,

$$F'(x) = \lim_{h \to 0} \frac{F(x + h) - F(x)}{h}$$

$$= \lim_{h \to 0} \frac{f(x + h)g(x + h) - f(x)g(x)}{h}$$

Now we use a "trick." Adding and subtracting $f(x + h)g(x)$ in the numerator, we have

$$F'(x) = \lim_{h \to 0} \frac{f(x + h)g(x + h) - f(x)g(x) + [f(x + h)g(x) - f(x + h)g(x)]}{h}$$

Regrouping gives

$$F'(x) = \lim_{h \to 0} \frac{[f(x + h)g(x + h) - f(x + h)g(x)] + [f(x + h)g(x) - f(x)g(x)]}{h}$$

$$= \lim_{h \to 0} \frac{f(x + h)[g(x + h) - g(x)] + g(x)[f(x + h) - f(x)]}{h}$$

$$= \lim_{h \to 0} \frac{f(x + h)[g(x + h) - g(x)]}{h} + \lim_{h \to 0} \frac{g(x)[f(x + h) - f(x)]}{h}$$

$$= \lim_{h \to 0} f(x + h) \cdot \lim_{h \to 0} \frac{g(x + h) - g(x)}{h} + \lim_{h \to 0} g(x) \cdot \lim_{h \to 0} \frac{f(x + h) - f(x)}{h}$$

Since we assumed that f and g are differentiable, then

$$\lim_{h \to 0} \frac{f(x + h) - f(x)}{h} = f'(x)$$

and $\quad \lim_{h \to 0} \frac{g(x + h) - g(x)}{h} = g'(x)$.

The differentiability of f implies that f is continuous, and from Sec. 11.4,

$$\lim_{h \to 0} f(x + h) = f(x).$$

Thus

$$F'(x) = f(x)g'(x) + g(x)f'(x).$$

EXAMPLE 1   If $F(x) = (x^2 + 3x)(4x + 5)$, find $F'(x)$.

Here F can be considered a product of two functions: $f(x) = x^2 + 3x$ and $g(x) = 4x + 5$. By Rule 5, the product rule,

$$F'(x) = f(x)g'(x) + g(x)f'(x)$$

$$= (x^2 + 3x) D_x(4x + 5) + (4x + 5) D_x(x^2 + 3x)$$

$$= (x^2 + 3x)(4) + (4x + 5)(2x + 3)$$

$$= 12x^2 + 34x + 15 \qquad \text{(simplifying)}.$$

This agrees with our previous result [see Eq. (1)].

Pitfall

We repeat: the derivative of the product of two functions is **not** the product of their derivatives. For example, $D_x(x^2 + 3x) = 2x + 3$ and $D_x(4x + 5) = 4$, but

$$D_x[(x^2 + 3x)(4x + 5)] = 12x^2 + 34x + 15 \neq (2x + 3)4.$$

EXAMPLE 2

a. *Find the slope of the graph of* $f(x) = (7x^3 - 5x + 2)(2x^4 + 7)$ *when* $x = 1$.

Here $f(x)$ is the product of $7x^3 - 5x + 2$ and $2x^4 + 7$. By the product rule,

$$f'(x) = (7x^3 - 5x + 2)D_x(2x^4 + 7) + (2x^4 + 7) D_x(7x^3 - 5x + 2)$$

$$= (7x^3 - 5x + 2)(8x^3) + (2x^4 + 7)(21x^2 - 5).$$

Evaluating $f'(x)$ at $x = 1$ gives the slope of the graph at that point:

$$f'(1) = 4(8) + 9(16) = 176.$$

Note: **We do not have to simplify the derivative before evaluating it.**

b. *If* $y = (x^{2/3} + 3)(x^{-1/3} + 5x)$, *find* $D_x y$.

$$D_x y = (x^{2/3} + 3) D_x(x^{-1/3} + 5x) + (x^{-1/3} + 5x) D_x(x^{2/3} + 3)$$

$$= (x^{2/3} + 3)(-\tfrac{1}{3}x^{-4/3} + 5) + (x^{-1/3} + 5x)(\tfrac{2}{3}x^{-1/3})$$

$$= \tfrac{25}{3}x^{2/3} + \tfrac{1}{3}x^{-2/3} - x^{-4/3} + 15.$$

c. *If* $y = (x + 2)(x + 3)(x + 4)$, *find* y'.

By grouping, we can consider y to be a product of two functions:

$$y = [(x + 2)(x + 3)](x + 4).$$

The product rule gives

$$y' = [(x + 2)(x + 3] D_x(x + 4) + (x + 4) D_x[(x + 2)(x + 3)]$$

$$= [(x + 2)(x + 3)](1) + (x + 4) D_x[(x + 2)(x + 3)].$$

Applying the product rule again, we have

$$y' = [(x + 2)(x + 3)(1) + (x + 4)[(x + 2) D_x(x + 3) + (x + 3) D_x(x + 2)]$$

$$= [(x + 2)(x + 3)](1) + (x + 4)[(x + 2)(1) + (x + 3)(1)].$$

After simplifying, we obtain

$$y' = 3x^2 + 18x + 26.$$

Usually, we do not use the product rule when simpler ways are obvious. For example, if $f(x) = 2x(x + 3)$, then it is quicker to write $f(x) = 2x^2 + 6x$, from which $f'(x) = 4x + 6$. Similarly, we do not usually use the product rule to differentiate $y = 4(x^2 - 3)$. Since the 4 is a constant multiplier, by Rule 3 we have $y' = 4(2x) = 8x$.

The next rule is used for differentiating a *quotient* of two functions.

Rule 6

QUOTIENT RULE   *If f and g are differentiable functions and $g(x) \neq 0$, then*

$$\frac{d}{dx}\left[\frac{f(x)}{g(x)}\right] = \frac{g(x)f'(x) - f(x)g'(x)}{[g(x)]^2}.$$

That is, the derivative of the quotient of two functions is the denominator times the derivative of the numerator, minus the numerator times the derivative of the denominator, all divided by the square of the denominator.

Proof.   *If $F(x) = \dfrac{f(x)}{g(x)}$, then*

$$F(x)g(x) = f(x).$$

By the product rule (Rule 5),

$$F(x)g'(x) + g(x)F'(x) = f'(x).$$

Solving for $F'(x)$, we have

$$F'(x) = \frac{f'(x) - F(x)g'(x)}{g(x)}.$$

But $F(x) = f(x)/g(x)$. Thus

$$F'(x) = \frac{f'(x) - \dfrac{f(x)g'(x)}{g(x)}}{g(x)}.$$

Simplifying, we have*

$$F'(x) = \frac{g(x)f'(x) - f(x)g'(x)}{[g(x)]^2}.$$

Pitfall

The derivative of the quotient of two functions is **not** the quotient of their derivatives.

---

* You may have observed that this proof assumes the existence of $F'(x)$. However, this rule can be proven without this assumption.

EXAMPLE 3

a. *If* $F(x) = \dfrac{4x^2 + 3}{2x - 1}$, *find* $F'(x)$.

Let $f(x) = 4x^2 + 3$ and $g(x) = 2x - 1$. Then $F(x) = f(x)/g(x)$ and by Rule 6, the quotient rule,

$$
\begin{aligned}
F'(x) &= \frac{g(x)f'(x) - f(x)g'(x)}{[g(x)]^2} \\[2mm]
&= \frac{(2x - 1)D_x(4x^2 + 3) - (4x^2 + 3)D_x(2x - 1)}{(2x - 1)^2} \\[2mm]
&= \frac{(2x - 1)(8x) - (4x^2 + 3)(2)}{(2x - 1)^2} \\[2mm]
&= \frac{8x^2 - 8x - 6}{(2x - 1)^2} = \frac{2(4x^2 - 4x - 3)}{(2x - 1)^2}.
\end{aligned}
$$

b. *Find* $D_x \dfrac{1}{x^2}$.

Although the quotient rule can be used, a simpler and more direct method is to write $1/x^2$ as x^{-2} and then apply the rule for differentiating x^n.

$$
D_x \frac{1}{x^2} = D_x x^{-2} = -2x^{-3} = -\frac{2}{x^3}.
$$

Alternatively, applying the quotient rule to this problem gives

$$
\begin{aligned}
D_x \frac{1}{x^2} &= \frac{(x^2)D_x(1) - (1)D_x(x^2)}{(x^2)^2} \\[2mm]
&= \frac{x^2(0) - 1(2x)}{x^4} = \frac{-2x}{x^4} = -\frac{2}{x^3}.
\end{aligned}
$$

c. *Find   an   equation   of   the   tangent   line   to   the   curve* $y = \dfrac{(x + 1)(x^2 + 2x + 5)}{1 - x}$ *at* $(0, 5)$.

By the quotient rule,

$$
y' = \frac{(1 - x)\, D_x[(x + 1)(x^2 + 2x + 5)] - [(x + 1)(x^2 + 2x + 5)]\, D_x(1 - x)}{(1 - x)^2}.
$$

Using the product rule to find $D_x[(x + 1)(x^2 + 2x + 5)]$, we have

$$
y' = \frac{(1 - x)[(x + 1)(2x + 2) + (x^2 + 2x + 5)(1)] - [(x + 1)(x^2 + 2x + 5)](-1)}{(1 - x)^2}.
$$

The slope of the curve at $(0, 5)$ is $y'(0) = 12$. An equation of the tangent line is

$$y - 5 = 12(x - 0),$$

$$y = 12x + 5.$$

EXAMPLE 4   *If the demand equation for a manufacturer's product is $p = 1000/(q + 5)$, find the marginal revenue function and evaluate it when $q = 45$.*

The revenue r received for selling q units is

$$\textbf{revenue} = \textbf{(price)(quantity)},$$

$$r = pq.$$

Thus the revenue function is

$$r = \left(\frac{1000}{q + 5}\right)q,$$

$$r = \frac{1000q}{q + 5}.$$

The marginal revenue function is dr/dq.

$$\frac{dr}{dq} = \frac{(q + 5) D_q(1000q) - (1000q) D_q(q + 5)}{(q + 5)^2}$$

$$= \frac{(q + 5)(1000) - (1000q)(1)}{(q + 5)^2} = \frac{5000}{(q + 5)^2}.$$

$$\left.\frac{dr}{dq}\right|_{q=45} = \frac{5000}{(45 + 5)^2} = \frac{5000}{2500} = 2.$$

This means that selling one additional unit beyond 45 results in approximately $2 more in revenue.

A function that plays an important role in economic analysis is the **consumption function.** The consumption function $C = f(I)$ expresses a relationship between the total national income I and the total national consumption C. Usually, both I and C are expressed in billions of dollars and I is restricted to some interval. The *marginal propensity to consume* is defined as the rate of change of consumption with respect to income. It is merely the derivative of C with respect to I.

$$\textbf{marginal propensity to consume} = \frac{dC}{dI}.$$

If we assume that the difference between income I and consumption C is savings S, then

$$S = I - C.$$

Differentiating both sides with respect to I gives

$$\frac{dS}{dI} = \frac{d}{dI}(I) - \frac{d}{dI}(C) = 1 - \frac{dC}{dI}.$$

We define dS/dI as the **marginal propensity to save.** Thus the marginal propensity to save indicates how fast savings change with respect to income.

EXAMPLE 5   *If the consumption function is given by*

$$C = \frac{5(2\sqrt{I^3} + 3)}{I + 10},$$

determine the marginal propensity to consume and the marginal propensity to save when $I = 100$.

$$\frac{dC}{dI} = \frac{(I + 10)\ D_I[5(2I^{3/2} + 3)] - 5(2\sqrt{I^3} + 3)\ D_I[I + 10]}{(I + 10)^2}$$

$$= \frac{(I + 10)[5(3I^{1/2})] - 5(2\sqrt{I^3} + 3)[1]}{(I + 10)^2}.$$

When $I = 100$ the marginal propensity to consume is

$$\left.\frac{dC}{dI}\right|_{I=100} = \frac{6485}{12,100} \approx 0.536.$$

The marginal propensity to save when $I = 100$ is $1 - 0.536 = 0.464$. This means that if a current income of \$100 billion increases by \$1 billion, the nation will consume approximately 53.6%(536/1000) and save 46.4%(464/1000) of that increase.

EXERCISE 11.5

In Problems **1–42,** *differentiate the functions.*

1. $f(x) = (4x + 1)(6x + 3)$.

2. $f(x) = (3x - 1)(7x + 2)$.

3. $s(t) = (8 - 7t)(t^2 - 2)$.

4. $Q(x) = (5 - 2x)(x^2 + 1)$.

5. $f(r) = (3r^2 - 4)(r^2 - 5r + 1)$.

6. $C(I) = (2I^2 - 3)(3I^2 - 4I + 1)$.

7. $y = (x^2 + 3x - 2)(2x^2 - x - 3)$.

8. $y = (2 - 3x + 4x^2)(1 + 2x - 3x^2)$.

9. $f(w) = (8w^2 + 2w - 3)(5w^3 + 2)$.

10. $f(x) = (3x - x^2)(3 - x - x^2)$.

11. $y = (x^2 - 1)(3x^3 - 6x + 5) - (x + 4)(4x^2 + 2x + 1)$.   **12.** $h(x) = 4(x^5 - 3)(2x^3 + 4) + 3(8x^2 - 5)(3x + 2)$.

13. $f(p) = \frac{3}{2}(\sqrt{p} - 4)(4p - 5)$.

14. $g(x) = (\sqrt{x} - 3x + 1)(\sqrt[4]{x} - 2\sqrt{x})$.

15. $y = 7 \cdot \frac{2}{3}$.

16. $y = (x - 1)(x - 2)(x - 3)$.

17. $y = (2x - 1)(3x + 4)(x + 7)$.

18. $y = \frac{2x - 3}{4x + 1}$.

19. $f(x) = \dfrac{x}{x-1}$.

20. $f(x) = \dfrac{-2x}{1-x}$.

21. $y = \dfrac{x+2}{x-1}$.

22. $h(w) = \dfrac{3w^2 + 5w - 1}{w - 3}$.

23. $h(z) = \dfrac{5 - 2z}{z^2 - 4}$.

24. $y = \dfrac{x^2 - 4x + 2}{x^2 + x + 1}$.

25. $y = \dfrac{8x^2 - 2x + 1}{x^2 - 5x}$.

26. $f(x) = \dfrac{x^3 - x^2 + 1}{x^2 + 1}$.

27. $y = \dfrac{x^2 - 4x + 3}{2x^2 - 3x + 2}$.

28. $F(z) = \dfrac{z^4 + 4}{3z}$.

29. $g(x) = \dfrac{1}{x^{100} + 1}$.

30. $y = \dfrac{3}{7x^3}$.

31. $u(v) = \dfrac{v^5 - 8}{v}$.

32. $y = \dfrac{x - 5}{2\sqrt{x}}$.

33. $y = \dfrac{3x^2 - x - 1}{\sqrt[3]{x}}$.

34. $y = \dfrac{x^{0.3} - 2}{2x^{2.1} + 1}$.

35. $y = 7 - \dfrac{4}{x - 8} + \dfrac{2x}{3x + 1}$.

36. $q(x) = 13x^2 + \dfrac{x - 1}{2x + 3} - \dfrac{4}{x}$.

37. $y = \dfrac{x - 5}{(x + 2)(x - 4)}$.

38. $y = \dfrac{(2s - 1)(3x + 2)}{4 - 5x}$.

39. $s(t) = \dfrac{t^2 + 3t}{(t^2 - 1)(t^3 + 7)}$.

40. $f(s) = \dfrac{17}{s(5s^2 - 10s + 4)}$.

41. $y = 3x - \dfrac{\dfrac{2}{x} - \dfrac{3}{x - 1}}{x - 2}$.

42. $y = 7 - 10x^2 + \dfrac{1 - \dfrac{7}{x^2 + 3}}{x + 2}$.

43. Find the slope of the curve $y = (4x^2 + 2x - 5)(x^3 + 7x + 4)$ at $(-1, 12)$.

44. Find the slope of the curve $y = \dfrac{x^3}{x^4 + 1}$ at $(1, \frac{1}{2})$.

In Problems **45–48,** *find an equation of the tangent line to the curve at the given point.*

45. $y = \dfrac{6}{x - 1}$; $(3, 3)$.

46. $y = \dfrac{4x + 5}{x^2}$; $(-1, 1)$.

47. $y = (2x + 3)[2(x^4 - 5x^2 + 4)]$; $(0, 24)$.

48. $y = \dfrac{x + 1}{x^2(x - 4)}$; $(2, -\frac{3}{8})$.

In Problems **49** *and* **50,** *determine the relative rate of change of y with respect to x for the given value of x.*

49. $y = \dfrac{x}{2x - 6}$; $x = 1$.

50. $y = \dfrac{1 - x}{1 + x}$; $x = 5$.

In Problems **51–54,** *each equation represents a demand function for a certain product where p denotes price per unit for q units. Find the marginal revenue function in each case. Recall that revenue = pq.*

51. $p = 25 - 0.02q$.   **52.** $p = 500/q$.   **53.** $p = \dfrac{108}{q + 2} - 3$.   **54.** $p = \dfrac{q + 750}{q + 50}$.

55. For the United States (1922–1942), the consumption function is estimated by[*]

$$C = 0.672I + 113.1.$$

Find the marginal propensity to consume.

56. Repeat Problem 55 if $C = 0.712I + 95.05$ for the United States for 1929–1941.[*]

In Problems **57–60,** *each equation represents a consumption function. Find the marginal propensity to consume and the marginal propensity to save for the given value of I.*

57. $C = 2 + 2\sqrt{I}$; $I = 9$.

58. $C = 6 + \dfrac{3I}{4} - \dfrac{\sqrt{I}}{3}$; $I = 25$.

59. $C = \dfrac{16\sqrt{I} + 0.8\sqrt{I^3} - 0.2I}{\sqrt{I} + 4}$; $I = 36$.

60. $C = \dfrac{20\sqrt{I} + 0.5\sqrt{I^3} - 0.4I}{\sqrt{I} + 5}$; $I = 100$.

61. If the total cost function for a manufacturer is given by

$$c = \frac{5q^2}{q + 3} + 5000,$$

find the marginal cost function.

62. In a discussion of social security benefits, Felstein[†] differentiates a function of the form

$$f(x) = \frac{a(1 + x) - b(2 + n)x}{a(2 + n)(1 + x) - b(2 + n)x},$$

where a, b, and n are constants. He determines that

$$f'(x) = \frac{-(1 + n)ab}{[a(1 + x) - bx]^2(2 + n)}.$$

Verify this. (*Hint:* For convenience, let $2 + n = c$.)

63. For a particular host-parasite relationship, it is determined that when the host density (number of hosts per unit of area) is x, the number of hosts that are parasitized is y, where

$$y = \frac{900x}{10 + 45x}.$$

At what rate is the number of hosts parasitized changing with respect to host density when $x = 2$?

64. The persistence of sound in a room after the sound source is turned off is called *reverberation*. The *reverberation time RT* of the room is the time it takes for the intensity level of the sound to fall 60 decibels. In the acoustical design of an auditorium, the following formula may be used to compute the *RT* of the room:[‡]

$$RT = \frac{0.05V}{A + xV},$$

where V is the room volume, A is the total room absorption, and x is the air absorption coefficient. Assuming that A and x are positive constants, show that the rate of change of *RT* with respect to V is always positive. If the total room volume increases by one unit, does reverberation time increase or decrease?

---

[*] T. Haavelmo, "Methods of Measuring the Marginal Propensity to Consume," *Journal of the American Statistical Association*, XLII (1947), 105–22.

[†] M. Feldstein, "The Optimal Level of Social Security Benefits," *The Quarterly Journal of Economics*, C, no. 2 (1985), 303–20.

[‡] L. L. Doelle, *Environmental Acoustics* (New York: McGraw-Hill Book Company, 1972).

65. In a predator-prey experiment* it was statistically determined that the number of prey consumed, y, by an individual predator was a function of prey density x (the number of prey per unit of area), where

$$y = \frac{0.7355x}{1 + 0.02744x}.$$

Determine the rate of change of prey consumed with respect to prey density.

11.6 THE CHAIN RULE AND POWER RULE

Our next rule, the chain rule, is one of the most important rules for finding derivatives. Before stating it, we shall consider the following situation. Suppose

$$y = u^2 \quad \text{and} \quad u = 2x + 1.$$

Here y is a function of u, and u is a function of x. If we substitute $2x + 1$ for u in the first equation, we can consider y to be a function of x:

$$y = (2x + 1)^2.$$

After expanding we can find dy/dx in the usual way.

$$y = 4x^2 + 4x + 1.$$

$$\frac{dy}{dx} = 8x + 4.$$

From this example you can see that finding dy/dx by first performing a substitution could be quite involved, especially if we had $y = u^{100}$ above instead of $y = u^2$. Fortunately, the chain rule will allow us to handle such situations with ease.

> **Rule 7**
> CHAIN RULE   *If y is a differentiable function of u and u is a differentiable function of x, then y is a differentiable function of x and*
> $$\frac{dy}{dx} = \frac{dy}{du} \cdot \frac{du}{dx}.$$

Let us see why the chain rule is reasonable. Suppose $y = 8u + 5$ and $u = 2x - 3$. Let x change by one unit. How does u change? Answer: $du/dx = 2$. But for *each* one-unit change in u there is a change in y of $dy/du = 8$. Therefore, what is the change in y if x changes by one unit, that is, what is dy/dx? Answer:

* C. S. Holling, "Some Characteristics of Simple Types of Predation and Parasitism," *The Canadian Entomologist*, XCI, no. 7 (1959), 385–98.

$8 \cdot 2$, which is $\dfrac{dy}{du} \cdot \dfrac{du}{dx}$. Thus $\dfrac{dy}{dx} = \dfrac{dy}{du} \cdot \dfrac{du}{dx}$.

EXAMPLE 1

a. *If* $y = 2u^2 - 3u - 2$ *and* $u = x^2 + 4$, *find* dy/dx.

By Rule 7, the chain rule,

$$\frac{dy}{dx} = \frac{dy}{du} \cdot \frac{du}{dx} = \frac{d}{du}(2u^2 - 3u - 2) \cdot \frac{d}{dx}(x^2 + 4)$$

$$= (4u - 3)(2x).$$

We can write our answer in terms of x alone by replacing u by $x^2 + 4$.

$$\frac{dy}{dx} = [4(x^2 + 4) - 3](2x) = [4x^2 + 13](2x) = 8x^3 + 26x.$$

b. *If* $y = \sqrt{w}$ *and* $w = 7 - t^3$, *find* dy/dt.

Here y is a function of w, and w is a function of t. Hence we can view y as a function of t. By the chain rule,

$$\frac{dy}{dt} = \frac{dy}{dw} \cdot \frac{dw}{dt} = \frac{d}{dw}(\sqrt{w}) \cdot \frac{d}{dt}(7 - t^3)$$

$$= \left(\frac{1}{2}w^{-1/2}\right)(-3t^2) = \frac{1}{2\sqrt{w}}(-3t^2)$$

$$= -\frac{3t^2}{2\sqrt{w}} = -\frac{3t^2}{2\sqrt{7 - t^3}}.$$

c. *If* $y = 4u^3 + 10u^2 - 3u - 7$ *and* $u = 4/(3x - 5)$, *find* dy/dx *when* $x = 1$.

By the chain rule,

$$\frac{dy}{dx} = \frac{dy}{du} \cdot \frac{du}{dx} = \frac{d}{du}(4u^3 + 10u^2 - 3u - 7) \cdot \frac{d}{dx}\left(\frac{4}{3x - 5}\right)$$

$$= (12u^2 + 20u - 3) \cdot \frac{(3x - 5) D_x(4) - 4 D_x(3x - 5)}{(3x - 5)^2}$$

$$= (12u^2 + 20u - 3) \cdot \frac{-12}{(3x - 5)^2}.$$

Even though dy/dx is in terms of x's and u's, we can evaluate it when $x = 1$ if we determine the corresponding value of u. When $x = 1$, then $u = \dfrac{4}{3(1) - 5} = -2$. Thus

$$\left.\frac{dy}{dx}\right|_{x=1} = [12(-2)^2 + 20(-2) - 3] \cdot \frac{-12}{[3(1) - 5]^2}$$

$$= 5 \cdot (-3) = -15.$$

The chain rule states that if $y = f(u)$ and $u = g(x)$, then

$$\frac{dy}{dx} = \frac{dy}{du} \cdot \frac{du}{dx}.$$

Actually, the chain rule applies to a composition function because

$$y = f(u) = f(g(x)) = (f \circ g)(x).$$

Thus y, as a function of x, is $f \circ g$. This means that we can use the chain rule to differentiate a function when we recognize the function as a composition. However, we must first break down the function into composite parts.

For example, to differentiate

$$y = (x^3 - x^2 + 6)^{100}$$

we think of the function as a composition. Let

$$y = f(u) = u^{100} \quad \text{and} \quad u = g(x) = x^3 - x^2 + 6.$$

Then $y = (x^3 - x^2 + 6)^{100} = [g(x)]^{100} = f(g(x))$. Now that we have a composition, we differentiate. Since $y = u^{100}$ and $u = x^3 - x^2 + 6$, by the chain rule

$$\frac{dy}{dx} = \frac{dy}{du} \cdot \frac{du}{dx}$$

$$= (100u^{99})(3x^2 - 2x)$$

$$= 100(x^3 - x^2 + 6)^{99}(3x^2 - 2x).$$

We have just used the chain rule to differentiate $y = (x^3 - x^2 + 6)^{100}$, which is a power of a *function* of x, not simply a power of x. The following rule, called the *power rule*, generalizes our result and is a special case of the chain rule.

Rule 8
POWER RULE   *If u is a differentiable function of x and n is any real number, then*

$$\frac{d}{dx}(u^n) = nu^{n-1}\frac{du}{dx}.$$

Proof. Let $y = u^n$. Since y is a differentiable function of u and u is a differentiable function of x, the chain rule gives

$$\frac{dy}{dx} = \frac{dy}{du} \cdot \frac{du}{dx}.$$

But $dy/du = nu^{n-1}$. Thus

$$\frac{dy}{dx} = nu^{n-1}\frac{du}{dx},$$

which is the power rule.

Another way of writing the power rule is

$$\frac{d}{dx}([u(x)]^n) = n[u(x)]^{n-1}\, u'(x).$$

EXAMPLE 2

a. *If* $y = (x^3 - 1)^7$, *find* y'.

Since y is a power of a *function* of x, the power rule applies. Letting $u(x) = x^3 - 1$ and $n = 7$, we have

$$y' = n[u(x)]^{n-1}u'(x)$$

$$= 7(x^3 - 1)^{7-1}\frac{d}{dx}(x^3 - 1)$$

$$= 7(x^3 - 1)^6(3x^2) = 21x^2(x^3 - 1)^6.$$

b. *If* $y = \sqrt[3]{(4x^2 + 3x - 2)^2}$, *find* dy/dx *when* $x = -2$.

Since $y = (4x^2 + 3x - 2)^{2/3}$ we use the power rule with $u = 4x^2 + 3x - 2$ and $n = \frac{2}{3}$.

$$\frac{dy}{dx} = \frac{2}{3}(4x^2 + 3x - 2)^{(2/3)-1} D_x(4x^2 + 3x - 2)$$

$$= \frac{2(8x + 3)}{3\sqrt[3]{4x^2 + 3x - 2}}.$$

$$\left.\frac{dy}{dx}\right|_{x=-2} = \frac{2(-13)}{3\sqrt[3]{8}} = -\frac{13}{3}.$$

c. *If* $y = \dfrac{1}{x^2 - 2}$, *find* $\dfrac{dy}{dx}$.

Although the quotient rule can be used here, we shall treat the right side as the power $(x^2 - 2)^{-1}$ and use the power rule. Let $u = x^2 - 2$. Then $y = u^{-1}$ and

$$\frac{dy}{dx} = nu^{n-1}\frac{du}{dx}$$

$$= (-1)(x^2 - 2)^{-1-1}D_x(x^2 - 2)$$

$$= (-1)(x^2 - 2)^{-2}(2x)$$

$$= -\frac{2x}{(x^2 - 2)^2}.$$

EXAMPLE 3

a. If $z = \left(\dfrac{2s + 5}{s^2 + 1}\right)^4$, find $\dfrac{dz}{ds}$.

Since z is a power of a function, we first use the power rule.

$$\frac{dz}{ds} = 4\left(\frac{2s + 5}{s^2 + 1}\right)^{4-1}D_s\left(\frac{2s + 5}{s^2 + 1}\right).$$

By the quotient rule,

$$\frac{dz}{ds} = 4\left(\frac{2s + 5}{s^2 + 1}\right)^3\frac{(s^2 + 1)(2) - (2s + 5)(2s)}{(s^2 + 1)^2}.$$

Simplifying, we have

$$\frac{dz}{ds} = 4 \cdot \frac{(2s + 5)^3}{(s^2 + 1)^3} \cdot \frac{(-2s^2 - 10s + 2)}{(s^2 + 1)^2}$$

$$= \frac{-8(s^2 + 5s - 1)(2s + 5)^3}{(s^3 + 1)^5}.$$

b. If $y = (x^2 - 4)^5(3x + 5)^4$, find y'.

Since y is a product, we first apply the product rule.

$$y' = (x^2 - 4)^5D_x[(3x + 5)^4] + (3x + 5)^4D_x[(x^2 - 4)^5].$$

Now we can use the power rule.

$$y' = (x^2 - 4)^5[4(3x + 5)^3(3)] + (3x + 5)^4[5(x^2 - 4)^4(2x)].$$

Simplifying gives

$$y' = 12(x^2 - 4)^5(3x + 5)^3 + 10x(3x + 5)^4(x^2 - 4)^4$$

$$= 2(x^2 - 4)^4(3x + 5)^3[6(x^2 - 4) + 5x(3x + 5)] \qquad \text{[factoring]}$$

$$= 2(x^2 - 4)^4(3x + 5)^3(21x^2 + 25x - 24).$$

Usually, the power rule should be used to differentiate $y = [u(x)]^n$. Although a function such as $y = (x^2 + 2)^2$ may be written $y = x^4 + 4x^2 + 4$ and differentiated easily, this method is impractical for a function such as $y = (x^2 + 2)^{1000}$. Since $y = (x^2 + 2)^{1000}$ is of the form $y = [u(x)]^n$, we have

$$y' = 1000(x^2 + 2)^{999}(2x).$$

Let us now use our knowledge of calculus to develop a concept relevant to economic studies. Suppose a manufacturer hires m employees who produce a total of q units of a product per day. We can think of q as a function of m. If r is the total revenue the manufacturer receives for selling these units, then r can also be considered a function of m. Thus we can look at dr/dm, the rate of change of revenue with respect to the number of employees. Since

$$\text{total revenue} = (\text{price per unit})(\text{number of units sold}),$$

we have

$$r = pq, \tag{1}$$

where p is the price per unit. Here p is a function of q and is determined by the product's demand equation. With Eq. (1) we can find dr/dm by the product rule:

$$\frac{dr}{dm} = p\frac{d}{dm}(q) + q\frac{d}{dm}(p) = p\frac{dq}{dm} + q\frac{dp}{dm}.$$

But by the chain rule,

$$\frac{dp}{dm} = \frac{dp}{dq} \cdot \frac{dq}{dm}.$$

Therefore,

$$\frac{dr}{dm} = p\frac{dq}{dm} + q\frac{dp}{dq} \cdot \frac{dq}{dm}$$

or

$$\frac{dr}{dm} = \frac{dq}{dm}\left(p + q\frac{dp}{dq}\right). \tag{2}$$

The derivative dr/dm is called the **marginal revenue product.** It is approximately the change in revenue that results when a manufacturer hires an extra employee.

EXAMPLE 4   *A manufacturer determines that m employees will produce a total of q units of a product per day, where $q = 10m^2/\sqrt{m^2 + 19}$. If the demand equation for the product is $p = 900/(q + 9)$, determine the marginal revenue product when $m = 9$.*

First we find dq/dm and dp/dq. Using the quotient and power rules, we obtain

$$\frac{dq}{dm} = \frac{(m^2 + 19)^{1/2}D_m(10m^2) - (10m^2)D_m[(m^2 + 19)^{1/2}]}{[(m^2 + 19)^{1/2}]^2}$$

$$= \frac{(m^2 + 19)^{1/2}(20m) - 10m^2[(1/2)(m^2 + 19)^{-1/2}(2m)]}{m^2 + 19}$$

$$= \frac{10m(m^2 + 19)^{-1/2}[(m^2 + 19)(2) - m(m)]}{m^2 + 19}$$

$$= \frac{10m(m^2 + 38)}{(m^2 + 19)^{3/2}}.$$

Since $p = 900(q + 9)^{-1}$, by the power rule,

$$\frac{dp}{dq} = 900[(-1)(q + 9)^{-2}(1)] = -\frac{900}{(q + 9)^2}.$$

Substituting into Eq. (2), we have the marginal revenue product:

$$\frac{dr}{dm} = \frac{10m(m^2 + 38)}{(m^2 + 19)^{3/2}}\left[p + q\left(-\frac{900}{[q + 9]^2}\right)\right].$$

When $m = 9$, then $q = 81$, which gives $p = 10$. Thus

$$\left.\frac{dr}{dm}\right|_{m=9} = 10.71.$$

If a tenth employee is hired, the extra revenue generated is approximately 10.71.

EXERCISE 11.6

In Problems **1–8**, *use the chain rule.*

1. If $y = u^2 - 2u$ and $u = x^2 - x$, find dy/dx.

2. If $y = 2u^3 - 8u$ and $u = 7x - x^3$, find dy/dx.

3. If $y = \dfrac{1}{w^2}$ and $w = 2 - x$, find dy/dx.

4. If $y = \sqrt[3]{z}$ and $z = x^6 - x^2 + 1$, find dy/dx.

5. If $w = u^2$ and $u = \dfrac{t + 1}{t - 1}$, find dw/dt when $t = 3$.

6. If $z = u^2 + \sqrt{u} + 9$ and $u = 2s^2 - 1$, find dz/ds when $s = -1$.

7. If $y = 3w^2 - 8w + 4$ and $w = 3x^2 + 1$, find dy/dx when $x = 0$.

8. If $y = 3u^3 - u^2 + 7u - 2$ and $u = 3x - 2$, find dy/dx when $x = 1$.

In Problems **9–44**, *find y′.*

9. $y = (3x + 2)^6$.

10. $y = (5 - x^2)^3$.

11. $y = 3(x^3 - 8x^2 + x)^{100}$.

12. $y = \dfrac{(2x^2 + 1)^4}{2}$.

13. $y = (x^2 - 2)^{-3}$.

14. $y = (7x - x^4)^{-3/2}$.

15. $y = \sqrt{5x^2 - x}$.

16. $y = \sqrt{3x^2 - 7}$.

17. $y = 2\sqrt[5]{(x^3 + 1)^2}$.

18. $y = 3\sqrt[3]{(x^2 + 1)^2}$.

19. $y = \dfrac{6}{2x^2 - x + 1}$.

20. $y = \dfrac{2}{x^4 + 2}$.

21. $y = \dfrac{1}{(x^2 - 3x)^2}.$

22. $y = \dfrac{1}{(1 - x)^3}.$

23. $y = \dfrac{2}{\sqrt{8x - 1}}.$

24. $y = \dfrac{1}{(3x^2 - x)^{2/3}}.$

25. $y = \sqrt[3]{7x} + \sqrt[3]{7}x.$

26. $y = \sqrt{2x} + \dfrac{1}{\sqrt{2x}}.$

27. $y = x^2(x - 4)^5.$

28. $y = x\sqrt{1 - x}.$

29. $y = 2x\sqrt{6x - 1}.$

30. $y = x^2(x^3 - 1)^4.$

31. $y = (8x - 1)^3(2x + 1)^4.$

32. $y = (6x + 1)^7(2x - 3)^3.$

33. $y = \left(\dfrac{x - 7}{x + 4}\right)^{10}.$

34. $y = \left(\dfrac{2x}{x + 2}\right)^4.$

35. $y = \sqrt{\dfrac{x - 2}{x + 3}}.$

36. $y = \sqrt[3]{\dfrac{8x^2 - 3}{x^2 + 2}}.$

37. $y = \dfrac{2x - 5}{(x^2 + 4)^3}.$

38. $y = \dfrac{(2x + 3)^3}{x^2 + 4}.$

39. $y = 6(5x^2 + 2)\sqrt{x^4 + 5}.$

40. $y = \sqrt{(x - 1)(x + 2)^3}.$

41. $y = 8t + \dfrac{t - 1}{t + 4} - \left(\dfrac{8t - 7}{4}\right)^2.$

42. $y = 6 + 3x - 4x(7x + 1)^2.$

43. $y = \dfrac{(8x - 1)^5}{(3x - 1)^3}.$

44. $y = \dfrac{(4x^2 - 2)(8x - 1)}{(3x - 1)^2}.$

In Problems **45** *and* **46,** *use the quotient rule and power rule to find* y'. *Do not simplify your answer.*

45. $y = \dfrac{(2x + 1)(3x - 5)^2}{(x^2 - 7)^4}.$

46. $y = \dfrac{\sqrt{x + 2}\,(4x^2 - 1)^2}{9x - 3}.$

47. If $y = (5u + 6)^3$ and $u = (x^2 + 1)^4$, find dy/dx when $x = 0$.

48. If $z = 2y^2 - 4y + 5$, $y = 6x - 5$, and $x = 2t$, find dz/dt when $t = 1$.

49. Find the slope of the curve $y = (x^2 - 7x - 8)^3$ at the point $(8, 0)$.

50. Find the slope of the curve $y = \sqrt{x + 1}$ at the point $(8, 3)$.

In Problems **51–54,** *find an equation of the tangent line to the curve at the given point.*

51. $y = \sqrt[3]{(x^2 - 8)^2};\quad (3, 1).$

52. $y = (2x + 3)^2;\quad (-2, 1).$

53. $y = \dfrac{\sqrt{7x + 2}}{x + 1};\quad (1, \tfrac{3}{2}).$

54. $y = \dfrac{-3}{(3x^2 + 1)^3};\quad (0, -3).$

In Problems **55** *and* **56,** *determine the percentage rate of change of* y *with respect to* x *for the given value of* x.

55. $y = (x^2 + 9)^3;\quad x = 4.$

56. $y = \dfrac{1}{(x^2 + 1)^2};\quad x = -3.$

In Problems **57–60,** q *is the total number of units produced per day by* m *employees of a manufacturer, and* p *is the price per unit at which the* q *units are sold. In each case find the marginal revenue product for the given value of* m.

57. $q = 2m,\ p = -0.5q + 20;\quad m = 5.$

58. $q = (200m - m^2)/20,\ p = -0.1q + 70;\quad m = 40.$

59. $q = 10m^2/\sqrt{m^2 + 9},\ p = 525/(q + 3);\quad m = 4.$

60. $q = 100m/\sqrt{m^2 + 19},\ p = 4500/(q + 10);\quad m = 9.$

61. Suppose $p = 100 - \sqrt{q^2 + 20}$ is a demand equation for a manufacturer's product. (a) Find the rate of change of p with respect to q. (b) Find the relative rate of change of p with respect to q. (c) Find the marginal revenue function.

62. If $p = k/q$, where k is a constant, is the demand equation for a manufacturer's product, and $q = f(m)$ defines a function that gives the total number of units produced per day by m employees, show that the marginal revenue product is always zero.

63. The cost c of producing q units of a product is given by $c = 4000 + 10q + 0.1q^2$. If the price per unit p is given by the equation $q = 800 - 2.5p$, use the chain rule to find the rate of change of cost with respect to price per unit when $p = 80$.

64. A governmental health agency examined the records of a group of individuals who were hospitalized with a particular illness. It was found that the total proportion who had been discharged at the end of t days of hospitalization is given by $f(t)$, where

$$f(t) = 1 - \left(\frac{300}{300 + t}\right)^3.$$

Find $f'(300)$ and interpret your answer.

65. If the total cost function for a manufacturer is given by

$$c = \frac{5q^2}{\sqrt{q^2 + 3}} + 5000,$$

find the marginal cost function.

66. For a certain population, if E is the number of years of a person's education and S represents a numerical value of the person's status based on that educational level, then $S = 4\left(\frac{E}{4} + 1\right)^2$. (a) How fast is status changing with respect to education when $E = 16$? (b) At what level of education does the rate of change of status equal 8?

67. The volume V of a spherical cell is given by $V = \frac{4}{3}\pi r^3$, where r is the radius. At time t seconds, the radius r (in centimeters) is given by $r = 10^{-8}t^2 + 10^{-7}t$. Use the chain rule to find dV/dt when $t = 10$.

68. Under certain conditions, the pressure p developed in body tissue by ultrasonic beams is given by a function of the intensity I:*

$$p = (2\rho VI)^{1/2},$$

where ρ (a Greek letter read "rho") is density and V is velocity of propagation. Here ρ and V are constants. (a) Find the rate of change of p with respect to I. (b) Find the relative rate of change.

69. Suppose that for a certain group of 20,000 births, the number l_x of people surviving to age x years is

$$l_x = 2000\sqrt{100 - x}, \qquad 0 \leq x \leq 100.$$

(a) Find the rate of change of l_x with respect to x and evaluate your answer for $x = 36$. (b) Find the relative rate of change of l_x when $x = 36$.

70. A muscle has the ability to shorten when a load, such as a weight, is imposed on it. The equation

$$(P + a)(v + b) = k$$

is called the "fundamental equation of muscle contraction".* Here P is the load imposed on the muscle, v is the velocity of the shortening of the muscle fibres, and a, b, and k are positive constants. Express v as a function of P. Use your result to find dv/dP.

* R. W. Stacy et al., *Essentials of Biological and Medical Physics* (New York: McGraw-Hill Book Company, 1955).

11.7 DERIVATIVES OF LOGARITHMIC FUNCTIONS

In this section, the derivatives of logarithmic functions will be found. We begin with the derivative of $\ln x$. Let $f(x) = \ln x$, where x is positive. By the definition of the derivative,

$$\frac{d}{dx}(\ln x) = \lim_{h \to 0} \frac{f(x + h) - f(x)}{h} = \lim_{h \to 0} \frac{\ln(x + h) - \ln x}{h}.$$

Using the property of logarithms that $\ln m - \ln n = \ln(m/n)$, we have

$$\frac{d}{dx}(\ln x) = \lim_{h \to 0} \frac{\ln\left(\dfrac{x + h}{x}\right)}{h}$$

$$= \lim_{h \to 0} \left[\frac{1}{h}\ln\left(\frac{x + h}{x}\right)\right] = \lim_{h \to 0}\left[\frac{1}{h}\ln\left(1 + \frac{h}{x}\right)\right].$$

Writing $\dfrac{1}{h}$ as $\dfrac{1}{x} \cdot \dfrac{x}{h}$ gives

$$\frac{d}{dx}(\ln x) = \lim_{h \to 0}\left[\frac{1}{x} \cdot \frac{x}{h}\ln\left(1 + \frac{h}{x}\right)\right]$$

$$= \lim_{h \to 0}\left[\frac{1}{x}\ln\left(1 + \frac{h}{x}\right)^{x/h}\right] \qquad \text{(since } r\ln m = \ln m^r\text{)}$$

$$= \frac{1}{x} \cdot \lim_{h \to 0}\left[\ln\left(1 + \frac{h}{x}\right)^{x/h}\right].$$

It can be shown that the limit of the logarithm is the logarithm of the limit ($\lim \ln u = \ln \lim u$), so

$$\frac{d}{dx}(\ln x) = \frac{1}{x}\ln\left[\lim_{h \to 0}\left(1 + \frac{h}{x}\right)^{x/h}\right]. \tag{1}$$

To evaluate $\lim\limits_{h \to 0}\left(1 + \dfrac{h}{x}\right)^{x/h}$, first note that as $h \to 0$, then $\dfrac{h}{x} \to 0$. Thus if we replace $\dfrac{h}{x}$ by k, the limit has the form

$$\lim_{k \to 0}(1 + k)^{1/k}.$$

As stated in Sec. 10.2, this limit is e. Thus Eq. (1) becomes

$$\frac{d}{dx}(\ln x) = \frac{1}{x}\ln e = \frac{1}{x}(1) = \frac{1}{x}.$$

Hence

$$\frac{d}{dx}(\ln x) = \frac{1}{x}. \qquad (2)$$

EXAMPLE 1   *Find y' if* $y = \dfrac{\ln x}{x^2}$.

By the quotient rule and Eq. (2),

$$y' = \frac{x^2\, D_x(\ln x) - (\ln x)\, D_x(x^2)}{(x^2)^2}$$

$$= \frac{x^2\left(\dfrac{1}{x}\right) - (\ln x)(2x)}{x^4} = \frac{x - 2x \ln x}{x^4} = \frac{1 - 2 \ln x}{x^3}.$$

We now extend Eq. (2) to cover a broader class of functions. Let $y = \ln u$, where u is a positive differentiable function of x. By the chain rule,

$$\frac{d}{dx}(\ln u) = \frac{dy}{du} \cdot \frac{du}{dx} = \frac{d}{du}(\ln u) \cdot \frac{du}{dx} = \frac{1}{u} \cdot \frac{du}{dx}.$$

Thus

$$\frac{d}{dx}(\ln u) = \frac{1}{u} \cdot \frac{du}{dx}. \qquad (3)$$

EXAMPLE 2   *Differentiate each of the following.*

a. $y = \ln (x^2 + 1)$.

This function has the form $\ln u$ with $u = x^2 + 1$. Using Eq. (3) gives

$$\frac{dy}{dx} = \frac{1}{x^2 + 1}\frac{d}{dx}(x^2 + 1) = \frac{1}{x^2 + 1}(2x) = \frac{2x}{x^2 + 1}.$$

b. $y = x^2 \ln(4x + 2)$.

Using the product rule and then Eq. (3) with $u = 4x + 2$, we obtain

$$\frac{dy}{dx} = x^2 D_x[\ln(4x + 2)] + [\ln(4x + 2)]D_x(x^2)$$

$$= x^2\left(\frac{1}{4x + 2}\right)(4) + [\ln(4x + 2)](2x)$$

$$= \frac{4x^2}{4x + 2} + 2x \ln(4x + 2).$$

c. $y = \ln(\ln x)$.

This has the form $y = \ln u$ where $u = \ln x$. Using Eqs. (3) and (2), we obtain

$$y' = \frac{1}{\ln x}\frac{d}{dx}(\ln x) = \frac{1}{\ln x}\left(\frac{1}{x}\right) = \frac{1}{x \ln x}.$$

To differentiate functions involving logarithms, like $y = \ln(2x + 5)^3$, it may be easier to simplify the function *before* the differentiation by using properties of logarithms. Example 3 will illustrate this.

EXAMPLE 3   *Differentiate each of the following.*

a. $y = \ln(2x + 5)^3$.

First we simplify the right side by using properties of logarithms.

$$y = \ln(2x + 5)^3 = 3 \ln(2x + 5).$$

$$\frac{dy}{dx} = 3\left(\frac{1}{2x + 5}\right)(2) = \frac{6}{2x + 5}.$$

Alternatively, if the simplification were not performed first,

$$\frac{dy}{dx} = \frac{1}{(2x + 5)^3} D_x[(2x + 5)^3]$$

$$= \frac{1}{(2x + 5)^3}(3)(2x + 5)^2(2) = \frac{6}{2x + 5}.$$

b. $f(p) = \ln[(p + 1)^2(p + 2)^2(p + 3)^4]$.

We simplify the right side and then differentiate.

$$f(p) = 2 \ln(p + 1) + 3 \ln(p + 2) + 4 \ln(p + 3).$$

$$f'(p) = 2\left(\frac{1}{p + 1}\right)(1) + 3\left(\frac{1}{p + 2}\right)(1) + 4\left(\frac{1}{p + 3}\right)(1)$$

$$= \frac{2}{p + 1} + \frac{3}{p + 2} + \frac{4}{p + 3}.$$

c. $f(w) = \ln\sqrt{\frac{1 + w^2}{w^2 - 1}}$.

Again, using properties of logarithms will simplify our work.

$$f(w) = \frac{1}{2}[\ln(1 + w^2) - \ln(w^2 - 1)].$$

$$f'(w) = \frac{1}{2}\left[\frac{1}{1 + w^2}(2w) - \frac{1}{w^2 - 1}(2w)\right]$$

$$= \frac{w}{1 + w^2} - \frac{w}{w^2 - 1} = -\frac{2w}{w^4 - 1}.$$

d. $f(x) = \ln^3(2x + 1)$.

The exponent 3 refers to the cubing of $\ln(2x + 1)$. That is,

$$f(x) = \ln^3(2x + 1) = [\ln(2x + 1)]^3.$$

By the power rule,

$$f'(x) = 3[\ln(2x + 1)]^2 D_x[\ln(2x + 1)]$$

$$= 3[\ln(2x + 1)]^2\left[\frac{1}{2x + 1}(2)\right]$$

$$= \frac{6}{2x + 1}[\ln(2x + 1)]^2 = \frac{6}{2x + 1}\ln^2(2x + 1).$$

We can generalize Eq. (3) to any base b. Since $\ln u = \dfrac{\log_b u}{\log_b e}$ (from the change of base formula in Sec. 5.3), then $\log_b u = (\log_b e) \ln u$. Hence

$$\frac{d}{dx}(\log_b u) = \frac{d}{dx}[(\log_b e) \ln u] = (\log_b e)\frac{d}{dx}(\ln u)$$

$$= (\log_b e)\left(\frac{1}{u}\frac{du}{dx}\right).$$

Thus

$$\boxed{\frac{d}{dx}(\log_b u) = \frac{1}{u}(\log_b e)\frac{du}{dx}. \qquad (4)}$$

Since the use of natural logarithms (that is, $b = e$) gives a value of 1 to the factor $\log_b e$ in Eq. (4), natural logarithms are used extensively in calculus.

EXAMPLE 4   *If $y = \log(2x + 1)$, find the rate of change of y with respect to x.*

We want to find dy/dx. By Eq. (4) with $u = 2x + 1$ and $b = 10$,

$$\frac{dy}{dx} = \frac{1}{2x + 1}(\log e) D_x(2x + 1) = \frac{1}{2x + 1}(\log e)(2) = \frac{2 \log e}{2x + 1}.$$

EXERCISE 11.7

In Problems **1–34,** *differentiate the functions. If possible, first use properties of logarithms to simplify the given function.*

1. $y = \ln(3x - 4)$.

2. $y = \ln(5x - 6)$.

3. $y = \ln x^2$.

4. $y = \ln(ax^2 + b)$.

5. $y = \ln(1 - x^2)$.

6. $y = \ln(-x^2 + 6x)$.

7. $f(p) = \ln(2p^3 + 3p)$.

8. $f(r) = \ln(2r^4 - 3r^2 + 2r + 1)$.

9. $f(t) = t \ln t$.

10. $y = x^2 \ln x$.

11. $y = \log_3(2x - 1)$.

12. $f(w) = \log(w^2 + w)$.

13. $f(z) = \dfrac{\ln z}{z}$.

14. $y = \dfrac{x^2 - 1}{\ln x}$.

15. $y = \ln(x^2 + 4x + 5)^3$.

16. $y = \ln x^{100}$.

17. $y = \ln\sqrt{1 + x^2}$.

18. $f(s) = \ln\left(\dfrac{s^2}{1 + s^2}\right)$.

19. $f(l) = \ln\left(\dfrac{1 + l}{1 - l}\right)$.

20. $y = \ln\left(\dfrac{2x + 3}{3x - 4}\right)$.

21. $y = \ln\sqrt[4]{\dfrac{1 + x^2}{1 - x^2}}$.

22. $y = \ln\sqrt{\dfrac{x^4 - 1}{x^4 + 1}}$.

23. $y = \ln[(x^2 + 2)^2(x^3 + x - 1)]$.

24. $y = \ln[(5x + 2)^4(8x - 3)^6]$.

25. $y = (x^2 + 1)\ln(2x + 1)$.

26. $y = (ax + b)\ln(ax)$.

27. $y = \ln x^3 + \ln^3 x$.

28. $y = x^{\ln 3}$.

29. $y = \ln^4(ax)$.

30. $y = \ln^2(2x + 3)$.

31. $y = x \ln\sqrt{x - 1}$.

32. $y = \ln(x^2\sqrt{3x - 2})$.

33. $y = \sqrt{4 + \ln x}$.

34. $y = \ln(x + \sqrt{1 + x^2})$.

35. Find an equation of the tangent line to the curve $y = \ln(x^2 - 2x - 2)$ when $x = 3$.

36. Find the slope of the curve $y = \dfrac{x}{\ln x}$ when $x = 2$.

37. Find the marginal revenue function if the demand function is $p = 25/\ln(q + 2)$.

38. A total cost function is given by $c = 25 \ln(q + 1) + 12$. Find the marginal cost when $q = 6$.

39. Show that the relative rate of change of $y = f(x)$ with respect to x is equal to the derivative of $y = \ln f(x)$.

11.8 DERIVATIVES OF EXPONENTIAL FUNCTIONS

We now obtain a formula for the derivative of the exponential function e^u, where u is a differentiable function of x. By letting $y = e^u$, in logarithmic form we have $u = \ln y$. Differentiating both sides with respect to x gives

$$\frac{d}{dx}(u) = \frac{d}{dx}(\ln y),$$

$$\frac{du}{dx} = \frac{1}{y}\frac{dy}{dx}.$$

Solving for dy/dx and replacing y by e^u give

$$\frac{dy}{dx} = y\frac{du}{dx} = e^u\frac{du}{dx}.$$

Thus

$$\frac{d}{dx}(e^u) = e^u\frac{du}{dx}. \tag{1}$$

As a special case, let $u = x$. Then $du/dx = 1$ and

$$\frac{d}{dx}(e^x) = e^x. \tag{2}$$

Pitfall

Do not use the power rule to find $D_x(e^x)$. That is, $D_x(e^x) \neq xe^{x-1}$.

Note that the function and its derivative are the same.

EXAMPLE 1

a. *Find* $\dfrac{d}{dx}(e^{x^3+3x})$.

The function has the form e^u with $u = x^3 + 3x$. From Eq. (1),

$$\frac{d}{dx}(e^{x^3+3x}) = e^{x^3+3x} D_x(x^3 + 3x) = e^{x^3+3x}(3x^2 + 3)$$

$$= 3(x^2 + 1)e^{x^3+3x}.$$

b. *If* $y = \dfrac{x}{e^x}$, *find* y'.

We *first* use the quotient rule and then use Eq. (2).

$$\frac{dy}{dx} = \frac{e^x D_x(x) - x D_x(e^x)}{(e^x)^2} = \frac{e^x(1) - x(e^x)}{(e^x)^2} = \frac{e^x(1 - x)}{e^{2x}} = \frac{1 - x}{e^x}.$$

c. *If* $f(w) = w^4 e^{2w}$, *find* $f'(w)$.

We *first* use the product rule and then use Eq. (1) with $u = 2w$.

$$f'(w) = w^4 D_w(e^{2w}) + e^{2w} D_w(w^4)$$

$$= w^4(e^{2w})(2) + e^{2w}(4w^3) = 2e^{2w}w^3(w + 2).$$

d. *Find* $D_x[e^{x+1} \ln (x^2 + 1)]$.

By the product rule,

$$D_x[e^{x+1} \ln(x^2 + 1)] = e^{x+1} D_x[\ln(x^2 + 1)] + [\ln(x^2 + 1)] D_x(e^{x+1})$$

$$= e^{x+1}\left(\frac{1}{x^2 + 1}\right)(2x) + [\ln(x^2 + 1)]e^{x+1}(1)$$

$$= e^{x+1}\left[\frac{2x}{x^2 + 1} + \ln(x^2 + 1)\right].$$

e. *If $y = e^2 + e^x + \ln 3$, find y'.*

Since e^2 and $\ln 3$ are constants, $y' = 0 + e^x + 0 = e^x$.

We can generalize Eq. (1) by considering the derivative of a^u where $a > 0$, $a \neq 1$, and u is a differentiable function of x. First we shall write a^u as an exponential function with base e. By Property 9 of Sec. 5.3, we have $a = e^{\ln a}$. Thus

$$D_x(a^u) = D_x[(e^{\ln a})^u] = D_x(e^{u \ln a})$$

$$= e^{u \ln a} D_x(u \ln a) \qquad \text{[by Eq. (1)]}$$

$$= e^{u \ln a}\left(\frac{du}{dx}\right) \ln a \qquad \text{[ln } a \text{ is constant]}$$

$$= a^u(\ln a)\frac{du}{dx} \qquad \text{[since } e^{u \ln a} = a^u\text{]}.$$

Thus

$$\frac{d}{dx}(a^u) = a^u(\ln a)\frac{du}{dx}. \qquad (3)$$

EXAMPLE 2

a. *Find dy/dx if $y = 4^{2x^3 + 5x}$.*

Using Eq. (3) with $a = 4$ and $u = 2x^3 + 5x$, we obtain

$$\frac{dy}{dx} = 4^{2x^3 + 5x}(\ln 4)\frac{d}{dx}(2x^3 + 5x)$$

$$= 4^{2x^3 + 5x}(\ln 4)(6x^2 + 5) = (\ln 4)(6x^2 + 5)4^{2x^3 + 5x}.$$

b. *Find $D_x y$ if $y = x^{100} + 100^x$.*

Note that this function involves a variable to a constant power and a constant raised to a variable power. Do not confuse these forms!

$$D_x y = 100x^{99} + 100^x(\ln 100) D_x(x) = 100x^{99} + 100^x \ln 100.$$

EXAMPLE 3   *An important function used in economic and business decisions is the **normal distribution density function***

$$y = f(x) = \frac{1}{\sigma\sqrt{2\pi}}e^{-(1/2)[(x-\mu)/\sigma]^2}$$

where σ (a Greek letter read "sigma") and μ (a Greek letter read "mu") are constants. Its graph, called the normal curve, is "bell-shaped" (see Fig. 11.15). Determine the rate of change of y with respect to x when $x = \mu$.
The rate of change of y with respect to x is dy/dx.

$$\frac{dy}{dx} = \frac{1}{\sigma\sqrt{2\pi}}[e^{-(1/2)[(x-\mu)/\sigma]^2}]\left[-\frac{1}{2}(2)\left(\frac{x-\mu}{\sigma}\right)\left(\frac{1}{\sigma}\right)\right].$$

Evaluating dy/dx when $x = \mu$, we obtain

$$\left.\frac{dy}{dx}\right|_{x=\mu} = 0.$$

Table 11.1 lists the differentiation formulas in this chapter. You should know these formulas, know the mechanics involved in applying them, and know both the definition and the interpretations of a derivative.

TABLE 11.1
Differentiation Formulas

$\frac{d}{dx}(c) = 0$, where c is any constant.

$\frac{d}{dx}(x^n) = nx^{n-1}$, where n is any real number.

$\frac{d}{dx}[cf(x)] = cf'(x)$.

$\frac{d}{dx}[f(x) \pm g(x)] = f'(x) \pm g'(x)$.

$\frac{d}{dx}[f(x)\,g(x)] = f(x)g'(x) + g(x)f'(x)$.

$\frac{d}{dx}\left[\frac{f(x)}{g(x)}\right] = \frac{g(x)f'(x) - f(x)g'(x)}{[g(x)]^2}$.

$\frac{dy}{dx} = \frac{dy}{du} \cdot \frac{du}{dx}$, where y is a function of u and u is a function of x.

$\frac{d}{dx}(u^n) = nu^{n-1}\frac{du}{dx}$.

$\frac{d}{dx}(\log_b u) = \frac{1}{u}(\log_b e)\frac{du}{dx}$.

$\frac{d}{dx}(\ln u) = \frac{1}{u}\frac{du}{dx}$.

$\frac{d}{dx}(a^u) = a^u(\ln a)\frac{du}{dx}$.

$\frac{d}{dx}(e^u) = e^u\frac{du}{dx}$.

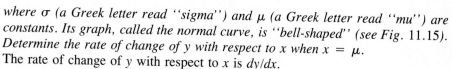

FIGURE 11.15

EXERCISE 11.8

In Problems **1–30,** *differentiate the functions.*

1. $y = e^{x^2+1}$.

2. $y = e^{2x^2+5}$.

3. $y = e^{3-5x}$.

4. $f(q) = e^{-q^3+6q-1}$.

5. $f(r) = e^{3r^2+4r+4}$.

6. $y = e^{9x^2+5x^3-6}$.

7. $y = xe^x$.

8. $y = x^2e^{-x}$.

9. $y = x^2e^{-x^2}$.

10. $y = xe^{2x}$.

11. $y = \dfrac{e^x + e^{-x}}{2}$.

12. $y = \dfrac{e^x - e^{-x}}{2}$.

13. $y = 4^{3x^2}$.

14. $y = 4^{3x+1}$.

15. $f(w) = \dfrac{e^{2w}}{w^2}$.

16. $y = 2^x x^2$.

17. $y = e^{1+\sqrt{x}}$.

18. $y = e^{x-\sqrt{x}}$.

19. $y = x^3 - 3^x$.

20. $y = (e^{3x} + 1)^4$.

21. $y = \dfrac{e^x - 1}{e^x + 1}$.

22. $f(z) = e^{1/z}$.

23. $y = e^{e^x}$.

24. $y = e^{2x}(x + 1)$.

25. $y = e^{\ln x}$.

26. $y = e^{\ln(x^2+1)}$.

27. $y = e^{x \ln x}$.

28. $y = e^{-x} \ln x$.

29. $y = (\log 2)^x$.

30. $y = \ln e^{4x+1}$.

31. Find an equation of the tangent line to the graph $y = e^x$ when $x = 2$.

32. Find the slope of the tangent line to the graph of $y = 2e^{-4x^2}$ when $x = 0$.

For each of the demand equations in Problems **33** *and* **34,** *find the rate of change of price p with respect to quantity q. What is the rate of change for the indicated value of q?*

33. $p = 15e^{-0.001q}$; $q = 500$.

34. $p = 8e^{-3q/800}$; $q = 400$.

In Problems **35** *and* **36,** $\bar{c}$ *is the average cost of producing q units of a product. Find the marginal cost function and the marginal cost for the given values of q.*

35. $\bar{c} = \dfrac{850}{q} + 4000\dfrac{e^{(2q+6)/800}}{q}$; $q = 97, q = 197$.

36. $\bar{c} = (7000e^{q/700})/q$; $q = 350, q = 700$.

37. For a firm the daily output q on the tth day of a production run is given by $q = 500(1 - e^{-0.2t})$. Find the rate of change of output q with respect to t on the tenth day.

38. For the normal density function

$$f(x) = \frac{1}{\sqrt{2\pi}} e^{-x^2/2},$$

find $f'(0)$.

39. The population P of a city t years from now is given by $P = 20,000e^{0.03t}$. Show that $dP/dt = kP$ where k is a constant. This means that the rate of change of population at any time is proportional to the population at that time.

40. In a discussion of diffusion of a new process into a market, Hurter and Rubenstein* refer to an equation of the form

$$Y = k\alpha^{\beta^t},$$

where Y is the cumulative level of diffusion of the new process at time t, and k, α, and β are positive constants. Verify their claim that

$$\frac{dY}{dt} = k\alpha^{\beta^t}(\beta^t \ln \alpha) \ln \beta.$$

---

* A. P. Hurter, Jr., A. H. Rubenstein, et al. "Market Penetration by New Innovations: The Technological Literature," *Technological Forecasting and Social Change,* 11 (1978), 197–221.

41. After t years, the value S of a principal of P dollars which is invested at the annual rate of r compounded continuously is given by $S = Pe^{rt}$. Show that the relative rate of change of S with respect to t is r.

42. In an article concerning predators and prey, Holling* refers to an equation of the form

$$y = K(1 - e^{-ax}),$$

where x is the prey density, y is the number of prey attacked, and K and a are constants. Verify his statement that

$$\frac{dy}{dx} = a(K - y).$$

43. According to Richter,† the number N of earthquakes of magnitude M or greater per unit of time is given by $N = 10^A 10^{-bM}$, where A and b are constants. Find dN/dM.

44. Short-term retention was studied by Peterson and Peterson.‡ They analyzed a procedure in which an experimenter verbally gave a subject a three-letter consonant syllable, such as CHJ, followed by a three-digit number, such as 309. The subject then repeated the number and counted backwards by 3's, such as 309, 306, 303, ... After a period of time the subject was signaled by a light to recite the three-letter consonant syllable. The time interval between the experimenter's completion of the last consonant to the onset of the light was called the *recall interval*. The time between the onset of the light and the completion of a response was referred to as *latency*. After many trials, it was determined that for a recall interval of t seconds, the approximate proportion of correct recalls with latency below 2.83 seconds was p, where

$$p = 0.89[0.01 + 0.99(0.85)^t].$$

a. Find dp/dt and interpret your result.
b. If you have a calculator, evaluate dp/dt when $t = 2$. Give your answer to two decimal places.

45. Suppose a tracer, such as a colored dye, is injected instantly into the heart at time $t = 0$ and mixes uniformly with blood inside the heart. Let the initial concentration of the tracer in the heart be C_0 and assume the heart has constant volume V. As fresh blood flows into the heart, assume that the diluted mixture of blood and tracer flows out at the constant positive rate r. Then the concentration $C(t)$ of the tracer in the heart at time t is given by

$$C(t) = C_0 e^{-(r/V)t}.$$

Show that $dC/dt = (-r/V)C(t)$.

46. In Problem 45, suppose the tracer is injected at a constant rate R. Then the concentration at time t is

$$C(t) = \frac{R}{r}[1 - e^{-(r/V)t}].$$

(a) Find $C(0)$. (b) Show that

$$\frac{dC}{dt} = \frac{R}{V} - \frac{r}{V}C(t).$$

47. Several models have been used to analyze the length of stay in a hospital. For a particular group of schizophrenics, one such model is§

$$f(t) = 1 - e^{-0.008t},$$

where $f(t)$ is the proportion of the group that was dis-

* C. S. Holling, "Some Characteristics of Simple Types of Predation and Parasitism," *The Canadian Entomologist*, XCI, no. 7 (1959), 385–98.

† C. F. Richter, *Elementary Seismology* (San Francisco: W. H. Freeman and Company, Publishers, 1958).

‡ L. R. Peterson and M. J. Peterson, "Short-Term Retention of Individual Verbal Items," *Journal of Experimental Psychology*, 58 (1959), 193–98.

§ W. W. Eaton and G. A. Whitmore, "Length of Stay as a Stocastic Process: A General Approach and Application to Hospitalization for Schizophrenia," *Journal of Mathematical Sociology*, 5 (1977), 273–92.

charged at the end of t days of hospitalization. Find the rate of discharge (proportion discharged per day) at the end of 100 days. Give your answer to four decimal places.

11.9 IMPLICIT DIFFERENTIATION

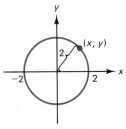

FIGURE 11.16

To introduce implicit differentiation, we shall find the slope of a tangent line to a circle. Let us take the circle of radius 2 whose center is at the origin (Fig. 11.16). Its equation is

$$x^2 + y^2 = 4,$$
$$x^2 + y^2 - 4 = 0. \tag{1}$$

The point $(\sqrt{2}, \sqrt{2})$ lies on the circle. To find the slope at this point, we need to find dy/dx there. Until now we have always had y given explicitly (directly) in terms of x before determining y'; that is, in the form $y = f(x)$. In Eq. (1) this is not so. We say that Eq. (1) has the form $F(x, y) = 0$, where $F(x, y)$ denotes a function of two variables. The obvious thing to do is solve Eq. (1) for y in terms of x:

$$x^2 + y^2 - 4 = 0,$$
$$y^2 = 4 - x^2,$$
$$y = \pm\sqrt{4 - x^2}. \tag{2}$$

A problem now occurs—Eq. (2) may give two values of y for a value of x. It does not define y explicitly as a function of x. We can, however, "consider" Eq. (1) as defining y as one of two different functions of x:

$$y = +\sqrt{4 - x^2} \quad \text{and} \quad y = -\sqrt{4 - x^2},$$

whose graphs are given in Fig. 11.17. Since $(\sqrt{2}, \sqrt{2})$ lies on the graph of $y =$

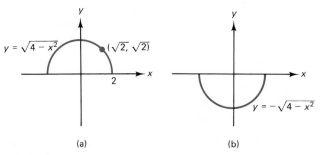

(a)   (b)

FIGURE 11.17

$\sqrt{4 - x^2}$, we should differentiate that function:

$$y = \sqrt{4 - x^2},$$
$$\frac{dy}{dx} = \frac{1}{2}(4 - x^2)^{-1/2}(-2x)$$

$$= -\frac{x}{\sqrt{4 - x^2}}.$$

$$\left.\frac{dy}{dx}\right|_{x=\sqrt{2}} = -\frac{\sqrt{2}}{\sqrt{4 - 2}} = -1.$$

Thus the slope of the circle $x^2 + y^2 - 4 = 0$ at the point $(\sqrt{2}, \sqrt{2})$ is -1.

Let us summarize the difficulties we had. First, y was not originally given explicitly in terms of x. Second, after we tried to find such a relation, we ended up with more than one function of x. In fact, depending on the equation given, it may be very complicated or even impossible to find an explicit expression for y. For example, it would be difficult to solve $ye^x + \ln(x + y) = 0$ for y. We shall now consider a method which avoids such difficulties.

An equation of the form $F(x, y) = 0$, such as we had originally, is said to express y *implicitly* as a function of x. The word "implicitly" is used since y is not given explicitly as a function of x. However, it is assumed or *implied* that the equation defines y as at least one differentiable function of x. Thus we assume that Eq. (1), $x^2 + y^2 - 4 = 0$, defines at least one function of x, say $y = f(x)$. Hence to find dy/dx we treat y as a function of x and differentiate both sides of Eq. (1) with respect to x.

$$\frac{d}{dx}(x^2 + y^2 - 4) = \frac{d}{dx}(0),$$

$$\frac{d}{dx}(x^2) + \frac{d}{dx}(y^2) - \frac{d}{dx}(4) = \frac{d}{dx}(0).$$

We know that $\frac{d}{dx}(x^2) = 2x$ and that both $\frac{d}{dx}(4)$ and $\frac{d}{dx}(0)$ are 0. But $\frac{d}{dx}(y^2)$ is **not** $2y$ because we are differentiating with respect to x, not y. That is, y is not the independent variable. Since y is assumed to be a function of x, the y^2-term has the form u^n, where y plays the role of u. Just as the power rule says that $\frac{d}{dx}(u^2) = 2u\frac{du}{dx}$, we have $\frac{d}{dx}(y^2) = 2y\frac{dy}{dx} = 2yy'$. Hence the equation above becomes

$$2x + 2yy' = 0.$$

Solving for y', we obtain

$$2yy' = -2x,$$

$$y' = -\frac{x}{y}. \tag{3}$$

Notice that the expression for y' involves the variable y as well as x. This means that to find y' at a point, both coordinates of the point must be substituted into y'. Thus

$$\left.y'\right|_{(\sqrt{2}, \sqrt{2})} = -\frac{\sqrt{2}}{\sqrt{2}} = -1 \text{ as before.}$$

This method of finding dy/dx is called **implicit differentiation.** We note that Eq. (3) is not defined when $y = 0$. Geometrically this is clear, since the tangent line to the circle at either $(2, 0)$ or $(-2, 0)$ is vertical and the slope is not defined.

EXAMPLE 1   *For each of the following, find y' by implicit differentiation.*

a. $y + y^3 = x$.

We treat y as a (differentiable) function of x and differentiate both sides with respect to x.

$$D_x(y) + D_x(y^3) = D_x(x).$$

Now, $D_x(y)$ can be written y', and $D_x(x) = 1$. By the power rule, $D_x(y^3) = 3y^2 \dfrac{dy}{dx}$ or $3y^2 y'$. Thus

$$y' + 3y^2 y' = 1.$$

Solving for y' gives

$$y'(1 + 3y^2) = 1,$$

$$y' = \frac{1}{1 + 3y^2}.$$

b. $x^3 + 4xy^2 - y^4 - 27 = 0$.

We assume that y is a function of x and differentiate both sides with respect to x.

$$D_x(x^3) + 4D_x(xy^2) - D_x(y^4) - D_x(27) = D_x(0).$$

To find $D_x(xy^2)$ we use the product rule.

$$[3x^2] + 4[x\, D_x(y^2) + y^2 D_x(x)] - [4y^3 y'] - 0 = 0,$$

$$[3x^2] + 4[x(2yy') + y^2(1)] - [4y^3 y'] = 0,$$

$$3x^2 + 8xyy' + 4y^2 - 4y^3 y' = 0.$$

Solving for y' gives

$$y'(8xy - 4y^3) = -3x^2 - 4y^2,$$

$$y' = \frac{-3x^2 - 4y^2}{8xy - 4y^3}$$

$$= \frac{3x^2 + 4y^2}{4y^3 - 8xy}.$$

EXAMPLE 2   *For each of the following, find y′ by implicit differentiation.*

a. $e^{xy} = x + y.$

$$D_x(e^{xy}) = D_x(x) + D_x(y),$$

$$e^{xy} D_x(xy) = 1 + y',$$

$$e^{xy}(x D_x y + y D_x x) = 1 + y',$$

$$e^{xy}(xy' + y) = 1 + y',$$

$$xe^{xy}y' + ye^{xy} = 1 + y',$$

$$y'(xe^{xy} - 1) = 1 - ye^{xy},$$

$$y' = \frac{1 - ye^{xy}}{xe^{xy} - 1}.$$

b. $x^3 = (y - x^2)^2.$

$$D_x(x^3) = D_x[(y - x^2)^2],$$

$$3x^2 = 2(y - x^2)(y' - 2x),$$

$$3x^2 = 2(yy' - 2xy - x^2y' + 2x^3),$$

$$3x^2 + 4xy - 4x^3 = 2y'(y - x^2),$$

$$y' = \frac{3x^2 + 4xy - 4x^3}{2(y - x^2)}.$$

For example, the slope of the curve $x^3 = (y - x^2)^2$ at the point $(1, 2)$ is

$$y'\Big|_{(1,2)} = \frac{3(1)^2 + 4(1)(2) - 4(1)^3}{2[2 - (1)^2]} = \frac{7}{2}.$$

EXAMPLE 3   *If $q - p = \ln q + \ln p$, find dq/dp, the rate of change of q with respect to p.*

We will assume that q is a function of p and differentiate implicitly with respect to p.

$$D_p(q) - D_p(p) = D_p(\ln q) + D_p(\ln p),$$

$$\frac{dq}{dp} - 1 = \frac{1}{q}\frac{dq}{dp} + \frac{1}{p},$$

$$\frac{dq}{dp}\left(1 - \frac{1}{q}\right) = \frac{1}{p} + 1,$$

$$\frac{dq}{dp}\left(\frac{q - 1}{q}\right) = \frac{1 + p}{p},$$

$$\frac{dp}{dq} = \frac{(1 + p)q}{p(q - 1)}.$$

EXERCISE 11.9

In Problems **1–22,** *find dy/dx by implicit differentiation.*

1. $x^2 + 4y^2 = 4$.

2. $3x^2 + 6y^2 = 1$.

3. $3y^4 - 5x = 0$.

4. $2x^2 - 3y^2 = 4$.

5. $\sqrt{x} + \sqrt{y} = 3$.

6. $x^{1/5} + y^{1/5} = 4$.

7. $x^{3/4} + y^{3/4} = 7$.

8. $y^3 = 4x$.

9. $xy = 4$.

10. $x + xy - 2 = 0$.

11. $xy - y - 4x = 5$.

12. $x^2 + y^2 = 2xy + 3$.

13. $x^3 + y^3 - 12xy = 0$.

14. $2x^3 + 3xy + y^3 = 0$.

15. $x = \sqrt{y} + \sqrt[3]{y}$.

16. $x^3y^3 + x = 9$.

17. $3x^2y^3 - x + y = 25$.

18. $y^2 + y = \ln x$.

19. $y \ln x = xe^y$.

20. $\ln(xy) + x = 4$.

21. $xe^y + y = 4$.

22. $ax^2 - by^2 = c$.

23. If $x + xy + y^2 = 7$, find y' at $(1, 2)$.

24. Find the slope of the curve $4x^2 + 9y^2 = 1$ at the point $(0, \frac{1}{3})$; at the point (x_0, y_0).

25. Find an equation of the tangent line to the curve $x^3 + y^2 = 3$ at the point $(-1, 2)$.

26. Repeat Problem 25 for the curve $y^2 + xy - x^2 = 5$ at the point $(4, 3)$.

For the demand equations in Problems **27–30,** *find the rate of change of q with respect to p.*

27. $p = 100 - q^2$.

28. $p = 400 - \sqrt{q}$.

29. $p = 20/(q + 5)^2$.

30. $p = 20/(q^2 + 5)$.

31. The magnitude M of an earthquake and its energy E are related by the equation*

$$1.5M = \log\left(\frac{E}{2.5 \times 10^{11}}\right).$$

Here M is given in terms of Richter's preferred scale of 1958 and E is in ergs. Determine the rate of change of energy with respect to magnitude.

32. The equation $(P + a)(v + b) = k$ is called the "fundamental equation of muscle contraction".† Here P is the load imposed on the muscle, v is the velocity of the shortening of the muscle fibres, and a, b, and k are positive constants. Use implicit differentiation to show that dv/dP, in terms of P, is given by

$$\frac{dv}{dP} = -\frac{k}{(P + a)^2}.$$

33. New products or technologies often tend to replace old ones. For example, today most commerical airlines use jet engines rather then prop engines. In discussing the forecasting of technological substitution, Hurter and Rubenstein‡ refer to the equation

$$\ln\frac{f(t)}{1 - f(t)} + \sigma\frac{1}{1 - f(t)} = C_1 + C_2t,$$

where $f(t)$ is the market share of the substitute over time t, and C_1, C_2, and σ (a Greek letter read "sigma") are constants. Verify their claim that the rate of substitution is

$$f'(t) = \frac{C_2f(t)[1 - f(t)]^2}{\sigma f(t) + [1 - f(t)]}.$$

---

* K. E. Bullen, *An Introduction to the Thoery of Seismology* (Cambridge at the University Press, 1963).

† R. W. Stacy et al., *Essentials of Biological and Medical Physics* (New York: McGraw-Hill Book Company, 1955).

‡ A. P. Hurter, Jr., A. H. Rubenstein, et al. "Market Penetration by New Innovations: The Technological Literature," *Technological Forecasting and Social Change*, 11 (1978), 197–221.

11.10 LOGARITHMIC DIFFERENTIATION

There is a technique that often simplifies the differentiation of $y = f(x)$ when $f(x)$ involves products, quotients, or powers. We first take the natural logarithm of both sides of $y = f(x)$. After simplifying $\ln [f(x)]$ by using properties of logarithms, we then differentiate both sides with respect to x. The next example illustrates this method of **logarithmic differentiation.**

EXAMPLE 1   *Find y' if $y = \dfrac{(2x - 5)^3}{x^2 \sqrt[4]{x^2 + 1}}$.*

Differentiating this function in the usual way is messy because it involves the quotient, power, and product rules. Logarithmic differentiation makes the work less of a chore. First, we take the natural logarithm of both sides and simplify.

$$\ln y = \ln \frac{(2x - 5)^3}{x^2 \sqrt[4]{x^2 + 1}} = \ln (2x - 5)^3 - \ln[x^2 \sqrt[4]{x^2 + 1}],$$

$$\ln y = 3 \ln(2x - 5) - 2 \ln x - \tfrac{1}{4}\ln(x^2 + 1).$$

Differentiating with respect to x gives

$$\frac{1}{y} y' = 3\left(\frac{1}{2x - 5}\right)(2) - 2\left(\frac{1}{x}\right) - \frac{1}{4}\left(\frac{1}{x^2 + 1}\right)(2x),$$

$$\frac{y'}{y} = \frac{6}{2x - 5} - \frac{2}{x} - \frac{x}{2(x^2 + 1)}.$$

Multiplying both sides by y and then substituting the original expression for y gives y' in terms of x only.

$$y' = y\left[\frac{6}{2x - 5} - \frac{2}{x} - \frac{x}{2(x^2 + 1)}\right],$$

$$y' = \frac{(2x - 5)^3}{x^2 \sqrt[4]{x^2 + 1}}\left[\frac{6}{2x - 5} - \frac{2}{x} - \frac{x}{2(x^2 + 1)}\right].$$

Logarithmic differentiation can also be used to differentiate a function of the form $y = u^v$, where both u and v are differentiable functions of x. Because both the base and exponent are not necessarily constants, the differentiation formulas for u^n and a^u do not apply here.

EXAMPLE 2   *Find y' for each of the following.*

a. $y = x^{4x}$

This has the form $y = u^v$, where u and v are functions of x. Taking the natural logarithm of both sides gives $\ln y = \ln x^{4x}$ or

$$\ln y = 4x \ln x.$$

Differentiating both sides with respect to x gives

$$\frac{1}{y}\, y' = 4x\left(\frac{1}{x}\right) + (\ln x)(4),$$

$$\frac{y'}{y} = 4(1 + \ln x).$$

Solving for y' and substituting x^{4x} for y,

$$y' = y[4(1 + \ln x)] = 4x^{4x}(1 + \ln x).$$

b. $y = x^{e^{-x^2}}$.

This has the form $y = u^v$ where $v = e^{-x^2}$. Using logarithmic differentiation, we have

$$\ln y = \ln x^{e^{-x^2}} = e^{-x^2} \ln x,$$

$$\frac{1}{y}y' = e^{-x^2}\left(\frac{1}{x}\right) + (\ln x)[(e^{-x^2})(-2x)],$$

$$\frac{y'}{y} = \frac{e^{-x^2}}{x} - 2xe^{-x^2}\ln x = e^{-x^2}\left(\frac{1}{x} - 2x\ln x\right),$$

$$y' = ye^{-x^2}\left(\frac{1}{x} - 2x\ln x\right)$$

$$= x^{e^{-x^2}}e^{-x^2}\left(\frac{1}{x} - 2x\ln x\right) \qquad \text{[by substitution]}.$$

Pitfall

When using properties of logarithms, you must at all times be able to justify your steps. For example,

$$\text{if } y = \ln(x + y), \quad \text{then} \quad \ln y \neq \ln(x + y).$$

Similarly,

$$\text{if } y = x^x + x^5, \quad \text{then} \quad \ln y \neq \ln x^x + \ln x^5.$$

Be sure you understand how to differentiate each of the following forms:

$$y = \begin{cases} [f(x)]^n, & \text{(a)} \\ a^{f(x)}, & \text{(b)} \\ [f(x)]^{g(x)}. & \text{(c)} \end{cases}$$

For type (a) you may use the power rule; for type (b) use the differentiation formula for exponential functions; for type (c) use logarithmic differentiation. It would be nonsense to write $D_x(x^x) = x \cdot x^{x-1}$. Be sure that all steps are justified by the basic concepts that have been developed.

EXERCISE 11.10

In Problems **1–20,** *find y' by using logarithmic differentiation.*

1. $y = (x + 1)^2(x - 1)(x^2 + 3)$.

2. $y = (3x + 4)(8x - 1)^2(3x^2 + 1)^4$.

3. $y = (3x^3 - 1)^2(2x + 5)^3$.

4. $y = (3x + 1)\sqrt{8x - 1}$.

5. $y = \sqrt{x + 1}\sqrt{x^2 - 2}\sqrt{x + 4}$.

6. $y = (x + 2)\sqrt{x^2 + 9}\sqrt[3]{2x + 1}$.

7. $y = \dfrac{\sqrt{1 - x^2}}{1 - 2x}$.

8. $y = \sqrt{\dfrac{x^2 + 5}{x + 9}}$.

9. $y = \dfrac{(2x^2 + 2)^2}{(x + 1)^2(3x + 2)}$.

10. $y = \sqrt{\dfrac{(x - 1)(x + 1)}{3x - 4}}$.

11. $y = \dfrac{(8x + 3)^{1/2}(x^2 + 2)^{1/3}}{(1 + 2x)^{1/4}}$.

12. $y = \dfrac{x(1 + x^2)^2}{\sqrt{2 + x^2}}$.

13. $y = x^{2x+1}$.

14. $y = x^{\sqrt{x}}$.

15. $y = x^{1/x}$.

16. $y = \left(\dfrac{2}{x}\right)^x$.

17. $y = (3x + 1)^{2x}$.

18. $y = x^{x^2}$.

19. $y = e^x x^{3x}$.

20. $y = (\ln x)^{e^x}$.

21. Find an equation of the tangent line to $y = (x + 1)(x + 2)^2(x + 3)^2$ at the point where $x = 0$.

22. If $y = x^{2x}$, find the relative rate of change of y with respect to x when $x = 2$.

23. Without using logarithmic differentiation, find the derivative of $y = x^x$. (*Hint:* First show that $y = x^x = e^{x \ln x}$.)

11.11 HIGHER-ORDER DERIVATIVES

As we said earlier, the derivative of a function $y = f(x)$ is itself a function, $f'(x)$. If we differentiate $f'(x)$, the resulting function is called the **second derivative** of f at x. It is denoted $f''(x)$, which is read "f double prime of x." Similarly, the derivative of the second derivative is called the **third derivative,** written $f'''(x)$. Continuing in this way, we get *higher-order derivatives*. Some notations for higher-order derivatives are given in Table 11.2. To avoid clumsy notation, primes are not used beyond the third derivative.

TABLE 11.2

First derivative:	y',	$f'(x)$,	$\dfrac{dy}{dx}$,	$\dfrac{d}{dx}[f(x)]$,	$D_x y$
Second derivative:	y'',	$f''(x)$,	$\dfrac{d^2y}{dx^2}$,	$\dfrac{d^2}{dx^2}[f(x)]$,	$D_x^2 y$
Third derivative:	y''',	$f'''(x)$,	$\dfrac{d^3y}{dx^3}$,	$\dfrac{d^3}{dx^3}[f(x)]$,	$D_x^3 y$
Fourth derivative:	$y^{(4)}$,	$f^{(4)}(x)$,	$\dfrac{d^4y}{dx^4}$,	$\dfrac{d^4}{dx^4}[f(x)]$,	$D_x^4 y$

Pitfall

The symbol $D_x^2 y$ represents the second derivative of y. It is not the same as $[D_x y]^2$, the square of the first derivative of y.

$$D_x^2 y \neq [D_x y]^2.$$

EXAMPLE 1

a. *If $f(x) = 6x^3 - 12x^2 + 6x - 2$, find all higher-order derivatives.*

Differentiating $f(x)$ gives

$$f'(x) = 18x^2 - 24x + 6.$$

Differentiating $f'(x)$ gives

$$f''(x) = 36x - 24.$$

Similarly,

$$f'''(x) = 36,$$
$$f^{(4)}(x) = 0.$$

All successive derivatives are also 0: $f^{(5)}(x) = 0$, and so on.

b. *If $f(x) = 7$, find $f''(x)$.*

$$f'(x) = 0,$$
$$f''(x) = 0.$$

EXAMPLE 2

a. *If $y = e^{x^2}$, find $\dfrac{d^2y}{dx^2}$.*

$$\frac{dy}{dx} = e^{x^2}(2x) = 2xe^{x^2}.$$

By the product rule,

$$\frac{d^2y}{dx^2} = 2[x(e^{x^2})(2x) + e^{x^2}(1)] = 2e^{x^2}(2x^2 + 1).$$

b. *If $y = f(x) = \dfrac{16}{x + 4}$, find $\dfrac{d^2y}{dx^2}$ and evaluate it when $x = 4$.*

Since $y = 16(x + 4)^{-1}$, the power rule gives

$$\frac{dy}{dx} = -16(x + 4)^{-2},$$

$$\frac{d^2y}{dx^2} = 32(x + 4)^{-3} = \frac{32}{(x + 4)^3}.$$

Evaluating when $x = 4$,

$$\frac{d^2y}{dx^2}\bigg|_{x=4} = \frac{32}{8^3} = \frac{1}{16}.$$

The second derivative evaluated at $x = 4$ is also denoted $f''(4)$ or $y''(4)$.

EXAMPLE 3   *If $f(x) = x \ln x$, find the rate of change of $f''(x)$.*

To find the rate of change of any function, we must find its derivative. Thus we want $D_x[f''(x)]$ which is $f'''(x)$.

$$f'(x) = x\left(\frac{1}{x}\right) + (\ln x)(1) = 1 + \ln x,$$

$$f''(x) = 0 + \frac{1}{x} = \frac{1}{x},$$

$$f'''(x) = D_x(x^{-1}) = (-1)x^{-2} = -\frac{1}{x^2}.$$

We shall now find a higher-order derivative by means of implicit differentiation. Keep in mind that we shall assume y to be a function of x.

EXAMPLE 4

a. *Find y'' if $x^2 + 4y^2 = 4$.*

Differentiating both sides with respect to x, we obtain

$$2x + 8yy' = 0,$$

$$y' = \frac{-x}{4y}. \tag{1}$$

$$y'' = \frac{4y\,D_x(-x) - (-x)\,D_x(4y)}{(4y)^2}$$

$$= \frac{4y(-1) - (-x)(4y')}{16y^2}$$

$$= \frac{-4y + 4xy'}{16y^2}.$$

$$y'' = \frac{-y + xy'}{4y^2}. \tag{2}$$

Since $y' = \dfrac{-x}{4y}$ from Eq. (1), by substituting into Eq. (2) we have

$$y'' = \frac{-y + x\left(\dfrac{-x}{4y}\right)}{4y^2} = \frac{-4y^2 - x^2}{16y^3} = -\frac{4y^2 + x^2}{16y^3}.$$

Since $x^2 + 4y^2 = 4$,

$$y'' = -\frac{4}{16y^3} = -\frac{1}{4y^3}.$$

b. *Find* y'' *if* $y^2 = e^{x+y}$.

$$y^2 = e^{x+y},$$

$$2yy' = e^{x+y}(1 + y').$$

Solving for y', we obtain

$$y' = \frac{e^{x+y}}{2y - e^{x+y}}.$$

Since $y^2 = e^{x+y}$.

$$y' = \frac{y^2}{2y - y^2} = \frac{y}{2 - y}.$$

$$y'' = \frac{(2 - y)(y') - y(-y')}{(2 - y)^2} = \frac{2y'}{(2 - y)^2}.$$

Since $y' = \dfrac{y}{2 - y}$,

$$y'' = \frac{2\dfrac{y}{2 - y}}{(2 - y)^2} = \frac{2y}{(2 - y)^3}.$$

EXERCISE 11.11

In Problems **1–20,** *find the indicated derivatives.*

1. $y = 4x^3 - 12x^2 + 6x + 2$, y'''.

2. $y = 2x^4 - 6x^2 + 7x - 2$, y'''.

3. $y = 7 - x$, $\dfrac{d^2y}{dx^2}$.

4. $y = -x - x^2$, $\dfrac{d^2y}{dx^2}$.

5. $y = x^3 + e^x$, $y^{(4)}$.

6. $f(q) = \ln q$, $f'''(q)$.

7. $f(x) = x^2 \ln x$, $D_x^2[f(x)]$.

8. $y = 1/x$, y'''.

9. $f(p) = \dfrac{1}{6p^3}$, $f'''(p)$.

10. $f(x) = \sqrt{x}$, $D_x^2[f(x)]$.

11. $f(r) = \sqrt{1 - r}$, $f''(r)$.

12. $y = e^{-4x^2}$, y''.

13. $y = \dfrac{1}{5x - 6}$, $\dfrac{d^2y}{dx^2}$.

14. $y = (2x + 1)^4$, y''.

15. $y = \dfrac{x + 1}{x - 1}$, y''.

16. $y = 2x^{1/2} + (2x)^{1/2}$, y''.

17. $y = \ln [x(x + 1)]$, y''.

18. $y = \ln\dfrac{(2x - 3)(4x - 5)}{x + 3}$, y''.

19. $f(z) = z^2 e^z$, $f''(z)$.

20. $y = \dfrac{x}{e^x}$, $\dfrac{d^2y}{dx^2}$.

In Problems **21–30,** *find y''.*

21. $x^2 + 4y^2 - 16 = 0$.

22. $x^2 - y^2 = 16$.

23. $y^2 = 4x$.

24. $4x^2 + 3y^2 = 4$.

25. $\sqrt{x} + 4\sqrt{y} = 4$.

26. $y^2 - 6xy = 4$.

27. $xy + y - x = 4$.

28. $xy + y^2 = 1$.

29. $y^2 = e^{x+y}$.

30. $e^x - e^y = x^2 + y^2$.

31. Find the rate of change of $f'(x)$ if $f(x) = (5x - 3)^4$.

32. Find the rate of change of $f''(x)$ if $f(x) = 6\sqrt{x} + \dfrac{1}{6\sqrt{x}}$.

33. If $c = 0.3q^2 + 2q + 850$ is a cost function, how fast is marginal cost changing when $q = 100$?

34. If $p = 1000 - 45q - q^2$ is a demand equation, how fast is marginal revenue changing when $q = 10$?

35. If $f(x) = x^4 - 6x^2 + 5x - 6$, determine the values of x for which $f''(x) = 0$.

11.12 REVIEW

Important Terms and Symbols

Section 11.1	secant line tangent line slope of a curve derivative
	$\lim\limits_{h \to 0} \dfrac{f(x + h) - f(x)}{h}$ $f'(x)$ y' $\dfrac{dy}{dx}$ $D_x y$
Section 11.3	Δx velocity rate of change total cost function marginal cost
	average cost total revenue function marginal revenue relative rate of change
	percentage rate of change
Section 11.5	product rule quotient rule consumption function marginal propensity to consume
	marginal propensity to save
Section 11.6	chain rule power rule marginal revenue product
Section 11.9	implicit differentiation
Section 11.10	logarithmic differentiation
Section 11.11	higher-order derivatives, $f''(x)$, $D_x^2 y$, $\dfrac{d^3y}{dx^3}$, $\dfrac{d^4}{dx^4}[f(x)]$, and so on

Summary

The tangent line (or tangent) to a curve at point P is the limiting position of secant lines PQ as Q approaches P along the curve. The slope of the tangent at P is called the slope of the curve at P.

If $y = f(x)$, the derivative of f at x is the function defined by the limit

$$f'(x) = \lim_{h \to 0} \frac{f(x + h) - f(x)}{h}.$$

Geometrically, the derivative gives the slope of the curve $y = f(x)$ at the point $(x, f(x))$. An equation of the tangent at a particular point (x_1, y_1) is obtained by evaluating $f'(x_1)$, which is the slope m of the tangent, and substituting into the point-slope form $y - y_1 = m(x - x_1)$. Any function that is differentiable at a point must also be continuous there.

The basic rules for finding derivatives are as follows.

$$\frac{d}{dx}(c) = 0, \text{ where } c \text{ is any constant.}$$

$$\frac{d}{dx}(x^n) = nx^{n-1}, \text{ where } n \text{ is any real number.}$$

$$\frac{d}{dx}[cf(x)] = cf'(x).$$

$$\frac{d}{dx}[f(x) + g(x)] = f'(x) + g'(x).$$

$$\frac{d}{dx}[f(x) - g(x)] = f'(x) - g'(x).$$

$$\frac{d}{dx}[f(x)g(x)] = f(x)g'(x) + g(x)f'(x).$$

$$\frac{d}{dx}\left[\frac{f(x)}{g(x)}\right] = \frac{g(x)f'(x) - f(x)g'(x)}{[g(x)]^2}.$$

$$\frac{dy}{dx} = \frac{dy}{du} \cdot \frac{du}{dx}, \text{ where } y \text{ is a function of } u \text{ and } u \text{ is a function of } x.$$

$$\frac{d}{dx}(u^n) = nu^{n-1}\frac{du}{dx}.$$

$$\frac{d}{dx}(\log_b u) = \frac{1}{u}(\log_b e)\frac{du}{dx}.$$

$$\frac{d}{dx}(\ln u) = \frac{1}{u}\frac{du}{dx}.$$

$$\frac{d}{dx}(a^u) = a^u(\ln a)\frac{du}{dx}.$$

$$\frac{d}{dx}(e^u) = e^u\frac{du}{dx}.$$

The derivative dy/dx can also be interpreted as giving the (instantaneous) rate of change of y with respect to x:

$$\frac{dy}{dx} = \lim_{\Delta x \to 0} \frac{\Delta y}{\Delta x} = \lim_{\Delta x \to 0} \frac{\text{change in } y}{\text{change in } x}.$$

In particular, if $s = f(t)$ is an equation of motion, where s is position at time t, then

$$\frac{ds}{dt} = \text{velocity at time } t.$$

In economics, the term *marginal* is used to describe derivatives of specific types of functions. If $c = f(q)$ is a total cost function (c is the total cost of q units of a product), then the rate of change

$$\frac{dc}{dq} \text{ is called marginal cost.}$$

We interpret marginal cost as the approximate cost of one additional unit of output. (Average cost per unit, $\bar{c}$, is related to total cost c by $\bar{c} = c/q$ or $c = \bar{c}q$.)

A total revenue function $r = f(q)$ gives a manufacturer's revenue r for selling q units of product. (Revenue r and price p are related by $r = pq$.) The rate of change

$$\frac{dr}{dq} \text{ is called marginal revenue,}$$

which is interpreted as the approximate revenue obtained from selling one additional unit of output.

If r is the revenue that a manufacturer receives when the total output q of m employees is sold at a price p per unit, then the derivative dr/dm is called the marginal revenue product and is given by

$$\frac{dr}{dm} = \frac{dq}{dm}\left(p + q\frac{dp}{dq}\right).$$

The marginal revenue product gives the approximate change in revenue that results when the manufacturer hires an extra employee.

If $C = f(I)$ is a consumption function, where I is national income and C is national consumption, then

$$\frac{dC}{dI} \text{ is marginal propensity to consume,}$$

$$1 - \frac{dC}{dI} \text{ is marginal propensity to save.}$$

For any function, the relative rate of change of $f(x)$ is

$$\frac{f'(x)}{f(x)},$$

which compares the rate of change of $f(x)$ with $f(x)$ itself. The percentage rate of change is

$$\frac{f'(x)}{f(x)} \cdot 100.$$

If an equation implicitly defines y as a function of x, rather than defining it explicitly in the form $y = f(x)$, then dy/dx can be found by implicit differentiation. With this method, we treat y as a function of x and differentiate both sides of the equation with respect to x. When doing this it is important to keep in mind that $D_x y^n = ny^{n-1}\frac{dy}{dx}$. Finally, we solve the resulting equation for dy/dx.

The method of logarithmic differentiation may be used to differentiate $y = f(x)$ when $f(x)$ consists of products, quotients, or powers. With that method, we take the natural logarithm of both sides of $y = f(x)$ to obtain $\ln y = \ln[f(x)]$. After simplifying $\ln[f(x)]$ by using properties of logarithms, we differentiate both sides of $\ln y = \ln[f(x)]$ with respect to x and then solve for y'. Logarithmic differentiation is also used to differentiate $y = u^v$ where both u and v are functions of x.

Because the derivative $f'(x)$ of a function $y = f(x)$ is itself a function, it can be successively differentiated to obtain the second derivative $f''(x)$, the third derivative $f'''(x)$, and other higher-order derivatives.

Review Problems

In Problems 1–54, differentiate.

1. $y = 6^3$.

2. $y = x$.

3. $y = 7x^4 - 6x^3 + 5x^2 + 1$.

4. $y = \sqrt{x} + 3$.

5. $y = 2e^x + e^2 + e^{x^2}$.

6. $y = 1/x^3$.

7. $y = \dfrac{x^2 + 3}{5}$.

8. $y = \dfrac{1}{2x + 1}$.

9. $f(r) = \ln(r^2 + 5r)$.

10. $y = e^{\ln x}$.

11. $y = (x^2 + 6x)(x^3 - 6x^2 + 4)$.

12. $y = (x^2 + 1)^{100}(x - 6)$.

13. $f(x) = (2x^2 + 4x)^{100}$.

14. $y = 2^{7x^2}$.

15. $y = (8 + 2x)(x^2 + 1)^4$.

16. $f(t) = \log_6 \sqrt{t^2 + 1}$.

17. $y = \sqrt[3]{4x - 1}$.

18. $y = \sqrt[3]{(1 - 3x^2)^2}$.

19. $y = e^x(x^2 + 2)$.

20. $f(w) = we^w + w^2$.

21. $f(z) = \dfrac{z^2 - 1}{z^2 + 1}$.

22. $y = \dfrac{x - 5}{(x + 2)^2}$.

23. $y = \dfrac{\ln x}{e^x}$.

24. $y = \dfrac{e^x + e^{-x}}{x^2}$.

25. $y = e^{x^2 + 4x + 5}$.

26. $y = (2x)^{3/5} + e$.

27. $y = \dfrac{x(x + 1)}{2x^2 + 3}$.

28. $g(z) = \dfrac{-7z}{(z - 1)^{-1}}$.

29. $2xy + y^2 = 6$ (find y').

30. $y = (x - 6)^4(x + 4)^3(6 - x)^2$.

31. $y = \sqrt{(x - 6)(x + 5)(9 - x)}$.

32. $4x^2 - 9y^2 = 4$ (find y').

33. $f(q) = \ln[(q + 1)^2(q + 2)^3]$.

34. $y = x^{x^3}$.

35. $y = \dfrac{1}{\sqrt{1 - x}}$.

36. $y = \sqrt{\dfrac{(x - 2)(x + 3)}{\sqrt{x - 1}}}$.

37. $y = \log_2(8x + 5)^2$.

38. $y + xy + y^2 = 1$ (find y').

39. $y = (x + 1)^{x + 1}$.

40. $y = (x + 2)^{\ln x}$.

41. $y = \dfrac{x^2 + 6}{\sqrt{x^2 + 5}}$.

42. $y = \dfrac{(x + 3)^5}{x}$.

43. $x^2y^2 = 1$ (find y').

44. $f(x) = 5x\sqrt{1 - 2x}$.

45. $y = 2x^{-3/8} + (2x)^{-3/8}$.

46. $f(t) = e^{\sqrt{t}}$.

47. $f(l) = \ln(1 + l + l^2 + l^3)$.

48. $y = \sqrt{\dfrac{x}{2}} + \sqrt{\dfrac{2}{x}}$.

49. $y = (x^3 + 6x^2 + 9)^{3/5}$.

50. $y = (e + e^2)^0$.

51. $f(u) = \ln(u^2\sqrt{1 - u})$.

52. $y = \dfrac{1 + e^x}{1 - e^x}$.

53. $y = \dfrac{(x^2 + 2)^{3/2}(x^2 + 9)^{4/9}}{(x^3 + 6x)^{4/11}}$.

54. $y = \dfrac{\ln x}{\sqrt{x}}$.

In Problems **55–62**, *find the indicated derivative at the given point. It is not necessary to simplify the derivative before substituting the coordinates.*

55. $y = x^4 - 2x^3 + 6x$, y''', $(1, 5)$.

56. $y = x^2 e^x$, y''', $(1, e)$.

57. $y = \dfrac{x}{\sqrt{x - 1}}$, y'', $(5, \frac{5}{2})$.

58. $y = \dfrac{2}{1 - x}$, y'', $(-2, \frac{2}{3})$.

59. $x + xy + y = 5$, y'', $(2, 1)$.

60. $xy + y^2 = 2$, y'', $(1, 1)$.

61. $y = \dfrac{4x}{x^2 + 4}$, y'', $(2, 1)$.

62. $y = (x + 1)^3(x - 1)$, y'', $(-1, 0)$.

In Problems **63–68**, *find an equation of the tangent line to the curve at the point corresponding to the given value of x.*

63. $y = x^2 - 6x + 4$, $x = 1$.

64. $y = -2x^3 + 6x + 1$, $x = 2$.

65. $y = e^x$, $x = \ln 2$.

66. $y = \dfrac{x}{1 - x}$, $x = 3$.

67. $x^2 - y^2 = 9$, $x = 7$, $y > 0$.

68. $xy = 6$, $x = 1$.

69. If $f(x) = 4x^2 + 2x + 8$, find the relative and percentage rates of change of $f(x)$ when $x = 1$.

70. If $f(x) = x/(x + 4)$, find the relative and percentage rates of change of $f(x)$ when $x = 1$.

71. If $r = q(20 - 0.1q)$ is a total revenue function, find the marginal revenue function.

72. If $c = 0.0001q^3 - 0.02q^2 + 3q + 6000$ is a total cost function, find the marginal cost when $q = 100$.

73. If $C = 7 + 0.6I - 0.25\sqrt{I}$ is a consumption function, find the marginal propensity to consume and the marginal propensity to save when $I = 16$.

74. If $p = (q + 14)/(q + 4)$ is a demand equation, find the rate of change of price p with respect to quantity q.

75. If $p = -0.5q + 450$ is a demand equation, find the marginal revenue function.

76. If $\bar{c} = (500/q)e^{q/300}$ is an average cost function, find the marginal cost function.

77. The total cost function for an electric light and power plant is estimated by*

$$c = 16.68 + 0.125q + 0.00439q^2, \qquad 20 \le q \le 90$$

where q is 8-hour total output (as percentage of capacity) and c is total fuel cost in dollars. Find the marginal cost function and evaluate it when $q = 70$.

78. A manufacturer determined that m employees will produce a total of q units of product per day where $q = m(50 - m)$. If the demand function is given by $p = -0.01q + 9$, find the marginal revenue product when $m = 10$.

79. Several models have been used to analyze the length of stay in a hospital. For a particular group of schizophrenics, one such model is†

$$f(t) = 1 - (0.8e^{-0.01t} + 0.2e^{-0.0002t}),$$

where $f(t)$ is the proportion of the group that was discharged at the end of t days of hospitalization. Deter-

* J. A. Nordin, "Note on a Light Plant's Cost Curves," *Econometrica*, 15 (1947), 231–35.

† Adapted from W. W. Eaton and G. A. Whitmore, "Length of Stay as a Stocastic Process: A General Approach and Application to Hospitalization for Schizophrenia," *Journal of Mathematical Sociology*, 5 (1977), 273–92.

mine the discharge rate (proportion discharged per day) at the end of t days.

80. According to Richter* the number N of earthquakes of magnitude M or greater per unit of time is given by log $N = A - bM$, where A and b are constants. He claims that

$$\log\left(-\frac{dN}{dM}\right) = A + \log\left(\frac{b}{q}\right) - bM,$$

where $q = \log e$. Verify this statement.

* C. F. Richter, *Elementary Seismology* (San Francisco: W. H. Freeman and Company, Publishers, 1958).

12

Curve Sketching

12.1 INTERCEPTS AND SYMMETRY

Examining the graphical behavior of equations is a basic part of mathematics and has applications to many areas of study. In this section we shall examine equations to determine whether their graphs have certain features. Specifically, we shall consider *intercepts* and *symmetry*.

A point where a graph intersects the x-axis is called an *x-intercept* of the graph and has the form $(x, 0)$. A *y-intercept* is a point $(0, y)$ where the graph intersects the y-axis.

EXAMPLE 1   *Find the x- and y-intercepts of the graphs of the following equations.*

a. $x^2 + y^2 = 25$.

If $(x, 0)$ is an x-intercept, its coordinates must satisfy $x^2 + y^2 = 25$. Replacing y by 0 and solving for x gives

$$x^2 + 0^2 = 25.$$

$$x = \pm 5.$$

The x-intercepts are thus $(5, 0)$ and $(-5, 0)$. Similarly, to determine the y-intercepts $(0, y)$, we replace x by 0 in $x^2 + y^2 = 25$ and solve for y.

$$0^2 + y^2 = 25.$$

$$y = \pm 5.$$

Thus the y-intercepts are $(0, 5)$ and $(0, -5)$ (see Fig. 12.1).

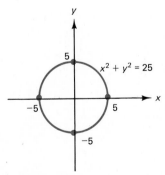

FIGURE 12.1

b. $y = \dfrac{1}{x}$.

Since x cannot be 0, the graph has no y-intercept. If y is 0, then $0 = 1/x$ and this equation has no solution. Thus no x-intercepts exist either (see Fig. 12.2).

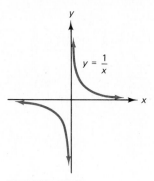

FIGURE 12.2

At times it may be quite difficult or even impossible to find intercepts. For example, the x-intercepts of the graph of $y - \sqrt{2}\,x^5 - 4x^2 - 7 = 0$ would be difficult to find, although the y-intercept is easily found to be $(0, 7)$. In cases such as this, we settle for those intercepts that we can find conveniently.

Some graphs may have *symmetry*. For example, consider the graph of $y = x^2$ in Fig. 12.3. The portion to the left of the y-axis is the reflection (or mirror image) through the y-axis of that portion to the right of the y-axis, and vice versa. More precisely, if (x_0, y_0) is any point on this graph, then the point $(-x_0, y_0)$ must also lie on the graph. We say that this graph is *symmetric about the y-axis*.

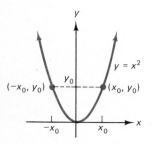

Symmetry about y-axis

FIGURE 12.3

Definition
*A graph is **symmetric about the y-axis** if and only if $(-x_0, y_0)$ lies on the graph when (x_0, y_0) does.*

EXAMPLE 2   *Use the definition above to show that the graph of $y = x^2$ is symmetric about the y-axis.*

Suppose (x_0, y_0) is *any* point on the graph of $y = x^2$. Then

$$y_0 = x_0^2.$$

We must show that the coordinates of $(-x_0, y_0)$ satisfy $y = x^2$:

$$y_0 = (-x_0)^2?$$

$$y_0 = x_0^2?$$

But from above we know that $y_0 = x_0^2$. Thus the graph *is* symmetric about the y-axis.

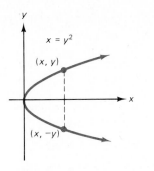

Symmetry about x-axis

FIGURE 12.4

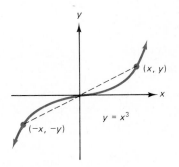

Symmetry about origin

FIGURE 12.5

When one is testing for symmetry in Example 2, (x_0, y_0) can be any point on the graph. In the future, for convenience we shall omit the subscripts. This means that a graph is symmetric about the y-axis if replacing x by $-x$ in its equation results in an equivalent equation.

Another type of symmetry is shown by the graph of $x = y^2$ in Fig. 12.4. Here the portion below the x-axis is the reflection through the x-axis of that portion above the x-axis, and vice versa. If the point (x, y) lies on the graph, then $(x, -y)$ also lies on it. This graph is said to be *symmetric about the x-axis*.

Definition
*A graph is **symmetric about the x-axis** if and only if $(x, -y)$ lies on the graph when (x, y) does.*

A third type of symmetry, *symmetry about the origin*, is illustrated by the graph of $y = x^3$ (Fig. 12.5). Whenever the point (x, y) lies on the graph, then $(-x, -y)$ also lies on it. As a result, the line segment joining points (x, y) and $(-x, -y)$ is bisected by the origin.

Definition
*A graph is **symmetric about the origin** if and only if $(-x, -y)$ lies on the graph when (x, y) does.*

Table 12.1 gives the tests for symmetry. When we know that a graph has symmetry, we can sketch it by plotting fewer points than would otherwise be needed.

TABLE 12.1
Tests for Symmetry

Symmetry about x-axis	Replace y by $-y$ in given equation. Symmetric if equivalent equation is obtained.
Symmetry about y-axis	Replace x by $-x$ in given equation. Symmetric if equivalent equation is obtained.
Symmetry about origin	Replace x by $-x$ and y by $-y$ in given equation. Symmetric if equivalent equation is obtained.

EXAMPLE 3   *Test $y = f(x) = 1 - x^4$ for symmetry about the x-axis, the y-axis, or the origin. Then find the intercepts and sketch the graph.*

Symmetry   *x-axis:*   Replacing y by $-y$ in $y = 1 - x^4$ gives
$$-y = 1 - x^4 \quad \text{or} \quad y = -1 + x^4,$$
which is not equivalent to the given equation. Thus the graph is *not* symmetric about the x-axis.

y-axis: Replacing x by $-x$ in $y = 1 - x^4$ gives
$$y = 1 - (-x)^4 \quad \text{or} \quad y = 1 - x^4,$$

which is equivalent to the given equation. Thus the graph *is* symmetric about the y-axis.

Origin: Replacing x by $-x$ and y by $-y$ in $y = 1 - x^4$ gives

$$-y = 1 - (-x)^4, \qquad -y = 1 - x^4, \qquad y = -1 + x^4,$$

which is not equivalent to the given equation. Thus the graph is *not* symmetric about the origin.

intercepts   Testing for x-intercepts, we set $y = 0$ in $y = 1 - x^4$. Then

$$1 - x^4 = 0,$$

$$(1 - x^2)(1 + x^2) = 0,$$

$$(1 - x)(1 + x)(1 + x^2) = 0,$$

$$x = 1 \text{ or } x = -1.$$

The x-intercepts are thus $(1, 0)$ and $(-1, 0)$. Testing for y-intercepts, we set $x = 0$. Then $y = 1$, so $(0, 1)$ is the only y-intercept.

Discussion   If the intercepts and some points (x, y) to the right of the y-axis are plotted, we can sketch the *entire* graph by using symmetry about the y-axis (Fig. 12.6).

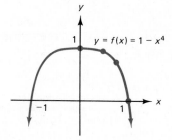

x	y
0	1
$\frac{1}{2}$	$\frac{15}{16}$
$\frac{3}{4}$	$\frac{175}{256}$
1	0
$\frac{3}{2}$	$-\frac{65}{16}$

FIGURE 12.6

In Example 3 we showed that the graph of $y = f(x) = 1 - x^4$ does not have x-axis symmetry. With the exception of the constant function $f(x) = 0$, *the graph of any **function** $y = f(x)$ cannot be symmetric about the x-axis* because such symmetry implies two y-values with the same x-value.

EXAMPLE 4   *Test the graph of $4x^2 + 9y^2 = 36$ for intercepts and symmetry. Sketch the graph.*

Intercepts   If $y = 0$, then $4x^2 = 36$, and so $x = \pm 3$. Thus the x-intercepts are $(3, 0)$ and $(-3, 0)$. If $x = 0$, then $9y^2 = 36$, and so $y = \pm 2$. Thus the y-intercepts are $(0, 2)$ and $(0, -2)$.

Symmetry   Testing for x-axis symmetry, we replace y by $-y$:

$$4x^2 + 9(-y)^2 = 36 \qquad \text{or} \qquad 4x^2 + 9y^2 = 36.$$

Since we obtain the original equation, there is symmetry about the x-axis. Testing for y-axis symmetry, we replace x by $-x$:

$$4(-x)^2 + 9y^2 = 36 \qquad \text{or} \qquad 4x^2 + 9y^2 = 36.$$

Again we have the original equation, so there is also symmetry about the y-axis. Testing for symmetry about the origin, we replace x by $-x$ and y by $-y$:

$$4(-x)^2 + 9(-y)^2 = 36 \qquad \text{or} \qquad 4x^2 + 9y^2 = 36.$$

Since this is the original equation, the graph is also symmetric about the origin.

Discussion In Fig. 12.7 the intercepts and some points in the first quadrant are plotted. The points in that quadrant are then connected by a smooth curve. By

x	y
± 3	0
0	± 2
1	$\dfrac{4\sqrt{2}}{3}$
2	$\dfrac{2\sqrt{5}}{3}$
$\dfrac{5}{2}$	$\dfrac{\sqrt{11}}{3}$

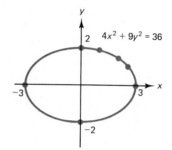

FIGURE 12.7

symmetry about the x-axis, the points in the fourth quadrant are obtained. Then by symmetry about the y-axis the complete graph is found. There are other ways of graphing the equation by using symmetry. For example, after plotting the intercepts and some points in the first quadrant, then by symmetry about the origin we can obtain the points in the third quadrant. By symmetry about the x-axis (or y-axis) we can then obtain the entire graph.

In Example 4 the graph is symmetric about the x-axis, the y-axis, and the origin. **For any graph, if any two of the three types of symmetry exist, then the remaining type must also exist.**

EXERCISE 12.1

In Problems 1–16, find the x- and y-intercepts of the graphs of the equations. Also test for symmetry about the x-axis, the y-axis, or the origin. Do not sketch the graphs.

1. $y = 5x$.

2. $y = f(x) = x^2 - 4$.

3. $2x^2 + y^2x^4 = 8 - y$.

4. $x = y^3$.

5. $4x^2 - 9y^2 = 36$.

6. $y = 7$.

7. $x = -2$.

8. $y = |2x| - 2$.

9. $x = -y^{-4}$.

10. $y = \sqrt{x^2 - 4}$.

11. $x - 4y - y^2 + 21 = 0$.

12. $x^3 - xy + y^2 = 0$.

13. $y = f(x) = x^3/(x^2 + 5)$.   14. $x^2 + xy + y^2 = 0$.   15. $e^{x^2+y^2} - 5 = 0$.

16. $y = e^{x^2}$.

In Problems **17–24,** find the x- and y-intercepts of the graphs of the equations. Also, test for symmetry about the x-axis, the y-axis, or the origin. Then sketch the graphs..

17. $2x + y^2 = 4$.   18. $x = y^4$.   19. $y = f(x) = x^3 - 4x$.   20. $y = x - x^3$.

21. $|x| - |y| = 0$.   22. $x^2 + y^2 = 16$.   23. $4x^2 + y^2 = 16$.   24. $x^2 - y^2 = 1$.

12.2 ASYMPTOTES

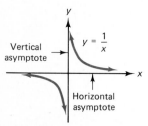

Vertical asymptote

$y = \dfrac{1}{x}$

Horizontal asymptote

FIGURE 12.8

In Example 1(b) of Sec. 12.1, we showed that the graph of the function $y = 1/x$ has no intercepts. Although this graph is symmetric with respect to the origin (as you may verify), it has other distinguishing features (see Fig. 12.8). As x approaches zero from the right, $1/x$ becomes positively infinite; as x approaches zero from the left, $1/x$ becomes negatively infinite. In terms of limits,

$$\lim_{x \to 0^+} \frac{1}{x} = \infty \qquad \text{and} \qquad \lim_{x \to 0^-} \frac{1}{x} = -\infty.$$

We say that the line $x = 0$ (the y-axis) is a *vertical asymptote* for the graph of $y = 1/x$. This means it is a vertical line near which the graph "explodes" (that is, the graph rises or falls without bound).

On the other hand, as x approaches ∞, as well as $-\infty$, $1/x$ approaches 0. That is,

$$\lim_{x \to \infty} \frac{1}{x} = 0 \qquad \text{and} \qquad \lim_{x \to -\infty} \frac{1}{x} = 0.$$

We say that the line $y = 0$ (the x-axis) is a *horizontal asymptote* for the graph of $y = 1/x$. This means that it is a horizontal line near which the graph "settles down" as $x \to \infty$ or $x \to -\infty$.

Although the graph of a horizontal line settles around itself as $x \to \infty$ or as $x \to -\infty$, a line is not considered to have asymptotes. In summary, we have the following definition.

Definition

*The line $x = a$ is a **vertical asymptote** for the graph of the function f if and only if either*

$$\lim_{x \to a^+} f(x) = \infty \ (\text{or} -\infty).$$

or $\qquad \lim_{x \to a^-} f(x) = \infty \ (\text{or} -\infty).$

*If f is a nonlinear function, the line $y = b$ is a **horizontal asymptote** for the graph of f if and only if either*

$$\lim_{x \to \infty} f(x) = b \qquad or \qquad \lim_{x \to -\infty} f(x) = b.$$

Because of the explosion around a vertical asymptote, a function cannot be continuous at a if its graph has a vertical asymptote $x = a$.

EXAMPLE 1   *Determine horizontal and vertical asymptotes for the graph of* $y = \dfrac{3x - 5}{x - 2}$.

To test for horizontal asymptotes, we find the limits of y as $x \to \infty$ and as $x \to -\infty$. Since y is a rational function (a quotient of two polynomials), the procedures of Sec. 10.2 may be used.

$$\lim_{x \to \infty} \frac{3x - 5}{x - 2} = \lim_{x \to \infty} \frac{3x}{x} = \lim_{x \to \infty} 3 = 3.$$

Thus the line $y = 3$ is a horizontal asymptote. Similarly,

$$\lim_{x \to -\infty} \frac{3x - 5}{x - 2} = 3.$$

Hence the graph will settle down near the line $y = 3$ as $x \to \infty$ and as $x \to -\infty$. To determine vertical asymptotes, we find where the values of $\dfrac{3x - 5}{x - 2}$ become unbounded. Note that the denominator $x - 2$ is 0 when x is 2. If x is slightly larger than 2, then $x - 2$ is both close to 0 and positive, and $3x - 5$ is close to 1. Thus $(3x - 5)/(x - 2)$ is very large, so

$$\lim_{x \to 2^+} \frac{3x - 5}{x - 2} = \infty.$$

This limit is sufficient to conclude that the line $x = 2$ is a vertical asymptote. Because we are ultimately interested in the behavior of a function around a vertical asymptote, it is worthwhile to examine what happens to this function as x approaches 2 from the left. If x is slightly less than 2, then $x - 2$ is very close to 0 but negative, and $3x - 5$ is close to 1. Thus $(3x - 5)/(x - 2)$ is "very negative," so

$$\lim_{x \to 2^-} \frac{3x - 5}{x - 2} = -\infty.$$

We conclude that the function increases without bound as $x \to 2^+$ and decreases without bound as $x \to 2^-$. The graph appears in Fig. 12.9. The dashed lines indicate the asymptotes and are not part of the graph. However, they are useful aids in sketching it because parts of the graph approach the asymptotes.

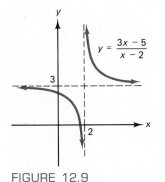

FIGURE 12.9

To determine vertical asymptotes, we must find values of x around which $f(x)$ increases or decreases without bound. For a rational function, these x-values are those for which the denominator is zero but the numerator is not zero. For instance, for the rational function $f(x) = \dfrac{3x - 5}{x - 2}$ in Example 1, when x is 2 the denominator is 0 but the numerator is not—and $x = 2$ is a vertical asymptote. In summary, we have a rule for vertical asymptotes for rational functions.

VERTICAL ASYMPTOTE RULE FOR RATIONAL FUNCTIONS

Suppose $f(x) = P(x)/Q(x)$ where P and Q are polynomial functions. If $Q(a) = 0$ and $P(a) \neq 0$, then $x = a$ is a vertical asymptote for the graph of f.

EXAMPLE 2   *Determine vertical and horizontal asymptotes for the graph of $f(x) = \dfrac{x^2 - 4x}{x^2 - 4x + 3}$.*

Since f is a rational function, the vertical asymptote rule applies. We have

$$f(x) = \frac{x^2 - 4x}{x^2 - 4x + 3} = \frac{x(x - 4)}{(x - 3)(x - 1)},$$

so the denominator is 0 when x is 3 or 1. Neither of these values makes the numerator 0. Thus the lines $x = 3$ and $x = 1$ are vertical asymptotes.

For horizontal asymptotes, we find the limits of $f(x)$ as $x \to \infty$ and as $x \to -\infty$.

$$\lim_{x \to \infty} \frac{x^2 - 4x}{x^2 - 4x + 3} = \lim_{x \to \infty} \frac{x^2}{x^2} = \lim_{x \to \infty} 1 = 1.$$

Thus the line $y = 1$ is a horizontal asymptote. The same result is obtained as $x \to -\infty$. Figure 12.10 shows the graph of f and the asymptotes.

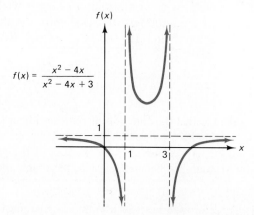

$$f(x) = \frac{x^2 - 4x}{x^2 - 4x + 3}$$

FIGURE 12.10

From Sec. 10.2, when the numerator of a rational function has degree greater than that of the denominator, no limit exists as $x \to \infty$ or $x \to -\infty$. From this we conclude that **whenever the degree of the numerator of a rational function is greater than the degree of the denominator, the graph of the function cannot have a horizontal asymptote.**

EXAMPLE 3   *Find vertical and horizontal asymptotes for the graph of* $y = f(x) = x^3 + 2x$.

This is a rational function with denominator 1, which is never zero. By the vertical asymptote rule, there are no vertical asymptotes.

Because the degree of the numerator (3) is greater than the degree of the denominator (0), there are no horizontal asymptotes. However, let us examine the behavior of the graph as $x \to \infty$ and $x \to -\infty$.

$$\lim_{x \to \infty} (x^3 + 2x) = \lim_{x \to \infty} \frac{x^3 + 2x}{1} = \lim_{x \to \infty} \frac{x^3}{1} = \lim_{x \to \infty} x^3 = \infty.$$

Similarly,

$$\lim_{x \to -\infty} (x^3 + 2x) = \lim_{x \to -\infty} x^3 = -\infty.$$

Thus as $x \to \infty$, the graph must extend indefinitely upward, and as $x \to -\infty$, the graph must extend indefinitely downard (see Fig. 12.11).

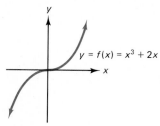

$y = f(x) = x^3 + 2x$

FIGURE 12.11

The results in Example 3 can be generalized to any polynomial function.

> A polynomial function has neither a horizontal nor a vertical asymptote.

EXAMPLE 4   *Find horizontal and vertical asymptotes for the graph of* $y = e^x - 1$.

Testing for horizontal asymptotes, we let $x \to \infty$. Then e^x increases without bound, so

$$\lim_{x \to \infty} (e^x - 1) = \infty.$$

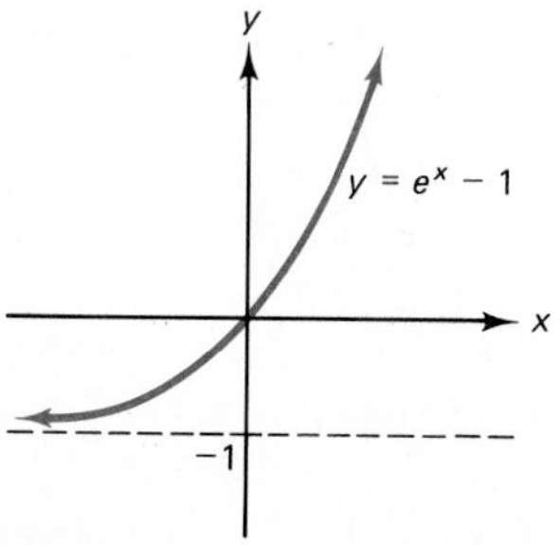

Thus the graph does not settle down as $x \to \infty$. However, as $x \to -\infty$, then $e^x \to 0$, so

$$\lim_{x \to -\infty} (e^x - 1) = \lim_{x \to -\infty} e^x - \lim_{x \to -\infty} 1 = 0 - 1 = -1.$$

Therefore, the line $y = -1$ is a horizontal asymptote. The graph has no vertical asymptotes, since $e^x - 1$ neither increases nor decreases without bound around any fixed value of x (see Fig. 12.12).

$y = e^x - 1$

-1

FIGURE 12.12

EXAMPLE 5   *Sketch the graph of* $y = \dfrac{x^2}{x^2 - 1}$ *with the aid of intercepts, symmetry, and asymptotes.*

Intercepts   If $x = 0$, then $y = 0$; if $y = 0$, then $x = 0$. Therefore, the x-intercept, as well as the y-intercept, is $(0, 0)$.

Symmetry   Since y is a function of x and is not the zero function, the graph is *not* symmetric about the x-axis.

Testing for y-axis symmetry, we replace x by $-x$:

$$y = \frac{(-x)^2}{(-x)^2 - 1}, \qquad y = \frac{x^2}{x^2 - 1}.$$

The graph is symmetric about the y-axis. *Symmetry about exactly one axis implies that the graph cannot be symmetric about the origin.* This follows from the last paragraph of Sec. 12.1.

Asymptotes
Horizontal: Since y is a rational function,

$$\lim_{x \to \infty} \frac{x^2}{x^2 - 1} = \lim_{x \to \infty} \frac{x^2}{x^2} = \lim_{x \to \infty} 1 = 1.$$

Therefore, as $x \to \infty$ the graph approaches the line $y = 1$, a horizontal asymptote. By symmetry, as $x \to -\infty$ the graph again approaches the line $y = 1$.

Vertical: We use the vertical asymptote rule. Since

$$y = \frac{x^2}{x^2 - 1} = \frac{x^2}{(x + 1)(x - 1)},$$

when x is -1 or 1 the denominator is zero and the numerator is not zero. Thus the lines $x = -1$ and $x = 1$ are vertical asymptotes. Let us analyze the behavior of the graph around these asymptotes.

$$\lim_{x \to 1^-} \frac{x^2}{(x - 1)(x + 1)} = -\infty \quad \text{and} \quad \lim_{x \to 1^+} \frac{x^2}{(x - 1)(x + 1)} = \infty.$$

Therefore, immediately to the left of the line $x = 1$, the function values are extremely negative, while to the immediate right, they are extremely positive. By symmetry

$$\lim_{x \to -1^+} \frac{x^2}{(x - 1)(x + 1)} = -\infty \quad \text{and} \quad \lim_{x \to -1^-} \frac{x^2}{(x - 1)(x + 1)} = \infty.$$

Thus immediately to the right of $x = -1$, the function values are extremely negative, while to the immediate left, they are extremely positive.

Discussion   We plot the intercept and some other points on the graph where $x > 0$, especially points near the asymptotes. By using properties of symmetry and asymptotes, it is relatively easy to sketch the graph (see Fig. 12.13).

x	y
0	0
$\frac{1}{2}$	$-\frac{1}{3}$
$\frac{3}{4}$	$-\frac{9}{7}$
$\frac{5}{4}$	$\frac{25}{9}$
$\frac{3}{2}$	$\frac{9}{5}$
2	$\frac{4}{3}$
3	$\frac{9}{8}$

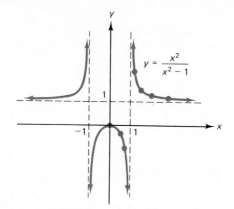

$y = \dfrac{x^2}{x^2 - 1}$

FIGURE 12.13

EXERCISE 12.2

In Problems **1–14,** *find the horizontal and vertical asymptotes for the graphs of the functions. Do not sketch the graphs.*

1. $f(x) = \dfrac{x - 1}{2x + 3}.$

2. $y = \dfrac{2x + 1}{2x - 1}.$

3. $y = \dfrac{4}{x}.$

4. $y = -\dfrac{4}{x^2}.$

5. $y = x^2 - 5x + 8.$

6. $y = \dfrac{x^3}{x^2 - 9}.$

7. $f(x) = \dfrac{2x^2}{x^2 + x - 6}.$

8. $f(x) = \dfrac{x^2}{5}.$

9. $y = \dfrac{4}{x - 6} + 4.$

10. $f(x) = \dfrac{5}{2x^2 - 9x + 4}.$

11. $f(x) = \sqrt[3]{x^2}.$

12. $y = \dfrac{x^2 + x}{x}.$

13. $y = 2e^{x+2} + 4.$

14. $f(x) = e^{x^3}.$

In Problems **15–26,** *find the x- and y-intercepts of the graphs of the functions; determine whether the graphs are symmetric about the x-axis, y-axis, or origin; determine horizontal and vertical asymptotes; sketch the graphs.*

15. $y = \dfrac{3}{x - 1}.$

16. $y = \dfrac{x}{4 - x}.$

17. $f(x) = \dfrac{8}{x^3}.$

18. $f(x) = \dfrac{1}{x^4}.$

19. $f(x) = \dfrac{1}{x^2 - 1}.$

20. $f(x) = \dfrac{x^2}{x^2 - 4}.$

21. $y = \dfrac{x^2 - 1}{x^2 - 4}.$

22. $y = \dfrac{x^3 - x}{x}.$

23. $y = \dfrac{x^2(x^2 - 9)}{x^2}.$

24. $f(x) = \begin{cases} 1/x, & \text{if } x > 0, \\ (x + 1)/x, & \text{if } x < 0. \end{cases}$

25. $y = 3 - e^{2x}.$

26. $y = e^{-x} - 1.$

27. In discussing the time pattern of purchasing, Mantell and Sing* use the curve

$$y = \dfrac{x}{a + bx}$$

as a mathematical model. They claim that $y = 1/b$ is an asymptote. Verify this.

* L.H. Mantell and F. P. Sing, *Economics for Business Decisions* (New York: McGraw-Hill Book Company, 1972), p. 107.

28. Sketch the graphs of $y = 6 - 3e^{-x}$ and $y = 6 + 3e^{-x}$. Show that they are asymptotic to the same line. What is the equation of this line?

29. For a new product the yearly number of thousand packages sold, y, after t years from its introduction is predicted to be

$$y = f(t) = 150 - 76e^{-t}.$$

Show that $y = 150$ is a horizontal asymptote for the graph. This shows that after the product is established with consumers, the market tends to be constant.

12.3 RELATIVE EXTREMA

In curve sketching, just plotting points may not give enough information about a curve's shape. For example, the points $(-1, 0)$, $(0, -1)$, and $(1, 0)$ satisfy the equation $y = (x + 1)^3(x - 1)$. Based on these points, you might hastily conclude that the graph should appear as in Fig. 12.14, but in fact the actual shape is given in Fig. 12.15. Even using information about symmetry and asymptotes

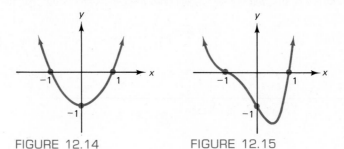

FIGURE 12.14   FIGURE 12.15

would be of little help here. In this section and the next one, we shall explore the powerful role that differentiation plays in analyzing a function so that we may determine the true shape and behavior of its graph.

We begin by analyzing the graph of the function $y = f(x)$ in Fig. 12.16.

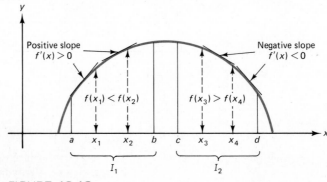

FIGURE 12.16

Notice that as x increases (goes from left to right) on the interval I_1 between a and b, the values of $f(x)$ increase and the curve is rising. Symbolically, this observation means that if x_1 and x_2 are any two points in I_1 such that $x_1 < x_2$, then $f(x_1) < f(x_2)$ Here f is said to be an *increasing function* on I_1. On the other hand, as x increases on the interval I_2 between c and d, the curve is falling. Here $x_3 < x_4$ implies $f(x_3) > f(x_4)$, and f is said to be a *decreasing function* on I_2. In general we have the following definition.

Definition

A function f is an **increasing** *[***decreasing***] function on the interval I if and only if for any points* x_1, x_2 *in I, where* $x_1 < x_2$, *then* $f(x_1) < f(x_2)$ [$f(x_1) > f(x_2)$].

A function is said to be increasing (decreasing) at a *point* x_0 if there is an open interval containing x_0 on which the function is increasing (decreasing). Thus in Fig. 12.16, f is increasing at x_1 and is decreasing at x_3.

Turning again to Fig. 12.16, we note that over the interval I_1, tangent lines to the curve have positive slopes, so $f'(x)$ must be positive for all x in I_1. Over the interval I_2, tangent lines have negative slopes, so $f'(x) < 0$ for all x in I_2. These facts lead to the following rule which allows us to use the derivative to determine when a function is increasing or decreasing.

> ### Rule 1
> *If* $f'(x) > 0$ *for all x in an interval I, then f is an increasing function on I. If* $f'(x) < 0$ *for all x on I, then f is a decreasing function on I.*

To illustrate these ideas, we shall use Rule 1 to find the intervals on which $y = 18x - \frac{2}{3}x^3$ is increasing or decreasing. Letting $y = f(x)$, we must determine when $f'(x)$ is positive and when $f'(x)$ is negative.

$$f'(x) = 18 - 2x^2 = 2(9 - x^2) = 2(3 + x)(3 - x).$$

Using the technique of Sec. 10.5, we can find the sign of $f'(x)$ by considering the intervals determined by the roots of $2(3 + x)(3 - x) = 0$, namely 3 and -3 (see Fig. 12.17). In each interval the sign of $f'(x)$ is determined by the signs

FIGURE 12.17

of its factors:

if $x < -3$, then $f'(x) = 2(-)(+) = (-)$ and f is decreasing;

if $-3 < x < 3$, then $f'(x) = 2(+)(+) = (+)$ and f is increasing;

if $x > 3$, then $f'(x) = 2(+)(-) = (-)$ and f is decreasing [see Fig. 12.18(a)].

Thus f is decreasing on $(-\infty, -3)$ and $(3, \infty)$, and is increasing on $(-3, 3)$ as seen in Fig. 12.18(b). This corresponds to the rising and falling nature of the graph. These results could be sharpened. Actually, by definition, f is decreasing

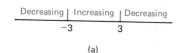

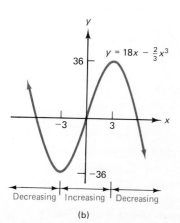

FIGURE 12.18

on $(-\infty, -3]$ and $[3, \infty)$, and increasing on $[-3, 3]$. However, for our purposes open intervals are sufficient. *It will be our practice to determine **open** intervals on which a function is increasing or decreasing.*

Look now at the graph of $y = f(x)$ in Fig. 12.19. Three observations can be made. First, there is something special about the points P_1, P_2, and P_3. Notice that P_1 is *higher* than any other "nearby" point on the curve—likewise for P_3. The point P_2 is *lower* than any other "nearby" point on the curve. Since P_1,

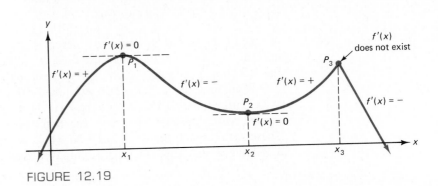

FIGURE 12.19

P_2, and P_3 may not necessarily be the highest or lowest points on the *entire* curve, we simply say that the graph of f has a *relative maximum (point)* when $x = x_1$ and when $x = x_3$, and has a *relative minimum (point)* when $x = x_2$. On the function level, f has a *relative maximum (value)* when $x = x_1$ and $x = x_3$, and has a *relative minimum (value)* when $x = x_2$. When we refer to a relative maximum or minimum, it is understood to refer to a point or value, depending on the context. Turning back to the graph, we see that there is an *absolute maximum* (highest point on the entire curve) when $x = x_1$, but there is no *absolute minimum* (lowest point on the entire curve), since the curve is assumed to extend downward indefinitely. We define these new terms as follows:

Definition

*A function f has a **relative maximum** [**relative minimum**] when $x = x_0$ if there is an open interval containing x_0 on which $f(x_0) \geq f(x)$ [$f(x_0) \leq f(x)$] for all x in the interval. The relative maximum [minimum] is $f(x_0)$.*

Definition

*A function f has an **absolute maximum** [**absolute minimum**] when $x = x_0$ if $f(x_0) \geq f(x)$ [$f(x_0) \leq f(x)$] for all x in the domain of f. The absolute maximum [minimum] is $f(x_0)$.*

We refer to either a relative maximum or a relative minimum as a **relative extremum** (plural: *relative extrema*). Similarly, we speak of **absolute extrema.**

When dealing with relative extrema, we compare the function value at a point to those of nearby points; however, when dealing with absolute extrema, we compare the function value at a point to all others determined by the domain.

Thus relative extrema are "local" in nature, while absolute extrema are "global" in nature.

Our second observation is that at a relative extremum the derivative may not be defined (as when $x = x_3$). But whenever it is defined, it is 0 (as when $x = x_1$ and $x = x_2$), and hence the tangent line is horizontal as shown in Fig. 12.19. We may state:

> **Rule 2**
>
> *If f has a relative extremum when $x = x_0$, then $f'(x_0) = 0$ or $f'(x_0)$ is not defined.*

Third, each relative extremum occurs at a point around which the sign of $f'(x)$ is changing, regardless of whether or not the derivative is defined at the point. For the relative maximum when $x = x_1$, $f'(x)$ goes from $+$ for $x < x_1$ to $-$ for $x > x_1$, as long as x is near x_1. At the relative minimum when $x = x_2$, $f'(x)$ goes from $-$ to $+$, and at the relative maximum when $x = x_3$, it again goes from $+$ to $-$. Thus *around relative maxima, f is increasing and then decreasing, and the reverse holds for relative minima.*

> **Rule 3**
>
> *If x_0 is in the domain of f and $f'(x)$ changes from positive to negative as x increases through x_0, then f has a relative maximum when $x = x_0$. If $f'(x)$ changes from negative to positive as x increases through x_0, then f has a relative minimum when $x = x_0$.*

From Rules 1–3, it should be clear that relative extrema may occur at points on the graph of f where $f'(x)$ is 0 or is not defined, for it is around these points that $f'(x)$ may change sign. These points are called *critical points* and their x-coordinates are called *critical values*. To find relative extrema, you should examine the signs of $f'(x)$ over the intervals determined by the critical values.

Definition

*If x_0 is in the domain of f and either $f'(x_0) = 0$ or $f'(x_0)$ is not defined, then x_0 is called a **critical value** of f. If x_0 is a critical value, then $(x_0, f(x_0))$ is called a **critical point.***

Pitfall

Not every critical value corresponds to a relative extremum. For example, if $y = f(x) = x^3$, then $f'(x) = 3x^2$. Since $f'(0) = 0$ and $f(0)$ is defined, 0 is a critical value. Now if $x < 0$, then $3x^2 > 0$. If $x > 0$, then $3x^2 > 0$. Since $f'(x)$ does not change sign, no relative maximum or minimum exists. Indeed, since $f'(x) \geq 0$ for all x, the graph of f never falls and f is said to be *nondecreasing* (see Fig. 12.20).

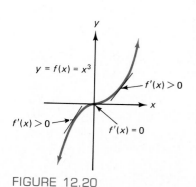

FIGURE 12.20

It is important to understand that not every value of x where $f'(x)$ does not exist is a critical value. For example, if $y = f(x) = 1/x^2$, then $f'(x) = -2/x^3$.

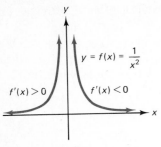

$$y = f(x) = \frac{1}{x^2}$$

$f'(x) > 0$ $f'(x) < 0$

FIGURE 12.21

Although $f'(x)$ is not defined when $x = 0$, 0 is not a critical value because 0 is not in the domain of f. That is, no y-value corresponds to $x = 0$. Thus a relative extrema cannot occur when $x = 0$. Nevertheless, the derivative may change sign around any x-value where $f'(x)$ is not defined, so such values are important in determining intervals over which f is increasing or decreasing. If $x < 0$, then $f'(x) = -2/x^3 > 0$. If $x > 0$, then $f'(x) = -2/x^3 < 0$. Thus f is increasing on $(-\infty, 0)$ and decreasing on $(0, \infty)$ (see Fig. 12.21).

From our discussions and the "Pitfall" above, you should realize that a critical value is only a "candidate" for a relative extremum. It may correspond to a relative maximum, a relative minimium, or neither.

Summarizing the results of this section, we have the *first-derivative test* for the relative extrema of $y = f(x)$:

First-Derivative Test for Relative Extrema

1. **Find $f'(x)$.**

2. **Determine all values of x where $f'(x) = 0$ or $f'(x)$ is not defined.**

3. **On the intervals suggested by the values in step 2, determine whether f is increasing ($f'(x) > 0$) or decreasing ($f'(x) < 0$).**

4. **For each critical value x_0, determine whether $f'(x)$ changes sign as x increases through x_0. There is a relative maximum when $x = x_0$ if $f'(x)$ changes from + to −, and a relative minimum if $f'(x)$ changes from − to +. If $f'(x)$ does not change sign, there is no relative extremum when $x = x_0$.**

EXAMPLE 1   *If $y = f(x) = x + \dfrac{4}{x + 1}$, use the first-derivative test to find when relative extrema occur.*

1. $f(x) = x + 4(x + 1)^{-1}$, so

$$f'(x) = 1 + 4(-1)(x + 1)^{-2} = 1 - \frac{4}{(x + 1)^2}$$

$$= \frac{(x + 1)^2 - 4}{(x + 1)^2} = \frac{x^2 + 2x - 3}{(x + 1)^2} = \frac{(x + 3)(x - 1)}{(x + 1)^2}.$$

2. Setting $f'(x) = 0$ gives $x = -3, 1$. The denominator of $f'(x)$ is 0 when x is -1, so $f'(-1)$ does not exist. The values -3 and 1 are critical values, but -1 is not because $f(-1)$ is not defined.

3. The three values in step 2 lead us to consider four intervals (Fig. 12.22).

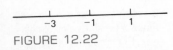

−3   −1   1

FIGURE 12.22

if $x < -3$, then $f'(x) = \dfrac{(-)(-)}{(+)} = +$, so f is increasing;

if $-3 < x < -1$, then $f'(x) = \dfrac{(+)(-)}{(+)} = -$, so f is decreasing;

$$\text{if } -1 < x < 1, \text{ then } f'(x) = \frac{(+)(-)}{(+)} = -, \text{ so } f \text{ is decreasing;}$$

$$\text{if } x > 1, \text{ then } f'(x) = \frac{(+)(+)}{(+)} = +, \text{ so } f \text{ is increasing (Fig. 12.23).}$$

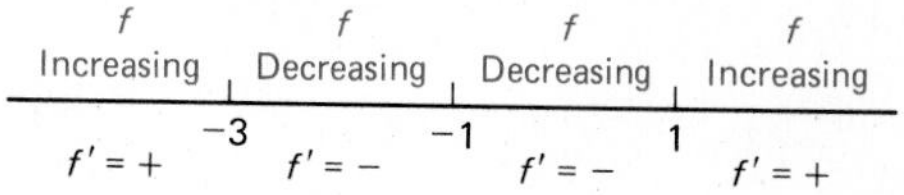

f	f	f	f
Increasing	Decreasing	Decreasing	Increasing

$$f' = + \qquad f' = - \qquad f' = - \qquad f' = +$$

with points at -3, -1, 1.

FIGURE 12.23

Thus f is increasing on the intervals $(-\infty, -3)$ and $(1, \infty)$, and is decreasing on $(-3, -1)$ and $(-1, 1)$.

4. When $x = -3$, there is a relative maximum since $f'(x)$ changes from $+$ to $-$. [This relative maximum value is $f(-3) = -3 + (4/-2) = -5$.] When $x = 1$, there is a relative minimum since $f'(x)$ changes from $-$ to $+$. We ignore $x = -1$ since -1 is not a critical value. The graph is shown in Fig. 12.24.

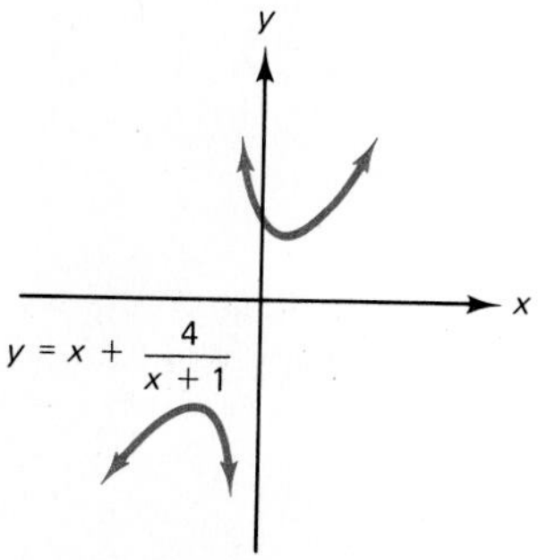

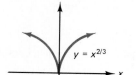

$$y = x + \frac{4}{x + 1}$$

FIGURE 12.24

EXAMPLE 2   Test $y = f(x) = x^{2/3}$ for relative extrema.

We have $f'(x) = \frac{2}{3}x^{-1/3} = 2/(3\sqrt[3]{x})$. When $x = 0$, then $f'(x)$ is not defined but $f(x)$ is defined. Thus 0 is a critical value. If $x < 0$, then $f'(x) < 0$. If $x > 0$, then $f'(x) > 0$. Therefore, there is a relative (as well as an absolute) minimum when $x = 0$ (see Fig. 12.25).

$$y = x^{2/3}$$

FIGURE 12.25

EXAMPLE 3   Test $y = f(x) = x^2 e^x$ for relative extrema.

By the product rule,

$$f'(x) = x^2 e^x + e^x(2x) = xe^x(x + 2).$$

Because e^x is always positive, $f'(x) = 0$ only for $x = 0, -2$. These are the only critical values of f. From the signs of $f'(x)$ given in Fig. 12.26, we conclude that there is a relative maximum when $x = -2$ and a relative minimum when $x = 0$.

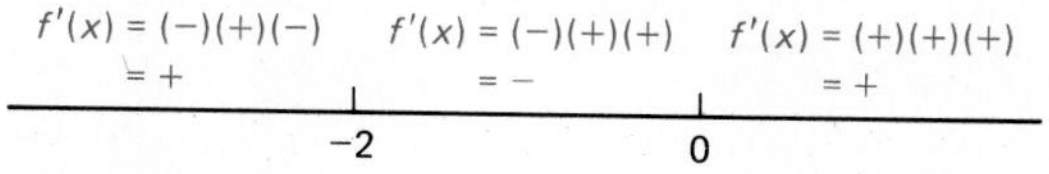

$$f'(x) = (-)(+)(-) \qquad f'(x) = (-)(+)(+) \qquad f'(x) = (+)(+)(+)$$
$$= + \qquad\qquad = - \qquad\qquad = +$$

with points at -2 and 0.

FIGURE 12.26

EXAMPLE 4   Sketch the graph of $y = f(x) = 2x^2 - x^4$.

Intercepts If $x = 0$, then $y = 0$. If $y = 0$, then

$$0 = 2x^2 - x^4 = x^2(2 - x^2) = x^2(\sqrt{2} + x)(\sqrt{2} - x),$$

and thus $x = 0, \pm\sqrt{2}$. The intercepts are $(0, 0)$ $(\sqrt{2}, 0)$, and $(-\sqrt{2}, 0)$.

Symmetry Testing for y-axis symmetry, we have

$$y = 2(-x)^2 - (-x)^4 \quad \text{or} \quad y = 2x^2 - x^4.$$

Since this is the original equation, there is y-axis symmetry. It can be shown that there is no x-axis symmetry and hence no symmetry about the origin.

Asymptotes No horizontal or vertical asymptotes exist, since f is a polynomial function.

First-Derivative Test

1. $y' = 4x - 4x^3 = 4x(1 - x^2) = 4x(1 + x)(1 - x)$.

2. Setting $y' = 0$ gives the critical values $x = 0, \pm 1$. The critical points are $(-1, 1)$, $(0, 0)$, and $(1, 1)$. The y-coordinates of these points were found by substituting $x = 0, \pm 1$ into the *original* equation, $y = 2x^2 - x^4$.

3. There are four intervals to consider in Fig. 12.27:

   if $x < -1$, then $y' = 4(-)(-)(+) = +$ and f is increasing;

   if $-1 < x < 0$, then $y' = 4(-)(+)(+) = -$ and f is decreasing;

   if $0 < x < 1$, then $y' = 4(+)(+)(+) = +$ and f is increasing;

   if $x > 1$, then $y' = 4(+)(+)(-) = -$ and f is decreasing (Fig. 12.28).

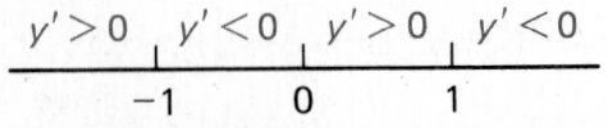

4. Relative maxima occur at $(-1, 1)$ and $(1, 1)$; a relative minimum occurs at $(0, 0)$.

Discussion In Fig. 12.29(a) we have plotted the horizontal tangents at the relative maximum and minimum points. We know the curve rises from the left, has a relative maximum, then falls, has a relative minimum, then rises to a relative maximum, and falls thereafter. A sketch is shown in Fig. 12.29(b).

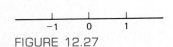

FIGURE 12.27

$y' > 0 \quad y' < 0 \quad y' > 0 \quad y' < 0$

FIGURE 12.28

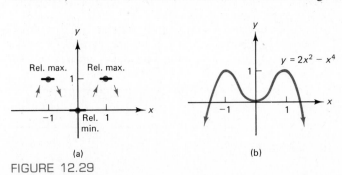

(a)   (b)

FIGURE 12.29

In Example 4 relative maxima, as well as absolute maxima, occur at $x = \pm 1$ [see Fig. 12.29(b)]. Although there is a relative minimum, there is no absolute minimum.

If the domain of a function is an interval that contains an endpoint, to determine *absolute* extrema we must not only examine the function for relative extrema, but we must also take into consideration the values of $f(x)$ at the endpoints. Although endpoints are not considered when we look for relative maxima or minima, they may yield *absolute* maxima or minima. Example 5 will illustrate.

EXAMPLE 5   *Find when extrema (relative and absolute) occur for $y = f(x) = x^2 - 4x + 5$ on the closed interval $[1, 4]$.*

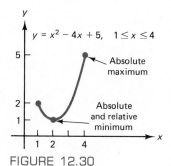

$y = x^2 - 4x + 5, \quad 1 \le x \le 4$

Absolute maximum

Absolute and relative minimum

FIGURE 12.30

1. $f'(x) = 2x - 4 = 2(x - 2)$.

2. Setting $f'(x) = 0$ gives the critical value $x = 2$.

3. The intervals to consider are when $x < 2$ and when $x > 2$. If $x < 2$, then $f'(x) < 0$ and f is decreasing; if $x > 2$, then $f'(x) > 0$ and f is increasing.

4. Thus there is a relative minimum when $x = 2$. It occurs on the graph at the point $(2, 1)$ (see Fig. 12.30).

5. Since f is decreasing for $x < 2$, an absolute maximum may *possibly* occur at the left-hand endpoint of the domain of f, that is, when $x = 1$. Similarly, since f is increasing for $x > 2$, an absolute maximum may *possibly* occur at the right-hand endpoint, that is, when $x = 4$. Testing the endpoints, we have $f(1) = 2$ and $f(4) = 5$. Noting that $f(4) > f(1)$, we conclude that an absolute maximum occurs when $x = 4$. When $x = 2$ there is an absolute, as well as a relative, minimum.

EXERCISE 12.3

In Problems **1–28** *determine when the function is increasing or decreasing and determine when relative maxima and minima occur. Do not sketch the graph.*

1. $y = x^2 + 2$.

2. $y = x^2 + 4x + 3$.

3. $y = x - x^2 + 2$.

4. $y = 4x - x^2$.

5. $y = -\dfrac{x^3}{3} - 2x^2 + 5x - 2$.

6. $y = 4x^3 - 3x^4$.

7. $y = x^4 - 2x^2$.

8. $y = -2 + 12x - x^3$.

9. $y = x^3 - 6x^2 + 9x$.

10. $y = x^3 - 6x^2 + 12x - 6$.

11. $y = 3x^5 - 5x^3$.

12. $y = 5x - x^5$.

13. $y = -x^5 - 5x^4 + 200$.

14. $y = 3x^4 - 4x^3 + 1$.

15. $y = \dfrac{1}{x - 1}$.

16. $y = \dfrac{3}{x}$.

17. $y = \dfrac{10}{\sqrt{x}}$.

18. $y = \dfrac{x}{x + 1}$.

19. $y = \dfrac{x^2}{1 - x}$.

20. $y = x + \dfrac{4}{x}$.

21. $y = (x + 2)^3(x - 5)^2$.

22. $y = x^2(x + 3)^4$.

23. $y = e^{-2x}$.

24. $y = x \ln x$.

25. $y = x^2 - 2 \ln x$.

26. $y = xe^x$.

27. $y = e^x + e^{-x}$.

28. $y = e^{-x^2}$.

In Problems **29–40,** *determine: intervals on which the functions are increasing or decreasing; relative maxima and minima; symmetry; horizontal and vertical asymptotes; those intercepts that can be obtained conveniently. Then sketch the graphs.*

29. $y = x^2 - 6x - 7$.

30. $y = 2x^2 - 5x - 12$.

31. $y = 3x - x^3$.

32. $y = x^4 - 16$.

33. $y = 2x^3 - 9x^2 + 12x$.

34. $y = x^3 - 9x^2 + 24x - 19$.

35. $y = x^4 + 4x^3 + 4x^2$.

36. $y = x^5 - \frac{5}{4}x^4$.

37. $y = \dfrac{x + 1}{x - 1}$.

38. $y = \dfrac{x^2}{x^2 + 1}$.

39. $y = \dfrac{x^2}{x + 3}$.

40. $y = x + \dfrac{1}{x}$.

In Problems **41–46,** *find when absolute maxima and minima occur for the given function on the given interval.*

41. $f(x) = x^2 - 2x + 3$, $[-1, 2]$.

42. $f(x) = -2x^2 - 6x + 5$, $[-2, 3]$.

43. $f(x) = \frac{1}{3}x^3 - x^2 - 3x + 1$, $[0, 2]$.

44. $f(x) = \frac{1}{4}x^4 - \frac{3}{2}x^2$, $[0, 1]$.

45. $f(x) = 4x^3 + 3x^2 - 18x + 3$, $[\frac{1}{2}, 3]$.

46. $f(x) = x^{4/3}$, $[-8, 8]$.

47. If $c_f = 25{,}000$ is a fixed cost function, show that the average fixed cost function $\overline{c}_f = c_f/q$ is a decreasing function for $q > 0$. Thus as output q increases, each unit's portion of fixed cost declines.

48. If $c = 4q - q^2 + 2q^3$ is a cost function, when is marginal cost increasing?

49. Given the demand function $p = 400 - 2q$, find when marginal revenue is increasing.

50. For the cost function $c = \sqrt{q}$, show that marginal and average costs are always decreasing for $q > 0$.

51. For a manufacturer's product, the revenue function is given by $r = 240q + 57q^2 - q^3$. Determine the output for maximum revenue.

52. Eswaran and Kotwal* consider agrarian economies in which there are two types of workers, permanent and casual. Permanent workers are employed on long-term contracts and may receive benefits such as holiday gifts and emergency aid. Casual workers are hired on a daily basis and perform routine and menial tasks such as weeding, harvesting, and threshing. The difference z in the present value cost of hiring a permanent worker over that of hiring a casual worker is given by

$$z = (1 + b)w_p - bw_c,$$

where w_p and w_c are wage rates for permanent labor and casual labor, respectively, b is a positive constant, and w_p is a function of w_c. (a) Show that

$$\frac{dz}{dw_c} = (1 + b)\left[\frac{dw_p}{dw_c} - \frac{b}{1 + b}\right].$$

(b) If $dw_p/dw_c < b/(1 + b)$, show that z is a decreasing function of w_c.

53. In Shonle's discussion of thermal pollution,† the efficiency E of a power plant is given by

$$E = 0.71\left(1 - \frac{T_c}{T_h}\right),$$

where T_c and T_h are the respective absolute temperatures of the hotter and colder reservoirs. Assume that T_c is a positive constant and that T_h is positive. Using calculus, show that as T_h increases, the efficiency increases.

* M. Eswaran and A. Kotwal, "A Theory of Two-Tier Labor Markets in Agrarian Economies," *The American Economic Review*, 75, no. 1 (1985), 162–77.

† J. I. Shonle, *Environmental Applications of General Physics* (Reading, Mass.: Addison-Wesley Publishing Company, Inc. 1975.

54. In a discussion of the pricing of local telephone service, Renshaw* determines that total revenue r is given by

$$r = 2F + \left(1 - \frac{a}{b}\right)p - p^2 + \frac{a^2}{b},$$

where p is an indexed price per call, and a, b, and F are constants. Determine the value of p that maximizes revenue.

55. In his model for storage and shipping costs of materials for a manufacturing process, Lancaster† derives the following cost function:

$$C(k) = 100\left(100 + 9k + \frac{144}{k}\right), \qquad 1 \le k \le 100,$$

where $C(k)$ is the total cost (in dollars) of storage and transportation for 100 days of operation if a load of k tons of material is moved every k days. (a) Find $C(1)$. (b) For what value of k does $C(k)$ have a minimum? (c) What is the minimum value?

12.4 CONCAVITY

You have seen that the first derivative provides much information for sketching curves. It is used to determine when a function is increasing or decreasing and to locate relative maxima and minima. However, to be sure we know the true shape of a curve, we may need more information. For example, consider the curve $y = f(x) = x^2$. Since $f'(x) = 2x$, $x = 0$ is a critical value. If $x < 0$, then $f'(x) < 0$ and f is decreasing; if $x > 0$, then $f'(x) > 0$ and f is increasing. Thus there is a relative minimum when $x = 0$. In Figure 12.31, both curves meet the preceding conditions. But which one truly describes the curve? This question will easily be settled by using the second derivative and the notion of *concavity*.

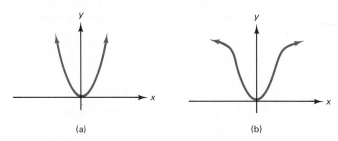

(a)   (b)

FIGURE 12.31

In Fig. 12.32 note that each curve $y = f(x)$ "bends" (or opens) upward. This means that if tangent lines are drawn to each curve, the curves lie above them. Moreover, the slopes of the tangent lines *increase* in value as x increases. In part (a) the slopes go from small positive values to larger values; in part (b) they are negative and approaching zero (thus increasing); in part (c) they pass from negative values to positive values. Since $f'(x)$ gives the slope at a point, an

* E. Renshaw, "A Note of Equity and Efficiency in the Pricing of Local Telephone Services," *The American Economic Review*, 75, no. 3 (1985), 515–18.

† P. Lancaster, *Mathematics: Models of the Real World* (Englewood Cliffs, N.J.: Prentice-Hall, Inc., 1976).

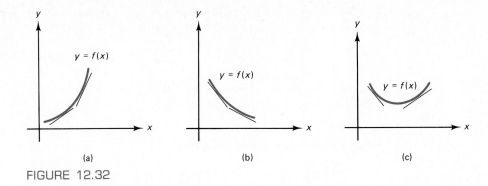

FIGURE 12.32

increasing slope means that f' must be an increasing function. To describe this, each curve (or function f) is said to be *concave up*. In Fig. 12.33 it can be seen that each curve lies below the tangent lines and the curves are bending downward. As x increases, the slopes of the tangent lines are *decreasing*. Thus f' must be a decreasing function here, and we say that f is *concave down*.

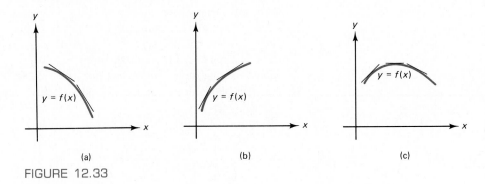

FIGURE 12.33

Definition
*A function f is said to be **concave up** [**concave down**] on an interval I if f' is increasing [decreasing] on I.*

Remember: If f is concave up on an interval I, then geometrically its graph is bending upward there. If f is concave down, then its graph is bending downward.

Pitfall

Concavity relates to whether f', not f, is increasing or decreasing. In Fig. 12.32(b), note that f is concave up and decreasing, but in Fig. 12.33(a), f is concave down and decreasing.

Since f' is increasing when its derivative $f''(x)$ is positive and f' is decreasing when $f''(x)$ is negative, we can state the following rule:

> **Rule 4**
> *If $f''(x) > 0$ for all x in an interval, then f is concave up on I. If $f''(x) < 0$ for all x in I, then f is concave down on I.*

A function f is also said to be concave up at a *point* x_0 if there exists an open interval around x_0 on which f is concave up. In fact, for the functions that

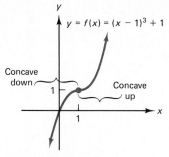

FIGURE 12.34

we shall consider, if $f''(x_0) > 0$, then f is concave up at x_0.* Similarly, f is concave down at x_0 if $f''(x_0) < 0$.

EXAMPLE 1 *Test for concavity.*

a. $y = f(x) = (x - 1)^3 + 1$.

To apply Rule 4, we must examine the signs of y''. Now, $y' = 3(x - 1)^2$, so $y'' = 6(x - 1)$. Thus f is concave up when $6(x - 1) > 0$; that is, when $x > 1$. And f is concave down when $6(x - 1) < 0$; that is, when $x < 1$ (see Fig. 12.34).

b. $y = x^2$.

We have $y' = 2x$ and $y'' = 2$. Because y'' is always positive, the graph of $y = x^2$ must always be concave up, as in Fig. 12.31(a). The graph cannot appear as in Fig. 12.31(b), for that curve is sometimes concave down.

A point on a graph, such as $(1, 1)$ in Fig. 12.34, where concavity changes from downward to upward, or vice versa, is called an *inflection point*. Around such a point the sign of $f''(x)$ must go from $-$ to $+$ or from $+$ to $-$.

Definition

*A function f has an **inflection point** when $x = x_0$ if and only if x_0 is in the domain of f and f changes concavity at x_0.*

To test a function for concavity and inflection points, first find the values of x where $f''(x)$ is 0 or undefined. These values of x determine intervals. On each interval determine whether $f''(x) > 0$ (f is concave up) or $f''(x) < 0$ (f is concave down). If $f''(x)$ is 0 or undefined at $x = x_0$, and x_0 also is in the domain of f, then f has an inflection point at $x = x_0$ provided that concavity changes around x_0.

EXAMPLE 2 *Test $y = 6x^4 - 8x^3 + 1$ for concavity and inflection points.*

We have $y' = 24x^3 - 24x^2$, so

$$y'' = 72x^2 - 48x = 24x(3x - 2).$$

FIGURE 12.35

To find when $y'' = 0$, we set each factor in y'' equal to 0. This gives $x = 0, \frac{2}{3}$. Because y'' is never undefined, there are three intervals to consider (Fig. 12.35):

if $x < 0$, then $y'' = 24(-)(-) = +$, so the curve is concave up;
if $0 < x < \frac{2}{3}$, then $y'' = 24(+)(-) = -$, so the curve is concave down;
if $x > \frac{2}{3}$, then $y'' = 24(+)(+) = +$, so the curve is concave up (see Fig. 12.36).

Concave up	Concave down	Concave up
$y'' = +$	$\quad 0 \quad y'' = -\quad \frac{2}{3} \quad$	$y'' = +$

FIGURE 12.36

Since concavity changes at $x = 0$ and $x = \frac{2}{3}$, which are in the domain of y, inflection points occur there (see Fig. 12.37). In summary, the curve is concave

---

* This is guaranteed for functions f such that f'' is continuous.

up on $(-\infty, 0)$ and $(\frac{2}{3}, \infty)$ and is concave down on $(0, \frac{2}{3})$. Inflection points occur when $x = 0$ or $x = \frac{2}{3}$. These points are $(0, 1)$ and $(\frac{2}{3}, -\frac{5}{27})$.

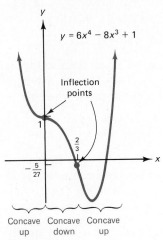

FIGURE 12.37

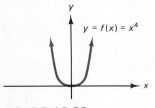

FIGURE 12.38

Pitfall

If $f''(x_0) = 0$, this does not prove that the graph of f has an inflection point when $x = x_0$. For example, if $f(x) = x^4$, then $f''(x) = 12x^2$ and $f''(0) = 0$. But $x < 0$ implies that $f''(x) > 0$, and $x > 0$ implies $f''(x) > 0$. Thus concavity does not change and there are no inflection points (see Fig. 12.38).

EXAMPLE 3   *Sketch the graph of $y = 2x^3 - 9x^2 + 12x$.*

Intercepts   If $x = 0$, then $y = 0$. Setting $y = 0$ gives $0 = x(2x^2 - 9x + 12)$. Clearly $x = 0$, and using the quadratic formula on $2x^2 - 9x + 12 = 0$ gives no real roots. Thus the only intercept is $(0, 0)$.

Symmetry   None.

Asymptotes   Because y is a polynomial function, there are no asymptotes.

Maxima and Minima   Letting $y = f(x)$, we have

$$f'(x) = 6x^2 - 18x + 12 = 6(x^2 - 3x + 2) = 6(x - 1)(x - 2).$$

The critical values are $x = 1, 2$ (see Fig. 12.39).

If $x < 1$, then $f'(x) = 6(-)(-) = +$, so f is increasing;

if $1 < x < 2$, then $f'(x) = 6(+)(-) = -$, so f is decreasing;

if $x > 2$, then $f'(x) = 6(+)(+) = +$, so f is increasing (see Fig. 12.40).

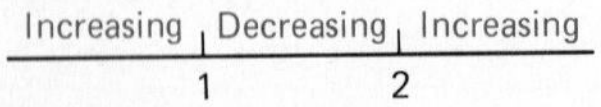

There is a relative maximum when $x = 1$ and a relative minimum when $x = 2$.

Concavity

$$f''(x) = 12x - 18 = 6(2x - 3).$$

FIGURE 12.39

FIGURE 12.40

FIGURE 12.41

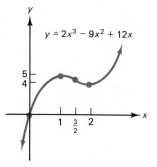

FIGURE 12.42

Setting $f''(x) = 0$ gives a possible inflection point at $x = \frac{3}{2}$. When $x < \frac{3}{2}$, then $f''(x) < 0$ and f is concave down. When $x > \frac{3}{2}$, then $f''(x) > 0$ and f is concave up (see Fig. 12.41).

Since concavity changes, there is an inflection point when $x = \frac{3}{2}$.

Discussion   We now find the coordinates of the important points on the graph (and any other points if there is doubt as to the behavior of the curve).

x	0	1	$\frac{3}{2}$	2
y	0	5	$\frac{9}{2}$	4

As x increases, the function is first concave down and increases to a relative maximum at $(1, 5)$; it then decreases to $(\frac{3}{2}, \frac{9}{2})$; it then becomes concave up but continues to decrease until it reaches a relative minimum at $(2, 4)$; thereafter it increases and is still concave up (see Fig. 12.42).

EXAMPLE 4   *Sketch the graph of* $y = \dfrac{1}{4 - x^2}$.

Intercepts   When $x = 0$, then $y = \frac{1}{4}$. If $y = 0$, then $0 = 1/(4 - x^2)$, which has no solution. Thus $(0, \frac{1}{4})$ is the only intercept.

Symmetry   There is symmetry only about the y-axis: replacing x by $-x$ gives

$$y = \frac{1}{4 - (-x)^2} \quad \text{or} \quad y = \frac{1}{4 - x^2},$$

which is the same as the original equation.

Asymptotes   Testing for horizontal asymptotes, we have

$$\lim_{x \to \infty} \frac{1}{4 - x^2} = \lim_{x \to \infty} \frac{1}{-x^2} = -\lim_{x \to \infty} \frac{1}{x^2} = 0.$$

Similarly,

$$\lim_{x \to -\infty} \frac{1}{4 - x^2} = 0.$$

Thus $y = 0$ (the x-axis) is a horizontal asymptote. Since the denominator of $1/(4 - x^2)$ is 0 when $x = \pm 2$, and the numerator is not 0 for these values of x, the lines $x = 2$ and $x = -2$ are vertical asymptotes.

Maxima and Minima   Since $y = (4 - x^2)^{-1}$,

$$y' = -1(4 - x^2)^{-2}(-2x) = \frac{2x}{(4 - x^2)^2}.$$

We see that y' is 0 when $x = 0$ and y' is undefined when $x = \pm 2$. However, only 0 is a critical value. If $x < -2$, then $y' < 0$; if $-2 < x < 0$, then $y' < 0$; if $0 < x < 2$, then $y' > 0$; if $x > 2$, then $y' > 0$. The function is decreasing on

$(-\infty, -2)$ and $(-2, 0)$ and increasing on $(0, 2)$ and $(2, \infty)$ (see Fig. 12.43). There is a relative minimum when $x = 0$.

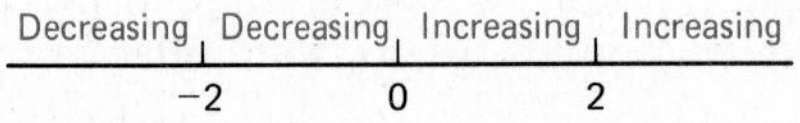

Decreasing	Decreasing	Increasing	Increasing
-2	0	2	

FIGURE 12.43

Concavity

$$y'' = \frac{(4 - x^2)^2(2) - (2x)2(4 - x^2)(-2x)}{(4 - x^2)^4} = \frac{2(4 - x^2)(4 + 3x^2)}{(4 - x^2)^4}$$

$$= \frac{8 + 6x^2}{(4 - x^2)^3}.$$

Setting $y'' = 0$, we get no real roots. However, y'' is undefined when $x = \pm 2$. Thus concavity may change around these values. If $x < -2$, then $y'' < 0$; if $-2 < x < 2$, then $y'' > 0$; if $x > 2$, then $y'' < 0$. The graph is concave up on $(-2, 2)$ and concave down on $(-\infty, -2)$ and $(2, \infty)$ (see Fig. 12.44). Although concavity changes around $x = \pm 2$, these values of x are not in the domain of the original function and hence do not give inflection points.

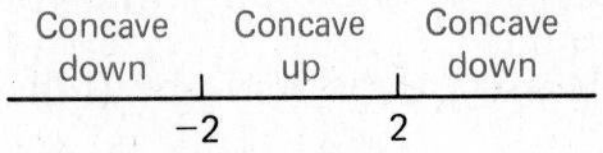

Concave down	Concave up	Concave down
-2		2

FIGURE 12.44

Discussion   Plotting the points in the table in Fig. 12.45, some arbitrarily chosen, and using the information above, we get the indicated graph. Due to symmetry, our table has only $x \geq 0$.

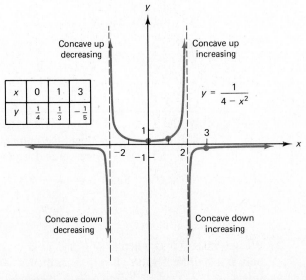

x	0	1	3
y	$\frac{1}{4}$	$\frac{1}{3}$	$-\frac{1}{5}$

$$y = \frac{1}{4 - x^2}$$

FIGURE 12.45

EXAMPLE 5   *Sketch the graph of* $y = \dfrac{4x}{x^2 + 1}$.

Intercepts   When $x = 0$, then $y = 0$; when $y = 0$, then $x = 0$. Thus $(0, 0)$ is the only intercept.

Symmetry   There is symmetry only about the origin: replacing x by $-x$ and y by $-y$ gives

$$-y = \frac{4(-x)}{(-x)^2 + 1} \qquad \text{or} \qquad y = \frac{4x}{x^2 + 1},$$

which is the same as the original equation.

Asymptotes   Testing for horizontal asymptotes, we have

$$\lim_{x \to \infty} \frac{4x}{x^2 + 1} = \lim_{x \to \infty} \frac{4x}{x^2} = \lim_{x \to \infty} \frac{4}{x} = 0,$$

and similarly,

$$\lim_{x \to -\infty} \frac{4x}{x^2 + 1} = 0.$$

Thus $y = 0$ (the x-axis) is a horizontal asymptote. Since the denominator of $4x/(x^2 + 1)$ is never 0, there is no vertical asymptote.

Maxima and Minima   Letting $y = f(x)$, we have

$$f'(x) = \frac{(x^2 + 1)(4) - 4x(2x)}{(x^2 + 1)^2} = \frac{4 - 4x^2}{(x^2 + 1)^2} = \frac{4(1 + x)(1 - x)}{(x^2 + 1)^2}.$$

From $f'(x)$, the critical values are $x = \pm 1$.

If $x < -1$, then $f'(x) = \dfrac{4(-)(+)}{(+)} = (-)$ and f is decreasing;

if $-1 < x < 1$, then $f'(x) = \dfrac{4(+)(+)}{(+)} = (+)$ and f is increasing;

if $x > 1$, then $f'(x) = \dfrac{4(+)(-)}{(+)} = (-)$ and f is decreasing (see Fig. 12.46).

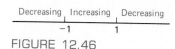

Decreasing Increasing Decreasing

FIGURE 12.46

There is a relative minimum when $x = -1$ and a relative maximum when $x = 1$.

Concavity   Since $f'(x) = \dfrac{4 - 4x^2}{(x^2 + 1)^2}$,

$$f''(x) = \frac{(x^2 + 1)^2(-8x) - (4 - 4x^2)(2)(x^2 + 1)(2x)}{(x^2 + 1)^4}$$

$$= \frac{8x(x^2 + 1)(x^2 - 3)}{(x^2 + 1)^4} = \frac{8x(x + \sqrt{3})(x - \sqrt{3})}{(x^2 + 1)^3}.$$

Setting $f''(x) = 0$, we see that the possible points of inflection are when $x = \pm\sqrt{3}, 0$.

If $x < -\sqrt{3}$, then $f''(x) = \dfrac{8(-)(-)(-)}{(+)} = (-)$ and f is concave down;

if $-\sqrt{3} < x < 0$, then $f''(x) = \dfrac{8(-)(+)(-)}{(+)} = (+)$ and f is concave up;

if $0 < x < \sqrt{3}$, then $f''(x) = \dfrac{8(+)(+)(-)}{(+)} = (-)$ and f is concave down;

if $x > \sqrt{3}$, then $f''(x) = \dfrac{8(+)(+)(+)}{(+)} = (+)$ and f is concave up (see Fig. 12.47).

Concave Concave Concave Concave
down   up   down   up

$-\sqrt{3}$ 0 $\sqrt{3}$

FIGURE 12.47

Inflection points occur when $x = 0, \pm\sqrt{3}$.

Discussion After consideration of all the above information, the graph of $y = 4x/(x^2 + 1)$ is given in Fig. 12.48 together with a table of important points.

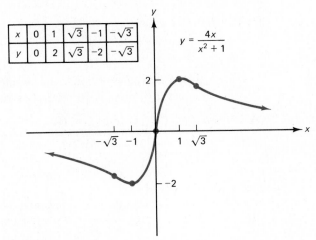

x	0	1	$\sqrt{3}$	-1	$-\sqrt{3}$
y	0	2	$\sqrt{3}$	-2	$-\sqrt{3}$

$y = \dfrac{4x}{x^2 + 1}$

FIGURE 12.48

EXERCISE 12.4

In Problems **1–14,** *determine concavity and the x-values where points of inflection occur. Do not sketch the graphs.*

1. $y = -2x^2 + 4x$.

2. $y = 3x^2 - 6x + 5$.

3. $y = 4x^3 + 12x^2 - 12x$.

4. $y = x^3 - 6x^2 + 9x + 1$.

5. $y = x^4 - 6x^2 + 5x - 6$.

6. $y = -\dfrac{x^4}{4} + \dfrac{9x^2}{2} + 2x$.

7. $y = \dfrac{x + 1}{x - 1}$.

8. $y = x + \dfrac{1}{x}$.

9. $y = \dfrac{x^2}{x^2 + 1}$.

10. $y = \dfrac{x^2}{x + 3}$.

11. $y = e^x$.

12. $y = e^x - e^{-x}$.

13. $y = xe^x$.

14. $y = xe^{-x}$.

In Problems **15–42,** *sketch each curve. Determine: intervals on which the function is increasing, decreasing, concave up, concave down; relative maxima and minima; inflection points; symmetry; horizontal and vertical asymptotes; those intercepts that can be obtained conveniently.*

15. $y = x^2 + 4x + 3$.

16. $y = x^2 + 2$.

17. $y = 4x - x^2$.

18. $y = x - x^2 + 2$.

19. $y = x^3 - 9x^2 + 24x - 19$.

20. $y = 3x - x^3$.

21. $y = \dfrac{x^3}{3} - 4x$.

22. $y = x^3 - 6x^2 + 9x$.

23. $y = x^3 - 3x^2 + 3x - 3$.

24. $y = 2x^3 - 9x^2 + 12x$.

25. $y = 4x^3 - 3x^4$.

26. $y = -\dfrac{x^3}{3} - 2x^2 + 5x - 2$.

27. $y = -2 + 12x - x^3$.

28. $y = (3 + 2x)^3$.

29. $y = x^3 - 6x^2 + 12x - 6$.

30. $y = \dfrac{x^5}{100} - \dfrac{x^4}{20}$.

31. $y = 5x - x^5$.

32. $y = x(1 - x)^3$.

33. $y = 3x^4 - 4x^3 + 1$.

34. $y = 3x^5 - 5x^3$.

35. $y = \dfrac{3}{x}$.

36. $y = \dfrac{1}{x - 1}$.

37. $y = \dfrac{x}{x + 1}$.

38. $y = \dfrac{10}{\sqrt{x}}$.

39. $y = x^2 + \dfrac{1}{x^2}$.

40. $y = \dfrac{x^2}{1 - x}$.

41. $y = 4x^2 - x^4$.

42. $y = x^4 - 2x^2$.

43. Show that the graph of the demand equation $p = 100/(q + 2)$ is decreasing and concave up for $q > 0$.

44. For the cost function $c = 3q^2 + 5q + 6$, show that the graph of the average cost function $\bar{c}$ is always concave up for $q > 0$.

45. The number of species of plants on a plot may depend on the size of the plot. For example, in Fig. 12.49 we

see that on 1-m^2 plots there are three species (A, B, and C on the left plot; A, B, and D on the right plot), and on a 2-m^2 plot there are four species (A, B, C, and D).

In a study of rooted plants in a certain geographic region,* it was determined that the average number of species, S, occurring on plots of size A (in square meters) is given by

$$S = f(A) = 12\sqrt[4]{A}, \qquad 0 \le A \le 625.$$

Sketch the graph of f.

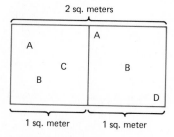

2 sq. meters

1 sq. meter 1 sq. meter

FIGURE 12.49

---

* Adapted from R. W. Poole, *An Introduction to Quantitative Ecology* (New York: McGraw-Hill Book Company, 1974).

46. In a discussion of an inferior good, Persky* considers a function of the form

$$g(x) = e^{(U_0/A)}e^{-x^2/(2A)},$$

where x is a quantity of a good, U_0 is a constant that represents utility, and A is a positive constant. Persky claims that the graph of g is concave down for $x < \sqrt{A}$ and concave up for $x > \sqrt{A}$. Verify this.

47. When a deep-sea diver undergoes decompression, or a pilot climbs to a high altitude, nitrogen may bubble out of the blood, causing what is commonly called the *bends*. Suppose the percentage P of people who suffer effects of the bends at an altitude of h thousand feet is given by†

$$P = \frac{100}{1 + 100,000e^{-0.36h}}.$$

Is P an increasing function of h?

48. In a study of the effects of food deprivation on hunger,‡ an insect was fed until its appetite was completely satisfied. Then it was deprived food for t hours (deprivation period). At the end of this period, the insect was refed until its appetite was again completely satisfied. The weight H (in grams) of the food that was consumed at this time was statistically found to be a function of t, where

$$H = 1.00[1 - e^{-(0.0464t + 0.0670)}].$$

Here H is a measure of hunger. Show that H is increasing with respect to t and is concave down.

49. In an experiment on dispersal of a particular insect,§ a large number of insects are placed at a release point in an open field. Surrounding this point are traps that are placed in a concentric circular arrangement at a distance of 1 m, 2 m, 3 m, and so on, from the release point. Twenty-four hours after the insects are released, the number of insects in each trap are counted. It is determined that at a distance of r meters from the release point, the average number of insects contained in a trap is n, where

$$n = f(r) = 0.1 \ln(r) + \frac{7}{r} - 0.8, \qquad 1 \le r \le 10.$$

(a) Show that the graph of f is always falling and concave up. (b) Sketch the graph of f. (c) When $r = 5$, at what rate is the average number of insects in a trap decreasing with respect to distance?

50. In a psychological experiment involving conditioned response,‖ subjects listened to four tones, denoted 0, 1, 2, and 3. Initially, the subjects were conditioned to tone 0 by receiving a shock whenever this tone was heard. Later, when each of the four tones (stimuli) were heard without shocks, the subjects' responses were recorded by means of a tracking device that measures galvanic skin reaction. The average response to each stimulus (without shock) was determined, and the results were plotted on a coordinate plane where the x- and y-axes represent the stimuli (0, 1, 2, 3) and the average galvanic responses, respectively. It was determined that the points fit a curve that is approximated by the graph of $y = 12.5 + 5.8(0.42)^x$. Show that this function is decreasing and concave up.

* A. L. Persky, "An Inferior Good and a Novel Indifference Map," *The American Economist*, XXIX, no. 1 (1985), 67–69.

† Adapted from G. E. Folk, Jr., *Textbook of Environmental Physiology*, 2nd ed. (Philadelphia: Lea & Febiger, 1974).

‡ C. S. Holling, "The Functional Response of Invertebrate Predators to Prey Density," *Memoirs of the Entomological Society of Canada*, no. 48 (1966).

§ Adapted from R. W. Poole, *An Introduction to Quantitative Ecology* (New York: McGraw-Hill Book Company, 1974).

‖ Adapted from C. I. Hovland, "The Generalization of Conditioned Responses: I. The Sensory Generalization of Conditioned Responses with Varying Frequencies of Tone," *Journal of General Psychology*, 17 (1937), 125–48.

12.5 THE SECOND-DERIVATIVE TEST

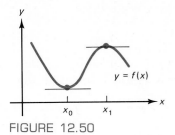

FIGURE 12.50

The second derivative may be used to test certain critical values for relative extrema. Observe in Fig. 12.50 that when $x = x_0$ there is a horizontal tangent; that is, $f'(x_0) = 0$. This implies the possibility of a relative maximum or minimum. Also, we see that the curve is bending upward there [that is, $f''(x_0) > 0$]. This leads us to conclude that there is a relative minimum at x_0. On the other hand, $f'(x_1) = 0$ but the curve is bending downward at x_1 (that is, $f''(x_1) < 0$). From this we conclude that a relative maximum exists there. This technique of examining the second derivative at points where the first derivative is 0 is called the *second-derivative test* for relative extrema.

Second-Derivative Test for Relative Extrema
Suppose $f'(x_0) = 0$.

If $f''(x_0) < 0$, then f has a relative maximum at x_0;

if $f''(x_0) > 0$, then f has a relative minimum at x_0.

We emphasize that **the second-derivative test does *not* apply when $f'(x_0) = 0$ and $f''(x_0) = 0$.** Under these conditions, at x_0 there may be a relative maximum, a relative minimum, or neither. In such cases, the first-derivative test should be used to analyze what is happening at x_0.

EXAMPLE 1   *Test the following for relative maxima and minima. Use the second-derivative test if possible.*

a. $y = 18x - \frac{2}{3}x^3$.

$$y' = 18 - 2x^2 = 2(9 - x^2) = 2(3 + x)(3 - x).$$
$$y'' = -4x.$$

Solving $y' = 0$ gives critical values $x = \pm 3$. If $x = 3$, then $y'' = -4(3) = -12 < 0$. So there is a relative maximum when $x = 3$. If $x = -3$, then $y'' = -4(-3) = 12 > 0$, so there is a relative minimum when $x = -3$ (see Fig. 12.18).

b. $y = 6x^4 - 8x^3 + 1$.

$$y' = 24x^3 - 24x^2 = 24x^2(x - 1).$$
$$y'' = 72x^2 - 48x.$$

Solving $y' = 0$ gives the critical values $x = 0, 1$. If $x = 1$, then $y'' > 0$, so there is a relative minimum when $x = 1$. If $x = 0$, then $y'' = 0$ and the second-derivative test does not apply. We now turn to the first-derivative test to analyze what is happening at 0. If $x < 0$, then $y' < 0$; if $0 < x < 1$, then $y' < 0$. Thus no relative maximum or minimum exists when $x = 0$ (see Fig. 12.37).

c. $y = x^4$.

$$y' = 4x^3.$$
$$y'' = 12x^2.$$

Solving $y' = 0$ gives the critical value $x = 0$. If $x = 0$, then $y'' = 0$ and the second-derivative test does not apply. Since $y' < 0$ for $x < 0$, and $y' > 0$ for $x > 0$, by the first-derivative test there is a relative minimum when $x = 0$ (see Fig. 12.38).

If a continuous function has *exactly one* relative extremum on an interval, it can be shown that the relative extremum must also be an *absolute* extremum on the interval. To illustrate, in Example 1(c), $y = x^4$ has a relative minimum when $x = 0$ and there are no other relative extrema. Since $y = x^4$ is continuous, this relative minimum is also an absolute minimum for the function.

EXERCISE 12.5

In Problems 1–10, test for relative maxima and minima. Use the second-derivative test if possible. In Problems 1–4, state whether the relative extrema are also absolute extrema.

1. $y = x^2 - 5x + 6$.

2. $y = -2x^2 + 6x + 12$.

3. $y = -4x^2 + 2x - 8$.

4. $y = 3x^2 - 5x + 6$.

5. $y = x^3 - 27x + 1$.

6. $y = x^3 - 12x + 1$.

7. $y = -x^3 + 3x^2 + 1$.

8. $y = x^4 - 2x^2 + 4$.

9. $y = 2x^4 + 2$.

10. $y = -x^7$.

12.6 REVIEW

Important Terms

Section 12.1	x-intercept y-intercept x-axis symmetry y-axis symmetry symmetry about origin
Section 12.2	vertical asymptote horizontal asymptote vertical asymptote rule for rational functions
Section 12.3	increasing function decreasing function relative maximum relative minimum relative extrema absolute extrema critical value critical point first-derivative test
Section 12.4	concave up concave down inflection point
Section 12.5	second-derivative text

Summary

There are many aids that can be used in sketching the graph of an equation. One is intercepts—points where a curve intersects the axes. The x-intercepts are of the form $(x, 0)$ and are found by setting $y = 0$ in the equation and solving for x. The y-intercepts are of the form $(0, y)$ and are found by setting $x = 0$ and solving for y.

If the graph of an equation has symmetry, the mirror-image effect allows us to sketch the graph by plotting fewer points than would otherwise be needed. The tests for symmetry are:

Symmetry about x-axis	Replace y by $-y$ in given equation. Symmetric if equivalent equation is obtained.
Symmetry about y-axis	Replace x by $-x$ in given equation. Symmetric if equivalent equation is obtained.
Symmetry about origin	Replace x by $-x$ and y by $-y$ in given equation. Symmetric if equivalent equation is obtained.

Asymptotes are also aids in curve sketching. Graphs "explode" near vertical asymptotes, and they "settle down" near horizontal asymptotes. The line $x = a$ is a vertical asymptote for the graph of a function f if $\lim f(x) = \infty$ or $-\infty$ as x approaches a from the right ($x \to a^+$) or from the left ($x \to a^-$). For the case of a rational function, $f(x) = P(x)/Q(x)$, we can find vertical asymptotes without evaluating limits. If $Q(a) = 0$ but $P(a) \neq 0$, then the line $x = a$ is a vertical asymptote. The line $y = b$ is a horizontal asymptote for the graph of a function f if either

$$\lim_{x \to \infty} f(x) = b \quad \text{or} \quad \lim_{x \to -\infty} f(x) = b.$$

In particular, a polynomial function has neither a horizontal nor a vertical asymptote. Moreover, a rational function whose numerator has degree greater than that of the denominator does not have a horizontal asymptote.

The first derivative is used to determine when a function is increasing or decreasing and to locate relative maxima and minima. If $f'(x)$ is positive throughout an interval, then over that interval f is increasing and its graph rises (from left to right). If $f'(x)$ is negative throughout an interval, then over that interval f is decreasing and its graph is falling.

A point (x_0, y_0) on the graph at which $f'(x)$ is 0 or is not defined is a candidate for a relative extremum, and x_0 is called a critical value. For a relative extremum to occur at x_0, the first derivative must change sign around x_0. The following procedure is the first-derivative test for the relative extrema of $y = f(x)$:

First-Derivative Test for Relative Extrema

1. Find $f'(x)$.

2. Determine all values of x where $f'(x) = 0$ or $f'(x)$ is not defined.

3. On the intervals suggested by the values in step 2, determine whether f is increasing ($f'(x) > 0$) or decreasing ($f'(x) < 0$).

4. For each critical value x_0, determine whether $f'(x)$ changes sign as x increases through x_0. There is a relative maximum when $x = x_0$ if $f'(x)$ changes from $+$ to $-$, and a relative minimum if $f'(x)$ changes from $-$ to $+$. If $f'(x)$ does not change sign, there is no relative extremum when $x = x_0$.

If the domain of f is a closed interval, then to locate absolute extrema we not only consider where relative extrema occur, but also examine $f(x)$ at the endpoints of the interval.

The second derivative is used to determine concavity and points of inflection. If $f''(x) > 0$ throughout an interval, then f is concave up over that interval and its graph bends upward. If $f''(x) < 0$ over an interval, then throughout that interval f is concave down and its graph bends downward. A point on the graph where concavity changes is an inflection point. The point (x_0, y_0) on the graph is a possible point of inflection if $f''(x_0)$ is 0 or is not defined.

The second derivative also provides a means for testing certain critical values for relative extrema.

Second-Derivative Test for Relative Extrema

Suppose $f'(x_0) = 0$.

If $f''(x_0) < 0$, then f has a relative maximum at x_0;

if $f''(x_0) > 0$, then f has a relative minimum at x_0.

Review Problems

In Problems **1** *and* **2**, *find intercepts and test for symmetry.*

1. $y = 2x - 3x^3$.

2. $\dfrac{xy^2}{x^2 + 1} = 4$.

In Problems **3** *and* **4**, *find horizontal and vertical asymptotes.*

3. $y = \dfrac{3x^2}{x^2 - 16}$.

4. $y = \dfrac{x + 1}{4x - 2x^2}$.

In Problems **5** *and* **6**, *find critical values.*

5. $f(x) = \dfrac{x^2}{2 - x}$.

6. $f(x) = (x - 1)^2(x + 6)^4$.

In Problems **7** *and* **8**, *find intervals on which the function is increasing or decreasing.*

7. $f(x) = -x^3 + 6x^2 - 9x$.

8. $f(x) = \dfrac{x^2}{(x + 1)^2}$.

In Problems **9** *and* **10**, *find intervals on which the function is concave or concave down.*

9. $f(x) = x^4 - x^3 - 14$.

10. $f(x) = \dfrac{x + 1}{x - 1}$.

In Problems **11** *and* **12**, *test for relative extrema.*

11. $f(x) = \dfrac{x^6}{6} + \dfrac{x^3}{3}$.

12. $f(x) = \dfrac{x^2}{x^2 - 4}$.

In Problems **13** *and* **14**, *find the x-values where inflection points occur.*

13. $y = x^5 - 5x^4 + 3x$.

14. $y = \dfrac{x^2 + 1}{x}$.

In Problems **15** *and* **16**, *test for absolute extrema on the given interval.*

15. $y = 3x^4 - 4x^3$, $[0, 2]$.

16. $y = 2x^3 - 15x^2 + 36x$, $[0, 3]$.

In Problems **17–26**, *sketch the graphs of the functions. Indicate intervals on which the function is increasing, decreasing, concave up, concave down; indicate relative maximum points, relative minimum points, points of inflection, horizontal asymptotes, vertical asymptotes, symmetry, and those intercepts that can be obtained conveniently.*

17. $y = x^2 - 2x - 24$.

18. $y = x^3 - 27x$.

19. $y = x^3 - 12x + 20$.

20. $y = x^4 - 4x^3 - 20x^2 + 150$.

21. $y = x^3 + x$.

22. $y = \dfrac{x + 2}{x - 3}$.

23. $f(x) = \dfrac{100(x + 5)}{x^2}$.

24. $y = \dfrac{x^2 - 4}{x^2 - 1}$.

25. $f(x) = \dfrac{e^x + e^{-x}}{2}$.

26. $f(x) = 1 + \ln(x^2)$.

27. Sketch the graph of the normal density function

$$f(x) = \frac{1}{\sqrt{2\pi}} e^{-x^2/2}.$$

Include relative extrema and inflection points.

28. In a model of the effect of contraception on birth rate,* the equation

$$R = f(x) = \frac{x}{4.4 - 3.4x}, \qquad 0 \le x \le 1$$

gives the proportional reduction R in the birth rate as a function of the efficiency x of a contraception method. An efficiency of 0.2 (or 20%) means that the probability of becoming pregnant is 80% of the probability of becoming pregnant without the contraceptive. Find the reduction (as a percentage) when efficiency is (a) 0, (b) 0.5, and (c) 1. Find dR/dx and d^2R/dx^2 and sketch the graph of the equation.

29. If you were to recite members of a category, such as four-legged animals, the words that you utter would probably occur in "chunks" with distinct pauses between such chunks. For example, you might say the following for the category of four-legged animals:

> dog, cat, mouse, rat,
> (pause)
>
> horse, donkey, mule,
> (pause)
>
> cow, pig, goat, lamb
> etc.

The pauses may occur because one may have to mentally search for subcategories (animals around the house, beasts of burden, farm animals, etc.)

The elapsed time between onsets of successive words is called *interresponse time*. A function has been used to analyze the length of time for pauses and chunk size (number of words in a chunk).† This function f is such that

$$f(t) = \begin{cases} \text{the average number of words} \\ \text{that occur in succession with} \\ \text{interresponse times less than } t. \end{cases}$$

The graph of f has a shape similar to that in Fig. 12.51 and is best fit by a third-degree polynomial, such as

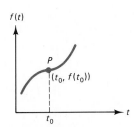

FIGURE 12.51

$$f(t) = At^3 + Bt^2 + Ct + D.$$

The point P has special meaning. It is such that the value t_0 separates interresponse times *within* chunks from those *between* chunks. Mathematically, P is a critical point that is also a point of inflection. Assume these two conditions and show that (a) $t_0 = -B/(3A)$ and (b) $B^2 = 3AC$.

---

* R. K. Leik and B. F. Meeker, *Mathematical Sociology* (Englewood Cliffs, N.J.: Prentice-Hall, Inc., 1975).

† A. Graesser and G. Mandler, "Limited Processing Capacity Constrains the Storage of Unrelated Sets of Words and Retrieval from Natural Categories," *Human Learning and Memory*, 4, no. 1 (1978), 86–100.

30. In a model for the market penetration of a new product, sales S of the product at time t is given by*

$$S = g(t) = \frac{m(p + q)^2}{p}\left[\frac{e^{-(p+q)t}}{\left(\frac{q}{p}e^{-(p+q)t} + 1\right)^2}\right],$$

where p, q, and m are nonzero constants.

a. Show that

$$\frac{dS}{dt} = \frac{\frac{m}{p}(p + q)^3 e^{-(p+q)t}\left[\frac{q}{p}e^{-(p+q)t} - 1\right]}{\left(\frac{q}{p}e^{-(p+q)t} + 1\right)^3}.$$

b. Determine the value of t for which maximum sales occur. You may assume that S attains a maximum when $dS/dt = 0$.

* A. P. Hurter, Jr., A. H. Rubenstein, et al. "Market Penetration by New Innovations: The Technological Literature," *Technological Forecasting and Social Change*, vol. 11 (1978), 197–221.

Applications of Differentiation

13.1 APPLIED MAXIMA AND MINIMA

By using techniques from the previous chapter, we can solve problems that involve maximizing or minimizing a quantity. For example, we might want to maximize profit or minimize cost. The crucial part is expressing the quantity to be maximized or minimized as a function of some variable involved in the problem. Then we differentiate and test the resulting critical values. For this, the first-derivative test or the second-derivative test may be used, although it is often obvious from the nature of the problem whether or not a critical value represents an appropriate answer. Because our interest is in *absolute* maxima and minima, sometimes we must examine endpoints of the domain of the function.

EXAMPLE 1   *A manufacturer's total cost function is given by* $c = \frac{q^2}{4} + 3q + 400$, *where q is the number of units produced. At what level of output will average cost per unit be a minimum? What is this minimum?*

The quantity to be minimized is average cost $\bar{c}$. The average cost function is

$$\bar{c} = \frac{c}{q} = \frac{\frac{q^2}{4} + 3q + 400}{q} = \frac{q}{4} + 3 + \frac{400}{q}. \tag{1}$$

Here q must be positive. To minimize $\bar{c}$ we differentiate.

$$D_q\bar{c} = \frac{1}{4} - \frac{400}{q^2} = \frac{q^2 - 1600}{4q^2}.$$

To get the critical values for $q > 0$, we solve $D_x \bar{c} = 0$.

$$q^2 - 1600 = 0,$$

$$(q - 40)(q + 40) = 0,$$

$$q = 40 \quad \text{(since } q > 0\text{)}.$$

To determine if this level of output gives a relative minimum, we shall use the second-derivative test.

$$D_q^2 \bar{c} = \frac{800}{q^3},$$

which is positive for $q = 40$. Thus $\bar{c}$ has a relative minimum when $q = 40$. We note that $\bar{c}$ is continuous for $q > 0$. Since $q = 40$ is the only relative extremum, we conclude that this relative minimum is indeed an absolute minimum. Substituting $q = 40$ in Eq. (1) gives the minimum average cost $\bar{c} = 23$.

EXAMPLE 2   *The demand equation for a manufacturer's product is $p = (80 - q)/4$, where q is the number of units and p is price per unit. At what value of q will there be maximum revenue? What is the maximum revenue?*

Let r be total revenue. Then revenue = (price)(quantity). Thus

$$r = pq = \frac{80 - q}{4} \cdot q = \frac{80q - q^2}{4},$$

where $q \geq 0$. Setting $dr/dq = 0$:

$$\frac{dr}{dq} = \frac{80 - 2q}{4} = 0,$$

$$q = 40.$$

Thus 40 is a critical value. Examining the first derivative, we have $dr/dq > 0$ for $0 \leq q < 40$, so r is increasing. If $q > 40$, then $dr/dq < 0$, so r is decreasing. Because to the left of 40 we have r increasing and to the right r is decreasing, we conclude that $q = 40$ gives the *absolute* maximum revenue. This revenue is $[80(40) - (40)^2]/4 = 400$.

Calculus can be applied to inventory decisions, as the following example shows.

EXAMPLE 3   *A company annually produces and sells 10,000 units of a product. Sales are uniformly distributed throughout the year. The company wishes to determine the number of units to be manufactured in each production run in order to minimize total annual setup costs and carrying costs. The same number of units is produced in each run. This number is referred to as the* **economic lot size** *or* **economic order quantity**. *The production cost of each unit is $20 and carrying costs (insurance, interest, storage, etc.) are estimated to be*

10% *of the value of the average inventory. Setup costs per production run are* $40. *Find the economic lot size.*

Let q be the number of units in a production run. Since sales are distributed at a uniform rate, we shall assume that inventory varies uniformly from q to 0 between production runs. Thus we take the average inventory to be $q/2$ units. The production costs are $20 per unit, so the value of the average inventory is $20(q/2)$. Carrying costs are 10% of this value:

$$0.10(20)\left(\frac{q}{2}\right).$$

The number of production runs per year is $10,000/q$. Thus the total setup costs are

$$40\left(\frac{10,000}{q}\right).$$

Hence the total annual carrying costs and setup costs C are

$$C = 0.10(20)\left(\frac{q}{2}\right) + 40\left(\frac{10,000}{q}\right),$$

$$C = q + \frac{400,000}{q}, \qquad (q > 0).$$

$$\frac{dC}{dq} = 1 - \frac{400,000}{q^2} = \frac{q^2 - 400,000}{q^2}.$$

Setting $dC/dq = 0$, we get

$$q^2 = 400,000.$$

Since $q > 0$, we choose

$$q = \sqrt{400,000} = 200\sqrt{10} \approx 632.5.$$

To determine if this value of q minimizes C, we shall examine the first derivative. If $0 < q < \sqrt{400,000}$, then $dC/dq < 0$. If $q > \sqrt{400,000}$, then $dC/dq > 0$. We conclude that there is an *absolute* minimum at $q = 632.5$. The number of production runs is $10,000/632.5 \approx 15.8$. For practical purposes, there would be 16 lots, each having an economic lot size of 625 units.

EXAMPLE 4   *The Vista TV Cable Co. currently has 3500 subscribers who are paying a monthly rate of* $8. *A survey reveals that there will be 50 more subscribers for each* $0.10 *decrease in the rate. At what rate will maximum revenue be obtained and how many subscribers will there be at this rate?*

Let x be the new rate (in dollars). Then the total decrease in the old rate is $8 - x$, and the number of $0.10 decreases is $\dfrac{8 - x}{0.10}$. For *each* of these decreases there will be 50 more subscribers. Thus the total number of *new* subscribers is

$50\left(\dfrac{8-x}{0.10}\right)$ and the total of all subscribers is

$$3500 + 50\left(\dfrac{8-x}{0.10}\right), \tag{2}$$

where $0 \le x \le 8$. The revenue r is given by $r =$ (rate)(number of subscribers):

$$r = x\left[3500 + 50\left(\dfrac{8-x}{0.10}\right)\right]$$

$$= x[3500 + 4000 - 500x]$$

$$= 7500x - 500x^2.$$

Setting $r' = 0$, we have

$$r' = 7500 - 1000x = 0.$$

$$x = 7.50.$$

If $0 \le x < 7.50$, then $r' > 0$; if $7.50 < x \le 8$, then $r' < 0$. We conclude that when the rate is \$7.50 there is an absolute maximum. Substituting $x = 7.50$ into expression (2) gives 3750 subscribers.

EXAMPLE 5   *If a particular health-care program for the elderly were initiated, then t years after its start, n thousand elderly people would receive direct benefits, where*

$$n = \dfrac{t^3}{3} - 6t^2 + 32t, \qquad 0 \le t \le 12.$$

For what value of t does the maximum number receive benefits?

Setting $dn/dt = 0$, we have

$$\dfrac{dn}{dt} = t^2 - 12t + 32 = 0,$$

$$(t - 4)(t - 8) = 0,$$

$$t = 4 \quad \text{or} \quad t = 8.$$

Now, $d^2n/dt^2 = 2t - 12$, which is negative for $t = 4$ and positive for $t = 8$. Thus there is a relative maximum when $t = 4$. This gives $n = 53\frac{1}{3}$. To determine whether this is an absolute maximum, we must find n at the endpoints of the domain. If $t = 0$, then $n = 0$. If $t = 12$, then $n = 96$. Thus an absolute maximum occurs when $t = 12$. A graph of the function is given in Fig. 13.1.

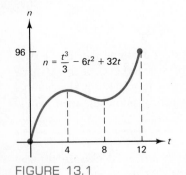

FIGURE 13.1

Pitfall
Example 5 illustrates that you should not ignore endpoints when finding absolute extrema on a closed interval.

In the next example we use the word *monopolist*. Under a situation of monopoly, there is only one seller of a product for which there are no similar substitutes, and the seller, that is, the monopolist, controls the market. By considering the demand equation for the product, the monopolist may set the price (or volume of output) so that maximum profit will be obtained.

EXAMPLE 6   *Suppose that the demand equation for a monopolist's product is $p = 400 - 2q$ and the average cost function is $\bar{c} = 0.2q + 4 + (400/q)$, where q is number of units, and both p and $\bar{c}$ are expressed in dollars per unit.*

a. *Determine the level of output at which profit is maximized.*

b. *Determine the price at which maximum profit occurs.*

c. *Determine the maximum profit.*

d. *If, as a regulatory device, the government imposes a tax of $22 per unit on the monopolist, what is the new price for profit maximization?*

$$\text{Profit} = \text{total revenue} - \text{total cost.}$$

Since total revenue $r = pq = 400q - 2q^2$ and total cost $c = q\bar{c} = 0.2q^2 + 4q + 400$, profit P is

$$P = r - c = 400q - 2q^2 - (0.2q^2 + 4q + 400).$$

$$P = 396q - 2.2q^2 - 400, \tag{3}$$

where $q > 0$.

a. Setting $dP/dq = 0$, we have

$$\frac{dP}{dq} = 396 - 4.4q = 0.$$

$$q = 90.$$

Since $d^2P/dq^2 = -4.4 < 0$, we conclude that $q = 90$ gives maximum profit.

b. From the demand equation, $p = 400 - 2(90) = 220$.

c. Replacing q by 90 in (3) gives $P = 17,420$.

d. The tax of $22 per unit means that for q units the total cost increases by $22q$. The new cost function is $c_1 = 0.2q^2 + 4q + 400 + 22q$, and the profit P_1 is given by

$$P_1 = 400q - 2q^2 - (0.2q^2 + 4q + 400 + 22q).$$

$$P_1 = 374q - 2.2q^2 - 400.$$

Setting $dP_1/dq = 0$ gives

$$\frac{dP_1}{dq} = 374 - 4.4q = 0.$$

$$q = 85.$$

Since $d^2P_1/dq^2 = -4.4 < 0$, we conclude that to maximize profit, the monopolist restricts output to 85 units at a higher price of $p_1 = 400 - 2(85) =$

230. Since this price is only $10 more than before, only part of the tax has been shifted to the consumer, and the monopolist must bear the cost of the balance. The profit now is $15,495, which is less than the former profit.

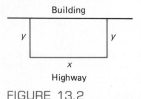

Building

y y

x

Highway

FIGURE 13.2

EXAMPLE 7   *For insurance purposes a manufacturer plans to fence in a 10,800-ft² rectangular storage area adjacent to a building by using the building as one side of the enclosed area (see Fig. 13.2). The fencing parallel to the building faces a highway and will cost $3 per foot installed, while the fencing for the other two sides costs $2 per foot installed. Find the amount of each type of fence so that the total cost of the fence will be a minimum. What is the minimum cost?*

In Fig. 13.2 we have labeled the length of the side parallel to the building as x and the lengths of the other two sides as y, where x and y are in feet. The cost (in dollars) of the fencing along the highway is $3x$, and along each of the other sides it is $2y$. Thus the total cost C of the fencing is

$$C = 3x + 2y + 2y = 3x + 4y.$$

We wish to minimize C. In order to differentiate, we first express C in terms of one variable only. To do this we find a relationship between x and y. Since the storage area xy must be 10,800,

$$xy = 10,800$$

or $$y = \frac{10,800}{x}.$$

By substitution, we have

$$C = 3x + 4\left(\frac{10,800}{x}\right) = 3x + \frac{43,200}{x},$$

where $x > 0$. To minimize C we set $dC/dx = 0$ and solve for x:

$$\frac{dC}{dx} = 3 - \frac{43,200}{x^2} = 0,$$

$$3 = \frac{43,200}{x^2},$$

from which

$$x^2 = \frac{43,200}{3} = 14,400.$$

$$x = 120 \quad (\text{since } x > 0).$$

Now, $d^2C/dx^2 = 86,400/x^3 > 0$ for $x = 120$, and we conclude that $x = 120$ indeed gives the minimum value of C. When $x = 120$, then $y = 10,800/120 = 90$. Thus 120 ft of the $3 fencing and 180 ft of the $2 fencing are needed. This gives a cost of $720.

We conclude this section by using calculus to develop an important principle in economics. Suppose $p = f(q)$ is the demand function for a firm's product, where p is price per unit and q is the number of units produced and sold. Then the total revenue $r = qp = q\,f(q)$ is a function of q. Let the total cost c of producing q units be given by the cost function $c = g(q)$. Thus the total profit P, which is total revenue $-$ total cost, is also a function of q:

$$P = r - c = q\,f(q) - g(q).$$

Let us consider the most profitable output for the firm. Ignoring special cases, we know that profit is maximized when $dP/dq = 0$ and $d^2P/dq^2 < 0$. By solving $dP/dq = 0$, we have

$$\frac{dP}{dq} = \frac{d}{dq}(r - c) = \frac{dr}{dq} - \frac{dc}{dq} = 0.$$

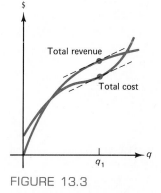

$

Total revenue

Total cost

q_1

q

FIGURE 13.3

Thus

$$\frac{dr}{dq} = \frac{dc}{dq}.$$

That is, at the level of maximum profit the slope of the tangent to the total revenue curve must equal the slope of the tangent to the total cost curve (Fig. 13.3). But dr/dq is marginal revenue MR, and dc/dq is marginal cost MC. Thus, under typical conditions, *to maximize profit it is necessary that*

$$MR = MC.$$

For this to indeed correspond to a maximum, it is necessary that $d^2P/dq^2 < 0$.

$$\frac{d^2P}{dq^2} = \frac{d^2}{dq^2}(r - c) = \frac{d^2r}{dq^2} - \frac{d^2c}{dq^2} < 0 \quad \text{or} \quad \frac{d^2r}{dq^2} < \frac{d^2c}{dq^2}.$$

That is, when $MR = MC$, in order to insure maximum profit the slope of the marginal revenue curve must be less than the slope of the marginal cost curve.

The condition that $d^2P/dq^2 < 0$ when $dP/dq = 0$ can be viewed another way. Equivalently, to have $MR = MC$ correspond to a maximum, dP/dq must go from $+$ to $-$; that is, from $dr/dq - dc/dq > 0$ to $dr/dq - dc/dq < 0$. Hence as output increases, we must have $MR > MC$ and then $MR < MC$. This means that at the point q_1 of maximum profit *the marginal cost curve must cut the marginal revenue curve from below* (Fig. 13.4). For production up to q_1, the

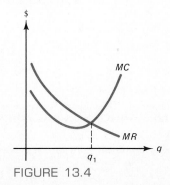

$

MC

MR

q_1

q

FIGURE 13.4

revenue from additional output would be greater than the cost of such output and total profit would increase. For output beyond q_1, $MC > MR$ and each unit of output would add more to total costs than to total revenue. Hence total profits would decline.

EXERCISE 13.1

In each of the following, p is price per unit (in dollars) and q is output per unit of time. Fixed costs refer to costs that remain constant at all levels of production in a given time period. (An example is rent.)

1. A manufacturer finds that the total cost c of producing a product is given by the cost function $c = 0.05q^2 + 5q + 500$. At what level of output will average cost per unit be a minimum?

2. The cost per hour C (in dollars) of operating an automobile is given by
$$C = 0.12s - 0.0012s^2 + 0.08, \qquad 0 \le s \le 60,$$
where s is the speed in miles per hour. At what speed is the cost per hour a minimum?

3. The demand equation for a monopolist's product is $p = -5q + 30$. At what price will revenue be maximized?

4. For a monopolist's product, the demand function is $q = 10,000e^{-0.02p}$. Find the value of p for which maximum revenue is obtained.

5. A group of biologists studied the nutritional effects on rats that were fed a diet containing 10% protein.* The protein consisted of yeast and cottonseed flour. By varying the percent p of yeast in the protein mix, the group found that the (average) weight gain (in grams) of a rat over a period of time was
$$f(p) = 160 - p - \frac{900}{p + 10}, \qquad 0 \le p \le 100.$$
Find (a) the maximum weight gain and (b) the minimum weight gain.

6. The severity R of the reaction of the human body to an initial dose D of a drug is given by[†]
$$R = f(D) = D^2\left(\frac{C}{2} - \frac{D}{3}\right),$$
where the constant C denotes the maximum amount of the drug that may be given. Show that R has a maximum *rate of change* when $D = C/2$.

7. For a monopolist's product, the demand function is $p = 72 - 0.04q$ and the cost function is $c = 500 + 30q$. At what level of output will profit be maximized? At what price does this occur and what is the profit?

8. For a monopolist, the cost per unit of producing a product is $3 and the demand equation is $p = 10/\sqrt{q}$. What price will give the greatest profit?

9. For a monopolist's product, the demand equation is $p = 42 - 4q$ and the average cost function is $\bar{c} = 2 + (80/q)$. Find the profit-maximizing price.

10. For a monopolist's product, the demand function is $p = 50/\sqrt{q}$ and the average cost function is $\bar{c} = 0.50 + (1000/q)$. Find the profit-maximizing price and output. At this level, show marginal revenue is equal to marginal cost.

11. For XYZ Manufacturing Co., total fixed costs are

* Adapted from R. Bressani, "The Use of Yeast in Human Foods," in *Single-Cell Protein*, ed. R. I. Mateles and S. R. Tannenbaum (Cambridge, Mass.: MIT Press, 1968).

† R. M. Thrall, J. A. Mortimer, K. R. Rebman, and R. F. Baum, eds., *Some Mathematical Models in Biology*, rev. ed., Report No. 40241-R-7. Prepared at University of Michigan, 1967.

$1200, material and labor costs combined are $2 per unit, and the demand equation is $p = 100/\sqrt{q}$. What level of output will maximize profit? Show that this occurs when marginal revenue is equal to marginal cost. What is the price at profit maximization?

12. A real estate firm owns 100 garden-type apartments. At $400 per month each apartment can be rented. However, for each $10 per month increase, there will be two vacancies with no possibility of filling them. What rent per apartment will maximize monthly revenue?

13. A TV cable company has 1000 subscribers who are each paying $5 per month. It can get 100 more subscribers for each $0.10 decrease in the monthly fee. What rate will yield maximum revenue and what will this revenue be?

14. A manufacturer of a product finds that for the first 500 units that are produced and sold, the profit is $50 per unit. The profit on each of the units beyond 500 is decreased by $0.10 times the number of additional units produced. For example, the total profit when 502 units are produced and sold is 500(50) + 2(49.80). What level of output will maximize profit?

15. Find two numbers whose sum is 40 and whose product is a maximum.

16. Find two nonnegative numbers whose sum is 20 and such that the product of twice one number and the square of the other number will be a maximum.

17. A company has set aside $3000 to fence in a rectangular portion of land adjacent to a stream by using the stream for one side of the enclosed area. The cost of the fencing parallel to the stream is $5 per foot installed, and the fencing for the remaining two sides is $3 per foot installed. Find the dimensions of the maximum enclosed area.

18. The owner of the Laurel Nursery Garden Center wants to fence in 1000 ft^2 of land in a rectangular plot to be used for different types of shrubs. The plot is to be divided into four equal plots with three fences parallel to the same pair of sides as shown in Fig. 13.5. What is the least number of feet of fence needed?

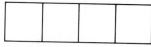

FIGURE 13.5

19. A container manufacturer is designing a rectangular box, open at the top and with a square base, that is to have a volume of 32 ft^3. If the box is to require the least amount of material, what must be the dimensions of the box? See Fig. 13.6.

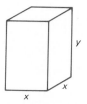

FIGURE 13.6

20. An open-top box with a square base is to be constructed from 192 ft^2 of material. What should be the dimensions of the box if the volume is to be a maximum? What is the maximum volume? See Fig. 13.6.

21. An open box is to be made by cutting equal squares from each corner of a 12-in.-square piece of cardboard and then folding up the sides. Find the length of the side of the square that must be cut out if the volume of the box is to be maximized. What is the maximum volume? See Fig. 13.7.

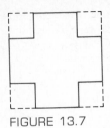

FIGURE 13.7

22. A rectangular cardboard poster is to have 150 in.^{2} for printed matter. It is to have a 3-in. margin at the top and bottom and a 2-in. margin on each side. Find the dimensions of the poster so that the amount of cardboard used is minimized (see Fig. 13.8). (*Hint:* First find the values of x and y in Fig. 13.8 that minimize the amount of cardboard.)

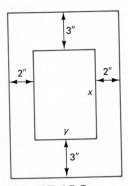

FIGURE 13.8

23. A cylindrical can, open at the top, is to have a fixed volume of K. Show that if the least amount of material is to be used, then both the radius and height are equal to $\sqrt[3]{K/\pi}$ (see Fig. 13.9).

Volume $= \pi r^2 h$
Surface area $= 2\pi rh + \pi r^2$

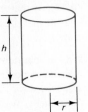

Open at top

FIGURE 13.9

24. A cylindrical can, open at the top, is to be made from a fixed amount of material, K. If the volume is to be a maximum, <u>show</u> that both the radius and height are equal to $\sqrt{K/(3\pi)}$ (see Fig. 13.9).

25. The demand equation for a monopolist's product is $p = 600 - 2q$ and the total cost function is $c = 0.2q^2 + 28q + 200$. Find the profit-maximizing output and price, and determine the corresponding profit. If the government were to impose a tax of $22 per unit on the manufacturer, what would be the new profit-maximizing output and price? What is the profit now?

26. Use the *original* data in Problem 25 and assume that the government imposes a license fee of $100 on the manufacturer. This is a lump-sum amount without regard to output. Show that the profit maximizing price and output remain the same. Show, however, that there will be less profit.

27. A manufacturer has to produce annually 1000 units of a product that is sold at a uniform rate during the year. The production cost of each unit is $10 and carrying costs (insurance, interest, storage, etc.) are estimated to be 12.8% of the value of average inventory. Setup costs per production run are $40. Find the economic lot size.

28. For a monopolist's product, the cost function is $c = 0.004q^3 + 20q + 5000$ and the demand function is $p = 450 - 4q$. Find the profit-maximizing output. At this level, show that marginal cost = marginal revenue.

29. Imperial Educational Services (I.E.S.) is considering offering a workshop in resource allocation to key personnel at Acme Corp. To make the offering economically feasible, I.E.S. feels that at least 30 persons must attend at a cost of $50 each. Moreover, I.E.S. will agree to reduce the charge for *everybody* by $1.25 for each person over the 30 who attends. How many people should be in the group for I.E.S. to maximize revenue? Assume that the maximum allowable number in the group is 40.

30. The Kiddie Toy Company plans to lease an electric motor to be used 90,000 horsepower-hours per year in manufacturing. One horsepower-hour is the work done in 1 hour by a 1-horsepower motor. The annual cost to lease a suitable motor is $150 plus $0.60 per horsepower. The cost per horsepower-hour of operating the motor is $0.006/N$, where N is the horsepower. What size motor, in horsepower, should be leased in order to minimize cost?

31. The cost of operating a truck on a throughway (excluding the salary of the driver) is $0.11 + (s/300)$ dollars per mile, where s is the (steady) speed of the truck in miles per hour. The truck driver's salary is $12 per hour. At what speed should the truck driver operate the truck to make a 700-mile trip most economical?

32. For a manufacturer, the cost of making a part is $3 per unit for labor and $1 per unit for materials; overhead is fixed at $2000 per week. If more than 5000 units are made each week, labor is $4.50 per unit for those units in excess of 5000. At what level of production will average cost per unit be a minimum?

33. Each day a firm makes x tons of chemical A ($x \le 4$) and y tons of chemical B with $y = (24 - 6x)/(5 - x)$. The profit on chemical A is $2000 per ton and on B it is $1000 per ton. How much of chemical A should be produced per day to maximize profit? Answer the same question if the profit on A is P per ton and that on B is $P/2$ per ton.

34. To erect an office building, fixed costs are $250,000 and include land, architect's fee, basement, foundation, etc. If x floors are constructed, the cost (excluding fixed costs) is $c = (x/2)[100{,}000 + 5000(x - 1)]$. The revenue per month is $5000 per floor. Find the number of floors that will yield a maximum rate of return on investment (rate of return = total revenue/total cost).

35. In a model by Smith[*] for power output P of an animal at a given speed as a function of its movement or *gait* j, the following relation is derived:

$$P(j) = Aj\frac{L^4}{V} + B\frac{V^3L^2}{1 + j}.$$

Here A and B are constants, j is a measure of the "jumpiness" of the gait, L is a constant representing linear dimension, and V is a constant forward speed. Assume that P is a minimum when $dP/dj = 0$. Show that when this occurs, then

$$(1 + j)^2 = \frac{BV^4}{AL^2}.$$

As a passing comment, Smith indicates, ". . . at top speed, j is zero for an elephant, 0.3 for a horse, and 1 for a greyhound, approximately."

[*] J. M. Smith, *Mathematical Ideas in Biology* (London: Cambridge University Press, 1968).

36. In a model of traffic flow on a lane of a freeway, the number N of cars the lane can carry per unit time is given by*

$$N = \frac{-2a}{-2at_r + v - \dfrac{2al}{v}},$$

where a is acceleration of a car when stopping ($a < 0$), t_r is reaction time to begin braking, v is average speed of the cars, and l is length of a car. Assume that a, t_r, and l are constant. To find at most how many cars a lane can carry, we want to find the speed v that maximizes N. To maximize N it suffices to minimize the denominator $-2at_r + v - (2al/v)$. (a) Find the value of v that minimizes the denominator. (b) Evaluate your answer in (a) when $a = -19.6(\text{ft/sec}^2)$, $l = 20(\text{ft})$ and $t_r = 0.5(\text{sec})$. Your answer will be in feet per second. (c) Find the corresponding value of N to one decimal place. Your answer will be in cars per second. Convert your answer to cars per hour.

13.2 DIFFERENTIALS

We shall soon give you a reason for using the symbol dy/dx to denote the derivative of y with respect to x. To do this, we introduce the notion of the *differential* of a function.

Definition

*Let $y = f(x)$ be a differentiable function of x and let Δx denote a change in x, where Δx can be any real number. Then the **differential of y,** denoted dy or $d[f(x)]$, is given by*

$$dy = f'(x)\Delta x.$$

Note that dy is a function of two variables, namely x and Δx.

EXAMPLE 1   *Find the differential of $y = x^3 - 2x^2 + 3x - 4$ and evaluate it when $x = 1$ and $\Delta x = 0.04$.*

$$dy = D_x(x^3 - 2x^2 + 3x - 4)\Delta x,$$

$$dy = (3x^2 - 4x + 3)\Delta x.$$

When $x = 1$ and $\Delta x = 0.04$, then

$$dy = [3(1)^2 - 4(1) + 3](0.04) = 0.08.$$

If $y = x$, then $dy = d(x) = 1\Delta x = \Delta x$. Hence the differential of x is Δx. We abbreviate $d(x)$ by dx. Thus $dx = \Delta x$. From now on, it will be our practice to write dx for Δx when finding a differential. For example,

$$d(x^2 + 5) = D_x(x^2 + 5)\,dx = 2x\,dx.$$

Summarizing, if $y = f(x)$ defines a differentiable function of x, then

$$\boxed{dy = f'(x)\,dx,}$$

---

* J. I. Shonle, *Environmental Applications of General Physics* (Reading, Mass.: Addison-Wesley Publishing Company, Inc., 1975).

where dx is any real number. Provided that $dx \neq 0$, we can divide both sides by dx:

$$\frac{dy}{dx} = f'(x).$$

That is, dy/dx can be viewed either as the quotient of two differentials, namely dy divided by dx, or as one symbol for the derivative of f at x. It is for this reason that we introduced the symbol dy/dx to denote the derivative.

EXAMPLE 2

a. If $f(x) = \sqrt{x}$, then

$$d(\sqrt{x}) = D_x(\sqrt{x})\, dx = \frac{1}{2}x^{-1/2}\, dx = \frac{1}{2\sqrt{x}}\, dx.$$

b. If $u = (x^2 + 3)^5$, then $du = 5(x^2 + 3)^4(2x)\, dx = 10x(x^2 + 3)^4\, dx.$

The differential can be interpreted geometrically. In Fig. 13.10 the point $P(x, f(x))$ is on the curve $y = f(x)$. Suppose x changes by dx, a real number, to the new value $x + dx$. Then the new function value is $f(x + dx)$, and the corresponding point on the curve is $Q(x + dx, f(x + dx))$. Passing through P and Q are horizontal and vertical lines, respectively, that intersect at S. A line L tangent to the curve at P intersects segment QS at R, forming the right triangle

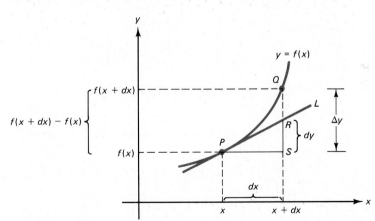

FIGURE 13.10

PRS. Observe that the graph of f near P is approximated by the tangent line at P. The slope of L is $f'(x)$ or, equivalently, it is $\overline{SR}/\overline{PS}$:

$$f'(x) = \frac{\overline{SR}}{\overline{PS}}.$$

Since $dy = f'(x)\, dx$, and $dx = \overline{PS}$,

$$dy = f'(x)\, dx = \frac{\overline{SR}}{\overline{PS}} \cdot \overline{PS} = \overline{SR}.$$

Thus if dx is a change in x at P, then dy is the corresponding vertical change along the **tangent line** at P. Note that for the same dx, the vertical change along the **curve** is $\Delta y = \overline{SQ} = f(x + dx) - f(x)$. Do not confuse Δy with dy. However, it is apparent from Fig. 13.10 that

when dx is close to 0, dy is an approximation to Δy.

Thus $\Delta y \approx dy$. This fact is useful in estimating Δy, a change in y, as Example 3 shows.

EXAMPLE 3   *A governmental health agency examined the records of a group of individuals who were hospitalized with a particular illness. It was found that the total proportion P that was discharged at the end of t days of hospitalization is given by*

$$P = P(t) = 1 - \left(\frac{300}{300 + t}\right)^3.$$

Use differentials to approximate the change in the proportion discharged if t changes from 300 to 305.

The change in t from 300 to 305 is $\Delta t = dt = 305 - 300 = 5$. The change in P is $\Delta P = P(305) - P(300)$. We approximate ΔP by dP.

$$\Delta P \approx dP = P'\, dt = -3\left(\frac{300}{300 + t}\right)^2\left[-\frac{300}{(300 + t)^2}\right]dt.$$

When $t = 300$ and $dt = 5$,

$$dP = -3\left(\frac{300}{600}\right)^2\left[-\frac{300}{(600)^2}\right]5$$

$$= -3\left(\frac{1}{2}\right)^2\left[-\frac{1}{2(600)}\right]5 = \frac{1}{320} \approx 0.0031.$$

For a comparison, the actual value of ΔP to 5 decimal places is 0.00307.

We said that if $y = f(x)$, then $\Delta y \approx dy$ if dx is small. Thus

$$\Delta y = f(x + dx) - f(x) \approx dy$$

or

$$\boxed{f(x + dx) \approx f(x) + dy.} \qquad (1)$$

This gives us a way of estimating a function value, $f(x + dx)$. For example, suppose we estimate $\ln(1.06)$. Letting $y = f(x) = \ln x$, we need to estimate $f(1.06)$. Since $d(\ln x) = (1/x)\, dx$, from (1) we have

$$f(x + dx) \approx f(x) + dy,$$

$$\ln(x + dx) \approx \ln x + \frac{1}{x} \, dx.$$

We know the exact value of ln 1, so we shall let $x = 1$ and $dx = 0.06$. Then $x + dx = 1.06$ and dx is small.

$$\ln(1 + 0.06) \approx \ln(1) + \frac{1}{1}(0.06),$$

$$\ln(1.06) \approx 0 + 0.06 = 0.06.$$

The actual value of ln(1.06) to five decimal places is 0.05827.

EXAMPLE 4   *The demand function for a product is given by $p = f(q) = 20 - \sqrt{q}$, where p is the price per unit in dollars for q units. By using differentials, approximate the price when 99 units are demanded.*

We want to approximate $f(99)$. By (1),

$$f(q + dq) \approx f(q) + dp,$$

where

$$dp = -\frac{1}{2\sqrt{q}} \, dq.$$

We choose $q = 100$ and $dq = -1$ because $q + dq = 99$, dq is small, and it is easy to compute $f(100) = 20 - \sqrt{100} = 10$.

$$f(99) = f[100 + (-1)] \approx f(100) - \frac{1}{2\sqrt{100}}(-1),$$

$$f(99) \approx 10 + 0.05 = 10.05.$$

Thus the price per unit when 99 units are demanded is approximately $10.05.

The equation $y = x^3 + 4x + 5$ defines y as a function of x. However, it also defines x implicitly as a function of y. Thus we can look at the derivative of x with respect to y, dx/dy. Since dx/dy can be considered a quotient of differentials, we are motivated to write (and it is indeed true) that

$$\frac{dx}{dy} = \frac{1}{\dfrac{dy}{dx}}, \quad dy/dx \neq 0.$$

But dy/dx is the derivative of y with respect to x and equals $3x^2 + 4$. Thus

$$\frac{dx}{dy} = \frac{1}{3x^2 + 4}.$$

This is the *reciprocal* of dy/dx.

EXAMPLE 5   Find dp/dq if $q = \sqrt{2500 - p^2}$.

Since $q = (2500 - p^2)^{1/2}$, then

$$\frac{dq}{dp} = \frac{1}{2}(2500 - p^2)^{-1/2}(-2p) = -\frac{p}{\sqrt{2500 - p^2}}.$$

Hence

$$\frac{dp}{dq} = \frac{1}{\dfrac{dq}{dp}} = -\frac{\sqrt{2500 - p^2}}{p}.$$

EXERCISE 13.2

In Problems 1–10, find the differentials of the functions in terms of x and dx.

1. $y = 3x - 4$.

2. $y = 2$.

3. $f(x) = \sqrt{x^4 + 2}$.

4. $f(x) = (4x^2 - 5x + 2)^3$.

5. $u = \dfrac{1}{x^2}$.

6. $u = \dfrac{1}{\sqrt{x}}$.

7. $p = \ln(x^2 + 7)$.

8. $p = e^{x^3 + 5}$.

9. $y = (4x + 3)e^{2x^2 + 3}$.

10. $y = \ln \sqrt{x^4 + 1}$.

In Problems 11–14, find Δy and dy for the given values of x and dx.

11. $y = 4 - 7x$; $x = 3$, $dx = 0.02$.

12. $y = 4x^2 - 3x + 10$; $x = -1$, $dx = 0.25$.

13. $y = \sqrt{25 - x^2}$; $x = 3$, $dx = -0.1$. (*Note:* $\sqrt{16.59} \approx 4.073$.)

14. $y = (3x + 2)^2$; $x = -1$, $dx = -0.03$.

In Problems 15–22, approximate each expression by using differentials.

15. $\sqrt{101}$.

16. $\sqrt{120}$.

17. $\sqrt[3]{63}$.

18. $\sqrt[4]{17}$.

19. $\ln 0.97$.

20. $\ln 1.01$.

21. $e^{0.01}$.

22. $e^{-0.01}$.

In Problems 23–28, find dx/dy or dp/dq.

23. $y = 2x - 1$.

24. $y = 5x^2 + 3x + 2$.

25. $q = (p^2 + 5)^3$.

26. $q = \sqrt{p + 5}$.

27. $q = \dfrac{1}{p}$.

28. $q = e^{5-p}$.

In Problems 29 and 30, find the rate of change of q with respect to p for the indicated value of q.

29. $p = \dfrac{500}{q + 2}$; $q = 18$.

30. $p = 50 - \sqrt{q}$; $q = 100$.

31. Suppose the profit P (in dollars) of producing q units of a product is

$$P = 396q - 2.2q^2 - 400.$$

Using differentials, find the approximate change in profit if the level of production changes from $q = 80$ to $q = 81$. Find the actual change.

32. Given the revenue function

$$r = 250q + 45q^2 - q^3,$$

use differentials to find the approximate change in revenue if the number of units increases from $q = 40$ to $q = 41$. Find the actual change.

33. The demand equation for a monopolist's product is $p = 10/\sqrt{q}$. Using differentials, approximate the price when 24 units are demanded.

34. Answer the same question in Problem 33 if 101 units are demanded.

35. If $y = f(x)$, then the *proportional change* in y is defined to be $\Delta y/y$, which can be approximated with differentials by dy/y. Use this last form to approximate the proportional change in the cost function $c = f(q) = (q^4/2) + 3q + 400$ when $q = 10$ and $dq = 2$. Give your answer to one decimal place.

36. Suppose S is a numerical value of status based on a person's annual income I (in thousands of dollars). For a certain population, suppose $S = 20\sqrt{I}$. Use differentials to approximate S for a person with an annual income of \$15,000, that is, $I = 15$.

37. The volume V of a spherical cell is given by $V = \frac{4}{3}\pi r^3$, where r is the radius. Estimate the change in volume when the radius changes from 6.5×10^{-4} cm to 6.6×10^{-4} cm.

38. The equation $(P + a)(v + b) = k$ is called the "fundamental equation of muscle contraction."[*] Here P is the load imposed on the muscle, v is the velocity of the shortening of the muscle fibers, and a, b, and k are positive constants. Find v in terms of P and then use the differential to approximate the change in v due to a small change in P.

39. In a study of rooted plants in a certain region,[†] it was determined that the average number of species S occurring on plots of size A (in square meters) was given by

$$S = 12\sqrt[4]{A}, \qquad 0 \le A \le 900.$$

Use differentials to approximate the average number of species in an 80-m^2 plot.

13.3 ELASTICITY OF DEMAND

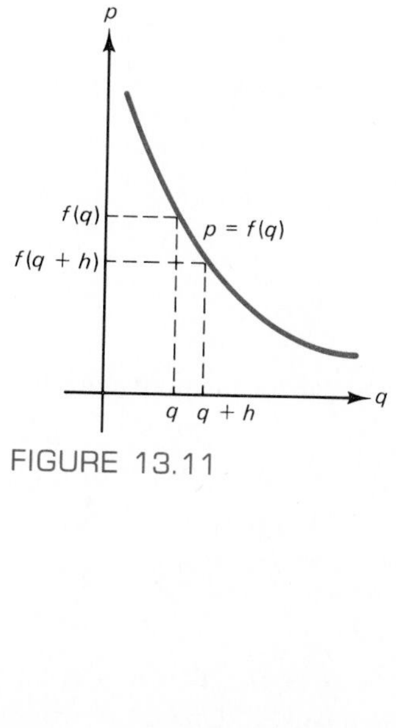

FIGURE 13.11

Elasticity of demand is a means by which economists measure how a change in the price of a product will affect the quantity demanded. That is, it refers to consumer response to price changes. Loosely speaking, elasticity of demand is the ratio of the resulting percentage change in quantity demanded to a given percentage change in price:

$$\frac{\text{percentage change in quantity}}{\text{percentage change in price}}.$$

For example, if for a price increase of 5%, quantity demanded were to decrease by 2%, we would *loosely say* that elasticity of demand is $-2/5$.

To be more general, suppose $p = f(q)$ is the demand function for a product. Consumers will demand q units at a price of $f(q)$ per unit, and will demand $q + h$ units at a price of $f(q + h)$ per unit (Fig. 13.11). The *percentage* change

[*] R. W. Stacy et al., *Essentials of Biological and Medical Physics* (New York: McGraw-Hill Book Company, 1955).

[†] R. W. Poole, *An Introduction to Quantitative Ecology* (New York: McGraw-Hill Book Company, 1974).

in quantity demanded from q to $q + h$ is $\frac{(q + h) - q}{q} \cdot 100 = \frac{h}{q} \cdot 100$. The

corresponding percentage change in price per unit is $\frac{f(q + h) - f(q)}{f(q)} \cdot 100$. The

ratio of these percentage changes is

$$\frac{\dfrac{h}{q} \cdot 100}{\dfrac{f(q + h) - f(q)}{f(q)} \cdot 100} = \frac{h}{q} \cdot \frac{f(q)}{f(q + h) - f(q)}$$

$$= \frac{f(q)}{q} \cdot \frac{h}{f(q + h) - f(q)}$$

$$= \frac{\dfrac{f(q)}{q}}{\dfrac{f(q + h) - f(q)}{h}}. \tag{1}$$

If f is differentiable, then as $h \to 0$ the limit of $[f(q + h) - f(q)]/h$ is $f'(q) = dp/dq$. Thus the limit of (1) is

$$\frac{\dfrac{f(q)}{q}}{\dfrac{dp}{dq}} \quad \text{or} \quad \frac{\dfrac{p}{q}}{\dfrac{dp}{dq}},$$

which is called *point elasticity*.

Definition
*If $p = f(q)$ is a differentiable demand function, the **point elasticity of demand**, denoted by the Greek letter η (eta), at (q, p) is given by*

$$\eta = \frac{\dfrac{p}{q}}{\dfrac{dp}{dq}}.$$

To illustrate, let us find the point elasticity of demand for the demand function $p = 1200 - q^2$.

$$\eta = \frac{\dfrac{p}{q}}{\dfrac{dp}{dq}} = \frac{\dfrac{1200 - q^2}{q}}{-2q} = -\frac{1200 - q^2}{2q^2} = -\left[\frac{600}{q^2} - \frac{1}{2}\right]. \tag{2}$$

For example, if $q = 10$, then $\eta = -[(600/10^2) - \frac{1}{2}] = -5\frac{1}{2}$. This means that if price were increased by 1% when $q = 10$, the quantity demanded would decrease by approximately $5\frac{1}{2}\%$. Similarly, increasing price by $\frac{1}{2}\%$ results in a decrease in demand of approximately 2.75%.

Note that when elasticity is evaluated, no units are attached to it—it is nothing more than a real number. For normal behavior of demand, a price increase (decrease) corresponds to a quantity decrease (increase). Thus dp/dq will always be negative or 0, and η (where defined) will always be negative or 0. Some economists disregard the minus sign; in the above situation they would consider the elasticity to be $5\frac{1}{2}$. We shall not adopt this practice.

There are three categories of elasticity:

1. When $|\eta| > 1$, demand is *elastic*.

2. When $|\eta| = 1$, demand has *unit elasticity*.

3. When $|\eta| < 1$, demand is *inelastic*.

In Eq. (2), since $|\eta| = 5\frac{1}{2}$ when $q = 10$, demand is elastic. If $q = 20$, then $|\eta| = |-[(600/20^2) - \frac{1}{2}]| = 1$, so demand has unit elasticity. If $q = 25$, then $|\eta| = |-\frac{23}{50}|$ and demand is inelastic.

Loosely speaking, for a given percentage change in price, there is a greater percentage change in quantity demanded if demand is elastic, a smaller percentage change if demand is inelastic, and an equal percentage change if demand has unit elasticity.

EXAMPLE 1   *Determine the point elasticity of the following demand equations for $q > 0$.*

a. $p = \dfrac{k}{q}$ where $k > 0$.

$$\eta = \frac{\dfrac{p}{q}}{\dfrac{dp}{dq}} = \frac{\dfrac{k}{q^2}}{\dfrac{-k}{q^2}} = -1.$$

Thus the demand has unit elasticity for all $q > 0$. The graph of $p = k/q$ is called an *equilateral hyperbola* and is often found in economics texts in discussions of elasticity. See Fig. 3.11 for a graph of such a curve.

b. $q = p^2 - 40p + 400$.

This equation defines p implicitly as a function of q. From Sec. 13.2,

$$\frac{dp}{dq} = \frac{1}{\dfrac{dq}{dp}}.$$

Therefore, $dp/dq = 1/(2p - 40)$ and

$$\eta = \frac{\dfrac{p}{q}}{\dfrac{dp}{dq}} = \frac{\dfrac{p}{q}}{2p - 40} = \frac{p(2p - 40)}{q}.$$

For example, if $p = 15$, then $q = 25$; hence $\eta = [15(-10)]/25 = -6$ and demand is elastic.

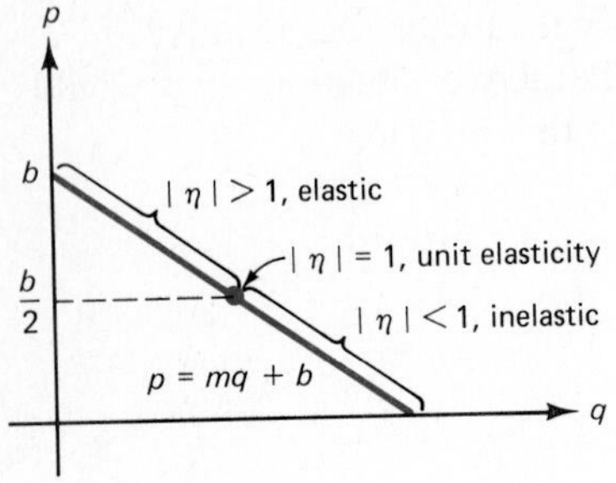

FIGURE 13.12

Point elasticity for a *linear* demand equation is quite interesting. Suppose the equation has the form

$$p = mq + b, \qquad \text{where } m < 0 \text{ and } b > 0.$$

See Fig. 13.12. We assume that $q > 0$; thus $p < b$. The point elasticity of demand is

$$\eta = \frac{\dfrac{p}{q}}{\dfrac{dp}{dq}} = \frac{\dfrac{p}{q}}{m} = \frac{p}{mq} = \frac{p}{p - b}.$$

By considering $d\eta/dp$, we shall show that η is a decreasing function of p. By the quotient rule,

$$\frac{d\eta}{dp} = \frac{(p - b) - p}{(p - b)^2} = -\frac{b}{(p - b)^2}.$$

Since $b > 0$ and $(p - b)^2 > 0$, then $d\eta/dp < 0$, so η is a decreasing function of p—as p increases, η must decrease. However, p ranges between 0 and b, and at the midpoint of this range, $b/2$,

$$\eta = \frac{\dfrac{b}{2}}{\dfrac{b}{2} - b} = \frac{\dfrac{b}{2}}{-\dfrac{b}{2}} = -1.$$

Therefore, if $p < b/2$, then $\eta > -1$; if $p > b/2$, then $\eta < -1$. Because we must have $\eta \le 0$, we can state these facts another way. When $p < b/2$, $|\eta| < 1$ and demand is inelastic; when $p = b/2$, $|\eta| = 1$ and demand has unit elasticity; when $p > b/2$, $|\eta| > 1$ and demand is elastic. This shows that the slope of a demand curve is not a measure of elasticity. The slope of the line above is m everywhere, but elasticity varies with the point on the line.

Turning to a different situation, we can relate how elasticity of demand affects changes in revenue (marginal revenue). If $p = f(q)$ is a manufacturer's demand function, total revenue r is given by

$$r = pq.$$

To find marginal revenue, dr/dq, we differentiate r by using the product rule.

$$\frac{dr}{dq} = p + q\frac{dp}{dq}. \tag{3}$$

Factoring the right side of Eq. (3), we have

$$\frac{dr}{dq} = p\left(1 + \frac{q}{p}\frac{dp}{dq}\right).$$

But

$$\frac{q}{p}\frac{dp}{dq} = \frac{\dfrac{dp}{dq}}{\dfrac{p}{q}} = \frac{1}{\eta}.$$

Thus

$$\frac{dr}{dq} = p\left(1 + \frac{1}{\eta}\right). \tag{4}$$

If demand is elastic, then $\eta < -1$ and $1 + \dfrac{1}{\eta} > 0$. If demand is inelastic, then $\eta > -1$ and $1 + \dfrac{1}{\eta} < 0$. Let us assume that $p > 0$. From Eq. (4) we can conclude that $dr/dq > 0$ on intervals for which demand is elastic; hence total revenue r is increasing there. On the other hand, marginal revenue is negative on intervals for which demand is inelastic; hence total revenue is decreasing there.

Thus we conclude from the above argument that as more units are sold, a manufacturer's total revenue increases if demand is elastic but decreases if demand is inelastic. That is, if demand is elastic, a lower price will increase revenue. This means that a lower price will cause a large enough increase in demand to actually increase revenue. If inelastic, a lower price will decrease revenue. For unit elasticity, a lower price leaves total revenue unchanged.

EXERCISE 13.3

In Problems 1–14, find the point elasticity of the demand equations for the indicated values of q or p and determine whether demand is elastic, inelastic, or has unit elasticity.

1. $p = 40 - 2q$; $q = 5$.

2. $p = 12 - 0.03q$; $q = 300$.

3. $p = \dfrac{1000}{q}$; $q = 288$.

4. $p = \dfrac{1000}{q^2}$; $q = 156$.

5. $p = \dfrac{500}{q + 2}$; $q = 100$.

6. $p = \dfrac{800}{2q + 1}$; $q = 25$.

7. $p = 150 - e^{q/100}$; $q = 100$.

8. $p = 100e^{-q/200}$; $q = 200$.

9. $q = 600 - 100p$; $p = 3$.

10. $q = 100 - p$; $p = 50$.

11. $q = \sqrt{2500 - p}$; $p = 900$.

12. $q = \sqrt{2500 - p^2}$; $p = 20$.

13. $q = \dfrac{(p - 100)^2}{2}$; $p = 20$.

14. $q = p^2 - 60p + 898$; $p = 10$.

15. For the linear demand equation $p = 13 - 0.05q$, verify that demand is elastic when $p = 10$, is inelastic when $p = 3$, and demand has unit elasticity when $p = 6.50$.

16. For what value (or values) of q do the following demand equations have unit elasticity?
    a. $p = 26 - 0.10q$.
    b. $p = 1200 - q^2$.

17. The demand equation for a product is
$$q = 500 - 40p + p^2,$$
where p is the price per unit (in dollars) and q is the quantity of units demanded (in thousands). Find the point elasticity of demand when $p = 15$. If this price of 15 is increased by $\frac{1}{2}\%$, what is the approximate change in demand?

18. The demand equation of a product is
$$q = \sqrt{2500 - p^2}.$$
Find the point elasticity of demand when $p = 30$. If the price of 30 decreases $\frac{2}{3}\%$, what is the approximate change in demand?

19. For the demand equation $p = 500 - 2q$ verify that demand is elastic and total revenue is increasing for $0 < q < 125$. Verify that demand is inelastic and total revenue is decreasing for $125 < q < 250$.

20. Verify that $\dfrac{dr}{dq} = p\left(1 + \dfrac{1}{\eta}\right)$ if $p = 40 - 2q$.

21. Repeat Problem 20 for $p = \dfrac{1000}{q^2}$.

22. Let $p = mq + b$ be a linear demand equation where $m \neq 0$ and $b > 0$.
    a. Show that $\lim\limits_{p \to b^-} \eta = -\infty$.
    b. Show that $\eta = 0$ when $p = 0$.

23. Given the demand equation $p = 1000 - q^2$, where $5 \leq q \leq 30$, for what value of q is $|\eta|$ a maximum? For what value is it a minimum?

24. Repeat Problem 23 for $p = 200/(q + 5)$ such that $5 \leq q \leq 95$.

13.4 REVIEW

Important Terms and Symbols

Section 13.1   economic lot size

Section 13.2   differential, dy, dx

Section 13.3   point elasticity of demand   elastic   inelastic   unit elasticity.

Summary

In a practical sense, the power of calculus is that it allows us to maximize or minimize quantities. For example, in the area of economics we can maximize profit or minimize cost. Some important relationships that are used in economics problems are:

$$\bar{c} = \frac{c}{q}, \qquad \frac{\text{average cost}}{\text{per unit}} = \frac{\text{total cost}}{\text{quantity}},$$

$$r = pq, \qquad \text{revenue} = (\text{price})(\text{quantity}),$$

$$p = r - c, \qquad \text{profit} = \text{total revenue} - \text{total cost}.$$

If $y = f(x)$ is a differentiable function of x, we define the differential dy by

$$dy = f'(x)\, dx,$$

where dx is any real number and dx represents Δx, a change in x. If dx is close to zero, then dy is an approximation to Δy, a change in y:

$$\Delta y \approx dy.$$

Moreover, dy can be used to estimate a function value. We use the relationship

$$f(x + dx) \approx f(x) + dy.$$

Here $f(x + dx)$ is the value to be estimated; x and dx are chosen so that $f(x)$ is easy to compute and dx is small.
If an equation defines y as a function of x, then the derivative of x with respect to y is given by

$$\frac{dx}{dy} = \frac{1}{\dfrac{dy}{dx}}, \qquad dy/dx \neq 0.$$

Point elasticity of demand is a number that measures how consumer demand is affected by price change. It is given by

$$\eta = \frac{p/q}{dp/dq},$$

where p is the price per unit at which q units are demanded. The three categories of elasticity are:

$$|\eta| > 1, \qquad \text{demand is elastic,}$$

$$|\eta| = 1, \qquad \text{unit elasticity,}$$

$$|\eta| < 1, \qquad \text{demand is inelastic,}$$

To put it simply, for a given percentage change in price, there is a greater percentage change in quantity demanded if demand is elastic, a smaller percentage change if demand is inelastic, and an equal percentage change if demand has unit elasticity.

Review Problems

1. A manufacturer determines that m employees on a certain production line will produce q units per month where $q = 80m^2 - 0.1m^4$. To obtain maximum monthly production, how many employees should be assigned to the production line?

2. The demand function for a manufacturer's product is given by $p = 100e^{-0.1q}$. For what value of q does the manufacturer maximize total revenue?

3. The demand function for a monopolist's product is $p = \sqrt{600 - q}$. If the monopolist wants to produce at least 100 units but not more than 300 units, how many units should be produced to maximize total revenue?

4. If $c = 0.01q^2 + 5q + 100$ is a cost function, find the average cost function. At what level of production q is there a minimum average cost?

5. The demand function for a monopolist's product is $p = 400 - 2q$ and the average cost per unit for producing q units is $\bar{c} = q + 160 + (2000/q)$, where p and $\bar{c}$ are in dollars per unit. Find the maximum profit that the monopolist can achieve.

6. A rectangular box is to be made by cutting out equal squares from each corner of a piece of cardboard 10 in. by 16 in. and then folding up the sides. What must be the length of the side of the square cut out if the volume of the box is to be a maximum?

7. A rectangular field is to be enclosed by a fence and divided equally into three parts by two fences parallel to one pair of the sides. If a total of 800 ft of fencing is to be used, find the dimensions of the field if its area is to be maximized.

8. A rectangular poster having an area of 500 in.^{2} is to have a 4-in. margin at each side and at the bottom and a 6-in. margin at the top. The remainder of the poster is for printed matter. Find the dimensions of the poster so that the area for the printed matter is maximized.

9. In a laboratory an experimental antibacterial agent is applied to a population of 100 bacteria. Data indicate that the number N of bacteria, t hours after the agent is introduced, is given by

$$N = \frac{14,400 + 120t + 100t^2}{144 + t^2}.$$

For what value of t does the maximum number of bacteria in the population occur? What is this maximum number?

In Problems **10** and **11**, determine the differentials of the functions in terms of x and dx.

10. $f(x) = (x^2 + 5)/(x - 7)$.

11. $f(x) = x^2 \ln(x + 5)$.

12. If $p = q^2 + 8q$, use differentials to estimate Δp if q changes from 4 to 4.02.

13. Fahrenheit temperature F and Celsius temperature C are related by $F = \frac{9}{5}C + 32$. Using differentials, find how much F would change due to a change in C of $\frac{1}{2}°$.

In Problems **14** and **15**, approximate the expressions by using differentials.

14. $\sqrt{25.5}$.

15. $e^{-0.01}$.

16. If $x = 4y^2 + 7y - 3$, find dy/dx.

For the demand equations in Problems **17–19**, determine whether demand is elastic, inelastic, or has unit elasticity for the indicated value of q.

17. $p = 18 - 0.02q$; $q = 600$.

18. $p = \dfrac{500}{q}$; $q = 200$.

19. $p = 900 - q^2$; $q = 10$.

14

Integration

Chapters 11–13 dealt with differential calculus. We differentiated a function and obtained another function, its derivative. *Integral calculus* is concerned with the reverse process. We are given the derivative of a function and must find the original function. The need for doing this arises in a natural way. For example, we may have a marginal revenue function and want to find the revenue function from it. Integral calculus also involves a limit concept that allows us to take the limit of a special kind of sum as the number of terms in the sum becomes infinite. This is the real power of integral calculus! With this notion we may find the area of a region that cannot be found by any other convenient method.

14.1 THE INDEFINITE INTEGRAL

Given a function f, if F is a function such that

$$F'(x) = f(x), \tag{1}$$

then F is called an *antiderivative* of f. Thus an antiderivative of f is simply a function whose derivative is f. Multiplying both sides of Eq. (1) by the differential dx gives $F'(x)\, dx = f(x)\, dx$. However, because $F'(x)\, dx$ is the differential of F, we have $dF = f(x)\, dx$. Thus we can think of an antiderivative of f as a function whose differential is $f(x)\, dx$.

Definition
An ***antiderivative*** of a function f is a function F such that

$$F'(x) = f(x),$$

or equivalently, in differential notation,

$$dF = f(x)\, dx.$$

For example, since $D_x(x^2) = 2x$, x^2 is an antiderivative of $2x$. However, it is not the only antiderivative of $2x$. Since

$$D_x(x^2 + 1) = 2x \quad \text{and} \quad D_x(x^2 - 5) = 2x,$$

both $x^2 + 1$ and $x^2 - 5$ are also antiderivatives of $2x$. It can be shown that *any* antiderivative of $2x$ must have the form $x^2 + C$, where C is a constant. Thus *any two antiderivatives of $2x$ differ only by a constant.*

An arbitrary antiderivative of $2x$ is denoted $\int 2x \, dx$, which is read "the *indefinite integral* of $2x$ with respect to x." Since all antiderivatives of $2x$ have the form $x^2 + C$, we write

$$\int 2x \, dx = x^2 + C.$$

The symbol $\int$ is called the **integral sign,** $2x$ is the **integrand,** and C is the **constant of integration.** The dx is part of the integral notation and indicates the variable involved. Here x is the **variable of integration.**

More generally, the **indefinite integral** of any function f with respect to x is written $\int f(x) \, dx$ and denotes an arbitrary antiderivative of f. It can be shown that all antiderivatives of f differ only by a constant. Thus if F is any antiderivative of f, then

$$\int f(x) \, dx = F(x) + C, \quad \text{where } C \text{ is a constant.}$$

To *integrate f* means to find $\int f(x) \, dx$. In summary,

$$\boxed{\int f(x) \, dx = F(x) + C \quad \text{if and only if} \quad F'(x) = f(x).}$$

EXAMPLE 1   *Find* $\int 5 \, dx$.

Pitfall

It is **incorrect** to write

$$\int 5 \, dx = 5x.$$

Do not forget the constant of integration.

First we must find (perhaps better words are "guess at") a function whose derivative is 5. Since we know that $D_x(5x) = 5$, $5x$ is an antiderivative of 5. Thus

$$\int 5 \, dx = 5x + C.$$

Using differentiation formulas from Chapter 11, we have compiled a list of basic integration formulas in Table 14.1. These formulas are easily verified. For example, Formula 2 is true because the derivative of $x^{n+1}/(n + 1)$ is x^n for $n \neq -1$. To verify Formula 4, we must show that the derivative of $k \int f(x) \, dx$

is $kf(x)$. Now, the derivative of $k \int f(x) \, dx$ is k times the derivative of $\int f(x) \, dx$. Because the derivative of $\int f(x) \, dx$ is $f(x)$, Formula 4 is verified. You should verify the other formulas. Formula 5 can be extended to any number of sums or differences.

TABLE 14.1
Basic Integration Formulas

1. $\int k \, dx = kx + C, \quad k$ a constant.

2. $\int x^n \, dx = \dfrac{x^{n+1}}{n+1} + C, \quad n \ne -1.$

3. $\int e^x \, dx = e^x + C.$

4. $\int k f(x) \, dx = k \int f(x) \, dx, \quad k$ a constant.

5. $\int [f(x) \pm g(x)] \, dx = \int f(x) \, dx \pm \int g(x) \, dx.$

Formula 2 states that the indefinite integral of a power of x (except x^{-1}) is obtained by increasing the exponent for x by one, dividing by the new exponent, and adding on the constant of integration. The case for x^{-1} will be discussed in Sec. 14.2.

EXAMPLE 2   *Find the following indefinite integrals.*

a. $\int 1 \, dx.$

By Formula 1 with $k = 1$,

$$\int 1 \, dx = 1x + C = x + C.$$

Usually, we write $\int 1 \, dx$ as $\int dx$. Thus $\int dx = x + C.$

b. $\int x^5 \, dx.$

By Formula 2 with $n = 5$,

$$\int x^5 \, dx = \frac{x^{5+1}}{5+1} + C = \frac{x^6}{6} + C.$$

c. $\int 7x \, dx.$

By Formula 4 with $k = 7$ and $f(x) = x$,

$$\int 7x \, dx = 7 \int x \, dx.$$

Since x is x^1, by Formula 2 we have

$$\int x^1 \, dx = \frac{x^{1+1}}{1+1} + C_1 = \frac{x^2}{2} + C_1,$$

where C_1 is the constant of integration. Therefore,

$$\int 7x \, dx = 7 \int x \, dx = 7 \left[\frac{x^2}{2} + C_1 \right] = \frac{7}{2}x^2 + 7C_1.$$

For simplicity we replace the constant $7C_1$ by C:

$$\int 7x \, dx = \frac{7}{2}x^2 + C.$$

It is not necessary to write all intermediate steps when integrating. More simply we write

$$\int 7x \, dx = (7)\frac{x^2}{2} + C = \frac{7}{2}x^2 + C.$$

Pitfall

Only a constant factor of the integrand can "jump" in front of an integral sign. Because x is not a constant, it is **incorrect** to write $\int 7x \, dx = 7x \int dx = (7x)(x + C) = 7x^2 + 7Cx.$

d. $\displaystyle \int -\frac{3}{5}e^x \, dx.$

$$\int -\frac{3}{5}e^x \, dx = -\frac{3}{5} \int e^x \, dx \qquad \text{(Formula 4)}$$

$$= -\frac{3}{5}e^x + C \qquad \text{(Formula 3)}.$$

EXAMPLE 3   *Find the following indefinite integrals.*

a. $\displaystyle \int \frac{1}{\sqrt{t}} \, dt.$

Here t is the variable of integration. We rewrite the integrand so that a basic formula can be used. Since $1/\sqrt{t} = t^{-1/2}$, applying Formula 2 gives

$$\int \frac{1}{\sqrt{t}} \, dt = \int t^{-1/2} \, dt = \frac{t^{(-1/2)+1}}{-\frac{1}{2}+1} + C = \frac{t^{1/2}}{\frac{1}{2}} + C = 2\sqrt{t} + C.$$

b. $\displaystyle \int \frac{1}{6x^3} \, dx.$

$$\int \frac{1}{6x^3} \, dx = \frac{1}{6} \int x^{-3} \, dx = \left(\frac{1}{6}\right) \frac{x^{-3+1}}{-3+1} + C$$

$$= -\frac{x^{-2}}{12} + C = -\frac{1}{12x^2} + C.$$

EXAMPLE 4   *Find the following indefinite integrals.*

a. $\int (x^2 + 2x)\, dx.$

By Formula 5,

$$\int (x^2 + 2x)\, dx = \int x^2\, dx + \int 2x\, dx.$$

Now,

$$\int x^2\, dx = \frac{x^{2+1}}{2+1} + C_1 = \frac{x^3}{3} + C_1,$$

and $$\int 2x\, dx = 2\int x\, dx = (2)\frac{x^{1+1}}{1+1} + C_2 = x^2 + C_2.$$

Thus

$$\int (x^2 + 2x)\, dx = \frac{x^3}{3} + x^2 + C_1 + C_2.$$

Replacing $C_1 + C_2$ by C, we have

$$\int (x^2 + 2x)\, dx = \frac{x^3}{3} + x^2 + C.$$

Omitting intermediate steps, we simply write

$$\int (x^2 + 2x)\, dx = \frac{x^3}{3} + (2)\frac{x^2}{2} + C = \frac{x^3}{3} + x^2 + C.$$

b. $\int (2\sqrt[5]{x^4} - 7x^3 + 10e^x - 1)\, dx.$

$$\int (2\sqrt[5]{x^4} - 7x^3 + 10e^x - 1)\, dx$$

$$= 2\int x^{4/5}\, dx - 7\int x^3\, dx + 10\int e^x\, dx - \int 1\, dx$$

$$= (2)\frac{x^{9/5}}{\frac{9}{5}} - (7)\frac{x^4}{4} + 10e^x - x + C$$

$$= \frac{10}{9}x^{9/5} - \frac{7}{4}x^4 + 10e^x - x + C.$$

Sometimes, in order to apply the basic integration formulas it is necessary to first perform algebraic manipulations on an integrand, as Example 5 shows.

EXAMPLE 5   *Find the following indefinite integrals.*

a. $\int y^2(y + \frac{2}{3})\, dy$.

By multiplying the integrand, we get

$$\int y^2(y + \tfrac{2}{3})\, dy = \int (y^3 + \tfrac{2}{3}y^2)\, dy$$

$$= \frac{y^4}{4} + \left(\frac{2}{3}\right)\frac{y^3}{3} + C = \frac{y^4}{4} + \frac{2y^3}{9} + C.$$

b. $\int \dfrac{(3x + \sqrt{x})(\sqrt[3]{x} - 2)}{6}\, dx$.

By factoring out $\frac{1}{6}$ and multiplying the binomials, we get

$$\int \frac{(3x + x^{1/2})(x^{1/3} - 2)}{6}\, dx$$

$$= \frac{1}{6}\int (3x^{4/3} + x^{5/6} - 6x - 2x^{1/2})\, dx$$

$$= \frac{1}{6}\left[(3)\frac{x^{7/3}}{\frac{7}{3}} + \frac{x^{11/6}}{\frac{11}{6}} - (6)\frac{x^2}{2} - (2)\frac{x^{3/2}}{\frac{3}{2}}\right] + C$$

$$= \frac{3x^{7/3}}{14} + \frac{x^{11/6}}{11} - \frac{x^2}{2} - \frac{2x^{3/2}}{9} + C.$$

Pitfall

In Example 5(a) we first multiplied the factors in the integrand. We point out that

$$\int y^2(y + \tfrac{2}{3})\, dy \neq \left[\int y^2\, dy\right]\left[\int (y + \tfrac{2}{3})\, dy\right].$$

More generally,

$$\int f(x)g(x)\, dx \neq \int f(x)\, dx \cdot \int g(x)\, dx.$$

Although there are many antiderivatives of a function, we may want to find a *particular* one that satisfies a certain condition. The following examples will illustrate.

EXAMPLE 6   *For a particular urban group, sociologists studied the current average yearly income y (in dollars) that a person can expect to receive with x years of education before seeking regular employment. They estimated that the rate at which income changes with respect to education is given by*

$$\frac{dy}{dx} = 10x^{3/2}, \qquad 4 \leq x \leq 16,$$

where $y = 5872$ *when* $x = 9$. *Find* y.

Since $dy/dx = 10x^{3/2}$, y is an antiderivative of $10x^{3/2}$. Thus

$$y = \int 10x^{3/2} \, dx = 10 \int x^{3/2} \, dx$$

$$= (10)\frac{x^{5/2}}{\frac{5}{2}} + C = 4x^{5/2} + C.$$

Thus *any* function of the form

$$y = 4x^{5/2} + C \qquad (2)$$

satisfies $dy/dx = 10x^{3/2}$. To determine the particular one for which $y = 5872$ when $x = 9$, we must find the value that C must assume. Substituting $y = 5872$ and $x = 9$ into Eq. (2), we obtain

$$5872 = 4(9)^{5/2} + C$$

$$= 4(243) + C.$$

$$5872 = 972 + C.$$

Therefore, $C = 4900$ and

$$y = 4x^{5/2} + 4900.$$

EXAMPLE 7   *Given that* $y'' = x^2 - 6$, $y'(0) = 2$, *and* $y(1) = -1$, *find* y. *[Note:* $y'(0) = 2$ *means that* $y' = 2$ *when* $x = 0$, *and* $y(1) = -1$ *means that* $y = -1$ *when* $x = 1$.*]*

Since $y'' = \dfrac{d}{dx}(y') = x^2 - 6$, y' is an antiderivative of $x^2 - 6$. Thus

$$y' = \int (x^2 - 6) \, dx = \frac{x^3}{3} - 6x + C_1. \qquad (3)$$

Since $y' = 2$ when $x = 0$, from Eq. (3) we have

$$2 = \frac{0^3}{2} - 6(0) + C_1.$$

Hence $C_1 = 2$ and

$$y' = \frac{x^3}{3} - 6x + 2.$$

By integration we can find y:

$$y = \int \left(\frac{x^3}{3} - 6x + 2 \right) dx$$

$$= \left(\frac{1}{3} \right) \frac{x^4}{4} - (6)\frac{x^2}{2} + 2x + C_2.$$

$$y = \frac{x^4}{12} - 3x^2 + 2x + C_2. \qquad (4)$$

Since $y = -1$ when $x = 1$, from Eq. (4) we have

$$-1 = \frac{1^4}{12} - 3(1)^2 + 2(1) + C_2.$$

Therefore, $C_2 = -\frac{1}{12}$ and

$$y = \frac{x^4}{12} - 3x^2 + 2x - \frac{1}{12}.$$

EXAMPLE 8   *If the marginal revenue function for a manufacturer's product is*

$$\frac{dr}{dq} = 2000 - 20q - 3q^2,$$

find the demand function.

Since dr/dq is the derivative of total revenue r,

$$r = \int (2000 - 20q - 3q^2)\, dq$$

$$= 2000q - (20)\frac{q^2}{2} - (3)\frac{q^3}{3} + C.$$

$$r = 2000q - 10q^2 - q^3 + C. \tag{5}$$

We assume that *when no units are sold, total revenue is* 0; that is, $r = 0$ when $q = 0$. Substituting these values into Eq. (5) gives

$$0 = 2000(0) - 10(0)^2 - 0^3 + C.$$

Hence $C = 0$ and

$$r = 2000q - 10q^2 - q^3.$$

To find the demand function, we use this result together with the general relationship that $r = pq$, where p is the price per unit. Solving $r = pq$ for p and substituting for r gives the demand function:

$$p = \frac{r}{q} = \frac{2000q - 10q^2 - q^3}{q}.$$

$$p = 2000 - 10q - q^2.$$

EXAMPLE 9   *In the manufacture of a product, fixed costs per week are $4000. Fixed costs are costs, such as rent and insurance, that remain constant at all levels of production in a given time period. If the marginal cost function dc/dq is*

$$\frac{dc}{dq} = 0.000001(0.002q^2 - 25q) + 0.2,$$

where c is the total cost (in dollars) of producing q pounds of product per week, find the cost of producing 10,000 lb in 1 week.

Since dc/dq is the derivative of total cost c,

$$c = \int [0.000001(0.002q^2 - 25q) + 0.2]\, dq$$

$$= 0.000001 \int (0.002q^2 - 25q)\, dq + \int 0.2\, dq.$$

$$c = 0.000001 \left(\frac{0.002q^3}{3} - \frac{25q^2}{2} \right) + 0.2q + C.$$

Fixed costs are constant regardless of output. Therefore, when $q = 0$, then $c = 4000$. Thus $C = 4000$ and

$$c = 0.000001 \left(\frac{0.002q^3}{3} - \frac{25q^2}{2} \right) + 0.2q + 4000. \tag{6}$$

From Eq. (6), when $q = 10,000$ then $c = 5416\frac{2}{3}$. The total cost for producing 10,000 pounds of product in 1 week is \$5416.67.

EXERCISE 14.1

In Problems 1–50, find the indefinite integrals.

1. $\int 5\, dx.$

2. $\int \frac{1}{2}\, dx.$

3. $\int x^8\, dx.$

4. $\int 2x^{25}\, dx.$

5. $\int 5x^{-7}\, dx.$

6. $\int \frac{z^{-3}}{3}\, dz.$

7. $\int \frac{1}{x^{10}}\, dx.$

8. $\int \frac{7}{x^4}\, dx.$

9. $\int \frac{1}{y^{11/5}}\, dy.$

10. $\int \frac{7}{2x^{9/4}}\, dx.$

11. $\int (8 + u)\, du.$

12. $\int (r^3 + 2r)\, dr.$

13. $\int (y^5 - 5y)\, dy.$

14. $\int (7 - 3w - 2w^2)\, dw.$

15. $\int (3t^2 - 4t + 5)\, dt.$

16. $\int (1 + u + u^2 + u^3)\, du.$

17. $\int (7 + e)\, dx.$

18. $\int (5 - 2^{-1})\, dx$

19. $\int \left(\frac{x}{7} - \frac{3}{4}x^4 \right) dx.$

20. $\int \left(\frac{2x^2}{7} - \frac{8}{3}x^4 \right) dx.$

21. $\int 3e^x\, dx.$

22. $\int \left(\frac{e^x}{3} + 2x \right) dx.$

23. $\int (x^{8.3} - 9x^6 + 3x^{-4} + x^{-3})\, dx.$

24. $\int (0.3y^4 - 8y^{-3} + 2)\, dy.$

25. $\int \frac{-2\sqrt{x}}{3}\, dx.$

26. $\int dw.$

27. $\int \frac{1}{4\sqrt[8]{x^7}}\, dx.$

28. $\int \frac{-3}{4\sqrt[8]{x}}\, dx.$

29. $\int \left(\frac{x^3}{3} - \frac{3}{x^3} \right) dx.$

30. $\int \left(\frac{1}{2x^3} - \frac{1}{x^4} \right) dx.$

31. $\int \left(\dfrac{3w^2}{2} - \dfrac{2}{3w^2} \right) dw.$

32. $\int \dfrac{2}{e^{-s}} \, ds.$

33. $\int (6 - \tfrac{5}{4}z^2 + 2e^z) \, dz.$

34. $\int \tfrac{1}{12}(\tfrac{1}{3}x^5) \, dx.$

35. $\int \left(\dfrac{e^u}{4} + 1 \right) du.$

36. $\int \left(3y^3 - 2y^2 + \dfrac{e^y}{6} \right) dy.$

37. $\int (2\sqrt{x} - 3\sqrt[4]{x}) \, dx.$

38. $\int 0 \, dx.$

39. $\int \left(-\dfrac{\sqrt[3]{x^2}}{5} - \dfrac{7}{2\sqrt{x}} + 6x \right) dx.$

40. $\int \left(\sqrt[3]{x} - \dfrac{1}{\sqrt[3]{x}} \right) dx.$

41. $\int (x^2 + 5)(x - 3) \, dx.$

42. $\int x^4(x^3 + 3x^2 + 7) \, dx.$

43. $\int \sqrt{x}(x + 3) \, dx.$

44. $\int (z + 2)^2 \, dz.$

45. $\int (2u + 1)^2 \, du.$

46. $\int \left(\dfrac{1}{\sqrt[3]{x}} + 1 \right)^2 dx.$

47. $\int v^{-2}(2v^4 + 3v^2 - 2v^{-3}) \, dv.$

48. $\int [6e^u - u^3(\sqrt{u} + 1)] \, du.$

49. $\int \dfrac{e^6 + e^x}{2} \, dx.$

50. $\int \dfrac{\sqrt{x}(x^5 - \sqrt[3]{x} + 2)}{3} \, dx.$

*In Problems **51–56**, find y subject to the given conditions.*

51. $dy/dx = 3x - 4;$ $y(-1) = \tfrac{13}{2}.$

52. $dy/dx = x^2 - x;$ $y(3) = 4.$

53. $y'' = -x^2 - 2x;$ $y'(1) = 0, y(1) = 1.$

54. $y'' = x + 1;$ $y'(0) = 0, y(0) = 5.$

55. $y''' = 2x;$ $y''(-1) = 3, y'(3) = 10, y(0) = 2.$

56. $y''' = e^x + 1;$ $y''(0) = 1, y'(0) = 2, y(0) = 3.$

*In Problems **57–60**, dr/dq is a marginal revenue function. Find the demand function.*

57. $dr/dq = 0.7.$

58. $dr/dq = 15 - \tfrac{1}{15}q.$

59. $dr/dq = 275 - q - 0.3q^2.$

60. $dr/dq = 10,000 - 2(2q + q^3).$

*In Problems **61–64**, dc/dq is a marginal cost function and fixed costs are indicated in braces. For Problems **61** and **62** find the total cost function. For Problems **63** and **64**, find the total cost for the indicated value of q.*

61. $dc/dq = 1.35;$ $\{200\}.$

62. $dc/dq = 2q + 50;$ $\{1000\}.$

63. $dc/dq = 0.09q^2 - 1.2q + 4.5;$ $\{7700\};$ $q = 10.$

64. $dc/dq = 0.000102q^2 - 0.034q + 5;$ $\{10,000\};$ $q = 100.$

65. A group of biologists studied the nutritional effects on rats that were fed a diet containing 10% protein.* The protein consisted of yeast and corn flour. Over a period of time, the group found that the (approximate) rate of change of the average weight gain G (in grams) of a rat with respect to the percentage P of yeast in the protein mix is

$$\frac{dG}{dP} = -\frac{P}{25} + 2, \qquad 0 \le P \le 100.$$

If $G = 38$ when $P = 10$, find G.

66. A study of the winter moth was made in Nova Scotia.† The prepupae of the moth fall onto the ground from

---

* Adapted from R. Bressani, "The Use of Yeast in Human Foods," in *Single-Cell Protein*, ed. R. I. Mateles and S. R. Tannenbaum (Cambridge, Mass.: MIT Press, 1968).

† Adapted from D. G. Embree, "The Population Dynamics of the Winter Moth in Nova Scotia, 1954–1962," *Memoirs of the Entomological Society of Canada*, no. 46 (1965).

host trees. It was found that the (approximate) rate at which prepupal density y (number of prepupae per square foot of soil) changes with respect to distance x (in feet) from the base of a host tree is

$$\frac{dy}{dx} = -1.5 - x, \qquad 1 \le x \le 9.$$

If $y = 57.3$ when $x = 1$, find y.

67. In the study of flow of fluid in a tube of constant radius R, such as blood flow in portions of the body, one can think of the tube as consisting of concentric tubes of radius r, where $0 \le r \le R$. The velocity v of the fluid is a function of r and is given by *

$$v = \int -\frac{(P_1 - P_2)r}{2l\eta}\, dr,$$

where P_1 and P_2 are pressures at the ends of the tube, η (a Greek letter read "eta") is fluid viscosity, and l is the length of the tube. If $v = 0$ when $r = R$, show that

$$v = \frac{(P_1 - P_2)(R^2 - r^2)}{4l\eta}.$$

68. The sole producer of a product has determined that the marginal revenue function is $dr/dq = 100 - 3q^2$. Determine the point elasticity of demand for the product when $q = 5$. (*Hint:* First find the demand function.)

69. A manufacturer has determined that the marginal cost function is $dc/dq = 0.003q^2 - 0.4q + 40$, where q is the number of units produced. If marginal cost is $27.50 when $q = 50$, and fixed costs are $5000, what is the *average* cost of producing 100 units?

14.2 MORE INTEGRATION FORMULAS

The formula

$$\int x^n\, dx = \frac{x^{n+1}}{n+1} + C, \quad \text{if } n \ne -1,$$

which applies to a power of x, can be generalized to handle a power of a *function* of x. Let u be a differentiable function of x. By the power rule, if $n \ne -1$ then

$$\frac{d}{dx}\left(\frac{[u(x)]^{n+1}}{n+1}\right) = \frac{(n+1)[u(x)]^n \cdot u'(x)}{n+1} = [u(x)]^n \cdot u'(x).$$

Thus

$$\int [u(x)]^n \cdot u'(x)\, dx = \frac{[u(x)]^{n+1}}{n+1} + C, \qquad n \ne -1.$$

We call this the *power rule for integration*. Since $u'(x)\, dx$ is the differential of u, namely du, for mathematical shorthand we can replace $u(x)$ by u and $u'(x)\, dx$ by du:

* R. W. Stacy et al., *Essentials of Biological and Medical Physics* (New York: McGraw-Hill, 1955).

POWER RULE FOR INTEGRATION

If u is differentiable, then

$$\int u^n \, du = \frac{u^{n+1}}{n+1} + C, \qquad \text{if } n \neq -1.$$

EXAMPLE 1   *Use the power rule for integration to find the following.*

a. $\int (x + 1)^{20} \, dx.$

Since we have a power of $x + 1$, we shall set $u = x + 1$. Then $du = dx$ and $\int (x + 1)^{20} \, dx$ has the form $\int u^{20} \, du$. By the power rule for integration,

$$\int (x + 1)^{20} \, dx = \int u^{20} \, du = \frac{u^{21}}{21} + C = \frac{(x+1)^{21}}{21} + C.$$

Note that we give our answer not in terms of u but explicitly in terms of x.

b. $\int 3x^2(x^3 + 7)^3 \, dx.$

Let $u = x^3 + 7$. Then $du = 3x^2 \, dx$. Fortunately, $3x^2$ appears as a factor in the integrand and can be used as part of du.

$$\int 3x^2(x^3 + 7)^3 \, dx = \int (x^3 + 7)^3 [3x^2 \, dx] = \int u^3 \, du$$

$$= \frac{u^4}{4} + C = \frac{(x^3 + 7)^4}{4} + C.$$

EXAMPLE 2   *Find* $\int x\sqrt{x^2 + 5} \, dx.$

We can write this as $\int x(x^2 + 5)^{1/2} \, dx$. If $u = x^2 + 5$, then $du = 2x \, dx$. Since the *constant* factor 2 in du does *not* appear in the integrand, this integral does not have the form $\int u^n \, du$. However, we can put it in this form by first multiplying and dividing the integrand by 2. This does not change its value. Thus

$$\int x(x^2 + 5)^{1/2} \, dx = \int \frac{2}{2} x(x^2 + 5)^{1/2} \, dx = \int \frac{1}{2}(x^2 + 5)^{1/2} [2x \, dx].$$

Moving the *constant* factor $\frac{1}{2}$ in front of the integral sign, we have

$$\int x(x^2 + 5)^{1/2} \, dx = \frac{1}{2} \int (x^2 + 5)^{1/2} [2x \, dx] \tag{1}$$

$$= \frac{1}{2} \int u^{1/2} \, du = \frac{1}{2} \left[\frac{u^{3/2}}{\frac{3}{2}} \right] + C.$$

Going back to x gives

$$\int x \sqrt{x^2 + 5} \, dx = \frac{(x^2 + 5)^{3/2}}{3} + C.$$

In Example 2 we needed the factor 2 in the integrand. In Eq. (1), it was inserted and the integral was simultaneously multiplied by $\frac{1}{2}$. More generally, if c is a nonzero constant, then

$$\int f(x) \, dx = \int \frac{c}{c} f(x) \, dx = \frac{1}{c} \int c f(x) \, dx.$$

In effect, we can multiply the integrand by a nonzero constant c as long as we compensate for this by multiplying the entire integral by $1/c$. Such a manipulation **cannot** be done with *variable* factors.

Pitfall

When using the form $\int u^n \, du$, do not neglect du. For example,

$$\int (4x + 1)^2 \, dx \neq \frac{(4x + 1)^3}{3} + C.$$

Letting $u = 4x + 1$, we have $du = 4 \, dx$. Thus

$$\int (4x + 1)^2 dx = \frac{1}{4} \int (4x + 1)^2 [4 \, dx] = \frac{1}{4} \int u^2 \, du$$

$$= \frac{1}{4} \cdot \frac{u^3}{3} + C = \frac{(4x + 1)^3}{12} + C.$$

EXAMPLE 3 *Find the following indefinite integrals.*

a. $\int \sqrt[3]{6y} \, dy$.

The integrand is $(6y)^{1/3}$. If we set $u = 6y$, then $du = 6 \, dy$. Since the factor 6 does not appear in the integrand, we insert a factor of 6 and adjust for it with a factor of $\frac{1}{6}$ in front of the integral.

$$\int \sqrt[3]{6y} \, dy = \int (6y)^{1/3} \, dy = \frac{1}{6} \int (6y)^{1/3} [6 \, dy] = \frac{1}{6} \int u^{1/3} \, du$$

$$= \left(\frac{1}{6} \right) \frac{u^{4/3}}{\frac{4}{3}} + C = \frac{(6y)^{4/3}}{8} + C.$$

b. $\int \dfrac{2x^3 + 3x}{(x^4 + 3x^2 + 7)^4} \, dx$.

We can write this as $\int (x^4 + 3x^2 + 7)^{-4}(2x^3 + 3x)\,dx$. If $u = x^4 + 3x^2 + 7$, then $du = (4x^3 + 6x)\,dx$, which is two times the quantity $(2x^3 + 3x)\,dx$ in the integral. Thus we insert a factor of 2 and adjust for it with a factor of $\frac{1}{2}$ in front of the integral.

$$\int (x^4 + 3x^2 + 7)^{-4}(2x^3 + 3x)\,dx$$

$$= \frac{1}{2}\int (x^4 + 3x^2 + 7)^{-4}[2(2x^3 + 3x)\,dx]$$

$$= \frac{1}{2}\int (x^4 + 3x^2 + 7)^{-4}[(4x^3 + 6x)\,dx]$$

$$= \frac{1}{2}\int u^{-4}\,du = \frac{1}{2}\cdot\frac{u^{-3}}{-3} + C = -\frac{1}{6u^3} + C$$

$$= -\frac{1}{6(x^4 + 3x^2 + 7)^3} + C.$$

When using the power rule for integration, take care when making your choice for u. In Example 3(b), you would *not* be able to proceed very far if, for instance, you let $u = 2x^3 + 3x$. At times you may find it necessary to try many different choices. **Skill at integration comes only after many hours of practice and conscientious study.**

EXAMPLE 4   Find $\int 4x^2(x^4 + 1)^2\,dx$.

If we set $u = x^4 + 1$, then $du = 4x^3\,dx$. To get du in the integral, we need an additional factor of the *variable* x. However, we can only adjust for **constant** factors. Thus we cannot use the power rule. To find the integral, we shall first expand $(x^4 + 1)^2$.

$$\int 4x^2(x^4 + 1)^2\,dx = 4\int x^2(x^8 + 2x^4 + 1)\,dx$$

$$= 4\int (x^{10} + 2x^6 + x^2)\,dx$$

$$= 4\left(\frac{x^{11}}{11} + \frac{2x^7}{7} + \frac{x^3}{3}\right) + C.$$

We now turn our attention to integrating exponential functions. If u is a differentiable function of x, then $D_x(e^u) = e^u\,du/dx$. Corresponding to this differentiation formula is the integration formula

$$\int e^u \frac{du}{dx}\,dx = e^u + C.$$

But $\dfrac{du}{dx} dx$ is the differential of u, namely du. Thus

$$\int e^u \, du = e^u + C. \qquad (2)$$

EXAMPLE 5   *Find the following integrals.*

a. $\displaystyle\int 2xe^{x^2} \, dx.$

Let $u = x^2$. Then $du = 2x \, dx$ and by Eq. (2),

$$\int 2xe^{x^2} \, dx = \int e^{x^2}[2x \, dx] = \int e^u \, du$$

$$= e^u + C = e^{x^2} + C.$$

b. $\displaystyle\int (x^2 + 1)e^{x^3 + 3x} \, dx.$

If $u = x^3 + 3x$, then $du = (3x^2 + 3) \, dx = 3(x^2 + 1) \, dx$. If the integrand contained a factor of 3, the integral would have the form $\int e^u \, du$. Thus we write

$$\int (x^2 + 1)e^{x^3 + 3x} \, dx = \frac{1}{3}\int e^{x^3 + 3x}[3(x^2 + 1) \, dx]$$

$$= \frac{1}{3}\int e^u \, du = \frac{1}{3}e^u + C$$

$$= \frac{1}{3}e^{x^3 + 3x} + C.$$

Pitfall
Do not apply the power rule formula for $\int u^n \, du$ to $\int e^u \, du$. For example,

$$\int e^x \, dx \neq \frac{e^{x+1}}{x+1} + C.$$

As you know, the power rule formula $\int u^n \, du = u^{n+1}/(n + 1) + C$ assumes that $n \neq -1$. To find $\int u^{-1} \, du = \int \dfrac{1}{u} \, du$, we first recall that

$$\frac{d}{dx}(\ln u) = \frac{1}{u}\frac{du}{dx}.$$

It would seem that $\int \dfrac{1}{u}\dfrac{du}{dx} \, dx = \int \dfrac{1}{u} \, du = \ln u + C$. However, the logarithm of u is defined if and only if u is positive. If $u < 0$, then $\ln u$ is not defined. Thus $\int \dfrac{1}{u} \, du = \ln u + C$ as long as $u > 0$. On the other hand, if $u < 0$, then $-u > 0$ and $\ln(-u)$ is defined. Moreover,

$$\frac{d}{dx}[\ln(-u)] = \frac{1}{-u}(-1)\frac{du}{dx} = \frac{1}{u}\frac{du}{dx}.$$

In this case ($u < 0$), $\int \frac{1}{u}\frac{du}{dx}\,dx = \int \frac{1}{u}\,du = \ln(-u) + C$. In summary, if $u > 0$, then $\int \frac{1}{u}\,du = \ln u + C$; if $u < 0$, then $\int \frac{1}{u}\,du = \ln(-u) + C$. Combining these cases, we have

$$\int \frac{1}{u}\,du = \ln|u| + C. \tag{3}$$

In particular, if $u = x$, then $du = dx$ and

$$\int \frac{1}{x}\,dx = \ln|x| + C. \tag{4}$$

EXAMPLE 6   *Find the following integrals.*

a. $\int \frac{7}{x}\,dx.$

From Eq. (4),

$$\int \frac{7}{x}\,dx = 7\int \frac{1}{x}\,dx = 7\ln|x| + C.$$

Using properties of logarithms, we can write this answer another way:

$$\int \frac{7}{x}\,dx = \ln|x^7| + C.$$

b. $\int \frac{2x}{x^2 + 5}\,dx.$

Let $u = x^2 + 5$. Then $du = 2x\,dx$. From Eq. (3),

$$\int \frac{2x}{x^2 + 5}\,dx = \int \frac{1}{x^2 + 5}[2x\,dx] = \int \frac{1}{u}\,du$$

$$= \ln|u| + C = \ln|x^2 + 5| + C.$$

Since $x^2 + 5$ is always positive we can omit the absolute-value bars:

$$\int \frac{2x}{x^2 + 5}\,dx = \ln(x^2 + 5) + C.$$

c. $\int \dfrac{(2x^3 + 3x)\,dx}{x^4 + 3x^2 + 7}.$

If $u = x^4 + 3x^2 + 7$, then $du = (4x^3 + 6x)\,dx$, which is two times the numerator. We insert a factor of 2 and adjust for it with a factor of $\frac{1}{2}$.

$$\int \frac{2x^3 + 3x}{x^4 + 3x^2 + 7}\,dx = \frac{1}{2}\int \frac{2(2x^3 + 3x)}{x^4 + 3x^2 + 7}\,dx$$

$$= \frac{1}{2}\int \frac{1}{x^4 + 3x^2 + 7}[(4x^3 + 6x)\,dx]$$

$$= \frac{1}{2}\int \frac{1}{u}\,du = \frac{1}{2}\ln|u| + C$$

$$= \frac{1}{2}\ln|x^4 + 3x^2 + 7| + C$$

$$= \ln\sqrt{x^4 + 3x^2 + 7} + C.$$

d. $\int \left[\dfrac{1}{(1 - w)^2} + \dfrac{1}{w - 1}\right]\,dw.$

$$\int \left[\frac{1}{(1 - w)^2} + \frac{1}{w - 1}\right]\,dw = \int (1 - w)^{-2}\,dw + \int \frac{1}{w - 1}\,dw$$

$$= -1\int (1 - w)^{-2}[-dw] + \int \frac{1}{w - 1}\,dw.$$

On the last line the first integral has the form $\int u^{-2}\,du$, and the second has the form $\int \dfrac{1}{v}\,dv$. Thus

$$\int \left[\frac{1}{(1 - w)^2} + \frac{1}{w - 1}\right]\,dw = -\frac{(1 - w)^{-1}}{-1} + \ln|w - 1| + C$$

$$= \frac{1}{1 - w} + \ln|w - 1| + C.$$

For your convenience we list in Table 14.2 the basic integration formulas so far discussed. We assume that u is a function of x.

TABLE 14.2
Basic Integration Formulas

1. $\int k \, du = ku + C, \quad k$ a constant.

2. $\int u^n \, du = \dfrac{u^{n+1}}{n+1} + C, \quad n \neq -1.$

3. $\int e^u \, du = e^u + C.$

4. $\int \dfrac{1}{u} \, du = \ln |u| + C, \quad u \neq 0.$

5. $\int kf(x) \, dx = k \int f(x) \, dx.$

6. $\int [f(x) \pm g(x)] \, dx = \int f(x) \, dx \pm \int g(x) \, dx.$

EXERCISE 14.2

In Problems **1–76,** *find the indefinite integrals.*

1. $\int (x + 4)^8 \, dx.$

2. $\int 2(x + 3)^3 \, dx.$

3. $\int 2x(x^2 + 16)^3 \, dx.$

4. $\int (3x^2 + 14x)(x^3 + 7x^2 + 1) \, dx.$

5. $\int (3y^2 + 6y)(y^3 + 3y^2 + 1)^{2/3} \, dy.$

6. $\int (-12z^2 - 12z + 1)(-4z^3 - 6z^2 + z)^{18} \, dz.$

7. $\int \dfrac{3}{(3x - 1)^3} \, dx.$

8. $\int \dfrac{4x}{(2x^2 - 7)^{10}} \, dx.$

9. $\int 3e^{3x} \, dx.$

10. $\int 2e^{2t+5} \, dt.$

11. $\int (2t + 1)e^{t^2 + t} \, dt.$

12. $\int -3w^2 e^{-w^3} \, dw.$

13. $\int \sqrt{x + 10} \, dx.$

14. $\int \dfrac{1}{\sqrt{x - 2}} \, dx.$

15. $\int (7x - 6)^4 \, dx.$

16. $\int x^2(3x^3 + 7)^3 \, dx.$

17. $\int x(x^2 + 3)^{12} \, dx.$

18. $\int x\sqrt{1 + 2x^2} \, dx.$

19. $\int x^4(27 + x^5)^{1/3} \, dx.$

20. $\int x^3 e^{4x^4} \, dx.$

21. $\int x e^{5x^2} \, dx.$

22. $\int (3 - 2x)^{10} \, dx.$

23. $\int 6e^{-2x} \, dx.$

24. $\int x^4 e^{-6x^5} \, dx.$

25. $\int \dfrac{1}{x + 5} \, dx.$

26. $\int \dfrac{2x + 1}{x + x^2} \, dx.$

27. $\int \dfrac{3x^2 + 4x^3}{x^3 + x^4} \, dx.$

28. $\int \dfrac{3x^2 - 2x}{1 - x^2 + x^3} \, dx.$

29. $\int \dfrac{6z}{(z^2 - 6)^5} \, dz.$

30. $\int \dfrac{1}{(8y - 3)^3} \, dy.$

31. $\int \dfrac{4}{x} \, dx.$

32. $\int \dfrac{3}{1 + 2y} \, dy.$

33. $\int \dfrac{s^2}{s^3 + 5} \, ds.$

34. $\int \dfrac{2x^2}{3 - 4x^3}\, dx.$

35. $\int \dfrac{7}{5 - 3x}\, dx.$

36. $\int \dfrac{7t}{5t^2 - 6}\, dt.$

37. $\int \sqrt{5x}\, dx.$

38. $\int \dfrac{1}{(4x)^7}\, dx.$

39. $\int \dfrac{x}{\sqrt{x^2 - 4}}\, dx.$

40. $\int \dfrac{7}{3 - 2x}\, dx.$

41. $\int 2y^3 e^{y^4 + 1}\, dy.$

42. $\int \sqrt{4x - 3}\, dx.$

43. $\int v^2 e^{-2v^3 + 1}\, dv.$

44. $\int \dfrac{x^2}{\sqrt[3]{2x^3 + 9}}\, dx.$

45. $\int (e^{-5x} + 2e^x)\, dx.$

46. $\int 4\sqrt[3]{y + 1}\, dy.$

47. $\int (x + 1)(3 - 3x^2 - 6x)^3\, dx.$

48. $\int 2ye^{3y^2}\, dy.$

49. $\int \dfrac{x^2 + 2}{x^3 + 6x}\, dx.$

50. $\int (e^x - e^{-x} + e^{2x})\, dx.$

51. $\int \dfrac{16s - 4}{3 - 2s + 4s^2}\, ds.$

52. $\int (t^2 + 4t)(t^3 + 6t^2)^6\, dt.$

53. $\int x(2x^2 + 1)^{-1}\, dx.$

54. $\int (w^3 - 8w^7 + 1)(w^4 - 4w^8 + 4w)^{-6}\, dw.$

55. $\int -(x^2 - 2x^5)(x^3 - x^6)^{-10}\, dx.$

56. $\int \tfrac{3}{7}(v - 2)e^{2 - 4v + v^2}\, dv.$

57. $\int (2x^3 + x)(x^4 + x^2)\, dx.$

58. $\int (e^{3.1})^2\, dx.$

59. $\int \dfrac{18 + 12x}{(4 - 9x - 3x^2)^5}\, dx.$

60. $\int (e^x - e^{-x})^2\, dx.$

61. $\int x(2x + 1)e^{4x^3 + 3x^2 - 4}\, dx.$

62. $\int (u^2 + 3 - ue^{7 - u^2})\, du.$

63. $\int x\sqrt{(7 - 5x^2)^3}\, dx.$

64. $\int e^{-x/4}\, dx.$

65. $\int \dfrac{dx}{\sqrt{2x}}.$

66. $\int \dfrac{x^3}{e^{x^4}}\, dx.$

67. $\int (x^2 + 1)^2\, dx.$

68. $\int \left[x(x^2 - 16)^2 - \dfrac{1}{2x + 5} \right] dx.$

69. $\int \left[\dfrac{x}{x^2 + 1} + \dfrac{x^5}{(x^6 + 1)^2} \right] dx.$

70. $\int \left[\dfrac{1}{x - 1} + \dfrac{1}{(x - 1)^2} \right] dx.$

71. $\int \left[\dfrac{1}{3x - 5} - (x^2 - 2x^5)(x^3 - x^6)^{-10} \right] dx.$

72. $\int (r^3 + 5)^2\, dr.$

73. $\int \left[\sqrt{2x + 3} - \dfrac{x}{x^2 + 3} \right] dx.$

74. $\int \left[\dfrac{2x}{x^2 + 3} - \dfrac{x^3}{(x^4 + 2)^2} \right] dx.$

75. $\int \dfrac{e^{\sqrt{x}}}{\sqrt{x}}\, dx.$

76. $\int (e^4 - 2^e)\, dx.$

In Problems 77–80, find y subject to the given conditions.

77. $D_x y = (3 - 2x)^2; \quad y(0) = 1.$

78. $D_x y = x/(x^2 + 4); \quad y(1) = 0.$

79. $y'' = 1/x^2; \quad y'(-1) = 1, y(1) = 0.$

80. $y'' = \sqrt{x + 2}; \quad y'(2) = \tfrac{1}{3}, y(2) = -\tfrac{7}{15}.$

81. In a discussion of diffusion of oxygen from capillaries,* concentric cylinders of radius *r* are used as a model for a capillary. The concentration *C* of oxygen in the capillary is given by

* W. Simon, *Mathematical Techniques for Physiology and Medicine* (New York: Academic Press, Inc., 1972).

$$C = \int \left(\frac{Rr}{2K} + \frac{B_1}{r} \right) dr,$$

where R is the constant rate at which oxygen diffuses from the capillary, and K and B_1 are constants. Find C. (Write the constant of integration as B_2.)

14.3 TECHNIQUES OF INTEGRATION

Now that you have had some practice in determining indefinite integrals, suppose we consider some problems of a greater degree of difficulty.

When one is integrating fractions, sometimes a preliminary division is needed to get familiar integration forms, as the next example shows.

EXAMPLE 1

a. $\int \dfrac{x^3 + x - 1}{x^2} \, dx.$

A familiar integration form is not apparent. However, we can break up the integrand into three fractions by dividing each term in the numerator by the denominator.

$$\int \frac{x^3 + x - 1}{x^2} \, dx = \int \left[\frac{x^3}{x^2} + \frac{x}{x^2} - \frac{1}{x^2} \right] dx = \int \left[x + \frac{1}{x} - \frac{1}{x^2} \right] dx$$

$$= \frac{x^2}{2} + \ln |x| - \int x^{-2} \, dx = \frac{x^2}{2} + \ln |x| + \frac{1}{x} + C.$$

b. $\int \dfrac{2x^3 + 3x^2 + x + 1}{2x + 1} \, dx.$

Here the integrand is a quotient of polynomials in which the degree of the numerator is greater than or equal to that of the denominator, and the denominator has more than one term. In such a situation, in order to integrate we first use long division until the degree of the remainder is less than that of the divisor.

$$\int \frac{2x^3 + 3x^2 + x + 1}{2x + 1} \, dx = \int \left(x^2 + x + \frac{1}{2x + 1} \right) dx$$

$$= \frac{x^3}{3} + \frac{x^2}{2} + \int \frac{1}{2x + 1} \, dx$$

$$= \frac{x^3}{3} + \frac{x^2}{2} + \frac{1}{2} \int \frac{1}{2x + 1} [2 \, dx]$$

$$= \frac{x^3}{3} + \frac{x^2}{2} + \frac{1}{2} \ln |2x + 1| + C.$$

EXAMPLE 2   *Find the following indefinite integrals.*

a. $\int \dfrac{1}{\sqrt{x}(\sqrt{x} - 2)^3}\, dx.$

We can write this integral as $\int \dfrac{(\sqrt{x} - 2)^{-3}}{\sqrt{x}}\, dx$. Let $u = \sqrt{x} - 2$. Then

$du = \dfrac{1}{2\sqrt{x}}\, dx$ and

$$\int \frac{(\sqrt{x} - 2)^{-3}}{\sqrt{x}}\, dx = 2\int (\sqrt{x} - 2)^{-3}\left[\frac{1}{2\sqrt{x}}\, dx\right]$$

$$= 2\int u^{-3}\, du = 2\left(\frac{u^{-2}}{-2}\right) + C$$

$$= -u^{-2} + C = -(\sqrt{x} - 2)^{-2} + C.$$

b. $\int \dfrac{1}{x \ln x}\, dx.$

If $u = \ln x$, then $du = \dfrac{1}{x}\, dx$ and

$$\int \frac{1}{x \ln x}\, dx = \int \frac{1}{\ln x}\left(\frac{1}{x}\, dx\right) = \int \frac{1}{u}\, du$$

$$= \ln |u| + C = \ln |\ln x| + C.$$

c. $\int \dfrac{5}{w(\ln w)^{3/2}}\, dw.$

If $u = \ln w$, then $du = \dfrac{1}{w}\, dw$ and

$$\int \frac{5}{w(\ln w)^{3/2}}\, dw = 5\int (\ln w)^{-3/2}\left(\frac{1}{w}\, dw\right)$$

$$= 5\int u^{-3/2}\, du = 5 \cdot \frac{u^{-1/2}}{-\frac{1}{2}} + C$$

$$= \frac{-10}{u^{1/2}} + C = \frac{-10}{(\ln w)^{1/2}} + C.$$

Since $D_x\left(\dfrac{a^u}{\ln a}\right) = \dfrac{1}{\ln a}\left[a^u(\ln a)\dfrac{du}{dx}\right] = a^u \dfrac{du}{dx}$, it follows that

$$\int a^u \frac{du}{dx}\, dx = \frac{a^u}{\ln a} + C.$$

But $\dfrac{du}{dx}\, dx$ is du, so we have the integration formula

$$\int a^u \, du = \frac{a^u}{\ln a} + C. \qquad (1)$$

EXAMPLE 3   *Find* $\int 2^{3-x} \, dx.$

Let $u = 3 - x$. Then $du = -dx$, and from Eq. (1) with $a = 2$ we have

$$\int 2^{3-x} \, dx = -\int 2^{3-x}[-dx] = -\int a^u \, du$$

$$= -\frac{a^u}{\ln a} + C = -\frac{2^{3-x}}{\ln 2} + C.$$

Alternatively, we can avoid Eq. (1) by writing 2 in terms of e. Since $2 = e^{\ln 2}$ (by Property 9 of Sec. 5.3), we have

$$\int 2^{3-x} \, dx = \int (e^{\ln 2})^{3-x} \, dx = \int e^{(\ln 2)(3-x)} \, dx$$

$$= -\frac{1}{\ln 2} \int e^{(\ln 2)(3-x)} [(-\ln 2) \, dx] \qquad \left(\text{form: } \int e^u \, du\right)$$

$$= -\frac{1}{\ln 2} e^{(\ln 2)(3-x)} + C = -\frac{1}{\ln 2} 2^{3-x} + C.$$

EXAMPLE 4   *For a certain country, the marginal propensity to consume is given by*

$$\frac{dC}{dI} = \frac{3}{4} - \frac{1}{2\sqrt{3I}},$$

where consumption C is a function of national income I. Here I is expressed in billions of slugs (50 slugs = 0.01). Determine the consumption function for the country if it is known that consumption is 10 billion slugs ($C = 10$) when $I = 12$.

Since the marginal propensity to consume is the derivative of C, we have

$$C = \int \left(\frac{3}{4} - \frac{1}{2\sqrt{3I}}\right) dI = \int \frac{3}{4} \, dI - \frac{1}{2} \int (3I)^{-1/2} \, dI$$

$$= \frac{3}{4} I - \frac{1}{2} \int (3I)^{-1/2} \, dI.$$

If we let $u = 3I$, then $du = 3 \, dI$ and

$$C = \frac{3}{4} I - \left(\frac{1}{2}\right) \frac{1}{3} \int (3I)^{-1/2} [3 \, dI]$$

$$= \frac{3}{4} I - \frac{1}{6} \frac{(3I)^{1/2}}{\frac{1}{2}} + C_1.$$

$$C = \frac{3}{4}I - \frac{\sqrt{3I}}{3} + C_1.$$

When $I = 12$, then $C = 10$, so

$$10 = \frac{3}{4}(12) - \frac{\sqrt{3(12)}}{3} + C_1,$$

$$10 = 9 - 2 + C_1.$$

Thus $C_1 = 3$ and the consumption function is

$$C = \frac{3}{4}I - \frac{\sqrt{3I}}{3} + 3.$$

EXERCISE 14.3

In Problems 1–42, determine the indefinite integrals.

1. $\int \dfrac{3x^3 + x^2 - x}{x^2}\, dx.$

2. $\int \dfrac{3x^2 - 7x}{4x}\, dx.$

3. $\int (3x^2 + 2)\sqrt{2x^3 + 4x + 1}\, dx.$

4. $\int \dfrac{x}{\sqrt[3]{x^2 + 5}}\, dx.$

5. $\int \dfrac{4}{\sqrt{2 - 3x}}\, dx.$

6. $\int \dfrac{xe^{x^2}\, dx}{e^{x^2} - 2}.$

7. $\int 4^{7x}\, dx.$

8. $\int 3^x\, dx.$

9. $\int 2x(7 - e^{x^2/4})\, dx.$

10. $\int \left(e^x + x^e + ex + \dfrac{e}{x}\right) dx.$

11. $\int \dfrac{3e^{2x}}{e^{2x} + 1}\, dx.$

12. $\int (e^{4 - 3x})^2\, dx.$

13. $\int \dfrac{e^{7/x}}{x^2}\, dx.$

14. $\int \dfrac{2x^4 - 6x^3 + x - 2}{x - 2}\, dx.$

15. $\int \dfrac{(\sqrt{x} + 2)^2}{3\sqrt{x}}\, dx.$

16. $\int \dfrac{3e^s}{6 + 5e^s}\, ds.$

17. $\int \dfrac{\ln x}{x}\, dx.$

18. $\int \sqrt{t}(5 - t\sqrt{t})^{0.4}\, dt.$

19. $\int \dfrac{\ln^2(r + 1)}{r + 1}\, dr.$

20. $\int \dfrac{8x^3 - 6x^2 - ex^4}{3x^3}\, dx.$

21. $\int x\sqrt{e^{x^2+3}}\, dx.$

22. $\int \dfrac{x + 3}{x + 6}\, dx.$

23. $\int \dfrac{1}{(x + 3)\ln(x + 3)}\, dx.$

24. $\int (x^{e^2} + 2x)\, dx.$

25. $\int \left(\dfrac{x^3}{\sqrt{x^4 - 1}} - \ln 4\right) dx.$

26. $\int \dfrac{x - x^{-2}}{x^2 + 2x^{-1}}\, dx.$

27. $\int \dfrac{2x^4 - 8x^3 - 6x^2 + 4}{x^3}\, dx.$

28. $\int \dfrac{e^x + e^{-x}}{e^x - e^{-x}}\, dx.$

29. $\int \dfrac{6x^2 - 11x + 5}{3x - 1}\, dx.$

30. $\int \dfrac{(2x - 1)(x + 3)}{x - 5}\, dx.$

31. $\int \dfrac{x}{x - 1}\, dx.$

32. $\int \dfrac{x}{(x^2 + 1)\ln(x^2 + 1)}\, dx.$

33. $\int \dfrac{xe^{x^2}}{\sqrt{e^{x^2} + 2}}\, dx.$

34. $\int \dfrac{7}{(2x\,+\,1)[1\,+\,\ln(2x\,+\,1)]^2}\,dx.$

35. $\int \dfrac{(e^{-x}\,+\,6)^2}{e^x}\,dx.$

36. $\int \left[\dfrac{1}{8x\,+\,1}\,-\,\dfrac{1}{e^x(8\,+\,e^{-x})^2}\right]dx.$

37. $\int \sqrt{x}\sqrt{(8x)^{3/2}\,+\,3}\,\,dx.$

38. $\int \dfrac{3}{x(\ln x)^{1/2}}\,dx.$

39. $\int \dfrac{\sqrt{s}}{e^{\sqrt{s^3}}}\,ds.$

40. $\int \dfrac{\ln^3 x}{3x}\,dx.$

41. $\int e^{\ln(x\,+\,2)}\,dx.$

42. $\int dx.$

In Problems 43 and 44, dr/dq is a marginal revenue function. Find the demand function.

43. $\dfrac{dr}{dq}\,=\,\dfrac{200}{(q\,+\,2)^2}.$

44. $\dfrac{dr}{dq}\,=\,\dfrac{900}{(2q\,+\,3)^3}.$

In Problems 45 and 46, dc/dq is a marginal cost function. Find the total cost function if fixed costs in each case are 2000.

45. $\dfrac{dc}{dq}\,=\,\dfrac{20}{q\,+\,5}.$

46. $\dfrac{dc}{dq}\,=\,2e^{0.001q}.$

In Problems 47–49, dC/dI represents marginal propensity to consume. Find the consumption function subject to the given condition.

47. $\dfrac{dC}{dI}\,=\,\dfrac{1}{\sqrt{I}};\quad C(9)\,=\,8.$

48. $\dfrac{dC}{dI}\,=\,\dfrac{3}{4}\,-\,\dfrac{1}{2\sqrt{3I}};\quad C(3)\,=\,\dfrac{11}{4}.$

49. $\dfrac{dC}{dI}\,=\,\dfrac{3}{4}\,-\,\dfrac{1}{6\sqrt{I}};\quad C(25)\,=\,23.$

14.4   SUMMATION

To prepare you for further applications of integration, we need to discuss certain sums.

Consider finding the sum S of the first n positive integers:

$$S = 1 + 2 + \cdots + (n - 1) + n. \tag{1}$$

Writing the right side of Eq. (1) in reverse order, we have

$$S = n + (n - 1) + \cdots + 2 + 1. \tag{2}$$

Adding the corresponding sides of Eqs. (1) and (2) gives

$$\begin{aligned}
S &= 1 &&+ 2 &&+ \cdots + (n - 1) + && n\\
S &= n &&+ (n - 1) &&+ \cdots + 2 &&+ 1\\
\hline
2S &= (n + 1) &&+ (n + 1) &&+ \cdots + (n + 1) &&+ (n + 1).
\end{aligned}$$

On the right side of the last equation the term $(n + 1)$ occurs n times. Thus $2S = n(n + 1)$, so

$$S = \dfrac{n(n + 1)}{2} \qquad \text{(the sum of the first } n \text{ positive integers).} \tag{3}$$

For example, the sum of the first 100 positive integers corresponds to $n = 100$ and is $100(100 + 1)/2$ or 5050.

For convenience, to indicate a sum we shall introduce *sigma notation,* so named because the Greek letter Σ (sigma) is used. For example,

$$\sum_{k=1}^{3} (2k + 5)$$

denotes the sum of those numbers obtained from the expression $2k + 5$ by first replacing k by 1, then by 2, and finally by 3. Thus

$$\sum_{k=1}^{3} (2k + 5) = [2(1) + 5] + [2(2) + 5] + [2(3) + 5]$$

$$= 7 + 9 + 11 = 27.$$

The letter k is called the *index of summation;* the numbers 1 and 3 are the *limits of summation* (1 is the *lower limit* and 3 is the *upper limit*). The values of the index begin at the lower limit and progress through integer values to the upper limit. The symbol used for the index is a "dummy" symbol in the sense that it does not affect the sum of the terms. Any other letter can be used. For example,

$$\sum_{j=1}^{3} (2j + 5) = 7 + 9 + 11 = \sum_{k=1}^{3} (2k + 5).$$

EXAMPLE 1   *Evaluate each of the following*

a. $\displaystyle\sum_{k=4}^{7} \frac{k^2 + 3}{2}.$

Here the sum begins with $k = 4$.

$$\sum_{k=4}^{7} \frac{k^2 + 3}{2} = \frac{4^2 + 3}{2} + \frac{5^2 + 3}{2} + \frac{6^2 + 3}{2} + \frac{7^2 + 3}{2}$$

$$= \frac{19}{2} + \frac{28}{2} + \frac{39}{2} + \frac{52}{2} = 69.$$

b. $\displaystyle\sum_{j=0}^{2} (-1)^{j+1}(j - 1)^2.$

$$\sum_{j=0}^{2} (-1)^{j+1}(j - 1)^2$$

$$= (-1)^{0+1}(0 - 1)^2 + (-1)^{1+1}(1 - 1)^2 + (-1)^{2+1}(2 - 1)^2$$

$$= (-1) + 0 + (-1) = -2.$$

To express the sum of the first n positive integers in sigma notation, we can write

$$\sum_{k=1}^{n} k = 1 + 2 + \cdots + n.$$

By Eq. (3),

$$\sum_{k=1}^{n} k = \frac{n(n + 1)}{2}. \qquad (4)$$

Note in Eq. (4) that $\sum_{k=1}^{n} k$ is a function of n alone, not of k.

EXAMPLE 2   *Evaluate each of the following.*

a. $\sum_{k=1}^{60} k.$

Here we must find the sum of the first sixty positive integers. By Eq. (4) with $n = 60$,

$$\sum_{k=1}^{60} k = \frac{60(60 + 1)}{2} = 1830.$$

b. $\sum_{k=1}^{n-1} k.$

Here we must add the first $n - 1$ positive integers. Replacing n by $n - 1$ in Eq. (4), we obtain

$$\sum_{k=1}^{n-1} k = \frac{(n - 1)[(n - 1) + 1]}{2} = \frac{(n - 1)n}{2}.$$

Another useful formula is that for the sum of the *squares* of the first n positive integers. We shall use it in Sec. 14.5.

$$\sum_{k=1}^{n} k^2 = \frac{n(n + 1)(2n + 1)}{6}. \qquad (5)$$

EXAMPLE 3   *Evaluate* $1 + 4 + 9 + 16 + 25 + 36.$

This sum can be written as $\sum_{k=1}^{6} k^2$. By Eq. (5) with $n = 6$,

$$\sum_{k=1}^{6} k^2 = \frac{6(6 + 1)[2(6) + 1]}{6} = 91.$$

We conclude with a property of sigma. If $x_1, x_2, \ldots, x_n$ are real numbers and c is a constant, then

$$\sum_i^n cx_i = cx_1 + cx_2 + \cdots + cx_n$$

$$= c(x_1 + x_2 + \cdots + x_n) = c\sum_{i=1}^n x_i.$$

Thus

$$\sum_{i=1}^n cx_i = c\sum_{i=1}^n x_i.$$

This means that a constant factor can "jump" before a sigma. For example,

$$\sum_{i=1}^5 3i^2 = 3\sum_{i=1}^5 i^2.$$

Pitfall

Although constant factors can "jump" before sigma, nothing else can.

By Eq. (5) we have

$$\sum_{i=1}^5 3i^2 = 3\sum_{i=1}^5 i^2 = 3\left[\frac{5(6)(11)}{6}\right] = 165.$$

EXERCISE 14.4

*In Problems **1–10**, evaluate the given sum.*

1. $\displaystyle\sum_{k=1}^5 (k + 4)$.

2. $\displaystyle\sum_{k=12}^{15} (5 - 2k)$.

3. $\displaystyle\sum_{j=1}^{10} (-1)^j$.

4. $\displaystyle\sum_{j=0}^5 2^j$.

5. $\displaystyle\sum_{n=2}^3 (3n^2 - 7)$.

6. $\displaystyle\sum_{n=2}^4 \frac{n + 1}{n - 1}$.

7. $\displaystyle\sum_{k=3}^4 \frac{(-1)^k(k + 1)}{2^k}$.

8. $\displaystyle\sum_{n=1}^5 1$.

9. $\displaystyle\sum_{k=1}^3 \frac{(-1)^{k-1}(1 - k^2)}{k}$.

10. $\displaystyle\sum_{n=1}^4 (n^2 + n)$.

*In Problems **11–16**, express the given sums in sigma notation.*

11. $1 + 2 + 3 + \cdots + 15$.

12. $7 + 8 + 9 + 10$.

13. $1 + 3 + 5 + 7$.

14. $2 + 4 + 6 + 8$.

15. $1^2 + 2^2 + 3^2 + \cdots + 12^2$.

16. $3 + 6 + 9 + 12$.

*In Problems **17–22**, by using Eqs. (4) and (5) evaluate the sums.*

17. $\displaystyle\sum_{k=1}^{450} k$.

18. $\displaystyle\sum_{k=1}^{10} k^2$.

19. $\displaystyle\sum_{j=1}^6 4j$.

20. $\displaystyle\sum_{i=1}^{40} \frac{i}{2}$.

21. $\displaystyle\sum_{i=1}^6 3i^2$.

22. $\displaystyle\sum_{j=1}^8 \left(\frac{j}{2}\right)^2$.

23. A company has an asset whose original value is $3200 and which has no salvage value. The maintenance cost each year is $100 and increases by $100 each year. Show that the average annual total cost C over a period of n years is

$$C = \frac{3200}{n} + 50(n + 1).$$

Find the value of n that minimizes C. What is the average annual cost at this value of n?

14.5   THE DEFINITE INTEGRAL

Figure 14.1 shows the region bounded by the lines $y = f(x) = 2x$, $y = 0$ (the x-axis), and $x = 1$. It is simply a right triangle. If b and h are the lengths of the base and the height, respectively, then from geometry the area A of the triangle is $A = \frac{1}{2}bh = \frac{1}{2}(1)(2) = 1$ square unit. We shall now find this area by another method which, as you will see later, applies to more complex regions. This method involves summation of areas of rectangles.

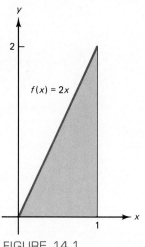

FIGURE 14.1

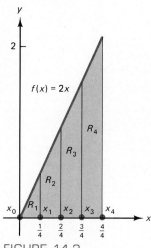

FIGURE 14.2

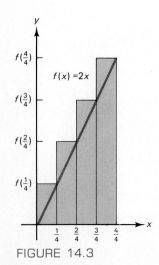

FIGURE 14.3

Let us divide the interval $[0, 1]$ on the x-axis into four subintervals of equal length by means of the equally spaced points $x_0 = 0$, $x_1 = \frac{1}{4}$, $x_2 = \frac{2}{4}$, $x_3 = \frac{3}{4}$, and $x_4 = \frac{4}{4} = 1$ (see Fig. 14.2). Each subinterval has length $\Delta x = \frac{1}{4}$. These subintervals determine four subregions: R_1, R_2, R_3, and R_4, as indicated.

With each subregion we can associate a *circumscribed* rectangle (Fig. 14.3); that is, a rectangle whose base is the corresponding subinterval and whose height is the *maximum* value of $f(x)$ on that subinterval. Since f is an increasing function, the maximum value of $f(x)$ on each subinterval occurs when x is the right-hand endpoint. Thus the areas of the circumscribed rectangles associated with regions R_1, R_2, R_3, and R_4 are $\frac{1}{4}f(\frac{1}{4})$, $\frac{1}{4}f(\frac{2}{4})$, $\frac{1}{4}f(\frac{3}{4})$, and $\frac{1}{4}f(\frac{4}{4})$, respectively. The area of each rectangle is an approximation to the area of its corresponding subregion. Thus the sum of the areas of these rectangles, denoted by $\overline{S}_4$, (read "S sub 4 upper bar" or "the fourth upper sum"), approximates the area A of the triangle.

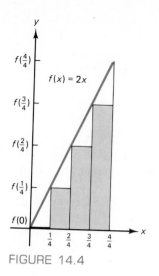

FIGURE 14.4

$$\overline{S}_4 = \tfrac{1}{4}f(\tfrac{1}{4}) + \tfrac{1}{4}f(\tfrac{2}{4}) + \tfrac{1}{4}f(\tfrac{3}{4}) + \tfrac{1}{4}f(\tfrac{4}{4})$$

$$= \tfrac{1}{4}[2(\tfrac{1}{4}) + 2(\tfrac{2}{4}) + 2(\tfrac{3}{4}) + 2(\tfrac{4}{4})] = \tfrac{5}{4}$$

You may verify that we can write $\overline{S}_4$ as $\overline{S}_4 = \sum\limits_{i=1}^{4} f(x_i)\,\Delta x$. The fact that $\overline{S}_4$ is greater than the actual area of the triangle might have been expected, since $\overline{S}_4$ includes areas of shaded regions that are not in the triangle (see Fig. 14.3).

On the other hand, with each subregion we can also associate an *inscribed* rectangle (see Fig. 14.4); that is, a rectangle whose base is the corresponding subinterval but whose height is the *minimum* value of $f(x)$ on that subinterval. Since f is an increasing function, the minimum value of $f(x)$ on each subinterval will occur when x is the left-hand endpoint. Thus the areas of the four inscribed rectangles associated with R_1, R_2, R_3, and R_4 are $\tfrac{1}{4}f(0)$, $\tfrac{1}{4}f(\tfrac{1}{4})$, $\tfrac{1}{4}f(\tfrac{2}{4})$, and $\tfrac{1}{4}f(\tfrac{3}{4})$, respectively. Their sum, denoted $\underline{S}_4$ (read "S sub 4 lower bar" or "the fourth lower sum"), is also an approximation to the area A of the triangle.

$$\underline{S}_4 = \tfrac{1}{4}f(0) + \tfrac{1}{4}f(\tfrac{1}{4}) + \tfrac{1}{4}f(\tfrac{2}{4}) + \tfrac{1}{4}f(\tfrac{3}{4})$$

$$= \tfrac{1}{4}[2(0) + 2(\tfrac{1}{4}) + 2(\tfrac{2}{4}) + 2(\tfrac{3}{4})] = \tfrac{3}{4}.$$

Using sigma notation, we can write $\underline{S}_4 = \sum\limits_{i=0}^{3} f(x_i)\Delta x$. Note that $\underline{S}_4$ is less than the area of the triangle because the rectangles do not account for that portion of the triangle which is not shaded in Fig. 14.4.

Since $\tfrac{3}{4} = \underline{S}_4 \leq A \leq \overline{S}_4 = \tfrac{5}{4}$, we say that $\underline{S}_4$ is an approximation to A from *below* and $\overline{S}_4$ is an approximation to A from *above*.

If [0, 1] is divided into more subintervals, we expect that better approximations to A will occur. To test this out, let us use six subintervals of equal length $\Delta x = \tfrac{1}{6}$. Then $\overline{S}_6$, the total area of six circumscribed rectangles (see Fig. 14.5), and $\underline{S}_6$, the total area of six inscribed rectangles (see Fig. 14.6) are

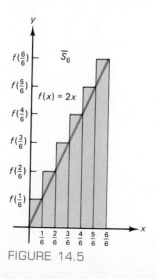

FIGURE 14.5

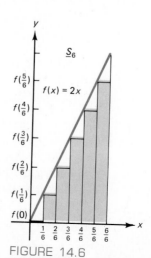

FIGURE 14.6

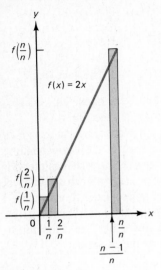

FIGURE 14.7

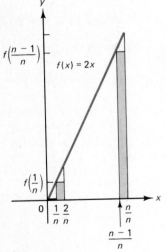

FIGURE 14.8

$$\overline{S}_6 = \tfrac{1}{6}f(\tfrac{1}{6}) + \tfrac{1}{6}f(\tfrac{2}{6}) + \tfrac{1}{6}f(\tfrac{3}{6}) + \tfrac{1}{6}f(\tfrac{4}{6}) + \tfrac{1}{6}f(\tfrac{5}{6}) + \tfrac{1}{6}f(\tfrac{6}{6})$$

$$= \tfrac{1}{6}[2(\tfrac{1}{6}) + 2(\tfrac{2}{6}) + 2(\tfrac{3}{6}) + 2(\tfrac{4}{6}) + 2(\tfrac{5}{6}) + 2(\tfrac{6}{6})] = \tfrac{7}{6}$$

and

$$\underline{S}_6 = \tfrac{1}{6}f(0) + \tfrac{1}{6}f(\tfrac{1}{6}) + \tfrac{1}{6}f(\tfrac{2}{6}) + \tfrac{1}{6}f(\tfrac{3}{6}) + \tfrac{1}{6}f(\tfrac{4}{6}) + \tfrac{1}{6}f(\tfrac{5}{6})$$

$$= \tfrac{1}{6}[2(0) + 2(\tfrac{1}{6}) + 2(\tfrac{2}{6}) + 2(\tfrac{3}{6}) + 2(\tfrac{4}{6}) + 2(\tfrac{5}{6})] = \tfrac{5}{6}.$$

Note that $\underline{S}_6 \le A \le \overline{S}_6$ and, with appropriate labelling, both $\overline{S}_6$ and $\underline{S}_6$ will be of the *form* $\Sigma f(x)\,\Delta x$. Using six subintervals gave better approximations to the area than did four subintervals, as expected.

More generally, if we divide [0, 1] into n subintervals of equal length Δx, then $\Delta x = 1/n$ and the endpoints of the subintervals are $x = 0,\ 1/n,\ 2/n,\ \ldots,$ $(n - 1)/n$, and $n/n = 1$ (see Fig. 14.7). The total area of n *circumscribed* rectangles is

$$\overline{S}_n = \frac{1}{n}f\left(\frac{1}{n}\right) + \frac{1}{n}f\left(\frac{2}{n}\right) + \cdots + \frac{1}{n}f\left(\frac{n}{n}\right) \tag{1}$$

$$= \frac{1}{n}\left[2\left(\frac{1}{n}\right) + 2\left(\frac{2}{n}\right) + \cdots + 2\left(\frac{n}{n}\right)\right]$$

$$= \frac{2}{n^2}[1 + 2 + \cdots + n] \qquad \left(\text{by factoring } \frac{2}{n} \text{ from each term}\right).$$

From Sec. 14.4, the sum of the first n positive integers is $\dfrac{n(n + 1)}{2}$. Thus

$$\overline{S}_n = \left(\frac{2}{n^2}\right)\frac{n(n + 1)}{2} = \frac{n + 1}{n}.$$

For n *inscribed* rectangles, the total area determined by the subintervals (see Fig. 14.8) is

$$\underline{S}_n = \frac{1}{n}f(0) + \frac{1}{n}f\left(\frac{1}{n}\right) + \cdots + \frac{1}{n}f\left(\frac{n - 1}{n}\right)$$

$$= \frac{1}{n}\left[2(0) + 2\left(\frac{1}{n}\right) + \cdots + 2\left(\frac{n - 1}{n}\right)\right] \tag{2}$$

$$= \frac{2}{n^2}[1 + \cdots + (n - 1)].$$

Summing the first $n - 1$ positive integers as we did in Example 2(b) of Sec. 14.4, we obtain

$$\underline{S}_n = \left(\frac{2}{n^2}\right)\frac{(n - 1)n}{2} = \frac{n - 1}{n}.$$

From Eqs. (1) and (2) we again see that both $\overline{S}_n$ and $\underline{S}_n$ are sums of the *form*

$\Sigma f(x)\ \Delta x$, namely $\bar{S}_n = \sum\limits_{k=1}^{n} f\left(\dfrac{k}{n}\right)\Delta x$ and $\underline{S}_n = \sum\limits_{k=0}^{n-1} f\left(\dfrac{k}{n}\right)\Delta x$.

From the nature of $\bar{S}_n$ and $\underline{S}_n$, it seems reasonable and it is indeed true that

$$\underline{S}_n \le A \le \bar{S}_n.$$

As n becomes larger, $\underline{S}_n$ and $\bar{S}_n$ become better approximations to A. In fact, let us take the limits of $\underline{S}_n$ and $\bar{S}_n$ as n approaches ∞ through positive integral values.

$$\lim_{n\to\infty} \underline{S}_n = \lim_{n\to\infty} \frac{n-1}{n} = \lim_{n\to\infty}\left(1 - \frac{1}{n}\right) = 1.$$

$$\lim_{n\to\infty} \bar{S}_n = \lim_{n\to\infty} \frac{n+1}{n} = \lim_{n\to\infty}\left(1 + \frac{1}{n}\right) = 1.$$

Since $\bar{S}_n$ and $\underline{S}_n$ have the same common limit, namely

$$\lim_{n\to\infty} \bar{S}_n = \lim_{n\to\infty} \underline{S}_n = 1, \tag{3}$$

and since

$$\underline{S}_n \le A \le \bar{S}_n,$$

we shall take this limit to be the area of the triangle. Thus $A = 1$ square unit which agrees with our prior finding.

We define the common limit of $\bar{S}_n$ and $\underline{S}_n$, namely 1, to be the **definite integral** of $f(x) = 2x$ on the interval from $x = 0$ to $x = 1$, and we denote this by writing

$$\int_0^1 2x\ dx = 1. \tag{4}$$

The reason for using the term "definite integral" and the symbolism in Eq. (4) will become apparent in the next section. The numbers 0 and 1 appearing with the integral sign $\int$ in Eq. (4) are called the **limits of integration**; 0 is the **lower limit** and 1 is the **upper limit**.

In general, for a function f defined on the interval from $x = a$ to $x = b$, where $a \le b$, we can form the sums $\bar{S}_n$ and $\underline{S}_n$, which are obtained by considering the maximum and minimum values, respectively, on each of n subintervals of equal length Δx.* Each sum has the form $\Sigma f(x)\ \Delta x$. The common limit of $\bar{S}_n$ and $\underline{S}_n$ as $n \to \infty$, if it exists, is called the definite integral of f over $[a, b]$ and is written

$$\int_a^b f(x)\ dx.$$

The symbol x is the **variable of integration** and $f(x)$ is the **integrand.** In terms of a limiting process we have

$$\Sigma f(x)\ \Delta x \to \int_a^b f(x)\ dx.$$

* Here we assume that the maximum and minimum values exist.

Two points must be made about the definite integral. First, the definite integral is a limit of a sum of the form $\Sigma f(x)\,\Delta x$. In fact, one can think of the integral sign as an elongated ''S'', the first letter of ''Summation.'' Second, for an arbitrary function f defined on an interval, we may be able to calculate sums $\overline{S}_n$ and $\underline{S}_n$, and determine their common limit if it exists. However, some terms in the sums may be negative if $f(x)$ is negative at points in the interval. These terms are not areas of rectangles (an area is never negative), and so the common limit may not represent area. Thus the definite integral is nothing more than a real number; it may or may not represent area.

As you saw in Eq. (3), $\lim\limits_{n\to\infty} \underline{S}_n$ is equal to $\lim\limits_{n\to\infty} \overline{S}_n$. For an arbitrary function this is not always true. However, for the functions that we shall consider, these limits will be equal and the definite integral will always exist. To save time we shall just use the **right-hand endpoint** of each subinterval in computing a sum. For the functions in this section, this sum will be denoted S_n and will correspond to either $\underline{S}_n$ or $\overline{S}_n$.

EXAMPLE 1

a. *Find the area of the region in the first quadrant bounded by $y = f(x) = 4 - x^2$ and the lines $x = 0$ and $y = 0$.*

A sketch of the region appears in Fig. 14.9. The interval over which x varies in this region is seen to be $[0, 2]$, which we divide into n subintervals of equal length Δx. Since the length of $[0, 2]$ is 2, we take $\Delta x = 2/n$. The endpoints of the subintervals are $x = 0, 2/n, 2(2/n), \ldots, (n - 1)(2/n)$, and $n(2/n) = 2$ (see Fig. 14.10).

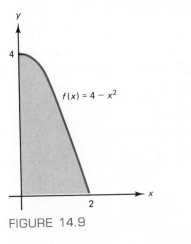

FIGURE 14.9

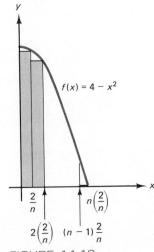

FIGURE 14.10

Using right-hand endpoints, we get

$$S_n = \frac{2}{n}f\left(\frac{2}{n}\right) + \frac{2}{n}f\left[2\left(\frac{2}{n}\right)\right] + \cdots + \frac{2}{n}f\left[n\left(\frac{2}{n}\right)\right]$$

$$= \frac{2}{n}\left[f\left(\frac{2}{n}\right) + f\left[2\left(\frac{2}{n}\right)\right] + \cdots + f\left[n\left(\frac{2}{n}\right)\right]\right]$$

$$= \frac{2}{n}\left[\left\{4 - \left[\frac{2}{n}\right]^2\right\} + \left\{4 - \left[2\left(\frac{2}{n}\right)\right]^2\right\} + \cdots + \left\{4 - \left[n\left(\frac{2}{n}\right)\right]^2\right\}\right].$$

Since the number 4 occurs n times in the sum, we can simplify S_n.

$$S_n = \frac{2}{n}\left[4n - \left(\frac{2}{n}\right)^2 - 2^2\left(\frac{2}{n}\right)^2 - \cdots - n^2\left(\frac{2}{n}\right)^2\right]$$

$$= \frac{2}{n}\left[4n - \left(\frac{2}{n}\right)^2\{1^2 + 2^2 + \cdots + n^2\}\right].$$

From Sec. 14.4, $\displaystyle\sum_{k=1}^{n} k^2 = \frac{n(n+1)(2n+1)}{6}$, so

$$S_n = \frac{2}{n}\left[4n - \left(\frac{2}{n}\right)^2 \frac{n(n+1)(2n+1)}{6}\right]$$

$$= 8 - \frac{4(n+1)(2n+1)}{3n^2}$$

$$= 8 - \frac{4}{3}\left(\frac{2n^2 + 3n + 1}{n^2}\right).$$

Finally we take the limit of S_n as $n \to \infty$.

$$\lim_{n\to\infty} S_n = \lim_{n\to\infty}\left[8 - \frac{4}{3}\left(\frac{2n^2 + 3n + 1}{n^2}\right)\right]$$

$$= \lim_{n\to\infty}\left[8 - \frac{4}{3}\left(2 + \frac{3}{n} + \frac{1}{n^2}\right)\right]$$

$$= 8 - \frac{8}{3} = \frac{16}{3}.$$

Hence the area of the region is $\frac{16}{3}$ square units.

b. Evaluate $\displaystyle\int_0^2 (4 - x^2)\,dx$.

Since $\displaystyle\int_0^2 (4 - x^2)\,dx = \lim_{n\to\infty} S_n$, from part (a) we conclude that

$$\int_0^2 (4 - x^2)\,dx = \frac{16}{3}.$$

EXAMPLE 2 *Integrate $f(x) = x - 5$ from $x = 0$ to $x = 3$; that is, evaluate $\displaystyle\int_0^3 (x - 5)\,dx$.*

A sketch of $f(x) = x - 5$ over $[0, 3]$ appears in Fig. 14.11. We divide $[0, 3]$

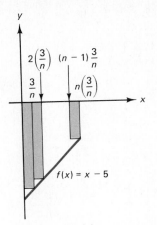

FIGURE 14.11

into n subintervals of equal length $\Delta x = 3/n$. The endpoints are $x = 0$, $3/n$, $2(3/n), \ldots, (n - 1)(3/n)$, and $n(3/n) = 3$. Note that $f(x)$ is negative at each endpoint. We form the sum

$$S_n = \frac{3}{n} f\left(\frac{3}{n}\right) + \frac{3}{n} f\left[2\left(\frac{3}{n}\right)\right] + \cdots + \frac{3}{n} f\left[n\left(\frac{3}{n}\right)\right].$$

Since all terms are negative, they do *not* represent areas of rectangles; in fact, they are the negatives of areas of rectangles. Simplifying, we have

$$S_n = \frac{3}{n}\left[\left\{\frac{3}{n} - 5\right\} + \left\{2\left(\frac{3}{n}\right) - 5\right\} + \cdots + \left\{n\left(\frac{3}{n}\right) - 5\right\}\right]$$

$$= \frac{3}{n}\left[-5n + \frac{3}{n}\{1 + 2 + \cdots + n\}\right]$$

$$= \frac{3}{n}\left[-5n + \left(\frac{3}{n}\right)\frac{n(n + 1)}{2}\right]$$

$$= -15 + \frac{9}{2} \cdot \frac{n + 1}{n}$$

$$= -15 + \frac{9}{2}\left(1 + \frac{1}{n}\right).$$

Taking the limit, we obtain

$$\lim_{n\to\infty} S_n = \lim_{n\to\infty}\left[-15 + \frac{9}{2}\left(1 + \frac{1}{n}\right)\right] = -15 + \frac{9}{2} = -\frac{21}{2}.$$

Thus

$$\int_0^3 (x - 5)\, dx = -\frac{21}{2}.$$

FIGURE 14.12

The definite integral is **not** the area of the region bounded by $f(x) = x - 5$, $y = 0$, $x = 0$, and $x = 3$. It represents the negative of that area.

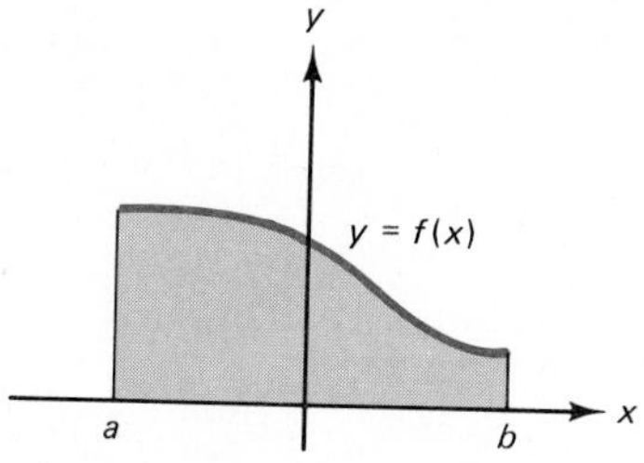

In Example 2 it was shown that *the definite integral does not have to represent area*. In fact, there the definite integral was negative. However, if f is continuous and $f(x) \geq 0$ on $[a, b]$, then $S_n \geq 0$ for all n. Hence $\lim_{n \to \infty} S_n \geq 0$ and so $\int_a^b f(x)\, dx \geq 0$. Furthermore, this definite integral gives the area of the region bounded by $y = f(x)$, $y = 0$, $x = a$ and $x = b$ (see Fig. 14.12).

Although the approach that we took to discuss the definite integral is sufficient for our purposes, it is by no means rigorous. **The important thing to remember about the definite integral is that it is the limit of a sum.**

EXERCISE 14.5

In Problems **1–4**, *sketch the region in the first quadrant that is bounded by the given curves. Approximate the area of the region by the indicated sum. Use the right-hand endpoint of each subinterval.*

1. $f(x) = x$, $y = 0$, $x = 1$; S_3.

2. $f(x) = 3x$, $y = 0$, $x = 1$; S_5.

3. $f(x) = x^2$, $y = 0$, $x = 1$; S_3.

4. $f(x) = x^2 + 1$, $y = 0$, $x = 0$, $x = 1$; S_2.

In Problems **5–10**, *sketch the region in the first quadrant that is bounded by the given curves. Determine the exact area of the region by considering the limit of S_n as $n \to \infty$. Use the right-hand endpoint of each subinterval.*

5. Region as described in Problem 1.

6. Region as described in Problem 2.

7. Region as described in Problem 3.

8. Region as described in Problem 4.

9. $f(x) = 2x^2$, $y = 0$, $x = 2$.

10. $f(x) = 9 - x^2$, $y = 0$, $x = 0$.

For each of the following problems, evaluate the given definite integral by taking the limit of S_n. Use the right-hand endpoint of each subinterval. Sketch the graph, over the given interval, of the function to be integrated.

11. $\int_0^2 3x\, dx$.

12. $\int_0^4 9\, dx$.

13. $\int_0^3 -4x\, dx$.

14. $\int_0^3 (2x - 9)\, dx$.

15. $\int_0^1 (x^2 + x)\, dx$.

14.6   THE FUNDAMENTAL THEOREM OF INTEGRAL CALCULUS

Until now the limiting processes of both the derivative and definite integral have been considered separately. We shall now bring these fundamental ideas together and develop the important relationship that exists between them. As a result, we may evaluate definite integrals more efficiently.

The graph of a function f is given in Fig. 14.13. Assume that f is continuous on the interval $[a, b]$ and its graph does not fall below the x-axis. That is,

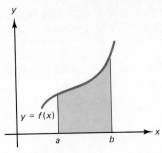

FIGURE 14.13

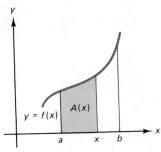

FIGURE 14.14

$f(x) \geq 0$. From the last section we know that the area of the region below the graph and above the x-axis from $x = a$ to $x = b$ is given by $\int_a^b f(x) \, dx$. We shall now consider another way to determine this area.

Suppose that there is a function $A = A(x)$, which we shall refer to as an "area" function, that gives the area of the region below the graph of f and above the x-axis from a to x, where $a \leq x \leq b$. This region is shaded in Fig. 14.14. Do not confuse $A(x)$, which is an area, with $f(x)$, which is the height of the graph at x.

From its definition we can state two properties of A immediately:

1. $A(a) = 0$ since there is no area from a to a;

2. $A(b)$ is the area from a to b; that is,

$$A(b) = \int_a^b f(x) \, dx.$$

If x is increased by h units, then $A(x + h)$ is the area of the shaded region in Fig. 14.15. Hence $A(x + h) - A(x)$ is the difference of the areas in Figs. 14.15 and 14.14: namely, the area of the shaded region in Fig. 14.16. For h

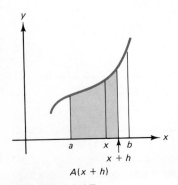

$A(x + h)$

FIGURE 14.15

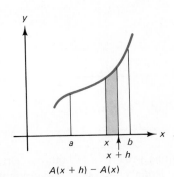

$A(x + h) - A(x)$

FIGURE 14.16

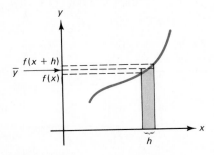

FIGURE 14.17

sufficiently close to zero, the area of this region is the same as the area of a rectangle (Fig. 14.17) whose base is h and whose height is some value $\bar{y}$ between

$f(x)$ and $f(x + h)$. Here $\bar{y}$ is a function of h. Thus the area of the rectangle is, on the one hand, $A(x + h) - A(x)$, and on the other hand it is $h\bar{y}$:

$$A(x + h) - A(x) = h\bar{y}$$

or

$$\frac{A(x + h) - A(x)}{h} = \bar{y} \qquad \text{(dividing by } h\text{)}.$$

As $h \to 0$, then $\bar{y}$ approaches the number $f(x)$, so

$$\lim_{h \to 0} \frac{A(x + h) - A(x)}{h} = f(x). \tag{1}$$

But the left side is merely the derivative of A. Thus Eq. (1) becomes

$$A'(x) = f(x).$$

We conclude that the area function A has the additional property that its derivative A' is f. That is, A is an antiderivative of f. Now, suppose that F is *any* antiderivative of f. Since both A and F are antiderivatives of the same function, they differ at most by a constant C:

$$A(x) = F(x) + C. \tag{2}$$

Recall that $A(a) = 0$. Evaluating both sides of Eq. (2) when $x = a$ gives

$$0 = F(a) + C$$

or

$$C = -F(a).$$

Thus Eq. (2) becomes

$$A(x) = F(x) - F(a). \tag{3}$$

If $x = b$, then from Eq. (3)

$$A(b) = F(b) - F(a). \tag{4}$$

But recall that

$$A(b) = \int_a^b f(x) \, dx. \tag{5}$$

From Eqs. (4) and (5) we get

$$\int_a^b f(x) \, dx = F(b) - F(a).$$

Thus a relationship between a definite integral and antidifferentiation has become clear. To find $\int_a^b f(x) \, dx$ it suffices to find an antiderivative of f, say F, and subtract the value of F at the lower limit a from its value at the upper limit b. We assumed here that f was continuous and $f(x) \geq 0$ so that we could appeal to the "area" concept. However, our result is true for any continuous function* and is known as the *Fundamental Theorem of Integral Calculus*.

FUNDAMENTAL THEOREM OF INTEGRAL CALCULUS.

If f is continuous on the interval $[a, b]$ and F is any antiderivative of f there, then

$$\int_a^b f(x) \, dx = F(b) - F(a).$$

It is important that you understand the difference between a definite integral and an indefinite integral. The **definite integral** $\int_a^b f(x) \, dx$ is a **number** defined to be the limit of a sum. The Fundamental Theorem states that the **indefinite integral** $\int f(x) \, dx$ (an antiderivative of f), which is a **function** of x and is related to the differentiation process, can be used to determine this limit.

Suppose we apply the Fundamental Theorem to evaluate $\int_0^2 (4 - x^2) \, dx$. Here $f(x) = 4 - x^2$, $a = 0$, and $b = 2$. Since an antiderivative of $4 - x^2$ is $F(x) = 4x - (x^3/3)$, then

$$\int_0^2 (4 - x^2) \, dx = F(2) - F(0) = \left(8 - \frac{8}{3}\right) - (0) = \frac{16}{3}.$$

This confirms our result in Example 1(b) of Sec. 14.5. If we had chosen $F(x)$ to be $4x - (x^3/3) + C$, then $F(2) - F(0) = [(8 - \frac{8}{3}) + C] - [0 + C] = \frac{16}{3}$ as before. Since the choice of the value of C is immaterial, for convenience we shall always choose it to be 0, as originally done. Usually, $F(b) - F(a)$ is abbreviated by writing

$$F(x)\Big|_a^b.$$

Hence we have

$$\int_0^2 (4 - x^2) \, dx = \left(4x - \frac{x^3}{3}\right)\Big|_0^2 = \left(8 - \frac{8}{3}\right) - 0 = \frac{16}{3}.$$

For a definite integral, we have the following convention:

$$\int_b^a f(x) \, dx = -\int_a^b f(x) \, dx.$$

---

* If f is continuous on $[a, b]$, it can be shown that $\int_a^b f(x) \, dx$ does indeed exist.

That is, interchanging the limits of integration changes the integral's sign. For example,

$$\int_2^0 (4 - x^2)\, dx = -\int_0^2 (4 - x^2)\, dx.$$

Some properties of the definite integral deserve mention. The first property restates more formally our comment from the preceding section concerning area.

1. If f is continuous and $f(x) \geq 0$ on $[a, b]$, then $\int_a^b f(x)\, dx$ can be interpreted as the area of the region bounded by the curve $y = f(x)$, the x-axis, and the lines $x = a$ and $x = b$.

2. $\int_a^b kf(x)\, dx = k\int_a^b f(x)\, dx$, where k is a constant.

3. $\int_a^b [f(x) \pm g(x)]\, dx = \int_a^b f(x)\, dx \pm \int_a^b g(x)\, dx.$

Properties 2 and 3 are similar to rules for indefinite integrals because a definite integral may be evaluated by the Fundamental Theorem in terms of an antiderivative. Two more properties of definite integrals are as follows.

4. $\int_a^b f(x)\, dx = \int_a^b f(t)\, dt.$ The variable of integration is a "dummy variable" in the sense that any other variable produces the same result, that is, the same number. You may verify, for example, that $\int_0^2 x^2\, dx = \int_0^2 t^2\, dt.$

5. If f is continuous on an interval I and a, b, and c are in I, then

$$\int_a^c f(x)\, dx = \int_a^b f(x)\, dx + \int_b^c f(x)\, dx.$$

This means that you may subdivide the interval over which a definite integral is to be evaluated. Thus

$$\int_0^2 (4 - x^2)\, dx = \int_0^1 (4 - x^2)\, dx + \int_1^2 (4 - x^2)\, dx.$$

We shall look at some examples of definite integration now and compute some areas in the next section.

EXAMPLE 1   *Evaluate each of the following definite integrals.*

a. $\int_{-1}^{3} (3x^2 - x + 6)\, dx.$

$$\int_{-1}^{3} (3x^2 - x + 6)\, dx$$

$$= \left(x^3 - \frac{x^2}{2} + 6x \right) \Big|_{-1}^{3}$$

$$= \left[3^3 - \frac{3^2}{2} + 6(3) \right] - \left[(-1)^3 - \frac{(-1)^2}{2} + 6(-1) \right]$$

$$= \left(\frac{81}{2} \right) - \left(-\frac{15}{2} \right) = 48.$$

b. $\int_{0}^{1} \frac{x^3}{\sqrt{1 + x^4}}\, dx.$

$$\int_{0}^{1} \frac{x^3}{\sqrt{1 + x^4}}\, dx = \int_{0}^{1} x^3 (1 + x^4)^{-1/2}\, dx$$

$$= \frac{1}{4} \int_{0}^{1} (1 + x^4)^{-1/2}[4x^3\, dx] = \left(\frac{1}{4} \right) \frac{(1 + x^4)^{1/2}}{\frac{1}{2}} \Big|_{0}^{1}$$

$$= \frac{1}{2}(1 + x^4)^{1/2} \Big|_{0}^{1} = \frac{1}{2}(2)^{1/2} - \frac{1}{2}(1)^{1/2}$$

$$= \frac{1}{2}(\sqrt{2} - 1).$$

Pitfall

In part (b), the value of the antiderivative $\frac{1}{2}(1 + x^4)^{1/2}$ at the lower limit 0 is $\frac{1}{2}(1)^{1/2}$. **Do not** assume that an evaluation at the limit zero will yield 0.

c. $\int_{1}^{2} [4t^{1/3} + t(t^2 + 1)^3]\, dt.$

$$\int_{1}^{2} [4t^{1/3} + t(t^2 + 1)^3]\, dt = 4\int_{1}^{2} t^{1/3}\, dt + \frac{1}{2}\int_{1}^{2} (t^2 + 1)^3[2t\, dt]$$

$$= (4)\frac{t^{4/3}}{\frac{4}{3}} \Big|_{1}^{2} + \left(\frac{1}{2} \right) \frac{(t^2 + 1)^4}{4} \Big|_{1}^{2}$$

$$= 3(2^{4/3} - 1) + \frac{1}{8}(5^4 - 2^4)$$

$$= 3 \cdot 2^{4/3} - 3 + \frac{609}{8}$$

$$= 6 \sqrt[3]{2} + \frac{585}{8}.$$

d. $\int_0^1 e^{3t}\, dt.$

$$\int_0^1 e^{3t}\, dt = \frac{1}{3}\int_0^1 e^{3t}[3\, dt]$$

$$= \left(\frac{1}{3}\right)e^{3t}\bigg|_0^1 = \frac{1}{3}(e^3 - e^0) = \frac{1}{3}(e^3 - 1).$$

EXAMPLE 2   *Evaluate* $\int_{-2}^1 x^3\, dx.$

$$\int_{-2}^1 x^3\, dx = \frac{x^4}{4}\bigg|_{-2}^1 = \frac{1^4}{4} - \frac{(-2)^4}{4} = \frac{1}{4} - \frac{16}{4} = -\frac{15}{4}.$$

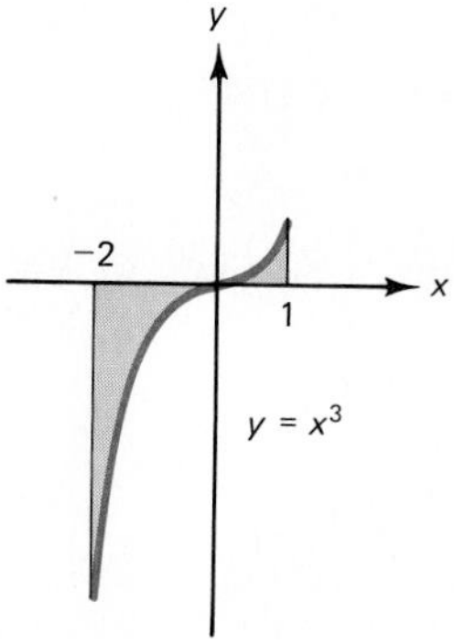

FIGURE 14.18

The reason the result is negative is clear from the graph of $y = x^3$ on the interval $[-2, 1]$ (see Fig. 14.18). For $-2 \le x < 0$, $f(x)$ is negative. Since a definite integral is a limit of a sum of the form $\Sigma f(x)\, \Delta x$, then $\int_{-2}^0 x^3\, dx$ is not only a negative number, but it is also the negative of the area of the shaded region in the third quadrant. On the other hand, $\int_0^1 x^3\, dx$ is the area of the shaded region in the first quadrant. However, the definite integral over the entire interval $[-2, 1]$ is the *algebraic* sum of these numbers since

$$\int_{-2}^1 x^3\, dx = \int_{-2}^0 x^3\, dx + \int_0^1 x^3\, dx.$$

Thus $\int_{-2}^1 x^3\, dx$ does not represent the area between the curve and the x-axis. However, the area can be given in the form

$$\left|\int_{-2}^0 x^3\, dx\right| + \int_0^1 x^3\, dx.$$

Pitfall

Remember that $\int_a^b f(x)\, dx$ is a limit of a sum. In some cases this limit represents area. In others it does not.

Since f is an antiderivative of f', by the Fundamental Theorem we have

$$\int_a^b f'(x)\, dx = f(b) - f(a). \tag{6}$$

But $f'(x)$ is the rate of change of f with respect to x. Thus, if we know the rate of change of f and want to find the difference in function values $f(b) - f(a)$, it suffices to evaluate $\int_a^b f'(x)\, dx$.

EXAMPLE 3   *A manufacturer's marginal cost function is*

$$\frac{dc}{dq} = 0.6q + 2.$$

If production is presently set at $q = 80$ units per week, how much more would it cost to increase production to 100 units per week?

The total cost function is $c = c(q)$, and we want to find the difference $c(100) - c(80)$. The rate of change of c is dc/dq, so by Eq. (6),

$$c(100) - c(80) = \int_{80}^{100} \frac{dc}{dq} \, dq = \int_{80}^{100} (0.6q + 2) \, dq$$

$$= \left[\frac{0.6q^2}{2} + 2q \right]\Bigg|_{80}^{100} = [0.3q^2 + 2q]\Bigg|_{80}^{100}$$

$$= [0.3(100)^2 + 2(100)] - [0.3(80)^2 + 2(80)]$$

$$= 3200 - 2080 = 1120.$$

If c is in dollars, then the cost of increasing production from 80 units to 100 units is $1120.

EXERCISE 14.6

In Problems 1–38, evaluate the definite integral.

1. $\int_0^3 4 \, dx.$

2. $\int_1^3 (2 + e) \, dx.$

3. $\int_1^2 3x \, dx.$

4. $\int_0^2 -5x \, dx.$

5. $\int_{-2}^1 (4x - 6) \, dx.$

6. $\int_{-1}^1 (5y + 2) \, dy.$

7. $\int_2^3 (y^2 - 2y + 1) \, dy.$

8. $\int_3^2 (2t - t^2) \, dt.$

9. $\int_{-2}^{-1} (3w^2 - w - 1) \, dw.$

10. $\int_8^9 dt.$

11. $\int_1^2 -4t^{-4} \, dt.$

12. $\int_1^2 \frac{x^{-2}}{2} \, dx.$

13. $\int_{-1}^1 \sqrt[3]{x^5} \, dx.$

14. $\int_{1/2}^{3/2} (x^2 + x + 1) \, dx.$

15. $\int_{1/2}^3 \frac{1}{x^2} \, dx.$

16. $\int_4^9 \left(\frac{1}{\sqrt{x}} - 2 \right) dx.$

17. $\int_{-1}^1 (z + 1)^5 \, dz.$

18. $\int_1^8 (x^{1/3} - x^{-1/3}) \, dx.$

19. $\int_0^1 2x^2(x^3 - 1)^3 \, dx.$

20. $\int_1^3 (x + 3)^3 \, dx.$

21. $\int_1^8 \frac{4}{y} \, dy.$

22. $\int_0^{e-1} \frac{1}{x + 1} \, dx.$

23. $\int_0^2 x^2 e^{x^3} \, dx.$

24. $\int_0^1 (3x^2 + 4x)(x^3 + 2x^2)^4 \, dx.$

25. $\int_4^5 \frac{2}{(x - 3)^3} \, dx.$

26. $\int_0^6 \sqrt{2x + 4} \, dx.$

27. $\int_{1/3}^2 \sqrt{10 - 3p} \, dp.$

28. $\int_{-1}^1 q\sqrt{q^2 + 3} \, dq.$

29. $\int_0^1 x^2\sqrt[3]{7x^3 + 1} \, dx.$

30. $\int_0^{\sqrt{7}} \left[2x - \frac{x}{(x^2 + 1)^{5/3}} \right] dx.$

31. $\int_0^1 \dfrac{2x^3 + x}{x^2 + x^4 + 1} \, dx.$

32. $\int_a^b (m + ny) \, dy.$

33. $\int_0^1 (e^x - e^{-2x}) \, dx.$

34. $\int_{-2}^1 |x| \, dx.$

35. $\int_1^e (x^{-1} + x^{-2} - x^{-3}) \, dx.$

36. $\int_1^2 \left(6\sqrt{x} - \dfrac{1}{\sqrt{2x}} \right) dx.$

37. $\int_1^3 (x + 1)e^{x^2 + 2x} \, dx.$

38. $\int_3^4 \dfrac{e^{\ln x}}{x} \, dx.$

39. In discussing traffic safety, Shonle[*] considers how much acceleration a person can tolerate in a crash so that there is no major injury. The *severity index* is defined as follows:

$$\text{severity index} = \int_0^T \alpha^{5/2} \, dt,$$

where α (a Greek letter read "alpha") is considered a constant involved with a weighted average acceleration, and T is the duration of the crash. Find the severity index.

40. In statistics, the mean μ (a Greek letter read "mu") of the continuous probability density function f defined on the interval $[a, b]$ is

$$\mu = \int_a^b [x \cdot f(x)] \, dx,$$

and the variance σ^2 (σ is a Greek letter read "sigma") is

$$\sigma^2 = \int_a^b (x - \mu)^2 f(x) \, dx.$$

Compute μ and then σ^2 if $a = 0$, $b = 1$, and $f(x) = 1$.

41. The economist Pareto[†] has stated an empirical law of distribution of higher incomes that gives the number N of persons receiving x or more dollars. If

$dN/dx = -Ax^{-B}$, where A and B are constants, set up a definite integral that gives the total number of persons having incomes between a and b, where $a < b$.

42. In a discussion of gene mutation[‡] the following integral occurs:

$$\int_0^{10^{-4}} x^{-1/2} \, dx.$$

Evaluate.

43. The present value (in dollars) of a continuous flow of income of \$2000 a year for 5 years at 6% compounded continuously is given by

$$\int_0^5 2000 e^{-0.06t} \, dt.$$

Evaluate the present value to the nearest dollar.

44. In biology, problems frequently arise involving transfer of a substance between compartments. An example would be transfer from the bloodstream to tissue. Evaluate the following integral which occurs in a two-compartment diffusion problem:[§]

$$\int_0^t (e^{-a\tau} - e^{-b\tau}) \, d\tau,$$

where τ (read "tau") is a Greek letter and a and b are constants.

[*] J. I. Shonle, *Environmental Applications of General Physics* (Reading, Mass.: Addison-Wesley Publishing Company, Inc., 1975).

[†] G. Tintner, *Methodology of Mathematical Economics and Econometrics* (Chicago: University of Chicago Press, 1967), p. 16.

[‡] W. J. Ewens, *Population Genetics* (London: Methuen & Company Ltd., 1969).

[§] W. Simon, *Mathematical Techniques for Physiology and Medicine* (New York: Academic Press, Inc., 1972).

45. For a certain population, suppose l is a function such that $l(x)$ is the number of persons who reach the age of x in any year of time. This function is called a *life table function*. Under appropriate conditions, the integral

$$\int_{x}^{x+n} l(t)\, dt$$

gives the expected number of people in the population between the exact ages of x and $x + n$, inclusive. If $l(x) = 10{,}000\sqrt{100 - x}$, determine the number of people between the exact ages of 36 and 64 inclusive. Give your answers to the nearest integer, since fractional answers make no sense.

46. If c_0 is the yearly consumption of a mineral at time $t = 0$, then under continuous consumption the total amount of the mineral used in the interval $[0, t_1]$ is

$$\int_{0}^{t_1} c_0 e^{kt}\, dt,$$

where k is the rate of consumption. For a rare-earth mineral it has been determined that $c_0 = 3000$ units and $k = 0.05$. Evaluate the integral above for these data.

47. A manufacturer's marginal cost function is $dc/dq = 0.2q + 3$. If c is in dollars, determine the cost involved to increase production from 60 to 70 units.

48. Repeat Problem 47 if $dc/dq = 0.003q^2 - 0.6q + 40$ and production increases from 100 to 200 units.

49. A manufacturer's marginal revenue function is $dr/dq = 1000/\sqrt{100q}$. If r is in dollars, find the change in the manufacturer's total revenue if production is increased from 400 to 900 units.

50. Repeat Problem 49 if $dr/dq = 250 + 90q - 3q^2$ and production is increased from 10 to 20 units.

51. A sociologist is studying the crime rate in a certain city. She estimates that t months after the beginning of next year, the total number of crimes committed will increase at the rate of $8t + 10$ crimes per month. Determine the total number of crimes that can be expected to be committed next year. How many crimes can be expected to be committed during the last 6 months of that year?

52. Taagepera* considers a "one-dimensional" country of length $2R$ (see Fig. 14.19). Suppose the production of

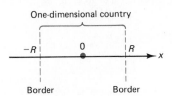

One-dimensional country

FIGURE 14.19

goods for this country is continuously distributed from border to border. If the amount produced each year per unit of distance is $f(x)$, then the country's total yearly production is given by

$$G = \int_{-R}^{R} f(x)\, dx.$$

Evaluate G if $f(x) = i$, where i is constant.

53. For the "one-dimensional" country of Problem 53, under certain conditions the amount E of the country's exports is given by

$$E = \int_{-R}^{R} \frac{i}{2}[e^{-k(R-x)} + e^{-k(R+x)}]\, dx,$$

where i and k are constants ($k \neq 0$). Evaluate E.

* R. Taagepera, "Why the Trade/GNP Ratio Decreases with Country Size," *Social Science Research*, 5 (1976), 385–404.

54. In a discussion of a delivered price of a good from a mill to a customer, DeCanio* claims that the average delivered price A paid by consumers is given by

$$A = \frac{\displaystyle\int_0^R (m + x)[1 - (m + x)] \, dx}{\displaystyle\int_0^R [1 - (m + x)] \, dx},$$

where m is mill price, x is distance, and R is the maxi-

mum distance to the point of sale. DeCanio determines that

$$A = \frac{m + \dfrac{R}{2} - m^2 - mR - \dfrac{R^2}{3}}{1 - m - \dfrac{R}{2}}.$$

Verify this.

14.7 AREA

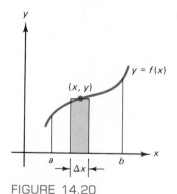

FIGURE 14.20

In Sec. 14.5, we saw that the area of a region could be found by evaluating the limit of a sum of the form $\Sigma f(x)\Delta x$, where $f(x)\,\Delta x$ represents the area of a rectangle. From Sec. 14.6, this limit is a special case of a definite integral, so it can easily be found by using the Fundamental Theorem.

When using the definite integral to determine area, you should make a rough sketch of the region involved. Let us consider the area of the region bounded by $y = f(x)$ and the x-axis from $x = a$ to $x = b$, as shown in Fig. 14.20. To set up the integral, a sample rectangle should be included in the sketch because the area of the region is a limit of sums of areas of rectangles. This will not only help you understand the integration process, it will also help you find areas of more complicated regions. Such a rectangle (see Fig. 14.20) is called a **vertical element of area** (or a **vertical strip**). In the diagram, the width of the vertical element is Δx. The length is the y-value of the curve. Hence the rectangle has area $y\,\Delta y$ or $f(x)\,\Delta x$. The area of the entire region is found by adding the areas of all such elements between $x = a$ and $x = b$ and finding the limit of this sum, which is the definite integral.

* S. J. DeCanio, "Delivered Pricing and Multiple Basing Point Equilibria: A Reevaluation," *The Quarterly Journal of Economics*, XCIX, no. 2 (1984), 329–49.

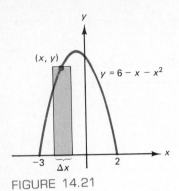

(x, y)

$y = 6 - x - x^2$

−3   2

Δx

FIGURE 14.21

$$\sum f(x)\ \Delta x \rightarrow \int_a^b f(x)\ dx = \text{area}.$$

Example 1 will illustrate.

EXAMPLE 1   *Find the area of the region bounded by the curve $y = 6 - x - x^2$ and the x-axis.*

First we must sketch the curve so that we can visualize the region. Since $y = -(x^2 + x - 6) = -(x - 2)(x + 3)$, the x-intercepts are (2, 0) and (−3, 0). Using techniques of graphing that were previously discussed, we obtain the graph shown in Fig. 14.21. With this region it is crucial that the x-intercepts of the curve be found because they determine the interval over which the areas of the elements must be summed. That is, these x-values are the limits of integration. For the vertical element shown, the width is Δx and the length is y. Hence the area of the element is $y\ \Delta x$. Summing the areas of these elements from $x = -3$ to $x = 2$ and taking the limit via the definite integral gives the area

$$\sum y\ \Delta x \rightarrow \int_{-3}^2 y\ dx = \text{area}.$$

To evaluate the integral, we must express the integrand in terms of the variable of integration, x. Since $y = 6 - x - x^2$,

$$\text{area} = \int_{-3}^2 (6 - x - x^2)\ dx = \left(6x - \frac{x^2}{2} - \frac{x^3}{3}\right)\Bigg|_{-3}^2$$

$$= \left(12 - \frac{4}{2} - \frac{8}{3}\right) - \left(-18 - \frac{9}{2} - \frac{-27}{3}\right) = \frac{125}{6} \text{ square units.}$$

$y = x^2 + 2x + 2$

−2   1

FIGURE 14.22

EXAMPLE 2   *Find the area of the region bounded by $y = x^2 + 2x + 2$, the x-axis, and the lines $x = -2$ and $x = 1$.*

A sketch of the region is given in Fig. 14.22.

$$\text{area} = \int_{-2}^1 y\ dx = \int_{-2}^1 (x^2 + 2x + 2)\ dx$$

$$= \left(\frac{x^3}{3} + x^2 + 2x\right)\Bigg|_{-2}^1 = \left(\frac{1}{3} + 1 + 2\right) - \left(-\frac{8}{3} + 4 - 4\right)$$

$$= 6 \text{ square units.}$$

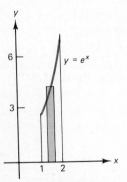

6

$y = e^x$

3

1   2

FIGURE 14.23

EXAMPLE 3   *Find the area between $y = e^x$ and the x-axis from $x = 1$ to $x = 2$.*

A sketch of the region is given in Fig. 14.23.

$$\text{area} = \int_1^2 y \, dx = \int_1^2 e^x \, dx = e^x \Big|_1^2 = e^2 - e = e(e - 1) \text{ square units.}$$

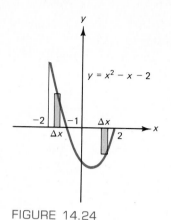

FIGURE 14.24

EXAMPLE 4 *Find the area of the region bounded by the curves* $y = x^2 - x - 2$ *and* $y = 0$ *(the x-axis) from* $x = -2$ *to* $x = 2$.

A sketch of the region is given in Fig. 14.24. Notice that the x-intercepts are $(-1, 0)$ and $(2, 0)$.

Pitfall

It is wrong to write hastily that the area is $\int_{-2}^2 y \, dx$ for the following reason. For the left rectangle the length is y. However, for the rectangle on the right, y is negative, so the rectangle has length $-y$. Remember that an area is never negative. This points out the importance of sketching the region.

On the interval $[-2, -1]$, the area of the element is

$$y \, \Delta x = (x^2 - x - 2) \, \Delta x.$$

On $[-1, 2]$ it is

$$-y \, \Delta x = -(x^2 - x - 2) \, \Delta x.$$

Thus

$$\text{area} = \int_{-2}^{-1} (x^2 - x - 2) \, dx + \int_{-1}^2 -(x^2 - x - 2) \, dx$$

$$= \left(\frac{x^3}{3} - \frac{x^2}{2} - 2x \right) \Big|_{-2}^{-1} - \left(\frac{x^3}{3} - \frac{x^2}{2} - 2x \right) \Big|_{-1}^2$$

$$= \left[\left(-\frac{1}{3} - \frac{1}{2} + 2 \right) - \left(-\frac{8}{3} - \frac{4}{2} + 4 \right) \right] -$$

$$\left[\left(\frac{8}{3} - \frac{4}{2} - 4 \right) - \left(-\frac{1}{3} - \frac{1}{2} + 2 \right) \right] = \frac{19}{3} \text{ square units.}$$

The next example shows the use of area as a probability in statistics.

EXAMPLE 5 *In statistics, a (probability) density function f of a variable* x*, where* x *assumes all values in the interval* $[a, b]$*, has the following properties:*

1. $f(x) \geq 0$.

2. $\int_a^b f(x) \, dx = 1$.

3. The probability that x assumes a value between c and d, which is written $P(c \le x \le d)$, where $a \le c \le d \le b$, is represented by the area of the region bounded by the graph of f and the x-axis between $x = c$ and $x = d$. Hence (see Fig. 14.25)

$$P(c \le x \le d) = \int_c^d f(x)\, dx.$$

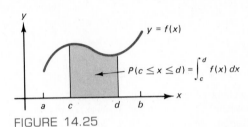

FIGURE 14.25

For the density function $f(x) = 6(x - x^2)$, where $0 \le x \le 1$, find

(a) $P(0 \le x \le \tfrac{1}{4})$ and   (b) $P(x \ge \tfrac{1}{2})$.

a. Here $[a, b]$ is $[0, 1]$, c is 0, and d is $\tfrac{1}{4}$. By property 3 we have

$$P(0 \le x \le \tfrac{1}{4}) = \int_0^{1/4} 6(x - x^2)\, dx = 6\int_0^{1/4} (x - x^2)\, dx$$

$$= 6\left(\frac{x^2}{2} - \frac{x^3}{3}\right)\Bigg|_0^{1/4} = (3x^2 - 2x^3)\Bigg|_0^{1/4}$$

$$= \left[3\left(\frac{1}{4}\right)^2 - 2\left(\frac{1}{4}\right)^3\right] - 0 = \frac{5}{32}.$$

b. Since the domain of f is $0 \le x \le 1$, to say that $x \ge \tfrac{1}{2}$ means that $\tfrac{1}{2} \le x \le 1$. Thus

$$P(x \ge \tfrac{1}{2}) = \int_{1/2}^1 6(x - x^2)\, dx = 6\int_{1/2}^1 (x - x^2)\, dx$$

$$= 6\left(\frac{x^2}{2} - \frac{x^3}{3}\right)\Bigg|_{1/2}^1 = (3x^2 - 2x^3)\Bigg|_{1/2}^1 = \frac{1}{2}.$$

EXERCISE 14.7

In Problems 1–34, use a definite integral to find the area of the region bounded by the given curve, the x-axis, and the given lines. In each case first sketch the region.

1. $y = 4x$, $x = 2$.

2. $y = 3x + 1$, $x = 0$, $x = 4$.

3. $y = 3x + 2$, $x = 2$, $x = 3$.

4. $y = x + 5$, $x = 2$, $x = 4$.

5. $y = x - 1$, $x = 5$.

6. $y = 2x^2$, $x = 1$, $x = 2$.

7. $y = x^2$, $x = 2$, $x = 3$.

8. $y = 2x^2 - x$, $x = -2$, $x = -1$.

9. $y = x^2 + 2$, $x = -1$, $x = 2$.

10. $y = 2x + x^3$, $x = 1$.

11. $y = x^2 - 2x$, $x = -3$, $x = -1$.

12. $y = 3x^2 - 4x$, $x = -2$, $x = -1$.

13. $y = 9 - x^2$.

14. $y = \dfrac{4}{x}$, $x = 1$, $x = 2$.

15. $y = 1 - x - x^3$, $x = -2$, $x = 0$.

16. $y = e^x$, $x = 1$, $x = 3$.

17. $y = 3 + 2x - x^2$.

18. $y = \dfrac{1}{x^2}$, $x = 2$, $x = 3$.

19. $y = \dfrac{1}{x}$, $x = 1$, $x = e$.

20. $y = \dfrac{1}{x}$, $x = 1$, $x = e^2$.

21. $y = \sqrt{x + 9}$, $x = -9$, $x = 0$.

22. $y = x^2 - 2x$, $x = 1$, $x = 3$.

23. $y = \sqrt{2x - 1}$, $x = 1$, $x = 5$.

24. $y = x^3 + 3x^2$, $x = -2$, $x = 2$.

25. $y = \sqrt[3]{x}$, $x = 2$.

26. $y = x^2 - 4$, $x = -2$, $x = 2$.

27. $y = e^x$, $x = 0$, $x = 2$.

28. $y = |x|$, $x = -2$, $x = 2$.

29. $y = x + \dfrac{2}{x}$, $x = 1$, $x = 2$.

30. $y = 6 - x - x^2$.

31. $y = x^3$, $x = -2$, $x = 4$.

32. $y = \sqrt{x - 2}$, $x = 2$, $x = 6$.

33. $y = 2x - x^2$, $x = 1$, $x = 3$.

34. $y = x^2 - x + 1$, $x = 0$, $x = 1$.

35. Given

$$f(x) = \begin{cases} 3x^2, & \text{if } 0 \leq x \leq 2, \\ 16 - 2x, & \text{if } x \geq 2, \end{cases}$$

find the area of the region bounded by the graph of $y = f(x)$, the x-axis, and the line $x = 3$. Include a sketch of the region.

36. Under conditions of a continuous uniform distribution, a topic in statistics, the proportion of persons with incomes between a and t, where $a \leq t \leq b$, is the area of the region between the curve $y = 1/(b - a)$ and the x-axis from $x = a$ to $x = t$. Sketch the graph of the curve and determine the area of the given region.

37. Suppose $f(x) = x/8$, where $0 \leq x \leq 4$. If f is a density function (see Example 5), find (a) $P(0 \leq x \leq 1)$, (b) $P(2 \leq x \leq 4)$, and (c) $P(x \geq 3)$.

38. Suppose $f(x) = 3(1 - x)^2$, where $0 \leq x \leq 1$. If f is a density function (see Example 5), find (a) $P(\frac{1}{2} \leq x \leq 1)$, (b) $P(\frac{1}{3} \leq x \leq \frac{1}{2})$, and (c) $P(x \leq \frac{1}{3})$. (d) Use your result from part (c) to determine $P(x \geq \frac{1}{3})$.

39. Suppose $f(x) = 1/x$, where $e \leq x \leq e^2$. If f is a density function (see Example 5), find (a) $P(3 \leq x \leq 5)$, (b) $P(x \leq 4)$, and (c) $P(x \geq 3)$. (d) Verify that $P(e \leq x \leq e^2) = 1$.

14.8 AREA BETWEEN CURVES

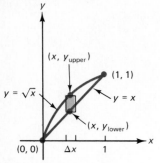

FIGURE 14.26

We shall now consider finding the area of a region enclosed by several curves. As before, our procedure will be to draw a sample element of area and use the definite integral to "add together" the areas of all such elements.

EXAMPLE 1   *Find the area of the region bounded by the curves* $y = \sqrt{x}$ *and* $y = x$.

A sketch of the region appears in Fig. 14.26. To determine where the curves intersect, we solve the system formed by the equations $y = \sqrt{x}$ and $y = x$. Eliminating y by substitution, we obtain

$$\sqrt{x} = x,$$

$$x = x^2 \quad \text{(squaring both sides)},$$

$$0 = x^2 - x = x(x - 1).$$

$$x = 0 \quad \text{or} \quad x = 1.$$

If $x = 0$, then $y = 0$; if $x = 1$, then $y = 1$. Thus the curves intersect at $(0, 0)$ and $(1, 1)$. The width of the indicated element of area is Δx. The length is the y-value on the upper curve minus the y-value on the lower curve. If we distinguish between the curves by writing $y_{\text{upper}} = \sqrt{x}$ and $y_{\text{lower}} = x$, then the length of the element is

$$y_{\text{upper}} - y_{\text{lower}} = \sqrt{x} - x.$$

Thus the area of the element is $(\sqrt{x} - x)\,\Delta x$. Summing all such areas from $x = 0$ to $x = 1$ by the definite integral, we get the area of the entire region.

$$\sum (\sqrt{x} - x)\,\Delta x \rightarrow \int_0^1 (\sqrt{x} - x)\,dx.$$

$$\text{area} = \int_0^1 (x^{1/2} - x)\,dx = \left(\frac{x^{3/2}}{\frac{3}{2}} - \frac{x^2}{2} \right) \Bigg|_0^1$$

$$= \left(\frac{2}{3} - \frac{1}{2} \right) - (0 - 0) = \frac{1}{6} \text{ square unit.}$$

It should be obvious to you that the points of intersection are important in determining the limits of integration.

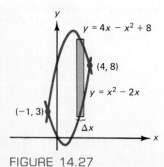

FIGURE 14.27

EXAMPLE 2   *Find the area of the region bounded by the curves* $y = 4x - x^2 + 8$ *and* $y = x^2 - 2x$.

A sketch of the region appears in Fig. 14.27. To find where the curves intersect, we solve the system of equations $y = 4x - x^2 + 8$ and $y = x^2 - 2x$.

$$4x - x^2 + 8 = x^2 - 2x,$$

$$-2x^2 + 6x + 8 = 0,$$

$$x^2 - 3x - 4 = 0,$$

$$(x + 1)(x - 4) = 0.$$

$$x = -1 \quad \text{or} \quad x = 4.$$

When $x = -1$, then $y = 3$; when $x = 4$, then $y = 8$. Thus the curves intersect at $(-1, 3)$ and $(4, 8)$. The width of the indicated element is Δx. The length is the y-value on the upper curve minus the y-value on the lower curve. By writing $y_{\text{upper}} = 4x - x^2 + 8$ and $y_{\text{lower}} = x^2 - 2x$, then the length of the element is

$$y_{\text{upper}} - y_{\text{lower}} = (4x - x^2 + 8) - (x^2 - 2x).$$

Thus the area of the element is

$$[(4x - x^2 + 8) - (x^2 - 2x)]\, \Delta x = (-2x^2 + 6x + 8)\, \Delta x.$$

Summing all such areas from $x = -1$ to $x = 4$, we have

$$\text{area} = \int_{-1}^{4} (-2x^2 + 6x + 8)\, dx = 41\tfrac{2}{3} \text{ square units.}$$

Sometimes area can more easily be determined by summing areas of horizontal elements rather than vertical elements. In the following example an area will be found by both methods. In each case the element of area determines the form of the integral.

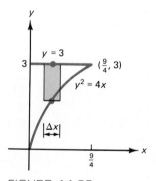

FIGURE 14.28

EXAMPLE 3   *Find the area of the region bounded by the curve $y^2 = 4x$ and the lines $y = 3$ and $x = 0$ (the y-axis).*

The region is sketched in Fig. 14.28. When the curves $y = 3$ and $y^2 = 4x$ intersect, then $9 = 4x$, so $x = \tfrac{9}{4}$. Thus the point of intersection is $(\tfrac{9}{4}, 3)$. Since the width of the vertical strip is Δx, we integrate with respect to the variable x. Thus y_{upper} and y_{lower} must be expressed as functions of x. For the curve $y^2 = 4x$, we have $y = \pm 2\sqrt{x}$. But for the portion of this curve that bounds the region, $y \geq 0$, so we use $y = 2\sqrt{x}$. Thus the length of the strip is $y_{\text{upper}} - y_{\text{lower}} = 3 - 2\sqrt{x}$. Hence the strip has an area of $(3 - 2\sqrt{x})\, \Delta x$, and we wish to sum up all such areas from $x = 0$ to $x = \tfrac{9}{4}$.

$$\text{area} = \int_0^{9/4} (3 - 2\sqrt{x})\, dx = \left(3x - \frac{4x^{3/2}}{3} \right) \Bigg|_0^{9/4}$$

$$= \left[3\left(\frac{9}{4}\right) - \frac{4}{3}\left(\frac{9}{4}\right)^{3/2} \right] - (0)$$

$$= \frac{27}{4} - \frac{4}{3}\left[\left(\frac{9}{4}\right)^{1/2} \right]^3 = \frac{27}{4} - \frac{4}{3}\left(\frac{3}{2}\right)^3 = \frac{9}{4} \text{ square units.}$$

Let us now approach this problem from the point of view of a **horizontal ele-**

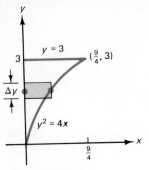

FIGURE 14.29

ment of area (or **horizontal strip**) as shown in Fig. 14.29. The width of the element is Δy. The length of the element is the *x-value on the right curve minus the x-value on the left curve.* Thus the area of the element is $(x_{\text{right}} - x_{\text{left}}) \Delta y$. We wish to sum all such areas from $y = 0$ to $y = 3$.

$$\sum (x_{\text{right}} - x_{\text{left}}) \Delta y \rightarrow \int_0^3 (x_{\text{right}} - x_{\text{left}}) \, dy.$$

Since the variable of integration is y, we must express x_{right} and x_{left} as functions of y. The right curve is $y^2 = 4x$ or, equivalently, $x = y^2/4$. The left curve is $x = 0$. Thus

$$\text{area} = \int_0^3 (x_{\text{right}} - x_{\text{left}}) \, dy$$

$$= \int_0^3 \left(\frac{y^2}{4} - 0 \right) dy = \frac{y^3}{12} \Big|_0^3 = \frac{9}{4} \text{ square units.}$$

Note that for this region, horizontal strips make the definite integral easier to evaluate (and set up) than an integral with vertical strips. In any case, remember that **the limits of integration are those limits for the variable of integration.**

EXAMPLE 4   *Find the area of the region bounded by $y^2 = x$ and $x - y = 2$.*

A sketch of the region appears in Fig. 14.30. The curves intersect when $y^2 - y = 2$. Thus $y^2 - y - 2 = 0$, or equivalently $(y + 1)(y - 2) = 0$, from which $y = -1$ or $y = 2$. The points of intersection are $(1, -1)$ and $(4, 2)$. Let us consider vertical elements of area [see Fig. 14.30(a)]. Solving $y^2 = x$ for y gives $y = \pm \sqrt{x}$. As seen in Fig. 14.30(a), to the *left* of $x = 1$ the upper end

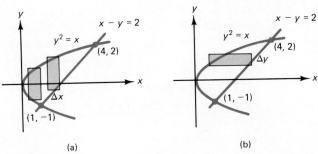

(a)   (b)

FIGURE 14.30

of the element lies on $y = \sqrt{x}$ and the lower end lies on $y = -\sqrt{x}$. To the *right* of $x = 1$, the upper curve is $y = \sqrt{x}$ and the lower curve is $x - y = 2$ (or $y = x - 2$). Thus with vertical strips *two* integrals are needed to evaluate the area.

$$\text{area} = \int_0^1 \left[\sqrt{x} - (-\sqrt{x}) \right] dx + \int_1^4 \left[\sqrt{x} - (x - 2) \right] dx.$$

Let us consider horizontal strips to see if we can simplify our work. In Fig.

14.30(b), the width of the strip is Δy. The rightmost curve is *always* $x - y = 2$ (or $x = y + 2$) and the leftmost curve is *always* $y^2 = x$ (or $x = y^2$). Thus the area of the horizontal strip is $[(y + 2) - y^2] \, \Delta y$ and the total area is

$$\text{area} = \int_{-1}^{2} (y + 2 - y^2) \, dy = \frac{9}{2} \text{ square units.}$$

Clearly, the use of horizontal strips is the more desirable approach for the problem.

EXERCISE 14.8

In Problems **1–22,** *find the area of the region bounded by the graphs of the given equations.*

1. $y = x^2, y = 2x$.

2. $y = x, y = -x + 3, y = 0$.

3. $y = x^2, x = 0, y = 4 \ (x \geq 0)$.

4. $y = x^2, y = x$.

5. $y = x^2 + 3, y = 9$.

6. $y^2 = x, x = 2$.

7. $x = 8 + 2y, x = 0, y = -1, y = 3$.

8. $y = x - 4, y^2 = 2x$.

9. $y = 4 - x^2, y = -3x$.

10. $x = y^2 + 2, x = 6$.

11. $y^2 = x, y = x - 2$.

12. $y = x^2, y = x + 2$.

13. $2y = 4x - x^2, 2y = x - 4$.

14. $y = \sqrt{x}, y = x^2$.

15. $y^2 = x, 3x - 2y = 1$.

16. $y = 2 - x^2, y = x$.

17. $y = 8 - x^2, y = x^2, x = -1, x = 1$.

18. $y^2 = 4 - x, y = x + 2$.

19. $y = x^2, y = 2, y = 5$.

20. $y = x^3 - x, x\text{-axis}$.

21. $y = x^3, y = x$.

22. $y = x^3, y = \sqrt{x}$.

23. A *Lorentz curve* is used in studying income distributions. If x is the cumulative percentage of income recipients, ranked from poorest to richest, and y is the cumulative percentage of income, then equality of income distribution is given by the line $y = x$ in Fig. 14.31, where x and y are expressed as decimals. For example, 10% of the people receive 10% of total income, 20% of the people receive 20% of the income, and so on. Suppose the actual distribution is given by the Lorentz curve defined by $y = \frac{20}{21}x^2 + \frac{1}{21}x$. Note, for example, that 30% of the people receive only 10% of total income. The degree of deviation from equality is mea-

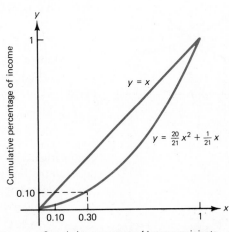

FIGURE 14.31

sured by the *coefficient of inequality** for a Lorentz curve. This coefficient is defined to be the area between the curve and the diagonal, divided by the area under the diagonal:

$$\frac{\text{area between curve and diagonal}}{\text{area under diagonal}}.$$

For example, when all incomes are equal, the coefficient of inequality is zero. Find the coefficient of inequality for the Lorentz curve defined above.

24. Find the coefficient of inequality as in Problem 23 for the Lorentz curve defined by $y = \frac{11}{12}x^2 + \frac{1}{12}x$.

14.9   CONSUMERS' AND PRODUCERS' SURPLUS

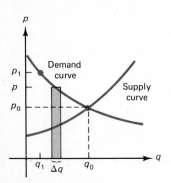

FIGURE 14.32

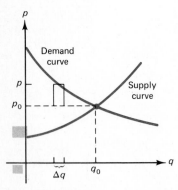

FIGURE 14.33

Determining the area of a region has applications in economics. Figure 14.32 shows the supply and demand curves for a product. The point (q_0, p_0) where these curves intersect is called the *point of equilibrium*. Here p_0 is the price per unit at which consumers will purchase the same quantity q_0 of a product that producers wish to sell at that price. In short, p_0 is the price at which stability in the producer-consumer relationship occurs.

Let us assume that the market is at equilibrium and the price per unit of the product is p_0. According to the demand curve, there are consumers who would be willing to pay *more* than p_0. For example, at the price per unit of p_1, consumers would buy q_1 units. These consumers are benefiting from the lower equilibrium price.

The vertical strip in Fig. 14.32 has area $p\,\Delta q$. This expression can also be thought of as the total amount of money that consumers would spend by buying Δq units of the product if the price per unit were p. Since the price is actually p_0, these consumers spend only $p_0\,\Delta q$ for these Δq units and thus benefit by the amount $p\,\Delta q - p_0\,\Delta q$. This can be written $(p - p_0)\,\Delta q$, which is the area of a rectangle of width Δq and length $p - p_0$ (see Fig. 14.33). Summing the areas of all such rectangles from $q = 0$ to $q = q_0$ by definite integration, we have $\int_0^{q_0} (p - p_0)\,dq$. This integral, under certain conditions, represents the total gain to consumers who are willing to pay more than the equilibrium price. This total gain is called **consumers' surplus,** abbreviated *CS*. If the demand function is given by $p = f(q)$, then

$$CS = \int_0^{q_0} [f(q) - p_0]\,dq.$$

Geometrically (see Fig. 14.34), consumers' surplus is represented by the area between the line $p = p_0$ and the demand curve $p = f(q)$ from $q = 0$ to $q = q_0$.

Some of the producers also benefit from the equilibrium price, since they are willing to supply the product at prices *less* than p_0. Under certain conditions

* G. Stigler, *The Theory of Price,* 3rd ed., (New York: The Macmillan Company, 1966), pp. 293–94.

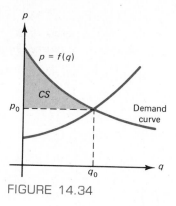

FIGURE 14.34

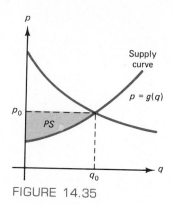

FIGURE 14.35

the total gain to the producers is represented geometrically in Fig. 14.35 by the area between the line $p = p_0$ and the supply curve $p = g(q)$ from $q = 0$ to $q = q_0$. This gain, called **producers' surplus** and abbreviated PS, is given by

$$PS = \int_0^{q_0} [p_0 - g(q)] \, dq.$$

EXAMPLE 1   *The demand function for a product is $p = f(q) = 100 - 0.05q$, where p is the price per unit (in dollars) for q units. The supply function is $p = g(q) = 10 + 0.1q$. Determine consumers' surplus and producers' surplus under market equilbrium.*

First we must find the equilibrium point by solving the system formed by $p = 100 - 0.05q$ and $p = 10 + 0.1q$.

$$10 + 0.1q = 100 - 0.05q,$$

$$0.15q = 90,$$

$$q = 600.$$

When $q = 600$, then $p = 10 + 0.1(600) = 70$. Thus $q_0 = 600$ and $p_0 = 70$. Consumers' surplus is

$$CS = \int_0^{q_0} [f(q) - p_0] \, dq = \int_0^{600} (100 - 0.05q - 70) \, dq$$

$$= \left(30q - 0.05\frac{q^2}{2} \right) \Bigg|_0^{600} = 18{,}000 - 9000 = 9000.$$

Producers' surplus is

$$PS = \int_0^{q_0} [p_0 - g(q)] \, dq = \int_0^{600} [70 - (10 + 0.1q)] \, dq$$

$$= \left(60q - 0.1\frac{q^2}{2} \right) \Bigg|_0^{600} = 36{,}000 - 18{,}000 = 18{,}000.$$

Thus consumers' surplus is $9000 and producers' surplus is $18,000.

EXAMPLE 2   *The demand equation for a product is $q = f(p) = (90/p) - 2$ and the supply equation is $q = g(p) = p - 1$. Determine the consumers' surplus and producers' surplus when market equilibrium has been established.*

Determining the equilibrium point, we have

$$p - 1 = \frac{90}{p} - 2,$$

$$p^2 + p - 90 = 0,$$

$$(p + 10)(p - 9) = 0.$$

Thus $p_0 = 9$ and $q_0 = 9 - 1 = 8$ (see Fig. 14.36). Note that the demand equation expresses q as a function of p. Since consumers' surplus can be consid-

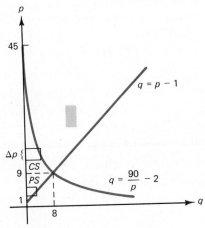

FIGURE 14.36

ered as an area, this area can be determined by means of horizontal strips of width Δp and length $q = f(p)$. These strips are summed from $p = 9$ to $p = 45$.

$$CS = \int_9^{45} \left(\frac{90}{p} - 2 \right) dp = (90 \ln |p| - 2p) \Big|_9^{45}$$

$$= 90 \ln 5 - 72 \approx 72.85.$$

Using horizontal strips for producers' surplus, we have

$$PS = \int_1^9 (p - 1) \, dp = \frac{(p - 1)^2}{2} \Big|_1^9 = 32.$$

EXERCISE 14.9

In Problems **1–6,** *the first equation is a demand equation and the second is a supply equation of a product. In each case determine the consumers' surplus and producers' surplus under market equilibrium.*

1. $p = 20 - 0.8q$,
   $p = 4 + 1.2q$.

2. $p = 900 - q^2$,
   $p = 100 + q^2$.

3. $p = \dfrac{50}{q + 5}$,

   $p = \dfrac{q}{10} + 4.5$.

4. $p = 400 - q^2$,
   $p = 20q + 100$.

5. $q = 100(10 - p)$,
   $q = 80(p - 1)$.

6. $q = \sqrt{100 - p}$,

   $q = \dfrac{p}{2} - 10$.

14.10 REVIEW

Important Terms and Symbols

Section 14.1   antiderivative   indefinite integral $\int f(x)\, dx$ integral sign   integrand

variable of integration   constant of integration

Section 14.2   power rule for integration

Section 14.4 $\sum$ index of summation   limits of summation

Section 14.5   definite integral $\int_a^b f(x)\, dx$ lower limit of integration   upper limit of integration

Section 14.6   Fundamental Theorem of Integral Calculus $F(x)\Big|_a^b$

Section 14.7   vertical element of area

Section 14.8   horizontal element of area

Section 14.9   consumers' surplus   producers' surplus

Summary

An antiderivative of a function f is a function F such that $F'(x) = f(x)$. Any two antiderivatives of f differ at most by a constant. An arbitrary antiderivative of f is called the indefinite integral of f and is denoted $\int f(x)\, dx$. Thus

$$\int f(x)\, dx = F(x) + C,$$

where C is called the constant of integration.

Some basic integration formulas are as follows:

$$\int k\, dx = kx + C, \quad k \text{ a constant,}$$

$$\int x^n \, dx = \frac{x^{n+1}}{n+1} + C, \quad n \neq -1,$$

$$\int e^x \, dx = e^x + C,$$

$$\int kf(x) \, dx = k \int f(x) \, dx, \quad k \text{ a constant,}$$

and $$\int [f(x) \pm g(x)] \, dx = \int f(x) \, dx \pm \int g(x) \, dx.$$

Another formula is the power rule for integration:

$$\int u^n \, du = \frac{u^{n+1}}{n+1} + C, \quad \text{if } n \neq -1.$$

Here u represents a differentiable function of x and du is its differential. When applying the power rule to a given integral, it is important that the integral is written in a form that precisely matches the power rule. Other integration formulas are

$$\int e^u \, du = e^u + C,$$

$$\int a^u \, du = \frac{a^u}{\ln a} + C,$$

and $$\int \frac{1}{u} \, du = \ln|u| + C, \quad u \neq 0.$$

If the rate of change of a function f is known, that is, f' is known, then f is an antiderivative of f'. If the value of $f(x)$ for a given value of x is also known, then we can find the particular antiderivative that satisfies this condition. For example, if a marginal cost function dc/dq is given to us, then by integration we can find c. The form of c that we obtain involves a constant of integration. However, if we are also given fixed costs (that is, costs involved when $q = 0$), then we can determine the value of the constant of integration and thus find the particular cost function c. Similarly, if we are given a marginal revenue function dr/dq, then by integration and by using the fact that $r = 0$ when $q = 0$, we can determine the particular revenue function r. Once r is known, the corresponding demand equation can be found by using the equation $p = r/q$.

Sigma notation is convenient for representing sums. This notation is especially useful in determining areas. To find the area of the region bounded by $y = f(x)$ [where $f(x) \geq 0$ and continuous] and the x-axis, from $x = a$ to $x = b$, we divide the interval $[a, b]$ into n subintervals of equal length Δx. If x_i is the right-hand endpoint of an arbitrary subinterval, then the product $f(x_i) \, \Delta x$ is the area of a rectangle. Denoting the sum of all such areas of rectangles for the n subintervals by S_n, then the limit of S_n as $n \to \infty$ is the area of the entire region.

$$\lim_{n \to \infty} S_n = \lim_{n \to \infty} \sum_{i=1}^{n} f(x_i) \, \Delta x = \text{area}.$$

If the restriction that $f(x) \geq 0$ is omitted, the limit above is defined as the definite integral of f over $[a, b]$.

$$\lim_{n \to \infty} \sum_{i=1}^{n} f(x_i) \, \Delta x = \int_{a}^{b} f(x) \, dx.$$

Instead of evaluating definite integrals by using limits, the Fundamental Theorem of Integral Calculus may be employed:

$$\int_{a}^{b} f(x) \, dx = F(x) \Big|_{a}^{b} = F(b) - F(a),$$

where F is any antiderivative of f.

Some properties of the definite integral are

$$\int_a^b kf(x)\,dx = k\int_a^b f(x)\,dx, \quad k \text{ is a constant,}$$

$$\int_a^b [f(x) \pm g(x)]\,dx = \int_a^b f(x)\,dx \pm \int_a^b g(x)\,dx,$$

and $\quad \displaystyle\int_a^c f(x)\,dx = \int_a^b f(x)\,dx + \int_b^c f(x)\,dx.$

If the rate of change of a function f is known, then a change in function values of f can be easily found by the formula

$$\int_a^b f'(x)\,dx = f(b) - f(a).$$

If $f(x) \geq 0$ and continuous on $[a, b]$, then the definite integral may be used to find the area of the region bounded by $y = f(x)$ and the x-axis from $x = a$ to $x = b$. The definite integral may also be used to find areas of more complicated regions. In these situations, an element of area should be drawn in the region. This will allow you to set up the proper definite integral. In some situations, vertical elements should be considered, while in others, horizontal elements are more advantageous.

One application of finding area involves consumers' surplus and producers' surplus. Suppose the market for a product is at equilibrium and (q_0, p_0) is the equilibrium point. Consumer's surplus, CS, corresponds to the area, from $q = 0$ to $q = q_0$, bounded above by the demand curve, and below by the line $p = p_0$. Thus

$$CS = \int_0^{q_0} [f(q) - p_0]\,dq,$$

where f is the demand function. Producers' surplus, PS, corresponds to the area, from $q = 0$ to $q = q_0$, bounded above by the line $p = p_0$, and below by the supply curve. Thus

$$PS = \int_0^{q_0} [p_0 - g(q)]\,dq,$$

where g is the supply function.

Review Problems

In Problems 1–32, determine the integrals.

1. $\displaystyle\int (x^3 + 2x - 7)\,dx.$

2. $\displaystyle\int dx.$

3. $\displaystyle\int_0^9 (\sqrt{x} + x)\,dx.$

4. $\displaystyle\int \frac{2}{5 - 3x}\,dx.$

5. $\displaystyle\int \frac{2}{(x + 5)^3}\,dx.$

6. $\displaystyle\int_4^{12} (y - 8)^{501}\,dy.$

7. $\displaystyle\int \frac{6x^2 - 12}{x^3 - 6x + 1}\,dx.$

8. $\displaystyle\int_0^2 xe^{4 - x^2}\,dx.$

9. $\displaystyle\int_0^1 \sqrt[3]{3t + 8}\,dt.$

10. $\displaystyle\int \frac{5 - 3x}{2}\,dx.$

11. $\displaystyle\int y(y + 1)^2\,dy.$

12. $\displaystyle\int_0^1 10^{-8}\,dx.$

13. $\displaystyle\int \frac{\sqrt[4]{z} - \sqrt[3]{z}}{\sqrt{z}}\,dz.$

14. $\displaystyle\int \frac{(0.5x - 0.1)^4}{0.4}\,dx.$

15. $\displaystyle\int_1^2 \frac{t^2}{2 + t^3}\,dt.$

16. $\displaystyle\int \frac{4x^2 - x}{x}\,dx.$

17. $\displaystyle\int x^2\sqrt{3x^3 + 2}\,dx.$

18. $\displaystyle\int (2x^3 + x)(x^4 + x^2)^{3/4}\,dx.$

19. $\int (e^{2y} - e^{-2y})\, dy.$

20. $\int \dfrac{8x}{3\sqrt[3]{7 - 2x^2}}\, dx.$

21. $\int \left(\dfrac{1}{x} + \dfrac{2}{x^2} \right) dx.$

22. $\int_0^1 \dfrac{e^{2x}}{1 + e^{2x}}\, dx.$

23. $\int_{-2}^1 (y^4 - y + 1)\, dy.$

24. $\int_7^{70} dx.$

25. $\int_{\sqrt{3}}^2 7x\sqrt{4 - x^2}\, dx.$

26. $\int_0^1 (2x + 1)(x^2 + x)^4\, dx.$

27. $\int_0^1 \left[2x - \dfrac{1}{(x + 1)^{2/3}} \right] dx.$

28. $\int_2^8 (\sqrt{2x} - x + 4)\, dx.$

29. $\int \dfrac{\sqrt{t} - 3}{t^2}\, dt.$

30. $\int \dfrac{z^2}{z - 1}\, dz.$

31. $\int_{-1}^0 \dfrac{x^2 + 4x - 1}{x + 2}\, dx.$

32. $\int \dfrac{(x^2 + 4)^2}{x^2}\, dx.$

*In Problems **33–40**, determine the area of the region bounded by the given curve, the x-axis, and the given lines.*

33. $y = x^2 - 1,\ x = 2\ (y \geq 0).$

34. $y = 4e^{2x},\ x = 0,\ x = 3.$

35. $y = \sqrt{x + 4},\ x = 0.$

36. $y = x^2 - x - 2,\ x = -2,\ x = 2.$

37. $y = 5x - x^2.$

38. $y = \sqrt[4]{x},\ x = 1,\ x = 16.$

39. $y = \dfrac{1}{x} + 3,\ x = 1,\ x = 3.$

40. $y = x^3 - 1,\ x = -1.$

*In Problems **41–48**, find the area of the region bounded by the given curves.*

41. $y^2 = 4x,\ x = 0,\ y = 2.$

42. $y = 2x^2,\ x = 0,\ y = 2\ (x \geq 0).$

43. $y = x^2 + 4x - 5,\ y = 0.$

44. $y = 2x^2,\ y = x^2 + 9.$

45. $y = x^2 - 2x,\ y = 12 - x^2.$

46. $y = \sqrt{x},\ x = 0,\ y = 3.$

47. $y = \ln x,\ x = 0,\ y = 0,\ y = 1.$

48. $y = 1 - x,\ y = x - 2,\ y = 0,\ y = 1.$

49. If marginal revenue is given by $dr/dq = 100 - (3/2)\sqrt{2q}$, determine the corresponding demand equation.

50. If marginal cost is given by $dc/dq = q^2 + 7q + 6$, and fixed costs are 2500, determine the total cost for producing 6 units.

51. A manufacturer's marginal revenue function is $dr/dq = 275 - q - 0.3q^2$. If r is in dollars, find the increase in the manufacturer's total revenue if production is increased from 10 to 20 units.

52. A manufacturer's marginal cost function is $dc/dq = 500/\sqrt{2q + 25}$. If c is in dollars, determine the cost involved to increase production from 100 to 300 units.

53. For a product the demand equation is $p = 0.01q^2 -$ $1.1q + 30$ and its supply equation is $p = 0.01q^2 + 8$. Determine consumers' surplus and producers' surplus when market equilibrium has been established.

54. The total expenditures (in dollars) of a business over the next 5 years is given by

$$\int_0^5 4000e^{0.05t}\, dt.$$

Evaluate the expenditures.

55. For a group of hospitalized individuals, suppose the discharge rate is given by $f(t) = 0.008e^{-0.008t}$, where $f(t)$ is the proportion discharged per day at the end of t days of hospitalization. What proportion of the group is discharged at the end of 100 days?

56. In a discussion of gene mutation,* the following equation occurs:

$$\int_{q_0}^{q_n} \frac{dq}{q - \hat{q}} = -(u + v)\int_0^n dt,$$

where u and v are gene mutation rates, the q's are gene frequencies, and n is the number of generations. Assume that all letters represent constants except q and t. Integrate both sides and then use your result to show that

$$n = \frac{1}{u + v} \ln \left| \frac{q_0 - \hat{q}}{q_n - \hat{q}} \right|.$$

57. In studying the flow of a fluid in a tube of constant radius R, such as blood flow in portions of the body, one can think of the tube as consisting of concentric tubes of radius r, where $0 \leq r \leq R$. The velocity v of the fluid is a function of r and is given by†

$$v = \frac{(P_1 - P_2)(R^2 - r^2)}{4\eta l},$$

where P_1 and P_2 are pressures at the ends of the tube, η (a Greek letter read "eta") is the fluid viscosity, and l is the length of the tube. The volume rate of flow, Q, through the tube is given by

$$Q = \int_0^R 2\pi r v \, dr.$$

Show that $Q = \dfrac{\pi R^4 (P_1 - P_2)}{8\eta l}$. Note that R occurs as a factor to the fourth power. Thus, doubling the radius of the tube has the effect of increasing the flow by a factor of 16. The formula that you derived for the volume rate of flow is called Poiseuille's law, after the French physiologist Jean Poiseuille.

58. In a discussion of inventory, Barbosa and Friedman‡ refer to the function

$$g(x) = \frac{1}{k} \int_1^{1/x} k u^r \, du,$$

where k and r are constants, $k > 0$ and $r > -2$, and $x > 0$. Verify the claim that

$$g'(x) = -\frac{1}{x^{r+2}}.$$

(*Hint:* Consider two cases: when $r \neq -1$, and when $r = -1$.)

---

* W. B. Mather, *Principles of Quantitative Genetics* (Minneapolis, Minn.: Burgess Publishing Company, 1964).

† R. W. Stacy et al., *Essentials of Biological and Medical Physics* (New York: McGraw-Hill Book Company, 1955).

‡ L. C. Barbosa and M. Friedman. "Deterministic Inventory Lot Size Models—A General Root Law," *Management Science*, 24, no. 8 (1978), 819–26.

CHAPTER 15

Methods and Applications of Integration

15.1 INTEGRATION BY PARTS*

Many integrals cannot be found by our previous methods. However, there are ways of changing certain integrals to forms that are easier to integrate. Of these methods, we shall discuss two: *integration by parts,* and (in Sec. 15.2) *integration using partial fractions.*

If u and v are differentiable functions of x, by the product rule we have

$$(uv)' = uv' + vu'.$$

Rearranging gives

$$uv' = (uv)' - vu'.$$

Integrating both sides with respect to x, we get

$$\int uv' \, dx = \int (uv)' \, dx - \int vu' \, dx. \tag{1}$$

For $\int (uv)' \, dx$, we must find a function whose derivative with respect to x is $(uv)'$. Clearly, uv is such a function. Hence $\int (uv)' \, dx = uv + C_1$ and Eq. (1) becomes

$$\int uv' \, dx = uv + C_1 - \int vu' \, dx.$$

Incorporating C_1 into the constant of integration for $\int vu' \, dx$ and replacing $v' \, dx$ by dv and $u' \, dx$ by du, we have the *integration by parts formula:*

* May be omitted without loss of continuity.

594

$$\boxed{\begin{array}{c} \text{INTEGRATION BY PARTS FORMULA} \\[6pt] \displaystyle \int u\,dv = uv - \int v\,du. \qquad (2) \end{array}}$$

This formula expresses an integral, $\displaystyle\int u\,dv$, in terms of another integral, $\displaystyle\int v\,du$, which may be easier to find.

To apply the formula to $\displaystyle\int f(x)\,dx$, we must write $f(x)\,dx$ as the product of two factors (or *parts*) by choosing a function u and a differential dv such that $f(x)\,dx = u\,dv$. For the formula to be useful, we must be able to integrate the part chosen for dv. To illustrate, consider

$$\int xe^x\,dx.$$

This integral cannot be determined by previous integration formulas. We can write $xe^x\,dx$ in the form $u\,dv$ by letting

$$u = x \qquad \text{and} \qquad dv = e^x\,dx.$$

To apply the integration by parts formula, we must find du and v:

$$du = dx \qquad \text{and} \qquad v = \int e^x\,dx = e^x + C_1.$$

Thus

$$\int \underbrace{x}_{u}\, \underbrace{e^x\,dx}_{dv} = uv - \int v\,du$$

$$= x(e^x + C_1) - \int (e^x + C_1)\,dx$$

$$= xe^x + C_1 x - e^x - C_1 x + C$$

$$= xe^x - e^x + C = e^x(x - 1) + C.$$

The first constant C_1 does not appear in the final answer. This is a characteristic of integration by parts and from now on this constant will not be written when finding v from dv.

When you are using the integration by parts formula, sometimes the "best choice" for u and dv may not be obvious. In some cases one choice may be as good as another; in other cases only one choice may be suitable. Insight into making a good choice (if any exists) will come only with practice and, of course, trial and error.

EXAMPLE 1 *Find* $\displaystyle\int \frac{\ln x}{\sqrt{x}}\,dx$ *by integration by parts.*

We try

$$u = \ln x \quad \text{and} \quad dv = \frac{1}{\sqrt{x}} \, dx.$$

Then

$$du = \frac{1}{x} \, dx \quad \text{and} \quad v = \int x^{-1/2} \, dx = 2x^{1/2}.$$

Thus

$$\int \underbrace{\ln x}_{u} \underbrace{\left(\frac{1}{\sqrt{x}} \, dx\right)}_{dv} = uv - \int v \, du$$

$$= (\ln x)(2\sqrt{x}) - \int (2x^{1/2})\left(\frac{1}{x} \, dx\right)$$

$$= 2\sqrt{x} \ln x - 2\int x^{-1/2} \, dx$$

$$= 2\sqrt{x} \ln x - 2(2\sqrt{x}) + C$$

$$= 2\sqrt{x} \, (\ln x - 2) + C$$

EXAMPLE 2   *Evaluate* $\int_1^2 x \ln x \, dx$.

Let $u = x$ and $dv = \ln x \, dx$. Then $du = dx$, but $v = \int \ln x \, dx$ is not apparent by inspection. We shall make a different choice for u and dv. Let

$$u = \ln x \quad \text{and} \quad dv = x \, dx.$$

Then

$$du = \frac{1}{x} \, dx \quad \text{and} \quad v = \int x \, dx = \frac{x^2}{2}.$$

Thus

$$\int_1^2 x \ln x \, dx = (\ln x)\left(\frac{x^2}{2}\right)\Big|_1^2 - \int_1^2 \left(\frac{x^2}{2}\right)\frac{1}{x} \, dx$$

$$= (\ln x)\left(\frac{x^2}{2}\right)\Big|_1^2 - \frac{1}{2}\int_1^2 x \, dx$$

$$= \frac{x^2 \ln x}{2}\Big|_1^2 - \frac{1}{2}\left(\frac{x^2}{2}\right)\Big|_1^2$$

$$= (2 \ln 2 - 0) - (1 - \tfrac{1}{4}) = 2 \ln 2 - \tfrac{3}{4}.$$

EXAMPLE 3   *Determine* $\int \ln y \, dy$.

Let $u = \ln y$ and $dv = dy$. Then $du = (1/y) \, dy$ and $v = y$.

$$\int \ln y \, dy = (\ln y)(y) - \int y \left(\frac{1}{y} \, dy \right)$$

$$= y \ln y - \int dy = y \ln y - y + C$$

$$= y(\ln y - 1) + C.$$

EXAMPLE 4   *Determine* $\int x e^{x^2} \, dx$.

Pitfall

Do not forget about basic integration forms. Integration by parts is not needed here!

$$\int x e^{x^2} \, dx = \frac{1}{2} \int e^{x^2} (2x \, dx)$$

$$= \frac{1}{2} \int e^u \, du \qquad (\text{where } u = x^2)$$

$$= \frac{1}{2} e^u + C = \frac{1}{2} e^{x^2} + C.$$

Sometimes integration by parts must be used more than once, as shown in the following example.

EXAMPLE 5   *Determine* $\int x^2 e^{2x+1} \, dx$.

Let $u = x^2$ and $dv = e^{2x+1} \, dx$. Then $du = 2x \, dx$ and $v = e^{2x+1}/2$.

$$\int x^2 e^{2x+1} \, dx = \frac{x^2 e^{2x+1}}{2} - \int \frac{e^{2x+1}}{2} (2x \, dx)$$

$$= \frac{x^2 e^{2x+1}}{2} - \int x e^{2x+1} \, dx.$$

To find $\int x e^{2x+1} \, dx$, we shall again use integration by parts. Here, let $u = x$ and $dv = e^{2x+1} \, dx$. Then $du = dx$ and $v = e^{2x+1}/2$.

$$\int x e^{2x+1} \, dx = \frac{x e^{2x+1}}{2} - \int \frac{e^{2x+1}}{2} \, dx$$

$$= \frac{x e^{2x+1}}{2} - \frac{e^{2x+1}}{4} + C_1.$$

Thus

$$\int x^2 e^{2x+1}\, dx = \frac{x^2 e^{2x+1}}{2} - \frac{x e^{2x+1}}{2} + \frac{e^{2x+1}}{4} + C \qquad (\text{where } C = -C_1)$$

$$= \frac{e^{2x+1}}{2}\left(x^2 - x + \frac{1}{2}\right) + C.$$

EXERCISE 15.1

In Problems **1–20,** *find the integrals.*

1. $\int x e^{-x}\, dx.$

2. $\int x e^{2x}\, dx.$

3. $\int y^3 \ln y\, dy.$

4. $\int x^2 \ln x\, dx.$

5. $\int \ln(4x)\, dx.$

6. $\int \frac{t}{e^t}\, dt.$

7. $\int x\sqrt{x+1}\, dx.$

8. $\int \frac{x}{\sqrt{1+4x}}\, dx.$

9. $\int \sqrt{x}\, \ln x\, dx.$

10. $\int \frac{\ln(x+1)}{2(x+1)}\, dx.$

11. $\int_1^2 x e^{2x}\, dx.$

12. $\int_0^1 x e^{-x}\, dx.$

13. $\int_0^1 x e^{-x^2}\, dx.$

14. $\int \frac{x^3}{\sqrt{4-x^2}}\, dx.$

15. $\int_1^2 \frac{x}{\sqrt{4-x}}\, dx.$

16. $\int (\ln x)^2\, dx.$

17. $\int x^2 e^x\, dx.$

18. $\int x^2 e^{-2x}\, dx.$

19. $\int (x - e^{-x})^2\, dx.$

20. $\int x^3 e^{x^2}\, dx.$

21. Find the area of the region bounded by the x-axis, the curve $y = \ln x$ and the line $x = e^3$.

22. Find the area of the region bounded by the x-axis and the curve $y = x e^{-x}$ between $x = 0$ and $x = 4$.

15.2 INTEGRATION BY PARTIAL FRACTIONS*

We now consider the integral of a rational function (quotient of two polynomials). Without loss of generality, we may assume that the numerator $N(x)$ and denominator $D(x)$ have no common polynomial factor and that the degree of $N(x)$ is less than the degree of $D(x)$ [that is, $N(x)/D(x)$ defines a *proper rational function*]. For if the numerator were not of lower degree, we could use long division to divide $N(x)$ by $D(x)$:

$$D(x) \overline{)N(x)} \begin{array}{c} P(x) \\ \\ \cdot \\ \cdot \\ \cdot \\ \hline R(x) \end{array}; \quad \text{thus } \frac{N(x)}{D(x)} = P(x) + \frac{R(x)}{D(x)}.$$

$P(x)$ would be a polynomial (easily integrable) and $R(x)$ would be a polynomial

---

* May be omitted without loss of continuity.

of lower degree than $D(x)$. Thus $R(x)/D(x)$ would define a proper rational function. For example,

$$\int \frac{2x^4 - 3x^3 - 4x^2 - 17x - 6}{x^3 - 2x^2 - 3x}\, dx = \int \left(2x + 1 + \frac{4x^2 - 14x - 6}{x^3 - 2x^2 - 3x} \right) dx$$

$$= x^2 + x + \int \frac{4x^2 - 14x - 6}{x^3 - 2x^2 - 3x}\, dx.$$

Therefore, we shall consider

$$\int \frac{4x^2 - 14x - 6}{x^3 - 2x^2 - 3x}\, dx = \int \frac{4x^2 - 14x - 6}{x(x + 1)(x - 3)}\, dx.$$

Observe that the denominator of the integrand consists only of **distinct linear factors,** each factor occurring exactly once. It can be shown that to each such factor $x - a$ there corresponds a *partial fraction* of the form

$$\frac{A}{x - a} \qquad (A \text{ a constant})$$

such that the integrand is the sum of the partial fractions. If there are n such *distinct* linear factors, there will be n such partial fractions, each of which is easily integrated. Applying these facts, we can write

$$\frac{4x^2 - 14x - 6}{x(x + 1)(x - 3)} = \frac{A}{x} + \frac{B}{x + 1} + \frac{C}{x - 3}. \tag{1}$$

To determine the constants A, B, and C, we first combine the terms on the right side:

$$\frac{4x^2 - 14x - 6}{x(x + 1)(x - 3)} = \frac{A(x + 1)(x - 3) + Bx(x - 3) + Cx(x + 1)}{x(x + 1)(x - 3)}.$$

Since the denominators of both sides are equal, we may equate their numerators:

$$4x^2 - 14x - 6 = A(x + 1)(x - 3) + Bx(x - 3) + Cx(x + 1). \tag{2}$$

Although Eq. (1) is not defined for $x = 0$, $x = -1$, and $x = 3$, we want to find values for A, B, and C that will make Eq. (2) true for all values of x. That is, it will be an identity. By successively setting x in Eq. (2) equal to any three different numbers, we can obtain a system of equations which can be solved for A, B, and C. In particular, the work can be simplified by letting x be the roots of $D(x) = 0$, in our case $x = 0$, $x = -1$, and $x = 3$. Using Eq. (2), if $x = 0$ we have

$$-6 = A(1)(-3) + B(0) + C(0) = -3A \qquad \text{and} \qquad A = 2.$$

If $x = -1$,

$$12 = A(0) + B(-1)(-4) + C(0) = 4B \qquad \text{and} \qquad B = 3.$$

If $x = 3$,

$$-12 = A(0) + B(0) + C(3)(4) = 12C \qquad \text{and} \qquad C = -1.$$

Thus Eq. (1) becomes

$$\frac{4x^2 - 14x - 6}{x(x + 1)(x - 3)} = \frac{2}{x} + \frac{3}{x + 1} - \frac{1}{x - 3}.$$

Hence

$$\int \frac{4x^2 - 14x - 6}{x(x + 1)(x - 3)} \, dx$$

$$= \int \left(\frac{2}{x} + \frac{3}{x + 1} - \frac{1}{x - 3} \right) dx$$

$$= 2 \int \frac{dx}{x} + 3 \int \frac{dx}{x + 1} - \int \frac{dx}{x - 3}$$

$$= 2 \ln |x| + 3 \ln |x + 1| - \ln |x - 3| + C$$

$$= \ln \left| \frac{x^2(x + 1)^3}{x - 3} \right| + C \qquad \text{(using properties of logarithms).}$$

For the *original* integral we can now state

$$\int \frac{2x^4 - 3x^3 - 4x^2 - 17x - 6}{x^3 - 2x^2 - 3x} \, dx = x^2 + x + \ln \left| \frac{x^2(x + 1)^3}{x - 3} \right| + C.$$

There is an alternative method of determining A, B, and C. It involves expanding the right side of Eq. (2) and combining similar terms:

$$4x^2 - 14x - 6 = A(x^2 - 2x - 3) + B(x^2 - 3x) + C(x^2 + x)$$

$$= Ax^2 - 2Ax - 3A + Bx^2 - 3Bx + Cx^2 + Cx.$$

$$4x^2 - 14x - 6 = (A + B + C)x^2 + (-2A - 3B + C)x + (-3A).$$

For this identity, coefficients of corresponding powers of x on the left and right sides of the equation must be equal:

$$\begin{cases} 4 = A + B + C, \\ -14 = -2A - 3B + C, \\ -6 = -3A. \end{cases}$$

Solving gives $A = 2$, $B = 3$, and $C = -1$ as before.

EXAMPLE 1   *Determine* $\int \dfrac{2x + 1}{3x^2 - 27} \, dx$.

Since the degree of $N(x)$ is less than the degree of $D(x)$, no long division is necessary. The integral can be written as

$$\frac{1}{3} \int \frac{2x + 1}{x^2 - 9} \, dx.$$

Expressing $(2x + 1)/(x^2 - 9)$ as a sum of partial fractions, we have

$$\frac{2x + 1}{x^2 - 9} = \frac{2x + 1}{(x + 3)(x - 3)} = \frac{A}{x + 3} + \frac{B}{x - 3}.$$

Combining terms and equating numerators gives

$$2x + 1 = A(x - 3) + B(x + 3).$$

If $x = 3$, then

$$7 = 6B \quad \text{and} \quad B = \frac{7}{6};$$

if $x = -3$, then

$$-5 = -6A \quad \text{and} \quad A = \frac{5}{6}.$$

Thus

$$\int \frac{2x + 1}{3x^2 - 27} \, dx = \frac{1}{3}\left[\int \frac{\frac{5}{6} \, dx}{x + 3} + \int \frac{\frac{7}{6} \, dx}{x - 3} \right]$$

$$= \frac{1}{3}\left[\frac{5}{6} \ln |x + 3| + \frac{7}{6} \ln |x - 3| \right] + C$$

$$= \frac{1}{18} \ln |(x + 3)^5(x - 3)^7| + C.$$

If the denominator of $N(x)/D(x)$ contains only linear factors, some of which are repeated, then for each factor $(x - a)^k$, where k is the maximum number of times $x - a$ occurs as a factor, there will correspond the sum of k partial fractions:

$$\frac{A}{x - a} + \frac{B}{(x - a)^2} + \cdots + \frac{K}{(x - a)^k}.$$

EXAMPLE 2   *Determine* $\int \dfrac{6x^2 + 13x + 6}{(x + 2)(x + 1)^2} \, dx.$

Since the degree of $N(x)$ is less than that of $D(x)$, no long division is necessary. In $D(x)$ the factor $x + 2$ occurs once and the factor $x + 1$ occurs twice. There will be three partial fractions and three constants to determine.

$$\frac{6x^2 + 13x + 6}{(x + 2)(x + 1)^2} = \frac{A}{x + 2} + \frac{B}{x + 1} + \frac{C}{(x + 1)^2}.$$

$$6x^2 + 13x + 6 = A(x + 1)^2 + B(x + 2)(x + 1) + C(x + 2).$$

Let us choose $x = -2$, $x = -1$, and for convenience $x = 0$.

For $x = -2$, we have

$$4 = A.$$

If $x = -1$, then

$$-1 = C.$$

If $x = 0$, then

$$6 = A + 2B + 2C = 4 + 2B - 2 = 2 + 2B,$$

$$2 = B.$$

Thus

$$\int \frac{6x^2 + 13x + 6}{(x + 2)(x + 1)^2} \, dx = 4 \int \frac{dx}{x + 2} + 2 \int \frac{dx}{x + 1} - \int \frac{dx}{(x + 1)^2}$$

$$= 4 \ln |x + 2| + 2 \ln |x + 1| + \frac{1}{x + 1} + C$$

$$= \ln [(x + 2)^4 (x + 1)^2] + \frac{1}{x + 1} + C.$$

Suppose a quadratic factor $x^2 + bx + c$ occurs in $D(x)$ and $x^2 + bx + c$ cannot be expressed as a product of two linear factors with real coefficients. Such a factor is called *irreducible over the real numbers*. To each irreducible quadratic factor that occurs exactly once in $D(x)$ there will correspond a partial fraction of the form

$$\frac{Ax + B}{x^2 + bx + c}.$$

EXAMPLE 3   *Determine* $\int \dfrac{-2x - 4}{x^3 + x^2 + x} \, dx.$

Since $x^3 + x^2 + x = x(x^2 + x + 1)$, we have the linear factor x and the quadratic factor $x^2 + x + 1$, which does not seem factorable on inspection. If it were factorable into $(x - r_1)(x - r_2)$, where r_1 and r_2 are real, then r_1 and r_2 would be roots of the equation $x^2 + x + 1 = 0$. By the quadratic formula, the roots are

$$x = \frac{-1 \pm \sqrt{1 - 4}}{2}.$$

Since there are no real roots, we conclude that $x^2 + x + 1$ is irreducible. Thus there will be two partial fractions and *three* constants to determine:

$$\frac{-2x - 4}{x(x^2 + x + 1)} = \frac{A}{x} + \frac{Bx + C}{x^2 + x + 1}.$$

$$-2x - 4 = A(x^2 + x + 1) + (Bx + C)x$$

$$= Ax^2 + Ax + A + Bx^2 + Cx.$$

$$0x^2 - 2x - 4 = (A + B)x^2 + (A + C)x + A.$$

Equating coefficients of like powers of x, we obtain

$$\begin{cases} 0 &= A + B, \\ -2 &= A + C, \\ -4 &= A. \end{cases}$$

Solving gives $A = -4$, $B = 4$, and $C = 2$. Thus

$$\int \frac{-2x - 4}{x(x^2 + x + 1)} \, dx = \int \left(\frac{-4}{x} + \frac{4x + 2}{x^2 + x + 1} \right) dx$$

$$= -4 \int \frac{dx}{x} + 2 \int \frac{2x + 1}{x^2 + x + 1} \, dx.$$

Both integrals have the form $\int \dfrac{du}{u}$, so

$$\int \frac{-2x - 4}{x(x^2 + x + 1)} \, dx = -4 \ln|x| + 2 \ln|x^2 + x + 1| + C$$

$$= \ln \left[\frac{(x^2 + x + 1)^2}{x^4} \right] + C.$$

Suppose $D(x)$ contains factors of the form $(x^2 + bx + c)^k$, where k is the maximum number of times the irreducible factor $x^2 + bx + c$ occurs. Then to each such factor there will correspond a sum of k partial fractions of the form

$$\frac{A + Bx}{x^2 + bx + c} + \frac{C + Dx}{(x^2 + bx + c)^2} + \cdots + \frac{M + Nx}{(x^2 + bx + c)^k}.$$

EXAMPLE 4   *Determine* $\int \dfrac{x^5}{(x^2 + 4)^2} \, dx$.

Since $N(x)$ has degree 5 and $D(x)$ has degree 4, we first divide $N(x)$ by $D(x)$.

$$\frac{x^5}{x^4 + 8x^2 + 16} = x - \frac{8x^3 + 16x}{(x^2 + 4)^2}.$$

The quadratic factor $x^2 + 4$ in the denominator of $(8x^3 + 16x)/(x^2 + 4)^2$ is irreducible and occurs as a factor twice. Thus to $(x^2 + 4)^2$ there correspond two partial fractions and *four* coefficients to be determined.

$$\frac{8x^3 + 16x}{(x^2 + 4)^2} = \frac{Ax + B}{x^2 + 4} + \frac{Cx + D}{(x^2 + 4)^2}.$$

$$8x^3 + 16x = (Ax + B)(x^2 + 4) + Cx + D.$$

$$8x^3 + 0x^2 + 16x + 0 = Ax^3 + Bx^2 + (4A + C)x + 4B + D.$$

Equating like powers of x, we obtain

$$\begin{cases} 8 = A, \\ 0 = B, \\ 16 = 4A + C, \\ 0 = 4B + D. \end{cases}$$

Solving gives $A = 8$, $B = 0$, $C = -16$, and $D = 0$. Thus

$$\int \frac{x^5}{(x^2 + 4)^2}\, dx = \int \left(x - \left[\frac{8x}{x^2 + 4} - \frac{16x}{(x^2 + 4)^2} \right] \right) dx$$

$$= \int x\, dx - 4 \int \frac{2x}{x^2 + 4}\, dx + 8 \int \frac{2x}{(x^2 + 4)^2}\, dx.$$

The second integral on the last line has the form $\int \dfrac{du}{u}$ and the third integral has

the form $\int \dfrac{du}{u^2}$.

$$\int \frac{x^5}{(x^2 + 4)^2}\, dx = \frac{x^2}{2} - 4 \ln(x^2 + 4) - \frac{8}{x^2 + 4} + C.$$

From our examples you may have deduced that the number of constants needed to express $N(x)/D(x)$ by partial fractions is equal to the degree of $D(x)$, if it is assumed that $N(x)/D(x)$ defines a proper rational function. This is indeed the case. It should be added that the representation of a proper rational function by partial fractions is unique; that is, there is only one choice of constants that can be made. Furthermore, regardless of the complexity of the polynomial $D(x)$, it can always (theoretically) be expressed as a product of linear and irreducible quadratic factors with real coefficients.

EXAMPLE 5   *Find* $\displaystyle\int \frac{2x + 3}{x^2 + 3x + 1}\, dx.$

Pitfall

Do not forget about basic integration forms.

This integral has the form $\int \dfrac{1}{u}\, du$. Thus

$$\int \frac{2x + 3}{x^2 + 3x + 1}\, dx = \ln |x^2 + 3x + 1| + C.$$

EXERCISE 15.2

*In Problems **1–22**, determine the integrals.*

1. $\int \dfrac{5x - 2}{x^2 - x}\, dx.$

2. $\int \dfrac{3x + 8}{x^2 + 2x}\, dx.$

3. $\int \dfrac{x + 10}{x^2 - x - 2}\, dx.$

4. $\int \dfrac{dx}{x^2 - 5x + 6}.$

5. $\int \dfrac{3x^3 - 3x + 4}{4x^2 - 4}\, dx.$

6. $\int \dfrac{4 - x^2}{(x - 4)(x - 2)(x + 3)}\, dx.$

7. $\int \dfrac{17x - 12}{x^3 - x^2 - 12x}\, dx.$

8. $\int \dfrac{4 - x}{x^4 - x^2}\, dx.$

9. $\int \dfrac{3x^5 + 4x^3 - x}{x^6 + 2x^4 - x^2 - 2}\, dx.$

10. $\int \dfrac{x^4 - 3x^3 - 5x^2 + 8x - 1}{x^3 - 2x^2 - 8x}\, dx.$

11. $\int \dfrac{2x^2 - 5x - 2}{(x - 2)^2(x - 1)}\, dx.$

12. $\int \dfrac{-3x^3 + 2x - 3}{x^2(x^2 - 1)}\, dx.$

13. $\int \dfrac{x^2 + 8}{x^3 + 4x}\, dx.$

14. $\int \dfrac{2x^3 - 6x^2 - 10x - 6}{x^4 - 1}\, dx.$

15. $\int \dfrac{-x^3 + 8x^2 - 9x + 2}{(x^2 + 1)(x - 3)^2}\, dx.$

16. $\int \dfrac{2x^4 + 9x^2 + 8}{x(x^2 + 2)^2}\, dx.$

17. $\int \dfrac{14x^3 + 24x}{(x^2 + 1)(x^2 + 2)}\, dx.$

18. $\int \dfrac{12x^3 + 20x^2 + 28x + 4}{(x^2 + 2x + 3)(x^2 + 1)}\, dx.$

19. $\int \dfrac{3x^3 + x}{(x^2 + 1)^2}\, dx.$

20. $\int \dfrac{3x^2 - 8x + 4}{x^3 - 4x^2 + 4x - 6}\, dx.$

21. $\int_0^1 \dfrac{2 - 2x}{x^2 + 7x + 12}\, dx.$

22. $\int_1^2 \dfrac{2x^2 + 1}{(x + 3)(x + 2)}\, dx.$

23. Find the area bounded by $y = (x^2 + 1)/(x + 2)^2$ and the *x*-axis from $x = 0$ to $x = 1$.

15.3 INTEGRATION BY TABLES

Certain forms of integrals that occur frequently may be found in standard tables of integration formulas.* A short table appears in Appendix E and its use will be illustrated in this section.

A given integral may have to be replaced by an equivalent form before it will fit a formula in the table. The equivalent form must match the formula *exactly*. Consequently, the steps that you perform should *not* be done mentally. *Write them down!* Failure to do this can easily lead to incorrect results. Before proceeding with the exercises, be sure you understand the illustrative examples *thoroughly*.

In the following examples the formula numbers refer to the Table of Selected Integrals given in Appendix E.

EXAMPLE 1   *Find* $\int \dfrac{x\, dx}{(2 + 3x)^2}.$

---

* See, for example, S. M. Selby, *Standard Mathematical Tables*, 22nd ed. (Cleveland, Ohio: Chemical Rubber Company, 1974).

Scanning the tables, we identify the integrand with Formula 7:

$$\int \frac{u\, du}{(a + bu)^2} = \frac{1}{b^2}\left(\ln |a + bu| + \frac{a}{a + bu} \right) + C.$$

Now we see if we can exactly match the given integrand with that of the formula. If we replace x by u, 2 by a, and 3 by b, then $du = dx$ and by substitution we have

$$\int \frac{x\, dx}{(2 + 3x)^2} = \int \frac{u\, du}{(a + bu)^2} = \frac{1}{b^2}\left(\ln |a + bu| + \frac{a}{a + bu} \right) + C.$$

Returning to the variable x and replacing a by 2 and b by 3, we obtain

$$\int \frac{x\, dx}{(2 + 3x)^2} = \frac{1}{9}\left(\ln |2 + 3x| + \frac{2}{2 + 3x} \right) + C.$$

EXAMPLE 2   Find $\int x^2 \sqrt{x^2 - 1}\, dx$.

This integral is identified with Formula 24:

$$\int u^2 \sqrt{u^2 \pm a^2}\, du = \frac{u}{8}(2u^2 \pm a^2)\sqrt{u^2 \pm a^2} - \frac{a^4}{8}\ln \left| u + \sqrt{u^2 \pm a^2} \right| + C.$$

In this formula, if the bottommost sign in the dual symbol "$\pm$" on the left side is used, then the bottommost sign in the dual symbols on the right side must also be used. In the original integral, we let $u = x$ and $a = 1$. Then $du = dx$ and by substitution the integral becomes

$$\int x^2 \sqrt{x^2 - 1}\, dx = \int u^2 \sqrt{u^2 - a^2}\, du$$

$$= \frac{u}{8}(2u^2 - a^2)\sqrt{u^2 - a^2} - \frac{a^4}{8}\ln \left| u + \sqrt{u^2 - a^2} \right| + C.$$

Since $u = x$ and $a = 1$,

$$\int x^2 \sqrt{x^2 - 1}\, dx = \frac{x}{8}(2x^2 - 1)\sqrt{x^2 - 1} - \frac{1}{8}\ln \left| x + \sqrt{x^2 - 1} \right| + C.$$

EXAMPLE 3   Find $\int \dfrac{dx}{x\sqrt{16x^2 + 3}}$.

The integrand can be identified with Formula 28:

$$\int \frac{du}{u\sqrt{u^2 + a^2}} = \frac{1}{a}\ln \left| \frac{\sqrt{u^2 + a^2} - a}{u} \right| + C.$$

If we let $u = 4x$ and $a = \sqrt{3}$, then $du = 4\, dx$. Watch closely how, by inserting 4's in the numerator and denominator, we transform the given integral into an equivalent form that matches Formula 28.

$$\int \frac{dx}{x\sqrt{16x^2 + 3}} = \int \frac{(4 \, dx)}{(4x)\sqrt{(4x)^2 + (\sqrt{3})^2}} = \int \frac{du}{u\sqrt{u^2 + a^2}}$$

$$= \frac{1}{a} \ln \left| \frac{\sqrt{u^2 + a^2} - a}{u} \right| + C$$

$$= \frac{1}{\sqrt{3}} \ln \left| \frac{\sqrt{16x^2 + 3} - \sqrt{3}}{4x} \right| + C.$$

EXAMPLE 4   *Find* $\displaystyle\int \frac{dx}{x^2(2 - 3x^2)^{1/2}}.$

The integrand is identified with Formula 21:

$$\int \frac{du}{u^2\sqrt{a^2 - u^2}} = -\frac{\sqrt{a^2 - u^2}}{a^2 u} + C.$$

Letting $u = \sqrt{3}x$ and $a^2 = 2$, we have $du = \sqrt{3} \, dx$. Hence by inserting two factors of $\sqrt{3}$ in both the numerator and denominator of the original integral, we have

$$\int \frac{dx}{x^2(2 - 3x^2)^{1/2}} = \sqrt{3} \int \frac{(\sqrt{3} \, dx)}{(\sqrt{3} \, x)^2[2 - (\sqrt{3} \, x)^2]^{1/2}} = \sqrt{3} \int \frac{du}{u^2(a^2 - u^2)^{1/2}}$$

$$= \sqrt{3} \left[-\frac{\sqrt{a^2 - u^2}}{a^2 u} \right] + C = \sqrt{3} \left[-\frac{\sqrt{2 - 3x^2}}{2(\sqrt{3} \, x)} \right] + C$$

$$= -\frac{\sqrt{2 - 3x^2}}{2x} + C.$$

EXAMPLE 5   *Find* $\displaystyle\int 7x^2 \ln(4x) \, dx.$

This is similar to Formula 42 with $n = 2$:

$$\int u^n \ln u \, du = \frac{u^{n+1} \ln u}{n + 1} - \frac{u^{n+1}}{(n + 1)^2} + C.$$

If we let $u = 4x$, then $du = 4 \, dx$. Hence

$$\int 7x^2 \ln(4x) \, dx = \frac{7}{4^3} \int (4x)^2 \ln(4x) \, (4 \, dx)$$

$$= \frac{7}{64} \int u^2 \ln u \, du = \frac{7}{64} \left(\frac{u^3 \ln u}{3} - \frac{u^3}{9} \right) + C$$

$$= \frac{7}{64} \left[\frac{(4x)^3 \ln(4x)}{3} - \frac{(4x)^3}{9} \right] + C$$

$$= 7x^3 \left[\frac{\ln(4x)}{3} - \frac{1}{9} \right] + C$$

$$= \frac{7x^3}{9} [3 \ln(4x) - 1] + C.$$

EXAMPLE 6   *Find* $\displaystyle\int \frac{e^{2x}\, dx}{7 + e^{2x}}.$

At first glance we do not identify the integrand with any form in the table. Perhaps rewriting the integral will help. Let $u = 7 + e^{2x}$; then $du = 2e^{2x}\, dx$.

$$\int \frac{e^{2x}\, dx}{7 + e^{2x}} = \frac{1}{2}\int \frac{(2e^{2x}\, dx)}{7 + e^{2x}} = \frac{1}{2}\int \frac{du}{u} = \frac{1}{2} \ln |u| + C$$

$$= \frac{1}{2} \ln |7 + e^{2x}| + C = \frac{1}{2} \ln (7 + e^{2x}) + C.$$

Thus we had only to use our knowledge of basic integration forms. Actually, this form appears as Formula 2 in the tables.

EXAMPLE 7   *Evaluate* $\displaystyle\int_1^4 \frac{dx}{(4x^2 + 2)^{3/2}}.$

We shall use Formula 32 to first get the indefinite integral:

$$\int \frac{du}{(u^2 \pm a^2)^{3/2}} = \frac{\pm u}{a^2\sqrt{u^2 \pm a^2}} + C.$$

Letting $u = 2x$ and $a^2 = 2$, then we have $du = 2\, dx$. Thus

$$\int \frac{dx}{(4x^2 + 2)^{3/2}} = \frac{1}{2}\int \frac{(2\, dx)}{[(2x)^2 + 2]^{3/2}} = \frac{1}{2}\int \frac{du}{(u^2 + 2)^{3/2}}$$

$$= \frac{1}{2}\left[\frac{u}{2\sqrt{u^2 + 2}} \right] + C.$$

Instead of substituting back to x and evaluating from $x = 1$ to $x = 4$, we can determine the corresponding limits of integration with respect to u and then evaluate the last expression between those limits. Since $u = 2x$, when $x = 1$ we have $u = 2$; when $x = 4$ we have $u = 8$. Thus

$$\int_1^4 \frac{dx}{(4x^2 + 2)^{3/2}} = \frac{1}{2}\int_2^8 \frac{du}{(u^2 + 2)^{3/2}}$$

$$= \frac{1}{2}\left(\frac{u}{2\sqrt{u^2 + 2}} \right)\Bigg|_2^8 = \frac{2}{\sqrt{66}} - \frac{1}{2\sqrt{6}}.$$

Pitfall

When changing the variable of integration x to the variable of integration u, be certain to change the limits of integration so that they agree with u. That is,

$$\int_1^4 \frac{dx}{(4x^2 + 2)^{3/2}} \neq \frac{1}{2}\int_1^4 \frac{du}{(u^2 + 2)^{3/2}}.$$

Tables of integrals are useful when dealing with integrals associated with annuities. Suppose that you must pay out $100 at the end of each year for the next two years. Recall from Chapter 6 that a series of payments over a period of time, such as this, is called an *annuity*. If you were to pay off the debt now instead, you would pay the present value of the $100 that is due at the end of the first year, plus the present value of the $100 that is due at the end of the second year. (Present value of an annuity is discussed in Sec. 6.3.) The sum of these present values is the present value of the annuity. We shall now consider the present value of payments made continuously over the time interval from $t = 0$ to $t = T$, t in years, when interest is compounded continuously at an annual rate of r.

Suppose a payment is made at time t such that on an annual basis this payment is $f(t)$. If we divide the interval $[0, T]$ into subintervals $[t_{i-1}, t_i]$ of length Δt (where Δt is small), then the total amount of all payments over such a subinterval is approximately $f(t_i)\Delta t$. [For example, if $f(t) = 2000$ and Δt were one day, then the total amount of the payments would be $2000(\frac{1}{365})$.] The present value of these payments is approximately $e^{-rt_i}f(t_i)\Delta t$ (see Sec. 10.3). Over the interval $[0, T]$, the total of all such present values is

$$\sum e^{-rt_i}f(t_i)\Delta t.$$

This sum approximates the present value A of the annuity. The smaller Δt is, the better is the approximation. That is, as $\Delta t \to 0$ the limit of the sum *is* the present value. However, this limit is also a definite integral. That is,

$$A = \int_0^T f(t)e^{-rt} \, dt. \qquad (1)$$

This gives the **present value of a continuous annuity** at an annual rate r (compounded continuously) for T years if a payment at time t is at the rate of $f(t)$ per year. Sometimes we say that Eq. (1) gives the **present value of a continuous income stream.** Equation (1) may also be used to find the present value of future profits of a business. In this situation, $f(t)$ is the annual rate of profit at time t.

We can also consider the *future* value of an annuity rather than its present value. If a payment is made at time t, then it has a certain value at the *end* of the period of the annuity, that is, $T - t$ years later. This value is

$$\begin{pmatrix} \text{amount of} \\ \text{payment} \end{pmatrix} + \begin{pmatrix} \text{interest on this} \\ \text{payment for } T - t \text{ years} \end{pmatrix}.$$

If S is the total of such values for all payments, then S is called the **accumulated amount of a continuous annuity** and is given by

$$S = \int_0^T f(t)e^{r(T-t)} \, dt.$$

EXAMPLE 8   *Find the present value (to the nearest dollar) of a continuous annuity at an annual rate of 8% for 10 years if the payment at time t is at the rate of t^2 dollars per year.*

The present value is given by

$$A = \int_0^T f(t)e^{-rt} \, dt = \int_0^{10} t^2 e^{-0.08t} \, dt.$$

We shall use Formula 39,

$$\int u^n e^{au} \, du = \frac{u^n e^{au}}{a} - \frac{n}{a} \int u^{n-1} e^{au} \, du,$$

called a *reduction formula* since it reduces an integral into an expression that involves an integral which is easier to determine. If $u = t$, $n = 2$, and $a = -0.08$, then $du = dt$ and we have

$$A = \frac{t^2 e^{-0.08t}}{-0.08} \bigg|_0^{10} - \frac{2}{-0.08} \int_0^{10} t e^{-0.08t} \, dt.$$

In the new integral the exponent of t has been reduced to 1. We can match this integral with Formula 38,

$$\int u e^{au} \, du = \frac{e^{au}}{a^2}(au - 1) + C,$$

by letting $u = t$ and $a = -0.08$. Then $du = dt$ and

$$A = \int_0^{10} t^2 e^{-0.08t} \, dt = \frac{t^2 e^{-0.08t}}{-0.08} \bigg|_0^{10} - \frac{2}{-0.08} \left[\frac{e^{-0.08t}}{(-0.08)^2}(-0.08t - 1) \right] \bigg|_0^{10}$$

$$= \frac{100 e^{-0.8}}{-0.08} - \frac{2}{-0.08} \left[\frac{e^{-0.8}}{(-0.08)^2}(-0.8 - 1) - \frac{1}{(-0.08)^2}(-1) \right]$$

$$= -1250 e^{-0.8} + 25[-281.25 e^{-0.8} + 156.25]$$

$$= -8281.25 e^{-0.8} + 3906.25 \approx -8281.25(0.44933) + 3906.25 \approx 185.$$

The present value is $185.

EXERCISE 15.3

In Problems **1–34,** *find the integrals by using the table in Appendix E.*

1. $\int \dfrac{dx}{x(6 + 7x)}.$

2. $\int \dfrac{x^2\,dx}{(1 + 2x)^2}.$

3. $\int \dfrac{dx}{x\sqrt{x^2 + 9}}.$

4. $\int \dfrac{dx}{(x^2 + 7)^{3/2}}.$

5. $\int \dfrac{x\,dx}{(2 + 3x)(4 + 5x)}.$

6. $\int 2^{5x}\,dx.$

7. $\int \dfrac{dx}{4 + 3e^{2x}}.$

8. $\int x^2\sqrt{1 + x}\,dx.$

9. $\int \dfrac{2\,dx}{x(1 + x)^2}.$

10. $\int \dfrac{dx}{x\sqrt{5 - 11x^2}}.$

11. $\int_0^1 \dfrac{x\,dx}{2 + x}.$

12. $\int \dfrac{x^2\,dx}{2 + 5x}.$

13. $\int \sqrt{x^2 - 3}\,dx.$

14. $\int \dfrac{dx}{(4 + 3x)(4x + 3)}.$

15. $\int_0^{1/12} xe^{12x}\,dx.$

16. $\int \sqrt{\dfrac{2 + 3x}{5 + 3x}}\,dx.$

17. $\int x^2 e^x\,dx.$

18. $\int_1^2 \dfrac{dx}{x^2(1 + x)}.$

19. $\int \dfrac{\sqrt{4x^2 + 1}}{x^2}\,dx.$

20. $\int \dfrac{dx}{x\sqrt{2 - x}}.$

21. $\int \dfrac{x\,dx}{(1 + 3x)^2}.$

22. $\int \dfrac{dx}{\sqrt{(1 + 2x)(3 + 2x)}}.$

23. $\int \dfrac{dx}{7 - 5x^2}.$

24. $\int x^2\sqrt{2x^2 - 9}\,dx.$

25. $\int x^5 \ln(3x)\,dx.$

26. $\int \dfrac{dx}{x^2(1 + x)^2}.$

27. $\int 2x\sqrt{1 + 3x}\,dx.$

28. $\int x^2 \ln x\,dx.$

29. $\int \dfrac{dx}{\sqrt{4x^2 - 13}}.$

30. $\int \dfrac{dx}{x \ln(2x)}.$

31. $\int x \ln(2x)\,dx.$

32. $\int \dfrac{\sqrt{2 - 3x^2}}{x}\,dx.$

33. $\int \dfrac{dx}{x^2\sqrt{9 - 4x^2}}.$

34. $\int_0^1 \dfrac{x^3\,dx}{1 + x^4}.$

In Problems **35–52,** *find the integrals by any method.*

35. $\int \dfrac{x\,dx}{x^2 + 1}.$

36. $\int \sqrt{x}\,e^{x^{3/2}}\,dx.$

37. $\int x\sqrt{2x^2 + 1}\,dx.$

38. $\int \dfrac{4x^2 - \sqrt{x}}{x}\,dx.$

39. $\int \dfrac{dx}{x^2 - 5x + 6}.$

40. $\int \dfrac{e^{2x}}{\sqrt{e^{2x} + 3}}\,dx.$

41. $\int x^3 \ln x\,dx.$

42. $\int_0^3 xe^{-x}\,dx.$

43. $\int xe^{2x}\,dx.$

44. $\int_1^2 x^2\sqrt{3 + 2x}\,dx.$

45. $\int \ln^2 x\,dx.$

46. $\int_1^e \ln x\,dx.$

47. $\int_1^2 \dfrac{x\,dx}{\sqrt{4 - x}}.$

48. $\int_1^2 x\sqrt{1 + 2x}\,dx.$

49. $\int_0^1 \dfrac{2x\,dx}{\sqrt{8 - x^2}}.$

50. $\int_0^{\ln 2} x^3 e^{2x}\,dx.$

51. $\int_1^2 x \ln(2x)\,dx.$

52. $\int_1^2 dx.$

53. In a discussion about gene frequency,* the following integral occurs:

$$\int_{q_0}^{q_n} \dfrac{dq}{q(1 - q)},$$

where the q's represent gene frequencies. Evaluate this integral.

* W. B. Mather, *Principles of Quantitative Genetics* (Minneapolis, Minn.: Burgess Publishing Company, 1964).

54. Under certain conditions, the number n of generations required to change the frequency of a gene from 0.3 to 0.1 is given by*

$$n = -\frac{1}{0.4}\int_{0.3}^{0.1} \frac{dq}{q^2(1-q)}.$$

Find n (to the nearest integer).

55. Find the present value, to the nearest dollar, of a continuous annuity at an annual rate of r for T years if the payment at time t is at the annual rate of $f(t)$ dollars given that

   a. $r = 0.06,\quad T = 10,\quad f(t) = 5000,$
   b. $r = 0.05,\quad T = 8,\quad f(t) = 200t.$

56. If $f(t) = k$, where k is a positive constant, show that the value of the integral in Eq. (1) of this section is

$$k\left(\frac{1 - e^{-rT}}{r}\right).$$

57. Find the accumulated amount, to the nearest dollar, of a continuous annuity at an annual rate of r for T years if the payment at time t is at an annual rate of $f(t)$ dollars given that

   a. $r = 0.06,\quad T = 10,\quad f(t) = 400,$
   b. $r = 0.04,\quad T = 5,\quad f(t) = 40t.$

58. Over the next 5 years the profits of a business at time t are estimated to be $20{,}000t$ dollars per year. The business is to be sold at a price equal to the present value of these future profits. If interest is compounded continuously at the annual rate of 10%, to the nearest 10 dollars at what price should the business be sold?

15.4 AVERAGE VALUE OF A FUNCTION

If we are given the three numbers 1, 2, and 9, then their average value, or *mean*, is their sum divided by 3. Calling this average $\bar{y}$, we have

$$\bar{y} = \frac{1 + 2 + 9}{3} = 4.$$

Similarly, suppose we are given a function f defined on the interval $[a, b]$ and the points $x_1, x_2, \ldots, x_n$ are in the interval. Then the average value of the n corresponding function values $f(x_1), f(x_2), \ldots, f(x_n)$ is

$$\bar{y} = \frac{f(x_1) + f(x_2) + \cdots + f(x_n)}{n} = \frac{\sum_{i=1}^{n} f(x_i)}{n}. \tag{1}$$

We can go a step further. Let us divide the interval $[a, b]$ into n subintervals of equal length. We shall choose x_1 to be in the first subinterval, x_2 to be in the second, etc. Since $[a, b]$ has length $b - a$, each subinterval has length $\dfrac{b - a}{n}$, which we shall call Δx. Thus (1) can be written

* E. O. Wilson and W. H. Bossert, *A Primer of Population Biology* (Stamford, Conn.: Sinauer Associates, Inc., 1971).

$$\bar{y} = \frac{\sum\limits_{i=1}^{n} f(x_i)\left(\dfrac{\Delta x}{\Delta x}\right)}{n} = \frac{\dfrac{1}{\Delta x}\sum\limits_{i=1}^{n} f(x_i)\,\Delta x}{n} = \frac{1}{n\,\Delta x}\sum_{i=1}^{n} f(x_i)\,\Delta x. \tag{2}$$

Since $\Delta x = \dfrac{b-a}{n}$, the expression $n\,\Delta x$ in Eq. (2) can be replaced by $b-a$. Moreover, as $n \to \infty$ the number of function values used in computing $\bar{y}$ increases and we get the so-called *average value of the function f,* denoted $\bar{f}$:

$$\bar{f} = \lim_{n\to\infty}\left[\frac{1}{b-a}\sum_{i=1}^{n} f(x_i)\,\Delta x\right] = \frac{1}{b-a}\lim_{n\to\infty}\sum_{i=1}^{n} f(x_i)\,\Delta x.$$

But the limit on the right is just the definite integral $\int_a^b f(x)\,dx$. Thus we have the following definition.

Definition

*The **average** (or **mean**) **value of a function** $y = f(x)$ over the interval $[a, b]$ is denoted $\bar{f}$ (or $\bar{y}$) and is given by*

$$\bar{f} = \frac{1}{b-a}\int_a^b f(x)\,dx.$$

EXAMPLE 1   *Find the average value of the function $f(x) = x^2$ over the interval $[1, 2]$.*

$$\bar{f} = \frac{1}{b-a}\int_a^b f(x)\,dx$$

$$= \frac{1}{2-1}\int_1^2 x^2\,dx = \frac{x^3}{3}\bigg|_1^2 = \frac{7}{3}.$$

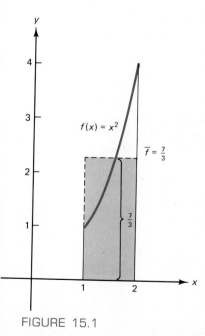

FIGURE 15.1

In Example 1 we found that the average value of $y = f(x) = x^2$ over the interval $[1, 2]$ is $\frac{7}{3}$. We can interpret this value geometrically. Since

$$\frac{1}{2-1}\int_1^2 x^2\,dx = \frac{7}{3},$$

by solving for the integral we have

$$\int_1^2 x^2\,dx = \frac{7}{3}(2-1).$$

However, this integral gives the area of the region bounded by $f(x) = x^2$ and the x-axis from $x = 1$ to $x = 2$ (see Fig. 15.1). This area also equals $(\frac{7}{3})(2-1)$, which is the area of a rectangle with height $\bar{f} = \frac{7}{3}$ and width $b - a = 2 - 1 = 1$.

EXAMPLE 2   *Suppose the flow of blood at time t in a system is given by*

$$F(t) = \frac{F_1}{(1 + \alpha t)^2}, \quad 0 \le t \le T,$$

where F_1 and α (a Greek letter read "alpha") are constant.* Find the average flow $\overline{F}$ on the interval $[0, T]$.

$$\overline{F} = \frac{1}{T - 0}\int_0^T F(t) \, dt$$

$$= \frac{1}{T}\int_0^T \frac{F_1}{(1 + \alpha t)^2} \, dt = \frac{F_1}{\alpha T}\int_0^T (1 + \alpha t)^{-2}(\alpha \, dt)$$

$$= \frac{F_1}{\alpha T}\left[\frac{(1 + \alpha t)^{-1}}{-1}\right]\Bigg|_0^T = \frac{F_1}{\alpha T}\left[-\frac{1}{1 + \alpha T} + 1\right]$$

$$= \frac{F_1}{\alpha T}\left[\frac{-1 + 1 + \alpha T}{1 + \alpha T}\right] = \frac{F_1}{\alpha T}\left[\frac{\alpha T}{1 + \alpha T}\right] = \frac{F_1}{1 + \alpha T}.$$

EXERCISE 15.4

In Problems **1–8**, *find the average value of the function over the given interval.*

1. $f(x) = x^2$; $[0, 4]$.

2. $f(x) = 3x - 1$; $[1, 2]$.

3. $f(x) = 2 - 3x^2$; $[-1, 2]$.

4. $f(x) = x^2 + x + 1$; $[1, 3]$.

5. $f(t) = 4t^3$; $[-2, 2]$.

6. $f(i) = i\sqrt{i^2 + 9}$; $[0, 4]$.

7. $f(x) = \sqrt{x}$; $[1, 9]$.

8. $f(x) = 1/x$; $[2, 4]$.

9. The profit P (in dollars) of a business is given by

$$P = P(q) = 396q - 2.1q^2 - 400,$$

where q is the number of units of the product sold. Find the average profit on the interval from $q = 0$ to $q = 100$.

10. Suppose the cost c (in dollars) of producing q units of a product is given by

$$c = 4000 + 10q + 0.1q^2.$$

Find the average cost on the interval from $q = 100$ to $q = 500$.

11. An investment of \$3000 earns interest at an annual rate of 10% compounded continuously. After t years, its value S (in dollars) is given by $S = 3000e^{0.10t}$. Find the average value of a 2-year investment.

12. Suppose that colored dye is injected into the bloodstream at a constant rate R.* Let $C(t)$ be the concentration at time t of dye at a location distant (distal) from the point of injection, where

$$C(t) = \frac{R}{F(t)}$$

---

* W. Simon, *Mathematical Techniques for Physiology and Medicine* (New York: Academic Press, Inc., 1972).

and $F(t)$ is given in Example 2. Show that the average concentration $\overline{C}$ on $[0, T]$ is

$$\overline{C} = \frac{R(1 + \alpha T + \frac{1}{3}\alpha^2 T^2)}{F_1}.$$

15.5 APPROXIMATE INTEGRATION

When using the Fundamental Theorem to evaluate $\int_a^b f(x)\ dx$, you may find it extremely difficult, or perhaps impossible, to find an antiderivative of f. Fortunately there are numerical methods that can be used to estimate a definite integral. These methods use values of $f(x)$ at various points and are especially suitable for computers or calculators. We shall consider two methods: the *trapezoidal rule* and *Simpson's rule*. In both cases we assume that f is continuous on $[a, b]$.

In developing the trapezoidal rule, for convenience we shall also assume that $f(x) \geq 0$ on $[a, b]$ so that we can think in terms of area. Basically, this rule involves approximating the graph of f by straight-line segments.

In Fig. 15.2 the interval $[a, b]$ is divided into n subintervals of equal length by the points $a = x_0, x_1, x_2, \ldots$, and $x_n = b$. Since the length of $[a, b]$ is

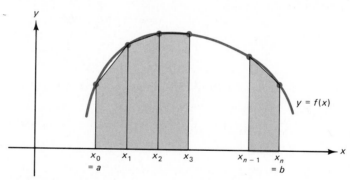

FIGURE 15.2

$b - a$, the length of each subinterval is $(b - a)/n$, which we shall call h. Clearly, $x_1 = a + h$, $x_2 = a + 2h$, $\ldots$, $x_n = a + nh = b$. With each subinterval we can associate a trapezoid (a four-sided figure with two parallel sides). The area of the region bounded by the curve, the x-axis, and the lines $x = a$ and $x = b$ is approximated by the sum of the areas of the trapezoids determined by the subintervals.

Consider the first trapezoid, which is redrawn in Fig. 15.3. Since the area of a trapezoid is equal to one-half the base times the sum of the lengths of the parallel sides, this trapezoid has area

$$\tfrac{1}{2}h[f(a) + f(a + h)].$$

Similarly, the second trapezoid has area

$$\tfrac{1}{2}h[f(a + h) + f(a + 2h)].$$

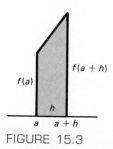

FIGURE 15.3

With n trapezoids the area A under the curve is approximated by

$$A \approx \tfrac{1}{2}h[f(a) + f(a + h)] + \tfrac{1}{2}h[f(a + h) + f(a + 2h)] +$$

$$\tfrac{1}{2}h[f(a + 2h) + f(a + 3h)] + \cdots + \tfrac{1}{2}h[f(a + (n - 1)h) + f(b)].$$

Since $A = \displaystyle\int_a^b f(x)\, dx$, by simplifying the above we have the trapezoidal rule:

THE TRAPEZOIDAL RULE

$$\int_a^b f(x)\, dx \approx \frac{h}{2}\{f(a) + 2f(a + h) + 2f(a + 2h) +$$

$$\cdots + 2f[a + (n - 1)h] + f(b)\},$$

where $h = (b - a)/n$.

Usually, the more subintervals, the better is the approximation. In our development, we assumed for convenience that $f(x) \geq 0$ on $[a, b]$. However, the trapezoidal rule is valid without this restriction.

EXAMPLE 1   *Use the trapezoidal rule to estimate the value of*

$$\int_0^1 \frac{1}{1 + x^2}\, dx$$

by using $n = 5$. Compute each term to four decimal places and round off the answer to three decimal places.

Here $f(x) = 1/(1 + x^2)$, $n = 5$, $a = 0$, and $b = 1$. Thus

$$h = \frac{b - a}{n} = \frac{1 - 0}{5} = \frac{1}{5} = 0.2.$$

The terms to be added are

$$
\begin{aligned}
f(a) &= f(0) &&= 1.0000 \\
2f(a + h) &= 2f(0.2) &&= 1.9231 \\
2f(a + 2h) &= 2f(0.4) &&= 1.7241 \\
2f(a + 3h) &= 2f(0.6) &&= 1.4706 \\
2f(a + 4h) &= 2f(0.8) &&= 1.2195 \\
f(b) &= f(1) &&= \underline{0.5000} \\
& && \ \ 7.8373 = \text{sum.}
\end{aligned}
$$

Thus our estimate for the integral is

$$\int_0^1 \frac{1}{1 + x^2}\, dx \approx \frac{0.2}{2}(7.8373) \approx 0.784.$$

The actual value of the integral is approximately 0.785.

Another method for estimating $\int_a^b f(x)\,dx$ is given by Simpson's rule, which involves approximating the graph of f by parabolic segments. We shall omit the derivation.

SIMPSON'S RULE (n even)

$$\int_a^b f(x)\,dx \approx \frac{h}{3}\{f(a) + 4f(a + h) + 2f(a + 2h) +$$
$$\cdots + 4f[a + (n - 1)h] + f(b)\},$$

where $h = (b - a)/n$ and n is even.

The pattern of coefficients inside the braces is 1, 4, 2, 4, 2, . . ., 2, 4, 1, and this requires that **n be even.** Let us use this rule for the integral in Example 1.

EXAMPLE 2   *Use Simpson's rule to estimate the value of $\int_0^1 \dfrac{1}{1 + x^2}\,dx$ by using $n = 4$. Compute each term to four decimal places and round off the answer to three decimal places.*

Here $f(x) = 1/(1 + x^2)$, $n = 4$, $a = 0$, and $b = 1$. Thus $h = (b - a)/n = 1/4 = 0.25$. The terms to be added are

$$\begin{aligned}
f(a) &= f(0) &= 1.0000 \\
4f(a + h) &= 4f(0.25) &= 3.7647 \\
2f(a + 2h) &= 2f(0.5) &= 1.6000 \\
4f(a + 3h) &= 4f(0.75) &= 2.5600 \\
f(b) &= f(1) &\approx \underline{0.5000} \\
& & 9.4247 = \text{sum.}
\end{aligned}$$

Thus by Simpson's rule,

$$\int_0^1 \frac{1}{1 + x^2}\,dx \approx \frac{0.25}{3}(9.4247) \approx 0.785.$$

This is a better approximation than that obtained in Example 1 with the trapezoidal rule.

Both Simpson's rule and the trapezoidal rule may be used if we know only $f(a)$, $f(a + h)$, and so on; we need not know f itself. Example 3 will illustrate.

EXAMPLE 3   *A function often used in demography (the study of births, marriages, mortality, etc., in a population) is the **life table function,** denoted l. In a population having 100,000 births in any year of time, $l(x)$ represents the* *number of persons who reach the age of x in any year of time. For example, if l(20) = 95,961, then the number of persons who attain age 20 in any year of time is 95,961. Suppose that the function l applies to all people born over an extended period of time. It can be shown that, at any time, the expected number of persons in the population between the exact ages of x and x + m inclusive is given by*

$$\int_x^{x+m} l(t) \, dt.$$

The following table gives values of l(x) for males and females in a certain population (for United States, 1967).* Approximate the number of women in the 20–35 age group by using the trapezoidal rule with n = 3.

Life Table

AGE, x	$l(x)$ MALES	$l(x)$ FEMALES	AGE, x	$l(x)$ MALES	$l(x)$ FEMALES
0	100,000	100,000	45	89,489	93,667
5	97,158	97,791	50	86,195	91,726
10	96,921	97,618	55	81,154	88,935
15	96,672	97,473	60	73,830	84,971
20	95,961	97,188	65	64,108	79,445
25	95,000	96,839	70	52,007	71,196
30	94,097	96,429	75	38,044	59,946
35	93,067	95,844	80	24,900	45,662
40	91,628	94,961			

We want to estimate

$$\int_{20}^{35} l(t) \, dt.$$

We have $h = \dfrac{b - a}{n} = \dfrac{35 - 20}{3} = 5$. The terms to be added are

$$l(20) = \quad 97,188$$
$$2l(25) = 2(96,839) = 193,678$$
$$2l(30) = 2(96,429) = 192,858$$
$$l(35) = \quad \underline{95,844}$$
$$579,568 = \text{sum.}$$

By the trapezoidal rule,

$$\int_{20}^{35} l(t) \, dt \approx \tfrac{5}{2}(579,568) = 1,448,920.$$

* *Source:* Adapted from *Population: Facts and Methods of Demography* by Nathan Keyfitz and William Flieger, W. H. Freeman and Company. Copyright © 1971.

There are formulas that are used to determine the accuracy of answers obtained by using the trapezoidal or Simpson's rule. They may be found in standard texts on numerical analysis.

EXERCISE 15.5

In each problem, compute each term to four decimal places and round off the answer to three decimal places.

*In Problems **1–6**, use the trapezoidal rule or Simpson's rule (as indicated) and the given value of n to estimate the integral. In Problems **1–4**, also find the answer by antidifferentiation (the Fundamental Theorem of Integral Calculus).*

1. $\int_0^1 x^2 \, dx$; trapezoidal rule, $n = 5$.

2. $\int_0^1 x^2 \, dx$; Simpson's rule, $n = 4$.

3. $\int_1^4 \dfrac{dx}{x}$; Simpson's rule, $n = 6$.

4. $\int_1^4 \dfrac{dx}{x}$; trapezoidal rule, $n = 6$.

5. $\int_0^2 \dfrac{x \, dx}{x + 1}$; trapezoidal rule, $n = 4$.

6. $\int_2^4 \dfrac{dx}{x + x^2}$; Simpson's rule, $n = 4$.

*In Problems **7** and **8**, use the life table in Example 3 to estimate the given integrals by the trapezoidal rule.*

7. $\int_{15}^{40} l(t) \, dt$, males, $n = 5$.

8. $\int_{35}^{55} l(t) \, dt$, females, $n = 4$.

*In Problems **9** and **10**, suppose the graph of a continuous function f, where $f(x) \geq 0$, contains the given points. Use Simpson's rule and all of the points to approximate the area between the graph and the x-axis on the given interval.*

9. (1, 0.4), (2, 0.6), (3, 1.2), (4, 0.8), (5, 0.5);   [1, 5].

10. (2, 0), (2.5, 3.6), (3, 10), (3.5, 19.9), (4, 34);   [2, 4].

11. Using all the information given in Fig. 15.4, estimate $\int_1^3 f(x) \, dx$ by Simpson's rule.

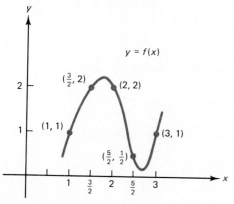

FIGURE 15.4

*Problems **12** and **13** are designed for students with calculators having the square-root function. Estimate the given integrals.*

12. $\int_4^6 \dfrac{1}{\sqrt{1 + x}} \, dx$; Simpson's rule, $n = 4$. Also find the answer by the Fundamental Theorem of Integral Calculus.

13. $\int_0^1 \sqrt{1 - x^2} \, dx$; Simpson's rule, $n = 4$.

15.6 DIFFERENTIAL EQUATIONS

Occasionally, you may have to solve an equation that involves the derivative of an unknown function. Such an equation is called a **differential equation.** An example is

$$y' = xy^2. \tag{1}$$

More precisely, Eq. (1) is a *first-order differential equation* since it involves a derivative of the first order and none of higher order. A solution of Eq. (1) is any function $y = f(x)$ that is defined on an interval and that satisfies the equation for all x in the interval.

To solve $y' = xy^2$ or, equivalently,

$$\frac{dy}{dx} = xy^2, \tag{2}$$

we consider dy/dx to be a quotient of differentials and algebraically "separate variables" by rewriting the equation so that each side contains only one variable and a differential is not in a denominator:

$$\frac{dy}{y^2} = x \, dx.$$

Integrating both sides and combining the constants of integration, we obtain

$$\int \frac{1}{y^2} \, dy = \int x \, dx,$$

$$-\frac{1}{y} = \frac{x^2}{2} + C_1,$$

$$-\frac{1}{y} = \frac{x^2 + 2C_1}{2}. \tag{3}$$

Replacing $2C_1$ by C and solving Eq. (3) for y, we have

$$y = -\frac{2}{x^2 + C}. \tag{4}$$

We can verify by substitution that y is a solution to differential equation (2):

$$\frac{dy}{dx} = xy^2?$$

$$\frac{4x}{(x^2 + C)^2} = x\left[-\frac{2}{x^2 + C} \right]^2 ?$$

$$\frac{4x}{(x^2 + C)^2} = \frac{4x}{(x^2 + C)^2}.$$

Note in Eq. (4) that for *each* value of C, a different solution is obtained. We call

Eq. (4) the **general solution** of the differential equation. The method that we used to find it is called **separation of variables.**

In the example above, suppose we are given the condition that $y = -\frac{2}{3}$ when $x = 1$; that is, $y(1) = -\frac{2}{3}$. Then the *particular* function that satisfies Eq. (2) and this condition can be found by substituting the values $x = 1$ and $y = -\frac{2}{3}$ into Eq. (4) and solving for C:

$$-\frac{2}{3} = -\frac{2}{1^2 + C},$$

$$C = 2.$$

Therefore, the solution of $dy/dx = xy^2$ such that $y(1) = -\frac{2}{3}$ is

$$y = -\frac{2}{x^2 + 2}. \tag{5}$$

We call Eq. (5) a **particular solution** to the differential equation.

EXAMPLE 1   *Solve* $y' = -\frac{y}{x}$ *if* $x, y > 0$.

Writing y' as dy/dx, separating variables, and integrating, we have

$$\frac{dy}{dx} = -\frac{y}{x},$$

$$\frac{dy}{y} = -\frac{dx}{x},$$

$$\int \frac{1}{y}\, dy = -\int \frac{1}{x}\, dx,$$

$$\ln |y| = C_1 - \ln |x|.$$

Since $x, y > 0$,

$$\ln y = C_1 - \ln x. \tag{6}$$

The constant of integration, C_1, can be any real number. Since the range of a logarithmic function is all real numbers, C_1 can be replaced by $\ln C$, where $C > 0$. Therefore, Eq. (6) becomes

$$\ln y = \ln C - \ln x,$$

$$\ln y = \ln \frac{C}{x}.$$

Thus

$$y = \frac{C}{x}, \qquad C, x > 0.$$

In Sec. 10.3 interest compounded continuously was developed. Let us now take a different approach to this topic. Suppose P dollars are invested at an annual rate r compounded n times a year. Let the function $S = S(t)$ give the compound amount S (or total amount present) after t years from the date of the initial investment. Then the initial principal is $S(0) = P$. Furthermore, since there are n interest periods per year, each period has length $1/n$ years, which we shall denote by Δt. At the end of the first period, the accrued interest for that period is added to the principal, and the sum acts as the principal for the second period, and so on. Hence if the beginning of an interest period occurs at time t, then the increase in the amount present (that is, the interest earned) at the end of a period of Δt is $S(t + \Delta t) - S(t)$, which we write as ΔS. Equivalently, the interest earned is principal times rate times time:

$$\Delta S = S \cdot r \cdot \Delta t.$$

Dividing both sides by Δt, we obtain

$$\frac{\Delta S}{\Delta t} = rS. \tag{7}$$

As $\Delta t \to 0$, then $n = \dfrac{1}{\Delta t} \to \infty$ and consequently interest is being *compounded continuously;* that is, the principal is subject to continuous growth at every instant. However, as $\Delta t \to 0$, then $\Delta S/\Delta t \to dS/dt$ and Eq. (7) takes the form

$$\frac{dS}{dt} = rS. \tag{8}$$

This differential equation means that *when interest is compounded continuously, the rate of change of the amount of money present at time t is proportional to the amount present at time t.* The constant of proportionality is r.

To determine the actual function S, we solve differential equation (8) by the method of separation of variables.

$$\frac{dS}{dt} = rS,$$

$$\frac{dS}{S} = r\, dt,$$

$$\int \frac{1}{S}\, dS = \int r\, dt,$$

$$\ln |S| = rt + C_1.$$

Since it can be assumed that $S > 0$, then $\ln |S| = \ln S$. Thus

$$\ln S = rt + C_1.$$

We can solve for S by converting to exponential form.

$$S = e^{rt + C_1} = e^{C_1} e^{rt}.$$

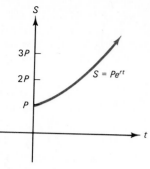

FIGURE 15.5

For simplicity, e^{C_1} can be replaced by C to obtain

$$S = Ce^{rt}.$$

Because of the condition that $S(0) = P$, we can determine the value of C:

$$P = Ce^{r(0)} = C \cdot 1.$$

Hence $C = P$ and

$$S = Pe^{rt}. \tag{9}$$

Equation (9) gives the total value after t years of an initial investment of P dollars compounded continuously at an annual rate r (see Fig. 15.5).

In our compound interest discussion, we saw from Eq. (8) that the rate of change in the amount present was proportional to the amount present. There are many natural quantities, such as population, whose rate of growth or decay at any time is considered proportional to the amount of that quantity present. If N denotes the amount of such a quantity at time t, then this rate of growth means that

$$\frac{dN}{dt} = kN,$$

where k is a constant. If we separate variables and solve for N as we did for Eq. (8), we get

$$N = N_0 e^{kt}, \tag{10}$$

where N_0 is a constant. Due to the form of Eq. (10), we say that the quantity follows an **exponential law of growth** if k is positive and **exponential decay** if k is negative.

EXAMPLE 2   *In a certain city the rate at which the population grows at any time is proportional to the size of the population. If the population was 125,000 in 1960 and 140,000 in 1980, what is the expected population in 2000?*

Let N be the size of the population at time t. Since the exponential law of growth applies,

$$N = N_0 e^{kt}.$$

We must first find the constants N_0 and k. Let the year 1960 correspond to $t = 0$. Then $t = 20$ in 1980 and $t = 40$ in 2000. Now, if $t = 0$, then $N = 125,000$. Thus

$$N = N_0 e^{kt},$$

$$125,000 = N_0 e^0 = N_0.$$

Hence $N_0 = 125,000$ and

$$N = 125,000e^{kt}.$$

But if $t = 20$, then $N = 140,000$. This means that

$$140,000 = 125,000e^{20k}.$$

Thus

$$e^{20k} = \frac{140,000}{125,000} = 1.12,$$

$$20k = \ln(1.12) \qquad \text{(logarithmic form)},$$

$$k = \tfrac{1}{20} \ln(1.12).$$

Therefore,

$$N = 125,000e^{(t/20) \ \ln \ 1.12} \tag{11}$$

$$= 125,000[e^{\ln \ 1.12}]^{t/20}.$$

$$N = 125,000(1.12)^{t/20}. \tag{12}$$

If $t = 40$,

$$N = 125,000(1.12)^2 = 156,800.$$

We can write Eq. (11) in a form different from Eq. (12). Because $\ln 1.12 \approx 0.11333$, we have $k \approx 0.11333/20 \approx 0.0057$. Thus

$$N \approx 125,000e^{0.0057t}.$$

The rate at which a radioactive element decays at any time is found to be proportional to the amount of that element present. If N is the amount of a radioactive substance at time t, then the rate of decay is given by

$$\frac{dN}{dt} = -\lambda N. \tag{13}$$

The positive constant λ (a Greek letter read "lambda") is called the **decay constant,** and the minus sign indicates that N is decreasing as t increases. Thus we have exponential decay. From Eq. (10), the solution of this differential equation is

$$N = N_0e^{-\lambda t}. \tag{14}$$

If $t = 0$, then $N = N_0 \cdot 1 = N_0$, so N_0 represents the amount of the radioactive substance present when $t = 0$.

The time for one-half of the substance to decay is called the **half-life** of the substance. It is the value of t when $N = N_0/2$. From Eq. (14),

$$\frac{N_0}{2} = N_0e^{-\lambda t},$$

$$\frac{1}{2} = e^{-\lambda t}.$$

In logarithmic form we have

$$-\lambda t = \ln \tfrac{1}{2} = \ln 1 - \ln 2 = -\ln 2,$$

$$t = \frac{\ln 2}{\lambda} \approx \frac{0.69315}{\lambda}. \tag{15}$$

Note that the half-life depends on λ. Figure 15.6 shows the graph of radioactive decay.

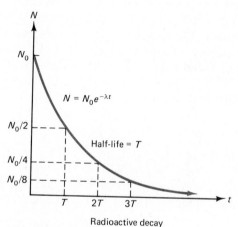

Radioactive decay

FIGURE 15.6

EXAMPLE 3   *If 60% of a radioactive substance remains after 50 days, find the decay constant and the half-life of the element.*

From Eq. (14),

$$N = N_0 e^{-\lambda t},$$

where N_0 is the amount of the element present at $t = 0$. When $t = 50$, then $N = 0.6N_0$ and we have

$$0.6N_0 = N_0 e^{-50\lambda},$$

$$0.6 = e^{-50\lambda},$$

$$-50\lambda = \ln(0.6) \quad \text{(logarithmic form)},$$

$$\lambda = -\frac{\ln(0.6)}{50} \approx -\frac{-0.51083^*}{50}$$

$$\approx 0.01022.$$

Thus $N \approx N_0 e^{-0.01022t}$. The half-life, from Eq. (15), is approximately

$$\frac{0.69315}{\lambda} \approx \frac{0.69315}{0.01022} \approx 67.82 \text{ days.}$$

---

* $\ln(0.6) = \ln(6/10) = \ln 6 - \ln 10 \approx 1.79176 - 2.30259 = -0.51083.$

Radioactivity is useful in dating such things as fossil plant remains and archaeological remains made from organic material. Plants and other living organisms contain a small amount of radioactive carbon 14 (C^{14}) in addition to ordinary carbon (C^{12}). The C^{12} atoms are stable, but the C^{14} atoms are decaying exponentially. However, C^{14} is formed in the atmosphere due to the effect of cosmic rays. Eventually, this C^{14} is taken up by plants during photosynthesis and replaces what has decayed. As a result, the ratio of C^{14} atoms to C^{12} atoms is considered constant over a long period of time. When a plant dies, it stops absorbing C^{14} and the remaining C^{14} atoms decay. By comparing the proportion of C^{14} to C^{12} in a fossil plant to that of plants found today, we can estimate the age of the fossil. The half-life of C^{14} is approximately 5600 years. Thus, for example, if a fossil is found to have a C^{14} to C^{12} ratio which is half that of a similar substance found today, we would estimate the fossil to be 5600 years old.

EXAMPLE 4   *A wood tool found in a Middle East excavation site is found to have a C^{14} to C^{12} ratio which is 0.6 of the corresponding ratio in a present-day tree. Estimate the age of the tool to the nearest hundred years.*

Let N be the amount of C^{14} present in the wood t years after the tool was made. Then $N = N_0 e^{-\lambda t}$ where N_0 is the amount of C^{14} when $t = 0$. Since the C^{14} to C^{12} ratio is 0.6 of the corresponding ratio in a present-day tree, this means that we want to find the value of t for which $N = 0.6 N_0$.

$$0.6 N_0 = N_0 e^{-\lambda t},$$

$$0.6 = e^{-\lambda t},$$

$$-\lambda t = \ln(0.6),$$

$$t = -\frac{1}{\lambda} \ln(0.6).$$

From Eq. (15), the half-life is (approximately) $0.69315/\lambda$, which equals 5600, so $\lambda \approx 0.69315/5600$. Thus

$$t \approx -\frac{1}{0.69315/5600} \ln(0.6)$$

$$\approx -\frac{5600}{0.69315}(-0.51083)$$

$$\approx 4100 \text{ years.}$$

EXERCISE 15.6

In Problems 1–8, solve the differential equations.

1. $y' = 2xy^2$.

2. $y' = x^3 y^3$.

3. $\dfrac{dy}{dx} - x\sqrt{x^2 + 1} = 0$.

4. $\dfrac{dy}{dx} = \dfrac{x}{y}$.

5. $\dfrac{dy}{dx} = y, \quad y > 0$.

6. $y' = e^x y^2$.

7. $y' = \dfrac{y}{x}, \quad x, y > 0$.

8. $\dfrac{dy}{dx} + xe^x = 0$.

In Problems **9–14,** *solve each of the differential equations subject to the given conditions.*

9. $y' = \dfrac{1}{y}$; $y > 0$, $y(2) = 2$.

10. $y' = e^{x-y}$; $y(0) = 0$. (*Hint:* $e^{x-y} = e^x/e^y$.)

11. $e^y y' - x^2 = 0$; $y = 0$ when $x = 0$.

12. $x^2 y' + \dfrac{1}{y^2} = 0$; $y(1) = 2$.

13. $(4x^2 + 3)^2 y' - 4xy^2 = 0$; $y(0) = \tfrac{3}{2}$.

14. $y' + x^2 y = 0$; $y > 0$, $y = 1$ when $x = 0$.

15. In a certain town the population at any time changes at a rate proportional to the population. If the population in 1975 was 20,000 and in 1985 it was 24,000, find an equation for the population at time t, where t is the number of years past 1975. Write your answer in two forms, one involving e. You may assume ln 1.2 = 0.18. What is the expected population in 1995?

16. The population of a town increases by natural growth at a rate which is proportional to the number N of persons present. If the population at time $t = 0$ is 10,000, find two expressions for the population N, t years later, if the population doubles in 50 years. Assume that ln 2 = 0.69. Also find N for $t = 100$.

17. Suppose that the population of the world in 1930 was 2 billion and in 1960 it was 3 billion. If the exponential law of growth is assumed, what is the expected population in 2000? Give your answer in terms of e.

18. If exponential growth is assumed, in approximately how many years will a population triple if it doubles in 50 years? (*Hint:* Let the population at $t = 0$ be N_0.)

19. If 30% of the initial amount of a radioactive sample remains after 100 seconds, find the decay constant and the half-life of the element.

20. If 30% of the initial amount of a radioactive sample has *decayed* after 100 seconds, find the decay constant and the half-life of the element.

21. An Egyptian scroll was found to have a C^{14} to C^{12} ratio that is 0.7 of the corresponding ratio in similar present-day material. Estimate the age of the scroll to the nearest hundred years.

22. A recently discovered archaeological specimen has a C^{14} to C^{12} ratio that is 0.2 of the corresponding ratio found in present-day organic material. Estimate the age of the specimen to the nearest hundred years.

23. Suppose a population follows exponential growth given by $dN/dt = kN$ for $t \geq t_0$, and $N = N_0$ when $t = t_0$. Find N, the population size at time t.

24. Radon has a half-life of 3.82 days. (a) Find the decay constant in terms of ln 2. (b) What fraction of the original amount of it remains after $2(3.82) = 7.64$ days?

25. Radioactive isotopes are used in medical diagnoses as tracers to determine abnormalities that may exist in an organ. For example, if radioactive iodine is swallowed, after some time it is taken up by the thyroid gland. With the use of a detector, the rate at which it is taken up can be measured and a determination can be made as to whether the uptake is normal. Suppose radioactive technetium-99m, which has a half-life of 6 hours, is to be used in a brain scan two hours from now. What should be its activity now if the activity when it is used is to be 10 units? Give your answer to one decimal place. [*Hint:* In Eq. (14), let N = activity t hours from now, and N_0 = activity now.]

26. A radioactive substance that has a half-life of 8 days is to be temporarily implanted in a hospital patient until there remains three-fifths of the amount originally present. How long should the implant remain in the patient?

27. In a forest natural litter occurs, such as fallen leaves and branches, dead animals, etc.* Let $A = A(t)$ denote the amount of litter present at time t, where $A(t)$ is expressed in grams per square meter and t is in years. Suppose that there is no litter at $t = 0$. Thus $A(0) = 0$. Assume that

1. Litter falls to the ground continuously at a constant rate of 200 grams per square meter per year.

2. The accumulated litter decomposes continuously at the rate of 50% of the amount present per year (which is 0.50A).

---

* R. W. Poole, *An Introduction to Quantitative Ecology* (New York: McGraw-Hill Book Company, 1974).

The difference of the two rates is the rate of change of the amount of litter present with respect to time:

$$\begin{pmatrix} \text{rate of change} \\ \text{of litter present} \end{pmatrix} = \begin{pmatrix} \text{rate of falling} \\ \text{to ground} \end{pmatrix} - \begin{pmatrix} \text{rate of} \\ \text{decomposition} \end{pmatrix}.$$

Thus

$$\frac{dA}{dt} = 200 - 0.50A.$$

Solve for A. To the nearest gram, determine the amount of litter per square meter after 1 year.

28. Suppose q is the amount of penicillin in the body at time t and let q_0 be the amount at $t = 0$. Assume that the rate of change of q with respect to t is proportional to q and that q decreases as t increases. Then we have $dq/dt = -kq$, where $k > 0$. Solve for q. What percentage of the original amount present is there when $t = 2/k$?

15.7 MORE APPLICATIONS OF DIFFERENTIAL EQUATIONS

Suppose that the number N of individuals in a population at time t follows an exponential law of growth. From the preceding section $N = N_0e^{kt}$, where $k > 0$ and N_0 is the population when $t = 0$. This law assumes that at time t the rate of growth, dN/dt, of the population is proportional to the number of individuals in the population. That is, $dN/dt = kN$.

Under exponential growth, a population would get infinitely large as time goes on. In reality, however, when the population gets large enough there are environmental factors that slow down the rate of growth. Examples are food supply, predators, overcrowding, and so on. These factors cause dN/dt to eventually decrease. It is reasonable to assume that population size is limited to some maximum number M, where $0 < N < M$, and as $N \to M$, then $dN/dt \to 0$ and the population size tends to be stable.

In summary, we want a population model that has exponential growth initially but which also includes the effects of environmental resistance to large population growth. Such a model is obtained by multiplying the right side of $dN/dt = kN$ by the factor $(M - N)/M$:

$$\frac{dN}{dt} = kN\left(\frac{M - N}{M}\right).$$

Notice that if N is small, then $(M - N)/M$ is close to 1 and we have growth that is approximately exponential. As $N \to M$, then $M - N \to 0$ and $dN/dt \to 0$ as we wanted in our model. Replacing k/M by K, we have

$$\frac{dN}{dt} = KN(M - N). \tag{1}$$

This states that the rate of growth is proportional to the product of the population size and the difference between the maximum size and the population size. We can solve for N in differential equation (1) by the method of separation of variables.

$$\frac{dN}{N(M - N)} = K \, dt,$$

$$\int \frac{1}{N(M - N)} \, dN = \int K \, dt. \tag{2}$$

The integral on the left side can be found by using Formula 5 in the table of integrals. Thus Eq. (2) becomes

$$\frac{1}{M} \ln \left| \frac{N}{M - N} \right| = Kt + C,$$

$$\ln \left| \frac{N}{M - N} \right| = Mkt + MC.$$

Since $N > 0$ and $M - N > 0$, we can write

$$\ln \frac{N}{M - N} = Mkt + MC.$$

In exponential form we have

$$\frac{N}{M - N} = e^{MKt + MC} = e^{MKt} e^{MC}.$$

Replacing the positive constant e^{MC} by A gives

$$\frac{N}{M - N} = Ae^{MKt},$$

$$N = (M - N)Ae^{MKt},$$

$$N = MAe^{MKt} - NAe^{MKt},$$

$$NAe^{MKt} + N = MAe^{MKt},$$

$$N(Ae^{MKt} + 1) = MAe^{MKt},$$

$$N = \frac{MAe^{MKt}}{Ae^{MKt} + 1}.$$

Dividing numerator and denominator by Ae^{MKt}, we have

$$N = \frac{M}{1 + \dfrac{1}{Ae^{MKt}}} = \frac{M}{1 + \dfrac{1}{A} e^{-MKt}}.$$

Replacing $1/A$ by b and MK by c gives

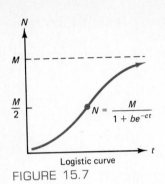

Logistic curve

FIGURE 15.7

$$N = \frac{M}{1 + be^{-ct}}. \qquad (3)$$

Equation (3) is called the **logistic function** or the **Verhulst-Pearl logistic function.** Its graph, called a *logistic curve,* is S-shaped and appears in Fig. 15.7. Notice in the graph that $N = M$ is a horizontal asymptote; that is,

$$\lim_{t \to \infty} \frac{M}{1 + be^{-ct}} = \frac{M}{1 + b(0)} = M.$$

Moreover, from Eq. (1) the rate of growth is

$$KN(M - N).$$

To find when the maximum rate of growth occurs, we solve

$$\frac{d}{dN}[KN(M - N)] = \frac{d}{dN}[K(MN - N^2)]$$

$$= K[M - 2N] = 0.$$

Thus $N = M/2$. The rate of growth increases until the population size is $M/2$ and decreases thereafter. The maximum rate of growth occurs when $N = M/2$ and corresponds to a point of inflection in the graph of N. To find the value of t for which this occurs, we substitute $M/2$ for N in Eq. (3) and solve for t.

$$\frac{M}{2} = \frac{M}{1 + be^{-ct}},$$

$$1 + be^{-ct} = 2,$$

$$e^{-ct} = \frac{1}{b},$$

$$e^{ct} = b,$$

$$ct = \ln b,$$

$$t = \frac{\ln b}{c}.$$

Thus the maximum rate of growth occurs at the point $([\ln b]/c, M/2)$.

We point out that in Eq. (3), we may replace e^c by C and then the logistic function has the form

$$N = \frac{M}{1 + bC^{-t}}.$$

EXAMPLE 1   *Suppose the membership in a new country club is to be a maximum of 800 persons due to limitations of the physical plant. One year ago, the initial membership was 50 persons and now there are 200. Provided that enrollment follows a logistic function, how many members will there be three years from now?*

Let N be the number of members enrolled t years after the formation of the club. Then

$$N = \frac{M}{1 + be^{-ct}}.$$

Here $M = 800$, and when $t = 0$ we have $N = 50$.

$$50 = \frac{800}{1 + b},$$

$$1 + b = \frac{800}{50} = 16,$$

$$b = 15.$$

Thus

$$N = \frac{800}{1 + 15e^{-ct}}. \tag{4}$$

When $t = 1$, then $N = 200$.

$$200 = \frac{800}{1 + 15e^{-c}},$$

$$1 + 15e^{-c} = \frac{800}{200} = 4,$$

$$e^{-c} = \frac{3}{15} = \frac{1}{5}.$$

Hence $c = -\ln \frac{1}{5} = \ln 5$. Rather that substituting this value of c into Eq. (4), it is more convenient to substitute the value of e^{-c} there.

$$N = \frac{800}{1 + 15(\frac{1}{5})^t}.$$

Three years from now, $t = 4$. Thus

$$N = \frac{800}{1 + 15(\frac{1}{5})^4} \approx 781.$$

Let us now consider a simplified model of how a rumor spreads in a population of size M. A similar situation would be the spread of an epidemic or new fad.

Let $N = N(t)$ be the number of persons who know the rumor at time t. We shall assume that those who know the rumor spread it randomly in the population and that those who are told the rumor become spreaders of the rumor. Furthermore, we shall assume that each knower tells the rumor to k individuals per unit of time. (Some of these k individuals may already know the rumor.) We want an expression for the rate of increase of the knowers of the rumor. Over a unit of time, each of approximately N persons will tell the rumor to k persons. Thus the total number of persons who are told the rumor over the unit of time is (approximately) Nk. However, we are interested only in *new* knowers. The proportion of the population who do not know the rumor is $(M - N)/M$. Thus the total number of new knowers of the rumor is

$$Nk\left(\frac{M - N}{M}\right),$$

which can be written $(k/M)N(M - N)$. Therefore,

$$\frac{dN}{dt} = \frac{k}{M} N(M - N)$$

$$= KN(M - N), \qquad \text{where } K = \frac{k}{M}.$$

This differential equation has the form of Eq. (1), so its solution, from Eq. (3), is a logistic function:

$$N = \frac{M}{1 + be^{-ct}}.$$

EXAMPLE 2   *In a large university of 45,000 students, a sociology major is researching the spread of a new campus rumor. When she begins her research, she determines that 300 students know the rumor. After one week she finds that 900 know it. Estimate the number who know it 4 weeks after the research begins by assuming logistic growth. Give the answer to the nearest thousand.*

Let N be the number of students who know the rumor after t weeks. Then

$$N = \frac{M}{1 + be^{-ct}}.$$

Here M, the size of the population, is 45,000, and when $t = 0$ we have $N = 300$.

$$300 = \frac{45{,}000}{1 + b},$$

$$1 + b = \frac{45{,}000}{300} = 150,$$

$$b = 149.$$

Thus

$$N = \frac{45{,}000}{1 + 149e^{-ct}}.$$

When $t = 1$, then $N = 900$.

$$900 = \frac{45{,}000}{1 + 149e^{-c}},$$

$$1 + 149e^{-c} = \frac{45,000}{900} = 50.$$

Therefore, $e^{-c} = \frac{49}{149}$, so

$$N = \frac{45,000}{1 + 149(\frac{49}{149})^t}.$$

When $t = 4$,

$$N = \frac{45,000}{1 + 149(\frac{49}{149})^4} \approx 16,000.$$

After 4 weeks, approximately 16,000 students know the rumor.

If a homicide is committed, the temperature of the victim's body will gradually decrease from 37°C (normal body temperature) to the temperature of the surroundings (ambient temperature). In general, the temperature of the cooling body changes at a rate proportional to the difference between the temperature of the body and the ambient temperature. This statement is known as **Newton's law of cooling.** Thus if $T(t)$ is the temperature of the body at time t and a is the ambient temperature, then

$$\frac{dT}{dt} = k(T - a),$$

where k is the constant of proportionality. Newton's law of cooling can be applied to determine the time at which a homicide was committed, as the next example illustrates.

EXAMPLE 3   *A wealthy industrialist was found murdered in his home. Police arrived on the scene at* 11:00 P.M. *The temperature of the body at that time was* 31°C, *and one hour later it was* 30°C. *The temperature of the room in which the body was found was* 22°C. *Determine the time at which the murder occurred.*

Let t be the number of hours after the body was discovered, and $T(t)$ be the temperature (in degrees Celsius) of the body at time t. We want to find the value of t for which $T = 37$ (normal body temperature). This value of t will, of course, be negative. By Newton's law of cooling,

$$\frac{dT}{dt} = k(T - a),$$

where k is a constant and a (the ambient temperature) is 22. Thus

$$\frac{dT}{dt} = k(T - 22).$$

Separating variables, we have

$$\frac{dT}{T - 22} = k \, dt,$$

$$\int \frac{dT}{T - 22} = \int k \, dt,$$

$$\ln |T - 22| = kt + C.$$

Because $T - 22 > 0$,

$$\ln(T - 22) = kt + C.$$

When $t = 0$, then $T = 31$. Thus

$$\ln(31 - 22) = k \cdot 0 + C,$$

$$C = \ln 9.$$

Hence

$$\ln(T - 22) = kt + \ln 9,$$

$$\ln(T - 22) - \ln 9 = kt,$$

$$\ln \frac{T - 22}{9} = kt.$$

When $t = 1$, then $T = 30$, so

$$\ln \frac{30 - 22}{9} = k \cdot 1,$$

$$k = \ln \frac{8}{9} \approx -0.11778.$$

Thus

$$\ln \frac{T - 22}{9} \approx -0.11778t.$$

Now we find t when $T = 37$:

$$\ln \frac{37 - 22}{9} \approx -0.11778t,$$

$$t \approx -\frac{\ln(15/9)}{0.11778} \approx -\frac{0.51083}{0.11778},$$

$$t \approx -4.34.$$

Thus the murder occurred about 4.34 hours *before* the time of discovery (11:00 P.M.). Since 4.34 hours is (approximately) 4 hours 20 minutes, the industrialist was murdered about 6:40 P.M.

EXERCISE 15.7

1. The population of a city follows logistic growth and is limited to 40,000. If the population in 1980 was 20,000 and in 1985 it was 25,000, what will be the population in 1990? Give your answer to the nearest hundred.

2. A company believes that the production of its product in present facilities will follow logistic growth. Presently, 200 units per day are produced, and production will increase to 300 units per day in 1 year. If production is limited to 500 units per day, what is the anticipated daily production in 2 years? Give your answer to the nearest unit.

3. In a country of 3,000,000 people the prime minister suffers a heart attack, which the government does not officially publicize. Initially, 50 governmental personnel know of the attack but are spreading this information as a rumor. At the end of 1 week 5000 people know the rumor. Assuming logistic growth, find how many people know the rumor after 2 weeks. Give your answer to the nearest thousand.

4. A new fad is sweeping a college campus of 30,000 students. The college newspaper feels that its readers would be interested in a series on the fad. It assigns a reporter when the number of faddists is 400. One week later there are 1200 faddists. Assuming logistic growth, find a formula for the number N of faddists t weeks after the assignment of the reporter.

5. In a city whose population is 100,000 an outbreak of flu occurs. When the city health department begins its record keeping, there are 500 infected persons. One week later there are 1000 infected persons. Assuming logistic growth, estimate the number of infected persons 2 weeks after record keeping begins.

6. The logistic curve for the U.S. population from 1790 to 1910 is estimated to be*

$$N = \frac{197.30}{1 + 35.60e^{-0.031186t}},$$

where N is the population in millions and t is in years counted from 1800. If this logistic function were valid for years after 1910, for what year would the point of inflection occur? Give your answer to one decimal place. Assume that $\ln 35.6 = 3.5723$.

7. In an experiment†, five *Paramecia* were placed in a test tube containing a nutritive medium. The number N of *Paramecia* in the tube at the end of t days is approximately given by

$$N = \frac{375}{1 + e^{5.2 - 2.3t}}.$$

(a) Show that this can be written as

$$N = \frac{375}{1 + 181.27e^{-2.3t}},$$

and hence is a logistic function. (b) Find $\lim_{t \to \infty} N$.

8. In the study of growth of a colony of unicellular organisms,‡ the following equation was obtained:

$$N = \frac{0.2524}{e^{-2.128x} + 0.005125}, \qquad 0 \le x \le 5,$$

where N is the estimated area of the growth in square centimeters and x is the age of the colony in days after being first observed. (a) Put this equation in the form of a logistic function. (b) Find the area when the age of the colony is 0.

9. A waterfront murder was committed, and the victim's body was discovered at 3:15 A.M. by police. At that time the temperature of the body was 32°C. One hour later the body temperature was 30°C. After checking with the weather bureau, it was determined that the temperature at the waterfront was 10°C from 10:00 P.M. to 5:00 A.M. About what time did the murder occur?

10. An enzyme is a protein that acts as a catalyst for increasing the rate of a chemical reaction that occurs in cells. In a certain reaction an enzyme A is converted to

---

* N. Keyfitz, *Introduction to the Mathematics of Population* (Reading, Mass.: Addison-Wesley Publishing Company, Inc., 1968).

† G. F. Gause, *The Struggle for Existence* (New York: Hafner Publishing Co., 1964).

‡ A. J. Lotka, *Elements of Mathematical Biology* (New York: Dover Publications, Inc. 1956).

another enzyme B. Enzyme B acts as a catalyst for its own formation. Let p be the amount of enzyme B at time t and I be the total amount of both enzymes when $t = 0$. Suppose the rate of formation of B is proportional to $p(I - p)$. Without directly using calculus, find the value of p for which the rate of formation will be a maximum.

11. A small town decides to conduct a fund-raising drive for a new fire engine whose cost is $70,000. The initial amount in the fund is $10,000. On the basis of past drives, it is determined that t months after the beginning of the drive, the rate dx/dt at which money is contributed to such a fund is proportional to the difference between the desired goal of $70,000 and the total amount x in the fund at that time. After 1 month a total of $40,000 is in the fund. How much will be in the fund after 3 months?

12. In a discussion of unexpected properties of mathematical models of population, Bailey* considers the case in which the birth rate per *individual* is proportional to the population size N at time t. Since the growth rate per individual is $\dfrac{1}{N}\dfrac{dN}{dt}$, this means that

$$\frac{1}{N}\frac{dN}{dt} = kN$$

or $\dfrac{dN}{dt} = kN^2$ (subject to $N = N_0$ at $t = 0$),

where $k > 0$. Show that

$$N = \frac{N_0}{1 - kN_0 t}.$$

Use this result to show that

$$\lim N = \infty \quad \text{as} \quad t \to \left(\frac{1}{kN_0}\right)^{-}.$$

This means that over a finite interval of time there is an infinite amount of growth. Such a model might be useful only for rapid growth over a short interval of time.

13. Suppose that the rate of growth of a population is proportional to the difference between some maximum size M and the number N of individuals in the population at time t. Suppose that when $t = 0$ the population size is N_0. Find a formula for N.

15.8 IMPROPER INTEGRALS†

Suppose $f(x)$ is nonnegative for $a \le x < \infty$ (see Fig. 15.8). Then the integral

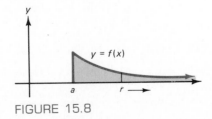

FIGURE 15.8

* N. T. J. Bailey, *The Mathematical Approach to Biology and Medicine* (New York: John Wiley & Sons, Inc., 1967).

† May be omitted if Chapter 16 is not covered.

$\int_a^r f(x)\ dx$ is the area between the curve and the x-axis from $x = a$ to $x = r$. As $r \to \infty$, we may think of

$$\lim_{r \to \infty} \int_a^r f(x)\ dx$$

as the area of the unbounded region that is shaded in Fig. 15.8. This limit is abbreviated by

$$\int_a^\infty f(x)\ dx, \tag{1}$$

called an **improper integral.** If this limit exists, $\int_a^\infty f(x)\ dx$ is said to be **convergent** or to *converge* to that limit. In this case the unbounded region is considered to have a finite area, and this area is represented by $\int_a^\infty f(x)\ dx$. If the limit does not exist, the improper integral is said to be **divergent** and the region does not have a finite area.

We can remove the restriction that $f(x) \geq 0$. In general, the improper integral $\int_a^\infty f(x)\ dx$ is defined by

$$\int_a^\infty f(x)\ dx = \lim_{r \to \infty} \int_a^r f(x)\ dx.$$

Other types of improper integrals are

$$\int_{-\infty}^b f(x)\ dx \tag{2}$$

and

$$\int_{-\infty}^\infty f(x)\ dx. \tag{3}$$

In each of the three cases, the interval over which the integral is evaluated has infinite length. The improper integral in (2) is defined by

$$\int_{-\infty}^b f(x)\ dx = \lim_{r \to -\infty} \int_r^b f(x)\ dx.$$

If this limit exists, $\int_{-\infty}^b f(x)\ dx$ is said to be convergent. Otherwise, it is divergent. We shall define the improper integral in (3) after the following example.

EXAMPLE 1   *Determine whether the following improper integrals are convergent or divergent. If convergent, determine the value of the integral.*

a. $\int_1^\infty \dfrac{1}{x^3}\ dx.$

$$\int_1^\infty \frac{1}{x^3}\ dx = \lim_{r \to \infty} \int_1^r x^{-3}\ dx = \lim_{r \to \infty} -\frac{x^{-2}}{2} \Big|_1^r$$

$$= \lim_{r \to \infty} \left[-\frac{1}{2r^2} + \frac{1}{2} \right] = -0 + \frac{1}{2} = \frac{1}{2}.$$

Therefore, $\int_1^\infty \frac{1}{x^3}\, dx$ converges to $\frac{1}{2}$.

b. $\int_{-\infty}^0 e^x\, dx.$

$$\int_{-\infty}^0 e^x\, dx = \lim_{r \to -\infty} \int_r^0 e^x\, dx = \lim_{r \to -\infty} e^x \Big|_r^0$$

$$= \lim_{r \to -\infty} (1 - e^r) = 1 - 0 = 1.$$

(Here we used the fact that, as $r \to -\infty$, then $e^r \to 0$.) Therefore, $\int_{-\infty}^0 e^x\, dx$ converges to 1.

c. $\int_1^\infty \frac{1}{\sqrt{x}}\, dx.$

$$\int_1^\infty \frac{1}{\sqrt{x}}\, dx = \lim_{r \to \infty} \int_1^r x^{-1/2}\, dx = \lim_{r \to \infty} 2x^{1/2} \Big|_1^r$$

$$= \lim_{r \to \infty} 2(\sqrt{r} - 1) = \infty.$$

Therefore, the improper integral diverges.

The improper integral $\int_{-\infty}^\infty f(x)\, dx$ is defined in terms of improper integrals of the forms (1) and (2):

$$\int_{-\infty}^\infty f(x)\, dx = \int_{-\infty}^0 f(x)\, dx + \int_0^\infty f(x)\, dx. \tag{4}$$

If *both* integrals on the right side of Eq. (4) are convergent, then $\int_{-\infty}^\infty f(x)\, dx$ is said to be convergent; otherwise, it is divergent.

EXAMPLE 2   *Determine whether* $\int_{-\infty}^\infty e^x\, dx$ *is convergent or divergent.*

$$\int_{-\infty}^\infty e^x\, dx = \int_{-\infty}^0 e^x\, dx + \int_0^\infty e^x\, dx.$$

By Example 1(b), $\int_{-\infty}^0 e^x\, dx = 1$. On the other hand,

$$\int_0^\infty e^x \, dx = \lim_{r \to \infty} \int_0^r e^x \, dx = \lim_{r \to \infty} e^x \Big|_0^r = \lim_{r \to \infty} (e^r - 1) = \infty.$$

Since $\int_0^\infty e^x \, dx$ is divergent, $\int_{-\infty}^\infty e^x \, dx$ is also divergent.

EXAMPLE 3   *In statistics, a function f is called a density function if* $f(x) \geq 0$ *and*

$$\int_{-\infty}^\infty f(x) \, dx = 1.$$

Suppose

$$f(x) = \begin{cases} ke^{-x}, & \text{for } x \geq 0, \\ 0, & \text{elsewhere} \end{cases}$$

is a density function. Find k.

We write the equation $\int_{-\infty}^\infty f(x) \, dx = 1$ as

$$\int_{-\infty}^\infty f(x) \, dx = \int_{-\infty}^0 f(x) \, dx + \int_0^\infty f(x) \, dx = 1.$$

Since $f(x) = 0$ for $x < 0$, $\int_{-\infty}^0 f(x) \, dx = 0$. Thus

$$\int_0^\infty ke^{-x} \, dx = 1,$$

$$\lim_{r \to \infty} \int_0^r ke^{-x} \, dx = 1,$$

$$\lim_{r \to \infty} -ke^{-x} \Big|_0^r = 1,$$

$$\lim_{r \to \infty} (-ke^{-r} + k) = 1,$$

$$0 + k = 1,$$

$$k = 1.$$

EXERCISE 15.8

*In Problems **1–12**, determine the integrals, if they exist. Indicate those that are divergent.*

1. $\int_3^\infty \dfrac{1}{x^2} \, dx.$

2. $\int_2^\infty \dfrac{1}{(2x - 1)^3} \, dx.$

3. $\int_1^\infty \dfrac{1}{x} \, dx.$

4. $\int_1^\infty \dfrac{1}{\sqrt[3]{x + 1}} \, dx.$

5. $\int_{1}^{\infty} e^{-x} \, dx.$

6. $\int_{0}^{\infty} (5 + e^{-x}) \, dx.$

7. $\int_{1}^{\infty} \frac{1}{\sqrt{x}} \, dx.$

8. $\int_{4}^{\infty} \frac{x \, dx}{\sqrt{(x^2 + 9)^3}}.$

9. $\int_{-\infty}^{-2} \frac{1}{(x + 1)^3} \, dx.$

10. $\int_{-\infty}^{3} \frac{1}{\sqrt{7 - x}} \, dx.$

11. $\int_{-\infty}^{\infty} xe^{-x^2} \, dx.$

12. $\int_{-\infty}^{\infty} (5 - 3x) \, dx.$

13. The density function for the life in hours x of an electronic component in a calculator is given by

$$f(x) = \begin{cases} \dfrac{k}{x^2}, & \text{for } x \geq 800, \\ 0, & \text{for } x < 800. \end{cases}$$

(a) If k satisfies the condition that $\int_{800}^{\infty} f(x) \, dx = 1$, find k. (b) The probability that the component will last at least 1200 hours is given by $\int_{1200}^{\infty} f(x) \, dx$. Evaluate this integral.

14. Given the density function

$$f(x) = \begin{cases} ke^{-4x}, & \text{for } x \geq 0, \\ 0, & \text{elsewhere}, \end{cases}$$

find k.

15. For a business the present value of all future profits at an annual interest rate r compounded continuously is given by

$$\int_{0}^{\infty} p(t)e^{-rt} \, dt,$$

where $p(t)$ is the profit per year in dollars at time t. If $p(t) = 240,000$ and $r = 0.06$, evaluate the integral above.

16. In a psychological model for signal detection,[*] the probability α (a Greek letter read "alpha") of reporting a signal when no signal is present is given by

$$\alpha = \int_{x_c}^{\infty} e^{-x} \, dx, \qquad x \geq 0.$$

The probability β (a Greek letter read "beta") of detecting a signal when it is present is

$$\beta = \int_{x_c}^{\infty} ke^{-kx} \, dx, \qquad x \geq 0.$$

In both integrals x_c is a fixed criterion value. Find α and β if $k = \frac{1}{8}$.

17. Find the area of the region in the first quadrant bounded by the curve $y = e^{-2x}$ and the x-axis.

18. In discussing entrance of a firm into an industry, Stigler[†] uses the equation

$$V = \pi_0 \int_{0}^{\infty} e^{\theta t}e^{-\rho t} \, dt,$$

where π_0, θ (a Greek letter read "theta"), and ρ (a Greek letter read "rho") are constants. Show that $V = \pi_0/(\rho - \theta)$ if $\theta < \rho$.

---

[*] D. Laming, *Mathematical Psychology* (New York: Academic Press, Inc., 1973).

[†] G. Stigler, *The Theory of Price*, 3rd ed. (New York: Macmillan Publishing Company, 1966), p. 344.

19. The predicted rate of growth per year of the population of a certain small city is given by $10,000/(t + 2)^2$, where t is the number of years from now. In the long run (that is, as $t \to \infty$), what is the expected change in population from today's level?

15.9 REVIEW

Important Terms and Symbols

Section 15.1	integration by parts
Section 15.2	proper rational function partial fractions
Section 15.3	present value of continous annuity accumulated amount of continuous annuity
Section 15.4	average value of function
Section 15.5	trapezoidal rule Simpson's rule
Section 15.6	first-order differential equation separation of variables exponential growth exponential decay decay constant half-life
Section 15.7	logistic function Newton's law of cooling
Section 15.8	improper integral, $\int_a^\infty f(x)\,dx$, $\int_{-\infty}^b f(x)\,dx$, $\int_{-\infty}^\infty f(x)\,dx$.

Summary

Sometimes we can easily determine an integral whose form is $\int u\,dv$, where u and v are functions, by applying the integration by parts formula:

$$\int u\,dv = uv - \int v\,du.$$

A proper rational function may be integrated by applying the technique of partial fractions. Here we express the rational function as a sum of fractions, each of which is easier to integrate.

To determine an integral that does not have a familiar form, you may be able to match it with a formula in a table of integrals. However, it may be necessary to transform the given integral into an equivalent form before the matching can occur.

An annuity is a series of payments over a period of time. Suppose payments are made continuously for T years such that a payment at time t is at the rate of $f(t)$ per year. If the rate of interest is r compounded continuously, then the present value A of the continuous annuity is given by

$$A = \int_0^T f(t)e^{-rt}\,dt,$$

and the accumulated amount S is given by

$$S = \int_0^T f(t)e^{r(T-t)}\,dt.$$

The average value $\bar{f}$ of a function f over the interval $[a, b]$ is given by

$$\bar{f} = \frac{1}{b-a}\int_a^b f(x)\,dx.$$

There are formulas that allow us to approximate the value of a definite integral. One formula is the trapezoidal rule:

Trapezoidal Rule

$$\int_a^b f(x)\,dx \approx \frac{h}{2}\{f(a) + 2f(a + h) + 2f(a + 2h) + \cdots + 2f\,[a + (n - 1)h] + f(b)\}, \text{ where } h = (b - a)/n.$$

Another formula is Simpson's rule:

Simpson's Rule

$$\int_a^b f(x)\,dx \approx \frac{h}{3}\{f(a) + 4f(a + h) + 2f(a + 2h) + \cdots + 4f\,[a + (n - 1)h] + f(b)\}, \text{ where } h = (b - a)/n \text{ and } n \text{ is even.}$$

An equation that involves the derivative of an unknown function is called a differential equation. If the highest-order derivative that occurs is the first, the equation is called a first-order differential equation. Some first order differential equations may be solved by the method of separation of variables. In that method, by considering the derivative to be a quotient of differentials, we rewrite the equation so that each side contains only one variable and a differential is not in a denominator. Integrating both sides of the resulting equation gives the solution. This solution involves a constant of integration and is called the general solution of the differential equation. If the unknown function must satisfy the condition that it has a specific function value for a given value of the independent variable, then a particular solution may be found.

Differential equations arise when we know a relation involving the rate of change of a function. For example, if a quantity N at time t is such that it changes at a rate proportional to the amount present, then

$$\frac{dN}{dt} = kN, \qquad \text{where } k \text{ is a constant.}$$

The solution of this differential equation is

$$N = N_0 e^{kt},$$

where N_0 is the quantity present at $t = 0$. The value of k may be determined when the value of N is known for a given value of t (other than $t = 0$). If k is positive, then N follows an exponential law of growth; if k is negative, N follows an exponential law of decay. When N represents a quantity of a radioactive element, then

$$\frac{dN}{dt} = -\lambda N, \qquad \text{where } \lambda \text{ is a positive constant.}$$

Thus N follows an exponential law of decay, and hence

$$N = N_0 e^{-\lambda t}.$$

The constant λ is called the decay constant. The time for one half of the element to decay is the half-life of the element and

$$\text{half-life} = \frac{\ln 2}{\lambda} \approx \frac{0.69315}{\lambda}.$$

A quantity N may follow a rate of growth given by

$$\frac{dN}{dt} = KN(M - N), \qquad \text{where } K, M \text{ are constants.}$$

Solving this differential equation gives a function of the form

$$N = \frac{M}{1 + be^{-ct}}, \qquad \text{where } b, c \text{ are constants,}$$

which is called a logistic function. Many population sizes can be described by a logistic function. In this case, M represents the limit of the size of the population. A logistic function is also used in analyzing the spread of a rumor.

Newton's law of cooling states that the temperature T of a cooling body at time t changes at a rate proportional to the difference $T - a$, where a is the ambient temperature. Thus

$$\frac{dT}{dt} = k(T - a), \qquad \text{where } k \text{ is a constant.}$$

The solution of this differential equation can be used to determine, for example, the time at which a homicide was committed.

An integral of the form

$$\int_a^\infty f(x)\,dx, \qquad \int_{-\infty}^b f(x)\,dx \quad \text{or} \quad \int_{-\infty}^\infty f(x)\,dx$$

is called an improper integral. The first two integrals are defined as follows:

$$\int_a^\infty f(x)\,dx = \lim_{r \to \infty} \int_a^r f(x)\,dx$$

$$\text{and} \qquad \int_{-\infty}^b f(x)\,dx = \lim_{r \to -\infty} \int_r^b f(x)\,dx.$$

If $\int_a^\infty f(x)\,dx$ $\left(\text{or } \int_{-\infty}^b f(x)\,dx\right)$ is a finite number, we say that the integral is convergent; otherwise, it is divergent. The improper integral $\int_{-\infty}^\infty f(x)\,dx$ is defined by

$$\int_{-\infty}^\infty f(x)\,dx = \int_{-\infty}^0 f(x)\,dx + \int_0^\infty f(x)\,dx.$$

If both integrals on the right side are convergent, then $\int_{-\infty}^\infty f(x)\,dx$ is said to be convergent; otherwise, it is divergent.

Review Problems

In Problems 1–18, determine the integrals.

1. $\displaystyle\int x \ln x\,dx.$

2. $\displaystyle\int \frac{1}{\sqrt{4x^2 + 1}}\,dx.$

3. $\displaystyle\int_0^2 \sqrt{4x^2 + 9}\,dx.$

4. $\displaystyle\int \frac{2x}{3 - 4x}\,dx.$

5. $\displaystyle\int \frac{x\,dx}{(2 + 3x)(3 + x)}.$

6. $\displaystyle\int_e^{e^2} \frac{1}{x \ln x}\,dx.$

7. $\displaystyle\int \frac{dx}{x(x + 2)^2}.$

8. $\displaystyle\int \frac{dx}{x^2 - 1}.$

9. $\displaystyle\int \frac{dx}{x^2\sqrt{9 - 16x^2}}.$

10. $\displaystyle\int x^2 \ln(4x)\,dx.$

11. $\displaystyle\int \frac{9\,dx}{x^2 - 9}.$

12. $\displaystyle\int \frac{3x}{\sqrt{1 + 3x}}\,dx.$

13. $\displaystyle\int xe^{7x}\,dx.$

14. $\displaystyle\int \frac{dx}{2 + 3e^{4x}}.$

15. $\displaystyle\int \frac{dx}{2x \ln 2x}.$

16. $\displaystyle\int \frac{dx}{x(2 + x)}.$

17. $\displaystyle\int \frac{2x}{3 + 2x}\,dx.$

18. $\displaystyle\int \frac{dx}{\sqrt{4x^2 - 9}}.$

19. Find the average value of $f(x) = 3x^2 + 2x$ over the interval $[2, 4]$.

20. Find the average value of $f(t) = te^{t^2}$ over the interval $[2, 5]$.

*In Problems **21** and **22**, use (a) the trapezoidal rule and (b) Simpson's rule to estimate the integral. Use the given value of n. Give your answer to three decimal places.*

21. $\int_0^3 \frac{1}{x+1}\,dx, \quad n = 6.$

22. $\int_0^1 \frac{1}{2-x^2}\,dx, \quad n = 4.$

*In Problems **23** and **24**, solve the differential equations.*

23. $y' = 3x^2y + 2xy, \quad y > 0.$

24. $y' - 2xe^{x^2-y+3} = 0, \quad y(0) = 3.$

*In Problems **25–28**, determine the improper integrals, if they exist.* Indicate those that are divergent.*

25. $\int_3^\infty \frac{1}{x^3}\,dx.$

26. $\int_{-\infty}^0 e^{3x}\,dx.$

27. $\int_1^\infty \frac{1}{2x}\,dx.$

28. $\int_{-\infty}^\infty xe^{1-x^2}\,dx.$

29. The population of a city in 1965 was 100,000 and in 1980 it was 120,000. Assuming exponential growth, project the population in 1995.

30. The population of a city doubles every 10 years due to exponential growth. At a certain time the population is 10,000. Find an expression for the number of people N at time t years later. Assume $\ln 2 = 0.69$.

31. If 95% of a radioactive substance remains after 100 years, find the decay constant and, to the nearest percent, give the percentage of the original amount present after 200 years.

32. For a group of hospitalized individuals, suppose

$$\int_0^t f(x)\,dx,$$

where $f(x) = 0.008e^{-0.01x} + 0.00004e^{-0.0002x}$,

gives the proportion that has been discharged at the end of t days. Evaluate $\int_0^\infty f(x)\,dx$.

33. Two organisms are initially placed in a medium and begin to multiply. The number N of organisms that are present after t days is recorded on a graph with the horizontal axis labeled t and the vertical axis labeled N. It is observed that the points lie on a logistic curve. The number of organisms present after 6 days is 300, and beyond 10 days the number approaches a limit of 450. Find the logistic equation.

34. A college believes that enrollment follows logistic growth. Last year, enrollment was 1000, and this year it is 1100. If the college can accommodate a maximum of 2000 students, what is the anticipated enrollment next year? Give your answer to the nearest hundred.

35. A coroner is called in on a murder case. He arrives at 6:00 P.M. and finds that the victim's temperature is 35°C. One hour later the body temperature is 34°C. The temperature of the room is 25°C. About what time was the murder committed? (Assume that normal body temperature is 37°C.)

36. Find the present value, to the nearest dollar, of a continuous annuity at an annual rate of 5% for 10 years if the payment at time t is at the annual rate of $f(t) = 40t$ dollars.

*37. Suppose $A(t)$ is the amount of a product that is consumed at time t and A follows an exponential law of growth. If $t_1 < t_2$ and at time t_2 the amount consumed, $A(t_2)$, is double the amount consumed at time t_1, $A(t_1)$, then $t_2 - t_1$ is called a doubling period. In a discussion of exponential growth, Shonle† states that under exponential growth, ". . . the amount of a product consumed during one doubling period is equal to the total used for all time up to the beginning of the doubling period in question." To justify this statement, reproduce his argument as follows. The amount of the product used up to time t_1 is given by

$$\int_{-\infty}^{t_1} A_0 e^{kt} \, dt, \qquad k > 0,$$

where A_0 is the amount when $t = 0$. Show that this is equal to $(A_0/k)e^{kt_1}$. Next, the amount used during the time interval from t_1 to t_2 is

$$\int_{t_1}^{t_2} A_0 e^{kt} \, dt.$$

Show that this is equal to

$$\frac{A_0}{k} e^{kt_1}[e^{k(t_2 - t_1)} - 1]. \tag{1}$$

If the interval $[t_1, t_2]$ is a doubling period, then

$$A_0 e^{kt_2} = 2A_0 e^{kt_1}.$$

Show that this implies $e^{k(t_2 - t_1)} = 2$. Substitute this into (1); your result should be the same as the total used during all time up to t_1, namely, $(A_0/k)e^{kt_1}$.

---

* Refers to Sec. 15.8.

† J. I. Shonle, *Environmental Applications of General Physics* (Reading, Mass.: Addison-Wesley Publishing Company, Inc., 1975).

16

Continuous Random Variables

16.1 CONTINUOUS RANDOM VARIABLES

In Chapter 7 the random variables that we considered were primarily discrete. Now we shall concern ourselves with *continuous* random variables. A random variable is continuous if it can assume any value in some interval or intervals. A continuous random variable usually represents data that are measured, such as heights, weights, distances, and time periods.

For example, the number of hours of life of a pocket-calculator battery is a continuous random variable, X. If the maximum possible life is 1000 hours, then X can assume any value in the interval [0, 1000]. In a practical sense, the likelihood that X will assume a single specified value, like 764.1238, is extremely remote. It is more meaningful to consider the likelihood of X lying within an *interval*, such as that between 764 and 765 (that is, $764 < X < 765$). In general, *with a continuous random variable our concern is the likelihood that it falls within an interval, and not that it assumes a particular value.*

As another example, consider an experiment in which a number X is randomly selected from the interval [0, 2]. Then X is a continuous random variable. What is the probability that X lies in the interval [0, 1]? Because we can loosely think of [0, 1] as being "half" the interval [0, 2], a reasonable (and correct) answer is $\frac{1}{2}$. Similarly, if we think of the interval [0, $\frac{1}{2}$] as being one-fourth of [0, 2], then $P(0 \le X \le \frac{1}{2}) = \frac{1}{4}$. Actually, each one of these probabilities is simply the length of the given interval divided by the length of [0, 2]. For example,

$$P\left(0 \le X \le \frac{1}{2}\right) = \frac{\text{length of } [0, \frac{1}{2}]}{\text{length of } [0, 2]} = \frac{\frac{1}{2}}{2} = \frac{1}{4}.$$

Let us now consider a similar experiment in which X denotes a number chosen at random from the interval [0, 1]. As you might expect, the probability that X will assume a value in any given interval within $[0, 1]$ is equal to the length of the given interval divided by the length of $[0, 1]$. Because $[0, 1]$ has length 1, we can simply say that the probability of X falling in an interval is the length of the interval. For example $P(0.2 \le X \le 0.5) = 0.5 - 0.2 = 0.3$, and $P(0.2 \le X \le 0.2001) = 0.0001$. Clearly, as the length of an interval approaches 0, the probability that X assumes a value in that interval approaches 0. Keeping this in mind, we can think of a single number like 0.2 as the limiting case of an interval as the length of the interval approaches 0 (think of $[0.2, 0.2 + x]$ as $x \to 0$). Thus $P(X = 0.2) = 0$. In general, *the probability that a continuous random variable X assumes a particular value is* 0. As a result, **the probability that X lies in some interval is not affected by whether or not either of the endpoints of the interval are included or excluded.** For example,

$$P(X \le 0.4) = P(X < 0.4) + P(X = 0.4)$$

$$= P(X < 0.4) + 0$$

$$= P(X < 0.4).$$

Similarly, $P(0.2 \le X \le 0.5) = P(0.2 < X < 0.5)$.

We can geometrically represent the probabilities associated with a continuous random variable X. This is done by means of the graph of a function $y = f(x)$ such that the area under this graph (and above the x-axis) between the lines $x = a$ and $x = b$ represents the probability that X assumes a value between a and b (see Fig. 16.1). Since this area is given by the definite integral $\int_a^b f(x)\, dx$, we have

$$P(a \le X \le b) = \int_a^b f(x)\, dx.$$

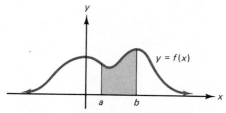

$P(a \le X \le b)$ = area of shaded region

FIGURE 16.1

We call the function f the *probability density function* for X (or simply the *density function* for X) and say that it defines the *distribution* of X. Because probabilities are always nonnegative, it is always true that $f(x) \ge 0$. Also, because the event $-\infty < X < \infty$ must occur, the total area under the density function curve must be 1. That is, $\int_{-\infty}^{\infty} f(x)\, dx = 1$. In summary we have the following.

Definition
*If X is a continuous random variable, then a function y = f(x) is called a (**probability) density function** for X if and only if it has the following properties:*

1. $f(x) \geq 0$.

2. $\int_{-\infty}^{\infty} f(x) \, dx = 1$.

3. $P(a \leq X \leq b) = \int_{a}^{b} f(x) \, dx$.

To illustrate a density function, we return to the previous experiment in which a number X is chosen at random from the interval $[0, 1]$. Recall that

$$P(a \leq X \leq b) = \text{length of } [a, b] = b - a, \tag{1}$$

where a and b are in $[0, 1]$. We shall show that the function

$$f(x) = \begin{cases} 1, & \text{if } 0 \leq x \leq 1, \\ 0, & \text{otherwise,} \end{cases} \tag{2}$$

whose graph appears in Fig. 16.2(a), is a density function for X. First, since $f(x)$

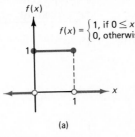

(a)   (b)

FIGURE 16.2

is either 0 or 1, we have $f(x) \geq 0$. Next, since $f(x) = 0$ for x outside $[0, 1]$,

$$\int_{-\infty}^{\infty} f(x) \, dx = \int_{0}^{1} 1 \, dx = x \Big|_{0}^{1} = 1.$$

Finally, to verify that $P(a \leq X \leq b) = \int_{a}^{b} f(x) \, dx$, we compute the area under the graph between $x = a$ and $x = b$ [Fig. 16.2(b)].

$$\int_{a}^{b} f(x) \, dx = \int_{a}^{b} 1 \, dx = x \Big|_{a}^{b} = b - a,$$

which, as stated in Eq. (1), is $P(a \leq X \leq b)$.

The function in Eq. (2) is called the **uniform density function** over $[0, 1]$, and X is said to have a **uniform distribution.** The word *uniform* is meaningful in the sense that the graph of the density function is horizontal, or "flat," over [0, 1]. As a result, X is just as likely to assume a value in one interval within [0, 1] as in another of equal length. A more general uniform distribution is given in Example 1.

EXAMPLE 1   The uniform density function over [a, b] for the random variable X is given by

$$f(x) = \begin{cases} \dfrac{1}{b-a}, & \text{if } a \leq x \leq b, \\ 0, & \text{otherwise.} \end{cases}$$

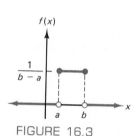

FIGURE 16.3

See Fig. 16.3. Note that over [a, b], the region under the graph is a rectangle with height $1/(b-a)$ and width $b-a$. Thus its area is $[1/(b-a)][b-a] = 1$; so $\int_{-\infty}^{\infty} f(x)\, dx = 1$, as must be the case for a density function. If [c, d] is any interval within [a, b], then

$$P(c \leq X \leq d) = \int_c^d f(x)\, dx = \int_c^d \frac{1}{b-a}\, dx$$

$$= \frac{x}{b-a}\bigg|_c^d = \frac{d-c}{b-a}.$$

For example, suppose X is uniformly distributed over the interval [1, 4] and we need to find $P(2 < X < 3)$. Then $a = 1$, $b = 4$, $c = 2$, and $d = 3$. Thus

$$P(2 < X < 3) = \frac{3-2}{4-1} = \frac{1}{3}.$$

EXAMPLE 2   *The density function for a random variable X is given by*

$$f(x) = \begin{cases} kx, & \text{if } 0 \leq x \leq 2, \\ 0, & \text{otherwise,} \end{cases}$$

where k is a constant.

a. *Find k.*

Since $\int_{-\infty}^{\infty} f(x)\, dx$ must be 1 and $f(x) = 0$ outside [0, 2], we have

$$\int_{-\infty}^{\infty} f(x)\, dx = \int_0^2 kx\, dx = \frac{kx^2}{2}\bigg|_0^2 = 2k = 1.$$

Thus $k = \frac{1}{2}$, so $f(x) = \frac{1}{2}x$ on [0, 2].

b. *Find $P(\frac{1}{2} < X < 1)$.*

$$P\left(\frac{1}{2} < X < 1\right) = \int_{1/2}^1 \frac{1}{2}x\, dx = \frac{x^2}{4}\bigg|_{1/2}^1 = \frac{1}{4} - \frac{1}{16} = \frac{3}{16}.$$

c. *Find $P(X < 1)$.*

Since $f(x) = 0$ for $x < 0$, we need only compute the area under the density function between 0 and 1.

$$P(X < 1) = \int_0^1 \frac{1}{2}x \, dx = \left.\frac{x^2}{4}\right|_0^1 = \frac{1}{4}.$$

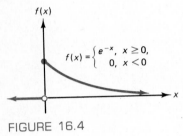

$f(x)$

$f(x) = \begin{cases} e^{-x}, & x \geq 0, \\ 0, & x < 0 \end{cases}$

FIGURE 16.4

EXAMPLE 3   The **exponential density function** *is defined by*

$$f(x) = \begin{cases} ke^{-kx}, & \text{if } x \geq 0, \\ 0, & \text{if } x < 0, \end{cases}$$

where k is a positive constant, called a **parameter,** *whose value depends on the experiment under consideration. If X is a random variable with this density function, then X is said to have an* **exponential distribution.** *Let $k = 1$. Then $f(x) = e^{-x}$ for $x \geq 0$, and $f(x) = 0$ for $x < 0$ (Fig. 16.4).*

a. *Find $P(2 < X < 3)$.*

$$P(2 < X < 3) = \int_2^3 e^{-x} \, dx = \left. -e^{-x}\right|_2^3$$

$$= -e^{-3} - (-e^{-2}) = e^{-2} - e^{-3}$$

$$= 0.13534 - 0.04979 = 0.086 \quad \text{(approximately)}.$$

b. *Find $P(X > 4)$.*

$$P(X > 4) = \int_4^\infty e^{-x} \, dx = \lim_{r \to \infty} \int_4^r e^{-x} \, dx$$

$$= \lim_{r \to \infty} \left. -e^{-x}\right|_4^r = \lim_{r \to \infty} (-e^{-r} + e^{-4})$$

$$= \lim_{r \to \infty} \left(-\frac{1}{e^r} + e^{-4} \right) = 0 + 0.01832$$

$$= 0.018 \quad \text{(approximately)}.$$

Alternatively, we can avoid an improper integral because

$$P(X > 4) = 1 - P(X \leq 4) = 1 - \int_0^4 e^{-x} \, dx.$$

The **cumulative distribution function** F for the continuous random variable X with density function f is defined by

$$F(x) = P(X \leq x) = \int_{-\infty}^x f(t) \, dt.$$

For example, $F(2)$ represents the entire area under the density curve that is to the left of the line $x = 2$ (Fig. 16.5). Under certain conditions of continuity, it can

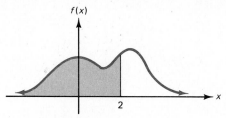

FIGURE 16.5

be shown that

$$F'(x) = f(x).$$

That is, the derivative of the cumulative distribution function is the density function. Thus F is an antiderivative of f, and by the Fundamental Theorem of Integral Calculus,

$$P(a < X < b) = \int_a^b f(x) \, dx = F(b) - F(a). \tag{3}$$

This means that the area under the density curve between a and b (Fig. 16.6) is simply the area to the left of b minus the area to the left of a.

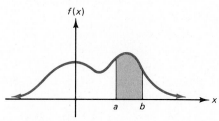

FIGURE 16.6

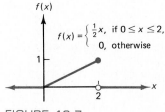

FIGURE 16.7

EXAMPLE 4   *Suppose X is a random variable with density function given by*

$$f(x) = \begin{cases} \frac{1}{2}x, & \text{if } 0 \leq x \leq 2, \\ 0, & \text{otherwise,} \end{cases}$$

as shown in Fig. 16.7.

a. *Find and sketch the cumulative distribution function.*

Because $f(x) = 0$ if $x < 0$, the area under the density curve to the left of $x = 0$ is 0. Thus $F(x) = 0$ if $x < 0$. If $0 \leq x \leq 2$, then

$$F(x) = \int_{-\infty}^x f(t) \, dt = \int_0^x \frac{1}{2} t \, dt = \left. \frac{t^2}{4} \right|_0^x = \frac{x^2}{4}.$$

Since f is a density function and $f(x) = 0$ for $x < 0$ and for $x > 2$, the area under the density curve from $x = 0$ to $x = 2$ is 1. Thus if $x > 2$, the area to the left of x is 1, so $F(x) = 1$. Hence the cumulative distribution function is

$$F(x) = \begin{cases} 0, & \text{if } x < 0, \\ \dfrac{x^2}{4}, & \text{if } 0 \le x \le 2, \\ 1, & \text{if } x > 2, \end{cases}$$

which is shown in Fig. 16.8.

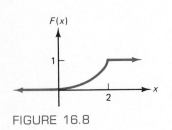

FIGURE 16.8

b. *Find $P(X < 1)$ and $P(1 < X < 1.1)$.*

Using the results of part (a), we have

$$P(X < 1) = F(1) = \frac{1^2}{4} = \frac{1}{4}.$$

From Eq. (3),

$$P(1 < X < 1.1) = F(1.1) - F(1) = \frac{1.1^2}{4} - \frac{1}{4} = 0.0525.$$

For a random variable X with density function f, the mean μ [or expectation $E(X)$] is given by

$$\mu = E(X) = \int_{-\infty}^{\infty} xf(x)\,dx,$$

and can be thought of as the "average" value of X in the long run. The variance σ^2 [or Var(X)] is given by

$$\sigma^2 = \text{Var}(X) = \int_{-\infty}^{\infty} (x - \mu)^2 f(x)\,dx.$$

You may have noticed that these formulas are similar to the corresponding ones in Chapter 7 for a discrete random variable. It can be shown that an alternative formula for variance is

$$\sigma^2 = \text{Var}(X) = \int_{-\infty}^{\infty} x^2 f(x)\,dx - \mu^2.$$

The standard deviation is σ, where

$$\sigma = \sqrt{\text{Var}(X)}.$$

For example, if X is exponentially distributed (see Example 3), it can be shown that $\mu = 1/k$ and $\sigma = 1/k$. As with a discrete random variable, the standard deviation of a continuous random variable X is small if X is likely to assume values close to the mean but unlikely to assume values far from the mean. It is large if the reverse is true.

EXAMPLE 5   *If X is a random variable with density function given by*

$$f(x) = \begin{cases} \frac{1}{2}x, & \text{if } 0 \le x \le 2, \\ 0, & \text{otherwise,} \end{cases}$$

find its mean and standard deviation.

The mean is given by

$$\mu = \int_{-\infty}^{\infty} xf(x)\, dx = \int_0^2 x \cdot \frac{1}{2}x\, dx = \frac{x^3}{6}\bigg|_0^2 = \frac{4}{3}.$$

By the alternative formula for variance, we have

$$\sigma^2 = \int_{-\infty}^{\infty} x^2 f(x)\, dx - \mu^2 = \int_0^2 x^2 \cdot \frac{1}{2}x\, dx - \left(\frac{4}{3}\right)^2$$

$$= \frac{x^4}{8}\bigg|_0^2 - \frac{16}{9} = 2 - \frac{16}{9} = \frac{2}{9}.$$

Thus the standard deviation is

$$\sigma = \sqrt{\frac{2}{9}} = \frac{\sqrt{2}}{3}.$$

We conclude this section by emphasizing that a density function for a continuous random variable must not be confused with a probability distribution function for a discrete random variable. Evaluating such a probability distribution function at a *point* gives a probability. But evaluating a density function at a point does not. Instead, the *area* under the density function curve over an *interval* is interpreted as a probability. That is, probabilities associated with a continuous random variable are given by integrals.

EXERCISE 16.1

1. Suppose X is a continuous random variable with density function given by

$$f(x) = \begin{cases} \frac{1}{6}(x + 1), & \text{if } 1 < x < 3, \\ 0, & \text{otherwise.} \end{cases}$$

   a. Find $P(1 < X < 2)$.
   b. Find $P(X < 2.5)$.
   c. Find $P(X \ge \frac{3}{2})$.
   d. Find c such that $P(X < c) = \frac{1}{2}$. Give your answer in radical form.

2. Suppose X is a continuous random variable with density function given by

$$f(x) = \begin{cases} \dfrac{1000}{x^2}, & \text{if } x > 1000, \\ 0, & \text{otherwise.} \end{cases}$$

   a. Find $P(3000 < X < 4000)$.
   b. Find $P(X > 2000)$.

3. Suppose X is a continuous random variable that is uniformly distributed on $[1, 4]$.
   a. What is the formula of the density function for X? Sketch its graph.
   b. Find $P(2 < X < 3)$.
   c. Find $P(0 < X < 1)$.
   d. Find $P(X \leq 3.5)$.
   e. Find $P(X > 2)$.
   f. Find $P(X = 3)$.
   g. Find $P(X < 5)$.
   h. Find μ.
   i. Find σ.
   j. Find the cumulative distribution function F and sketch its graph. Use F to find $P(X < 2)$ and $P(1 < X < 3)$.

4. Suppose X is a continuous random variable that is uniformly distributed on $[0, 5]$.
   a. What is the formula of the density function for X? Sketch its graph.
   b. Find $P(1 < X < 3)$.
   c. Find $P(4.5 \leq X < 5)$.
   d. Find $P(X = 4)$.
   e. Find $P(X > 1)$.
   f. Find $P(X < 5)$.
   g. Find $P(X > 5)$.
   h. Find μ.
   i. Find σ.
   j. Find the cumulative distribution function F and sketch its graph. Use F to find $P(1 < X < 3.5)$.

5. Suppose X is uniformly distributed on $[a, b]$.
   a. What is the density function for X?
   b. Find μ.
   c. Find σ^2 and σ.

6. Suppose X is a continuous random variable with density function given by

$$f(x) = \begin{cases} k, & \text{if } a \leq x \leq b, \\ 0, & \text{otherwise.} \end{cases}$$

   a. Show that $k = \dfrac{1}{b - a}$ and thus X is uniformly distributed.
   b. Find the cumulative distribution function F.

7. Suppose the random variable X is exponentially distributed with $k = 2$.
   a. Find $P(1 < X < 3)$.
   b. Find $P(X < 2)$.
   c. Find $P(X > 2.5)$.
   d. Find $P(\mu - \sigma < X < \mu + \sigma)$.
   e. Show that the area under the density function is 1.

8. Suppose the random variable X is exponentially distributed with $k = 0.5$.
   a. Find $P(X > 4)$.
   b. Find $P(0.5 < X < 2.6)$.
   c. Find $P(X < 5)$.
   d. Find $P(X = 4)$.
   e. Find c such that $P(0 < X < c) = \frac{1}{2}$.

9. The density function for a random variable X is given by

$$f(x) = \begin{cases} kx, & \text{if } 0 \leq x \leq 4, \\ 0, & \text{otherwise.} \end{cases}$$

   a. Find k.
   b. Find $P(2 < X < 3)$.
   c. Find $P(X > 2.5)$.
   d. Find $P(X > 0)$.
   e. Find μ.
   f. Find σ.
   g. Find c such that $P(X < c) = \frac{1}{2}$.
   h. Find $P(3 < X < 5)$.

10. The density function for a random variable X is given by

$$f(x) = \begin{cases} \frac{1}{2}x + k, & \text{if } 2 \leq x \leq 4, \\ 0, & \text{otherwise.} \end{cases}$$

   a. Find k.
   b. Find $P(X \geq 2.5)$.
   c. Find μ.
   d. Find $P(2 < X < \mu)$.

11. At a bus stop, the time X (in minutes) that a randomly arriving person must wait for a bus is uniformly distributed with density function given by $f(x) = \frac{1}{10}$ where $0 \le x \le 10$ and $f(x) = 0$ otherwise. What is the probability that such a person must wait at most 7 minutes? What is the average time that a person must wait?

12. An automatic soft-drink dispenser at a fast-food restaurant dispenses X ounces of cola in a 12-ounce drink. Suppose X is uniformly distributed over [11.92, 12.08]. What is the probability that less than 12 ounces will be dispensed? What is the probability that exactly 12 ounces will be dispensed? What is the average amount dispensed?

13. At a particular hospital, the length of time X (in hours) between successive arrivals at the emergency room is exponentially distributed with $k = 3$. What is the probability that more than 1 hour passes without an arrival?

14. The length of life X (in years) of an electronic component has an exponential distribution with $k = \frac{1}{5}$. What is the probability that such a component will fail within 4 years of use? What is the probability that it will last more than 6 years?

16.2 THE NORMAL DISTRIBUTION

Quite often, measured data in nature—such as heights of individuals in a population—are represented by a random variable whose density function may be approximated by the bell-shaped curve in Fig. 16.9. The curve extends indefinitely to the right and left and never touches the x-axis, although it appears to do so at points where the ordinates are close to zero. This curve, called the **normal curve**, is the graph of the most important of all density functions, the *normal density function*.

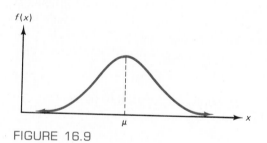

FIGURE 16.9

Definition

*A continuous random variable X is a **normal random variable** or has a **normal (or Gaussian*) distribution** if its density function is given by*

$$f(x) = \frac{1}{\sigma\sqrt{2\pi}} e^{-(1/2)[(x-\mu)/\sigma]^2}, \qquad -\infty < x < \infty,$$

*called the **normal density function**. The parameters μ and σ are the mean and standard deviation of X, respectively.*

Observe in Fig. 16.9 that $f(x) \to 0$ as $x \to \pm\infty$. That is, the normal curve has the x-axis as a horizontal asymptote. Also note that the normal curve is symmetric about the vertical line $x = \mu$. That is, the height of a point on the

* After the German mathematician Carl Friedrich Gauss (1777–1855).

curve d units to the right of $x = \mu$ is the same as the height of the point on the curve that is d units to the left of $x = \mu$. Because of this symmetry and the fact that the area under the normal curve is 1, the area to the right (left) of the mean must be $\frac{1}{2}$.

Each choice of values for μ and σ determines a different normal curve. The value of μ determines where the curve is "centered," and σ determines how "spread out" the curve is. The smaller the value of σ, the less spread out is the area near μ. For example, Fig. 16.10 shows normal curves C_1, C_2, and C_3, where C_1 has mean μ_1 and standard deviation σ_1, C_2 has mean μ_2, etc. Here

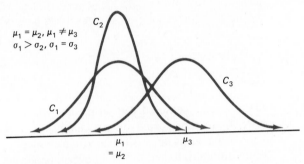

FIGURE 16.10

C_1 and C_2 have the same mean but different standard deviations: $\sigma_1 > \sigma_2$. C_1 and C_3 have the same standard deviation but different means: $\mu_1 < \mu_3$. Curves C_2 and C_3 have different means and different standard deviations.

The standard deviation plays a significant role in describing probabilities associated with a normal random variable X. More precisely, the probability that X will lie within one standard deviation of the mean is approximately 0.68:

$$P(\mu - \sigma < X < \mu + \sigma) = 0.68.$$

In other words, approximately 68 percent of the area under a normal curve is within one standard deviation of the mean (Fig. 16.11). Between $\mu \pm 2\sigma$ is

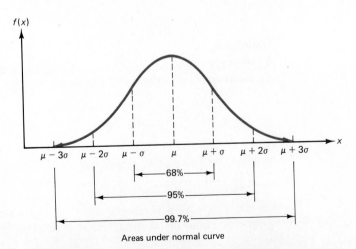

Areas under normal curve

FIGURE 16.11

about 95% of the area, and between $\mu \pm 3\sigma$ is about 99.7%:

$$P(\mu - 2\sigma < X < \mu + 2\sigma) = 0.95,$$
$$P(\mu - 3\sigma < X < \mu + 3\sigma) = 0.997.$$

Thus it is highly likely that X will lie within three standard deviations of the mean.

EXAMPLE 1   Let X be a random variable whose values are the test scores obtained on a nationwide test given to high school seniors. Suppose, for modeling purposes, X is normally distributed with mean 600 and standard deviation 90. Then the probability that X lies within $2\sigma = 2(90) = 180$ points of 600 is 0.95. In other words, 95% of the scores lie between 420 and 780. Similarly, 99.7% of the scores are within $3\sigma = 3(90) = 270$ points of 600—that is, between 330 and 870.

If Z is a normally distributed random variable with $\mu = 0$ and $\sigma = 1$, we obtain the normal curve, as in Fig. 16.12, called the **standard normal curve.**

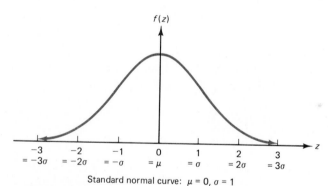

Standard normal curve: $\mu = 0, \sigma = 1$

FIGURE 16.12

Definition

*A continuous random variable Z is a **standard normal random variable** (or has a **standard normal distribution**) if its density function is given by*

$$f(z) = \frac{1}{\sqrt{2\pi}}e^{-z^2/2},$$

*called the **standard normal density function.** The variable Z has mean 0 and standard deviation 1.*

Because a standard normal random variable Z has mean 0 and standard deviation 1, its values are in units of standard deviations from the mean, which are called **standard units.** For example, if $0 < Z < 2.54$, then Z lies within 2.54 standard deviations to the right of 0, the mean. That is, $0 < Z < 2.54\sigma$.

To find $P(0 < Z < 2.54)$, we have

$$P(0 < Z < 2.54) = \int_0^{2.54} \frac{e^{-z^2/2}}{\sqrt{2\pi}}\, dz.$$

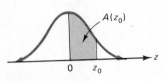

FIGURE 16.13

This integral cannot be evaluated by elementary methods. However, values for integrals of this kind have been computed and put in table form.

One such table is given in Appendix F. This table gives the area under a standard normal curve between $z = 0$ and $z = z_0$, where $z_0 \geq 0$. This area is shaded in Fig. 16.13 and is denoted by $A(z_0)$. In the left-hand columns of the table are z-values to the nearest tenth. The numbers across the top are the hundredths' values. For example, the entry in the row for 2.5 and column under 0.04 corresponds to $z = 2.54$ and is 0.4945. Thus the area under a standard normal curve between $z = 0$ and $z = 2.54$ is 0.4945:

$$P(0 < Z < 2.54) = A(2.54) = 0.4945.$$

Similarly, you should verify that $A(2) = 0.4772$ and $A(0.33) = 0.1293$.

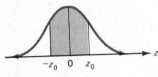

FIGURE 16.14

Using symmetry, we compute an area to the left of $z = 0$ by computing the corresponding area to the right of $z = 0$. For example,

$$P(-z_0 < Z < 0) = P(0 < Z < z_0) = A(z_0),$$

as shown in Fig. 16.14. Thus $P(-2.54 < Z < 0) = A(2.54) = 0.4945$.

When computing probabilities for a standard normal variable, you may have to add or subtract areas. A useful aid for doing this properly is a rough sketch of a standard normal curve in which you have shaded the entire area that you want to find, as Example 2 shows.

EXAMPLE 2   *Suppose Z is a standard normal variable.*

a. *Find $P(Z > 1.5)$.*

This probability is the area to the right of $z = 1.5$ (Fig. 16.15). This area is equal to the difference between the total area to the right of $z = 0$, which is 0.5, and the area between $z = 0$ and $z = 1.5$, which is $A(1.5)$. Thus

$$P(Z > 1.5) = 0.5 - A(1.5)$$

$$= 0.5 - 0.4332 = 0.0668.$$

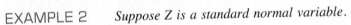

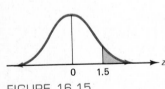

FIGURE 16.15

b. *Find $P(0.5 < Z < 2)$.*

This probability is the area between $z = 0.5$ and $z = 2$ (Fig. 16.16). This area is the difference of two areas. It is the area between $z = 0$ and $z = 2$, or $A(2)$, minus the area between $z = 0$ and $z = 0.5$, or $A(0.5)$. Thus

$$P(0.5 < Z < 2) = A(2) - A(0.5)$$

$$= 0.4772 - 0.1915 = 0.2857.$$

FIGURE 16.16

c. *Find $P(Z \leq 2)$.*

This probability is the area to the left of $z = 2$ (Fig. 16.17). This area is

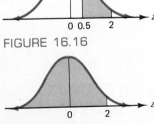

FIGURE 16.17

equal to the sum of the area to the left of $z = 0$, which is 0.5, and the area between $z = 0$ and $z = 2$, or $A(2)$. Thus

$$P(Z \le 2) = 0.5 + A(2)$$

$$= 0.5 + 0.4772 = 0.9772.$$

d. *Find* $P(-2 < Z < -0.5)$.

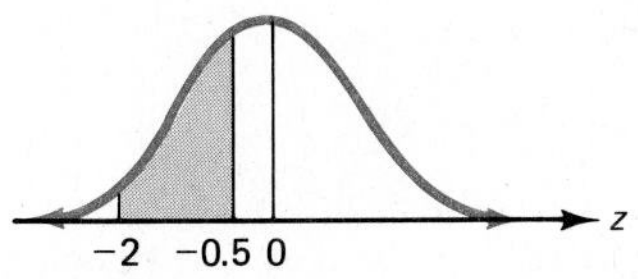

This probability is the area between $z = -2$ and $z = -0.5$ (Fig. 16.18). By symmetry, this is equal to the area between $z = 0.5$ and $z = 2$, which was computed in Part (b). We have

$$P(-2 < Z < -0.5) = P(0.5 < Z < 2)$$

$$= A(2) - A(0.5) = 0.2857.$$

e. *Find* z_0 *such that* $P(-z_0 < Z < z_0) = 0.9642$.

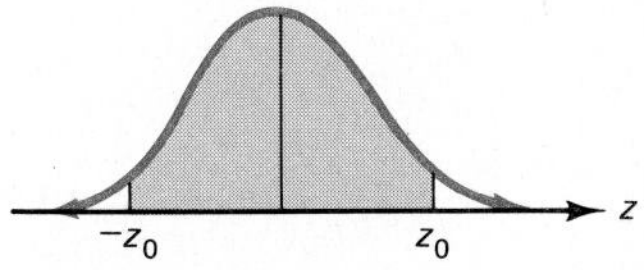

Figure 16.19 shows the corresponding area. Because the total area is 0.9642, by symmetry the area between $z = 0$ and $z = z_0$ is $\frac{1}{2}(0.9642) = 0.4821$, which is $A(z_0)$. Looking at the body of the table in Appendix F, we see that 0.4821 corresponds to a Z-value of 2.1. Thus $z_0 = 2.1$.

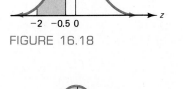

FIGURE 16.18

FIGURE 16.19

If X is normally distributed with mean μ and standard deviation σ, you might think that a table of areas is needed for each pair of values of μ and σ. Fortunately this is not the case. Appendix F is still used. But you must first express a given area as an equivalent area under a standard normal curve. This involves transforming X into a standard variable Z (with mean 0 and standard deviation 1) by using the following change of variable formula:

$$Z = \frac{X - \mu}{\sigma}. \tag{1}$$

On the right side, subtracting μ from X gives the distance from μ to X. Dividing by σ expresses this distance in terms of units of standard deviation. Thus Z is the number of standard deviations that X is from μ. That is, formula (1) converts units of X to standard units (Z-values). For example, if $X = \mu$, then using formula (1) gives $Z = 0$. Hence μ is zero standard deviations from μ.

Suppose X is normally distributed with $\mu = 4$ and $\sigma = 2$. To find—for example—$P(0 < X < 6)$, we first use formula (1) to convert the X-values 0 and 6 to Z-values (standard units).

$$z_1 = \frac{x_1 - \mu}{\sigma} = \frac{0 - 4}{2} = -2,$$

$$z_2 = \frac{x_2 - \mu}{\sigma} = \frac{6 - 4}{2} = 1.$$

It can be shown that

$$P(0 < X < 6) = P(-2 < Z < 1).$$

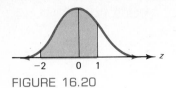

FIGURE 16.20

This means that the area under a normal curve with $\mu = 4$ and $\sigma = 2$ between $x = 0$ and $x = 6$ is equal to the area under a standard normal curve between $z = -2$ and $z = 1$ (Fig. 16.20). This area is the sum of the area A_1 between $z = -2$ and $z = 0$ and the area A_2 between $z = 0$ and $z = 1$. Using symmetry for A_1, we have

$$P(-2 < Z < 1) = A_1 + A_2 = A(2) + A(1)$$

$$= 0.4772 + 0.3413 = 0.8185.$$

EXAMPLE 3   *The weekly salaries of 5000 employees of a large corporation are assumed to be normally distributed with mean $300 and standard deviation $40. How many employees earn less than $250 per week?*

Converting to standard units, we have

$$P(X < 250) = P\left(Z < \frac{250 - 300}{40}\right)$$

$$= P(Z < -1.25).$$

This probability is the area shown in Fig. 16.21(a). By symmetry, this is equal to the area in Fig. 16.21(b) that corresponds to $P(Z > 1.25)$. This area is the

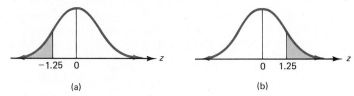

(a)   (b)

FIGURE 16.21

difference between the total area to the right of $z = 0$, which is .5, and the area between $z = 0$ and $z = 1.25$, which is $A(1.25)$. Thus

$$P(X < 250) = P(Z < -1.25) = P(Z > 1.25)$$

$$= 0.5 - A(1.25) = 0.5 - 0.3944$$

$$= 0.1056.$$

This means that 10.56% of the employees have salaries less than $250. This corresponds to $0.1056(5000) = 528$ employees.

EXERCISE 16.2

1. If Z is a standard normal random variable, find each of the following probabilities.
   a. $P(0 < Z < 1.8)$.
   b. $P(0.45 < Z < 2.81)$.
   c. $P(Z > -1.22)$.
   d. $P(Z \leq 2.93)$.
   e. $P(-2.61 < Z \leq 1.4)$
   f. $P(Z > 0.07)$.

2. If Z is a standard normal random variable, find each of the following.
   a. $P(-1.96 < Z < 1.96)$.
   b. $P(-2.11 < Z < -1.25)$.

c. $P(Z < -1.05)$.

e. $P(|Z| > 2)$.

d. $P(Z > 3\sigma)$.

f. $P(|Z| < \frac{1}{2})$.

In Problems 3–8, find z_0 such that the given statement is true. Assume that Z is a standard normal random variable.

3. $P(Z < z_0) = 0.5517$.

4. $P(Z < z_0) = 0.0668$.

5. $P(Z > z_0) = 0.8599$.

6. $P(Z > z_0) = 0.4960$.

7. $P(-z_0 < Z < z_0) = 0.2662$.

8. $P(|Z| > z_0) = 0.2186$.

9. If X is normally distributed with $\mu = 16$ and $\sigma = 4$, find each of the following probabilities.
   a. $P(X < 22)$.
   b. $P(X < 10)$.
   c. $P(10.8 < X < 12.4)$.

10. If X is normally distributed with $\mu = 200$ and $\sigma = 40$, find each of the following probabilities.
    a. $P(X > 150)$.
    b. $P(210 < X < 250)$.

11. If X is normally distributed with $\mu = -3$ and $\sigma = 2$, find $P(X > -2)$.

12. If X is normally distributed with $\mu = 0$ and $\sigma = 1.5$, find $P(X < 3)$.

13. If X is normally distributed with $\mu = 25$ and $\sigma^2 = 9$, find $P(19 < X \leq 28)$.

14. If X is normally distributed with $\mu = 8$ and $\sigma = 1$, find $P(X > \mu - \sigma)$.

15. If X is normally distributed with $\mu = 40$ and $P(X > 54) = 0.0401$, find σ.

16. If X is normally distributed with $\mu = 16$ and $\sigma = 2.25$, find x_0 such that the probability that X is between x_0 and 16 is 0.4641.

17. The scores on a national achievement test are normally distributed with mean 500 and standard deviation 100.

What percentage of those who took the test had a score greater than 630?

18. In a test given to a large group of people, the scores were normally distributed with mean 70 and standard deviation 10. What is the least whole-number score that a person could get and yet score in about the top 15%?

19. The heights (in inches) of adults in a large population are normally distributed with $\mu = 68$ and $\sigma = 3$. What percentage of the group is under 6 feet tall?

20. The yearly income for a group of 10,000 professional people is normally distributed with $\mu = \$30,00$ and $\sigma = \$2500$.
    a. What is the probability that a person from this group has a yearly income of less than $28,000?
    b. How many of these people have yearly incomes of over $35,000?

21. The IQs for a large population of children are normally distributed with mean 100.4 and standard deviation 11.6.
    a. What percentage of the children have IQs greater than 125?
    b. About 90% of the children have IQs greater than what value?

22. Suppose X is a random variable with $\mu = 10$ and $\sigma = 2$. If $P(4 < X < 16) = 0.25$, can X be normally distributed?

16.3 THE NORMAL APPROXIMATION TO THE BINOMIAL DISTRIBUTION

We conclude this chapter by bringing together the notions of a discrete random variable and a continuous random variable. Recall from Chapter 7 that if X is a binomial random variable (which is discrete), and if the probability of success on any trial is p, then for n independent trials,

$$P(X = x) = C_{n,x}p^x q^{n-x},$$

where $q = 1 - p$. You would no doubt agree that calculating probabilities for a binomial random variable can be quite tedious when the number of trials is large. For example, just imagine trying to compute $C_{100,40} (0.3)^{40}(0.7)^{60}$. To handle expressions like this, we can approximate a binomial distribution by a normal distribution and then use a table of areas to estimate a binomial probability.

To show how this is done, let us take a simple example. Figure 16.22 gives a probability histogram for a binomial experiment with $n = 10$ and $p = 0.5$.

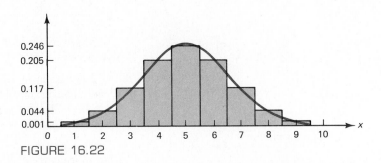

FIGURE 16.22

The rectangles centered at $x = 0$ and $x = 10$ are not shown because their heights are very close to 0. Superimposed on the histogram is a normal curve, which approximates it. The approximation would even be better if n were larger. That is, as n gets larger, then the width of each unit interval appears to get smaller and the outline of the histogram tends to take on the appearance of a smooth curve. In fact, *it is not unusual to think of a density curve as the limiting case of a probability histogram.* In spite of the fact that in our case n is only 10, the approximation shown does not seem too bad. The question that now arises is, "Which normal distribution approximates the binomial distribution?" Since the mean and standard deviation are measures of central tendency and dispersion of a random variable, we choose the approximating normal distribution to have the same mean and standard deviation as that of the binomial distribution. For this choice we can estimate the areas of rectangles in the histogram (that is, the binomial probabilities) by finding the corresponding area under the normal curve. In summary, we have the following:

> If X is a binomial random variable and n is sufficiently large, then the distribution of X can be approximated by a normal random variable whose mean and standard deviation are the same as for X, which are np and $\sqrt{npq}$, respectively.

Perhaps a word of explanation is appropriate concerning the phrase "n is sufficiently large." Generally speaking, a normal approximation to a binomial distribution is not good if n is small and p is near 0 or 1, because much of the area in the binomial histogram would be concentrated at one end of the distribution (that is, at 0 or n). Thus the distribution would not be fairly symmetric and a normal curve would not "fit" well. A general rule that you can follow is that the normal approximation to the binomial distribution is reasonable if np and nq are at least 5. This is the case in our example: $np = 10(0.5) = 5$ and $nq = 10(0.5) = 5$.

Let us now use the normal approximation to estimate a binomial probability for $n = 10$ and $p = 0.5$. If X denotes the number of successes, then its mean is $np = 10(0.5) = 5$ and its standard deviation is $\sqrt{npq} = \sqrt{10(0.5)(0.5)} = 1.58$. The probability function for X is given by

$$f(x) = C_{10,x}(0.5)^x(0.5)^{10-x}.$$

We approximate this distribution by the normal distribution with $\mu = 5$ and $\sigma = 1.58$.

Suppose we estimate the probability that there are between 4 and 7 successes, inclusive, which is given by

$$P(4 \leq X \leq 7) = P(X = 4) + P(X = 5) + P(X = 6) + P(X = 7)$$

$$= \sum_{x=4}^{7} C_{10,x}(0.5)^x(0.5)^{10-x}.$$

This probability is the sum of the areas of the *rectangles* for $X = 4, 5, 6,$ and 7 in Fig. 16.23. Under the normal curve we have shaded the corresponding area

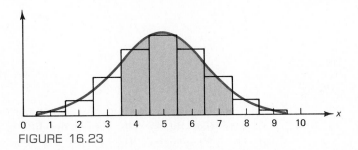

FIGURE 16.23

that we shall compute as an approximation to this probability. Note that the shading extends not from 4 to 7, but from $4 - \frac{1}{2}$ to $7 + \frac{1}{2}$, that is, from 3.5 to 7.5. This "continuity correction" of 0.5 on each end of the interval allows most of the area in the appropriate rectangles to be included in the approximation, and *such a correction must always be made*. The phrase *continuity correction* is used because X is treated as though it were a continuous random variable. We now convert the X-values 3.5 and 7.5 to Z-values.

$$z_1 = \frac{3.5 - 5}{1.58} = -0.95,$$

$$z_2 = \frac{7.5 - 5}{1.58} = 1.58.$$

Thus

$$P(4 \leq X \leq 7) \approx P(-0.95 \leq Z \leq 1.58),$$

which corresponds to the area under a standard normal curve between $z =$

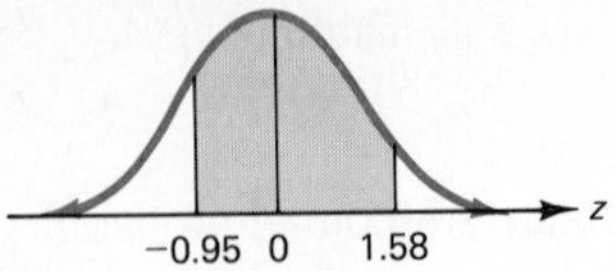

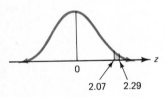

FIGURE 16.24

-0.95 and $z = 1.58$ (Fig. 16.24). This area is the sum of the area between $z = -0.95$ and $z = 0$, which by symmetry is $A(0.95)$, and the area between $z = 0$ and $z = 1.58$, which is $A(1.58)$. Hence

$$P(4 \le X \le 7) \approx P(-0.95 \le Z \le 1.58)$$
$$= A(0.95) + A(1.58)$$
$$= 0.3289 + 0.4429 = 0.7718.$$

This result is close to the true value 0.7734.

EXAMPLE 1   *Suppose X is a binomial random variable with $n = 100$ and $p = 0.3$. Estimate $P(X = 40)$ using the normal approximation.*

We have

$$P(X = 40) = C_{100,40}(0.3)^{40}(0.7)^{60},$$

which was mentioned at the beginning of this section. We use a normal distribution with $\mu = np = 100(0.3) = 30$ and $\sigma = \sqrt{npq} = \sqrt{100(0.3)(0.7)} = 4.58$. Converting the corrected X-values 39.5 and 40.5 to Z-values gives

$$z_1 = \frac{39.5 - 30}{4.58} = 2.07,$$

$$z_2 = \frac{40.5 - 30}{4.58} = 2.29.$$

Thus

$$P(X = 40) \approx P(2.07 \le Z \le 2.29).$$

FIGURE 16.25

This probability is the area under a standard normal curve between $z = 2.07$ and $z = 2.29$ (Fig. 16.25). This area is the difference of the area between $z = 0$ and $z = 2.29$, which is $A(2.29)$, and the area between $z = 0$ and $z = 2.07$, which is $A(2.07)$. Thus

$$P(X = 40) \approx P(2.07 \le Z \le 2.29)$$
$$= A(2.29) - A(2.07)$$
$$= 0.4890 - 0.4808 = 0.0082.$$

EXAMPLE 2   *In a quality-control experiment, a sample of 500 items is taken from an assembly line. Customarily, 8% of the items produced are defective. What is the probability that more than 50 defective items appear in the sample?*

If X is the number of defective items in the sample, then we shall consider X to be binomial with $n = 500$ and $p = 0.08$. To find $P(X \ge 51)$, we use the normal approximation to the binomial distribution with $\mu = np = 500(0.08) = 40$ and $\sigma = \sqrt{npq} = \sqrt{500(0.08)(0.92)} = 6.066$. Converting the corrected value 50.5

to a Z-value gives

$$z = \frac{50.5 - 40}{6.066} = 1.73$$

Thus

$$P(X \geq 51) \approx P(Z \geq 1.73).$$

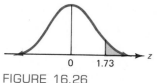

FIGURE 16.26

This probability is the area under a standard normal curve to the right of $z = 1.73$ (Fig. 16.26). This area is the difference of the area to the right of $z = 0$, which is 0.5, and the area between $z = 0$ and $z = 1.73$, which is $A(1.73)$. Thus

$$P(X \geq 51) \approx P(Z \geq 1.73)$$

$$= 0.5 - A(1.73) = 0.5 - 0.4582 = 0.0418.$$

EXERCISE 16.3

In Problems 1–4, X is a binomial random variable with the given values of n and p. Calculate the indicated probabilities by using the normal approximation.

1. $n = 150, p = 0.4.$ $P(X \leq 52), P(X \geq 74).$

2. $n = 50, p = 0.3.$ $P(X = 18), P(X \leq 18).$

3. $n = 200, p = 0.6.$ $P(X = 125), P(110 \leq X \leq 135).$

4. $n = 25, p = 0.25.$ $P(X \geq 5).$

5. Suppose a fair die is tossed 300 times. What is the probability that a 5 turns up between 45 and 60 times inclusive?

6. For a biased coin, $P(H) = 0.4$ and $P(T) = 0.6$. If the coin is tossed 200 times, what is the probability of getting between 90 and 100 heads, inclusive?

7. A delivery service has a fleet of 60 trucks. At any given time the probability of a truck being out of use due to factors such as breakdowns and maintenance is 0.1. What is the probability that 7 or more trucks are out of service at any time?

8. In a manufacturing plant, a sample of 100 items is taken from the assembly line. For each item in the sample, the probability of being defective is 0.06. What is the probability that there are 3 or more defective items in the sample?

9. In a true-false exam with 20 questions, what is the probability of getting at least 12 correct answers by just guessing on all the questions? If there are 100 questions

instead of 20, what is the probability of getting at least 60 correct answers by just guessing?

10. In a multiple-choice test with 50 questions, each question has four answers, only one of which is correct. If a student guesses on the last 20 questions, what is the probability of getting at least half of them correct?

11. In a poker game, the probability of being dealt a hand consisting of three cards of one suit and two cards of another suit (in any order) is about 0.1. In 100 dealt hands, what is the probability that 16 or more of them will be as described above?

12. A major cola company sponsors a national taste test, in which subjects sample its cola as well as the best-selling brand. Neither cola is identified by brand. The subjects are then asked to choose the cola that tastes better. If each of the 25 subjects in a supermarket actually have no preference and arbitrarily chose one of the colas, what is the probability that 15 or more of them choose the cola from the sponsoring company?

16.4 REVIEW

Important Terms and Symbols

Section 16.1   continuous random variable   density function   uniform density function
uniform distribution   exponential density function   exponential distribution
cumulative distribution function   mean, μ variance, σ^2 standard deviation, σ

Section 16.2   normal random variable   normal distribution   normal density function
standard normal curve   standard normal random variable
standard normal distribution   standard normal density function   standard units

Section 16.3   continuity correction

Summary

A continuous random variable X can assume any value in an interval or intervals. A density function for X is a function that has the following properties:

$$1.\ f(x) \geq 0, \qquad 2.\ \int_{-\infty}^{\infty} f(x)\ dx = 1, \qquad 3.\ P(a \leq X \leq b) = \int_{a}^{b} f(x)\ dx.$$

Property 3 means that the area under the graph of f and above the x-axis from $x = a$ to $x = b$ is $P(a \leq X \leq b)$. The probability that X assumes a particular value is 0.

The continuous random variable X has a uniform distribution over $[a, b]$ if its density function is given by

$$f(x) = \begin{cases} \dfrac{1}{b - a}, & \text{if } a \leq x \leq b \\ 0, & \text{otherwise.} \end{cases}$$

X has an exponential density function f if

$$f(x) = \begin{cases} ke^{-kx}, & x \geq 0, \\ 0, & x < 0, \end{cases}$$

where k is a positive constant.

The cumulative distribution function F for the continuous random variable X with density function f is given by

$$F(x) = P(X \leq x) = \int_{-\infty}^{x} f(t)\ dt.$$

Geometrically, $F(x)$ represents the area under the density curve to the left of x. By using F, we can find $P(a \leq x \leq b)$:

$$P(a \leq x \leq b) = F(b) - F(a).$$

The mean μ of X [or expectation $E(X)$] is given by

$$\mu = E(X) = \int_{-\infty}^{\infty} xf(x)\ dx;$$

the variance σ^2 is given by

$$\sigma^2 = \text{Var}(X) = \int_{-\infty}^{\infty} (x - \mu)^2 f(x)\ dx = \int_{-\infty}^{\infty} x^2 f(x)\ dx - \mu^2;$$

the standard deviation σ is given by

$$\sigma = \sqrt{\text{Var}(X)}.$$

The graph of the normal density function

$$f(x) = \frac{1}{\sigma\sqrt{2\pi}} e^{-(1/2)[(x-\mu)/\sigma]^2}$$

is called a normal curve and is bell-shaped. If X has a normal distribution, then the probability that X lies within one standard deviation of the mean μ is (approximately) 0.68; within two standard deviations the probability is 0.95; and within three standard deviations it is 0.997. If Z is a normal random variable with $\mu = 0$ and $\sigma = 1$, then Z is called a standard normal random variable. The probability $P(0 < Z < z_0)$ is the area under the graph of the standard normal curve from $z = 0$ to $z = z_0$ and is denoted $A(z_0)$. Values of $A(z_0)$ appear in Appendix F.

If X is normally distributed with mean μ and standard deviation σ, then X may be transformed into a standard normal random variable by the change of variable formula

$$Z = \frac{X - \mu}{\sigma}.$$

With this formula, probabilities for X may be found by using areas under the standard normal curve.

If X is a binomial random variable and the number n of independent trials is large, then the distribution of X may be approximated by using a normal random variable with mean np and with standard deviation $\sqrt{npq}$, where p is the probability of success on any trial and $q = 1 - p$. It is important that continuity corrections are considered when estimating binomial probabilities by a normal random variable.

Review Problems

1. Suppose X is a continuous random variable with density function given by
$$f(x) = \begin{cases} \frac{1}{3} + kx^2, & \text{if } 0 \le x \le 1, \\ 0, & \text{otherwise.} \end{cases}$$

   a. Find k.   **b.** Find $P(\frac{1}{2} < X < \frac{3}{4})$.
   c. Find $P(X \ge \frac{1}{2})$.   **d.** Find the cumulative distribution function.

2. Suppose X is exponentially distributed with $k = \frac{1}{4}$. Find $P(X > 1)$.

3. Suppose X is a random variable with density function given by
$$f(x) = \begin{cases} \frac{2}{9}x, & \text{if } 0 \le x \le 3, \\ 0, & \text{otherwise.} \end{cases}$$

   a. Find μ.   **b.** Find σ.

4. Suppose X is uniformly distributed over the interval $[2, 6]$. Find $P(X < 5)$.

Let X be normally distributed with mean 20 and standard deviation 4. In Problems 5–10, determine the given probabilities.

5. $P(X > 22)$.   6. $P(X < 21)$.   7. $P(12 < X < 18)$.

8. $P(X > 10)$.   9. $P(X < 16)$.   10. $P(22 < X < 32)$.

In Problems 11 and 12, X is a binomial random variable with $n = 100$ and $p = 0.35$. Find the given probabilities by using the normal approximation.

11. $P(25 \le X \le 47)$.   12. $P(X = 48)$.

13. The heights (in inches) of individuals in a certain group are normally distributed with mean 68 and standard deviation 2. Find the probability that an individual from this group is taller than 6 ft.

14. If a fair coin is tossed 400 times, use the normal approximation to the binomial distribution to estimate the probability that a head comes up at least 185 times.

CHAPTER 17

Multivariable Calculus

17.1 FUNCTIONS OF SEVERAL VARIABLES

Suppose a manufacturer produces two products, X and Y. Then the total cost depends on the levels of production of *both* X and Y. Table 17.1 is a schedule

TABLE 17.1

NO. OF UNITS OF X PRODUCED, x	NO. OF UNITS OF Y PRODUCED, y	TOTAL COST OF PRODUCTION, c
5	6	17
5	7	19
6	6	18
6	7	20

that indicates total cost at various levels. For example, when 5 units of X and 6 units of Y are produced, the total cost c is 17. In this situation, it seems natural to associate the number 17 with the *ordered pair* (5, 6):

$$(5, 6) \rightarrow 17.$$

The first element of the ordered pair, 5, represents the number of units of X produced, while the second element, 6, represents the number of units of Y produced. Corresponding to the other production situations, we have

$$(5, 7) \rightarrow 19,$$

$$(6, 6) \rightarrow 18,$$

and $\quad (6, 7) \rightarrow 20.$

This correspondence can be considered an input-output relation where the inputs are ordered pairs. With each input we associate exactly one output. Thus the correspondence defines a function f where

the domain consists of (5, 6), (5, 7), (6, 6), (6, 7),

and   the range consists of 17, 19, 18, 20.

In function notation,

$$f(5, 6) = 17, \quad f(5, 7) = 19,$$
$$f(6, 6) = 18, \quad f(6, 7) = 20.$$

We say that the total cost schedule can be described by $c = f(x, y)$, a function of the two independent variables x and y. The letter c is the dependent variable.

Turning to another function of two variables, we see that the equation

$$z = \frac{2}{x^2 + y^2}$$

defines z as a function of x and y:

$$z = f(x, y) = \frac{2}{x^2 + y^2}.$$

The domain of f is all ordered pairs of real numbers (x, y) for which the equation has meaning when the first and second elements of (x, y) are substituted for x and y, respectively, in the equation. Thus the domain of f is all ordered pairs except (0, 0). To find $f(2, 3)$, for example, we substitute $x = 2$ and $y = 3$ into $2/(x^2 + y^2)$. Hence $f(2, 3) = 2/(2^2 + 3^2) = 2/13$.

EXAMPLE 1

a. $f(x, y) = \dfrac{x + 3}{y - 2}$ is a function of two variables. Because the denominator is zero when $y = 2$, the domain of f is all (x, y) such that $y \neq 2$. Some function values are

$$f(0, 3) = \frac{0 + 3}{3 - 2} = 3,$$

$$f(3, 0) = \frac{3 + 3}{0 - 2} = -3.$$

Note that $f(0, 3) \neq f(3, 0)$.

b. $h(x, y) = 4x$ defines h as a function of x and y. The domain is all ordered pairs of real numbers. Some function values are

$$h(2, 5) = 4(2) = 8,$$
$$h(2, 6) = 4(2) = 8.$$

c. If $z^2 = x^2 + y^2$ and $x = 3$ and $y = 4$, then $z^2 = 3^2 + 4^2 = 25$. Consequently, $z = \pm 5$. Thus with the ordered pair (3, 4) we *cannot* associate exactly one output number. Hence z is *not* a function of x and y.

EXAMPLE 2   *On hot and humid days, many people tend to feel uncomfortable. The degree of discomfort is numerically given by the temperature-humidity index, THI, which is a function of two variables, t_d and t_w:*

$$\text{THI} = f(t_d, t_w) = 15 + 0.4(t_d + t_w),$$

where t_d is the dry-bulb temperature (in degrees Fahrenheit) and t_w is the wet-bulb temperature (in degrees Fahrenheit) of the air. Evaluate the THI when $t_d = 90$ and $t_w = 80$.

We want to find $f(90, 80)$.

$$f(90, 80) = 15 + 0.4(90 + 80) = 15 + 68 = 83.$$

When the THI is greater than 75, most people are uncomfortable. In fact, the THI was once called the "discomfort index." Many electric utilities closely follow this index so that they can anticipate the demand of air conditioning on their systems.

If $y = f(x)$ is a function of one variable, the domain of f can be geometrically represented by points on the real number line. The function itself can be represented by its graph in a coordinate plane, sometimes called a two-dimensional coordinate system. However, for a function of two variables, $z = f(x, y)$, its domain (consisting of ordered pairs of real numbers) can be geometrically represented by a *region* in the plane. The function itself can be geometrically represented in a **three-dimensional coordinate system.** Such a system is formed when three mutually perpendicular real number lines in space intersect at the origin of each line as in Fig. 17.1. The three number lines are called the x-, y-, and z-axes, and their point of intersection is called the origin of the system.

To each point P in space we can assign a unique ordered triple of numbers, called the *coordinates* of P. To do this [see Fig. 17.2(a)], from P we construct a line perpendicular to the x,y-plane, that is, the plane determined by the x- and y-axes. Let Q be the point where the line intersects this plane. From Q we construct

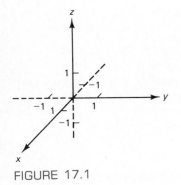

FIGURE 17.1

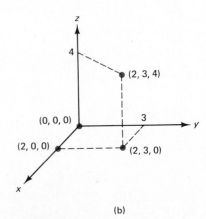

(a)   (b)

FIGURE 17.2

perpendiculars to the x- and y-axes. These lines intersect the x- and y-axes at x_0 and y_0, respectively. From P a perpendicular to the z-axis is constructed which intersects it at z_0. Thus to P we assign the ordered triple (x_0, y_0, z_0). It should also be evident that with each ordered triple of numbers we can assign a unique point in space. Due to this one-to-one correspondence between points in space and ordered triples, an ordered triple may be called a point. In Fig. 17.2(b) the points $(2, 0, 0)$, $(2, 3, 0)$, and $(2, 3, 4)$ are shown. Note that the origin corresponds to $(0, 0, 0)$.

We can represent geometrically a function of two variables, $z = f(x, y)$. To each ordered pair (x, y) in the domain of f we assign the point $(x, y, f(x, y))$. The set of all such points is called the *graph* of f. Such a graph appears in Fig. 17.3. You can consider $z = f(x, y)$ as representing a surface in space.*

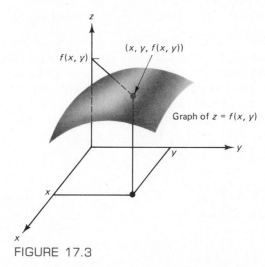

FIGURE 17.3

In Chapter 10, continuity of a function of one variable was discussed. If $y = f(x)$ is continuous, then the graph of f has no break in it. Extending this concept, we say that a function of two variables is continuous if its graph is an "unbroken surface."

Until now we have considered only functions of either one or two variables. In general, a **function of n variables** is one whose domain consists of ordered n-tuples $(x_1, x_2, \ldots, x_n)$. For example, $f(x, y, z) = 2x + 3y + 4z$ is a function of three variables with a domain consisting of all ordered triples. The function $g(x_1, x_2, x_3, x_4) = x_1 x_2 x_3 x_4$ is a function of four variables with a domain consisting of all ordered 4-tuples. Although functions of several variables are extremely important and useful, we cannot geometrically represent functions of more than two variables.

We now give a brief discussion of sketching surfaces in space. We begin with planes that are parallel to a coordinate plane. By a "coordinate plane" we mean a plane containing two coordinate axes. For example, the plane determined by the x- and y- axes is the x,y-**plane.** Similarly, we speak of the x,z-**plane** and

---

* We shall freely use the term "surface" in the intuitive sense.

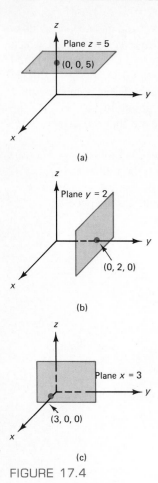

(a)

(b)

(c)

FIGURE 17.4

the **y,z-plane.** The coordinate planes divide space into eight parts, called *octants*. In particular, the part containing all points (x, y, z) where x, y, and $z > 0$ is called the **first octant.**

Suppose S is a plane that is parallel to the x,y-plane and passes through the point $(0, 0, 5)$ [see Fig. 17.4(a)]. Then the point (x, y, z) will lie on S if and only if $z = 5$; that is, x and y can be any real numbers, but z must equal 5. For this reason we say that $z = 5$ is an equation of S. Similarly, an equation of the plane parallel to the x,z-plane and passing through the point $(0, 2, 0)$ is $y = 2$ [Fig. 17.4(b)]. The equation $x = 3$ is an equation of the plane passing through $(3, 0, 0)$ and parallel to the y,z-plane [Fig. 17.4(c)]. Now let us look at planes in general.

In space the graph of an equation of the form

$$Ax + By + Cz + D = 0,$$

where D is a constant and A, B and C are constants that are not all zero, is a plane. Since three distinct points (not lying on the same line) determine a plane, a convenient way to sketch a plane is to first determine the points, if any, where the plane intersects the x-, y-, or z-axes. These points are called *intercepts*.

EXAMPLE 3   *Sketch the plane $2x + 3y + z = 6$.*

The plane intersects the x-axis when $y = 0$ and $z = 0$. Thus $2x = 6$, which gives $x = 3$. Similarly, if $x = z = 0$, then $y = 2$; if $x = y = 0$, then $z = 6$. Thus the intercepts are $(3, 0, 0)$, $(0, 2, 0)$, and $(0, 0, 6)$. The portion of the plane in the first octant is shown in Fig. 17.5(a).

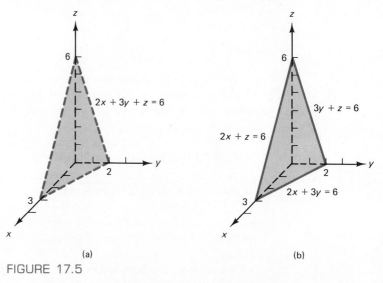

(a)   (b)

FIGURE 17.5

A surface can be sketched with the aid of its **traces.** These are the intersections of the surface with the coordinate planes. For the plane $2x + 3y + z = 6$ in Example 3, the trace in the x,y-plane is obtained by setting $z = 0$. This gives $2x + 3y = 6$, which is an equation of a *line* in the x,y-plane. Similarly, setting

$x = 0$ gives the trace in the y,z-plane: the line $3y + z = 6$. The x,z-trace is the line $2x + z = 6$ [see Fig. 17.5(b)].

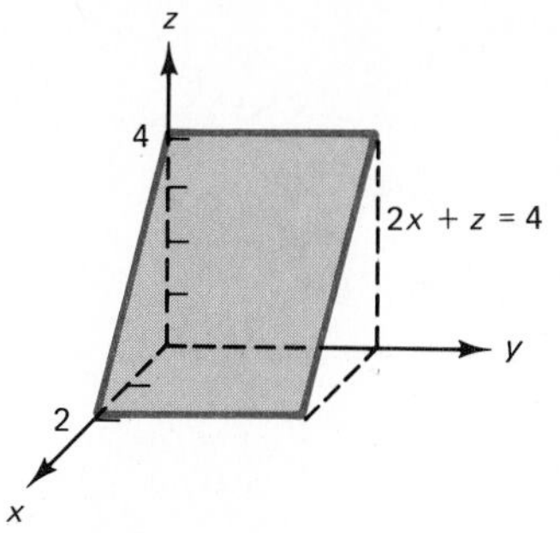

EXAMPLE 4   *Sketch the surface $2x + z = 4$.*

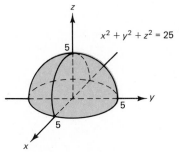

FIGURE 17.6

This equation has the form of a plane. The x- and z-intercepts are $(2, 0, 0)$ and $(0, 0, 4)$, and there is no y-intercept since x and z cannot both be zero. Setting $y = 0$ gives the x, z-trace $2x + z = 4$, which is a line in the x, z-plane. In fact, the intersection of the surface with *any* plane $y = k$ is also $2x + z = 4$. Hence the plane appears as in Fig. 17.6.

Our final examples deal with surfaces that are not planes but whose graphs can be easily obtained.

EXAMPLE 5   *Sketch the surface $z = x^2$.*

The x,z-trace is the curve $z = x^2$, which is a parabola. In fact, for *any* fixed value of y we get $z = x^2$. Thus the graph appears as in Fig. 17.7.

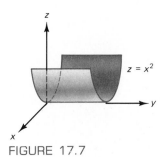

FIGURE 17.7

EXAMPLE 6   *Sketch the surface $x^2 + y^2 + z^2 = 25$.*

Setting $z = 0$ gives the x,y-trace $x^2 + y^2 = 25$, which is a circle of radius 5. Similarly, the y,z- and x,z-traces are the circles $y^2 + z^2 = 25$ and $x^2 + z^2 = 25$, respectively. Note also that since $x^2 + y^2 = 25 - z^2$, the intersection of the surface with the plane $z = k$, where $-5 \le k \le 5$, is a circle. For example, if $z = 3$, the intersection is the circle $x^2 + y^2 = 16$. If $z = 4$, the intersection is $x^2 + y^2 = 9$. That is, cross sections of the surface that are parallel to the x, y-plane are circles. A portion of the surface appears in Fig. 17.8. The entire surface is a sphere.

FIGURE 17.8

EXERCISE 17.1

In Problems 1–12, determine the indicated function values for the given functions.

1. $f(x, y) = 3x + y - 1$; $f(0, 4)$.

2. $f(x, y) = xy^2 + 2$; $f(1, -4)$.

3. $g(x, y, z) = ze^{x+y}$; $g(-2, 2, 6)$.

4. $g(x, y, z) = xy + xz + yz$; $g(1, 2, -3)$.

5. $h(r, s, t, u) = \dfrac{r + s^2}{t - u}$; $h(-3, 3, 5, 4)$.

6. $h(r, s, t, u) = \ln(ru)$; $h(1, 5, 3, 1)$.

7. $g(p_A, p_B) = 2p_A(p_A^2 - 5)$; $g(4, 8)$.

8. $g(p_A, p_B) = p_A\sqrt{p_B} + 10$; $g(8, 4)$.

9. $F(x, y, z) = 3$; $F(2, 0, -1)$.

10. $F(x, y, z) = \dfrac{x}{yz}$; $F(0, 0, 3)$.

11. $f(x, y) = 2x - 5y + 4$; $f(x_0 + h, y_0)$.

12. $f(x, y) = x^2y - 3y^3$; $f(r + t, r)$.

13. A method of ecological sampling to determine animal populations in a given area involves first marking all the animals obtained in a sample of R animals from the area and then releasing them so that they can mix with un-marked animals. At a later date a second sample is taken of M animals and the number of these which are marked, S, are noted. Based on R, M, and S an estimate of the total population of animals, N, in the sample area is given by

$$N = f(R, M, S) = \frac{RM}{S}.$$

Find $f(400, 400, 80)$. This method is called the *mark and recapture procedure*,*

14. Under certain conditions, if two brown-eyed parents have exactly k children, the probability $P = P(r, k)$ that there will be exactly r blue-eyed children is given by

$$P(r, k) = \frac{k!(\frac{1}{4})^r(\frac{3}{4})^{k-r}}{r!(k - r)!}, \qquad r = 0, 1, 2, \ldots, k.$$

Find the probability that out of a total of four children exactly three will be blue-eyed.

In Problems **15–18**, *find equations of the planes that satisfy the given conditions.*

15. Parallel to the x,z-plane and passes through the point $(0, -4, 0)$.

16. Parallel to the y,z-plane and passes through the point $(8, 0, 0)$.

17. Parallel to the x,y-plane and passes through the point $(2, 7, 6)$.

18. Parallel to the y,z-plane and passes through the point $(-4, -2, 7)$.

In Problems **19–28**, *sketch the given surfaces.*

19. $x + y + z = 1$.

20. $2x + y + 2z = 6$.

21. $3x + 6y + 2z = 12$.

22. $x + 2y + 3z = 4$.

23. $x + 2y = 2$.

24. $y + z = 1$.

25. $z = 4 - x^2$.

26. $y = x^2$.

27. $x^2 + y^2 + z^2 = 1$.

28. $x^2 + y^2 = 1$.

17.2 PARTIAL DERIVATIVES

Figure 17.9 shows the surface $z = f(x, y)$ and a plane that is parallel to the x,z-plane and that passes through the point $(x_0, y_0, f(x_0, y_0))$ on the surface. An equation of this plane is $y = y_0$. Hence any point on the curve that is the inter-section of the surface with the plane must have the form $(x, y_0, f(x, y_0))$. Thus the curve can be described by $z = f(x, y_0)$. Since y_0 is constant, $z = f(x, y_0)$

* E. P. Odum, *Ecology* (New York: Holt, Rinehart and Winston, 1966).

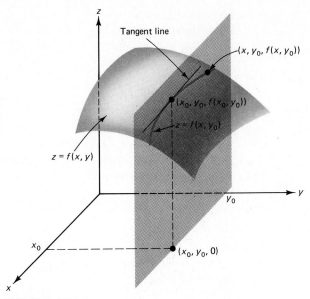

FIGURE 17.9

can be considered a function of one variable, x. When the derivative of this function is evaluated at x_0, it gives the slope of the tangent line to this curve at $(x_0, y_0, f(x_0, y_0))$ (see Fig. 17.9). This slope is called the *partial derivative of f with respect to x* at (x_0, y_0) and is denoted $f_x(x_0, y_0)$. In terms of limits,

$$f_x(x_0, y_0) = \lim_{h \to 0} \frac{f(x_0 + h, y_0) - f(x_0, y_0)}{h}. \tag{1}$$

On the other hand, in Fig. 17.10 the plane $x = x_0$ is parallel to the y,z-

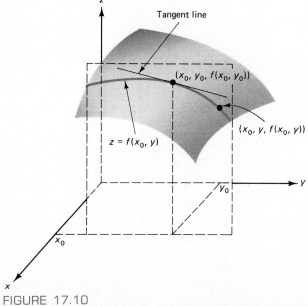

FIGURE 17.10

plane and cuts the surface $z = f(x, y)$ in a curve given by $z = f(x_0, y)$, a function of y. When the derivative of this function is evaluated at y_0, it gives the slope of the tangent line to this curve at the point $(x_0, y_0, f(x_0, y_0))$. This slope is called the *partial derivative of f with respect to y* at (x_0, y_0) and is denoted $f_y(x_0, y_0)$. In terms of limits,

$$f_y(x_0, y_0) = \lim_{h \to 0} \frac{f(x_0, y_0 + h) - f(x_0, y_0)}{h}. \tag{2}$$

Sometimes $f_x(x_0, y_0)$ is said to be the slope of the tangent line to the graph of f at $(x_0, y_0, f(x_0, y_0))$ *in the x-direction*; similarly, $f_y(x_0, y_0)$ is the slope of the tangent line *in the y-direction*.

For generality, by replacing x_0 and y_0 in Eqs. (1) and (2) by x and y, respectively, we get the following definition.

Definition

*If $z = f(x, y)$, the **partial derivative of f with respect to x**, denoted f_x, is the function given by*

$$f_x(x, y) = \lim_{h \to 0} \frac{f(x + h, y) - f(x, y)}{h},$$

provided this limit exists.
*The **partial derivative of f with respect to y**, denoted f_y, is the function given by*

$$f_y(x, y) = \lim_{h \to 0} \frac{f(x, y + h) - f(x, y)}{h},$$

provided this limit exists.

From the definition, we see that to find f_x we treat y as a constant and differentiate f with respect to x in the usual way. Similarly, to find f_y we treat x as a constant and differentiate f with respect to y.

EXAMPLE 1   *If $f(x, y) = xy^2 + x^2y$, find $f_x(x, y)$ and $f_y(x, y)$. Also find $f_x(3, 4)$ and $f_y(3, 4)$.*

To find $f_x(x, y)$, we treat y as a constant and differentiate f with respect to x:

$$f_x(x, y) = (1)y^2 + (2x)y = y^2 + 2xy.$$

To find $f_y(x, y)$ we treat x as a constant and differentiate with respect to y.

$$f_y(x, y) = x(2y) + x^2(1) = 2xy + x^2.$$

Note that $f_x(x, y)$ and $f_y(x, y)$ are each functions of the two variables x and y. To find $f_x(3, 4)$ we evaluate $f_x(x, y)$ when $x = 3$ and $y = 4$.

$$f_x(3, 4) = 4^2 + 2(3)(4) = 40.$$

Similarly,

$$f_y(3, 4) = 2(3)(4) + 3^2 = 33.$$

Notations for partial derivatives of $z = f(x, y)$ are in Table 17.2. Table 17.3 gives notations for partial derivatives evaluated at (x_0, y_0).

TABLE 17.2

PARTIAL DERIVATIVE OF f(OR z) WITH RESPECT TO x	PARTIAL DERIVATIVE OF f(OR z) WITH RESPECT TO y
$f_x(x, y)$	$f_y(x, y)$
$\dfrac{\partial}{\partial x}[f(x, y)]$	$\dfrac{\partial}{\partial y}[f(x, y)]$
$\dfrac{\partial z}{\partial x}$	$\dfrac{\partial z}{\partial y}$

TABLE 17.3

PARTIAL DERIVATIVE OF f (OR z) WITH RESPECT TO x EVALUATED AT (x_0, y_0)	PARTIAL DERIVATIVE OF f (OR z) WITH RESPECT TO y EVALUATED AT (x_0, y_0)
$f_x(x_0, y_0)$	$f_y(x_0, y_0)$
$\dfrac{\partial z}{\partial x}\bigg|_{(x_0, y_0)}$	$\dfrac{\partial z}{\partial y}\bigg|_{(x_0, y_0)}$
$\dfrac{\partial z}{\partial x}\bigg|_{\substack{x=x_0 \\ y=y_0}}$	$\dfrac{\partial z}{\partial y}\bigg|_{\substack{x=x_0 \\ y=y_0}}$

EXAMPLE 2

a. *If $z = 3x^3y^3 - 9x^2y + xy^2 + 4y$, find $\dfrac{\partial z}{\partial x}, \dfrac{\partial z}{\partial y}, \dfrac{\partial z}{\partial x}\bigg|_{(1,0)}$ and $\dfrac{\partial z}{\partial y}\bigg|_{(1,0)}$.*

To find $\partial z/\partial x$ we differentiate z with respect to x while treating y as a constant:

$$\frac{\partial z}{\partial x} = 3(3x^2)y^3 - 9(2x)y + (1)y^2 + 0$$

$$= 9x^2y^3 - 18xy + y^2.$$

Evaluating at $(1, 0)$, we obtain

$$\frac{\partial z}{\partial x}\bigg|_{(1,0)} = 9(1)^2(0)^3 - 18(1)(0) + 0^2 = 0.$$

To find $\partial z/\partial y$ we differentiate z with respect to y while treating x as a constant:

$$\frac{\partial z}{\partial y} = 3x^3(3y^2) - 9x^2(1) + x(2y) + 4(1)$$

$$= 9x^3y^2 - 9x^2 + 2xy + 4.$$

Thus

$$\left.\frac{\partial z}{\partial y}\right|_{(1,0)} = 9(1)^3(0)^2 - 9(1)^2 + 2(1)(0) + 4 = -5.$$

b. *If* $w = x^2 e^{2x+3y}$, *find* $\partial w/\partial x$ *and* $\partial w/\partial y$.

To find $\partial w/\partial x$, we treat y as a constant and differentiate with respect to x. Since $x^2 e^{2x+3y}$ is a product of two functions, each involving x, we use the product rule.

$$\frac{\partial w}{\partial x} = x^2 \frac{\partial}{\partial x}(e^{2x+3y}) + e^{2x+3y}\frac{\partial}{\partial x}(x^2)$$

$$= x^2(2e^{2x+3y}) + e^{2x+3y}(2x)$$

$$= 2x(x + 1)e^{2x+3y}.$$

To find $\partial w/\partial y$, we treat x as a constant and differentiate with respect to y.

$$\frac{\partial w}{\partial y} = x^2 \frac{\partial}{\partial y}(e^{2x+3y}) = 3x^2 e^{2x+3y}.$$

We have seen that for a function of two variables, two partial derivatives can be considered. Actually the concept of partial derivatives can be extended to functions of more than two variables. For example, with $w = f(x, y, z)$ we have three partial derivatives:

the partial with respect to x, denoted $f_x(x, y, z)$, $\partial w/\partial x$, etc.;

the partial with respect to y, denoted $f_y(x, y, z)$, $\partial w/\partial y$, etc.;

and   the partial with respect to z, denoted $f_z(x, y, z)$, $\partial w/\partial z$, etc.

To determine $\partial w/\partial x$, treat y and z as constants and differentiate w with respect to x. For $\partial w/\partial y$, treat x and z as constants and differentiate with respect to y. For $\partial w/\partial z$, treat x and y as constants and differentiate with respect to z. With a function of n variables we have n partial derivatives, which are determined in the obvious way.

EXAMPLE 3

a. *If* $f(x, y, z) = x^2 + y^2 z + z^3$, *find* $f_x(x, y, z)$, $f_y(x, y, z)$, *and* $f_z(x, y, z)$.

To find $f_x(x, y, z)$, we treat y and z as constants and differentiate f with respect to x.

$$f_x(x, y, z) = 2x.$$

Treating x and z as constants and differentiating with respect to y, we have

$$f_y(x, y, z) = 2yz.$$

Treating x and y as constants and differentiating with respect to z, we have

$$f_z(x, y, z) = y^2 + 3z^2.$$

b. *If* $p = g(r, s, t, u) = \dfrac{rsu}{rt^2 + s^2t}$, *find* $\dfrac{\partial p}{\partial s}$, $\dfrac{\partial p}{\partial t}$, *and* $\dfrac{\partial p}{\partial t}\bigg|_{(0,1,1,1)}$.

To find $\partial p/\partial s$, first note that p is a quotient of two functions, each involving the variable s. Thus we use the quotient rule and treat r, t, and u as constants.

$$\frac{\partial p}{\partial s} = \frac{(rt^2 + s^2t)\dfrac{\partial}{\partial s}(rsu) - rsu\dfrac{\partial}{\partial s}(rt^2 + s^2t)}{(rt^2 + s^2t)^2}$$

$$= \frac{(rt^2 + s^2t)(ru) - (rsu)(2st)}{(rt^2 + s^2t)^2}.$$

Simplifying gives

$$\frac{\partial p}{\partial s} = \frac{ru(rt - s^2)}{t(rt + s^2)^2}.$$

To find $\partial p/\partial t$ we can first write p as

$$p = rsu(rt^2 + s^2t)^{-1}.$$

Next we use the power rule and treat r, s, and u as constants.

$$\frac{\partial p}{\partial t} = rsu(-1)(rt^2 + s^2t)^{-2}\frac{\partial}{\partial t}(rt^2 + s^2t)$$

$$= -rsu(rt^2 + s^2t)^{-2}(2rt + s^2).$$

$$\frac{\partial p}{\partial t} = -\frac{rsu(2rt + s^2)}{(rt^2 + s^2t)^2}.$$

Letting $r = 0$, $s = 1$, $t = 1$ and $u = 1$ gives

$$\frac{\partial p}{\partial t}\bigg|_{(0,1,1,1)} = -\frac{0(1)(1)[2(0)(1) + (1)^2]}{[0(1)^2 + (1)^2(1)]^2} = 0.$$

EXERCISE 17.2

In each of Problems 1–26, find all partial derivatives.

1. $f(x, y) = x - 5y + 3$.

2. $f(x, y) = 4 - 5x^2 + 6y^3$.

3. $f(x, y) = 3x - 4$.

4. $f(x, y) = \sqrt{7}$.

5. $g(x, y) = x^5y^4 - 3x^4y^3 + 7x^3 + 2y^2 - 3xy + 4$.

6. $g(x, y) = x^8 - 2x^6y^5 + 3x^5y^3 + x^3y^3 + 3x - 4$.

7. $g(p, q) = \sqrt{pq}$.

8. $g(w, z) = \sqrt[3]{w^2 + z^2}$.

9. $h(s, t) = \dfrac{s^2 + 4}{t - 3}$.

10. $h(u, v) = \dfrac{4uv^2}{u^2 + v^2}$.

11. $u(q_1, q_2) = \frac{3}{4} \ln q_1 + \frac{1}{4} \ln q_2$.

12. $Q(l, k) = 3l^{0.41}k^{0.59}$.

13. $h(x, y) = \dfrac{x^2 + 3xy + y^2}{\sqrt{x^2 + y^2}}$.

14. $h(x, y) = \dfrac{\sqrt{x + 4}}{x^2y + y^2x}$.

15. $z = e^{5xy}$.

16. $z = (x^2 + y)e^{3x + 4y}$.

17. $z = 5x \ln(x^2 + y)$.

18. $z = \ln(3x^2 + 4y^4)$.

19. $f(r, s) = \sqrt{r + 2s}(r^3 - 2rs + s^2)$.

20. $f(r, s) = \sqrt{rs}\, e^{2+r}$.

21. $f(r, s) = e^{3-r} \ln(7 - s)$.

22. $f(r, s) = (5r^2 + 3s^3)(2r - 5s)$.

23. $g(x, y, z) = 3x^2y + 2xy^2z + 3z^3$.

24. $g(x, y, z) = x^2y^3z^5 - 3x^2y^4z^3 + 5xz$.

25. $g(r, s, t) = e^{s+t}(r^2 + 7s^3)$.

26. $g(r, s, t, u) = rs \ln(2t + 5u)$.

In Problems **27–32,** *evaluate the given partial derivatives.*

27. $f(x, y) = x^3y + 7x^2y^2$; $f_x(1, -2)$.

28. $z = \sqrt{5x^2 + 3xy + 2y}$; $\left. \dfrac{\partial z}{\partial x} \right|_{\substack{x=0 \\ y=2}}$.

29. $g(x, y, z) = e^x\sqrt{y + 2z}$; $g_z(0, 1, 4)$.

30. $g(x, y, z) = \dfrac{3x^2 + 2y}{xy + xz}$; $g_y(1, 1, 1)$.

31. $h(r, s, t, u) = (s^2 + tu) \ln(2r + 7st)$; $h_s(1, 0, 0, 1)$.

32. $h(r, s, t, u) = \dfrac{7r + 3s^2u^2}{s}$; $h_t(4, 3, 2, 1)$.

33. In a discussion of inventory theory of money demand, Swanson* considers the function

$$F(b, C, T, i) = \frac{bT}{C} + \frac{iC}{2}$$

and determines that $\dfrac{\partial F}{\partial C} = -\dfrac{bT}{C^2} + \dfrac{i}{2}$. Verify this partial derivative.

34. In a discussion of stock prices of a dividend cycle, Palmon and Yaari† consider the function f given by

$$u = f(t, r, z) = \frac{(1 + r)^{1-z} \ln(1 + r)}{(1 + r)^{1-z} - t},$$

where u is the instantaneous rate of ask-price appreciation, r is an annual opportunity rate of return, z is the fraction of a dividend cycle over which a share of stock

is held by a midcycle seller, and t is the effective rate of capital gains tax. They claim that

$$\frac{\partial u}{\partial z} = \frac{t(1 + r)^{1-z} \ln^2(1 + r)}{[(1 + r)^{1-z} - t]^2}.$$

Verify this.

35. In an analysis of advertising and profitability, Swales‡ considers a function f given by

$$R = f(r, a, n) = \frac{r}{1 + a\,\dfrac{n - 1}{2}},$$

where R is adjusted rate of profit, r is accounting rate of profit, a is a measure of advertising expenditures, and n is the number of years that advertising fully depreciates. In the analysis Swales determines $\partial R/\partial n$. Find this partial derivative.

* P. E. Swanson, "Integer Constraints on the Inventory Theory of Money Demand," *Quarterly Journal of Business and Economics*, 23, no. 1 (1984), 32–37.

† D. Palmon and U. Yaari, "Taxation of Capital Gains and the Behavior of Stock Prices over the Dividend Cycle," *The American Economist*, XXVII, no. 1 (1983), 13–22.

‡ J. K. Swales, "Advertising as an Intangible Asset: Profitability and Entry Barriers: A Comment on Reekie and Bhoyrub," *Applied Economics*, 17, no. 4 (1985), 603–17.

36. In an article on interest rate deregulation, Christofi and Agapos* arrive at the equation

$$r_L = r + D\frac{\partial r}{\partial D} + \frac{dC}{dD},$$ (3)

where r is the deposit rate paid by commercial banks, r_L is the rate earned by commercial banks, C is the administrative cost of transforming deposits into return-earning assets, and D is the savings deposits level.

Christofi and Agapos state that

$$r_L = r\left[\frac{1 + \eta}{\eta}\right] + \frac{dC}{dD},$$ (4)

where η is the deposit elasticity with respect to the deposit rate and is given by $\eta = \dfrac{r/D}{\partial r/\partial D}$. Express Eq. (3) in terms of η to verify Eq. (4).

17.3 APPLICATIONS OF PARTIAL DERIVATIVES _____

Suppose a manufacturer produces x units of product X and y units of product Y. Then the total cost c of these units is a function of x and y and is called a **joint-cost function.** If such a function is $c = f(x, y)$, then $\partial c/\partial x$ is called the **(partial) marginal cost with respect to x.** It is the rate of change of c with respect to x when y is held fixed. Similarly, $\partial c/\partial y$ is the **(partial) marginal cost with respect to y.** It is the rate of change of c with respect to y when x is held fixed.

For example, if c is expressed in dollars and $\partial c/\partial y = 2$, then the cost of producing an extra unit of Y when the level of production of X is fixed is approximately two dollars.

If a manufacturer produces n products, the joint-cost function is a function of n variables and there are n (partial) marginal cost functions.

EXAMPLE 1 *A company manufactures two types of skis, the Lightning and the Alpine models. Suppose the joint-cost function for producing x pairs of the Lightning model and y pairs of the Alpine model per week is $c = f(x, y) = 0.06x^2 + 7x + 15y + 1000$, where c is expressed in dollars. Determine the marginal costs $\partial c/\partial x$ and $\partial c/\partial y$ when $x = 100$ and $y = 50$ and interpret the results.*

The marginal costs are

$$\frac{\partial c}{\partial x} = 0.12x + 7 \quad \text{and} \quad \frac{\partial c}{\partial y} = 15.$$

---

* A. Christofi and A. Agapos, ''Interest Rate Deregulation: An Empirical Justification,'' *Review of Business and Economic Research*, XX (1984), 39–49.

Thus

$$\left.\frac{\partial c}{\partial x}\right|_{(100,50)} = 0.12(100) + 7 = 19 \tag{1}$$

and $\left.\dfrac{\partial c}{\partial y}\right|_{(100,50)} = 15.$ $\tag{2}$

Equation (1) means that increasing the output of the Lightning model from 100 to 101, while maintaining production of the Alpine model at 50, increases costs by approximately \$19. Equation (2) means that increasing output of the Alpine model from 50 to 51 and holding production of the Lightning model at 100 will increase costs by approximately \$15. In fact, since $\partial c/\partial y$ is a constant function, the marginal cost with respect to y is \$15 at all levels of production.

EXAMPLE 2   *On a cold day a person may feel colder when the wind is blowing than when the wind is calm because the rate of heat loss is a function of both temperature and wind speed. The equation*

$$H = (10.45 + 10\sqrt{w} - w)(33 - t)$$

indicates the rate of heat loss H (in kilocalories per square meter per hour) when the air temperature is t (in degrees Celsius) and the wind speed is w (in meters per second). For H = 2000, exposed flesh will freeze in one minute.[*]

a. *Evaluate H when $t = 0$ and $w = 4$.*

b. *Evaluate $\partial H/\partial w$ and $\partial H/\partial t$ when $t = 0$ and $w = 4$, and interpret the results.*

c. *When $t = 0$ and $w = 4$, which has a greater effect on H: a change in wind speed of 1 m/s or a change in temperature of 1°C?*

a. When $t = 0$ and $w = 4$, then

$$H = (10.45 + 10\sqrt{4} - 4)(33 - 0) = 872.85.$$

b. $\dfrac{\partial H}{\partial w} = \left(\dfrac{5}{\sqrt{w}} - 1\right)(33 - t), \qquad \left.\dfrac{\partial H}{\partial w}\right|_{\substack{t=0 \\ w=4}} = 49.5;$

$\dfrac{\partial H}{\partial t} = (10.45 + 10\sqrt{w} - w)(-1), \qquad \left.\dfrac{\partial H}{\partial t}\right|_{\substack{t=0 \\ w=4}} = -26.45.$

This means that when $t = 0$ and $w = 4$, then increasing w by a small amount while keeping t fixed will make H increase approximately 49.5 times as much as w increases. Increasing t by a small amount while keeping w fixed will make H *decrease* approximately 26.45 times as much as t increases.

c. Since the partial derivative of H with respect to w is greater in magnitude than the partial with respect to t when $t = 0$ and $w = 4$, a change in wind speed of 1 m/s has a greater effect on H.

---

[*] G. E. Folk, Jr., *Textbook of Environmental Physiology*, 2nd ed. (Philadelphia: Lea & Febiger, 1974).

Output of a product depends on many factors of production. Among these may be labor, capital, land, machinery, and so on. Suppose output depends only on labor and capital. If the function $P = f(l, k)$ gives the output P when the producer uses l units of labor and k units of capital, then this function is called a **production function.** We define the **marginal productivity with respect to l** to be $\partial P/\partial l$. This is the rate of change of P with respect to l when k is held fixed. Likewise, the **marginal productivity with respect to k** is $\partial P/\partial k$. It is the rate of change of P with respect to k when l is held fixed.

EXAMPLE 3   *A manufacturer of a popular toy has determined that the production function is $P = \sqrt{lk}$, where l is the number of labor-hours per week and k is the capital (expressed in hundreds of dollars per week) required for a weekly production of P gross of the toy. Determine the marginal productivity functions and evaluate them when $l = 400$ and $k = 16$. Interpret the results.*

Since $P = (lk)^{1/2}$,

$$\frac{\partial P}{\partial l} = \frac{1}{2}(lk)^{-1/2}k = \frac{k}{2\sqrt{lk}}$$

and $$\frac{\partial P}{\partial k} = \frac{1}{2}(lk)^{-1/2}l = \frac{l}{2\sqrt{lk}}.$$

Evaluating when $l = 400$ and $k = 16$, we obtain

$$\frac{\partial P}{\partial l}\bigg|_{\substack{l=400\\k=16}} = \frac{16}{2\sqrt{400(16)}} = \frac{1}{10}$$

and $$\frac{\partial P}{\partial k}\bigg|_{\substack{l=400\\k=16}} = \frac{400}{2\sqrt{400(16)}} = \frac{5}{2}.$$

Thus if $l = 400$ and $k = 16$, increasing l to 401 and holding k at 16 will increase output by approximately $\frac{1}{10}$ gross. But if k is increased to 17 while l is held at 400, the output increases by approximately $\frac{5}{2}$ gross.

Sometimes two products may be related so that changes in the price of one of them can affect the demand for the other. A typical example is that of butter and margarine. If such a relationship exists between products A and B, then the demand for each product is dependent on the prices of both. Suppose q_A and q_B are the quantities demanded for A and B respectively, and p_A and p_B are their respective prices. Then both q_A and q_B are functions of p_A and p_B:

$$q_A = f(p_A, p_B), \quad \text{demand function for A}$$

$$q_B = g(p_A, p_B), \quad \text{demand function for B.}$$

We can find four partial derivatives:

$$\frac{\partial q_A}{\partial p_A}, \quad \text{the marginal demand for A with respect to } p_A;$$

$$\frac{\partial q_A}{\partial p_B}, \quad \textit{the marginal demand for A with respect to } p_B;$$

$$\frac{\partial q_B}{\partial p_A}, \quad \textit{the marginal demand for B with respect to } p_A;$$

$$\frac{\partial q_B}{\partial p_B}, \quad \textit{the marginal demand for B with respect to } p_B.$$

Under typical conditions, if the price of B is fixed and the price of A increases, then the quantity of A demanded will decrease. Thus $\partial q_A/\partial p_A < 0$. Similarly, $\partial q_B/\partial p_B < 0$. However, $\partial q_A/\partial p_B$ and $\partial q_B/\partial p_A$ may be either positive or negative. If

$$\frac{\partial q_A}{\partial p_B} > 0 \quad \text{and} \quad \frac{\partial q_B}{\partial p_A} > 0,$$

then A and B are said to be **competitive products** or **substitutes.** In this situation, an increase in the price of B causes an increase in the demand for A, if it is assumed that the price of A does not change. Likewise, an increase in the price of A causes an increase in the demand for B when the price of B is held fixed. Butter and margarine are examples of substitutes.

Proceeding to a different situation, we say that if

$$\frac{\partial q_A}{\partial p_B} < 0 \quad \text{and} \quad \frac{\partial q_B}{\partial p_A} < 0,$$

then A and B are **complementary products.** In this case an increase in the price of B causes a decrease in the demand for A if the price of A does not change. Similarly, an increase in the price of A causes a decrease in the demand for B when the price of B is held fixed. For example, cameras and film are complementary products. An increase in the price of film will make picture-taking more expensive. Hence the demand for cameras will decrease.

EXAMPLE 4   *The demand functions for products* A *and* B *are each a function of the prices of* A *and* B *and are given by*

$$q_A = \frac{50 \sqrt[3]{p_B}}{\sqrt{p_A}} \quad \textit{and} \quad q_B = \frac{75 p_A}{\sqrt[3]{p_B^2}},$$

respectively. Find the four marginal demand functions and also determine whether A *and* B *are competitive products, complementary products, or neither.*

Writing $q_A = 50 p_A^{-1/2} p_B^{1/3}$ and $q_B = 75 p_A p_B^{-2/3}$, we have

$$\frac{\partial q_A}{\partial p_A} = 50 \left(-\frac{1}{2} \right) p_A^{-3/2} p_B^{1/3} = -25 p_A^{-3/2} p_B^{1/3},$$

$$\frac{\partial q_A}{\partial p_B} = 50 p_A^{-1/2} \left(\frac{1}{3} \right) p_B^{-2/3} = \frac{50}{3} p_A^{-1/2} p_B^{-2/3},$$

$$\frac{\partial q_B}{\partial p_A} = 75(1)p_B^{-2/3} = 75p_B^{-2/3},$$

$$\frac{\partial q_B}{\partial p_B} = 75p_A\left(-\frac{2}{3}\right)p_B^{-5/3} = -50p_A p_B^{-5/3}.$$

Since p_A and p_B represent prices, they are both positive. Hence $\partial q_A/\partial p_B > 0$ and $\partial q_B/\partial p_A > 0$. We conclude that A and B are competitive products.

EXERCISE 17.3

For the joint-cost functions in Problems 1–3, find the indicated marginal cost at the given production level.

1. $c = 4x + 0.3y^2 + 2y + 500$; $\dfrac{\partial c}{\partial y}$, $x = 20$, $y = 30$.   **2.** $c = x\sqrt{x + y} + 1000$; $\dfrac{\partial c}{\partial x}$, $x = 40$, $y = 60$.

3. $c = 0.03(x + y)^3 - 0.6(x + y)^2 + 4.5(x + y) + 7700$; $\dfrac{\partial c}{\partial x}$, $x = 50$, $y = 50$.

For the production functions in Problems 4 and 5, find the marginal production functions $\partial P/\partial k$ and $\partial P/\partial l$.

4. $P = 20lk - 2l^2 - 4k^2 + 800$.   **5.** $P = 1.582l^{0.192}k^{0.764}$.

6. A Cobb-Douglas production function is a production function of the form $P = Al^\alpha k^\beta$ where A, α, and β are constants and $\alpha + \beta = 1$. For such a function, show that
a. $\partial P/\partial l = \alpha P/l$.   **b.** $\partial P/\partial k = \beta P/k$.
c. $l\dfrac{\partial P}{\partial l} + k\dfrac{\partial P}{\partial k} = P$. This means that summing the products of the marginal productivity of each factor and the amount of that factor results in the total product P.

In Problems 7–9, q_A and q_B are demand functions for products A and B, respectively. In each case find $\partial q_A/\partial p_A$, $\partial q_A/\partial p_B$, $\partial q_B/\partial p_A$, $\partial q_B/\partial p_B$ and determine whether A and B are competitive, complementary, or neither.

7. $q_A = 1000 - 50p_A + 2p_B$; $q_B = 500 + 4p_A - 20p_B$.

8. $q_A = 20 - p_A - 2p_B$; $q_B = 50 - 2p_A - 3p_B$.

9. $q_A = \dfrac{100}{p_A\sqrt{p_B}}$; $q_B = \dfrac{500}{p_B\sqrt[3]{p_A}}$.

10. The production function for the Canadian manufacturing industries for 1927 is estimated by* $P = 33.0l^{0.46}k^{0.52}$, where P is product, l is labor, and k is capital. Find the marginal productivities for labor and capital and evaluate when $l = 1$ and $k = 1$.

$$P = A^{0.27}B^{0.01}C^{0.01}D^{0.23}E^{0.09}F^{0.27},$$

where P is product, A is land, B is labor, C is improvements, D is liquid assets, E is working assets, and F is cash operating expenses. Find the marginal productivities for labor and improvements.

11. An estimate of the production function for dairy farming in Iowa (1939) is given by†

* P. Daly and P. Douglas. "The Production Function for Canadian Manufactures," *Journal of the American Statistical Association,* 38 (1943), 178–86.

† G. Tintner and O. H. Brownlee. "Production Functions Derived from Farm Records," *American Journal of Agricultural Economics,* 26 (1944), 566–71.

12. A person's general status, S_g, is believed to be a function of status attributable to education, S_e, and status attributable to income, S_i, where S_g, S_e, and S_i are represented numerically. If $S_g = 7\sqrt[3]{S_e}\sqrt{S_i}$, determine $\partial S_g / \partial S_e$ and $\partial S_g / \partial S_i$ when $S_e = 125$ and $S_i = 100$, and interpret your results.*

13. In a study of success among master of business administration (M.B.A.) graduates, it was estimated that for staff managers (which includes accountants, analysts, etc.) current annual compensation z in dollars) was given by

$$z = 10{,}990 + 1120x + 873y,$$

where x and y are the number of years of work experience before and after receiving the M.B.A. degree, respectively.† Find $\partial z / \partial x$ and interpret your result.

14. The study of frequency of vibrations of a taut wire is useful in considering such things as an individual's voice. Suppose

$$\omega = \frac{1}{bL}\sqrt{\frac{\tau}{\pi \rho}},$$

where ω (a Greek letter read "omega") is frequency, b is diameter, L is length, ρ (a Greek letter read "rho") is density, and τ (a Greek letter read "tau") is tension.‡ Find $\partial \omega / \partial b$, $\partial \omega / \partial L$, $\partial \omega / \partial \rho$, and $\partial \omega / \partial \tau$.

15. Sometimes we want to evaluate the degree of readability of a piece of writing. Rudolf Flesch§ developed a function of two variables that will do this:

$$R = f(w, s) = 206.835 - (1.015w + 0.846s),$$

where R is called the *reading ease score*, w is the average number of words per sentence in 100-word samples, and s is the average number of syllables in such samples. Flesch says that an article for which $R = 0$ is "practically unreadable," but one with $R = 100$ is "easy for any literate person." (a) Find $\partial R / \partial w$ and $\partial R / \partial s$. (b) Which is "easier" to read: an article for which $w = w_0$ and $s = s_0$, or one for which $w = w_0 + 1$ and $s = s_0$?

16. Consider the following traffic-flow situation. On a highway where two lanes of traffic flow in the same direction, there is a maintenance vehicle blocking the left lane (see Fig. 17.11). Two vehicles (*lead* and *follow-*

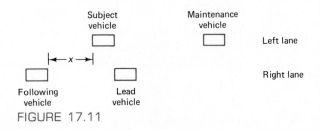

FIGURE 17.11

ing) are in the right lane with a gap between them. The *subject* vehicle can choose either to fill or not to fill the gap. That decision may be based not only on the distance x shown in the diagram, but on other factors (such as the velocity of the *following* vehicle). A *gap index*,

* Adapted from R. K. Leik and B. F. Meeker, *Mathematical Sociology* (Englewood Cliffs, N.J.: Prentice-Hall, Inc., 1975).

† A. G. Weinstein and V. Srinivasen. "Predicting Managerial Success of Master of Business Administration (M.B.A.) Graduates," *Journal of Applied Psychology*, 59, no. 2 (1974), 207–12.

‡ R. M. Thrall, J. A. Mortimer, K. R. Rebman, and R. F. Baum, eds., *Some Mathematical Models in Biology*, rev. ed., Report No. 40241-R-7. Prepared at University of Michigan, 1967.

§ R. Flesch, *The Art of Readable Writing* (New York: Harper & Row Publishers, Inc., 1949).

g, has been used in analyzing such a decision.[*][†] The greater the g-value, the greater is the propensity for the *subject* vehicle to fill the gap. Suppose

$$g = \frac{x}{V_F} - \left(0.75 + \frac{V_F - V_S}{19.2} \right),$$

where x (in feet) is as before, V_F is the velocity of the *following* vehicle (in feet per second), and V_S is the velocity of the *subject* vehicle (in feet per second). From the diagram it seems reasonable that if both V_F and V_S are fixed and x increases, then g should increase. Show that this is true by applying calculus to the function g given above. Assume that x, V_F, and V_S are positive.

17. For the congressional elections of 1974, the Republican percentage, R, of the Republican-Democratic vote in a district is given (approximately) by[‡]

$R = f(E_r, E_d, I_r, I_d, N)$

$\quad = 15.4725 + 2.5945E_r - 0.0804E_r^2 - 2.3648E_d +$

$\qquad 0.0687E_d^2 + 2.1914I_r - 0.0912I_r^2 -$

$\qquad 0.8096I_d + 0.0081I_d^2 - 0.0277E_rI_r +$

$\qquad 0.0493E_dI_d + 0.8579N - 0.0061N^2.$

Here E_r and E_d are the campaign expenditures (in units of $10,000) by Republicans and Democrats, respectively; I_r and I_d are the number of terms served in Congress, *plus* one, for the Republican and Democratic candidates, respectively; and N is the percentage of the two-party presidential vote that Richard Nixon received in the district for 1968. The variable N gives a measure of Republican strength in the district.

a. In the Federal Election Campaign Act of 1974, Congress set a limit of $188,000 on campaign expenditures. By analyzing $\partial R/\partial E_r$, would you have advised a Republican candidate who served nine terms in Congress to spend $188,000 on his campaign?

b. Find the percentage above which the Nixon vote had a negative effect on R; that is, determine when $\partial R/\partial N < 0$. Give your answer to the nearest percent.

Let f define a demand function for product A and $q_A = f(p_A, p_B)$ where q_A is the quantity of A demanded when the price per unit of A is p_A and the price per unit of product B is p_B. The partial elasticity of demand for A with respect to p_A, denoted η_{p_A}, is defined as $\eta_{p_A} = (p_A/q_A)(\partial q_A/\partial p_A)$. The partial elasticity of demand for A with respect to p_B, denoted η_{p_B}, is defined as $(p_B/q_A)(\partial q_A/\partial p_B)$. Loosely speaking, η_{p_A} is the ratio of a percentage change in the quantity of A demanded to a percentage change in the price of A when the price of B is fixed. Similarly, η_{p_B} can be loosely interpreted as the ratio of a percentage change in the quantity of A demanded to a percentage change in the price of B when the price of A is fixed. In Problems 18–20, find η_{p_A} and η_{p_B} for the given values of p_A and p_B.

18. $q_A = 1000 - 50p_A + 2p_B;$ $\quad p_A = 2, p_B = 10.$

19. $q_A = 100/(p_A\sqrt{p_B});$ $\quad p_A = 1, p_B = 4.$

20. $q_A = 20 - p_A - 2p_B;$ $\quad p_A = 2, p_B = 2.$

* P. M. Hurst, K. Perchonok, and E. L. Seguin, "Vehicle Kinematics and Gap Acceptance," *Journal of Applied Psychology*, 52, no. 4 (1968), 321–24.

† K. Perchonok and P. M. Hurst, "Effect of Lane-Closure Signals upon Driver Decision Making and Traffic Flow," *Journal of Applied Psychology*, 52, no. 5 (1968), 410–13.

‡ J. Silberman and G. Yochum. "The Role of Money in Determining Election Outcomes," *Social Science Quarterly*, 58, no. 4 (1978), 671–82.

17.4 IMPLICIT PARTIAL DIFFERENTIATION* _____

For the equation

$$z^2 - x^2 - y^2 = 0, \tag{1}$$

if $x = 1$ and $y = 1$, then $z^2 - 1 - 1 = 0$, so $z = \pm\sqrt{2}$. Thus Eq. (1) does not define z as a function of x and y. However, solving Eq. (1) for z gives

$$z = \sqrt{x^2 + y^2} \quad \text{or} \quad z = -\sqrt{x^2 + y^2},$$

each of which defines z as a function of x and y. Although Eq. (1) does not explicitly express z as a function of x and y, it can be thought of as expressing z *implicitly* as one of two different functions of x and y. Note that $z^2 - x^2 - y^2 = 0$ has the form $F(x, y, z) = 0$. Any equation of the form $F(x, y, z) = 0$ can be thought of as expressing z implicitly as one of a set of possible functions of x and y.

To find $\partial z/\partial x$ where

$$z^2 - x^2 - y^2 = 0, \tag{2}$$

we first differentiate both sides of Eq. (2) with respect to x while treating z as a function of x and y and treating y as a constant

$$\frac{\partial}{\partial x}(z^2 - x^2 - y^2) = \frac{\partial}{\partial x}(0),$$

$$\frac{\partial}{\partial x}(z^2) - \frac{\partial}{\partial x}(x^2) - \frac{\partial}{\partial x}(y^2) = 0,$$

$$2z\frac{\partial z}{\partial x} - 2x - 0 = 0.$$

Solving for $\partial z/\partial x$, we obtain

$$2z\frac{\partial z}{\partial x} = 2x,$$

$$\frac{\partial z}{\partial x} = \frac{x}{z}.$$

To find $\partial z/\partial y$ we differentiate both sides of Eq. (2) with respect to y while treating z as a function of x and y and treating x as a constant.

$$\frac{\partial}{\partial y}(z^2 - x^2 - y^2) = \frac{\partial}{\partial y}(0),$$

$$2z\frac{\partial z}{\partial y} - 0 - 2y = 0,$$

$$2z\frac{\partial z}{\partial y} = 2y.$$

_____
* May be omitted without loss of continuity.

Hence

$$\frac{\partial z}{\partial y} = \frac{y}{z}.$$

The method we used to find $\partial z/\partial x$ and $\partial z/\partial y$ is called *implicit (partial) differentiation*.

EXAMPLE 1

a. *If* $\dfrac{xz^2}{x + y} + y^2 = 0$, *evaluate* $\partial z/\partial x$ *when* $x = -1$, $y = 2$, *and* $z = 2$.

We treat z as a function of x and y and differentiate both sides of the equation with respect to x.

$$\frac{\partial}{\partial x}\left(\frac{xz^2}{x + y}\right) + \frac{\partial}{\partial x}(y^2) = \frac{\partial}{\partial x}(0).$$

Using the quotient rule for the first term on the left side, we have

$$\frac{(x + y)\dfrac{\partial}{\partial x}(xz^2) - xz^2\dfrac{\partial}{\partial x}(x + y)}{(x + y)^2} + 0 = 0.$$

Using the product rule for $\dfrac{\partial}{\partial x}(xz^2)$ gives

$$\frac{(x + y)\left[x\left(2z\dfrac{\partial z}{\partial x}\right) + z^2(1)\right] - xz^2(1)}{(x + y)^2} = 0.$$

Solving for $\partial z/\partial x$, we obtain

$$2xz(x + y)\frac{\partial z}{\partial x} + z^2(x + y) - xz^2 = 0,$$

$$\frac{\partial z}{\partial x} = \frac{xz^2 - z^2(x + y)}{2xz(x + y)} = -\frac{yz}{2x(x + y)}, \qquad z \neq 0.$$

Thus

$$\frac{\partial z}{\partial x}\bigg|_{(-1,2,2)} = 2.$$

b. *If* $se^{r^2 + u^2} = u \ln(t^2 + 1)$, *determine* $\partial t/\partial u$.

We consider t as a function of r, s, and u. By differentiating both sides with respect to u while treating r and s as constants, we get

$$\frac{\partial}{\partial u}(se^{r^2 + u^2}) = \frac{\partial}{\partial u}[u \ln(t^2 + 1)],$$

$$2sue^{r^2+u^2} = u\,\frac{\partial}{\partial u}\,[\ln(t^2 + 1)] + \ln(t^2 + 1)\frac{\partial}{\partial u}(u) \qquad \text{(product rule)},$$

$$2sue^{r^2+u^2} = u\,\frac{2t}{t^2 + 1}\frac{\partial t}{\partial u} + \ln(t^2 + 1).$$

Thus

$$\frac{\partial t}{\partial u} = \frac{(t^2 + 1)[2sue^{r^2+u^2} - \ln(t^2 + 1)]}{2ut}.$$

EXERCISE 17.4

*In Problems **1–11**, by the method of implicit partial differentiation find the indicated partial derivatives.*

1. $x^2 + y^2 + z^2 = 9$; $\partial z/\partial x$.

2. $z^2 - 3x^2 + y^2 = 0$; $\partial z/\partial x$.

3. $2z^3 - x^2 - 4y^2 = 0$; $\partial z/\partial y$.

4. $3x^2 + y^2 + 2z^3 = 9$; $\partial z/\partial y$.

5. $x^2 - 2y - z^2 + x^2yz^2 = 20$; $\partial z/\partial x$.

6. $z^3 - xz - y = 0$; $\partial z/\partial x$.

7. $e^x + e^y + e^z = 10$; $\partial z/\partial y$.

8. $xyz + 2y^2x - z^3 = 0$; $\partial z/\partial x$.

9. $\ln(z) + z - xy = 1$; $\partial z/\partial x$.

10. $\ln x + \ln y - \ln z = e^y$; $\partial z/\partial x$.

11. $(z^2 + 6xy)\sqrt{x^3 + 5} = 2$; $\partial z/\partial y$.

*In Problems **12–18**, evaluate the indicated partial derivatives for the given values of the variables.*

12. $xz + xyz - 5 = 0$; $\partial z/\partial x$, $x = 1$, $y = 4$, $z = 1$.

13. $xz^2 + yz - 12 = 0$; $\partial z/\partial x$, $x = 2$, $y = -2$, $z = 3$.

14. $e^{zx} = xyz$; $\partial z/\partial y$, $x = 1$, $y = -e^{-1}$, $z = -1$.

15. $\ln z = x + y$; $\partial z/\partial x$, $x = 5$, $y = -5$, $z = 1$.

16. $\sqrt{xz + y^2} - xy = 0$; $\partial z/\partial y$, $x = 2$, $y = 2$, $z = 6$.

17. $\dfrac{s^2 + t^2}{rs} = 10$; $\partial t/\partial r$, $r = 1$, $s = 2$, $t = 4$.

18. $\dfrac{rs}{s^2 + t^2} = t$; $\partial r/\partial t$, $r = 0$, $s = 1$, $t = 0$.

17.5 HIGHER-ORDER PARTIAL DERIVATIVES

If $z = f(x, y)$, then not only is z a function of x and y, but also f_x and f_y are each functions of x and y. Hence we may differentiate f_x and f_y to obtain **second-order partial derivatives** of f. Symbolically,

$$f_{xx} \quad \text{means} \quad (f_x)_x, \qquad f_{xy} \quad \text{means} \quad (f_x)_y,$$
$$f_{yx} \quad \text{means} \quad (f_y)_x, \qquad f_{yy} \quad \text{means} \quad (f_y)_y.$$

In terms of ∂-notation,

$$\frac{\partial^2 z}{\partial x^2} \quad \text{means} \quad \frac{\partial}{\partial x}\left[\frac{\partial z}{\partial x}\right], \qquad \frac{\partial^2 z}{\partial y\partial x} \quad \text{means} \quad \frac{\partial}{\partial y}\left[\frac{\partial z}{\partial x}\right]$$

$$\frac{\partial^2 z}{\partial x\partial y} \quad \text{means} \quad \frac{\partial}{\partial x}\left[\frac{\partial z}{\partial y}\right], \qquad \frac{\partial^2 z}{\partial y^2} \quad \text{means} \quad \frac{\partial}{\partial y}\left[\frac{\partial z}{\partial y}\right].$$

Note that to find f_{xy}, first differentiate f with respect to x. For $\partial^2 z/\partial x \partial y$, first differentiate with respect to y.

We can extend our notation beyond second-order partial derivatives. For example, f_{xyx} (or $\partial^3 z/\partial x \partial y \partial x$) is a third-order partial derivative of f. It is the partial derivative of f_{xy} (or $\partial^2 z/\partial y \partial x$) with respect to x. A generalization regarding higher-order partial derivatives to functions of more than two variables should be obvious.

EXAMPLE 1   *Find the four second-order partial derivatives of $f(x, y) = x^2 y + x^2 y^2$.*

Since

$$f_x(x, y) = 2xy + 2xy^2,$$

we have

$$f_{xx}(x, y) = \frac{\partial}{\partial x}(2xy + 2xy^2) = 2y + 2y^2$$

and

$$f_{xy}(x, y) = \frac{\partial}{\partial y}(2xy + 2xy^2) = 2x + 4xy.$$

Since

$$f_y(x, y) = x^2 + 2x^2 y,$$

we have

$$f_{yy}(x, y) = \frac{\partial}{\partial y}(x^2 + 2x^2 y) = 2x^2$$

and

$$f_{yx}(x, y) = \frac{\partial}{\partial x}(x^2 + 2x^2 y) = 2x + 4xy.$$

The derivatives f_{xy} and f_{yx} are called **mixed partial derivatives.** Observe in Example 1 that $f_{xy}(x, y) = f_{yx}(x, y)$. Under suitable conditions, mixed partial derivatives for a function are equal; that is, the order of differentiation is of no concern. You may assume this is the case for all the functions that we consider.

EXAMPLE 2   *Find the value of $\left.\dfrac{\partial^3 w}{\partial z \partial y \partial x}\right|_{(1,2,3)}$ if $w = (2x + 3y + 4z)^3$.*

$$\frac{\partial w}{\partial x} = 3(2x + 3y + 4z)^2 \frac{\partial}{\partial x}(2x + 3y + 4z)$$

$$= 6(2x + 3y + 4z)^2.$$

$$\frac{\partial^2 w}{\delta y \partial x} = 6 \cdot 2(2x + 3y + 4z) \frac{\partial}{\partial y}(2x + 3y + 4z)$$

$$= 36(2x + 3y + 4z).$$

$$\frac{\partial^3 w}{\partial z \partial y \partial x} = 36 \cdot 4 = 144.$$

Thus

$$\left.\frac{\partial^3 w}{\partial z \partial y \partial x}\right|_{(1,2,3)} = 144.$$

EXAMPLE 3*   *Determine $\partial^2 z/\partial x^2$ if $z^2 = xy$.*

By implicit differentiation we first determine $\partial z/\partial x$:

$$\frac{\partial}{\partial x}(z^2) = \frac{\partial}{\partial x}(xy),$$

$$2z\frac{\partial z}{\partial x} = y,$$

$$\frac{\partial z}{\partial x} = \frac{y}{2z}, \quad z \neq 0.$$

Differentiating both sides with respect to x, we obtain

$$\frac{\partial}{\partial x}\left[\frac{\partial z}{\partial x}\right] = \frac{\partial}{\partial x}\left[\frac{1}{2}yz^{-1}\right],$$

$$\frac{\partial^2 z}{\partial x^2} = -\frac{1}{2}yz^{-2}\frac{\partial z}{\partial x}.$$

Substituting $y/(2z)$ for $\partial z/\partial x$, we have

$$\frac{\partial^2 z}{\partial x^2} = -\frac{1}{2}yz^{-2}\left(\frac{y}{2z}\right) = -\frac{y^2}{4z^3}, \quad z \neq 0.$$

EXERCISE 17.5

In Problems **1–10,** *find the indicated partial derivatives.*

1. $f(x, y) = 3x^2y^2;\quad f_x(x, y), f_{xy}(x, y).$

2. $f(x, y) = 3x^2y + 2xy^2 - 7y;\quad f_x(x, y), f_{xx}(x, y).$

3. $f(x, y) = e^{3xy} + 4x^2y;\quad f_y(x, y), f_{yx}(x, y), f_{yxy}(x, y).$

4. $f(x, y) = 7x^2 + 3y;\quad f_y(x, y), f_{yy}(x, y), f_{yyx}(x, y).$

5. $f(x, y) = (x^2 + xy + y^2)(x^2 + xy + 1);\quad f_x(x, y), f_{xy}(x, y).$

6. $f(x, y) = \ln(x^2 + y^2) + 2;\quad f_x(x, y), f_{xx}(x, y), f_{xy}(x, y).$

7. $f(x, y) = (x + y)^2(xy);\quad f_x(x, y), f_y(x, y), f_{xx}(x, y), f_{yy}(x, y).$

8. $f(x, y, z) = xy^2z^3;\quad f_x(x, y, z), f_{xz}(x, y, z), f_{xy}(x, y, z).$

9. $z = \sqrt{x^2 + y^2};\quad \dfrac{\partial z}{\partial x}, \dfrac{\partial^2 z}{\partial x^2}.$

10. $z = \dfrac{\ln(x^2 + 5)}{y};\quad \dfrac{\partial z}{\partial x}, \dfrac{\partial^2 z}{\partial y \partial x}.$

* Omit if Sec. 17.4 was not covered.

11. If $f(x, y, z) = 7$, find $f_{yxx}(4, 3, -2)$.

12. If $f(x, y, z) = z^2(3x^2 - 4xy^3)$, find $f_{xyz}(1, 2, 3)$.

13. If $f(l, k) = 5l^3k^6 - lk^7$, find $f_{kkl}(2, 1)$.

14. If $f(x, y) = 2x^2y + xy^2 - x^2y^2$, find $f_{xxy}(0, 1)$.

15. If $f(x, y) = y^2e^x + \ln(xy)$, find $f_{xyy}(1, 1)$.

16. If $f(x, y) = x^3 - 3xy^2 + x^2 - y^3$, find $f_{xy}(1, -1)$.

17. For $f(x, y) = 8x^3 + 2x^2y^2 + 5y^4$, show that $f_{xy}(x, y) = f_{yx}(x, y)$.

18. For $f(x, y) = x^4y^4 + 3x^3y^2 - 7x + 4$, show that $f_{xyx}(x, y) = f_{xxy}(x, y)$.

19. For $z = \ln(x^2 + y^2)$, show that $\dfrac{\partial^2 z}{\partial x^2} + \dfrac{\partial^2 z}{\partial y^2} = 0$.

*20. If $2z^2 - x^2 - 4y^2 = 0$, find $\dfrac{\partial^2 z}{\partial x^2}$.

*21. If $z^2 - 3x^2 + y^2 = 0$, find $\dfrac{\partial^2 z}{\partial y^2}$.

17.6 CHAIN RULE†

Suppose a manufacturer of two related products A and B has a joint-cost function given by

$$c = f(q_A, q_B),$$

where c is the total cost of producing quantities q_A and q_B of A and B, respectively. Furthermore, suppose the demand functions for the products are

$$q_A = g(p_A, p_B) \quad \text{and} \quad q_B = h(p_A, p_B),$$

where p_A and p_B are the prices per unit of A and B, respectively. Since c is a function of q_A and q_B and both q_A and q_B are themselves functions of p_A and p_B, then c can be viewed as a function of p_A and p_B. (Appropriately, the variables q_A and q_B are called *intermediate variables* of c.) Consequently, we should be able to determine $\partial c/\partial p_A$, the rate of change of total cost with respect to the price of A. One way to do this is to substitute the expressions $g(p_A, p_B)$ and $h(p_A, p_B)$ for q_A and q_B, respectively, into $c = f(q_A, q_B)$. Then c is a function of p_A and p_B and we can differentiate c with respect to p_A directly. This approach has some drawbacks—especially when f, g, or h is given by a complicated expression. Another way to approach the problem would be to use the chain rule (actually *a* chain rule), which we now state without proof.

Chain Rule

Let $z = f(x, y)$, where both x and y are functions of r and s given by $x = x(r, s)$ and $y = y(r, s)$. If f, x, and y have continuous partial derivatives, then z is a function of r and s and

$$\frac{\partial z}{\partial r} = \frac{\partial z}{\partial x}\frac{\partial x}{\partial r} + \frac{\partial z}{\partial y}\frac{\partial y}{\partial r}$$

and

$$\frac{\partial z}{\partial s} = \frac{\partial z}{\partial x}\frac{\partial x}{\partial s} + \frac{\partial z}{\partial y}\frac{\partial y}{\partial s}.$$

---

* Omit if Sec. 17.4 was not covered.

† May be omitted without loss of continuity.

Note that in the chain rule the number of intermediate variables of z (two) is the same as the number of terms that compose each of $\partial z / \partial r$ and $\partial z / \partial s$.

Returning to the original situation concerning the manufacturer, we see that if f, q_A, and q_B have continuous partial derivatives, then by the chain rule

$$\frac{\partial c}{\partial p_A} = \frac{\partial c}{\partial q_A} \frac{\partial q_A}{\partial p_A} + \frac{\partial c}{\partial q_B} \frac{\partial q_B}{\partial p_A}.$$

EXAMPLE 1   *For a manufacturer of cameras and film, the total cost c of producing q_C cameras and q_F units of film is given by*

$$c = 30q_C + 0.015q_C q_F + q_F + 900.$$

The demand functions for the cameras and film are given by

$$q_C = \frac{9000}{p_C \sqrt{p_F}} \qquad and \qquad q_F = 2000 - p_C - 400p_F,$$

where p_C is the price per camera and p_F is the price per unit of film. Find the rate of change of total cost with respect to the price of the camera when $p_C = 50$ and $p_F = 2$.

We must first determine $\partial c / \partial p_C$. By the chain rule,

$$\frac{\partial c}{\partial p_C} = \frac{\partial c}{\partial q_C} \frac{\partial q_C}{\partial p_C} + \frac{\partial c}{\partial q_F} \frac{\partial q_F}{\partial p_C}$$

$$= (30 + 0.015q_F) \left[\frac{-9000}{p_C^2 \sqrt{p_F}} \right] + (0.015q_C + 1)(-1).$$

When $p_C = 50$ and $p_F = 2$, then $q_C = 90\sqrt{2}$ and $q_F = 1150$. Substituting these values into $\partial c / \partial p_C$ and simplifying, we have

$$\left. \frac{\partial c}{\partial p_C} \right|_{\substack{p_C=50 \\ p_F=2}} = -123.2 \qquad \text{(approximately)}.$$

The chain rule can be extended. For example, suppose $z = f(v, w, x, y)$ and v, w, x, and y are all functions of r, s, and t. Then, if certain conditions of continuity are assumed, z is a function of r, s, and t and

$$\frac{\partial z}{\partial r} = \frac{\partial z}{\partial v} \frac{\partial v}{\partial r} + \frac{\partial z}{\partial w} \frac{\partial w}{\partial r} + \frac{\partial z}{\partial x} \frac{\partial x}{\partial r} + \frac{\partial z}{\partial y} \frac{\partial y}{\partial r},$$

$$\frac{\partial z}{\partial s} = \frac{\partial z}{\partial v} \frac{\partial v}{\partial s} + \frac{\partial z}{\partial w} \frac{\partial w}{\partial s} + \frac{\partial z}{\partial x} \frac{\partial x}{\partial s} + \frac{\partial z}{\partial y} \frac{\partial y}{\partial s},$$

and $$\frac{\partial z}{\partial t} = \frac{\partial z}{\partial v} \frac{\partial v}{\partial t} + \frac{\partial z}{\partial w} \frac{\partial w}{\partial t} + \frac{\partial z}{\partial x} \frac{\partial x}{\partial t} + \frac{\partial z}{\partial y} \frac{\partial y}{\partial t}.$$

Observe that the number of intermediate variables of z (four) is the same as the number of terms that form each of $\partial z / \partial r$, $\partial z / \partial s$, and $\partial z / \partial t$.

Now consider the situation where $z = f(x, y)$ and $x = x(t)$ and $y = y(t)$. Then

$$\frac{dz}{dt} = \frac{\partial z}{\partial x}\frac{dx}{dt} + \frac{\partial z}{\partial y}\frac{dy}{dt}.$$

Here we use the symbol dz/dt rather than $\partial z/\partial t$, since z can be considered a function of the *one* variable t. Likewise, the symbols dx/dt and dy/dt are used rather than $\partial x/\partial t$ and $\partial y/\partial t$. As is typical, the number of terms that compose dz/dt equals the number of intermediate variables of z. Other situations would be treated in a similar way.

EXAMPLE 2

a. *If $w = f(x, y, z) = 3x^2y + xyz - 4y^2z^3$, where $x = 2r - 3s$, $y = 6r + s$, and $z = r - s$, determine $\partial w/\partial r$ and $\partial w/\partial s$.*

Since x, y, and z are functions of r and s, then by the chain rule,

$$\frac{\partial w}{\partial r} = \frac{\partial w}{\partial x}\frac{\partial x}{\partial r} + \frac{\partial w}{\partial y}\frac{\partial y}{\partial r} + \frac{\partial w}{\partial z}\frac{\partial z}{\partial r}$$

$$= (6xy + yz)(2) + (3x^2 + xz - 8yz^3)(6) + (xy - 12y^2z^2)(1)$$

$$= x(18x + 13y + 6z) + 2yz(1 - 24z^2 - 6yz).$$

Also,

$$\frac{\partial w}{\partial s} = \frac{\partial w}{\partial x}\frac{\partial x}{\partial s} + \frac{\partial w}{\partial y}\frac{\partial y}{\partial s} + \frac{\partial w}{\partial z}\frac{\partial z}{\partial s}$$

$$= (6xy + yz)(-3) + (3x^2 + xz - 8yz^3)(1) + (xy - 12y^2z^2)(-1)$$

$$= x(3x - 19y + z) - yz(3 + 8z^2 - 12yz).$$

b. *If $z = \dfrac{x + e^y}{y}$, where $x = rs + se^{rt}$ and $y = 9 + rt$, evaluate $\partial z/\partial s$ when $r = -2$, $s = 5$, and $t = 4$.*

Since x and y are functions of r, s, and t (note that we can write $y = 9 + rt + 0 \cdot s$), by the chain rule,

$$\frac{\partial z}{\partial s} = \frac{\partial z}{\partial x}\frac{\partial x}{\partial s} + \frac{\partial z}{\partial y}\frac{\partial y}{\partial s}$$

$$= \left(\frac{1}{y}\right)(r + e^{rt}) + \frac{\partial z}{\partial y}\cdot(0) = \frac{r + e^{rt}}{y}.$$

If $r = -2$, $s = 5$, and $t = 4$, then $y = 1$. Thus

$$\left.\frac{\partial z}{\partial s}\right|_{\substack{r=-2 \\ s=5 \\ t=4}} = \frac{-2 + e^{-8}}{1} = -2 + e^{-8}.$$

c. *Determine $\partial y/\partial r$ if $y = x^2 \ln(x^4 + 6)$ and $x = (r + 3s)^6$.*

By the chain rule,

$$\frac{\partial y}{\partial r} = \frac{dy}{dx}\frac{\partial x}{\partial r}$$

$$= \left[x^2 \cdot \frac{4x^3}{x^4 + 6} + 2x \cdot \ln(x^4 + 6)\right][6(r + 3s)^5]$$

$$= 12x(r + 3s)^5\left[\frac{2x^4}{x^4 + 6} + \ln(x^4 + 6)\right].$$

EXAMPLE 3   *Given that $z = e^{xy}$, $x = r - 4s$, and $y = r - s$, find $\partial z/\partial r$ in terms of r and s.*

$$\frac{\partial z}{\partial r} = \frac{\partial z}{\partial x}\frac{\partial x}{\partial r} + \frac{\partial z}{\partial y}\frac{\partial y}{\partial r}$$

$$= (ye^{xy})(1) + (xe^{xy})(1)$$

$$= (x + y)e^{xy}.$$

Since $x = r - 4s$ and $y = r - s$,

$$\frac{\partial z}{\partial r} = [(r - 4s) + (r - s)]e^{(r-4s)(r-s)}$$

$$= (2r - 5s)e^{r^2 - 5rs + 4s^2}.$$

EXERCISE 17.6

In Problems **1–12,** *find the indicated derivatives by using the chain rule.*

1. $z = 5x + 3y$, $x = 2r + 3s$, $y = r - 2s$; $\partial z/\partial r$, $\partial z/\partial s$.

2. $z = x^2 + 3xy + 7y^3$, $x = r^2 - 2s$, $y = 5s^2$; $\partial z/\partial r$, $\partial z/\partial s$.

3. $z = e^{x+y}$, $x = t^2 + 3$, $y = \sqrt{t^3}$; dz/dt.

4. $z = \sqrt{8x + y}$, $x = t^2 + 3t + 4$, $y = t^3 + 4$; dz/dt.

5. $w = x^2z^2 + xyz + yz^2$, $x = 5t$, $y = 2t + 3$, $z = 6 - t$; dw/dt.

6. $w = \ln(x^2 + y^2 + z^2)$, $x = 2 - 3t$, $y = t^2 + 3$, $z = 4 - t$; dw/dt.

7. $z = (x^2 + xy^2)^3$, $x = r + s + t$, $y = 2r - 3s + t$; $\partial z/\partial t$.

8. $z = \sqrt{x^2 + y^2}$, $x = r^2 + s - t$, $y = r - s + t$; $\partial z/\partial r$.

9. $w = x^2 + xyz + y^3z^2$, $x = r - s^2$, $y = rs$, $z = 2r - 5s$; $\partial w/\partial s$.

10. $w = e^{xyz}$, $x = r^2s^3$, $y = r - s$, $z = rs^2$; $\partial w/\partial r$.

11. $y = x^2 - 7x + 5$, $x = 15rs + 2s^2t^2$; $\partial y/\partial r$.

12. $y = 4 - x^2$, $x = 2r + 3s - 4t$; $\partial y/\partial t$.

13. If $z = (4x + 3y)^3$, where $x = r^2s$ and $y = r - 2s$, evaluate $\partial z/\partial r$ when $r = 0$ and $s = 1$.

14. If $z = \sqrt{5x + 2y}$, where $x = 4t + 7$ and $y = t^2 - 3t + 4$, evaluate dz/dt when $t = 1$.

15. If $w = e^{3x-y}(x^2 + 4z^3)$, where $x = rs$, $y = 2s - r$, and $z = r + s$, evaluate $\partial w/\partial s$ when $r = 1$ and $s = -1$.

16. If $y = x/(x - 5)$, where $x = 2t^2 - 3rs - r^2t$, evaluate $\partial y/\partial t$ when $r = 0$, $s = 2$, and $t = -1$.

17. In considering a production function $P = f(l, k)$ where l is labor input and k is capital input, Fon, Boulier, and Goldfarb* assume that l is given by $l = Lg(h)$. Here L is number of workers, h is the number of hours per day per worker, and $g(h)$ is a labor effectiveness function. In maximizing profit p given by

$$p = aP - whL,$$

where a is the price per unit of output and w is the hourly wage per worker, Fon, Boulier, and Goldfarb determine $\partial p/\partial L$ and $\partial p/\partial h$. Assume that k is independent of L and h and determine these partial derivatives.

17.7 MAXIMA AND MINIMA FOR FUNCTIONS OF TWO VARIABLES

We now extend to functions of two variables the notion of relative maxima and minima (or relative extrema).

Definition

*A function $z = f(x, y)$ is said to have a **relative maximum** at the point (x_0, y_0), that is, when $x = x_0$ and $y = y_0$, if for all points (x, y) in the plane that are sufficiently close to (x_0, y_0) we have*

$$f(x_0, y_0) \geq f(x, y). \tag{1}$$

*For a **relative minimum**, in (1) we replace $\geq$ by $\leq$.*

To say that $z = f(x, y)$ has a relative maximum at (x_0, y_0) means geometrically that the point (x_0, y_0, z_0) on the graph of f is higher than (or is as high as) all other points on the surface that are "near" (x_0, y_0, z_0). In Fig. 17.12(a), f has a relative maximum at (x_1, y_1). Similarly, the function f in Fig. 17.12(b) has a

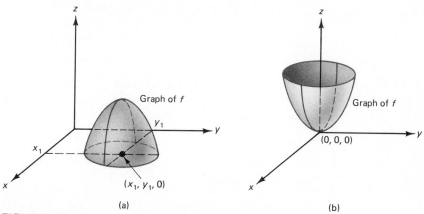

Graph of f

Graph of f

$(0, 0, 0)$

(a)

(b)

FIGURE 17.12

* V. Fon, B. L. Boulier, and R. S. Goldfarb, "The Firm's Demand for Daily Hours of Work: Some Implications," *Atlantic Economic Journal*, XIII, no. 1 (1985), 36–42.

relative minimum when $x = y = 0$, which corresponds to a *low* point on the surface.

Recall that in locating extrema for a function $y = f(x)$ of one variable, we examined those values of x in the domain of f for which $f'(x) = 0$ or $f'(x)$ does not exist. For functions of two (or more) variables, a similar procedure is followed. However, for the functions that concern us, extrema will not occur where a derivative does not exist, and such situations will be excluded from considerations.

Suppose $z = f(x, y)$ has a relative maximum at (x_0, y_0), as indicated in Fig. 17.13(a). Then the curve where the plane $y = y_0$ intersects the surface must have a relative maximum when $x = x_0$. Hence the slope of the tangent line to the surface in the x-direction must be 0 at (x_0, y_0). Equivalently, $f_x(x, y) = 0$ at

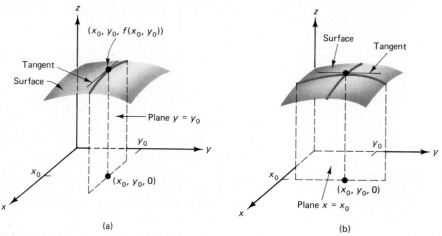

FIGURE 17.13

(x_0, y_0). Similarly, on the curve where the plane $x = x_0$ intersects the surface [Fig. 17.13(b)], there must be a relative maximum when $y = y_0$. Thus in the y-direction, the slope of the tangent to the surface must be 0 at (x_0, y_0). Equivalently, $f_y(x, y) = 0$ at (x_0, y_0). Since a similar discussion can be given for a relative minimum, we can combine these results as follows.

Rule 1
If $z = f(x, y)$ has a relative maximum or minimum at (x_0, y_0) and if both f_x and f_y are defined for all points close to (x_0, y_0), it is necessary that (x_0, y_0) be a solution of the system

$$\begin{cases} f_x(x, y) = 0, \\ f_y(x, y) = 0. \end{cases}$$

A point (x_0, y_0) for which $f_x(x, y) = f_y(x, y) = 0$ is called a **critical point** of f. Thus from Rule 1 we infer that to locate relative extrema for a function we should examine its critical points.

Pitfall

Rule 1 does not imply that there must be an extremum at a critical point. Just as in the case of functions of one variable, a critical point can give rise to a relative maximum, a relative minimum, or neither.

Two additional comments: First, Rule 1, as well as the notion of a critical point, can be extended to functions of more than two variables. Thus to locate possible extrema for $w = f(x, y, z)$ we would examine those points for which $w_x = w_y = w_z = 0$. Second, for a function whose domain is restricted, a thorough examination for absolute extrema would include consideration of boundary points.

EXAMPLE 1   *Find the critical points of the following functions.*

a. $f(x, y) = 2x^2 + y^2 - 2xy + 5x - 3y + 1$.

Since $f_x(x, y) = 4x - 2y + 5$ and $f_y(x, y) = 2y - 2x - 3$, we solve the system

$$\begin{cases} 4x - 2y + 5 = 0, \\ -2x + 2y - 3 = 0. \end{cases}$$

This gives $x = -1$ and $y = \frac{1}{2}$. Thus, $(-1, \frac{1}{2})$ is the only critical point.

b. $f(l, k) = l^3 + k^3 - lk$.

$$\begin{cases} f_l(l, k) = 3l^2 - k = 0, & (2) \\ f_k(l, k) = 3k^2 - l = 0. & (3) \end{cases}$$

From Eq. (2), $k = 3l^2$. Substituting for k in Eq. (3) gives $0 = 27l^4 - l = l(27l^3 - 1)$. Hence, $l = 0$ or $l = \frac{1}{3}$. If $l = 0$, then $k = 0$; if $l = \frac{1}{3}$, then $k = \frac{1}{3}$. The critical points are thus $(0, 0)$ and $(\frac{1}{3}, \frac{1}{3})$.

c. $f(x, y, z) = 2x^2 + xy + y^2 + 100 - z(x + y - 100)$.

Solving the system

$$\begin{cases} f_x(x, y, z) = 4x + y - z = 0, \\ f_y(x, y, z) = x + 2y - z = 0, \\ f_z(x, y, z) = -x - y + 100 = 0 \end{cases}$$

gives the critical point $(25, 75, 175)$, as you may verify.

EXAMPLE 2   *Find the critical points of $f(x, y) = x^2 - 4x + 2y^2 + 4y + 7$.*

We have $f_x(x, y) = 2x - 4$ and $f_y(x, y) = 4y + 4$. The system

$$\begin{cases} 2x - 4 = 0, \\ 4y + 4 = 0 \end{cases}$$

gives the critical point $(2, -1)$. Observe that the given function can be written

$$f(x, y) = x^2 - 4x + 4 + 2(y^2 + 2y + 1) + 1$$
$$= (x - 2)^2 + 2(y + 1)^2 + 1,$$

and $f(2, -1) = 1$. Clearly, if $(x, y) \neq (2, -1)$, then $f(x, y) > 1$. Hence a relative minimum occurs at $(2, -1)$. Moreover, there is an *absolute minimum* at $(2, -1)$, since $f(x, y) > f(2, -1)$ for *all* $(x, y) \neq (2, -1)$.

Although in Example 2 we were able to show that the critical point gave rise to a relative extremum, in many cases this is not so easy to do. There is, however, a second-derivative test that gives conditions under which a critical point will be a relative maximum or minimum. We state it now, omitting the proof.

Rule 2
SECOND-DERIVATIVE TEST FOR FUNCTIONS OF TWO VARIABLES
Suppose $z = f(x, y)$ has continuous partial derivatives $f_{xx}, f_{yy},$ and f_{xy} at all points (x, y) near the critical point (x_0, y_0). Let D be the function defined by

$$D(x, y) = f_{xx}(x, y)f_{yy}(x, y) - [f_{xy}(x, y)]^2.$$

Then

1. if $D(x_0, y_0) > 0$ and $f_{xx}(x_0, y_0) < 0$, f has a relative maximum at (x_0, y_0);
2. if $D(x_0, y_0) > 0$ and $f_{xx}(x_0, y_0) > 0$, f has a relative minimum at (x_0, y_0);
3. if $D(x_0, y_0) < 0$, f has neither a relative maximum nor a relative minimum at (x_0, y_0);
4. if $D(x_0, y_0) = 0$, no conclusion about extrema at (x_0, y_0) can be drawn and further analysis is required.

EXAMPLE 3   *Examine $f(x, y) = x^3 + y^3 - xy$ for relative maxima or minima by using the second-derivative test.*

First we find critical points.

$$f_x(x, y) = 3x^2 - y, \qquad f_y(x, y) = 3y^2 - x.$$

In the same manner as in Example 1(b), solving $f_x(x, y) = f_y(x, y) = 0$ gives the critical points $(0, 0)$ and $(\frac{1}{3}, \frac{1}{3})$.

Now

$$f_{xx}(x, y) = 6x, \qquad f_{xy}(x, y) = -1, \qquad f_{yy}(x, y) = 6y.$$

Thus

$$D(x, y) = (6x)(6y) - (-1)^2 = 36xy - 1.$$

Since $D(0, 0) = 36(0)(0) - 1 = -1 < 0$, there is no relative extremum at $(0, 0)$.

Since $D(\frac{1}{3}, \frac{1}{3}) = 36(\frac{1}{3})(\frac{1}{3}) - 1 = 3 > 0$ and $f_{xx}(\frac{1}{3}, \frac{1}{3}) = 6(\frac{1}{3}) = 2 > 0$, there is a relative minimum at $(\frac{1}{3}, \frac{1}{3})$. At this point the value of the function is

$$f(\tfrac{1}{3}, \tfrac{1}{3}) = (\tfrac{1}{3})^3 + (\tfrac{1}{3})^3 - (\tfrac{1}{3})(\tfrac{1}{3}) = -\tfrac{1}{27}.$$

EXAMPLE 4   *Examine $f(x, y) = y^2 - x^2$ for relative extrema.*

Solving

$$f_x(x, y) = -2x = 0 \qquad \text{and} \qquad f_y(x, y) = 2y = 0,$$

we get the critical point $(0, 0)$. Moreover, at $(0, 0)$, and indeed at any point,

$$f_{xx}(x, y) = -2, \qquad f_{yy}(x, y) = 2, \qquad f_{xy}(x, y) = 0.$$

Hence $D(0, 0) = (-2)(2) - (0)^2 = -4 < 0$ and no relative extrema exist. A sketch of $z = f(x, y) = y^2 - x^2$ appears in Fig. 17.14. Note that for the surface curve cut by the plane $y = 0$ there is a *maximum* at $(0, 0)$; but for the surface curve cut by the plane $x = 0$ there is a *minimum* at $(0, 0)$. Thus on the *surface* no relative extremum can exist at the origin, although $(0, 0)$ is a critical point. Around the origin the curve is saddle-shaped and $(0, 0)$ is called a *saddle point* of f.

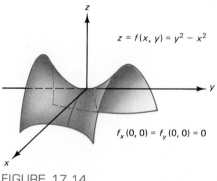

z

$z = f(x, y) = y^2 - x^2$

y

$f_x(0, 0) = f_y(0, 0) = 0$

x

FIGURE 17.14

EXAMPLE 5   *Examine $f(x, y) = x^4 + (x - y)^4$ for relative extrema.*

If we set

$$f_x(x, y) = 4x^3 + 4(x - y)^3 = 0 \tag{4}$$

$$\text{and} \qquad f_y(x, y) = -4(x - y)^3 = 0, \tag{5}$$

then from Eq. (5) we have $x - y = 0$, or $x = y$. Substituting into Eq. (4) gives $4x^3 = 0$, or $x = 0$. Thus $x = y = 0$ and $(0, 0)$ is the only critical point. At $(0, 0)$, $f_{xx}(x, y) = 12x^2 + 12(x - y)^2 = 0$, $f_{yy}(x, y) = 12(x - y)^2 = 0$, and $f_{xy}(x, y) = -12(x - y)^2 = 0$. Hence $D(0, 0) = 0$ and the second-derivative test gives no information. However, for all $(x, y) \neq (0, 0)$ we have $f(x, y) > 0$ while $f(0, 0) = 0$. Hence at $(0, 0)$ the graph of f has a low point and we conclude that f has a relative (and absolute) minimum at $(0, 0)$.

In many situations involving functions of two variables, and especially in their applications, the nature of the given problem is an indicator of whether a critical point is in fact a relative (or absolute) maximum or a relative (or absolute) minimum. In such cases the second-derivative test is not needed. Often, in mathematical studies of applied areas the appropriate second-order conditions are assumed to hold.

EXAMPLE 6   *Let P be a production function given by*

$$P = f(l, k) = 0.54l^2 - 0.02l^3 + 1.89k^2 - 0.09k^3,$$

where l and k are the amounts of labor and capital, respectively, and P is the quantity of output produced. Find the values of l and k that maximize P.

$$P_l = 1.08l - 0.06l^2 \qquad\qquad P_k = 3.78k - 0.27k^2$$

$$\qquad = 0.06l(18 - l) = 0. \qquad\qquad = 0.27k(14 - k) = 0.$$

$$\qquad l = 0, l = 18. \qquad\qquad\qquad k = 0, k = 14.$$

The crticial points are $(0, 0)$, $(0, 14)$, $(18, 0)$, and $(18, 14)$.

Now,

$$P_{ll} = 1.08 - 0.12l, \qquad P_{kk} = 3.78 - 0.54k, \qquad P_{lk} = 0.$$

Thus

$$D(l, k) = P_{ll}P_{kk} - [P_{lk}]^2$$

$$\qquad = (1.08 - 0.12l)(3.78 - 0.54k).$$

At $(0, 0)$,

$$D(0, 0) = 1.08(3.78) > 0.$$

Since $D(0, 0) > 0$ and $P_{ll} = 1.08 > 0$, there is a relative minimum at $(0, 0)$.

At $(0, 14)$,

$$D(0, 14) = 1.08(-3.78) < 0.$$

Since $D(0, 14) < 0$, there is no relative extremum at $(0, 14)$.

At $(18, 0)$,

$$D(18, 0) = (-1.08)(3.78) < 0.$$

Since $D(18, 0) < 0$, there is no relative extremum at $(18, 0)$.

At $(18, 14)$,

$$D(18, 14) = (-1.08)(-3.78) > 0.$$

Since $D(18, 14) > 0$ and $P_{ll} = -1.08 < 0$, there is a relative maximum at $(18, 14)$. The maximum output is obtained when $l = 18$ and $k = 14$.

EXAMPLE 7   *A food manufacturer produces two types of candy, A and B, for which the average costs of production are constant at 70 and 80 cents per pound, respectively. The quantities q_A, q_B (in pounds) of A and B that can be sold each week are given by the joint-demand functions*

$$q_A = 240(p_B - p_A)$$

and $$q_B = 240(150 + p_A - 2p_B),$$

where p_A and p_B are the selling prices (in cents per pound) of A and B, respectively. Determine the selling prices that will maximize the manufacturer's profit P.

For A and B the profits per pound are $p_A - 70$ and $p_B - 80$, respectively. Hence total profit P is given by

$$P = (p_A - 70)q_A + (p_B - 80)q_B$$

$$= (p_A - 70)[240(p_B - p_A)] + (p_B - 80)[240(150 + p_A - 2p_B)].$$

To maximize P we set its partial derivatives equal to 0:

$$\frac{\partial P}{\partial p_A} = (p_A - 70)[240(-1)] + [240(p_B - p_A)](1) +$$

$$(p_B - 80)[(240)(1)] = 0, \qquad (6)$$

$$\frac{\partial P}{\partial p_B} = (p_A - 70)[240(1)] + (p_B - 80)[240(-2)] +$$

$$[240(150 + p_A - 2p_B)](1) = 0. \qquad (7)$$

Simplifying the preceding two equations gives

$$\begin{cases} p_B - p_A - 5 & = 0, \\ -2p_B + p_A + 120 = 0, \end{cases}$$

whose solution is $p_A = 110$ and $p_B = 115$ (both in cents). Moreover,

$$\frac{\partial^2 P}{\partial p_A^2} = -480 < 0, \qquad \frac{\partial^2 P}{\partial p_B^2} = -960, \qquad \frac{\partial^2 P}{\partial p_B \partial p_A} = 480.$$

Thus $D(110, 115) = (-480)(-960) - (480)^2 > 0$. Since $\partial^2 P/\partial p_A^2 < 0$, we indeed have a maximum. The manufacturer should sell candy A at $1.10 per pound and B at $1.15 per pound.

EXAMPLE 8*

Suppose a monopolist is practicing price discrimination by selling the same product in two separate markets at different prices. Let q_A be the number of units sold in market A, where the demand function is $p_A = f(q_A)$, and let q_B be the number of units sold in market B, where the demand function is $p_B = g(q_B)$.

*Omit if Sec. 17.6 was not covered.

Then the revenue functions for the two markets are

$$r_A = q_A f(q_A) \quad \text{and} \quad r_B = q_B g(q_B).$$

Assume that all units are produced at one plant and let the cost function for producing q ($= q_A + q_B$) units be $c = c(q)$. Keep in mind that r_A is a function of q_A, and r_B is a function of q_B. The monopolist's profit P is

$$P = r_A + r_B - c.$$

To maximize P with respect to outputs q_A and q_B, we set its partial derivatives equal to 0. To begin with,

$$\frac{\partial P}{\partial q_A} = \frac{dr_A}{dq_A} + 0 - \frac{\partial c}{\partial q_A}$$

$$= \frac{dr_A}{dq_A} - \frac{dc}{dq}\frac{\partial q}{\partial q_A} = 0 \quad \text{(chain rule)}.$$

Because

$$\frac{\partial q}{\partial q_A} = \frac{\partial}{\partial q_A}(q_A + q_B) = 1,$$

we have

$$\frac{\partial P}{\partial q_A} = \frac{dr_A}{dq_A} - \frac{dc}{dq} = 0. \tag{8}$$

Similarly,

$$\frac{\partial P}{\partial q_B} = \frac{dr_B}{dq_B} - \frac{dc}{dq} = 0. \tag{9}$$

From Eqs. (8) and (9) we get

$$\frac{dr_A}{dq_A} = \frac{dc}{dq} = \frac{dr_B}{dq_B}.$$

But dr_A/dq_A and dr_B/dq_B are marginal revenues, and dc/dq is marginal cost. Hence, to maximize profit it is necessary to charge prices (and distribute output) so that the marginal revenues in both markets will be the same and, loosely speaking, will also be equal to the cost of the last unit produced in the plant.

EXERCISE 17.7

In Problems 1–6, find the critical points of the functions.

1. $f(x, y) = x^2 + y^2 - 5x + 4y + xy.$

2. $f(x, y) = x^2 + 4y^2 - 6x + 16y.$

3. $f(x, y) = 2x^3 + y^3 - 3x^2 + 1.5y^2 - 12x - 90y.$

4. $f(x, y) = xy - \frac{1}{x} - \frac{1}{y}.$

5. $f(x, y, z) = 2x^2 + xy + y^2 + 100 - z(x + y - 200).$

6. $f(x, y, z, w) = x^2 + y^2 + z^2 - w(x - y + 2z - 6).$

In Problems **7–18,** *find the critical points of the functions. Determine, by the second-derivative test, whether each point corresponds to a relative maximum, to a relative minimum, to neither, or whether the test gives no information.*

7. $f(x, y) = x^2 + 3y^2 + 4x - 9y + 3$.

8. $f(x, y) = -2x^2 + 8x - 3y^2 + 24y + 7$.

9. $f(x, y) = y - y^2 - 3x - 6x^2$.

10. $f(x, y) = x^2 + y^2 + xy - 9x + 1$.

11. $f(x, y) = x^3 - 3xy + y^2 + y - 5$.

12. $f(x, y) = \dfrac{x^3}{3} + y^2 - 2x + 2y - 2xy$.

13. $f(x, y) = \frac{1}{3}(x^3 + 8y^3) - 2(x^2 + y^2) + 1$.

14. $f(x, y) = x^2 + y^2 - xy + x^3$.

15. $f(l, k) = 2lk - l^2 + 264k - 10l - 2k^2$.

16. $f(l, k) = l^3 + k^3 - 3lk$.

17. $f(p, q) = pq - \dfrac{1}{p} - \dfrac{1}{q}$.

18. $f(x, y) = (x - 3)(y - 3)(x + y - 3)$.

In Problems **19–26,** *unless otherwise indicated the variables p_A and p_B denote selling prices of products A and B, respectively. Similarly, q_A and q_B denote quantities of A and B which are produced and sold during some time period. In all cases, the variables employed will be assumed to be units of output, input, money, etc.*

19. Suppose $P = f(l, k) = 1.08l^2 - 0.03l^3 + 1.68k^2 - 0.08k^3$ is a production function for a firm. Find the quantities of inputs, l and k, so as to maximize output P.

20. In a certain automated manufacturing process, machines M and N are utilized for m and n hours, respectively. If daily output Q is a function of m and n, namely $Q = 4.5m + 5n - 0.5m^2 - n^2 - 0.25mn$, find the values of m and n that maximize Q.

21. A candy company produces two varieties of candy, A and B, for which the constant average costs of production are 60 and 70 (cents per lb), respectively. The demand functions for A and B are respectively given by $q_A = 5(p_B - p_A)$ and $q_B = 500 + 5(p_A - 2p_B)$. Find the selling prices p_A and p_B that maximize the company's profit.

22. Repeat Problem 21 if the constant costs of production of A and B are a and b (cents per lb), respectively.

23. Suppose a monopolist is practicing price discrimination in the sale of a product by charging different prices in two separate markets. In market A the demand function is $p_A = 100 - q_A$ and in B it is $p_B = 84 - q_B$, where q_A and q_B are the quantities sold per week in A and B, and p_A and p_B are the respective prices per unit. If the monopolist's cost function is $c = 600 + 4(q_A + q_B)$, how much should be sold in each market to maximize profit? What selling prices give this maximum profit? Find the maximum profit.

24. A monopolist sells two competitive products, A and B, for which the demand functions are $q_A = 1 - 2p_A + 4p_B$ and $q_B = 11 + 2p_A - 6p_B$. If the constant average cost of producing a unit of A is 4 and for B it is 1, how many units of A and B should be sold to maximize the monopolist's profit?

25. For products A and B, the joint-cost function for a manufacturer is $c = 1.5q_A^2 + 4.5q_B^2$ and the demand functions are $p_A = 36 - q_A^2$ and $p_B = 30 - q_B^2$. Find the level of production that maximizes profit.

26. For a monopolist's products, A and B, the joint-cost function is $c = (q_A + q_B)^2$ and the demand functions are $q_A = 26 - p_A$ and $q_B = 10 - 0.25p_B$. Find the values of p_A and p_B that maximize profit. What are the quantities of A and B that correspond to these prices? What is the total profit?

27. An open-top rectangular box is to have a volume of 6 ft³. The cost per sq ft of materials is \$3 for the bottom, \$1 for the front and back, and \$0.50 for the other two sides. Find the dimensions of the box so that the cost of materials is minimized (see Fig. 17.15).

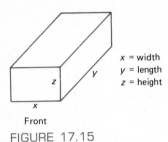

x = width
y = length
z = height

Front

FIGURE 17.15

28. Suppose A and B are the only two firms in the market selling the same product (we say that they are *duopolists*). The industry demand function for the product is $p = 92 - q_A - q_B$ where q_A and q_B denote the output produced and sold by A and B, respectively. For A the cost function is $c_A = 10q_A$; for B it is $c_B = 0.5q_B^2$. Suppose the firms decide to enter into an agreement on output and price control by jointly acting as a monopoly. In this case we say they enter into *collusion*. Show that the profit function for the monopoly is given by

$$P = pq_A - c_A + pq_B - c_B.$$

Express P as a function of q_A and q_B and determine how output should be allocated so as to maximize the profit of the monopoly.

29. Suppose $f(x, y) = -2x^2 + 5y^2 + 7$, where x and y must satisfy the equation $3x - 2y = 7$. Find the relative extrema of f subject to the given conditions on x and y by first solving the second equation for y. Substitute the result for y in the given equation. Thus f is expressed as a function of one variable for which extrema may be found in the usual way.

30. Repeat Problem 29 if $f(x, y) = x^2 + 4y^2 + 6$ subject to the condition that $2x - 8y = 20$.

17.8 LAGRANGE MULTIPLIERS

We shall now find relative maxima and minima for a function on which certain *constraints* are imposed. Such a situation could arise if a manufacturer wished to minimize the total cost of factors of input and yet obtain a particular level of output.

Suppose we want to find the relative extrema of

$$w = x^2 + y^2 + z^2 \qquad (1)$$

subject to the constraint that x, y, and z must satisfy

$$x - y + 2z = 6. \qquad (2)$$

We can transform w, which is a function of three variables, into a function of two variables such that the new function reflects constraint (2). Solving Eq. (2) for x, we get

$$x = y - 2z + 6, \qquad (3)$$

which when substituted for x in Eq. (1) gives

$$w = (y - 2z + 6)^2 + y^2 + z^2. \qquad (4)$$

Since w is now expressed as a function of two variables, to find relative extrema we follow the usual procedure of setting its partial derivatives equal to 0:

$$\frac{\partial w}{\partial y} = 2(y - 2z + 6) + 2y = 4y - 4z + 12 = 0, \tag{5}$$

$$\frac{\partial w}{\partial z} = -4(y - 2z + 6) + 2z = -4y + 10z - 24 = 0. \tag{6}$$

Solving Eqs. (5) and (6) simultaneously gives $y = -1$ and $z = 2$. Substituting in Eq. (3), we get $x = 1$. Hence the only critical point of (1) subject to constraint (2) is $(1, -1, 2)$. By using the second-derivative test on (4) when $y = -1$ and $z = 2$, we have

$$\frac{\partial^2 w}{\partial y^2} = 4, \qquad \frac{\partial^2 w}{\partial z^2} = 10, \qquad \frac{\partial^2 w}{\partial z \partial y} = -4,$$

$$D(-1, 2) = 4(10) - (-4)^2 = 24 > 0.$$

Thus w, subject to the constraint, has a relative minimum at $(1, -1, 2)$.

This solution was found by using the constraint to express one of the variables in the original function in terms of the other variables. Often this is not practical, but there is another technique, called the method of **Lagrange multipliers,** * that avoids this step and yet allows us to obtain critical points.

The method is as follows. Suppose we have a function $f(x, y, z)$ subject to the constraint $g(x, y, z) = 0$. We construct a new function F of four variables defined by the following (where λ is a Greek letter read "lambda"):

$$F(x, y, z, \lambda) = f(x, y, z) - \lambda g(x, y, z).$$

It can be shown that if (x_0, y_0, z_0) is a critical point of f subject to the constraint $g(x, y, z) = 0$, there exists a value of λ, say λ_0, such that $(x_0, y_0, z_0, \lambda_0)$ is a critical point of F. The number λ_0 is called a *Lagrange multiplier*. Also, if $(x_0, y_0, z_0, \lambda_0)$ is a critical point of F, then (x_0, y_0, z_0) is a critical point of f subject to the constraint. Thus to find critical points of f subject to $g(x, y, z) = 0$, we instead find critical points of F. These are obtained by solving the simultaneous equations

$$\begin{cases} F_x(x, y, z, \lambda) = 0, \\ F_y(x, y, z, \lambda) = 0, \\ F_z(x, y, z, \lambda) = 0, \\ F_\lambda(x, y, z, \lambda) = 0. \end{cases}$$

At times, ingenuity must be used to do this. Once we obtain a critical point $(x_0, y_0, z_0, \lambda_0)$ of F, we can conclude that (x_0, y_0, z_0) is a critical point of f subject to the constraint $g(x, y, z) = 0$. Although f and g are functions of three variables, the method of Lagrange multipliers can be extended to n variables.

Let us illustrate the method of Lagrange multipliers for the original situation:

$$f(x, y, z) = x^2 + y^2 + z^2 \quad \text{subject to} \quad x - y + 2z = 6.$$

* After the French mathematician, Joseph-Louis Lagrange (1736–1813).

First, we write the constraint as $g(x, y, z) = x - y + 2z - 6 = 0$. Second, we form the function

$$F(x, y, z, \lambda) = f(x, y, z) - \lambda g(x, y, z)$$
$$= x^2 + y^2 + z^2 - \lambda(x - y + 2z - 6).$$

Next we set each partial derivative of F equal to 0. For convenience we shall write $F_x(x, y, z, \lambda)$ as F_x, and so on.

$$\begin{cases} F_x = 2x - \lambda = 0, & (7) \\ F_y = 2y + \lambda = 0, & (8) \\ F_z = 2z - 2\lambda = 0, & (9) \\ F_\lambda = -x + y - 2z + 6 = 0. & (10) \end{cases}$$

From Eqs. (7)–(9) we see immediately that

$$x = \frac{\lambda}{2}, \qquad y = -\frac{\lambda}{2}, \qquad \text{and} \qquad z = \lambda. \tag{11}$$

Substituting these values in Eq. (10), we obtain

$$-\frac{\lambda}{2} - \frac{\lambda}{2} - 2\lambda + 6 = 0,$$

$$\lambda = 2.$$

Thus from Eq. (11), $x = 1$, $y = -1$, and $z = 2$. Hence the only critical point of f subject to the constraint is $(1, -1, 2)$ at which there may exist a relative maximum, a relative minimum, or neither of these. The method of Lagrange multipliers does not directly indicate which of these possibilities occurs, although from our previous work we saw that it is indeed a relative minimum. In applied problems the nature of the problem itself may give a clue as to how a critical point is to be regarded. Often the existence of either a relative minimum or a relative maximum is assumed and a critical point is treated accordingly. Actually, sufficient second-order conditions for relative extrema are available, but we shall not consider them.

EXAMPLE 1   *Find the critical points for $z = f(x, y) = 3x - y + 6$ subject to the constraint $x^2 + y^2 = 4$.*

We write the constraint as $g(x, y) = x^2 + y^2 - 4 = 0$ and construct the function

$$F(x, y, \lambda) = f(x, y) - \lambda g(x, y) = 3x - y + 6 - \lambda(x^2 + y^2 - 4).$$

Setting $F_x = F_y = F_\lambda = 0$:

$$\begin{cases} 3 - 2x\lambda = 0, & (12) \\ -1 - 2y\lambda = 0, & (13) \\ -x^2 - y^2 + 4 = 0. & (14) \end{cases}$$

From Eqs. (12) and (13),

$$x = \frac{3}{2\lambda} \quad \text{and} \quad y = -\frac{1}{2\lambda}.$$

Substituting in Eq. (14), we obtain

$$-\frac{9}{4\lambda^2} - \frac{1}{4\lambda^2} + 4 = 0,$$

$$\lambda = \pm\frac{\sqrt{10}}{4}.$$

If $\lambda = \sqrt{10}/4$, then

$$x = \frac{3}{2\left(\dfrac{\sqrt{10}}{4}\right)} = \frac{3\sqrt{10}}{5}, \qquad y = -\frac{1}{2\left(\dfrac{\sqrt{10}}{4}\right)} = -\frac{\sqrt{10}}{5}.$$

Similarly, if $\lambda = -\sqrt{10}/4$,

$$x = -\frac{3\sqrt{10}}{5}, \qquad y = \frac{\sqrt{10}}{5}.$$

Therefore, the critical points of f subject to the constraint are $(3\sqrt{10}/5, -\sqrt{10}/5)$ and $(-3\sqrt{10}/5, \sqrt{10}/5)$. Note that the values of λ do not appear in the answer. They are simply a means to obtain it.

EXAMPLE 2   *Find critical points for* $f(x, y, z) = xyz$, *where* $xyz \neq 0$, *subject to the constraint* $x + 2y + 3z = 36$.

Set

$$F(x, y, z, \lambda) = xyz - \lambda(x + 2y + 3z - 36).$$

Then

$$\begin{cases} F_x = yz - \lambda = 0, \\ F_y = xz - 2\lambda = 0, \\ F_z = xy - 3\lambda = 0, \\ F_\lambda = -x - 2y - 3z + 36 = 0. \end{cases}$$

We can write the system as

$$\begin{cases} yz = \lambda, & (15) \\ xz = 2\lambda, & (16) \\ xy = 3\lambda, & (17) \\ x + 2y + 3z - 36 = 0. & (18) \end{cases}$$

Dividing each side of Eq. (15) by the corresponding side of Eq. (16), we get

$$\frac{yz}{xz} = \frac{\lambda}{2\lambda} \qquad \text{or} \qquad y = \frac{x}{2}.$$

This division is valid since $xyz \neq 0$. Similarly, from Eqs. (15) and (17) we get

$$z = \frac{x}{3}.$$

Substituting into Eq. (18) gives

$$x + 2\left(\frac{x}{2}\right) + 3\left(\frac{x}{3}\right) - 36 = 0,$$

$$x = 12.$$

Thus $y = 6$ and $z = 4$. Hence (12, 6, 4) is the only critical point satisfying the given conditions.

EXAMPLE 3   *Suppose a firm has an order for* 200 *units of its product and wishes to distribute their manufacture between two of its plants, plant* 1 *and plant* 2. *Let* q_1 *and* q_2 *denote the outputs of plants* 1 *and* 2, *respectively, and suppose the total cost function is given by* $c = f(q_1, q_2) = 2q_1^2 + q_1q_2 + q_2^2 + 200$. *How should the output be distributed in order to minimize costs?*

We must minimize $c = f(q_1, q_2)$ subject to the constraint $q_1 + q_2 = 200$.

$$F(q_1, q_2, \lambda) = 2q_1^2 + q_1q_2 + q_2^2 + 200 - \lambda(q_1 + q_2 - 200).$$

$$\frac{\partial F}{\partial q_1} = 4q_1 + q_2 - \lambda = 0, \tag{19}$$

$$\frac{\partial F}{\partial q_2} = q_1 + 2q_2 - \lambda = 0, \tag{20}$$

$$\frac{\partial F}{\partial \lambda} = -q_1 - q_2 + 200 = 0. \tag{21}$$

Solving Eqs. (19) and (20) simultaneously for q_1 and q_2 gives

$$q_1 = \frac{\lambda}{7}, \qquad q_2 = \frac{3\lambda}{7}.$$

Substituting these values in Eq. (21) gives $\lambda = 350$. Thus $q_1 = 50$ and $q_2 = 150$. Plant 1 should produce 50 units and plant 2 should produce 150 units, in order to minimize costs.

An interesting observation can be made concerning Example 3. From Eq. (19), $\lambda = 4q_1 + q_2 = \partial c/\partial q_1$, the marginal cost of plant 1. From Eq. (20), $\lambda = q_1 + 2q_2 = \partial c/\partial q_2$, the marginal cost of plant 2. Hence $\partial c/\partial q_1 = \partial c/\partial q_2$, and we conclude that to minimize cost it is necessary that the marginal costs of each plant be equal to each other.

EXAMPLE 4   *Suppose a firm must produce a given quantity P_0 of output in the cheapest possible manner. If there are two input factors l and k, and their prices per unit are fixed at p_l and p_k respectively, discuss the economic significance of combining input to achieve least cost. That is, describe the least-cost input combination.*

Let $P = f(l, k)$ be the production function. Then we must minimize the cost function

$$c = lp_l + kp_k$$

subject to

$$P_0 = f(l, k).$$

We construct

$$F(l, k, \lambda) = lp_l + kp_k - \lambda[f(l, k) - P_0].$$

We have

$$\frac{\partial F}{\partial l} = p_l - \lambda \frac{\partial}{\partial l}[f(l, k)] = 0, \tag{22}$$

$$\frac{\partial F}{\partial k} = p_k - \lambda \frac{\partial}{\partial k}[f(l, k)] = 0, \tag{23}$$

$$\frac{\partial F}{\partial \lambda} = -f(l, k) + P_0 = 0.$$

From Eqs. (22) and (23),

$$\lambda = \frac{p_l}{\dfrac{\partial}{\partial l}[f(l, k)]} = \frac{p_k}{\dfrac{\partial}{\partial k}[f(l, k)]}. \tag{24}$$

Hence

$$\frac{p_l}{p_k} = \frac{\dfrac{\partial}{\partial l}[f(l, k)]}{\dfrac{\partial}{\partial k}[f(l, k)]}.$$

We conclude that when the least-cost combination of factors is used, the ratio of the marginal products of the input factors must be equal to the ratio of their corresponding prices.

The method of Lagrange multipliers is by no means restricted to problems involving a single constraint. For example, suppose $f(x, y, z, w)$ were subject to constraints $g_1(x, y, z, w) = 0$ and $g_2(x, y, z, w) = 0$. Then there would be two lambdas, λ_1 and λ_2 (one for each constraint), and we would construct the function $F = f - \lambda_1 g_1 - \lambda_2 g_2$. We would then solve the system $F_x = F_y = F_z = F_w = F_{\lambda_1} = F_{\lambda_2} = 0$.

EXAMPLE 5   *Find critical points for $f(x, y, z) = xy + yz$ subject to the constraints $x^2 + y^2 = 8$ and $yz = 8$.*

Set

$$F(x, y, z, \lambda_1, \lambda_2) = xy + yz - \lambda_1(x^2 + y^2 - 8) - \lambda_2(yz - 8).$$

Then

$$\begin{cases} F_x = y - 2x\lambda_1 = 0, \\ F_y = x + z - 2y\lambda_1 - z\lambda_2 = 0, \\ F_z = y - y\lambda_2 = 0, \\ F_{\lambda_1} = -x^2 - y^2 + 8 = 0, \\ F_{\lambda_2} = -yz + 8 = 0. \end{cases}$$

We can write the system as

$$\begin{cases} \dfrac{y}{2x} = \lambda_1, & (25) \\ x + z - 2y\lambda_1 - z\lambda_2 = 0, & (26) \\ \lambda_2 = 1, & (27) \\ x^2 + y^2 = 8, & (28) \\ z = \dfrac{8}{y}. & (29) \end{cases}$$

Substituting $\lambda_2 = 1$ from Eq. (27) into Eq. (26) and simplifying give the equation $x - 2y\lambda_1 = 0$, so

$$\lambda_1 = \frac{x}{2y}.$$

Substituting into Eq. (25) gives

$$\frac{y}{2x} = \frac{x}{2y},$$
$$y^2 = x^2. \qquad (30)$$

Substituting into Eq. (28) gives $x^2 + x^2 = 8$ from which $x = \pm 2$. If $x = 2$, then from Eq. (30) we have $y = \pm 2$. Similarly, if $x = -2$, then $y = \pm 2$. Thus if $x = 2$ and $y = 2$, then from Eq. (29) we obtain $z = 4$. Continuing in this manner, we obtain four critical points:

$$(2, 2, 4), \quad (2, -2, -4), \quad (-2, 2, 4), \quad (-2, -2, -4).$$

EXERCISE 17.8

In Problems **1–12** find, by the method of Lagrange multipliers, the critical points of the functions subject to the given constraints.

1. $f(x, y) = x^2 + 4y^2 + 6$; $2x - 8y = 20$.

2. $f(x, y) = -2x^2 + 5y^2 + 7$; $3x - 2y = 7$.

3. $f(x, y, z) = x^2 + y^2 + z^2$; $2x + y - z = 9$.

4. $f(x, y, z) = x + y + z$; $xyz = 27$.

5. $f(x, y, z) = x^2 + xy + 2y^2 + z^2$; $x - 3y - 4z = 16$.

6. $f(x, y, z) = xyz^2$; $x - y + z = 20$, $(xyz^2 \neq 0)$.

7. $f(x, y, z) = xyz$; $x + 2y + 3z = 18$, $(xyz \neq 0)$.

8. $f(x, y, z) = x^2 + y^2 + z^2$; $x + y + z = 1$.

9. $f(x, y, z) = x^2 + 2y - z^2$; $2x - y = 0, y + z = 0$.

10. $f(x, y, z) = x^2 + y^2 + z^2$; $x + y + z = 1, x - y + z = 1$.

11. $f(x, y, z) = xyz$; $x + y + z = 12, x + y - z = 0$, $(xyz \neq 0)$.

12. $f(x, y, z, w) = 2x^2 + 2y^2 + 3z^2 - 4w^2$; $4x - 8y + 6z + 16w = 6$.

13. To fill an order for 100 units of its product, a firm wishes to distribute the production between its two plants, plant 1 and plant 2. The total cost function is given by $c = f(q_1, q_2) = 0.1q_1^2 + 7q_1 + 15q_2 + 1000$, where q_1 and q_2 are the number of units produced at plants 1 and 2, respectively. How should the output be distributed in order to minimize costs?

14. Repeat Problem 13 if the cost function is $c = 3q_1^2 + q_1q_2 + 2q_2^2$ and a total of 200 units are to be produced.

15. The production function for a firm is $f(l, k) = 12l + 20k - l^2 - 2k^2$. The cost to the firm of l and k is 4 and 8 per unit, respectively. If the firm wants the total cost of input to be 88, find the greatest output possible subject to this budget constraint.

16. Repeat Problem 15, given that $f(l, k) = 60l + 30k - 2l^2 - 3k^2$ and the budget constraint is $2l + 3k = 30$.

Problems **17–20** refer to the following definition. A **utility function** is a function that attaches a measure to the satisfaction or utility a consumer gets from the consumption of products per unit of time. Suppose $U = f(x, y)$ is such a function, where x and y are the amounts of two products, X and Y. The **marginal utility** of X is $\partial U/\partial x$ and approximately represents the change in total utility resulting from a one-unit change in consumption of product X per unit of time. We define the marginal utility of Y in similar fashion. If the prices of X and Y are p_x and p_y, respectively, and the consumer has an income or budget of I to spend, then the budget constraint is $xp_x + yp_y = I$. In Problems **17–19,** find the quantities of each product that the consumer should buy, subject to the budget, that will allow maximum satisfaction. That is, in Problems **17** and **18,** find values of x and y that maximize $U = f(x, y)$ subject to $xp_x + yp_y = I$. Similarly for Problem **19.** Assume that such a maximum exists.

17. $U = x^3y^3$; $p_x = 2, p_y = 3, I = 48$, $(x^3y^3 \neq 0)$.

18. $U = 46x - (5x^2/2) + 34y - 2y^2$; $p_x = 5, p_y = 2, I = 30$.

19. $U = f(x, y, z) = xyz$; $p_x = 2, p_y = 1, p_z = 4, I = 60$, $(xyz \neq 0)$.

20. Let $U = f(x, y)$ be a utility function subject to the budget constraint $xp_x + yp_y = I$, where p_x, p_y, and I are constant. Show that to maximize satisfaction it is necessary that

$$\lambda = \frac{f_x(x, y)}{p_x} = \frac{f_y(x, y)}{p_y},$$

where $f_x(x, y)$ and $f_y(x, y)$ are the marginal utilities of X and Y, respectively. Deduce that $f_x(x, y)/p_x$ is the marginal utility of one dollar's worth of X. Hence, maximum satisfaction is obtained when the consumer allocates the budget so that the marginal utility of a dollar's worth of X is equal to the marginal utility per dollar's worth of Y. Performing the same procedure as above, verify that this is true for $U = f(x, y, z, w)$ subject to the corresponding budget equation. In each case, λ is called the *marginal utility of income*.

17.9 LINES OF REGRESSION*

To study the influence of advertising on sales, a firm compiled the data in Table 17.4. The variable x denotes advertising expenditures in hundreds of dollars and

TABLE 17.4

Expenditures, x	2	3	4.5	5.5	7
Revenue, y	3	6	8	10	11

the variable y denotes the resulting sales revenue in thousands of dollars. If each pair (x, y) of data is plotted, the result is called a *scatter diagram* [Fig. 17.16(a)].

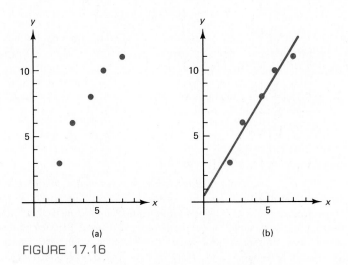

(a)   (b)

FIGURE 17.16

From an observation of the distribution of the points, it is reasonable to assume that a relationship exists between x and y and that it is approximately linear. On this basis we may fit "by eye" a straight line that approximates the given data [Fig. 17.16(b)], and from this line predict a value of y for a given value of x. This line seems consistent with the trend of the data, although other lines could be drawn as well. Unfortunately, determining a line "by eye" is not very objective. We want to apply criteria in specifying what we shall call a line of "best fit." A frequently used technique is called the **method of least squares.**

* May be omitted without loss of continuity.

To apply the method of least squares to the data in Table 17.4, we first assume that x and y are approximately linearly related and that we can fit a straight line

$$\hat{y} = \hat{a} + \hat{b}x \tag{1}$$

that approximates the given points by a suitable objective choice of the constants $\hat{a}$ and $\hat{b}$ (read "a hat" and "b hat," respectively). For a given value of x in Eq. (1), $\hat{y}$ is the corresponding predicted value of y, and $(x, \hat{y})$ will be on the line. Our aim is that $\hat{y}$ be near y.

When $x = 2$, the observed value of y is 3. Our predicted value of y is obtained by substituting $x = 2$ in Eq. (1), which yields $\hat{y} = \hat{a} + 2\hat{b}$. The error of estimation, or vertical deviation of the point $(2, 3)$ from the line, is $\hat{y} - y$, or

$$\hat{a} + 2\hat{b} - 3.$$

This vertical deviation is indicated (although exaggerated for clarity) in Fig. 17.17. Similarly, the vertical deviation of $(3, 6)$ from the line is $\hat{a} + 3\hat{b} - 6$,

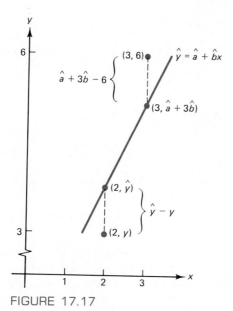

FIGURE 17.17

as is also illustrated. To avoid possible difficulties associated with positive and negative deviations, we shall consider the squares of the deviations and shall form the sum S of all such squares for the given data.

$$S = (\hat{a} + 2\hat{b} - 3)^2 + (\hat{a} + 3\hat{b} - 6)^2 + (\hat{a} + 4.5\hat{b} - 8)^2 +$$

$$(\hat{a} + 5.5\hat{b} - 10)^2 + (\hat{a} + 7\hat{b} - 11)^2.$$

The method of least squares requires that we choose as the line of "best fit" the one obtained by selecting $\hat{a}$ and $\hat{b}$ so as to minimize S. We can minimize

S with respect to $\hat{a}$ and $\hat{b}$ by solving the system

$$\begin{cases} \dfrac{\partial S}{\partial \hat{a}} = 0, \\[2mm] \dfrac{\partial S}{\partial \hat{b}} = 0. \end{cases}$$

We have

$$\frac{\partial S}{\partial \hat{a}} = 2(\hat{a} + 2\hat{b} - 3) + 2(\hat{a} + 3\hat{b} - 6) + 2(\hat{a} + 4.5\hat{b} - 8) +$$

$$2(\hat{a} + 5.5\hat{b} - 10) + 2(\hat{a} + 7\hat{b} - 11) = 0,$$

$$\frac{\partial S}{\partial \hat{b}} = 4(\hat{a} + 2\hat{b} - 3) + 6(\hat{a} + 3\hat{b} - 6) + 9(\hat{a} + 4.5\hat{b} - 8) +$$

$$11(\hat{a} + 5.5\hat{b} - 10) + 14(\hat{a} + 7\hat{b} - 11) = 0,$$

which when simplified gives

$$\begin{cases} 5\hat{a} + 22\hat{b} = 38, \\ 44\hat{a} + 225\hat{b} = 384. \end{cases}$$

Solving for $\hat{a}$ and $\hat{b}$, we obtain

$$\hat{a} = \frac{102}{157} \approx 0.65, \qquad \hat{b} = \frac{248}{157} \approx 1.58.$$

It can be shown that these values of $\hat{a}$ and $\hat{b}$ lead to a minimum value of S. Hence in the sense of least squares, the line of best fit $\hat{y} = \hat{a} + \hat{b}x$ is

$$\hat{y} = 0.65 + 1.58x. \tag{2}$$

This is, in fact, the line indicated in Fig. 17.16(b). It is called the **least squares line of y on x** or the **linear regression line of y on x.** The constants $\hat{a}$ and $\hat{b}$ are called **linear regression coefficients.** With Eq. (2) we would predict that when $x = 5$, the corresponding value of y is $\hat{y} = 0.65 + 1.58(5) = 8.55$.

More generally, suppose we are given the following n pairs of observations:

$$(x_1, y_1), (x_2, y_2), \ldots, (x_n, y_n).$$

If we assume that x and y are approximately linearly related and that we can fit a straight line $\hat{y} = \hat{a} + \hat{b}x$ that approximates the data, the sum of the squares of the errors $\hat{y} - y$ is

$$S = (\hat{a} + \hat{b}x_1 - y_1)^2 + (\hat{a} + \hat{b}x_2 - y_2)^2 + \cdots + (\hat{a} + \hat{b}x_n - y_n)^2.$$

Since S must be minimized with respect to $\hat{a}$ and $\hat{b}$,

$$\frac{\partial S}{\partial \hat{a}} = 2(\hat{a} + \hat{b}x_1 - y_1) + 2(\hat{a} + \hat{b}x_2 - y_2) + \cdots + 2(\hat{a} + \hat{b}x_n - y_n) = 0,$$

$$\frac{\partial S}{\partial \hat{b}} = 2x_1(\hat{a} + \hat{b}x_1 - y_1) + 2x_2(\hat{a} + \hat{b}x_2 - y_2) + \cdots + 2x_n(\hat{a} + \hat{b}x_n - y_n) = 0.$$

Dividing both equations by 2 and using sigma notation, we have

$$\begin{cases} \hat{a}n + \hat{b} \displaystyle\sum_{i=1}^{n} x_i - \sum_{i=1}^{n} y_i = 0, \\[2em] \hat{a} \displaystyle\sum_{i=1}^{n} x_i + \hat{b} \sum_{i=1}^{n} x_i^2 - \sum_{i=1}^{n} x_i y_i = 0. \end{cases}$$

Equivalently, we have the system of so-called *normal equations:*

$$\begin{cases} \displaystyle\sum_{i=1}^{n} y_i = \hat{a}n + \hat{b} \sum_{i=1}^{n} x_i, & (3) \\[2em] \displaystyle\sum_{i=1}^{n} x_i y_i = \hat{a} \sum_{i=1}^{n} x_i + \hat{b} \sum_{i=1}^{n} x_i^2. & (4) \end{cases}$$

To solve for $\hat{b}$ we first multiply Eq. (3) by $\displaystyle\sum_{i=1}^{n} x_i$ and Eq. (4) by n:

$$\begin{cases} \left(\displaystyle\sum_{i=1}^{n} x_i \right)\left(\sum_{i=1}^{n} y_i \right) = \hat{a}n \sum_{i=1}^{n} x_i + \hat{b}\left(\sum_{i=1}^{n} x_i \right)^2, & (5) \\[2em] n \displaystyle\sum_{i=1}^{n} x_i y_i = \hat{a}n \sum_{i=1}^{n} x_i + \hat{b}n \sum_{i=1}^{n} x_i^2. & (6) \end{cases}$$

Subtracting Eq. (5) from Eq. (6), we obtain

$$n \sum_{i=1}^{n} x_i y_i - \left(\sum_{i=1}^{n} x_i \right)\left(\sum_{i=1}^{n} y_i \right) = \hat{b}n \sum_{i=1}^{n} x_i^2 - \hat{b}\left(\sum_{i=1}^{n} x_i \right)^2$$

$$= \hat{b}\left[n \sum_{i=1}^{n} x_i^2 - \left(\sum_{i=1}^{n} x_i \right)^2 \right].$$

Thus

$$\hat{b} = \frac{n \displaystyle\sum_{i=1}^{n} x_i y_i - \left(\displaystyle\sum_{i=1}^{n} x_i \right)\left(\displaystyle\sum_{i=1}^{n} y_i \right)}{n \displaystyle\sum_{i=1}^{n} x_i^2 - \left(\displaystyle\sum_{i=1}^{n} x_i \right)^2}. \qquad (7)$$

Solving Eqs. (3) and (4) for $\hat{a}$ gives

$$\hat{a} = \frac{\left(\sum\limits_{i=1}^{n} x_i^2\right)\left(\sum\limits_{i=1}^{n} y_i\right) - \left(\sum\limits_{i=1}^{n} x_i\right)\left(\sum\limits_{i=1}^{n} x_i y_i\right)}{n \sum\limits_{i=1}^{n} x_i^2 - \left(\sum\limits_{i=1}^{n} x_i\right)^2}. \tag{8}$$

It can be shown that these values of $\hat{a}$ and $\hat{b}$ minimize S.

Computing the linear regression coefficients $\hat{a}$ and $\hat{b}$ by the formulas of Eqs. (7) and (8) gives the linear regression line of y on x, namely $\hat{y} = \hat{a} + \hat{b}x$, which can be used to estimate y for a given value of x.

In the next example, as well as in the exercises, you will encounter *index numbers*. They are used to relate a variable in one period of time to the same variable in another period, this latter period called the *base period*. An index number is a *relative* number that describes data that are changing over time. Such data are referred to as *times series*.

For example, consider the time series data of total production of widgets in the United States for 1982–86 indicated in Table 17.5. If we choose 1983 as the base year and assign to it the index number 100, then the other index numbers are obtained by dividing each year's production by the 1983 production of 900 and multiplying the result by 100. We can, for example, interpret the index 106 for 1986 as meaning that production for that year was 106% of the production in 1983.

TABLE 17.5

YEAR	PRODUCTION (IN THOUSANDS)	INDEX [1983 = 100]
1982	828	92
1983	900	100
1984	936	104
1985	891	99
1986	954	106

In time series analysis, index numbers are obviously of great advantage if the data involve numbers of great magnitude. But regardless of the magnitude of the data, index numbers simplify the task of comparing changes in data over periods of time.

EXAMPLE 1   *By means of the linear regression line, represent the trend for the Index of Industrial Production from 1963 to 1968 (1967 = 100).*

YEAR	1963	1964	1965	1966	1967	1968
INDEX	79	84	91	99	100	105

Source: Economic Report of the President, 1971, U.S. Government Printing Office, Washington, D.C., 1971.

We shall let x denote time, y denote the index, and treat y as a linear function of x. Also, we shall designate 1963 by $x = 1$, 1964 by $x = 2$, and so on. There are $n = 6$ pairs of measurements. To determine the linear regression coefficients by using Eqs. (7) and (8), we first perform the arithmetic:

YEAR	x_i	y_i	$x_i y_i$	x_i^2
1963	1	79	79	1
1964	2	84	168	4
1965	3	91	273	9
1966	4	99	396	16
1967	5	100	500	25
1968	6	105	630	36
Total	21	558	2046	91
	$= \sum_{i=1}^{6} x_i$	$= \sum_{i=1}^{6} y_i$	$= \sum_{i=1}^{6} x_i y_i$	$= \sum_{i=1}^{6} x_i^2$

Hence by Eq. (8),

$$\hat{a} = \frac{91(558) - 21(2046)}{6(91) - (21)^2} = \frac{7812}{105} = 74.4,$$

and by Eq. (7),

$$\hat{b} = \frac{6(2046) - 21(558)}{6(91) - (21)^2} = \frac{558}{105} = 5.31 \text{ (approximately)}.$$

Thus the regression line of y on x is

$$\hat{y} = 74.4 + 5.31x,$$

whose graph, as well as a scatter diagram, appears in Fig. 17.18.

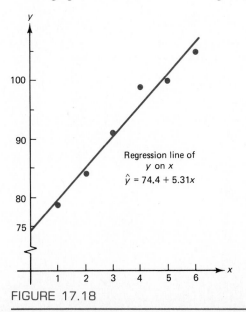

Regression line of
y on x

$\hat{y} = 74.4 + 5.31x$

FIGURE 17.18

EXERCISE 17.9

In Problems **1–4,** *find an equation of the least squares linear regression line of y on x for the given data and sketch both the line and the data. Predict the value of y corresponding to x =* 3.5.

1.

x	1	2	3	4	5	6
y	1.5	2.3	2.6	3.7	4.0	4.5

2.

x	1	2	3	4	5	6	7
y	1	1.8	2	4	4.5	7	9

3.

x	2	3	4.5	5.5	7
y	3	5	8	10	11

4.

x	2	3	4	5	6	7
y	2.4	2.9	3.3	3.8	4.3	4.9

5. A firm finds that when the price of its product is p dollars per unit, the number of units sold is q, as indicated below. Find an equation of the regression line of q on p.

PRICE, p	10	30	40	50	60	70
DEMAND, q	70	68	63	50	46	32

6. On a farm an agronomist finds that the amount of water applied (in inches) and the corresponding yield of a certain crop (in tons per acre) are as given below. Find an equation of the regression line of y on x. Predict y when $x = 12$.

WATER, x	8	16	24	32
YIELD, y	4.1	4.5	5.1	6.1

7. A rabbit was injected with a virus, and x hours after the injection the temperature y (in degrees Fahrenheit) of the rabbit was measured.* The data are given below. Find an equation of the regression line of y on x, and estimate the rabbit's temperature 40 hours after the injection.

ELAPSED TIME, x	24	32	48	56
TEMPERATURE, y	102.8	104.5	106.5	107.0

* R. R. Sokal and F. J. Rohlf, *Introduction to Biostatistics* (San Francisco: W. H. Freeman & Company, Publishers, 1973).

8. In a psychological experiment, four persons were subjected to a stimulus. Both before and after the stimulus, the systolic blood pressure (in millimeters of mercury) of each subject was measured. The data are given below. Find an equation of the regression line of y on x where x and y are defined below.

BEFORE STIMULUS, x	130	132	136	140
AFTER STIMULUS, y	139	140	144	146

*For the time series in Problems **9** and **10** fit a linear regression line by least squares; that is, find an equation of the linear regression line of y on x. In each case let the first year in the table correspond to $x = 1$.*

9. Production of Product A, 1982–1986 (in thousands of units)

YEAR	PRODUCTION
1982	10
1983	15
1984	16
1985	18
1986	21

10. In the following, let 1961 correspond to $x = 1$, 1963 correspond to $x = 3$, and so on.

Wholesale Price Index—
Lumber and Wood Products
[1967 = 100]

YEAR	INDEX
1961	91
1963	94
1965	96
1967	100

Source: Economic Report of the President, 1971, U.S. Government Printing Office, Washington, D.C., 1971.

11. **a.** Find an equation of the least squares line of y on x for the following data. Refer to 1981 as year $x = 1$, and so on.

Overseas Shipments of Computers
by Acme Computer Co. (in thousands)

YEAR	QUANTITY
1981	35
1982	31
1983	26
1984	24
1985	26

b. For the data in part (a), refer to 1981 as year $x = -2$, 1982 as year $x = -1$, 1983 as year $x = 0$, and so on. Then $\sum_{i=1}^{5} x_i = 0$. Fit a least squares line and observe how the calculation is simplified.

12. For the following time series, find an equation of the linear regression line that best fits the data. Refer to 1965 as year $x = -2$, 1966 as year $x = -1$, and so on.

Consumer Price Index—Medical Care
1965–1969 [1967 = 100]

YEAR	INDEX
1965	90
1966	93
1967	100
1968	106
1969	113

Source: Economic Report of the President, 1971, U.S. Government Printing Office, Washington, D.C., 1971.

17.10 A COMMENT ON HOMOGENEOUS FUNCTIONS*

Many of the functions that are useful in economic analysis share the property of being homogeneous.

Definition

*A function $z = f(x, y)$ is said to be **homogeneous of degree n** (n being a constant) if, for **all** positive real values of λ,*

$$f(\lambda x, \lambda y) = \lambda^n f(x, y).$$

Verbally, if both x and y are multiplied by the same positive real number, then the resulting function value is a power of the number times the function value $f(x, y)$. For example, if

$$f(x, y) = x^3 - 2xy^2,$$

then

$$f(\lambda x, \lambda y) = (\lambda x)^3 - 2(\lambda x)(\lambda y)^2 = \lambda^3 x^3 - 2\lambda^3 xy^2$$
$$= \lambda^3 (x^3 - 2xy^2) = \lambda^3 f(x, y).$$

Thus f is homogeneous of degree three.

An important homogeneous function in economics is the Cobb-Douglas production function:

$$P = f(l, k) = Al^\alpha k^{1-\alpha} \qquad (\alpha \text{ and } A \text{ are constants}).$$

We have

$$f(\lambda l, \lambda k) = A(\lambda l)^\alpha (\lambda k)^{1-\alpha} = A\lambda^\alpha l^\alpha \lambda^{1-\alpha} k^{1-\alpha}$$
$$= \lambda Al^\alpha k^{1-\alpha} = \lambda f(l, k).$$

Thus f is homogeneous of degree one. For example, $f(l, k) = 2l^{0.3}k^{0.7}$ is a homogeneous function of degree one.

Homogeneous production functions of degree one have an interesting property. If f is such a function, then

$$f(\lambda l, \lambda k) = \lambda f(l, k).$$

Thus if all inputs are doubled, then

$$f(2l, 2k) = 2f(l, k),$$

and output is doubled. Similarly, if all inputs are tripled, output is tripled, etc. In short, the same proportional change in each input factor of production results in the same proportional change in output.

By considering the partial derivatives of a homogeneous function, an important result can be obtained. Let $f(l, k)$ be a homogeneous production function

---

* This section contains material from Sec. 17.6 and may be omitted without loss of continuity.

of degree n. Then we have the identity

$$f(\lambda l, \lambda k) = \lambda^n f(l, k). \tag{1}$$

Consider the left side of Eq. (1). If we set $r = \lambda l$ and $s = \lambda k$, then Eq. (1) becomes

$$f(r, s) = \lambda^n f(l, k). \tag{2}$$

Now, for each side we shall take the partial with respect to λ. For the left side, $f(r, s)$, by the chain rule we have

$$\frac{\partial}{\partial \lambda}[f(r, s)] = \frac{\partial}{\partial r}[f(r, s)]\frac{\partial r}{\partial \lambda} + \frac{\partial}{\partial s}[f(r, s)]\frac{\partial s}{\partial \lambda}$$

$$= \frac{\partial}{\partial r}[f(r, s)]l + \frac{\partial}{\partial s}[f(r, s)]k. \tag{3}$$

For the right side of Eq. (2),

$$\frac{\partial}{\partial \lambda}[\lambda^n f(l, k)] = n\lambda^{n-1}f(l, k). \tag{4}$$

Setting Eqs. (3) and (4) equal to each other, we have

$$l\frac{\partial}{\partial r}[f(r, s)] + k\frac{\partial}{\partial s}[f(r, s)] = n\lambda^{n-1}f(l, k).$$

In particular, if $\lambda = 1$, then $r = l$ and $s = k$, and so $f(r, s) = f(l, k)$. Thus, $\frac{\partial}{\partial r}[f(r, s)] = \frac{\partial}{\partial l}[f(l, k)]$ and $\frac{\partial}{\partial s}[f(r, s)] = \frac{\partial}{\partial k}[f(l, k)]$. Hence we have what is called *Euler's Theorem* for homogeneous functions:

$$l\frac{\partial}{\partial l}[f(l, k)] + k\frac{\partial}{\partial k}[f(l, k)] = nf(l, k). \tag{5}$$

Now, if f is homogeneous of degree one, such as the Cobb-Douglas function, then $n = 1$ and Eq. (5) becomes

$$l\frac{\partial}{\partial l}[f(l, k)] + k\frac{\partial}{\partial k}[f(l, k)] = f(l, k).$$

Thus if we multiply the marginal product of each input by the quantity of the input, the sum is equal to the total product.

17.11 MULTIPLE INTEGRALS

Recall that the definite integral of a function of one variable is concerned with integration over an *interval*. There are also definite integrals of functions of two variables, called (definite) **double integrals.** These involve integration over a *region* in the plane.

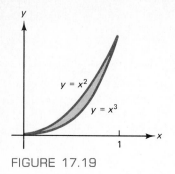

FIGURE 17.19

For example, the symbol

$$\int_0^1 \int_{x^3}^{x^2} (x^3 - xy)\, dy\, dx, \quad \text{or equivalently} \quad \int_0^1 \left[\int_{x^3}^{x^2} (x^3 - xy)\, dy \right] dx,$$

is the double integral of $f(x,\ y) = x^3 - xy$ over a region determined by the limits of integration. That region is all points (x,y) in the x,y-plane such that $x^3 \le y \le x^2$ and $0 \le x \le 1$, which is shown in Fig. 17.19. Essentially, a double integral is a limit of a sum of the form $\Sigma f(x,\ y)\ \Delta y\ \Delta x$, where in our case the points $(x,\ y)$ are in the shaded region. A geometric interpretation of a double integral will be given later.

To evaluate

$$\int_0^1 \int_{x^3}^{x^2} (x^3 - xy)\, dy\, dx \quad \text{or} \quad \int_0^1 \left[\int_{x^3}^{x^2} (x^3 - xy)\, dy \right] dx,$$

we use successive integrations starting with the innermost integral. First, we evelute

$$\int_{x^3}^{x^2} (x^3 - xy)\, dy$$

by treating x as a constant and integrating with respect to y between the limits x^3 and x^2:

$$\int_{x^3}^{x^2} (x^3 - xy)\, dy = \left(x^3 y - \frac{xy^2}{2} \right) \Bigg|_{x^3}^{x^2}.$$

Substituting the limits for the variable y, we have

$$\left[x^3(x^2) - \frac{x(x^2)^2}{2} \right] - \left[x^3(x^3) - \frac{x(x^3)^2}{2} \right]$$

$$= x^5 - \frac{x^5}{2} - x^6 + \frac{x^7}{2} = \frac{x^5}{2} - x^6 + \frac{x^7}{2}.$$

Now we integrate this result with respect to x between the limits 0 and 1.

$$\int_0^1 \left(\frac{x^5}{2} - x^6 + \frac{x^7}{2} \right) dx = \left(\frac{x^6}{12} - \frac{x^7}{7} + \frac{x^8}{16} \right) \Bigg|_0^1$$

$$= \left(\frac{1}{12} - \frac{1}{7} + \frac{1}{16} \right) - 0 = \frac{1}{336}.$$

Thus

$$\int_0^1 \int_{x^3}^{x^2} (x^3 - xy)\, dy\, dx = \frac{1}{336}.$$

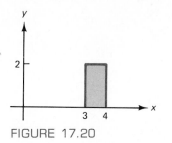

FIGURE 17.20

Now consider the double integral

$$\int_0^2 \int_3^4 xy \, dx \, dy \qquad \text{or} \qquad \int_0^2 \left[\int_3^4 xy \, dx \right] dy.$$

The region over which the integration takes place is all points (x, y) for which $3 \leq x \leq 4$ and $0 \leq y \leq 2$ (see Fig. 17.20). This double integral is evaluated by first treating y as a constant and integrating xy with respect to x between 3 and 4. Then we integrate the result with respect to y between 0 and 2.

$$\int_0^2 \int_3^4 xy \, dx \, dy = \int_0^2 \left[\int_3^4 xy \, dx \right] dy = \int_0^2 \left(\frac{x^2 y}{2} \right) \Big|_3^4 dy$$

$$= \int_0^2 \left(8y - \frac{9y}{2} \right) dy = \int_0^2 \left(\frac{7}{2} y \right) dy$$

$$= \frac{7y^2}{4} \Big|_0^2 = 7 - 0 = 7.$$

EXAMPLE 1   *Evaluate* $\int_{-1}^1 \int_0^{1-x} (2x + 1) \, dy \, dx.$

Here we first integrate with respect to y.

$$\int_{-1}^1 \int_0^{1-x} (2x + 1) \, dy \, dx$$

$$= \int_{-1}^1 \left[\int_0^{1-x} (2x + 1) \, dy \right] dx$$

$$= \int_{-1}^1 (2xy + y) \Big|_0^{1-x} dx = \int_{-1}^1 \{ [2x(1 - x) + (1 - x)] - 0 \} \, dx$$

$$= \int_{-1}^1 (-2x^2 + x + 1) \, dx = \left(-\frac{2x^3}{3} + \frac{x^2}{2} + x \right) \Big|_{-1}^1$$

$$= \left(-\frac{2}{3} + \frac{1}{2} + 1 \right) - \left(\frac{2}{3} + \frac{1}{2} - 1 \right) = \frac{2}{3}.$$

EXAMPLE 2   *Evaluate* $\int_1^{\ln 2} \int_{e^y}^2 dx \, dy.$

Here we first integrate with respect to x.

$$\int_1^{\ln 2} \int_{e^y}^2 dx \, dy = \int_1^{\ln 2} \left[\int_{e^y}^2 dx \right] dy = \int_1^{\ln 2} x \Big|_{e^y}^2 dy$$

$$= \int_1^{\ln 2} (2 - e^y) \, dy = (2y - e^y) \Big|_1^{\ln 2}$$

$$= (2 \ln 2 - 2) - (2 - e) = 2 \ln 2 - 4 + e$$

$$= \ln 4 - 4 + e.$$

A double integral can be interpreted in terms of the volume of a region between the x,y-plane and a surface $z = f(x, y)$ if $z \geq 0$. In Fig. 17.21 is a

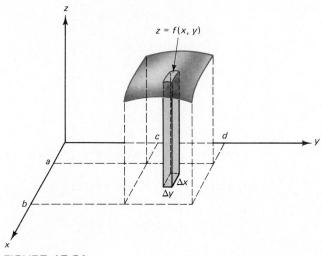

FIGURE 17.21

region whose volume we shall consider. The element of volume for this region is a vertical column. It has height $z = f(x, y)$ and a base area of $\Delta y \, \Delta x$. Thus its volume is $f(x, y) \, \Delta y \, \Delta x$. The volume of the entire region can be found by summing the volumes of all such elements for $a \leq x \leq b$ and $c \leq y \leq d$ via a double integral. Thus

$$\text{volume} = \int_a^b \int_c^d f(x, y) \, dy \, dx.$$

Triple integrals are handled by successively evaluating three integrals, as the next example shows.

EXAMPLE 3   *Evaluate* $\int_0^1 \int_0^x \int_0^{x-y} x \, dz \, dy \, dx.$

$$\int_0^1 \int_0^x \int_0^{x-y} x \, dz \, dy \, dx = \int_0^1 \int_0^x \left[\int_0^{x-y} x \, dz \right] dy \, dx$$

$$= \int_0^1 \int_0^x (xz) \Big|_0^{x-y} dy \, dx = \int_0^1 \int_0^x [x(x - y) - 0] \, dy \, dx$$

$$= \int_0^1 \int_0^x (x^2 - xy)\, dy\, dx = \int_0^1 \left[\int_0^x (x^2 - xy)\, dy \right] dx$$

$$= \int_0^1 \left(x^2 y - \frac{xy^2}{2} \right) \Big|_0^x dx = \int_0^1 \left[\left(x^3 - \frac{x^3}{2} \right) - 0 \right] dx$$

$$= \int_0^1 \frac{x^3}{2}\, dx = \frac{x^4}{8} \Big|_0^1 = \frac{1}{8}.$$

EXERCISE 17.11

In Problems 1–22, evaluate the multiple integrals.

1. $\int_0^3 \int_0^4 x\, dy\, dx.$

2. $\int_0^2 \int_1^2 y\, dy\, dx.$

3. $\int_0^1 \int_0^1 xy\, dx\, dy.$

4. $\int_0^2 \int_0^3 x^2\, dy\, dx.$

5. $\int_1^3 \int_1^2 (x^2 - y)\, dx\, dy.$

6. $\int_{-1}^2 \int_1^4 (x^2 - 2xy)\, dy\, dx.$

7. $\int_0^1 \int_0^2 (x + y)\, dy\, dx.$

8. $\int_0^3 \int_0^x (x^2 + y^2)\, dy\, dx.$

9. $\int_0^6 \int_0^{3x} y\, dy\, dx.$

10. $\int_1^2 \int_0^{x-1} y\, dy\, dx.$

11. $\int_0^1 \int_{3x}^{x^2} 2x^2 y\, dy\, dx.$

12. $\int_0^2 \int_0^{x^2} xy\, dy\, dx.$

13. $\int_0^2 \int_0^{\sqrt{4-y^2}} x\, dx\, dy.$

14. $\int_0^1 \int_y^{\sqrt{y}} y\, dx\, dy.$

15. $\int_{-1}^1 \int_x^{1-x} (x + y)\, dy\, dx.$

16. $\int_0^3 \int_{y^2}^{3y} x\, dx\, dy.$

17. $\int_0^1 \int_0^y e^{x+y}\, dx\, dy.$

18. $\int_2^3 \int_0^2 e^{x-y}\, dx\, dy.$

19. $\int_{-1}^0 \int_{-1}^2 \int_1^2 6xy^2 z^3\, dx\, dy\, dz.$

20. $\int_0^1 \int_0^x \int_0^{x-y} x\, dz\, dy\, dx.$

21. $\int_0^1 \int_{x^2}^x \int_0^{xy} dz\, dy\, dx.$

22. $\int_0^2 \int_{y^2}^{3y} \int_0^x dz\, dx\, dy.$

23. In statistics a joint density function $z = f(x,y)$ defined on a region in the x,y-plane is represented by a surface in space. The probability of $a \le x \le b$ and $c \le y \le d$ is given by

$$P(a \le x \le b,\ c \le y \le d) = \int_c^d \int_a^b f(x,\ y)\, dx\, dy$$

and is represented by the volume between the graph of f and the rectangular region given by $a \le x \le b$ and c

$\le y \le d$. If $f(x,\ y) = e^{-(x+y)}$ is a joint density function, where $x \ge 0$ and $y \ge 0$, find $P(0 \le x \le 2, 1 \le y \le 2)$ and give your answer in terms of e.

24. In Problem 23, let $f(x,y) = 12e^{-4x-3y}$ for $x,y \ge 0$. Find $P(3 \le x \le 4, 2 \le y \le 6)$ and give your answer in terms of e.

25. In Problem 23, let $f(x,\ y) = x/8$, where $0 \le x \le 2$ and $0 \le y \le 4$. Find $P(x \ge 1, y \ge 2)$.

26. In Problem 23, let f be the uniform density function $f(x, y) = 1$ defined over the unit square $0 \le x \le 1$, $0 \le y \le 1$. Find the probability that $0 \le x \le \frac{1}{3}$ and $\frac{1}{4} \le y \le \frac{3}{4}$.

17.12 REVIEW

Important Terms and Symbols

Section 17.1   three dimensional coordinate system $f(x_1, x_2, \ldots, x_n)$ function of n variables
x,y-plane x,z-plane y,z-plane   octant   traces

Section 17.2   partial derivative $\dfrac{\partial z}{\partial x}$ $f_x(x, y)$ $\dfrac{\partial z}{\partial x}\Big|_{(x_0,y_0)}$ $f_x(x_0, y_0)$

Section 17.3   joint-cost function   production function   marginal productivity   competitive products   complementary products

Section 17.4   implicit partial differentiation

Section 17.5 $\dfrac{\partial^2 z}{\partial y\, \partial x}$ $\dfrac{\partial^2 z}{\partial x\, \partial y}$ $\dfrac{\partial^2 z}{\partial x^2}$ $\dfrac{\partial^2 z}{\partial y^2}$ f_{xy} f_{yx} f_{xx} f_{yy}

Section 17.6   chain rule   intermediate variable

Section 17.7   relative maxima and minima   critical point   second-derivative test for functions of two variables

Section 17.8   method of Lagrange multipliers

Section 17.9   scatter diagram   method of least squares   linear regression line of y on x index numbers

Section 17.10   homogeneous function of degree n

Section 17.11   double integral   triple integral

Summary

We can extend the concept of a function of one variable to functions of several variables. The inputs for functions of n variables are n-tuples. Generally, the graph of a function of two variables is a surface in a three-dimensional coordinate system. Functions of more than two variables cannot be geometrically represented.

For a function of n variables, we can consider n partial derivatives. For example, if $w = f(x, y, z)$, we have the partial derivatives of f with respect to x, with respect to y, and with respect to z, denoted f_x, f_y, and f_z, or $\partial f/\partial x$, $\partial f/\partial y$, and $\partial f/\partial z$, respectively. To find $f_x(x, y, z)$, treat y and z as constants and differentiate f with respect to x in the usual way. The other partial derivatives are found in a similar fashion. We can interpret $f_x(x, y, z)$ as the approximate change in w that results from a one-unit change in x when y and z are held fixed. There are similar interpretations for the other partial derivatives.

A function of several variables may be defined implicitly. In this case, its partial derivatives are found by implicit (partial) differentiation.

Functions of several variables occur frequently in business and economic analysis as well as other areas of study. If a manufacturer produces x units of product X and y units of product Y, then the total cost c of these units is a function of x and y and is called a joint-cost function. The partial derivatives $\partial c/\partial x$ and $\partial c/\partial y$ are called the marginal costs with respect to x and y, respectively. We can interpret, for example, $\partial c/\partial x$ as the approximate cost of producing an extra unit of X while the level of production of Y is held fixed.

If l units of labor and k units of capital are used to produce P units of a product, then the function $P = f(l, k)$ is called a production function. The partial derivatives of P are called marginal productivity functions.

Suppose two products, A and B, are such that the quantity demanded of each is dependent on the prices of both. If q_A and q_B are the quantities of A and B demanded when the prices of A and B are p_A and p_B, respectively, then q_A and q_B are each functions of p_A and p_B. When $\partial q_A/\partial p_B > 0$ and $\partial q_B/\partial p_A > 0$, then A and B are called competitive products (or substitutes). When $\partial q_A/\partial p_B < 0$ and $\partial q_B/\partial p_A < 0$, then A and B are called complementary products.

If $z = f(x, y)$ where $x = x(r, s)$ and $y = y(r, s)$, then z can be considered as a function of r and s. To find, for example, $\partial z/\partial r$, a chain rule may be used:

$$\frac{\partial z}{\partial r} = \frac{\partial z}{\partial x}\frac{\partial x}{\partial r} + \frac{\partial z}{\partial y}\frac{\partial y}{\partial r}.$$

A partial derivative of a function of n variables is itself a function of n variables. By successively taking partial derivatives of partial derivatives, we obtain high-order partial derivatives. For example, if f is a function of x and y, then f_{xy} denotes the partial derivative of f_x with respect to y; f_{xy} is called the second-partial derivative of f, first with respect to x and then with respect to y.

If the function $f(x, y)$ has a relative extremum at (x_0, y_0), then (x_0, y_0) must be a solution of the system

$$f_x(x_0, y_0) = 0, \qquad f_y(x_0, y_0) = 0.$$

Any solution of this system is called a critical point of f. Thus critical points are the candidates at which a relative extremum may occur. The second-derivative test for functions of two variables gives conditions under which a critical point corresponds to a relative maximum or a relative minimum. It states that if (x_0, y_0) is a critical point of f and

$$D(x, y) = f_{xx}(x, y)f_{yy}(x, y) - [f_{xy}(x, y)]^2,$$

then

1. if $D(x_0, y_0) > 0$ and $f_{xx}(x_0, y_0) < 0$, f has a relative maximum at (x_0, y_0);

2. if $D(x_0, y_0) > 0$ and $f_{xx}(x_0, y_0) > 0$, f has a relative minimum at (x_0, y_0);

3. if $D(x_0, y_0) < 0$, f has neither a relative maximum nor a relative minimum at (x_0, y_0);

4. if $D(x_0, y_0) = 0$, no conclusion about extrema at (x_0, y_0) can be drawn and further analysis is required.

To find critical points of a function of several variables subject to a constraint, we may use the method of Lagrange multipliers. For example, to find the critical points of $f(x, y, z)$ subject to the constraint $g(x, y, z) = 0$, we first form the function

$$F(x, y, z, \lambda) = f(x, y, z) - \lambda g(x, y, z).$$

By solving the system

$$F_x = 0, \quad F_y = 0, \quad F_z = 0, \quad F_\lambda = 0,$$

we obtain the critical points of F. If $(x_0, y_0, z_0, \lambda_0)$ is such a critical point, then (x_0, y_0, z_0) is a critical point of f subject to the constraint. It is important to write the constraint in the form $g(x, y, z) = 0$. For example, if the constraint is $2x + 3y - z = 4$, then $g(x, y, z) = 2x + 3y - z - 4$ [or $g(x, y, z) = 4 - 2x - 3y + z$]. If $f(x, y, z)$ is subject to two constraints, $g_1(x, y, z) = 0$ and $g_2(x, y, z) = 0$, then we would form the function $F = f - \lambda_1 g_1 - \lambda_2 g_2$ and solve the system

$$F_x = 0, \quad F_y = 0, \quad F_z = 0, \quad F_{\lambda_1} = 0, \quad F_{\lambda_2} = 0.$$

Sometimes two variables, say x and y, may be related in such a way that the relationship is approximately linear. When the data points (x_i, y_i), where $i = 1, 2, 3, \ldots, n$, are given to us, we can fit a straight line that approximates them. Such a line is the linear regression line (or least squares line) of y on x and is given by $\hat{y} = \hat{a} + \hat{b}x$ where

$$\hat{a} = \frac{\left(\sum_{i=1}^{n} x_i^2\right)\left(\sum_{i=1}^{n} y_i\right) - \left(\sum_{i=1}^{n} x_i\right)\left(\sum_{i=1}^{n} x_i y_i\right)}{n\sum_{i=1}^{n} x_i^2 - \left(\sum_{i=1}^{n} x_i\right)^2}$$

and

$$\hat{b} = \frac{n\sum_{i=1}^{n} x_i y_i - \left(\sum_{i=1}^{n} x_i\right)\left(\sum_{i=1}^{n} y_i\right)}{n\sum_{i=1}^{n} x_i^2 - \left(\sum_{i=1}^{n} x_i\right)^2}.$$

The $\hat{y}$-values can be used to predict y-values for given values of x.

When working with functions of several variables, we can consider their multiple integrals. These are determined by successive integration. For example, the double integral

$$\int_1^2 \int_0^y (x + y)\, dx\, dy$$

is determined by first treating y as a constant and integrating $x + y$ with respect to x. After evaluating between the limits 0 and y, we integrate that result with respect to y from $x = 1$ to $x = 2$. Thus

$$\int_1^2 \int_0^y (x + y)\, dx\, dy = \int_1^2 \left[\int_0^y (x + y)\, dx\right] dy.$$

Triple integrals involve functions of three variables and are also evaluated by successive integration.

Review Problems

In Problems 1–4, sketch the given surfaces.

1. $2x + 3y + z = 9$.   2. $z = x$.   3. $z = y^2$.   4. $x^2 + z^2 = 1$.

In Problems 5–16, find the indicated partial derivatives.

5. $f(x, y) = 2x^2 + 3xy + y^2 - 1$; $f_x(x, y), f_y(x, y)$.

6. $P = l^3 + k^3 - lk$; $\partial P/\partial l, \partial P/\partial k$.

7. $z = x/(x + y)$; $\partial z/\partial x, \partial z/\partial y$.

8. $w = \dfrac{\sqrt{x^2 + y^2}}{y}$; $\partial w/\partial x$.

9. $w = e^{x^2yz}$; $w_{xy}(x, y, z)$.

10. $f(x, y) = xy \ln(xy)$; $f_{xy}(x, y)$.

11. $f(x, y) = \ln\sqrt{x^2 + y^2}$; $\dfrac{\partial}{\partial y}[f(x, y)]$.

12. $f(p_A, p_B) = (p_A - 20)q_A + (p_B - 30)q_B$; $f_{p_A}(p_A, p_B)$.

13. $f(x, y, z) = (x + y)(y + z^2)$; $\dfrac{\partial^2}{\partial z^2}[f(x, y, z)]$.

14. $z = (x^2 - y)(y^2 - 2xy)$; $\partial^2 z/\partial y^2$.

15. $w = xe^{yz} \ln z$; $\partial w/\partial y, \partial^2 w/\partial x \partial z$.

16. $P = 2.4l^{0.11}k^{0.89}$; $\partial P/\partial k$.

*17. If $w = x^2 + 2xy + 3y^2$, $x = e^r$, and $y = \ln(r + s)$, find $\partial w/\partial r$ and $\partial w/\partial s$.

*18. If $z = \ln(x/y) + e^y - xy$, $x = r^2s^2$, and $y = r + s$, find $\partial z/\partial s$.

*19. If $x^2 + 2xy - 2z^2 + xz + 2 = 0$, find $\partial z/\partial x$.   *20. If $z^2 - e^{yz} + \ln z + e^{xz} = 0$, find $\partial z/\partial y$.

* Refers to Sec. 17.4 or 17.6.

21. If a manufacturer's production function is defined by $P = 20l^{0.7}k^{0.3}$, determine the marginal productivity functions.

22. A manufacturer's cost for producing x units of product X and y units of product Y is given by $c = 5x + 0.03xy + 7y + 200$. Determine the (partial) marginal cost with respect to x when $x = 100$ and $y = 200$.

23. If $q_A = 200 - 3p_A + p_B$ and $q_B = 50 - 5p_B + p_A$, where q_A and q_B are the number of units demanded of products A and B, respectively, and p_A and p_B are their respective prices per unit, determine whether A and B are competitive or complementary products.

24. For industry there is a model that describes the rate α (a Greek letter read "alpha") at which a new innovation substitutes for an established process. It is given by*

$$\alpha = Z + 0.530P - 0.027S,$$

where Z is a constant that depends on the particular industry, P is an index of profitability of the new innovation, and S is an index of the extent of the investment necessary to make use of the innovation. Find $\partial\alpha/\partial P$ and $\partial\alpha/\partial S$.

25. Examine $f(x, y) = x^2 + 2y^2 - 2xy - 4y + 3$ for relative extrema.

26. Examine $f(w, z) = 2w^3 + 2z^3 - 6wz + 7$ for relative extrema.

27. An open-top rectangular cardboard box is to have a volume of 32 cubic feet. Find the dimensions of the box so that the amount of cardboard used is minimized.

28. Find all critical points of $f(x, y, z) = xyz$ subject to $3x + 2y + 4z - 120 = 0$ $(xyz \neq 0)$.

29. Find all critical points of $f(x, y, z) = x^2 + y^2 + z^2$ subject to the constraint $3x + 2y + z = 14$.

30. In an experiment† a group of fish were injected with living bacteria. Of those fish maintained at 28°C, the percentage p that survived the infection t hours after the injection is given below. Find the linear regression line of p on t.

t	8	10	18	20	48
p	82	79	78	78	64

31. Find the least squares linear regression line of y on x for the data given below. Refer to year 1981 as year $x = 1$, etc.

Equipment Expenditures of Allied
Computer Company, 1981–1986
(in millions of dollars)

YEAR	EXPENDITURES
1981	15
1982	22
1983	21
1984	27
1985	26
1986	34

In Problems 32–35, evaluate the double integrals.

32. $\int_{1}^{2}\int_{0}^{y} x^2y^2 \, dx \, dy$.

33. $\int_{0}^{4}\int_{y/2}^{2} xy \, dx \, dy$.

34. $\int_{0}^{3}\int_{y^2}^{3y} x \, dx \, dy$.

35. $\int_{0}^{1}\int_{\sqrt{x}}^{x^2} (x^2 + 2xy - 3y^2) \, dy \, dx$.

* A. P. Hurter, Jr., A. H. Rubenstein, et al. "Market Penetration by New Innovations: The Technological Literature," *Technological Forecasting and Social Change,* 11 (1978), 197–221.

† J. B. Covert and W. W. Reynolds, "Survival Value of Fever in Fish," *Nature,* 267, no. 5606 (1977), 43–45.

Tables of Powers-
Roots-
Reciprocals

n	n^2	$\sqrt{n}$	$\sqrt{10n}$	n^3	$\sqrt[3]{n}$	$\sqrt[3]{10n}$	$\sqrt[3]{100n}$	$1/n$
1.0	1.0000	1.0000	3.1623	1.0000	1.0000	2.1544	4.6416	1.0000
1.1	1.2100	1.0488	3.3166	1.3310	1.0323	2.2240	4.7914	0.9091
1.2	1.4400	1.0954	3.4641	1.7280	1.0627	2.2894	4.9324	0.8333
1.3	1.6900	1.1402	3.6056	2.1970	1.0914	2.3513	5.0658	0.7692
1.4	1.9600	1.1832	3.7417	2.7440	1.1187	2.4101	5.1925	0.7143
1.5	2.2500	1.2247	3.8730	3.3750	1.1447	2.4662	5.3133	0.6667
1.6	2.5600	1.2649	4.0000	4.0960	1.1696	2.5198	5.4288	0.6250
1.7	2.8900	1.3038	4.1231	4.9130	1.1935	2.5713	5.5397	0.5882
1.8	3.2400	1.3416	4.2426	5.8320	1.2164	2.6207	5.6462	0.5556
1.9	3.6100	1.3784	4.3589	6.8590	1.2386	2.6684	5.7489	0.5263
2.0	4.0000	1.4142	4.4721	8.0000	1.2599	2.7144	5.8480	0.5000
2.1	4.4100	1.4491	4.5826	9.2610	1.2806	2.7589	5.9439	0.4762
2.2	4.8400	1.4832	4.6904	10.6480	1.3006	2.8020	6.0368	0.4545
2.3	5.2900	1.5166	4.7958	12.1670	1.3200	2.8439	6.1269	0.4348
2.4	5.7600	1.5492	4.8990	13.8240	1.3389	2.8845	6.2145	0.4167
2.5	6.2500	1.5811	5.0000	15.6250	1.3572	2.9240	6.2996	0.4000
2.6	6.7600	1.6125	5.0990	17.5760	1.3751	2.9625	6.3825	0.3846
2.7	7.2900	1.6432	5.1962	19.6830	1.3925	3.0000	6.4633	0.3704
2.8	7.8400	1.6733	5.2915	21.9520	1.4095	3.0366	6.5421	0.3571
2.9	8.4100	1.7029	5.3852	24.3890	1.4260	3.0723	6.6191	0.3448
3.0	9.0000	1.7321	5.4772	27.0000	1.4422	3.1072	6.6943	0.3333
3.1	9.6100	1.7607	5.5678	29.7910	1.4581	3.1414	6.7679	0.3226
3.2	10.2400	1.7889	5.6569	32.7680	1.4736	3.1748	6.8399	0.3125
3.3	10.8900	1.8166	5.7446	35.9370	1.4888	3.2075	6.9104	0.3030
3.4	11.5600	1.8439	5.8310	39.3040	1.5037	3.2396	6.9795	0.2941
3.5	12.2500	1.8708	5.9161	42.8750	1.5183	3.2711	7.0473	0.2857
3.6	12.9600	1.8974	6.0000	46.6560	1.5326	3.3019	7.1138	0.2778
3.7	13.6900	1.9235	6.0828	50.6530	1.5467	3.3322	7.1791	0.2703
3.8	14.4400	1.9494	6.1644	54.8720	1.5605	3.3620	7.2432	0.2632
3.9	15.2100	1.9748	6.2450	59.3190	1.5741	3.3912	7.3061	0.2564

n	n^2	$\sqrt{n}$	$\sqrt{10n}$	n^3	$\sqrt[3]{n}$	$\sqrt[3]{10n}$	$\sqrt[3]{100n}$	$1/n$
4.0	16.0000	2.0000	6.3246	64.0000	1.5874	3.4200	7.3681	0.2500
4.1	16.8100	2.0248	6.4031	68.9210	1.6005	3.4482	7.4290	0.2439
4.2	17.6400	2.0494	6.4807	74.0880	1.6134	3.4760	7.4889	0.2381
4.3	18.4900	2.0736	6.5574	79.5070	1.6261	3.5034	7.5478	0.2326
4.4	19.3600	2.0976	6.6333	85.1840	1.6386	3.5303	7.6059	0.2273
4.5	20.2500	2.1213	6.7082	91.1250	1.6510	3.5569	7.6631	0.2222
4.6	21.1600	2.1448	6.7823	97.3360	1.6631	3.5830	7.7194	0.2174
4.7	22.0900	2.1679	6.8557	103.823	1.6751	3.6088	7.7750	0.2128
4.8	23.0400	2.1909	6.9282	110.592	1.6869	3.6342	7.8297	0.2083
4.9	24.0100	2.2136	7.0000	117.649	1.6985	3.6593	7.8837	0.2041
5.0	25.0000	2.2361	7.0711	125.000	1.7100	3.6840	7.9370	0.2000
5.1	26.0100	2.2583	7.1414	132.651	1.7213	3.7084	7.9896	0.1961
5.2	27.0400	2.2804	7.2111	140.608	1.7325	3.7325	8.0415	0.1923
5.3	28.0900	2.3022	7.2801	148.877	1.7435	3.7563	8.0927	0.1887
5.4	29.1600	2.3238	7.3485	157.464	1.7544	3.7798	8.1433	0.1852
5.5	30.2500	2.3452	7.4162	166.375	1.7652	3.8030	8.1932	0.1818
5.6	31.3600	2.3664	7.4833	175.616	1.7758	3.8259	8.2426	0.1786
5.7	32.4900	2.3875	7.5498	185.193	1.7863	3.8485	8.2913	0.1754
5.8	33.6400	2.4083	7.6158	195.112	1.7967	3.8709	8.3396	0.1724
5.9	34.8100	2.4290	7.6811	205.379	1.8070	3.8930	8.3872	0.1695
6.0	36.0000	2.4495	7.7460	216.000	1.8171	3.9149	8.4343	0.1667
6.1	37.2100	2.4698	7.8102	226.981	1.8272	3.9365	8.4809	0.1639
6.2	38.4400	2.4900	7.8740	238.328	1.8371	3.9579	8.5270	0.1613
6.3	39.6900	2.5100	7.9372	250.047	1.8469	3.9791	8.5726	0.1587
6.4	40.9600	2.5298	8.0000	262.144	1.8566	4.0000	8.6177	0.1563
6.5	42.2500	2.5495	8.0623	274.625	1.8663	4.0207	8.6624	0.1538
6.6	43.5600	2.5690	8.1240	287.496	1.8758	4.0412	8.7066	0.1515
6.7	44.8900	2.5884	8.1854	300.763	1.8852	4.0615	8.7503	0.1493
6.8	46.2400	2.6077	8.2462	314.432	1.8945	4.0817	8.7937	0.1471
6.9	47.6100	2.6268	8.3066	328.509	1.9038	4.1016	8.8366	0.1449
7.0	49.0000	2.6458	8.3666	343.000	1.9129	4.1213	8.8790	0.1429
7.1	50.4100	2.6646	8.4261	357.911	1.9220	4.1408	8.9211	0.1408
7.2	51.8400	2.6833	8.4853	373.248	1.9310	4.1602	8.9628	0.1389
7.3	53.2900	2.7019	8.5440	389.017	1.9399	4.1793	9.0041	0.1370
7.4	54.7600	2.7203	8.6023	405.224	1.9487	4.1983	9.0450	0.1351
7.5	56.2500	2.7386	8.6603	421.875	1.9574	4.2172	9.0856	0.1333
7.6	57.7600	2.7568	8.7178	438.976	1.9661	4.2358	9.1258	0.1316
7.7	59.2900	2.7749	8.7750	456.533	1.9747	4.2543	9.1657	0.1299
7.8	60.8400	2.7928	8.8318	474.552	1.9832	4.2727	9.2052	0.1282
7.9	62.4100	2.8107	8.8882	493.039	1.9916	4.2908	9.2443	0.1266
8.0	64.0000	2.8284	8.9443	512.000	2.0000	4.3089	9.2832	0.1250
8.1	65.6100	2.8460	9.0000	531.441	2.0083	4.3267	9.3217	0.1235
8.2	67.2400	2.8636	9.0554	551.368	2.0165	4.3445	9.3599	0.1220
8.3	68.8900	2.8810	9.1104	571.787	2.0247	4.3621	9.3978	0.1205
8.4	70.5600	2.8983	9.1652	592.704	2.0328	4.3795	9.4354	0.1190
8.5	72.2500	2.9155	9.2195	614.125	2.0408	4.3968	9.4727	0.1176

n	n^2	$\sqrt{n}$	$\sqrt{10n}$	n^3	$\sqrt[3]{n}$	$\sqrt[3]{10n}$	$\sqrt[3]{100n}$	$1/n$
8.0	64.0000	2.8284	8.9443	512.000	2.0000	4.3089	9.2832	0.1250
8.6	73.9600	2.9326	9.2736	636.056	2.0488	4.4140	9.5097	0.1163
8.7	75.6900	2.9496	9.3274	658.503	2.0567	4.4310	9.5464	0.1149
8.8	77.4400	2.9665	9.3808	681.472	2.0646	4.4480	9.5828	0.1136
8.9	79.2100	2.9833	9.4340	704.969	2.0723	4.4647	9.6190	0.1124
9.0	81.000	3.0000	9.4868	729.000	2.0801	4.4814	9.6549	0.1111
9.1	82.8100	3.0166	9.5394	573.571	2.0878	4.4979	9.6905	0.1099
9.2	84.6400	3.0332	9.5917	778.688	2.0954	4.5144	9.7259	0.1087
9.3	86.4900	3.0496	9.6436	804.357	2.1029	4.5307	9.7610	0.1075
9.4	88.3600	3.0659	9.6954	830.584	2.1105	4.5468	9.7959	0.1064
9.5	90.2500	3.0822	9.7468	857.375	2.1179	4.5629	9.8305	0.1053
9.6	92.1600	3.0984	9.7980	884.736	2.1253	4.5789	9.8648	0.1042
9.7	94.0900	3.1145	9.8489	912.673	2.1327	4.5947	9.8990	0.1031
9.8	96.0400	3.1305	9.8995	941.192	2.1400	4.6014	9.9329	0.1020
9.9	98.0100	3.1464	9.9499	970.299	2.1472	4.6261	9.9666	0.1010
10.0	100.000	3.1623	10.000	1000.00	2.1544	4.6416	10.0000	0.1000

Table of e^x and e^{-x}

x	e^x	e^{-x}	x	e^x	e^{-x}
0.00	1.0000	1.00000	0.35	1.4191	.70469
0.01	1.0101	0.99005	0.36	1.4333	.69768
0.02	1.0202	.98020	0.37	1.4477	.69073
0.03	1.0305	.97045	0.38	1.4623	.68386
0.04	1.0408	.96079	0.39	1.4770	.67706
0.05	1.0513	.95123	0.40	1.4918	.67032
0.06	1.0618	.94176	0.41	1.5068	.66365
0.07	1.0725	.93239	0.42	1.5220	.65705
0.08	1.0833	.92312	0.43	1.5373	.65051
0.09	1.0942	.91393	0.44	1.5527	.64404
0.10	1.1052	.90484	0.45	1.5683	.63763
0.11	1.1163	.89583	0.46	1.5841	.63128
0.12	1.1275	.88692	0.47	1.6000	.62500
0.13	1.1388	.87809	0.48	1.6161	.61878
0.14	1.1503	.86936	0.49	1.6323	.61263
0.15	1.1618	.86071	0.50	1.6487	.60653
0.16	1.1735	.85214	0.51	1.6653	.60050
0.17	1.1853	.84366	0.52	1.6820	.59452
0.18	1.1972	.83527	0.53	1.6989	.58860
0.19	1.2092	.82696	0.54	1.7160	.58275
0.20	1.2214	.81873	0.55	1.7333	.57695
0.21	1.2337	.81058	0.56	1.7507	.57121
0.22	1.2461	.80252	0.57	1.7683	.56553
0.23	1.2586	.79453	0.58	1.7860	.55990
0.24	1.2712	.78663	0.59	1.8040	.55433
0.25	1.2840	.77880	0.60	1.8221	.54881
0.26	1.2969	.77105	0.61	1.8404	.54335
0.27	1.3100	.76338	0.62	1.8589	.53794
0.28	1.3231	.75578	0.63	1.8776	.53259
0.29	1.3364	.74826	0.64	1.8965	.52729
0.30	1.3499	.74082	0.65	1.9155	.52205
0.31	1.3634	.73345	0.66	1.9348	.51685
0.32	1.3771	.72615	0.67	1.9542	.51171
0.33	1.3910	.71892	0.68	1.9739	.50662
0.34	1.4049	.71177	0.69	1.9937	.50158

x	e^x	e^{-x}	x	e^x	e^{-x}
0.70	2.0138	.49659	2.50	12.182	.08208
0.71	2.0340	.49164	2.60	13.464	.07427
0.72	2.0544	.48675	2.70	14.880	.06721
0.73	2.0751	.48191	2.80	16.445	.06081
0.74	2.0959	.47711	2.90	18.174	.05502
0.75	2.1170	.47237	3.00	20.086	. 04979
0.76	2.1383	.46767	3.10	22.198	.04505
0.77	2.1598	.46301	3.20	24.533	.04076
0.78	2.1815	.45841	3.30	27.113	.03688
0.79	2.2034	.45384	3.40	29.964	.03337
0.80	2.2255	.44933	3.50	33.115	.03020
0.81	2.2479	.44486	3.60	36.598	.02732
0.82	2.2705	.44043	3.70	40.447	.02472
0.83	2.2933	.43605	3.80	44.701	.02237
0.84	2.3164	.43171	3.90	49.402	.02024
0.85	2.3396	.42741	4.00	54.598	.01832
0.86	2.3632	.42316	4.10	60.340	.01657
0.87	2.3869	.41895	4.20	66686	.01500
0.88	2.4109	.41478	.430	73.700	.01357
0.89	2.4351	.41066	4.40	81.451	.01227
0.90	2.4596	.40657	4.50	90.107	. 01111
0.91	2.4843	.40252	4.60	99.484	.01005
0.92	2.5093	.39852	4.70	109.95	.00910
0.93	2.5345	.39455	4.80	121.51	.00823
0.94	2.5600	.39063	4.90	134.29	.00745
0.95	2.5857	.38674	5.00	148.41	.00674
0.96	2.6117	.38289	5.10	164.02	.00610
0.97	2.6379	.37908	5.20	181.27	.00552
0.98	2.6645	.37531	5.30	200.34	.00499
0.99	2.6912	.37158	5.40	221.41	.00452
1.00	2.7183	.36788	5.50	244.69	.00409
1.10	3.0042	.33287	5.60	270.43	.00370
1.20	3.3201	.30119	5.70	298.87	.00335
1.30	3.6693	.27253	5.80	330.30	.00303
1.40	4.0552	.24660	5.90	365.04	.00274
1.50	4.4817	.22313	6.00	403.43	.00248
1.60	4.9530	.20190	6.25	518.01	.00193
1.70	5.4739	.18268	6.50	665.14	.00150
1.80	6.0496	.16530	6.75	854.06	.00117
1.90	6.6859	.14957	7.00	1096.6	.00091
2.00	7.3891	.13534	7.50	1808.0	.00055
2.10	8.1662	.12246	8.00	2981.0	.00034
2.20	9.0250	.11080	8.50	4914.8	.00020
2.30	9.9742	.10026	9.00	8103.1	.00012
2.40	11.023	.09072	9.50	13360.	.00007
			10.00	22026.	.00005

Table of Natural Logarithms

In the body of the table the first two digits (and decimal point) of most entries are carried over from a preceding entry in the first column. For example, ln 3.32 ≈ 1.19996. However, an asterisk (*) indicates that the first two digits are those of a following entry in the first column. For example, ln 3.33 ≈ 1.20297.

To extend this table for a number less than 1.0 or greater than 10.09, write the number in the form $x = y \cdot 10^n$, where $1.0 \leq y < 10$ and use the fact that $\ln x = \ln y + n \ln 10$. Some values of $n \ln 10$ are

$$1 \ln 10 \approx 2.30259, \qquad 6 \ln 10 \approx 13.81551,$$
$$2 \ln 10 \approx 4.60517, \qquad 7 \ln 10 \approx 16.11810,$$
$$3 \ln 10 \approx 6.90776, \qquad 8 \ln 10 \approx 18.42068,$$
$$4 \ln 10 \approx 9.21034, \qquad 9 \ln 10 \approx 20.72327,$$
$$5 \ln 10 \approx 11.51293, \qquad 10 \ln 10 \approx 23.02585.$$

For example,
$$\ln 332 = \ln[(3.32)(10^2)] = \ln 3.32 + 2 \ln 10$$
$$\approx 1.19996 + 4.60517 = 5.80513$$

and
$$\ln 0.0332 = \ln[(3.32)(10^{-2})] = \ln 3.32 - 2 \ln 10$$
$$\approx 1.19996 - 4.60517 = -3.40521.$$

Properties of logarithms may be used to find the logarithm of a number such as $\frac{3}{8}$:

$$\ln \tfrac{3}{8} = \ln 3 - \ln 8 \approx 1.09861 - 2.07944$$
$$= -0.98083.$$

N	0	1	2	3	4	5	6	7	8	9
1.0	0.0 0000	0995	1980	2956	3922	4879	5827	6766	7696	8618
1.1	9531	*0436	*1333	*2222	*3103	*3976	*4842	*5700	*6551	*7395
1.2	0.1 8232	9062	9885	*0701	*1511	*2314	*3111	*3902	*4686	*5464
1.3	0.2 6236	7003	7763	8518	9267	*0010	*0748	*1481	*2208	*2930
1.4	0.3 3647	4359	5066	5767	6464	7156	7844	8526	9204	9878

N	0	1	2	3	4	5	6	7	8	9
1.5	0.4 0547	1211	1871	2527	3178	3825	4469	5108	5742	6373
1.6	7000	7623	8243	8858	9470	*0078	*0672	*1282	*1879	*2473
1.7	0.5 3063	3649	4232	4812	5389	5962	6531	7098	7661	8222
1.8	8779	9333	9884	*0432	*0977	*1519	*2058	*2594	*3127	*3658
1.9	0.6 4185	4710	5233	5752	6269	6783	7294	7803	8310	8813
2.0	9315	9813	*0310	*0804	*1295	*1784	*2271	*2755	*3237	*3716
2.1	0.7 4194	4669	5142	5612	6081	6547	7011	7473	7932	8390
2.2	8846	9299	9751	*0200	*0648	*1093	*1536	*1978	*2418	*2855
2.3	0.8 3291	3725	4157	4587	5015	5442	5866	6289	6710	7129
2.4	7547	7963	8377	8789	9200	9609	*0016	*0422	*0826	*1228
2.5	0.9 1629	2028	2426	2822	3216	3609	4001	4391	4779	5166
2.6	5551	5935	6317	6698	7078	7456	7833	8208	8582	8954
2.7	9325	9695	*0063	*0430	*0796	*1160	*1523	*1885	*2245	*2604
2.8	1.0 2962	3318	3674	4028	4380	4732	5082	5431	5779	6126
2.9	6471	6815	7158	7500	7841	8181	8519	8856	9192	9527
3.0	9861	*0194	*0526	*0856	*1186	*1514	*1841	*2168	*2493	*2817
3.1	1.1 3140	3462	3783	4103	4422	4740	5057	5373	5688	6002
3.2	6315	6627	6938	7248	7557	7865	8173	8479	8784	9089
3.3	9392	9695	9996	*0297	*0597	*0896	*1194	*1491	*1788	*2083
3.4	1.2 2378	2671	2964	3256	3547	3837	4127	4415	4703	4990
3.5	5276	5562	5846	6130	6413	6695	6976	7257	7536	7815
3.6	8093	8371	8647	8923	9198	9473	9746	*0019	*0291	*0563
3.7	1.3 0833	1103	1372	1641	1909	2176	2442	2708	2972	3237
3.8	3500	3763	4025	4286	4547	4807	5067	5325	5584	5841
3.9	6098	6354	6609	6864	7118	7372	7624	7877	8128	8379
4.0	8629	8879	9128	9377	9624	9872	*0118	*0364	*0610	*0854
4.1	1.4 1099	1342	1585	1828	2070	2311	2552	2792	3031	3270
4.2	3508	3746	3984	4220	4456	4692	4927	5161	5395	5629
4.3	5862	6094	6326	6557	6787	7018	7247	7476	7705	7933
4.4	8160	8387	8614	8840	9065	9290	9515	9739	9962	*0185
4.5	1.5 0408	0630	0851	1072	1293	1513	1732	1951	2170	2388
4.6	2606	2823	3039	3256	3471	3687	3902	4116	4330	4543
4.7	4756	4969	5181	5393	5604	5814	6025	6235	6444	6653
4.8	6862	7070	7277	7485	7691	7898	8104	8309	8515	8719
4.9	8924	9127	9331	9534	9737	9939	*0141	*0342	*0543	*0744
5.0	1.6 0944	1144	1343	1542	1741	1939	2137	2334	2531	2728
5.1	2924	3120	3315	3511	3705	3900	4094	4287	4481	4673
5.2	4866	5058	5250	5441	5632	5823	6013	6203	6393	6582
5.3	6771	6959	7147	7335	7523	7710	7896	8083	8269	8455
5.4	8640	8825	9010	9194	9378	9562	9745	9928	*0111	*0293
5.5	1.7 0475	0656	0838	1019	1199	1380	1560	1740	1919	2098
5.6	2277	2455	2633	2811	2988	3166	3342	3519	3695	3871
5.7	4047	4222	4397	4572	4746	4920	5094	5267	5440	5613
N	0	1	2	3	4	5	6	7	8	9

N	0	1	2	3	4	5	6	7	8	9
5.8	5786	5958	6130	6302	6473	6644	6815	6985	7156	7326
5.9	7495	7665	7834	8002	8171	8339	8507	8675	8842	9009
6.0	1.7 9176	9342	9509	9675	9840	*0006	*0171	*0336	*0500	*0665
6.1	1.8 0829	0993	1156	1319	1482	1645	1808	1970	2132	2294
6.2	2455	2616	2777	2938	3098	3258	3418	3578	3737	3896
6.3	4055	4214	4372	4530	4688	4845	5003	5160	5317	5473
6.4	5630	5786	5942	6097	6253	6408	6563	6718	6872	7026
6.5	7180	7334	7487	7641	7794	7947	8099	8251	8403	8555
6.6	8707	8858	9010	9160	9311	9462	9612	9762	9912	*0061
6.7	1.9 0211	0360	0509	0658	0806	0954	1102	1250	1398	1545
6.8	1692	1839	1986	2132	2279	2425	2571	2716	2862	3007
6.9	3152	3297	3442	3586	3730	3874	4018	4162	4305	4448
7.0	4591	4734	4876	5019	5161	5303	5445	5586	5727	5869
7.1	6009	6150	6291	6431	6571	6711	6851	6991	7130	7269
7.2	7408	7547	7685	7824	7962	8100	8238	8376	8513	8650
7.3	8787	8924	9061	9198	9334	9470	9606	9742	9877	*0013
7.4	2.0 0148	0283	0418	0553	0687	0821	0956	1089	1223	1357
7.5	1490	1624	1757	1890	2022	2155	2287	2419	2551	2683
7.6	2815	2946	3078	3209	3340	3471	3601	3732	3862	3992
7.7	4122	4252	4381	4511	4640	4769	4898	5027	5156	5284
7.8	5412	5540	5668	5796	5924	6051	6179	6306	6433	6560
7.9	6686	6813	6939	7065	7191	7317	7443	7568	7694	7819
8.0	7944	8069	8194	8318	8443	8567	8691	8815	8939	9063
8.1	9186	9310	9433	9556	9679	9802	9924	*0047	*0169	*0291
8.2	2.1 0413	0535	0657	0779	0900	1021	1142	1263	1384	1505
8.3	1626	1746	1866	1986	2106	2226	2346	2465	2585	2704
8.4	2823	2942	3061	3180	3298	3417	3535	3653	3771	3889
8.5	4007	4124	4242	4359	4476	4593	4710	4827	4943	5060
8.6	5176	5292	5409	5524	5640	5756	5871	5987	6102	6217
8.7	6332	6447	6562	6677	6791	6905	7020	7134	7248	7361
8.8	7475	7589	7702	7816	7929	8042	8155	8267	8380	8493
8.9	8605	8717	8830	8942	9054	9165	9277	9389	9500	9611
9.0	9722	9834	9944	*0055	*0166	*0276	*0387	*0497	*0607	*0717
9.1	2.2 0827	0937	1047	1157	1266	1375	1485	1594	1703	1812
9.2	1920	2029	2138	2246	2354	2462	2570	2678	2786	2894
9.3	3001	3109	3216	3324	3431	3538	3645	3751	3858	3965
9.4	4071	4177	4284	4390	4496	4601	4707	4813	4918	5024
9.5	5129	5234	5339	5444	5549	5654	5759	5863	5968	6072
9.6	6176	6280	6384	6488	6592	6696	6799	6903	7006	7109
9.7	7213	7316	7419	7521	7624	7727	7829	7932	8034	8136
9.8	8238	8340	8442	8544	8646	8747	8849	8950	9051	9152
9.9	9253	9354	9455	9556	9657	9757	9858	9958	*0058	*0158
10.0	2.3 0259	0358	0458	0558	0658	0757	0857	0956	1055	1154
N	0	1	2	3	4	5	6	7	8	9

Compound
Interest
Tables

$r = 0.005$

n	$(1 + r)^n$	$(1 + r)^{-n}$	$a_{\overline{n}\rfloor r}$	$s_{\overline{n}\rfloor r}$
1	1.005000	0.995025	0.995025	1.000000
2	1.010025	0.990075	1.985099	2.005000
3	1.015075	0.985149	2.970248	3.015025
4	1.020151	0.980248	3.950496	4.030100
5	1.025251	0.975371	4.925866	5.050251
6	1.030378	0.970518	5.896384	6.075502
7	1.035529	0.965690	6.862074	7.105879
8	1.040707	0.960885	7.822959	8.141409
9	1.045911	0.956105	8.779064	9.182116
10	1.051140	0.951348	9.730412	10.228026
11	1.056396	0.946615	10.677027	11.279167
12	1.061678	0.941905	11.618932	12.335562
13	1.066986	0.937219	12.556151	13.397240
14	1.072321	0.932556	13.488708	14.464226
15	1.077683	0.927917	14.416625	15.536548
16	1.083071	0.923300	15.339925	16.614230
17	1.088487	0.918707	16.258632	17.697301
18	1.093929	0.914136	17.172768	18.785788
19	1.099399	0.909588	18.082356	19.879717
20	1.104896	0.905063	18.987419	20.979115
21	1.110420	0.900560	19.887979	22.084011
22	1.115972	0.896080	20.784059	23.194431
23	1.121552	0.891622	21.675681	24.310403
24	1.127160	0.887186	22.562866	25.431955
25	1.132796	0.882772	23.445638	26.559115
26	1.138460	0.878380	24.324018	27.691911
27	1.144152	0.874010	25.198028	28.830370
28	1.149873	0.869662	26.067689	29.974522
29	1.155622	0.865335	26.933024	31.124395
30	1.161400	0.861030	27.794054	32.280017
31	1.167207	0.856746	28.650800	33.441417
32	1.173043	0.852484	29.503284	34.608624
33	1.178908	0.848242	30.351526	35.781667
34	1.184803	0.844022	31.195548	36.960575
35	1.190727	0.839823	32.035371	38.145378
36	1.196681	0.835645	32.871016	39.336105
37	1.202664	0.831487	33.702504	40.532785
38	1.208677	0.827351	34.529854	41.735449
39	1.214721	0.823235	35.353089	42.944127
40	1.220794	0.819139	36.172228	44.158847
41	1.226898	0.815064	36.987291	45.379642
42	1.233033	0.811009	37.798300	46.606540
43	1.239198	0.806974	38.605274	47.839572
44	1.245394	0.802959	39.408232	49.078770
45	1.251621	0.798964	40.207196	50.324164
46	1.257879	0.794989	41.002185	51.575785
47	1.264168	0.791034	41.793219	52.833664
48	1.270489	0.787098	42.580318	54.097832
49	1.276842	0.783182	43.363500	55.368321
50	1.283226	0.779286	44.142786	56.645163

$r = 0.0075$

n	$(1 + r)^n$	$(1 + r)^{-n}$	$a_{\overline{n}|r}$	$s_{\overline{n}|r}$
1	1.007500	0.992556	0.992556	1.000000
2	1.015056	0.985167	1.977723	2.007500
3	1.022669	0.977833	2.955556	3.022556
4	1.030339	0.970554	3.926110	4.045225
5	1.038067	0.963329	4.889440	5.075565
6	1.045852	0.956158	5.845598	6.113631
7	1.053696	0.949040	6.794638	7.159484
8	1.061599	0.941975	7.736613	8.213180
9	1.069561	0.934963	8.671576	9.274779
10	1.077583	0.928003	9.599580	10.344339
11	1.085664	0.921095	10.520675	11.421922
12	1.093807	0.914238	11.434913	12.507586
13	1.102010	0.907432	12.342345	13.601393
14	1.110276	0.900677	13.243022	14.703404
15	1.118603	0.893973	14.136995	15.813679
16	1.126992	0.887318	15.024313	16.932282
17	1.135445	0.880712	15.905025	18.059274
18	1.143960	0.874156	16.779181	19.194718
19	1.152540	0.867649	17.646830	20.338679
20	1.161184	0.861190	18.508020	21.491219
21	1.169893	0.854779	19.362799	22.652403
22	1.178667	0.848416	20.211215	23.822296
23	1.187507	0.842100	21.053315	25.000963
24	1.196414	0.835831	21.889146	26.188471
25	1.205387	0.829609	22.718755	27.384884
26	1.214427	0.823434	23.542189	28.590271
27	1.223535	0.817304	24.359493	29.804698
28	1.232712	0.811220	25.170713	31.028233
29	1.241957	0.805181	25.975893	32.260945
30	1.251272	0.799187	26.775080	33.502902
31	1.260656	0.793238	27.568318	34.754174
32	1.270111	0.787333	28.355650	36.014830
33	1.279637	0.781472	29.137122	37.284941
34	1.289234	0.775654	29.912776	38.564578
35	1.298904	0.769880	30.682656	39.853813
36	1.308645	0.764149	31.446805	41.152716
37	1.318460	0.758461	32.205266	42.461361
38	1.328349	0.752814	32.958080	43.779822
39	1.338311	0.747210	33.705290	45.108170
40	1.348349	0.741648	34.446938	46.446482
41	1.358461	0.736127	35.183065	47.794830
42	1.368650	0.730647	35.913713	49.153291
43	1.378915	0.725208	36.638921	50.521941
44	1.389256	0.719810	37.358730	51.900856
45	1.399676	0.714451	38.073181	53.290112
46	1.410173	0.709133	38.782314	54.689788
47	1.420750	0.703854	39.486168	56.099961
48	1.431405	0.698614	40.184782	57.520711
49	1.442141	0.693414	40.878195	58.952116
50	1.452957	0.688252	41.566447	60.394257

$r = 0.01$

n	$(1 + r)^n$	$(1 + r)^{-n}$	$a_{\overline{n}|r}$	$s_{\overline{n}|r}$
1	1.010000	0.990099	0.990099	1.000000
2	1.020100	0.980296	1.970395	2.010000
3	1.030301	0.970590	2.940985	3.030100
4	1.040604	0.960980	3.901966	4.060401
5	1.051010	0.951466	4.853431	5.101005
6	1.061520	0.942045	5.795476	6.152015
7	1.072135	0.932718	6.728195	7.213535
8	1.082857	0.923483	7.651678	8.285671
9	1.093685	0.914340	8.566018	9.368527
10	1.104622	0.905287	9.471305	10.462213
11	1.115668	0.896324	10.367628	11.566835
12	1.126825	0.887449	11.255077	12.682503
13	1.138093	0.878663	12.133740	13.809328
14	1.149474	0.869963	13.003703	14.947421
15	1.160969	0.861349	13.865053	16.096896
16	1.172579	0.852821	14.717874	17.257864
17	1.184304	0.844377	15.562251	18.430443
18	1.196147	0.836017	16.398269	19.614748
19	1.208109	0.827740	17.226008	20.810895
20	1.220190	0.819544	18.045553	22.019004
21	1.232392	0.811430	18.856983	23.239194
22	1.244716	0.803396	19.660379	24.471586
23	1.257163	0.795442	20.455821	25.716302
24	1.269735	0.787566	21.243387	26.973465
25	1.282432	0.779768	22.023156	28.243200
26	1.295256	0.772048	22.795204	29.525631
27	1.308209	0.764404	23.559608	30.820888
28	1.321291	0.756836	24.316443	32.129097
29	1.334504	0.749342	25.065785	33.450388
30	1.347849	0.741923	25.807708	34.784892
31	1.361327	0.734577	26.542285	36.132740
32	1.374941	0.727304	27.269589	37.494068
33	1.388690	0.720103	27.989693	38.869009
34	1.402577	0.712973	28.702666	40.257699
35	1.416603	0.705914	29.408580	41.660276
36	1.430769	0.698925	30.107505	43.076878
37	1.445076	0.692005	30.799510	44.507647
38	1.459527	0.685153	31.484663	45.952724
39	1.474123	0.678370	32.163033	47.412251
40	1.488864	0.671653	32.834686	48.886373
41	1.503752	0.665003	33.499689	50.375237
42	1.518790	0.658419	34.158108	51.878989
43	1.533978	0.651900	34.810008	53.397779
44	1.549318	0.645445	35.455454	54.931757
45	1.564811	0.639055	36.094508	56.481075
46	1.580459	0.632728	36.727236	58.045885
47	1.596263	0.626463	37.353699	59.626344
48	1.612226	0.620260	37.973959	61.222608
49	1.628348	0.614119	38.588079	62.834834
50	1.644632	0.608039	39.196118	64.463182

$r = 0.0125$

n	$(1 + r)^n$	$(1 + r)^{-n}$	$a_{\overline{n}\mid r}$	$s_{\overline{n}\mid r}$
1	1.012500	0.987654	0.987654	1.000000
2	1.025156	0.975461	1.963115	2.012500
3	1.037971	0.963418	2.926534	3.037656
4	1.050945	0.951524	3.878058	4.075627
5	1.064082	0.939777	4.817835	5.126572
6	1.077383	0.928175	5.746010	6.190654
7	1.090850	0.916716	6.662726	7.268038
8	1.104486	0.905398	7.568124	8.358888
9	1.118292	0.894221	8.462345	9.463374
10	1.132271	0.883181	9.345526	10.581666
11	1.146424	0.872277	10.217803	11.713937
12	1.160755	0.861509	11.079312	12.860361
13	1.175264	0.850873	11.930185	14.021116
14	1.189955	0.840368	12.770553	15.196380
15	1.204829	0.829993	13.600546	16.386335
16	1.219890	0.819746	14.420292	17.591164
17	1.235138	0.809626	15.229918	18.811053
18	1.250577	0.799631	16.029549	20.046192
19	1.266210	0.789759	16.819308	21.296769
20	1.282037	0.780009	17.599316	22.562979
21	1.298063	0.770379	18.369695	23.845016
22	1.314288	0.760868	19.130563	25.143078
23	1.330717	0.751475	19.882037	26.457367
24	1.347351	0.742197	20.624235	27.788084
25	1.364193	0.733034	21.357269	29.135435
26	1.381245	0.723984	22.081253	30.499628
27	1.398511	0.715046	22.796299	31.880873
28	1.415992	0.706219	23.502518	33.279384
29	1.433692	0.697500	24.200018	34.695377
30	1.451613	0.688889	24.888906	36.129069
31	1.469759	0.680384	25.569290	37.580682
32	1.488131	0.671984	26.241274	39.050441
33	1.506732	0.663688	26.904962	40.538571
34	1.525566	0.655494	27.560456	42.045303
35	1.544636	0.647402	28.207858	43.570870
36	1.563944	0.639409	28.847267	45.115505
37	1.583493	0.631515	29.478783	46.679449
38	1.603287	0.623719	30.102501	48.262942
39	1.623328	0.616019	30.718520	49.866229
40	1.643619	0.608413	31.326933	51.489557
41	1.664165	0.600902	31.927835	53.133177
42	1.684967	0.593484	32.521319	54.797341
43	1.706029	0.586157	33.107475	56.482308
44	1.727354	0.578920	33.686395	58.188337
45	1.748946	0.571773	34.258168	59.915691
46	1.770808	0.564714	34.822882	61.664637
47	1.792943	0.557742	35.380624	63.435445
48	1.815355	0.550856	35.931481	65.228388
49	1.838047	0.544056	36.475537	67.043743
50	1.861022	0.537339	37.012876	68.881790

$r = 0.015$

n	$(1 + r)^n$	$(1 + r)^{-n}$	$a_{\overline{n}\rvert r}$	$s_{\overline{n}\rvert r}$
1	1.015000	0.985222	0.985222	1.000000
2	1.030225	0.970662	1.955883	2.015000
3	1.045678	0.956317	2.912200	3.045225
4	1.061364	0.942184	3.854385	4.090903
5	1.077284	0.928260	4.782645	5.152267
6	1.093443	0.914542	5.697187	6.229551
7	1.109845	0.901027	6.598214	7.322994
8	1.126493	0.887711	7.485925	8.432839
9	1.143390	0.874592	8.360517	9.559332
10	1.160541	0.861667	9.222185	10.702722
11	1.177949	0.848933	10.071118	11.863262
12	1.195618	0.836387	10.907505	13.041211
13	1.213552	0.824027	11.731532	14.236830
14	1.231756	0.811849	12.543382	15.450382
15	1.250232	0.799852	13.343233	16.682138
16	1.268986	0.788031	14.131264	17.932370
17	1.288020	0.776385	14.907649	19.201355
18	1.307341	0.764912	15.672561	20.489376
19	1.326951	0.753607	16.426168	21.796716
20	1.346855	0.742470	17.168639	23.123667
21	1.367058	0.731498	17.900137	24.470522
22	1.387564	0.720688	18.620824	25.837580
23	1.408377	0.710037	19.330861	27.225144
24	1.429503	0.699544	20.030405	28.633521
25	1.450945	0.689206	20.719611	30.063024
26	1.472710	0.679021	21.398632	31.513969
27	1.494800	0.668986	22.067617	32.986678
28	1.517222	0.659099	22.726717	34.481479
29	1.539981	0.649359	23.376076	35.998701
30	1.563080	0.639762	24.015838	37.538681
31	1.586526	0.630308	24.646146	39.101762
32	1.610324	0.620993	25.267139	40.688288
33	1.634479	0.611816	25.878954	42.298612
34	1.658996	0.602774	26.481728	43.933092
35	1.683881	0.593866	27.075595	45.592088
36	1.709140	0.585090	27.660684	47.275969
37	1.734777	0.576443	28.237127	48.985109
38	1.760798	0.567924	28.805052	50.719885
39	1.787210	0.559531	29.364583	52.480684
40	1.814018	0.551262	29.915845	54.267894
41	1.841229	0.543116	30.458961	56.081912
42	1.868847	0.535089	30.994050	57.923141
43	1.896880	0.527182	31.521232	59.791988
44	1.925333	0.519391	32.040622	61.688868
45	1.954213	0.511715	32.552337	63.614201
46	1.983526	0.504153	33.056490	65.568414
47	2.013279	0.496702	33.553192	67.551940
48	2.043478	0.489362	34.042554	69.565219
49	2.074130	0.482130	34.524683	71.608698
50	2.105242	0.475005	34.999688	73.682828

$r = 0.02$

n	$(1 + r)^n$	$(1 + r)^{-n}$	$a_{\overline{n}\rceil r}$	$s_{\overline{n}\rceil r}$
1	1.020000	0.980392	0.980392	1.000000
2	1.040400	0.961169	1.941561	2.020000
3	1.061208	0.942322	2.883883	3.060400
4	1.082432	0.923845	3.807729	4.121608
5	1.104081	0.905731	4.713460	5.204040
6	1.126162	0.887971	5.601431	6.308121
7	1.148686	0.870560	6.471991	7.434283
8	1.171659	0.853490	7.325481	8.582969
9	1.195093	0.836755	8.162237	9.754628
10	1.218994	0.820348	8.982585	10.949721
11	1.243374	0.804263	9.786848	12.168715
12	1.268242	0.788493	10.575341	13.412090
13	1.293607	0.773033	11.348374	14.680332
14	1.319479	0.757875	12.106249	15.973938
15	1.345868	0.743015	12.849264	17.293417
16	1.372786	0.728446	13.577709	18.639285
17	1.400241	0.714163	14.291872	20.012071
18	1.428246	0.700159	14.992031	21.412312
19	1.456811	0.686431	15.678462	22.840559
20	1.485947	0.672971	16.351433	24.297370
21	1.515666	0.659776	17.011209	25.783317
22	1.545980	0.646839	17.658048	27.298984
23	1.576899	0.634156	18.292204	28.844963
24	1.608437	0.621721	18.913926	30.421862
25	1.640606	0.609531	19.523456	32.030300
26	1.673418	0.597579	20.121036	33.670906
27	1.706886	0.585862	20.706898	35.344324
28	1.741024	0.574375	21.281272	37.051210
29	1.775845	0.563112	21.844385	38.792235
30	1.811362	0.552071	22.396456	40.568079
31	1.847589	0.541246	22.937702	42.379441
32	1.884541	0.530633	23.468335	44.227030
33	1.922231	0.520229	23.988564	46.111570
34	1.960676	0.510028	24.498592	48.033802
35	1.999890	0.500028	24.998619	49.994478
36	2.039887	0.490223	25.488842	51.994367
37	2.080685	0.480611	25.969453	54.034255
38	2.122299	0.471187	26.440641	56.114940
39	2.164745	0.461948	26.902589	58.237238
40	2.208040	0.452890	27.355479	60.401983
41	2.252200	0.444010	27.799489	62.610023
42	2.297244	0.435304	28.234794	64.862223
43	2.343189	0.426769	28.661562	67.159468
44	2.390053	0.418401	29.079963	69.502657
45	2.437854	0.410197	29.490160	71.892710
46	2.486611	0.402154	29.892314	74.330564
47	2.536344	0.394268	30.286582	76.817176
48	2.587070	0.386538	30.673120	79.353519
49	2.638812	0.378958	31.052078	81.940590
50	2.691588	0.371528	31.423606	84.579401

$r = 0.025$

n	$(1 + r)^n$	$(1 + r)^{-n}$	$a_{\overline{n}|r}$	$s_{\overline{n}|r}$
1	1.025000	0.975610	0.975610	1.000000
2	1.050625	0.951814	1.927424	2.025000
3	1.076891	0.928599	2.856024	3.075625
4	1.103813	0.905951	3.761974	4.152516
5	1.131408	0.883854	4.645828	5.256329
6	1.159693	0.862297	5.508125	6.387737
7	1.188686	0.841265	6.349391	7.547430
8	1.218403	0.820747	7.170137	8.736116
9	1.248863	0.800728	7.970866	9.954519
10	1.280085	0.781198	8.752064	11.203382
11	1.312087	0.762145	9.514209	12.483466
12	1.344889	0.743556	10.257765	13.795553
13	1.378511	0.725420	10.983185	15.140442
14	1.412974	0.707727	11.690912	16.518953
15	1.448298	0.690466	12.381378	17.931927
16	1.484506	0.673625	13.055003	19.380225
17	1.521618	0.657195	13.712198	20.864730
18	1.559659	0.641166	14.353364	22.386349
19	1.598650	0.625528	14.978891	23.946007
20	1.638616	0.610271	15.589162	25.544658
21	1.679582	0.595386	16.184549	27.183274
22	1.721571	0.580865	16.765413	28.862856
23	1.764611	0.566697	17.332110	30.584427
24	1.808726	0.552875	17.884986	32.349038
25	1.853944	0.539391	18.424376	34.157764
26	1.900293	0.526235	18.950611	36.011708
27	1.947800	0.513400	19.464011	37.912001
28	1.996495	0.500878	19.964889	39.859801
29	2.046407	0.488661	20.453550	41.856296
30	2.097568	0.476743	20.930293	43.902703
31	2.150007	0.465115	21.395407	46.000271
32	2.203757	0.453771	21.849178	48.150278
33	2.258851	0.442703	22.291881	50.354034
34	2.315322	0.431905	22.723786	52.612885
35	2.373205	0.421371	23.145157	54.928207
36	2.432535	0.411094	23.556251	57.301413
37	2.493349	0.401067	23.957318	59.733948
38	2.555682	0.391285	24.348603	62.227297
39	2.619574	0.381741	24.730344	64.782979
40	2.685064	0.372431	25.102775	67.402554
41	2.752190	0.363347	25.466122	70.087617
42	2.820995	0.354485	25.820607	72.839808
43	2.891520	0.345839	26.166446	75.660803
44	2.963808	0.337404	26.503849	78.552323
45	3.037903	0.329174	26.833024	81.516131
46	3.113851	0.321146	27.154170	84.554034
47	3.191697	0.313313	27.467483	87.667885
48	3.271490	0.305671	27.773154	90.859582
49	3.353277	0.298216	28.071369	94.131072
50	3.437109	0.290942	28.362312	97.484349

$r = 0.03$

n	$(1 + r)^n$	$(1 + r)^{-n}$	$a_{\overline{n}\rvert r}$	$s_{\overline{n}\rvert r}$
1	1.030000	0.970874	0.970874	1.000000
2	1.060900	0.942596	1.913470	2.030000
3	1.092727	0.915142	2.828611	3.090900
4	1.125509	0.888487	3.717098	4.183627
5	1.159274	0.862609	4.579707	5.309136
6	1.194052	0.837484	5.417191	6.468410
7	1.229874	0.813092	6.230283	7.662462
8	1.266770	0.789409	7.019692	8.892336
9	1.304773	0.766417	7.786109	10.159106
10	1.343916	0.744094	8.530203	11.463879
11	1.384234	0.722421	9.252624	12.807796
12	1.425761	0.701380	9.954004	14.192030
13	1.468534	0.680951	10.634955	15.617790
14	1.512590	0.661118	11.296073	17.086324
15	1.557967	0.641862	11.937935	18.598914
16	1.604706	0.623167	12.561102	20.156881
17	1.652848	0.605016	13.166118	21.761588
18	1.702433	0.587395	13.753513	23.414435
19	1.753506	0.570286	14.323799	25.116868
20	1.806111	0.553676	14.877475	26.870374
21	1.860295	0.537549	15.415024	28.676486
22	1.916103	0.521893	15.936917	30.536780
23	1.973587	0.506692	16.443608	32.452884
24	2.032794	0.491934	16.935542	34.426470
25	2.093778	0.477606	17.413148	36.459264
26	2.156591	0.463695	17.876842	38.553042
27	2.221289	0.450189	18.327031	40.709634
28	2.287928	0.437077	18.764108	42.930923
29	2.356566	0.424346	19.188455	45.218850
30	2.427262	0.411987	19.600441	47.575416
31	2.500080	0.399987	20.000428	50.002678
32	2.575083	0.388337	20.388766	52.502759
33	2.652335	0.377026	20.765792	55.077841
34	2.731905	0.366045	21.131837	57.730177
35	2.813862	0.355383	21.487220	60.462082
36	2.898278	0.345032	21.832252	63.275944
37	2.985227	0.334983	22.167235	66.174223
38	3.074783	0.325226	22.492462	69.159449
39	3.167027	0.315754	22.808215	72.234233
40	3.262038	0.306557	23.114772	75.401260
41	3.359899	0.297628	23.412400	78.663298
42	3.460696	0.288959	23.701359	82.023196
43	3.564517	0.280543	23.981902	85.483892
44	3.671452	0.272372	24.254274	89.048409
45	3.781596	0.264439	24.518713	92.719861
46	3.895044	0.256737	24.775449	96.501457
47	4.011895	0.249259	25.024708	100.396501
48	4.132252	0.241999	25.266707	104.408396
49	4.256219	0.234950	25.501657	108.540648
50	4.383906	0.228107	25.729764	112.796867

$r = 0.035$

n	$(1 + r)^n$	$(1 + r)^{-n}$	$a_{\overline{n}|r}$	$s_{\overline{n}|r}$
1	1.035000	0.966184	0.966184	1.000000
2	1.071225	0.933511	1.899694	2.035000
3	1.108718	0.901943	2.801637	3.106225
4	1.147523	0.871442	3.673079	4.214943
5	1.187686	0.841973	4.515052	5.362466
6	1.229255	0.813501	5.328553	6.550152
7	1.272279	0.785991	6.114544	7.779408
8	1.316809	0.759412	6.873956	9.051687
9	1.362897	0.733731	7.607687	10.368496
10	1.410599	0.708919	8.316605	11.731393
11	1.459970	0.684946	9.001551	13.141992
12	1.511069	0.661783	9.663334	14.601962
13	1.563956	0.639404	10.302738	16.113030
14	1.618695	0.617782	10.920520	17.676986
15	1.675349	0.596891	11.517411	19.295681
16	1.733986	0.576706	12.094117	20.971030
17	1.794676	0.557204	12.651321	22.705016
18	1.857489	0.538361	13.189682	24.499691
19	1.922501	0.520156	13.709837	26.357180
20	1.989789	0.502566	14.212403	28.279682
21	2.059431	0.485571	14.697974	30.269471
22	2.131512	0.469151	15.167125	32.328902
23	2.206114	0.453286	15.620410	34.460414
24	2.283328	0.437957	16.058368	36.666528
25	2.363245	0.423147	16.481515	38.949857
26	2.445959	0.408838	16.890352	41.313102
27	2.531567	0.395012	17.285365	43.759060
28	2.620172	0.381654	17.667019	46.290627
29	2.711878	0.368748	18.035767	48.910799
30	2.806794	0.356278	18.392045	51.622677
31	2.905031	0.344230	18.736276	54.429471
32	3.006708	0.332590	19.068865	57.334502
33	3.111942	0.321343	19.390208	60.341210
34	3.220860	0.310476	19.700684	63.453152
35	3.333590	0.299977	20.000661	66.674013
36	3.450266	0.289833	20.290494	70.007603
37	3.571025	0.280032	20.570525	73.457869
38	3.696011	0.270562	20.841087	77.028895
39	3.825372	0.261413	21.102500	80.724906
40	3.959260	0.252572	21.355072	84.550278
41	4.097834	0.244031	21.599104	88.509537
42	4.241258	0.235779	21.834883	92.607371
43	4.389702	0.227806	22.062689	96.848629
44	4.543342	0.220102	22.282791	101.238331
45	4.702359	0.212659	22.495450	105.781673
46	4.866941	0.205468	22.700918	110.484031
47	5.037284	0.198520	22.899438	115.350973
48	5.213589	0.191806	23.091244	120.388257
49	5.396065	0.185320	23.276564	125.601846
50	5.584927	0.179053	23.455618	130.997910

$r = 0.04$

n	$(1 + r)^n$	$(1 + r)^{-n}$	$a_{\overline{n}\rvert r}$	$s_{\overline{n}\rvert r}$
1	1.040000	0.961538	0.961538	1.000000
2	1.081600	0.924556	1.886095	2.040000
3	1.124864	0.888996	2.775091	3.121600
4	1.169859	0.854804	3.629895	4.246464
5	4.216653	0.821927	4.451822	5.416323
6	1.265319	0.790315	5.242137	6.632975
7	1.315932	0.759918	6.002055	7.898294
8	1.368569	0.730690	6.732745	9.214226
9	1.423312	0.702587	7.435332	10.582795
10	1.480244	0.675564	8.110896	12.006107
11	1.539454	0.649581	8.760477	13.486351
12	1.601032	0.624597	9.385074	15.025805
13	1.665074	0.600574	9.985648	16.626838
14	1.731676	0.577475	10.563123	18.291911
15	1.800944	0.555265	11.118387	20.023588
16	1.872981	0.533908	11.652296	21.824531
17	1.947900	0.513373	12.165669	23.697512
18	2.025817	0.493628	12.659297	25.645413
19	2.106849	0.474642	13.133939	27.671229
20	2.191123	0.456387	13.590326	29.778079
21	2.278768	0.438834	14.029160	31.969202
22	2.369919	0.421955	14.451115	34.247970
23	2.464716	0.405726	14.856842	36.617889
24	2.563304	0.390121	15.246963	39.082604
25	2.665836	0.375117	15.622080	41.645908
26	2.772470	0.360689	15.982769	44.311745
27	2.883369	0.346817	16.329586	47.084214
28	2.998703	0.333477	16.663063	49.967583
29	3.118651	0.320651	16.983715	52.966286
30	3.243398	0.308319	17.292033	56.084938
31	3.373133	0.296460	17.588494	59.328335
32	3.508059	0.285058	17.873551	62.701469
33	3.648381	0.274094	18.147646	66.209527
34	3.794316	0.263552	18.411198	69.857909
35	3.946089	0.253415	18.664613	73.652225
36	4.103933	0.243669	18.908282	77.598314
37	4.268090	0.234297	19.142579	81.702246
38	4.438813	0.225285	19.367864	85.970336
39	4.616366	0.216621	19.584485	90.409150
40	4.801021	0.208289	19.792774	95.025516
41	4.993061	0.200278	19.993052	99.826536
42	5.192784	0.192575	20.185627	104.819598
43	5.400495	0.185168	20.370795	110.012382
44	5.616515	0.178046	20.548841	115.412877
45	5.841176	0.171198	20.720040	121.029392
46	6.074823	0.164614	20.884654	126.870568
47	6.317816	0.158283	21.042936	132.945390
48	6.570528	0.152195	21.195131	139.263206
49	6.833349	0.146341	21.341472	145.833734
50	7.106683	0.140713	21.482185	152.667084

$r = 0.05$

n	$(1 + r)^n$	$(1 + r)^{-n}$	$a_{\overline{n}|r}$	$s_{\overline{n}|r}$
1	1.050000	0.952381	0.952381	1.000000
2	1.102500	0.907029	1.859410	2.050000
3	1.157625	0.863838	2.723248	3.152500
4	1.215506	0.822702	3.545951	4.310125
5	1.276282	0.783526	4.329477	5.525631
6	1.340096	0.746215	5.075692	6.801913
7	1.407100	0.710681	5.786373	8.142008
8	1.477455	0.676839	6.463213	3.549109
9	1.551328	0.644609	7.107822	11.026564
10	1.628895	0.613913	7.721735	12.577893
11	1.710339	0.584679	8.306414	14.206787
12	1.795856	0.556837	8.863252	15.917127
13	1.885649	0.530321	9.393573	17.712983
14	1.979932	0.505068	9.898641	19.598632
15	2.078928	0.481017	10.379658	21.578564
16	2.182875	0.458112	10.837770	23.657492
17	2.292018	0.436297	11.274066	25.840366
18	2.406619	0.415521	11.689587	28.132385
19	2.526950	0.395734	12.085321	30.539004
20	2.653298	0.376889	12.462210	33.065954
21	2.785963	0.358942	12.821153	35.719252
22	2.925261	0.341850	13.163003	38.505214
23	3.071524	0.325571	13.488574	41.430475
24	3.225100	0.310068	13.798642	44.501999
25	3.386355	0.295303	14.093945	47.727099
26	3.555673	0.281241	14.375185	51.113454
27	3.733456	0.267848	14.643034	54.669126
28	3.920129	0.255094	14.898127	58.402583
29	4.116136	0.242946	15.141074	62.322712
30	4.321942	0.231377	15.372451	66.438848
31	4.538039	0.220359	15.592811	70.760790
32	4.764941	0.209866	15.802677	75.298829
33	5.003189	0.199873	16.002549	80.063771
34	5.253348	0.190355	16.192904	85.066959
35	5.516015	0.181290	16.374194	90.320307
36	5.791816	0.172657	16.546852	95.836323
37	6.081407	0.164436	16.711287	101.628139
38	6.385477	0.156605	16.867893	107.709546
39	6.704751	0.149148	17.017041	114.095023
40	7.039989	0.142046	17.159086	120.799774
41	7.391988	0.135282	17.294368	127.839763
42	7.761588	0.128840	17.423208	135.231751
43	8.149667	0.122704	17.545912	142.993339
44	8.557150	0.116861	17.662773	151.143006
45	8.985008	0.111297	17.774070	159.700156
46	9.434258	0.105997	17.880066	168.685164
47	9.905971	0.100949	17.981016	178.119422
48	10.401270	0.096142	18.077158	188.025393
49	10.921333	0.091564	18.168722	198.426663
50	11.467400	0.087204	18.255925	209.347996

$r = 0.06$

n	$(1 + r)^n$	$(1 + r)^{-n}$	$a_{\overline{n}|r}$	$s_{\overline{n}|r}$
1	1.060000	0.943396	0.943396	1.000000
2	1.123600	0.889996	1.833393	2.060000
3	1.191016	0.839619	2.673012	3.183600
4	1.262477	0.792094	3.465106	4.374616
5	1.338226	0.747258	4.212364	5.637093
6	1.418519	0.704961	4.917324	6.975319
7	1.503630	0.665057	5.582381	8.393838
8	1.593848	0.627412	6.209794	9.897468
9	1.689479	0.591898	6.801692	11.491316
10	1.790848	0.558395	7.360087	13.180795
11	1.898299	0.526788	7.886875	14.971643
12	2.012196	0.496969	8.383844	16.869941
13	2.132928	0.468839	8.852683	18.882138
14	2.260904	0.442301	9.294984	21.015066
15	2.396558	0.417265	9.712249	23.275970
16	2.540352	0.393646	10.105895	25.672528
17	2.692773	0.371364	10.477260	28.212880
18	2.854339	0.350344	10.827603	30.905653
19	3.025600	0.330513	11.158116	33.759992
20	3.207135	0.311805	11.469921	36.785591
21	3.399564	0.294155	11.764077	39.992727
22	3.603537	0.277505	12.041582	43.392290
23	3.819750	0.261797	12.303379	46.995828
24	4.048935	0.246979	12.550358	50.815577
25	4.291871	0.232999	12.783356	54.864512
26	4.549383	0.219810	13.003166	59.156383
27	4.822346	0.207368	13.210534	63.705766
28	5.111687	0.195630	13.406164	68.528112
29	5.418388	0.184557	13.590721	73.639798
30	5.743491	0.174110	13.764831	79.058186
31	6.088101	0.164255	13.929086	84.801677
32	6.453387	0.154957	14.084043	90.889778
33	6.840590	0.146186	14.230230	97.343165
34	7.251025	0.137912	14.368141	104.183755
35	7.686087	0.130105	14.498246	111.434780
36	8.147252	0.122741	14.620987	119.120867
37	8.636087	0.115793	14.736780	127.268119
38	9.154252	0.109239	14.846019	135.904206
39	9.703507	0.103056	14.949075	145.058458
40	10.285718	0.097222	15.046297	154.761966
41	10.902861	0.091719	15.138016	165.047684
42	11.557033	0.086527	15.224543	175.950545
43	12.250455	0.081630	15.306173	187.507577
44	12.985482	0.077009	15.383182	199.758032
45	13.764611	0.072650	15.455832	212.743514
46	14.590487	0.068538	15.524370	226.508125
47	15.465917	0.064658	15.589028	241.098612
48	16.393872	0.060998	15.650027	256.564529
49	17.377504	0.057546	15.707572	272.958401
50	18.420154	0.054288	15.761861	290.335905

$r = 0.07$

n	$(1 + r)^n$	$(1 + r)^{-n}$	$a_{\overline{n}|r}$	$s_{\overline{n}|r}$
1	1.070000	0.934579	0.934579	1.000000
2	1.144900	0.873439	1.808018	2.070000
3	1.225043	0.816298	2.624316	3.214900
4	1.310796	0.762895	3.387211	4.439943
5	1.402552	0.712986	4.100197	5.750739
6	1.500730	0.666342	4.766540	7.153291
7	1.605781	0.622750	5.389289	8.654021
8	1.718186	0.582009	5.971299	10.259803
9	1.838459	0.543934	6.515232	11.977989
10	1.967151	0.508349	7.023582	13.816448
11	2.104852	0.475093	7.498674	15.783599
12	2.252192	0.444012	7.942686	17.888451
13	2.409845	0.414964	8.357651	20.140643
14	2.578534	0.387817	8.745468	22.550488
15	2.759032	0.362446	9.107914	25.129022
16	2.952164	0.338735	9.446649	27.888054
17	3.158815	0.316574	9.763223	30.840217
18	3.379932	0.295864	10.059087	33.999033
19	3.616528	0.276508	10.335595	37.378965
20	3.869684	0.258419	10.594014	40.995492
21	4.140562	0.241513	10.835527	44.865177
22	4.430402	0.225713	11.061240	49.005739
23	4.740530	0.210947	11.272187	53.436141
24	5.072367	0.197147	11.469334	58.176671
25	5.427433	0.184249	11.653583	63.249038
26	5.807353	0.172195	11.825779	68.676470
27	6.213868	0.160930	11.986709	74.483823
28	6.648838	0.150402	12.137111	80.697691
29	7.114257	0.140563	12.277674	87.346529
30	7.612255	0.131367	12.409041	94.460786
31	8.145113	0.122773	12.531814	102.073041
32	8.715271	0.114741	12.646555	110.218154
33	9.325340	0.107235	12.753790	118.933425
34	9.978114	0.100219	12.854009	128.258765
35	10.676581	0.093663	12.947672	138.236878
36	11.423942	0.087535	13.035208	148.913460
37	12.223618	0.081809	13.117017	160.337402
38	13.079271	0.076457	13.193473	172.561020
39	13.994820	0.071455	13.264928	185.640292
40	14.974458	0.066780	13.331709	199.635112
41	16.022670	0.062412	13.394120	214.609570
42	17.144257	0.058329	13.452449	230.632240
43	18.344355	0.054513	13.506962	247.776496
44	19.628460	0.050946	13.557908	266.120851
45	21.002452	0.047613	13.605522	285.749311
46	22.472623	0.044499	13.650020	306.751763
47	24.045707	0.041587	13.691608	329.224386
48	25.728907	0.038867	13.730474	353.270093
49	27.529930	0.036324	13.766799	378.999000
50	29.457025	0.033948	13.800746	406.528929

$$r = 0.08$$

n	$(1 + r)^n$	$(1 + r)^{-n}$	$a_{\overline{n}\rvert r}$	$s_{\overline{n}\rvert r}$
1	1.080000	0.925926	0.925926	1.000000
2	1.166400	0.857339	1.783265	2.080000
3	1.259712	0.793832	2.577097	3.246400
4	1.360489	0.735030	3.312127	4.506112
5	1.469328	0.680583	3.992710	5.866601
6	1.586874	0.630170	4.622880	7.335929
7	1.713824	0.583490	5.206370	8.922803
8	1.850930	0.540269	5.746639	10.636628
9	1.999005	0.500249	6.246888	12.487558
10	2.158925	0.463193	6.710081	14.486562
11	2.331639	0.428883	7.138964	16.645487
12	2.518170	0.397114	7.536078	18.977126
13	2.719624	0.367698	7.903776	21.495297
14	2.937194	0.340461	8.244237	24.214920
15	3.172169	0.315242	8.559479	27.152114
16	3.425943	0.291890	8.851369	30.324283
17	3.700018	0.270269	9.121638	33.750226
18	3.996019	0.250249	9.371887	37.450244
19	4.315701	0.231712	9.603599	41.446263
20	4.660957	0.214548	9.818147	45.761964
21	5.033834	0.198656	10.016803	50.422921
22	5.436540	0.183941	10.200744	55.456755
23	5.871464	0.170315	10.371059	60.893296
24	6.341181	0.157699	10.528758	66.764759
25	6.848475	0.146018	10.674776	73.105940
26	7.396353	0.135202	10.809978	79.954415
27	7.988061	0.125187	10.935165	87.350768
28	8.627106	0.115914	11.051078	95.338830
29	9.317275	0.107328	11.158406	103.965936
30	10.062657	0.099377	11.257783	113.283211
31	10.867669	0.092016	11.349799	123.345868
32	11.737083	0.085200	11.434999	134.213537
33	12.676050	0.078889	11.513888	145.950620
34	13.690134	0.073045	11.586934	158.626670
35	14.785344	0.067635	11.654568	172.316804
36	15.968172	0.062625	11.717193	187.102148
37	17.245626	0.057986	11.775179	203.070320
38	18.625276	0.053690	11.828869	220.315945
39	20.115298	0.049713	11.878582	238.941221
40	21.724521	0.046031	11.924613	259.056519
41	23.462483	0.042621	11.967235	280.781040
42	25.339482	0.039464	12.006699	304.243523
43	27.366640	0.036541	12.043240	329.583005
44	29.555972	0.033834	12.077074	356.949646
45	31.920449	0.031328	12.108402	386.505617
46	34.474085	0.029007	12.137409	418.426067
47	37.232012	0.026859	12.164267	452.900152
48	40.210573	0.024869	12.189136	490.132164
49	43.427419	0.023027	12.212163	530.342737
50	46.901613	0.021321	12.233485	573.770156

Table of Selected Integrals

Rational Forms Containing $(a + bu)$

1. $\displaystyle\int u^n \, du = \frac{u^{n+1}}{n+1} + C, \quad n \neq -1.$

2. $\displaystyle\int \frac{du}{a + bu} = \frac{1}{b} \ln |a + bu| + C.$

3. $\displaystyle\int \frac{u \, du}{a + bu} = \frac{u}{b} - \frac{a}{b^2} \ln |a + bu| + C$

4. $\displaystyle\int \frac{u^2 \, du}{a + bu} = \frac{u^2}{2b} - \frac{au}{b^2} + \frac{a^2}{b^3} \ln |a + bu| + C.$

5. $\displaystyle\int \frac{du}{u(a + bu)} = \frac{1}{a} \ln \left| \frac{u}{a + bu} \right| + C.$

6. $\displaystyle\int \frac{du}{u^2(a + bu)} = -\frac{1}{au} + \frac{b}{a^2} \ln \left| \frac{a + bu}{u} \right| + C.$

7. $\displaystyle\int \frac{u \, du}{(a + bu)^2} = \frac{1}{b^2} \left(\ln |a + bu| + \frac{a}{a + bu} \right) + C.$

8. $\displaystyle\int \frac{u^2 \, du}{(a + bu)^2} = \frac{u}{b^2} - \frac{a^2}{b^3(a + bu)} - \frac{2a}{b^3} \ln |a + bu| + C.$

9. $\displaystyle\int \frac{du}{u(a + bu)^2} = \frac{1}{a(a + bu)} + \frac{1}{a^2} \ln \left| \frac{u}{a + bu} \right| + C.$

10. $\displaystyle\int \frac{du}{u^2(a + bu)^2} = -\frac{a + 2bu}{a^2 u(a + bu)} + \frac{2b}{a^3} \ln \left| \frac{a + bu}{u} \right| + C.$

11. $\displaystyle\int \frac{du}{(a + bu)(c + ku)} = \frac{1}{bc - ak} \ln \left| \frac{a + bu}{c + ku} \right| + C.$

12. $\displaystyle\int\frac{u\ du}{(a + bu)(c + ku)} = \frac{1}{bc - ak}\left[\frac{c}{k}\ln|c + ku| - \frac{a}{b}\ln|a + bu|\right] + C.$

Forms Containing $\sqrt{a + bu}$

13. $\displaystyle\int u\sqrt{a + bu}\ du = \frac{2(3bu - 2a)(a + bu)^{3/2}}{15b^2} + C.$

14. $\displaystyle\int u^2\sqrt{a + bu}\ du = \frac{2(8a^2 - 12abu + 15b^2u^2)(a + bu)^{3/2}}{105b^3} + C.$

15. $\displaystyle\int\frac{u\ du}{\sqrt{a + bu}} = \frac{2(bu - 2a)\sqrt{a + bu}}{3b^2} + C.$

16. $\displaystyle\int\frac{u^2\ du}{\sqrt{a + bu}} = \frac{2(3b^2u^2 - 4abu + 8a^2)\sqrt{a + bu}}{15b^3} + C.$

17. $\displaystyle\int\frac{du}{u\sqrt{a + bu}} = \frac{1}{\sqrt{a}}\ln\left|\frac{\sqrt{a + bu} - \sqrt{a}}{\sqrt{a + bu} + \sqrt{a}}\right| + C,\ a > 0.$

18. $\displaystyle\int\frac{\sqrt{a + bu}\ du}{u} = 2\sqrt{a + bu} + a\int\frac{du}{u\sqrt{a + bu}}.$

Forms Containing $\sqrt{a^2 - u^2}$

19. $\displaystyle\int\frac{du}{(a^2 - u^2)^{3/2}} = \frac{u}{a^2\sqrt{a^2 - u^2}} + C.$

20. $\displaystyle\int\frac{du}{u\sqrt{a^2 - u^2}} = -\frac{1}{a}\ln\left|\frac{a + \sqrt{a^2 - u^2}}{u}\right| + C.$

21. $\displaystyle\int\frac{du}{u^2\sqrt{a^2 - u^2}} = -\frac{\sqrt{a^2 - u^2}}{a^2 u} + C.$

22. $\displaystyle\int\frac{\sqrt{a^2 - u^2}\ du}{u} = \sqrt{a^2 - u^2} - a\ln\left|\frac{a + \sqrt{a^2 - u^2}}{u}\right| + C,\ a > 0.$

Forms Containing $\sqrt{u^2 \pm a^2}$

23. $\displaystyle\int\sqrt{u^2 \pm a^2}\ du = \frac{1}{2}(u\sqrt{u^2 \pm a^2} \pm a^2\ln|u + \sqrt{u^2 \pm a^2}|) + C.$

24. $\displaystyle \int u^2 \sqrt{u^2 \pm a^2}\, du = \frac{u}{8}(2u^2 \pm a^2)\sqrt{u^2 \pm a^2} -$
$$\frac{a^4}{8} \ln \left| u + \sqrt{u^2 \pm a^2} \right| + C.$$

25. $\displaystyle \int \frac{\sqrt{u^2 + a^2}\, du}{u} = \sqrt{u^2 + a^2} - a \ln \left| \frac{a + \sqrt{u^2 + a^2}}{u} \right| + C.$

26. $\displaystyle \int \frac{\sqrt{u^2 \pm a^2}\, du}{u^2} = -\frac{\sqrt{u^2 \pm a^2}}{u} + \ln \left| u + \sqrt{u^2 \pm a^2} \right| + C.$

27. $\displaystyle \int \frac{du}{\sqrt{u^2 \pm a^2}} = \ln \left| u + \sqrt{u^2 \pm a^2} \right| + C.$

28. $\displaystyle \int \frac{du}{u\sqrt{u^2 + a^2}} = \frac{1}{a} \ln \left| \frac{\sqrt{u^2 + a^2} - a}{u} \right| + C.$

29. $\displaystyle \int \frac{u^2\, du}{\sqrt{u^2 \pm a^2}} = \frac{1}{2}(u\sqrt{u^2 \pm a^2} \mp a^2 \ln \left| u + \sqrt{u^2 \pm a^2} \right|) + C.$

30. $\displaystyle \int \frac{du}{u^2\sqrt{u^2 \pm a^2}} = -\frac{\pm\sqrt{u^2 \pm a^2}}{a^2 u} + C.$

31. $\displaystyle \int (u^2 \pm a^2)^{3/2}\, du = \frac{u}{8}(2u^2 \pm 5a^2)\sqrt{u^2 \pm a^2} +$
$$\frac{3a^4}{8} \ln \left| u + \sqrt{u^2 \pm a^2} \right| + C.$$

32. $\displaystyle \int \frac{du}{(u^2 \pm a^2)^{3/2}} = \frac{\pm u}{a^2\sqrt{u^2 \pm a^2}} + C.$

33. $\displaystyle \int \frac{u^2\, du}{(u^2 \pm a^2)^{3/2}} = \frac{-u}{\sqrt{u^2 \pm a^2}} + \ln \left| u + \sqrt{u^2 \pm a^2} \right| + C.$

Rational Forms Containing $a^2 - u^2$ and $u^2 - a^2$

34. $\displaystyle \int \frac{du}{a^2 - u^2} = \frac{1}{2a} \ln \left| \frac{a + u}{a - u} \right| + C.$

35. $\displaystyle \int \frac{du}{u^2 - a^2} = \frac{1}{2a} \ln \left| \frac{u - a}{u + a} \right| + C.$

Exponential and Logarithmic Forms

36. $\displaystyle \int e^u\, du = e^u + C.$

37. $\displaystyle \int a^u\, du = \frac{a^u}{\ln a} + C, \quad a > 0, \quad a \neq 1.$

38. $\int ue^{au}\,du = \dfrac{e^{au}}{a^2}(au - 1) + C.$

39. $\int u^n e^{au}\,du = \dfrac{u^n e^{au}}{a} - \dfrac{n}{a}\int u^{n-1}e^{au}\,du.$

40. $\int \dfrac{e^{au}\,du}{u^n} = -\dfrac{e^{au}}{(n-1)u^{n-1}} + \dfrac{a}{n-1}\int \dfrac{e^{au}\,du}{u^{n-1}}.$

41. $\int \ln u\,du = u \ln u - u + C.$

42. $\int u^n \ln u\,du = \dfrac{u^{n+1}\ln u}{n+1} - \dfrac{u^{n+1}}{(n+1)^2} + C,\quad n \neq -1.$

43. $\int u^n \ln^m u\,du = \dfrac{u^{n+1}}{n+1}\ln^m u - \dfrac{m}{n+1}\int u^n \ln^{m-1} u\,du,\quad m,\ n \neq -1.$

44. $\int \dfrac{du}{u \ln u} = \ln |\ln u| + C.$

45. $\int \dfrac{du}{a + be^{cu}} = \dfrac{1}{ac}(cu - \ln |a + be^{cu}|) + C.$

Miscellaneous Forms

46. $\int \sqrt{\dfrac{a+u}{b+u}}\,du = \sqrt{(a+u)(b+u)} +$
$$(a - b)\ln(\sqrt{a+u} + \sqrt{b+u}) + C.$$

47. $\int \dfrac{du}{\sqrt{(a+u)(b+u)}} = \ln\left|\dfrac{a+b}{2} + u + \sqrt{(a+u)(b+u)}\right| + C.$

48. $\int \sqrt{a + bu + cu^2}\,du = \dfrac{2cu + b}{4c}\sqrt{a + bu + cu^2} -$
$$\dfrac{b^2 - 4ac}{8c^{3/2}}\ln|2cu + b + 2\sqrt{c}\sqrt{a + bu + cu^2}| + C,\quad c > 0.$$

Areas under the Standard Normal Curve

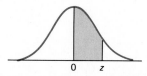

$$A(z) = \int_0^z \frac{1}{\sqrt{2\pi}} e^{-x^2/2} \, dx$$

$$A(-z) = A(z)$$

z	.00	.01	.02	.03	.04	.05	.06	.07	.08	.09
0.0	.0000	.0040	.0080	.0120	.0160	.0199	.0239	.0279	.0319	.0359
0.1	.0398	.0438	.0478	.0517	.0557	.0596	.0636	.0675	.0714	.0754
0.2	.0793	.0832	.0871	.0910	.0948	.0987	.1026	.1064	.1103	.1141
0.3	.1179	.1217	.1255	.1293	.1331	.1368	.1406	.1443	.1480	.1517
0.4	.1554	.1591	.1628	.1664	.1700	.1736	.1772	.1808	.1844	.1879
0.5	.1915	.1950	.1985	.2019	.2054	.2088	.2123	.2157	.2190	.2224
0.6	.2258	.2291	.2324	.2357	.2389	.2422	.2454	.2486	.2518	.2549
0.7	.2580	.2612	.2642	.2673	.2704	.2734	.2764	.2794	.2823	.2852
0.8	.2881	.2910	.2939	.2967	.2996	.3023	.3051	.3078	.3106	.3133
0.9	.3159	.3186	.3212	.3238	.3264	.3289	.3315	.3340	.3365	.3389
1.0	.3413	.3438	.3461	.3485	.3508	.3531	.3554	.3577	.3599	.3621
1.1	.3643	.3665	.3686	.3708	.3729	.3749	.3770	.3790	.3810	.3820
1.2	.3849	.3869	.3888	.3907	.3925	.3944	.3962	.3980	.3997	.4015
1.3	.4032	.4049	.4066	.4082	.4099	.4115	.4131	.4147	.4162	.4177
1.4	.4192	.4207	.4222	.4236	.4251	.4265	.4279	.4292	.4306	.4319
1.5	.4332	.4345	.4357	.4370	.4382	.4394	.4406	.4418	.4429	.4441
1.6	.4452	.4463	.4474	.4484	.4495	.4505	.4515	.4525	.4535	.4545
1.7	.4554	.4564	.4573	.4582	.4591	.4599	.4608	.4616	.4625	.4633
1.8	.4641	.4649	.4656	.4664	.4671	.4678	.4686	.4693	.4699	.4706
1.9	.4713	.4719	.4726	.4732	.4738	.4744	.4750	.4756	.4761	.4767
2.0	.4772	.4778	.4783	.4788	.4793	.4798	.4803	.4808	.4812	.4817
2.1	.4821	.4826	.4830	.4834	.4838	.4842	.4846	.4850	.4854	.4857
2.2	.4861	.4864	.4868	.4871	.4875	.4878	.4881	.4884	.4887	.4890
2.3	.4893	.4896	.4898	.4901	.4904	.4906	.4909	.4911	.4913	.4916
2.4	.4918	.4920	.4922	.4925	.4927	.4929	.4931	.4932	.4934	.4936

z	.00	.01	.02	.03	.04	.05	.06	.07	.08	.09
2.5	.4938	.4940	.4941	.4943	.4945	.4946	.4948	.4949	.4951	.4952
2.6	.4953	.4955	.4956	.4957	.4959	.4960	.4961	.4962	.4963	.4964
2.7	.4965	.4966	.4967	.4968	.4969	.4970	.4971	.4972	.4973	.4974
2.8	.4974	.4975	.4976	.4977	.4977	.4978	.4979	.4979	.4980	.4981
2.9	.4981	.4982	.4982	.4983	.4984	.4984	.4985	.4985	.4986	.4986
3.0	.4987	.4987	.4987	.4988	.4988	.4989	.4989	.4989	.4990	.4990
3.1	.4990	.4991	.4991	.4991	.4992	.4992	.4992	.4992	.4993	.4993
3.2	.4993	.4993	.4994	.4994	.4994	.4994	.4994	.4995	.4995	.4995
3.3	.4995	.4995	.4995	.4996	.4996	.4996	.4996	.4996	.4996	.4997
3.4	.4997	.4997	.4997	.4997	.4997	.4997	.4997	.4997	.4997	.4998
3.5	.4998	.4998	.4998	.4998	.4998	.4998	.4998	.4998	.4998	.4998

Answers to Odd-Numbered Problems

Exercise 0.2

1. True. **3.** False; the natural numbers are 1, 2, 3, and so on. **5.** True. **7.** False; $\frac{4}{2} = 2$, a positive integer.

9. True. **11.** True.

Exercise 0.3

1. False. **3.** False. **5.** True. **7.** True. **9.** False. **11.** Distributive. **13.** Associative.

15. Commutative. **17.** Definition of subtraction. **19.** Distributive.

Exercise 0.4

1. -6. **3.** 2. **5.** 11. **7.** -2. **9.** -63. **11.** -6. **13.** $6 - x$.

15. $-12x + 12y$ (or $12y - 12x$). **17.** $-\frac{1}{3}$. **19.** -2. **21.** 18. **23.** 25. **25.** $3x - 12$. **27.** $-x + 2$.

29. $\frac{8}{11}$. **31.** $-\frac{5x}{7y}$. **33.** $\frac{2}{3x}$. **35.** 3. **37.** $\frac{7}{xy}$. **39.** $\frac{5}{6}$. **41.** $-\frac{1}{6}$. **43.** $\frac{x - y}{9}$.

45. $\frac{1}{24}$. **47.** $\frac{x}{6y}$. **49.** Not defined. **51.** Not defined.

Exercise 0.5

1. 2^5 ($= 32$). **3.** w^{12}. **5.** $\frac{x^8}{y^{17}}$. **7.** $\frac{x^{10}}{y^{50}}$. **9.** $8x^6y^9$. **11.** x^6. **13.** x^{14}. **15.** 5. **17.** -2.

19. $\frac{1}{2}$. **21.** 10. **23.** 8. **25.** $\frac{1}{4}$. **27.** $\frac{1}{32}$. **29.** $4\sqrt{2}$. **31.** $x\sqrt[3]{2}$. **33.** $4x^2$. **35.** $3z^2$. **37.** $\frac{9t^2}{4}$.

39. $\dfrac{x^3}{y^2z^2}$.   **41.** $\dfrac{2}{x^4}$.   **43.** $\dfrac{1}{9t^2}$.   **45.** $7^{1/3}s^{2/3}$.   **47.** $x^{1/2} - y^{1/2}$.   **49.** $\dfrac{x^{9/4}z^{3/4}}{y^{1/2}}$.   **51.** $\sqrt[5]{(8x-y)^4}$.   **53.** $\dfrac{1}{\sqrt[5]{x^4}}$.

55. $\dfrac{2}{\sqrt[5]{x^2}} - \dfrac{1}{\sqrt[5]{4x^2}}$.   **57.** $\dfrac{3\sqrt{7}}{7}$.   **59.** $\dfrac{2\sqrt{2x}}{x}$.   **61.** $\dfrac{\sqrt[3]{9x^2}}{3x}$.   **63.** 4.   **65.** $\dfrac{\sqrt[12]{8x^8y^4}}{xy}$.   **67.** $\dfrac{2x^6}{y^3}$.   **69.** $t^{2/3}$.

71. $\dfrac{64y^6x^{1/2}}{x^2}$.   **73.** xyz.   **75.** $\dfrac{1}{9}$.   **77.** $\dfrac{4y^4}{x^2}$.   **79.** $x^2y^{5/2}$.   **81.** $\dfrac{y^{10}}{z^2}$.   **83.** $\dfrac{1}{x^4}$.   **85.** $-\dfrac{4}{s^5}$.   **87.** $\dfrac{4x^4z^4}{9y^4}$.

Exercise 0.6

1. $11x - 2y - 3$.   **3.** $6t^2 - 2s^2 + 6$.   **5.** $2\sqrt{x} + \sqrt{2y} + \sqrt{3z}$.   **7.** $6x^2 - 9xy - 2z + \sqrt{2} - 4$.
9. $\sqrt{2y} - \sqrt{3z}$.   **11.** $-7x + 14y - 19$.   **13.** $x^2 + 9y^2 + xy$.   **15.** $6x^2 + 96$.   **17.** $-6x^2 - 18x - 18$.
19. $x^2 + 9x + 20$.   **21.** $x^2 + x - 6$.   **23.** $10x^2 + 19x + 6$.   **25.** $x^2 + 6x + 9$.   **27.** $x^2 - 10x + 25$.
29. $2y + 6\sqrt{2y} + 9$.   **31.** $4s^2 - 1$.   **33.** $x^3 + 4x^2 - 3x - 12$.   **35.** $2x^4 + 2x^3 - 5x^2 - 2x + 3$.
37. $5x^3 + 5x^2 + 6x$.   **39.** $3x^2 + 2y^2 + 5xy + 2x - 8$.   **41.** $x^3 + 15x^2 + 75x + 125$.
43. $8x^3 - 36x^2 + 54x - 27$.   **45.** $z - 4$.   **47.** $3x^3 + 2x - \dfrac{1}{2x^2}$.   **49.** $x + \dfrac{-1}{x+3}$.   **51.** $3x^2 - 8x + 17 + \dfrac{-37}{x+2}$.
53. $t + 8 + \dfrac{64}{t-8}$.   **55.** $x - 2 + \dfrac{7}{3x+2}$.

Exercise 0.7

1. $2(3x + 2)$.   **3.** $5x(2y + z)$.   **5.** $4bc(2a^3 - 3ab^2d + b^3cd^2)$.   **7.** $(x-5)(x+5)$.   **9.** $(p+3)(p+1)$.
11. $(4x - 3)(4x + 3)$.   **13.** $(z+4)(z+2)$.   **15.** $(x+3)^2$.   **17.** $2(x+4)(x+2)$.   **19.** $3(x-1)(x+1)$.
21. $(6y + 1)(y + 2)$.   **23.** $2s(3s+4)(2s-1)$.   **25.** $x^{2/3}y(1-2xy)(1+2xy)$.   **27.** $2x(x+3)(x-2)$.
29. $4(2x+1)^2$.   **31.** $x(xy-5)^2$.   **33.** $(x-2)^2(x+2)$.   **35.** $(y-1)(y+1)(y^4+4)^2$.   **37.** $(x+2)(x^2-2x+4)$.
39. $(x+1)(x^2-x+1)(x-1)(x^2+x+1)$.   **41.** $2(x+3)^2(x+1)(x-1)$.   **43.** $P(1+r)^2$.
45. $(x^2+4)(x+2)(x-2)$.   **47.** $(y^4+1)(y^2+1)(y+1)(y-1)$.   **49.** $(x^2+2)(x+1)(x-1)$.   **51.** $x(x+1)^2(x-1)^2$.

Exercise 0.8

1. $-\dfrac{y^2}{(y-3)(y+2)}$.   **3.** $\dfrac{3-2x}{3+2x}$.   **5.** $\dfrac{2(x+4)}{(x-4)(x+2)}$.   **7.** $\dfrac{x}{2}$.

9. $\dfrac{1}{2n}$.   **11.** $\dfrac{2}{3}$.   **13.** $-27x^2$.   **15.** 1.

17. $\dfrac{2x^2}{x-1}$.   **19.** 1.   **21.** $-\dfrac{(2x+3)(1+x)}{x+4}$.   **23.** $x+2$.   **25.** $\dfrac{5}{3t}$.   **27.** $-\dfrac{1}{p^2-1}$.
29. $\dfrac{2x^2+3x+12}{(2x-1)(x+3)}$.   **31.** $\dfrac{2x-3}{(x-2)(x+1)(x-1)}$.   **33.** $\dfrac{35-8x}{(x-1)(x+5)}$.   **35.** $\dfrac{x^2+2x+1}{x^2}$.   **37.** $\dfrac{x}{1-xy}$.
39. $\dfrac{x+1}{3x}$.   **41.** $\dfrac{(x+2)(6x-1)}{2x^2(x+3)}$.   **43.** $\dfrac{2\sqrt{x}-2\sqrt{x+h}}{\sqrt{x}\sqrt{x+h}}$.   **45.** $2 - \sqrt{3}$.   **47.** $-\dfrac{\sqrt{6}+2\sqrt{3}}{3}$.
49. $-4 - 2\sqrt{6}$.   **51.** $\dfrac{x-\sqrt{5}}{x^2-5}$.   **53.** $\dfrac{5\sqrt{3}-4\sqrt{2}-13}{2}$.

Exercise 1.1

1. 0.   **3.** $\dfrac{10}{3}$.   **5.** Does not satisfy equation.   **7.** Adding 5 to both sides; equivalence guaranteed.   **9.** Squaring both sides; equivalence *not* guaranteed.   **11.** Dividing both sides by x; equivalence *not* guaranteed.   **13.** Multiplying both sides by $x - 1$; equivalence *not* guaranteed.   **15.** Multiplying both sides by $(x - 5)/x$; equivalence *not* guaranteed.   **17.** $\frac{5}{2}$.   **19.** 0.

21. 1.   **23.** $\frac{12}{5}$.   **25.** -1.   **27.** 2.   **29.** $\frac{10}{3}$.   **31.** 90.   **33.** 8.   **35.** $-\frac{26}{9}$.   **37.** $-\frac{37}{18}$.   **39.** $\frac{60}{17}$.

41. $\frac{14}{3}$.   **43.** 3.   **45.** $\frac{7}{8}$.   **47.** $P = \frac{I}{rt}$.   **49.** $q = \frac{p + 1}{8}$.   **51.** $r = \frac{S - P}{Pt}$.   **53.** $a_1 = \frac{2S - na_n}{n}$.

55. 3.   **57.** $y = \frac{ax}{1 + abx}$.

Exercise 1.2

1. $\frac{1}{5}$.   **3.** $\varnothing$.   **5.** $\frac{8}{3}$.   **7.** $\frac{3}{2}$.   **9.** 0.   **11.** $\frac{5}{3}$.   **13.** $\frac{1}{8}$.   **15.** 3.   **17.** $\frac{5}{13}$.   **19.** $\varnothing$.   **21.** 3.

23. $\frac{262}{5}$.   **25.** $-\frac{10}{9}$.   **27.** 2.   **29.** 7.   **31.** $\frac{49}{36}$.   **33.** $-\frac{9}{4}$.   **35.** $d = \frac{r}{1 + rt}$.   **37.** $n = \frac{2mI}{rB} - 1$.

39. 10.   **41.** 67 ft.

Exercise 1.3

1. 2.   **3.** 4, 3.   **5.** 3, -1.   **7.** 6.   **9.** ± 2.   **11.** 0, 8.   **13.** $\frac{1}{2}$.   **15.** 1, $-\frac{5}{2}$.   **17.** 5, -2.

19. 0, $\frac{3}{2}$.   **21.** 0, 1, -2.   **23.** 0, ± 8.   **25.** 0, $\frac{1}{2}$, $-\frac{4}{3}$.   **27.** $-3, -1, 2$.   **29.** 3, 4.   **31.** 4, -6.

33. $\frac{3}{2}$.   **35.** $\frac{5 \pm \sqrt{13}}{2}$.   **37.** No real roots.   **39.** $\frac{1}{2}, -\frac{5}{3}$.   **41.** 4, $-\frac{5}{2}$.   **43.** $\frac{-2 \pm \sqrt{14}}{2}$.   **45.** $\frac{3}{2}, -1$.

47. 6, -2.   **49.** $\frac{1}{2}$.   **51.** 5, -2.   **53.** $\frac{3}{2}$.   **55.** -2.   **57.** 7.   **59.** 4, 8.   **61.** 2.   **63.** 0, 4.

65. 4.   **69.** **(a)** 1, $\frac{1}{2n - 1}$; **(b)** $\frac{2n + 1 - \sqrt{4n^2 + 1}}{2n}$.

Review Problems—Chapter 1

1. $\frac{1}{4}$.   **3.** $-\frac{2}{15}$.   **5.** $-\frac{1}{2}$.   **7.** $\varnothing$.   **9.** $\frac{5}{2}$.   **11.** $\frac{1}{3}$.   **13.** $-\frac{9}{7}$.   **15.** $-\frac{5}{3}, 1$.   **17.** 0, $\frac{7}{5}$.   **19.** 5.

21. $\pm\frac{\sqrt{15}}{3}$.   **23.** $\frac{5}{8}, -3$.   **25.** $\frac{5 \pm \sqrt{13}}{6}$.   **27.** 4, ± 3.   **29.** $\frac{1}{2}$.   **31.** $\frac{4 \pm \sqrt{13}}{3}$.   **33.** 10.   **35.** 5.

37. No solution.   **39.** 10.   **41.** 4, 8.

Exercise 2.1

1. 181,250.   **3.** $4000 at 6%, $16,000 at $7\frac{1}{2}$%.   **5.** $4.25.   **7.** 4%.   **9.** 80.   **11.** $8000.   **13.** 1600.
15. $72.50.   **17.** 40.   **19.** 46,000 units.   **21.** Either $440 or $460.   **23.** $100.   **25.** 77.
27. 80 ft by 140 ft.   **29.** 9 cm long, 4 cm wide.   **31.** $112,000.   **33.** 60.
35. Either 125 units of A and 100 units of B, or 150 units of A and 125 units of B.

Exercise 2.2

1. $x > 4$.   **3.** $x \leq 5$.   **5.** $x \leq -\dfrac{1}{2}$.   **7.** $s < -\dfrac{2}{5}$.   **9.** $y > 0$.   **11.** $x \geq -\dfrac{7}{5}$.   **13.** $x > -\dfrac{2}{7}$.   **15.** $\varnothing$.

17. $x < \dfrac{\sqrt{3} - 2}{2}$.   **19.** $x < 6$.   **21.** $y \leq -5$.   **23.** $-\infty < x < \infty$.   **25.** $t > \dfrac{17}{9}$.   **27.** $x \geq -\dfrac{14}{3}$.   **29.** $r > 0$.

31. $y < 0$.   **33.** $x \leq -2$.   **35.** $444{,}000 < S < 636{,}000$.

Exercise 2.3

1. At least 120,001.   **3.** 12,400.   **5.** 60,000.   **7.** \$25,714.29.   **9.** 1000.   **11.** $t > 36.5$.   **13.** \$4.50, \$1160.

Exercise 2.4

1. 13.   **3.** 6.   **5.** 5.   **7.** $-3 < x < 3$.   **9.** $\sqrt{5} - 2$.   **11.** **(a)** $|x - 7| < 3$,   **(b)** $|x - 2| < 3$,
(c) $|x - 7| \leq 5$,   **(d)** $|x - 7| = 4$,   **(e)** $|x + 4| < 2$,   **(f)** $|x| < 3$,   **(g)** $|x| > 6$,   **(h)** $|x - 6| > 4$,   **(i)** $|x - 105| < 3$,
(j) $|x - 850| < 100$.   **13.** $|p_1 - p_2| \leq 2$.   **15.** ± 7.   **17.** ± 6.   **19.** $-3, 13$.   **21.** $\dfrac{2}{5}$.   **23.** $\dfrac{1}{2}, 3$.
25. $-4 < x < 4$.   **27.** $x < -8, x > 8$.   **29.** $-9 < x < -5$.   **31.** $x < 0, x > 1$.   **33.** $2 \leq x \leq 3$.
35. $x \leq 0, x \geq \dfrac{16}{3}$.   **37.** $x < \mu - h\sigma, x > \mu + h\sigma$.

Review Problems—Chapter 2

1. $x \leq 0$.   **3.** $x > \dfrac{2}{3}$.   **5.** $\varnothing$.   **7.** $x \leq \dfrac{13}{2}$.   **9.** $-\infty < s < \infty$.   **11.** $-2, 5$.   **13.** $0 < t < \dfrac{1}{2}$.
15. $x \leq -\dfrac{1}{2}, x \geq \dfrac{7}{2}$.   **17.** 542.   **19.** 6000.

Exercise 3.1

1. All real numbers except 0.   **3.** All real numbers ≥ 5.   **5.** All real numbers.   **7.** All real numbers except $-\dfrac{5}{2}$.

9. All real numbers except 0 and 1.   **11.** All real numbers except 4 and $-\dfrac{1}{2}$.   **13.** $0, 15, -20$.

15. $-62, 2 - u^2, 2 - u^4$.   **17.** $2, (2v)^2 + 2v = 4v^2 + 2v, (-x^2)^2 + (-x^2) = x^4 - x^2$.
19. $4, 0, (x + h)^2 + 2(x + h) + 1 = x^2 + 2xh + h^2 + 2x + 2h + 1$.
21. $0, \dfrac{3x - 5}{(3x)^2 + 4} = \dfrac{3x - 5}{9x^2 + 4}, \dfrac{(x + h) - 5}{(x + h)^2 + 4} = \dfrac{x + h - 5}{x^2 + 2xh + h^2 + 4}$.   **23.** $0, 256, \dfrac{1}{16}$.   **25.** **(a)** $3x + 3h - 4$; **(b)** 3.

27. (a) $x^2 + 2hx + h^2 + 2x + 2h$; (b) $2x + h + 2$.   **29.** y is a function of x; x is a function of y.   **31.** y is a function of x; x is not a function of y.   **33.** Yes.   **35.** $V = f(t) = 10,000 + 400t$.   **37.** Yes; P; q.   **39.** (a) $C = 850 + 3q$; (b) 250.

Exercise 3.2

1. All real numbers.   **3.** All real numbers.   **5.** (a) 3; (b) 2.   **7.** (a) 4; (b) -3.   **9.** 12, 12, 12.

11. 1, -1, 0, -1.   **13.** 8, 3, 3, 1.   **15.** (a) $C = 850 + 3q$; (b) 250.   **17.** $\dfrac{9}{64}$.

19. (a) All T such that $30 \le T \le 39$; (b) 4, $\dfrac{17}{4}$, $\dfrac{33}{4}$.

Exercise 3.3

1. (a) $2x + 5$; (b) 5; (c) -3; (d) $x^2 + 5x + 4$; (e) -2; (f) $\dfrac{x+1}{x+4}$; (g) $x + 5$; (h) 8;

(i) $x + 5$.   **3.** (a) $2x^2 + x$; (b) $-x$; (c) $\dfrac{1}{2}$; (d) $x^4 + x^3$; (e) $\dfrac{x^2}{x^2+x} = \dfrac{x}{x+1}$; (f) -1;

(g) $(x^2 + x)^2 = x^4 + 2x^3 + x^2$, (h) $x^4 + x^2$; (i) 90.   **5.** 53; -32.   **7.** $\dfrac{4}{(t-1)^2} + \dfrac{6}{t-1} + 1$; $\dfrac{2}{t^2+3t}$.

9. $\dfrac{1}{v+3}$, $\sqrt{\dfrac{2w^2+3}{w^2+1}}$.   **11.** $f(x) = x^4$, $g(x) = 3x + 1$.   **13.** $f(x) = \dfrac{1}{x}$, $g(x) = x^2 - 2$.

15. $f(x) = \sqrt[5]{x}$, $g(x) = \dfrac{x+1}{3}$.   **17.** $400m - 10m^2$; the total revenue received when the total output of m employees is sold.

Exercise 3.4

1.

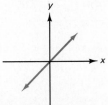

3. (a) 1, 2, 3, 0;
(b) All real numbers;
(c) All real numbers.

5. (a) 0, -1, -1;
(b) All real numbers;
(c) All nonpositive reals.

7. Function; all real numbers; all real numbers.

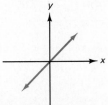

9. Function; all real numbers; all real numbers.

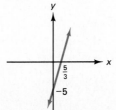

11. Function; all real numbers; all nonnegative real numbers.

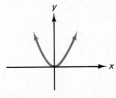

13. Not a function of x.

15. Function; all real numbers; all real numbers.

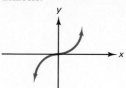

17. Not a function of x.

19. Function; all real numbers; all real numbers.

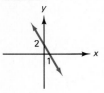

21. All real numbers; all reals ≤ 4.

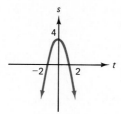

23. All real numbers; 2.

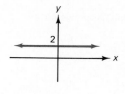

25. All real numbers; all reals ≥ -3.

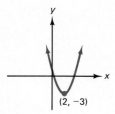

27. All real numbers; all real numbers.

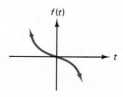

29. All real numbers ≥ 5; all nonnegative reals.

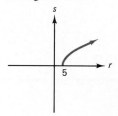

31. All real numbers; all nonnegative reals.

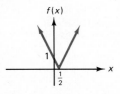

33. All nonzero real numbers; all positive real numbers.

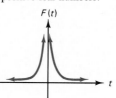

35. All nonnegative reals; all reals x where $0 \leq x \leq 2$.

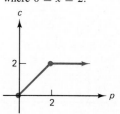

37. All real numbers; all nonnegative reals.

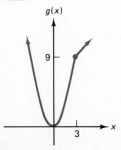

39. a, b, d.

41.

As price decreases, quantity increases; p is a function of q.

43.

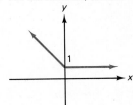

Review Problems—Chapter 3

1. All real numbers except 1 and 2.   **3.** All real numbers.   **5.** All nonnegative reals except 1.

7. $7, 46, 62, 3t^2 - 4t + 7$.   **9.** $0, 3, \sqrt{t}, \sqrt{x^2 - 1}$.   **11.** $\dfrac{3}{5}, 0, \dfrac{\sqrt{x + 4}}{x}, \dfrac{\sqrt{u}}{u - 4}$.   **13.** $-8, 4, 4, -92$.

15. (a) $3 - 7x - 7h$; (b) -7.   **17.** (a) $5x + 2$; (b) 22; (c) $x - 4$; (d) $6x^2 + 7x - 3$; (e) 10; (f) $\dfrac{3x - 1}{2x + 3}$;

(g) $3(2x + 3) - 1 = 6x + 8$; (h) 38; (i) $2(3x - 1) + 3 = 6x + 1$.   **19.** $\dfrac{1}{x - 1}, \dfrac{1}{x} - 1 = \dfrac{1 - x}{x}$.   **21.** $x^3 + 2, (x + 2)^3$.

23.

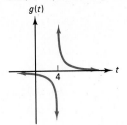

25. All $u \geq -4$; all reals ≥ 0.

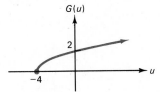

27. All real numbers; all reals ≥ 1.

29. All $t \neq 4$; all nonzero real numbers.

31. a, c.

Exercise 4.1

1. 2.   **3.** $-\dfrac{8}{13}$.   **5.** Undefined.   **7.** 0.   **9.** $6x - y - 4 = 0$.   **11.** $x + 4y - 18 = 0$.

13. $3x - 7y + 25 = 0$.   **15.** $8x - 5y - 29 = 0$.   **17.** $2x - y - 4 = 0$.   **19.** $x + 2y + 6 = 0$.

21. $y + 2 = 0$.   **23.** $x - 2 = 0$.   **25.** $2; -1$.   **27.** $-\dfrac{1}{2}; \dfrac{3}{2}$.   **29.** Slope undefined; no y-intercept.   **31.** $3; 0$.

33. $0; 1$.   **35.** $x + 2y - 4 = 0; y = -\dfrac{1}{2}x + 2$.   **37.** $4x + 9y - 5 = 0; y = -\dfrac{4}{9}x + \dfrac{5}{9}$.

39. $3x - 2y + 24 = 0; y = \dfrac{3}{2}x + 12$.   **41.** $(5, -4)$.

Exercise 4.2

1. $-4; 0.$ **3.** $2; -4.$ **5.** $-\dfrac{1}{2}, \dfrac{7}{2}.$

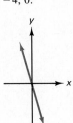

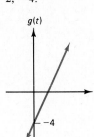

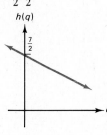

7. $f(x) = 5x - 14.$ **9.** $f(x) = -3x + 9.$ **11.** $f(x) = -\dfrac{1}{2}x + \dfrac{15}{4}.$

13. $f(x) = x - 1.$ **15.** $p = -\dfrac{2}{5}q + 28; \$16.$ **17.** $c = 3q + 10; \$115.$ **19.** $v = -800t + 8000; \text{slope} = -800.$

21. $x + 10y = 100.$ **23.** **(a)** $y = \dfrac{5}{11}x + \dfrac{600}{11};$ **(b)** 12.   **25.** **(a)** $p = 0.059t + 0.025;$ **(b)** 0.556.

27. **(a)** $t = \dfrac{1}{4}c + 37;$ **(b)** add 37 to the number of chirps in 15 seconds.

Exercise 4.3

1. Not quadratic.   **3.** Quadratic.   **5.** Not quadratic.   **7.** Quadratic.   **9.** **(a)** $(1, 11);$ **(b)** Highest.
11. **(a)** $-8;$ **(b)** $-4, 2;$ **(c)** $(-1, -9).$
13. Vertex: $(3, -4);$ intercepts: $(1, 0),$ **15.** Vertex: $\left(-\dfrac{3}{2}, \dfrac{9}{2}\right);$ intercepts: $(0, 0),$ **17.** Vertex: $(-1, 0);$ intercepts:
  $(5, 0), (0, 5);$ range: all $y \geq -4.$ $(-1, 0), (0, 1);$ range: all $s \geq 0.$
  $(-3, 0);$ range: all $y \leq \dfrac{9}{2}.$

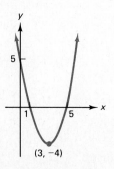

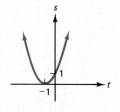

19. Vertex: $(2, -1)$; intercept: $(0, -9)$; range: all $y \le -1$.

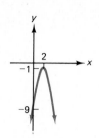

21. Vertex: $(4, -3)$; intercepts: $(4 + \sqrt{3}, 0)$, $(4 - \sqrt{3}, 0)$, $(0, 13)$; range: all $t \ge -3$.

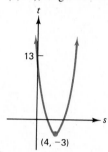

23. Minimum; 24.   **25.** Maximum; -10.   **27.** $q = 200$; $r = \$120{,}000$.   **29.** 70 grams.

Exercise 4.4

1. $x = 4$, $y = -5$.   **3.** $x = 3$, $y = -1$.   **5.** $v = 0$, $w = 18$.   **7.** No solution.   **9.** $x = 12$, $y = -12$.

11. The coordinates of any point on the line $q = -\dfrac{1}{3}p + \dfrac{1}{2}$.   **13.** $x = \dfrac{1}{2}$, $y = \dfrac{1}{2}$, $z = \dfrac{1}{4}$.   **15.** $x = 1$, $y = 1$, $z = 1$.

17. 420 gal of 20% solution, 280 gal of 30% solution.   **19.** 240 units (Early American), 200 units (Contemporary).

21. 800 calculators from Exton plant, 700 from Whyton plant.   **23.** 4% on first $100,000, 6% on remainder.

25. 60 units of Argon I, 40 units of Argon II.   **27.** 100 chairs, 100 rockers, 200 chaise lounges.   **29.** 40 semiskilled workers, 20 skilled workers, 10 shipping clerks.

Exercise 4.5

1. $x = 4$, $y = -12$; $x = -1$, $y = 3$.   **3.** $p = -3$, $q = -5$; $p = 2$, $q = 0$.   **5.** $x = 0$, $y = 0$; $x = 1$, $y = 1$.

7. $x = 4$, $y = 8$; $x = -1$, $y = 3$.   **9.** $p = 0$, $q = 0$; $p = 1$, $q = 1$.

11. $x = 3\sqrt{2}$, $y = 2$; $x = -3\sqrt{2}$, $y = 2$; $x = \sqrt{15}$, $y = -1$; $x = -\sqrt{15}$, $y = -1$.   **13.** $x = -2$, $y = -\dfrac{1}{3}$.

Exercise 4.6

1.

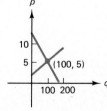

3. $(5, 212.50)$.   **5.** $(9, 38)$.   **7.** $(15, 5)$.   **9.**

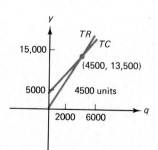

11. Cannot break even at any level of production.   **13.** 10 units or 40 units.   **15.** (a) \$12;   (b) \$12.18.

17. 5840 units; 840 units; 1840 units.   **19.** \$4.   **21.** Total cost always exceeds total revenue—no break-even point.

23. Decreases by \$0.70.   **25.** $p_A = 5$; $p_B = 10$.

Review Problems—Chapter 4

1. 9.   **3.** $y = -x + 1$; $x + y - 1 = 0$.   **5.** $y = \frac{1}{2}x - 1$; $x - 2y - 2 = 0$.   **7.** $y = 4$; $y - 4 = 0$.

9. $y = \frac{3}{2}x - 2$; $\frac{3}{2}$.   **11.** $y = \frac{4}{3}$; 0.   **13.** -2; $(0, 4)$.   **15.** $(3, 0)$, $(-3, 0)$, $(0, 9)$; $(0, 9)$.

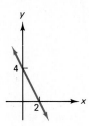

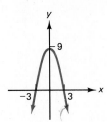

17. $(5, 0)$, $(-1, 0)$, $(0, -5)$; $(2, -9)$.   **19.** 3; $(0, 0)$.   **21.** $(0, -3)$; $(-1, -2)$.

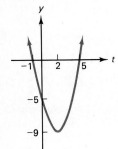

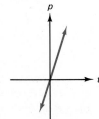

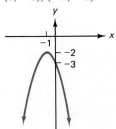

23. $x = \frac{17}{7}$, $y = -\frac{8}{7}$.   **25.** $x = 2$, $y = -1$.   **27.** $x = 8$, $y = 4$.   **29.** $x = 0$, $y = 1$, $z = 0$.

31. $x = -3$, $y = -4$; $x = 2$, $y = 1$.   **33.** $a + b - 3 = 0$; 0.   **35.** $f(x) = -\frac{4}{3}x + \frac{19}{3}$.   **37.** 50 units; $5000.

39. 6.   **41.** (a) $R = 75L + 1310$; (b) 1385 milliseconds; (c) the slope is 75, the time necessary to travel from one level to the next level is 75 milliseconds.

Exercise 5.1

1.

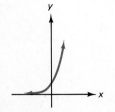

3.

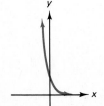

5.

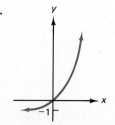

7. 4.4817.   **9.** 0.67032   **11.** 140,000.   **13.** 0.2241.   **15.** 0.399; 0.242; 0.242.   **17.** 0.1466.   **19.** 50.
21. 6065

Exercise 5.2

1. $\log 10{,}000 = 4$.   **3.** $2^6 = 64$.   **5.** $\ln 7.3891 = 2$.   **7.** $e^{1.09861} = 3$.   **9.**   **11.** 2.

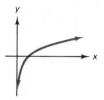

13. 3.   **15.** 1.   **17.** -2.   **19.** 0.   **21.** -3.   **23.** 9.   **25.** 125.   **27.** $\dfrac{1}{10}$.   **29.** e^2.   **31.** 2.

33. 6.   **35.** $\dfrac{1}{81}$.   **37.** 2.   **39.** $\dfrac{5}{3}$.   **41.** $\log_2 5$.   **43.** $\dfrac{\ln 2}{3}$.   **45.** $\log_3 8$.   **47.** $\dfrac{5 + \ln 3}{2}$.   **49.** 1.60944.

51. 2.00013.   **53.** 41.50.   **55.** $E = 2.5 \times 10^{11 + 1.5M}$.   **57.** $225 \ln \dfrac{9}{4} \approx 182$.   **59.** $e^{[u_0 - (x_2^2/2)]/A}$.

Exercise 5.3

1. 1.1761.   **3.** 0.4260.   **5.** 1.5564.   **7.** 3.3010.   **9.** 48.   **11.** $5x$.   **13.** 1.5850.   **15.** -1.   **17.** 4.
19. $\ln x + 2\ln(x + 1)$.   **21.** $2\ln x - 3\ln(x + 1)$.   **23.** $3[\ln x - \ln(x + 1)]$.   **25.** $\ln x - \ln(x + 1) - \ln(x + 2)$.
27. $\dfrac{1}{2}\ln x - 2\ln(x + 1) - 3\ln(x + 2)$.   **29.** $\dfrac{2}{5}\ln x - \dfrac{1}{5}\ln(x + 1) - \ln(x + 2)$.   **31.** $\log 28$.   **33.** $\log_2 \dfrac{2x}{x + 1}$.

35. $\log[7^9(23)^5]$.   **37.** $\log[100(1.05)^{10}]$.   **39.** 2.   **41.** $\dfrac{1}{12}$.   **43.** $\dfrac{5}{2}$.   **45.** ± 2.   **47.** 5.   **49.** $\dfrac{4}{3}$.   **51.** 8.

53. $\dfrac{\ln(x + 8)}{\ln 10}$.   **55.** $\log y = \log a + x \log b$.   **57.** $S = 12.4A^{0.26}$.   **59.** $p = \dfrac{\log(80 - q)}{\log 2}$; 4.32.

Review Problems—Chapter 5

1. $\log_3 81 = 4$.   **3.** 3.   **5.** -4.   **7.** -2.   **9.** 3.   **11.** $\dfrac{1}{100}$.   **13.** 3.   **15.** 3.   **17.** 1.8295.

19. $\log \dfrac{25}{27}$.   **21.** $\ln \dfrac{x^2 y}{z^3}$.   **23.** $\log_2 \dfrac{x^{9/2}}{(x + 1)^3(x + 2)^4}$.   **25.** $2\ln x + \ln y - 3\ln z$.   **27.** $\dfrac{1}{3}(\ln x + \ln y + \ln z)$.

29. $\dfrac{1}{2}(\ln y - \ln z) - \ln x$.   **31.** $2y + \dfrac{1}{2}x$.   **33.** $2x$.   **35.** $y = e^{x^2 + 2}$.   **37.** 134,064; 109,762.

Exercise 6.1

1. (a) \$6014.52; (b) \$2014.52.   **3.** (a) \$1964.76; (b) \$1264.76.   **5.** (a) \$19,606.76; (b) 9,606.76.
7. (a) \$6256.36; (b) \$1256.36.   **9.** (a) \$11,105.58; (b) \$5105.58.   **11.** \$14,124.86.   **13.** \$9649.69.   **15.** 8.24%.
17. 8.32776%.   **19.** 9.0 years.   **21.** \$10,446.14.   **23.** \$16,117.63.   **25.** (a) 18%; (b) 19.56%.
27. \$3198.54.   **29.** 8% compounded annually.   **31.** (a) 5.47%; (b) 5.39%.   **33.** 11.61%.   **35.** 11.11%.

Exercise 6.2

1. \$2261.33.   **3.** \$1751.83.   **5.** \$1598.37.   **7.** \$3813.94.   **9.** \$4862.31.   **11.** \$6838.95.   **13.** \$14,091.11.
15. \$1238.58.   **17.** \$1963.28.   **19.** (a) \$515.63; (b) profitable.   **21.** Savings account.   **23.** \$103.56.
25. 9.55%.

Exercise 6.3

1. 64, 32, 16, 8, 4.   **3.** 100, 102, 104.04.   **5.** $\dfrac{422}{243}$.   **7.** 1.11111.   **9.** 18.664613.   **11.** 8.213180.
13. $2050.10.   **15.** $29,984.06   **17.** $8001.24.   **19.** $90,231.01.   **21.** $204,977.46.   **23.** $24,594.36.
25. $1937.14.   **27.** $458.40.   **29.** (a) $3048.85; (b) $648.85.   **31.** $3474.12.   **33.** $1725.   **35.** 102.91305.
37. 55,360.30.   **39.** $131.34.   **41.** $418,288.84.

Exercise 6.4

1. $69.33.   **3.** $1565.56.   **5.** (a) $249.11; (b) $75; (c) $174.11.

7.

PERIOD	PRIN. OUTS. AT BEGINNING	INTEREST FOR PERIOD	PMT. AT END	PRIN. REPAID AT END
1	5000.00	350.00	1476.14	1126.14
2	3873.86	271.17	1476.14	1204.97
3	2668.89	186.82	1476.14	1289.32
4	1379.57	96.57	1476.14	1379.57
		904.56	5904.56	5000.00

9.

PERIOD	PRIN. OUTS. AT BEGINNING	INTEREST FOR PERIOD	PMT. AT END	PRIN. REPAID AT END
1	900.00	22.50	193.72	171.22
2	728.78	18.22	193.72	175.50
3	553.28	13.83	193.72	179.89
4	373.39	9.33	193.72	184.39
5	189.00	4.71	193.72	189.00
		68.60	968.60	900.00

11. 11.   **13.** $12.73.   **15.** (a) $415.28; (b) $382.50; (c) $32.78; (d) $79,584.   **17.** 23.   **19.** $74,417.
21. $38.63.

Review Problems—Chapter 6

1. $\dfrac{63}{16}$.   **3.** (a) $3829.05; (b) $1229.05.   **5.** 8.5% compounded annually.   **7.** $586.60.   **9.** (a) $1997.13;
(b) $3325.37.   **11.** $1036.85.   **13.** $886.98   **15.** $314.00

17.

PERIOD	PRIN. OUTS. AT BEGINNING	INTEREST FOR PERIOD	PMT. AT END	PRIN. REPAID AT END
1	15,000.00	112.50	3067.84	2955.34
2	12,044.66	90.33	3067.84	2977.51
3	9,067.15	68.00	3067.84	2999.84
4	6,067.31	45.50	3067.84	3022.34
5	3,044.97	22.84	3067.84	3045.00
		339.17	15,339.20	15,000.03

19. $32,527.80.

Exercise 7.1

1.

Assembly line	Finishing line	Production route
A	D	AD
	E	AE
B	D	BD
	E	BE
C	D	CD
	E	CE

Start — A, B, C

3. 20. **5.** 720. **7.** 15. **9.** 1. **13.** 20.
15. 96. **17.** 1024. **19.** 336. **21.** 216.
23. 2520; 5040. **25.** 66. **27.** 45. **29.** 56.
31. 624. **33.** 11,880; 19,008. **35.** (a) 24;
(b) 64. **37.** 234,000. **39.** 17,325.

Exercise 7.2

1. {9D, 9H, 9C, 9S}. **3.** {1H, 1T, 2H, 2T, 3H, 3T, 4H, 4T, 5H, 5T, 6H, 6T}.
5. {lo, lv, le, ov, oe, ve, ol, vl, el, vo, eo, ev}. **7.** 64. **9.** 312. **11.** $C_{52,13}$. **13.** {1, 3, 5, 7, 9}. **15.** {3,5}.
17. {1, 2, 4, 6, 8, 10}. **19.** S. **21.** E_1 and E_4, E_2 and E_3, E_3 and E_4.
23. (a) {RR, RW, RB, WR, WW, WB, BR, BW, BB}; **(b)** {RW, RB, WR, WB, BR, BW}.
25. (a) {HHH, HHT, HTH, HTT, THH, THT, TTH, TTT}; **(b)** {HHH, HHT, HTH, HTT, THH, THT, TTH};
(c) {HHT, HTH, HTT, THH, THT, TTH, TTT}; **(d)** S; **(e)** {HHT, HTH, HTT, THH, THT, TTH}; **(f)** $\varnothing$;
(g) (HHH, TTT}. **27. (a)** {ABC, ACB, BAC, BCA, CAB, CBA}; **(b)** {ABC, ACB}; **(c)** {BAC, BCA, CAB, CBA}.

Exercise 7.3

1. (a) $\dfrac{5}{36}$; **(b)** $\dfrac{1}{12}$; **(c)** $\dfrac{1}{4}$; **(d)** $\dfrac{1}{36}$; **(e)** $\dfrac{1}{2}$; **(f)** $\dfrac{1}{2}$; **(g)** $\dfrac{5}{6}$.

3. (a) $\dfrac{1}{52}$; **(b)** $\dfrac{1}{4}$; **(c)** $\dfrac{1}{13}$; **(d)** $\dfrac{1}{2}$; **(e)** $\dfrac{1}{2}$; **(f)** $\dfrac{1}{52}$; **(g)** $\dfrac{4}{13}$; **(h)** $\dfrac{1}{26}$; **(i)** 0.

5. (a) $\dfrac{1}{624}$; **(b)** $\dfrac{4}{624} = \dfrac{1}{156}$; **(c)** $\dfrac{8}{624} = \dfrac{1}{78}$; **(d)** $\dfrac{39}{624} = \dfrac{1}{16}$. **7. (a)** $\dfrac{12}{2652} = \dfrac{1}{221}$; **(b)** $\dfrac{338}{2652} = \dfrac{13}{102}$.

9. (a) $\dfrac{1}{8}$; **(b)** $\dfrac{3}{8}$; **(c)** $\dfrac{1}{8}$; **(d)** $\dfrac{7}{8}$. **11.** $\dfrac{1}{9}$. **13. (a)** $\dfrac{4}{5}$; **(b)** $\dfrac{1}{5}$.

15. (a) 0.1; **(b)** 0.35; **(c)** 0.7; **(d)** 0.95; **(e)** 0.1, 0.35, 0.7, 0.95.

17. $\dfrac{2}{20} = \dfrac{1}{10}$. **19. (a)** $\dfrac{1}{2^{10}} = \dfrac{1}{1024}$; **(b)** $\dfrac{11}{1024}$. **21.** $\dfrac{13 \cdot 12 \cdot C_{4,3} \cdot C_{4,2}}{C_{52,5}}$.

Exercise 7.4

1. $\mu = 1.7$; $\mathrm{Var}(X) = 1.01$; $\sigma = 1.00$. **3.** $\mu = \dfrac{9}{4} = 2.25$; $\mathrm{Var}(X) = \dfrac{11}{16} = 0.6875$; $\sigma = 0.83$.

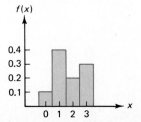

5. $E(X) = \dfrac{3}{2} = 1.5; \sigma^2 = \dfrac{3}{4} = 0.75; \sigma = 0.87.$ **7.** $E(X) = \dfrac{4}{5} = 0.8; \sigma^2 = \dfrac{9}{25} = 0.36; \sigma = 0.6.$ **9.** $101.43.

11. $3.00.   **13.** $66.   **15.** Loss of $0.25; $1.

Exercise 7.5

1. $f(0) = \dfrac{9}{16}, f(1) = \dfrac{3}{8}, f(2) = \dfrac{1}{16}; \mu = \dfrac{1}{2}; \sigma = \dfrac{\sqrt{6}}{4}.$ **3.** 0.001536.   **5.** **(a)** $\dfrac{9}{64}$; **(b)** $\dfrac{5}{32}.$ **7.** $\dfrac{13}{16}.$ **9.** 0.1536.

11. 0.002.

Review Problems—Chapter 7

1. 336.   **3.** 36.   **5.** 608,400.   **7.** 32.   **9.** 210.   **11.** 42.   **13.** **(a)** 2024; **(b)** 253.

15. **(a)** {1,2,3,4,5,6,7}; **(b)** {4,5,6}; **(c)** {4,5,6,7,8}; **(d)** ∅; **(e)** {4,5,6,7,8}; **(f)** No.

17. **(a)** {$R_1R_2R_3$, $R_1R_2G_3$, $R_1G_2R_3$, $R_1G_2G_3$, $G_1R_2R_3$, $G_1R_2G_3$, $G_1G_2R_3$, $G_1G_2G_3$};   **(b)** {$R_1R_2G_3$, $R_1G_2R_3$, $G_1R_2R_3$};

(c) {$R_1R_2R_3$, $G_1G_2G_3$}.   **19.** 0.2.   **21.** **(a)** $\dfrac{4}{25}$; **(b)** $\dfrac{2}{15}.$ **23.** **(a)** $\dfrac{1}{4}$; **(b)** $\dfrac{1}{4}.$ **25.** $\mu = 1.5$, $\mathrm{Var}(X) = 0.65$, $\sigma = 0.81.$

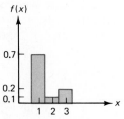

27. **(a)** $f(1) = \dfrac{1}{12}, f(2) = f(3) = f(4) = f(5) = f(6) = \dfrac{1}{6}, f(7) = \dfrac{1}{12}$; **(b)** 4.   **29.** Loss of $0.10 per play.

31. $f(0) = 0.729, f(1) = 0.243, f(2) = 0.027, f(3) = 0.001; \mu = 0.3; \sigma = \sqrt{0.27} \approx 0.52.$ **33.** $\dfrac{33}{81}.$

Exercise 8.1

1. **(a)** 2×3, 3×3, 3×2, 2×2, 4×4, 1×2, 3×1, 3×3, 1×1;   **(b)** **B, D, E, H, J**;

(c) **H, J** upper triangular; **D, J** lower triangular; **(d)** **F, J**; **(e)** **G, J**.   **3.** 2.   **5.** 4.   **7.** 6.   **9.** 7, 2, 1, 0.

11. $\begin{bmatrix} 5 & 8 & 11 & 14 \\ 7 & 10 & 13 & 16 \\ 9 & 12 & 15 & 18 \end{bmatrix}.$ **13.** 120 entries, 1, 0, 1, 0.   **15.** **(a)** $\begin{bmatrix} 0 & 0 & 0 & 0 \\ 0 & 0 & 0 & 0 \\ 0 & 0 & 0 & 0 \\ 0 & 0 & 0 & 0 \end{bmatrix}$ **(b)** $\begin{bmatrix} 0 & 0 & 0 & 0 & 0 & 0 \\ 0 & 0 & 0 & 0 & 0 & 0 \\ 0 & 0 & 0 & 0 & 0 & 0 \\ 0 & 0 & 0 & 0 & 0 & 0 \\ 0 & 0 & 0 & 0 & 0 & 0 \\ 0 & 0 & 0 & 0 & 0 & 0 \end{bmatrix}.$

17. $x = 6, y = \dfrac{2}{3}, z = \dfrac{7}{2}.$ **19.** $x = 0, y = 0.$ **21.** **(a)** 7; **(b)** 3; **(c)** February; **(d)** deluxe blue; **(e)** February;

(f) February; **(g)** 35.

Exercise 8.2

1. $\begin{bmatrix} 4 & -3 & 1 \\ -2 & 10 & 5 \\ 10 & 5 & 3 \end{bmatrix}.$ **3.** $\begin{bmatrix} -5 & 5 \\ -9 & 5 \\ 5 & 9 \end{bmatrix}.$ **5.** $[-9 \quad -7 \quad 6 \quad 11].$ **7.** Not defined.   **9.** $\begin{bmatrix} -12 & 36 & -42 & -6 \\ -42 & -6 & -36 & 12 \end{bmatrix}.$

11. $\begin{bmatrix} 5 & -4 & 1 \\ 0 & 7 & -2 \\ -3 & 3 & 13 \end{bmatrix}$.   **13.** $\begin{bmatrix} 6 & 5 \\ -2 & 3 \end{bmatrix}$.   **15.** **O.**   **17.** $\begin{bmatrix} 28 & 22 \\ -2 & 6 \end{bmatrix}$.   **19.** Not defined.   **21.** $\begin{bmatrix} -22 & -15 \\ -11 & 9 \end{bmatrix}$.

23. $\begin{bmatrix} 21 & \frac{29}{2} \\ \frac{19}{2} & \frac{15}{2} \end{bmatrix}$.   **29.** $x = \dfrac{146}{13}, y = -\dfrac{28}{13}$.   **31.** $x = 6, y = \dfrac{4}{3}$.   **33.** $x = -6, y = -14, z = 1$.   **35.** 1.1.

Exercise 8.3

1. -12.   **3.** 19.   **5.** 7.   **7.** 2×2, 4.   **9.** 3×5, 15.   **11.** 2×1, 2.   **13.** 3×3, 9.   **15.** 3×1, 3.

17. $\begin{bmatrix} 1 & 0 & 0 & 0 \\ 0 & 1 & 0 & 0 \\ 0 & 0 & 1 & 0 \\ 0 & 0 & 0 & 1 \end{bmatrix}$.   **19.** $\begin{bmatrix} 10 & -16 \\ 7 & 8 \end{bmatrix}$.   **21.** $\begin{bmatrix} 23 \\ 50 \end{bmatrix}$.   **23.** $\begin{bmatrix} -3 & 4 & 2 \\ 2 & 2 & 4 \\ 5 & 0 & 3 \end{bmatrix}$.   **25.** $[-6 \quad 16 \quad 10 \quad -6]$.

27. $\begin{bmatrix} 4 & 6 & -4 & 6 \\ 6 & 9 & -6 & 9 \\ -8 & -12 & 8 & -12 \\ 2 & 3 & -2 & 3 \end{bmatrix}$.   **29.** $\begin{bmatrix} 78 & 84 \\ -21 & -12 \end{bmatrix}$.   **31.** $\begin{bmatrix} -5 & -8 \\ -5 & -20 \end{bmatrix}$.   **33.** $\begin{bmatrix} x \\ y \\ z \end{bmatrix}$.   **35.** $\begin{bmatrix} 2x_1 + x_2 + 3x_3 \\ 4x_1 + 9x_2 + 7x_3 \end{bmatrix}$.

37. $\begin{bmatrix} -4 & 11 & -2 \\ 3 & -12 & 3 \end{bmatrix}$.   **39.** $\begin{bmatrix} -1 \\ 3 \\ 8 \end{bmatrix}$.   **41.** $\begin{bmatrix} 3 & 0 & 0 \\ 0 & 6 & 3 \\ 3 & 12 & 3 \end{bmatrix}$.   **43.** $[7, 23]$.   **45.** $\begin{bmatrix} 0 & 0 & 0 \\ 0 & -1 & 1 \\ 1 & 2 & 0 \end{bmatrix}$.

47. $\begin{bmatrix} -1 & -20 \\ -2 & 23 \end{bmatrix}$.   **49.** $\begin{bmatrix} \frac{3}{2} & 0 & 0 \\ 0 & \frac{3}{2} & 0 \\ 0 & 0 & \frac{3}{2} \end{bmatrix}$.   **51.** $\begin{bmatrix} -1 & 5 \\ 2 & 17 \\ 1 & 31 \end{bmatrix}$.   **53.** $\begin{bmatrix} 3 & 1 \\ 7 & -2 \end{bmatrix}\begin{bmatrix} x \\ y \end{bmatrix} = \begin{bmatrix} 6 \\ 5 \end{bmatrix}$.   **55.** $\begin{bmatrix} 4 & -1 & 3 \\ 3 & 0 & -1 \\ 0 & 3 & 2 \end{bmatrix}\begin{bmatrix} r \\ s \\ t \end{bmatrix} = \begin{bmatrix} 9 \\ 7 \\ 15 \end{bmatrix}$.

57. $735,300.   **59.** (a) $180,000, $520,000, $400,000, $270,000, $380,000, $640,000;   (b) $390,000, $100,000, $800,000;
(c) $2,390,000;   (d) $\dfrac{110}{239}, \dfrac{129}{239}$

Exercise 8.4

1. Not reduced.   **3.** Reduced.   **5.** Not reduced.   **7.** $\begin{bmatrix} 1 & 0 \\ 0 & 1 \end{bmatrix}$.   **9.** $\begin{bmatrix} 1 & 2 & 3 \\ 0 & 0 & 0 \\ 0 & 0 & 0 \end{bmatrix}$.

11. $\begin{bmatrix} 1 & 0 & 0 & 0 \\ 0 & 1 & 0 & 0 \\ 0 & 0 & 1 & 0 \\ 0 & 0 & 0 & 1 \end{bmatrix}$.   **13.** $x = 1, y = 1$.   **15.** No solution.   **17.** $x = -\dfrac{2}{3}z + \dfrac{5}{3}, y = -\dfrac{1}{6}z + \dfrac{7}{6}, z = z$.
19. No solution.   **21.** $x = -3, y = 1, z = 0$.   **23.** $x = 2, y = -5, z = -1$.
25. $x_1 = 0, x_2 = -x_5, x_3 = -x_5, x_4 = -x_5, x_5 = x_5$.   **27.** Federal, $72,000; state, $24,000.
29. A, 2000; B, 4000; C, 5000.   **31.** (a) 3 of X, 4 of Z; 2 of X, 1 of Y, 5 of Z; 1 of X, 2 of Y, 6 of Z; 3 of Y, 7 of Z.
(b) 3 of X, 4 of Z   (c) 3 of X, 4 of Z; 3 of Y, 7 of Z.

Exercise 8.5

1. $w = -y - 3z + 2, x = -2y + z - 3, y = y, z = z$.   **3.** $w = -z, x = -3y - 4z + 2, y = y, z = z$.
5. $w = -2y + z - 2, x = -y + 4, y = y, z = z$.
7. $x_1 = -2x_3 + x_4 - 2x_5 + 1, x_2 = -x_3 - 2x_4 + x_5 + 4, x_3 = x_3 \ x_4 = x_4, x_5 = x_5$.   **9.** Infinite.   **11.** Trivial.

13. Infinite.   **15.** $x = 0, y = 0.$ **17.** $x = -\dfrac{6}{5}z, y = \dfrac{8}{15}z, z = z.$ **19.** $x = 0, y = 0.$

21. $x = z, y = -2z, z = z.$ **23.** $w = -2z, x = -3z, y = z, z = z.$

Exercise 8.6

1. $\begin{bmatrix} 1 & -1 \\ -5 & 6 \end{bmatrix}.$ **3.** Not invertible.   **5.** $\begin{bmatrix} 1 & 0 & 0 \\ 0 & -\frac{1}{3} & 0 \\ 0 & 0 & \frac{1}{4} \end{bmatrix}.$ **7.** Not invertible.

9. Not invertible (not a square matrix).   **11.** $\begin{bmatrix} 1 & -1 & 0 \\ 0 & 1 & -1 \\ 0 & 0 & 1 \end{bmatrix}.$ **13.** $\begin{bmatrix} 1 & 0 & 2 \\ 0 & 1 & 0 \\ 3 & 0 & 7 \end{bmatrix}.$

15. $\begin{bmatrix} 1 & -\frac{2}{3} & \frac{5}{3} \\ -1 & \frac{4}{3} & -\frac{10}{3} \\ -1 & 1 & -2 \end{bmatrix}.$ **17.** $\begin{bmatrix} -\frac{11}{3} & -3 & \frac{13}{3} \\ -\frac{7}{3} & 3 & -\frac{2}{3} \\ \frac{2}{3} & -1 & \frac{1}{3} \end{bmatrix}.$ **19.** $x = 17, y = -20.$ **21.** $x = 1, y = 3.$

23. $x = -3y + 1, y = y.$ **25.** $x = 0, y = 1, z = 2.$ **27.** $x = 1, y = \dfrac{1}{2}, z = \dfrac{1}{2}.$

29. No solution.   **31.** $w = 1, x = 3, y = -2, z = 7.$ **33.** $\begin{bmatrix} -\frac{2}{3} & -\frac{1}{3} \\ \frac{1}{3} & -\frac{1}{3} \end{bmatrix}.$

35. **(a)** 40 of first model, 60 of second model;   **(b)** 45 of first model, 50 of second model.

Exercise 8.7

1. 1.   **3.** 0.   **5.** $y.$ **7.** $-\dfrac{2}{7}.$ **9.** 12.   **11.** $-12.$ **13.** 6.   **15.** $\begin{vmatrix} a_{11} & a_{13} & a_{14} \\ a_{21} & a_{23} & a_{24} \\ a_{41} & a_{43} & a_{44} \end{vmatrix}.$ **17.** $\begin{vmatrix} a_{21} & a_{22} & a_{24} \\ a_{31} & a_{32} & a_{34} \\ a_{41} & a_{42} & a_{44} \end{vmatrix}.$

19. $-16.$ **21.** 98.   **23.** $-89.$ **25.** $-1.$ **27.** 2.   **29.** $-90.$ **31.** 1.   **33.** 24.   **35.** 3, 4.
37. 192.

Exercise 8.8

1. $x = \dfrac{9}{5}, y = -\dfrac{2}{5}.$ **3.** $x = \dfrac{7}{16}, y = \dfrac{13}{8}.$ **5.** $x = -\dfrac{1}{3}, y = -1.$ **7.** $x = \dfrac{6}{5}, z = \dfrac{16}{5}.$ **9.** $x = 4, y = 2, z = 0.$

11. $x = \dfrac{2}{3}, y = -\dfrac{28}{15}, z = -\dfrac{26}{15}.$ **13.** $x = 3 - z, y = 0, z = z.$ **15.** $x = 1, y = 3, z = 5.$ **17.** $y = 6, w = 1.$

19. Since $\Delta = \begin{vmatrix} 1 & 1 \\ 1 & 1 \end{vmatrix} = 0$, Cramer's rule does not apply. But the equations in $\begin{cases} x + y = 2, \\ x + y = -3 \end{cases}$ represent distinct parallel lines and hence no solution exists.

Exercise 8.9

1. $\begin{bmatrix} \frac{1}{4} & \frac{1}{4} \\ -\frac{1}{8} & \frac{3}{8} \end{bmatrix}.$ **3.** $\begin{bmatrix} 4 & -9 \\ 0 & 6 \end{bmatrix}.$ **5.** $\begin{bmatrix} 7 & -8 & 5 \\ -4 & 5 & -3 \\ 1 & -1 & 1 \end{bmatrix}.$ **7.** $\begin{bmatrix} 2 & 1 & 0 \\ 4 & -1 & 5 \\ 1 & -1 & 2 \end{bmatrix}.$ **9.** $\begin{bmatrix} 2 & -1 & 3 \\ 0 & 2 & 0 \\ 2 & 1 & 1 \end{bmatrix}.$ **11.** $\begin{bmatrix} 1 & 2 & -1 \\ 0 & 1 & 4 \\ 1 & -1 & 2 \end{bmatrix}$

Exercise 8.10

1. $\begin{bmatrix} 1290 \\ 1425 \end{bmatrix}$; 1405.   **3. (a)** $\begin{bmatrix} 297.80 \\ 349.54 \\ 443.12 \end{bmatrix}$; **(b)** $\begin{bmatrix} 102.17 \\ 125.28 \\ 175.27 \end{bmatrix}$.

Review Problems—Chapter 8

1. $\begin{bmatrix} 7 & 12 \\ -19 & -5 \end{bmatrix}$.   **3.** $\begin{bmatrix} 1 & 35 & 5 \\ 2 & -15 & -7 \\ 1 & 0 & -2 \end{bmatrix}$.   **5.** $\begin{bmatrix} -1 & -2 \\ 5 & 22 \end{bmatrix}$.   **7.** $x = 3, y = 6$.   **9.** $\begin{bmatrix} 1 & 0 \\ 0 & 1 \end{bmatrix}$.   **11.** $\begin{bmatrix} 1 & 2 & 0 \\ 0 & 0 & 1 \\ 0 & 0 & 0 \end{bmatrix}$.

13. $x = 0, y = 0$.   **15.** No solution.   **17.** $\begin{bmatrix} -\frac{3}{2} & \frac{5}{6} \\ \frac{1}{2} & -\frac{1}{6} \end{bmatrix}$.   **19.** No inverse exists.   **21.** $x = 0, y = 1, z = 0$.

23. 18.   **25.** 3.   **27.** rich.   **29.** $x = 1, y = 2$.   **31.** $\begin{bmatrix} \frac{1}{2} & -1 & \frac{1}{2} \\ -\frac{1}{2} & 0 & \frac{1}{2} \\ 1 & 1 & -1 \end{bmatrix}$.   **33.** $\begin{bmatrix} 3.6 \\ 3.2 \end{bmatrix}$.

Exercise 9.1

1.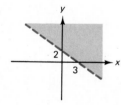

3.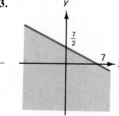

5.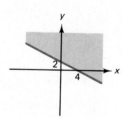

7.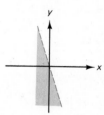

9.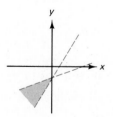

11.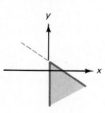

13.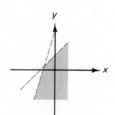

15.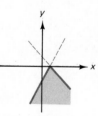

17.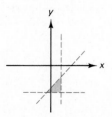

19.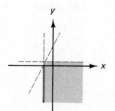

21.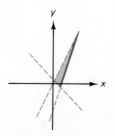

23.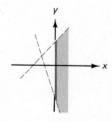

25.

27.

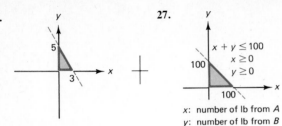

$x + y \leq 100$
$x \geq 0$
$y \geq 0$

x: number of lb from A
y: number of lb from B

Exercise 9.2

1. $P = 640$ when $x = 40$, $y = 20$. **3.** $Z = -10$ when $x = 2$, $y = 3$. **5.** No optimum solution (empty feasible region).

7. $Z = 3$ when $x = 0$, $y = 1$. **9.** $C = 2.4$ when $x = \frac{3}{5}$, $y = \frac{6}{5}$. **11.** No optimum solution (unbounded).

13. 15 widgets, 25 wadgits; $210. **15.** 4 units of food A, 4 units of food B; $8. **17.** 10 tons of ore I, 10 tons of ore II; $1100.

Exercise 9.3

1. $Z = 33$ when $x = (1 - t)(2) + 5t = 2 + 3t$, $y = (1 - t)(3) + 2t = 3 - t$, and $0 \leq t \leq 1$.

3. $Z = 72$ when $x = (1 - t)(3) + 4t = 3 + t$, $y = (1 - t)(2) + 0t = 2 - 2t$, and $0 \leq t \leq 1$.

Exercise 9.4

1. $Z = 8$ when $x_1 = 0$, $x_2 = 4$. **3.** $Z = 14$ when $x_1 = 1$, $x_2 = 5$. **5.** $Z = 28$ when $x_1 = 3$, $x_2 = 2$.

7. $Z = 20$ when $x_1 = 0$, $x_2 = 5$, $x_3 = 0$. **9.** $Z = 2$ when $x_1 = 1$, $x_2 = 0$, $x_3 = 0$. **11.** $Z = \frac{16}{3}$ when $x_1 = \frac{2}{3}$, $x_2 = \frac{14}{3}$.

13. $W = 13$ when $x_1 = 1$, $x_2 = 0$, $x_3 = 3$. **15.** $Z = 600$ when $x_1 = 4$, $x_2 = 1$, $x_3 = 4$, $x_4 = 0$.

17. 400 from A, 1600 from B; $1100. **19.** 0 chairs, 300 rockers, 100 chaise lounges; $3600.

Exercise 9.5

1. Yes; for the tableau, x_2 is the entering variable and the quotients $\frac{6}{2}$ and $\frac{3}{1}$ tie for being the smallest. **3.** No optimum solution (unbounded). **5.** $Z = 12$ when $x_1 = (1 - t) \cdot 4 + 5t = 4 + t$, $x_2 = (1 - t) \cdot 0 + 1 \cdot t = t$, and $0 \leq t \leq 1$. **7.** No optimum solution (unbounded). **9.** $Z = 13$ when $x_1 = (1 - t)\frac{3}{2} + 0t = \frac{3}{2} - \frac{3}{2}t$, $x_2 = (1 - t)0 + 6t = 6t$, $x_3 = (1 - t)4 + 1 \cdot t = 4 - 3t$, and $0 \leq t \leq 1$. **11.** $3800. If x_1, x_2, and x_3 denote the number of chairs, rockers, and chaise lounges produced, respectively, then $x_1 = (1 - t)100 + 0t = 100 - 100t$, $x_2 = (1 - t)100 + 250t = 100 + 150t$, $x_3 = (1 - t)200 + 150t = 200 - 50t$, and $0 \leq t \leq 1$.

Exercise 9.6

1. $Z = 7$ when $x_1 = 1$, $x_2 = 5$. **3.** $Z = 4$ when $x_1 = 1$, $x_2 = 2$, $x_3 = 0$. **5.** $Z = \frac{58}{3}$ when $x_1 = \frac{14}{3}$, $x_2 = \frac{2}{3}$, $x_3 = 0$.

7. $Z = -17$ when $x_1 = 3$, $x_2 = 2$. **9.** No optimum solution (empty feasible region). **11.** $Z = 2$ when $x_1 = 6$, $x_2 = 10$.

13. 255 contemporary tables, 0 traditional tables. **15.** 30% in A, 0% in AA, 70% in AAA; 6.6%.

Exercise 9.7

1. $Z = 54$ when $x_1 = 2, x_2 = 8$.   **3.** $Z = 36$ when $x_1 = 9, x_2 = 0, x_3 = 0$.   **5.** $Z = 4$ when $x_1 = 0, x_2 = 0, x_3 = 4$.
7. $Z = 0$ when $x_1 = 3, x_2 = 0, x_3 = 1$.   **9.** $Z = 28$ when $x_1 = 3, x_2 = 0, x_3 = 5$.   **11.** Install device A on kilns producing 700,000 barrels annually, and device B on kilns producing 2,600,000 barrels annually.   **13.** To Exton, 10 from A and 20 from B; to Whyton, 30 from A; $760.   **15.** **(a)** Column 3: 1, 3, 3; column 4: 0, 4, 8.   **(b)** $x_1 = 10, x_2 = 0, x_3 = 20, x_4 = 0$.   **(c)** 90 in.

Exercise 9.8

1. Minimize
$$W = 6y_1 + 4y_2$$
subject to
$$y_1 - y_2 \geq 2,$$
$$y_1 + y_2 \geq 3,$$
$$y_1, y_2 \geq 0.$$

3. Maximize
$$W = 8y_1 + 2y_2$$
subject to
$$y_1 - y_2 \leq 1,$$
$$y_1 + 2y_2 \leq 8,$$
$$y_1 + y_2 \leq 5,$$
$$y_1, y_2 \geq 0.$$

5. Minimize
$$W = 13y_1 - 3y_2 - 11y_3$$
subject to
$$-y_1 + y_2 - y_3 \geq 1,$$
$$2y_1 - y_2 - y_3 \geq -1,$$
$$y_1, y_2, y_3 \geq 0.$$

7. Maximize
$$W = -3y_1 + 3y_2$$
subject to
$$-y_1 + y_2 \leq 4,$$
$$y_1 - y_2 \leq 4,$$
$$y_1 + y_2 \leq 6,$$
$$y_1, y_2 \geq 0.$$

9. $Z = 11$ when $x_1 = 0, x_2 = \dfrac{1}{2}, x_3 = \dfrac{3}{2}$.   **11.** $Z = 26$ when $x_1 = 6, x_2 = 1$.   **13.** $Z = 14$ when $x_1 = 1, x_2 = 2$.
15. $25 on newspaper advertising, $140 on radio advertising; $165.   **17.** 20 shipping clerk apprentices, 40 shipping clerks, 90 semiskilled workers, 0 skilled workers; $600.

Review Problems—Chapter 9

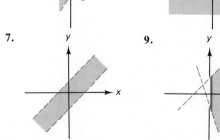

1.   **3.**   **5.**

7.   **9.**

11. $Z = 3$ when $x = 3, y = 0$.   **13.** $Z = -2$ when $x = 0, y = 2$.   **15.** No optimum solution (empty feasible region).
17. $Z = 36$ when $x = (1 - t)(2) + 4t = 2 + 2t, y = (1 - t)(3) + 0t = 3 - 3t$, and $0 \leq t \leq 1$.
19. $Z = 32$ when $x_1 = 8, x_2 = 0$.   **21.** $Z = 2$ when $x_1 = 0, x_2 = 0, x_3 = 2$.   **23.** $Z = 24$ when $x_1 = 0, x_2 = 12$.
25. $Z = \dfrac{7}{2}$ when $x_1 = \dfrac{5}{4}, x_2 = 0, x_3 = \dfrac{9}{4}$.   **27.** No optimum solution (unbounded).

29. $Z = 70$ when $x_1 = 35$, $x_2 = 0$, $x_3 = 0$.   **31.**   0 units of X, 6 units of Y, 14 units of Z; \$398.   **33.**   500,000 gal from A to D, 100,000 gal from A to C, 400,000 gal from B to C; \$19,000.

Exercise 10.1

1. 16.   **3.** 7.   **5.** 20.   **7.** -1.   **9.** $-\dfrac{5}{2}$.   **11.** 0.   **13.** 5.   **15.** -2.   **17.** 3.   **19.** 0.

21. $\dfrac{1}{6}$.   **23.** $-\dfrac{1}{5}$.   **25.** $\dfrac{11}{9}$.   **27.** 4.   **29.** $2x$.   **31.** -1.   **33.** $2x$.   **35.** (a) 1; (b) 0.

Exercise 10.2

1. (a) 2; (b) 3; (c) does not exist; (d) $-\infty$; (e) ∞; (f) ∞; (g) ∞; (h) 0; (i) 1; (j) 1; (k) 1.
3. 1.   **5.** $-\infty$.   **7.** $-\infty$.   **9.** ∞.   **11.** 0.   **13.** Does not exist.   **15.** 0.   **17.** 1.   **19.** 0.   **21.** ∞.
23. 0.   **25.** $-\dfrac{2}{5}$.   **27.** $-\infty$.   **29.** $\dfrac{2}{5}$.   **31.** $\dfrac{11}{5}$.   **33.** $-\dfrac{1}{2}$.   **35.** ∞.   **37.** ∞.   **39.** Does not exist.
41. $-\infty$.   **43.** 0.   **45.** 1.   **47.** (a) 1; (b) 2; (c) does not exist; (d) 1; (e) 2.   **49.** (a) 0; (b) 0; (c) 0;
(d) $-\infty$; (e) $-\infty$.   **51.**   **53.** 20,000.   **55.** 1, 0.5, 0.525, 0.631, 0.912, 0.986, 0.998; conclude limit is 1.

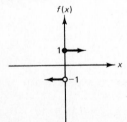

Exercise 10.3

1. \$5564; \$1564.   **3.** \$1456.88.   **5.** 4.08%.   **7.** 10.52%.   **9.** \$111.63.   **11.** \$670,320.   **13.** 4.88%.
15. \$927.   **17.** 16.

Exercise 10.4

1. Continuous at -2 and 0.   **3.** Discontinuous at ± 3.   **5.** f is a polynomial function.   **7.** f is a rational function and the denominator is never zero.   **9.** None.   **11.** $x = 4$.   **13.** None.   **15.** $x = -5, 3$.   **17.** $x = 0, \pm 1$.   **19.** None.
21. $x = 0$.   **23.** None.

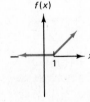

25. Discontinuities at $t = 1, 2, 3, 4$.

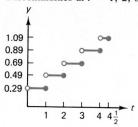

27. Yes, no, no.

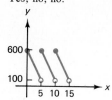

Exercise 10.5

1. $x < -1, x > 4$. **3.** $2 \leq x \leq 3$. **5.** $-\dfrac{7}{2} < x < -2$. **7.** No solution. **9.** $x \leq -6, -2 \leq x \leq 3$.

11. $x < -4, 0 < x < 5$. **13.** $x \geq 0$. **15.** $-3 < x < 0, x > 1$. **17.** $x < -1, 0 < x < 1$. **19.** $x > 1$.

21. $x < -5, -2 \leq x < 1, x \geq 3$. **23.** $-4 < x < -2$. **25.** $x \leq -1 - \sqrt{3}, x \geq -1 + \sqrt{3}$. **27.** Between 50 and 150, inclusive. **29.** 17 in. by 17 in.

Review Problems—Chapter 10

1. -5. **3.** 2. **5.** x. **7.** $-\dfrac{8}{3}$. **9.** 0. **11.** $\dfrac{3}{5}$. **13.** Does not exist. **15.** -1. **17.** 0. **19.** $\dfrac{1}{9}$.

21. $-\infty$. **23.** (a) $\$6661.25$; (b) $\$938.28$. **25.** 6.18%. **27.** Continuous everywhere; f is a polynomial function.

29. $x = -3$. **31.** None. **33.** $x = -4, 1$. **35.** $x = -2$. **37.** $x < -6, x > 2$. **39.** $x \geq 2, x = 0$.

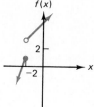

41. $x < -5, -1 < x < 1$. **43.** $x < -4, -3 \leq x \leq 0, x > 2$.

Exercise 11.1

1. 1. **3.** 3. **5.** -4. **7.** 0. **9.** $2x + 4$. **11.** $4q + 5$. **13.** $-1/x^2$. **15.** $1/(2\sqrt{x + 2})$.

17. -4. **19.** 0. **21.** $y = x + 4$. **23.** $y = -3x - 7$. **25.** $y = -\dfrac{1}{3}x + \dfrac{5}{3}$. **27.** $\dfrac{r}{r_L - r - \dfrac{dC}{dD}}$.

Exercise 11.2

1. 0. **3.** $5x^4$. **5.** $32x^3$. **7.** $-7w^{-8}$. **9.** $-\dfrac{56}{5}x^{-19/5}$. **11.** 3. **13.** $\dfrac{13}{5}$. **15.** $6x - 5$.

17. $42x^2 - 12x + 7$. **19.** $-9q^2 + 9q + 9 = 9(1 + q - q^2)$. **21.** $1002x^{500} - 12{,}500x^{99} + 0.68x^{2.4}$. **23.** $-8x^3$.

25. $-\dfrac{4}{3}x^3$.   **27.** $-4x^{-5} - 3x^{-2/3} - 2x^{-7/5}$.   **29.** $-2(27 - 70x^4) = 2(70x^4 - 27)$.   **31.** $-4x + \dfrac{3}{2} + x^3$.

33. $-x^{-2} = -\dfrac{1}{x^2}$.   **35.** $-\dfrac{5}{4}s^{-6}$.   **37.** $2t^{-1/2} = \dfrac{2}{\sqrt{t}}$.   **39.** $-\dfrac{1}{5}x^{-6/5}$.   **41.** $9x^2 - 14x + 7$.   **43.** $t + 4t^{-3}$.

45. $45x^4$.   **47.** $\dfrac{1}{3}x^{-2/3} - \dfrac{10}{3}x^{-5/3} = \dfrac{1}{3}x^{-5/3}(x - 10)$.   **49.** $8q + \dfrac{4}{q^2}$.   **51.** $2(x + 2)$.   **53.** 1.   **55.** 4, 16, -14.

57. 0, 0, 0.   **59.** $y = 13x - 2$.   **61.** $y = x + 3$.   **63.** $(0, 0), (2, -\tfrac{4}{3})$.

Exercise 11.3

1. **(a)** 4 m; **(b)** 5 m/s.   **3.** **(a)** 8 m; **(b)** 6 m/s.   **5.** **(a)** 2 m; **(b)** 9 m/s.   **7.** $dy/dx = 10x^{3/2}$; 270.   **9.** 0.27.

11. $dc/dq = 10$; 10.   **13.** $dc/dq = 0.6q + 2$; 3.8.   **15.** $dc/dq = 2q + 50$; 80, 82, 84.   **17.** $dc/dq = 0.02q + 5$; 6, 7.

19. $dc/dq = 0.00006q^2 - 0.02q + 6$; 4.6, 11.   **21.** $dr/dq = 0.7$; 0.7, 0.7, 0.7.

23. $dr/dq = 250 + 90q - 3q^2$; 625, 850, 625.   **25.** $dc/dq = 6.750 - 0.000656q$; 3.47.   **27.** $dP/dR = -4,650,000R^{-1.93}$.

29. **(a)** -7.5; **(b)** 4.5.   **31.** **(a)** 1; **(b)** $\dfrac{1}{x + 4}$; **(c)** 1; **(d)** $\dfrac{1}{9} \approx 0.111$; **(e)** 11.1%.   **33.** **(a)** $6x$; **(b)** $\dfrac{2x}{x^2 + 2}$; **(c)** 12;

(d) $\dfrac{2}{3} \approx 0.667$; **(e)** 66.7%.   **35.** **(a)** $-3x^2$; **(b)** $-\dfrac{3x^2}{8 - x^3}$; **(c)** -3; **(d)** $-\dfrac{3}{7} \approx -0.429$; **(e)** -42.9%.   **37.** 3.2; 21.3%.

39. **(a)** $dr/dq = 30 - 0.6q$; **(b)** $\dfrac{4}{45} \approx 0.089$; **(c)** 9%.   **41.** $\dfrac{0.432}{t}$.

Exercise 11.5

1. $(4x + 1)(6) + (6x + 3)(4) = 48x + 18 = 6(8x + 3)$.   **3.** $(8 - 7t)(2t) + (t^2 - 2)(-7) = 14 + 16t - 21t^2$.

5. $(3r^2 - 4)(2r - 5) + (r^2 - 5r + 1)(6r) = 12r^3 - 45r^2 - 2r + 20$.

7. $(x^2 + 3x - 2)(4x - 1) + (2x^2 - x - 3)(2x + 3) = 8x^3 + 15x^2 - 20x - 7$.

9. $(8w^2 + 2w - 3)(15w^2) + (5w^3 + 2)(16w + 2) = 200w^4 + 40w^3 - 45w^2 + 32w + 4$.

11. $(x^2 - 1)(9x^2 - 6) + (3x^3 - 6x + 5)(2x) - [(x + 4)(8x + 2) + (4x^2 + 2x + 1)(1)] = 15x^4 - 39x^2 - 26x - 3$.

13. $\dfrac{3}{2}\left[(p^{1/2} - 4)(4) + (4p - 5)\left(\dfrac{1}{2}p^{-1/2}\right)\right] = \dfrac{3}{4}(12p^{1/2} - 5p^{-1/2} - 32)$.   **15.** 0.   **17.** $18x^2 + 94x + 31$.

19. $\dfrac{(x - 1)(1) - (x)(1)}{(x - 1)^2} = -\dfrac{1}{(x - 1)^2}$.   **21.** $\dfrac{(x - 1)(1) - (x + 2)(1)}{(x - 1)^2} = \dfrac{-3}{(x - 1)^2}$.

23. $\dfrac{(z^2 - 4)(-2) - (5 - 2z)(2z)}{(z^2 - 4)^2} = \dfrac{2(z - 4)(z - 1)}{(z^2 - 4)^2}$.

25. $\dfrac{(x^2 - 5x)(16x - 2) - (8x^2 - 2x + 1)(2x - 5)}{(x^2 - 5x)^2} = \dfrac{-38x^2 - 2x + 5}{(x^2 - 5x)^2}$.

27. $\dfrac{(2x^2 - 3x + 2)(2x - 4) - (x^2 - 4x + 3)(4x - 3)}{(2x^2 - 3x + 2)^2} = \dfrac{5x^2 - 8x + 1}{(2x^2 - 3x + 2)^2}$.

29. $\dfrac{-100x^{99}}{(x^{100} + 1)^2}$.   **31.** $\dfrac{4(v^5 + 2)}{v^2}$.   **33.** $\dfrac{15x^2 - 2x + 1}{3x^{4/3}}$.   **35.** $\dfrac{4}{(x - 8)^2} + \dfrac{2}{(3x + 1)^2}$.

37. $\dfrac{[(x + 2)(x - 4)](1) - (x - 5)(2x - 2)}{[(x + 2)(x - 4)]^2} = \dfrac{-(x^2 - 10x + 18)}{[(x + 2)(x - 4)]^2}$.

39. $\dfrac{[(t^2 - 1)(t^3 + 7)](2t + 3) - (t^2 + 3t)(5t^4 - 3t^2 + 14t)}{[(t^2 - 1)(t^3 + 7)]^2} = \dfrac{-3t^6 - 12t^5 + t^4 + 6t^3 - 21t^2 - 14t - 21}{[(t^2 - 1)(t^3 + 7)]^2}$.

41. $3 - \dfrac{2x^3 + 3x^2 - 12x + 4}{[x(x-1)(x-2)]^2}.$ **43.** $-6.$ **45.** $y = -\dfrac{3}{2}x + \dfrac{15}{2}.$ **47.** $y = 16x + 24.$ **49.** $1.5.$

51. $\dfrac{dr}{dq} = 25 - 0.04q.$ **53.** $\dfrac{dr}{dq} = \dfrac{216}{(q+2)^2} - 3.$ **55.** $\dfrac{dC}{dI} = 0.672.$ **57.** $\dfrac{1}{3}; \dfrac{2}{3}.$ **59.** $0.615; 0.385.$

61. $\dfrac{dc}{dq} = \dfrac{5q(q+6)}{(q+3)^2}.$ **63.** $\dfrac{9}{10}.$ **65.** $\dfrac{0.7355}{(1 + 0.02744x)^2}.$

Exercise 11.6

1. $(2u - 2)(2x - 1) = 4x^3 - 6x^2 - 2x + 2.$ **3.** $\left(-\dfrac{2}{w^3}\right)(-1) = \dfrac{2}{(2-x)^3}.$

5. $-2.$ **7.** $0.$ **9.** $18(3x + 2)^5.$ **11.** $300(3x^2 - 16x + 1)(x^3 - 8x^2 + x)^{99}.$ **13.** $-6x(x^2 - 2)^{-4}.$

15. $\dfrac{1}{2}(10x - 1)(5x^2 - x)^{-1/2}.$ **17.** $\dfrac{12}{5}x^2(x^3 + 1)^{-3/5}.$ **19.** $-6(4x - 1)(2x^2 - x + 1)^{-2}.$ **21.** $-2(2x - 3)(x^2 - 3x)^{-3}.$

23. $-8(8x - 1)^{-3/2}.$ **25.** $\dfrac{7}{3}(7x)^{-2/3} + \sqrt[3]{7}.$ **27.** $(x^2)[5(x - 4)^4(1)] + (x - 4)^5(2x) = x(x - 4)^4(7x - 8).$

29. $(2x)\left[\dfrac{1}{2}(6x - 1)^{-1/2}(6)\right] + (\sqrt{6x - 1})(2) = 6x(6x - 1)^{-1/2} + 2\sqrt{6x - 1}.$

31. $(8x - 1)^3[4(2x + 1)^3(2)] + (2x + 1)^4[3(8x - 1)^2(8)] = 16(8x - 1)^2(2x + 1)^3(7x + 1).$

33. $10\left(\dfrac{x - 7}{x + 4}\right)^9\left[\dfrac{(x + 4)(1) - (x - 7)(1)}{(x + 4)^2}\right] = \dfrac{110(x - 7)^9}{(x + 4)^{11}}.$

35. $\dfrac{1}{2}\left(\dfrac{x - 2}{x + 3}\right)^{-1/2}\left[\dfrac{(x + 3)(1) - (x - 2)(1)}{(x + 3)^2}\right] = \dfrac{5}{2(x + 3)^2}\left(\dfrac{x - 2}{x + 3}\right)^{-1/2}.$

37. $\dfrac{(x^2 + 4)^3(2) - (2x - 5)[3(x^2 + 4)^2(2x)]}{(x^2 + 4)^6} = \dfrac{-2(5x^2 - 15x - 4)}{(x^2 + 4)^4}.$

39. $6\{(5x^2 + 2)[2x^3(x^4 + 5)^{-1/2}] + (x^4 + 5)^{1/2}(10x)\} = 12x(x^4 + 5)^{-1/2}(10x^4 + 2x^2 + 25).$

41. $8 + \dfrac{5}{(t + 4)^2} - (8t - 7) = 15 - 8t + \dfrac{5}{(t + 4)^2}.$

43. $\dfrac{(3x - 1)^3[40(8x - 1)^4] - (8x - 1)^5[9(3x - 1)^2]}{(3x - 1)^6} = \dfrac{(8x - 1)^4(48x - 31)}{(3x - 1)^4}.$

45. $\dfrac{(x^2 - 7)^4[(2x + 1)(2)(3x - 5)(3) + (3x - 5)^2(2)] - (2x + 1)(3x - 5)^2[4(x^2 - 7)^3(2x)]}{(x^2 - 7)^8}.$

47. $0.$ **49.** $0.$ **51.** $y = 4x - 11.$ **53.** $y = -\dfrac{1}{6}x + \dfrac{5}{3}.$ **55.** $96\%.$ **57.** $20.$ **59.** $13.99.$

61. **(a)** $-\dfrac{q}{\sqrt{q^2 + 20}};$ **(b)** $-\dfrac{q}{100\sqrt{q^2 + 20} - q^2 - 20};$ **(c)** $100 - \dfrac{q^2}{\sqrt{q^2 + 20}} - \sqrt{q^2 + 20}.$ **63.** $-325.$

65. $\dfrac{dc}{dq} = \dfrac{5q(q^2 + 6)}{(q^2 + 3)^{3/2}}.$ **67.** $48\pi(10)^{-19}.$ **69.** **(a)** $-\dfrac{1000}{\sqrt{100 - x}}, -125;$ **(b)** $-\dfrac{1}{128}.$

Exercise 11.7

1. $\dfrac{3}{3x - 4}.$ **3.** $\dfrac{2}{x}.$ **5.** $-\dfrac{2x}{1 - x^2}.$ **7.** $\dfrac{6p^2 + 3}{2p^3 + 3p} = \dfrac{3(2p^2 + 1)}{p(2p^2 + 3)}.$ **9.** $t\left(\dfrac{1}{t}\right) + (\ln t)(1) = 1 + \ln t.$

11. $\dfrac{2 \log_3 e}{2x - 1}$.   **13.** $\dfrac{z\left(\dfrac{1}{z}\right) - (\ln z)(1)}{z^2} = \dfrac{1 - \ln z}{z^2}$.   **15.** $\dfrac{3(2x + 4)}{x^2 + 4x + 5} = \dfrac{6(x + 2)}{x^2 + 4x + 5}$.   **17.** $\dfrac{x}{1 + x^2}$.   **19.** $\dfrac{2}{1 - l^2}$.

21. $\dfrac{x}{1 - x^4}$.   **23.** $\dfrac{4x}{x^2 + 2} + \dfrac{3x^2 + 1}{x^3 + x - 1}$.   **25.** $\dfrac{2(x^2 + 1)}{2x + 1} + 2x \ln(2x + 1)$.   **27.** $\dfrac{3(1 + \ln^2 x)}{x}$.   **29.** $\dfrac{4 \ln^3(ax)}{x}$.

31. $\dfrac{x}{2(x - 1)} + \ln\sqrt{x - 1}$.   **33.** $\dfrac{1}{2x\sqrt{4 + \ln x}}$.   **35.** $y = 4x - 12$.   **37.** $\dfrac{dr}{dq} = 25\dfrac{(q + 2) \ln(q + 2) - q}{(q + 2) \ln^2(q + 2)}$.

Exercise 11.8

1. $2xe^{x^2+1}$.   **3.** $-5e^{3-5x}$.   **5.** $(6r + 4)e^{3r^2 + 4r + 4} = 2(3r + 2)e^{3r^2 + 4r + 4}$.   **7.** $x(e^x) + e^x(1) = e^x(x + 1)$.

9. $2xe^{-x^2}(1 - x^2)$.   **11.** $\dfrac{e^x - e^{-x}}{2}$.   **13.** $(6x)4^{3x^2} \ln 4$.   **15.** $\dfrac{2e^{2w}(w - 1)}{w^3}$.   **17.** $\dfrac{e^{1+\sqrt{x}}}{2\sqrt{x}}$.   **19.** $3x^2 - 3^x \ln 3$.

21. $\dfrac{2e^x}{(e^x + 1)^2}$.   **23.** $e^x e^x = e^{e^x + x}$.   **25.** 1.   **27.** $e^{x \ln x}(1 + \ln x)$.   **29.** $(\log 2)^x \ln(\log 2)$.

31. $y - e^2 = e^2(x - 2)$ or $y = e^2 x - e^2$.   **33.** $\dfrac{dp}{dq} = -0.015e^{-0.001q}; -0.015e^{-0.5}$.   **35.** $\dfrac{dc}{dq} = 10e^{(q+3)/400}; 10e^{0.25}, 10e^{0.5}$.

37. $100e^{-2}$.   **43.** $-b(10^{A - bM})\ln 10$ **47.** 0.0036

Exercise 11.9

1. $-\dfrac{x}{4y}$.   **3.** $\dfrac{5}{12y^3}$.   **5.** $-\dfrac{\sqrt{y}}{\sqrt{x}}$.   **7.** $-\dfrac{y^{1/4}}{x^{1/4}}$.   **9.** $-\dfrac{y}{x}$.   **11.** $\dfrac{4 - y}{x - 1}$.   **13.** $\dfrac{4y - x^2}{y^2 - 4x}$.   **15.** $\dfrac{6y^{2/3}}{3y^{1/6} + 2}$.

17. $\dfrac{1 - 6xy^3}{1 + 9x^2y^2}$.   **19.** $\dfrac{xe^y - y}{x(\ln x - xe^y)}$.   **21.** $-\dfrac{e^y}{xe^y + 1}$.   **23.** $-\dfrac{3}{5}$.   **25.** $y = -\dfrac{3}{4}x + \dfrac{5}{4}$.   **27.** $\dfrac{dq}{dp} = -\dfrac{1}{2q}$.

29. $\dfrac{dq}{dp} = -\dfrac{(q + 5)^3}{40}$.   **31.** $\dfrac{1.5E}{\log e}$.

Exercise 11.10

1. $(x + 1)^2(x - 1)(x^2 + 3)\left[\dfrac{2}{x + 1} + \dfrac{1}{x - 1} + \dfrac{2x}{x^2 + 3}\right]$.   **3.** $(3x^3 - 1)^2(2x + 5)^3\left[\dfrac{18x^2}{3x^3 - 1} + \dfrac{6}{2x + 5}\right]$.

5. $\dfrac{\sqrt{x + 1}\sqrt{x^2 - 2}\sqrt{x + 4}}{2}\left[\dfrac{1}{x + 1} + \dfrac{2x}{x^2 - 2} + \dfrac{1}{x + 4}\right]$.   **7.** $\dfrac{\sqrt{1 - x^2}}{1 - 2x}\left[\dfrac{x}{x^2 - 1} + \dfrac{2}{1 - 2x}\right]$.

9. $\dfrac{(2x^2 + 2)^2}{(x + 1)^2(3x + 2)}\left[\dfrac{4x}{x^2 + 1} - \dfrac{2}{x + 1} - \dfrac{3}{3x + 2}\right]$.   **11.** $\dfrac{(8x + 3)^{1/2}(x^2 + 2)^{1/3}}{(1 + 2x)^{1/4}}\left[\dfrac{4}{8x + 3} + \dfrac{2x}{3(x^2 + 2)} - \dfrac{1}{2(1 + 2x)}\right]$.

13. $x^{2x+1}\left(\dfrac{2x + 1}{x} + 2 \ln x\right)$.   **15.** $\dfrac{x^{1/x}(1 - \ln x)}{x^2}$.   **17.** $2(3x + 1)^{2x}\left[\dfrac{3x}{3x + 1} + \ln(3x + 1)\right]$.   **19.** $e^x x^{3x}(4 + 3 \ln x)$.

21. $y = 96x + 36$.   **23.** $x^x(1 + \ln x)$.

Exercise 11.11

1. 24. **3.** 0. **5.** e^x. **7.** $3 + 2 \ln x$. **9.** $-\dfrac{10}{p^6}$. **11.** $-\dfrac{1}{4(1 - r)^{3/2}}$. **13.** $\dfrac{50}{(5x - 6)^3}$. **15.** $\dfrac{4}{(x - 1)^3}$.

17. $-\left[\dfrac{1}{x^2} + \dfrac{1}{(x + 1)^2}\right]$. **19.** $e^z(z^2 + 4z + 2)$. **21.** $-\dfrac{1}{y^3}$. **23.** $-\dfrac{4}{y^3}$. **25.** $\dfrac{1}{8x^{3/2}}$. **27.** $\dfrac{2(y - 1)}{(1 + x)^2}$.

29. $\dfrac{2y}{(2 - y)^3}$. **31.** $300(5x - 3)^2$. **33.** 0.6. **35.** ± 1.

Review Problems—Chapter 11

1. 0. **3.** $28x^3 - 18x^2 + 10x = 2x(14x^2 - 9x + 5)$. **5.** $2e^x + e^x(2x) = 2(e^x + xe^x)$. **7.** $\dfrac{2x}{5}$.

9. $\dfrac{1}{r^2 + 5r}(2r + 5) = \dfrac{2r + 5}{r(r + 5)}$. **11.** $(x^2 + 6x)(3x^2 - 12x) + (x^3 - 6x^2 + 4)(2x + 6) = 5x^4 - 108x^2 + 8x + 24$.

13. $100(2x^2 + 4x)^{99}(4x + 4) = 400(x + 1)[(2x)(x + 2)]^{99}$.

15. $(8 + 2x)(4)(x^2 + 1)^3(2x) + (x^2 + 1)^4(2) = 2(x^2 + 1)^3(9x^2 + 32x + 1)$. **17.** $\dfrac{4}{3}(4x - 1)^{-2/3}$.

19. $e^x(2x) + (x^2 + 2)e^x = e^x(x^2 + 2x + 2)$. **21.** $\dfrac{(z^2 + 1)(2z) - (z^2 - 1)(2z)}{(z^2 + 1)^2} = \dfrac{4z}{(z^2 + 1)^2}$.

23. $\dfrac{e^x\left(\dfrac{1}{x}\right) - (\ln x)(e^x)}{e^{2x}} = \dfrac{1 - x \ln x}{xe^x}$. **25.** $e^{x^2 + 4x + 5}(2x + 4) = 2(x + 2)e^{x^2 + 4x + 5}$.

27. $\dfrac{(2x^2 + 3)(2x + 1) - (x^2 + x)(4x)}{(2x^2 + 3)^2} = \dfrac{-2x^2 + 6x + 3}{(2x^2 + 3)^2}$. **29.** $-\dfrac{y}{x + y}$.

31. $\dfrac{y}{2}\left[\dfrac{1}{x - 6} + \dfrac{1}{x + 5} - \dfrac{1}{9 - x}\right] = \dfrac{y}{2}\left[\dfrac{1}{x - 6} + \dfrac{1}{x + 5} + \dfrac{1}{x - 9}\right]$, where $y = \sqrt{(x - 6)(x + 5)(9 - x)}$.

33. $\dfrac{2}{q + 1} + \dfrac{3}{q + 2}$. **35.** $-\dfrac{1}{2}(1 - x)^{-3/2}(-1) = \dfrac{1}{2}(1 - x)^{-3/2}$. **37.** $\dfrac{16 \log_2 e}{8x + 5}$. **39.** $(x + 1)^{x+1}[1 + \ln(x + 1)]$.

41. $\dfrac{\sqrt{x^2 + 5}\,(2x) - (x^2 + 6)(1/2)(x^2 + 5)^{-1/2}(2x)}{x^2 + 5} = \dfrac{x(x^2 + 4)}{(x^2 + 5)^{3/2}}$. **43.** $-\dfrac{y}{x}$.

45. $2\left(-\dfrac{3}{8}\right)x^{-11/8} + \left(-\dfrac{3}{8}\right)(2x)^{-11/8}(2) = -\dfrac{3}{4}(1 + 2^{-11/8})x^{-11/8}$. **47.** $\dfrac{1 + 2l + 3l^2}{1 + l + l^2 + l^3}$.

49. $\left(\dfrac{3}{5}\right)(x^3 + 6x^2 + 9)^{-2/5}(3x^2 + 12x) = \dfrac{9}{5}x(x + 4)(x^3 + 6x + 9)^{-2/5}$. **51.** $2\left(\dfrac{1}{u}\right) + \dfrac{1}{2}\left(\dfrac{1}{1 - u}\right)(-1) = \dfrac{5u - 4}{2u(u - 1)}$.

53. $y\left[\dfrac{3}{2}\left(\dfrac{1}{x^2 + 2}\right)(2x) + \dfrac{4}{9}\left(\dfrac{1}{x^2 + 9}\right)(2x) - \dfrac{4}{11}\left(\dfrac{1}{x^3 + 6x}\right)(3x^2 + 6)\right] = y\left[\dfrac{3x}{x^2 + 2} + \dfrac{8x}{9(x^2 + 9)} - \dfrac{12(x^2 + 2)}{11x(x^2 + 6)}\right]$, where

$y = \dfrac{(x^2 + 2)^{3/2}(x^2 + 9)^{4/9}}{(x^3 + 6x)^{4/11}}$. **55.** 12. **57.** $-\dfrac{1}{128}$. **59.** $\dfrac{4}{9}$. **61.** $-\dfrac{1}{4}$. **63.** $y = -4x + 3$.

65. $y = 2x + 2(1 - \ln 2)$ or $y = 2x + 2 - \ln 4$. **67.** $7x - 2\sqrt{10}\,y - 9 = 0$. **69.** $\dfrac{5}{7} \approx 0.714$; 71.4%.

71. $\dfrac{dr}{dq} = 20 - 0.2q$. **73.** 0.569, 0.431. **75.** $\dfrac{dr}{dq} = 450 - q$. **77.** $\dfrac{dc}{dq} = 0.125 + 0.00878q$; 0.7396.

79. $f'(t) = 0.008e^{-0.01t} + 0.00004e^{-0.0002t}$.

Exercise 12.1

1. (0, 0); sym. about origin.   **3.** (± 2, 0), (0, 8); sym. about y-axis.   **5.** (± 3, 0); sym. about x-axis, y-axis, origin.
7. (-2, 0); sym. about x-axis.   **9.** Sym. about x-axis.   **11.** (-21, 0), (0, -7), (0, 3).   **13.** (0, 0); sym. about origin.
15. ($\pm \sqrt{\ln 5}$, 0), (0, $\pm \sqrt{\ln 5}$); sym. about x-axis, y-axis, origin.   **17.** (2, 0), (0, ± 2); sym. about x-axis.

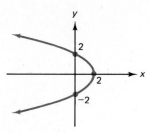

19. (± 2, 0), (0, 0); sym. about origin.   **21.** (0, 0); sym. about x-axis, y-axis, origin.

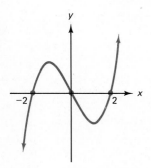   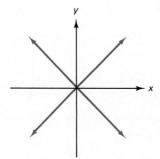

23. (± 2, 0), (0, ± 4); sym. about x-axis, y-axis, origin.

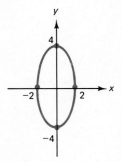

Exercise 12.2

1. $y = \dfrac{1}{2}$, $x = -\dfrac{3}{2}$.   **3.** $y = 0$, $x = 0$.   **5.** None.   **7.** $y = 2$, $x = -3$, $x = 2$.   **9.** $y = 4$, $x = 6$.
11. None.   **13.** $y = 4$.

15. $(0, -3)$; $y = 0$, $x = 1$.

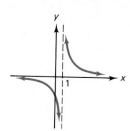

17. Sym. about origin;
$y = 0$, $x = 0$.

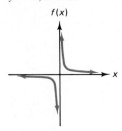

19. $(0, -1)$; sym. about y-axis;
$y = 0$, $x = 1$, $x = -1$.

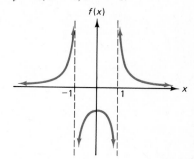

21. $(\pm 1, 0)$, $\left(0, \dfrac{1}{4}\right)$;

sym. about y-axis;
$y = 1$, $x = 2$, $x = -2$.

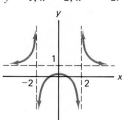

23. $(\pm 3, 0)$; sym. about y-axis.

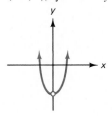

25. $((\ln 3)/2, 0)$, $(0, 2)$; $y = 3$.

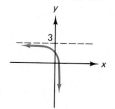

Exercise 12.3

1. Dec. on $(-\infty, 0)$; inc. on $(0, \infty)$; rel. min. when $x = 0$.   **3.** Inc. on $\left(-\infty, \dfrac{1}{2}\right)$; dec. on $\left(\dfrac{1}{2}, \infty\right)$; rel. max. when $x = \dfrac{1}{2}$.

5. Dec. on $(-\infty, -5)$ and $(1, \infty)$; inc. on $(-5, 1)$; rel. min. when $x = -5$; rel. max. when $x = 1$.

7. Dec. on $(-\infty, -1)$ and $(0, 1)$; inc. on $(-1, 0)$ and $(1, \infty)$; rel. max. when $x = 0$; rel. min. when $x = \pm 1$.

9. Inc. on $(-\infty, 1)$ and $(3, \infty)$; dec. on $(1, 3)$; rel. max. when $x = 1$; rel. min. when $x = 3$.

11. Inc. on $(-\infty, -1)$ and $(1, \infty)$; dec. on $(-1, 0)$ and $(0, 1)$; rel. max. when $x = -1$; rel. min. when $x = 1$.

13. Dec. on $(-\infty, -4)$ and $(0, \infty)$; inc. on $(-4, 0)$; rel. min. when $x = -4$; rel. max. when $x = 0$.

15. Dec. on $(-\infty, 1)$ and $(1, \infty)$; no rel. max. or min.   **17.** Dec. on $(0, \infty)$; no rel. max. or min.

19. Dec. on $(-\infty, 0)$ and $(2, \infty)$; inc. on $(0, 1)$ and $(1, 2)$; rel. min. when $x = 0$; rel. max. when $x = 2$.

21. Inc. on $(-\infty, -2)$, $\left(-2, \dfrac{11}{5}\right)$, and $(5, \infty)$; dec. on $\left(\dfrac{11}{5}, 5\right)$; rel. max. when $x = \dfrac{11}{5}$; rel. min. when $x = 5$.

23. Dec. on $(-\infty, \infty)$; no rel. max. or min.   **25.** Dec. on $(0, 1)$; inc. on $(1, \infty)$; rel. min. when $x = 1$.

27. Dec. on $(-\infty, 0)$; inc. on $(0, \infty)$; rel. min. when $x = 0$.

29. Dec. on $(-\infty, 3)$; inc. on $(3, \infty)$; rel. min. when $x = 3$;
intercepts: $(7, 0)$, $(-1, 0)$, $(0, -7)$.

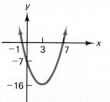

31. Dec. on $(-\infty, -1)$ and $(1, \infty)$; inc. on $(-1, 1)$; rel. min.
when $x = -1$; rel. max. when $x = 1$; sym. to origin;
intercepts: $(\pm\sqrt{3}, 0)$, $(0, 0)$.

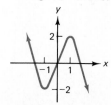

33. Inc. on $(-\infty, 1)$ and $(2, \infty)$; dec. on $(1, 2)$; rel. max. when $x = 1$; rel. min. when $x = 2$; intercept: $(0, 0)$.

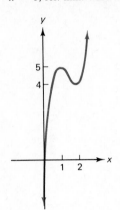

35. Inc. on $(-2, -1)$ and $(0, \infty)$; dec. on $(-\infty, -2)$ and $(-1, 0)$; rel. max. when $x = -1$; rel. min. when $x = -2$, 0; intercepts $(0, 0)$, $(-2, 0)$.

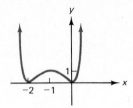

37. Dec. on $(-\infty, 1)$ and $(1, \infty)$; asym. $y = 1$, $x = 1$; intercepts: $(0, -1)$, $(-1, 0)$.

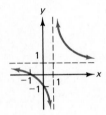

39. Inc. on $(-\infty, -6)$ and $(0, \infty)$; dec. on $(-6, -3)$ and $(-3, 0)$; rel. max. when $x = -6$; rel. min. when $x = 0$; asym. $x = -3$; intercept: $(0, 0)$.

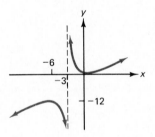

41. Ab. max. when $x = -1$; ab. min. when $x = 1$.   **43.** Ab. max. when $x = 0$; ab. min. when $x = 2$.

45. Ab. max. when $x = 3$; ab. min. when $x = 1$.   **49.** Never.   **51.** 40.   **55.** (a) 25,300; (b) 4; (c) 17,200.

Exercise 12.4

1. Conc. down $(-\infty, \infty)$.   **3.** Conc. down $(-\infty, -1)$; conc. up $(-1, \infty)$; inf. pt. when $x = -1$.

5. Conc. up $(-\infty, -1)$, $(1, \infty)$; conc. down $(-1, 1)$; inf. pt. when $x = \pm 1$.   **7.** Conc. down $(-\infty, 1)$; conc. up $(1, \infty)$.

9. Conc. down $(-\infty, -1/\sqrt{3})$, $(1/\sqrt{3}, \infty)$; conc. up $(-1/\sqrt{3}, 1/\sqrt{3})$; inf. pt. when $x = \pm 1/\sqrt{3}$.   **11.** Conc. up $(-\infty, \infty)$.

13. Conc. down $(-\infty, -2)$; conc. up $(-2, \infty)$; inf. pt. when $x = -2$.

15. Int. $(-3, 0)$, $(-1, 0)$, $(0, 3)$; dec. $(-\infty, -2)$; inc. $(-2, \infty)$; rel. min. when $x = -2$; conc. up $(-\infty, \infty)$.

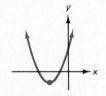

17. Int. $(0, 0)$, $(4, 0)$; inc. $(-\infty, 2)$; dec. $(2, \infty)$; rel. max. when $x = 2$; conc. down $(-\infty, \infty)$.

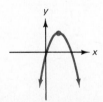

19. Int. $(0, -19)$; inc. $(-\infty, 2)$, $(4, \infty)$; dec. $(2, 4)$; rel. max. when $x = 2$; rel. min. when $x = 4$; conc. down $(-\infty, 3)$; conc. up $(3, \infty)$; inf. pt. when $x = 3$.

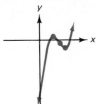

21. Int. $(0, 0)$, $(\pm 2\sqrt{3}, 0)$; inc. $(-\infty, -2)$, $(2, \infty)$; dec. $(-2, 2)$; rel. max. when $x = -2$; rel. min. when $x = 2$; conc. down $(-\infty, 0)$; conc. up $(0, \infty)$; inf. pt. when $x = 0$; sym. about origin.

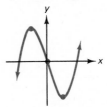

23. Int. $(0, -3)$; inc. $(-\infty, 1)$, $(1, \infty)$; no rel. max. or min.; conc. down $(-\infty, 1)$; conc. up $(1, \infty)$; inf. pt. when $x = 1$.

25. Int. $(0, 0)$, $(4/3, 0)$; inc. $(-\infty, 0)$, $(0, 1)$; dec. $(1, \infty)$; rel. max. when $x = 1$; conc. up $(0, 2/3)$; conc. down $(-\infty, 0)$, $(2/3, \infty)$; inf. pt. when $x = 0$, $x = 2/3$.

27. Int. $(0, -2)$; dec. $(-\infty, -2)$, $(2, \infty)$; inc. $(-2, 2)$; rel. min. when $x = -2$; rel. max. when $x = 2$; conc. up $(-\infty, 0)$; conc. down $(0, \infty)$; inf. pt. when $x = 0$.

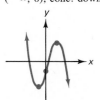

29. Int. $(0, -6)$; inc. $(-\infty, 2)$, $(2, \infty)$; conc. down $(-\infty, 2)$; conc. up $(2, \infty)$; inf. pt. when $x = 2$.

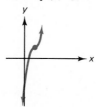

31. Int. $(0, 0)$, $(\pm\sqrt[4]{5}, 0)$; dec. $(-\infty, -1)$, $(1, \infty)$; inc. $(-1, 1)$; rel. min. when $x = -1$; rel. max. when $x = 1$; conc. up $(-\infty, 0)$; conc. down $(0, \infty)$; inf. pt. when $x = 0$; sym. about origin.

33. Int. $(0, 1)$, $(1, 0)$; dec. $(-\infty, 0)$, $(0, 1)$; inc. $(1, \infty)$; rel. min. when $x = 1$; conc. up $(-\infty, 0)$, $(2/3, \infty)$; conc. down $(0, 2/3)$; inf. pt. when $x = 0$, $x = 2/3$.

35. Dec. $(-\infty, 0)$, $(0, \infty)$; conc. down $(-\infty, 0)$; conc. up $(0, \infty)$; sym. about origin; asymptotes $x = 0$, $y = 0$.

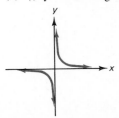

37. Int. $(0, 0)$; inc. $(-\infty, -1)$, $(-1, \infty)$; conc. up $(-\infty, -1)$; conc. down $(-1, \infty)$; asymptotes $x = -1$, $y = 1$.

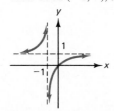

39. Dec. $(-\infty, -1)$, $(0, 1)$; inc. $(-1, 0)$, $(1, \infty)$; rel. min. when $x = \pm 1$; conc. up $(-\infty, 0)$, $(0, \infty)$; sym. about y-axis; asymptote $x = 0$.

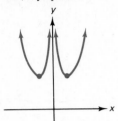

41. Int. $(0, 0)$, $(\pm 2, 0)$; inc. $(-\infty, -\sqrt{2})$, $(0, \sqrt{2})$; dec. $(-\sqrt{2}, 0)$, $(\sqrt{2}, \infty)$; rel. max. when $x = \pm\sqrt{2}$; rel. min. when $x = 0$; conc. down $(-\infty, -\sqrt{2/3})$, $(\sqrt{2/3}, \infty)$; conc. up $(-\sqrt{2/3}, \sqrt{2/3})$; inf. pt. when $x = \pm\sqrt{2/3}$; sym. about y-axis.

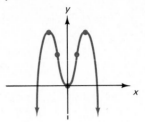

45.

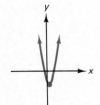

47. Yes

Exercise 12.5

1. Rel. min. when $x = \dfrac{5}{2}$; abs. min.   **3.** Rel max. when $x = \dfrac{1}{4}$; abs. max.   **5.** Rel. max. when $x = -3$, rel. min. when $x = 3$.

7. Rel. min. when $x = 0$, rel. max. when $x = 2$.   **9.** Test fails, when $x = 0$ there is rel. min. by first-deriv. test.

Review Problems—Chapter 12

1. $(0, 0)$, $(\pm\sqrt{2/3}, 0)$; sym. about origin.   **3.** $y = 3$, $x = 4$, $x = -4$.   **5.** $x = 0, 2, 4$.

7. Inc. on $(1, 3)$; dec. on $(-\infty, 1)$ and $(3, \infty)$.   **9.** Conc. up on $(-\infty, 0)$ and $(\frac{1}{2}, \infty)$; conc. down on $(0, \frac{1}{2})$.

11. Rel. min. at $x = -1$.   **13.** At $x = 3$.   **15.** Abs. max. at $x = 2$; abs. min. at $x = 1$.

17. Int. $(-4, 0)$, $(6, 0)$, $(0, -24)$; inc. $(1, \infty)$; dec. $(-\infty, 1)$; rel. min. when $x = 1$; conc. up $(-\infty, \infty)$.

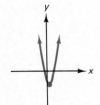

19. Int. $(0, 20)$; inc. $(-\infty, -2)$, $(2, \infty)$; dec. $(-2, 2)$; rel. max. when $x = -2$; rel. min. when $x = 2$; conc. up $(0, \infty)$; conc. down $(-\infty, 0)$; inf. pt. when $x = 0$.

21. Int. (0, 0); inc. $(-\infty, \infty)$; conc. down $(-\infty, 0)$; conc. up $(0, \infty)$; inf. pt. when $x = 0$; sym. about origin.

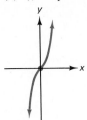

23. Int. $(-5, 0)$; inc. $(-10, 0)$; dec. $(-\infty, -10)$, $(0, \infty)$; rel. min. when $x = -10$; conc. up $(-15, 0)$, $(0, \infty)$; conc. down $(-\infty, -15)$; inf. pt. when $x = -15$; horiz. asym. $y = 0$; vert. asym. $x = 0$.

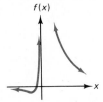

25. Int. (0, 1); inc. $(0, \infty)$; dec. $(-\infty, 0)$; rel. min. when $x = 0$; conc. up $(-\infty, \infty)$; sym. about y-axis.

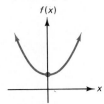

27. Rel. max when $x = 0$; inf. pt. when $x = \pm 1$.

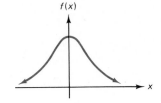

Exercise 13.1

1. 100.   **3.** \$15.   **5. (a)** 110 grams; **(b)** $51\frac{9}{11}$ grams.   **7.** 525, \$51, \$10,525.   **9.** \$22.   **11.** 625, \$4.
13. \$3, \$9000.   **15.** 20 and 20.   **17.** 300 ft by 250 ft.   **19.** 4 ft by 4 ft by 2 ft.   **21.** 2 in.; 128 in.^{3}.
25. 130, $p = 340$, $P = 36,980$; 125, $p = 350$, $P = 34,175$.   **27.** 250 per lot (4 lots).   **29.** 35.   **31.** 60 mi/h.
33. $5 - \sqrt{3}$ tons, $5 - \sqrt{3}$ tons.

Exercise 13.2

1. $3\,dx$.   **3.** $\dfrac{2x^3}{\sqrt{x^4 + 2}}\,dx$.   **5.** $-\dfrac{2}{x^3}\,dx$.   **7.** $\dfrac{2x}{x^2 + 7}\,dx$.   **9.** $4e^{2x^2+3}(4x^2 + 3x + 1)\,dx$.

11. $\Delta y = -0.14$, $dy = -0.14$.   **13.** $\Delta y = 0.073$, $dy = \dfrac{3}{40} = 0.075$.   **15.** 10.05.   **17.** $3\frac{47}{48}$.   **19.** -0.03.

21. 1.01.   **23.** $\dfrac{1}{2}$.   **25.** $\dfrac{1}{6p(p^2 + 5)^2}$.   **27.** $-p^2$.   **29.** $-\dfrac{4}{5}$.   **31.** 44; 41.80.   **33.** 2.04.   **35.** 0.7.
37. $(1.69 \times 10^{-11})\pi$.   **39.** $35\frac{8}{9}$.

Exercise 13.3

1. -3, elastic.   **3.** -1, unit elasticity.   **5.** -1.02, elastic.   **7.** $-(150e^{-1} - 1)$, elastic.   **9.** -1, unit elasticity.
11. $-\dfrac{9}{32}$, inelastic.   **13.** $-\dfrac{1}{2}$, inelastic.   **15.** $|\eta| = \dfrac{10}{3}$ when $p = 10$, $|\eta| = \dfrac{3}{10}$ when $p = 3$, $|\eta| = 1$ when $p = 6.50$.
17. -1.2, 0.6% decrease.   **23.** 5, 30.

Review Problems—Chapter 13

1. 20.   **3.** 300.   **5.** \$2800.   **7.** 200 ft by 100 ft.   **9.** 12; 105.   **11.** $\left[\dfrac{x^2}{x+5} + 2x\,\ln(x+5)\right]dx.$

13. $\left(\dfrac{9}{10}\right)^{\circ}.$ **15.** 0.99.   **17.** Inelastic.   **19.** Elastic.

Exercise 14.1

1. $5x + C.$ **3.** $\dfrac{x^9}{9} + C.$ **5.** $-\dfrac{5}{6x^6} + C.$ **7.** $-\dfrac{1}{9x^9} + C.$ **9.** $-\dfrac{5}{6y^{6/5}} + C.$ **11.** $8u + \dfrac{u^2}{2} + C.$

13. $\dfrac{y^6}{6} - \dfrac{5y^2}{2} + C.$ **15.** $t^3 - 2t^2 + 5t + C.$ **17.** $(7 + e)x + C.$ **19.** $\dfrac{x^2}{14} - \dfrac{3x^5}{20} + C.$ **21.** $3e^x + C.$

23. $\dfrac{x^{9.3}}{9.3} - \dfrac{9x^7}{7} - \dfrac{1}{x^3} - \dfrac{1}{2x^2} + C.$ **25.** $-\dfrac{4x^{3/2}}{9} + C.$ **27.** $2\sqrt[8]{x} + C.$ **29.** $\dfrac{x^4}{12} + \dfrac{3}{2x^2} + C.$ **31.** $\dfrac{w^3}{2} + \dfrac{2}{3w} + C.$

33. $6z - \dfrac{5z^3}{12} + 2e^z + C.$ **35.** $\dfrac{e^u}{4} + u + C.$ **37.** $\dfrac{4x^{3/2}}{3} - \dfrac{12x^{5/4}}{5} + C.$ **39.** $-\dfrac{3x^{5/3}}{25} - 7x^{1/2} + 3x^2 + C.$

41. $\dfrac{x^4}{4} - x^3 + \dfrac{5x^2}{2} - 15x + C.$ **43.** $\dfrac{2x^{5/2}}{5} + 2x^{3/2} + C.$ **45.** $\dfrac{4u^3}{3} + 2u^2 + u + C.$ **47.** $\dfrac{2v^3}{3} + 3v + \dfrac{1}{2v^4} + C.$

49. $\dfrac{1}{2}(e^6x + e^x) + C.$ **51.** $y = \dfrac{3x^2}{2} - 4x + 1.$ **53.** $y = -\dfrac{x^4}{12} - \dfrac{x^3}{3} + \dfrac{4x}{3} + \dfrac{1}{12}.$ **55.** $y = \dfrac{x^4}{12} + x^2 - 5x + 2.$

57. $p = 0.7.$ **59.** $p = 275 - 0.5q - 0.1q^2.$ **61.** $c = 1.35q + 200.$ **63.** 7715.   **65.** $G = -\dfrac{P^2}{50} + 2P + 20.$

69. \$80. $(dc/dq = 27.50$ when $q = 50$ is not relevant to problem.)

Exercise 14.2

1. $\dfrac{(x+4)^9}{9} + C.$ **3.** $\dfrac{(x^2+16)^4}{4} + C.$ **5.** $\dfrac{3}{5}(y^3 + 3y^2 + 1)^{5/3} + C.$ **7.** $-\dfrac{(3x-1)^{-2}}{2} + C.$ **9.** $e^{3x} + C.$

11. $e^{t^2+t} + C.$ **13.** $\dfrac{2(x+10)^{3/2}}{3} + C.$ **15.** $\dfrac{(7x-6)^5}{35} + C.$ **17.** $\dfrac{(x^2+3)^{13}}{26} + C.$ **19.** $\dfrac{3}{20}(27 + x^5)^{4/3} + C.$

21. $\dfrac{1}{10}e^{5x^2} + C.$ **23.** $-3e^{-2x} + C.$ **25.** $\ln|x + 5| + C.$ **27.** $\ln|x^3 + x^4| + C.$ **29.** $-\dfrac{3}{4}(z^2 - 6)^{-4} + C.$

31. $4\ln|x| + C.$ **33.** $\dfrac{1}{3}\ln|s^3 + 5| + C.$ **35.** $-\dfrac{7}{3}\ln|5 - 3x| + C.$ **37.** $\dfrac{2}{15}(5x)^{3/2} + C = \dfrac{2}{3}x\sqrt{5x} + C.$

39. $\sqrt{x^2 - 4} + C.$ **41.** $\dfrac{1}{2}e^{y^4+1} + C.$ **43.** $-\dfrac{1}{6}e^{-2v^3+1} + C.$ **45.** $-\dfrac{1}{5}e^{-5x} + 2e^x + C.$

47. $-\dfrac{1}{24}(3 - 3x^2 - 6x)^4 + C.$ **49.** $\dfrac{1}{3}\ln|x^3 + 6x| + C.$ **51.** $2\ln|3 - 2s + 4s^2| + C.$ **53.** $\dfrac{1}{4}\ln(2x^2 + 1) + C.$

55. $\dfrac{1}{27}(x^3 - x^6)^{-9} + C.$ **57.** $\dfrac{1}{4}(x^4 + x^2)^2 + C.$ **59.** $\dfrac{1}{2}(4 - 9x - 3x^2)^{-4} + C.$ **61.** $\dfrac{1}{6}e^{4x^3+3x^2-4} + C.$

63. $-\dfrac{1}{25}(7 - 5x^2)^{5/2} + C.$ **65.** $\sqrt{2x} + C.$ **67.** $\dfrac{x^5}{5} + \dfrac{2x^3}{3} + x + C.$ **69.** $\dfrac{1}{2}\ln(x^2 + 1) - \dfrac{1}{6(x^6 + 1)} + C.$

71. $\dfrac{1}{3}\ln|3x - 5| + \dfrac{1}{27}(x^3 - x^6)^{-9} + C.$ **73.** $\dfrac{1}{3}(2x + 3)^{3/2} - \ln\sqrt{x^2 + 3} + C.$ **75.** $2e^{\sqrt{x}} + C.$

77. $y = -\dfrac{1}{6}(3 - 2x)^3 + \dfrac{11}{2}.$ **79.** $y = -\ln|x| = \ln|1/x|.$ **81.** $\dfrac{Rr^2}{4K} + B_1 \ln r + B_2.$

Exercise 14.3

1. $\frac{3}{2}x^2 + x - \ln|x| + C.$ **3.** $\frac{1}{3}(2x^3 + 4x + 1)^{3/2} + C.$ **5.** $-\frac{8}{3}\sqrt{2 - 3x} + C.$ **7.** $\frac{4^{7x}}{7 \ln 4} + C.$

9. $7x^2 - 4e^{x^2/4} + C.$ **11.** $\frac{3}{2}\ln(e^{2x} + 1) + C.$ **13.** $-\frac{1}{7}e^{7/x} + C.$ **15.** $\frac{2}{9}(\sqrt{x} + 2)^3 + C.$ **17.** $\frac{1}{2}(\ln^2 x) + C.$

19. $\frac{1}{3}\ln^3 (r + 1) + C.$ **21.** $e^{(x^2 + 3)/2} + C.$ **23.** $\ln|\ln(x + 3)| + C.$ **25.** $\frac{1}{2}\sqrt{x^4 - 1} - (\ln 4)x + C.$

27. $x^2 - 8x - 6\ln|x| - \frac{2}{x} + C.$ **29.** $x^2 - 3x + \frac{2}{3}\ln|3x - 1| + C.$ **31.** $x + \ln|x - 1| + C.$

33. $\sqrt{e^{x^2} + 2} + C.$ **35.** $-\frac{(e^{-x} + 6)^3}{3} + C.$ **37.** $\frac{1}{36\sqrt{2}}[(8x)^{3/2} + 3]^{3/2} + C.$ **39.** $-\frac{2}{3}e^{-\sqrt{s^3}} + C.$

41. $\frac{x^2}{2} + 2x + C.$ **43.** $p = \frac{100}{q + 2}.$ **45.** $c = 20 \ln|(q + 5)/5| + 2000.$ **47.** $C = 2(\sqrt{I} + 1).$

49. $C = \frac{3}{4}I - \frac{1}{3}\sqrt{I} + \frac{71}{12}.$

Exercise 14.4

1. 35.   **3.** 0.   **5.** 25.   **7.** $-\frac{3}{16}.$ **9.** $-\frac{7}{6}.$ **11.** $\sum_{k=1}^{15} k.$ **13.** $\sum_{k=1}^{4}(2k - 1).$ **15.** $\sum_{k=1}^{12} k^2.$

17. 101,475.   **19.** 84.   **21.** 273.   **23.** 8; $850.

Exercise 14.5

1. $\frac{2}{3}$ square unit.   **3.** $\frac{14}{27}$ square unit.   **5.** $\frac{1}{2}$ square unit.   **7.** $\frac{1}{3}$ square unit.   **9.** $\frac{16}{3}$ square units.   **11.** 6.

13. $-18.$ **15.** $\frac{5}{6}.$

Exercise 14.6

1. 12.   **3.** $\frac{9}{2}.$ **5.** $-24.$ **7.** $\frac{7}{3}.$ **9.** $\frac{15}{2}.$ **11.** $-\frac{7}{6}.$ **13.** 0.   **15.** $\frac{5}{3}.$ **17.** $\frac{32}{3}.$ **19.** $-\frac{1}{6}.$

21. $4 \ln 8.$ **23.** $\frac{1}{3}(e^8 - 1).$ **25.** $\frac{3}{4}.$ **27.** $\frac{38}{9}.$ **29.** $\frac{15}{28}.$ **31.** $\frac{1}{2}\ln 3.$ **33.** $e + \frac{1}{2e^2} - \frac{3}{2}.$

35. $\frac{3}{2} - \frac{1}{e} + \frac{1}{2e^2}.$ **37.** $\frac{e^3}{2}(e^{12} - 1).$ **39.** $\alpha^{5/2}T.$ **41.** $\int_b^a -Ax^{-B}\, dx.$ **43.** $8639.   **45.** 1,973,333.

47. $160.   **49.** $2000.   **51.** 696; 492.   **53.** $\frac{i}{k}(1 - e^{-2kR}).$

Exercise 14.7

*In Problems **1–33**, answers are assumed to be expressed in square units.*

1. 8.   **3.** $\frac{19}{2}.$ **5.** 8.   **7.** $\frac{19}{3},.$ **9.** 9.   **11.** $\frac{50}{3}.$ **13.** 36.   **15.** 8.   **17.** $\frac{32}{3}.$ **19.** 1.   **21.** 18.

23. $\dfrac{26}{3}$. **25.** $\dfrac{3}{2}\sqrt[3]{2}$. **27.** $e^2 - 1$. **29.** $\dfrac{3}{2} + 2\ln 2 = \dfrac{3}{2} + \ln 4$. **31.** 68. **33.** 2. **35.** 19 square units.

37. (a) $\dfrac{1}{16}$; **(b)** $\dfrac{3}{4}$; **(c)** $\dfrac{7}{16}$. **39. (a)** $\ln\dfrac{5}{3}$; **(b)** $\ln(4) - 1$; **(c)** $2 - \ln 3$.

Exercise 14.8

*In Problems **1–21**, the answers are assumed to be expressed in square units.*

1. $\dfrac{4}{3}$. **3.** $\dfrac{16}{3}$. **5.** $8\sqrt{6}$. **7.** 40. **9.** $\dfrac{125}{6}$. **11.** $\dfrac{9}{2}$. **13.** $\dfrac{125}{12}$. **15.** $\dfrac{32}{81}$. **17.** $\dfrac{44}{3}$.

19. $\dfrac{4}{3}(5\sqrt{5} - 2\sqrt{2})$. **21.** $\dfrac{1}{2}$. **23.** $\dfrac{20}{63}$.

Exercise 14.9

1. $CS = 25.6$, $PS = 38.4$. **3.** $CS = 50\ln(2) - 25$, $PS = 1.25$. **5.** $CS = 800$, $PS = 1000$.

Review Problems—Chapter 14

1. $\dfrac{x^4}{4} + x^2 - 7x + C$. **3.** $\dfrac{117}{2}$. **5.** $-(x + 5)^{-2} + C$. **7.** $2\ln|x^3 - 6x + 1| + C$. **9.** $\dfrac{11\sqrt[3]{11}}{4} - 4$.

11. $\dfrac{y^4}{4} + \dfrac{2y^3}{3} + \dfrac{y^2}{2} + C$. **13.** $\dfrac{4z^{3/4}}{3} - \dfrac{6z^{5/6}}{5} + C$. **15.** $\dfrac{1}{3}\ln\dfrac{10}{3}$. **17.** $\dfrac{2}{27}(3x^3 + 2)^{3/2} + C$.

19. $\dfrac{1}{2}(e^{2y} + e^{-2y}) + C$. **21.** $\ln|x| - \dfrac{2}{x} + C$. **23.** 11.1. **25.** $\dfrac{7}{3}$. **27.** $4 - 3\sqrt[3]{2}$. **29.** $\dfrac{3}{t} - \dfrac{2}{\sqrt{t}} + C$.

31. $\dfrac{3}{2} - 5\ln 2$.

*In Problems **33–47**, answers are assumed to be expressed in square units.*

33. $\dfrac{4}{3}$. **35.** $\dfrac{16}{3}$. **37.** $\dfrac{125}{6}$. **39.** $6 + \ln 3$. **41.** $\dfrac{2}{3}$. **43.** 36. **45.** $\dfrac{125}{3}$. **47.** $e - 1$.

49. $p = 100 - \sqrt{2q}$. **51.** $\$1900$. **53.** $CS = 166\dfrac{2}{3}$, $PS = 53\dfrac{1}{3}$. **55.** 0.5507.

Exercise 15.1

1. $-e^{-x}(x + 1) + C$. **3.** $\dfrac{y^4}{4}\left[\ln(y) - \dfrac{1}{4}\right] + C$. **5.** $x[\ln(4x) - 1] + C$.

7. $\dfrac{2x}{3}(x + 1)^{3/2} - \dfrac{4}{15}(x + 1)^{5/2} + C = \dfrac{2}{15}(x + 1)^{3/2}(3x - 2) + C$. **9.** $\dfrac{2}{3}x^{3/2}\ln(x) - \dfrac{4}{9}x^{3/2} + C$. **11.** $\dfrac{1}{4}e^2(3e^2 - 1)$.

13. $\dfrac{1}{2}(1 - e^{-1})$, parts not needed. **15.** $\dfrac{2}{3}(9\sqrt{3} - 10\sqrt{2})$. **17.** $e^x(x^2 - 2x + 2) + C$.

19. $\dfrac{x^3}{3} + 2e^{-x}(x + 1) - \dfrac{e^{-2x}}{2} + C$. **21.** $2e^3 + 1$ square units.

Exercise 15.2

1. $2 \ln |x| + 3 \ln |x - 1| + C = \ln |x^2(x - 1)^3| + C.$ **3.** $-3 \ln |x + 1| + 4 \ln |x - 2| + C = \ln |(x - 2)^4/(x + 1)^3| + C.$

5. $\frac{1}{4}\left[\frac{3x^2}{2} + 2 \ln |x - 1| - 2 \ln |x + 1|\right] + C = \frac{1}{4}\left(\frac{3x^2}{2} + \ln\left[\frac{x - 1}{x + 1}\right]^2\right) + C.$

7. $\ln |x| + 2 \ln |x - 4| - 3 \ln |x + 3| + C = \ln |x(x - 4)^2/(x + 3)^3| + C.$ **9.** $\frac{1}{2}\ln|x^6 + 2x^4 - x^2 - 2| + C$, partial fractions

not required.   **11.** $[4/(x - 2)] - 5 \ln |x - 1| + 7 \ln |x - 2| + C. = [4/(x - 2)] + \ln|(x - 2)^7/(x - 1)^5| + C.$

13. $2 \ln |x| - \frac{1}{2}\ln(x^2 + 4) + C = \frac{1}{2}\ln\left[\frac{x^4}{x^2 + 4}\right] + C.$ **15.** $-\frac{1}{2}\ln(x^2 + 1) - \frac{2}{x - 3} + C.$

17. $5 \ln(x^2 + 1) + 2 \ln(x^2 + 2) + C = \ln [(x^2 + 1)^5(x^2 + 2)^2] + C.$ **19.** $\frac{3}{2}\ln(x^2 + 1) + \frac{1}{x^2 + 1} + C.$

21. $18 \ln (4) - 10 \ln (5) - 8 \ln (3).$ **23.** $\frac{11}{6} + 4 \ln \frac{2}{3}$ square units.

Exercise 15.3

1. $\frac{1}{6} \ln \left|\frac{x}{6 + 7x}\right| + C.$ **3.** $\frac{1}{3} \ln \left|\frac{\sqrt{x^2 + 9} - 3}{x}\right| + C.$ **5.** $\frac{1}{2}\left[\frac{4}{5} \ln |4 + 5x| - \frac{2}{3} \ln |2 + 3x|\right] + C.$

7. $\frac{1}{8}(2x - \ln[4 + 3e^{2x}]) + C.$ **9.** $2\left[\frac{1}{1 + x} + \ln \left|\frac{x}{1 + x}\right|\right] + C.$ **11.** $1 + \ln \frac{4}{9}.$

13. $\frac{1}{2}(x \sqrt{x^2 - 3} - 3 \ln |x + \sqrt{x^2 - 3}|) + C.$ **15.** $\frac{1}{144}.$ **17.** $e^x(x^2 - 2x + 2) + C.$

19. $2\left(-\frac{\sqrt{4x^2 + 1}}{2x} + \ln |2x + \sqrt{4x^2 + 1}|\right) + C.$ **21.** $\frac{1}{9}\left(\ln |1 + 3x| + \frac{1}{1 + 3x}\right) + C.$

23. $\frac{1}{\sqrt{5}}\left(\frac{1}{2\sqrt{7}} \ln \left|\frac{\sqrt{7} + \sqrt{5} x}{\sqrt{7} - \sqrt{5} x}\right|\right) + C.$ **25.** $\frac{1}{3^6}\left[\frac{(3x)^6 \ln(3x)}{6} - \frac{(3x)^6}{36}\right] + C = \frac{x^6}{36}[6 \ln(3x) - 1] + C.$

27. $\frac{4(9x - 2)(1 + 3x)^{3/2}}{135} + C.$ **29.** $\frac{1}{2} \ln|2x + \sqrt{4x^2 - 13}| + C.$ **31.** $\frac{1}{4}[2x^2 \ln(2x) - x^2] + C.$

33. $-\frac{\sqrt{9 - 4x^2}}{9x} + C.$ **35.** $\frac{1}{2} \ln(x^2 + 1) + C.$ **37.** $\frac{1}{6}(2x^2 + 1)^{3/2} + C.$ **39.** $\ln \left|\frac{x - 3}{x - 2}\right| + C.$

41. $\frac{x^4}{4}\left[\ln(x) - \frac{1}{4}\right] + C.$ **43.** $\frac{e^{2x}}{4}(2x - 1) + C.$ **45.** $x(\ln x)^2 - 2x \ln(x) + 2x + C.$ **47.** $\frac{2}{3}(9\sqrt{3} - 10\sqrt{2}).$

49. $2(2\sqrt{2} - \sqrt{7}).$ **51.** $\frac{7}{2} \ln(2) - \frac{3}{4}.$ **53.** $\ln\left|\frac{q_n(1 - q_0)}{q_0(1 - q_n)}\right|.$ **55. (a)** \$37,599;   **(b)** \$4924.

57. (a) \$5481;   **(b)** \$535.

Exercise 15.4

1. $\frac{16}{3}.$ **3.** $-1.$ **5.** $0.$ **7.** $\frac{13}{6}.$ **9.** \$12,400.   **11.** \$3321.

Exercise 15.5

1. 0.340; 0.333.　　**3.** 1.388; 1.386.　　**5.** 0.883.　　**7.** 2,361,375.　　**9.** 2.967.　　**11.** $\dfrac{8}{3}$.　　**13.** 0.771.

Exercise 15.6

1. $y = -\dfrac{1}{x^2 + C}$.　　**3.** $y = \dfrac{1}{3}(x^2 + 1)^{3/2} + C$.　　**5.** $y = Ce^x, C > 0$.　　**7.** $y = Cx, C > 0$.　　**9.** $y = \sqrt{2x}$.

11. $y = \ln\dfrac{x^3 + 3}{3}$.　　**13.** $y = \dfrac{4x^2 + 3}{2(x^2 + 1)}$.　　**15.** $N = 20{,}000e^{0.018t}$; $N = 20{,}000(1.2)^{t/10}$; 28,800.　　**17.** $2e^{0.946}$ billion.

19. 0.01204; 57.57 sec.　　**21.** 2900 years.　　**23.** $N = N_0 e^{k(t - t_0)}, t \geq t_0$.　　**25.** 12.6 units.

27. $A = 400(1 - e^{-t/2})$; 157 grams.

Exercise 15.7

1. 29,400.　　**3.** 430,000.　　**5.** 1990.　　**7.** **(b)** 375.　　**9.** 1:06 A.M.　　**11.** $62,500.

13. $N = M - (M - N_0)e^{-kt}$.

Exercise 15.8

1. $\dfrac{1}{3}$.　　**3.** Div.　　**5.** $\dfrac{1}{e}$.　　**7.** Div.　　**9.** $-\dfrac{1}{2}$.　　**11.** 0.　　**13.** **(a)** 800; **(b)** $\dfrac{2}{3}$.　　**15.** 4,000,000.

17. $\dfrac{1}{2}$ square unit.　　**19.** 5000 increase.

Review Problems—Chapter 15

1. $\dfrac{x^2}{4}[2 \ln(x) - 1] + C$.　　**3.** $5 + \dfrac{9}{4} \ln 3$.　　**5.** $\dfrac{1}{21}(9 \ln |3 + x| - 2 \ln |2 + 3x|) + C$.　　**7.** $\dfrac{1}{2(x + 2)} + \dfrac{1}{4} \ln \left| \dfrac{x}{x + 2} \right| + C$.

9. $-\dfrac{\sqrt{9 - 16x^2}}{9x} + C$.　　**11.** $\dfrac{3}{2} \ln \left| \dfrac{x - 3}{x + 3} \right| + C$.　　**13.** $\dfrac{e^{7x}}{49}(7x - 1) + C$.　　**15.** $\dfrac{1}{2} \ln |\ln 2x| + C$.

17. $x - \dfrac{3}{2} \ln |3 + 2x| + C$.　　**19.** 34.　　**21.** **(a)** 1.405; **(b)** 1.388.　　**23.** $y = Ce^{x^3 + x^2}, C > 0$.　　**25.** $\dfrac{1}{18}$.

27. Div.　　**29.** 144,000.　　**31.** 0.0005; 90%.　　**33.** $N = \dfrac{450}{1 + 224e^{-1.02t}}$.　　**35.** 4:16 P.M.

Exercise 16.1

1. **(a)** $\dfrac{5}{12}$; **(b)** $\dfrac{11}{16} = 0.6875$; **(c)** $\dfrac{13}{16} = 0.8125$; **(d)** $-1 + \sqrt{10}$.　　**3.** **(a)** $f(x) = \begin{cases} \dfrac{1}{3}, & \text{if } 1 \leq x \leq 4, \\ 0, & \text{otherwise}; \end{cases}$

(b) $\dfrac{1}{3}$; **(c)** 0; **(d)** $\dfrac{5}{6}$; **(e)** $\dfrac{2}{3}$; **(f)** 0; **(g)** 1, **(h)** $\dfrac{5}{2}$; **(i)** $\dfrac{\sqrt{3}}{2}$;

(j) $F(x) = \begin{cases} 0, & \text{if } x < 1, \\ \dfrac{x-1}{3}, & \text{if } 1 \le x \le 4, \\ 1, & \text{if } x > 4, \end{cases}$

$P(X < 2) = \dfrac{1}{3}, \; P(1 < X < 3) = \dfrac{2}{3}.$

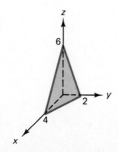

5. **(a)** $f(x) = \begin{cases} \dfrac{1}{b-a}, & \text{if } a \le x \le b, \\ 0, & \text{otherwise;} \end{cases}$ **(b)** $\dfrac{a+b}{2}$; **(c)** $\sigma^2 = \dfrac{(b-a)^{12}}{12}$, $\sigma = \dfrac{b-a}{\sqrt{12}}$.

7. **(a)** 0.133; **(b)** 0.982; **(c)** 0.007; **(d)** 0.865.   **9.** **(a)** $\dfrac{1}{8}$; **(b)** $\dfrac{5}{16}$; **(c)** $\dfrac{39}{64} = 0.609$; **(d)** 1; **(e)** $\dfrac{8}{3}$; **(f)** $\dfrac{2\sqrt{2}}{3}$;

(g) $2\sqrt{2}$;   **(h)** $\dfrac{7}{16}$.   **11.** $\dfrac{7}{10}$; 5 min.   **13.** 0.050.

Exercise 16.2

1. **(a)** 0.4641; **(b)** 0.3239; **(c)** 0.8888; **(d)** 0.9983; **(e)** 0.9147; **(f)** 0.4721.   **3.** 0.13.   **5.** -1.08.   **7.** 0.34.
9. **(a)** 0.9332; **(b)** 0.0668; **(c)** 0.0873.   **11.** 0.3085.   **13.** 0.8185.   **15.** 8.   **17.** 9.68%.   **19.** 90.82%.
21. **(a)** 1.7%; **(b)** 85.6.

Exercise 16.3

1. 0.1056; 0.0122.   **3.** 0.0430; 0.9232.   **5.** 0.7507.   **7.** 0.4129.   **9.** 0.2514; 0.0287.   **11.** 0.0336.

Review Problems—Chapter 16

1. **(a)** 2; **(b)** $\dfrac{9}{32}$; **(c)** $\dfrac{3}{4}$; **(d)** $F(x) = \begin{cases} 0, & \text{if } x < 0, \\ \dfrac{x}{3} + \dfrac{2x^3}{3}, & \text{if } 0 \le x \le 1, \\ 1, & \text{if } x > 1. \end{cases}$ **3.** **(a)** 2; **(b)** $\dfrac{1}{\sqrt{2}} = 0.71$.   **5.** 0.3085.

7. 0.2857.   **9.** 0.1587.   **11.** 0.9817.   **13.** 0.0228.

Exercise 17.1

1. 3.   **3.** 6.   **5.** 6.   **7.** 88.   **9.** 3.   **11.** $2x_0 + 2h - 5y_0 + 4$.   **13.** 2000.   **15.** $y = -4$.
17. $z = 6$.

19.

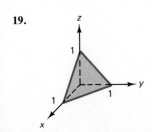

21.

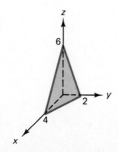

23.

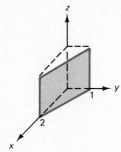

25.

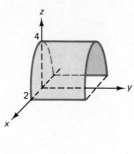

27. Surface is a sphere (top hemisphere shown).

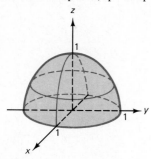

Exercise 17.2

1. $f_x(x, y) = 1$; $f_y(x, y) = -5$. **3.** $f_x(x, y) = 3$; $f_y(x, y) = 0$.

5. $g_x(x, y) = 5x^4y^4 - 12x^3y^3 + 21x^2 - 3y$; $g_y(x, y) = 4x^5y^3 - 9x^4y^2 + 4y - 3x$.

7. $g_p(p, q) = \dfrac{q}{2\sqrt{pq}}$; $g_q(p, q) = \dfrac{p}{2\sqrt{pq}}$. **9.** $h_s(s, t) = \dfrac{2s}{t - 3}$; $h_t(s, t) = -\dfrac{s^2 + 4}{(t - 3)^2}$.

11. $u_{q_1}(q_1, q_2) = \dfrac{3}{4q_1}$; $u_{q_2}(q_1, q_2) = \dfrac{1}{4q_2}$.

13. $h_x(x, y) = (x^3 + xy^2 + 3y^3)(x^2 + y^2)^{-3/2}$; $h_y(x, y) = (3x^3 + x^2y + y^3)(x^2 + y^2)^{-3/2}$.

15. $\dfrac{\partial z}{\partial x} = 5ye^{5xy}$; $\dfrac{\partial z}{\partial y} = 5xe^{5xy}$. **17.** $\dfrac{\partial z}{\partial x} = 5\left[\dfrac{2x^2}{x^2 + y} + \ln(x^2 + y)\right]$; $\dfrac{\partial z}{\partial y} = \dfrac{5x}{x^2 + y}$.

19. $f_r(r, s) = \sqrt{r + 2s}\,(3r^2 - 2s) + \dfrac{r^3 - 2rs + s^2}{2\sqrt{r + 2s}}$; $f_s(r, s) = 2(s - r)\sqrt{r + 2s} + \dfrac{r^3 - 2rs + s^2}{\sqrt{r + 2s}}$.

21. $f_r(r, s) = -e^{3-r}\ln(7 - s)$; $f_s(r, s) = \dfrac{e^{3-r}}{s - 7}$.

23. $g_x(x, y, z) = 6xy + 2y^2z$; $g_y(x, y, z) = 3x^2 + 4xyz$; $g_z(x, y, z) = 2xy^2 + 9z^2$.

25. $g_r(r, s, t) = 2re^{s+t}$; $g_s(r, s, t) = (7s^3 + 21s^2 + r^2)e^{s+t}$; $g_t(r, s, t) = e^{s+t}(r^2 + 7s^3)$. **27.** 50.

29. $\dfrac{1}{3}$. **31.** 0. **35.** $-\dfrac{ra}{\left[1 + a\dfrac{n - 1}{2}\right]^2}$.

Exercise 17.3

1. 20.   **3.** 784.5.   **5.** $\dfrac{\partial P}{\partial k} = 1.208648l^{0.192}k^{-0.236}$; $\dfrac{\partial P}{\partial l} = 0.303744l^{-0.808}k^{0.764}$.

7. $\dfrac{\partial q_A}{\partial p_A} = -50$; $\dfrac{\partial q_A}{\partial p_B} = 2$; $\dfrac{\partial q_B}{\partial p_A} = 4$; $\dfrac{\partial q_B}{\partial p_B} = -20$; competitive.

9. $\dfrac{\partial q_A}{\partial p_A} = -\dfrac{100}{p_A^2 p_B^{1/2}}$; $\dfrac{\partial q_A}{\partial p_B} = -\dfrac{50}{p_A p_B^{3/2}}$; $\dfrac{\partial q_B}{\partial p_A} = -\dfrac{500}{3 p_B p_A^{4/3}}$; $\dfrac{\partial q_B}{\partial p_B} = -\dfrac{500}{p_B^2 p_A^{1/3}}$; complementary.

11. $\dfrac{\partial P}{\partial B} = 0.01A^{0.27}B^{-0.99}C^{0.01}D^{0.23}E^{0.09}F^{0.27}$; $\dfrac{\partial P}{\partial C} = 0.01A^{0.27}B^{0.01}C^{-0.99}D^{0.23}E^{0.09}F^{0.27}$.

13. 1120; if a staff manager with an M.B.A. degree had an extra year of work experience before the degree, the manager would receive $1120 per year in extra compensation.   **15.** (a) -1.015; -0.846.   (b) one for which $w = w_0$ and $s = s_0$.

17. (a) no;   (b) 70%.   **19.** $\eta_{p_A} = -1$, $\eta_{p_B} = -\dfrac{1}{2}$.

Exercise 17.4

1. $-\dfrac{x}{z}$.   **3.** $\dfrac{4y}{3z^2}$.   **5.** $\dfrac{x(yz^2 + 1)}{z(1 - x^2 y)}$.   **7.** $-e^{y-z}$.   **9.** $\dfrac{yz}{1 + z}$.   **11.** $-\dfrac{3x}{z}$.   **13.** $-\dfrac{9}{10}$.   **15.** 1.   **17.** $\dfrac{5}{2}$.

Exercise 17.5

1. $6xy^2$; $12xy$.   **3.** $3xe^{3xy} + 4x^2$; $9xye^{3xy} + 3e^{3xy} + 8x$; $9x(3xy + 2)e^{3xy}$.

5. $(2x + y)(2x^2 + 2xy + y^2 + 1)$; $6x^2 + 8xy + 3y^2 + 1$.

7. $3x^2y + 4xy^2 + y^3$; $3xy^2 + 4x^2y + x^3$; $6xy + 4y^2$; $6xy + 4x^2$.   **9.** $x(x^2 + y^2)^{-1/2}$; $y^2(x^2 + y^2)^{-3/2}$.

11. 0.   **13.** 1758.   **15.** $2e$.   **21.** $-\dfrac{y^2 + z^2}{z^3} = -\dfrac{3x^2}{z^3}$.

Exercise 17.6

1. $\dfrac{\partial z}{\partial r} = 13$; $\dfrac{\partial z}{\partial s} = 9$.   **3.** $\left[2t + \dfrac{3\sqrt{t}}{2}\right]e^{x+y}$.   **5.** $5(2xz^2 + yz) + 2(xz + z^2) - (2x^2z + xy + 2yz)$.

7. $3(x^2 + xy^2)^2(2x + y^2 + 2xy)$.   **9.** $-2s(2x + yz) + r(xz + 3y^2z^2) - 5(xy + 2y^3z)$.   **11.** $15s(2x - 7)$.   **13.** 324.

15. -1.   **17.** $\dfrac{\partial p}{\partial L} = a\dfrac{\partial P}{\partial l}g(h) - wh$; $\dfrac{\partial p}{\partial h} = a\dfrac{\partial P}{\partial l}Lg'(h) - wL$.

Exercise 17.7

1. $\left(\dfrac{14}{3}, -\dfrac{13}{3}\right)$.   **3.** $(2, 5)$, $(2, -6)$, $(-1, 5)$, $(-1, -6)$.   **5.** $(50, 150, 350)$.   **7.** $\left(-2, \dfrac{3}{2}\right)$, rel. min.

9. $\left(-\frac{1}{4}, \frac{1}{2}\right)$, rel. max.   **11.** (1, 1), rel. min.; $\left(\frac{1}{2}, \frac{1}{4}\right)$, neither.

13. (0, 0), rel. max.; $\left(4, \frac{1}{2}\right)$, rel. min.; $\left(0, \frac{1}{2}\right)$, (4, 0), neither.   **15.** (122, 127), rel. max.   **17.** $(-1, -1)$, rel. min.

19. $l = 24, k = 14$.   **21.** $p_A = 80, p_B = 85$.   **23.** $q_A = 48, q_B = 40, p_A = 52, p_B = 44$, profit $= 3304$.

25. $q_A = 3, q_B = 2$.   **27.** 1 ft by 2 ft by 3 ft.   **29.** $\left(\frac{105}{37}, \frac{28}{37}\right)$, rel. min.

Exercise 17.8

1. $(2, -2)$.   **3.** $\left(3, \frac{3}{2}, -\frac{3}{2}\right)$.   **5.** $\left(\frac{4}{3}, -\frac{4}{3}, -\frac{8}{3}\right)$.   **7.** (6, 3, 2).   **9.** $\left(\frac{2}{3}, \frac{4}{3}, -\frac{4}{3}\right)$.   **11.** (3, 3, 6).

13. Plant 1, 40 units; plant 2, 60 units.   **15.** 74 units (when $l = 8, k = 7$).   **17.** $x = 12, y = 8$.
19. $x = 10, y = 20, z = 5$.

Exercise 17.9

1. $\hat{y} = 0.98 + 0.61x; 3.12$.   **3.** $\hat{y} = 0.057 + 1.67x; 5.90$.   **5.** $\hat{q} = 82.6 - 0.641p$.   **7.** $\hat{y} = 100 + 0.13x; 105.2$.
9. $\hat{y} = 8.5 + 2.5x$.   **11.** **(a)** $\hat{y} = 35.9 - 2.5x$;   **(b)** $\hat{y} = 28.4 - 2.5x$.

Exercise 17.11

1. 18.   **3.** $\frac{1}{4}$.   **5.** $\frac{2}{3}$.   **7.** 3.   **9.** 324.   **11.** $-\frac{58}{35}$.   **13.** $\frac{8}{3}$.   **15.** $-\frac{1}{3}$.   **17.** $\frac{e^2}{2} - e + \frac{1}{2}$.

19. $-\frac{27}{4}$.   **21.** $\frac{1}{24}$.   **23.** $e^{-4} - e^{-2} - e^{-3} + e^{-1}$.   **25.** $\frac{3}{8}$.

Review Problems—Chapter 17

1.   **3.**   **5.** $4x + 3y; 3x + 2y$.   **7.** $\frac{y}{(x+y)^2}; -\frac{x}{(x+y)^2}$.

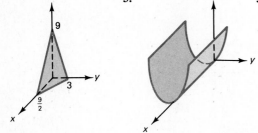

9. $2xze^{x^2yz}(1 + x^2yz)$.   **11.** $\dfrac{y}{x^2 + y^2}$.   **13.** $2(x + y)$.   **15.** $xze^{yz} \ln z; \dfrac{e^{yz}}{z} + ye^{yz} \ln z = e^{yz}\left(\dfrac{1}{z} + y \ln z\right)$.

17. $2(x + y)e^r + 2\left(\dfrac{x + 3y}{r + s}\right); 2\left(\dfrac{x + 3y}{r + s}\right)$.   **19.** $\dfrac{2x + 2y + z}{4z - x}$.   **21.** $\dfrac{\partial P}{\partial l} = 14l^{-0.3}k^{0.3}; \dfrac{\partial P}{\partial k} = 6l^{0.7}k^{-0.7}$.

23. Competitive.   **25.** $(2, 2)$, rel. min.   **27.** 4 ft by 4 ft by 2 ft.   **29.** $(3, 2, 1)$.   **31.** $\hat{y} = 12.87 + 3.23x$.

33. 8.   **35.** $\dfrac{1}{210}$.

Index